BASIC MARKETING

RESEARCH

GILBERT A. CHURCHILL, JR.
Arthur C. Neilsen, Jr., Chair of Marketing Research
University of Wisconsin

THE DRYDEN PRESS A Division of Harcourt College Publishers

Fort Worth   Philadelphia   San Diego   New York   Orlando   Austin   San Antonio
Toronto   Montreal   London   Sydney   Tokyo

PUBLISHER ....Mike Roche

ACQUISITIONS EDITOR.....Bill Schoof

MARKET STRATEGIST ......Beverly Dunn

DEVELOPMENTAL EDITOR...Bobbie Bochenko

PROJECT EDITOR ....Christy Goldfinch

ART DIRECTOR ....Garry Harman

PRODUCTION MANAGER ....Lois West

Globe Photo: Paul Taylor–Photonica

ISBN: 0-03-021104-2
Library of Congress Catalog Card Number: 00-102808

Address for Domestic Orders
Harcourt, Inc., 6277 Sea Harbor Drive, Orlando, FL 32887-6777
800-782-4479

Address for International Orders
International Customer Service
Harcourt, Inc., 6277 Sea Harbor Drive, Orlando, FL 32887-6777
407-345-3800
(fax) 407-345-4060
(e-mail) hbintl@harcourtbrace.com

Address for Editorial Correspondence
Harcourt College Publishers, 301 Commerce Street, Suite 3700, Fort Worth, TX 76102

Web Site Address
http://www.hbcollege.com

THE DRYDEN PRESS, DRYDEN, and the DP LOGO are registered trademarks of Harcourt, Inc.

Printed in the United States of America

0 1 2 3 4 5 6 7 8 9   048   9 8 7 6 5 4 3 2 1

The Dryden Press
A Division of Harcourt College Publishers

To our grandchildren—

Kayla Marie

Johnathan Winston

Kelsey Lynn

Sean Jeffrey

THE
DRYDEN PRESS SERIES IN MARKETING

PREFACE

Basic Marketing Research is designed for the introductory, undergraduate course in marketing research and can be used either in one- or two-quarter sequences or in semester courses.

The topic of marketing research is a complex one. It involves a number of questions that need to be answered and a number of decisions that need to be made with respect to the choice of techniques used to solve a research problem. Without some overriding framework, which this book attempts to provide, it is easy for students to become lost in a maze; that is, to become so overwhelmed by the bits and pieces that they fail to see the interrelationships of the parts to the whole. Yet, an understanding of these interrelationships is essential both to the aspiring manager and the aspiring researcher, for in a very real sense, marketing research is one big trade-off.

Decisions made with respect to one stage in the research process have consequences for other stages. Managers need an appreciation of the subtle and pervasive interactions among the parts of the research process so that they can have the appropriate degree of confidence in a particular research result. Researchers also need to appreciate the interactions among the parts. The parts serve as the "pegs" on which to hang the knowledge accumulated about research methods. Researchers need to resist the temptation of becoming enamored of the parts to the detriment of the whole.

This book attempts to serve both the aspiring manager and the aspiring researcher by breaking the research process down into some basic stages that must be completed when answering a research question. The specific stages are

1. Formulate problem.
2. Determine research design.
3. Determine data-collection method.
4. Design data-collection forms.
5. Design sample and collect data.
6. Analyze and interpret the data.
7. Prepare the research report.

The organization of the book parallels these stages in the research process. Thus, the book is organized into seven corresponding parts. Each part (or stage) is then broken into smaller parts, so that a given stage is typically discussed in multiple chapters. This modular treatment allows students to negotiate the maze. It also allows instructors some latitude with respect to the order in which they cover topics.

Organization

Part I consists of four chapters and an appendix. Chapter 1 provides an overview of the subject of marketing research and describes the kinds of problems for which it is used, who is doing research, and how the research function is organized. Chapter 1 also provides a perspective on career opportunities available in marketing research. Chapter 2 provides an overview of the various ways of gathering marketing intelligence. It emphasizes the increasingly important role played by decision support systems and the Internet in providing business and competitive intelligence and contrasts the information system approaches to the project emphasis taken in the book. Chapter 3 then overviews the research process. The appendix to Chapter 3 discusses various ethical frameworks for viewing marketing research techniques. Chapter 4 discusses the problem-formulation stage of the research process and explains the issues that must be addressed in translating a marketing decision problem into one or more questions that research can address productively. It also covers the preparation of a research proposal.

Part II concerns the choice of research design and consists of two chapters. Chapter 5 overviews the role of various research designs and discusses one of the basic types, the exploratory design. Chapter 6 then discusses the two other basic types, descriptive and causal designs.

Part III discusses the general issue of selecting a data-collection method and contains five chapters and an appendix. Chapter 7 focuses on secondary data as an information resource, while the appendix to Chapter 7 discusses the many sources of secondary data. Chapter 8 discusses the operations of and data supplied by standardized marketing information services. Chapter 9 describes the issues involved when choosing between the two primary means by which marketing information can be collected—through observing or questioning subjects. Chapter 10 then describes the main alternatives and the advantages and disadvantages of each when subjects are to be questioned. Chapter 11 does the same for observational techniques.

Part IV addresses the actual design of the data-collection forms that will be used in a study. Chapter 12 discusses a sequential procedure that can be used to design a questionnaire or observation form. Chapter 13 then discusses some basic measurement issues that researchers and managers need to be aware of so that they will neither mislead others nor be misled themselves when interpreting the findings. Chapter 14 describes some of the most popular techniques marketers currently use to measure customers' attitudes, perceptions, and preferences.

Part V, which consists of four chapters, examines sample design and deals with the actual collection of data needed to answer questions. Chapter 15 overviews the main types of samples that can be used to determine the population elements from which data should be collected. It also describes the main types of nonprobability samples and simple random sampling, the most basic probability sampling technique. Chapter 16 discusses the use of stratified sampling and cluster sampling, which are more sophisticated probability sampling techniques. Chapter 17 treats the question of how many population elements need to be sampled for research questions to be answered with precision and confidence in the results. Chapter 18 discusses data collection and the many errors that can occur in completing this task from a perspective that allows managers to better assess the quality of information they receive from research.

Once the data have been collected, emphasis in the research process logically turns to analysis, which is a search for meaning in the collected information. The search for meaning involves many questions and several steps, and the three chapters in Part VI attempt to overview these steps and questions. Chapter 19 reviews the preliminary analysis steps of editing, coding, and tabulating the data. Chapter 20 discusses the procedures that are appropriate for examining whether the differences between groups are statistically significant. Chapter 21 describes the statistical procedures that can be used to examine the degree of relationship between variables.

Part VII, which consists of two chapters and an epilogue, discusses the last, yet critically important, part of he research process: the research report. Because it often becomes the standard by which any research effort is judged, the research report must contribute positively to that evaluation. Chapter 22 discusses the criteria a written research report should satisfy and a form it can follow so that it does contribute positively to the research effort. Chapter 23 provides a similar perspective for oral reports. Chapter 23 also discusses some graphic techniques that can be used to communicate the important findings more forcefully. The epilogue ties together the elements of the research process by demonstrating their interrelationships in overview fashion.

Organizing the material in this book around the stages in the research process produces several significant benefits. First, it allows the subject of marketing research to be broken into very digestible bites. Second, it demonstrates and continually reinforces how the individual bits and pieces of research technique fit into a larger whole. Students can see readily, for example, the relationship between statistics and marketing research, or where they might pursue additional study to become research specialists. Third,

the organization permits the instructor some flexibility with respect to the order in which the parts of the process may be covered.

Special Features

In addition to its pedagogically sound organization, *Basic Marketing Research* has several special features that deserve mention. First, the book is relatively complete with respect to its coverage of the most important techniques available for gathering marketing intelligence. The general approach employed when discussing topics is not only to provide students with the pros and cons of the various methods by which a research problem can be addressed, but also to develop an appreciation of why these advantages and disadvantages occur. The hope is that through this appreciation students will be able to creatively apply and critically evaluate the procedures of marketing research. Other important features include the following:

1. A set of learning objectives highlights the most important topics discussed in the chapter. The chapter summary then recaps the learning objectives point by point.

2. A "Case in Marketing Research" opens each chapter. These scenarios are adapted form actual situations and should prove to be very interesting to students. Furthermore, an end-of-chapter reference to the introductory case ("Back to the Case") illustrates how the scenario can be brought into sharper focus using the methods described in the chapter.

3. A running glossary appears throughout the text. Key terms in each chapter are boldfaced, and their definitions appear in the margin where the terms are discussed. Each key term is also indexed.

4. The "Research Windows" provide a view of what is happening in the world of marketing research. "Research Windows" describe what is going on at specific companies and offer some specific "how to" tips. Like the "Case in Marketing Research" features, they serve to breathe life into the subject and strongly engage the students' interest.

5. Extensive use of photos provides visual reinforcement to important concepts. Appearing throughout the book, the photos provide students with a tangible understanding of how various aspects of the research process are conducted.

6. Discussion questions, problems, and/or projects are found at the end of each chapter. This feature allows students the opportunity to apply the chapter topics to focused situations, thereby honing their analytical skills and developing firsthand knowledge of the strengths and weaknesses of various research techniques.

7. A worked-out research project is discussed throughout the book. This project is found at the end of each part and concerns retailers' attitudes toward advertising in various media. The project represents an actual situation faced by a group of radio stations in one community. It begins with a description of the radio stations' concerns and objectives. Each of the sections then describes how the research was designed and carried out, demonstrating the interrelationships of the stages in the research process and providing students with a real, hands-on perspective as to how research is actually conducted.

8. Several cases occur at the end of each part and deal with a stage in the research process. The 38 cases assist students in developing their own evaluation and analytical skills. They are also useful in demonstrating the universal application of marketing research techniques. The methods of marketing research can be used not only by manufacturers and distributors of products, as is commonly assumed, but also by the private and public sectors to address other issues. The cases include such diverse entities or issues as the Big Brothers program, education, banking, and theater, among others. All cases represent actual situations, although some of them have been disguised to protect the proprietary nature of the information.

9. Raw data are provided for eight of the cases to allow students to perform their own analyses to answer questions. The data are available on computer disk to adopters. The disk allows those who have statistical packages available to use them for analyses. To obtain a copy of the disk, which is available for the IBM platform, adopters must send the insert card in the *Instructor's Manual* to the nearest Dryden regional sales office.

10. The fourth edition also contains the description, questionnaire, coding form, and raw data for a ground coffee study conducted by NFO. The study was used to generate a number of discussion questions and problems for the chapters, which give students the opportunity to work with "live" data. This should hone their skills in translating research problems into data analysis issues and in interpreting computer output. Moreover, the database is rich enough for instructors to design their own application problems and exercises for their classes, thereby allowing even more opportunity for "hands-on" learning.

Distance Learning

For professors interested in supplementing classroom presentations with online content or who are interested in setting up a distance learning course, Harcourt College Publishers, along with WebCT, can provide you with the industry's leading online courses.

WebCT facilitates the creation of sophisticated Web-based educational environments by providing tools to help you manage course content, facilitate online classroom collaboration, and track your students' progress. If you are using WebCT in your class but not a Harcourt Online Course or textbook, you may adopt the *Student's Guide to the World Wide Web and WebCT* (ISBN 0-03-045503-0). This manual gives step-by-step instructions on using WebCT tools and features.

In conjunction with WebCT, Harcourt College Publishers also offers information on adopting a Harcourt online course, WebCT testing service, free access to a blank WebCT template, and customized course creation. For more information, please contact your local sales representative. To view a demo of any of our online courses, go to webct.harcourtcollege.com.

Changes in the Fourth Edition

Although it looks similar to the first three editions, the new edition contains some major changes. The primary change is increased emphasis in the use of the Internet for marketing research. The emphasis is most clearly reflected in Chapter 2, Gathering Marketing Intelligence, where there is expanded discussion of the Internet, the Intranet, the role of the chief information officer, and the networking of modern information systems. However, it can also be seen throughout the book in the discussion of issues and the new examples.

Another major change involves the cases. More than 20 percent of the cases are new and over 25 percent of the others have been revised. At the same time, the video case that was added to the third edition has been retained. The video case, which uses an original script and professional actors, allows students to view short segments illustrating the points being discussed. There is a special icon at the end of the chapters in the *Instructor's Manual* that indicates the questions that might be asked after students view a segment of the video case. The video case makes for a very interactive learning environment.

Finally, all of the chapters have been subjected to thorough scrutiny and rewrite.

Acknowledgments

While writing a book is never the work of a single person, one always runs the risk of omitting some important contributions when attempting to acknowledge the help of others. Nonetheless, the attempt must be made because this book benefited immensely from the many helpful comments I received along the way from interested colleagues.

I especially wish to acknowledge the following people who reviewed the manuscript for this or one of the earlier editions. While much of the credit for the strength of this book is theirs, the blame for any weaknesses is strictly mine. Thank you one and all for your most perceptive and helpful comments.

David Andrus
Kansas State University

Joseph Ballenger
Stephin R. Austin State University

Edward Bond
Bradley University

Donald Bradley
University of Central Arkansas

Terry Childers
University of Minnesota

James S. Chow
East Carolina University

C. Anthony Di Benedetto
Temple University

Elizabeth Ferrell
Southwestern Oklahoma State University

David Gourley
Arizona State University

Dhruv Grewal
University of Miami

Thomas S. Gruca
University of Iowa

D. S. Halfhill
California State University, Fresno

James E. Hansz
Lehigh University

Doug Hausknecht
University of Akron

Vince Howe
University of North Carolina–Wilmington

Deborah Roedder John
University of Minnesota

Glen Jarboe
University of Texas, Arlington

Leonard Jensen
Southern Illinois University, Carbondale

Roland Jones
Mississipi State University

Ram Kesavan
University of Detroit

Richard H. Kolbe
Kent State University

Elizabeth K. La Fleur
Nicholls State University

Subhash Lonial
University of Louisville

Daulatram Lund
University of Nevada

Douglas Mac Lachlan
University of Washington

Tridib Mazumdar
Syracuse University

Donald J. Messmer
College of William and Mary

Thomas Noordewier
University of Vermont

Pradeep A. Rau
The George Washington University

Debra Ringold
Williamette University

Abhijit Roy
Plymouth State College

Bruce Stern
Portland State University

R. Sukumar
University of Houston

John H. Summey
Southern Illinois University–Carbondale

David Urban
Virginia Commonwealth University

Joe Welch
North Texas State University

My colleagues at the University of Wisconsin have my thanks for the intellectual stimulation and psychological support they have always provided.

I also wish to thank Janet Christopher who did most of the typing on the manuscript. She was efficient in her efforts and patient with mine. I also wish to thank students Tom Brown, Beth Bubon, Jennifer Markkanen, Joseph Kuester, Jayashree Mahajan, Kay Powers, and David Szymanski for their help with many of the tasks involved in completing a book such as this. I would like to thank the editorial and production staff of The Dryden Press for their professional efforts on my behalf. I am also grateful to the Literary Executor of the late Sir Ronald A. Fisher, F.R.S., to Dr. Frank Yates, F.R.S., and to Longman Group Ltd., for permission to reprint Table III from their book *Statistical Tables for Biological, Agricultural and Medical Research* (6th Edition, 1974).

Finally, I once again owe a special debt of thanks to my wife, Helen, and our children. Their unyielding support and generous love not only made this book possible but worthwhile doing in the first place.

Gilbert A. Churchill, Jr.

Madison, Wisconsin
July 2000

Gilbert A. Churchill, Jr., received his DBA from Indiana University in 1966 and joined the University of Wisconsin faculty upon graduation. Churchill was named Distinguished Marketing Educator by the American Marketing Association in 1986—only the second individual so honored. The lifetime achievement award recognizes and honors a living marketing educator for distinguished service and outstanding contributions in the field of marketing education. Professor Churchill was also awarded the Academy of Marketing Science's lifetime achievement award in 1993 for his significant scholarly contributions. In 1996, he received a Paul D. Converse Award, given to the most influential marketing scholars as judged by a national jury drawn from universities, business, and government. Also in 1996, the Marketing Research Group of the American Marketing Association established the Gilbert A. Churchill, Jr., lifetime achievement award, to be given each year to a person judged to have made significant lifetime contributions to marketing research.

Professor Churchill is a past recipient of the William O'Dell Award for the outstanding article appearing in the *Journal of Marketing Research* during the year. He has also been a finalist for the award five other times. He was named Marketer of the Year by the South Central Wisconsin Chapter of the American Marketing Association in 1981. He is a member of the American Marketing Association and has served as vice-president of publications and on its board of directors as well as on the association's Advisory Committee to the Bureau of the Census. In addition, he has served as consultant to a number of companies, including Oscar Mayer, Western Publishing Company, and Parker Pen.

Professor Churchill's articles have appeared in such publications as the *Journal of Marketing Research,* the *Journal of Marketing,* the *Journal of Consumer Research,* the *Journal of Retailing,* the *Journal of Business Research, Decision Sciences, Technometrics,* and *Organizational Behavior and Human Performance,* among others. He is co-author of several books, including *Marketing: Creating Value for Customers,* Second Edition (Burr Ridge, IL.: Irwin McGraw Hill, 1998), *Sales Force Management: Planning, Implementation, and Control,* Sixth Edition (Burr Ridge, IL.: Irwin McGraw Hill, 2000), and *Salesforce Performance* (Lexington Books, 1984); and he is also the author of *Marketing Research: Methodological Foundations,* Seventh Edition (Fort Worth, TX.: Dryden 1999) in addition to *Basic Marketing Research,* Fourth Edition (Fort Worth, TX.: Harcourt College Publishers, 2001). He is a former editor of the *Journal of Marketing Research* and has served on the editorial boards of *Journal of Marketing Research, Journal of Marketing, Journal of Business Research, Journal of Health Care Marketing* and the *Asian Journal of Marketing.* Professor Churchill is a past recipient of the Lawrence J. Larson Excellence in Teaching Award.

TABLE OF CONTENTS

Introduction to Marketing Research and Problem Definition

Part One gives an overview of marketing research. Chapter 1 looks at the kinds of problems for which marketing research is used, who is doing it, and how it is organized. Chapter 2 discusses alternative ways of providing marketing intelligence: through marketing information systems, decision support systems, or projects designed to get at specific issues. Chapter 3 provides an overview of the research process, and the appendix to Chapter 3 discusses some of the ethical questions that can arise when gathering information. Chapter 4 discusses in detail problem formulation, the first stage in the research process.

SOMETHING TO "YAHOO!" ABOUT Here's an ambitious corporate vision: becoming "the only place anyone in the world would have to go to find and get connected to anything or anybody." It sounds like a description of the Library of Congress, AT&T, and the world's greatest singles bar all rolled into one. Yet these words, taken from the company's 1998 annual report, may become a fitting description of one of the nation's fastest-growing businesses.

That business is an Internet portal site called Yahoo!. (The exclamation point, according to company cofounder Jerry Yang, is simply "pure marketing hype.") Travelers in cyberspace use Yahoo! as a starting point, where they can find links to weather reports, maps, news stories, e-mail, stock prices, real estate listings, on-line retailers, chat rooms, and much, much more.

Yahoo!'s strategy requires it to get as many Internet users as possible to visit its World Wide Web site, then keep them there as long as possible. This helps the company's bottom line in several ways. First, Yahoo! gets most of its revenues from selling advertising space on its Web site. The more users that visit, the more advertising dollars Yahoo! can attract. Likewise, the longer people stay on the site, the more valuable the advertising space is, because consumers who stick around for a while are more likely to spend more time noticing the advertising.

Heavy traffic also helps an area of revenue that is expected to be increasingly important in the future: e-commerce. Yahoo! enters partnerships with on-line vendors. The vendors get links on the Yahoo! site, so consumers can easily find and purchase their products. Yahoo! in exchange gets a share of their sales dollars. A greater number of site visitors should translate into more buyers generating commissions for Yahoo!. And because a customer who buys is more valuable than a Web visitor who merely glances at an ad, companies pay more for this service. For example, Yahoo! might get 2 cents whenever someone clicks on a link that causes a banner advertisement to pop up and 30 cents whenever someone fills out a loan application.

The number of Web users and on-line advertising dollars are both growing at a breathtaking rate (the 1998 numbers were double those of 1997, for example.). With this trend in its favor, Yahoo! could sit back and wait for the earnings to flow in. However, that would ignore the competitive threat of other software leaders, such as America Online and Microsoft, which are redefining their own roles to encompass more and more of what Yahoo! does. If Yahoo! is to succeed in its strategy of giving consumers everything they want, it must be an expert in knowing what they want.

Consequently, Yahoo! is a gatherer as well as a provider of information. One way it gathers customer information is by collecting hundreds of billions of bytes of data every day about how its site is used. It tracks which sites customers visit, as well as the paths they follow to get to those sites. The company uses the data to develop offerings in areas in which users have shown the most interest. The information also helps the company identify which ads and business links get the best response, helping the company target its efforts to sell advertising and set up e-commerce deals. For example, SmarterKids.com, a retailer of educational products, found that a few sites, including Yahoo!, attracted the most response. Therefore, the company directed more of its advertising dollars to those Web sites.

Usage numbers are much more useful if the company knows something about the consumers themselves. To gather such data, as well as to encourage people to linger, Yahoo! encourages users to personalize their Yahoo! page. Users can, for instance, set up the site so that it automatically provides news from particular sources and about particular areas of interest, as well as quotes on the stocks in their portfolio. They can also sign up for a club in which people who share an interest can schedule on-line chats, share ideas, and post links to sites that might interest other club members. They can even ask Yahoo! to send updated stock quotes or other data to their pagers. In its most recent annual report, Yahoo! reported that it has 50 million users worldwide. Of these, 35 million had registered for services, and their number continues to grow rapidly. Upon registering, each user provides information for Yahoo!'s preferences database, making it one of the Web's largest.

In addition, Yahoo! subscribes to information services such as Nielsen/NetRatings. This service provides basic measurements, such as rankings of Web sites by reach (the percent visiting a site relative to the total number of Internet users who logged on to the Internet at least once during the survey period). Nielsen/NetRatings also provides more detailed site statistics, including audience exposure to advertising, response to advertising, and audience demographics. Data in these reports let Yahoo! track which pages in its site are most popular, which sites its visitors come from, and which sites they head for when they leave Yahoo!'s site. The Nielsen/NetRatings data come from a panel of consumers who gave information about themselves when they agreed to participate in the study, so Yahoo! can learn demographics of its visitors.

Other marketing research firms provide information related to aspects of Yahoo!'s strategy. Generating heavy traffic at the Web site requires high recognition of the Yahoo! name, so the company uses brand research. IntelliQuest, a research firm that specializes in brand recognition, has studied unaided recall of the Yahoo! name. Recent results placed brand awareness at 18 percent, triple the awareness of three years earlier—not just a step, but a leap, in the right direction.

Yahoo!'s strategy of giving customers what they want continues to attract computer users and advertisers. In recent years, revenues have tripled annually, as advertisers make more and longer-term purchases. A recent Nielsen/NetRatings report of the top 25 Web sites placed Yahoo! number two in terms of reach and first in terms of time spent at the site. Good reason for the company's owners to shout "Yahoo!"

Sources: Yahoo!, Annual Report, 1998 (downloaded from Yahoo! Web site, www.yahoo.com, August 18, 1999); Jane Hodges, "5 Winning and Keeping Web Surfers: Yahoo," Fortune (May 24, 1999), pp. 121–122; Randall E. Stross, "How Yahoo! Won the Search Wars," Fortune (March 2, 1998, downloaded from the Northern Light Internet site, www.northernlight.com, August 18, 1999); Heather Green, "The Information Gold Mine," Business Week (July 26, 1999, downloaded from America Online, August 3, 1999); Jeffrey M. O'Brien, "Behind the Yahoo!" Adweek (June 28, 1999), pp. 16–18+; UPI, "AOL and Yahoo Tops on Net," news wire (April 22, 1999, downloaded from Northern Light Internet site, www.northernlight.com, August 18, 1999); Nielsen/NetRatings Web site, www.nielsen-netratings.com (downloaded August 18, 1999).

Chapter 1

ROLE OF MARKETING RESEARCH

Upon Completing This Chapter, You Should Be Able to

1. Define marketing research.

2. Cite the two factors that are most responsible for how the research function is organized in any given firm.

3. List some of the skills that are important for careers in marketing research.

Case in Marketing Research

Sarah, Erik, and Kelly, like other students across the country, were in cyberspace on a recent afternoon. Sarah was researching her term paper on Apple Computer Company, and she started with a visit to the World Wide Web.

She cruised over to Mercury Center, the Web site for the *San Jose Mercury News,* to see what Apple had been up to lately. She had subscribed to the site's membership program, called Passport, by giving her name, address, and credit card information. She also selected comic strips to receive: "Bizarro," "Sherman's Lagoon," "Boondocks," and "Garfield."

After reading the day's comics, Sarah got to work. While she was checking out the site's NewsLibrary Archives, the *Mercury News* gathered more information. It saved data on what articles she ordered, then charged her credit card for each.

Erik prepared to start his statistics homework. First, however, he made a detour to Amazon.com to order John Grisham's novel *The Testament.* He typed in the title at the Web site. The relevant Web page came up, displaying facts about the book, along with the advice that customers who had ordered *The Testament* had also ordered *Rainbow Six* by Tom Clancy and *No Safe Place* by Richard North Patterson.

Erik was a frequent shopper at Amazon.com, partly because of information he had provided to the company. He asked to receive Special Occasion Reminders for Mother's Day, Father's Day, and his girlfriend's birthday. He'd entered information about their age, sex, and interests so that Amazon.com could recommend gifts. In addition, he had asked the company to send him reviews, articles, and recommendations related to several book topics: computer games, home audio, and mysteries and thrillers.

Kelly logged on to the Internet and smiled when the familiar voice crowed, "You've got mail!" She clicked on the mailbox icon and saw a list of three messages, including one titled "Survey Opportunity! Enter to Win $500!" Enticed by the chance to win prizes, Kelly had given a research firm permission to e-mail occasional marketing research questionnaires.

Today's survey consisted of 60 questions about automobiles. Kelly answered questions about the kind of car she owned, her satisfaction with it, her plans to buy another car in the future, and her opinions about automobiles and their manufacturers. At the end of the survey, Kelly provided facts about herself, including her household size, income, and attitudes toward driving. Ten minutes later, she finished the survey and clicked on a message from her friend at a campus in Florida.

Discussion Issues

1. What types of marketing activities were present in Sarah, Erik, and Kelly's experiences?

2. What kinds of information did they provide?

3. How might marketers use this information?

Marketing research is a much broader activity than most people realize. There is much more to it than simply asking ultimate consumers what they think or feel about some product or ad. To be sure, consumer surveys and focus groups are very important marketing research tools. However, in an effort to learn about the consumer and compete effectively in the marketplace, an organization may need to employ other methods. Consider the following examples:

Example When Julia Knight launched Growing Healthy, Inc., to sell a line of frozen baby food, she was an experienced marketing executive but not a parent. She gained a mom's perspective by personally conducting research into how parents shop. Knight cruised the aisles of supermarkets, often accompanied by friends and their children. She observed children complaining about the cold in the frozen-food aisle and saw parents rush them through. Knight therefore developed a marketing strategy that included convincing supermarket managers to put cutaway freezers in the warmer environs of the baby food section. Her attention to buying habits helped Knight build Growing Healthy into a $2.8 million firm.[1]

Example In order to get a better fix on how households use their home personal computers, NPD Group monitored the habits of 10,076 households in its panel of computer users. Much to the dismay of PC manufacturers, the results indicated that the machines sat idle 54 percent of the time they were switched on, not counting the short pauses between keystrokes. Moreover, much of the "productive time" was spent in more trivial activities such as organizing files, selecting "wallpaper," and playing games.[2]

Example In the United Kingdom, Levi's coupled industry and population data with its own consumer studies to identify a need for change in its marketing strategy. The company observed that the market for denim and Levi's share of that market peaked in 1996 and then declined. In addition, population trends indicated that the size of the company's core age group of 18- to 25-year-olds has been declining in Europe. Levi's research into attitudes revealed a possible cause of the decline in market share: Young adults in the U.K. want more innovation from the company. Levi's responded by setting up groups to develop new products for each of three markets, called "urban opinion formers," "extreme sports," and "regular girls and guys."[3]

Example Dorothy Lane Market in Dayton, Ohio, recently initiated a frequent-shopper program. Customers sign up for the discount program by providing some personal information, such as name and address, in exchange for a card, which the company uses to track buying habits. Price discounts go only to club members, and the company's direct mail promotions are customized to reflect the individual's shopping habits. Not only are the store's customers happier in that they don't have to clip coupons to save, Dorothy Lane is more profitable. Moreover, the card has also helped to cut inventory and speed distribution. Because the card quickly reveals which products are selling and how fast, the stores are more likely to get just what they need and when they need it from its suppliers.[4]

As the preceding examples demonstrate, the scope of marketing research activities goes beyond simply asking individual consumers for their likes and dislikes. Observation, either personal observation (as was done by Julia Knight) or electronic observation (à la NPD Group and Dorothy Lane Markets), is also a legitimate marketing research activity. At the same time, some very productive research involves no more than the study of readily available data (e.g., population trends), and some involves the systematic testing of an ad, a new package, or a product. The fundamental point is that marketing research is a pervasive activity that can take *many forms,* because its basic purpose is to help marketing managers make better decisions in any of their areas of responsibility.

Role of Marketing Research

Anyone planning a career in business and in many other fields as well should understand what marketing research can do. Simply put, effective decision making depends on the quality of the information input, and marketing research plays an essential role in providing accurate and useful information. For example, salespeople use the results of marketing research studies to better sell their products. Land planners use marketing research to better understand the desires of their constituents. Politicians use marketing research to plan campaign strategies. Even clergy use marketing research to determine when to hold services! The accompanying advertisement shows how Gerber used market research to develop a new line of products.

You may recall from your introductory course in marketing that the principal task of marketing is to create value for customers, where customer value is the difference between customer perceptions of the benefits they receive from purchasing and using products and services, and their perceptions of the costs they incur to exchange for them.

Gerber used marketing research to develop its twenty new varieties of "Tender Harvest™" line of baby foods and juices. In this ad directed to the supermarket industry, the company states that "extensive consumer testing" shows that the Tender Harvest line "made with certified organic fruits, vegetables, whole grains and no sugar or salt added" is just the "unique product your customers want. . . ."

Customers who are willing and able to make exchanges will do so when (1) the benefits of exchanges exceed the costs of exchanges and (2) the products or services offer superior value compared with alternatives.[5]

In their attempts to create customer value, marketing managers generally focus their efforts on the elements of the marketing mix or the four Ps—namely, the *p*roduct or service, its *p*rice, its *p*lacement or the channels in which it is distributed, and its *p*romotion or communications mix.

The marketing manager's essential task is to develop a marketing strategy which involves combining the marketing mix elements in such a way that they complement each other and positively influence customers' value perceptions and behaviors. This task would be much simpler if all the elements that affect customers' perceptions of value were under the manager's control and if customer reaction to any contemplated change could be predicted. Usually, however, a number of factors affecting the success of the marketing effort, including economic, political and legal, social, natural, technological, and competitive environments, are beyond the marketing manager's control, and the behavior of individual customers is largely unpredictable.

Figure 1.1 summarizes the task of marketing management. Customers are the target because they are the focus of the firm's activities. Their satisfaction is achieved through simultaneous adjustments in the elements of the marketing mix, but the results of these adjustments are uncertain because the marketing task takes place within an uncontrollable environment (see Figure 1.2). Consequently, as director of the firm's marketing activities, the marketing manager has an urgent need for information—and marketing research is traditionally responsible for providing it. Marketing research is the firm's formal communication link with the environment. It is the means by which the firm generates, transmits, and interprets information from the environment about or relating to the success of the firm's marketing plans.

The communication link that marketing research serves is becoming increasingly critical and difficult as the world moves to a global economy. What works in one environment does not necessarily work in another (see Research Window 1.1).

FIGURE 1.1   The Task of Marketing Management

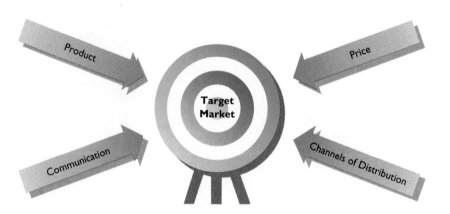

Source: Gilbert A. Churchill, Jr., and J. Paul Peter, *Marketing: Creating Value for Customers,* 2nd ed. (Burr Ridge, Ill.: Irwin/McGraw Hill, 1998), p. 22.

FIGURE 1.2   **The Environments Affecting Marketing**

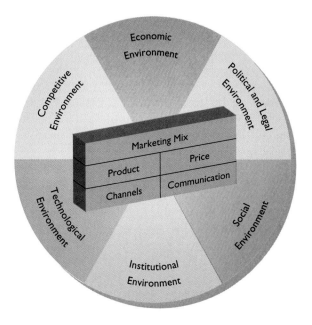

Source: Gilbert A. Churchill, Jr., and J. Paul Peter, *Marketing: Creating Value for Customers,* 2nd ed. (Burr Ridge, Ill.: Irwin/McGraw Hill, 1998), p. 29.

Marketing research
The function that links the consumer to the marketer through information—information used to identify and define marketing problems; generate, define, and evaluate marketing actions; monitor marketing performance; and improve understanding of marketing as a process.

The definition of **marketing research** emphasizes its information-linkage role.

Marketing research is the function which links the consumer, customer, and public to the marketer through information—information used to identify and define marketing opportunities and problems; generate, refine, and evaluate marketing actions; monitor marketing performance; and improve our understanding of marketing as a process.[6]

Note that this definition indicates that marketing research provides information to the organization for use in at least four areas: (1) the generation of ideas for marketing action, including the identification of marketing problems and opportunities, (2) the evaluation of marketing actions, (3) the comparison of performance versus objectives, and (4) the development of general understanding of marketing phenomena and processes. Further, marketing research is involved with all phases of the information-management process, including (1) the specification of what information is needed, (2) the collection and analysis of the information, and (3) the interpretation of that information with respect to the objectives that motivated the study in the first place.

A periodic survey (Exhibit 1.1) conducted by the American Marketing Association details more specifically how many organizations use marketing research.[7] Much research, for example, is done to measure consumer wants and needs. Other research assesses the impact of previous adjustments in the marketing mix or gauges the potential impact of new changes. Some research deals directly with the environment, such as studies of legal constraints on advertising and promotion and studies of social values, business policy, and business trends.

Another way of looking at the function of marketing research is to consider how management uses it. Some marketing research is used for planning, some for problem solving,

Example An American manufacturer of cornflakes tried to introduce its product in Japan but failed miserably. Since the Japanese were not interested in the general concept of breakfast cereals, how could the manufacturer expect them to purchase cornflakes?

Example After learning that ketchup was not available in Japan, a U.S. company is reported to have shipped the Japanese a large quantity of its popular brand-name ketchup. Unfortunately, the firm did not first determine why ketchup was not already marketed in Japan. The large, affluent Japanese market was so tempting that the company feared any delay would permit its competition to spot the "opportunity" and capture the market. A marketing research study would have revealed the reason behind the lack of availability of ketchup: Soy sauce is the preferred condiment in Japan.

Example Unilever was forced to withdraw temporarily from one of its foreign markets when it learned the hard way that the French were not interested in frozen foods.

Example CPC International met some resistance when it first tried to sell its Knorr soups in the Untied States. The company had test-marketed the product by serving passersby a small portion of its already prepared warm soup. After the taste test, the individuals were questioned about buying the product. The research revealed U.S. interest, but sales were very low once the packages were placed on grocery store shelves. Further investigation uncovered that the market tests had not taken into account the American tendency to avoid dry soups. During the testing, those individuals interviewed were unaware that they were tasting a dried soup. Finding the taste quite acceptable, the interviewees indicated they would be willing to buy the product. Had they known that the soup was sold in a dry form and that the preparation required 15 to 20 minutes of occasional stirring, they would have lost interest in the product. In this case, the soup's method of preparation was extremely important to the consumer, and the company's failure to test for this unique product difference resulted in an unpredicted sluggish market.

Example Warner encountered difficulties when it tried to sell cinnamon-flavored Freshen-Up gum in Chile. Because the gum's taste was unacceptable there, the product fared poorly in the marketplace. Coca-Cola also had little success in marketing a product in Chile. When the company attempted to introduce a new grape-flavored drink, it soon discovered that the Chileans were not interested. Apparently, the Chileans prefer wine as their grape drink.

Example Chase and Sanborn met resistance when it tried to introduce its instant coffee in France. In the French home, the consumption of coffee plays a more significant role than in the English home. Since the preparation of "real" coffee is a ritual in the life of the French consumer, he or she will generally reject instant coffee because of its impromptu characteristics.

Example Dutch building company Fomabo agreed to form a strategic alliance with two Malaysian companies to build prefabricated housing in Malaysia. Following numerous bureaucratic delays in obtaining the proper licenses from regional authorities, the green light was finally given and the first group of houses was built. However, sales soon proved discouraging and subsequently the reasons for this were uncovered. It turned out that the walls of the Fomabo houses were made of reinforced concrete, just like those in the Netherlands. Traditional Malaysian houses, however, were made of wood, a feature that permitted Malaysians to hang pictures and other objects on their walls. Naturally, it was difficult to hammer nails into the concrete walls of the new ones. Not only did this require home buyers to obtain boring tools in order to decorate their homes, but the general "feeling" of the new homes was perceived as less comfortable than that of traditional housing.

Sources: David A. Ricks, *Blunders in International Business* (Cambridge, Mass.: Blackwell Publishers, 1993), pp. 133–136; Tevfik Dalgic and Ruud Heijblom, "Educator Insights: International Marketing Blunders Revisited—Some Lessons for Managers," *Journal of International Marketing* 4 (No. 1, 1996), pp. 81–91.

and some for control. When used for planning, it deals largely with determining which marketing opportunities are viable and which are not promising for the firm. Also, when viable opportunities are uncovered, marketing research provides estimates of their size and scope, so that marketing management can better assess the resources needed to develop them. Problem-solving marketing research focuses on the short- or long-term

EXHIBIT 1.1 Research Activities of 435 Companies

	PERCENTAGE DOING		PERCENTAGE DOING

A. Business/Economic and Corporate Research

1. Industry/market characteristics and trends	92%
2. Acquisition/diversification studies	50
3. Market share analyses	85
4. Internal employee studies (morale, communications, etc.)	72

B. Pricing

1. Cost analysis	57%
2. Profit analysis	55
3. Price elasticity	56
4. Demand analysis:	
a. market potential	78
b. sales potential	75
c. sales forecasts	71
5. Competitive pricing analyses	71

C. Product

1. Concept development and testing	78%
2. Brand name generation and testing	55
3. Test market	55
4. Product testing of existing products	63
5. Packaging design studies	48
6. Competitive product studies	54

D. Distribution

1. Plant/warehouse location studies	25%
2. Channel performance studies	39
3. Channel coverage studies	31
4. Export and international studies	32

E. Promotion

1. Motivation research	56%
2. Media research	70
3. Copy research	68
4. Advertising effectiveness testing	
a. prior to marketplace airing	67
b. during marketplace airing	66
5. Competitive advertising studies	43
6. Public image studies	65
7. Sales force compensation studies	34
8. Sales force quota studies	28
9. Sales force territory structure	32
10. Studies of premiums, coupons, deals, etc.	47

F. Buying Behavior

1. Brand preference	78%
2. Brand attitudes	76
3. Product satisfaction	87
4. Purchase behavior	80
5. Purchase intentions	79
6. Brand awareness	80
7. Segmentation studies	84

Source: Thomas C. Kinnear and Ann R. Root, *1994 Survey of Marketing Research, 1995*, p. 49. Reprinted with permission from American Marketing Association, Chicago, Ill. 60606.

decisions that the firm must make with respect to the elements of the marketing mix. Control-oriented marketing research helps management to isolate trouble spots and to keep abreast of current operations. The kinds of questions marketing research can address with regard to planning, problem solving, and control decisions are listed in Exhibit 1.2. The relationship between each of these questions and a marketing manager's area of responsibility is easy to see.

Firms operating in the international arena often use marketing research to get a perspective on what it is like to do business in specific countries. Some of the questions they might use marketing research to investigate are listed in Exhibit 1.3.

Marketing research helped McDonald's adjust its positioning as attitudes toward the company changed in the United Kingdom. When the company first crossed the Atlantic in the mid-1970s, customers were drawn in by its American origins and the novelty of fast food. Reflecting this appeal, McDonald's first U.K. ad slogan announced, "There's a difference at McDonald's you'll enjoy."

The fast-food giant used consumer research to keep tabs on opinions as the market matured. Fifteen years after McDonald's began serving the British market, consumers were

EXHIBIT 1.2   Kinds of Questions Marketing Research Can Help Answer

I. Planning
  A. What kinds of people buy our products? Where do they live? How much do they earn? How many of them are there?
  B. Are the markets for our products increasing or decreasing? Are there promising markets that we have not yet reached?
  C. Are the channels of distribution for our products changing? Are new types of marketing institutions likely to evolve?

II. Problem Solving
  A. Product
    1. Which of various product designs is likely to be the most successful?
    2. What kind of packaging should we use?
  B. Price
    1. What price should be charge for our products?
    2. As production costs decline, should we lower our prices or try to develop higher-quality products?
  C. Place
    1. Where, and by whom, should our products be sold?
    2. What kinds of incentives should we offer the trade to push our products?
  D. Promotion
    1. How much should we spend on promotion? How should it be allocated to products and to geographic areas?
    2. What combination of media—newspapers, radio, television, magazines, the Internet—should we use?

III. Control
  A. What is our market share overall? In each geographic area? By each customer type?
  B. Are customers satisfied with our products? How is our record for service? Are there many returns?
  C. How does the public perceive our company? What is our reputation with the trade?

- What is the nature of competition in the foreign market?

- Who are the major direct and indirect competitors?

- What are the major characteristics of the competition?

- What are the firm's competitive strengths and weaknesses in product quality, product lines, warranties, services, brands, packaging, distribution, sales force, advertising, prices, experience, technology, capital and human resources, and market share?

- What attitudes do different governments (domestic and foreign) have toward foreign trade?

- Are there any foreign trade incentives and barriers?

- Is there any prejudice against imports or exports?

- What are different governments doing specifically do encourage or discourage international trade?

- What specific requirements—for example, import or export licenses—have to be met to conduct international trade?

- How difficult are certain government regulations for the firm?

- How well developed are the foreign mass communication media?

- Are the print and electronics media abroad efficient and effective?

- Are there adequate transportation and storage or warehouse facilities in the foreign market?

- Does the foreign market offer efficient channels of distribution for the firm's products?

- What are the characteristics of the existing domestic and foreign distributors?

- How effectively can the distributors perform specific marketing functions?

- What is the state of retailing institutions?

Source: Vinay Kothari, "Researching for Export Marketing," in Michael Czinkota, ed., *Export Promotion: The Public and Private Sector Interaction* (New York: Praeger Publishers, 1983), pp. 169–172. Reprinted with permission of Greenwood Publishing Group, Inc., Westport, Conn., copyright © 1983. See also Philip R. Cateora, *International Marketing*, 8th ed. (Burr Ridge, Ill.: McGraw/Irwin, 1993), pp. 339–370; Johnny K. Johansson, *Global Marketing: Foreign Entry, Local Marketing, and Global Management* (Burr Ridge, Ill.: McGraw/Irwin, 1997), pp. 272–304 for discussion of the insights to be gained from and the problems involved in researching foreign markets.

describing McDonald's as inflexible and arrogant—a negative take on the efficiency consumers associated with the company's American heritage. McDonald's therefore adjusted its ad campaigns to use softer messages depicting McDonald's at the center of British family life. The company's ability to detect and adapt to changing customer attitudes helps it maintain an impressive 75 percent share of the U.K. hamburger market.[8]

Who Does Marketing Research?

Marketing research, as a sizable business activity, owes its existence to this country's shift from a production-oriented to a consumption-oriented economy at the end of World War II. However, some marketing research was conducted before the war, and the origins of formal marketing research predate the war by a good number of years.

> More by accident than foresight, N. W. Ayer & Son applied marketing research to marketing and advertising problems. In 1879, in attempting to fit a proposed advertising schedule to the needs of the Nichols-Shepard Company, manufacturers of agricultural machinery, the agency wired state officials and publishers throughout the country requesting information on expected grain production. As a result, the agency was able to construct a crude but formal market survey by states and counties. This attempt to construct a market survey is probably the first real instance of marketing research in the United States.[9]

There were even formal marketing research departments and marketing research firms before World War II.[10] However, marketing research really began to grow when firms found they could no loner sell all they could produce, but rather had to gauge market needs and produce accordingly. Marketing research was called upon to estimate these needs. As consumer discretion became more important, many firms shifted their orientation to accommodate the new business climate. Marketing began to assume a more dominant role and production a less important one. The marketing concept emerged, and

Peter Zollo is president of Teenage Research Unlimited. Since 1982, Zollo's firm has been interviewing teens about what's hot and what's not. Zollo assists the marketing departments in companies such as MTV, Nike, and Procter & Gamble by selling insights on the teen mind. He claims that teenagers are not a homogenous group but are highly stratified into groups—the "edge" teens, who set trends but have no interest in anything mainstream; the "influencers," who edit the trends of the edgy teens; and the "conformers" or the mainstream teens, the biggest group, who follow the trends set by the influencers.

Source: Tribune photo by Jim Robinson.

along with it a reorganization of the marketing effort. Many marketing research departments were born in these reorganizations. The growth of these departments was stimulated by a number of factors, including past successes, increased management sophistication, and the data revolution created by the computer. The success of firms with marketing research departments caused still other firms to establish departments.

Although the growth in the number of new marketing research departments has slowed recently, the firm that does not have a formal department, or at least a person assigned specifically to the marketing research activity, is now the exception rather than the rule (see Figure 1.3). Marketing research departments are very prevalent among industrial and consumer manufacturing companies, but they also exist in other types of companies. Publishers and broadcasters, for example, do a good deal of research. They attempt to measure the size of the market reached by their message and construct a demographic profile of this audience. These data are then used to sell advertising space or time. Also, financial institutions such as banks and brokerage houses do research involving forecasting, measurement of market potentials, determination of market characteristics, market share analyses, sales analyses, location analyses, and product-mix studies.

Much of the research conducted by advertising agencies deals directly with creating the advertisement itself. This may involve testing alternative approaches to the wording or art used in the ad or investigating the effectiveness of various celebrity spokespersons. However, many agencies also do marketing research for their clients to determine the market potential of a proposed new product or the client's market share.

FIGURE 1.3   **Organization for Marketing Research**

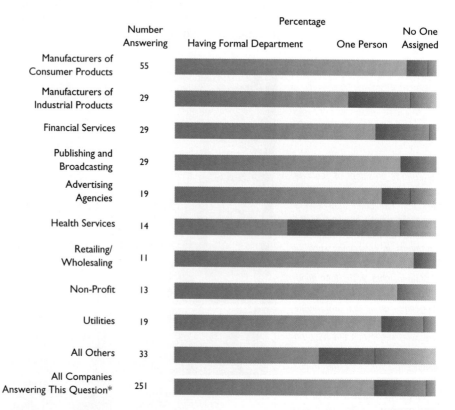

*Excludes marketing research and consulting firms.

Source: Thomas C. Kinnear and Ann R. Root, 1994 *Survey of Marketing Research*, p. 7. Reprinted with permission from American Marketing Association, Chicago, Ill. 60606.

The enterprises included in the "All Others" category shown in Figure 1.3 include public utilities, transportation companies, and trade associations, among others. Public utilities and transportation companies often provide their customers with useful marketing information, particularly statistics dealing with area growth and potential. Trade associations often collect and disseminate operating data gathered from members.

The entire spectrum of marketing research activity also includes specialized marketing research and consulting firms, government agencies, and universities. Although most specialized marketing research firms are small, a few are sizable enterprises. Research Window 1.2, for example, shows the revenues of the 10 largest marketing research firms in the world and the proportion of their revenues generated outside their home countries. Some firms provide syndicated research; they collect certain information on a regular basis, which they then sell to interested clients. The syndicated services include such operations as ACNielsen, which provides product-movement data for grocery stores and drugstores, and the NPD, which operates a consumer panel. Such services are distinguished by the fact that their research is not custom designed except in the limited sense that the firm will perform special analyses for a client from the data it regularly collects. Other firms, though, specialize in custom-designed research. Some of these provide only a field service; they collect data and return the data-collection instruments directly to the research sponsor. Some are limited-service firms, which not only collect the data but also analyze them for the client. And some are full-service research suppliers, which help the client in the design of the research as well as in collecting and analyzing data.

Government agencies provide much marketing information in the form of published statistics. Indeed, the federal government is the largest producer of marketing facts through its various censuses and other publications.

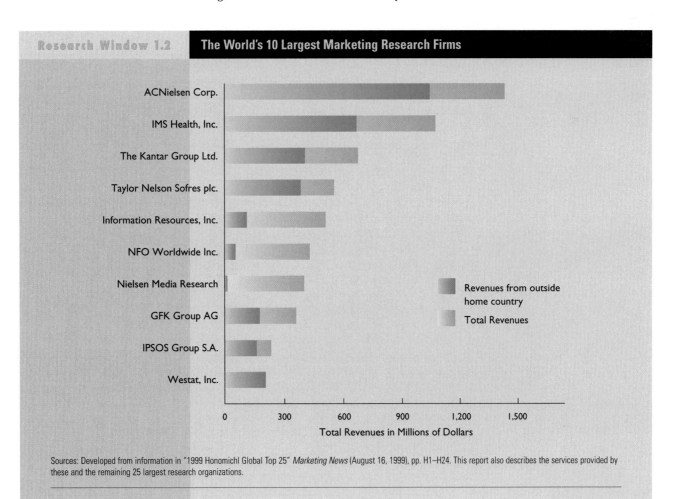

Research Window 1.2 — **The World's 10 Largest Marketing Research Firms**

Sources: Developed from information in "1999 Honomichl Global Top 25" *Marketing News* (August 16, 1999), pp. H1–H24. This report also describes the services provided by these and the remaining 25 largest research organizations.

Much university-sponsored research of interest to marketers is produced by the marketing faculty or by the bureaus of business research found in many schools of business. Faculty research is often reported in marketing journals, while research bureaus often publish monographs on various topics of interest.

Organization of Marketing Research

The organizational form of marketing research depends largely on the size and organizational structure of the individual company. In small firms, where one person often handles all the organization's research needs, there are few organizational questions other than determining to whom the research director will report. Most often, this will be the sales or marketing manager, although some marketing research managers report directly to the president or the executive vice president. Although larger research units can take a variety of organizational forms, three types are common.

1. Organization by areas of application, such as by product line, by brand, by market segment, or by geographic area.

2. Organization by marketing function performed, such as field sales analysis, advertising research, or product planning.

3. Organization by research technique or approach, such as sales analysis, mathematical and/or statistical analysis, field interviewing, or questionnaire design.

Many firms with very large marketing research departments combine two or more of these organizational structures.

Whether the firm is centralized or decentralized also affects the organization of the marketing research function. With decentralized companies—those in which authority and decision making are spread among a fairly large number of people—each division or operating unit might have its own marketing research department, or a single department in central headquarters might serve all operating divisions, or research departments might exist at both levels. The primary advantages of a corporate-level location are greater coordination and control of corporate research activity, economy, increased capability from an information system perspective, and greater usefulness to corporate management in planning. The primary advantage of a division or group-level location is that it allows research personnel to acquire valuable knowledge about divisional markets, products, practices, and problems. Although shifting between the corporate and divisional structures occurs quite frequently, the recent emphasis is on a mixed arrangement, in an attempt to secure the advantages of each.

For example, Kodak has a combination centralized/decentralized marketing research function. The research people in the divisions work directly with the managers of those business units. The centralized group is responsible for staying abreast of industry trends and changing technology, since changes here could affect a number of business units. Researchers assigned to corporate marketing research are also responsible for competitive analysis in order to ensure the most objective view. Finally, they serve as a quality-control center for the decentralized research activity, so division-initiated projects are passed before this group for possible changes in method. One benefit of this review is that it develops institutional memory in terms of better ways to approach specific tasks.

The Japanese are more likely to view research as a "line" function performed by all involved in the decision process rather than as a "staff" function performed by professional marketing researchers. Those involved in the decision team might play a role in gathering and interpreting information. For example, in developing its "Pro Mavica" professional still-video system, which, unlike conventional 35mm still cameras, records images on a two-inch-square floppy disk, Sony did extensive marketing research. This research involved a mail survey, personal and telephone interviews, and on-site tests to elicit user response to the product during its development. A unique aspect was that the Pro Mavica task force included both engineers and sales/marketing representatives from Sony's medical systems and broadcast units. In addition to working with their marketing peers, Sony's engineers gained insights from talking with prospects; they then incorporated user comments into product modifications.[11]

The organization of the marketing research function thus depends on the relative importance of the function within the firm and on the scale and complexity of the research activities to be undertaken. Moreover, the organizational form is subject to changes from time to time, often arising from changes within the firm. As the firm's size and market position change, the emphasis and organization of the marketing research function must also change, so that it is continually tailored to suit the firm's information needs.

One important change that has been occurring in marketing research in recent years is the transition from a specific-problem perspective to a total-marketing-intelligence perspective. This perspective is usually called a marketing information system (MIS) or decision support system (DSS). The emphasis in these systems is on diagnosing the information needs of each of the marketing decision makers so that they have the kinds of information they need, when they need it, to make the kinds of decisions they must make. We will discuss marketing intelligence systems in the next chapter.

Job Opportunities in Marketing Research

It is hard to generalize about the kinds of tasks a marketing researcher might perform. As previously suggested, the tasks will depend upon the type, size, organizational structure, and philosophy of the firm with which the individual is employed. They will also depend upon whether the person works for a research supplier or for a consumer of research information.

The responsibilities of a marketing researcher could range from the simple tabulation of questionnaire responses to the management of a large research department. Research Window 1.3, for example, lists some common job titles and the functions typically performed by occupants of these positions. Figure 1.4 illustrates what they are likely to be paid and how that compares with salaries of those in similar positions in 1988.

As these job descriptions reveal, there are opportunities in marketing research for people with a variety of skills. There is room for technical specialists, such as statisticians, as well as for research generalists, whose skills are relevant to managing the people and resources needed for a research project rather than the mathematical detail any study may involve. The skills required to perform each job satisfactorily will, of course, vary.

In consumer-goods companies, the typical entry-level position is research analyst, usually for a specific brand. While learning the characteristics and details of the industry, the analyst will receive on-the-job training from a research manager. The usual career path for an analyst is to advance to senior analyst, then research supervisor, and on to research manager for a specific brand. At that time the researcher's responsibilities often broaden to include a group of brands.

Among research suppliers, the typical entry-level position is research trainee, a position in which the person will be exposed to the types of studies in which the supplier specializes and to the procedures required for completing them. Quite often, trainees will spend some time actually conducting interviews, coding completed data-collection forms, or possibly even assisting with the analysis. The goal is to expose trainees to the processes the firm follows so that when they become account representatives, they will be familiar enough with the firm's capabilities to respond intelligently to clients' needs for research information.

The requirements for entering the marketing research field include human-relation, communication, conceptual, and analytical skills. Marketing researchers need to be able to interact effectively with others, for they rarely, if ever, work in isolation. They need to be good communicators, both orally and with the written word. They need to understand

Research Window 1.3 **Marketing Research Job Titles and Responsibilities**

1. **Research Director/Vice President of Marketing Research:** This is the senior position in research. The director is responsible for the entire research program of his company. Accepts assignments from superiors, from clients, or may, on own initiative, develop and propose research undertakings to company executives. Employs personnel and executes general supervision of research department. Presents research findings to clients or to company executives.

2. **Assistant Director of Research:** This position usually represents a defined "second in command," a senior staff member having responsibilities above those of other staff members.

3. **Statistician/Data Processing Specialist:** Duties are usually those of an expert consultant on theory and applications of statistical technique to specific research problems. Usually responsible for experimental design and data processing.

4. **Senior Analyst:** Usually found in larger research departments. Participates with superior in initial planning of research projects, and directs execution of projects assigned. Operates with minimum supervision. Prepares or works with analysts in preparing questionnaires. Selects research techniques, makes analyses, and writes final report. Budgetary control over projects and primary responsibility for meeting time schedules rests with the senior analyst.

5. **Analyst:** The analyst usually handles the bulk of the work required for execution of research projects. Often works under senior analyst's supervision. The analyst assists in questionnaire preparation, pretests them, and makes preliminary analyses of results. Most of the library research or work with company data is handled by the analyst.

6. **Junior Analyst:** Working under rather close supervision, junior analysts handle routine assignments. Editing and coding of questionnaires, statistical calculations above the clerical level, and simpler forms of library research are among their duties. A large portion of the junior analyst's time is spent on tasks assigned by superiors.

7. **Librarian:** The librarian builds and maintains a library of reference sources adequate to the needs of the research department.

8. **Clerical Supervisor:** In larger departments, the central handling and processing of statistical data are the responsibilities of one or more clerical supervisors. Duties include work scheduling and responsibility for accuracy.

9. **Field Work Director:** Usually only larger departments have a field work director, who hires, trains, and supervises field interviewers.

10. **Full-time Interviewer:** The interviewer conducts personal interviews and works under direct supervision of the field work director. Few companies employ full-time interviewers.

11. **Tabulating and Clerical Help:** The routine, day-to-day work of the department is performed by these individuals.

Source: Thomas C. Kinnear and Ann R. Root, *1994 Survey of Marketing Research*, 1995, p. 93. Reprinted with permission from American Marketing Association, Chicago, Ill. 60606.

business in general and marketing processes in particular. When dealing with brand, advertising, sales, or other types of managers, they need to have some understanding of the issues with which these managers contend and the types of mental models the managers use to make sense of situations. Marketing researchers also should have basic numerical and statistical skills, or at least they should have the capacity to develop those skills. They must be comfortable with numbers and with the techniques of marketing research. Their growth as professionals and their advancement within their organization will depend upon their use of these skills and their acquiring other technical, management, and financial skills.

FIGURE 1.4   Mean Compensation for All Marketing Research Positions

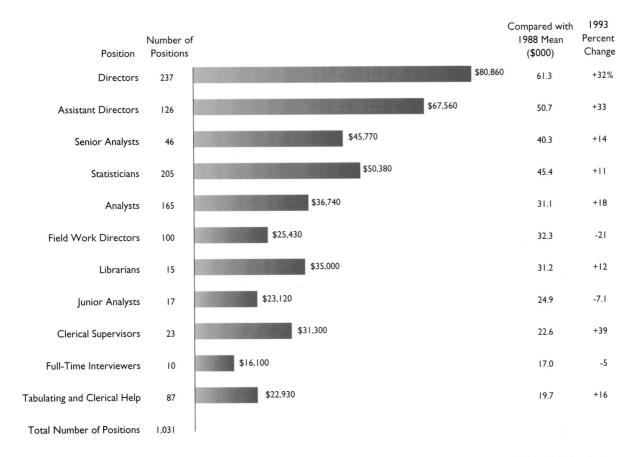

Position	Number of Positions		Compared with 1988 Mean ($000)	1993 Percent Change
Directors	237	$80,860	61.3	+32%
Assistant Directors	126	$67,560	50.7	+33
Senior Analysts	46	$45,770	40.3	+14
Statisticians	205	$50,380	45.4	+11
Analysts	165	$36,740	31.1	+18
Field Work Directors	100	$25,430	32.3	-21
Librarians	15	$35,000	31.2	+12
Junior Analysts	17	$23,120	24.9	-7.1
Clerical Supervisors	23	$31,300	22.6	+39
Full-Time Interviewers	10	$16,100	17.0	-5
Tabulating and Clerical Help	87	$22,930	19.7	+16
Total Number of Positions	1,031			

Source: Thomas C. Kinnear and Ann R. Root, *1994 Survey of Marketing Research,* 1995, p. 77. Reprinted with permission from American Marketing Association, Chicago, Ill. 60606.

An increasingly common career path for those working in divisionalized structures is a switch from research to product or brand management. One advantage these people possess is that after working so intimately with marketing intelligence, they often know more about the customers, the industry, and the competitors than anyone in the company with the same years of experience. Note, though, that researchers desiring such a switch need more substantive knowledge about marketing phenomena and greater business acumen in general than those planning on staying in marketing research, although all researchers need a good foundation of business and marketing knowledge if they are going to succeed.

Successful marketing researchers tend to be proactive rather than reactive; that is, they tend to identify and lead the direction in which the individual studies and overall programs go rather than simply respond to the explicit requests for information given them. Successful marketing researchers realize that marketing research is conducted for one primary reason—to help make better marketing decisions. Thus, they are comfortable in the role of staff person making recommendations to others rather than having responsibility for the decisions themselves.

Back to the Case

While people like Sarah, Erik, and Kelly are using the Internet for research, e-mail, and entertainment, marketers are gathering information about them. The Internet lets marketers extend traditional forms of marketing research and innovate with new forms.

When Kelly filled out the on-line questionnaire, she was responding to an electronic version of the familiar marketing survey. On-line surveys efficiently deliver questions that a researcher also might ask in a telephone call or in person at a mall. An automobile manufacturer could use the results of the survey Kelly answered to plan marketing communications or product development.

Sarah and Erik also provided information actively, when they entered personal data in order to receive services at the Web sites they visited. Now whenever they visit those Web sites, the sites automatically collect more data, recording what they look up and what they buy.

When Sarah visited the Mercury Center, the *San Jose Mercury News* had a chance to communicate directly with a potential customer. It used this opportunity not only to promote the sale of subscriptions and archived articles but also to gather data. Sarah was lured into signing up for the Mercury Center's Passport by the invitation to receive her choice of "nearly 100 free comics." Giving information about herself—

her e-mail address, zip code, and country—seemed a small price to pay for receiving her favorite comic strips every day.

Whenever Sarah visits Mercury Center, the site can link her activities to her e-mail address and zip code. The company can use that data to tailor future communications to her at her e-mail address. It also can see which of its articles and comic strips are most requested, and by people in which zip code or country. It can determine where in the country—and in the world—most of its on-line subscribers come from. This information can help the company plan future marketing activities.

Similarly, Erik provided information about himself to Amazon.com. The on-line retailer knows something about where he lives, what books and other products he buys, what his interests are, and who besides himself he shops for. The company can use this rich collection of data to create personalized advertising messages. In fact, Erik invited advertising by requesting Special Occasion Reminders. When the company sends such a "reminder," it is targeting someone who already is interested in the message. Amazon.com can also pool data about its customers to identify buying patterns and forecast trends.

Sources: Based on Amazon.com Web site (www.amazon.com, July 13, 1999); "Mercury Center," Web site of *San Jose Mercury News* (www.mercurycenter.com, July 13, 1999); e-mail from Millward Brown Interactive (www.mbinteractive.com, July 8, 1999).

Summary

Learning Objective 1

Define marketing research.

Marketing research is the function that links the consumer to the marketer through information. The information is used to identify and define marketing problems; generate, refine, and evaluate marketing actions; monitor marketing performance; and improve understanding of marketing as a process.

Learning Objective 2

Cite the two factors that are most responsible for how the research function is organized in any given firm.

The two factors that are most significant in determining the organization of a firm's research function are the firm's size and the degree of centralization or decentralization of its operations.

Learning Objective 3

List some of the skills that are important for careers in marketing research.

Most positions in marketing research require analytical, communication, and human-relation skills. In addition, marketing researchers must be comfortable working with numbers and statistical techniques, and they must be familiar with a great variety of marketing research methods.

R e v i e w   Q u e s t i o n s

1. What is marketing management? What is marketing research's task? Is there any relation between the two tasks?

2. How is marketing research defined? What are the key elements of this definition?

3. Who does marketing research? What are the primary kinds of research done by each enterprise?

4. How would you explain the facts that production research started in the 1860s but marketing research did not develop formally until the 1910s and did not experience real growth until after World War II?

5. What factors influence the internal organization of the marketing research department and its reporting location within the company?

6. In a large research department, who would be responsible for specifying the objective of a research project? For deciding on specific procedures to be followed? For designing the questionnaire? For analyzing the results? For reporting the results to top management?

7. What are the necessary skills for employment in a junior or entry-level marketing research position? Do the skills change as one changes job levels? If so, what new skills are necessary at these higher levels?

D i s c u s s i o n   Q u e s t i o n s ,   P r o b l e m s ,   a n d   P r o j e c t s

1. Indicate whether marketing research is relevant to each of the following organizations and, if so, how each might use it.
   (a) Pepsico, Inc.
   (b) Your university
   (c) The Chase Manhattan Bank
   (d) The American Cancer Society
   (e) A small dry cleaner

2. Specify some useful sources of marketing research information for the following situation.

   Ethan Moore has worked for several years as the head chef in a restaurant specializing in ethnic cuisine. Dissatisfied with his income, he has decided to start his own business. Based on his experiences in the restaurant, he recognizes a need for a local wholesale distributor specializing in hard-to-find ethnic foodstuffs. He envisions starting a firm that will handle items commonly used in Asian and African recipes.
   With the help of a local accountant, Moore prepared a financial proposal that revealed the need for $150,000 in start-up capital for Ethan's Ethnic Foods. The proposal was presented to a local bank for review by their commercial loan committee, and Moore subsequently received the following letter from the bank:

   Mr. Moore:

   We have received and considered your request for start-up financing for your proposed business. While the basic idea seems sound, we find that your sales projections are based solely on your own experience and do not include any hard documentation concerning the market potential for the products you propose to carry. Until such information is made available for our consideration, we have no choice but to reject your loan application.

Bitten hard by the entrepreneurial bug, Moore views this rejection as a minor setback. Given his extremely limited financial resources, where and how might he obtain the needed information? (Hint: First determine what types of information would be useful.)

3. What do the following two research situations have in common?

Situation I: The Bugs-Away Company marketed successful insect repellents. The products were effective and leaders in the market. They were available in blue aerosol cans with red caps. The instructions, in addition to a warning to keep the product away from children, were clearly specified on the container. Most of the company's range of products were also produced in similar containers by competitors. The CEO was worried because of declining sales and shrinking profit margins. Another issue that perturbed her was that companies such as hers were being severely criticized by government and consumer groups for their use of aerosol cans. The CEO contacted the company's advertising agency and requested that it do the necessary research to find out what was happening.

Situation II: In early 1990 the directors of Adams University were considering an expansion of the business school due to increasing enrollments over the past 10 years. Their plans included constructing a new wing, hiring five new faculty members, and increasing the number of scholarships from 100 to 120. The funding for this ambitious project was to be provided by some private sources, internally generated funds, and the state and federal governments. A prior research study (completed in 1981), using a sophisticated forecasting methodology, indicated that student enrollment would peak in 1989. Another study, conducted in November 1983, indicated universities could expect gradual declining enrollments during the mid-1990s. The directors were concerned about the results of the later study and the talk it stimulated about budget cuts by the government. A decision was made to conduct a third and final study to determine likely student enrollment.

4. What do the following two research situations have in common?

Situation I: The sales manager of Al-Can, an aluminum can manufacturing company, was delighted with the increase in sales over the past few months. He was wondering whether the company's new cans, which would be on the market in two months, should be priced higher than the traditional products. He confidently commented to the vice president of marketing, "Nobody in the market is selling aluminum cans with screw-on tops. We can get a small portion of the market and yet make substantial profits." The product manager disagreed with this strategy. In fact, she was opposed to marketing these new cans. The cans might present problems in preserving the contents. She though to herself, "Aluminum cans are recycled, so nobody is going to keep them as containers." There was little she could do formally because these cans were the president's own idea. She strongly recommended to the vice president of marketing that the cans should be priced in line with the other products. The vice president thought a marketing research study would resolve this issue.

Situation II: A large toy manufacturer was in the process of developing a tool kit for children in the five-to-10-year age group. The tool kit included a small saw, screwdriver, hammer, chisel, and drill. This tool kit was different from the competitors', as it included an instruction manual with "101 things to do." The product manager was concerned about the safety of the kit and recommended the inclusion of a separate booklet for parents. The sales manager recommended that the tool kit be made available in a small case, as this would increase its marketability. The advertising manager recommended that a special promotional campaign be launched in order to distinguish it from the competitor's products. The vice president thought that all the recommendations were worthwhile but that the costs would increase drastically. He consulted the marketing research manager, who further recommended that a study be conducted.

5. List the key attributes that an individual occupying the following positions must possess. Why are these attributes essential?
   (a) Senior analyst
   (b) Full-time interviewer
   (c) Research director

6. Suppose that you have decided to pursue a career in the field of marketing research. In general, what types of courses should you take in order to help yourself achieve your goal? Why? What types of part-time jobs and/or volunteer work would look good on your resume? Why?

Endnotes

1. Joshua Macht, "The New Market Research," *Inc.* (July 1998), pp. 87–94.

2. Joan Indiana Rigdon, "The Letter P in Your Home PC Just Might Mean Potted Plant," *The Wall Street Journal* (February 28, 1997), p. B1.

3. Julian Lee, "Can Levi's Ever Be Cool Again?" *Marketing* (downloaded from www.marketing.haynet.com, June 3, 1999).

4. Calmetta Y. Coleman, "Finally, Supermarkets Find Ways to Increase Their Profit Margins," *The Wall Street Journal* (May 29, 1997), pp. A1, A6.

5. Gilbert A. Churchill, Jr., and J. Paul Peter, *Marketing: Creating Value for Customers*, 2nd ed. (Burr Ridge, Ill.: Irwin/McGraw-Hill, 1998), p. 15.

6. Peter Bennett, *Glossary of Marketing Terms* 2nd ed. (Chicago: American Marketing Association, 1995), p. 169.

7. Thomas C. Kinnear and Ann R. Root, *1994 Survey of Marketing Research* (Chicago: American Marketing Association, 1995). This survey is the ninth in a series begun in 1947.

8. "How McDonald's Conquered the UK," *Marketing* (downloaded from www.marketing.haynet.com, June 3, 1999).

9. Lawrence C. Lockley, "History and Development of Marketing Research," Section 1, p. 4, in Robert Ferber, ed., *Handbook of Marketing Research,* Copyright © 1974 by McGraw-Hill, 1974. Used with permission of McGraw-Hill Book Company.

10. The Curtis Publishing Company is generally conceded to have formed the first formal marketing research department with the appointment of Charles Parlin as manager of the Commercial Research Division of the Advertising Department in 1911, while ACNielsen, the largest marketing research firm in the world, began operation in 1934. For a detailed treatment of the development of marketing research, see Robert Bartels, *The Development of Marketing Thought* (Homewood, Ill.: Richard D. Irwin, 1962), pp. 106–124, or Jack J. Honomichl, *Marketing Research People: Their Behind-the-Scenes Stories* (Chicago: Crain Books, 1984), especially Part II on pages 95–184.

11. Michael Czinkota and Masaaki Kotabe, "Product Development the Japanese Way," *The Journal of Business Strategy* 11 (November/December 1990), p. 36.

Suggested Additional Readings

For a discussion of what is happening in the world of marketing research, see
Jack J. Honomichl, "1997 Honomichl Business Report on The Marketing Research Industry," *Marketing News,* 31 (June 9, 1997), pp. H1–H43.
Thomas C. Kinnear and Ann R. Root, *1994 Survey of Marketing Research* (Chicago: American Marketing Association, 1995).

For a historical perspective on the evolution of the marketing research industry, see
Jack J. Honomichl, *Marketing Research People: Their Behind-the-Scenes Stories* (Chicago: Crain Books, 1984).

Chapter 2

GATHERING MARKETING INTELLIGENCE

Upon Completing This Chapter, You Should Be Able to

1. Explain the difference between a project emphasis in research and a systems emphasis.

2. Define what is meant by a marketing information system (MIS) and a decision support system (DSS).

3. Describe the networking of modern information systems.

4. Identify the components of a decision support system.

5. Discuss trends in the gathering of marketing intelligence.

Case in Marketing Research

Stan was worried. The numbers on the sales report for the Asia Pacific Division showed that the recession in Southeast Asia was hurting sales of his company's printers. His competitors' sales were down as well. What to do?

"Well," Stan mused, "I know that Printer Tech isn't going to single-handedly end this recession. But if we can keep selling toner and parts to all the customers who have our printers, and if we can turn more of our prospects into sales, I think we can meet this year's sales targets."

Stan fired off an e-mail message to May, his top sales rep in South Korea: "We need to keep our overall sales on target. If printer sales are down, let's focus on toner, etc. How can we get our customers to buy all their toner from us?"

Before long, May replied: "I can make a schedule to call all our customers regularly to see if they need toner. Is this what you have in mind?" Stan read her message and smiled wearily. Clearly, she was not enthusiastic. And for good reason. Selling toner would not generate commissions for May. It was sold through local suppliers, not through the company's sales force.

Stan pondered his problem. His monthly sales reports gave him enough information to see a need to adjust the region's sales strategy. But to execute those adjustments, his salespeople needed more specific information, including quick access to data about individual customers and prospects. When he had started out as a salesperson years ago, he couldn't have dreamed of such a database, but maybe now . . .

Stan clicked his mouse and returned to a Web site he had been browsing a few days ago, that of Rubric, Inc. The company was offering something it called "Enterprise Marketing Automation" (EMA). Maybe it could help Printer Tech get the information it needed.

Stan read several Web pages about Enterprise Marketing Automation. He saw that Rubric's EMA system would create a database of information about prospects, customers, and promotional campaigns. He and the sales force could use Internet-style tools for retrieving information from the system. In addition, the system could automatically schedule mailings or calls based on when customers purchased products, and it could schedule follow-up calls to prospects. "Maybe it's time to try this," thought Stan.

Discussion Issues

1. What kinds of information might help Stan improve the sales performance of Printer Tech's Asia Pacific Division?

2. What kinds of information might help the individual salespeople in the division improve their sales performance?

3. Why might an Internet-based information system be advantageous for gathering and delivering this information?

The preceding chapter suggested that the fundamental purpose of marketing research is to help managers make decisions they face each day in their various areas of responsibility. As directors of firms' marketing activities, marketing managers urgently need information, or marketing intelligence. They might need to know about the changes that can be expected in customer purchasing patterns, the types of marketing intermediaries that might evolve, which of several alternative product designs might be the most successful, the shape of the firm's demand curve, or any of a number of other issues that could affect the way they plan, solve problems, or evaluate and control the marketing effort. We suggested that marketing research is traditionally responsible for this intelligence function. As the formal link with the environment, marketing research generates, transmits, and interprets feedback regarding the success of the firm's marketing plans and the strategies and tactics employed in implementing those plans.

Marketing research can meet the need for marketing intelligence in two basic ways:

1. By developing and executing projects that answer a specific problem;

2. By establishing systems that provide marketing intelligence and guide decision making on an ongoing basis.

Most of this book describes the first approach, called the project approach. The next chapter provides an overview of the steps involved in using research to address a specific problem. The remainder of the book then explores each step in detail. In contrast, this chapter examines the second approach, typically called the systems approach. The chapter begins by distinguishing a systems approach to marketing research from a project approach. The remainder of the chapter describes the kinds of systems marketers use for obtaining information and making decisions.

The Project Approach and the Systems Approach

Although most discussions of marketing research focus on the project approach, both approaches are valuable. Both contribute information, but in different ways. Robert J. Williams, who created the first recognized marketing information system at the Mead Johnson division of the Edward Dalton Company, explains the difference with an analogy. Williams says both sources of marketing intelligence illuminate the darkness, but the project approach is like a flashbulb, and the systems approach is like a candle.[1] A marketing research project can shed intense light on a particular issue at a particular time. In contrast, a marketing information system rarely shows all the details of a particular situation, but its glow is continuous, even as conditions change.

As this analogy suggests, one of the problems of the project emphasis has been its nonrecurring nature. Often projects are devised in times of crisis and carried out with urgency. This pattern has led to an emphasis on data collection and analysis instead of the development of pertinent information on a regular basis. One suggestion for closing the gap is to think of management in terms of an ongoing process of decision making that requires a flow of regular inputs rather than in terms of waiting for crises. Today the usual mechanisms for doing this are some form of marketing information system and/or decision support system.

The earliest attempts at providing a steady flow of information inputs (that is, candlelight) were **marketing information systems (MIS).** An MIS is "a set of procedures and methods for the regular, planned collection, analysis, and presentation of information for

Marketing Information System (MIS)
A set of procedures and methods for the regular, planned collection, analysis, and presentation of information for use in making marketing decisions.

use in making marketing decisions."[2] The key word in the definition is *regular*, since the emphasis in an MIS is to produce information on a recurring basis rather than on the basis of one-time research studies.

In contrast to an MIS, which emphasizes the preparation of routine reports, a **decision support system (DSS)** includes software to assist in making certain kinds of decisions. Formally defined, a DSS is "a coordinated collection of data, systems, tools, and techniques with supporting software and hardware, by which an organization gathers and interprets relevant information from business and the environment and turns it into a basis for marketing decisions.[3] Thus, besides storing information, the DSS provides models for analyzing that information—for example, creating tables or graphs of key data and seeing how a forecast changes if assumptions are changed.

DSSs and MISs are both concerned with improving information processing to enable better marketing decisions. A DSS differs from an MIS, though, in a number of ways:

Decision Support System (DSS)
A coordinated collection of data, systems, tools, and techniques with supporting software and hardware, by which an organization gathers and interprets relevant information from business and environment and turns it into a basis for marketing decisions.

- A DSS tends to be aimed at the less well structured, underspecified problems that managers face rather than at problems that can be investigated using a relatively standard set of procedures and comparisons.

- A DSS combines the use of models and analytical techniques and procedures with the more traditional data access and retrieval functions of an MIS.

- A DSS specifically incorporates features that make it easy to use in an interactive mode by noncomputer people. These features include menu-driven procedures for doing an analysis and graphic display of the results. Regardless of how the interaction is structured, the systems can respond to users' ad hoc requests in real time, meaning the time available for making the decision.

- A DSS emphasizes flexibility and adaptability. It can accommodate different decision makers with diverse styles as well as changing environmental conditions.

Ideally, a marketing information system regularly provides the information marketers need for making decisions. Designers of such an MIS start with a detailed analysis of each decision maker who might use the system. They attempt to secure an accurate, objective assessment of each manager's decision-making responsibilities, capabilities, and style. They identify types of decisions each decision maker routinely makes, the types of information needed to make those decisions, the types of information the individual receives regularly, and the special studies that are periodically needed. The analysis also considers the improvements decision makers would like in the current information system, not only in the types of information they receive but also in the form in which they receive it.

Given these information specifications, system designers then attempt to specify, get approval for, and subsequently generate a series of reports that would go to the various decision makers. To complete these tasks, systems designers need to specify the data to be input to the system, how to secure and store the data, how to access and combine the data, and what the report formats will look like. Only after these analysis and design steps are completed can the system be constructed. Programmers write and document the programs, making data retrieval as efficient as possible in terms of computer time and memory. When all the procedures are debugged, it is put on-line, so managers with authorized access can ask for a report.

Limitations of Marketing Information Systems

When they were first proposed, MISs were held up as an information panacea. The reality, however, often fell short of the promise. The primary reasons are as much behavioral as they are technical. People tend to resist change, and with an MIS the changes are often substantial. Also many decision makers are reluctant to disclose to others what factors they use and how they combine these factors when making a decision about a particular issue, and without such disclosure it is next to impossible to design reports that will give them the information they need in the form they need it.

Even when managers are willing to disclose their decision-making calculus and information needs, there are problems. Different managers typically emphasize different things and, consequently, have different data needs. There are very few report formats that are optimal for different users. Either the developers have to design "compromise" reports that are satisfactory for a number of users, although not ideal for any single user, or they have to engage in the laborious task of programming to meet each user's needs, one at a time.

Moreover, the costs and time required to establish such systems are often underestimated. This is cause by underestimating the size of the task, changes in organizational structure, key personnel, and electronic data-processing systems they require. By the time these systems can be developed, the personnel for which they are designed often have different responsibilities or the economic and competitive environments around which they are designed have changed. Thus, they are often obsolete soon after being put on-line, meaning that the whole process of analysis, design, development, and implementation has to be repeated anew.

Another fundamental problem with MISs is that the systems do not lend themselves to the solution of the kinds of problems managers typically face. Many of the activities performed by managers cannot be programmed, nor can they be performed routinely or delegated, because they involve personal choices. Since a manager's decision making is often ad hoc and addressed to unexpected choices, standardized reporting systems lack the necessary scope and flexibility to be useful. Nor can managers, even if they are willing to, specify in advance what they want from programmers and model builders, because decision making and planning are often exploratory. As decision makers and their staffs learn more about a problem, their information needs and methods of analysis evolve. Further, decision making often involves exceptions and qualitative issues that are not easily programmed.

Networking Information Systems

In the earliest days of MISs, managers obtained reports by requesting them from the company's computer or information systems department. Someone in the department would print out the report and deliver it to the manager. Modern computer systems allow authorized users at all levels of the organization to get the information themselves, usually through some form of computer network. This empowers decision makers to get the types of information they need, when they need it, even if they suddenly and unexpectedly face new situations with new information requirements.

The older computer networks linked terminals or personal computers to a database in a mainframe. Such networks still exist in many companies, especially those with massive databases. Today's computer networks may also link a series of personal computers. In addition, most companies now offer access to that network of networks, the Internet.

The *Internet*—an extensive global network of computers at government agencies, universities, businesses, and Internet access providers—was once limited to academicians and government employees sharing technological information. It has grown explosively in terms of the number of users and the kinds of information available. The Internet links more than 100 million people from many countries.[4] Its popularity is due in part to the fact that access requires only a personal computer with the right software and modem plus an account with a service provider (a commercial on-line service such as America Online or a direct provider such as Netcom).

Many Internet users browse the *World Wide Web*, a hypertext system that allows users to receive text, graphics, video, and sound. *Hypertext* is a method for jumping to text and graphics by clicking on highlighted words and images. The Web's hypertext links may send users from the documents of one organization to those of another, perhaps in another part of the world. The World Wide Web boasts hundreds of millions of Web sites, a number that continues to grow rapidly.

The familiarity and capabilities of the Internet have inspired many organizations to apply its tools to their own computer networks. A growing number of organizations are setting up *intranets,* which apply such Web tools as hypertext links to internal computer net-

U.S. Census Bureau
United States Department of Commerce

Subjects A to Z **A B C D E F G H I** **J K L M N O P Q** **R S T U V W X Y Z**	**United States** **Census** **2000**	Jobs · Census in Schools · Advertising · Local Offices · Questionnaires · More	**Earn Extra Money**
New on the Site	People	Estimates · Projections · Housing · Income · International · Poverty · Genealogy · More	**Population Clocks** U.S. 274,105,983 World 6,038,620,213 13:59 EST Jan 17, 2000
Search	Business	Economic Census · Government · NAICS · Foreign Trade · More	
Access Tools	Geography	Maps · TIGER · Gazetteer · More	**State & County** **QuickFacts**
Catalog	News	Releases · Webcasts · Minority Links · Contacts · More	Select a State ⬍
Publications (PDF)			*Go!*
Jobs@Census	Special Topics	Conversations with America · FedStats · American Community Survey	**Latest Economic** **Indicators**
About the Bureau			Total
Related Sites			Business
American FactFinder			Sales

U S C E N S U S B U R E A U
Helping You Make Informed Decisions

Accessibility | Privacy |
Quality | Confidentiality |
About our new look

The U.S. Census Bureau maintains a Web site at www.census.gov. At this site, users can access online data as well as order printed reports.

works. Similarly, *extranets* link authorized users in the organization, its suppliers, and customers, allowing them to share information as easily as they browse the World Wide Web. With both intranets and extranets, users can look up a variety of company data, from the past week's sales or the inventory level of a particular product to the production status of a particular order. The search engines that have been designed to search the Web have proven to be so useful that many companies have begun using them to manage their intranets and extranets. Companies use software called "firewalls" to prevent unauthorized computer users from accessing confidential data in the network. However, those using the intranet or extranet can use links that carry them outside the firewall to the rest of the Internet.

The Internet, and its intranet and extranet offspring, have given a whole new meaning to the idea of an information system. Today's computer users can look up not only data stored on the company's proprietary system but an astounding variety of free data from the government and, usually for a fee, data from industry and trade groups, publishers, and many other sources.[5] Chapter 7 offers a more detailed look at some of these sources of data.

Decision Support Systems

As the problems with traditional MISs became more apparent, the emphasis in regularly supplied marketing intelligence changed from the production of preformatted batch reports to a decision support system (DSS). A DSS combines data systems, model systems, and dialog systems that can be used interactively (see Figure 2.1).

Data Systems

Data System
The part of a decision support system that includes the processes used to capture and the methods used to store data coming from a number of external and internal sources.

The **data system** in a DSS includes the processes used to capture and the methods used to store data coming from marketing, finance, and manufacturing, as well as information coming from any number of external or internal sources. The typical data system has modules containing customer information, general economic and demographic information, competitor information, and industry information, including market trends. Especially in companies that once set up an MIS and later expanded to a decision support system, the DSS may use the existing MIS as part of its data system. In other words, the DSS retrieves data from the marketing information system and uses it to support decision making.

The exponential growth in computing power and the emergence of increasingly sophisticated data processing capabilities has led to a commensurate increase in the size of databases. While historically a business's databases contained current information, many new ones contain historical information as well. These "data warehouses" literally dwarf those available even a few years ago. For example, Wal-Mart has a data warehouse with 43 terabytes (terabyte = 1,000 gigabytes) of data storage. The system provides information about each of Wal-Mart's over 3,000 stores in eight countries. Wal-Mart plans to use the information to select products that need replenishment, analyze seasonal buying patterns, examine customer buying trends, select markdowns, and react to merchandise volume and movement.[6]

Besides company data, the data system may retrieve information from on-line databases. A significant trend affecting DDSs is the explosion in the number of such databases. Thousands of databases can now be accessed on-line via computer, as compared with less than nine hundred in 1980. The insights managers can gather from commercially available databases are mindboggling, and dwarf the possibilities of even a half-dozen years ago. Research Window 2.1, for example, highlights some of the information available on the Internet.

Lycos and IntelliSeek recently teamed up to offer Internet users access to over 7,000 databases and other information sources. To retrieve information with this service, called Invisible Web Catalog, you visit the Lycos Web site (www.lycos.com) and type in the terms you want to look up. The service then displays a list of documents and databases containing that term. Invisible Web Catalog differs from other Internet search engines in its use of IntelliSeek's technology for indexing databases with formats that had not previously been indexable (for example, those with a proprietary format).[7]

FIGURE 2.1   **Components of a Decision Support System**

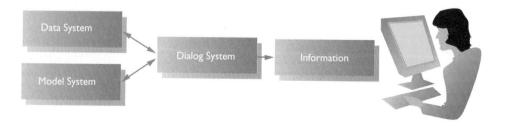

From the U.S. Bureau of the Census to Dun & Bradstreet, most of the traditional suppliers of marketing and other business information now provide access to that information on the Internet. Some of the information can be downloaded free. You can download other data in exchange for a subscription fee or item-by-item charges. In still other cases, you can order print publications or CD-ROMs and have them shipped to you.

Web Portals Most visitors to the Internet start at a Web portal, an indexing and search site where users enter the World Wide Web. Examples are CompuServe.com (www.compuserve.com), the Microsoft Network (http://home.microsoft.com), Netscape Netcenter (http://home.netscape.com/), and Yahoo! (www.yahoo.com). At the portal, you can type in the URL (Internet "address") for a Web site you want to visit or use hypertext links to selected information sources. You can also use a search engine such as HotBot or Lycos to find information about particular companies or topics.

CEO Express A portal designed especially for businesspeople is CEO Express (www.ceoexpress.com). This site is especially helpful for novice Internet researchers, because it lists a wealth of links to major business-related sites such as these:

- Newspapers, news magazines, television networks, and news wires

- Business and technology magazines

- Search engines for researching particular topics or locating organizations' Web sites

- Sources of company data, including annual reports, listings of the Fortune 500 and Inc. 100, rating services, and stock quotes

- Government agencies, including the Census Bureau, Patent and Trademark Office, and Library of Congress

- Reports of research into Internet usage and on-line marketing.

Yellow Pages To find names and addresses of companies, such as competitors or potential distributors, you can visit an on-line yellow pages. For example, at the Netscape Netcenter's yellow pages service (at http://home.netscape.com), you can look up addresses and phone numbers by company name or category (for example, autos or computers). You can also specify that the search be

limited to a particular geographic region (city, state, country).

Dowjones.com At the Web site of Dow Jones, publisher of *The Wall Street Journal* (www.dowjones.com), you can read headlines from Dow Jones and Associated Press, specify industries about which you would like to receive news, or use the Business Search function. Business Search lets you specify a topic and will search for articles in the news wires, an index of 2,000 Web sites, and 250 news and business publications. Dowjones.com also offers Quotes Plus Lookup, which checks the price of stocks when you enter the company's symbol or name, and Market Indicators, which tracks major stock averages.

Securities and Exchange Commission If you want information about particular companies, you can start with the reports they file with the Securities and Exchange Commission. Visit the SEC's Web site (www.sec.gov).

Dun and Bradstreet For more company details—including facts about privately held companies, which don't have to file documents with the SEC—visit the Dun & Bradstreet Web site (www.dnb.com). You can order CD-ROMs and directories drawn from D&B's database on more than 11 million U.S. companies or from its global database about more than 53 million companies in 200 countries. D&B also offers publications on a variety of topics, including marketing and particular industries.

Moody's Rating firms such as Moody's Investors Service examine company performance and industry trends and rate companies for investment purposes. You can get ratings and other information from Moody's at its Web site (www.moodys.com).

Patents and Trademarks If you are developing a new product, you will need information about patents and trademarks. You can get reports, forms, and other information from the U.S. Patent and Trademark Office at its Web site (www.uspto.gov).

The Census Bureau Vast amounts of data collected from the various U.S. Censuses are available on-line at www.census.gov or by placing an order at the Web site. Want to know the number of pharmacies in Rankin County, Mississippi? You can find the number here. Also contains updated reports since the last census.

As the number of databases has expanded, so too has public concern with the issue of privacy and if, and how, people's right to privacy is being violated in the generation and sharing of these databases. For example, Research Window 2.2 describes the controversy over automated generation of detailed data about individuals' Internet usage. Much of this controversy arises because people are asked to provide data without full information about how it will be used. For example, the Federal Trade Commission recently surveyed commercial Web sites and learned that most ask for personal information, yet fewer than 17 percent publish an information disclosure statement at the Web site. Only 2 percent publish a comprehensive, easy-to-find privacy policy at the site. Furthermore, among sites that post a policy, only a fraction offer a choice as to how the information will be used, or even a chance to look at and correct personal data.[8]

The privacy problem is not limited to consumers, either. Companies in extranets and other information-sharing arrangements routinely share detailed data. Like consumers, they do not always know every use to which the data are put.

Boston-based Newbury Comics depends on its forward-looking knowledge of music to keep its 20 music stores competitive with the retailing giants. Mike Dreese, co-owner of the business, was therefore shocked to learn that he was inadvertently sharing his insights. He was reporting each store's weekly sales, by label and artist, to SoundScan, a firm that specializes in gathering such data from most of the music retailers in the United States. Retailers providing data to SoundScan receive more favorable treatment from the recording companies. Dreese knew that SoundScan uses the data to prepare reports for recording labels, promoters, and managers. What surprised him were comments from a rack jobber (a type of intermediary), boasting that his company was buying detailed data from Sound-Scan to support giant retailers like Wal-Mart and Kmart by stocking what would be the hottest albums in particular regions. Especially because of its position as a trendsetter, Newbury Comics was apparently providing data that helped its toughest competitors.

RF (radio frequency) systems are a wireless form of data capture that is evolving rapidly. Today's state-of-the-art systems, attached to lift trucks or wrists, pinpoint deliveries, control inventories, and provide marketing information better than ever before. "A good RF system will improve productivity within a warehouse, as well as the timeliness and speed with which information is collected," says Keith Stickell, executive vice president of Atlanta-based Commercial Cold Storage. And for the past two years at Hannaford Bros., a 150-store supermarket chain headquartered in Scarborough, Maine, shoppers have been market testing RF technology. Shoppers use portable self-scanning handheld scanners to record purchases as they fill their carts (photo). "The customers who use it love it" according to Bill Homa, vice president and chief information officer.

Source: Photo by Warren Roos/Executive Technology

Privacy advocates howled when Intel launched its Pentium III computer chips. Expected to power the latest generation of personal computers, the chips were designed to contain so-called processor serial numbers that could uniquely identify each computer's on-line communications.

Intel expected that the 96-digit serial number would be a boon to marketers by providing extra security, because it could be used to verify computer users' identity. The company also thought consumers might be glad to get the feature. The serial number could prevent problems arising from mistakes when the consumer enters personal information. It could also discourage fraudulent use of consumers' credit card numbers or passwords. In addition, Intel thought the serial number would help organizations manage their computer networks.

Nevertheless, many consumers were upset that they would be providing information about themselves without first being asked for it. Intel quickly responded to the deluge of criticism. It modified its chip to deactivate the ID system. The computer user now decides whether or not to turn it on.

A spokesperson for the American Civil Liberties Union praised Intel's decision. Still, the criticism has continued in other quarters. The Center for Democracy and Technology filed a complaint with the Federal Trade Commission. The center and other privacy advocates worry that popular Web sites may deny access to computers with a deactivated ID. They also contend that consumers may get so used to the idea of the serial numbers that they may eventually treat them as a routine aspect of life in cyberspace—disclosing their on-line habits without much thought.

Sources: Robert O'Harrow, Jr., and Elizabeth Corcoran, "Intel Drops Plans to Activate Chip IDs," *Washington Post* (January 26, 1999, downloaded from the Washington Post Internet archives, http://search.washingtonpost.com, February 9, 1999); James Lardner, "Intel Even More Inside," *U.S. News & World Report* (February 8, 1999), p. 43; Dan Goodin, "More Support for Pentium III Complaint," CNET News.com (April 8, 1999, downloaded from CNET Web site, www.news.com, June 7, 1999).

After some hard thinking about the consequences, Dreese decided that Newbury Comics would no longer provide data to SoundScan.[9]

There is little doubt that as the ability to gather and organize detailed data expands, so will the controversy regarding individual versus company rights. Companies planning on collecting particular types of data need to be sensitive to privacy issues. Research Window 2.3, for example, offers a privacy checklist companies might use when developing their databases.

Beyond protection of privacy, an important criterion for adding a particular piece of data to the database is whether it is useful for marketing decision making. The basic task of a DSS is to capture relevant marketing data in reasonable detail and to put that data in a truly accessible form. It is crucial that the database management capabilities built into the system can logically organize the data the same way a manager does, regardless of the form that organization assumes.

Model Systems

Model System
The part of a decision support system that includes all the routines that allow the user to manipulate the data so as to conduct the kind of analysis the individual desires.

The **model system** in a DSS includes all the routines that allow the user to manipulate the data so as to conduct the kind of analysis the individual desires. Whenever managers look at data, they have a preconceived idea of how something works and, therefore, what is interesting and worthwhile in the data. These ideas are called *models*.[10] Most managers also want to manipulate data to gain a better understanding of a marketing issue. These manipulations are called *procedures*. The routines for manipulating the data may run the gamut from summing a set of numbers to conducting a complex statistical analysis to finding an optimization strategy using some kind of nonlinear programming routine. At the same time, "the most frequent operations are basic ones: segregating numbers into relevant groups, aggregating them, taking ratios, ranking them, picking out exceptional cases, plotting and making tables."[11]

In the long run, ensuring a customer's privacy can improve a company's profitability. Privacy is really about earning the customer's trust, and trust is a central component of relationship marketing.

Anyone who uses personal information to target customers can stay on top of the privacy issue by writing a formal privacy policy. If you need to create a policy or review your old one, here are some basic guidelines:

Remember "knowledge, notice, and no." Tell your customers how you will use their personal information. If you plan to share the information with a third party, tell your customers and give them a chance to drop out of the database. Even if you don't sell your customer lists, tell them so. The practice of renting customer lists has become so widespread that a customer may assume you share your lists unless you explicitly tell them otherwise.

Look before you cross-market. Do your customers believe that personal information collected for one purpose is being used for a different unrelated purpose without their consent? If so, improve your communication with them. Be sure the "knowledge, notice, no" rule applies to both your internal cross-marketing and your frequent-buyers programs, especially if these programs involve

unrelated products. Consumers may not know that responding to one of your offers may trigger subsequent offers. The customer should never have to ask anyone, "How did you get my name?"

Don't be tempted by incidental information. Information about a transaction typically passes through many hands. Credit-card companies, insurance companies, and others usually serve as brokers for transactions between consumers and other businesses. If this is your role, take care to protect the content of that transaction.

Exercise conscience and common sense. So far, few legal restrictions apply to the gathering and use of personal information by the private sector. That's why privacy is more about "should" than "must." Clearly, some medical, financial, and lifestyle data are more sensitive than others. Apply a "sniff test" to any proposed reuse of your customer database. Would you be comfortable sending a member of your family the same offers that you propose to mail to your customers? If your company is identified as a sponsor of this mailing, will your 800-number be clogged with complaints?

Source: Mary J. Culnan, "The Privacy Checklist," in Judith Waldrop, "The Business of Privacy," *American Demographics,* 16 (October 1994), p. 55.

The explosion in recent years in the number of databases available and the size of some of them has triggered a commensurate need for ways to efficiently analyze them. For example, store scanners provide massive amounts of data to marketing managers in packaged goods companies. The huge amounts of data require a great amount of time for even an astute analyst to come up with simple summaries that show the major trends. In response, a number of firms have developed **expert systems**—computer-based, artificial intelligence systems that attempt to model how experts in the area process information to solve the problem at hand.[12]

For example, Figure 2.2 displays the type of output provided by The Partners, an expert system developed by Information Resources, Inc., for the analysis of its scanner-generated data. The Partners can provide highlights of the performance of a brand and competitors' brands within minutes. It can sort through all the data and provide a comparison of current results with past results, by brand and by category as well as by markets, regions, or key accounts. It can also produce a memo highlighting the major findings.

Expert System
A computer-based, artificial intelligence system that attempts to model how experts in the area process information to solve the problem at hand.

Dialog System
The part of a decision support system that permits users to explore the databases by employing the system models to produce reports that satisfy their particular information needs. Also called language system.

Dialog Systems

The element of a DSS that clearly differentiates it from an MIS is its **dialog system,** also called a *language system.* Dialog systems permit managers who are not programmers themselves to explore the databases by using the system models to produce reports that satisfy their own particular information needs. The reports can be tabular or graphical,

FIGURE 2.2   **Example Report Produced by the Expert System The Partners**

SECRET's share has declined 0.7 points, from 11.1 to 10.4.

Among the components of SECRET, the top share gainer is SECRET STICK/SOLID (+0.7). The 2 products with the largest share loss are SECRET AEROSOL (-0.7) and SECRET ROLL-ON (-0.6).

Total US - Food's largest 3 share declines were posted in Boston, MA (-2.0), Los Angeles, CA (-1.3), and Detroit, MI (-1.2).

Among SECRET's major competitors, the 3 principal share gainers are MNEN LSpSt (+2.1), DEGREE (+0.9), and SUAVE (+0.5). The largest 3 share losses occurred for DRY IDEA (-1.5), BAN (-0.9), and SOFT & DRI (-0.9).

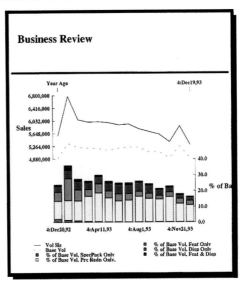

Sales Trend Review

	Volume Share		Base Volume Share		Incrm Volume Share	
	Current	Change	Current	Change	Current	Change
SECRET	10.4	-0.7	9.7	-0.1	0.8	-0.6
SECRET STICK/SOLID	5.5	0.7	4.8	0.7	0.7	-0.0
SECRET AEROSOL	3.2	-0.7	3.1	-0.4	0.0	-0.4
SECRET ROLL-ON	1.8	-0.6	1.7	-0.4	0.1	-0.2
Competitors						
MNEN LSpSt	5.3	2.1	4.2	1.4	1.2	0.7
DEGREE	4.5	0.9	4.1	0.8	0.4	0.0
SUAVE	4.9	0.5	4.6	0.6	0.3	-0.0
DRY IDEA	2.6	-1.5	2.2	-1.0	0.3	-0.5
BAN	4.3	-0.9	4.0	-0.9	0.3	-0.0
SOFT & DRI	4.6	-0.9	4.1	-0.8	0.5	-0.1
Total US - Food	10.4	-0.7	9.7	-0.1	0.8	-0.6
Boston, MA	11.1	-2.0	9.5	-0.9	1.5	-1.1
Los Angeles, CA	8.8	-1.3	8.3	-1.4	0.5	0.1
Detroit, MI	9.2	-1.2	8.5	-1.3	0.6	0.1

Share Reference	DEODORANT/ANTI-PERSPIRANT		
Time	4 Wks Ending Dec 19, 93		
Comparison Period	4 Wks Ending Dec 20, 92		
Title	Business Review	08-29-1994	Source: Infoscan

and the report formats can be specified by individual managers. The dialog systems can be passive, which means that the analysis possibilities are presented to the decision makers for selection via menu, a few simple keystrokes, light pen, or a mouse, or they can be active, requiring the users to state their requests in a command mode.

A key feature is that managers and employees, instead of funneling their data requests through a team of programmers, can conduct their analyses by themselves sitting at a computer terminal using the dialog system. This allows them to target the information they want and not be overwhelmed with irrelevant data. They can ask a question and, on the basis of the answer, ask a subsequent question, and then another, and another, and so on.

As the availability of on-line databases has increased, so too has the need for better dialog systems. The dialog systems are what puts data at the decision maker's fingertips. While that sounds simple enough, it is in fact a difficult task because of the large amount of data available, the speed with which they hit a company, and the fact that they come from a variety of sources.

One way to handle these problems is distributed network computing. Such systems make use of a common interface or server. Through that server, the analyst can do data entry, data query, spreadsheet analysis, plots, statistical analysis, or even report preparation, all through simple commands (see Figure 2.3). The technical term for this capability is *data mining,* and businesses hope it will allow them to boost sales and profits by better understanding their customers.

A typical approach to data mining uses a supercomputer to link a number of personal computers. Decision makers at their PCs pose their questions, and the supercomputer tackles them with parallel processing, which breaks down questions into smaller computational tasks to perform simultaneously. A computer using parallel processing can readily work through trillions of pieces of data, slashing problem-solving time from weeks or months to days or hours. For example, Fingerhut Companies, a Minnetonka, Minnesota, catalog retailer, used data mining to target a promotional effort. The company's computer sorted through six trillion characters of data to learn which of its 25 million customers had recently purchased outdoor furniture and thus might also be interested in a new gas grill.[13]

FIGURE 2.3   **Use of Dialog Systems with Common Server or Interface Using Simplified, Standardized Instructions to Perform Multiple Tasks**

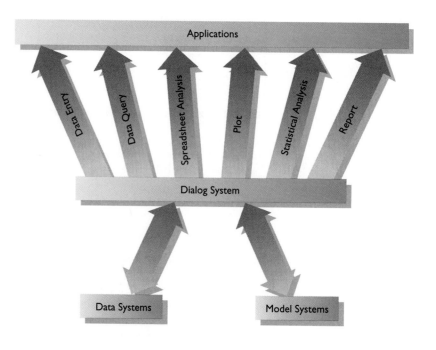

Trends in Obtaining Marketing Intelligence

There is no question that the explosion in databases, computer hardware and software or accessing those databases, and the Internet are all changing the way marketing intelligence is obtained. Not only are more companies building DSSs, but those that have them are becoming more sophisticated in using them for general business and competitive intelligence.

Chief Information Officers and Chief Knowledge Officers

The sophistication in the design and uses of decision support systems opens up access to so much data that higher-level management of information becomes critical. An executive in charge of information can ensure that it is used in support of strategic thinking. In many organizations, this function is now the responsibility of a chief information officer, or CIO.

The CIO's major role is to run the company's information and computer systems like a business. The CIO serves as the liaison between the firm's top management and its information systems department. He or she has the responsibility for planning, coordinating, and controlling the use of the firm's information resources, and is much more concerned with the firm's outlook than with the daily activities of the department. CIOs typically know more about the business in general than the managers of the information system departments, who are often stronger technically. In many cases, the managers of the information system department will report directly to the CIO.

Falling sales have awakened Levi Strauss to the need to build closer ties to consumers, and CIO Linda Glick is in the midst of that effort. Her group started with the ways in which individual consumers interact directly with the company—at its Web site and through its Original Spin service, which allows customers in stores to have their measurements taken so that they can order individually customized jeans. In addition, Glick is overseeing the restructuring of the information technology divisions in North America, Europe, and Asia so that its people work more directly with Levi's employees in business departments such as design and marketing. The objective of the restructuring is to have IT employees act as internal consultants to the departments.[14]

A growing number of companies are extending the idea of information systems management to include management of the knowledge that resides inside its employees' heads. One of an organization's greatest assets can be what its people know about customers, its products, and its marketplace. However, few companies yet have a way to make that information widely available to those who can use it. *Knowledge management* is an effort to systematically collect that information and make it accessible to others.

Oil giant BP Amoco has documented hundreds of millions of dollars in savings from applying knowledge management. Its strategy is to identify projects that can most benefit from the effort and then to apply a variety of tactics. Before launching a project, the company conducts a two-day meeting at which people who have done a similar project describe what they have learned. After the project, brief and in-depth reviews analyze what happened and what was learned. Information from the meeting and reviews go into a Web-based folder that includes hypertext links to people who have relevant information to share. In addition, the company's intranet offers an in-house yellow pages of people who have volunteered to share information on specific topics.[15]

Companies that adopt knowledge management may assign responsibility for the effort to a chief knowledge officer, or CKO. Typically, a CKO is responsible for the ways an organization manages and shares, not just explicit information, but also those bits of knowledge that experienced people may use without giving much conscious thought to them. Carrying out this type of information sharing requires getting the organization's people to recognize and communicate what they know. Thus, it is not surprising that a study by the London Business School found that technological skills are less important to a CKO than to a traditional CIO, and people-related skills are more important.[16]

Linking Marketing Intelligence to Other Business Intelligence

Another way in which powerful information systems are influencing the direction of marketing intelligence is in the blurring of distinctions between types of information management. When an organization's computer could handle only enough data for a single function's decision support system, each function needed a separate system with a separate database. However, today more and more companies are enjoying the benefits of sharing data among the various functions and levels of the organization.

For example, an enterprise resource planning (ERP) system monitors and controls all of an organization's resource requirements, such as inventory, human resources, and production capacity. This sophisticated software system tracks financial data, schedules, inventory levels, and more, all in an effort to ensure that the organization has just the resources it needs to meet anticipated demand as efficiently as possible. Marketing intelligence can support ERP by helping managers prepare accurate sales forecasts. In addition, a promotional effort or new-product launch will affect all of an organization's functions and many of its resource needs. ERP can support marketing efforts by providing information about a marketing decision's impact on the entire organization.

Intelligence Gathering in the Organization of the Future

Although one might expect they would, the explosion in databases and the emergence of DSSs have not eliminated traditional marketing research projects for gathering marketing

---

Back to the Case

Stan was surprised to find that installing Rubric's Enterprise Marketing Automation system was relatively painless—especially compared with the installation of an information system at his first job. Back then, he'd spent months working with computer programmers and systems analysts to create a system that would deliver useful reports. In contrast, Rubric installed its EMA at Printer Tech and let the marketing decision makers themselves specify what they needed and when they needed it.

Printer Tech's salespeople in Asia were already used to regular e-mail communication with Stan and one another. Furthermore, they all browsed the World Wide Web every morning and evening to get information about their competitors and market. So the Rubric EMA's on-line access to data and Web-based search tools were familiar. Within days, some salespeople were trying system capabilities that Stan had only begun to absorb.

"This is great!" May e-mailed Stan. "I've been using the system to see which types of businesses and which types of sales calls—phone, in-person, and so on—are generating the most business."

"Good for you," Stan wrote back. "Check your results every week or two. You can adjust your follow-up as you learn more about each customer."

"You know what else I like?" added May. "The EMA system faxes a local supplier every six months after each customer bought a printer, alerting the supplier that my customer might need more toner. The customers say WE'RE on the ball, and I can focus on selling printers."

Stan clicked through more e-mail from his sales force. Several of the salespeople told of deals they were closing as the system helped them keep track of each customer and prospect. To each customer that purchased a printer five years earlier, the system sent a note offering a special on an upgrade. It also sent the customer's salesperson an e-mail reminder to follow up with the customer. When a prospect visited Printer Tech's Web site and requested more information, the system immediately forwarded the request to the nearest sales rep.

Stan smiled. He couldn't wait to set up the system to tell him the results of the latest promotional campaign. Printer Tech would offer a special service contract to customers that bought a printer by April 30. The EMA system would track the promotion's cost and measure its impact on sales as a return on investment. As soon as the campaign launched, Stan would be able to observe the results. Printer Tech could launch the campaign in a few cities and, if the return was good, quickly expand it.

Source: The Printer Tech case is based on a description of the EMA system at Rubric's Web site, www.rubricsoft.com, and background on the company (and a customer, Hewlett-Packard) in Elizabeth Weise, "Start-Up Bets Big on Computer Age," *USA Today* (November 16, 1998), pp. 18E–19E.

intelligence nor the need to understand their strengths and weaknesses. This is be-cause the two activities are not competitive mechanisms for marketing intelligence but, rather, complementary ones. For one thing, many of the project-oriented techniques discussed in this book are used to generate the information that goes into the databases that businesses use in their DSSs. Thus, the value of the insights gained from these databases depends directly on the quality of the underlying data, and users need to be able to assess their quality. For another, while DSSs provide valuable input for board strategic decisions, allow managers to stay in tune with what is happening in their external environments, and serve as excellent early-warning systems, they sometimes do not provide enough information as to what to do in specific instances, such as when the firm is faced with introducing a new product, changing distribution channels, evaluating a promotional campaign, and so on. When actionable information is required to address specific marketing problems or opportunities, the research project will likely continue to play a major role.

In sum, both traditional, or project-based, and DSS-based approaches to marketing intelligence can be expected to remain important. In an increasingly competitive world, information is vital, and a company's ability to obtain and analyze information will largely determine its future. The light from both flashbulbs and candles is necessary.

Summary

Learning Objective 1

Explain the difference between a project emphasis in research and a systems emphasis.

The difference between the project emphasis to research and the marketing information system (MIS) or decision support system (DSS) emphasis is that both of the latter rely on the continual monitoring of the firm's activities, competitors, and environment, while the former emphasizes the in-depth, but nonrecurring, study of some specific problem or environmental condition.

Learning Objective 2

Define what is meant by a marketing information system (MIS) and a decision support system (DSS).

A marketing information system is a set of procedures and methods for the regular, planned collection, analysis, and presentation of information for use in making marketing decisions. A decision support system expands the capabilities of an MIS to include tools that assist in decision making. A DSS is a coordinated collection of data, systems tools, and techniques with supporting software and hardware, by which an organization gathers and interprets relevant information from business and the environment and turns it into a basis for marketing action. A DSS encompasses data systems, model systems, and dialog systems.

Learning Objective 3

Describe the networking of modern information systems.

Modern information systems are usually linked in a network that allows decision makers at personal computers to get information themselves, without making requests through an information systems department. The data may reside in a central computer, in personal computers, or on the Internet. Many networks incorporate Internet search tools and data into an intranet (for internal users only) or an extranet (for internal users and authorized external users such as customers or suppliers).

Learning Objective 4

Identify the components of a decision support system.

A decision support system has three major components: a data system, a model system, and a dialog system. The data system collects and stores data from internal and external sources. The model system consists of routines that allow the user to manipulate data in order to analyze it as desired. Software in the model system may include expert systems, which make information-processing decisions based on models of how experts solve similar problems. Finally, the dialog system permits marketers to use the system models to produce reports based on criteria they specify themselves.

Learning Objective 5

Discuss trends in the gathering of marketing intelligence.

So much information is readily available from modern information systems and decision support systems that managing it has become a strategic challenge. Many organizations have placed a chief information officer (CIO) in charge of how the organization gathers data and makes it available to support decision making. Others have broadened this role to the gathering and management of all the organization's knowledge, sometimes under the oversight of a chief knowledge officer (CKO). This person's responsibilities include developing ways for individuals in the organization to identify and share what they have learned. In addition, many organizations are creating information and decision support systems that serve entire organizations, linking the various functions. Systems such as enterprise resource planning (ERP) systems show decision makers how their decisions affect the organization's resource levels and needs. ERP therefore can provide marketers with information about how a marketing decision will affect the entire organization. The explosion in the number and availability of databases heightens the potential of intelligence gathering to support marketing decisions, but it does not substitute for traditional marketing research projects to answer specific questions.

Review Questions

1. How does a project emphasis in marketing research differ from a systems emphasis?

2. What are the steps in developing an MIS?

3. What are the main differences between a marketing information system and a decision support system?

4. In a decision support system, what is a data system? A model system? A dialog system? Which of these is most important? Why?

5. How does knowledge management expand the concept of an information system? What additional kinds of marketing intelligence can it provide?

Discussion Questions, Problems, and Projects

1. How is the growth in the Internet and the World Wide Web changing the way researchers use management information systems and decision support systems?

Consider opportunities and challenges of researching on the Internet, as opposed to using a traditional marketing information system.

2. You have been requested to design a DSS for a manufacturer of automotive parts.
   (a) What data should be included in the system (e.g., sales by sales area or by product line, age, and type of automobile driven)?
   (b) What data sources might be used to create the information system?
   (c) How will you structure the system conceptually, including the elements you will build into each of the subsystems?

3. You are responsible for deciding whether to adopt an MIS or a DSS for the following situations. Which system approach would you choose? Why?
   (a) Production of profit and loss statements for Kool Aid sugar-free flavored drink mixes.
   (b) Introduction of a new product line extension for Smucker's preserves and jellies.
   (c) Determination of seasonal pricing schedules for Johnson outboard motors.
   (d) Identification of the amount of time spent on hold by consumers on a toll-free, customer-service assistance telephone line.

4. Arrange an interview with a manager of a local business to discuss a DSS, intranet, extranet, or knowledge management system.
   (a) Complete the following:
       Name of the company: _____
       Name and title of the manager you interviewed: _____
   (b) Briefly describe the system that the company is currently using, emphasizing especially the functions that are served by it (e.g., production, sales management, etc.).
   (c) Write a brief assessment of the manager's familiarity with the concept. Is the manager more concerned with the technical questions (e.g., how information is stored) or with the over-all concept and its impact on the organization's decision-making capabilities?
   (d) Briefly describe the company's use of the system, including how it determines who gets what access to what data and how, its experience with the system, and so on.

5. Your company is in the process of installing its first DSS. The system has been designed and the hardware installed, and it is due to be up and running in two weeks. Your task is to provide system users with orientation and training. It is your feeling that the company's people initially will resist using the DSS. To help overcome this resistance, what specific capabilities of the DSS will you emphasize in your initial orientation presentations?

Endnotes

1. Robert J. Williams, "Marketing Intelligence Systems: A DEW Line for Marketing Men," *Business Management* (January 1966), p. 32.
2. Peter D. Bennett, ed., *Dictionary of Marketing Terms,* 2nd ed. (Chicago: American Marketing Association, 1995), p. 167.
3. Ibid., p. 77.
4. Nielsen//Net Ratings, "Internet Usage Statistics for the Week Ending May 30, 1999" (downloaded from http://209.249.142.16/nnpm/owa/ on June 7, 1999).
5. For discussion of how to develop an industry overview, for example, using the Internet, see Marydee Ojala, "Industry Overviews: Turning Industry Question Marks into Answers," *Online User* (July/August 1996), pp. 14–19. For a general discussion of doing marketing research online, see Reva Basch, "A Strategy for Market Research Online," *Online User* (May/June 1996), pp. 42–43.
6. Jeremy Kahn, "Wal-Mart Goes Shopping in Europe," *Fortune* (June 7, 1999), pp. 105–1061; Wal-Mart Web site (www.wal-mart.com, downloaded July 20, 1999).
7. "Lycos Aligns with IntelliSeek to Reveal the Invisible Web Catalog—The Largest Collection of Searchable Databases" (Lycos press release, downloaded from http://biz.yahoo.com on June 7, 1999).
8. "New Media: What the FTC Really Discovered about Privacy on the Net," *PR & Marketing Network* (September 14, 1998, downloaded from the PR and Marketing Web site, www.prandmarketing.com, May 6, 1999).

9. Thea Singer, "Sharer Beware," *Inc. Technology* (March 16, 1999), pp. 38–401.

10. John D. C. Little and Michael N. Cassettari, *Decision Support Systems for Marketing Managers* (New York: American Management Association, 1984), p. 14.

11. Ibid., p. 15.

12. For general discussions of expert systems, see Judy Bayer and Rachel Harter, "'Miner,' 'Manager,' and 'Researcher': Three Modes of Analysis of Scanner Data," *International Journal of Research in Marketing* 8 (April 1991), pp. 17–27; Paul Alpar, "Knowledge-Based Modeling of Marketing Managers' Problem Solving Behavior," International Journal of Research in Marketing 8 (April 1991), pp. 5–16; Arvind Rangaswamy, Bari A. Harlam, and Leonard M. Lodish, "Infer: An Expert System for Automatic Analysis of Scanner Data," *International Journal of Research in Marketing* 8 (April 1991), pp. 29–40; Louis Moutinho, Bruce Curry, Fiona Davis, and Paulo Rita, *Computer Modeling and Expert Systems in Marketing* (New York: Routledge, 1994); Clive Couldwell, "Tapping the Data Revolution," Marketing (August 8, 1996), pp. 22–25.

13. Laurie Hays, "Using Computers to Decide Who Might Buy a Gas Grill," *The Wall Street Journal* (August 16, 1994), pp. B1, B6. See also John Verity, "Silicon and Software that Mine for Gold," *Business Week* (September 5, 1994), p. 62.

14. Tom Field, "Great Expectations," *CIO Magazine* (May 1, 1999, downloaded from the CIO Web site, www.cio.com, June 7, 1999).

15. Thomas A. Stewart, "Telling Tales at BP Amoco," *Fortune* (June 7, 1999), pp. 220, 222, 224.

16. Stowe Boyd, "The Role of the Chief Knowledge Officer," *Knowledge Management Review* (September/October 1998, downloaded from the Modus Operandi Web site, www.modusoperandi.com, June 7, 1999).

Suggested Additional Readings

For useful discussions of the structure and use of decision support systems, see

Robert C. Blattberg, Rashi Glazer and John D. C. Little, eds., *The Marketing Information Revolution* (Boston: Harvard Business School Press, 1994).

Louis Moutinho, Bruce Curry, Fiona Davies, and Paulo Rita, *Computer Modeling and Expert Systems in Marketing* (New York: Routledge, 1994).

Chapter 3

PROCESS OF MARKETING RESEARCH

Upon Completing This Chapter, You Should Be Able to

1. Explain the difference between a program strategy and a project strategy in marketing research.

2. Outline the steps in the research process and show how the steps are interrelated.

3. Cite the most critical error in marketing research.

Case in Marketing Research

Tempers flared within the expensively appointed, oak-paneled offices of Waring, Weatherell & Hough in Chicago. Management of the 400-attorney international law firm was debating the merits of spending money to learn more about the firm's clients.

"This is a wholly inappropriate use of funds," growled Bernard Lowenthal, who, as head of the firm's finance committee, held the purse strings. It was Lowenthal who last month had attempted to discontinue the firm's traditional year-end bonuses for nonattorney personnel—this despite the fact that WW&H was on the way to its most profitable year ever. Lowenthal had been overruled on the bonuses by Charles "Chip" Shepherd, the firm's managing partner. Now, Shepherd disagreed with the tightfisted tax attorney on marketing research.

"Bernie, I'm going to be blunt: Sometimes you can be pretty ignorant," Shepherd asserted. "Just how much longer do you think we can sustain profitability without learning everything we can about our clients? Right now, we know almost nothing. Let's bite the bullet, for heaven's sake, and begin the research before this whole thing gets any further out of hand.

"You and I both know that some people here are spending marketing dollars without any rationale. When we know more about our clients, we'll be able to impose stricter controls on that spending," Shepherd added.

"Setting aside costs for the moment," interrupted trial attorney Janet Lathrop, "I agree that we should know more about our clients. But specifically, what is it we hope to learn from this research? How will we go about it? And who will conduct it?

"I hope you don't think that my attorneys have time to do this sort of thing, Chip. With caseloads being what they are, we can barely keep our heads above water now."

"No, Janet," Shepherd began, massaging his brow wearily, "this is not a project for attorneys. I don't know exactly how we'll go about it. But I think, at a minimum, we ought to be able to create some profiles of our most typical clients—how much they're spending with us, how many and what types of matters they're giving us, which other firms they use and why.

"I suggest we ask Lauren how to start. I don't know if this is a project she can handle by herself, but she can get it going."

Shepherd was referring to Lauren Greene, the firm's marketing director. Greene, WW&H's first marketing director, came from a Big Six accounting firm the year before. When she arrived, she discovered an organization in disarray: a few gung-ho marketers spending money without a rationale or any thought to measurement; some lawyers roundly condemning marketing—and her; and others in the middle, knowing little about marketing but willing to learn as long as it didn't require any commitment on their part.

"So, it's settled," Shepherd stated. "I'll talk to Lauren first thing in the morning."

Discussion Issues

1. If you were Lauren Greene, what would you tell Chip Shepherd when he asks you for advice on marketing research?

2. Does Waring, Weatherell & Hough have a research strategy? Does it need one?

3. What would you tell the lawyers to assure them of the value of marketing research to the firm?

Chapter 1 highlighted the many kinds of problems that marketing research can be used to solve. It emphasized that marketing research is a firm's communication link with the environment and can help the marketing manager in planning, problem solving, and control. Every company has its own way of using marketing research. Some use it on a continuous basis to track sales or to monitor the firm's market share. Others resort to it only when a problem arises or an important decision—such as the launching of a new product—needs to be made.

A company's overall philosophy of how marketing research fits into its marketing plan determines its **program strategy** for marketing research.[1] A program strategy specifies the types of studies that are to be conducted and for what purposes. It might even specify how often these studies are to take place. Program strategy typically answers such questions as "Should we do marketing research?" and "How often?" and "What kind?"

How the individual studies are designed is the basis of a firm's **project strategy.** Project strategy addresses the issue of "Now that we've decided to go ahead with marketing research, how should we proceed? Should we use in-store surveys, self-administered printed questionnaires, or perhaps electronically administered questionnaires? Should we question more people or fewer? More often or less often?" In sum, project strategy deals with how a study should be conducted, whereas program strategy addresses the question of what type of studies the firm should conduct.

A look at how marketing research is handled at Procter & Gamble (P&G), one of the nation's leading consumer manufacturers, should help to clarify the difference between a program strategy and a project strategy.

It is P&G's policy that at least once a year marketing research will be conducted on each of its brands. These studies assess people's likes and dislikes about P&G products, the products' names, packaging, and hundreds of other details. This mountain of information is then funneled to every major segment of the company, including the executive suite, where it is sifted and resifted for implications for P&G's marketing, advertising, manufacturing, and research and development operations. This ongoing process may be thought of as P&G's *program* strategy for marketing research.

The *project* strategies P&G employs vary widely, however. In addition to the usual types of marketing research—such as extensive questionnaires about existing products and test-marketing in supermarkets—P&G takes some further steps. For example, P&G's researchers might follow homemakers around while they do the laundry, noting how they sort the clothes, how many loads they do, and what temperature settings they use on their washing machines. This kind of research has led to some breakthroughs. Cheer, for example, was formulated in response to researchers' observations that homemakers needed one detergent that could handle all fabrics and all water temperatures. The details of this type of research, as well as the specific design of consumer questionnaires or the format in which a new product is sampled to customers in supermarkets, all reflect the company's project strategy.

Research Window 3.1 outlines the kinds of studies that constitute the Gillette Company's program strategy for marketing research. As you can see, each type of study is planned to meet a certain objective. The design of individual studies defines the firm's project strategy—for example, the use of personal interviews in the national consumer studies, mail questionnaires in the brand-tracking studies, and telephone interviews when

Program strategy
A company's philosophy of how marketing research fits into its marketing plan.

Project strategy
The design of individual marketing research studies that are to be conducted.

1. Annual National Consumer Studies

The objectives of these annual studies are to determine what brand of razor and blade was used for the respondents' last shave, to collect demographic data, and to examine consumer attitudes toward the various blade and razor manufacturers. These studies rely on personal interviews with national panels of male and female respondents, who are selected using probability sampling methods.

2. National Brand-Tracking Studies

The purpose of these studies is to track the use of razors and blades so as to monitor brand loyalty and brand switching tendencies over time. These studies are also conducted annually and use panels of male and female shavers. However, the information is collected via mail questionnaires.

3. Annual Brand-Awareness Studies

These studies are aimed at determining the "share of mind" Gillette products have. This information is collected by annual telephone surveys that employ unaided as well as aided recall of brand names and advertising campaigns.

4. Consumer-Use Tests

The key objectives of the use-testing studies are to ensure that "Gillette remains state of the art in the competitive arena, that our products are up to our desired performance standards, and that no claims in our advertising, packaging, or display materials are made without substantiation." At least two consumer-use tests are conducted each month by Gillette. In these tests, consumers are asked to use a single variation of a product for an extended period of time, at the end of which their evaluation of the product is secured.

5. Continuous Retail Audits

The purpose of the retail audits is to provide top management with monthly market share data, along with information regarding distribution, out-of-stock, and inventory levels of the various Gillette products. This information is purchased from the commercial information services providing syndicated retail sales data. The information is supplemented by special retail audits that Gillette itself conducts, which look at product displays and the extent to which Gillette blades and razors are featured in retailer advertisements.

6. Laboratory Research Studies

These studies are designed to test the performance of existing Gillette products and to help in the design of new products. They include having people shave with Gillette and competitor products and measuring the results, as well as determining the number of whiskers on a man's face, how fast whiskers grow, and how many shaves a man can get from a single blade.

Sources: Adapted from "Mature Products Remain as the Mainstays in the Gillette Company," *Marketing News* 17 (June 10, 1983), p. 17; Lourdes Lee Valeriano, "Marketing: Western Firms Poll Estern Europeans to Discern Tastes of Nascent Consumers," *The Wall Street Journal* (April 27, 1992), p. B1; Lawrence Ingrassia, "Gillette Holds Its Edge by Endlessly Searching for a Better Shave," *The Wall Street Journal* (December 10, 1992), pp. A1, A6; Barbara Carton, "To Make Gillette Bristle, Ask about the Razor's Edge," *The Wall Street Journal* (July 30, 1996), p. A1.

Research process
The sequence of steps in the design and implementation of a research study, including problem formulation, determination of research design, determination of data collection method, design of data collection forms, design of the sample and collection of the data, analysis and interpretation of the data, and preparation of the research report.

measuring brand awareness. The goal of all this research is to help Gillette maintain its 60 percent share of the blade and razor market.

All research problems require their own special emphases and approaches. Since every marketing research problem is unique in some ways, the research procedure is usually custom tailored. Nonetheless, there is a sequence of steps called the **research process** (see Figure 3.1), which can be followed when designing the research project. This chapter overviews the research process, and the remaining chapters discuss the stages in the process in more detail.

FIGURE 3.1   **Stages in the Research Process**

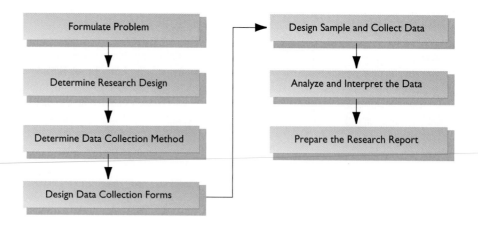

Sequence of Steps in Marketing Research

Formulate Problem

One of the more valuable roles of marketing research is to help define the marketing problem to be solved. Only when the problem is precisely defined can research be designed to provide pertinent information. Part of the process of problem definition includes specifying the *objectives* of the specific research project or projects that might be undertaken. Each project should have one or more objectives, and the next step in the process should not be taken until these can be explicitly stated.

Determine Research Design

The choice of research design depends on how much is known about the problem. If relatively little is known about the phenomenon to be investigated, *exploratory research* will be warranted. Typically, exploratory research is used when the problem to be solved is broad or vague. It may involve reviewing published data, interviewing knowledgeable people, conducting focus groups, or investigating trade literature that discusses similar cases. In any event, one of the most important characteristics of exploratory research is its flexibility. Since researchers know little about the problem at this point, they must be ready to follow their intuition about possible areas and tactics of investigation.

If, instead of being broad or vague, a problem is precisely and unambiguously formulated, *descriptive* or *causal* research is needed. In these research designs, data collection is not flexible but rigidly specified, both with respect to the data collection forms and the sample design. The descriptive design emphasizes determining the frequency with which something occurs or the extent to which two variables covary. The causal design uses experiments to identify cause-and-effect relationships between variables.

Secondary Data
Statistics not gathered for the immediate study at hand but for some other purpose.

Determine Data Collection Method

Often the information that a firm needs to solve its problem already exists in the form of **secondary data,** or data that have already been collected for some purpose other than

Nissan Design International, Inc., in San Diego, California, used new technology and effective marketing research to design a new type of vehicle. It crossed a sport-utility vehicle and a pickup truck to develop this innovative SUT, or sport-utility truck. The Nissan SUT is designed for people who need the passenger space of an SUV but also occasionally need extra cargo space. Focus groups liked the SUT concept so much that the company gave the OK for production. The product may be in showrooms as early as January 2001.

Source: Copyright Nissan (1999). Nissan and the Nissan logo are registered trademarks of Nissan.

Annual | Design | Awards DESIGN EXPLORATION

Nissan Comes Up with a SUT for Sore Eyes

Primary Data
Information collected specifically for the investigation at hand.

the question at hand. Such data may exist in the firm's own internal information system as feedback on warranty cards, call reports from the sales force, or orders from wholesalers. If the firm itself does not have the necessary information, it may be readily available from a good business library, in the form of government statistics or trade association reports. Finally, if neither of these sources proves fruitful, the data may have been collected already by a commercial research supplier. Although the firm must pay for such information, the fee is usually less than the cost of an original study. In any case, for reasons of both cost and time, researchers should always look first at existing sources of data before launching a research project.

If the information needed is not readily available, or if it is available only in a form unsuitable for the problem at hand, then the research must depend on **primary data,** which are collected specifically for the study. The research questions here are several, including: Should the data be collected by observation or questionnaire? How should these observations be made—personally or electronically? How should the questions be administered—in person, over the telephone, or through the mail?

Design Data Collection Forms

Once the researchers have settled on the method to be used for the study, they must decide on the type of observation form or questionnaire that will best suit the needs of the project. Suppose a questionnaire is being used. Should it be structured as a fixed set of alternative answers, or should the responses be open-ended, to allow respondents to reply in their own words? Should the purpose be made clear to the respondents, or should the study objectives be disguised? Should some kind of rating scale be used? What type?

Design Sample and Collect Data

After determining how the needed information will be collected, the researchers must decide what group will be observed or questioned. Depending on the study, this group might be homemakers, preschoolers, sports car drivers, Pennsylvanians, or tennis players. The particular subset of the population chosen for study is known as a *sample.*

Sampling Frame
The list of sampling units from which a sample will be drawn; the list could consist of geographic areas, institutions, individuals, or other units.

In designing the sample, researchers must specify (1) the **sampling frame,** which is the list of population elements from which the sample will be drawn, (2) the sample-selection process, and (3) the size of the sample. Although people often assume the frame is implicit in the research problem and thus take it for granted, that assumption can be dangerous.

> Take the case of the manufacturer of dog food . . . who went out and did an intensive market study. He tested the demand for dog food; he tested the package size, the design, the whole advertising program. Then he launched the product with a big campaign, got the proper distribution channels, put it on the market and had tremendous sales. But two months later, the bottom dropped out—no follow-up sales. So he called in an expert, who took the dog food out to the local pound, put it in front of the dogs—and they would not touch it. For all the big marketing study, no one had tried the product on the dogs.[2]

As this old but classic example illustrates, the dog population was not part of the sampling frame, probably because it is people who buy dog food and not the dogs themselves. Nevertheless, the careless specification of population elements had dire consequences. Although the consequences may be less dire in other cases, it is important to realize that when we sample from, say, a phone book or a mailing list, we are not sampling from the population as a whole, but are only sampling from people whose names appear in the phone book or on the mailing list. Answers to a questionnaire on frequency of air travel would clearly be quite different if the sample were selected from the New York City phone book than if it were selected from the book covering rural West Virginia.

Probability sample
A sample in which each population element has a known, nonzero chance of being included in the sample.

Nonprobability sample
A sample that relies on personal judgment somewhere in the element selection process and therefore prohibits estimating the probability that any population element will be included in the sample.

The sample-selection process requires that the form of the sample be specified. Will it be a **probability sample,** in which each member of the population has a known chance of being selected? Or will it be a **nonprobability sample,** in which the researchers subjectively decide which particular group will be part of the study?

Sample size addresses the issue of how many institutions or subjects it is necessary to use in the project in order to get reliable answers without exceeding the time and money budgeted for it.

Once the dimensions of the sample design are specified, data collection can begin. Data collection requires a field force of some type, although field methods are largely dictated by the data collection method, the kinds of information to be obtained, and the sampling requirements. The use of personnel to collect data raises a host of questions with respect to selection, training, and control of the field staff. For example, what kind of background should interviewers have in order to glean the most information from respondents? What specific training is necessary to ensure that interviewers administer the questionnaires accurately? How often, and in what way, should the accuracy of the answers on the questionnaires be checked by validation studies? These questions should be anticipated in designing the research.

Editing
Inspection and correction, if necessary, of each questionnaire or observation form.

Coding
The technical procedure by which data are categorized; it involves specifying the alternative categories or classes into which the responses are to be placed and assigning code numbers to the classes.

Tabulation
The procedure by which the cases that fall into each of a number of categories are counted.

Analyze and Interpret the Data

Researchers may amass a mountain of data, but it is useless unless the findings are analyzed and the results interpreted in light of the problem at hand. Data analysis generally involves several steps. First, the data collection forms must be scanned to be sure that they are complete and consistent and that the instructions were followed. This process is called **editing.** After being edited, the forms must be **coded,** which involves assigning numbers to each of the answers so that they may be analyzed by a computer. The final step in analyzing the data is **tabulation.** This refers to the orderly arrangement of data in a table or other summary format achieved by counting the frequency of responses to each question. At this point the data may also be cross-classified by other variables. Suppose researchers asked women if they like a certain new cosmetic. Their responses may be cross-classified by age-group, income level, and so forth.

The editing, coding, and tabulation functions are common to most research studies. Any statistical tests applied to the data are generally unique to the particular sampling procedures and data collection instruments used in the research. These tests should be anticipated before data collection is begun, if possible, to ensure that the data and analyses will be appropriate for the problem as specified.

Prepare the Research Report

The research report is the document submitted to management that summarizes the research results and conclusions. It is all that many executives will see of the research effort, and it becomes the standard by which that research is judged. Thus, it is imperative that the research report be clear and accurate, since no matter how well all previous steps have been completed, the project will be no more successful than the research report. One empirical study that investigated the factors determining the extent to which research results are used by firms found that the research report was one of the five most important determinants.[3]

Additional Comments on Marketing Research Steps

While the above discussion should provide some understanding of the steps in the research process, five additional points need to be made. First, each step in the process is more complex than the above discussion suggests. Each involves a number of issues rather than a single decision or even a few decisions. Exhibit 3.1, for example, lists some of the typical questions that need to be resolved at each stage.

Second, although the stages have been presented as if one would proceed through them in a lockstep fashion when designing a research project, nothing could be further from the truth. Rather, Figure 3.1 could be drawn with a number of feedback loops suggesting a possible need to rethink, redraft, or revise the various elements in the process as the study proceeds. The process would begin with problem formulation and then could take any direction. The problem may not be specified explicitly enough to allow the development of the research design, in which case the researchers would need to return to stage one to define the research objectives more clearly. Alternatively, the process may proceed smoothly to the design of the data collection forms, the pretest of which may require a revision of the research objectives or the research design. Still further, the sample necessary to answer the problem as specified may be prohibitively costly, again requiring a revision of the earlier steps. Once the data are collected, no revision of the procedure is possible. It is possible, though, to revise the earlier steps on the basis of the *anticipated* analysis, so it is critical that the methods used to analyze the data be determined before the data are collected.

Although it is hard for beginning researchers to understand, the steps in the research process are highly interrelated. A decision made at one stage will affect decisions at each of the other stages, and a revision of the procedure at any stage often requires modifications of procedures at each of the other stages. Unfortunately, it seems that this lesson is understood only by those who have experienced the frustrations and satisfactions of being involved in an actual research project.

Third, the important error to be concerned about when designing a research project is the *total error* likely to be associated with the project. All the steps are necessary and vital, and it is dangerous to emphasize one to the exclusion of one or more others. Many beginning students of research, for example, argue for large sample sizes. What they fail to realize is that an increase in the sample size to reduce sampling error can often lead to an increase in the total error of the research effort, since other errors increase more than proportionately with sample size. For example, a study may require researchers to call people from a list of randomly selected phone numbers. Even if the numbers themselves represent an excellent cross section of the population, a funny thing may happen on the way to the study's results. Researchers working a nine-to-five day will doubtlessly have trouble connecting with families in which both spouses work or with households made up of single working people. If this potential error is not accounted for, the study may overly represent the homebound—the elderly, families with a baby or an invalid, or the unemployed. The larger the sample size, of course, the larger would be the weight of this

EXHIBIT 3.1	Questions Typically Addressed at the Various Stages of the Research Process
Stage in the Process	**Typical Questions**
Formulate problem	What is the purpose of the study—to solve a problem? Identify an opportunity? Is additional background information necessary? What information is needed to make the decision at hand? How will the information be utilized? Should research be conducted?
Determine research design	How much is already known? Can a hypothesis be formulated? What types of questions need to be answered? What type of study will best address the research questions?
Determine data collection method	Can existing data be used to advantage? What is to be measured? How? What is the source of the data to be collected? Are there any cultural factors that need to be taken into account in designing the data collection method? What are they? Are there any legal restrictions on data collection methods? What are they? Can objective answers be obtained by asking people? How should people be questioned? Should the questionnaires be administered in person, over the phone, or through the mail? Should electronic or mechanical means be used to make the observations?
Design data collection forms	Should structured or unstructured items be used to collect the data? Should the purpose of the study be made known to the respondents? Should rating scales be used in the questionnaires? What specific behaviors should the observers record?
Design sample and collect data	Who is the target population? Is a list of population elements available? Is a sample necessary? Is a probability sample desirable? How large should the sample be? How should the sample be selected? Who will gather the data? How long will the data gathering take? How much supervision is needed? What operational procedures will be followed? What methods will be used to ensure the quality of the data collected?
Analyze and interpret the data	Who will handle the editing of the data? How will the data be coded? Who will supervise the coding? Will computer or hand tabulation be utilized? What tabulations are called for? What analysis techniques will be used?
Prepare the research report	Who will read the report? What is their technical level of sophistication? What is their involvement with the project? Are managerial recommendations called for? What will be the format of the written report? Is an oral report necessary? How should the oral report be structured?

group's opinions. The magnitude of the error caused by a large sample would then have a significant effect on the total error associated with the project.

Total error, rather than errors incurred in any single stage, is the important error in research work, except insofar as those individual errors increase total error. Quite often, *part error,* or *stage error,* will be increased so that total error may be decreased. Questions such as those in Exhibit 3.1 must be addressed so that total error can be minimized.

Fourth, the stages in the research process serve to structure the remainder of this book. The next chapter, for example, discusses the first stage, problem formulation, while each of the remaining stages warrants a special section in the book.

Fifth, the stages in the research process can also be used to direct additional study in research method. The aspiring research student needs more sophistication in at least some of the stages than this book could possibly provide. The sections and chapters will indicate where in-depth study might be most useful.

Back to the Case

Shepherd called Lauren Greene into his office in the morning. "Lauren," he began, "we're going to do some marketing research. We need to know more about who our clients are. How do we begin?"

Greene replied, "You and I have had many discussions about research, Chip, so forgive me if today I go back to the beginning. We need first to articulate the problem: Specifically, what do we need to know and why do we need to know it? Then, let's outline what we hope to achieve with the research."

"Well, as you know, Lauren, some of our partners are spending money on marketing activities without any idea of whether it's effective. We need to get control of these expenditures, and fast.

"Obviously, we've got some accounting controls in place, but that doesn't do much to help us understand the value of the expenditure. To really get a handle on our marketing effort, we need to obtain as complete a picture of our clients as possible. That will help us determine whether we're spending money intelligently on some of these marketing projects," her boss answered.

"And," Greene interjected, "it will give us a yardstick for the marketing activities we want to undertake in the future."

"OK, so how do we go about this?" asked Shepherd.

"There are all kinds of research possibilities," Greene began. "Let's look first at what we can learn from the data the firm already maintains. I'm talking about our financial information, Chip. We have a wealth of secondary data stored in our billing system, and we've never really tapped it for marketing purposes.

"We can extract and organize this information and learn a lot about who our biggest clients are, how often they use us, and how many of our practice groups they use. We can also create profiles on the types of clients we have, all from info we can pull from the billing system.

"Depending on how detailed our attorneys or their secretaries have gotten with the 'Comments' section of the billing system, we may also be able to spot patterns in other things, such as which firms are getting the business we can't handle. For example, when there's a conflict of interest, we may be able to determine what business is being lost and to which firms we are losing it to.

"At some point in the process, we'll want to collect some primary data as well. We'll obtain that kind of information from clients themselves. There are many ways to do this. For now, however, let's assess what's on hand and how we can learn from it."

The discussion continued, with Greene and Shepherd identifying the research problem and outlining the objectives of proposed research. Greene agreed to prepare a memo summarizing their discussion, which Shepherd would use in a report to management on how the research program would proceed.

For more information about marketing to the legal profession, see William J. Winston, ed., *Marketing for Attorneys and Law Firms* (New York: Haworth, 1993).

Summary

Learning Objective 1

Explain the difference between a program strategy and a project strategy in marketing research.

A company's overall philosophy of how marketing research fits into its marketing plan determines its program strategy for marketing research. A program strategy specifies the types of studies that are to be conducted, and for what purposes. It might even specify how often these studies are to take place. The design of the individual studies themselves constitutes the firm's project strategy.

Learning Objective 2

Outline the steps in the research process and show how the steps are interrelated.

The steps in the research process are: (1) formulate the problem, (2) determine the research design, (3) determine the data collection method, (4) design the data collection forms, (5) design the sample and collect the data, (6) analyze and interpret the data, and (7) prepare the research report. These steps are highly interrelated in that a decision made at one stage will affect decisions in every other stage, and a revision of the procedure in any stage often requires modification of procedures in every other stage.

Learning Objective 3

Cite the most critical error in marketing research.

Total error, rather than the size of an error that occurs in any single stage, is the most critical error in research work.

Review Questions

1. What is the difference between a program strategy for research and a project strategy?

2. What is the research process?

3. What is the most important error in research? Explain.

Discussion Questions, Problems, and Projects

1. What advantages are gained by marketing researchers who follow the research process illustrated in Figure 3.1?

2. For each of the situations described below, which type of research design is most appropriate? Why?
   (a) Frank's Flies is a fishing lure manufacturer. Frank's management has decided to enter the lucrative market for trout flies, an area in which the company has little experience. The fly development department has decided that it needs more information concerning trout fishing in general before it can begin designing the new product line.
   (b) The management team at Aardvark Audio strongly suspects that the company's current advertising campaign is not achieving its stated goal of raising consumer awareness of the company's name to a 75 percent recognition level in the target

market. The team has decided to commission a research project to test the effectiveness of the various ads in the current campaign.

(c) Ace Fertilizer Company is trying to decide where advertisements for its vegetable garden fertilizers should be placed. Management is contemplating a research project to determine which publications home gardeners read on a regular basis.

3. Using the steps of the research process to structure your thinking, evaluate the following marketing research effort.

The FlyRight Airline Company was interested in altering the interior layout of its aircraft to suit the tastes and needs of an increasing segment of its market— businesspeople. Management was planning to reduce the number of seats and install small tables to enable businesspeople to work during long flights. Prior to the renovation, management decided to do some research to ensure that these changes would suit the needs of the passengers. To keep expenses to a minimum, the following strategy was employed.

Questionnaires were completed by passengers during flights. Due to the ease of administration and collection, the questionnaires were distributed only on the short flights (those less than one hour). The study was conducted during the second and third week of December, as that was when flights were full. To increase the response rate, each flight attendant was responsible for a certain number of questionnaires. Management thought this was a good time to acquire as much information as possible; hence, the questionnaire included issues apart from the new seating arrangement. As a result, the questionnaire took 20 minutes to complete.

4. Schedule an interview with the marketing research director of a firm near your home or where you go to school. In the interview, try to develop an exhaustive list of the general types of studies the firm conducts and for what purposes. Pick two of the studies and secure as much detail as you can on their specifics, such as the type and size of the sample, the data collection instruments used, what is done with the data after they are collected, and so on. Report on what you find, organizing that report according to the firm's program and project strategies for research.

Endnotes

1. Walter B. Wentz, *Marketing Research: Management and Methods* (New York: Harper and Row, 1972), pp. 19–24. For an example of a program strategy for marketing research, see Robert Johnson, "In the Chips: At Frito-Lay, the Consumer Is an Obsession," *The Wall Street Journal,* March 22, 1991, pp. B1–B2. See also Robert Frank, "Frito-Lay Devours Snack-Food Business," *The Wall Street Journal,* (October 27, 1995, pp. B1, B4; Chad Rubel, "Research Results Must Justify Brand Spending," *Marketing News* 30 (February 26, 1996), p. 12.

2. Joseph R. Hochstim, "Practical Uses of Sampling Surveys in the Field of Labor Relations," *Proceedings of the Conference on Business Application of Statistical Sampling Methods* (Monticello, Ill.: The Bureau of Business Management, University of Illinois, 1950), pp. 181–182. As should be obvious from the example, researchers need to access both constituencies (dogs *and* dogs' purchasing agents) when assessing the appeal of a product like dog food. See Nancy J. Church, "Get the Dog's Opinion When Researching Dog Food," *Marketing News* 22 (August 29, 1988), p. 41, for suggestions on how to go about this.

3. Rohit Deshpande and Gerald Zaltman, "A Comparison of Factors Affecting Researcher and Manager Perceptions of Market Research Use," *Journal of Marketing Research* 21 (February 1984), pp. 32–38. See also Christine Moorman, Gerald Zaltman, and Rohit Deshpande, "Relationships between Providers and Users of Market Research: The Dynamics of Trust within and between Organizations," *Journal of Marketing Research* 29 (August 1992), pp. 314–328.

MARKETING RESEARCH ETHICS

Much of this text discusses the techniques for doing marketing research. Most of the time, the act of choosing a particular technique will involve an implicit judgment about the ethics of the proposed procedure. **Ethics** are the moral principles and values that govern the way an individual or group conduct its activities. Ethics applies to all situations in which there can be actual or potential harm of any kind (e.g., economic, physical, or mental) to an individual or group. **Marketing ethics** are the principles, values, and standards of conduct followed by marketers.

Many researchers (and managers as well) fail to confront the issue of whether it is morally acceptable to proceed in a particular way or whether they are acting in a socially responsible manner by doing so. Many take the view that if it is legal, it is ethical. They fail to appreciate that there can be differences between what is ethical and what is legal. Even among those who do appreciate the distinction, there is often a reluctance to evaluate the ethical implications of their decisions, because they feel ill-equipped to do so. Like most professionals, they simply do not know how or where to start.

Although ignorance may seem like bliss, ignoring ethics issues simply because they are difficult presents real and growing dangers to individual researchers and the marketing research profession itself. One of the most notorious cases in recent years involved research in support of marketing cigarettes to young smokers. During the pretrial fact-finding phase of a California lawsuit against R. J. Reynolds Tobacco Company, company documents about such research came to light. For example, a 1980 memo discussed efforts to research "the demographics and smoking behavior of 14–17 year olds." Other documents referred to efforts to target the 14–24 age group. When the documents became public, they generated a storm of negative publicity, not only for R. J. Reynolds, but for the tobacco industry as a whole.[1]

Other causes for concern rest with the increasing use of the Internet, since once information is on a computer linked to the Internet, it is vulnerable to theft or intentional misuse. For example, General Mills sued a former food scientist, alleging he misappropriated eight breakfast-cereal recipes, including those for Wheaties, Cocoa Puffs, and Cheerios, through unauthorized access to the company's computers before quitting to join a rival cereal maker.[2] Some companies use the Internet to spy on competitors. Some computer manufacturers including Dell and Compaq, for example, use the Internet to check up on rival PC makers, looking for discussion of bugs and product delays, and even joining in chat group discussions of hot products and ideas for competitive products.[3] The Internet has also raised some serious issues regarding invasion of privacy (see Research Window 3A.1).

As mentioned, ethics is not simply a matter of compliance with laws and regulations. Rather, a particular act may be legal but not ethical. For example, even though it is perfectly legal to observe people without their consent when they are shopping, some would argue that it is unethical to do so. Ethics are more proactive than the law. They attempt to anticipate problems, whereas most laws and regulations emerge from social pressure for change in a slow, reactive fashion. Ethics are concerned with the development of moral standards by which situations can be judged. They ask such questions as the following:

- Is the action or anticipated action arbitrary or capricious? Does it unfairly single out an individual or group?

- Does the action or anticipated action violate the moral or legal rights of any individual or group?

Ethics
A concern with the development of moral standards by which situations can be judged; applies to all situations in which there can be actual or potential harm of any kind (e.g., economic, physical, or mental) to an individual or group.

Marketing ethics
The principles, values, and standards of conduct followed by marketers.

Source: This appendix is based largely on the unpublished paper by Jacqueline C. Hitchon and Gilbert A. Churchill, Jr., "The Three Domains of Ethical Concern for the Marketing Researcher."

Research Window 3A.1   **Web Threats to Privacy**

There is no question that the Web has the ability to be extremely nosy.

For instance, Web marketers can determine, without permission, your "domain," the portion of your e-mail address that follows the @ symbol. That can tell marketers whether you reached their site via a consumer service such as America Online or a corporate connection. Internet marketers can thus target specific domains for their ads.

More controversial are the whimsically dubbed *cookies*, a technology that allows Web sites to track individual users. For a long time, Web sites could tally requests for information made each day, but they couldn't tell whether one visitor made 100 requests or 100 users made one request each.

With cookies, a Web site places a tiny file on a visitor's computer that serves as a kind of tracking beacon. The site doesn't know your name or e-mail address, but it does know that you represent a distinct user. (Curious? Search your hard drive for a file called "cookies" and open it in a word-processing program to see who has served you a cookie.)

Cookies feed some of the more dire privacy scenarios. With them, a Web magazine will see which articles you read; a merchant can tell not only which products you bought, but also which product descriptions you simply viewed. (Imagine a supermarket scanner that monitors everything you look at in a store.) Similarly, the merchant knows not only which ads work but which don't.

Still, some of these fears are no doubt overblown. You can set your computer to refuse to accept cookies. When you visit a Web site, the computer maintaining that site may know your domain, but it can't know your e-mail address unless you volunteer it. Of course, plenty of sites that sell products on-line require names, addresses, e-mail addresses, and credit-card information. Providing it, however, is your choice.

Source: Thomas E. Weber, "Browsers Beware: The Web Is Watching," *The Wall Street Journal* (June 27, 1996), pp, B10, B12. See also Walter S. Mossberg, "Threats to Privacy On-Line Become More Worrisome," *The Wall Street Journal* (October 24, 1996), p. B1; Gautam Naik, "Do I Have Privacy On-Line?" *The Wall Street Journal* (December 9, 1996), p. R12.

- Does the action or anticipated action conform to accepted moral standards?

- Are there alternative courses of action that are less likely to cause actual or potential harm?[4]

Marketing researchers need to recognize that (1) the effective practice of their profession depends a great deal on the goodwill of and participation by the public, and (2) currently, the American public is becoming more and more protective of its privacy. This makes it more difficult and costly to approach, recruit, and survey participants. "Bad" research experiences that violate the implicit trust of the participants in a study can only accentuate the trend. In addition to moral fairness issues, then, self-preservation issues dictate that marketing researchers develop a sense for the ethical issues involved in particular choices. The fact that good ethics is good business is one reason associations whose members are involved in marketing research have developed codes of ethics to guide the behaviors of their members.

The purpose of this appendix is to provide marketing researchers with a framework and some guidelines for making ethical judgments. To this end, the appendix first reviews two main approaches from moral philosophy for making ethical judgments—*deontology* and *teleology*. The two approaches offer different perspectives on ethical problems. They illustrate that a judgment about the ethicality of some approach depends not only on the researcher's awareness of the ethical dilemma but also on his or her philosophical orientation or value system.[5] Then the appendix discusses some of the major ethical issues that arise within the researcher's three domains of ethical responsibility: (1) the researcher–participant relationship, (2) the researcher–client relationship, and (3) the researcher–research team relationship. It is recognized that all these interactions take place within a larger environment and that they have potential implications for society as well as for the research profession itself.

One of the many things that make ethical decisions difficult is that the researcher's duties and responsibilities toward one party in the three domains often conflict with the individual's responsibilities toward another, including one's self. The individual then must somehow balance these opposing obligations. Consider, for example, the dilemma faced by a researcher deciding whether to expose the true purpose of a study to potential respondents. The researcher believes that exposing the true purpose beforehand would increase noncooperation and would lower the accuracy and reliability of the data collected from those who participate. The researcher's obligation to the client suggests that the research purpose should be disguised. But that could be unfair to the respondents. As a compromise, the researcher might decide to withhold the purpose initially but then debrief each respondent after securing the data. Even though this might be perceived as being more fair than keeping the purpose hidden, it might also cause some of the respondents to feel that they have been duped. This, in turn, could cause them to refuse to participate in any research investigation in the future, thereby hurting the profession.

Ethical Frameworks

Deontology
An ethical or moral reasoning framework that focuses on the welfare of the individual and that uses means, intentions, and features of an act itself in judging its ethicality; sometimes referred to as the rights, or entitlements, model.

Teleology
An ethical or moral reasoning framework that focuses on the net consequences that an action may have. If the net result of benefits minus all costs is positive, the act is morally acceptable; if the net result is negative, the act is not morally acceptable.

As mentioned previously, there are currently two major traditions providing different bases for evaluating the ethics of a given act that tend to dominate ethical reasoning in general and marketing ethics in particular: **deontology** and **teleology.**[6]

Deontology

Deontological ethics focus on the welfare of the individual and emphasize means and intentions for justifying the act. Deontologists believe that features of the act itself make it right or wrong. Deontological thinking rests on two fundamental principles—the rights principle and the justice principle.

The *rights principle* focuses on two criteria for judging an action: (1) universality, which means that every act should be based on principles that everyone could act on, and (2) reversibility, which means that every act should be based on reasons that the actor would be willing to have all others use, even as a basis for how they treat the actor. The rights principle is the philosophical source of specific, generally acknowledged rights in society, such as the "right to know." Several rights have acquired the force of law and have become established in the literature with respect to the treatment of research participants.

The *justice principle* reflects three categories of justice: (1) distributive, whereby resources are distributed according to some evaluation of just desserts; (2) retributive, whereby the wrongdoer is punished proportionally to the wrong, provided that it was committed knowingly and freely; and (3) compensatory, whereby the injured party is restored to his or her original position. An example of the justice principle applied in a marketing research setting concerns the compensatory measures that researchers take in debriefing research participants who have been significantly changed by the research experience.

With its emphasis on the issue that every individual has a right to be treated in ways that ensure the person's dignity, respect, and autonomy, the deontological model is sometimes referred to as the rights, or entitlements, model.

Teleology

The most well known branch of teleological ethics is *utilitarianism,* which focuses on society as the unit of analysis and stresses the consequences of an act, rather than the intentions behind it, in evaluating ethical status. The utilitarian model emphasizes the consequences that an action may have on all those directly or indirectly affected by it. The utilitarian perspective holds that the correct course of action is the one that promotes "the greatest good for the greatest number." Utilitarianism requires that a social cost/benefit analysis be conducted for the contemplated action. All benefits and costs to all persons affected by the particular act need to be considered to "the degree possible and summarized as the net of all benefits minus all costs. If the net result is positive, the act is morally acceptable; if the net result is negative, the act is not."[7] Net benefits can be assessed by focusing on the questions listed in Exhibit 3A.1.

Historically, social scientists for the most part have assumed that a cost/benefit analysis is appropriate in deciding whether or not to conduct a research study.[8] Usually, the costs of conducting the study, in terms of time, money, and harm to participants, are weighed against its benefits in terms of useful and valid information to society. Marketing researchers have operated similarly, but they have typically focused on the benefits to the client rather than to society as a whole. Both have tended to neglect, or have seemingly been unaware of, other ethical perspectives or the possibility that the decision reached from applying a utilitarian perspective could conflict with one reached from applying some other perspective. This type of situation is illustrated in the ethical dilemmas in Exhibit 3A.2.

EXHIBIT 3A.1   **Questions That Need Asking to Apply the Utilitarian Model**

What are the viable courses of action available?

What are the alternatives?

What are the harms and benefits associated with the courses of action available?

Can these harms and benefits be measured? Can they be compared?

How long will these harms and benefits last?

When will these harms and benefits begin?

Who will be directly harmed? Who will be indirectly harmed?

Who will be directly benefited? Who will be indirectly benefited?

What are the social and/or economic costs attached to each alternative course of action?

Which alternatives will most likely yield the greatest net benefit to all individuals affected by the decision? Or if no alternative yields a net benefit, which one will lead to the least overall harm?

Source: Robert A. Cooke, *Ethics in Business: A Perspective* (Chicago: Arthur Andersen, 1988), p. 5.

EXHIBIT 3A.2   **Two Ethical Dilemmas to Contrast Deontological and Teleological Analysis**

Consider the situation of a small-town sheriff in a "grade-B" Western movie: Twelve individual men are being held as suspects in a murder case. The town is upset, and a mob threatens to kill all 12, unless the individual who committed the heinous crime comes forward. The sheriff can't stop the mob, so he picks one person at random and turns him over to the crowd, thus saving the other 11.

Or consider this case: The CEO of a company is under attack because the company recently experienced some setbacks, which were caused entirely by external circumstances. Stockholders stand to lose much of their investments, and the entire leadership of the company is threatened. The CEO decides to blame one of his vice presidents, picked at random and without any reason. The entire company is saved.

Here's the issue: Did the sheriff or the CEO act rightly in either or both cases?

Source: Taken from the comments made by Myles Brand, provost and vice president for academic affairs at The Ohio State University, while serving as a moderator for the session "Academia: Fostering Values" at the Fourth Biannual W. Arthur Cullman Symposium, The Ohio State University, Columbus, Ohio, April 25, 1988.

The utilitarian (teleological) perspective, with its focus on the greatest good for the greatest number, would suggest that both the sheriff and the CEO acted correctly. By acting the way they did, they saved the most people. The deontological view, with its emphasis on fairness and justice to the individual, would suggest that both men acted unethically. The dilemmas illustrate one of the fundamental problems with the utilitarian view—namely, that individuals or small groups can suffer major harm because their "large costs" are averaged with small gains to a large number of other people, with the result that the net benefit for the act is positive.

Partly because small segments can pay a high price for a slight benefit to large numbers, the suggestion has recently been made that utilitarianism is appropriate only to very general planning when no specific harm to individuals is expected and that marketing activities having a foreseeable and potentially serious impact on individuals should be regulated by deontological reasoning.[9] This implies that since research participants, clients, and team members are identifiable individuals and the effect of the research on them can be anticipated, the criteria of universality and reversibility, rather than a broad cost/benefit analysis, should be applied.

Readers also need to be aware that although the two frameworks emphasize different perspectives by which the ethicality of some contemplated act can be evaluated, neither approach provides precise answers to ethical decisions. In a utilitarian analysis, for example, one still needs to quantify costs and benefits; in deontological reasoning, one needs to evaluate the seriousness of a right's infringement. What constitutes ethical conduct in the eyes of the marketing research profession is ultimately going to be a matter of consensus. That consensus can be reached only if individual researchers think about ethical issues and exchange views.

In part to redress the unbalance in a field dominated by a utilitarian approach to ethical decision making, deontological reasoning underlies the remainder of the discussion in this appendix—specifically, identifying rights violations and conflicts and evaluating their severity. As a student of marketing research, you should form the habit of interpreting a rights violation, as identified here, as a cost to be integrated into a utilitarian cost/benefit analysis. Interpreting the issues from both perspectives should make you a more informed researcher who is better able to see and to evaluate the ethical trade-offs in particular situations.

Researcher—Research Participant Relationship

One useful way of viewing the ethical dilemmas that arise in the domain of the researcher–research participant relationship is by discussing them from the perspective of the rights of research participants. The advantage of discussing these issues within such a framework is that the emphasis is on identifying why a procedure might be unethical (e.g., it violates participants' rights to safety) and learning which procedures cause ethical controversy. Researchers are then in a better position to generalize to new situations as they arise.

On March 15, 1962, President Kennedy delivered a special message on protecting consumers' interests, in which he outlined the Consumers' Bill of Rights, enumerating the right to safety, the right to be informed, the right to choose, and the right to be heard. These four rights were given the force of law in the Privacy Act of 1974, which applies to the abuse of respondents in federal government surveys.[10] Moreover, because most marketing research participants are acting in their role as consumers, these rights are ethically (even where they are not legally) applicable to our discussion. Other rights have since been advocated by various groups (e.g., the right to a consumer education, the right to representation, the right to a healthy physical environment), but one right in particular has been generally accepted and seems appropriate within the domain of the researcher–research participant relationship: the right to redress.[11]

Not all rights violations are grievous, so once an infringement has been identified, subjective judgment is required to evaluate the seriousness of the offense. For example, many researchers have pointed out that the degree of deception involved in concealing the true purpose of an experiment (and disregarding the subjects' right to be informed) is usually of the same trivial order as the degree of deception involved in the "white lies" that are an inherent part of everyone's social and family life.

Figure 3A.1 shows the eight areas of ethical concern that seem most relevant to the domain of the researcher–research participant relationship.[12] Each key issue primarily violates one of three rights: the right to safety, to be informed, or to choose. The fourth right, the right to be heard, is violated whenever a participant is not allowed to ask questions during and after the research procedure or to voice anxieties and misgivings. Moreover, compliance with the subject's right to be heard can sometimes compensate for an infringement of other rights, such as with the use of debriefing procedures after experiments. Where the right to be heard stresses the fundamental need for self-expression, the right to redress emphasizes restoration to an original or comparable position.

Preserving Participants' Anonymity

Maintaining subjects' anonymity ensures that they are safe from invasions of privacy. The preservation of participants' anonymity is often a more serious obligation in the field of

---

FIGURE 3A.1 Ethical Issues in the Researcher-Respondent Relationship

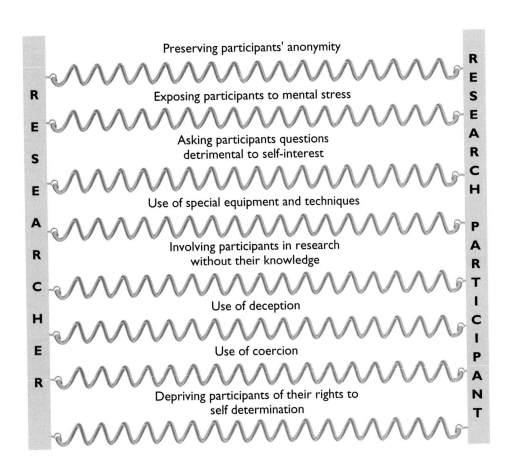

marketing research than in other behavioral disciplines because the information obtained by marketing researchers can be extremely useful to other agents. Purchase-related data, for example, are of interest to all kinds of sellers.[13] Further, knowledge of participants' identities is often desirable for the client who wishes to compile a mailing list of survey respondents, particularly those who feel favorably disposed to the product concept being tested. Unless respondents agree ahead of time to have their identities disclosed to the sponsor, however, such information should not be provided.

Exposing Participants to Mental Stress

An effort should be made at all times to minimize any mental stress that the research procedures may inflict on participants. On an everyday procedural level, this includes arriving punctually for a prearranged interview, showing the subject consideration and respect, and promptly fulfilling one's commitments (e.g., payment for participating). In addition, subjects may be exposed to stress as a result of the subject matter of an experiment. For example, taste tests can be humiliating for participants who pride themselves on their ability to identify a certain brand, when they find themselves unable to do so in a blind taste test.

Debriefing is usually recognized as essential if the research experience is stressful or if deception is used, but it can be undertaken in other circumstances because it is consistent with the subject's right to be heard. Its main purpose is to give participants the opportunity to voice their views on the research experience and to have any anxieties dispelled.

Asking Participants Questions Detrimental to Their Self-Interest

Consider the situation in which a marketing researcher is hired to ask respondents how acceptable certain prices are for a product, when the client's objective is to raise the current price to the highest acceptable level. If respondents are informed of the purpose of the research and its sponsor, they are likely to hedge in their answers, which will reduce the quality of the research. If, on the other hand, they are not informed about the purpose and sponsor, their responses may be against their own self-interest.

Situations like this, which put the researcher's ethical standards against his or her technical standards, are particularly distressing. Although the simplest solution may be to refuse to undertake the project, it is up to the individual to consider all the issues involved and reach an informed decision with which he or she feels comfortable.

Using Special Equipment and Techniques

Special equipment and techniques deserve separate mention largely because they threaten subjects' safety in ways that other procedures do not. Recording devices, for example, make later identification of individual subjects much easier and thus threaten their anonymity. The potential audience for a participant's response is also broadened when recordings are used. In certain cases, such techniques may even render blackmail a possibility. Another class of special techniques to cause ethical concern is projective techniques, the renewed use of which is increasingly being advocated in consumer research.[14] Projective techniques are believed to be means of revealing unconscious thoughts and motives. In situations in which the subject is not even aware of what he or she is revealing, it is evident that the researcher is doubly obliged to act discreetly and responsibly.

If safety is interpreted primarily in physical rather than privacy terms, then equipment used to measure participants' physiological reactions is more likely to violate the right to safety. Although most measures in marketing research have traditionally been either self-report or human observation, there is growing interest in the use of physiological measures, particularly to measure the response to advertising.[15] When testing physiological reactions, the researcher is under obligation to ensure that the machines are used and maintained properly so that there is no threat to the participant's physical safety. In addition, it is important that the subject be psychologically comfortable with the procedure.

Involving Participants in Research without Their Knowledge

The importance of gaining subjects' "informed, expressed consent" was first articulated at the Nuremburg Trials in protest against the inhuman treatment of prisoners involved in research in Nazi concentration camps. The criterion of "informed, expressed consent" has subsequently been incorporated into many codes of ethics and has been amended to allow incompletely informed consent provided that (1) the research involves minimal risk to subjects and (2) the research could not be practically carried out otherwise.

Three common procedures exist that involve subjects in research without their knowledge and therefore without their consent:

First, *participant observation* is the name given to procedures in which the researcher participates in the activity of interest in order to observe people's behavior in their natural environment. A relevant example would be a marketer living among and studying young white American males (18–25 years old) for 18 months in order to better understand their consumption behavior. Few clear guidelines exist on how participant observers should balance ethical concerns against greater validity in observation. One suggestion is to reveal one's true identity and purpose to subjects once the data have been collected and to allow the subjects to read the final report on their activities.[16] This course of action is consistent with participants' right to be heard. It rests on the hope that they will endorse the researcher's efforts and conclusions. If they do not support the study's findings, however, the researcher is faced with two competing obligations: promoting the use of the research versus respecting the subjects' right to redress (i.e., to refuse to participate after the fact).

A second procedure, *observing people in public places,* is less intrusive than participant observation and is also more common among marketing researchers. It is helpful to watch shopper's reactions to new floor displays in a store, for example. For many researchers, any activity or conversation occurring in a public place is fair game and arouses no ethical scruples. Strictly speaking, however, the research participants are being involved without their knowledge or consent, and their rights are being infringed on. If the research cannot be practically carried out by any other means, the violation can be minimized in two ways: (1) by posting an obvious notice over the whole area (e.g., the store), stating that it is under observation by researchers, or (2) by approaching subjects individually once the data have been collected and asking their permission to use the information.

Withholding benefits from control groups is an issue of particular concern in running field experiments. Burroughs-Wellcome's AIDS-combating drug AZT was released for general use before testing was complete, precisely because it seemed ethically indefensible to deprive the tests' control groups of the hope of delaying the disease's progress. Researchers in other AIDS-related studies have handled the situation differently, however. In Uganda, the U.S. National Institutes of Health is funding a study to test an AIDS vaccine. Half the subjects will get the vaccine, and half will get a placebo. And in Zimbabwe, a joint research project sponsored by Johns Hopkins, the University of Zimbabwe, and Montreal General Hospital Research Institute involves giving vitamin A supplements to HIV-positive mothers and/or their babies shortly after birth. (Vitamin A deficiency has been associated with high concentrations of HIV in breast milk.) A computer randomly assigns the subjects to receive either vitamin A or a placebo.[17] Issues to consider in deciding whether to run a field experiment with a control group include the importance of the possible benefit to the participants and the crucial nature of the information to be provided by running the study. In the case of AIDS research, the deadliness of the disease makes these issues difficult to weigh. In Zimbabwe, for example, AIDS has driven average life expectancy down from 65 years to just 39, according to a worldwide population survey by the U.S. Census Bureau.[18]

In an international context, the issues become even more complex. Many people in developing countries may be unfamiliar with how scientific research works. A reporter who talked to some of the subjects of the Zimbabwe AIDS research, for example, asked them if they knew they might be receiving a placebo. Some subjects appeared to be confused by that possibility, although the researchers had tried to obtain informed consent.[19]

Using Deception

Deception is commonly used in research with human participants in the belief that subjects try to guess what behavior the researcher is expecting to see and alter their behavior accordingly.[20] Even procedural information can provoke dysfunctional responses. If the researcher announces that a recall test will be given later, for example, subjects may make a conscious effort to memorize the stimuli, whereas the recall test may well have been intended to tap noneffortful remembrance. Because of such concerns, most research is given a cover story or guise, and subjects in experiments are not informed about what kinds of tests will be given to them later.

These precautions seem sensible from the point of view of preserving the validity of the research, but they violate the subjects' right to know. Once again, there is no single correct decision that can be generalized to all research. A legal framework is available in this instance to supplement other frameworks, however. The 1981 amendment to the Privacy Act sanctions incompletely informed consent, provided that the research involves minimal risk to the subject and cannot be practicably carried out any other way.

Using Coercion

The use of coercion by Nazi doctors in World War II concentration camps to get subjects for their research experiments has been well publicized. Less overt forms of coercion operate frequently in today's research with human subjects, and researchers need to be alert to them.

Captive Subject Pools Unlike many social scientists, marketers usually do not recruit prisoners or hospital patients, subjects who tend to think that it will count against them in their own institution if they refuse to participate. But marketing researchers do commonly use employees who may think that their success in the company is partially dependent on their compliance.

Persistent Harassment Telephone interviewing currently is a popular data collection technique among marketing researchers. Unfortunately, its high usage level has provoked an ethical dispute that may lead to government regulation. Consumers are being harassed by an overload of telephone surveys, many of which are merely sales ploys in disguise and an increasing number of which, though genuine, are irritatingly impersonal computer-voiced interviews.[21] As with all forms of coercion used in recruiting research subjects, harassment by telephone tends to result not only in an ethical dilemma but also in poor data. If people agree to answer questions, they will do so resentfully and without due care; it is also likely that many will refuse to participate at all, with the result that the final sample of respondents will be skewed and will have been relatively costly to obtain.

Status of the Researcher As an expert and authority figure, the researcher can use this status as another subtle source of coercion. Sometimes individuals who initially agree to take part in the research later wish to change their minds but are too intimidated to voice their reluctance. Marketing researchers need to be particularly sensitive to this issue when dealing with children, the elderly, the poor, or the uneducated.

Depriving Participants of Their Right to Self-Determination

The experience of participating in research always has some effect on the individual, but usually it is of a trivial nature, such as when a person fills in a questionnaire in order to kill time before supper. In some instances, however, the subject is substantially changed by the research experience in ways that he or she could not have foreseen. The subject has thereby been deprived of choice in the matter of self-determination. For example, the objective of taste tests is to find the alternative that is preferred by most people or a particular segment of subjects, not to demonstrate to subjects that many of them cannot identify their "favorite" brand when the typical identification symbols (such as the label) have been removed. One nagging question is what this does to the individual's self-confidence. In situations like this, it is the experimenter's responsibility to restore the subject to his or her original, or a comparable, condition.

Exhibit 3A.3 summarizes the discussion regarding the areas of ethical concern involving research participants.

Researcher–Client Relationship

The ethical issues surrounding the researcher's interactions with the study's subjects are difficult in their own right, and they become even more troublesome when the researcher's obligations to the client are introduced into the picture. Many times the demands of how to best serve the client will compete with the demands placed on the researcher regarding the moral rights of participants. Ethical concerns in the domain of

EXHIBIT 3A.3   **Areas of Ethical Concern Regarding Research Participants**

Area of Concern	Example	Ethical Standards
Preserving participant's anonymity	Keeping the names of survey respondents anonymous, even though the client would like to use them to create a mailing list	This is a basic standard of ethical research
Exposing participants to mental stress	Arriving late for a scheduled interview; conducting experiments in which subjects are embarrassed at their lack of knowledge about products	When stress is unavoidable, researcher should debrief subjects afterward.
Asking participants questions against their self-interest	Asking about the acceptability of various prices in order to plan a price increase	Such issues tend to place ethical standards in conflict with technical standards for accurate research.
Using special equipment and techniques	Using equipment to measure physiological responses to a product or promotional message	These must be properly maintained to avoid injury.
Involving participants in research without their knowledge	Secretly observing the behavior of shoppers	Informed consent is a basic ethical standard unless minimal risk to subjects is involved and the research could not be practically carried out with consent.
Using deception	Showing subjects sample advertisements without telling them that they will have to take a recall test afterward	Incompletely informed consent is considered ethical only if there is minimal risk to subjects and research cannot be practically carried out an other way.
Using coercion	Harassing consumers by repeatedly requesting telephone interviews	Coercion is unethical and tends to bias results.
Depriving participants of their right to self-determination	Changing participants in ways they could not expect, such as a taste test in which they cannot identify their preferred brand and unexpectedly lose confidence in their ability to judge	Researchers should try to restore participants to their original condition when this occurs.

the marketing researcher–client relationship can be usefully organized around four main issues: confidentiality, technical integrity, administrative integrity, and research utilization.

Confidentiality

The researcher is obliged to be discreet in at least two respects: (1) in not revealing one client's affairs to another client who is a competitor, and (2) in some circumstances, in not revealing the sponsor of the research to participants. In both cases, the researcher's loyalties can be torn and compromise may be necessary.

It is difficult to serve well several clients who have similar business interests. Even if one keeps one's list of clients confidential so that overt inquiries from one customer about another are avoided, it is not always possible to keep information acquired about one client's interests from affecting work for another client. The collection of basic demographic and socioeconomic information on a particular area is a case in point. What if that information, gathered for one client, is useful in designing a study for another client? Should researchers ignore the knowlede they have when this can raise the quoted cost of the research to the second client and thereby jeopardize the business for the researcher? The issue of when "background knowledge" stops and an ethical conflict begins because of the need for client confidentiality is a real one for independent research agencies.

A conflict of loyalties also exists if the sponsor of the research does not want to be identified to the research participants for fear of biasing their responses or indirectly tipping off a competitor. Participants' right to be informed, however, includes knowledge of the research sponsor as well as of the research purpose. Not every obligation can be fulfilled in this instance, and the researcher must make decisions tailored to each situation. For example, greater weight can be given to participants' rights if they are providing information that could be used against their interests.

Technical Integrity

As Research Window 3A.2 indicates, marketing researchers personally feel that maintaining research integrity is the most difficult ethical problem they face. Violations of research integrity extend from designing studies without due care through the unnecessary use of complex analytical procedures to the deliberate fudging of data. It cannot be emphasized enough that in this pioneering stage of the profession's development, researchers must maintain the strictest technical integrity if they are to have credibility as professional experts. It is not only unethical but also shortsighted to take advantage of the client's lack of expertise in research design and methodology, because where trust fails, funding eventually does also.

Administrative Integrity

Research Window 3A.2 indicates that treating clients fairly is also a difficult ethical problem for marketing researchers. Unfair practices that have received particular mention can be generally grouped under the term *administrative integrity,* as distinguished from technical integrity. For independent research agencies, passing hidden charges to the client and conflicts in pricing are common problems.

Research Utilization

A researcher's ethical obligations to the client extend beyond the mere completion of the project. After the project is finished, the researcher has the responsibility to promote the correct use of the research and to prevent the misuse of the findings. To some extent, these obligations are fulfilled if the contributions and limitations of the research are clearly articulated in the research report. In addition to inadvertent misuse, however, the client might deliberately suppress or distort the research results. Empirical evidence, for example, indicates that dishonesty in reporting to higher-ups is perverting the results of market tests and that potentially successful products have been dropped and unwanted ones have been introduced because of the manipulation of marketing research results.[22]

Research Window 3A.2	Researchers' Own Perceptions of the Four Most Difficult Ethical Problems They Face*	
Activity	**Examples**	**Frequency**
Maintaining their research integrity	Deliberately withholding information, falsifying figures, altering research results, misusing statistics, ignoring pertinent data	33%
Treating outside clients fairly	Passing hidden charges to clients, overlooking violations of the project requirements when subcontracting parts of the project	11
Maintaining research confidentiality	Sharing information among subsidiaries in the same corporation, using background data developed in a previous project to reduce the cost of a current project	9
Balancing marketing and social considerations	Conducting research for companies that produce products hazardous to one's health or research that improves the effectiveness of advertising to children	8

*Based on responses to the question, "In all professions (e.g., law, medicine, education, accounting, marketing, etc.), managers are exposed to at least some situations that pose a moral or ethical problem. Would you briefly describe the job situation that poses the most difficult ethical or moral problem for you?"

Source: Developed from the information in Shelby D. Hunt, Lawrence B. Chonko, and James B. Wilcox, "Ethical Problems of Marketing Researchers," *Journal of Marketing Research* 21 (August 1984), pp. 309–324.

Distortion of the findings can create a serious dilemma for the researcher, because it raises the issue of with whom the researcher's loyalties rest: the manager who hired the researcher and to whom the research report was delivered but who is now distorting the findings to support his or her preconceived beliefs, or the firm for which the manager works. In situations like this, the researcher will often want to set the record straight because it is the firm's (not the manager's) money that paid for the research, and the researcher's own integrity and reputation are also at stake.

Researcher–Research Team Relationship

At this point it may appear that researchers operate as individuals when making research decisions. That is incorrect. Rather, an authority structure that constrains the individual researcher's decision-making latitude is likely to exist. When subordinates are acting according to instructions, the supervisor is partly responsible for their ethical conduct. Moreover, in addition to the official hierarchy, there exists an unofficial sphere of influence that renders every team member partially responsible for the others' moral behavior. Three areas of primary concern in the domain of the researcher–research team are the individual's own belief system, association with others at work, and the opportunity to behave unethically.[23]

Researcher's Own Beliefs

Surprisingly, only a small correlation has been found between people's ethical behavior in organizations and their own ethical beliefs. Indeed, associations with other people who are behaving unethically and the opportunity to behave likewise are better predictors of an individual's conduct than his or her own belief system.[24]

Association with Others at Work

Many studies indicate that superiors have a great deal of influence over juniors' ethical conduct. In fact, actions of top management have been found to be the best predictor of perceived ethical problems for marketing researchers.[25] The source of the boss's influence probably resides in subordinates' fear of reprisals for not conforming and in their acceptance of legitimate authority. As a consequence of poor examples seen by them, marketing practitioners do not see themselves as being under pressure to improve their own ethics. Indeed, they view themselves as more ethical than their peers, top management, and corporate policy. When frequency of contact with superiors is low, peers will have more influence than superiors on ethical conduct.

Opportunity to Behave Unethically

Evidence suggests that the opportunity to engage in unethical behavior affects its occurrence; more behaviors are likely to be unethical when there is greater opportunity to engage in unethical behavior.[26] Moreover, the opportunity to behave unethically is greater for marketing researchers than for many workers because of their boundary-spanning roles. Marketers, in general, span the boundary between the company and the public; marketing researchers, specifically, bridge the gap between the participant and the client, and there is a great deal of room for dishonesty while playing the go-between. Punishments and rewards might be used to reduce the attractiveness of opportunities for unethical conduct, such as a special raise for acting ethically or a delayed promotion for acting unethically. Management could also issue a corporate code of ethics to announce its concern with ethical issues and to voice standards of conduct that it considers desirable. Other suggestions to reduce the acceptability of unethical conduct within the organization include the use of consultants and seminars on ethics.

Needed: A Balanced Perspective

You are probably sensitive by now to the fact that ethical issues are indeed difficult to deal with. Even when one wants to do what is morally right, the correct course of action is not always intuitively obvious. Actions that might benefit one of the parties in the three domains of ethical responsibility might harm another. Whose rights or what benefits should take precedence? There are no easy answers to this question, but there are some things researchers can do to assure themselves that they are operating ethically when making decisions on techniques.

Sensitivity to the issue helps in itself. Asking oneself about the ethical implications of each contemplated course of action is a useful posture in its own right. Those who do that regularly should behave more ethically because their actions then entail explicit rather than implicit judgments. It is also useful to develop experience and expertise in handling difficult ethical situations. To that end, each of the following chapters contains two or more ethical situations that you are asked to evaluate. These Ethical Dilemmas are strategically placed within the chapters to expose you to the technical elements of the situations before confronting you with the ethical issues.

You are strongly urged to evaluate formally each of these Ethical Dilemmas, using both deontological and teleological moral philosophies and taking into account the typical parties with whom researchers deal.

Summary

Ethics is concerned with the development of moral standards that can be applied to situations in which there can be actual or potential harm of any kind (economic, physical, or mental) to an individual or group. When contemplating some action, the marketing researcher needs to be concerned with at least three parties: participants or subjects, clients, and members of the research team.

There are two major traditions providing different bases for evaluating the ethics of a given act that tend to dominate marketing ethics: deontology and teleology. Deontological ethics focuses on the welfare of the individual and emphasizes means and intentions in justifying an act. Deontologists argue that every individual has certain rights, and it is the features of the act itself, with regard to how the act affects these rights, that make the act right or wrong.

Teleological ethics focuses on the benefits to be derived from the act. The various teleological theories differ on the issue of whose benefits to focus on. The most well known branch of teleological ethics, utilitarianism, focuses on society as the unit of analysis. It holds that the correct course of action is the one that promotes the greatest good for the greatest number.

If researchers are to behave ethically, they need to be vigilant. They must be aware that the use of certain techniques in certain instances may be morally questionable. A recommended posture is to evaluate each contemplated action from both the deonological and the teleological perspectives. That, at least, will make the judgment explicit rather than implicit.

Discussion Questions, Problems, and Projects

1. The opinion has sometimes been voiced, "If it's legal, it's ethical." Is there any difference between what is legally right and what is morally right? Explain.

2. What are the essential differences between the deontological and the teleological perspectives? Which do you embrace? Why?

3. What questions would need to be asked to apply the teleological perspective?

4. What are the basic rights of participants in research?

5. What are the areas of most ethical concern within the domain of the researcher–research participant relationship, from a deontological perspective? What rights are at issue in each area?

6. What are the chief ethical concerns of marketing researchers when dealing with clients?

7. What factors most affect a researcher's ethics when dealing with other research team members? What are the implications for how researchers behave?

Endnotes

1. Milo Geyelin, "Reynolds Sought Specifically to Lure Young Smokers Years Ago, Data Suggest," *The Wall Street Journal* (January 15, 1998, p. A4, downloaded from Dow Jones Publications Library, at the Dow Jones Web site, www.dowjones.com, July 26, 1999).

2. Milo Geyelin, "Legal Beat: Why Many Businesses Can't Keep Their Secrets," *The Wall Street Journal* (November 20, 1995), p. B1. See also Joan Indiana Rigdon, "Curbing Digital Dillydalling on the Job," *The Wall Street Journal* (November 25, 1996), pp. B1, B2.

3. Scott McCartney, "Companies Go On-Line to Chat, Spy and Rebut," *The Wall Street Journal* (September 15, 1994), pp. B1, B6. The increasing availability of more electronic equipment such as faxes and portable computers is also causing problems for businesses when trying to protect their trade secrets.

See Carl Quintanilla, "Travel: Tiny Cameras, Bugs and Secret Agents May Be Snooping on Your Business Trip," *The Wall Street Journal* (November 10, 1995), p B1.

4. Robert A. Cooke, *Ethics in Business: A Perspective* (Chicago: Arthur Andersen, 1988), p. 2. See also Lawrence B. Chonko, *Ethical Decision Making in Marketing* (Thousand Oaks, Calif.: Sage Publications, 1995).

5. This appendix approaches ethics from the micro, or individual, level. It can also be approached from a macro perspective, in which the focus is on the ethical rightness or wrongness of the system itself, or from a company or firm perspective. For discussion of the types of questions that arise from these alternative perspectives, see Cooke, *Ethics in Business*.

6. For general discussions of the differences between the perspectives, see Cooke, *Ethics in Business*; O. C. Ferrell and Larry G. Gresham, "A Contingency Framework for Understanding Ethical Decision Making in Marketing," *Journal of Marketing* 49 (Summer 1985), pp. 87–96; Shelby D. Hunt and Scott Vitell, "A General Theory of Marketing Ethics," *Journal of Macromarketing* 6 (Spring 1986), pp. 5–16; and Donald P. Robin and R. Eric Reidenbach, "Social Responsibility, Ethics, and Marketing Strategy: Closing the Gap between Concept and Application," *Journal of Marketing* 51 (January 1987), pp. 44–58. For a general treatment of ethics in marketing, including separate discussions of ethics in advertising, field sales, and marketing research, see Gene R. Laczniak and Patrick E. Murphy, eds., *Marketing Ethics: Guidelines for Managers* (Lexington, Mass.: D. C. Heath, 1985). Gene R. Laczniak and Patrick E. Murphy, *Ethical Marketing Decisions: The Higher Road* (Boston: Allyn and Bacon, 1993).

7. Robin and Reidenbach, "Social Responsibility, Ethics, and Marketing Strategy," p. 46.

8. Louise H. Kidder and Charles M. Judd, *Research Methods in Social Relations*, 5th ed. (New York: Holt, Rinehart and Winston, 1986), pp. 452–510.

9. Robin and Reidenbach, "Social Responsibility, Ethics, and Marketing Strategy."

10. Cynthia J. Frey and Thomas C. Kinnear, "Legal Constraints and Marketing Research: Review and Call to Action," *Journal of Marketing Research* 16 (August 1979), pp. 295–302.

11. David A. Aaker and George S. Day, "A Guide to Consumerism," in David A. Aaker and George S. Day, eds., *Consumerism: Search for the Consumer Interest* (New York: Macmillan Publishing Co., Inc., 1982), pp. 4–8; and Lee E. Preston and Paul N. Bloom, "The Concerns of the Rich/Poor Consumer," in Paul N. Bloom and Ruth Belk Smith, eds., *The Future of Consumerism* (Lexington, Mass.: D. C. Heath, 1986), pp. 38–40.

12. For an alternative classification of issues, see Patrick E. Murphy and Gene R. Laczniak, "Traditional Ethical Issues Facing Marketing Researchers," *Marketing Research: A Magazine of Management & Applications* 4 (March 1992), pp. 8–21.

13. For a discussion of the pros and cons involved in protecting confidentiality, see Richard G. Mitchell, *Secrecy and Fieldwork* (Thousand Oaks, Calif.: Sage Publications, 1993); Stephen Fienberg, "Conflicts between the Needs for Access to Statistical Information and Demands for Confidentiality," *Journal of Official Statistics* 10, pp. 115–132.

14. David G. Mick, "Consumer Research and Semiotics: Exploring the Morphology of Signs, Symbols, and Significance," *Journal of Consumer Research* 13 (September 1986), pp. 196–213; Sidney J. Levy, "Interpreting Consumer Mythology: Structural Approach to Consumer Behavior Focuses on Story Telling," *Marketing Management* 2 (No. 4, 1994), pp. 4–9.

15. David W. Stewart, "Physiological Measurement of Advertising Effects," *Psychology and Marketing* 1 (Spring 1984), pp. 43–48; John T. Cacioppo and Richard E. Petty, "Physiological Responses and Advertising Effects: Is the Cup Half Full or Half Empty?" *Psychology and Marketing* 2 (Summer 1985), pp. 115–126; Joanne M. Klebba, "Physiological Measures of Research: A Review of Brain Activity, Electrodermal Response, Pupil Dilation and Voice Analysis Methods and Studies," in *Current Issues and Research in Advertising* (Ann Arbor: University of Michigan, 1985), pp. 53–76; Scott S. Liu, "Picture-Image Memory of TV Advertising in Low-Involvement Situations: A Psychophysiological Analysis," in *Current Issues and Research in Advertising*, pp. 27–66; Lee S. Weinblatt, "The Evolution of Technology in Pretesting," *Marketing Research: A Magazine of Management & Applications* 6 (Spring 1994), pp. 42–44.

16. Elizabeth C. Hirschman, "Humanistic Inquiry in Marketing Research: Philosophy, Method, and Criteria," *Journal of Marketing Research* 23 (August 1986), p. 243.

17. Brenda Wilson, "AIDS in Zimbabwe, Part II," *Morning Edition* (February 26, 1999, downloaded from the National Public Radio Web site, www.npr.org, July 26, 1999); Associated Press, "Test of AIDS Vaccine Beginning in Uganda," *Boston Globe* (February 9, 1999, downloaded from Knight-Ridder's NewsLibrary, http://newslibrary.krmediastream.com, July 26, 1999); D. Grady, "Look, Doctor, I'm Dying. Give Me the Drug," *Discover* (August 1986), pp. 78–86.

18. Neely Tucker, "AIDS Drastically Cuts Life Spans in Southern African Nations," *Philadelphia Inquirer* (March 19, 1999, downloaded from Knight-Ridder's NewsLibrary, http://newslibrary.krmediastream.com, July 26, 1999).

19. Wilson, "AIDS in Zimbabwe, Part II."

20. Alan G. Sawyer, "Demand Artifacts in Laboratory Experiments," *Journal of Consumer Research* 1 (March 1975), pp. 20–30; Leonard Berkowitz and Edward Donnerstein, "External Validity Is More Than Skin Deep: Some Answers to Criticisms of Laboratory Experiments," *American Psychologist* 37 (March 1982), pp. 245–257.

21. The practice of "sugging" (selling under the guise of research) should decrease because the Telemarketing and Consumer Fraud and Abuse Prevention Act, passed in 1994, requires telemarketers to divulge that they are selling something when they contact consumers by telephone. See Diane K. Bowers, "Sugging Banned, At Last," *Marketing Research: A Magazine of Management & Applications* 7 (Fall/Winter 1995), p. 40.

22. Calvin L. Hodock, "Intellectual Dishonesty Is Perverting the Results from Various Market Tests," *Marketing News* 18 (January 1984), p. 1; "Respondents Assail Quality of Research," *Marketing News* 29 (May 8, 1995), p. 14.

23. Ferrell and Gresham, "A Contingency Framework for Understanding Ethical Decision Making in Marketing."

24. Mary Zey-Ferrell and O. C. Ferrell, "Role-Set Configurations and Opportunities as Predictors of Unethical Behavior in Organizations," *Human Relations* 35 (July 1982), pp. 587–604; O. C. Ferrell, Mary Zey-Ferrell, and Dean Krugman, "A Comparison of Predictors of Ethical and Unethical Behavior among Corporate and Agency Advertising Managers," *Journal of Macromarketing* 3 (Spring 1983), pp. 19–27.

25. Shelby D. Hunt, Lawrence B. Chonko, and James B. Wilcox, "Ethical Problems of Marketing Researchers," *Journal of Marketing Research* 21 (August 1984), p. 314.

26. Zey-Ferrell and Ferrell, "Role-Set Configurations and Opportunities"; Ferrell and Gresham, "A Contingency Framework for Understanding Ethical Decision Making."

Chapter 4

PROBLEM FORMULATION

Upon Completing This Chapter, You Should Be Able to

1. Specify the three sources of marketing problems or opportunities.

2. Describe the main purpose of marketing research for each of the three sources of marketing problems.

3. Describe a decision situation.

4. List the factors that make up a decision maker's environment.

5. Describe the various elements a researcher must understand in order to address the real decision problem.

6. Distinguish between a decision problem and a research problem.

7. Explain why a decision tree can be useful in problem solving.

8. Outline the various elements of the research proposal.

Case in Marketing Research

Elizabeth Silver didn't like what she was hearing from her ad agency, BBDO Worldwide. Silver, senior vice president of advertising at Visa USA, had asked BBDO to run focus groups to learn consumers' image of the Visa credit card. What they said was a little embarrassing.

Charles Miesmer, vice chairman and senior executive creative director of BBDO, put it this way: "We heard 'garden hose.'" In other words, people thought of Visa when it came time to pay for mundane items.

Silver, Miesmer, and their teams agreed that this was not an image that served the company well.

They wanted the brand to stand apart from its major rival, MasterCard. They wanted people to think of using a Visa card in more situations. And they wanted people to feel good about using their Visa card—not to feel awkward pulling it out on a special date or with an important client.

To fulfill those plans, Visa needed a makeover—a more exciting image.

Silver and Miesmer agreed that their strategy would be to reposition Visa. They wanted Visa to be more prestigious, even potentially a card that businesses would issue to their executives and salespeople. "But how can we tell people that Visa is something different?" mused a member of Silver's group.

Miesmer promised that his team would soon be back with a proposal. He already had an idea to explore.

Discussion Issues

1. What is the decision problem Elizabeth Silver faces?

2. What specific research problems emerge from this decision problem?

3. How should the Visa and BBDO teams proceed?

Problem Formulation

An old adage says, "A problem well defined is half solved." This is especially true in marketing research, for it is only when the problem has been clearly defined and the objectives of the research precisely stated that research can be designed properly. "Properly" here means not only that the research will generate the kinds of answers needed, but that it will do so efficiently.

Problem definition (or problem formulation) is being used in the broadest sense of the term. It refers to those situations that might indeed represent real problems to the marketing decision maker, as well as to those situations that might be better described as opportunities. In order to understand the problem definition stage of the marketing research process, it is helpful to have some appreciation of how problems and opportunities arise.

There seem to be three fundamental sources for marketing problems or opportunities and, consequently, research problems: (1) unanticipated change, (2) planned change, and (3) serendipity in the form of new ideas.[1] Change in one form or another is the most important source by far.

One of the great sources of unanticipated change is the environment in which firms operate. There are many elements in a firm's external environment that can create problems or opportunities. These include demographic, economic, technological, competitive, political, and legal changes that can impact, often significantly, the marketing function. How the firm responds to new technology or a new product introduced by a competitor or a change in demographics or lifestyles largely determines whether the change turns out to be a problem or an opportunity. In recent years, many change-driven problems and opportunities have resulted from the widespread adoption of Internet technology. For example, the executives and editors of the business world's prestigious *Fortune* magazine noticed a growing amount of advertising in on-line rivals such as *Business 2.0* and *Red Herring*. They conducted an analysis and found that three-quarters of that advertising came from advertisers that don't buy space in *Fortune*. The magazine's management therefore began evaluating whether to launch the company's own cyberpublication.[2]

Not all change is unanticipated. Much of it is planned. Most firms want to increase their business and contemplate various marketing actions for doing so. These actions include the introduction of new products, improved distribution, more effective pricing, and advertising. Planned change is oriented more toward the future, while unanticipated change is oriented more toward the past. The former is more proactive, while the latter is more reactive. Planned change is change that the firm wishes to bring about—the basic issue is *how*. The role of marketing research here is to investigate the feasibility of the alternatives being considered.

A third source of marketing problems or opportunities is serendipity, or chance ideas. The new idea might come from a customer in a complaint letter or by some other means. For example, Rubbermaid makes it a practice for its executives to read customer letters to find out how people like the company's products. These letters often lead to new product ideas. For example, complaints about the difficulty of storing traditional rack-and-mat sets because of their bulk led the company to develop a one-piece dish drainer for washing dishes by hand. Strict attention to detail, including suggestions like this, has allowed the company to introduce hundreds of new products a year and over 30 percent of the company's sales in recent years have come from new products.[3] Marketing research plays an important role in the company's development process. Besides customers, other sources of good ideas are salespeople and their call reports. Similarly, comments from the trade might serve as the impetus for planned change, for which research might play a role.

E-corporations are companies built around the Internet. Change for these companies is not only anticipated and planned but planned overnight. Amazon.com is an e-corporation whose business is in retail sales. Begun in 1994, the company is built on innovation credited to encouraging e-mail feedback, sorting through purchase histories, conducting focus groups, and even buying companies like PlanetAll.com (an online community site chock full of good data). With 16 million items for sale, Amazon.com has "Earth's biggest selection," says chief executive Jeffrey Bezos (photo). Change at Amazon.com has included adding music, videos, toys and games, electronics, greeting cards, and auctions to the books it offers some 8.4 million customers—plus links to drugstore goods, pet supplies, and more.

Source: © 1999 Tina Hager—Focus Matrix

Regardless of how problems or opportunities arise, most of them will require additional information for resolution. The information needed for their resolution will need to be identified and approaches for securing it determined. This requires good communication between the decision maker and the marketing researcher. The decision maker needs to understand what research can and cannot accomplish. The researcher needs to understand the nature of the decision the manager faces and what he or she hopes to learn from research—that is, the project objectives.

Researchers must avoid simply responding to managers' requests for information. To do so is akin to a doctor letting a patient perform his or her own diagnosis and prescribe the treatment as well. Rather, the researcher needs to work with the manager much like a doctor works with a patient; both need to communicate openly in translating symptoms into underlying causal factors.

Sometimes marketers confuse problems with symptoms. A problem is a situation requiring some type of action, whereas a symptom is merely evidence that a problem exists. For example, Xerox became concerned a number of years ago that it was rapidly losing photocopier sales to Japanese competitors. That was the symptom. An investigation revealed that while Xerox was focusing on which features it could add to its copiers to make them more desirable, the problem was product quality. Customers wanted copiers that would break down less often.[4]

There is a general tendency to assume that managers have a clear understanding of the problems they face and that the only real difficulty lies in communicating that understanding. This assumption is false. To many managers, the problem is primarily a lack of important facts. They tend to define it as a broad area of ignorance. "They say in effect: 'Here are some things I don't know. When the results come in, I'll know more. And when I know more, then I can figure out what to do.'"[5] Research results based on such a mode of operation most often turn out to be "interesting," but not very actionable. All the results do is reduce the level of uncertainty, but they provide little understanding of the true problem. Both managers and researchers need to recognize that marketing research does not produce answers or strategies. It produces data—data that must be interpreted and converted into action plans by management. In order for the interpretation to be on target, the research needs to reflect management's business priorities and concerns, for "it is far better to resolve the right . . . problem partially than to resolve the wrong problem fully."[6]

Managers need to play an active role in communicating their information needs to researchers. They also need to be semiactive participants in the research process itself, interacting with the researchers when necessary to ensure that the research will provide the information they truly need to make the decisions with which they are faced. Sometimes this may mean using their own intuition when interpreting the research findings, as Research Window 4.1 demonstrates.

In other cases it means managers getting directly involved in the research process. One factor, for example, that plays an important part in Japan's new product development is that the Japanese consider marketing research to be a line function executed by all participants in the product development process and not a staff function performed only by marketing researchers. One upshot of their perspective is a more hands-on approach that looks at the context in which things occur and that emphasizes softer or less formal data collection methods to a greater extent. For example, Toyota sent a group of its engineers and designers to southern California to nonchalantly observe how women got into and operated their cars. Their observations suggested that women with long fingernails had trouble opening the door and operating various knobs on the dashboard. Using this knowledge, they were able to redraw some of their automobile and interior designs.[7]

A proper understanding of the basic structure of decisions can help researchers do a better job of determining the information needs of managers. The simplest of decision situations can be characterized by the following conditions (see Figure 4.1).

"My mistake was in ignoring the effect that global marketing imperatives would have on local hot dog sales."

Source: Drawing by Ed Fisher. © 1990 *Advertising Age*. Reprinted by permission of Ed Fisher.

In the early days of pay-cable services, a television company was considering the establishment of a cultural cable channel as a logical extension of its business. A company executive commissioned a survey to determine the demand for such a channel, which would have carried a monthly fee similar to that charged by Home Box Office (HBO), at the time the only existing pay-cable outlet.

The survey appeared to give a green light to the project, indicating that 20 percent of all cable users would subscribe. But the executive, even though he could find no technical flaw in the questionnaire or the sampling technique, remained skeptical of the results. He remembered from his years of experience how focus group participants would often claim to be fans of public television but would rarely admit to watching *Dallas, Dynasty,* or other top-rated network shows. This phenomenon suggested to him that the survey data might not be realistic.

Pursuing his hunch, the executive hired another research firm to investigate the channel's potential. This firm knew that consumers have been known to tell white lies to an interviewer. They tend, for example to exaggerate their involvement in socially desirable activities such as voting. Similarly, they are apt to overestimate their willingness to purchase attractive or glamorous new products or services. They may wish to please the interviewer, to appear open to new experiences, to appear financially capable of purchasing the offering, or—as in the case of the cable station—to appear intelligent and cultured. The new

research team constructed its study to account for such tendencies.

Although the researchers asked many of the same questions that appeared in the first survey, they also included seemingly unrelated questions about respondents' recent participation in a range of activities, from attending the opera to going to the zoo to watching a ball game. Again, 20 percent said they were willing to pay for the cultural channel. But when respondents who had never before patronized cultural events were eliminated from the "yea sayers"—on the assumption that they were unlikely to undergo a sudden metamorphosis into highbrows—the research predicted that less than 1 percent of cable users were likely to subscribe. The company scrapped its plan for the station.

How did this cable executive avoid a calamity? First, his understanding of the market allowed him to recognize shortcomings in the initial research. Second, he was able to find a research company experienced in gauging consumers' real interest in new products. Obviously, had he commissioned the research only to support a decision he had already made, he would never have questioned the encouraging findings of the first study. His success underscores the importance of direct management's involvement in market research.

Source: Robert S. Duboff, "The Real Magic of Market Research," *Viewpoint* 17 (Summer 1988), pp. 19–20.

1. Person or organization X has a problem. That problem is the result of something that is taking place in X's environment (E).

2. There are at least two courses of action, A_1 and A_2, that X can follow.

3. If X chooses to follow A_2, for example, there are at least two possible outcomes of that choice (O_1 and O_2). Of these outcomes, one is preferred to the other, so the decision process must have an objective.

4. There is a chance, but not an equal chance, that each course of action will lead to the desired outcome. If the chances were equal, the choice would not matter.[8]

To sum up, a person faces a decision situation if he or she has a problem, knows several good, but not equally good, ways of solving it, and must pick between the various choices available. Research can assist in clarifying any of these characteristics of the decision situation. Let us briefly consider how.

FIGURE 4.1   **A Sample Decision Situation**

Barbara B., a high school student interested in a broadcasting career, must decide whether to go to **College A₁**—*an inexpensive community college nearby, which will allow her to live at home and work part-time as a secretary at a local radio station in hopes of getting experience that will lead to a good job in her field, or* **College A₂**—*an expensive but excellent private college far from home, with a well-known communications department and a good track record in job placement and in percentage of students accepted to graduate school. What might be the advantages—and disadvantages—of each choice?*

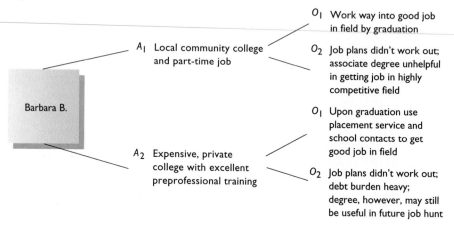

Barbara B.

A_1 Local community college and part-time job

O_1 Work way into good job in field by graduation

O_2 Job plans didn't work out; associate degree unhelpful in getting job in highly competitive field

A_2 Expensive, private college with excellent preprofessional training

O_1 Upon graduation use placement service and school contacts to get good job in field

O_2 Job plans didn't work out; debt burden heavy; degree, however, may still be useful in future job hunt

The Decision Maker and the Environment

It is important that the researcher understand the personality of the decision maker and the environment in which that person operates. Sometimes a decision maker will have preset ideas about a particular situation, and surprisingly, his or her position may not change, regardless of what is found by the researcher. Research merely represents "conscience money" in these cases. The results are readily accepted when they are consistent with the decision the individual wants to make, or with the person's perceptions of the environment or the consequences of alternative actions. Otherwise, the results are questioned at best, or discarded as being inaccurate at worst. The reason, of course, is that the individual's view of the situation is so strongly held that the research will do little to change it. When this is the case, research will be a waste of the firm's resources. The first task of the researcher, therefore, is to discover whether the decision maker is truly willing to consider the results of the research.

Often the task of determining whether management's preferred opinion might change with research information is complicated by the fact that the researcher's contact is not the final decision maker but a liaison. Yet, this determination should be made before the researcher begins work.

As previously mentioned, the researcher also needs to understand the environment of the enterprise in which the decision maker operates. What are the constraints on that person's actions? What are the resources at the decision maker's disposal? What is the time frame in which the manager is operating? It does little good to design a study, however accurate, that costs $20,000 and takes six months to complete when the decision maker needs the results within one month and has only $2,000 for the research. Obviously, some compromises must be made, and it is the researcher's responsibility to anticipate them by carefully examining the decision environment.

The corporate culture, of course, is an important factor in the environment and should be carefully studied by the researcher. In some firms, the process by which decisions are made is dominant, while in other firms the personality of management is more important. At General Mills, for example, the emphasis is on research that evaluates alternatives. Thus, instead of asking the question, "What proportion of potato chips is eaten at meals?" General Mills would ask, "How can we advertise our potato chips for meal consumption?" or "Will a 'meal commercial' sell more chips than our present commercial?" (both action questions). To design effective research for General Mills, therefore, a researcher would need to be aware of this aspect of the general corporate culture.

The environment will include the state of the economy in general and also the economic situation of the particular industry involved and the company itself. In the 1990s, for example, the environment for manufacturers of fast-selling products like personal computers and cell phones was quite different from that for the steel industry, despite the fact that they were both part of the same national economy.

Alternative Courses of Action

Research can be properly designed only when the alternative courses of action being considered are known. The more obvious ones are typically given to the researcher by the decision maker, and the researcher's main task is to determine whether the list provided indeed exhausts the alternatives. Quite often the researcher will not be informed of some of the options being considered. The researcher should check to see that all implicit options have been made explicit, since it is important that the research be relevant to all alternatives.

As an example of the types of alternative courses of action that a company may weigh, consider the Campbell Soup Company, which has a strong commitment to keeping pace with consumer and technological trends. As part of its ongoing research, the company's product managers team up with in-house and outside researchers to probe for openings in the market. Research teams have investigated the preferences and eating habits of growing consumer market segments and noted the preference for easier-to-prepare items. Thus, some of the company's newest products are based on convenient packaging: tomato soup in resealable plastic bottles and microwaveable soup in single-serving containers. The company is also testing a type of vending machine for soup, which could be installed in convenience stores.[9]

Researchers at times must adopt the role of detective in order to uncover the hidden agendas and alternatives lurking beneath the surface in any decision situation. If a critical piece of information remains undiscovered, even the most sophisticated research techniques cannot solve the problem. Attempting to impress the company president, researchers at Pillsbury discovered this fact belatedly—to their embarrassment (Figure 4.2).

FIGURE 4.2	The Best-Laid Models of Mice and Men . . .

The late Bob Keith, while president of the Pillsbury Company, was once persuaded by Pillsbury's operations researchers to review one of his major marketing decisions using a formal decision model. He agreed to the outcomes, their values, and their probabilities, and chose the decision rule he felt most appropriate. The computer then calculated the expectations, compared them, and reported the alternative that should be chosen according to that rule. Keith disagreed, noting that another alternative was obviously the only correct choice—indeed, it was the choice that had been made not long before. "How can that be?" the researchers asked. "You accepted all the values and probabilities and chose the decision rule yourself. The rest is just arithmetic." "That's fine," Keith replied, "but you forgot to ask me about a few other things that were more important."

Source: Adapted from Charles Raymond, *The Art of Using Science in Marketing* (New York: Harper and Row, 1974), p. 17.

Objectives of the Decision Maker

As a part of understanding the decision maker, the researcher should be aware that individuals differ in their attitudes toward risk and that these differences influence their choices. Some people are willing to assume a good deal of risk for the chance of even a small gain.[10] Others are unwilling to assume any risk, even when the potential gain is great. And some individuals walk a middle ground.

A person's attitude toward risk changes with the situation. When feeling secure in his or her position in the company, a person may take greater risks than at another time, when feeling less secure.

It is the researcher's task to discover what attitude toward risk the decision maker has. Often some hint of the decision maker's posture can be gained from intensive probing, using "what if" hypothetical outcomes of the research.

Closely allied to the need to determine the decision maker's attitude toward risk is the need to determine the decision maker's specific objectives. It is unfortunate, but true, that these are rarely explicitly stated.

> Despite a popular misconception to the contrary, objectives are seldom given to the researcher. The decision maker seldom formulates his objectives accurately. He is likely to state his objectives in the form of platitudes which have no operational significance. Consequently, objectives usually have to be extracted by the researcher. In so doing, the researcher may well be performing his most useful service to the decision maker.[11]

The researcher must transform the platitudes into specific operational objectives that the research can be designed to serve.

> One effective technique for uncovering these objectives consists of confronting the decision maker with each of the possible solutions to a problem and asking him whether he would follow that course of action. Where he says "no," further probing will usually reveal objectives which are not served by the course of action.[12]

Another useful technique for uncovering objectives is to get the decision maker to agree to a single-sentence statement specifying the primary objectives to guide the research.[13]

Once the objectives for the research are finally decided upon, they should be committed to writing. In the course of this effort, additional clarity in thinking and in communication between the decision maker and researcher is often achieved. They should then agree formally on their written expression (by initialing each statement of purpose, by initialing the entire document, or by some other means). This tends to prevent later misunderstandings.

Consequences of Alternative Courses of Action

A great deal of marketing research is intended to determine the consequences of various courses of action. Much of the research highlighted in the tables in Chapter 1, for example, deals with the impact of manipulating one of the elements in the marketing mix. This is not surprising since, as we have seen, the marketing manager's task basically involves manipulating the elements of the mix to achieve customer satisfaction. What is a more natural marketing research activity than seeking answers to such questions as, What will be the change in sales occasioned by a change in the product's package? If we change the sales compensation plan, what will be the effect on the sales representatives' performance and on their attitudes toward the job and company? Which ad is likely to generate the most favorable customer response?

Researchers are primarily responsible for designing research that accurately assesses the outcomes of past or contemplated marketing actions. In this capacity, they must gauge the actions against all the outcomes management deems relevant. Management, for example, may want to know the impact of the proposed change on sales as well as on consumer attitudes. If the research addresses only consumer attitudes, management will most assuredly ask for the relationship between attitudes and sales. Embarrassing questions of this nature can only be avoided if researchers painstakingly probe for all relevant outcomes before designing the research.

Translating the Decision Problem into a Research Problem

Decision problem
The problem facing the decision maker for which the research is intended to provide answers.

Research problem
A restatement of the decision problem in research terms.

A detailed understanding of the decision maker's personality, environment, objectives, and preconceived ideas of possible alternative courses of action should enable researchers to translate the **decision problem** into a **research problem.** A research problem is essentially a restatement of the decision problem in research terms. Consider, for example, the new product introduction for which sales are below target. The decision problem faced by the marketing manager is what to do about the shortfall. Should the target be revised? Should the product be withdrawn? Should one of the other elements in the marketing mix, such as advertising, be altered? Suppose the manager suspects that the advertising campaign supporting the new product introduction has been ineffective. This suspicion could serve as the basis for a research problem. The product manager who believes that advertising was not creating sufficient customer awareness for a successful non-product launch might wish to have some evidence that either confirmed or denied that suspicion before changing the advertising program. The research problem would then become the assessment of product awareness among potential customers.

Some illustrations of the distinctions between decision problems and research problems can be found in Exhibit 4.1. Though the two problems are obviously related, they are not the same. The decision problem involves what needs to be done. The research problem involves determining what information should be provided in order to make the decision on what needs to be done—and how that information can best be secured.

In making the determination, the researcher must make certain that the real decision problem, not just the symptoms, is being addressed. The landscape is dotted with examples where poor decision problem definition led to poor research problem definition with unfortunate consequences, some more dire than others. The debacle with Coca-Cola Classic is well known. What is perhaps less well known is that Miller did not invent Lite beer. Rather, it was first developed by Meister Bräu.[14] The taste tests indicated that people

EXHIBIT 4.1	Examples of the Relationship Between Decision Problems and Research Problems

Decision Problems	Research Problems
Develop package for a new product	Evaluate effectiveness of alternative package designs
Increase market penetration through the opening of new stores	Evaluate prospective locations
Increase store traffic	Measure current image of the store
Increase amount of repeat purchasing behavior	Assess current amount of repeat purchasing behavior
Develop more equitable sales territories	Assess current and proposed territories with respect to their potential and workload
Allocate advertising budget geographically	Determine current level of market penetration in the respective areas
Introduce new product	Design a test market through which the likely acceptance of the new product can be assessed
Expand into other countries	Assess market potential for firm's products in each of the countries being considered
Select foreign distribution channels	Evaluate current channel structures and channel members in each of the countries being considered

like the beer. When it was introduced by Meister Bräu, though, it failed. The company in turn sold it to Miller, who defined the decision problem and subsequently the research problem as something more than having a preferred taste. Rather, Miller's research suggested that the big beer drinkers tried to project macho images, and the very concept of a diet beer connoted "wimp." Miller's emphasis thus became one of changing the image of the brand through its use of famous sports personalities.

Another instance of poor problem definition leading to poor interpretation of research involved RJR Nabisco's attempt to develop a smokeless cigarette. After much hard work to develop a cigarette with an acceptable taste but no visible smoke, the company launched Eclipse. Unfortunately, smokers didn't care to buy the product; they liked the smoke of a cigarette. Cigarettes' smokiness was a problem only for nonsmokers—and they, by definition, were not the company's target market. The company's $100 million development effort went to correct something its customers didn't view as a problem by developing a product they didn't want.[15]

How does one avoid the trap of researching the wrong decision problem? The main way is to delay research until the decision problem is properly defined.

There is an old saying that applies here: "If you do not know where you want to go, any road will get you there." It is the same in decision making. If the decision maker does not know what he or she wants to achieve, any alternative will be satisfactory and research will be of little use. Too often the researcher's initial step is to write a proposal describing the methods that will be used to conduct the research. Instead, the researcher should take the time to examine the situation carefully so as to acquire the necessary appreciation for (1) the decision maker and the environment, (2) the alternative courses of action, (3) the objectives of the decision maker, and (4) the consequences of alternative actions. As Figure 4.3 indicates, even marketing managers believe that researchers should take an active role in helping to define the decision problem and in specifying the information that will be useful for solving it.

One useful mechanism for making sure that the real decision problem will be addressed by the research is to execute a **research request step** before preparing the research proposal.[16] This step requires that the decision maker and researcher have a meeting in which the decision maker describes the problem and the information that is needed. The researcher then drafts a statement describing his or her understanding of the problem. The statement should include, but is not limited to, the following items:

Research request step
The initial step that sets the research process in motion; this statement, which is prepared by the researcher after meeting with the decision maker, summarizes the problem and the information that is needed to address it.

Ethical Dilemma 4.1

The president of a small bank approaches you with plans to launch a special program of financial counseling and support for women and asks you to establish whether there is sufficient public interest to justify starting the program. No other bank in the city caters specifically to women, and you think that professional women, in particular, might be enthused. The president believes that if news of the plan leaks out, competitors may try to preempt her, so she asks you to keep the bank's identity secret from respondents and to inquire only into general levels of interest in increased financial services for women. However, as you read through the literature that she has left on your desk, you notice that the bank is located in the most depressed area of the city, where women might be harassed and feel unsafe.

- Would it be unethical to research the general problem of how much demand exists for a women's banking program, when the bank in question will interpret the demand as encouragement to launch such a program itself?

- What might be the costs to the researcher in voicing misgivings about the suitability of this particular bank's launching of the program? Would you voice your misgivings?

- Does it violate respondents' rights if you do not reveal the identity of the research sponsor? If so, is it a serious violation in this case? Is there a conflict of interest here with respect to respondents' right to be informed versus the client's right to confidentiality?

Case I.A Big Brothers of Fairfax County

Big Brothers of America is a social service program designed to meet the needs of boys ages six to 18 from single-parent homes. Most of the boys served by the program live with their mothers and rarely see or hear from their fathers. The purpose of the program is to give these boys the chance to establish a friendship with an interested adult male. Big Brothers of America was founded on the belief that association with a responsible adult can help program participants become more responsible citizens and better adjusted young men.

The program was started in Cincinnati in 1903. Two years later, the organization was granted its first charter in New York State through the efforts of Mrs. Cornelius Vanderbilt. By the end of World War II, there were 30 Big Brothers agencies. Today there are 300 agencies across the United States, and more than 120,000 boys are matched with Big Brothers.

The Fairfax County chapter of Big Brothers of America was founded in Fairfax in 1966. In 1971, United Way of Fairfax County accepted the program as part of its umbrella organization and now provides about 85 percent of its funding. The remaining 15 percent is raised by the local Big Brothers agency.

Information about the Big Brothers program in Fairfax County reaches the public primarily through newspapers (feature stories and classified advertisements), radio, public service announcements, posters (on buses and in windows of local establishments), and word-of-mouth advertising. The need for volunteers is a key message emanating from these sources. The agency phone number is always included so that people wanting to know more about the program can call for information. Those calling in are given basic information over the telephone and are invited to attend one of the monthly orientation sessions organized by the Big Brothers program staff. At these meetings, men get the chance to talk to other volunteers and to find out what will be expected of them should they decide to join the program. At the end of the session, prospective volunteers are asked to complete two forms. One is an application form and the other is a questionnaire in which the person is asked to describe the type of boy he would prefer to be matched with, as well as his own interests.

The files on potential Little Brothers are then reviewed in an attempt to match boys with the volunteers. A match is made only if both partners agree. The agency stays in close contact with the pair and monitors its progress. The three counselors for the Big Brothers program serve as resources for the volunteer.

The majority of the inquiry calls received by the Fairfax County agency are from women who are interested in becoming Big Sisters or from people desiring information on the Couples Program. Both programs are similar to the Big Brothers program and are administered by it. In fact, of 55 calls concerning a recent orientation meeting, only five were from males. Only three of the five callers actually attended the meeting, a typical response.

Although the informational campaigns and personal appeals thus seem to have some effect, the results were also generally disappointing and did little to alleviate the shortage of volunteer Big Brothers. There are currently 250 boys waiting to be matched with Big Brothers, and the shortage grows weekly.

Big Brothers of Fairfax County believed that a lack of awareness and accurate knowledge could be the cause of the shortage of volunteers. Are there men who would volunteer if only they were made aware of the program and its needs? Or is the difficulty a negative program image? Do people think of Little Brothers as problem children, boys who have been in trouble with the law or who have severe behavioral problems? Or could there be a misconception of the type of man who would make a good Big Brother? Do people have stereotypes with respect to the volunteers—for example, that the typical volunteer is a young, single, professional male?

Questions

1. What is (are) the marketing decision problem(s)?

2. What is (are) the marketing research problem(s)?

3. What types of information would be useful to answer these questions?

4. How would you go about securing this information?

Case I.B   Transitional Housing, Inc. (A)[1]

Transitional Housing, Inc. (THI), is a local nonprofit organization located in Madison, Wisconsin. THI provides assistance to homeless and very low income individuals and families in finding emergency shelter, food, employment, transitional housing, and affordable apartment housing. These services are provided through four basic THI programs (see exhibit below for details):

1. *The Drop-In Shelter:* An emergency drop-in shelter for men located at Grace Episcopal Church.

2. *The Hospitality House:* A day shelter for homeless and very low income men and women.

3. *The Transitional Housing Program:* Provides transitional living arrangements for families and single men for six months or more depending on the needs of the individual/family and the unit.

4. *The Housing Opportunity Program:* Helps families in obtaining a lease.

As part of its planning, the board of directors of THI was interested in determining ways to improve the organization's services. Their original thought was to conduct a survey of the organization's paid staff, volunteers, and guests (the homeless staying at THI or using its facilities or services), to determine which programs of THI they found particularly useful, which should be revised, and what other programs or services might be of more assistance to guests.

[1]The contributions of Monika Wingate to the development of this case are gratefully acknowledged.

However, the analysis of THI's internal statistics and other published data indicated the need for THI to narrow its focus. Specifically, internal information indicated the number of agencies serving the male homeless population was decreasing, and the number of homeless families was increasing. Moreover, THI was currently the only Madison shelter that served the male homeless population, and this community appeared to be underserved. In fact, the number of homeless men staying at THI's Drop-In Shelter had increased 89 percent, from 607 three years ago to 1,146 the past year. This was partly due to the closing of other Madison male shelters in the last three years. Finally, the THI shelter was filled beyond its capacity of 66 men per night. During the winter, there were frequently more than 90 men staying at the Drop-In Shelter on any given night, with many of them sleeping on the hallway floor.

Given this information, the board of directors decided to use the organization's limited resources to focus first on the Drop-In Shelter. More specifically, the board asked for an evaluation of THI's current facilities and the services for the homeless as well as a determination of what future services and facilities it should try to provide.

Questions

1. What is the decision problem?

2. What is the research problem?

3. Discuss in general terms how you would address the board of directors' concerns. Specifically, who would you obtain information from and how would you access these people?

Programs Offered by Transitional Housing, Inc.

Drop-In Shelter

Located at the Grace Episcopal Church in the downtown area, the Drop-In Shelter (DIS) is a 46-person-capacity emergency drop-in shelter for men. Overflow capacity for 20 additional people is provided at St. John's Lutheran Church from October through April. The basic services provided at DIS are shelter, food, personal grooming supplies, and counseling. Medical and legal services are also provided once a week through volunteers. The shelter is open to all men who are not incapacitated by drugs or alcohol and agree to abide by the rules of DIS. Operating hours are from 8:00 P.M. to 8:00 A.M. seven days per week, 365 days per year. Both dinner and breakfast are provided for DIS guests through the support of approximately 1,200 volunteers (churches, community groups, and other interested individuals) who offer their help to DIS.

Hospitality House

Hospitality House (HH), located on the near west side, is a day shelter and resource center for homeless and very low income men, women, and children. HH is generally regarded as a warm, safe place for the homeless to congregate, where services are provided but are not mandatory. The basic services provided at HH are: assistance with finding employment and housing, help for obtaining benefits from other social service agencies, and mental health services. Telephones are available for the guests' use, and guests may also use HH as a mailing address while they are staying at DIS.

Transitional Housing Program

The Transitional Housing Program (THP) operates 15 traditional housing sites throughout Dane County. There are 20 family units

EXHIBIT 1.B.1   Programs Offered by Transitional Housing, Inc., continued

and 39 single units. Residents of THP may stay in the units for a period of six months to "permanent," depending on the unit and the needs of the individual or family. Services provided to the residents of the THP include: money management, employment counseling, case management, and referrals to agencies involved in providing services needed by the individual or family. DIS is often the first step in the process of single men involved in THP.

Housing Opportunity Program

The Housing Opportunity Program (HOP) is a service provided by THI that is designed to aid families in obtaining a lease in their own name and staying in the site on a permanent basis. THI leases apartments from area landlords and subleases the units to homeless families, whoa are referred to THI through area shelters. During this time, THI assumes responsibility for any unpaid rent or repairs that may accrue. Maintenance checks are performed monthly and outreach services are provided to families involved in the program.

Case I.C   Supervisory Training at the Management Institute

University of Wisconsin–Extension is the outreach campus of the University of Wisconsin system. Its mission is to extend high-quality education to people who are not necessarily "college students" in the usual sense. The Management Institute is one of the departments within UW–Extension. It conducts programs aimed at providing education and training in at least a dozen areas of business and not-for-profit management.

The supervisory training area within the Management Institute designs and conducts continuing education training programs for first-level supervisors. The training programs are designed to improve a trainee's managerial, communication, decision-making, and human-relation skills. They consequently cover a broad range of topics.

A continuing decline in enrollments in the various programs during the past several years had become a problem of increasing concern to the three supervisory program directors. They were at a loss to explain the decline, although informal discussions among the supervisors raised a number of questions to which they did not know the answers. Have people's reasons for attending

supervisory training programs changed? What are their reasons for attending them? Was the decline caused by economic factors? Was it because of increased competition among continuing education providers? Was it due to the content or structure of MI's programs themselves? Was it because of the way the programs were structured or promoted? Were the programs targeted at the right level of supervisor?

Typically, the major promotion for any program involved mailed brochures that described the content and structure of the course. The mailing list for the brochures was all past attendees of any supervisory training program conducted by the Management Institute.

Questions

1. What is the decision problem?

2. What is (are) the research problem(s)?

3. How would you recommend MI go about addressing the research problem(s)? That is, what data would you collect and how might those data be used to answer the research question(s) posed?

Case I.D   Department of Administration

Consistent with its general policy of stimulating economic development in the area, the Department of Administration (DOA) of a U.S. state wishes to give more state business to small vendors. Assuming that state contracts benefit small businesses financially, it should be within the power of the DOA to help small businesses prosper by facilitating the procurement of state contracts on their behalf. To explore this idea further, the DOA solicits bids from the local marketing research firms—themselves small businesses—to investigate the issue.

Hobbes Research is a newly formed company in the region with a small, specialized staff. Hobbes is not a "full-service" marketing firm in that it does not employ its own telephone interviewers or field workers. Rather, it concentrates on the planning and supervision of research projects. Hobbes Research is eager to submit a proposal for the DOA's small-business development scheme, based upon the following information obtained during discussions with the DOA.

Background Information

The general problem of promoting small-business development by means of the procurement of state contracts seemed to encompass several subproblems. The DOA had no idea what the financial impact of selling to the state was for small businesses. It seemed likely that small vendors would make less profit from their dealings with the state than with private companies, but no actual data were available, and there was no indication whether small businesses were satisfied with their dealings with the state. Similarly, the DOA was ignorant of any problem small vendors encountered in obtaining state contracts. Presumably, there must be advantages in selling to the state, but these were likewise unclear.

Hobbes Research felt that exploratory interviews with small-business owners, DOA personnel, and perhaps one or two academics in the field might clarify these issues. In addition, the State Bureau of Procurement provided information packets for small-business owners, and annual reports of the state's purchasing activities were published regularly, all of which might be informative.

Meanwhile DOA staff were happy to impart their preliminary ideas about state–small-business interactions. They believed that being a vendor to the state had positive impact on small businesses and that the level of economic impact on individual businesses varied. They were also convinced that small businesses bid lower for state deals than for private-industry contracts and that profit margins on sales to the state were lower than profit margins on other sales. Finally, they felt that small businesses derived satisfaction from dealing with the state but that they experienced recurring, common problems in procuring state contracts.

Hobbes Research needed some clarification of definitional issues before they could plan further. It appeared that a business that reported less than $1.5 million in gross sales in the 2000 calendar year could officially be classified as small. Moreover, such a business would be termed a current vendor to the state in the eyes of the DOA only if it had sold to the state during the 2000 fiscal year (July 1, 1999–June 30, 2000). For 1,000 out of an estimated 2,500 firms thus qualifying as small vendors, the DOA wanted gross sales and profit figures for 2000 and wished to know the number of employees hired for the express purpose of working on state contracts in 2000.

Listings of relevant companies were available on state tapes. Specifically, the State Department of Revenue possessed one tape listing the addresses of all businesses located in the state and another that contained gross sales figures for all businesses situated in the state. Further, the State Bureau of Procurement kept a purchase-order tape that identified vendors to the state for any given year.

The DOA wanted to work closely with whichever marketing research firm they selected to undertake the study. They were enthusiastic about having their staff help with administrative duties such as typing and printing, and requested that their premises be considered the research center. Indeed, they were glad to provide an office equipped with personal computers for the purposes of data analysis. In addition, the DOA was adamant that its staff would need to see an interim report before any large-scale study commenced. In this way, they could review the questionnaire and have a clear idea of the tabulations that the researchers were planning to generate.

It was already January 6, 2001, and the DOA wanted the entire project completed and a full, written report by the end of April 2001. The closing date for submission of proposals was January 15. They promised that they would announce their choice of marketing research firm by the end of that month.

Questions

1. Prepare a research proposal to submit to the DOA on behalf of Hobbes Research.

2. Evaluate your approach to data collection versus other approaches that could be used.

Case I.E   Wisconsin Power & Light (A)[1]

Recent changes in the utility industry have led to a more deregulated and competitive environment. In response, Wisconsin Power & Light (WP&L) has been shifting its focus from that of a product-driven company to one of a market- and information-driven company. Management has increasingly relied on information from marketing studies and has been incorporating the external data in their decision-making processes. WP&L's espousal of a market-sensitive mentality has helped to shape the company's overall business strategies. One current area of concern for WP&L involves environmental issues, so much so that one of the company's goals is "to be a responsible corporate citizen, promoting the social, economic, and environmental well-being of the communities that it serves."

[1]The contributions of Kavita Maini and Paul Metz to the development of this case are gratefully acknowledged as is the permission of Wisconsin Power & Light to use the material included.

WP&L, in an effort to realize its environmental goals, developed several programs for its residential, commercial, and industrial customers to foster the conservation of energy. The programs, which were classified under the BuySmart umbrella of WP&L's Demand-Side Management Programs, consisted of such specific programs as Appliance Rebates, Energy Analysis, Weatherization Help, and the Home Energy Improvement Loan (HEIL) program. All previous marketing research and information gathering focused primarily on issues from the customer's perspective, such as an evaluation of net program impacts in terms of energy and demand savings and an estimation of the levels of free ridership (individuals who would have undertaken the conservation actions promoted by the program, even if there was no program in place). In addition, a study has been designed and is currently being conducted to evaluate and identify customer attitudes and opinions concerning the design, implementation, features, and delivery of the residential programs. Having examined the consumer perspective, WP&L's current goal is to focus on obtaining information from other participants in the programs, namely employees and lenders.

The next task for the management of WP&L to undertake is a study of the Home Energy Improvement Loan (HEIL) program of the BuySmart umbrella. The HEIL program was designed to make low-interest-rate financing available to residential gas and electric WP&L customers for conservation and weatherization measures. The low-interest guaranteed loans are delivered through WP&L account representatives in conjunction with participating financial institutions and trade allies. The procedures for obtaining a loan begin with an energy "audit" of the interested customer's residence to determine the appropriate conservation measures. Once the customer decides on which measures to have installed, the WP&L representative assists in arranging the low-interest-rate financing through one of the participating local banking institutions. At the completion of the projects, WP&L representatives conduct an inspection of the work by checking a random sample of participants. Conservation measures eligible under the HEIL program include the installation of natural gas furnaces/boilers, automatic vent dampers, intermittent ignition devices, heat pumps, and heat pump water heaters. Eligible structural improvements include the addition of attic/wall/basement insulation, storm windows and doors, sillbox insulation, window weather-stripping, and caulking.

Purpose

The primary goal of the current study is to identify ways of improving the HEIL program from the lenders' point of view. Specifically, the following issues need to be addressed:

- Identify the lenders' motivation for participating in the program.

- Determine how lenders get their information regarding various changes/updates in the program.

- Identify how lenders promote the program.

- Assess the current programs with respect to administrative and program features.

- Determine the type of credit analysis conducted by the lenders.

- Identify ways of minimizing the default rate from the lenders' point of view.

- Identify lenders' opinions of the overall program.

- Assess the lenders' commitment to the program.

- Identify if the reason for loan inactivity in some lending institutions is due to lack of a customer base.

Question

1. Prepare a research request that will address WP&L's study objectives.

Research Design

Part II deals with the general issue of designing research so that it addresses the appropriate questions efficiently. Chapter 5 provides an overview of various research designs and discusses the exploratory design at some length. Chapter 6 then discusses descriptive and causal designs, two other primary types of research design.

RESEARCH HELPS HEAL GRIFFIN HOSPITAL Griffin Hospital's comfortable business environment was shattered by the opening of a highway. This seemingly mundane change transformed Derby, Connecticut, a small community served by the hospital for almost eight decades. The new highway passed through Derby as it linked two major commuter routes, making Derby a convenient commute from New York City and Hartford. Businesses moved in, and housing prices tripled. The rubber mills left, and so did their workers, replaced by young families with no traditional ties to Griffin Hospital.

Admissions at Griffin dropped precipitously. Apparently, the new residents of Derby preferred to drive ten to thirty miles to visit one of Griffin's seven competitors. The business problem for the hospital was to bring people back to Griffin. The research problem was to find out why they weren't coming. The initial research design: a survey of local residents.

Griffin hired a research firm to ask people their impressions of the hospital. What the hospital's administration learned was far from encouraging. Over one-quarter of the respondents categorized Griffin as a hospital they "would avoid." As weaknesses, they cited the caliber of the medical staff, the condition of the facilities, and the inadequacy of parking. However, the survey also asked whether respondents had actually been to the hospital. This turned out to be important, because the most critical respondents included people who had never seen Griffin. This gave administrators a clue that they had an image problem fueled by negative word of mouth.

Now they could define a new research problem requiring a new research design. At first, the design seemed obvious. They would ask potential customers to provide more details about what they wanted. This called for another survey. But right away, the administrators got stuck on a design basic: Who would they survey? Talking to everyone in the community not only would be expensive, but they were likely to get so many ideas that the hospital wouldn't be able to implement them all or measure which changes mattered most to the hospital's bottom line. They needed to focus on one group. Deciding which group to start with was a business decision. The hospital's board of directors noted a population trend—that the population was aging—and recommended a survey focusing on geriatric care. Assistant administrator Patrick Charmel (who has since been promoted to chief executive officer) had a different idea. He observed the young married couples moving to Derby and saw an opportunity to build long-term relationships. If they came to Griffin for obstetrical and maternity care, assuming it was a good experience, Griffin could keep them coming back as they aged.

Charmel's view prevailed, and the hospital's administration agreed to a combination of detailed questionnaires and focus groups. The survey population consisted of obstetrics patients at Griffin and other hospitals. Subjects were asked to describe what they wanted in terms of obstetrical and maternity care.

Research participants had no trouble thinking up ideas. They wanted their families—husbands, parents, children—with them in the birthing room. They wanted rooms that bore no resemblance to hospital rooms. They wanted double beds and skylights, fresh flowers and Jacuzzis. They wanted comfortable lounges. They wanted plenty of follow-up and attention from their doctors and nurses.

The survey results in, the research was far from over. Now the hospital's administration had to determine how to implement the ideas. This required researching what other hospitals were doing. The initial plan was to identify hospitals doing what patients wanted so that Griffin could copy them. The design for this phase of the research coupled visits to observe local hospitals with a search of the literature about hospitals nationwide. A female manager wearing a pillow under her dress went with Charmel to all the obstetrics departments within an hour's drive. Pretending to be expectant parents, they asked to tour each hospital's facilities. Other managers reviewed the hospital industry literature. Neither the literature nor the visits uncovered any hospital doing everything patients wanted.

With those results, the administrators prepared to make another business decision. First, they agreed, they should set priorities among the ideas, then try out the ones that seemed most feasible. However, as they argued about the merits of skylights versus Jacuzzis, Charmel had a radical idea: let's just give the patients what they say they want.

Once the administrators recovered from their shock, they decided to try Charmel's idea. It required changing staff members' expectations about how to run a maternity ward. Some obstetricians left, but the hospital found that it had become an attractive employer for talented young doctors eager to be part of a "patient-driven" environment. Turnover among the nursing staff dropped. More importantly, in terms of the hospital's objectives, obstetrics admissions doubled over the first few years after the changes were made. Applying the results of the research had enabled Griffin to transform its obstetrics unit.

The hospital's executives therefore shouldn't have been surprised at Charmel's next idea: to build an entire hospital the same way. They *were* surprised, but they launched the next research effort: conducting surveys and focus groups of the area's elderly population. The list of ideas was again staggering; however, the hospital building was due for a renovation. The administration drew up plans, modified them based on focus group results, and revamped the entire building for a homier atmosphere. Today the hospital boasts a patient satisfaction rate of 96 percent and annual growth in admissions despite its stiff competition, all while managing to keeps its cash flow healthy.

Source: Adapted from David H. Freedman, "Intensive Care," *Inc.* (February 1999), pp. 72–80.

Chapter 5

TYPES OF RESEARCH DESIGN AND EXPLORATORY RESEARCH

LEARNING OBJECTIVES

Upon Completing This Chapter, You Should Be Able to

1. Explain what a research design is.

2. List the three basic types of research design.

3. Describe the major emphasis of each type of research design.

4. Cite the crucial principle of research.

5. Describe the basic uses of exploratory research.

6. Specify the key characteristic of exploratory research.

7. Discuss the various types of exploratory research and identify the characteristics of each.

8. Identify the key person in a focus group.

Case in Marketing Research

"If these ventures succeed, we'll open up vast new markets for picture taking," crowed Paul Hartwell, vice president of marketing of consumer imaging at Western Kodiak Film Company.

Paul was referring to two new products the company had been developing. The first it called Photos on CD. This is a processing service in which consumers get their pictures back on a compact disk, along with the traditional set of prints and negatives.

The other new product, Pictures Online, is an offering through a joint venture between Western Kodiak and a major Internet service provider, Internet America. Consumers who sign up for Pictures Online can download their developed photos when they log on to Internet America.

"Great," said Jane Bright, a regional sales manager at Western Kodiak, in response to Paul's prediction. "But why do you think consumers will want these services when they seem to have lost interest in taking pictures?" The company had been struggling because consumers were spending less on traditional photography in favor of digital cameras. (Digital cameras don't require film.)

"The idea is that we'll get people excited about taking pictures again because of all the new ways they can use their pictures. With Photos on CD and Pictures Online, they can make adjustments to their pictures and play around with them."

"What kind of adjustments?" asked John Sterling, another sales manager.

"They can crop them or enlarge them. They can add borders or messages. They can reduce the red-eye effect. Also, they can attach them to e-mail."

"Hey, that sounds like fun," said John. "I can't wait to try the demo."

"Yeah, but do we have enough reason to believe that most consumers will think it's fun?" probed Jane. "What research have we done so far into their opinions of these products? And what about their computer use? Will they want to hang out at their computers, cropping photos?"

"Sure they will," responded John. "Just think about all the people who are going on-line—there's more of them every day."

"I wonder," said Jane. "Didn't you see the report on our intranet about that study—the one that says fewer consumers are using their computer these days? Do we really know how people feel about playing with photos on their computer?"

"Maybe we need some more research," said Paul. "It sounds like we need to keep a closer eye on consumer behavior, especially what people are doing with their computers. Is any research already being done on this? I hope we don't have to commission our own study."

"Let's see what's out there and put it on the agenda for next week's meeting," John proposed. The others agreed.

Discussion Issues

1. What research problems does Western Kodiak face?

2. How can Western Kodiak benefit from exploratory research?

3. How should the research be structured?

Research Design as a Plan of Action

Research design
The framework or plan for a study that guides the collection and analysis of the data.

A **research design** is simply the framework or plan for a study used as a guide in collecting and analyzing data. It is the blueprint that is followed in completing a study. It resembles the architect's blueprint for a house. While it is possible to build a house without a detailed blueprint, the final product will more than likely be somewhat different from what was originally envisioned by the buyer. A certain room is too small; the traffic pattern is poor; some things really wanted are omitted; other, less important things are included; and so on. It is also possible to conduct research without a detailed blueprint. The research findings are also likely to differ widely from what was desired by the consumer or user of the research. "These results are interesting, but they do not solve the basic problem" is a common lament. Further, just as the house built without a blueprint is likely to cost more because of midstream alterations in construction, research conducted without a research design is likely to cost more than research properly executed using a research design.

Thus, a research design ensures that the study (1) will be relevant to the problem and (2) will use economical procedures. It would help the student learning research methods if there were a single procedure to follow in developing the framework or if there were a single framework to be learned. Unfortunately, this is not the case.[1]

> There is never a single, standard, correct method of carrying out research. Do not wait to start your research until you find out the proper approach, because there are many ways to tackle a problem—some good, some bad, but probably several good ways. There is no single perfect design. A research method for a given problem is not like the solution to a problem in algebra. It is more like a recipe for beef stroganoff; there is no one best recipe.

Rather, there are many research design frameworks, just as there are many unique house designs. Fortunately though, just as house designs can be broken into basic types (for example, ranch, split-level, two-story), research designs can be classified into some basic types. One very useful classification is in terms of the fundamental objective of the research: exploratory, descriptive, or causal.[2]

Types of Research Design

Exploratory research
Research design in which the major emphasis is on gaining ideas and insights; it is particularly helpful in breaking broad, vague problem statements into smaller, more precise subproblem statements.

Descriptive research
Research design in which the major emphasis is on determining the frequency with which something occurs or the extent to which two variables covary.

The major emphasis in **exploratory research** is on the discovery of *ideas* and *insights*.[3] The soft drink manufacturer faced with decreased sales might conduct an exploratory study to generate possible explanations. **Descriptive research** is typically concerned with determining the *frequency* with which something occurs or the relationship between two variables. It is typically guided by an initial hypothesis. Suppose the soft drink manufacturer thinks that sales of its diet cola are slipping because the number of teenage girls who constitute the company's primary market has declined over the past five years. The company might decide to commission a study to see if trends in soft drink consumption are related to such characteristics as age or sex. This would be a descriptive study.

A **causal research** design is concerned with determining cause-and-effect relationships. Causal studies typically take the form of experiments, since experiments are best suited to determine cause and effect. For instance, our soft drink manufacturer may be interested in determining which of several different advertising appeals is most effective. One way for such a company to proceed would be to use different ads in different geo-

Causal research
Research design in which the major emphasis is on determining cause-and-effect relationships.

graphic areas and investigate which ad generated the highest sales. In effect, the company would perform an experiment, and if it was designed properly, the company would be in a position to conclude that one specific appeal caused the higher rate of sales.

Although it is useful to divide research designs into these neat categories—exploratory, descriptive, and causal research—as a way of helping to explain the research process, three warnings are in order. First, the distinctions among the three are not absolute. Any given study may serve several purposes. Nevertheless, certain types of research designs are better suited for some purposes than others. The crucial principle of research is that *the design of the investigation should stem from the problem.* Each of these types is appropriate to specific kinds of problems.

Second, in the remainder of this chapter and in the next chapter, we shall discuss each of the design types in more detail. The emphasis will be on their *basic characteristics* and *generally fruitful approaches.* Whether the designs are useful in a given problem setting depends on how imaginatively they are applied. Architects can be taught basic design principles; whether they then design attractive, well-built houses depends on how they apply these principles. So it is with research. The general characteristics of each design can be taught. Whether they are productive in a given situation depends on how skillfully they are applied. There is no single best way to proceed, just as there is no single best floor plan for, say, a ranch-type house. It all depends on the specific problem to be solved. Research analysts, then, need an understanding of the basic designs so that they can modify them to suit specific purposes.

Finally, it should be noted that the three basic research designs can be viewed as stages in a continuous process. Figure 5.1 shows the interrelationships. Exploratory studies are often seen as the initial step. When researchers begin an investigation, it stands to reason that they lack a great deal of knowledge about the problem. Consider: Store X's share of book sales is slipping. Why? This statement is too broad to serve as a guide for research. To narrow and refine it would logically be accomplished with exploratory research, in which the emphasis would be on finding possible explanations for the sales decrease. These tentative explanations, or **hypotheses,** would then serve as specific guides for descriptive or causal studies. Suppose the tentative explanation that emerged was that "Store X sells books in superstores. Consumers today are pressed for time, and a growing number prefer to shop on-line at home. Store X is losing sales to Internet booksellers." The hypothesis that consumers are buying books on-line as a substitute for shopping in bookstores such as Store X could be examined in a descriptive study of trends in book retailing.

Suppose the descriptive study did support the hypothesis. The company might then wish to determine whether consumers would buy more books from Store X if it were to offer them on-line and, if so, what features of an on-line bookstore would be most important to them. This might be accomplished through a test market study, a causal design.

Hypothesis
A statement that specifies how two or more measurable variables are related.

⬛ **FIGURE 5.1**   **Relationships among Research Designs**

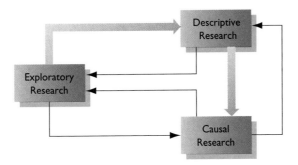

Ethical Dilemma 5.1

Marketing Research Insights was asked to carry out the data collection and analysis procedures for a study designed by a consumer goods company. After studying the research purpose and design, a consultant for Marketing Research Insights concluded that the design was poorly conceived. First, she thought that the design was more complex than was necessary since some of the data could be obtained through secondary sources, precluding the necessity of much primary data collection. Second, the proposed choice of primary data collection would not produce the kinds of information sought by the company.

Although the consultant advised the company of her opinions, the company insisted on proceeding with

the proposed design. Marketing Research Insights' management was reluctant to undertake the study, as it believed that the firm's reputation would be harmed if its name were associated with poor research.

- What decision would you make if you were a consultant for Marketing Research Insights?

- In general, should a researcher advance his or her opinion of a proposed design, or should the researcher remain silent and simply do the work?

- Is it ethical to remain silent in such situations?

Each stage in the process thus represents the investigation of a more detailed statement of the problem. Although we have suggested that the sequence would be from exploratory to descriptive to causal research, alternative sequences might occur. The hypothesis that Internet retailing is taking business away from superstores might be so generally accepted that the sequence would be from exploratory directly to causal. This sequence better describes what actually happened in the early stages of the battle between Barnes & Noble and Amazon.com.

The Barnes & Noble bookstore chain grew first through a series of acquisitions, most notably the 1986 purchase of B. Dalton. In the 1990s the company began building superstores with amenities like reading areas and coffee. It eventually became the nation's top bookseller, with about 1,000 stores and 15 percent of U.S. book sales. In the meantime, however, Amazon.com saw the potential of the Internet and began offering books on-line. That year, 1995, Barnes & Noble's annual report described plans to open new stores but didn't even mention the Internet.

Amazon.com quickly began attracting media attention, investor capital, and sales. Barnes & Noble saw its share slipping and couldn't afford to waste time. The company launched its own Web site, barnesandnoble.com, but it was more than a year and a half after Amazon.com's start-up—a huge lag by Internet standards. At the end of the first big Internet retailing season, the last five weeks of 1998, Amazon.com was bragging that it had signed up a million new customers, compared with just 320,000 for barnesandnoble.com. A few months later, Amazon.com announced it would offer best-sellers at 50 percent off the list price. Although this strategy eliminated any profit on those titles, barnesandnoble.com matched Amazon.com's pricing.[4] In the still-new and fast-changing business environment of the Internet, the costs of falling further behind were not worth the benefits of waiting for the results of causal research. Eventually, perhaps, Barnes & Noble will use marketing research to carve out a distinctive position for its Web site. For example, as Amazon.com branches into selling other kinds of merchandise, barnesandnoble.com may test a strategy of positioning itself as the Web site that specializes in books.

The potential for conducting research in the reverse direction also exists. If a hypothesis is disproved by causal research (e.g., the product bombs in taste tests), the analyst may then decide that another descriptive study, or even another exploratory study, is needed. Also, not every research problem will begin with an exploratory study. It depends on how specific researchers can be in formulating the problem before them. A general,

Leonard Riggio, chief executive of Barnes & Noble, is the man who made bookstores fun, turning them into modern village greens where people flock as much for the entertainment value as the huge selection. Barnes & Noble, whose stores have been reported to ring up one in eight books sold in America, has recently ventured on-line. The barnesand noble.com site recently ranked as the third most popular Web retailer, behind only first-place Amazon.com and second-place CDNOW. This was measured by the 1,884,013 U.S. in-dividuals who visited the site during a one-month period (Amazon.com measured 6,380,044 visits) reported by Nielsen/NetRatings. Riggio sees the Internet as much more than just another place to sell books. He envisions it as a place to meet all types of consumer needs: a book research center, a database, an ad vehicle, and, most of all, a tool to help people weed through an onslaught of information.

Source: © Josef Astor.

vague statement leads naturally to exploratory work, while a specific, cause-effect hypothesis lends itself to experimental work.

Exploratory Research

As previously stated, the general objective in exploratory research is to gain insights and ideas. The exploratory study is particularly helpful in breaking broad, vague problem statements into smaller, more precise subproblem statements, ideally in the form of specific hypotheses. In effect, a hypothesis is a statement that specifies how two or more measurable variables are related.[5]

In the early stages of research, we usually lack sufficient understanding of the problem to formulate a specific hypothesis. Further, there are often several tentative explanations for a given marketing phenomenon. For example, sales are off because our price is too high, our dealers or sales representatives are not doing the job they should or our advertising is weak, and so on. Exploratory research can be used to establish priorities in studying these competing explanations. Top priority would usually be given to whichever hypothesis appeared most promising in the exploratory study. Priorities may also be established according to the feasibility of researching the hypotheses. Exploratory studies should help to eliminate ideas that are not practical.

An exploratory study is also used to increase the analyst's familiarity with a problem. This is particularly true when the analyst is new to the problem arena—for example, a marketing research consultant going to work for a company for the first time.

The exploratory study may also be used to clarify concepts. For instance, if management is considering a change in service policy intended to increase dealer satisfaction, an exploratory study could be used to (1) clarify what is meant by dealer satisfaction and (2) develop a method by which dealer satisfaction could be measured.

When Congress discusses revising the tax code in order to make it "more fair" (so as to increase taxpayer compliance), a problem that often surfaces is determining what fairness in the tax code means. Is it tax enforcement that bothers people? Tax avoidance by other people? The way tax laws are written? Tax rates? That people believe their tax dollars are being poorly spent? Exploratory research would play a particularly important role in clarifying a concept such as this.

In sum, an exploratory study is used for any or all of the following purposes:[6]

- Formulating a problem for more precise investigation

- Developing hypotheses

- Establishing priorities for further research

- Gathering information about the practical problems of carrying out research on particular issues

- Increasing the analyst's familiarity with the problem

- Clarifying concepts

In general, exploratory research is appropriate for any problem about which little is known. It becomes the foundation for a good study.

Because so much is typically unknown at the beginning of an inquiry, exploratory studies are generally very flexible with regard to the methods used for gaining insight and developing hypotheses. Exploratory studies rarely use detailed questionnaires or involve probability sampling plans. Rather, investigators frequently change the research procedure as the vaguely defined initial problem is transformed into one with more precise meaning. Investigators often follow where their noses lead them in an exploratory study. Ingenuity, judgment, and good luck inevitably play a part in leading to the one or two key hypotheses that, it is hoped, will account for the phenomenon. While exploratory research may be conducted in a variety of ways, experience has shown that literature searches, experience surveys, focus groups, and the analysis of selected cases are particularly productive (see Figure 5.2).[7]

FIGURE 5.2   Types of Exploratory Studies

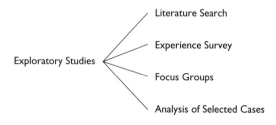

Literature Search

Literature search
A search of statistics, trade journal articles, other articles, magazines, newspapers, and books for data or insight into the problem at hand.

One of the quickest and cheapest ways to discover hypotheses is in the work of others, through a **literature search.** The search may involve conceptual literature, trade literature, or, quite often, published statistics. The literature that is searched depends naturally on the problem being addressed. Miller Business Systems, Inc., of Dallas, for example, routinely monitors trade literature in order to keep track of its competitors. The information on each competitor is entered into the "competitor profiles" it keeps in its database. The company regularly scans these profiles for insights on what the competition might be doing. One such scan indicated that a competitor had hired nine furniture salespeople in a ten-day period. This was a tip-off to a probable push by the competitor in the office-furniture market. With this early notice, Miller was able to schedule its salespeople to make extra calls on their accounts, thereby blunting the competitor's sales drive.[8]

Sometimes conceptual literature is more valuable than trade literature. For example, a firm with a dissatisfied field sales force would probably begin its study with a search of literature on concepts and ideas related to satisfaction in such personnel. The search might include research studies in psychology, sociology, and personnel management, in addition to marketing journals. The focus would be on the factors determining employee satisfaction and dissatisfaction. The analyst would keep a keen eye for those factors also found in the company's environment. The question of how to measure an employee's satisfaction would be researched at the same time.

Suppose a firm's problem was one that typically triggers much marketing research: "Sales are off. Why?" Exploratory insights into this problem could easily and cheaply be gained by analyzing published data and trade literature. Such an analysis would quickly indicate whether the problem was an industry problem or a firm problem. For example, it was readily apparent to Barnes & Noble that the decline in its market share was a company problem, since book sales industry wide showed no signs of weakening.

Very different research is in order if the firm's sales are down but (1) the company's market share is up, since industry sales are down further; (2) the company's market share has remained stable; or (3) the company's market share has declined. The last situation would trigger an investigation of the firm's marketing mix variables, while the first condition would prompt an analysis to determine why industry sales are off.

A company's own internal data should be included in the literature examined in exploratory research, as Mosinee Paper Company found to its pleasant surprise. The company was contemplating dropping one of its products because of its dismal sales performance. Before doing so, though, the company tallied sales of the product per salesperson and found that only a single salesperson was selling that specific grade of industrial paper. Upon further investigation, Mosinee discovered how the buyers were using the paper—an application that had been known only to the one salesman and his customers. This information enabled management to educate the rest of its sales force as to the potential market for the paper and sales rose substantially.

It is important to remember that in a literature search, as in any exploratory research, the major emphasis is on the discovery of ideas and tentative explanations of the phenomenon and not on demonstrating which explanation is *the* explanation. The demonstration is better left to descriptive and causal research. Thus, the analyst must be alert to the hypotheses that can be derived from available material, both published material and the company's internal records.

Experience Survey

Experience survey
Interviews with people knowledgeable about the general subject being investigated.

Sometimes called the *key informant survey,* the **experience survey** attempts to tap the knowledge and experience of those familiar with the general subject being investigated. Some marketing researchers get ideas for new products by hiring "cool hunters" to spot the latest trends. For example, a marketing research firm called Youth Intelligence pays several part-timers aged 14 to 30 whom the firm has identified as having avant-garde tastes. The cool hunters use the field study approach of anthropology, observing settings such as night clubs and basketball courts, and writing reports about what they see. The research firm can then follow up this exploratory effort with other research techniques such as focus groups. Several years ago, based on a Youth Intelligence prediction that tattoos would become popular, Sprint used temporary tattoos in promoting its calling cards to students. The promotion sold double the cards Sprint had forecast.[9]

In studies concerned with the marketing of a product, anyone who has any association with the marketing effort is a potential source of information. This would include the top executives of the company, the sales manager, product manager, and sales representatives. It would also include wholesalers and retailers who handle the product, as well as consumers who use the product. It might even include individuals who are not part of the chain of distribution but who might, nevertheless, possess some insight into the phenomenon. For example, a children's book publisher gained valuable insights into the reason for a sales decline by talking with librarians and schoolteachers. These discussions indicated that an increased use of library facilities, both public and school, coincided with the product's drop in sales. The increase in library usage was, in turn, traced to an increase in federal funds, which had enabled libraries to buy more books for their children's collections. Similarly, when designing the Louisville, a medium-duty conventional truck intended for beverage distribution among other things, Ford Motor sought feedback from fleet owners, mechanics, and drivers.[10]

Usually, a great many people know something about the general subject of any given problem. However, not all of them should be contacted.

> Research economy dictates that the respondents in an experience survey be carefully selected. The aim of the experience survey is to obtain insight into the relationships between variables rather than to get an accurate picture of current practices or a simple consensus as to best practices. One is looking for provocative ideas and useful insights, not for the statistics of the profession. Thus the respondents must be chosen because of the likelihood that they will offer the contributions sought. In other words, a selected sample of people working in the area is called for.[11]

Never, therefore, should a probability sample, in which respondents are chosen by some random process, be used in an experience survey. Moreover, it is a waste of time to interview those who have little competence or little relevant experience in the subject under investigation. It is also a waste of time to interview those who cannot articulate their experience and knowledge. It is important, though, to include people with differing points of view. The children's book publisher mentioned earlier interviewed company executives, key people in the product group, sales representatives, managers of retail outlets in which the books were sold, teachers, and librarians in the process of investigating the sales decline.

The interviews were all unstructured and informal. The emphasis in each interview among those immediately concerned with the distribution of the product was, "How do you explain the sales decrease? In your opinion, what is needed to reverse the downward slide?"[12] Most of the time in each interview was then devoted to exploring in detail the various rationales and proposed solutions. A number of sometimes conflicting hypotheses emerged. This provided the researchers with an opportunity to "bounce" some of the hypotheses off groups with differing vantage points and, in the process, get a feel for which of the hypotheses would be most fruitful to research. The interviews with librarians and teachers approached the problem from a different angle. Here the emphasis was on discovering changes in children's reading habits.

The respondents were given a great deal of freedom in choosing the factors to be discussed. This is consistent with the notion that the emphasis in exploratory research is on developing tentative explanations and not on demonstrating the viability of a given explanation.

Focus Groups

Focus groups are another useful method for gathering ideas and insights. In a **focus group,** a small number of individuals are brought together in a room to sit and talk about

Focus group
A personal interview simultaneously conducted among a small number of individuals; the interview relies more on group discussion than on directed questions to generate data.

some topic of interest to the focus group sponsor. The discussion is directed by a moderator. The moderator attempts to follow a rough outline of issues while simultaneously having the comments made by each person considered in group discussion. Each individual is thereby exposed to the ideas of the others and submits his or her ideas to the group for consideration.

Focus groups are one of the more frequently used techniques in marketing research; they have proved to be productive for a variety of purposes, including the following:

- Generating hypotheses that can be further tested quantitatively.

- Generating information helpful in structuring consumer questionnaires.

- Providing overall background information on a product category.

- Securing impressions on new product concepts.

When Brendan Boyle and Fern Mandelbaum pooled their marketing experience to start Skyline Products, a company that develops and licenses children's toys, they wanted to get regular feedback directly from children. Their solution was to set up focus groups in the form of six-week-long play groups. Parents were happy to sign up their children in exchange for the one-hour break each week; in fact, they pay $30 for the privilege. The groups meet at a local park or school. Boyle and Mandelbaum show up with toys and watch the children play, observing which toys they choose and which are hard to handle. During the session they also ask children why they prefer one toy over another. Afterward, they follow up with parents to learn what the children said they liked. Mandelbaum credits the focus groups with helping them develop a "kid sense" that has enabled the company to license 70 products in its first few years.[13] In designing its Z3 roadster, BMW conducted focus groups in Japan, the United States, the United Kingdom and Germany; the Americans' influence is visible in the dual cupholders, the coinholder, and the third brake light.[14] Research Window 5.1 discusses the insights Harley-Davidson gleaned from focus groups.

Although focus groups do vary in size, most consist of eight to twelve members. Smaller groups are too easily dominated by one or two members; with larger groups, frustration and boredom can set in, as individuals have to wait their turn to respond or get involved. Respondents are generally selected so that the groups are relatively homogeneous, minimizing both conflicts among group members on issues not relevant to the study objectives and differences in perceptions, experiences, and verbal skills. Differences that are too great with respect to any of these characteristics can intimidate some of the group participants and stifle discussion. For example, the group for a project that involved a mixed group of architects, roofing contractors, and building owners included a person whose company was called Tony the Roofer. "Tony had all the experience and involvement with the product category the other participants had. But he was so intimidated by all the other people, he just would not say anything. Every so often we would ask what he thought of some subject, but he just would mumble that he agreed with what one of the 'bigger' people had said."[15]

Most firms conducting focus groups use screening interviews to determine the individuals who will compose a particular group. One type they try to avoid is the individual who has participated before in a focus group, since some of these people tend to behave as "experts." Their presence can cause the group to behave in dysfunctional ways as experienced participants continually try to make their presence felt. Firms also try to avoid groups in which some of the participants are friends or relatives, because this tends to inhibit spontaneity in the discussion as the acquaintances begin talking to each other.

Given that the participants in any one group should be reasonably homogeneous, how can a firm ensure that it is getting a wide spectrum of insights? The key way is by having multiple groups. Not only can the characteristics of the participants vary across groups, but so can the issue outline. Ideas discovered in one group session can be introduced in subsequent group sessions for reaction. A typical project has four groups, but some may

Research Window 5.1 **Experience of Harley-Davidson with Focus Groups**

After making a remarkable comeback in the 1980s, motorcycle manufacturer Harley-Davidson had buyers on two-year-long waiting lists all over the country. But that success placed the company in a familiar quandary: Should Harley expand and risk a market downturn, or should it stay the course, content with its good position in the industry?

"To invest or not to invest, that was the question," said Frank Cimermancic, Harley's director of business planning. "Dealers were begging us to build more motorcycles," he said. "But you have to understand our history. One of the things that caused past problems was a lack of quality, and that was the result of a too-rapid expansion. We did not want to relive that situation."

The company's dilemma was complicated by the fact that the market for heavyweight bikes was shrinking. "We were doing fine, but look at the market," Cimermancic said. "Maybe, we thought, we could reverse these trends and become an industry leader, something we hadn't been for a long time."

A new kind of customer seemed to hold the keys to market growth. White-color motorcycle enthusiasts, or "Rubbies" (Rich Urban Bikers), started to shore up Harley sales in the middle '80s, adding to the company's success and image. But whether these Lenos and Forbeses were reliable, long-term customers was another question.

"Are those folks going to stay with us, or are they going to move on when the next fad comes along?" Cimermancic asked. "If we got the answer right, we could become a force in the industry. If we got it wrong, we would go right back to the early '80s. Nobody wanted to make the wrong decision and watch 20 percent of our employees walk away with their possessions in a cardboard box."

Harley also needed to know if it should market its products differently to different audiences. A core clientele of traditional "bikers" had kept Harley afloat during its leanest years, and they could not be alienated. "We had to understand the customer mindset," Cimermancic said. "Was there a universal appeal to owning a Harley?"

To find out, the company first invited focus groups made up of current owners, would-be owners, and owners of other brands to make cut-and-paste collages that expressed their feelings about Harley-Davidsons. Whether long-time Harley riders or fresh prospects, common themes emerged in the artwork: enjoyment, the great outdoors, freedom.

Harley-Davidson then mailed more than 16,000 surveys "with a typical battery of psychological, sociological, and demographic questions you typically see in studies," Cimermancic said, as well as subjective questions such as "Is Harley typified more by a brown bear or a lion?" The questionnaire got a 30 percent response rate, with no incentive for return.

From the responses, Harley identified seven core customer types: the Adventure-Loving Traditionalist, the Sensitive Pragmatist, the Stylish Status-Seeker, the Laid-Back Camper, the Classy Capitalist, the Cool-Headed Loner, and the Cocky Misfit. All of them appreciated Harley-Davidson products for the same reasons.

"Independence, freedom, and power were universal Harley appeals," Cimermancic said. "It didn't matter if you were the guy who swept the floor of the factory or if you were the CEO at that factory, the attraction to Harley-Davidson was very similar. We were surprised by a tremendous amount of loyalty across the board."

That loyalty meant the company could build and sell more motorcycles, without having to overextend itself. In 1990, Harley-Davidson expanded to build 62,800 bikes; last year, it built more than 105,000. Based on research, and the fact that names are again piling up on waiting lists, Harley expects its phenomenal growth to continue.

Source: Ian P. Murphy, "Aided by Research, Harley Goes Whole Hog," *Marketing News* 30 (December 2, 1996), pp. 16–17.

have up to twelve. The guiding criterion is whether the later groups are generating additional insight into the phenomenon under study. When they show diminishing returns, the groups are stopped.

The typical focus group session lasts from 1½ to 2 hours. Most groups are held at facilities designed especially for them, although they can be held at other places.[16] One advantage of these facilities is that they can incorporate the latest in technology because of the large number of groups held there. For example, videoconferencing technology can be used to link groups in different locations, allowing participants at the various locations to interact directly with each other.

The moderator in the focus group has a key role.[17] For one thing, the moderator typically translates the study objectives into a discussion guide. To do so, he or she needs to understand the background of the problem and the most important information the client hopes to glean from the research process. The moderator also needs to understand the parameters of all the focus groups in terms of their number, size, and composition, as well as how they might be structured to build on one another. Moreover, the moderator must lead the discussion so that all objectives of the study are met and do so in such a way that *interaction* among the group members is stimulated and promoted. The focus group session should not be allowed to dissolve into nothing more than a set of concurrent interviews in which the participants each take turns responding to a predetermined set of questions. This is an extremely delicate role. It requires someone who is intimately familiar with the purpose and objectives of the research and at the same time possesses good interpersonal communication skills. One important measure of a focus group's success is whether the participants talk to each other, rather than the moderator, about the items on the discussion guide.

Some of the key qualifications moderators must have are described in Exhibit 5.1. Moderating an industrial focus group is even more difficult than moderating one involving a consumer product. A moderator for a consumer good typically knows something about the product or service at issue. After all, moderators are consumers too. Not so with many industrial goods. This means that the moderator's briefing for an industrial good has to be longer and more detailed. It also means that many of the group participants will know a great deal more about the product or service being discussed than the moderator. Directing group discussion under these conditions can be a taxing job indeed.[18]

Sponsors can realize several advantages from the proper conduct of focus groups. For one thing, they allow for serendipity. Ideas can simply drop "out of the blue" during a focus group discussion. Further, the group setting allows ideas to be developed to their full significance, because it allows for snowballing. A comment by one individual can trigger a chain of responses from other participants. Often after a brief introductory warm-up period, respondents can "turn on" to the discussion. They become sufficiently involved that they want to express their ideas and expose their feelings. Some feel more secure in the group environment than if they were being interviewed alone, since they soon realize that they can expose an idea without necessarily having to defend or elaborate on it. Consequently, responses are often more spontaneous and less conventional than they might be in a one-on-one interview.

Group interviews do offer certain benefits not obtainable with individual depth interviews (see Exhibit 5.2), but they also have weaknesses. Although they are easy to set up, they are difficult to moderate and to interpret. It is easy to find evidence in one or more of the group discussions that supports almost any preconceived position. Because executives have the ability to observe the discussions through one-way mirrors or the opportunity to listen to tape recordings of the sessions, focus groups seem more susceptible to executive and even researcher biases than do other data collection techniques, although sometimes the ability to study the tapes can be an advantage. Not only does the systematic study of the tapes allow those doing so to get a firsthand sense of what the target group is feeling, but the tape also provides a vehicle for communicating that feeling to others. For example, Time, Inc., used focus groups when it noticed signs of rising dissatisfaction with customer service, which threatened renewal rates.

Readers who had received poor service were invited to hour-long sessions to voice their complaints.

"All of the people had some complaint about what had happened to them," McDonald (the director of research) said. "A premium promised but not delivered, a mix-up in billing, a payment not credited, an erroneous referral to a collection agency."

EXHIBIT 5.1   **Seven Characteristics of Good Focus Group Moderators**

Superior Listening Ability.   It is essential that the moderator be able to listen to what the participants are saying. A moderator must not miss the participants' comments because of lack of attention or misunderstanding. The effective moderator knows how to paraphrase, to restate the comments of a participant when necessary, to ensure that the content of the comments is clear.

Excellent Short-Term Auditory Memory.   The moderator must be able to remember comments that participants make early in a group, then correlate them with comments made later by the same or other participants. A participant might say that she rarely watches her weight, for example, then later indicate that she always drinks diet soft drinks. The moderator should remember the first comment and be able to relate it to the later one so that the reason for her diet soft drink consumption is clarified.

Well Organized.   The best moderators see things in logical sequence from general to specific and keep similar topics organized together. A good moderator guide should be constructed logically, as should the final report. An effective moderator can keep track of all the details associated with managing the focus group process, so that nothing "falls through the cracks" that impacts negatively on the overall quality of the groups.

A Quick Learner.   Moderators become intimately involved in a large number of different subject areas—and for only a very short time in each. An effective moderator is able to learn enough about a subject quickly in order to develop an effective moderator guide and conduct successful group sessions. Moderators normally have only a short period of time to study subject areas about which they will be conducting groups. Therefore, the most effective moderators can identify the key points in any topic area, then focus on them, so that they know enough to listen and/or probe for the nuances that make the difference between an extremely informative and an average group discussion.

High Energy Level.   Focus groups can be very boring, both for the participants and for the client observers. When the tenor of a group gets very laid back and lifeless, it dramatically lowers the quality of the information that the participants generate. The best moderators find a way to inject energy and enthusiasm into the group so that both the participants and the observers are energized throughout the session. This ability tends to be most important during the second group of an evening (the eight to ten o'clock session), when observers and participants are frequently tired because of the late hour, and can become listless if they are not motivated to keep their energy and interest levels high. The moderator must be able to keep his or her own energy level high so that the discussion can continue to be very productive to the end.

Personable.   The most effective moderators are people who can develop an instant rapport with participants, so that the people become actively involved in the discussion in order to please the moderator. Participants who don't establish rapport with the moderator are much less likely to "open up" during the discussion, and the output from the group is not as good.

Well-Above-Average Intelligence.   This is a vital characteristic of the effective moderator, because no one can plan for every contingency that may occur in a focus group session. The moderator must be able to think on his or her feet: to process the information that the group is generating, then determine what line of questioning will most effectively generate further information needed to achieve the research objectives.

Source: Thomas L. Greenbaum, *The Handbook for Focus Group Research*, 2nd ed. (Thousand Oaks, Calif.: Sage Publications, 1998) pp. 77–78.

Because of the bad service, he said, the readers were furious.

McDonald taped the focus groups, edited the tape to a 25-minute video, and used it as a propaganda device to change the attitudes of the customer service staff.

"Its impact upon the Time, Inc., staff was incredibly powerful," he said. "Suddenly, all of the faceless millions had faces. The customers became real people rather than abstractions."[19]

Putting faces on the faceless worked to advantage for Time, but it can just as easily become a disadvantage, for it makes it very easy to forget that the discussion, and conse-

EXHIBIT 5.2   **The Advantages/Disadvantages of Focus Groups versus Individual Depth Interviews**

Advantages of Individual Depth Interviews versus Focus Groups

- They permit the interviewer to delve much deeper into a topic, because all the attention during the 1½-hour session is concentrated on one individual rather than a group of ten.

- They allow more candid discussion on the part of the interviewee, who might be intimidated to talk about a particular topic in a group of his or her peers. This is particularly the case for sensitive topics such as personal-care products, financial behavior, or attitudes toward sex, religion, and politics.

- They eliminate negative group influences that can occur in a focus group. Because there is only one person being interviewed in the room, it is not possible for the individual's comments to be influenced by others.

- They are essential for certain situations where competitors would otherwise be placed in the same room. For example, it might be very difficult to do an effective focus group with managers from competing department stores or restaurants. Therefore, research with these people must be done on a one-to-one basis.

Limitations of Individual Depth Interviews versus Focus Groups

- They are typically much more expensive than focus groups, particularly when viewed on a per-interview basis. This is because the time of the moderator, which is the biggest cost in qualitative research, is the same for a two-hour focus group as it is for two hours of one-on-ones. Thus, for the same budget, the client gains input from significantly more people in a focus group.

- They generally do not get the same degree of client involvement as focus groups. It is difficult to convince most clients to sit through multiple hours of one-on-ones; this can be a problem if one of the objectives is to get the clients to view the research so they benefit firsthand from the information.

- They are physically exhausting for the moderator, so it is difficult to cover as much ground in one day as can be covered with groups. Most moderators will not do more than four or five interviews in a day, yet in two focus groups they can cover 20 people.

- Focus groups give the moderator the ability to leverage the dynamics of the group to obtain reactions that might not otherwise be generated in a one-on-one session.

Source: Adapted from Thomas L. Greenbaum, "Focus Groups vs. One-on-Ones: The Controversy Continues," *Marketing News* 25 (September 2, 1991), p. 16. Reprinted with permission of American Marketing Association.

quently the results, are greatly influenced by the moderator and the specific direction he or she provides. Moderators possessing all of the desired skills listed in Exhibit 5.1 are extremely rare. One has to remember that the results are not representative of what would be found in the general population and thus are *not* projectable. Further, the unstructured nature of the responses makes coding, tabulation, and analysis difficult. Focus groups should *not* be used, therefore, to develop head counts of the proportion of people who feel a particular way. Focus groups are better for generating ideas and insights than for systematically examining them.

With the increasing tendency of companies to offer their products and services for sale worldwide, many U.S. companies are relying on foreign focus groups to research global markets. Firms considering doing so need to be aware of some of the more important differences between focus groups conducted in foreign countries versus those held in the United States and Canada. See Research Window 5.2.

Research Window 5.2 — Major Differences between Focus Groups Held in Foreign Countries and Those Held in the United States and Canada

- **Timeframe.** Whereas many companies are accustomed to developing a project on a Monday and having it completed by the end of the following week, this is almost impossible to do in foreign countries. Lead times tend to be much longer, especially in the Far East. If it takes two weeks to set up groups in the United States, expect almost double that in most of Europe and even more than that for Asia.

- **Structure.** Eight to ten people in a group is a large number for most foreign groups, which often consist of four to six people. Further, the length of groups outside the United States can be up to four hours. Be very specific when arranging for international focus groups. Most foreign research organizations seem to adapt well to our format if properly informed and supervised.

- **Recruiting and recreating.** In general, the United States is much more rigid in adhering to specifications both in recruiting and screening. These processes must be monitored very carefully.

- **Approach.** Foreign moderators tend to be much less structured and authoritative, which can result in a great deal of down time during the sessions. Foreign moderators feel this is necessary to make group members feel comfortable with each other and build the rapport necessary to get the desired information.

Also, they tend to use fewer writing exercises and external stimuli such as concept boards and photos. This must be considered when planning foreign sessions.

- **Project length.** Projects can take much longer to execute. In the United States we are accustomed to doing two, sometimes three or four, groups a day, but in many overseas markets, one group is the limit because of the time they are scheduled, the length of the sessions, or the demands of the moderators. Also, some moderators have a break in the middle of the group, which would be very unusual in U.S. sessions.

- **Facilities.** The facility environment outside the United States and Canada is much like the setup here 20 years ago. For example, it is more common than not to watch a group in a residential setting on a television that is connected to the group room by cable. Further, many of the facilities with one-way mirror capabilities simply do not have the amenities we are accustomed to in the United States.

- **Costs.** Though costs vary considerably by region and country, it would not be unusual to pay almost twice as much per group for sessions conducted in Europe and almost three times as much for many areas in Asia.

Source: Thomas L. Greenbaum, "Understanding Focus Group Research Abroad," *Marketing News* 30 (June 30, 1996), pp. H14, H36.

Analysis of Selected Cases

Analysis of selected cases
Intensive study of selected examples of the phenomenon of interest.

Sometimes referred to as the analysis of *insight-stimulating examples*, the **analysis of selected cases** involves the intensive study of selected cases of the phenomenon under investigation. Researchers may examine existing records, observe the phenomenon as it occurs, conduct unstructured interviews, or use any one of a variety of other approaches to analyze what is really happening in a given situation. The focus may be on entities (individual people or institutions) or groups of entities (sales representatives or distributors in various regions).

The method is characterized by several features.[20] First, the attitude of the investigator is the key. The most productive attitude is one of alert receptivity, of seeking explanations rather than testing explanations. The investigator is likely to make frequent changes in direction as new information emerges. He or she may have to search for new cases or secure more data from previously contacted cases. Second, the success of the method depends heavily on how well the investigator can integrate the diverse bits of information he or she has amassed into a unified interpretation. Finally, the method is characterized by its intensity. The analyst attempts to obtain sufficient information to characterize and explain both the unique features of the case being studied and the features it has in common with other cases.

In one study to improve the productivity of the sales force of a particular company, the investigator studied intensively two or three of the best sales representatives and two or three of the worst. Data was collected on the background and experience of each representative and then several days were spent making sales calls with them. As a result, a hypothesis was developed. It was that checking the stock of retailers and suggesting items on which they were low were the most important differences between the successful and the poor sales representatives.[21]

In this example, the key insight that good sales representatives had in common, and in which they differed from poor sales representatives, led them to check retailer inventory. The following situations are particularly productive of hypotheses:

1. *Cases reflecting changes and, in particular, abrupt changes.* For example, the way a market adjusts to the entrance of a new competitor can reveal a great deal about the structure of an industry.

2. *Cases reflecting extremes of behavior.* The case of the best and worst sales representatives just cited is an example. Similarly, to determine the factors responsible for the differences in sales performance among a company's territories, one could learn more by comparing the best and worst territories than by looking at all territories.

3. *Cases reflecting the order in which events occurred over time.* For example, in the case of the differing sales performance by territory, it may be that in one territory a branch office replaced a manufacturer's agent, while in another it replaced an industrial distributor.

Which cases will be most valuable depends, of course, on the problem in question. It is generally true, though, that cases that display sharp contrasts or have striking features are most useful. This is because minute differences are usually difficult to discern. Thus, instead of trying to determine what distinguishes the average case from the slightly above-average case, it is better to contrast the best and worst and thereby magnify whatever differences may exist.

Benchmarking

Using organizations that excel at some function as sources of ideas for improvement.

A frequently used example of the use of selected cases to develop insights is benchmarking. **Benchmarking** involves identifying one or more organizations that excel at carrying out some function and using their practices as a source of ideas for improvement. For example, L. L. Bean is noted for its excellent order fulfillment. During one spring, the company mailed 500,000 packages, with every order filled correctly. Even during the busy Christmas season, the company fills 99.9 percent of its orders correctly.[22] Therefore, other organizations have sought to improve their own order fulfillment by benchmarking L. L. Bean.

Ethical Dilemma 5.2

Prompted by an increasing incidence of homes for sale by owner, the president of a local real estate company asks you to undertake exploratory research to ascertain what kind of image Realtors enjoy in the community. Unbeknownst to your current client, you undertook a similar research study for a competitor two years ago and, based on your findings, have formed specific hypotheses about why some homeowners are reluctant to sell their houses through Realtors.

Is it ethical to give information obtained while working for one client to another client who is a competitor? What should you definitely not tell your current client about the earlier project?

Is it ethical to undertake a research project when you think that you already know what the findings will be? Can you generalize findings from two years ago to today?

Should you help this company define its problem, and if so, how?

Organizations carry out benchmarking through activities such as reading about other organizations, visiting or calling them, and taking apart competing products to see how they are made. The process of benchmarking varies according to the information needs of the organization and the resources available.

Benchmarking is most useful for learning about existing rather than new products and about business practices, including ways of providing better value to customers. Benchmarked organizations are less likely to reveal information about new products or to disclose their strategies to competitors.

Xerox is widely credited with the first benchmarking project in the United States. In 1979, Xerox studied Japanese competitors to learn how they could sell midsize copiers for less than what it cost Xerox to make them. Today many companies including AT&T, Eastman Kodak, and Motorola use benchmarking as a standard research tool. Pittsburgh's Mellon Bank started benchmarking to improve the way it handled customer complaints about its credit card billing. Mellon benchmarked seven companies, including credit card operations, an airline, and a competing bank, by visiting three companies and phoning four. By applying what it learned, the bank cut its complaint-resolution time from an average of 45 days to 25 days.[23]

Back to the Case

At the next week's meeting, the Western Kodiak sales and marketing managers were again discussing the company's planned new products, Photos on CD and Pictures Online. They had invited Estella Ramos, the company's director of research, to fill them in on background information the company had obtained regarding consumer use of information technology.

"In addition to doing research projects," Estella explained, "we routinely conduct exploratory research by reviewing published studies, news stories, and so on. For example, we track the extent to which Internet usage has been growing."

"What exactly do you mean by 'Internet usage'?" asked Jane.

"Good question. I mean the number of households with Internet access. We have somewhat less in the way of data about what those households are doing, but we're working on that. For example, one of the media services has been tracking usage of home personal computers. They've found that although people keep buying PCs, the percent that actually turns them on has been falling over the last few years."

"Do we have any research establishing why that is?" asked Paul.

"Some people have hypothesized reasons," Stella replied. "They think consumers use computers at work and are tired of them by the time they get home. We're watching the literature for research into this."

"It sounds to me as though we still have a lot to learn about people's computer use," said Jane.

"That's right," Estella replied, "and it's an exciting area of research. We're also watching for the results of a big study into how the Internet is affecting people's behavior. The Center for Communication Policy at UCLA is working with universities in Singapore and Italy to observe consumer behavior and measure attitudes of thousands of households on an international scale over several years. The study will look at social relationships, as well as e-mail and e-commerce. The researches will observe consumers at home as well as conduct surveys."

"Whoa," said John, "we could never fund a study like that here at Western Kodiak."

"Exactly," said Estella. "And this is a groundbreaking study, because it looks at how the Internet is changing lifestyles and attitudes. That's why we combine the results of other people's exploratory research with our own data to give you information and help you identify questions to answer with our own studies."

"Thanks, Estella," Paul said. "With your group's help, we can adjust our plans whenever we need to so that Photos on CD and Pictures Online help consumers do what they really want to do."

Source: The Western Kodiak case is based on David Goetzl, "Kodak Sets Assault on 'Photo Use' with Three New Campaigns," *Advertising Age* (June 28, 1999), p. 4; Margaret Kane, "UCLA Launches Wide-Ranging Net Study," ZDNet Tech News (downloaded from Excite Web site, www.excite.com, June 8, 1999); Michael Miller, "Researchers to Study Internet's Impact on Society," Reuters Internet Report (downloaded from Excite Web site, www.excite.com, June 8, 1999); David Plotnikoff, "Study Asks How Wired World Has Changed the Way We Live," *San Jose Mercury News* (June 13, 1999), pp. 1F, 7F; "Use of Household PCs Is on the Wane," *Chicago Tribune* (June 22, 1999), sec. 3, p. 4.

Summary

Learning Objective 1

Explain what a research design is.

> A research design is the framework or plan for a study and guides the collection and analysis of data.

Learning Objective 2

List the three basic types of research design.

> One basic way of classifying designs is in terms of the fundamental objective of the research: exploratory, descriptive, or causal.

Learning Objective 3

Describe the major emphasis of each type of research design.

> The major emphasis in exploratory research is on the discovery of ideas and insights. Descriptive research is typically concerned with determining the frequency with which something occurs or the relationship between variables. A causal research design is concerned with determining cause-and-effect relationships.

Learning Objective 4

Cite the crucial principle of research.

> The crucial principle of research is that the design of the investigation should stem from the problem.

Learning Objective 5

Describe the basic uses of exploratory research.

> Exploratory research is basically "general picture" research. It is quite useful in becoming familiar with a phenomenon, in clarifying concepts, in developing but not testing "if-then" statements, and in establishing priorities for further research. The output from exploratory research is ideas and insights, not answers.

Learning Objective 6

Specify the key characteristic of exploratory research.

> Exploratory studies are characterized by their flexibility.

Learning Objective 7

Discuss the various types of exploratory research and identify the characteristics of each.

Among the various types of exploratory research are literature searches, experience surveys, focus groups, and analyses of selected cases. Literature searches may involve conceptual literature, trade literature, or, quite often, published statistics. Experience surveys, sometimes known as key informant surveys, attempt to tap the knowledge and experience of those familiar with the general subject being investigated. Focus groups are in a sense personal interviews conducted among a small number of individuals, normally 8 to 12, simultaneously. However, the interview relies more on group discussion than on a series of directed questions to generate data. The analysis of selected cases is sometimes referred to as the analysis of insight-stimulating examples. By either label, the approach involves the intensive study of selected cases of the phenomenon under investigation.

Learning Objective 8

Identify the key person in a focus group.

The moderator is key to successful functioning of a focus group. The moderator must not only lead the discussion so that all objectives of the study are met but must do so in such a way that interaction among group members is stimulated and promoted.

Review Questions

1. What is a research design? Is a research design necessary to conduct a study?

2. What are the different types of research designs? What is the basic purpose of each?

3. What is the crucial tenet of research?

4. What are the basic uses for exploratory research?

5. What is the key characteristic of exploratory research?

6. What are some of the more productive types of exploratory research? What are the characteristics of each type?

Discussion Questions, Problems, and Projects

1. The Communicon Company was a large supplier of residential telephones and related services in the southeast United States. The Department of Research and Development recently designed a prototype with a memory function that could store the number of calls and the contents of the calls for a period of 48 hours. A similar model, introduced by Communicon's competitor three months earlier, was marginally successful. However, both the models suffered from a technical flaw. It was found that a call lasting for over 20 minutes would result in a loss of the dial tone for 90 seconds. This was mainly attributable to the activation of the memory function. Notwithstanding the flaw, management was excited about the efforts of the research and development department. They decided to do a field study to gauge consumer reaction to the memory capability. A random sample of 1,000 respondents was to be chosen from three major metropolitan centers in the Southeast. The questionnaires were designed to find out respondents' attitudes and opinions toward this new instrument.

   In this situation, is the research design appropriate? If yes, why? If no, why not?

2. A medium-sized manufacturer of high-speed copiers and duplicators was introducing a new desktop model. The vice president of communications had to decide between two advertising programs for this product. He preferred advertising program Gamma and was sure it would generate more sales than its counterpart, advertising program Beta. The next day he was to meet with the senior vice president of marketing to plan

an appropriate research design for a study that would aid in the final decision as to which advertising program to implement.

What research design would you recommend? Justify your choice.

3. A local mail-order firm was concerned with improving its service. In particular, management wanted to assess if customers were dissatisfied with current service and the nature of this dissatisfaction.

What research design would you recommend? Justify your choice.

4. The Write-It Company was a manufacturer of writing instruments such as fountain pens, ballpoint pens, soft-tip pens, and mechanical pencils. Typically, these products were retailed through small and large chains, drugstores, and grocery stores. The company had recently diversified into the manufacture of disposable cigarette lighters. The distribution of this product was to be restricted to drugstores and grocery stores because management believed that its target market of low- and middle-income classes would use these outlets. Your expertise is required in order to decide on an appropriate research design to determine if this would indeed be the case.

What research design would you recommend? Justify your choice.

5. Feather-Tote Luggage is a producer of cloth-covered luggage, one of the primary advantages of which is its light weight. The company distributes its luggage through major department stores, mail-order houses, clothing retailers, and other retail outlets such as stationery stores, leather goods stores, and so on. The company advertises rather heavily, but it also supplements this promotional effort with a large field staff of sales representatives, numbering around 400. The number of sales representatives varies, and one of the historical problems confronting Feather-Tote Luggage has been the large number of sales representatives' resignations. It is not unusual for 10 to 20 percent of the sales force to turn over every year. Since the cost of training a new person is estimated at $5,000 to $10,000, not including the lost sales that might result because of a personnel switch, Mr. Harvey, the sales manager, is rightly concerned. He has been concerned for some time and, therefore, has been conducting exit interviews with each departing sales representative. On the basis of these interviews, he has formulated the opinion that the major reason for this high turnover is general sales representatives' dissatisfaction with company policies, promotional opportunities, and pay. But top management has not been sympathetic to Harvey's pleas regarding the changes needed in these areas of corporate policy. Rather, it has tended to counter Harvey's pleas with arguments that too much of what he is suggesting is based on his gut reactions and little hard data. Before it would be willing to change things, top management desires more systematic evidence that job satisfaction, in general, and these dimensions of job satisfaction, in particular, are the real reasons for the high turnover. Harvey has called on the Marketing Research Department at Feather-Tote Luggage to assist him in solving his problem.
   (a) As a member of this department, identify the general hypothesis that would guide your research efforts.
   (b) What type of research design would you recommend to Harvey? Justify your answer.

6. Cynthia Gaskill is the owner of a clothing store that caters to college students. Through informal conversations with her customers, she has begun to suspect that a video-rental store specifically targeting college students as customers would do quite well in the local market. While her informal conversations with students have revealed an overall sense of dissatisfaction with existing rental outlets, she hasn't been able to isolate specific areas of concern. Gaskill, thinking back to a marketing research course she took in school, has decided that focus group research would be an appropriate method to gather information that might be useful in deciding whether to pursue further development of her idea (e.g., a formal business plan, store policies, etc.).

(a) What is the decision problem and resulting research problem apparent in this situation?

(b) Who should Gaskill select as participants for the focus group?

(c) Where should the focus group session be conducted?

(d) Who should be the moderator of the focus group?

(e) Develop a discussion outline for the focus group.

7. The exploratory techniques of focus group research and experience surveys are similar in many ways, yet each offers distinct advantages, depending on the objectives of the research project. What are some of the similarities and differences in these techniques?

Endnotes

1. Julian L. Simon, *Basic Research Methods in Social Science: The Art of Empirical Investigation* (New York: Random House, 1969), p. 4.

2. Claire Selltiz, Lawrence S. Wrightsman, and Stuart W. Cook, *Research Methods in Social Relations*, 3rd ed. (New York: Holt, Rinehart and Winston, 1976), pp. 90–91. See also Fred N. Kerlinger, *Foundations of Behavioral Research*, 3rd ed. (New York: Holt, Rinehart and Winston, 1986), pp. 347–390; John W. Creswell, *Research Design: Qualitative and Quantitative Approaches* (Thousand Oaks, Calif.: Sage Publications, 1994).

3. The basic purposes are those suggested by Selltiz, Wrightsman, and Cook, *Research Methods*.

4. Nina Munk, "Title Fight," *Fortune* (June 21, 1999, downloaded from Northern Light Web site, www.northernlight.com, July 29, 1999).

5. See Kerlinger, *Foundations of Behavioral Research*, for a discussion of the criteria of good hypotheses and of the value of hypotheses in guiding research.

6. Selltiz, Wrightsman, and Cook, *Research Methods*, p. 91.

7. Selltiz, Wrightsman, and Cook, *Research Methods*. Chapter 4 has a particularly informative discussion of the types of research that are productive at the exploratory stages of an investigation.

8. Steven P. Galante, "More Firms Quiz Customers for Clues About Competition," *The Wall Street Journal* (March 3, 1986), p. 17. See also Thomas L'egare, "Acting on Customer Feedback," *Marketing Research: A Magazine of Management & Applications* 8 (Spring 1996), pp. 46–51.

9. Roy Furchgott, "Trend Spotting," *San Jose Mercury News* (July 6, 1998), pp. 1C, 4C.

10. Bob Deierlein, "A New Louisville Slugger," *Beverage World*, 114 (June 1995), pp. 116–117.

11. Selltiz, Wrightsman, and Cook, *Research Methods*, p. 94.

12. Selltiz, Wrightsman, and Cook suggest that it is often useful in an exploratory study to orient questions toward "what works." That is, they recommend that questions be of the following form: "If (a given effect) is desired, what influences or what methods will, in your experience, be most likely to produce it?" (p. 95).

13. Joshua Macht, "The New Market Research," *Inc.* (July 1998), pp. 87–94.

14. Tim Neenan, "007's BMW Z3," *Ward's Auto World* 32 (March 1996), pp. 75–76.

15. Robert C. Inglis, "In-Depth Data: Using Focus Groups to Study Industrial Markets," *Business Marketing* 72 (November 1987), p. 80.

16. Goldman and McDonald discuss the pros and cons of the various sites as well as a number of other operational questions that arise with the conduct of focus groups. See Alfred E. Goldman and Susan Schwartz McDonald, *The Group Interview: Principles and Practice* (Englewood Cliffs, N.J.: Prentice-Hall, 1987). See also David W. Stewart and Prem N. Shamdasani, *Focus Groups: Theory and Practice* (Newbury Park, Calif.: Sage Publications, 1990); David L. Morgan, ed., *Successful Focus Groups: Advancing the State of the Art* (Thousand Oaks, Calif.: Sage Publications, 1993).

17. See Thomas L. Greenbaum, *The Handbook for Focus Group Research*, 2nd ed. (Thousand Oaks, Calif.: Sage Publications, 1998); Richard A. Krueger, *Focus Groups: A Practical Guide for Applied Research* (Thousand Oaks, Calif.: Sage Publications, 1994); Jane Farley Templeton, *The Focus Group: A Strategic Guide to Organizing, Conducting, and Analyzing the Focus Group Interview* (Thousand Oaks, Calif.: Sage Publications, 1994) regarding the requirements for moderators and how to go about selecting them.

18. Inglis, "In-Depth Data," has a useful discussion of the extra difficulties moderators of industrial focus groups face. For discussions of the use of focus groups for industrial goods, see Edward F. McQuarrie and Shelby H. McIntyre, "Focus Groups and the Development of New Products by Technologically Driven Companies: Some Guidelines," *Journal of Product Innovation Management* 3 (March 1986), pp. 40–46. Curtis J. Fedder, "Biz-to-Biz Focus Groups Require a Special Touch," *Marketing News* 24 (January 8, 1990), p. 46.

19. Scott C. McDonald, Nancy E. Dince, and Larry P. Stanek, "Focus Groups Being Subverted by Clients," *Marketing News* 18 (August 28, 1987), p. 48. See also Thomas L., Greenbaum, "Observing a Focus Group Takes as Much Skill as Moderating It," *Marketing News* 22 (August 29, 1994), p. 17.

20. These features are detailed further in Selltiz, Wrightsman, and Cook, *Research Methods,* pp. 98–99. See also Thomas V. Bonoma, "Case Research in Marketing: Opportunities, Problems, and a Process," *Journal of Marketing Research* 22 (May 1985), pp. 199–208; Robert K. Yin, *Case Study Research: Design and Methods* (Thousand Oaks, Calif.: Sage Publications, 1994); Robert E. Stake, *The Art of Case Study Research* (Thousand Oaks, Calif.: Sage Publications, 1993).

21. Harper W. Boyd, Ralph Westfall, and Stanley F. Stasch, *Marketing Research: Text and Cases,* 6th ed. (Homewood, Ill.: Richard D. Irwin, 1985), p. 51.

22. Otis Port, "Quality: Small and Midsize's Companies Seize the Challenge—Not a Moment too Soon," *Business Week* (November 30, 1992), pp. 66–72.

23. Jeremy Main, "How to Steal the Best Ideas Around," *Fortune* 126 (October 19, 1992), pp. 102–106. See also Douglas Brownlie, "The Conduct of Marketing Audits," *Industrial Marketing Management* 25 (January 1996), pp. 11–22; Subra Balakrishnan, "Benefits of Customer and Competitive Orientations in Industrial Markets," *Industrial Marketing Management* 25 (July 1996), pp. 257–269.

Suggested Additional Readings

For an excellent discussion of the three types of research designs, their basic purposes, and generally fruitful approaches, see
Claire Selltiz, Lawrence S. Wrightsman, and Stuart W. Cook, *Research Methods in Social Relations,* 3rd ed. (New York: Holt, Rinehart and Winston, 1976).
Fred N. Kerlinger, *Foundations of Behavioral Research,* 3rd ed. (New York: Holt, Rinehart and Winston, 1986).

For detailed discussion on conducting focus groups, see
Thomas L. Greenbaum, *The Handbook for Focus Group Research,* 2nd ed. (Thousand Oaks, Calif.: Sage Publishers, 1998).
Richard A. Krueger, *Focus Groups: A Practical Guide for Applied Research,* (Thousand Oaks, Calif.: Sage Publications, 1994).
Jane Farley Templeton, *The Focus Group: A Strategic Guide to Organizing, Conducting, and Analyzing the Focus Group Interview* (Thousand Oaks, Calif.: Sage Publications, 1994).

Chapter 6

DESCRIPTIVE AND CAUSAL RESEARCH DESIGNS

LEARNING OBJECTIVES

Upon Completing This Chapter, You Should Be Able to

1. Cite three major purposes of descriptive research.

2. List the six specifications of a descriptive study.

3. Explain what a dummy table is.

4. Discuss the difference between cross-sectional and longitudinal designs.

5. Explain what is meant by a *panel* in marketing research and explain the difference between a traditional panel and an omnibus panel.

6. Explain what is meant by a *turnover table,* or brand-switching matrix.

7. Describe the emphasis in sample surveys.

8. Distinguish between the commonsense notion of causality and the scientific notion.

9. Define *concomitant variation.*

10. List three ways of determining a causal relationship.

11. Clarify the difference between laboratory experiments and field experiments.

12. Explain which of the two types of experiments has greater internal validity and which has greater external validity.

13. List the three major problems in test-marketing.

14. Discuss the advantages and disadvantages of simulated test-marketing.

15. Distinguish between a standard test market and a controlled test market.

Case in Marketing Research

The telephone business just isn't what it used to be. Once, AT&T was benevolent "Ma Bell." Together with its local subsidiaries, it was the company that let people talk to each other down the street, across the United States, and around the world. Then the U.S. phone business was segmented into local service providers and a handful of long-distance carriers.

Today's environment is far more complex—and competitive. Communication isn't just making a traditional phone call; it can include sending faxes, sending e-mail via the Internet, watching cable television, or using a wireless phone. Furthermore, the local companies are being allowed to enter the more profitable long-distance marketplace, but only if they first let the long-distance players compete in the local markets. At the same time, AT&T is laying the groundwork to enter the market for local telephone service.

Probably the company's grandest plan is to use cable TV lines as a gateway for delivering a variety of communications services. AT&T in 1999 merged with Tele-Communications Inc. (TCI) to obtain a so-called broadband connection to millions of homes. Through this new business unit, named AT&T Broadband & Internet Services, consumers who sign up with AT&T are to receive local and long-distance phone service, high-speed Internet connections, and digital cable TV. They get all that through one company, with one bill.

But this is a high-risk strategy. It requires heavy investment in technology and infrastructure. AT&T has already spent billions of dollars acquiring and upgrading the cable services. To get a satisfactory return on that investment, the company must be sure that consumers understand and want this new type of service package.

Entering the thicket of the modern communications marketplace requires enormous technical know-how coupled with in-depth marketing data. AT&T must ensure that its technology will perform well enough to meet and exceed consumers' expectations—preferably without the expense of setting up the whole system nationwide. The company must know what consumers want their communications provider to do for them and how to explain a new service to them. Presumably, obtaining this information requires that AT&T offer the service and measure consumers' reaction. However, doing so invites a response from competitors.

AT&T cannot afford to let the information technology revolution pass it by. Someday plain-vanilla phone service will be as passé as black-and-white television.

Discussion Issues

1. What questions should AT&T answer through marketing research?

2. What kinds of research can help AT&T answer these marketing questions?

3. How might the company prepare for competitors' reactions when its research becomes public?

In the preceding chapter we learned that research designs typically fall into one of three categories: exploratory, descriptive, or causal research. We examined exploratory research and noted that one of its primary uses is to generate ideas and insights for additional, more targeted research. In this chapter we will see how descriptive and causal research might be used to test the validity of the hypotheses that exploratory studies generate.

Descriptive Research Designs

A great deal of marketing research can be considered descriptive research, which is used for the following purposes:

1. To describe the characteristics of certain groups. For example, based on information gathered from known users of our particular product, we might attempt to develop a profile of the "average user" with respect to income, sex, age, educational level, and so on.

2. To estimate the proportion of people in a specified population who behave in a certain way. We might be interested, say, in estimating the proportion of people within a specified radius of a proposed shopping complex who would shop at the center.

3. To make specific predictions. We might be interested in predicting the level of sales for each of the next five years so that we could plan for the hiring and training of new sales representatives.

Descriptive research encompasses an array of research objectives. However, a descriptive study is more than a fact-gathering expedition.

> Facts do not lead anywhere. Indeed, facts, as facts, are the commonest, cheapest, and most useless of all commodities. Anyone with a questionnaire can gather thousands of facts a day—and probably not find much real use for them. What makes facts practical and valuable is the glue of explanation and understanding, the framework of theory, the tie-rod of conjecture. Only when facts can be fleshed to a skeletal theory do they become meaningful in the solution of problems.[1]

The researcher should not fall prey to the temptation of beginning a descriptive research study with the vague thought that the data collected should be interesting. A good descriptive study presupposes much prior knowledge about the phenomenon being studied. It rests on one or more specific hypotheses. These conjectural statements guide the research in specific directions. In this respect, a descriptive study design is very different from an exploratory study design. Whereas an exploratory study is characterized by its flexibility, descriptive studies can be considered rigid. Descriptive studies require a *clear specification* of the *who, what, when, where, why,* and *how* of the research.

Suppose a chain of convenience food stores is planning to open a new outlet, and the company wants to determine how people usually come to patronize a new outlet. Consider some of the questions that would need to be answered before data collection for this descriptive study could begin. Who is to be considered a patron? Anyone who enters the store? What if they do not buy anything but just participate in the grand-opening prize

Recent descriptive research regarding use of the Internet by Media Metrix, a leading market researcher whose Web site is pictured, found that men 18 years or older are at least as likely to shop on-line as women of the same age. Blue Mountain Arts Electronic Greeting Cards was the most visited site by both genders, followed by Amazon.com and Ebay.com. For women, the fourth most visited spot is barnesand noble.com, while for men Cnet Software Download Services ranks fourth. Coupon sites such as Cool-Savings and ValuPage rank in fifth and sixth places with women and nowhere in the top 10 with men.

Source: Media Metrix, Inc., is a pioneer in the field of Internet and digital media measurement services.

giveaway? Perhaps a patron should be defined as anyone who purchases anything from the store.

Should patrons be defined on the basis of the family unit, or should they be defined as individuals, even though the individuals come from the same family? What characteristics of these patrons should be measured? Are we interested in their age and sex, or perhaps in where they live and how they came to know about our store? When shall we measure them—while they are shopping or later? Should the study take place during the first weeks of operation of the store, or should it be delayed until the situation has stabilized somewhat? Certainly if we are interested in word-of-mouth influence, we must wait at least until that influence has a chance to operate.

Where shall we measure the patrons? Should it be in the store, immediately outside the store, or should we attempt to contact them at home? Why do we want to measure them? Are we going to use these measurements to plan promotional strategy? In that case the emphasis might be on measuring how people become aware of the store. Or are we going to use these measurements as a basis for locating other stores? In that case the emphasis might shift more to determining the trading area of the store.

How shall we measure the patrons? Shall we use a questionnaire, or shall we observe their purchasing behavior? If we use a questionnaire, what form will it take? Will it be highly structured? Will it be in the form of a scale? How will it be administered? By telephone? By mail? Perhaps by personal interview?

These questions are not the only ones that would be or should be asked. Certainly, some of the answers will be implicit in the hypothesis or hypotheses that guide the descriptive research. Others, though, will not be obvious. The researcher will be able to specify them only after some labored thought or even after a small pilot or exploratory study. In either case, the researcher is well advised to delay collecting that first item of information with which to test the hypotheses until clear judgments of the who, what, when, where, why, and how of descriptive research have been made.

The researcher should also delay data collection until it has been clearly determined how the data are to be analyzed. Ideally, a set of dummy tables should be prepared before

Dummy table
A table that will be used to catalog the collected data.

beginning the collection process. A **dummy table** is used to catalog the data that is to be collected. It shows how the analysis will be structured and conducted. Complete in all respects save for filling in the actual numbers, it contains a title, headings, and specific categories for the variables making up the table. All that remains after collecting the data is to count the number of cases of each type. Exhibit 6.1 shows a dummy table that might be used by a women's specialty store preparing to investigate whether its customers are predominantly from one age group and, if so, how that group differs from the customers who frequent competitors' stores.

Note that the table lists the particular age segments the store's owner wishes to compare. It is crucial that the exact variables and categories to be investigated be specified before researchers begin to collect the data. The statistical tests that will be used to uncover the relationship between age and store preference in this case should also be specified before data collection begins. Inexperienced researchers often question the need for such hard, detailed decisions before collecting the data. They assume that delaying these decisions until after the data are collected will somehow make the decisions easier. Just the opposite is true, as any experienced researcher will attest.

> Most difficult for the beginning researcher to anticipate will be the analytical problems he may face after the data are gathered. He tends to believe that a wide variety of facts will be enough to solve anything. Only after struggling with sloppy, stubborn, and intractable facts, with data not adequate for the testing of hypotheses and with data that are interesting but incapable of supporting practical recommendations for action will he be fully aware that the big "mistakes" of research usually are made in the early stages. Each definition of a problem or problem variable will create different facts or findings, and a formulation once made serves to restrict the scope of analysis. No problem is definitively formulated until the researcher can specify how he will make his analysis and how the results will contribute to a practical solution.[2]

Once the data have been collected and analysis is begun, it is too late to lament, "If only we had collected information on that variable," or "If only we had measured the Y variable using a finer scale." Correcting such mistakes at this time is next to impossible. Rather, the analyst must take such considerations into account when planning the study. And dummy tables make such planning easier.

Another way of ensuring that the information collected in a descriptive study will address the objectives of the research is to specify in advance the objective each question addresses, the reason the question is included in the study, and the particular analysis in which the question will be used, although not going so far as laying out all of the cross-classification tables. Although output planning like this is extremely valuable, there is added merit in specifying all anticipated dummy tables in advance. Dummy tables are particularly valuable in providing clues on how to phrase the individual questions and code the responses.

Cross-sectional study
Investigation involving a sample of elements selected from the population of interest that are measured at a single point in time.

Figure 6.1 is an overview of the various types of descriptive studies. The basic distinction is between *cross-sectional designs,* which are the most common and most familiar, and *longitudinal designs.* Typically, a **cross-sectional study** involves researching a sam-

---

EXHIBIT 6.1   Dummy Table

	STORE PREFERENCE BY AGE		
Age	Prefer A	Prefer B	Prefer C
Less than 30			
30–39			
40 or more			

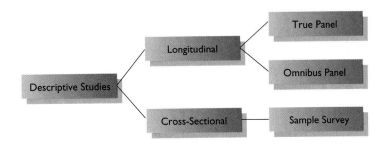

ple of elements from the population of interest. Most characteristics of the elements, or sample members, are measured only once.

A **longitudinal study,** on the other hand, involves a *panel,* which is a fixed sample of elements. The elements may be stores, dealers, individuals, or other entities. The panel, or sample, remains relatively constant through time, although members may be added to replace dropouts or to keep it representative. The sample members in a panel are measured repeatedly, in contrast with the one-time measurement in a cross-sectional study. Both cross-sectional and longitudinal studies have weaknesses and advantages.

Longitudinal study
Investigation involving a fixed sample of elements that is measured repeatedly through time.

Longitudinal Analysis

There are two types of panels: true panels and omnibus panels. **True panels,** which are older, rely on repeated measurements of the same variables. Nielsen maintains a panel of 52,000 households nationwide as a basis of its HOMESCAN service. The panel households use a handheld scanner to record every UPC-coded item they purchase. They simply pass the scanner across the Universal Product Codes on the packages of the purchased items when they return from shopping and then answer a programmed set of questions (e.g., store where purchased, price paid) by responding to a series of prompts from the machine. Similarly, National Purchase Diary (NPD) maintains a consumer panel of families who record their purchases in a paper diary when they return from shopping. The operations of these panels will be detailed when discussing standardized marketing information services in Chapter 8. The important point to note now is that each panel member is measured with respect to the same characteristics at each time—purchases.

In recent years, a new type of panel, called the **omnibus panel,** has sprung up. The information collected from the members selected for this type of panel varies. At one time, it may be attitudes with respect to a new product. At another time, the panel members might be asked to evaluate alternative advertising copy. In each case, a sample might be selected from the larger group, which is in turn a sample of the population. The subsample might be drawn randomly. More likely, though, participants with the desired characteristics will be chosen from a total panel. For example, the Parker Pen Company maintains a panel of 1,100 individuals who were chosen because they expressed some interest in writing instruments and, of course, because of their willingness to participate. Parker Pen uses selected members of this panel to evaluate new writing instruments. If the new instrument is a fountain pen, the company will probably choose individuals who prefer fountain pens to test the product. Those chosen and the information sought varies from project to project.

As Research Window 6.1 reveals, the children's cable television network Nickelodeon uses a panel of children to help it evaluate its programming and magazine ideas. In an interesting twist, it uses on-line computer connections to gather their reactions.

The distinction between the traditional panel and the omnibus panel is important. True longitudinal analysis, also called *time series analysis,* can be performed only on the

Panel (true)
A fixed sample of respondents who are measured repeatedly over time with respect to the same variables.

Panel (omnibus)
A fixed sample of respondents who are measured repeatedly over time but on variables that change from measurement to measurement.

Research Window 6.1   Use of an On-Line Computer Panel by Nickelodeon

After reading an article in a new magazine, a child pans it, calling the article "stupid." Another says: "It was boring." A third: "A lot of it was a little too weird for me." For market researchers, these sorts of spontaneous comments are priceless, but they're tough to obtain, because kids are often intimidated when they talk to adults. Now Nickelodeon, the children's cable television network, has gotten around that problem by setting up one of the first consumer product testing panels established over a computer network.

"It's a great tool because it gives a real sense of immediacy with the kids," says Michael Hainey, an editor of the *Nickelodeon Magazine* prototype that was skewered by the children. "We liked it because it was a sounding board for kids across the country." The children responded favorably to the magazine overall, Hainey says, but "We'll be rethinking" parts, such as a confusing table of contents and an article on a boy from North Dakota.

The children—75 of them between the ages of 8 and 12 in a dozen areas from Boston to Los Angeles—have been recruited for a two-year stint as participants in "Get hooked on Nick" by Nickelodeon's researchers. Nickelodeon wants to make sure that TV shows, often created by childless New Yorkers, will actually appeal to boys and girls of all races who are between the ages of 2 and 14 and who come from all over the country.

Other TV and movie people also are getting in touch with their fans on services such as CompuServ, Prodigy, and Genie. Show publicists and directors sometimes go on-line to see how people reacted to a show that ran the night before. In other fields, computer software companies have been doing market research on-line in CompuServ forums for years, asking early testers to report problems as they find them.

But Nickelodeon seems to be the first network to formalize on-line research. The children that it selected all had computers and VCRs. Half are minorities, and half are girls. Family incomes in the group range from $20,000 to $120,000.

The children, who aren't paid, can go on-line and chat informally with each other or with Nickelodeon researchers three afternoons a week. Sometimes, they post jokes on a bulletin board or contribute a sentence to a fantasy story started by one child. When Nickelodeon wants reaction to a new show or to the magazine, it sends videos or a prototype to 20 kids and asks them to sign on to a special conference at a set time for one to two hours.

If a special research project comes up, the children are there. In one case, Nickelodeon sent 12 children videotapes of a new show called "The Tomorrow People" and then asked them their opinions. One conclusion: Many children didn't realize that action was shifting among several countries. Producers inserted graphics in the show to clarify the changes in location.

In December, when the network had just started the on-line project, it used the kids' group to decide whether to produce a special news show on Somalia. Researchers found that the children already understood the issues, and Nickelodeon dropped the idea.

On-line isn't perfect, Nickelodeon researchers concede. "You'd prefer to see them in person," says Hainey. On-line "tends to be a lot of monosyllabic typing." It also doesn't work for younger children, who reveal more by their body language than by their spoken or written words.

Therefore, Nickelodeon continues more traditional research, including analyzing Nielsen and Arbitron ratings, in-person focus groups, interviews at schools, and tracking letters and calls about shows. But the on-line group eliminates travel costs and lets people in New York get reaction in a few hours to questions such as preferred sneaker styles or what music children consider oldies— "Beatoven," one boy replied. It has already become "an unbelievable research resource to us," says Rande Price, manager of research.

Source: William M. Bulkeley, "Nickelodeon Sets Up Online Focus Group," *The Wall Street Journal* (March 29, 1993), p. B4. Reprinted by permission of Wall Street Journal, © Dow Jones & Company, Inc. All Rights Reserved Worldwide.

first type of data, repeated measurements of the same variables for the same entities over time. We shall see why when we discuss the method of analysis unique to panel data—the turnover table. The turnover table can be used only when individuals and variables are held constant through time. This is not to deny the value of omnibus panels. Rather, we wish only to raise a cautionary flag, because in other respects (for example, sample design, information collection) both types of panels have about the same advantages and disadvantages when compared with cross-sectional studies. Consequently, we shall treat both types of panel studies together when discussing these general advantages and disadvantages.

Probably the single most important advantage of true panel data is the way it lends itself to analysis. Suppose we are presently subscribing to the type of service that generates consumer purchase data from a panel of 1,000 families. Suppose further that we manufacture a laundry detergent, which we will call Brand A, and our brand has two main competitors, Brands B and C. There are also a number of other smaller competitors, which we will classify together in the single category Brand D.

We have recently changed the package design of our product, and we are now interested in determining what impact the new design has on sales. Let us consider the performance of our brand before the change (time period t_1) and after the package change (time period t_2).

We could perform several types of analyses on these data.[3] We could look at the proportion of those in the panel who bought our brand in period t_1. We could also calculate the proportion of those who bought our brand in period t_2. Suppose these calculations generated the data shown in Exhibit 6.2, which indicates that the package change was successful. Brand A's market share increased from 20 percent to 25 percent. Further, Brand A seemed to make its gain at the expense of its two major competitors, whose market shares decreased.

But that is not the whole story or even a completely accurate picture of the market changes that occurred. Look at what happens when, in assessing the impact of the package change, we maintain the identity of the sample members. Since we have repeated measures of the same individuals, we can count the number of families who bought Brand A in both periods, those who bought B or C or one of the miscellaneous brands in both periods, and those who switched brands between the two periods. Suppose Exhibit 6.3 resulted from these tabulations. This table, which is a **turnover table,** or a **brand-switching matrix,** contains the same basic information as Exhibit 6.2. That is, we see that 200, or 20 percent, of the families bought Brand A in period t_1, while 250, or 25 percent, did so in period t_2. But Exhibit 6.3 also shows that Brand A did not make its market share gains at the expense of Brands B and C, as originally suggested, but rather captured some of the families who previously bought one of the miscellaneous brands; 75 families

Brand-switching matrix
A two-way table that indicates which brands a sample of people purchased in one period and which brands they purchased in a subsequent period, thus highlighting the switches occurring among and between brands as well as the number of persons that purchased the same brand in both periods.

EXHIBIT 6.2   Number of Families in Panel Purchasing Each Brand

Brand Purchased	During First Time Period (t_1)	During Second Time Period (t_2)
A	200	250
B	300	270
C	350	330
D	150	150
Total	1,000	1,000

EXHIBIT 6.3   Number of Families in Panel Buying Each Brand in Each Period

		DURING SECOND TIME PERIOD (t_2)				
		Bought A	**Bought B**	**Bought C**	**Bought D**	**Total**
During First Time Period (t_1)	Bought A	175	25	0	0	200
	Bought B	0	225	50	25	300
	Bought C	0	0	280	70	350
	Bought D	75	20	0	55	150
	Total	250	270	330	150	1,000

switched from Brand D in period t_1 to Brand A in period t_2. And, as a matter of fact, Brand A lost some of its previous users to Brand B during the period; 25 families switched from Brand A in period t_1 to Brand B in period t_2.

Exhibit 6.3 also allows the calculation of brand loyalty. Consider Brand A, for example: 175 of the 200, or 87.5 percent, of those who bought Brand A in period t_1 remained "loyal to it" (bought it again) in period t_2. By dividing each cell entry by the row or previous period totals, one can assess these brand loyalties and can also throw the basic changes that occurred in the market into bolder relief. Exhibit 6.4, produced by such calculations, suggests, for example, that among the three major brands, Brand A exhibited the greatest buying loyalty and Brand B the least. This is important to know because it indicates whether families like the brand when they try it.[4]

Whether we can conclude that those who switched from one of the miscellaneous brands to Brand A were prompted to do so by the package change is open to question, for reasons that we will discuss later in the chapter. The point is that turnover, or brand-switching, analysis can be performed only when there are repeated measures over time for the same variables for the same subjects. It is not appropriate for omnibus panel data, in which the variables being measured are constantly changing, nor is it appropriate for cross-sectional studies, even if successive cross-sectional samples are taken.

Thus, the unique advantage of true longitudinal analysis is that since it reveals changes in individual members' behavior, researchers can determine the effect of a change in a particular marketing variable—a package design, for example—better than if they had conducted separate studies using samples made up of different individuals. Had two different groups been used to study a change in a particular variable, it would not be clear whether variations in the data were due to changes in the marketing variable or to differences between the two groups.

Although the major advantage of a panel is analytical, a panel also provides some advantages in the kind of information it yields. Panels are probably a researcher's best format for collecting classification information, such as respondents' incomes, ages, education levels, and occupations. And this information allows a more sophisticated analysis of a study's results.

Cross-sectional studies are limited in this respect, since respondents being contacted for the first and only time are rarely willing to give lengthy, time-consuming interviews. Panel members are usually compensated for their participation, so their interviews can be longer and more exacting, or there can be several interviews. Further, the sponsoring firm can afford to spend more time and effort securing accurate classification information, as this information can be used in a number of studies.

Panel data are also believed to be more accurate than cross-sectional data because panel data tend to be freer from the errors associated with reporting past behavior. Errors arise in reporting past behavior because humans tend to forget, partly because time has elapsed, but partly for other reasons. In particular, research has shown that events and experiences are forgotten more readily if they are inconsistent with attitudes or beliefs that are important to the person or that threaten the person's self-esteem. If, for example, subjects are asked how often they brush their teeth, they might overstate the number of

EXHIBIT 6.4   **Brand Loyalty and Brand-Switching Probabilities among Families in Panel**

		DURING SECOND TIME PERIOD (t_2)				
		Bought A	Bought B	Bought C	Bought D	Total
During First Time Period (t_1)	Bought A	.875	.125	.000	.000	1.000
	Bought B	.000	.750	.167	.083	1.000
	Bought C	.000	.000	.800	.200	1.000
	Bought D	.500	.133	.000	.367	1.000

times—either because they genuinely do not remember or because they fear the interviewer will think less of them for brushing too seldom. In a panel, on the other hand, behavior is recorded as it occurs, so less reliance is placed on a respondent's memory. When diaries are used to record purchases, the problems should be virtually eliminated because the respondent is instructed to record the purchases immediately upon returning home. When other behaviors, such as television viewing, are of interest, respondents are asked to record those behaviors as they occur, thus minimizing the possibility that they will be

EXHIBIT 6.5   **Arbitron Radio Listening Diary**

THURSDAY

Time			Station			Place			
	Start	Stop	Call letters, dial setting or station name *Don't know? Use program name.*	Mark (✗) one AM	FM	Mark (✗) one At Home	In a Car	At Work	Other Place
Early Morning (from 5 AM)									
Midday									
Late Afternoon									
Night (to 5 AM Friday)									

If you didn't hear a radio today, please mark (✗) here. ☐

Source: © 2000 The Arbitron Company

forgotten or distorted when they are eventually asked about. Exhibit 6.5, for example, shows a page out of an Arbitron radio listening diary. These diaries, which are used to determine radio station listening audiences, are used by the stations to make programming decisions and by advertisers to figure out which programs to sponsor. Every person over the age of 12 in each of the participating households receives a new diary for each week they participate. A key advantage of the diary is that it is completely portable and can be filled out anywhere, which tends to increase its accuracy.

The main disadvantage of panels is that they are nonrepresentative. The agreement to participate involves a commitment on the part of the designated sample member, and many individuals refuse this commitment. They do not wish to be bothered with testing products, evaluating advertising copy, or filling out consumer diaries. Because these activities require a sizable time commitment, families in which both husband and wife work, for example, may be less well represented than those in which one partner works and the other is at home. Consumer panels that require households to keep a record of their purchases generally have cooperation rates of about 60 percent when members are contacted in person and lower participation rates if telephone or mail is used for the initial contact.[5]

The better ongoing panel operations select prospective participants very systematically. They attempt to generate and maintain panels that are representative of the total population of interest with respect to such characteristics as age, occupation, education, and so on. Quite often, to create a representative panel, they will use *quota samples,* in which the proportion of sample members possessing a certain characteristic is approximately the same as the proportion possessing that characteristic in the general population. As a very simplified example of this, consider an organization that wishes to study sports car owners. If the organization knows that in the general population of interest, 52 percent are men and 48 percent are women, then it will want its quota sample to reflect that percentage.

All the research organization can do, however, is designate the families or respondents that are to be included in the sample. Researchers cannot force individuals to participate, nor can they require continued participation from those who initially agreed to cooperate. True, they often encourage participation by offering some premium or by paying panel members for their cooperation. Nevertheless, a significant percentage of the individuals the organization may have hoped to include often refuse to cooperate—or drop out quickly once the panel has begun. Some individuals are lost to the panel because they move away or die. Depending on the type of cooperation needed, the refusal and *mortality,* or drop-out, rate might run over 50 percent. And, of course, the question then arises as to whether the panel is still representative of the population. Further, the payment of a reward for cooperation raises the question of whether particular types of people are attracted to such panels. It is generally accepted, for example, that panel samples underrepresent African Americans, persons with poor English language skills, and those at the extremes of the socioeconomic spectrum.[6] Unrepresentativeness may not be a problem in every study. It depends on the purpose of the study and the particular variables of interest.

In a series of studies investigating the "representativeness" of a continuing household panel, Market Facts compared data gathered from a mail panel against data gathered from randomly selected telephone samples. Research Window 6.2 displays some of the results of its findings with respect to such characteristics as product ownership, lifestyle, and leisure activities. As the sample of comparisons suggest, the evidence led Market Facts to conclude that "mail panels are likely to parallel the population in most, if not all, dimensions of leisure activity and lifestyle."[7] The series of studies also, though "revealed instances of significant differences between data generated by mail panel and through telephone interviewing. . . . What these experiments strongly suggest, therefore, is that great care must continue to be exercised in the selection of research method, when methodological options exist. But they also suggest that many . . . marketing questions can be addressed very effectively through controlled mail panels."[8] The trouble with bias due to unrepresentativeness, of course, is that one never knows in advance whether it will affect the results, much less how.

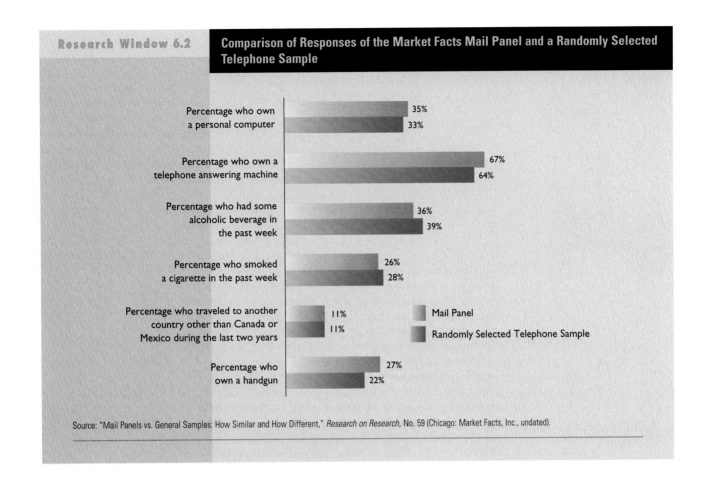

Source: "Mail Panels vs. General Samples: How Similar and How Different," *Research on Research*, No. 59 (Chicago: Market Facts, Inc., undated).

Cross-Sectional Analysis

Despite the advantages of longitudinal analysis, in actual practice cross-sectional designs are the best known and most important descriptive designs. The cross-sectional study has two distinguishing features. First, the study provides a snapshot of the variables of interest at a single point in time, as contrasted with the longitudinal study, which provides a series of pictures that, when pieced together, provide a movie of the situation and the changes that are occurring. Second, in the cross-sectional study, the sample of elements is typically selected to be representative of some known universe. Therefore, a great deal of emphasis is placed on selecting sample members, usually with a probability sampling plan. That is one reason that the technique is often called **sample survey.** The probability sampling plan allows the determination of the sampling error associated with the statistics, which are generated from the sample but used to describe the universe. Most sample surveys involve enough observations to allow for cross-classification of the variables.

The objective of cross-classification analysis is to establish categories such that classification in one category implies classification in one or more other categories. The method of cross-classification analysis will be detailed later, in the discussion of tabulation. For the moment, simply note that it involves counting the *simultaneous occurrence* of the variables of interest. For example, suppose management feels that occupation is an important factor in determining the consumption of its product. Further, suppose the proposition to be examined is that white-collar workers are more apt to use the product than blue-collar workers. If this hypothesis were examined in a cross-sectional study, measurements would be taken from a representative sample of the population with respect to their occupation and use of the product. In cross tabulation, researchers would count the number of cases that fell in each of the following classes:

Sample survey

Cross-sectional study in which the sample is selected to be representative of the target population and in which the emphasis is on the generation of summary statistics such as averages and percentages.

- White-collar and use the product

- Blue-collar and use the product

- White-collar and do not use the product

- Blue-collar and do not use the product

That is, the emphasis would be on the relative frequency of occurrence of the joint phenomenon "white-collar occupation and user of the product." If the hypothesis is to be supported by the sample data, the proportion of white-collar workers using the product should exceed the proportion of blue-collar workers using the product.

Although the sample survey is commonly used, it has several disadvantages. These include superficial analysis of the phenomenon, high cost, and the technical sophistication required to conduct survey research. Let us consider each disadvantage in turn.

One common criticism of survey data is that they typically do not penetrate very deeply below the surface, since breadth is often emphasized at the expense of depth. There is ordinarily an emphasis on the calculation of statistics that efficiently summarize the wide variety of data collected from the sometimes large cross section of subjects. Yet the very process of generating summary statistics to describe the phenomenon suggests that the eventual "average" might not accurately describe any individual entity making up the aggregate. The situation is much like that of "the guy who slept with his feet in the refrigerator and his head in the stove and who, on the average, was comfortable."

Second, a survey is expensive in terms of time and money. It will often be months before a single hypothesis can be tested because of the necessary preliminaries so vital to survey research. The entire research process—from problem definition through measuring instrument development, design of the sample, collecting the data, and editing, coding, and tabulating the data—must be executed before an analyst can begin to examine the hypotheses that guide the study. As parts of the remainder of this book will show, each of these tasks can be formidable in its own right. Each can require large investments of time, energy, and money.

Survey research also requires a good deal of technical skill. The research analyst must either have the skills required at each stage of the process or have access to such skills in, say, the form of technical consultants. It is the rare individual indeed who has the technical sophistication both to develop an attitude scale and to design a complex probability sample.

Causal Research Designs

Often exploratory or descriptive research will turn up several cause-and-effect hypotheses that a marketing manager may want to examine. For example, if a price change is planned, a manager may want to test this hypothesis: "A 5 percent increase in the price of the product will have no significant effect on the amount of the product that customers will buy." If the marketing department is considering a change in packaging, planners may first want to test this hypothesis: "A redesign of the cereal package so that it is shorter and less likely to tip over will improve consumer attitudes toward the product."

When the research question can be framed this explicitly, the researcher is dealing with a situation ripe for causal analysis. Descriptive research works okay for testing hypotheses, but it is not as effective as causal designs for testing cause-and-effect relationships. To understand why, one must understand the notion of causality, the types of evidence that establish causality, and the effect of outside variables in a research setting.

Concept of Causality

The concept of causality is complex, and a detailed discussion of it would take us too far afield. However, a few essentials will allow us to properly determine the role of the experiment in establishing the validity of a hypothesis that X causes Y.

The regional sales manager for a large chain of men's clothing stores asks you to establish whether increasing her salespeople's commission will result in better sales performance. Specifically, she wants to know whether increasing the commission on limited lines of clothing will result in better sales on those lines but with the penalty of fewer sales on the remaining lines, and whether raising the commission on all lines will produce greater sales on all lines. Suppose that you think that the best way to investigate the issue is through a field experiment in which some salespeople receive increased commission on a single line, others receive increased commission across the board, and still others make up a control group, whose members receive no increase in commission.

- Are there ethical problems inherent in such a design?

- Is the control group being deprived of any benefits?

In nontechnical language, the statement that one thing (X) is the cause of another thing (Y) suggests that there is a single cause of an event. The scientific notion of causality differs from this commonsense notion in three respects. First, the scientific notion holds that X would be only one of a number of determining conditions rather than the single one. Second, it holds that X does not make the occurrence of Y certain but just makes it more likely. Finally, the scientific notion holds that we can never prove that X really is a cause of Y, but rather we only *infer* from some observed data (perhaps acquired in a very controlled experimental setting) that such a relationship exists.[9]

The scientific notion recognizes the fallibility of the procedures used to obtain data, or evidence, and for that reason, a causal statement is never demonstrated conclusively. Three basic kinds of evidence can be used to support scientific inferences: concomitant variation, time order of occurrence of variables, and elimination of other possible causal factors.[10]

Evidence of Causality

Concomitant variation

The extent to which a cause, X, and an effect, Y, occur together or vary together in the way predicted by the hypothesis.

One type of evidence for the scientific inference "X is a cause of Y" is **concomitant variation**—the extent to which a cause, X, and an effect, Y, occur together or vary together in the way predicted by the hypothesis.

Consider the example of a foreign car manufacturer who wants to test the relationship between the quality of its dealers and the company's market share in an area. The manufacturer's hypothesis is, "The success of our marketing efforts is highly dealer dependent. Where we have good dealers, we have good market penetration, and where we have poor dealers, we have unsatisfactory market penetration." Now if X is to be considered a cause of Y, we should expect to find the following: In those territories where our good dealers are located, we should have satisfactory market shares, while in those territories where our poor dealers are located, we should have unsatisfactory market shares. However, if we find that in a large number of territories with good dealers we also have unsatisfactory market shares, we must conclude that our hypothesis is faulty.

Perfect evidence of concomitant variation would be provided, of course, if all good dealers were located in territories with satisfactory market shares, and all poor dealers were located in territories with unsatisfactory market shares. The "pure" case will rarely be found in practice, as other causal factors will produce some deviation from a one-to-one relationship between X and Y. Some good dealers, for example, may be located in territories where "Buy American" sentiment is very strong and hence foreign car sales are very low. A poor dealer may have no nearby competition in a territory where foreign cars are popular and thus have an excellent market share despite a reputation for poor service.

Suppose that when we analyzed the relationship between X and Y, we found evidence of concomitant variation. What can we say? All we can say is that *the association makes the hypothesis more likely; it does not prove it.*[11] We are always inferring, rather than proving, that a causal relationship exists. Similarly, the lack of an association between X and Y cannot be taken as conclusive evidence that there is no causal relationship between them.

We will explore the idea of concomitant variation more closely in a later chapter. For the moment, let us emphasize that concomitant variation is one type of evidence supporting the existence of a causal relationship between X and Y; but its absence does not necessarily negate a relationship between X and Y, nor does its presence guarantee one.

The time order of occurrence of variables is another type of evidence of a causal relationship between two variables. This evidence is based on the following simple concept:

> One event cannot be considered the "cause" of another if it occurs after the other event. The occurrence of a causal factor may precede or may be simultaneous with the occurrence of an event; by definition, an effect cannot be produced by an event that occurs only after the effect has taken place. However, it is possible for each term in the relationship to be both a "cause" and an "effect" of the other term.[12]

Though conceptually simple, time-order evidence requires the close attention of researchers. Sometimes it is difficult to establish the time sequence governing a phenomenon. For example, consider the relationship between a firm's annual advertising expenditures and its sales. Marketing managers often attribute a sales increase to an increase in spending on advertising. However, some companies follow a rule of thumb that uses past sales as a guide to allocating resources to advertising. For example, an amount equal to 10 percent of last year's sales may be earmarked for this year's advertising budget. This practice confuses the issue of which event is the cause and which is the effect. Does advertising lead to higher sales, or do higher sales lead to an increased ad budget? An intimate understanding of the way the company establishes the ad budget should resolve the dilemma in this situation.

The *elimination of other possible causal factors* is very much like the Sherlock Holmes approach to analysis. Just as Sherlock Holmes holds that "when you have eliminated the impossible, whatever remains, however improbable, must be the truth,"[13] this type of evidence of causality focuses on the elimination of possible explanations other than the one being studied. This may mean physically holding other factors constant, or it may mean adjusting the results to remove the effects of factors that do vary.

Take the situation of the divisional manager of a chain of supermarkets investigating the effects of end-of-aisle displays on orange sales. Suppose that the manager found that per-store sales of oranges increased during the past week and that a number of stores were using end-of-aisle displays for oranges. To conclude that the end displays were indeed the factor responsible for the sales increase, the manager would need to eliminate other possible variables, such as price, size of store, and orange type and quality. This might involve looking at orange sales for stores of approximately the same size, checking to see if prices were the same in stores having an increase in sales and stores with no increase, and checking to determine if the type and quality of oranges were consistent with the previous week's.

Experimentation as Causal Research

Experiment
Scientific investigation in which an investigator manipulates and controls one or more independent variables and observes the dependent variable or variables for variation concomitant to the manipulation of the independent variables.

Because of the control it affords investigators, an **experiment** can provide more convincing evidence of causal relationships than an exploratory or descriptive design can. For this reason, experiments are often called causal research.

> An experiment is taken to mean a scientific investigation in which an investigator manipulates and controls one or more independent variables and observes the dependent variable or variables for variation concomitant to the manipulation of the

independent variables. An *experimental design*, then, is one in which the investigator *manipulates* at least one independent variable.[14]

Because investigators are able to control at least some manipulations of the presumed causal factor, they can be more confident that the relationships discovered are so-called true relationships.

Two types of experiments can be distinguished—the *laboratory experiment* and the *field experiment*. Since each has its own advantages and disadvantages, research analysts need to be familiar with both. A **laboratory experiment** is one in which an investigator creates a situation with the desired conditions and then manipulates some variables while controlling others. The investigator is thus able to observe and measure the effect of the manipulation of the variables while the effect of other factors is minimized.

Laboratory experiment
Research investigation in which investigators create a situation with exact conditions so as to control some, and manipulate other, variables.

In one laboratory experiment designed to measure the effect of price on the demand for coffee and cola, for example, 135 homemakers in a small town in Illinois were asked to take part in simulated shopping trips.[15] On each of the eight simulated trips, which were conducted in subjects' homes, the homemakers could choose their favorite brands from a full assortment of coffees and colas listed on index cards. The only change on each trip was the products' prices. Each homemaker was free to switch brands to obtain the best product for the money. In this respect, the trial purchase was not unlike an actual purchase. In other respects, however, this trial was unlike conditions in a real supermarket. In the laboratory experiment, the homemakers were free from the distractions of other variables such as packaging, position on the shelf, and in-store promotions.

Field experiment
Research study in a realistic situation in which one or more independent variables are manipulated by the experimenter under as carefully controlled conditions as the situation will permit.

A **field experiment** is a research study in a realistic or natural situation, although it, too, involves the manipulation of one or more variables under as carefully controlled conditions as the situation will permit. The laboratory experiment is distinguished from the field experiment, then, primarily in terms of environment, although the distinction is one more of degree than of kind, as both involve some manipulation. The degree of control and precision afforded by each individual field or laboratory experiment varies.[16]

A similar investigation to test the effect of price on the demand for coffee and cola was also conducted in a field experiment. In this case, the experiment was conducted in two small towns in Illinois, ten miles apart. The manipulations here involved actual changes in price for the respective brands.

Four supermarkets were used in all, two from each town. Two units in one town were designated as control stores, where the price of each brand was maintained at its regular level throughout the experiment. In the experimental town, the prices were systematically varied in the two stores during the experiment. Prices were marked on the package of each brand so as to be clearly visible but not conspicuous. After each price change, a cooling-off period was introduced to offset any surplus accumulated by consumers. The impact of the price change was monitored by recording weekly sales for each brand. This allowed brand market shares for each price condition to be determined. No displays, special containers, or other devices were used to draw consumer attention to the fact that the relative prices of the brands had been altered. All other controllable factors were also held as constant as possible.

Note the distinction between the two studies. In the field experiment, no attempt was made to set up special conditions. The situation was accepted as found, and manipulation of the experimental variable—price—was imposed in this natural environment. The laboratory experiment, on the other hand, was contrived. Subjects were told to behave as if they were actively shopping for the product. The prices of the respective brands were varied for each of these simulated shopping trips.

The results of the two experiments were consistent for one product and inconsistent for the other. The laboratory experiment generated reasonably valid estimates of consumers' reactions to real-world (field experiment) price changes for brands of cola. However, the data for coffee was considered invalid since it tended to overstate the effects of the price changes.

Internal and External Validity of Experiments

Internal validity

One criterion by which an experiment is evaluated; the criterion focuses on obtaining evidence demonstrating that the variation in the criterion variable was the result of exposure to the treatment, or experimental, variable.

Certain advantages and disadvantages result from the difference in procedure in laboratory and field experiments. The laboratory experiment typically has the advantage of greater **internal validity** because of the greater control of the variables that it affords. To the extent that we are successful in eliminating the effects of other factors that may obscure or confound the relationships under study, either by physically holding these other factors constant or by allowing for them statistically, we may conclude that the observed effect was due to the manipulation of the experimental variable. That is, we may conclude the experiment is internally valid. Thus, internal validity refers to our ability to attribute the effect that was observed to the experimental variable and not other factors. In the pricing experiment, internal validity focused on the need to obtain data demonstrating that the variation in the criterion variable—brand demanded—was the result of exposure to the experimental variable—relative price of the brand—rather than other factors, such as advertising, display space, store traffic, and so on. These other factors were nonexistent in the simulated shopping trips.

External validity

One criterion by which an experiment is evaluated; the extent, to what populations and settings, to which the observed experimental effect can be generalized.

Whereas the laboratory experiment has the advantage in internal validity, the field experiment has the advantage in **external validity,** which focuses on how well the results of the experiment can be generalized to other situations. The artificiality of laboratory experiments limits the extent to which the results can be generalized to other populations and settings.[17] In the simulated shopping trips, no real purchases took place. Further, we might suppose that the experimenter's calling attention to the price may have caused people to be more price conscious than they would have been in a supermarket. They may have attempted to act more "rationally" than they normally would. Further, those who agreed to participate in the laboratory experiment may not be representative of the larger population of shoppers, either because the location of the study was not typical or because those who willingly participated in such a study may be different in some significant way from those who declined to participate. Such problems would seriously jeopardize the external validity of the findings.

The controls needed for internal validity often conflict with the controls needed for external validity. A control or procedure required to establish internal validity may lessen the ability to generalize the results. The conditions needed to establish external validity may cast doubt on a study's internal validity. Both internal and external validity are matters of degree rather than all-or-nothing propositions.

Role of Experimentation in Marketing Research

Market test (test- marketing)

A controlled experiment done in a limited but carefully selected sector of the marketplace; its aim is to predict the sales or profit consequences, either in absolute or relative terms, of one or more proposed marketing actions.

Experiments in marketing were rare before 1960, but their growth since then has been steady. One of the most significant growth areas has been in market testing, or *test-marketing*. Although some writers make a distinction between the terms, the essential feature of the **market test** is that "it is a controlled experiment, done in a limited but carefully selected part of the marketplace, whose aim is to predict the sales or profit consequences, either in absolute or relative terms, of one or more proposed marketing actions."[18] Very often the action in question is the marketing of a new product or an improved version of an old product. For example, Blockbuster Video in 1999 launched test marketing of CD-ROM rentals. At stores in Anchorage, Alaska, and Austin, Texas, Blockbuster began offering ten computer games on CD-ROM to complement its rentals of movies and Nintendo and Sony PlayStation games. Consumers who rent the CD-ROMs get a coupon that they activate on-line, permitting them to play the game for three days. They keep the CD-ROM and may choose to renew the rental or buy the game.[19] As another example, consider Wendy's development of the "Big Classic" hamburger, an experience described in Research Window 6.3.

Notwithstanding previous tests of the product concept, the product package, the advertising copy, and so on, the test market is still the final gauge of consumer acceptance of the product. ACNielsen data, for example, indicate that roughly three out of four products that have been test-marketed succeed, while four out of five that have not been test-marketed fail.[20] The benefits to be gained from test marketing are illustrated in the

| Research Window 6.3 | Research Conducted by Wendy's for the "Big Classic" Hamburger |

To find out what people want, Wendy's spent $1 million over nine months doing taste tests with 5,200 people in six cities. They tested:

Nine different buns: some hard, some soft; with sesame seeds or poppy seeds; cold, toasted, or warmed; square or round; and even croissants

Forty special sauces, including steak sauce, hot sauce, mustard, and salad dressing

Three types of lettuce: chopped, shredded, and leaf

Two sizes of tomato slices

Four boxes in ten earth-tone colors

The final product is a quarter-pound square beef patty topped with leaf lettuce, two tomato slices, raw onion rings, dill pickles, and extra dabs of ketchup and mayonnaise on a corn-dusted, hearth-baked kaiser bun. It comes in an almond-colored Styrofoam box with a dome sculpted to resemble the bun's top. It can cost up to 10 cents more than the old burger, which is still on the menu.

The big news research showed was that the order of the condiments "makes a tremendous difference to consumers," Denny Lynch, a spokesperson for Wendy's, said, "Which is why the Big Classic will taste different rightside up or upside down, depending on the way the toppings hit your taste buds."

Wendy's came up with a color code to help its employees remember the correct order: white, red, green, white, red, green (mayonnaise, ketchup, pickle, onion, tomato, lettuce).

Source: "Wendy's Discovers—Old Burger," *The Wisconsin State Journal* (September 19, 1986), p. 6. Reprinted with permission.

experience of Pillsbury in developing its Oven Lovin' refrigerated cookie dough, which was packaged in resealable tubs. In focus groups, consumers raved about Oven Lovin', which was loaded with Hershey's chocolate chips, Reese's Pieces, or Brach's candies. Based on the rave reactions, the company omitted test marketing and immediately rolled out the product, supporting it with heavy television advertising and some 200 million coupons. Sales took off like a rocket, rising from zero to almost $6 million a month. After three months, though, they began to crumble and were almost nonexistent two years later. While consumers still maintained they liked the product and resealable package, "many shoppers found they ended up baking the entire package at once—or gobbling up left-over raw dough instead of saving it—eliminating the need for the . . . package." In sum, the package provided a benefit consumers didn't really need, particularly given the fact that it contained only 18 ounces of dough, compared with 20 ounces in a tube of Pillsbury Best dough that was priced comparably.[21]

Test-marketing is not restricted to testing the sales potential of new products; it has been used to examine the sales effectiveness of almost every element of the marketing mix: General Motors, for example, used its Cadillac car division to test market a proposed alteration in the distribution strategy for all its car lines. The Florida test involved keeping 1,200 new cars at a regional distribution center in Orlando for delivery to the state's 42 dealerships within 24 hours of an order. The approach was intended to whittle down the costly inventory that dealers have to maintain, improve manufacturing efficiency, and increase sales by allowing consumers to take quick possession of precisely the Cadillac model they wanted. GM and most other car makers have long been criticized for the waste associated with their typical practice of loading up dealership lots with an assortment of cars they think people will buy. This practice saddles dealers with high-cost inventory and does little to encourage just-in-time production practices at the factory level. Moreover, dealers often find themselves stuck with models that customers really don't want and short of the ones in demand.[22]

Market tests have also been employed to measure the sales effectiveness of new displays, the responsiveness of sales to shelf-space changes, the impact of changes in retail prices on market shares, the price elasticity of demand for products, the effect of different commercials on sales of products, and the differential effects of price and advertising on demand.

Experimentation is not restricted to test-marketing. Rather, it can be used whenever the manager has some specific mix alternatives to consider—for example, package design A versus B—and when the researcher can control the conditions sufficiently to allow an adequate test of the alternatives. Experiments are often used, therefore, when testing product or package concepts and advertising copy, although they have also been used for such things as determining the optimal number of sales calls to be made upon industrial distributors.[23]

Future and Problems of Experimentation

Although marketing experiments will continue to be used, particularly when the research problem is one of determining which is the best of an available set of limited marketing alternatives, experimentation is not without its problems. Test-marketing, which has been described as a double-edged sword, is a useful vehicle for illustrating these problems. As Larry Gibson, former director of corporate marketing research for General Mills, states: "It costs a mint, tells the competition what you're doing, takes forever, and is not always accurate. . . . For the moment, it's the only game in town."[24] Although Gibson is referring specifically to test-marketing, similar problems beset other types of experiments as well. Three of the more critical problems of experimentation in general, and test-marketing in particular, are cost, time, and control.

Cost Always a major consideration in test-marketing, the cost includes the normal research costs associated with designing the data-collection instruments and the sample, the wages paid to the field staff that collects the data, and a number of other indirect expenses as well. General Mills, for example, spent $2.8 million testing and refining its chain of Olive Garden restaurants.[25] Moreover, the test market should reflect the marketing strategy to be employed on the national scale if the results are to be useful. So the test also includes marketing costs for advertising, personal selling, displays, and so on.

With new product introductions, there are also the costs associated with producing the merchandise. To produce the product on a small scale is typically inefficient. Yet to gear up immediately for large-scale production can be tremendously wasteful if the product proves a failure.

Time The time required for an adequate test market can also be substantial. In the 1960s, Procter & Gamble devoted eight years to testing Pampers disposable diapers before launching the product in the United States. In today's faster-paced global environment, this approach simply leaves a company much too vulnerable to attack from more agile competitors.

There is pressure to extend the period of test-marketing because the empirical evidence indicates that a test market's accuracy increases directly with time. Experiments conducted over short periods do not allow the cumulative impact of marketing actions. Consequently, a year is often recommended as a minimum before any kind of "go–no go" decision is made. The year allows researchers to account for possible seasonal variations and to study repeat-purchasing behavior. Such lengthy experiments are costly, though, and raise additional problems of control and competitive reaction. Procter & Gamble has committed itself to speeding product introductions worldwide. Its test marketing of the Dryel home dry-cleaning kit and the Swiffer sweeper system each took less than a year and a half. Furthermore, the test markets were international—Columbus, Ohio, and Ireland for Dryel and Iowa and France for Swiffer. This enables the company to launch products globally, rather than waiting for U.S. success before moving overseas.[26]

Control The problems associated with control manifest themselves in several ways. First, there are the control problems in the experiment itself. What specific test markets will be used? How will product distribution be organized in those markets? Can the firm elicit the necessary cooperation from wholesalers? From retailers? Can the test markets and control cities be matched sufficiently to rule out market characteristics as the primary reason for different sales results? Can the rest of the elements of the marketing strategy be controlled so as not to cause unwanted aberrations in the experimental setting? Too much control can often be as much a problem as too little. Precisely because the product is being test-marketed, it may receive more attention than it would ever receive on a national scale. In the test market, for example, store shelves may be better stocked, the sales force more diligent, and the advertising more prominent than would normally be the case.

One example of this phenomenon is Pringle's potato chips, which were very successful in the test market but bombed nationally. Their failure has often been attributed to a decline in quality that occurred when the product had to be produced in quantities large enough for national distribution.

There are control problems associated with competitive reaction, too. Although the firm might be able to coordinate its own marketing activities, and even those of intermediaries in the distribution channel, so as not to contaminate the experiment, it can exert little control over its competitors. Competitors can, and do, sabotage marketing experiments by cutting the prices of their own products, gobbling up quantities of the test marketer's product—thereby creating a state of euphoria and false confidence on the part of the test marketer—and by other devious means. Test-marketing has been called the most dangerous game in all of marketing because of the great opportunity it affords for misfires, as shown by the examples in Exhibit 6.6.

One could argue that the misfires reflected in the first two examples in Exhibit 6.6 represent one fundamental reason why test markets are desirable. Indeed, it seems better to find out about product performance problems like this in a test market than after a product is introduced nationally. Consider, for example, the losses in company prestige that would have resulted if the following problems had not been discovered in test markets.[27]

- Sunlight dishwashing liquid was confused with Minute Maid lemon juice by at least 33 adults and 45 children, who became ill after drinking it.

- When a large packaged goods company set out to introduce a squirtable soft drink concentrate for children, it held focus groups to monitor user reaction. In the sessions children squirted the product neatly into cups. Yet once at home, few could resist the temptation to decorate their parents' floors and walls with colorful liquid. After a flood of parental complaints, the product was withdrawn from development.

Other companies, however, could not avoid embarrassment when they implemented faulty plans nationwide. A mid-1990s effort to merge television and computers flopped when NetTV was offered at $3,000 for a 29-inch monitor coupled with a personal computer. Consumers couldn't figure out why they wanted a computer in their living room, especially considering how frustrating a computer can be to operate.[28] Apple Computer's notorious mistake was introducing an early palmtop computer, the Newton, which failed miserably at one of its featured tasks: reading the user's handwriting. Newton quickly became the butt of jokes, and although Apple later improved the product, it sank under the weight of poor publicity.[29]

The remaining examples in Exhibit 6.6, however, are of a different sort. By exposing the product to competitors through a test market, each of the firms lost much of its differential development advantage.

The simple point is that the marketing manager contemplating a market test must weigh the costs of such a test against its anticipated benefits. While it may serve as the final yardstick for consumer acceptance of the product, in some cases it may be less effective and more expensive than a carefully controlled laboratory or in-home test.

EXHIBIT 6.6 **Examples of Misfires in Test-Marketing**

- A few years ago, Snell (Booz Allen's design and development division, which does product development and work under contract) developed a nonliquid temporary hair coloring that consumers used by inserting a block of solid hair dye into a special comb. "It went to market and it was a bust," the company's Mr. Schoenholz recalls. On hot days when people perspired, any hair dye excessively applied ran down their necks and foreheads. "It just didn't occur to us to look at this under conditions where people perspire," he says.

- Frito-Lay test marketed its Max potato, corn, and tortilla chips containing the Olestra fat substitutes in Grand Junction, Colorado; Eau Claire, Wisconsin; and Cedar Rapids, Iowa. A TV crew sampled the chips and succumbed to diarrhea, and then broadcast a report about it, creating lots of bad publicity for the chips.

- When Campbell Soup first test-marketed Prego spaghetti sauce, Campbell marketers say they noticed a flurry of new Ragu ads and cents-off deals that they feel were designed to induce shoppers to load up on Ragu and to skew Prego's test results. They also claim that Ragu copied Prego when it developed Ragu Homestyle spaghetti sauce, which was thick, red, flecked with oregano and basil, and which Ragu moved into national distribution before Prego.

- Procter & Gamble claims that competitors stole its patented process for Duncan Hines chocolate chip cookies when they saw how successful the product was in test market.

- A health and beauty aids firm developed a deodorant containing baking soda. A competitor spotted the product in test market, rolled out its own version of the deodorant nationally before the first firm completed its testing, and later successfully sued the product originator for copyright infringement when it launched its deodorant nationally.

- When Procter & Gamble introduced its Always brand sanitary napkin in a test market in Minnesota, Kimberly-Clark Corporation and Johnson & Johnson countered with free products, lots of coupons, and big dealer discounts, which caused Always not to do as well as expected.

- Campbell Soup spent 18 months developing a blended fruit juice called Juiceworks. By the time the product reached the market, three competing brands were already on store shelves. Campbell dropped its product.

- Spurred by its incredible success with Fruit 'N' Juice Bars, Dole worked hard to create a new fruity ice cream novelty product with the same type of appeal. Company officials expected that the product that resulted from this development activity, Fruit and Cream Bars, which it test-marketed in Orlando, Florida, would do slightly less well because it was more of an indulgence-type product. However, the test market results were so positive that Dole became the number-one brand in the market within three months. The company consequently shortened the test market to six months. When it rolled out the product, though, the company unhappily found four unexpected entrants in the ice cream novelty category. Due to the intense competition, Fruit and Cream sales fell short of expectations.

Source: Example 1—Roger Recklefs, "Success Comes Hard in the Tricky Business of Creating Products," *The Wall Street Journal* (August 23, 1978), pp. 1, 27; Example 2—Annetta Miller and Karen Springen, "Will Fake Fat Play in Peoria?" *Newsweek* (June 3, 1996), p. 50; Example 3—Betty Morris, "New Campbell Entry Sets Off a Big Spaghetti Sauce Battle," *The Wall Street Journal* (December 2, 1982), p. 31; Example 4—Eleanor Johnson Tracy, "Testing Time for Test Marketing," *Fortune* 110 (October 29, 1984), pp. 75–76; Example 5—Kevin Wiggins, "Simulated Test Marketing Winning Acceptance," *Marketing News* 19 (March 1, 1985), pp. 15, 19; Example 6—Damon Darden, "Faced with More Competition, P&G Sees New Products as Crucial to Earnings Growth," *The Wall Street Journal* (September 13, 1983), pp. 37, 53; Example 7—Annetta Miller and Dody Tsiantor, "A Test for Market Research," *Newsweek* 110 (December 28, 1987), pp. 32–33; Example 8—Leslie Brennan, "Test Marketing Put to the Test," *Sales and Marketing Management* 138 (March 1987), pp. 65–68.

Types of Test Markets

Standard test market
A test market in which the company sells the product through its normal distribution channels.

Controlled test market
An entire test program conducted by an outside service in a market in which it can guarantee distribution.

Figure 6.2 shows some popular **standard test markets,** markets in which companies sell the product through their normal distribution channels. The results are typically monitored by one of the standard distribution services discussed in Chapter 8.

An alternative to the standard test market is the **controlled test market,** sometimes called the *forced-distribution test market.* In the controlled market, the entire test program is conducted by an outside service. The service pays retailers for shelf space and can therefore guarantee distribution to those stores that represent a predetermined percentage of the marketer's total food store sales volume. A number of research firms operate controlled test markets, including Audits & Surveys and Burgoyne.

FIGURE 6.2   Some Popular Standard Test Markets

Source: Steve Lohr, "Test It in Tulsa, It'll Play in Peoria," *Chicago Tribune* (June 7, 1992), sec. 7, p. 1. See also Judith Waldrop, "Markets with Attitude," *American Demographics* (July 1994), pp. 22–33 for the "most typical" and "most surveyed" American cities.

Electronic test market

A market test done in a limited geographic area in which a supplier maintains a panel of households from which it collects demographic information, who are given an identification card, whose purchases are scanned, and whose television-viewing behavior is electronically monitored, thereby allowing the supplier to link demographic information with television-viewing and purchase behavior.

An increasingly popular variation of the controlled test market is the **electronic test market.** Electronic test markets differ from traditional controlled test markets in several ways. First, providers of the electronic services recruit a panel of households in the test market area from which they secure a great deal of demographic information. These households are given identification cards, which they show when checking out at grocery stores. Everything they purchase is automatically recorded and associated with the household through scanners found in all supermarkets in the area. Second, suppliers of the electronic services also have the capability to monitor each household's television-viewing behavior. They thus have the capability to correlate exposure to test commercials to purchase behavior, which in turn allows users of the electronic services to test not only consumer acceptance of a new or modified product but also various other parts of the marketing program. Del Monte, for example, uses electronic test markets for media-weight, pricing, and promotion tests, in addition to new product evaluations. The leading suppliers of electronic test-marketing services are Nielsen and BehaviorScan. Research Window 6.4 illustrates how the link between the demographic information of households and their purchase behavior can be used to advantage.

Simulated test market

A study in which interviews are conducted to determine consumer ratings of products: then consumers are given the opportunity to purchase the product in a simulated store environment.

Another variation in test-marketing is the **simulated test market (STM).** STM studies are usually employed prior to a full-scale test market. Typically an STM study begins with consumer interviews, either in shopping malls or occasionally in their homes. During the interview, consumers are shown the new product and asked to rate its features. They are then shown commercials for it and for competitors' products. In a simulated store environment, they are then given the opportunity to buy the product, often at a reduced price or with a cents-off coupon. Those who choose not to purchase the test product are typically given free samples.

After a predetermined use period, researchers conduct follow-up telephone interviews with the participants to assess their reactions to the product and their repeat-purchase intentions.

In an attempt to be perceived more broadly, Ocean Spray developed a totally new fruit beverage, Mauna La'i Hawaiian Guava Drink. The product represented a significant departure for Ocean Spray, in that it was different in color, taste, and aroma from any other fruit drink on the market.

Concerned about how consumers might respond to the product, Ocean Spray decided to test-market it using BehaviorScan's facilities in Eau Claire, Wisconsin, and Midland, Texas. Ocean Spray believed that the target market for Mauna La'i was similar to that for its cranberry drink: older children and adults with average education and income.

After six months in test market, initial trial for Mauna La'i was good, but the rate of repurchase was far below what was needed to be profitable. It did not appear that Mauna La'i would survive the test to go national. But on analyzing BehaviorScan's data more closely, Ocean Spray found a few surprises: (1) the buyer base was smaller than expected, but these consumers were buying the product more frequently than was projected; (2) the product was

not selling to the target market—yuppies (young urban professionals) were buying the Mauna La'i.

After analyzing this pattern for nearly a year, Ocean Spray decided that it would be profitable to market the product as long as it was marketed toward the heavily beverage-consuming yuppies. Mauna La'i's media plan was altered to reach the more upscale market, and the juice was rolled out nationally. After only three months in the national market, consumer demand was so high that Ocean Spray started to produce a 64-ounce size. John Tarsa, Ocean Spray's manager of marketing research, believes that the use of an electronic test market was key to Mauna La'i's success. "In a traditional test market, we wouldn't be rolling with Mauna La'i at all, because our repeat number was no good. The electronic test market was instrumental in helping us decide what we needed to change to make it a success."

Source: Leslie Brennan, "Test Marketing Put to the Test," *Sales and Marketing Management* 138 (March 1987), p. 68. Electronic test markets are also used to test the effects of advertising strategy. See Leonard M. Lodish, et al., "How TV Advertising Works: A Meta-Analysis of 389 Real World Split Cable T.V. Advertising Experiments," *Journal of Marketing Research* 32 (May 1995), pp. 125–139 for an integration of the findings.

All the information is fed into a computer model, which has equations for the repeat purchase and market share likely to be achieved by the test model. The key to the simulation is the equations built into the computer model. Studies have indicated that in 80 percent of the cases, STM models can come within 10 percent of predicting actual sales.[30]

Choosing a Test-Market Procedure

Those faced with the need to test market a new product or to fine-tune another element of the marketing program need to make a choice about which type of test market to use. One useful way to view that choice is to look at the alternatives as stages in a sequential process, with simulated test markets preceding controlled test markets, which in turn come before standard test markets (see Figure 6.3). The sequence is not always as pictured, however. A very promising STM or controlled test market can cause a firm to skip one or more intermediate stages, and perhaps to move directly to national rollout.

A prime advantage of STMs is the protection from competitors they provide. They are also good for assessing trial and repeat-purchasing behavior. They are faster and cheaper than full-scale tests and are particularly good for spotting weak products, which allows firms to avoid full-scale testing of these products. The Achilles' heel of STMs is that they do not provide any information about the firm's ability to secure trade support for the product or about what competitive reaction is likely to be. Thus, they are more suited for evaluating product extensions than for examining the likely success of radically different new products.

Controlled test markets are more expensive than simulated test markets but less costly than standard test markets. One reason why they cost less than standard test markets is that the research supplier secures distribution. The manufacturer does not need to use its

FIGURE 6.3   **A Perspective on the Various Types of Test Markets**

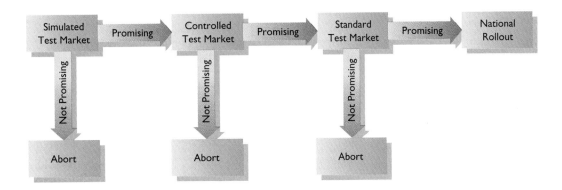

own sales force to convince the trade that stocking the product is worthwhile. The manufacturer can rest assured that the new product will obtain the right level of store acceptance, will be positioned in the correct aisle in each store, will receive the right number of facings on the shelf, will have the correct everyday price, will not experience any out-of-stock problems, and will receive the planned level of promotional displays and price features.

This perfect implementation of the marketing plan also represents one of the weaknesses of the controlled test market. Acceptance or rejection of the new product by the trade in the "real world" is typically critical to the success of any new product. A controlled test market guarantees acceptance by the trade for the duration of the test, but acceptance will not be guaranteed during the actual marketing of the product. When the manufacturer does not need to worry about this because the new product fits in nicely with its existing line, for which the company already has distribution, the controlled test market is a fairly good indicator. However, the problem of overcontrol of the marketing effort during the test market does need to be taken into account. At times, the real situation is still going to have out-of-stocks, poor aisle locations, inadequate displays, and less-than-perfect cooperation from the trade on pricing and trade promotions. When the manufacturer has

Ethical Dilemma 6.2

The promotions manager of a soft drink company asks you to help him run an experiment to determine whether he should start advertising in cinemas showing movies rated R or NC-17. He explains that he has read a journal article indicating that viewers' responses to upbeat commercials are more favorable if the commercials follow very arousing film clips, and he believes that his soft drink commercial will stimulate more sales of the drink in the cinema if it follows previews of very violent or erotic films, such as are shown before the feature film.

If you ran a laboratory experiment for this client, what kinds of manipulations would you use, and what are the ethical issues involved in their use?

Is it feasible to run a field experiment, and would the ethical issues change if a field experiment were run rather than a laboratory experiment?

If you found that increasing viewers' arousal levels did indeed make them more favorably disposed toward products advertised through upbeat commercials, what are the ultimate ethical implications for influencing television programming?

sufficient experience to account for these adjustments, the controlled test market provides a useful laboratory for testing acceptance of the product and for fine-tuning the marketing program. When the product is novel or represents a radical departure for the manufacturer, the question of trade support is much more problematic, and the controlled test is much less useful under these circumstances.

The traditional, or standard, test market provides a more natural environment than either the simulated or the controlled test market. The standard test market plays a more vital role when

1. It is important for the firm to test its ability to actually sell to the trade and get distribution for the product.

2. The capital investment is significant and the firm needs a prolonged test market to accurately assess its capital needs or its technical ability to manufacture the product.

3. The firm is entering new territory and needs to build its experience base so that it can play for real, but it wants to learn how to do so on a limited scale.

Back to the Case

To support its complex expansion plans, AT&T has adopted equally sophisticated marketing research. As it expands the scope of its services, it conducts test marketing of its technology and consumer response.

Regulations limit exactly which services the company can offer in a given area at a given time. Thus, as services vary, so do the kinds of test markets and tests the company undertakes.

On the East Coast, near the time Bell Atlantic was expected to be authorized to offer long-distance service, AT&T tested its own ability to offer local service. The initial test was a three-month campaign to obtain 6,000 residential subscribers to AT&T's local phone service. The company leased portions of Bell Atlantic's network and had telemarketers call a cross-section of AT&T's long-distance customers in New York, offering them a package deal: long-distance plus local service at a discount.

The objective was to test how well AT&T's systems work with the Bell Atlantic lines. If the transition went smoothly, AT&T would offer the same package deal statewide.

The company also made plans for a similar trial in Texas.

While AT&T was testing its ability to provide local phone service in some markets, in others it launched tests of its broadband technology. In Fremont, California, the company began offering residents local phone service over their cable TV lines. The company invited current long-distance customers to try the new service and fill out customer satisfaction surveys. In exchange for their participation, AT&T pays them $150 a month.

In the first few months of the Fremont test, AT&T observed some patterns in the response. One was that interest in the service was high, with about one-fifth of those contacted signing up for the service. Another observation came as a surprise: the number of people buying multiple phone lines. Almost half have ordered multiple lines, more than the company had predicted before launching the test.

Fremont customer Jessica Schieve is typical in that regard. Before joining the trial, Schieve had two phone lines—one for family use and one for her home office. When AT&T called, she was delighted to learn she could get three phone lines for less than she was paying to get two from Pacific Bell, so she signed on right away. Now she doesn't have to unplug her phone when she wants to use her fax machine.

With customers like Schieve already signed on, AT&T is optimistic about expanding its trials. The next cities slated for test marketing include Seattle, Portland, Denver, Chicago, and Salt Lake City.

Sources: "AT&T Begins Cable Brand Transition on August 3," AT&T press release, July 27, 1999 (downloaded from AT&T Web site, www.att.com, August 6, 1999); "AT&T Fact Book," AT&T Web site, www.att.com, downloaded August 6, 1999; Jeff May, "AT&T Tiptoeing into Local Service: N.Y. Effort Called 'a Test of Readiness,'" Star-Ledger (Newark, N.J.), August 4, 1999 (downloaded from Dow Jones Web site, www.dowjones.com, August 4, 1999); Chris O'Brien, "AT&T Likes the Sound of Local Test," San Jose Mercury News, July 31, 1999 (downloaded from the Mercury News Web site, www.mercurycenter.com, August 4, 1999).

Summary

Learning Objective 1

Cite three major purposes of descriptive research.

Descriptive research is used when the purpose is (1) to describe the characteristics of certain groups, (2) to estimate the proportion of people in a specified population who behave in a certain way, and (3) to make specific predictions.

Learning Objective 2

List the six specifications of a descriptive study.

Descriptive studies require a clear specification of the answers to who, what, when, where, why, and how in the research.

Learning Objective 3

Explain what a dummy table is.

A dummy table is used to catalog the data that are to be collected. It serves as a statement of how the analysis will be structured and conducted. Complete in all respects save for filling in the actual numbers, it contains a title, headings, and specific categories for the variables making up the table.

Learning Objective 4

Discuss the difference between cross-sectional and longitudinal designs.

A cross-sectional design involves researching a sample of elements from the population of interest. Various characteristics of the elements are measured once. Longitudinal studies involve panels of people or other entities whose responses are measured repeatedly over a span of time.

Learning Objective 5

Explain what is meant by a panel in marketing research and explain the difference between a traditional panel and an omnibus panel.

A panel is a fixed sample of elements. In a traditional panel, a fixed sample of subjects is measured repeatedly with respect to the same type of information. In an omnibus panel, a sample of elements is still selected and maintained, but the information collected from the members varies with the project.

Learning Objective 6

Explain what is meant by a turnover table, or brand-switching matrix.

A turnover table, or brand-switching matrix, is a two-way table that indicates which brands a sample of people purchased in one period and which brands they purchased in a subsequent period, thus highlighting the switches occurring among brands as well as the number of persons who purchased the same brand in both periods.

Learning Objective 7

Describe the emphasis in sample surveys.

The sample survey involves the study of a number of cases at the same point in time. The survey attempts to be representative of some known universe, both in terms of the number of cases included and in the manner of their selection.

Learning Objective 8

Distinguish between the commonsense notion of causality and the scientific notion.

The commonsense notion of causality suggests that there is a single cause of an event. The scientific notion of causality holds that there may be a number of determining conditions that are probable causes for an event, but that said relationship can be only inferred, never proven conclusively.

Learning Objective 9

Define concomitant variation.

Concomitant variation is the extent to which a cause and an effect occur together or vary together in the way predicted by the hypothesis.

Learning Objective 10

List three ways of determining a causal relationship.

Three ways of determining a causal relationship are (1) through concomitant variation, (2) through time order of occurrence of variables, and (3) by eliminating other possible sources of explanation.

Learning Objective 11

Clarify the difference between laboratory experiments and field experiments.

Laboratory experiments are distinguished from field experiments primarily in terms of environment. The analyst creates a setting for a laboratory experiment, while a field experiment is conducted in a natural setting. The distinction is one more of degree than of kind, as both involve control and manipulation of one or more presumed causal factors.

Learning Objective 12

Explain which of the two types of experiments has greater internal validity and which has greater external validity.

The laboratory experiment typically has the advantage of greater internal validity because of the greater control of the variables that it affords. Field experiments are generally considered more externally valid, meaning that their results are better able to be generalized to other situations.

Learning Objective 13

List the three major problems in test-marketing.

Three of the more critical problems in experimentation in general, and in test-marketing in particular, are cost, time, and control.

Learning Objective 14

Discuss the advantages and disadvantages of simulated test-marketing.

Simulated test-marketing studies provide the following advantages: (1) they protect a marketer from competitors, (2) they are faster and cheaper than full-scale tests, and (3) they are particularly good for spotting weak products. However, they do have disadvantages in that they cannot provide any information about the firm's ability to secure trade support for a product, nor do they indicate what competitive reaction is likely to be.

Learning Objective 15

Distinguish between a standard test market and a controlled test market.

A standard test market is one in which companies sell the product through their normal distribution channels, and results are typically monitored by a standard distribution service. In a controlled test market, the entire program is conducted by an outside service. The service pays retailers for shelf space and therefore can guarantee distribution to those stores that represent a predetermined percentage of the marketer's total store sales volume.

Review Questions

1. What are the basic uses of descriptive research?

2. What is the key characteristic of descriptive research?

3. What are the main types of descriptive studies, and what do their differences mean?

4. What are the basic types of panels, and of what importance are the differences that exist?

5. What is the turnover table? How is it read? What kinds of analyses does a turnover table allow that cannot be done with other types of studies?

6. What is the fundamental thrust of a sample survey? What are its advantages and disadvantages?

7. What is a cross-tabulation table? What is the objective of cross-classification analysis?

8. How do the scientific notion and commonsense notion of causality differ?

9. What types of evidence can be employed to support an inference of causality?

10. What is an experiment?

11. What is the distinction between a laboratory and a field experiment?

12. What is the difference between internal and external validity?

13. How would you explain marketing's infrequent use of experimental research before 1960 and its steadily increasing use since then?

14. What is a test market? For what kinds of investigations can test markets be used? What are the problems associated with test markets?

15. What is the primary difference between a standard test market and a controlled test market?

16. How does an electronic test market work? What are its advantages compared to a traditional test market?

17. How does simulated test-marketing (STM) work? What are its main advantages and disadvantages compared to full market tests?

18. Under what conditions is a standard test market a better choice than either simulated or controlled test markets?

Discussion Questions, Problems, and Projects

1. The management of a national book club was convinced that the company's market segment consisted of individuals in the 25- to 35-year-old age group, while its major competitor's market segment seemed more widely distributed with respect to age. It attributed this difference to the type of magazines in which the competitor advertised. Management decided to do a study to determine the socioeconomic characteristics of its own market segment. Management formed a panel of 800 heads of households who had previously shown a strong interest in reading. Mail questionnaires would be sent to all the panel members. One month after receiving all the questionnaires, the company would again send similar questionnaires to all the panel members. In this situation is the research design appropriate? If yes, why? If no, why not?

2. Mr. Pennymarch, as the advertising manager for *Chemistry Today* magazine, is charged with the responsibility for selling advertising space in the magazine. The magazine deals primarily with chemical processing technology and is distributed solely by subscription. Major advertisers in the magazine are the producers of chemical processing equipment, since the magazine is primarily directed at engineers and other technical people concerned with the design of chemical processing units.

   Since the size and composition of the target audience for *Chemistry Today* are key concerns for prospective advertisers, Pennymarch is interested in collecting more detailed data on the readership. While he presently has total circulation figures, he feels that these understate the potential exposure of an advertisement in *Chemistry Today*. In particular, he feels that for every subscriber, there are several others in the subscriber's firm to whom the magazine is routed for their perusal. He wishes to determine how large this secondary audience is and also wishes to develop more detailed data on *Chemistry Today* readers, such as degree of technical training, level in the administrative hierarchy, and so forth.
   (a) Does Pennymarch have a specific hypothesis? If yes, state the hypothesis.
   (b) What type of research design would you recommend? Justify your answer.

3. The Allure Company, a large manufacturer of women's beauty aids, conducted a study in 1999 in order to assess how its brand of hair dye was faring in the market. Questionnaires were mailed to a panel of 1,260 families. The Allure brand of hair dye had three major competitors: Brand A, Brand B, and Brand C. A similar study conducted in 1998 had indicated the following market shares: Allure, 31.75 percent (i.e., 400 families); Brand A, 25 percent (315 families); Brand B, 32.54 percent (410 families); and Brand C, 10.71 percent (135 families). The present study indicated that its market share had not changed during the one-year period, although Brand B had increased its market share to 36.5 percent (460 families). However, this increase

could be accounted for by a decrease in Brand A's and Brand C's market shares. (Brand A now had a market share of 22.23 percent, or 280 families; Brand C now had a market share of 9.52 percent, or 120 families.) The management of the Allure Company decided it had little to worry about.

The study of 1999 also revealed some additional facts. Over the one-year period 70 families from Brand A and 30 families from Brand C had switched to Allure. Five families from Brand B and 30 families from Brand C had switched to Brand A, while none of the Allure users had switched to Brand A. These facts further reassured management. Finally, 45 families switched from Brand B to Brand C, but none of the families using Allure or Brand A had switched to Brand C. Brand C's loyalty was estimated to be .556.

(a) Do you think that management of the Allure Company was accurate in analyzing the situation? Justify your answer.

(b) You are called upon to do some analysis. From the data given above, construct the brand-switching matrix. (Hint: Begin by filling in the row and column totals.)

(c) Indicate what this matrix reveals for each of the brands over the one-year period.

(d) Complete the following table and compute the brand loyalties.

		AT TIME (t_2)			
	Bought Allure	**Bought A**	**Bought B**	**Bought C**	**Total**
At Time (t_1): Bought Allure					
Bought A					
Bought B					
Bought C					

(e) What can be said about the degree of brand loyalty for each of the four products?

4. The Nutri Company was a medium-sized manufacturer of highly nutritional food products. The products were marketed as diet foods with high nutritional content. The company was considering marketing these products as snack foods but was concerned about its present customer's reaction to the change in the products' images. The company decided to assess customers' reaction by conducting a study using one of the established types of consumer panels.

(a) What type of panel would you recommend in this situation? Why?

(b) Would you recommend a sample survey instead? Why?

5. Super Savers is a chain of department stores located in large towns and metropolitan centers in the northeastern United States. In order to improve its understanding of the market, management has decided to develop a profile of the so-called average customer. You are requested to design the study.

(a) What kind of research design will you select? Justify your choice.

(b) List at least ten relevant variables.

(c) Specify at least four hypotheses. (Note: A hypothesis is a conjecture as to how two or more variables are related. You should indicate the direction of the suggested relationship and how each of the variables would be measured.)

(d) Construct dummy tables using four of the variables that you specified in part (b) of this problem.

6. Consider the following statement: "The increase in sales is due to the new sales personnel that we recruited from the vocational school over the last several years. Sales of the new salespeople are up substantially, while sales for longer-term salespeople have not increased."

(a) Identify the causal factor (X) and the effect factor (Y) in the above statement.

7. The research department of the company in Question 6 investigated the change in sales for each of the company's salespeople. Using criteria supplied by management, the department categorized all territory sales changes as "increased substantially," "increased marginally," or "no increase." Consider the following table, in which 260 sales personnel have been classified as old or new:

TERRITORY SALES CHANGE

Salesperson Assigned	Increased Substantially	Increased Marginally	No Increase	Total
New	75	30	5	110
Old	50	40	60	150

(a) Does this table provide evidence of concomitant variation? Justify your answer.
(b) What conclusions can be drawn about the relationship between X and Y on the basis of the preceding table?

8. Six months later, the research department in Question 7 investigated the situation once again. However, a new variable was considered in the analysis, namely, the type of territory to which the salesperson was assigned—more specifically, whether the salesperson was assigned to an essentially metropolitan or nonmetropolitan territory. The following table summarizes the research department's findings:

METROPOLITAN TERRITORY
TERRITORY SALES CHANGE

Salesperson Assigned	Increased Substantially	Increased Marginally	No Increase	Total
New	70	20	—	90
Old	54	16	—	70

NONMETROPOLITAN TERRITORY
TERRITORY SALES CHANGE

Salesperson Assigned	Increased Substantially	Increased Marginally	No Increase	Total
New	5	10	5	20
Old	20	40	20	80

(a) If the type of territory to which the salesperson was assigned is ignored, does this table provide evidence of concomitant variation between change in sales and whether the salespeople were new or old? Justify your answer.
(b) If type of territory is considered, does the table provide evidence of concomitant variation between sales changes and whether the salespeople were new or old? Justify your answer.

9. The product development team at Busby's Briquets has been working on several modifications of Busby's highly successful line of charcoal briquets. The most promising development is a new briquet that imparts a unique smoky flavor to grilled meat. Management, based on favorable feedback from a few employees who have tested the product in their homes, feels that the new briquet has the potential to become a major seller.

At a recent strategy session, the vice president of marketing suggested a test-marketing program before committing to introduction of the new briquet. He pointed out that a test market would be a good way to evaluate the effectiveness of two alternative advertising and promotional campaigns that have been proposed by Busby's ad agency. He feels that effectiveness should be evaluated in terms of the trial and repeat-purchasing behavior engendered by each program. He also wants to gauge Busby's current distributors' acceptance of the new product.

The CEO of Busby's, however, is not very enthusiastic about the idea of test-marketing. She pointed out several of her concerns, among them the fact that Busby's competitors could easily duplicate the new briquet, the fact that the company is nearing the limit of budgeted costs for developing the new briquet, and the fact that the seasonal nature of briquet sales makes it imperative to reach a "go–no go" decision on the new briquet by early April, only four months away.

The director of marketing research stated that she felt a test-marketing plan could be devised that would satisfy both the vice president of marketing and the CEO. She was instructed to submit a preliminary proposal at the next strategy session.
(a) What information should be obtained from the test market in order to satisfy the vice president of marketing?
(b) Under what constraints must the test-marketing plan operate in order to satisfy the CEO?
(c) Given your answers to (a) and (b), what method of test marketing should the director recommend? Why?

10. Schedule an interview with the marketing manager of a firm near your home or your school. In the interview, discuss the use of test-marketing by the firm. Attempt to find answers to the following questions: How important is test-marketing in the firm's product-development process? Does the firm normally progress through different types of test-marketing for a specific product (as suggested in this text), or is only one type commonly used? What does your contact see as the advantages and disadvantages of various methods of test-marketing? Have successful test-marketing episodes always led to successful product introductions for the firm? What does your contact perceive as the most promising avenue for future development of test-marketing procedures?

Write a report of your interview, highlighting information that you obtained that was not discussed in the text, or that seems at odds with the textbook discussion.

Endnotes
1. Robert Ferber, Donald F. Blankertz, and Sidney Hollander, Jr., *Marketing Research* (New York: Ronald Press, 1964), p. 153. See also Thomas T. Semon, "Marketing Research Needs Basic Research," *Marketing News* (March 14, 1994), p. 12.

2. Ferber, Blankertz, and Hollander, *Marketing Research* p. 171.

3. Hans Zeisel, *Say It With Figures*, 5th ed. (New York: Harper and Row, 1968), pp. 200–239, has a highly readable version of the analyses that can be performed with panel data. See also Gregory B. Markus, *Analyzing Panel Data* (Thousand Oaks, Calif.: Sage Publications, 1979); Steven E. Finkel, *Causal Analysis with Panel Data* (Thousand Oaks, Calif.: Sage Publications, 1995).

4. Exhibit 6.4 can also be viewed as a transition matrix, because it depicts the brand-buying changes occurring from period to period. Knowing the proportion switching allows early prediction of the ultimate success of some new product or some change in market strategy. See, for example, Seymour Sudman and Robert Ferber, *Consumer Panels* (Chicago: American Marketing Association, 1979), pp. 19–27, which also provides an excellent review of the literature on such facets of consumer panels as their uses, sampling and sampling biases, data collection methods, conditioning, data processing and file maintenance, costs of operating, and choosing a consumer panel service. See also Scott Menard, *Longitudinal Research* (Thousand Oaks, Calif.: Sage Publications, 1991).

5. See Sudman and Ferber, *Consumer Panels*, p. 31. See also B. Golany, F. Y. Phillips, and J. J. Rousseau, "Few-Wave vs. Continuous Consumer Panels: Some Issues of Attrition, Bias, and Variance," *International Journal of Research in Marketing* 8 (September 1991), pp. 273–280.

6. "Mail Panels vs. General Samples: How Similar and How Different," *Research on Research,* No. 59 (Chicago: Market Facts, Inc., undated).

7. Ibid.

8. Verne B. Churchill, "Learning to Live with Continuing Household Panels," *TeleNation Reports* (Summer 1988), p. 2.

9. See Claire Selltiz, Lawrence S. Wrightsman, and Stuart W. Cook, *Research Methods in Social Relations,* rev. Ed. (New York: Holt, Rinehart and Winston, 1959), pp. 80–82, for a brief but helpful discussion of the differences between the commonsense and scientific notions of causality. See also David A. Kenny, *Correlation and Causality* (New York: John Wiley, 1979); Earl R. Babbie, *The Practice of Social Research,* 7th ed. (Belmont, Calif.: Wadsworth Publishing, 1995).

10. Selltiz, Wrightsman, and Cook, *Research Methods,* pp. 83–88.

11. In Chapter 19 we will discuss the various conditions that can arise when looking at evidence of concomitant variation. For the moment, we simply wish to emphasize through example that association between X and Y does not mean there is causality between X and Y and that the absence of such association does not mean there is no causality.

12. Selltiz, Wrightsman, and Cook, *Research Methods,* p. 85.

13. Arthur Conan Doyle, "The Sign of the Four," in *The Complete Sherlock Holmes* (Garden City, N.Y.: Garden City Publishing Company, 1938), p. 94.

14. Fred N. Kerlinger, *Foundations of Behavioral Research,* 3rd ed. (New York: Holt, Rinehart and Winston, 1986), p. 293. See also Geoffrey Keppel, *Design and Analysis: A Researcher's Handbook,* 2nd ed. (Englewood Cliffs, N.J.: Prentice-Hall, 1982), especially Chapter 1 for a description of the essential ingredients in experiments.

15. John R. Nevin, "Using Controlled Experiments to Estimate and Analyze Brand Demand," unpublished Ph.D. Dissertation, University of Illinois, 1972. See also John R. Nevin, "Laboratory Experiments for Estimating Consumer Demand: A Validation Study," *Journal of Marketing Research* 11 (August 1974), pp. 261–268. For comparison of consumer choice processes in a laboratory versus an actual grocery store, see Raymond R. Burke, Barbara E. Kahn, and Leonard M. Lodish, "Comparing Dynamic Consumer Choice in Real and Computer-Simulated Environments," *Journal of Consumer Research* 19 (June 1992), pp. 71–82.

16. Laboratory and field experiments typically play complementary roles in providing managerially useful marketing information. For a discussion of their respective roles, see Alan G. Sawyer, Parker M. Worthing, and Paul E. Sendak, "The Role of Laboratory Experiments to Test Marketing Strategies," *Journal of Marketing* 43 (Summer 1979), pp. 60–67.

17. For a general discussion of how the usefulness of experimental results is affected by the researcher's treatment of unmanipulated background factors in the experiment, see John G. Lynch, Jr., "On the External Validity of Experiments in Consumer Research," *Journal of Consumer Research* 9 (December 1982), pp. 225–244. See also Raymond R. Burke, Bari A. Harlam, Barbara E. Kahn, and Leonard M. Lodish, "Comparing Dynamic Consumer Choice in Real and Computer-Simulated Environments," *Journal of Consumer Research* 19 (June 1992), 71–82.

18. Alvin R. Achenbaum, "Market Testing: Using the Marketplace as a Laboratory," in Robert Ferber, ed., *Handbook of Marketing Research* (New York: McGraw-Hill, 1974), pp. 4–31 to 4–54. See also James F. Donues, "Marketplace Measurement: The Evolution of Market Testing," *Journal of Advertising Research* 27 (December 1987/January 1988), pp. RC3–RC5; Madhav N. Segal and J. S. Johar, "On Improving the Effectiveness of Test Marketing Decisions," *European Journal of Marketing* 26 (No. 4, 1992), pp. 21–33.

19. Omar L. Gallaga, "Blockbuster Video Tests Rental of Desktop-Computer Games," *Austin American-Statesman* (April 26, 1999, downloaded from Dow Jones Publications Library at the Dow Jones Web site, www.dowjones.com, August 4, 1999).

20. "Test Marketing: What's in Store," *Sales and Marketing Management* 128 (March 15, 1982), pp. 57–85. See also Richard Gibson, "Pinning Down Costs of Product Introductions," *The Wall Street Journal* (November 26, 1990), p. B1.

21. Kathleen Deveny, "Failure of Its Oven Lovin' Cookie Dough Shows Pillsbury Pitfalls of New Products," *The Wall Street Journal* (June 17, 1993), pp. B1, B8.

22. Gabriele Stern, "GM Expands Its Experiment to Improve Cadillac's Distribution, Cut Inefficiency," *The Wall Street Journal* (February 8, 1995), p. A12.

23. There are several references that provide useful overviews of marketing's use of experiments in general and test markets in particular. See, for example, David M. Gardner and Russell W. Belk, *A Basic Bibliography on Experimental Design in Marketing* (Chicago: American Marketing Association, 1980); John R. Dickinson, *The Bibliography of Marketing Research Methods,* 3rd ed. (Lexington, Mass.: Lexington Books, 1990), pp. 148–150.

24. "To Test or Not to Test Seldom the Question," *Advertising Age* 55 (February 20, 1984), pp. M10–M11.

25. Annetta Miller and Karen Springen, "Egg Rolls for Peoria," *Newsweek* (October 12, 1992), pp. 59–60.

26. Suzanne Vranica, "P&G Puts Two Cleaning Products on Its New Marketing Fast Track," *The Wall Street Journal* (May 18, 1999, downloaded from Dow Jones Publications Library at the Dow Jones Web site, www.dowjones.com, August 4, 1999).

27. The first problem is found in Lynn G. Reiling, "Consumer Misuse Mars Sampling for Sunlight Dishwashing Liquid," *Marketing News* 16 (September 3, 1982), pp. 1 and 12; the second problem is discussed in Annetta Miller and Dody Tsiantor, "A Test for Market Research," *Newsweek* 110 (December 28, 1987), pp. 32–33.

28. Lee Gomes, "It Sounded So Good . . . : The History of Consumer Electronics Is Littered with Failure," *The Wall Street Journal* (June 15, 1998, downloaded from Dow Jones Publications Library at the Dow Jones Web site, www.dowjones.com, August 7, 1999).

29. Jim Carlton, "Apple Drops Newton, an Idea Ahead of Its Time," *The Wall Street Journal* (March 2, 1998, downloaded from Dow Jones Publications Library at the Dow Jones Web site, www.dowjones.com, August 7, 1999).

30. "Simulated Test Marketing Winning Acceptance," *Marketing News* 19; Allan D. Shocker and William G. Hall, "Pretest Market Models: A Critical Evaluation," *Journal of Product Innovation Management* 3 (September 1986), pp. 86–107; Kevin J. Clancy and Robert S. Shulman, "It's Better to Fly a New Product Simulator than Crash the Real Thing," *Planning Review* 20 (July/August 1992), pp. 10–17; Christopher Power, "Will It Sell in Podunk? Hard to Say," *Business Week* (August 10, 1992), pp. 46–47; Burke, Harlam, Kahn, and Lodish, "Comparing Dynamic Consumer Choice in Real and Computer-Simulated Environments," pp. 71–82; Kevin J. Clancy, Robert S. Schulman, and Marianne Wolf, *Simulated Test Marketing: Technology for Launching Successful New Products* (New York: Lexington Books, 1994).

Suggested Additional Readings

For discussion of the operation and the advantages and disadvantages of panels, see
Frank J. R. Pol, *Issues of Design and Analysis of Panels* (Amsterdam, The Netherlands: Sociometric Research Foundation, 1989).

For general discussion regarding the design of experiments, see
Geoffrey Keppel, *Design and Analysis: A Researcher's Handbook,* 2d ed. (New York: W. H. Freeman and Company, 1995).

The second stage in the research process is to determine the research design. As we have seen in Chapters 5 and 6, the design may take one of three forms, depending on the objective of the research. In these chapters we discussed the three basic types of research: exploratory, descriptive, and causal.

You will recall that the major emphasis in exploratory research is on the discovery of ideas and insights. A descriptive study is typically concerned with determining the frequency with which something occurs or the relationship between two variables, and it is generally guided by an initial hypothesis. A causal research design is concerned with determining cause-and-effect relationships.

Researchers for the Centerville Area Radio Association (CARA) decided to begin their study by conducting some exploratory research. This research consisted primarily of two types: (1) a literature review and (2) experience surveys.

They began the literature review by reading articles dealing with the positive and negative perceptions held by users of television, radio, and newspaper advertising. This secondary information was found in marketing research studies, general articles, and reference works dealing with the three major advertising media.

They found "The Radio Marketing Consultants Guide to Media," published by the Radio Advertising Bureau, to be a particularly helpful source. This source provided extensive coverage of the advantages and problems associated with each of the three major media.

They supplemented what they had found in the literature review with an experience survey. They began by interviewing various people who had specialized knowledge and experience with these media and then used their input to develop a revised list of advantages and problems associated with each medium.

Next, they discussed each of the media attribute items on the list with a group of CARA advertising sales representatives in order to obtain their input. Although the sales reps' feedback and suggestions were valued highly and weighed heavily, researchers also recognized that the group's opinions were not free of bias. Consequently, the final list of attribute items included in the study were determined by the researchers alone.

The resulting criteria decided upon were then discussed with three local retail businesses. This was done in order to determine the relevancy of each of the items and to make any appropriate additions, corrections, or deletions. In these interviews, it was obvious that individuals were going to have strong opinions and biases about the effectiveness of one medium versus another. However, there was virtually total agreement that the criteria chosen would be sufficient and broad enough in scope to assess the three media and respective sales representatives accurately.

The information gleaned from the literature review and experience survey were then used to develop the various hypotheses that would guide further research. A complete list of these hypotheses was given at the end of Part One. Among them were the hypotheses that there would be differences in businesspeople's attitudes toward television, radio, and newspaper, and that differences would also exist in attitudes toward sales representatives of each of the media.

As we pointed out in Chapter 3, the stages in the research process should not be viewed as discrete entities, but rather as elements in a continuous process. Information uncovered at one stage in the process is often used to refine decisions made earlier in the study. The information researchers for CARA discovered in the course of their exploratory research may well have been used to formulate the research problem more clearly.

In this case, once the hypotheses were formed, the decision was made to test them by examining the perceptions of a cross section of retailers.

Discussion Issues

Given the hypotheses, if you were one of the researchers for CARA,

1. What kinds of information would you attempt to secure from retailers?

2. How would you go about selecting retailers to contact?

CASES TO PART II

Case II.A Rumstad Decorating Centers (A)

In 1929, Joseph Rumstad opened a small paint and wallpaper supply store in downtown Rockford, Illinois. For the next 45 years the store enjoyed consistent, although not spectacular, success. Sales and profits increased steadily but slowly as, to keep pace with the competition, the original line of products was expanded to include unpainted furniture, mirrors, picture framing material, and other products. In 1974, because of a declining neighborhood environment, Jack Rumstad, who had taken over management of the store from his father in 1970, decided to close the downtown store and open a new outlet on the far west side of the city. The west side was chosen because it was experiencing a boom in new home construction. In 1999, a second store was opened on the east side of the city, and the name of the business was changed to Rumstad Decorating Centers. The east side store was staffed with salesclerks but was basically managed by Rumstad himself from the west side location. All ordering, billing, inventory

control, and even the physical storage of excess inventory were concentrated at the west side store.

In 2000, the east side store was made an independent profit center. Rumstad personally took over the management of the outlet and hired a full-time manager for the west side store. With the change in accounting procedures occasioned by this organizational change, it became possible to examine the profitability of each outlet separately.

Rumstad conducted such an examination early in 2001, using the profit and loss figures shown in the exhibit below, and became very concerned with what he discovered. Both stores had suffered losses for 2000, and, although he had anticipated incurring a loss during the first couple of years of operation of the east side store, he was not at all prepared for a second successive loss at the west side outlet. He blamed the 1999 loss on the disruptions caused by the change in organizational structure. Further, from 1999

EXHIBIT II.A.1 Profit and Loss Statement for Rumstad Decorating Centers

	EAST SIDE STORE		WEST SIDE STORE	
	2000	1999	2000	1999
Total Sales	$114,461	$91,034	$ 87,703	$108,497
Cash sale discounts	4,347	2,971	4,165	2,930
Net sales	110,114	88,063	83,538	105,567
Beginning inventory	53,369	49,768	1,936	0
Purchases	64,654	56,528	163,740	59,366
Total	118,023	106,206	165,676	59,366
Ending inventory	51,955	53,369	115,554	1,936
Cost of sales	66,068	52,837	50,122	57,430
Gross profit or (loss)	44,046	35,226	33,416	48,137
Direct Costs				
Salaries	24,068	19,836	24,549	26,583
Payroll taxes	2,025	1,814	1,764	2,060
Depreciation—furniture and fixtures	92	92	92	92
Freight	6	43	511	800
Store supplies	694	828	607	4,153
Accounting and legal expenses	439	433	439	433
Advertising	2,977	4,890	4,820	5,252
Advertising—Yellow Pages	1,007	618	1,387	956
Convention and seminar expenses	0	33	83	216
Insurance	226	139	1,271	1,643
Office expense and supplies	4,466	4,393	5,327	5,010
Personal property tax	139	139	140	140
Rent	7,000	7,000	4,900	4,900
Utilities	2,246	1,651	2,746	2,359
Total direct costs	45,385	41,909	48,636	54,597
Profit or (loss)	(1,339)	(6,683)	(15,220)	(6,460)

to 2000, the east side had a 25 percent increase in net sales, a 25 percent increase in gross profits, and an 8 percent increase in total direct costs. Also, although the east side store still showed a net loss, it was 80 percent less than the previous year's loss. The west side store, on the other hand, had shown a 21 percent decrease in net sales, a 31 percent decrease in gross profit, an 11 percent decrease in direct costs, and a 136 percent increase in net loss. Rumstad is very concerned about the survival of the business and is particularly concerned with the west side store. He has called you in as a research consultant to help him pinpoint what is happening so that he might take corrective action.

West Side Store

The west side store is located in the heart of the census tract with the highest per capita income in the city. Most of the residents in the area are professional people or white-collar workers. The store is a freestanding unit located on a frontage road with the word "Rumstad" printed across the front. Since Rumstad's transfer to the east side store, there has been a succession of managers at the west side store. The first one lasted for six months and the second and third for four months. The current manager, previously a salesclerk at the store for four years, has held the job for

ten months. Even though the products carried and the prices charged are the same in both stores, there is some difference in advertising emphasis. The west side store does all of its advertising in the *Shopper's World,* a weekly paper devoted exclusively to advertising, which is distributed free to all households in the community. Paper delivery is by and large door-to-door, although it is quite typical for a stack of newspapers to be placed at the entrance to apartment buildings for residents to pick up a copy if they so choose.

East Side Store

The east side store is located in a small shopping center in a predominantly blue-collar area. Most of the residents in the immediate vicinity work for one of the various machine tool manufacturers that compose one of the basic industries in Rockford. The store has a large window display area with a readily visible "Rumstad Decorating Center" sign above the store. The east side store advertises periodically in the *Rockford Morning Star* in addition to its Yellow Pages advertising.

Question
1. How would you proceed to answer Rumstad's problem?

Case II.B   Riverside County Humane Society (A)

The demands on the Riverside County Humane Society (RCHS) had increased rather dramatically over the past several years, while the tax dollars the society received to provide services had remained relatively unchanged. In an effort to halt further decline in the quality of its services and to provide better care for the pets at the center, the membership committee of the board of directors began making plans for a member/contributor drive. The organized drive was to be the first of its kind for the local chapter, and the committee members wanted it to be as productive as possible.

As the plans began to evolve, the committee realized that the organization had only scattered bits and pieces of information about its current members. It did have a list of members and contributors for the last five years that had been compiled by the RCHS staff. In addition, it had access to the results of a survey done by a staff member several years previous that focused on member usage of shelter facilities and their opinions of shelter services and programs. However, the organization had only sparse knowledge of the profile of its typical member and contributor, why they belonged or contributed, how long they had been associated with the Humane Society, how the

services of the Humane Society could be improved, and so on. The committee members believed information on these issues was important to the conduct of a successful membership drive, and thus they commissioned some research to secure it.

One of the first things the researchers did was to contact other Humane Society chapters to determine what kinds of research they had done, particularly with respect to identifying the characteristics of their members. The researchers also interviewed key Riverside County Humane Society staff members and several board members for their thoughts and ideas regarding RCHS membership. The researchers also held a focus group among members of the Membership Committee.

These research activities produced the following general ideas about membership and contributions:

1. The people who use the center's facilities are not necessarily the same people who would become members. Members love their own pets, take good care of them, and want other animals to be treated humanely.

2. Most contributors do not care about being a "member" because membership does not confer any rights

or privileges, except a newsletter. Members are very different from contributors.

3. The female member of the household is probably making the decision regarding membership or contribution to the RCHS.

4. The majority of members in the RCHS are female and are at least 35 years old.

5. Many retired or elderly people are contributing to or joining the RCHS.

6. The average contribution is about $15 to $25.

7. People in the community have a generally positive perception of the RCHS.

8. An emotional appeal in a membership drive is likely to have the best chance for success.

9. Most people have heard about the RCHS primarily through education programs conducted by the society.

10. The greatest benefit associated with membership is the warm feeling that people get from belonging to the RCHS.

The research firm planned to select a sample of names from the current lists of members and contributors and to send them mail questionnaires to explore these ideas further.

Questions

1. What kind of research design is being used?

2. Is it a good choice?

3. Design a questionnaire that addresses the issues raised and that also gathers helpful demographic information on members and contributors.

Case II.C   HotStuff Computer Software (A)[1]

Simpson, Edwards and Associates has had considerable success with a computer software package that it designed to enable government agencies to manage their database systems. The firm is currently developing a second product, a more specialized version of its first endeavor. Called HotStuff, its latest computer software concept is targeted at the firefighting industry. Researchers at Simpson, Edwards and Associates have a hunch that fire departments are a prime market for database software because of their extensive information-handling responsibilities—equipment inventories, building layouts, hazardous materials data, budget records, personnel files, and so on.

At this embryonic stage in the new product's development, the company is following the same game plan that helped it launch its previous success. Responsibilities have been broadly divided: Jean Edwards has assumed command of the production side and Craig Simpson has taken charge of marketing and promotion. Craig's first move was to reassemble the original team of staff members who had researched the market for government agency software. At their first orientation meeting, he submitted the following objectives for their deliberation:

1. Determine market potential.

2. Identify important product attributes.

3. Develop an effective promotional strategy.

4. Identify competitors in the market.

By the close of discussion, the group had decided that its first task would be exploratory research. Specifically, it decided to conduct experience surveys involving local fire chiefs, informal telephone interviews with state and national fire officials, and a literature search. Based on findings from the exploratory research effort, the group hoped to be able to pursue descriptive research to fulfill the four objectives.

Exploratory Research

The first finding to emerge from the exploratory research affected the target market for HotStuff. There are two broad categories of fire departments: municipal departments with full staffs of paid firefighters, and volunteer departments consisting of a paid chief and remaining members who may or may not be paid firefighters. The team quickly discovered that the two kinds of departments differ in two important ways. First, from the point of view of funding, municipal departments receive the majority of their funds from taxes, so the money is tightly controlled and tends to be earmarked for specific uses. Volunteer fire departments, on the other hand, rely heavily on donors and special events as sources of income, to the extent that fund-raising may account for more than 50 percent of their total receipts. Since money obtained through fund-raising is not technically part of the budget, it is not subject to budgetary controls per se.

The second key difference between municipal and volunteer departments concerned purchasing procedures. Local municipal departments tended to route all purchases through a central purchasing agent, who would then apply for approval from the data-processing center at city hall before acquiring computer hardware and software. Fire

[1]The contributions of Jacqueline C. Hitchon to the development of this case are gratefully acknowledged.

chiefs interviewed in volunteer departments, however, reported that they had sole authority to purchase any hardware or software required.

Telephone calls to out-of-state fire officials indicated that these differences were consistent across the nation. As a result, Simpson, Edwards and Associates decided to restrict its target market to volunteer fire departments.

A second finding uncovered in the exploratory research concerned the extent to which the needs of the target market were already being met. Inquiries within the state revealed that only a few volunteer departments had already purchased computers. Further, those with computers had not possessed them for long and were still in the process of automating manual databases. The general feeling among fire officials was that computerization would be an inevitable development in the industry in the near future. Indeed, four specialized software packages were already being advertised in fire prevention journals: Chief's Helper, Fire Organizer, Spread Systems, and JLT Software. Spread Systems differed from the others in that it consisted of separate programs, each of which sold individually and covered a particular information type, such as inventory records or hazardous materials. The strategy followed by Spread Systems allowed fire departments to reduce their expenditure on software because they could select only those programs that they needed. It was conjectured at Simpson, Edwards and Associates that specific programs for specific functions may help overcome initial consumer caution toward spending several thousand dollars for computer software, because the expenditure would not be made all at one time. It was also believed that some makers of generic software packages that perform spreadsheet or database management analysis should be included in the list of competitors, although users of generic software packages needed some proficiency with computers in order to tailor these basic packages to their specific applications.

A third finding of interest from the exploratory research was that the term *volunteer* was offensive to departments officially classified as volunteer because they thought that it implied a lack of professionalism. In fact, their staffs were as well trained as members of municipal departments. This sentiment led the researchers to conclude that the label *volunteer* should not be used in the future promotion of HotStuff.

Based on what it had learned from the exploratory research, Simpson, Edwards and Associates decided to conduct a more formal investigation to address the following objectives:

1. Determine the market potential for its new software by
   a. establishing the incidence of computer use and planned computer purchases in volunteer fire departments, and
   b. obtaining more information about volunteer fire departments' funding and authority structures.

2. Identify important product attributes—that is, the types of information that needed to be handled by volunteer fire departments and that therefore needed to be incorporated into the software.

3. Secure ideas for promotional strategy by
   a. determining which fire publications are read by the target market, and
   b. determining which association conventions are most well attended by the target market.

4. Identify competitors in the market by
   a. establishing which brands of software are currently used in volunteer fire departments, and
   b. establishing how satisfactory existing software packages are perceived to be.

Study Design

Simpson, Edwards and Associates' researchers believed that the best way to address these objectives was through a national survey of volunteer fire departments. They decided on a structured–disguised telephone survey using team members as interviewers. The state fire marshall informed the group that most volunteer fire departments were located in communities with populations under 25,000. Consequently, it was decided to sample towns with populations under 25,000 that were situated within a 20-mile radius of cities of at least 100,000 people. Volunteer fire departments within those towns could then be contacted by telephone by means of directory assistance. Two large cities were randomly selected from each state in the United States, excluding Alaska and Hawaii, and then a town located near each city was randomly selected. An atlas and the most recent *Current Population Reports* were used to identify cities and towns of the right specification.

A questionnaire was devised and pretested twice. The first pretest was conducted through personal interviews and was meant to test the questionnaire; the second pretest was performed by telephone and was meant to test the mode of administration. In each case, inquiries were directed to the fire chiefs as representatives of the departments. The actual survey was conducted between April 13 and April 24. It would have taken less time to administer the survey had there not been a national fire convention the week that the phone survey began. Because the national fire convention coincided with Easter week, many fire chiefs were not at their departments; they attended the convention with their families, as their children did not have school. Nonetheless, the interviewer team was able to increase the response rate to 85 percent by numerous callbacks.

Questions

1. Evaluate Simpson, Edwards and Associates' decision to focus on volunteer fire departments as its target market, based on the exploratory research.

2. Do you consider that exploratory research was productive in this case? Do you think that further useful insights could have been gained without significantly greater expenditure of resources? Is so, what and how?

3. Comment on the differences between the four objectives as originally formulated and as reformulated after exploratory research.

4. Was the choice of phone interviews a good one?

Case II.D   Student Computer Lab (A)[1]

A major university served over 2,000 undergraduate and graduate students majoring in business administration. The large number of students enrolled in the Business School coupled with increasing utilization of computer technology by faculty and students created overwhelming demands on the Business School's computer center. In order to respond, the Business School decided to upgrade its computer facilities.

Rod Stevenson, director of the Student Computer Center (SCC), opened a new computer lab in the fall of 2000. The new lab offered specialized software required by student courses, both IBM compatible and Macintosh machines, and the latest technology in hardware and software.

Computer Lab Project

After operating for six months, Stevenson recognized some potential problems with the new computer lab. Although the number of computers had doubled with the new lab, student suggestions and complaints indicated that the demand for computers at times exceeded the available resources. To address this problem, Stevenson established a task force to investigate the level of student satisfaction with the computer lab. The task force was made up of four graduate students and was established in January 2001. The task force aimed to help the computer lab identify student needs and provide suggestions on how those needs could be most effectively met.

The first activity of the task force was to examine available information on the lab and its functions and resources. A layout of the lab is displayed in Figure II.D.1. Students are divided into two rooms, one for Macintosh (MAC) users and one for IBM-compatible users. The MAC room supported 18 computers, all loaded with the latest software. The IBM room had a total of 42 computers. Services offered by the computer lab included network and printer access. The lab usually had three to four lab monitors to collect money for printouts and answer any of the

[1]The contributions of Monika E. Wingate to the development of this case are gratefully acknowledged.

student's questions. Lab hours were 8:00 A.M. to 9:30 P.M. on weekdays and 8:00 A.M. to 5:00 P.M. on Saturdays and Sundays.

After reviewing available information on the lab, the task force decided it needed to conduct some research before making recommendations on the services offered. Exhibit II.D.1 displays a proposal written by the task force outlining the information to be obtained and the time frame for the research.

Focus Group Study

Stevenson received the proposal and approved it. He agreed with the task force's use of focus groups to gain a preliminary understanding of the students' attitudes. The focus groups would identify existing problems better than secondary research, although the process of collecting and analyzing the data would be more time consuming. After receiving approval, the task force posted information around the Business School to alert students that focus groups were being conducted. Free laser copies were offered as an incentive for participation. Students were selected based on their interest. The student focus group was held on March 10, 2001. Seven students participated, of whom five were graduate and two were undergraduate students. Transcripts are provided in Exhibit II.D.2.

Because one of the responsibilities of the lab monitors is to assist students with questions and problems, separate focus groups were also conducted on March 9, 2001, and March 11, 2001, with eight lab monitors. Information from both the student and lab monitor focus groups was used as a guide to develop questions for the second phase, a student survey. Information from the focus groups was reduced to a list of key issues, which were then categorized. An exhaustive list of statements was devised to address potential user attitudes with respect to each issue. When the list was complete, statements were revised, combined, or eliminated to a set that succinctly covered the original key issue categories. The questionnaire was then pretested, and finally administered to a sample of students attending class in the Business School.

FIGURE II.D.1 **Student Computer Lab**

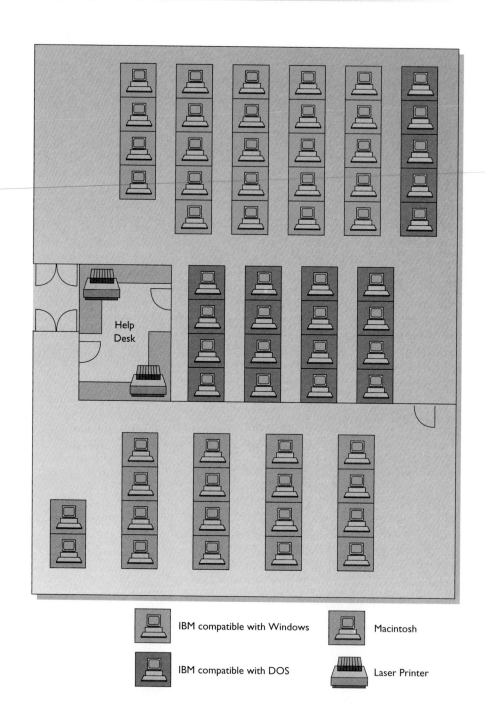

Questions

1. Did the moderator do an adequate job of getting the information needed by the SCC?

2. Do you think it was wise to have a group with both graduate and undergraduate students included, and with both MAC and IBM users?

3. Analyze the focus group transcript very thoroughly. Make a list of problems and ideas generated for the student computer lab.

4. What do you see as the benefits and limitations of the focus group findings? Do you think the task force plan for utilizing the focus groups is appropriate?

EXHIBIT II.D.1   Task Force Proposal

DATE: February 1, 2001
TO: Rod Stevenson
FROM: Computer Center Improvement Task Force
ARE: Computer Lab Research Proposal

Background: In 2000, the Business School opened a new student computer lab. Through suggestions and complaints, the SCC realizes that there is a resource allocation problem in this lab. Specifically, there is a service delivery problem in that student demand for computers at times exceeds available resources. The aim of this research is to help the SCC identify student needs and provide suggestions on how those needs can be most effectively met. The results of this research will be limited to the student computer lab. Other Business School computer facilities, such as the computer classrooms and the multimedia lab, are outside the scope of this project.

Objectives: The research objectives are as follows:

• Determine overall student satisfaction with the lab
• Identify current problem areas
• Collect student recommendations for improvements

Methodology: The research design is divided into two parts, exploratory research followed by descriptive research. The exploratory research would attempt to gain a better understanding of students' perceptions of the computer lab and to identify the issues that concern them. The student survey would aim to quantify the magnitude of these problems and to develop recommendations.

Focus Groups: The task force feels that focus groups would be the most appropriate method for exploratory research. Two sets of focus groups are recommended. One set will focus on students who use the computer lab, while the other will address the lab monitors who deal with student problems on a daily basis.

Student Survey: The focus group information would be used to develop questions for a subsequent survey. Since the population of interest is students enrolled in the School of Business, this survey would be administered to students attending classes within the Business School, both graduates and undergraduates.

Time Schedule	Completed By
Focus Groups	March 11
Questionnaire Design	April 2
Pretest Questionnaire	April 9
Survey	April 23
Data Analysis	May 10

EXHIBIT II.D.2   Student Focus Group Transcript

Moderator: I'm Robert from Professional Interviewing. I really appreciate your participation in this group session. As you can see, I am taping this session so I can review all of your comments. We are here tonight to talk about the computer lab at the Business School. As business students, you all have access to the lab for your class assignments. How do you think the computer lab is meeting your needs?

Lisa: I think that there is a problem with the lab because the folks that are using computers don't know about computers. That's been reflected in the fact that you go to one computer and you pick up a virus and these people don't know anything about viruses, they're transmitting them all over the place, nobody is scanning for viruses and there's something that could be easily put on the systems.

Oliver: I think there has to be training for the people who are watching the computers. They are ignorant. You ask them any question and they don't know. It's a computer lab and this computer doesn't seem to be doing the thing that it should be doing, why? Why is this network different from the rest? How are we supposed to handle this network? They don't know.

Lisa: Not only that, they don't know any of the software.

Oliver: Absolutely!

Lisa: This is like I have Word at home and this is WordPerfect, "How do I do XYZ in WordPerfect?" They don't know. They say let me go check with John and it takes three of them.

Marion: And there are three of them!

Lisa: I know!

Oliver: There is always a big queue so you cannot get onto a Windows machine, you have to go to Pagemaker Plus if you need to make a presentation. You cannot go to these WordPerfect machines that have just keyboard entries. But there are very few computers and a lot of lines in the peak times and they are just not equipped to handle it. They have so many staff over there, five people, all of these people, but not one of them will help anyone.

EXHIBIT II.D.2   **Student Focus Group Transcript,** *continued*

Moderator:	How about you, Jennifer, have you experienced this?
Jennifer:	Yeah, I even had it today. I just don't have time to wait in line to get a computer. It's a half hour sometimes to go in and get one.
Lisa:	And that's now. At the end of the semester it's worse.
Jennifer:	Yeah, it gets worse.
Lisa:	It takes an hour and there's no sign-up. There's no regular sign-up.
Mike:	They truncated the hours the last two weeks of the semester.
Jennifer:	You could take these four people and turn that into one educated person or take the four people and have one uneducated person there 24 hours a day. That would be nice. If all they're going to do is take your card and give you your copy, why do you have to have four of them? That's all they're doing. And studying.
Moderator:	How about you, I didn't get your name?
Tammy:	Tammy.
Moderator:	Welcome, Tammy, how about you. What kind of things have you come across?
Tammy:	What I'm hearing are a lot of the problems I've seen too. I just think there needs to be more computers in the lab and the hours need to be longer.
Mike:	I don't think they need more computers. They just need to expand the hours and the computing labs.
Oliver:	I had an idea where they don't need more computers. One suggestion I already put in the suggestion box, have people come with their own computers. Why doesn't a grad student who is going to be here for two years, going to interface with technology when he leaves here, spend a thousand dollars and go buy his own system? They should do that. Have your own computer here, I'm saying it's a requirement. It's a requirement at a lot of universities that you come with your own system. Then you don't have to worry about it, you don't need to access to our labs. Now for undergraduates we still have similar problems but it would put less of a stress on the system.
Moderator:	What would you suggest for people that would say, okay I can get this computer system, but I have to get this software for this class, and this software for this class, and this software. That is a lot of money.
Oliver:	Yeah, we can already jump into the network from home. All you need is the software.
Lisa:	I don't think so.
Oliver:	You can get in. I can check my mail and stuff.
Lisa:	But not software.
Oliver:	Oh, software. I haven't tried and so I don't know.
Tammy:	Getting back to the machine. I'd love to have my own machine but I don't want to have it if I don't have to. As long as we have all these other computers, why not use what we've got?
Mike:	I can't afford it. If you want to buy a good computer, a decent printer, a decent monitor, you are still going to spend between $1,600 and $2,000.
Oliver:	I think while you're in school the school should support us with computers.
Mike:	I think one of the reasons there aren't enough computers is that people who aren't in the business school have access to come and use the lab. In the old building, they always checked your ID.
Tammy:	Yeah. Why don't we use the card machines? They were working, weren't they? They had the doors closed and you used a key card.
Oliver:	I think the old lab was better because they controlled people coming and going.
Mike:	Yeah. Gatekeeping.
Tammy:	They had hours when only graduate students could come in. I think that's something that should be started again because they have a lot more papers to type up.
Mike:	I don't see why this lab isn't 24 hours. I really don't. Why aren't the labs 24 hours?
Lisa:	Monitor problem, they need someone to monitor them, to work with them.
Jennifer:	Three people, 3 eight-hour shifts.
Mike:	They don't have a budget to increase their hours. They need to double the hours, like not having four monitors at one time.
Moderator:	There are peak hours and there are hours that there are a lot of open computers, where people don't generally come in. If there was a way to monitor those times and put a schedule up and people could come in and say that's a time when we could go there. Continually monitor that, what do you think about that?
Mike:	Every hour is a peak hour, particularly at the end of the semester.

EXHIBIT II.D.2   Student Focus Group Transcript, *continued*

Oliver:	*I think it would be a good way of trying to smooth it out, because that's what you are trying to do. Have people go there when it's not so frequented. But then what about times like today? I happened to get out of class one-half hour early and went downstairs and utilized it. But if I hadn't signed up early, there were a million folks in there. There are some trade-offs, but I think it's a great idea to try and smooth it out. This morning there were four of us in there at 8:00 or 8:15 when it opened and I don't think anybody showed up until 10:00.*
Mike:	*One of the other problems in the lab right now, there are a lot of computers that are broken at one time.*
Oliver:	*Oh yeah!*
Mike:	*There are six of them right now that aren't working.*
Oliver:	*That's from people not knowing what they are doing. I was sitting down there on one of the old machines and there was a gentleman sitting next to me who couldn't figure out why it wouldn't work. He took his disk out and shut the computer off and it came back on and got a boot error. Then he got scared and he just left. He didn't go tell anyone. The monitors are looking from the other side, so they don't know there is anything wrong. Someone comes in, they just look around, and see that the computer is broken, or it's not booted up, and so on. That's why I am saying, it's the students themselves. People need to know how to work the system.*
Ira:	*I think there should be a small note pasted next to the computers saying the ways to handle each computer.*
Marion:	*Even a template for the word processing.*
Ira:	*Even a small hint for troubleshooting, please don't do this and do this.*
Tammy:	*I think an excellent model for this are the computer labs in the dorms. Those are run, the first time you use it, they scan everyone's ID to be sure you are a dorm resident, they know if it's the first time you are using it, they ask you to make sure you know how to use the software. They have a rack with every different kind of title and anything you need to use the software. They tell you exactly what's going to come up on the machine and what you have to do. I'm sure the Business School can get copies of it all and then just copy it.*
Marion:	*We have no reference guides for the software.*
Tammy:	*And then they have the guides there. The little orange books.*
Moderator:	*Are there any other concerns we haven't talked about?*
Ira:	*Is there any way the cost for a laser print can be reduced?*
Tammy:	*It kills me.*
Ira:	*It should be 7 cents. It is 6 cents in the library.*
Tammy:	*You used to have the option to go to a dot matrix printer. They changed that this semester. The only way to go to the dot matrix was to go to an AT&T machine. Don't tell me someone is looking at cost.*
Ira:	*I think the initial cost is pretty high, that is why they're keeping it at 10 cents.*
Jennifer:	*If they are planning on getting more printers, I think they should have at least one or two individual print stations where you can grab your stuff. If you're working on your resume and you want to print on bond paper or do envelopes, the people behind the desk won't let you do it because they don't know if other people are going to send it, they don't know what is going to come out.*
Oliver:	*Or they waste your paper because they can't coordinate it.*
Jennifer:	*So I think there should be some individual workstations.*
Oliver:	*I have something to say and maybe I'm the only one with this problem. I always find that when I go there and I am working alone I have these groups creating a racket, so it's really frustrating. I'm working on a project, I need to think. I don't need this kind of heavy distraction, this loud talk. I go and work in groups too, we try to whisper. There should be some kind of discipline in the computer lab. I think I may be the only one being that sensitive, but I think there has to be silence maintained. It is a computer lab, it is a place for people working, if you're having a fun time go have it outside.*
Moderator:	*How effective do you think their waiting lists system is?*
Tammy:	*It sucks.*
Ira:	*I didn't even know they had one.*
Oliver:	*At the end of the last semester no one knew if the list was for the MAC side or the IBM side of the room.*
Tammy:	*It would be better to set up a physical waiting list where there would be chairs or a bench or something like that.*
Ira:	*Or like a number.*
Tammy:	*Or six chairs in a row and you come down and sit down next to the computers and that means you are next to get on and then if you leave the next person can move down and then you can see that no one is getting in front of you.*

EXHIBIT II.D.2   **Student Focus Group Transcript,** *continued*

Oliver: It worked pretty well for me. Every time I used the waiting list I had to wait for maybe a half hour and my name was called and I could get a computer. I have no complaints. This happened every time. There was no problem. I had no problems at all.

Mike: Until this time I didn't even know there was a waiting list. If there was an open computer I just would sit down.

Tammy: I found out the hard way, I went down and sat down and someone told me.

Jennifer: It's not very consistent. It's kind of whenever they feel like.

Moderator: Anything else?

Jennifer: I have one comment about the resources, since we are able to use the resources like e-mail and the Internet. The Internet's great but if you don't know any of the numbers to call out, it's kind of a useless thing. But there are books out there with the numbers that cost about $30 and if you keep one of the books as a reference copy at the desk for people to look at, I think it would be a great resource. I looked at the bookstore once and it's incredible the different things you can call up on it.

Tammy: Good point. I think they could put it down there with all the reference items.

Jennifer: I think they need more computers and longer hours. They're not meeting the demands.

Ira: At least the building hours.

Tammy: Match the library's hours. They're open 100 and some hours a week. Sunday night. They could close earlier on Friday and Saturday night (like 8 A.M. to 11 P.M.).

Jennifer: And do it during exams too—all of a sudden it's close to 5:00 and even Memorial Library is open later.

Moderator: We're close to wrapping up. Is there anything else?

Tammy: Oh, can I get templates? For the word processing, I don't know how to use them. You have to use control that, shift that.

Ira: They used to have them. Just photocopy them.

Moderator: Is there anything else? I want to thank all of you. Your concerns will definitely be evaluated and considered. I have some printout cards for all of you. I knew I would give you $5.00 for each copy but as it turned out there's $9.75 on each card.

Case II.E   Chestnut Ridge Country Club (A)[1]

The Chestnut Ridge Country Club has long maintained a distinguished reputation as one of the outstanding country clubs in the Elma, Tennessee, area. The club's golf facilities are said by some to be the finest in the state, and its dining and banquet facilities are highly regarded as well. This reputation is due in part to the commitment by the board of directors of Chestnut Ridge to offer the finest facilities of any club in the area. For example, several negative comments by club members regarding the dining facilities prompted the board to survey members to get their feelings and perceptions of the dining facilities and food offerings at the club. Based on the survey findings, the board of directors established a quality control committee to oversee the dining room, and a new club manager was hired.

Most recently, the board became concerned about the number of people seeking membership to Chestnut Ridge. Although no records are kept on the number of membership applications received each year, the board sensed that this figure was declining. They also believed that membership applications at the three competing country clubs in

the area—namely, Alden, Chalet, and Lancaster—were not experiencing similar declines. Because Chestnut Ridge had other facilities, such as tennis courts and a pool, that were comparable to the facilities at these other clubs, the board was perplexed as to why membership applications would be falling at Chestnut Ridge.

To gain insight into the matter, the board of directors hired an outside research firm to conduct a study of the country clubs in Elma, Tennessee. The goals of the research were: (1) to outline areas in which Chestnut Ridge fared poorly in relation to other clubs in the area; (2) to determine people's overall perception of Chestnut Ridge; and (3) to provide recommendations for ways to increase membership applications at the club.

Research Method

The researchers met with the board of directors and key personnel at Chestnut Ridge to gain a better understanding of the goals of the research and the types of services and facilities offered at a country club. A literature search of published research relating to country clubs uncovered no studies. Based solely on their contact with individuals at Chestnut Ridge, therefore, the research team developed

[1]The contributions of David M. Szymanski to the development of this case are gratefully acknowledged.

the survey contained in Exhibit II.E.1. Because personal information regarding demographics and attitudes would be asked of those contacted, the researchers decided to use a mail questionnaire.

The researchers thought it would be useful to survey members from Alden, Chalet, and Lancaster country clubs in addition to those from Chestnut Ridge for two reasons. One, members of these other clubs would be knowledge-able about the levels and types of services and facilities desired from a country club, and, two, they had at one time represented potential members of Chestnut Ridge. Hence, their perceptions of Chestnut Ridge might reveal why they chose to belong to a different country club.

No public documents were available that contained a list-ing of each club's members. Consequently, the researchers decided to contact each of the clubs personally to try to

---

EXHIBIT II.E.1   Questionnaire Used to Survey Alden, Chalet, and Lancaster Country Club Members

1. Of which club are you curently a member? _____
2. How long have you been a member of this club? _____
3. How familiar are you with each of the following country clubs?

Alden Country Club

_____ very familiar (I am a member or I have visited the club as a guest)
_____ somewhat familiar (I have heard about the club from others)
_____ unfamiliar

Chalet Country Club

_____ very familiar
_____ somewhat familiar
_____ unfamiliar

Chestnut Ridge Country Club

_____ very familiar
_____ somewhat familiar
_____ unfamiliar

Lancaster Country Club

_____ very familiar
_____ somewhat familiar
_____ unfamiliar

4. The following is a list of factors that may be influential in the decision to join a country club. Please rate the factors according to their importance to you in joining your country club. Circle the appropriate response, where 1 = not at all important and 5 = extremely important.

Golf facilities	1	2	3	4	5
Tennis facilities	1	2	3	4	5
Pool facilities	1	2	3	4	5
Dining facilities	1	2	3	4	5
Social events	1	2	3	4	5
Family activities	1	2	3	4	5
Number of friends who are members	1	2	3	4	5
Cordiality of members	1	2	3	4	5
Prestige	1	2	3	4	5
Location	1	2	3	4	5

5. The following is a list of phrases pertaining to **Alden Country Club.** Please place an X in the space that best describes your impressions of Alden. The ends represent extremes; the center position is neutral. Do so even if you are only vaguely familiar with Alden.

Club landscape is attractive.	:__:__:__:__:__:__:	Club landscape is unattractive.
Clubhouse facilities are poor.	:__:__:__:__:__:__:	Clubhouse facilities are excellent.
Locker room facilities are excellent.	:__:__:__:__:__:__:	Locker room facilities are poor.
Club management is ineffective.	:__:__:__:__:__:__:	Club management is effective.
Dining room atmosphere is pleasant.	:__:__:__:__:__:__:	Dining room atmosphere is unpleasant.
Food prices are unreasonable.	:__:__:__:__:__:__:	Food prices are reasonable.
Golf course is poorly maintained.	:__:__:__:__:__:__:	Golf course is well maintained.
Golf course is challenging.	:__:__:__:__:__:__:	Golf course is not challenging.
Membership rates are too high.	:__:__:__:__:__:__:	Membership rates are too low.

6. The following is a list of phrases pertaining to **Chalet Country Club.** Please place an X in the space that best describes your impressions of Chalet. Do so even if you are only vaguely familiar with Chalet.

Club landscape is attractive.	:__:__:__:__:__:__:	Club landscape is unattractive.
Clubhouse facilities are poor.	:__:__:__:__:__:__:	Clubhouse facilities are excellent.
Locker room facilities are excellent.	:__:__:__:__:__:__:	Locker room facilities are poor.
Club management is effective.	:__:__:__:__:__:__:	Club management is ineffective.
Dining room atmosphere is pleasant.	:__:__:__:__:__:__:	Dining room atmosphere is unpleasant.
Food prices are unreasonable.	:__:__:__:__:__:__:	Food prices are reasonable.
Food quality is excellent.	:__:__:__:__:__:__:	Food quality is poor.
Golf course is poorly maintained.	:__:__:__:__:__:__:	Golf course is well maintained.
Golf course is challenging.	:__:__:__:__:__:__:	Golf course is not challenging.
Tennis courts are in excellent condition.	:__:__:__:__:__:__:	Tennis courts are in poor condition.
There are too many tennis courts.	:__:__:__:__:__:__:	There are too few tennis courts.
Membership rates are too high.	:__:__:__:__:__:__:	Membership rates are too low.

7. The following is a list of phrases pertaining to **Chestnut Ridge Country Club.** Please place an X in the space that best describes your impressions of Chestnut Ridge. Do so even if you are only vaguely familiar with Chestnut Ridge.

Club landscape is attractive.	:__:__:__:__:__:__:	Club landscape is unattractive.
Clubhouse facilities are poor.	:__:__:__:__:__:__:	Clubhouse facilities are excellent.
Locker room facilities are excellent.	:__:__:__:__:__:__:	Locker room facilities are poor.
Club management is ineffective.	:__:__:__:__:__:__:	Club management is effective.
Dining room atmosphere is pleasant.	:__:__:__:__:__:__:	Dining room atmosphere is unpleasant.
Food prices are unreasonable.	:__:__:__:__:__:__:	Food prices are reasonable.
Food quality is excellent.	:__:__:__:__:__:__:	Food quality is poor.
Golf course is poorly maintained.	:__:__:__:__:__:__:	Golf course is well maintained.
Tennis courts are in poor condition.	:__:__:__:__:__:__:	Tennis courts are in excellent condition.
There are too many tennis courts.	:__:__:__:__:__:__:	There are too few tennis courts.
Swimming pool is in poor condition.	:__:__:__:__:__:__:	Swimming pool is in excellent condition.
Membership rates are too high.	:__:__:__:__:__:__:	Membership rates are too low.

8. The following is a list of phrases pertaining to **Lancaster Country Club.** Please place an X in the space that best describes your impressions of Lancaster. Do so even if you are only vaguely familiar with Lancaster.

Club landscape is attractive.	:__:__:__:__:__:__:	Club landscape is unattractive.
Clubhouse facilities are poor.	:__:__:__:__:__:__:	Clubhouse facilities are excellent.
Locker room facilities are excellent.	:__:__:__:__:__:__:	Locker room facilities are poor.
Club management is ineffective.	:__:__:__:__:__:__:	Club management is effective.
Dining room atmosphere is pleasant.	:__:__:__:__:__:__:	Dining room atmosphere is unpleasant.
Food prices are unreasonable.	:__:__:__:__:__:__:	Food prices are reasonable.

EXHIBIT II.E.1   Questionnaire Used to Survey Alden, Chalet, and Lancaster Country Club Members, *continued*

Food quality is excellent.	:__:__:__:__:__:	Food quality is poor.
Golf course is poorly maintained.	:__:__:__:__:__:	Golf course is well maintained.
Tennis courts are in poor condition.	:__:__:__:__:__:	Tennis courts are in excellent condition.
There are too many tennis courts.	:__:__:__:__:__:	There are too few tennis courts.
Swimming pool is in poor condition.	:__:__:__:__:__:	Swimming pool is in excellent condition.
Membership rates are too high.	:__:__:__:__:__:	Membership rates are too low.

9. Overall, how would you rate each of the country clubs? Circle the appropriate response, where 1 = poor and 5 = excellent.

Alden	1	2	3	4	5
Chalet	1	2	3	4	5
Chestnut Ridge	1	2	3	4	5
Lancaster	1	2	3	4	5

10. The following questions are designed to give a better understanding of the members of country clubs.

Have you ever been a member of another club in the Elma area?
_____yes   _____no

Approximately what is the distance of your residence from your club in miles?
_____0–2 miles   _____3–5 miles   _____6–10 miles   _____10+ miles

Age: _____21–30   _____31–40   _____41–50   _____51–60   _____61 or over

Sex: _____male   _____female

Marital status: _____married   _____single   _____widowed   _____divorced

Number of dependents including yourself:
_____2 or less   _____3–4   _____5 or more

Total family income:
_____Less than $20,000
_____$20,000–$29,999
_____$30,000–$49,999
_____$50,000–$99,999
_____$100,000 or more
_____Do not know/Refuse to answer

obtain a mailing list. Identifying themselves as being affiliated with an independent research firm conducting a study on country clubs in the Elma area, the researchers first spoke to the chairman of the board at Alden Country Club. The researchers told the chairman that they could not reveal the organization sponsoring the study but that the results of their study would not be made public. The chairman was not willing to provide the researchers with the mailing list. The chairman cited an obligation to respect the privacy of the club's members as his primary reason for turning down the research team's request.

The researchers then made the following proposal to the board chairman: In return for the mailing list, the researchers would provide the chairman a report on Alden members' perceptions of Alden Country Club. In addition, the mailing list would be destroyed as soon as the surveys were sent. The proposal seemed to please the chairman, for he agreed to give the researchers a listing of the members and their addresses in exchange for the report. The researchers told the chairman they must check with their sponsoring organization for approval of this arrangement.

EXHIBIT II.E.2   Average Overall Ratings of Each Club by Club Membership of the Respondent

Club Rated	Club Membership			Composite Ratings Across All Members
	Alden	Chalet	Lancaster	
Alden	4.57	3.64	3.34	3.85
Chalet	2.87	3.63	2.67	3.07
Chestnut Ridge	4.40	4.44	4.20	4.35
Lancaster	3.60	3.91	4.36	3.95

EXHIBIT II.E.3   Average Ratings of the Respective Country Clubs across Dimensions

Dimension	Country Club			
	Alden	Chalet	Chestnut Ridge	Lancaster
Club landscape	6.28	4.65	6.48	5.97
Clubhouse facilities	5.37	4.67	6.03	5.51
Locker room facilities	4.99	4.79	5.36	4.14
Club management	5.38	4.35	5.00	5.23
Dining room atmosphere	5.91	4.10	5.66	5.48
Food prices	5.42	4.78	4.46	4.79
Food quality	a	4.12	5.48	4.79
Golf course maintenance	6.17	5.01	6.43	5.89
Golf course challenge	5.14	5.01	a	4.77
Condition of tennis courts	b	5.10	4.52	5.08
Number of tennis courts	b	4.14	4.00	3.89
Swimming pool	b	b	4.66	5.35
Membership rates	4.49	3.97	5.00	4.91

[a]Question not asked.
[b]Not applicable.

EXHIBIT II.E.4   Attitudes toward Chestnut Ridge by Members of the Other Country Clubs

Dimension	Alden	Chalet	Lancaster
Club landscape	6.54	6.54	6.36
Clubhouse facilities	6.08	6.03	5.98
Locker room facilities	5.66	5.35	5.07
Club management	4.97	5.15	4.78
Dining room atmosphere	5.86	5.70	5.41
Food prices	4.26	4.48	4.63
Food quality	5.52	5.75	5.18
Golf course maintenance	6.47	6.59	6.22
Condition of tennis courts	4.55	4.46	4.55
Number of tennis courts	4.00	4.02	3.98
Swimming pool	5.08	4.69	4.26
Membership rates	5.09	5.64	4.24

The research team made similar proposals to the chairmen of the boards of directors of both the Chalet and Lancaster country clubs. In return for a mailing list of the club's members, they promised each chairman a report outlining their members' perceptions of their clubs, contingent on approval from the research team's sponsoring organization. Both chairmen agreed to supply the requested list of members.

The researchers subsequently met with the Chestnut Ridge board of directors. In their meeting, the researchers outlined the situation and asked for the board's approval to provide each of the clubs with a report in return for the mailing lists. The researchers emphasized that the report would contain no information regarding Chestnut Ridge nor information by which each of the other clubs could compare itself to any of the other clubs in the area, in contrast to the information to be provided to the Chestnut Ridge board of directors. The report would only contain a small portion of the overall study's results. After carefully considering the research team's arguments, the board of directors agreed to the proposal.

Membership Surveys

A review of the lists subsequently provided by each club showed Alden had 114 members, Chalet had 98 members, and Lancaster had 132 members. The researchers believed that 69 to 70 responses from each membership group would be adequate. Anticipating a 70 to 75 percent response rate because of the unusually high involvement and familiarity of each group with the subject matter, the research team decided to mail 85 to 90 surveys to each group; a simple random sample of members was chosen

from each list. In all, 87 members from each country club were mailed a questionnaire (348 surveys in total). Sixty-three usable surveys were returned from each group (252 in total) for a response rate of 72 percent.

Summary results of the survey are presented in the exhibits. Exhibit II.E.2 gives people's overall ratings of the country clubs, and Exhibit II.E.3 shows people's ratings of the various clubs on an array of dimensions. Exhibit II.E.4 is a breakdown of attitudes toward Chestnut Ridge by the three different membership groups: Alden, Chalet, and Lancaster. The data are average ratings of respondents. Exhibit II.E.2 scores are based on a five-point scale, where "1" is poor and "5" is excellent. The last two are based on seven-point scales in which "1" represents an extremely negative rating and "7" an extremely positive rating.

Questions

1. What kind of research design is being used? Is it a good choice?

2. Do you think it was ethical for the researchers not to disclose the identity of the sponsoring organization? Do you think it was ethical for the boards of directors to release the names of their members in return for a report that analyzes their members' perceptions toward their own club?

3. Overall, how does Chestnut Ridge compare to the other three country clubs (Alden, Chalet, and Lancaster)?

4. In what areas might Chestnut Ridge consider making improvements to attract additional members?

Data-Collection Methods

Part III covers the third stage in the research process, determination of the methods used to collect data. Chapter 7 focuses on secondary data as an information resource; and Chapter 8, on the data available from commercial suppliers. Chapter 9 compares the two methods marketing researchers have available for collecting marketing data—communication and observation. Chapter 10 then discusses the main alternatives if communication methods are used, and Chapter 11 explains the alternatives if observation methods are used.

TRACKING DOWN IDEAS FOR RADIOSHACK When RadioShack wanted to figure out how to attract women by positioning itself as America's favorite phone store, it called in . . . an anthropologist?

Well, yes, but not any anthropologist. RadioShack hired Paco Underhill, who calls himself a "retail anthropologist." His marketing research firm, Envirosell, specializes in applying the techniques of anthropology to the study of retailing.

An Envirosell study is based on observing shoppers in and around stores. The researchers in the field are trackers, people trained to observe without being observed. Trackers record their observations on a track sheet carried on a clipboard. A typical track sheet includes a map of the area being studied and plenty of space to describe a shopper and precisely what he or she does while in the area. For most studies, Envirosell dispatches several trackers to each of three or four sites on a series of weekends. Each tracker observes up to 50 shoppers in the course of a day. The trackers also perform a "density check" every hour on the hour. One tracker hurries through the entire store, noting how many shoppers are in each section. In addition, Envirosell collects data by videotaping and photographing shoppers in the store.

Why all that observation? Wouldn't a survey tell you more about what consumers want? Wouldn't the cash register tape tell you more about what they actually buy?

Those tried-and-true research methods do serve an important purpose, says Underhill. But they don't tell enough. A survey might tell you that people are excited about the latest electronic gizmo, but it might not show that they are too mystified by the store display to make a purchase decision. Also, as Karen Hyatt, category development manager for Hewlett-Packard, told a reporter for *Fortune,* "People tend to be overly polite and tell you what they think you want to hear."

Similarly, sales volume doesn't tell why some things are *not* selling. Underhill describes a bookstore that piled discounted books on a big table near the entrance. Many people who entered the store bought books from the table, so it was apparently a success. However, Envirosell's trackers noted that relatively few shoppers explored the rest of the store. The bookstore was selling its cheap books at the expense of its full-priced stock. Deducing this from the cash register tapes would have been difficult.

Envirosell provides clients with some standard measurements. One of these is the conversion rate: of the people who enter a store, the proportion who actually buy something. Over the years Envirosell has collected data indicating which conversion rates are typical for different kinds of retailers and products. The company has also noted factors that tend to improve the conversion rate. For example, the longer a person stays in a store, the more likely that person is to buy something. A purchase is also more likely if a shopper speaks to a store employee. Thus, Envirosell's measurements include the average time shoppers spend in the store and the interception rate (percentage who speak to an employee), as well as an important measure of satisfaction, the time spent waiting for help.

The way Envirosell helped RadioShack was to watch how customers behaved in its stores, particularly how they interacted with its telephones. Trackers watched shopper after shopper approach the wall display of phones, scan the display, and check prices. Then they saw that almost all the customers picked up the receiver and held it to their ear.

At first, this behavior seemed puzzling. After all, you can't call a friend with a display phone. But Envirosell's researchers well knew shoppers' desire to test a product with their senses. If they can't call someone, they can at least experience handling the phone.

Envirosell advised RadioShack to hook up the phones to a recorded message so that lifting the receiver would start the message playing. The retailer agreed, and Envirosell watched the results of the test. They saw shoppers picking up phones, listening, and handing the receivers to their companions. The retailer was delighted; when shoppers discuss a product, they are more likely to buy it.

Envirosell also taught RadioShack about the importance of the front of its stores. Experience has shown that what people see in the front of a store plays a large role in determining which shoppers go in. Therefore, RadioShack positioned its telephone displays near store entrances. The percentage of female shoppers in Radio Shack rose significantly. And not only did women buy phones, they picked up products they had previously purchased elsewhere—batteries, toys, computer peripherals, and so on.

Envirosell even helped RadioShack cater to another market segment: older shoppers. As is common in retailing, RadioShack stocked the slowest-moving items on the lowest shelves. In the case of batteries, this meant that hearing aid batteries went on the bottom tier of the spinning racks. Envirosell pointed out that this placed them essentially out of reach of older shoppers, who have more difficulty bending and stooping. RadioShack tried moving them up higher, and sales increased—without any loss to sales of batteries now stocked nearer the floor.

RadioShack and other happy Envirosell clients agree, there's a lot you can learn just by watching people.

Sources: Paco Underhill, *Why We Buy: The Science of Shopping* (New York: Simon & Schuster, 1999); Kenneth Labich, "Attention Shoppers: This Man Is Watching You," *Fortune* (July 19, 1999), pp. 131–134.

Chapter 7

SECONDARY DATA

LEARNING OBJECTIVES

Upon Completing This Chapter, You Should Be Able to

1. Explain the difference between primary and secondary data.

2. Cite two advantages offered by secondary data.

3. Specify two problems common to secondary data.

4. List the three criteria researchers should use in judging the accuracy of secondary data.

5. State the most fundamental rule in using secondary data.

6. Explain the difference between internal and external data.

7. List some of the key sources researchers should consider in conducting a search process.

8. Describe the roles of the database producer, database vendor, and data user in the operations of on-line computer search services.

Case in Marketing Research

Banks are not generally known as marketing innovators. Sometimes, however, the need to change becomes impossible to ignore.

At NationsBank (now part of Bank of America), executives saw such a need when they reviewed demographic data from the federal government. They saw projections that the Hispanic segment of the U.S. population would grow by 49 percent through 2010, becoming the largest minority group in the United States. The company examined the market area it would serve along with Bank of America and determined that it already had a potential market of 20 million Hispanic consumers and over a million Hispanic-owned businesses. Furthermore, the buying power of Hispanics has been growing faster than the national average: an 84.5 percent increase since 1990 versus 56.7 for the nation as a whole. NationsBank and Bank of America executives saw the obvious: This was a market to target.

Other bankers have been reaching similar conclusions, especially in areas of the country where the Hispanic presence is greater than average. In Texas, according to census forecasts, Hispanic people will constitute 43 percent of the population by 2030. Chase Bank executive vice president Alice Rodriguez spoke for many Texas banks when she observed, "We recognize the buying power in the minority community is significant, and we want to capture that market."

In Bethany, Oklahoma, near Oklahoma City, Peter and Chris Pierce view the Hispanic population as an uptapped market for their small, privately owned bank, First Bethany Bank and Trust. Peter Pierce told a reporter, "It's like finding a city of about 80,000 people which doesn't have a local financial institution." The Pierce brothers hired Jorge Esperilla, who served for two years as director of diversity programs at Southern Nazarene University, to consult on developing a new division that would serve the area's Hispanic residents. First Bethany is betting its future on a strategy of targeting underserved niche markets, including the Hispanic population.

To Alex López Negrete, president of marketing firm López Negrete, targeting Hispanic consumers and businesses is an immensely practical strategy. "It's common knowledge," he told a reporter. "Whoever wins the multicultural race will win, period."

But how to target that group effectively? In the past, banks have simply printed some literature in Spanish to include in their displays and maybe hired a translator in neighborhoods with a sizable population of non-English-speaking people. However, these tactics do not really reach out beyond the bank's walls and bring in new customers.

Furthermore, the banks don't want to make mistakes based on stereotypes or misuse of data. (Even sophisticated marketers like Frito-Lay can make mistakes. Consider that company's evaluation a decade ago of data suggesting Hispanic consumers are very brand loyal. The company decided to build Frito-Lay parks in Hispanic communities—a nice gesture, but the connection to buying corn chips was not exactly obvious to the communities' residents.)

Successfully targeting Hispanic consumers and businesses will require a great deal of information about those new markets. This is information that banks sorely lack, claims Bill Strunk, a banking consultant based in Houston: "Eighty-five percent of the growth between now and 2015 in Texas will be Hispanics, and everyone is waking up and wanting to market to this, but only a handful know how to do it."

Discussion Issues

1. What kinds of information will banks need in order to target Hispanic consumers and businesses?

2. Where can banks get such information (external sources, company data, published reports, commissioning their own research projects)?

3. Whom should the banks include in their research process?

Once the research problem is defined and clearly specified, the research effort logically turns to data collection. The natural temptation among beginning researchers is to advocate some sort of survey among appropriate respondent groups. This should be a last, rather than a first, resort. "A good operating rule is to consider a survey akin to surgery—to be used only after other possibilities have been exhausted."[1] First attempts at data collection should logically focus on **secondary data,** which are statistics not gathered for the immediate study at hand but previously gathered for some other purpose. Information originated by the researcher for the purpose of the investigation at hand is called **primary data.** The purpose therefore defines the distinction.

If General Electric conducted a survey on the demographic characteristics of refrigerator purchasers to determine who buys the various sizes of refrigerators, this would be primary data. If, instead, the company used its existing files and compiled the same data from warranty cards its customers had returned, or if it used already-published industry statistics on refrigerator buyers, the information would be considered secondary data.

Beginning researchers are apt to underestimate the amount of secondary data available. Exhibit 7.1, for example, lists some of the information on people and households that is collected by the U.S. Census Bureau and which is readily available for use by re-

Secondary data
Information not gathered for the immediate study at hand but for some other purpose.

Primary data
Information collected specifically for the purpose of the investigation at hand.

EXHIBIT 7.1 | **Information Items Available from the Census of Population**

POPULATION HOUSING

100-Percent Component

Household relationship	Number of units in structure
Sex	Number of rooms in unit
Race	Tenure—owned or rented
Age	Vacancy characteristics
Marital status	Value of owned unit or rent paid
Hispanic origin	

Sample Component

Education—enrollment and attainment	Source of water and method of sewage disposal
Place of birth, citizenship, and year of entry	Autos, light trucks, and vans
Ancestry	Kitchen facilities
Language spoken at home	Year structure built
Migration	Year moved into residence
Disability	Number of bedrooms
Fertility	Farm residence
Veteran status	Shelter costs, including utilities
Employment and unemployment	Condominium status
Occupation, industry, and class of worker	Plumbing
Place of work and commuting to work	Telephone
Work experience and income	Utilities and fuels

Note: Subjects covered in the 100-percent component apply to all persons and housing units. Those covered by the sample component apply to a portion of the population and housing units.

searchers. It is important for researchers to know what is available in secondary sources, not just to avoid "reinventing the wheel," but because secondary data possess some significant advantages over primary data. Further, because of the ongoing "information explosion," such an oversight will have even greater consequences in the future.

Advantages of Secondary Data

The most significant advantages of secondary data are the time and money they save the researcher. If the information being sought is available as secondary data, the researcher need simply go to the library or go online, locate the appropriate source or sources, and extract and record the information desired. This should take no more than a few days and involve little cost. If instead the information were to be collected in a sample survey, the following steps would have to be taken: data-collection form designed and pretested; field interviewing staff selected and trained; sampling plan devised; data gathered and then checked for accuracy and omissions; data coded and tabulated. As a conservative estimate, this process would take two to three months and could cost thousands of dollars, since it would include expenses and wages for a number of additional field and office personnel.

With secondary data, the expenses incurred in collecting the data have already been paid by the original compiler of the information. Even if there is a charge for using the data (unlike statistics compiled by government or trade associations, commercial data are not free), the cost is still substantially less than if the firm collected the information itself.

Given the substantial amount of time and money at stake, we offer this advice: *Do not bypass secondary data. Begin with secondary data, and only when the secondary data are exhausted or show diminishing returns, proceed to primary data.* Sometimes the secondary data are sufficient, especially when all the analyst needs is a ballpark estimate, which is often the case. For example, a common question that confronts marketing research analysts is: What is the market potential for the product or service? Are there enough people or organizations interested in it to justify providing it?

Exhibit 7.2 illustrates how secondary data were used to advantage to answer this question, in this case by a manufacturer of pet foods to assess the potential demand for a dog

---

EXHIBIT 7.2   Use of Secondary Data by a Manufacturer of Pet Foods to Assess the Potential Demand for a Dog Food That Included Both Moist Chunks and Hard, Dry Chunks

The question was, "Is there currently a significant number of persons who mix moist or canned dog food with dry dog food?" At this early stage in the exploration of this product concept, the firm did not want to expend funds for primary research. While an actual survey of pet owners would have yielded the best answer, such a survey would have required the expenditure of several thousand dollars. In addition, further development of the idea would have required a delay of several weeks to obtain the survey results. An effort to develop an acceptable first answer to the question of demand using secondary sources was initiated.

The firm identified the following information:

1. From published literature on veterinary medicine, the firm identified the amount (in ounces) of food required to feed a dog each day by type of food (dry, semimoist, moist), age, size, and type of dog.

2. From an existing survey conducted annually by the firm's advertising agency the firm obtained information on
   (a) the percentage of U.S. households owning dogs;
   (b) the number, sizes, and types of dogs owned by each household in the survey;
   (c) the type(s) of dog food fed to the dogs; and
   (d) the frequency of use of various types of dog food.

It was assumed that dog owners who reported feeding their dogs two or more different types of dog food each day were good prospects for a product that provided premixed moist and dry food. Combining the information in the survey with the information from the literature on veterinary medicine and doing some simple multiplication produced a demand figure for the product concept. The demand exceeded 20 percent of the total volume of dog food sales, a figure sufficiently large to justify proceeding with product development and testing.

Source: David W. Stewart and Michael A. Kamins, *Secondary Research: Information Sources and Methods*, 2d ed. (Thousand Oaks, Calif.: Sage Publications, © 1993), p. 129. Reprinted by permission of Sage Publications, Inc.

food that included both moist chunks and hard, dry chunks. As the example indicates, when using secondary data, it is often necessary to make some assumptions in order to use the data effectively (e.g., the number of owners who were good prospects). The key is to make reasonable assumptions and then to vary these assumptions to determine how sensitive a particular conclusion is to variations in them. In the dog food example, "altering the assumption regarding the number of owners who were good prospects for the new product to include as few as one-tenth of the original number did not alter the decision to proceed with the product. Under such circumstances, the value of additional information would be quite small."[2]

Although it is rare that secondary data completely solve the particular problem under study, they usually will (1) help the investigator to better state the problem under investigation, (2) suggest improved methods or further data that should be collected, and/or (3) provide comparative data by which primary data can be more insightfully interpreted.

Disadvantages of Secondary Data

Two problems that commonly arise with secondary data are (1) they do not completely fit the problem, and (2) they are not totally accurate.

Problems of Fit

Since secondary data are collected for other purposes, it is rare when they perfectly fit the problem as defined. The problems of fit are particularly acute in cross-country studies, as the various censuses are inconsistent in the information they collect, when they collect it, and how they present it (see Research Window 7.1). In some cases, the fit will be so poor as to render the data completely inappropriate. Usually the poor fit is due to unsuitable (1) units of measurement, (2) class definitions, or (3) publication currency.

The size of a retail store, for instance, can be expressed in terms of gross sales, profits, square feet, and number of employees. Consumer income can be expressed by individual, family, household, and spending unit. So it is with many variables, and a recurring source of frustration in using secondary data is that the source containing the basic information desired presents that information in units of measurement different from that needed.

Assuming the units are consistent, we find that the class boundaries presented are often different from those needed. If the problem demands income by individual in increments of $5,000 (0–$4,999, $5,000–$9,999, and so on), it does the researcher little good if the data source offers income by individual using boundaries $7,500 apart (0–$7,499, $7,500–$14,999, and so on).

Finally, secondary data are often out of date. The time from data collection to data dissemination is often long, sometimes as much as two to three years, as, for example, with much government census data. Although census data have great value while current, this value diminishes rapidly with time. Most marketing decisions require current, rather than historical, information.

Problems of Accuracy

The accuracy of much secondary data is also questionable. As this book indicates, there are a number of sources of error possible in the collection, analysis, and presentation of marketing information. When a researcher is collecting primary data, firsthand experience helps in judging the accuracy of the information being collected. But when using secondary data, the researcher's task in assessing accuracy is more difficult.[3] It may help in this task to consider the primacy of the source, the purpose of publication, and the general quality of the data-collection methods and presentation.[4]

Inconsistencies in the Information Collected in Country Censuses

Language English-speaking countries, of course, present no language barriers to U.S. market researchers. And a number of nations offer bilingual census tabulations. Nations publishing census reports containing English include the Scandinavian countries, Japan, South Korea, Taiwan, Singapore, and Thailand.

Other countries offer only their native language. This is not too serious a problem if the language is French, Italian, Spanish, or Portuguese. Demographic terms in these languages are fairly close to English and the format of the tables, along with a little guesswork, is often enough to let researchers find what they need. German, Hungarian, Polish, and languages using different alphabets, such as Russian, are much more difficult to decipher unless one has been trained in these languages.

Data Content What a researcher can get from a census depends on what is on the census form. The content is typically a mixture of traditional questions and some new items of interest to government bureaucrats and policymakers. These same forces, further modified by budget constraints, shape the form and content of the printed results.

European countries such as Switzerland and Germany print a good deal of information on noncitizens. Canada collects data on religion. Both of these topics are ignored in the U.S. censuses. What this suggests is that one cannot expect to find the same range of data topics from one country to the next; this can complicate a researcher's life enormously.

Consider income data, the lifeblood of most U.S. segmentation studies. Most nations do not include an income question in their censuses. Britain doesn't. Japan doesn't. Nor do France, Spain, and Italy. Among the few countries that have asked about income are Canada, Australia, New Zealand, Mexico, Sweden, and Finland.

Educational attainment can be used for socioeconomic status. However, educational systems vary enough among countries that comparisons can be fairly crude. Some countries report graduates of vocational-technical schools, while in this country education is reported simply by the number of years of school attended.

Data concerning marital status also varies from country to country. Ireland, for example, recognizes only three marital statuses: single, married, and widowed. Other countries tabulate the separated population, but sometimes lump it in with divorced or married populations. Latin American censuses often have "cohabitating" or "consensual union" as marital categories. Sweden cross-tabulates its cohabiting population by marital status. Although most countries gather data on marital status, few cross-tabulate it with household headship. Nor is headship often cross-tabulated by educational attainment.

Census Frequency The United States takes a census every ten years, which is the typical frequency. Japan and Canada conduct their censuses every five years, but the mid-decade counts are not as complete as the ones done at the end of each decade. France takes a census irregularly; since the 1960s, the interval has been about seven years. In what used to be West Germany, the most recent census was taken in 1987, but the previous one was in 1970, the same year of the last Dutch census.

Some northern and western European nations seem to be abandoning the census as a data collection tool. Instead, they hope to rely on population registers to account for births, deaths, and changes in marital status or place of residence. One result of this appears to be less hard-copy data. Assuming that government databases can be tapped for market research purposes, this would present no serious problem where research budgets are robust. However, government bureaucrats aren't always friendly to market researchers.

Source: Donald B. Pittenger, "Gathering Foreign Demographics Is No Easy Task," *Marketing News* 24 (January 8, 1990), pp. 23, 25. Reprinted with permission of American Marketing Association.

Primary source
The originating source of secondary data.

Secondary source
A source of secondary data that did not originate the data but rather secured them from another source.

Primary of Source Consider the source first. Secondary data can be secured from either a primary source or a secondary source. A **primary source** is the source that originated the data. A **secondary source** is a source that in turn secured the data from a primary source. The *Statistical Abstract of the United States,* for example, which is published each year and contains a great deal of useful information for many research projects, is a secondary source of secondary data. All of its data are taken from other government and trade sources. The researcher who *terminated* a search for secondary data with the *Statistical Abstract* would violate the most fundamental rule in using secondary data—*always use the primary source of secondary data.*

Irene Viento violated that rule when she planned the launch of her store Grand Kids Ltd. in Pelham, New York. She thought her upscale suburb was an ideal location for a store catering to grandparents eager to spoil their grandchildren. After all, specialty stores of this type were the largest segment of the clothing market for infants and toddlers. She checked data from the school district and a company that produces advertising circulars, and estimated that there were about 10,000 families in Pelham—enough, she reasoned to support her store. But three years after the founding, she closed for lack of business. She had grossly overestimated her market. Census data recorded 12,000 residents and fewer than 3,500 families. Furthermore, less than one-third of Pelham's residents were in her targeted age group of people 50 and older.[5]

There are two main reasons for using a primary source. First and foremost, the researcher will need to search for general evidence of quality (e.g., the methods of data collection and analysis). The primary source will typically be the only source that describes the process of collection and analysis, and thus it is the only source by which this judgment can be made. Second, a primary source is usually more accurate and complete than a secondary source. Secondary sources often fail "to reproduce significant footnotes, or textual comments, by which the primary source had qualified the data or the definition of units."[6] Errors in transcription can also occur in copying the data from a primary source. Once made, transcription errors seem to hold on tenaciously, as the following example illustrates.

In 1901 Napoleon Lajoie produced the highest batting average ever attained in the American League when he batted .422 on 229 hits in 543 times at bat. In setting the type for the record book after that season, a printer correctly reported Lajoie's .422 average, but incorrectly reported his hits, giving him 220 instead of 229. A short time later, someone pointed out that 220 hits in 543 at-bats yields a batting average of .405, and so Lajoie's reported average was changed. The error persisted for some 50 years, until an energetic fan checked all the old box scores and discovered the facts.[7]

Purpose of Publication A second criterion by which the accuracy of secondary data can be assessed is the purpose of publication. Consider the examples in Research Window 7.2. After reading them, do you think any of the following: (A) The Food and Drug Administration should give pharmaceutical companies wide latitude in advertising drugs directly to consumers; (B) home handymen are an important group of innovators that marketers need to target in their communications; (C) Americans take their cars very seriously? Are your reactions any different if you are told: The survey in Example A was sponsored by *Prevention* magazine, which publishes health-related articles and is therefore a magazine in which prescription drug marketers advertise; the survey in Example B was sponsored by *Popular Mechanics* magazine; and the survey in Example C was sponsored by Bridgestone/Firestone, a tire manufacturer? Do you now have the same confidence in the objectivity of the results? Probably not, which suggests that the source is one criterion for evaluating the accuracy of secondary data.

> Sources published to promote sales, to advance the interests of an industrial or commercial or other group, to present the cause of a political party, or to carry on any sort of propaganda are suspect. Data published anonymously, or by an organization which is on the defensive, or under conditions which suggest a controversy, or in a form which reveals a strained attempt at "frankness," or to controvert inferences from other data are generally suspect.[8]

Using the Source to Evaluate the Accuracy of Secondary Data

A. Advertising Medicine to Consumers

According to a recent survey, almost one-third of respondents have talked to a doctor about a treatment they saw advertised. Of those who asked their doctor for a drug they saw advertised, half were given a prescription for it. Three-quarters of respondents said ads for prescription drugs showed both the risks and benefits of the medicine. The survey was released at a time when the Food and Drug Administration was preparing new guidelines for advertising prescription drugs directly to consumers (rather than promoting them just to physicians).

B. Home Handymen

Home handymen play a significant role in millions of purchasing decisions, a new study finds. According to the study, 18 million "must-know" men affect what is bought by as many as 85 million other consumers. The study says that such men—independent do-it-yourselfers who have

a compulsion to know what makes things tick and enjoy fiddling with gadgets—are sought out for their advice by buyers of products in such areas as home improvement and electronics.

C. Americans and Their Cars

How strong are Americans' love affairs with their cars? A surprising 38 percent of the men surveyed recently by a Nashville research firm declared that they love their cars more than women. Nearly 8 percent of the women surveyed said that men who drove nice cars are more appealing, and roughly 15 percent of the respondents had even gone so far as to name their cars.

Source: Example A: David Goetzl, "Second Magazine Study Touts Value of DTC Drug Ads," *Advertising Age* (June 28, 1999), p. 22; Example B: "Just Ask the Man Who Has Taken One Apart," *The Wall Street Journal* (September 20, 1991), p. B1; Example C: "The 'Other Woman' May Be His Volvo," *The Wall Street Journal* (June 24, 1994), p. B1.

This is not to say that data collected or sponsored by an interested party cannot be used by the researcher. Rather, it is simply to suggest that such data should be viewed most critically by the research user. A source that has no ax to grind but, rather, publishes secondary data as its primary function deserves confidence. If data publication is a source's raison d'être, high quality must be maintained. Inaccurate data offer such a firm no competitive advantage, and their publication represents a potential loss of confidence and eventual demise. The success of any organization supplying data as its primary purpose depends on the long-run satisfaction on the part of its users that the information supplied is indeed accurate.

General Evidence of Quality The third criterion by which the accuracy of secondary data can be assessed is through the general evidence of quality. One way of determining this quality is to evaluate the ability of the supplying organization to collect the data. The Internal Revenue Service, for example, has greater leverage in securing income data than an independent marketing research firm. However, researchers also have to weigh whether this additional leverage may introduce bias. Would a respondent be more likely to hedge in estimating her income in completing her tax return or in responding to a consumer survey?

In judging the quality of secondary data, a user also needs to understand how the data were collected. A primary source should provide a detailed description of the data-collection process, including definitions, data-collection forms, method of sampling, and so forth. If it does not, researcher beware! Such omissions are usually indicative of sloppy methods.

When the details of data collection are provided, the user of secondary data should examine them thoroughly. Was the sampling plan sound? Was this type of data best collected through questionnaire or by observational methods? What about the quality of the field force? What kind of training was provided? What kinds of checks of the fieldwork were employed? What was the extent of nonresponse, due to refusals, not at homes, and by item? Are these statistics reported? Is the information presented in a well-organized manner? Are the tables properly labeled, and are the data within them internally consistent? Are the conclusions supported by the data? As these questions suggest, the user of secondary data must be familiar with the research process and the potential sources of error. The remainder of this book should provide much of the needed insight for evaluating secondary data. For the moment, though, let us examine some of the main types of secondary data.

Types of Secondary Data: Internal and External

Internal data

Data that originate within the organization for which the research is being done.

External data

Data that originate outside the organization for which the research is being done.

The most common way of classifying data is by source, whether internal or external. **Internal data** are those found within the organization for whom the research is being done, while **external data** are those obtained from outside sources. The external sources can be further split into those that regularly publish statistics and make them available to the user at no charge (e.g., the U.S. government), and those commercial organizations that sell their services to various users (e.g., ACNielsen). In the remainder of this chapter and its appendix we will review some of the main types and sources of published statistics; in the next chapter we will review some of the more important sources of commercial statistics. Together they represent some of the most commonly used sources of secondary data, the ones with which the researcher would typically begin a search. Figure 7.1 provides an overview of these sources.

FIGURE 7.1   **Types of Secondary Data**

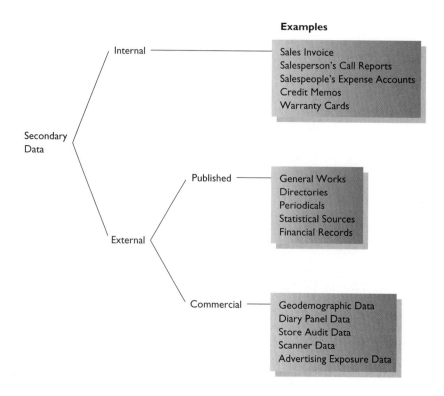

An independent marketing research firm was hired by a manufacturer of power equipment, including lawn mowers, snowblowers, and chain saws, to study the Minneapolis market. The manufacturer wanted to determine (1) whether there was sufficient market potential to warrant opening a new dealership, and (2) if so, where the dealership should be located in the metropolitan area. The research firm went about the task by scouring secondary data on the Minneapolis market, particularly statistics published by the Census Bureau. In less than two months, the research firm was able to develop a well-documented recommendation as to what the power equipment manufacturer should do.

Approximately six months after completing this study, the research firm has been approached by a manufacturer of electric power tools to do a similar study concerning the location of a distribution center through which it could more effectively serve the many hardware stores in the area.

- Is it ethical for the research firm to use the information it collected in the first study to reduce its cost quote to the client in the second?

- Does it make any difference if the firm making electric power tools also manufactures electric lawn mowers and chain saws?

- Suppose some of the data were collected through personal interviews that the first client paid for. Should that affect the situation in any way?

Internal Secondary Data

Internal data that were collected for some purpose other than the study at hand are *internal secondary data.* For example, the sales and cost data compiled in the normal accounting cycle represent promising internal secondary data for many research problems—such as evaluation of past marketing strategy or assessment of the firm's competitive position in the industry. Such data are less helpful in guiding future-oriented decisions, such as evaluating a new product or a new advertising campaign, but even here they can serve as a foundation for planning other research.

Generally, the one most productive source document is the sales invoice. From this, the following information can usually be extracted:

- Customer name and location
- Product(s) or service(s) sold
- Volume and dollar amount of the transaction
- Salesperson (or agent) responsible for the sale
- End use of the product sold
- Location of customer facility where product is to be shipped and/or used
- Customer's industry, class of trade, and/or channel of distribution
- Terms of sale and applicable discount
- Freight paid and/or to be collected
- Shipment point for the order
- Transportation used in shipment

Other documents provide more specialized input. Some of the more important of these are listed in Exhibit 7.3. Most companies are likely to use only two or three of these

EXHIBIT 7.3	Some Useful Sources of Internal Secondary Data

Document	Information Provided
Cash register receipts	Type (cash or credit) and dollar amount of transaction by department by salesperson
Salespeople's call reports	Customers and prospects called on (company and individual seen; planned or unplanned calls)
	Products discussed
	Orders obtained
	Customer's product needs and usage
	Other significant information about customers
	Distribution of salespeople's time among customer calls, travel, and office work
	Sales-related activities: meetings, conventions, etc.
Salespeople's expense accounts	Expenses by day by item (hotel, meals, travel, etc.)
Individual customer (and prospect) records	Name and location and customer number
	Number of calls by company salespeople (agents)
	Sales by company (in dollars and/or units, by product or service, by location of customer facility)
	Customer's industry, class of trade, and/or trade channel
	Estimated total annual usage of each product or service sold by the company
	Estimated annual purchases from the company of each such product or service
	Location (in terms of company sales territory)
Financial records	Sales revenue (by products, geographic markets, customers, class of trade, unit of sales organization, etc.)
	Direct sales expenses (similarly classified)
	Overhead sales costs (similarly classified)
	Profits (similarly classified)
Credit memos	Returns and allowances
Warranty cards	Indirect measures of dealer sales
	Customer service

sources of sales information in addition to the sales invoice. The particular ones used depend on the company and the types of analyses used to plan and evaluate the marketing effort. Even something as simple as a product registration card can be used to advantage for marketing intelligence, as Research Window 7.3 indicates.

Another useful, but often overlooked, source of internal secondary data is prior marketing research studies on related topics. While each study typically addresses a number of specific questions, most also involve only one or two key learnings. There can be great synergy when these key learnings are studied and combined. As Larry Stanek, while director of marketing research at Kraft, commented:

> Combining key learnings can help you develop a competitive advantage for your company. By examining your combined learnings you may discover things that other companies have yet to learn. Or you can learn to be more productive or cost effective and lower your research costs. Or you may learn something that helps you skip steps or speeds your development process.[9]

Internal secondary data are the least costly (and most readily available) of any type of marketing research. If maintained in an appropriate form, internal sales data can be used to analyze the company's past sales performance by product, geographic location, customer, channel of distribution, and so on, while cost data help in determining how profitable these segments of the business are. This type of information typically forms the basis

Targeting: It's in the Cards

When the Skil Corporation was launching a cordless power screwdriver, management was worried. It believed that the company had designed a useful product, but it wondered whether consumers would think the new tool was just a gimmick. Using information from product registration cards and follow-up interviews, Skil was quickly able to prove to itself that the screwdriver was not a fad.

The registration card research revealed something else, however. Although do-it-yourselfers were the primary market for the new product, a substantial portion of the purchases were elderly people for whom the screwdriver's ease of operation was the chief advantage. "We hadn't realized the arthritis implications," says Skil's Ron Techter. In response, Skil began advertising in publications geared to older Americans.

Almost everyone has filled out a product registration card. As they slip the card into the mailbox, few consumers realize that they have just completed a questionnaire. Yet for National Demographics & Lifestyles (NDL), the information from product registration cards has been pure gold. NDL compiles information from these "mini-questionnaires" to feed its comprehensive data base, which includes demographics and participation information covering 57 activities, interests, and lifestyles.

According to Jock Bickert, the company's founder, NDL data offer no special advantage at a national level, because a marketer can survey 1,500 or 2,000 consumers to obtain national projections. However, NDL's data base is very powerful when one moves down to individual markets, neighborhoods, or even postal routes.

One company that has made effective use of NDL's data is Amana Appliance. One day Bill Packard, domestic sales manager for an independent Amana Appliance distributor in Fort Lauderdale was talking with Amana's manager of marketing services, Dave Collins. Collins mentioned that Amana could provide Packard with profiles of Amana purchasers from his territory for the past year and a half based on NDL product-registration cards. When the NDL profile arrived, Packard got an idea.

He took the information to the marketing director of a Boca Raton real estate developer who was trying to decide what brand of appliances to put into his $200,000 homes. Packard pointed out that the purchaser profile of high-end Amana products perfectly matched the developer's profile of potential customers. Initially skeptical, the marketing director polled 100 potential home buyers himself. These homebuyer profiles so closely matched Amana's that the developer decided to use Amana appliances in the kitchens.

"If you look at one of our completed questionnaires," says NDL's Bickert, "you really begin to get a picture of the individual. You are able to say, 'This person is a likely candidate for these kinds of offers and promotions and appeals and is very unlikely for other kinds.' You can't do that if you are looking at demography alone."

Source: Wally Wood, "Targeting: It's in the Cards," *Marketing & Media Decisions* 23 (September 1988), pp. 121–122. See also Robert Bengen, "Teamwork: Its in the Bag," *Marketing Research: A Magazine of Management & Applications* 5 (Winter 1993), pp. 30–33, for discussion of how Samsonite uses warranty cards along with other information to improve its marketing.

of a firm's marketing intelligence system. We shall not go into the details of this type of analysis here because it is a somewhat specialized topic and is extensively reported elsewhere.[10] Most studies should begin with internal secondary data.

Searching for Published External Secondary Data

There is such a wealth of external data that beginning researchers typically underestimate what is available. The statement that there is *some relevant* external secondary data on almost any problem a marketer might confront is not an exaggeration. The fundamental problem is not availability; it is identifying and accessing what is there. Even those researchers who do have an inkling of how much valuable secondary data there is are typically unsure of how to go about searching for it. Figure 7.2 provides some guidelines that can be used to get started on a search of secondary data on a particular topic.[11]

FIGURE 7.2   **How to Get Started When Searching Published Sources of Secondary Data**

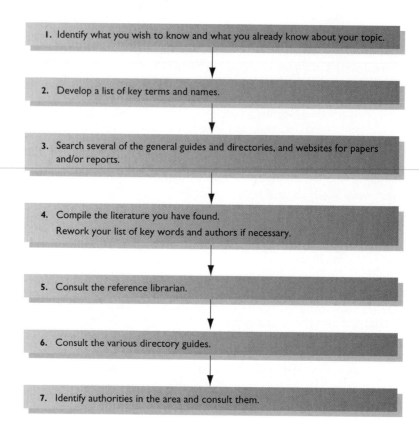

FIGURE 7.2   **How to Get Started When Searching Published Sources of Secondary Data**

1. Identify what you wish to know and what you already know about your topic.

2. Develop a list of key terms and names.

3. Search several of the general guides and directories, and websites for papers and/or reports.

4. Compile the literature you have found.
   Rework your list of key words and authors if necessary.

5. Consult the reference librarian.

6. Consult the various directory guides.

7. Identify authorities in the area and consult them.

Step 1 The first step in the process is to identify what you wish to know and what you already know about your topic. This may include relevant facts, names of researchers or organizations associated with the topic, key papers and other publications with which you are already familiar, and any other information you may have.

Step 2 A useful second step is to develop a list of key terms and authors. These terms and names will provide access to secondary sources. Unless you have a very specific topic of interest, it is better to keep this initial list long and quite general.

Step 3 In Step 3, you are ready to use the library or the Internet for the first time. It is useful to begin your search with several of the directories and guides listed in Appendix 7A or websites that deal with the subject. A relatively new way to identify information sources on the Internet is to start with an InfoTech Marketing Web site called The Marketing Source (www.infotechmarketing.net/thesource.htm). It offers hundreds of links to sites that InfoTech has reviewed for relevancy to marketing issues, including published reports, newspapers and magazines, government data sources, and sources of data about specific companies. Some of the links are to free data.[12]

Step 4 Now it is time to compile the literature you have found. Is it relevant to your needs? Perhaps you are overwhelmed by information. Perhaps you have found little that is relevant. If so, rework your list of key words and authors and expand your search to include a few more years and a few additional sources. Once again evaluate your findings. By the end of Step 4, you should have a clear idea of the nature of the information you are seeking and sufficient background to use more specialized sources.

Step 5 One very useful specialized source is a reference librarian. Reference librarians are specialists who have been trained to know the contents of many of the key information sources in a library and on the Web, as well as how to search those sources most effectively. It is a rare problem indeed for which a reference librarian cannot uncover some relevant published information. While the reference librarian can help you if you wish to consider a computer-assisted information search, he or she will need your help, though, in the form of a carefully constructed list of key words or topics. You need to remember that the reference librarian cannot be of much help until you can provide some rather specific details about what you want to know.

Step 6 If you have had little success or your topic is highly specialized, consult one of the general guides to information listed in Appendix 7A. These are really directories of directories, which means that this level of search will be very general. You will first need to identify potentially useful primary directories, which will then lead you to other sources.

Step 7 If you are unhappy with what you have found or are otherwise having trouble, and the reference librarian has not been able to identify sources, use an authority. Identify some individual or organization that might know something about the topic. The various *Who's Who* publications, *Consultants and Consulting Organizations Directory, Encyclopedia of Associations, Industrial Research Laboratories in the United States,* or *Research Centers Directory* may help you identify sources. The Bureau of the Census puts out a list of department specialists whom users can contact for information on any of the bureau's studies. These people are often quite knowledgeable about related studies in their areas of expertise. Faculty at universities, government officials, and business executives can also be useful sources of information.

Some Key General Sources of External Secondary Data

In addition to the key role played by reference librarians, some other particularly important sources of external secondary data are associations, general guides to useful marketing information, and on-line computer searches.

Associations Most associations gather and often publish detailed information on such things as industry shipments and sales, growth patterns, environmental factors affecting the industry, operating characteristics, and the like. Trade associations are often able to secure information from members that other research organizations cannot, because of the working relationships that exist between the association and the firms that belong to it. Two useful sources for locating associations serving a particular industry are the *Directory of Directories* and the *Encyclopedia of Associations,* described in Appendix 7A.

General Guides to Secondary Data Other useful sources for locating information on a particular topic are the general guides to secondary data described in Appendix 7A. Exhibit 7.4, for example, lists what the *Encyclopedia of Business Information Sources* has to say about data sources on the electric appliance industry. Aspiring researchers are also well advised to acquaint themselves with the more important general sources of marketing information so that they know what statistics are available and where they can be found. Many of the most important of these are listed and briefly described in Appendix 7A.

On-line Computer Searches On-line computer searches have become increasingly popular for locating published information and data in the past 20 years, as computer-readable storage systems for databases have come into their own. Many public libraries, as well as college and university libraries, have invested in the equipment and personnel that are

EXHIBIT 7.4   Sources of Data on the Electric Appliance Industry

ELECTRIC APPLIANCE INDUSTRY
See also: Consumer Electronics

CD-ROM DATABASES

Business Indicators. Slater Hall Information Products. Monthly. $2,200.00 per year. On CD-ROM, includes 1) National Income and Product Accounts from 1929; 2) State Income and Employment data from 1958; and 3) Business Statistics from 1961 corresponding to the *Survey of Current Business.*

DIRECTORIES

Appliance—Appliance Industry Purchasing Directory. Dana Chase Publications, Inc. Annual. $40.00.

Appliance Manufacturer Buyers Guide. Business News Publishing Co. Annual. $25.00.

European Electrical Appliances Marketing Directory. Available from Gale Research Inc. 1993. $335.00. Second edition. Published by Euromonitor. Provides detailed information on approximately 3,600 manufacturers, retailers, and wholesalers of consumer electrical appliances in Europe. Industry trends are reviewed, and about 1,500 information sources relating to European appliance marketing are included.

FINANCIAL RATIOS

Almanac of Business and Industrial Financial Ratios. Leo Troy. Prentice Hall. Annual. $89.95. Contains financial ratios derived from federal tax returns. Ratios for each of about 200 industries are arranged according to company asset size.

Annual Statement Studies, Including Comparative Historical Data and Other Sources of Composite Financial Data. Robert Morris Associates: The Association of Bank Loan and Credit Officers. Annual. $119.00. Median and quartile financial ratios are given for over 400 kinds of manufacturing, wholesale, retail, construction, and consumer finance establishments. Data is sorted by both asset size and sales volume. Includes a clearly written "Definition of Ratios," a bibliography of financial ratio sources, and an alphabetical industry index.

NARDA's Cost of Doing Business Survey. North American Retailer Dealers Association. Annual. $150.00.

Tax and Financial Statement Benchmarks. Neil Sheflin. John Wiley and Sons, Inc. Annual. $145.00 Based on Internal Revenue Service data. Provides financial ratio information relating to a wide variety of factors for 235 specific industries. Ratio information is classified within each industry by company asset size.

ONLINE DATABASES

CITIBASE (Citicorp Economic Database). FAME Software Corp. Presents over 6,000 statistical series relating to business, industry, finance, and economics. Includes series from *Survey of Current Business* and many other sources. Time period is 1947 to date, with daily updates. Inquire as to online cost and availability.

PERIODICALS AND NEWSLETTERS

Appliance. Dana Chase Publications, Inc. Monthly. $60.00 per year.

Appliance Manufacturer. Business News Publishing Co. Monthly. $55.00 per year.

Appliance Service News. Gamit Enterprises, Inc. Monthly. $15.25.

Chilton's Product Design and Development. Chilton Co. Monthly. $50.00 per year.

Dealerscope Merchandising: The Marketing Magazine for Consumer Electronics and Major Appliance Retailing. North American Publishing Co. Free to qualified personnel; others, $65.00 per year. Formed by the merger *Dealerscope and Merchandising.*

Global Appliance Report: A Monthly Digest of International News Affecting the Home Appliance Industry. Association of Home Appliance Manufacturers. Monthly. Members, $250.00 per year; non-members, $350.00 per year.

NARDA News. North American Retail Dealers Association. Monthly. $36.00.

STATISTICS SOURCES

Business Statistics. Available from U.S. Government Printing Office. Biennial. $20.00. Issued by Bureau of Economic Analysis, U.S. Department of Commerce. Shows annual data for 29 years and monthly data for a recent four-year period. Statistics correspond to the Survey of Current Business.

Major Home Appliance Industry Fact Book: A Comprehensive Reference on the United States Major Home Appliance Industry. Association of Home Appliance Manufacturers. Biennial. $35.00. Includes statistical data on manufacturing, industry shipments, distribution, and ownership.

Major Household Appliances. U.S. Bureau of the Census. Annual. (Current Industrial Reports MA-36F.)

Survey of Current Business. Available from U.S. Government Printing Office. Monthly. $41.00 per year. Issued by Bureau of Economic Analysis, U.S. Department of Commerce. Presents a wide variety of business and economic data.

TRADE ASSOCIATIONS AND PROFESSIONAL SOCIETIES

Appliance Parts Distributors Association, 228 E. Baltimore St., Detroit, MI 48202. Phone: (313) 872-3658. Fax: (313) 872-5312.

Association of Home Appliance Manufacturers. 20 N. Wacker Dr., Suite 1500, Chicago, IL 60606. Phone: (312) 984-5800. Fax: (312) 984-5823.

National Appliance Service Association. 9247 Meridan St., Suite 216, Indianapolis, IN 46260. Phone: (317) 844-1602. Fax: (317) 844-4745.

National Association of Retail Dealers of America. 10 E. 22nd St., Lombard, IL 60148. Phone: (708) 953-8950. Fax: (708) 953-8957.

National Housewares Manufacturers Association, 6400 Shafer Court, Suite 650, Rosemont, IL 60018. Phone: (847) 292-4200. Members are manufacturers of housewares and small appliances.

Source: James Woy, ed., *Encyclopedia of Business Information Services,* 1997–98 (Detroit: Gale, 1996), p. 248.

necessary to make database searching available to their patrons. There are now more than 3,000 databases to pick from, with 200 to 300 of them applying to business.

The operation of the on-line services is as follows: There are a database producer, a database vendor, and a data user. The database producer collects and edits the information according to its own criteria. The producer then puts it on tape or compact disk and sells it to the vendor for a fee. The vendor mounts the tape or disk on a computer or may sell copies outright on CD-ROM disks. The vendor might combine or split the information to fit his or her own needs. Thus, the same database from different vendors might have different structures.

When accessing the database on-line, users pay whether they get the answer or not. The more information one gets, the more one pays. The user also pays for the use of the telephone lines, connect charges, and printing charges. Printing charges vary as a function of how much is printed and whether the printing occurs on-line or off-line at a more convenient time, in which case the output is mailed to the user. In sum, the costs of using a database on-line include: (1) planning and executing the search, (2) telephone-line charges, (3) connect charges, and (4) citation and printing charges. The big advantage of on-line searching is time savings. Some of the more well known database vendors are Compuserve, Data-Star (a subsidiary of Knight/Ridder), Knight/Ridder, Lexis/Nexis, and Questal-Orbit.

Databases are typically defined by the type of information they contain. For example, bibliographic databases provide references to magazine or journal articles. They will list the name of the article, the author, the title of the journal, and the date of publication. They are likely to include some key words that describe the contents of the article. Most bibliographic databases also provide an abstract or summary of the article. Some of the useful bases for marketers are those that contain the following:

- *Specific company or industry information*—The information in these databases comes primarily from reports filed with the Securities and Exchange Commission, stockholder reports, and stock market information. The databases cover financial, marketing, and product information, some company profiles, and the usual directory information, such as name of an organization, its address, and its phone number. Typical examples are *Moody's Corporate Profiles* and *Standard & Poor's Corporate Descriptions*.

- *Mergers, affiliations, ownership information*—These databases typically list by name the institutions and people that own a stock, and the ownership changes, including the mergers and acquisitions, that have taken place in the recent past or are pending. Typical examples are *Disclosure/Spectrum Ownership* and *Insider Trading Monitor*.

- *Company directory information*—There are a number of directories. They differ in the types of companies covered, and their geographic coverage. In addition to the name, address, and telephone number, many of the directories will list the primary and secondary Standard Industrial Classification (SIC) codes for the business. Typical examples are *Dun's Business Locator* and *Standard & Poor's Corporate Register*.

- *U.S. government contract information*—These databases are particularly useful to businesses dealing with the government. They contain information on whether a specific company has any government contracts and recent contract awards. Typical examples are *Commerce Business Daily* and *DMS Contract Awards*.

- *Economic information*—These databases contain general economic and demographic information. Some of it comes from U.S. census materials and some from the private sector. Many of these databases contain forecasts of future economic activity. Typical examples are *Cendata* and *PTS U.S. Forecasts*.

- *General business information*—These databases cover companies, industries, people, and products. The information from them comes primarily from trade and business-oriented journals, selected newspapers, and various reports. Typical examples are *ABI/Inform* and *Harvard Business Review*.

- *Brand name information*—These databases contain information on specific products, including what competitors might be doing with respect to new product introductions or expenditures on advertising and what company owns a specific trademark. Typical examples are *New Product Announcements* and *Thomas Register Online.*

- *People information*—These databases contain information on people who have been noted in the literature for their accomplishments in the arts, sciences, business, or other fields of endeavor. These databases are used to track people in the business world or inventors and the patents they hold. Typical examples are *American Men & Women of Science* and *Standard & Poor's Register—Biographical.*

As the preceding list indicates, companies use on-line databases to search for journal articles, reports, speeches, marketing data, economic trends, legislation, inventions, and

---

Ethical Dilemma 7.2

A marketing manager for a dog food manufacturer stumbled onto an important piece of competitive intelligence while visiting a local printer near her company's plant. While waiting to speak with the salesperson that handled her company's account, the manager noticed some glossy advertising proofs for one of its competitor's products. The ad highlighted some new low prices. When she mentioned the prices to the printer, she was told that they were part of a new advertising campaign. On her return to headquarters, the marketing manager called a meeting of her own company's management. As a result of that meeting, the company initiated a preemptive, price-cutting campaign of its own that effectively neutralized the competitor's strategy.

Did the marketing manager act ethically in reporting the information back to her own company?

Would your judgment be different if the proofs were in a folder and the marketing manager casually and somewhat inadvertently opened the folder while standing there? What if she did so on purpose after noticing that the folder pertained to the competitor?

Should information like this be entered into the firm's decision support system?

EXHIBIT 7.5 **How to Conduct a Database Search**

STEP 1 Specify the information to be sought and develop a "search strategy." The search strategy is a set of words that will be entered into the computer for the actual search. If the database being searched is unfamiliar, it is often valuable to develop the search strategy with the help of a specialist familiar with the database.

STEP 2 Log on to the database, either by loading the appropriate CD-ROM or by dialing the database computer via a modem. If dialing, the database computer will ask for identification to determine whether the searcher is an authorized user of the system. The user will reply by typing in a code. If it is accepted, the database computer will ask for the name of the database or file to be searched.

STEP 3 Input the search strategy. When the search strategy has been entered, the computer will begin the search and will report the number of matches. If the number of matches is large, the user may wish to add further qualifications to the terms used in the search to find the specific information he or she needs.

STEP 4 If the results are satisfactory, the user must decide the level of detail he or she wishes to see for each match made. The choices may include a simple bibliography, an annotated bibliography, a bibliography with abstracts, or the full text. The more detail the user wants, the more costly the search will be because of printing charges. Users doing a search via modem connections with the database computer will also need to decide whether to have the information printed at the computer site and delivered later by mail or United Parcel Service, or printed immediately at the terminal. Having the results delivered by mail or UPS is usually cheaper, since charges for the services are partially based on the amount of time the computer is connected to the user's terminal.

The Start Button
YAHOO!
http://www.yahoo.com

Yahoo! was cited repeatedly by members of our panel as the best all-around starting point for conducting research on the Web. Fans say it's the fastest way to find Web sites dedicated to any given subject.

But to get the most out of Yahoo, it's important to understand exactly how the site works. Unlike AltaVista and other so-called search engines, which use computers to automatically index every word at a Web site, Yahoo is a true directory. The sites it catalogs have been sorted by Yahoo's staff into subject categories, subcategories, and sub-subcategories.

That means you can click your way down through successive levels of subjects to find sites that interest you. For instance, choosing the category "Business and Economy" calls up a new set of selections, including "Employment," "Finance and Investment," and "Real Estate."

Here's where the directory vs. search engine difference comes in. Say you need to find the Web site for General Motors Corp. quickly but you aren't sure of the address. If you type "General Motors" into Yahoo's search box, the site comes back immediately with a category that lists all of GM's sites. But searching on the same phrase at a search engine would call up a list of Web pages that merely contain the words "General Motors," forcing a user to sift through dozens of pages before finding the actual GM corporate site.

One caveat: Because the Web is constantly changing, Yahoo's listings aren't always completely up-to-date. Don't be surprised if it turns out that a site listed in the directory has disappeared.

Desperately Seeking Something

ALTAVISTA
http://altavista.digital.com
EXCITE
http://www.excite.com
HOTBOT
http://www.hotbot.com

INFOSEEK
http://infoseek.go.com
LYCOS
http://www.lycos.com

Where Yahoo's directory-style guide is speedy, search engines are thorough—almost unbelievably so. And for that reason, nearly all of our experts said they keep at least one of these massive indexes in their arsenal of Web tools.

Generally, the time to enlist a search engine is when searches at a directory haven't panned out, when you are seeking something that may not be directly related to a Web site's topic or you just want to cast as wide a net as possible.

Favorite search engines varied among our group. But all of them operate on the same basic premise: Instead of categorizing complete sites the way Yahoo does, search engines operate by indexing individual words or groups of words found on the pages at Web sites. Think of a catalog that would index every word found in all the books of a library's collection.

As a result, search engines turn up word matches in the most unlikely places. Search for "General Motors" at Infoseek, for example, and you'll soon stumble upon the Web site for the Vancouver Canucks hockey team. Why? The pages contain multiple references to the Canucks' home arena: General Motors Place.

That kind of find may be serendipitous. Or, more likely, it may be completely irrelevant to the task at hand. Searching at one of these indexes may turn up tens of thousands of Web pages, requiring you to slog through page after page of results before locating something useful.

One tip for alleviating the tedium: Set aside 10 minutes to read through the "help" pages at the search engine you're using. All of these sites offer advanced search commands that can significantly narrow your results. For instance, at most sites, typing in two words would call up a list of pages that contain either word. But placing the two words within quotation marks will force the search engine to look for the words as one phrase ("fish food").

Source: Thomas E. Weber, "Watching the Web: Experts Pick Their Most Useful Sites," *The Wall Street Journal*, August 28, 1997, p. B26.

many other types of information on a particular topic. Some especially useful guides to on-line databases are described in Appendix 7a. Exhibit 7.5 explains how to conduct a database search.

In addition to using on-line databases, researchers can use the Internet to execute general searches of the World Wide Web to locate secondary data on a subject. To do so requires Web access through an access provider and one or more search engines. Search engines are needed because the Internet contains well over 10 billion words in documents that are not arranged for retrieval. Creators of search engines compile and index an electronic catalog of web contents, then provide the software needed to search through the index for key words or concepts specified by the user. The indices may be directory or word based or a combination of the two. The differences in perspective are described in Research Window 7.4, which also contains the recommendations of a panel of experts as to how to go about the task of searching the Web using some of the more popular search engines.

Back to the Case

For such a significant move as targeting what may become the largest minority group in the United States, banks are getting marketing research data from a variety of sources.

They are starting with government census data. This is what highlighted the opportunity in the first place, and it details where the market potential is greatest.

They are getting further insight and help from companies that specialize in marketing to Hispanics. Bank of America hired López Negrete, which is advising the company to take a three-pronged approach: identifying and providing relevant products, communicating in both English and Spanish, and "earning the right to do business with the community" through support of the community's interests.

Bank of America has also reviewed published research reports on Hispanic consumers, in particular their use of banking services. For example, the bank learned from a firm called EPM Communications that half of Hispanic consumers would use more banking services if they had a clearer understanding of their choices. Almost two-thirds told the researchers that they wished for better financial advice from their banks.

Some of the actions Bank of America has taken include staffing a customer service line with Spanish-speaking representatives, offering a choice of language at ATMs, seeking branch employees that reflect the area's demographics, and funding scholarships for minority students at the University of Dallas.

Wells Fargo & Company, based in San Francisco, sponsored a study to learn more about the needs of Hispanic-owned businesses. The study report, titled "Latino Owned Businesses: Access to Capital," told bank management that Hispanic business owners are much less likely than other business owners to have enough capital.

The bank determined that this was a business opportunity and launched a joint program with the United States

Hispanic Chamber of Commerce, in which the bank committed to lending $1 billion to Hispanic-owned businesses over a six-year period. The lending process is designed to be simple, and applications are available in a choice of English or Spanish. Wells Fargo's first year of experience with the program showed that a real demand exists. Lending through the program exceeded the bank's first-year forecast by 10 percent.

In Oklahoma, First Bethany's consultant, Jorge Esperilla, has contributed insights into Mexican culture and banking practices. (Most Hispanics in the area are of Mexican descent.) Esperilla observed that banks are less central to Hispanics than to other Americans, and that Hispanics have tended to avoid credit. Based on the results of his consulting work, and in his more recent role as president of First Bethany's new facility for Hispanic customers, Esperilla has developed a strategy. He emphasizes building ties to the local Hispanic community and educating them about the services the bank offers.

The combination of government data, published research, commissioned studies, and work by consultants and marketing specialists has equipped banks for their race to grab a share of the important Hispanic market.

Sources: Barbara Powell, "Texas Banks Want to Reach Minority Markets, But Not All Know How," *Fort Worth Star-Telegram* (April 5, 1999, downloaded from Dow Jones Publications Library at the Dow Jones Web site, www.dowjones.com, August 5, 1999); "Bank of America Hires Ad Agencies to Target Ethnic Segments," press release (July 1, 1999, downloaded from Bank of America Web site, www.bankofamerica.com, August 10, 1999); "Wells Fargo Exceeds Expectations, Lends $184 Million to Hispanic Business Owners in First Year of Latino Loan Program," press release (December 1, 1998, downloaded from Wells Fargo & Company Web site, www.wellsfargo.com, August 10, 1999); Gregory Potts, "Banking on the Hispanic Market," *The Journal Record* (May 26, 1998, downloaded from the Northern Light Internet site, www.northernlight.com, August 10, 1999); Gene Taylor, "Remarks at Hispanic Association on Corporate Responsibility," President's Breakfast Keynote, speech delivered June 12, 1998, in Miami, Florida (downloaded from Bank of America Web site, www.bankofamerica.com, August 10, 1999); Hugh Graham, "Annals of Marketing: Don't Go Changin'," *Globe and Mail* (September 25, 1998, downloaded from Dow Jones Publications Library at the Dow Jones Web site, www.dowjones.com, August 10, 1999).

Summary

Learning Objective 1

Explain the difference between primary and secondary data.

Secondary data are statistics not gathered for the immediate study at hand, but for some other purpose. Primary data are originated by the researcher for the purpose of the investigation at hand.

Learning Objective 2

Cite two advantages offered by secondary data.

The most significant advantages offered by secondary data are time savings and money savings for the researcher.

Learning Objective 3

Specify two problems common to secondary data.

Two problems that commonly arise when secondary data are used are (1) they do not completely fit the problem, and (2) they are not completely accurate.

Learning Objective 4

List the three criteria researchers should use in judging the accuracy of secondary data.

The three criteria researchers should use in judging the accuracy of secondary data are (1) the source, (2) the purpose of publication, and (3) general evidence regarding the quality of the data.

Learning Objective 5

State the most fundamental rule in using secondary data.

The most fundamental rule in using secondary data is to always use the primary source of secondary data.

Learning Objective 6

Explain the difference between internal and external data.

Internal data are those found within the organization for which the research is being done, while external data are those obtained from outside sources.

Learning Objective 7

List some of the key sources researchers should consider in conducting a search process.

The key sources researchers should keep in mind in conducting a search process are reference librarians, associations, on-line computer searches, and general guides to useful marketing information.

Learning Objective 8

Describe the roles of the database producer, database vendor, and data user in the operations of on-line computer search services.

The database producer collects and edits the information according to its own criteria, puts it on a computer tape or disk, and sells it to the vendor for a fee. The vendor mounts the tape or disk on a computer and sells access to it to the data user. The data user pays for citation and printing charges, connect charges, and telephone-line charges, and also incurs the cost of planning and executing the computer search. The vendor also pays the database producer a fee every time the database is used and a fee for all citations from it.

Review Questions

1. What is the difference between primary and secondary data?

2. What are the advantages and disadvantages of secondary data?

3. What criteria can be employed to judge the accuracy of secondary data?

4. What is the difference between a primary source and a secondary source of secondary data? Which is preferred? Why?

5. What distinguishes internal secondary data from external secondary data?

6. How would you go about searching the secondary data on a particular topic?

7. How would you perform an on-line computer search? What types of information would you be hoping to find?

Discussion Questions, Problems, and Projects

1. List some major secondary sources of information for the following situations:
   (a) The marketing research manager of a national soft-drink manufacturer has to prepare a comprehensive report on the soft-drink industry.
   (b) Mr. Baker has several ideas for instant cake mixes and is considering entering this industry. He needs to find the necessary background information to assess its potential.
   (c) Mr. Adams has heard that the profit margins in the fur business are high. The fur industry has always intrigued him, and he decides to do some research to determine if the claim is true.
   (d) A recent graduate hears that condominiums are the homes of the future. She decides to collect some information on the condominium market.
   (e) Owning a grocery store has been Mrs. Smith's dream. She finally decides to make this a reality. The first step she wishes to take is to collect information on the grocery business in her hometown.

2. Assume that you are interested in opening a fast-food Mexican restaurant in St. Louis, Missouri. You are unsure of its acceptance by consumers and are considering doing a marketing research study to evaluate their attitudes and opinions. In your search for information you find the following studies:
   Study A was recently conducted by a research agency for a well-known fast-food chain. To secure a copy of this study, you would be required to pay the agency $225. The study evaluated consumers' attitudes toward fast food in general based on a sample of 500 housewives for the cities of Springfield, Illinois; St. Louis and Kansas City, Missouri; and Topeka, Kansas. The findings indicated that respondents did not

view fast food favorably. The major reason for the unfavorable attitude was the low nutritional value of the food.

Study B was completed by a group of students as a requirement for an MBA marketing course. This study would not cost you anything, as it is available in your university library. The study evaluated consumers' attitudes toward various ethnic fast foods. The respondents consisted of a convenience sample of 200 students from St. Louis. The findings indicated a favorable attitude toward two ethnic fast foods, Italian and Mexican. Based on these results, one of the students planned to open a pizza parlor in 1997 but instead accepted a job as sales representative for General Foods Corporation.

(a) Critically evaluate the two sources of data.

(b) Which do you consider to be better? Why?

(c) Assume that you decide it will be profitable to become a franchisee in fast food. Identify five specific secondary sources of data and evaluate the data.

3. For many years, Home Decorating Products had been a leading producer of paint and painting-related equipment such as brushes, rollers, turpentine, and so on. The company is now considering adding wallpaper to its line. At least initially, it did not intend to actually manufacture the wallpaper but, rather, planned to subcontract the manufacturing. Home Decorating Products would assume the distribution and marketing functions.

Before adding wallpaper to its product line, however, Home Decorating secured some secondary data assessing the size of the wallpaper market. One mail survey made by a trade association showed that, on the average, families in the United States wallpapered two rooms in their homes each year. Among these families, 60 percent did the task themselves. Another survey, which had also been done by mail but by one of the major home magazines, found that 70 percent of the subscribers answering the questionnaire had wallpapered one complete wall or more during the last 12 months. Among this 70 percent of the families, 80 percent had done the wallpapering themselves. Home Decorating Products thus has two sets of secondary data on the same problem, but the data are not consistent.

Discuss the data in terms of the criteria one would use to determine which set, if either, is correct. Assume that you are forced to make the determination on the basis of the information in front of you. Which would you choose?

4. Assume that your school is interested in developing a marketing plan to boost sagging attendance at major athletic events, particularly home football games. As an initial step in developing the new marketing plan, the athletic department has decided that it needs demographic and lifestyle profiles of people who currently attend games on a regular (season-ticket) basis. Fortunately, the ticket office maintains a listing of all season-ticket purchasers (including names and addresses) from year to year. What potential sources of internal secondary data might the athletic department first investigate before considering the collection of primary data?

5. Using the 1996 U.S. *Statistical Abstract* answer the following questions.

(a) Which metropolitan statistical area in the United States has the largest population (based on 1994 numbers)?

(b) What is the population of this metropolitan area?

(c) What was the estimated median age of the U.S. population in 1995?

(d) Complete the following table:

MARITAL STATUS OF U.S. POPULATION	1995 (MILLION)	PERCENT OF TOTAL
Total		
Never Married		
Married		
Widowed		
Divorced		

(e) Complete the following table on school enrollment for 1994.

18–19 years old	20–24 years old	25–34 years old

(f) Complete the following table:

INCOME CATEGORY	TOTAL HOUSEHOLDS 1994
Under $5,000	
$5,000 to $9,999	
$10,000 to $14,999	
$15,000 to $19,999	
$20,000 to $24,999	
$25,000 to $34,999	
$35,000 to $49,999	
$50,000 to $74,999	
$75,000 and over	

(g) What was the consumer price index for all items in 1995? What was the base year? What does that indicate?

(h) Complete the following table:

INDUSTRY GROUP	RATIO OF PROFITS TO EQUITY (1995) (PERCENT)	PROFITS PER DOLLAR OF SALES (1995) (PERCENT)
Nondurable goods industries		
Food and kindred products		
Textile mill products		
Paper and allied products		

6. The *Statistical Abstract* is a secondary source of secondary data. Since it is always better to use the primary source, identify the primary source for the following data:
   (a) The estimated median age of the U.S. population for 1995.
   (b) The height of males and females ages 18–24.
   (c) The Consumer Price Indexes by major groups.
   (d) The manufacturing corporations' profits, stockholders' equity, sales, and debt ratios.

7. John Smith is interested in becoming a wholesaler in household appliances. He has collected some general information but requires your help in finding answers to the following questions.
   (a) What is the SIC code for household appliance manufacturers?
   (b) How many retail establishments sell household appliances in the United States?
   (c) What are the total sales of all the retail establishments?

   Instead of attempting to handle all household appliances, John is considering specializing in household refrigerators and freezers.
   (d) What are the total number of establishments manufacturing household refrigerators and freezers?
   (e) How many wholesale establishments are there in the United States dealing in this category?

   John thinks that Dayton, Ohio, would be a profitable place to locate. He needs to know the following:
   (f) What is the total population of Dayton, Ohio?
   (g) What is the total civilian labor force in Dayton, Ohio?

(h) How many persons are employed in Dayton, Ohio?
(i) What is the total number of furniture and home furnishing stores that have a payroll in Dayton, Ohio?
(Hint: To complete this exercise, refer to the *Census of Manufacturers, Census of Retail Trade, Census of Wholesale Trade,* and *County and City Databook.*)

8. Suppose you are interested in introducing a four-by-two-inch FM/AM radio that could be carried in a person's pocket.
    (a) What data would be useful in making your decision?
    (b) Identify the specific secondary sources and the data they would provide that would assist you in making your decisions.
    (c) Develop a brief report on the data you find.

9. In addition to on-line computer searches, many university and public libraries now offer off-line database search capability, using CD-ROM technology. Prepare a brief report outlining availability of both types of these information resources (on-line and off-line) in your area. Be sure to include the following information for each available service in your report:
    (a) name of service and type of information (e.g., bibliographic, statistical) available
    (b) location(s) of access point(s)
    (c) times available for use
    (d) name of contact person(s) for further information
    (e) any special skills required for use and availability of training, if needed
    (f) access fees, if any
    (g) report formats available (e.g., hard copy, transfer to diskette)

10. Interview representatives of your local media outlets (e.g., radio stations, television stations, and newspapers) and determine the extent to which they utilize sources of standardized marketing information. You may wish to use the following questions as a guideline for your interviews:
    (a) Which sources do they use?
    (b) What specific types of information do they obtain?
    (c) How do they use the information?
    (d) How important is the information in the conduct of their business?
    (e) How do they rate the accuracy of the information?
    (f) Do they supplement the standardized information with locally collected primary data?

11. Assume that you have recently begun work as a researcher with a very large management consulting organization. One of your first assignments is to prepare a thorough profile of a specific industry based on secondary data. For a significant industry of your choosing, develop such a profile. Your report should contain industry information related to major products, largest producers, primary inputs on the supply side, SIC codes, unions, trade magazines, and other information you feel is useful (including financial information). The information should be addressed to other businesspeople—not academicians—and should be presented in a readable manner using a format similar to the following:

     I   Executive Summary (including a synopsis of your opinion on the state of the industry along with the reasons for your opinion)
     II   Major Industry Competitors (including financial information)
     III   Major Industry Products (including export information)
     IV   Primary Industry Inputs (including import information)
     V   Human Resource/Labor Unions
     VI   Ownership Trends
     VII   Technology
     VIII   Governmental Regulation

Include two special exhibits with your profile—a chronology showing important events in the history of the industry, especially during the past ten years; and a flowchart of a typical firm in the industry showing inputs, primary products, channels of distribution, major customers, and so on.

You are encouraged to use as many sources as possible, including financial databases, business periodicals, and government reports. Prepare a complete bibliography of all sources used in preparing your report. In addition, carefully identify all sources throughout your report, including sources for graphs and charts.

Endnotes

1. Robert Ferber and P. J. Verdoorn, *Research Methods in Economics and Business* (New York: Macmillan, 1962), p. 208.

2. David W. Stewart and Michael A. Kamins, *Secondary Research: Information Sources and Methods,* 2d ed. (Thousand Oaks, Calif.: Sage Publications, 1993), p. 130. See also Kathy Friedman, *Case Studies for Better Business Decisions* (Washington, D.C.: U.S. Department of Commerce, 1992); and Richard E. Barrett, *Using the 1990 Census for Research* (Thousand Oaks, Calif.: Sage Publications, Inc., 1994) for discussion of the marketing-related information that is available from the federal and state governments and how that information can be used for such marketing tasks as market potential estimation, establishing sales quotas, allocating advertising budgets, and locating retail outlets.

3. Jacob has a particularly helpful discussion on the various errors that are present in published data and what remedies are available to the analyst for treating these errors. See Herbert Jacob, *Using Published Data: Errors and Remedies* (Thousand Oaks, Calif.: Sage Publications, 1984). The problem of accuracy in secondary data seems to be getting worse as the ability to generate and capture data expands. See William J. Bulkeley, "Databases Are Plagued by Reign of Error," *The Wall Street Journal* (May 26, 1992), p. 36.

4. For an alternative list of criteria, see Stewart and Kamins, *Secondary Research,* pp. 17–31.

5. Phaedra Hise, "Grandma Got Run Over by Bad Research," *Inc.* (January 1998), p. 27.

6. Erwin Esser Nemmers and John H. Myers, Business Research: *Text and Cases* (New York: McGraw-Hill, 1966), p. 38. See also William G. Zikmund, *Business Research Methods,* 4th ed. (Fort Worth: The Dryden Press, 1994).

7. *The Chicago Tribune,* September 19, 1960. If there had not been a cult of "baseball superfans whose passion is to dig up obscure facts about the erstwhile national pastime," the error might never have been discovered. See "You May Not Care but 'Nappie' Lajoie Batted .422 in 1901," *The Wall Street Journal* (September 13, 1974), p. 1.

8. Nemmers and Myers, *Business Research,* p. 43. For other illustrations of how knowledge of the source provides insights into the accuracy of the data, see Marilyn Chose, "Mixing Science, Stocks Raises Question of Bias in the Testing of Drugs," *The Wall Street Journal* (January 26, 1989), p. A1; Michael Miller, "High-Tech Hype Reaches New Heights," *The Wall Street Journal* (January 12, 1989), p. B1; Jeff Bailey, "How Two Industries Created a Fresh Spin on the Dioxin Debate," *The Wall Street Journal* (February 20, 1992), pp. A1, A6; "Leading Researchers Invite Criticism and They Get It," *Marketing News* 26 (June 22, 1992), p. 5; Cynthia Crossen, "How 'Tactical Research' Muddied Diaper Debate," *The Wall Street Journal* (May 17, 1994), pp. B1, B8.

9. Larry P. Stanek, "Keeping Focused on the Consumer While Managing Tons of Information," in *Presentations from the 9th Annual Marketing Research Conference* (Chicago: American Marketing Association, 1988), pp. 66–67. See also Joel D. Raphael and Richard Kitaeff, "The Research Information Center," *Marketing Research: A Magazine of Management & Applications* 2 (September 1990), pp. 50–52.

10. See, for example, Charles H. Sevin, *Marketing Productivity Analysis* (New York: McGraw-Hill, 1965), or Sanford R. Simon, *Managing Marketing Profitability* (New York: American Management Association, Inc., 1969), for two of the best treatments of sales and profitability analysis.

11. The figure and surrounding discussion are adapted from Stewart and Kamins, *Secondary Research.* See also Robert I. Berkman, *Find It Fast: How to Uncover Export Information on Any Subject,* 4th ed. (New York: Harper Collins, 1997).

12. "Complete Reference for Marketers' Web Site Launched," InfoTech Marketing press release (June 2, 1999, downloaded from the Yahoo! Finance Internet site, http://biz.yahoo.com, June 2, 1999); "The Marketing Source," InfoTech Marketing Web site, www.infotechmarketing.net/thesource.htm (downloaded August 11, 1999).

Suggested Additional Readings

For a general discussion of secondary data sources and how to go about finding secondary data, see
David W. Stewart and Michael A. Kamins, *Secondary Research: Information Sources and Methods*, 2d ed. (Thousand Oaks, Calif.: Sage Publications, 1993).

For discussion of the marketing-related information that is available from the federal and state governments and how that information can be used for such marketing tasks as estimating market potential, establishing sales quotas, allocating advertising budgets, locating retail outlets, and so on, see
Richard E. Barrett, *Using the 1990 Census for Research* (Thousand Oaks, Calif.: Sage Publications, 1994).
Kathy Friedman, *Case Studies for Better Business Decisions* (Washington, D.C.: U.S. Department of Commerce, 1992).

SECONDARY DATA SOURCES

There is so much published secondary data that it is impossible to mention all of it in a single appendix. For this reason, only a representative cross section of the available material is presented.[1] These secondary sources are organized into six sections, according to the type of information they contain. Several sources of electronic on-line search services are included. First, however, a brief discussion of governmental sources of secondary data is presented.

Census Data and Other Government Publications: Overview

The Bureau of the Census of the United States Department of Commerce is the largest gatherer of statistical information in the world. The original census was the Census of Population, which was required by the Constitution to serve as a basis for apportioning representation in the House of Representatives. The first censuses were merely head counts. Not only has the Census of Population been expanded, but the whole census machinery has also been enlarged. At this point there are nine different censuses, all of which are of interest to the marketing researcher. Exhibit 7.1, for example, listed some of the most useful data on population and housing that are available in the Census of Population. Exhibit 7A.1 lists some of the most useful data that are collected in the various economic censuses described in the following sections.

Census data are of generally high quality. Further, they are quite often available on the detailed level that the researcher needs. When data are not available in this form, researchers can create their own tabulations by purchasing either computer tapes or flexible diskettes from the Bureau of the Census for a nominal fee. Alternatively, researchers can contract with one of the private companies that market census-related products for information on a particular issue. Not only does this allow getting the information tailored to one's own needs, but it is also one of the fastest ways to get census data. Further, many of the private providers update the census data at a detailed geographic level for the between-census years.

There are two major drawbacks to the use of census data: (1) censuses are not taken every year, and (2) the delay from time of collection to time of publication is quite substantial, often two years or more. This last weakness, however necessary because of the massive editing, coding, and tabulation tasks involved, renders the data obsolete for many research problems. The first difficulty requires that the researcher supplement the census data with current data. Unfortunately, current data are rarely available in the detail the researcher desires. This is particularly true with respect to detailed classifications by small geographic area, unless one takes advantage of the services of a private provider with update capability.

The federal government also collects and publishes a great deal of statistical information in addition to the censuses. Some of this material is designed to supplement the various censuses and is gathered and published for this purpose (e.g., *Current Population Reports),* whereas other data are generated in the normal course of operations, such as collecting taxes, social security payments, claims for unemployment benefits, and so forth. Some publications also result from the desire to make the search for information more convenient.

---

[1]For more detailed treatment, see David W. Stewart and Michael A. Kamins, *Secondary Research: Information Sources and Methods,* 2nd ed. (Beverly Hills, Calif.: Sage Publications, 1993).
Source: The wonderful assistance of Eunice Graupner, Reference and Bibliographic Instruction Librarian in the University of Wisconsin School of Business Library, in revising this appendix is gratefully acknowledged.

Major Data Items	Retail Trade	Wholesale Trade	Service Industries	Construction Industries	Manufacturers	Mineral Industries
Number of Establishments and Firms						
All establishments	X			X		
Establishments with payroll	X	X	X	X	X	X
Establishments by legal form of organization	X	X	X	X	X	X
Firms	X	X	X		X	X
Single-unit and multi-unit firms	X	X	X		X	X
Concentration by major firms	X	X	X		X	
Employment						
All employees	X	X	X	X	X	X
Production (construction) workers				X	X	X
Employment size of establishments	X	X	X	X	X	X
Employment size of firms	X	X	X			
Production (construction) worker hours				X	X	X
Payrolls						
All employees, entire year	X	X	X	X	X	X
Production (construction) workers				X	X	X
Supplemental labor costs, legally required and voluntary	X	X	X	X	X	X
Sales Receipts, or Value of Shipments						
All establishments	X			X	X	X
Establishments with payroll	X	X	X	X		
By product or line or type of construction	X	X	X	X	X	X
By class of customer	X	X				
By size of establishments	X	X	X	X	X	X
By size of firm	X	X	X			
Operating Expenses						
Total	X	X	X			
Cost of materials, etc.	X	X		X	X	X
Specific materials consumed (quantity and cost)	X	X			X	X
Cost of fuels	X	X	X	X	X	X
Electric energy consumed (quantity and cost)	X	X	X		X	X
Contract work		X		X	X	X
Products bought and sold					X	X
Advertising	X	X	X			
Rental payments, total	X	X	X	X	X	X
Buildings and structures	X	X	X	X	X	X
Machinery and equipment	X	X	X	X	X	X
Communications services	X	X	X	X	X	X
Purchased repairs	X	X	X	X	X	
Capital Expenditures						
Total	X	X	X	X	X	X
New, total	X	X	X	X	X	X
Buildings/equipment	X	X	X	X	X	X
Used, total	X	X	X	X	X	X
Buildings/equipment				X		X

Industry Information

***Almanac of Business and Industrial Financial Ratios* (Englewood Cliffs, N.J.: Prentice-Hall)**   This publication contains the number of establishments, sales, and selected operating ratios for various industries (e.g., food stores). The figures are derived from tax return data supplied by the Internal Revenue Service and are reported for 12 categories, based on assets, within each industry. The data thus allow the comparison of a particular company's financial ratios with competitors of similar size.

***KR Information Ondisc: Business & Industry* (Beachwood, Ohio: Responsive Database Services, Inc.)**   Updated monthly, this CD-ROM database provides access to over 600 business journals and trade publications. All articles have extensive abstracts and over 60 percent contain the full text as well.

***Census of Agriculture* (U.S. Bureau of the Census: Government Printing Office)**
The *Census of Agriculture* was formerly taken in the years ending in "4" and "9." Since 1982, it has been taken in years ending in "2" and "7." This census offers detailed breakdowns by state and county on the number of farms, farm types, acreage, land-use practices, employment, livestock produced and products raised, and value of products. It is supplemented by the annual publications *Agriculture Statistics* and *Commodity Yearbook.* In addition, the Department of Agriculture issues a number of bulletins, which often contain data not otherwise published.

***Census of Construction Industries* (U.S. Bureau of the Census: Government Printing Office)**   Taken every five years (in the years ending with "2" and "7"), this census covers establishments primarily engaged in contract construction, in construction for sale, or in subdividing real property into lots. Statistics are provided for such things as value of inventories, total assets, and employment by state.

***Census of Government* (U.S. Bureau of the Census: Government Printing Office)**
The *Census of Government* presents information on the general characteristics of state and local governments, including such things as employment, size of payroll, amount of indebtedness, and operating revenues and costs. The census is authorized in the years ending in "2" and "7."

***Census of Manufacturers* (U.S. Bureau of the Census: Government Printing Office)**   The *Census of Manufacturers* has been taken somewhat irregularly in the past, but it is now authorized for the years ending in "2" and "7." It categorizes manufacturing establishments by type, using some 450 classes, and contains detailed industry and geographic statistics for such items as the number of establishments, quantity of output, value added in manufacture, capital expenditures, employment, wages, inventories, sales by customer class, and fuel, water, and energy consumption. *The Annual Survey of Manufacturers* covers the years between publications of the census, and *Current Industrial Reports* contains the monthly and annual production figures for some commodities.

***Census of Mineral Industries* (U.S. Bureau of the Census: Government Printing Office)**   The *Census of Mineral Industries* is taken in the years ending in "2" and "7." The information here parallels that for the *Census of Manufacturers* but is for the mining industry. The census offers detailed geographic breakdowns for some 50 mineral industries on such things as the number of establishments, production, value of shipments, capital expenditures, cost of supplies, employment, payroll, power equipment, and water use. The *Minerals Yearbook,* published by the Bureau of Mines of the Department of the Interior, supplements the *Census of Mineral Industries* by providing annual data, although the two are not completely comparable because they employ different classifications—an industrial classification for the Census Bureau data and a product classification for the Bureau of Mines data.

***Census of Retail Trade* (U.S. Bureau of the Census: Government Printing Office)**
The *Census of Retail Trade*, taken every five years in the years ending in "2" and "7," contains detailed statistics on the retail trade. Retail stores are classified by type of business, and statistics are presented on such things as the number of stores, total sales, employment, and payroll. The statistics are broken down by small geographic areas such as counties, cities, and standard metropolitan statistical areas. Current data pertaining to some of the information can be found in *Monthly Retail Trade*.

***Census of Service Industries* (U.S. Bureau of the Census: Government Printing Office)**   The *Census of Service Industries* is taken every five years in the years ending in "2" and "7." The service trade census provides data on receipts, employment, type of business (for example, hotel, laundry, and so on), and number of units by small geographic areas. Current data can be found in *Monthly Selected Services Receipts*.

***Census of Transportation* (U.S. Bureau of the Census: Government Printing Office)**   The *Census of Transportation* is taken in the years ending in "2" and "7." It covers three major areas: passenger travel, truck and bus inventory and use, and the transport of commodities by the various classes of carriers.

***Census of Wholesale Trade* (U.S. Bureau of the Census: Government Printing Office)**   The *Census of Wholesale Trade*, taken every five years in the years ending in "2" and "7," contains detailed statistics on the wholesale trade. For instance, it classifies wholesalers into over 150 business groups and contains statistics on the functions they perform, sales volume, warehouse space, expenses, and so forth. It presents these statistics for counties, cities, and standard metropolitan statistical areas. Current data can be found in *Monthly Wholesale Trade*.

***Commodity Yearbook* (New York: Commodity Research Bureau)**   Produced annually, this publication contains data on prices, production, exports, stocks, and so on for approximately 100 individual commodities.

***Guide to Industrial Statistics* (Washington, D.C.: U.S. Bureau of the Census)**   A guide to the Census Bureau's programs relating to industry, including the types of statistics gathered and where these statistics are published.

***Industry Norms and Key Business Ratios* (Murray Hill, N.J.: Dun & Bradstreet)**
This annual publication provides industry norm statistics for over 800 types of businesses.

***Inside U.S. Business: A Concise Encyclopedia of Leading Industries* (Burr Ridge, Ill.: Irwin Professional Publishing, 1994)**   Twenty-five major industries are discussed in detail, along with a description of top companies, recent trends, and key issues.

***Manufacturing USA: Industry Analyses, Statistics, and Leading Companies* (Detroit: Gale Research)**   This two-volume set provides comprehensive information on 458 manufacturing industries.

***Moody's Industry Review* (New York: Moody's Investors Service)**   This publication provides financial information on 137 industry groups and compares the performance of top companies within each industry.

***Predicast's Basebook* (Foster City, Calif.: Information Access Co.)**   Arranged by SIC code, this publication provides a wide array of statistical information on U.S. industries.

***Predicast's F&S Index Plus Text* (New York: Information Access Co.)**   This database provides citations, abstracts, and some full-text articles from over 2,400 business and trade publications. Coverage is international.

***RMA Annual Statement Studies* (Philadelphia: Robert Morris Associates)** This volume provides composite financial data on over 400 manufacturers, wholesalers, retailers, service providers, and agricultural endeavors.

***Service Industries USA: Industry Analyses, Statistics, and Leading Organizations* (Detroit: Gale Research)** Similar in format to *Manufacturing USA,* this volume provides comprehensive information on 150 service industries.

***Standard & Poor's Industry Surveys* (New York: Standard & Poor's Corporation)** Organized by broad industry headings, this quarterly publication consists of detailed articles as well as charts and graphs depicting trends in 52 areas.

***Standard Industrial Classification Manual* (Springfield, Va.: Office of Management and Budget, National Technical Information Service)** The *Standard Industrial Classification Manual* provides the basic system used for classifying industries into 11 major divisions. The SIC system is used for federal economic statistics classified by industry.

***U.S. Industry Profiles: The Leading 100* (Detroit Gale Research)** The 100 leading U.S. industries are described along with an industry outlook, the names of relevant associations, trade journals, statistical sources, and other sources of information.

***Worldcasts* (Foster City, Calif.: Information Access Co.)** Published quarterly, *Worldcasts* provides worldwide forecast information for regions and products. Forecast data are drawn from over 800 publications.

Company Information

***Directory of Corporate Affiliations Library* (Wilmette, Ill.: National Register Publishing)** An annual publication, the *directory of Corporate Affiliations* provides a description of which companies own more than 117,000 U.S. and international corporations.

***Fortune Directory* (New York: Time, Inc.)** Published annually by the editors of *Fortune* magazine, this directory provides information on sales, assets, profits, invested capital, and employees for the 500 largest industrial corporations in the United States.

***Hoover's Handbook of American Business* (Austin, Tex.: Hoover's Business Press)** This two-volume set profiles over 700 of the largest and fastest-growing companies in the United States. A useful "List-Lover's Compendium" is also included.

***How to Find Information About Companies* (Washington, D.C.: Washington Researchers, 1994)** A useful guide to locating information about specific companies.

***Million Dollar Directory* (New York: Dun & Bradstreet)** Published annually, this reference source lists the offices, products, sales, and number of employees for United States companies with assets of at least $500,000.

***Moody's Manuals* (New York: Moody's Investors Service)** Published annually, these eight sets of manuals contain balance sheets and income statements for individual companies and governmental units.

***Notable Corporate Chronologies* (New York: Gale Research, 1995)** This two-volume set compiles company histories for over 1,150 corporations worldwide and includes article citations for further reading.

Standard & Poor's Corporate Records **(New York: Standard & Poor's Corp.)** *Corporate Records* provides current financial statistics, news items, and background information on approximately 12,000 publicly traded companies.

Standard & Poor's Register of Corporations, Directors and Executives **(New York: Standard & Poor's Corp.)** This annual publication lists officers, products, sales, addresses, telephone numbers, and employees for more than 56,000 United States and Canadian public companies.

Thomas Food Industry Register **(New York: Thomas Publishing Co.)** This three-volume set provides detailed information on more than 40,000 food-related companies.

Thomas Register of American Manufacturers and Thomas Register Catalog File **(New York: Thomas Publishing Co.)** Published annually in paper and CD-ROM format, this multivolume publication lists the specific manufacturers of individual products and provides information on their addresses, branch offices, and subsidiaries.

Value Line Investment Survey **(New York: Value Line Publishing** This quarterly publication provides current information on 1,700 publicly traded companies. Although written with investors in mind, it offers concise yet comprehensive company information.

Market and Consumer Information

A Guide to Consumer Markets **(New York: The Conference Board)** Issued annually, this publication contains data on the behavior of consumers in the marketplace. It includes statistics on population, employment, income, expenditure, and prices.

Aging America—Trends and Projections **(U.S. Senate Special Committee on Aging and the American Association of Retired Persons: Government Printing Office)** This chartbook describes the sustained growth in America's elderly population expected during the next 30 years. Graphs and tables cover such areas as demographics, employment, health, and income.

Census of Housing **(U.S. Bureau of the Census: Government Printing Office)** The *Census of Housing* is published decennially for the years ending in "0." It was first taken in 1940 in conjunction with the *Census of Population* and lists such things as type of structure, size, building condition, occupancy, water and sewage facilities, monthly rent, average value, and equipment including stoves, dishwashers, air conditioners, and so on. For large metropolitan areas, it provides detailed statistics by city block. The periods between publications of the *Census of Housing* are covered by the bureau's annual *American Housing Survey.*

Census of Population **(U.S. Bureau of the Census: Government Printing Office)** The *Census of Population* is taken every ten years, in the years ending with "0." The census reports the population by geographic region. It also provides detailed breakdowns on such characteristics as sex, marital status, age, education, race, national origin, family size, employment and unemployment, income, and other demographic characteristics. The *Current Population Reports,* which are published annually and make use of the latest information on migrations, birth and death rates, and so forth, update the information in the *Census of Population.*

1990 Census of Population and Housing: User's Guide **(U.S. Bureau of the Census: Government Printing Office)** The *User's Guide* provides information about how the data were collected and the scope of every subject, discusses how to locate all the statistics for a given geographical area, and provides a glossary of terms used in the census. An index to summary tape files is also available.

County and City Databook **(U.S. Bureau of the Census: Government Printing Office)**   Published every five years, the *County and City Databook* serves as a convenient source of statistics gathered in the various censuses and provides breakdowns on a city and county basis. Included are statistics on such things as population, education, employment, income, housing, banking, manufacturing output and capital expenditures, retail and wholesale sales, and mineral and agricultural output.

County Business Patterns **(U.S. Department of Commerce: Government Printing Office)**   This annual publication contains statistics on a number of businesses by type and their employments and payrolls broken down by county. These data are often quite useful in industrial market potential studies.

Data Sources for Business and Market Analysis, **4th ed., Nathalie D. Frank (Metuchen, N.J.: Scarecrow Press, 1994)**   An annotated guide to original statistical sources arranged by source of information rather than by topic.

Editor and Publisher Market Guide **(New York: Editor and Publisher Magazine)**   Published annually, this guide contains data on some 265 metropolitan statistical areas, including location, population, number of households, principal industries, retail sales and outlets, and climate.

Marketing Economics Guide **(New York: Marketing Economics Institute)**   Issued annually, this publication provides detailed operating information on 1,500 retailing centers throughout the country on a regional, state, county, and city basis. It contains information on population, percent of households by income class, disposable income, total retail sales, and retail sales by store group.

Rand McNally Commercial Atlas and Marketing Guide **(Chicago: Rand McNally Company)**   Published annually, this atlas contains marketing data and maps for some 100,000 cities and towns in the United States. Included are such things as population, auto registrations, and retail trade.

Sales and Marketing Management Survey of Buying Power **(New York: Sales and Marketing Management)**   Published annually, this survey contains market data for states, a number of counties, cities, and standard metropolitan statistical areas. Included are statistics on population, retail sales, and household income, and a combined index of buying power for each reported geographic area.

State and Metropolitan Area Databook **(U.S. Department of Commerce: Government Printing Office)**   This book is a *Statistical Abstract* supplement put out by the Department of Commerce. It contains information on population, housing, government, manufacturing, retail and wholesale trade, and selected services by state and standard metropolitan statistical areas.

General Economic and Statistical Information

Business Statistics **(U.S. Department of Commerce: Government Printing Office)**   Published every two years, this publication provides a historical record of the data series appearing monthly in the *Survey of Current Business.*

***Economic Indicators* (Council of Economic Advisers: Government Printing Office)**   This monthly publication contains charts and tables of general economic data, such as gross national product, personal consumption expenditures, and other series important in measuring general economic activity. An annual supplement presenting historical and descriptive material on the sources, uses, and limitations of the data is also issued.

***Economic Report of the President* (U.S. Government: Government Printing Office)**   This publication results from the president's annual address to Congress about the general economic well-being of the country. The back portion of the report contains summary statistical tables using data collected elsewhere.

***Federal Reserve Bulletin* (Washington, D.C.: Federal Reserve System Board of Governors)**   Published monthly, this publication is an important source of financial data, including statistics on banking activity, interest rates, savings, the index of industrial production, an index of department store sales, prices, and international trade and finance.

***The Handbook of Basic Economic Statistics* (Washington, D.C.: Economic Statistics Bureau of Washington, D.C.)**   This monthly publication provides a compilation of more than 1,800 statistical series related to the national economy condensed from the volumes of information released by the federal government.

***Handbook of Cyclical Indicators* (Washington, D.C.: U.S. Department of Commerce)**   This monthly publication contains at least 70 indicators of business activity designed to serve as a key to general economic conditions.

***Historical Statistics of the United States from Colonial Times to 1970* (U.S. Bureau of the Census: Government Printing Office)**   This volume was prepared by the Bureau of the Census to supplement the *Statistical Abstract*. The *Statistical Abstract* is one of the more important general sources for the marketing researcher, since it contains data on many social, economic, and political aspects of life in the United States. One problem a user of *Statistical Abstract* data faces is incomparability of figures at various points in time because of the changes in definitions and classifications occasioned by a dynamic economy. *Historical Statistics* contains annual data on some 12,500 different series, using consistent definitions and going back to the inception of the series.

***Monthly Labor Review* (U.S. Bureau of Labor Statistics: Government Printing Office)**   This monthly publication contains statistics on employment and unemployment, labor turnover, earnings and hours worked, wholesale and retail prices, and work stoppages.

***Statistical Abstract of the United States* (U.S. Bureau of the Census: Government Printing Office)**   This annual publication reproduces more than 1,500 tables originally published elsewhere that cover such areas as the economic, demographic, social, and a political structure of the United States. The publication is intended to serve as a convenient statistical reference and as a guide to more detailed statistics. The latter function is fulfilled through references to the original sources in the introductory comments to each section, the table footnotes, and a bibliography of sources. The *Statistical Abstract* is a source with which many researchers begin the search for external secondary data.

***Statistics of Income* (Internal Revenue Service: Government Printing Office)**   This annual publication is prepared from federal income tax returns of corporations and individuals. There are different publications for each type of tax report—one for corporations, one for sole proprietorships and partnerships, and one for individuals. The

Corporate Income Tax Return volume, for example, contains balance sheet and income statement statistics compiled from corporate tax returns and broken down by major industry, asset size, and so on.

Survey of Current Business (U.S. Bureau of Economic Analysis: Government Printing Office)   This monthly publication provides a comprehensive statistical summary of the national income and product accounts of the United States. There are some 2,600 different statistical series reported, covering such topics as general business indicators, commodity prices, construction and real estate activity, personal consumption expenditures by major type, foreign transactions, income and employment by industry, transportation and communications activity, and so on. Most of the statistical series present data on the last four years.

United Nations Statistical Yearbook (New York: United Nations)   This annual United Nations publication contains statistics on a wide range of foreign and domestic activities, including forestry, transportation, manufacturing, consumption, and education.

World Almanac and Book of Facts (New York: Newspaper Enterprise Association)   Issued annually by the Newspaper Enterprise Association, this publication serves as a well-indexed handbook on a wide variety of subjects. Included are industrial, financial, religious, social, and political statistics.

General Guides to Business Information

American Marketing Association Bibliography Series (Chicago: American Marketing Association)   Published periodically, each of the publications provides an indepth annotated bibliography of a topic of interest in marketing.

Business Information: How to Find It, How to Use It, 2d ed., Michael R. Lavin (Phoenix, Ariz.: Oryx Press, 1992)   A general guide to searching for business information, this book provides useful information for the development of search strategies.

Business Information Sources, 3d ed., Lorna M. Daniells (Berkeley: University of California Press, 1993)   A guide to the basic sources of business information organized by subject area.

Census Catalog and Guide (U.S. Bureau of the Census: Government Printing Office)   This annual, cumulative catalog describes all products (reports, maps, microfiche, computer tapes, diskettes, and on-line items) that the Census Bureau has issued since 1980, including information about how to order the material. Also included is an appendix that includes, among other things, a directory of telephone numbers of Census Bureau specialists by area of expertise.

Encyclopedia of Business Information Sources, 11th ed. (Detroit: Gale Research, 1997)   A guide to the information available on various subjects, including basic statistical sources, associations, periodicals, directories, handbooks, and general literature.

Factfinder for the Nation (U.S. Bureau of the Census: Government Printing Office)   Issued irregularly, this series of publications describes the range of Census Bureau materials that are available on a variety of subjects and suggests some of their uses. A few of the subjects included are population statistics, housing statistics, statistics on race and ethnicity, availability of census records about individuals, and more.

***The Federal Database Finder* (Chevy Case, Md.: Information USA Inc.)** This useful resource provides a directory of over 4,200 no-cost and fee-based databases and data files that are available through the federal government.

***Guide to American Directories,* 13th ed., Bernard Klein (Coral Springs, Fla.: Todd Publications, 1993)** This guide provides information on directories published in the United States, categorized under 300 technical, mercantile, industrial, scientific, and professional headings.

***Guide to Foreign Trade Statistics* (Washington, D.C.: U.S. Bureau of the Census, 1991)** A guide to the published and unpublished sources of foreign trade statistics.

***A Handbook on the Use of Government Statistics* (Charlottesville, Va.: Taylor Murphy Institute)** This publication is designed to assist the businessperson with the use of government statistics. A series of brief case descriptions are presented.

***Statistics Sources,* 20th ed., Paul Wasserman, et al. (Detroit: Gale Research, 1997)** A guide to federal, state, and private sources of statistics on a wide variety of subjects.

***A User's Guide to BEA Information* (U.S. Bureau of Economic Analysis: Government Printing Office)** This booklet provides a directory for Bureau of Economic Analysis publications, computer tapes, diskettes, and other information sources.

Indexes

***ABI/Inform* (Ann Arbor, Mich.: UMI)** This core business database indexes 800 scholarly, trade, and popular business journals. The full text of some articles is available.

***American Statistics Index* (Washington, D.C.: Congressional Information Service)** Published annually and updated monthly, the publication is intended to serve as a comprehensive index of statistical data available to the public from any agency of the federal government.

***Business Index* (Foster City, Calif.: Information Access Company)** The *Business Index* is an index to over 460 business periodicals, *The Wall Street Journal, Barrons, The New York Times,* and business information from more than 1,100 general and legal periodicals. Index entries are arranged by subject and author in alphabetic order.

***Business Periodicals Index* (Bronx, N.Y.: The H. W. Wilson Company)** The *Business Periodicals Index* is a general purpose business index published monthly (with quarterly and annual compilations) and is composed of subject entries covering approximately 350 business periodicals.

***Communications Abstracts* (Thousand Oaks, Calif.: Sage Publications, Inc.)** *Communications Abstracts* provides an index to communications-related articles, books, and reports. It is issued quarterly and covers such topics as marketing, advertising, and mass communication.

***Dissertation Abstracts International* (Ann Arbor, Mich.: University Microfilms International)** Issued monthly, this publication contains descriptions of doctoral dissertations from nearly 500 participating institutions in North America and around the world. The approximately 35,000 annual entries are divided into three divisions: the humanities and social sciences, the sciences and engineering, and European abstracts.

The Information Catalog (**New York: FIND/SVP**)   *The Information Catalog* is a bimonthly publication of FIND/SVP, a business information and research firm. This resource contains overviews of reports, directories, reference works, and so on, that may be of interest to businesses. The reports have been produced by FIND/SVP and other research companies, publishers, and brokerage firms.

Journal of Marketing, "Marketing Literature Review" (**Chicago: American Marketing Association**)   Each quarterly issue of the *Journal of Marketing* includes a "Marketing Literature Review" section that indexes a selection of article abstracts related to marketing from the business literature. Abstracts are drawn from over 125 business journals; entries are indexed under a variety of marketing subject headings.

Social Sciences Citation Index (**Philadelphia: Institute for Scientific Information**)   Published three times yearly, with annual cumulations, this publication indexes all articles in about 1,400 social science periodicals and selected articles in approximately 3,300 periodicals in other disciplines.

Statistical Reference Index (**Washington, D.C.: Congressional Information Service**)   Published monthly with annual cumulations, this publication is a selective guide to American statistical publications from private organizations and state government sources.

The Wall Street Journal Index (**Princeton, N.J.: Dow Jones Books**)   Published monthly, *The Wall Street Journal Index* provides a subject index of information appearing in *The Wall Street Journal* in two sections—general news and corporate news.

▌Specialized Directories

American Business Locations Directory (**Detroit: Gale Research**)   This unique directory provides 50,000 site locations for 1,000 of the largest American corporations. Sites include manufacturing plants, branch offices, R&D centers, and subsidiaries.

American Marketing Association International Membership Directory & Marketing Services Guide (**Chicago: American Marketing Association**)   This directory, produced annually, contains an international directory of AMA members and member companies as well as a guide to providers of marketing services.

Business Organizations, Agencies, and Publications Directory (**Detroit: Gale Research**)   This directory serves as a guide to approximately 30,000 organizations, agencies, and publications related to foreign and domestic business, trade, and industry.

Consultants and Consulting Organizations Directory, **18th ed.** (**Detroit: Gale Research, 1997**)   This directory lists approximately 24,000 firms and individuals who are active in consulting and briefly describes their services and fields of interest.

Directories in Print, **13th ed.** (**Detroit: Gale Research, 1996**)   This directory is a descriptive guide to over 15,000 print and nonprint directories and includes a valuable keyword index

Directory of American Research and Technology, **31st ed.** (**New York: Bowker, 1997**)   A guide to research and development capabilities of more than 11,000 industrial organizations in the United States. It contains an alphabetical listing of the organizations, addresses of facilities, sizes of staffs, and fields of research.

***Encyclopedia of Associations* (Detroit: Gale Research)**   Published annually, this encyclopedia lists the active trade, business, and professional associations, and briefly describes their activities and lists their publications. Also available on CD-ROM.

***FINDEX, The Directory of Market Research Reports, Studies and Surveys* (Bethesda, Md.: Cambridge Information Group)**   This publication indexes and provides abstracts to more than 10,000 research reports produced by top U.S. and international research firms.

***Gale Directory of Databases* (Detroit: Gale Research)**   Published twice a year, this comprehensive guide describes more than 11,500 databases, 3,700 database producers, and 2,100 online services.

***Hoover's Masterlist of Major U.S. Companies* (Austin, Tex.: Hoover's Business Press)**   This annual volume gives brief histories and key statistics for the largest U.S. companies.

***Information Industry Directory* (Detroit: Gale Research)**   This directory lists and describes over 4,000 producers and vendors of electronic information.

***International Directory of Marketing Research Companies and Services* (New York: American Marketing Association, New York Chapter)**   This publication provides an alphabetic listing of domestic and international marketing research companies. A geographic listing is also provided, along with an index of principal personnel.

***Standard Directory of Advertisers* (Wilmette, Ill.: National Register Publishing Company)**   This annual directory lists over 25,000 companies with allotments for advertising campaigns of more than $75,000. Included are individual listings containing information on type of business, address, key personnel, advertising agency relationship, products advertised, media utilized, etc. The directory is published in two editions, one by product classification and one by geographic location.

***Standard Directory of Advertising Agencies* (Wilmette, Ill.: National Register Publishing)**   This annual directory lists approximately 10,000 advertising agencies and provides such information as personnel by title, key accounts, addresses, and telephone numbers.

Chapter 8

STANDARDIZED MARKETING INFORMATION SERVICES

L E A R N I N G   O B J E C T I V E S

Upon Completing This Chapter, You Should Be Able to

1. List three common uses of the information supplied by standardized marketing information services.

2. Define *geodemography*.

3. Describe the operation of a diary panel.

4. Describe the operation of store audits.

5. Define *UPC*.

6. Define *single-source measurement*.

7. Discuss the purpose and operation of people meters.

Case in Marketing Research

Marcie Chandler drives an hour each way, past all the region's big supermarket chains, in order to do her grocery shopping. Her destination is the Whole Foods Market in Plano, Texas. "I'd rather drive all this way and spend more—I mean, it costs a lot more to feed your family fresher products," Chandler, a college student, told a newspaper reporter.

Driving an hour to spend more? What's going on here? The attraction for Chandler is the desire to buy the most healthful food. Whole Foods specializes in natural and certified organic products, as well as hormone-free meat. Chandler explained, "I have a lot of heart disease in my family. It's a big concern for me. . . . It's worth knowing that you don't have the chemicals in your products."

Consumers like Chandler have fueled impressive growth for Whole Foods. The first Whole Foods Market opened in Austin, Texas, in 1980, when fewer than half a dozen natural food supermarkets existed in the United States. Expanding through acquisitions and construction, the chain now operates close to 100 stores. Sales of $1.4 billion in 1998 made Whole Foods the market leader among natural foods retailers. Furthermore, sales in Whole Foods's comparable stores (a comparison of year-to-year performance) rose 11 percent that year, compared with less than 2 percent growth for the supermarket industry overall. The company's plans call for continuing that pattern of growth.

Some nationwide trends are in Whole Foods's favor. Its specialty, natural foods, represents a fast-growing sector of the retailing industry nationwide. Industry analysts at the Salomon Smith Barney investment firm conservatively forecast 12 percent growth in annual sales of "natural" products, following several years of gains ranging from 15 to 20 percent.

But the industry growth is also attractive to competitors, including mainline supermarkets, which are adding natural and organic offerings to their product mix. Boston's Star Markets did so well when it introduced a section devoted to natural foods that it launched its own natural foods store, called Wild Harvest. In the Midwest, Dominick's has trained pharmacists to serve as "health solutions experts," providing advice on vitamins and homeopathic remedies as well as dispensing pills.

Traditional supermarkets have had the price advantage, but this may be changing. Whole Foods once charged 30 percent more than mainstream grocers, but as it has grown and expanded distribution channels, that price difference has fallen by half. Eventually, economies of scale may drive prices down even closer to those of traditional stores.

Other competition comes from rival natural foods chains. On the East Coast, Whole Foods competes with Wild Harvest and Nature's Heartland. Wild Oats Market has a significant presence in the western United States and Canada. Although it is still a smaller company than Whole Foods, it has doubled in size to 78 stores between 1996 and 1999. Wild Oats has also launched a new format, called People's Market. These stores offer a more limited selection and plainer stores. They lure customers with lower prices (5 to 15 percent below Wild Oats) and the tongue-in-cheek slogan "Good food for the masses."

With competition as colorful and varied as a Whole Foods produce display, how can the retailer stay at the top of the heap?

Discussion Issues

1. To maintain its competitive strength, what does Whole Foods need to know about its customers?

2. What does it need to know about how its customers respond to its product selection and other marketing decisions, including pricing and advertising?

3. How can Whole Foods obtain this information?

The many standardized marketing information services that are available are another important source of secondary data for the marketing researcher. These services are available at some cost to the user and in this respect are a more expensive source of secondary data than published information. However, they are also typically much less expensive than primary data, because purchasers of these data share the costs incurred by the supplier in collecting, editing, coding, and tabulating them. Because it must be suitable for a number of users, though, what is collected and how the data are gathered must be uniform. Thus, the data may not always ideally fit the needs of the user, which is their main disadvantage over primary data.

This chapter describes some of the main types and sources of standardized marketing information service data.

Profiling Customers

Market segmentation is common among businesses seeking to improve their marketing efforts. Effective segmentation demands that firms group their customers into relatively homogeneous groups. That enables them to tailor marketing programs to the individual groups, thereby making the programs more effective. A common segmentation base for firms selling industrial goods takes into account the industry designation or designations of its customers, most typically by means of the Standard Industrial Classification (SIC) codes. The SIC codes are a system developed by the U.S. Census Bureau for organizing the reporting of business information, such as employment, value added in manufacturing, capital expenditures, and total sales. Each major industry in the United States is assigned a two-digit number, indicating the group to which it belongs. The types of businesses making up each industry are further identified by additional digits. Figure 8.1 displays a partial breakdown of the construction industry.

One of the commercial services that is especially popular among industrial goods and service suppliers is Dun's Business Locator, an index on CD-ROM that provides basic data on over 10 million U.S. businesses including the SIC code of each establishment. These records allow sales management to construct sales prospect files, define sales territories and measure territory potentials, and isolate potential new customers with particular characteristics. They allow advertising management to select potential customers by size and location; to analyze and select the media to reach them; to build, maintain, and structure current mailing lists; to generate sales leads qualified by size, location, and quality, and to locate new markets for testing. Finally, they allow marketing research professionals to assess market potential by territory, to measure market penetration in terms of numbers of prospects and numbers of customers, and to make comparative analyses of overall performance by districts and sales territories and in individual industries.

Firms selling consumer goods can ill afford to target individual customers, because no single customer is likely to buy much of any product or service. Rather, firms need to target groups of customers. Their ability to do this has increased substantially since the 1970 census, which was the first electronic census. Since that time, the Census Bureau has made available computer tapes of the facts that have been gathered and, more recently, CD-ROMs, which also make the data usable by those with personal computers. Having the data available in electronic form allows their tabulation by arbitrary geographic boundaries, and an entire industry has developed to take advantage of this capability. The **geodemographers,** as they are typically called, combine census data with their own survey

Geodemography
The availability of demographic, consumer-behavior, and lifestyle data by arbitrary geographic boundaries that are typically quite small.

FIGURE 8.1   **Partial Breakdown of Standard Industrial Classification (SIC) Codes**

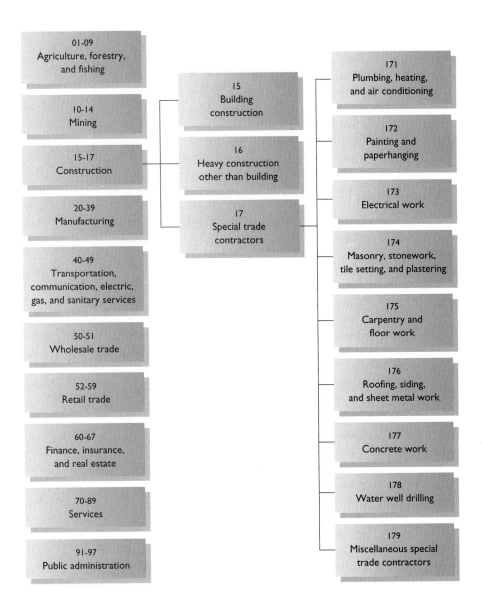

data or data that they gather from administrative records, such as motor vehicle registrations or credit transactions, to produce customized products for their clients.

For example, R. L. Polk has a product for retailers called the Vehicle Origin Survey. Polk gathers license-plate numbers from cars parked in shopping centers and matches them against Polk's National Vehicle Registration Database to find out where these retail customers live. The shopping center can then use plots of its customers' residences to determine its trading area.[1] Moreover, the locations can be computer matched with the Census Bureau's demographics for the area using its TIGER files, thereby providing a demographic profile of the people who shop there.

Mapping software, at its most sophisticated called a geographic information system (GIS), combines various kinds of demographic data with geographic information on maps. The user can draw a map showing average income levels of a county, then zoom

Maps, Inc., is the marketing research division of a large credit card company. The division specializes in the preparation of geodemographic maps. To prepare these maps, it combines information from customers' credit card transactions with the demographic data it collected when the customers applied for a credit card. Then, with its profiles of who is purchasing what, in combination with census data on small geographic areas, Maps, Inc., is able to develop maps that display by ZIP Code area the potential market for various types of products and services. The company in turn sells this information to various manufacturers, wholesalers, and retailers after customizing the data to the geographic boundaries specified by the client.

- Is it ethical to use credit card transaction information in this way?

- Do the credit card users have a right to know this research is being conducted?

- Should it be necessary for Maps, Inc., to get signed releases from individual cardholders before incorporating the individuals' purchase transactions in the database? What might happen to the quality of the data with the requirement of signed releases?

closer to look at particular towns in more detail. Most GIS programs on the market can show information as detailed as a single block; some programs can show individual buildings. Seeing the information on a map can be more useful than merely reading tables of numbers. At PepsiCo, a GIS enabled marketers to analyze traffic patterns and consumer demographics to identify the best sites for new Taco Bell and Pizza Hut restaurants.[2]

GISs once required mainframe computers and could cost more than $100,000, but today's applications are usually off-the-shelf programs that can run on personal computers. Microsoft's Excel, the popular spreadsheet program, contains a GIS function. Programs designed specifically for use as GISs include EasyStreet (by OverPlay Data company), Maptitude (Caliper Corporation), MapInfo (MapInfo), MapLinx (MapLinx) and GeoWizard (GeoDemX); some of these cost less than $500.

Another thing that the geodemographers do is regularly update the census data through statistical extrapolation. The data can consequently be used with much more confidence during the years intervening between the censuses. Another value-added feature that has had a great deal to do with the success of the industry has been the analysis performed on the census data. Firms supplying geodemographic information have cluster-analyzed the census-produced data to produce "homogeneous groups" that describe the American population.

For example, Claritas (the first firm to do this and still one of the leaders in the industry) used over 500 demographic variables in its PRIZM (Potential Ratings for Zip Markets) system when classifying residential neighborhoods. This system breaks the 250,000 neighborhood areas in the United States into 40 types based on consumer behavior and lifestyle. Each of the types has a fancy name that theoretically describes the type of people living there, such as Urban Gold Coast, Shotguns and Pickups, Pools and Patios, and so on. Figure 8.2, for example, describes the Towns and Gowns cluster.

Claritas or the other suppliers will do a customized analysis for whatever geographic boundaries a client specifies. Alternatively, a client can send the ZIP Code addresses of some customer database, and the geodemographer will attach the cluster codes. Researchers can request information, ranging from four-page descriptions of Prizm clusters to detailed maps, by submitting requests via an on-line connection with Claritas. A somewhat more limited set of information is available over the Internet at the Claritas Web site.[3,4]

FIGURE 8.2 Sample Cluster Profile from the PRIZM System

The **Towns and Gowns** cluster describes most of our college towns and university campus neighborhoods. With a typical mix of half locals (Towns) and half students (Gowns), it is wholly unique, with thousands of penniless 18–24 year-old kids, plus highly educated professionals, all with a taste for products beyond their evident means.

Predominant Characteristics

- Household (%U.S.): 1,290,200 (1.4%)
- Population: 3,542,500
- Demographic Caption: College Town Singles
- Ethnic Diversity: Dominant White, High Asian
- Family Type: Singles
- Predominant Age Ranges: Under 24, 25–34
- Education: College Graduates
- Employment Level: White-Collar/Service
- Housing Type: Renters/Multi-Unit 10+
- Density Centile: 58 (1=Sparse, 99=Dense)

Lifestyle

More Likely To:
Go to college football games
Play racquetball
Go skiing
Play billiards/pool
Use cigarette rolling paper
Use a charter/tour bus

Products and Services

More Likely To:
Have a personal education loan
Use an ATM card
Own a Honda
Buy 3+ pairs of jeans annually
Drink Coca-Cola Classic
Eat Kraft Macaroni and Cheese

Radio/TV

More Likely To:
Listen to CHR/rock radio
Watch VH1
Watch *Jeopardy*
Listen to variety radio
Watch *The Simpsons*

Print

More Likely To:
Read *Self*
Read newspaper comics section
Read *Rolling Stone*
Read *GQ*

Applying geodemographics to cyberspace has been tricky, because people can visit any Internet address from just about anywhere in the world. However, a company called ZDNet, which offers advertising space on dozens of Web sites, offers the ability to target ads based on a rudimentary form of geodemographic data. Whereas some e-mail addresses (such as those from America Online) don't tell much, others are associated with Internet service providers in particular geographic areas or computer users at particular companies. ZDNet combines this general information about the user's location with a database on 2.5 million users who have registered with the firm, thereby providing information about themselves and their interests. On-line wine retailer Evineyard has used ZDNet data to target Internet advertising to users in the states where it is permitted to ship wine.[5]

Measuring Product Sales and Market Share

A critical need in today's increasingly competitive environment is for firms to have an accurate assessment of how they are doing. A common yardstick for that assessment is sales and market share. Firms selling industrial goods or services typically track their own sales and market shares through analyses of their sales invoices. They also obtain feedback from the sales department in terms of how they did in various product or system proposal competitions. An alternative source that companies use to measure their market share is one of the on-line bibliographic data sources discussed in the preceding chapter. Many times a search of an appropriate database will turn up published studies containing product, company, and market information, including market share statistics.

Manufacturers of consumer goods also monitor their sales by account through the examination of sales invoices. For them, though, that is only part of the equation to determine how they are doing. Using factory shipments as a sales barometer neglects the filling or depleting of distribution pipelines that may be occurring. The other part of the equation involves the measurement of sales to final consumers. Historically there are several ways that such measurements have been handled, including the use of diary panels of households and the measurement of sales at the store level.

Diary Panels

The diary panels operate similarly. For example, the NPD Group panel, which is the largest in the United States, comprises more than 13,000 reporting households, who use a preprinted diary to record their monthly purchases in approximately 30 product categories. Figure 8.3 illustrates the sample diary for Toys & Games/Hobby & Craft Purchases. Note that the diary asks for considerable detail about the toy purchased, including the price paid, store where purchased, age and sex of both the recipient and the purchaser, as well as other specific characteristics of the purchase.

The households composing NPD are geographically dispersed but demographically balanced so they can be projected onto the population of the United States. Panel members are recruited quarterly and are added to the active panel after they have satisfactorily met NPD's reporting standards. Panel members are compensated for their participation with gifts, and families are dropped from the panel at their request or if they fail to return three of their last six diaries.

The diaries are returned to NPD monthly, the purchase histories are aggregated, and reports prepared. Using these reports, the subscribing company is able to assess (among other things) the following:

- The size of the market, the proportion of households buying over time, and the amount purchased per buyer

- Manufacturer and brand shares over time

- Brand loyalty and brand-switching behavior

- Frequency of purchase and amount purchased per transaction

- Influence of price and special price deals, as well as average price paid

- Characteristics of heavy buyers

- Impact of a new manufacturer or brand on the established brands

- Effect of a change in advertising or distribution strategy[6]

For example, the Toy Manufacturers of America, the industry trade group, found through analysis of NPD data that a fundamental shift occurred in where toys are purchased. There has been a decline in use of toy departments in department and discount stores and an increasing use of toy supermarkets like Toys "R" Us and Child World.

FIGURE 8.3   Sample Page from the NPD Group, Inc.

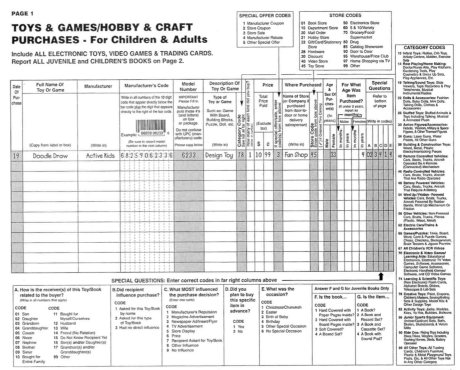

Source: Courtesy of The NPD Group, Inc., Port Washington, N.Y.

Store Audits

Another historically popular way of measuring sales to ultimate customers is at the store level using either store audits or scanners. Scanners reflect the new way; store audits, the old. However, audits are still used in some stores that do not as yet use scanners, primarily because the products they sell do not lend themselves to scanner processing or the stores have not made the investment in scanner equipment.

The basic concept of a store audit is very simple. The research firm sends field workers, called auditors, to a select group of retail stores at fixed intervals. On each visit the auditors take a complete inventory of all products designated for the audit. The auditors also note the merchandise moving into the store by checking wholesale invoices, warehouse withdrawal records, and direct shipments from manufacturers. Sales to consumers are then determined by the following calculation:

Beginning inventory + Net purchases (from wholesalers and manufacturers)
– Ending inventory = Sales

The store audit was pioneered by ACNielsen and served as the backbone of the *Nielsen Retail Index* for many years. The method is still used to measure sales for small, independent grocery stores, convenience stores, and liquor stores and to gather other information. The company takes the auditing records and generates the following information for each brand of each of the products audited:

According to store audit figures recently released by ACNielsen, toy industry sales, including video games, hit $27.2 billion in 1998, with dollar sales up 16.6 percent and unit sales up 11 percent. With the success of toys such as Beanie Babies, electronic games, and Furby, even grocery marketers found themselves in the toy business. The Shop-Rite chain piles up Beanie Babies in special bins throughout the store, and Barbie has debuted at other chains. Wal-Mart nabbed the top-selling retail position for toys in general, selling 17.4 percent of all toys.

Source: Courtesy of *Progressive Grocer.*

- Sales to consumers

- Purchases by retailers

- Retail inventories

- Number of days' supply

- Out-of-stock stores

- Prices (wholesale and retail)

- Special factory packs

- Dealer support (displays, local advertising, coupon redemption)

Subscribers to the ACNielsen service can get these data broken down by competitor, geographic area, or store type. ACNielsen will also provide special reports to clients for a fee. These special reports include such things as the effect of shelf facings on sales; the sales impact of different promotional strategies, premiums, or prices; or the analysis of sales by client-specified geographic areas. The stores pinpointed for inclusion in the panel are contacted personally to secure their cooperation. Further, the stores are compensated for their cooperation on a per-audit basis.

Scanners

Scanner
An electronic device that automatically reads the Universal Product Code imprinted on a product, looks up the price in an attached computer, and instantly prints the description and price of the item on the cash register receipt.

Since the late 1970s, ACNielsen has been replacing its *Retail Index* service with its SCAN-TRACK service. The SCANTRACK service emerged from the revolutionary development in the grocery industry brought about by the installation of scanning equipment to read Universal Product Codes (UPCs). Universal Product Codes are 11-digit numbers imprinted on each product sold in a supermarket. The first digit, called the number system character, indicates the type of product it is (e.g., grocery or drug). The next five digits identify the manufacturer and the last five a particular product of the manufacturer, be it a different size, variety, or flavor. See Figure 8.4.

There is a unique 11-digit code for each product. As the product with its bar code is pulled across the **scanner,** the scanner identifies the 11-digit number, looks up the price in the attached computer, and immediately prints the description and price of the item on

FIGURE 8.4 **Universal Product Codes**

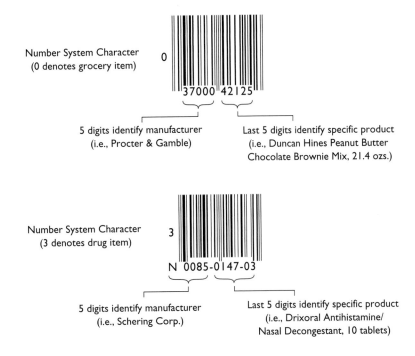

Number System Character
(0 denotes grocery item) 0

37000 42125

5 digits identify manufacturer
(i.e., Procter & Gamble)

Last 5 digits identify specific product
(i.e., Duncan Hines Peanut Butter
Chocolate Brownie Mix, 21.4 ozs.)

Number System Character
(3 denotes drug item) 3

N 0085-0147-03

5 digits identify manufacturer
(i.e., Schering Corp.)

Last 5 digits identify specific product
(i.e., Drixoral Antihistamine/
Nasal Decongestant, 10 tablets)

Ethical Dilemma 8.2

Toys-4-Kids, a major toy manufacturer, wishes to monitor changes in its sales, market share, and household penetration through the establishment and maintenance of a panel of households having children ages 12 and under. The households will be asked to record their purchases of all toys and games. Jean Blue, the marketing research director, believes it will be best to withhold the sponsor's name when recruiting households for the panel. She thinks that if the panel members know the research is being conducted by Toys-4-Kids, their reporting behavior could be biased.

- If the panel members are volunteers, do they have a right to know who is sponsoring the panel?

- If they are compensated for their participation, do they have a right to know who is sponsoring the panel?

- Do you think a household's reporting behavior will be biased if the household knows Toys-4-Kids is sponsoring the research?

the cash register receipt. At the same time, the computer can keep track of the movement of every item that is scanned.

Scanners are now so pervasive that the majority of retail-sales information today is based on scanner data. Utilizing either a sample of stores to represent a channel or a census of all stores to represent a retail organization, scanning data is available across multiple outlets, including grocery, mass merchant, drug, special warehouse clubs, and selected convenience stores. Where scanning is available, weekly sales (units sold at what price) are collected from a retailer's system. ACNielsen takes this data and matches the UPC to a description to make the information analytically useful (e.g. share of category, full fat versus low fat, etc.). Additionally, other "causal" data sources are combined with this information.

Causal data is collected to help explain the "causes" of sales fluctuations. Causal data includes:

* Display information—stores are audited and items on display are recorded;

* Feature information—features are collected and coded to identify items being advertised;

* Price decreases—the system identifies decreases via comparisons to historical prices.

By combining the retail sales and causal data, the effectiveness of various marketing actions can be assessed. This is accomplished by estimating what "base" sales would have been without the presence of the action. The data allow clients to evaluate the effectiveness of short-term promotions, to evaluate pricing changes, to follow new product introductions, and to monitor unexpected events, such as product recalls and shortages.

Scanners' effect on the collection of sales and market share data has been profound. Research Window 8.1 provides an example. Scanners also provide an ability to link purchase behavior with demographic information. Before the advent of scanners, the link was made using diaries. A problem with diaries is that they depend for their accuracy on the conscientiousness of those in the panel to record their purchases as they occur. Scanner data are not subject to such recording biases. Several firms have developed systems over the last few years to take advantage of this fact, including Information Resources and Nielsen. A key feature of the new systems is the ability to link television-viewing behavior with product-purchasing behavior to produce what has become known as *single-source* data.

The basics of single-source research are straightforward. As an example, consider the operation of the Information Resources BehaviorScan system. In each of the markets in which BehaviorScan operates, more than 3,000 households have been recruited by Information Resources to present identification cards at each of the grocery stores or drugstores every time their members make a purchase. Almost all the supermarkets and drugstores in each area are provided scanners by Information Resources.[7] Each household member presents his or her identification card when checking out. The card is scanned along with the purchases, allowing Information Resources to relate a family's purchase by brand, size, and price to the family's demographic characteristics and the household's known exposure to coupons, newspaper ads, free samples, and point-of-purchase displays.

Information Resources also is able to direct different TV advertising spots to different households through the "black boxes" that have been attached to the television sets in each test household, in cooperation with the cable television systems serving the markets. This allows Information Resources to monitor the buying reactions to different advertisements or to the same advertisement in different types of households (e.g., whether the buying reactions to a particular ad are the same or different among past users and nonusers of the product). This targetable television capability allows Information Resources to balance the panel of members for each ad test within each market according to the criteria the sponsor chooses (e.g., past purchases of the product), thereby minimizing the problem of having comparable experimental and control groups.

Nielsen's system is designed to measure natural consumer behavior rather than test the effects of different promotions or advertising. Its Homescan Service maintains a panel of 52,000 participating households whose purchases are measured through an electronic wand they are asked to pass over the UPC codes on products brought into the house. The electronic unit then queries them with respect to where the purchase was made, age and sex of the shopper, price paid, and deal type if any, among other things. The information from each household is downloaded once a week to Nielsen's computer simply by transmitting the data over the telephone.[8] Some of the other types of analyses that are possible with Homescan are described in Exhibit 8.1.

As retailers get used to single-source measurement and see a return on using it, and as companies like ACNielsen gain experience in collecting the data, these services are expanding. For example, ACNielsen has recently adapted Homescan to cover fresh foods sold

An Example of the Impact of Scanners

HARTSDALE, N.Y.—TVT Records President Steve Gottlieb spends his Wednesday mornings hunched over a computer screen, studying numbers that tell him whether he's having a good week.

Most music industry executives are doing the same thing, since that's the day SoundScan transmits data showing how many albums Alanis Morissette, Stone Temple Pilots, and other artists have sold.

SoundScan, a company that didn't exist at the dawn of the 1990s, in five years has transformed the record business simply by providing an accurate accounting of how the product is selling.

Information provided by SoundScan has changed the way music is marketed, rerouted concert tours and leveled the playing field between major record companies and independents.

SoundScan's leaders, Michael Fine and Michael Shalett, formed a partnership in the late 1980s to set up focus groups of music consumers. Fine had a background in political polling and Shalett in radio and record promotion. They decided to compete with Billboard, the music industry's chief trade paper, which was trying to establish a computerized system for tracking music sales to make its record charts more accurate.

For all the money at stake, compiling the weekly Top 40 list was unscientific. Trade publications would ask selected record stores to phone in reports of their top sellers. It was susceptible to manipulation—a store owner might be persuaded to inflate the sales of a certain disc in return for, say, tickets to a hot concert.

SoundScan signed major retail chains like Musicland, Trans World, and Camelot to exclusive deals letting the company keep track of sales through bar codes. The system went on-line in January 1991.

It took until the middle of that year to establish a market. But when Sony became the first major record company to sign up for SoundScan's service, most of the others quickly followed suit. So did artist managers, concert promoters,

and the ABC Radio network. Billboard abandoned its own efforts and began basing its charts on SoundScan's data.

Suddenly, the industry had a comprehensive record of what was selling and where. Not only could it tell how many discs Madonna really sold, it could also see if opera was hot in Omaha or alternative rock big in Albuquerque.

SoundScan showed that many discs sell the most copies in their first week of release, with only the true hits growing in sales as time went on. It's the sort of information that guides advertising and marketing decisions; many record stores now host events on the release data of a much-awaited album.

Record companies tend to show more patience in supporting new artists if SoundScan data shows these musicians are making an impact, said Geoff Mayfield, Billboard's charts director.

Artists such as Sheryl Crow, Hootie & the Blowfish, and Morissette might not have been a success in the pre-SoundScan era, he said.

Large record companies, no longer able to manipulate charts to help their artists, now face tougher competition from nimble independent labels like Tommy Boy, he said.

Marketers use SoundScan's information in very specific ways. Concert promoters are able to see where an artist is doing well and are using that information in scheduling tours.

SoundScan measures sales in close to 13,000 music outlets in the United States representing between 85 percent and 90 percent of the total music sold, Shalett said.

Many independent stores are missing from SoundScan's count. Mayfield's heard his share of gripes from industry officials who see this as a crucial weakness; they believe their discs are selling big in the stores not counted. He discounts most complaints as sour grapes.

Source: David Bauder, "Tracking Sales by Computer Transforms Music Industry," *Wisconsin State Journal* (May 28, 1996), p. 5B.

EXHIBIT 8.1	Types of Analyses Possible Using ACNielsen's Homescan Service	

Type	Purpose	Key measures
Market Overview/Trend Analysis	To provide a general overview of consumer purchasing for a particular product category, its major segments, and major brands. Measures are compared between brands and over time to identify changes and developments in the marketplace. Data can be analyzed for any period, can be looked at across/within outlet types, or can be looked at for specific consumer groups (e.g., heavy buyers, microwave owners, etc.).	Volume and market share. Percentage of households purchasing (penetration). Volume per buyer (buying rate). Volume per purchase occasion. Purchase occasion per buyer (frequency). Pricing (total, deal, nondeal). Percentage of volume on deal (coupon vs. store special). Distribution of volume by outlet (e.g., grocery, drug, club warehouse, etc.).
Demographic Analysis	To target advertising and promotional efforts most effectively by determining the demographic profile of particular buyer groups (e.g., brand buyers, heavy buyers, frequent commercial viewers). By evaluating the absolute sales importance of one demographic segment versus another, along with the importance of each demographic segment relative to the general population, the overall profile of each buyer group can be identified.	Across all demographic characteristics, the following measures are produced: Distribution of buyers. Distribution of volume. Market share (within demo group). Percentage of volume on deal (within demo group) Buyer Index (distribution of buyers vs. distribution of population). Volume Index (distribution of volume vs. distribution of population).
Loyalty/Combination Purchase Analysis	To understand the extent to which buyers are loyal to a brand or retailer, to determine the competitive set in which brands operate; and to identify size/flavor/form preference. The report also looks at the importance of price and dealing when buyers purchase competitive items.	Percentage of brand buyers purchasing competitive items. Percentage of brand volume accounted for by buyers who purchase competitive brands. Percentage of competitive brand volume purchased on deal by Brand A buyers. Price paid for competitive brand by Brand A buyers. Brand A buyers' total category volume (distribution). Interaction Index—index of Brand A's interaction with competitive brands versus expectations.
Brand-Shifting Analysis	To identify the sources of growth or decline in a brand's sales. By looking at changes from period to period on a household-by-household basis, we can see if volume changes were attributed to consumers switching to/from other brands, increasing/decreasing their overall category purchasing, and/or entering/leaving the market.	Brand-shifting volume. Increased/decreased category purchasing. New/lost category buyers. Percentage of shifting gains/loss. Gain/loss index. Interaction index.
Trial and Repeat Analysis	Trial measures consumer interest in a new product by evaluating the percentage of households of the product. Trial also measures the ability of a marketing plan to translate interest into purchasing. Repeat purchasing evaluates product satisfaction by determining the percentage of triers and repurchasing the brand—the ability of a product to deliver on its promise.	Cumulative trial. Cumulative repeat. Depth of repeat. Package rate (volume on trial, on repeat). Percentage volume on deal (total on trial vs. on repeat). Market share (total from trial vs. from repeat).

Source: ACNielsen

by the pound or the piece, such as produce, meat, and deli items. Consumers who participate in the Homescan Fresh Foods Consumer Index use scanners and a book of scannable codes for items sold by weight or in bulk. They scan the codes in the book to record how much of each item they purchased, whether or not the items carry UPC labels.[9]

The impact of single-source measurement on the conduct of marketing activities has been and promises to be so profound that it may "ultimately rival the importance of the microscope to scientists," according to a report by J. Walter Thompson USA.[10] For example, ACNielsen recently recruited a panel of 500 Hispanic households to use its Homescan system, thereby providing marketers with much greater insight into the buying behavior of that demographic group. Data compare purchases by Hispanic households whose preferred language is Spanish, English, or bilingual with purchases by non-Hispanic households. Early results show marketers that it is important to consider various types of Hispanic households. Spanish-speaking households are heavy buyers of diapers, cereal, and yogurt, but in Hispanic households where English is the preferred language, these items are purchased even less than in non-Hispanic households.[11]

Although single-source measurement offers the opportunity for new market insights, firms subscribing to these services need to prepare themselves for the incredible amounts of data these services produce. Without proper planning, firms literally can drown in these data. That is why decision support systems for analyzing data (particularly expert systems, which were discussed in Chapter 2) are becoming increasingly important in marketing research.

Measuring Advertising Exposure and Effectiveness

Another area in which there is a great deal of commercial information available for marketers relates to the assessment of exposure to, and effectiveness of, advertising. Most suppliers of industrial goods advertise most heavily in trade publications. To sell space more effectively, the various trade publications typically sponsor readership studies that they make available to potential advertisers. Suppliers of consumer goods and services also have access to media-sponsored readership studies. In addition, a number of services have evolved to measure consumer exposure to the various media.

Television and Radio

The Nielsen Television Index is probably the most generally familiar commercial information service. The most casual television watcher has probably heard of the Nielsen ratings and their impact on which television shows are canceled by the networks and which are allowed to continue. The index itself is designed to provide estimates of the size and nature of the audience for individual television programs. For a long time, the basic data were gathered through the use of Audimeter instruments, which were electronic devices attached to the television sets in cooperating households. Each Audimeter was connected to a central computer, which recorded when the set was on and to what channel it was tuned. Beginning in the fall of 1988, Nielsen started measuring television audiences through the use of people meters.

People meter
A device used to measure when a television is on, to what channel it is tuned, and who in the household is watching it.

People meters attempt to measure not only the channel to which a set is tuned, but who in the household is watching. Each member of the family has his or her own viewing number. Whoever turns on the set, sits down to watch, or changes the channel is supposed to enter his or her number into the people meter. All of this information is transmitted immediately to the central computer for processing.

Through the data provided by these basic records, Nielsen develops estimates of the number and percentage of all television households viewing a given television show. Nielsen also breaks down these aggregate ratings by ten socioeconomic and demographic characteristics, including territory, education of head of house, county size, time zones, household income, age of woman of house, color-television ownership, occupation of head of house, presence of nonadults, and household size. These breakdowns assist the network, of course, in selling advertising on particular programs, while they assist the advertiser in choosing to sponsor programs that reach households with the desired characteristics.[12]

Advertisers buying radio time are also interested in the size and demographic composition of the audiences they will be reaching. Radio-listening statistics are typically gathered using diaries that are placed in a panel of households. Arbitron, for example, generates telephone numbers randomly to ensure that it is reaching households with unlisted numbers. Those household members who agree to participate when called are sent diaries similar to that illustrated in Chapter 6, in which they are asked to record their radio-listening behavior for a short period. Most radio markets are rated only once or twice a year, although some of the larger ones are rated four times a year. The April/May survey is conducted in every Arbitron market and consequently is known as the "sweeps" period. Radio ratings are typically broken down by age and sex and focus more on individual than household behavior, in contrast with television ratings.

Print Media

There are several services that measure exposure to, and readership of, print media. For example, the Starch Readership Service measures the reading of advertisements in magazines and newspapers. Some 50,000 advertisements in 1,000 issues of consumer and farm magazines, business publications, and newspapers are assessed each year using over 75,000 personal interviews.

The Starch surveys employ the *recognition method* to assess a particular ad's effectiveness. With the magazine open, the respondent is asked to indicate whether he or she had read each ad. Three degrees of reading are recorded:

1. Noted—a person who remembered seeing any part of the advertisement in that particular issue.

2. Associated—a person who not only noted the advertisement but also saw or read some part of it that clearly indicates the brand or advertiser.

3. Read most—a person who read 50 percent or more of the written material in the ad.[13]

During the course of the interview, reading data are also collected on the component parts of each ad, such as the headlines, subheadings, pictures, copy blocks, and so forth.

Interviewing begins a short time after the issue of the magazine is placed on sale. For weekly and biweekly consumer magazines, interviewing begins three to six days after the on-sale date and continues for one to two weeks. For monthly magazines, interviewing begins two weeks after the on-sale date and continues for two weeks.

The interviews are conducted by a trained staff of field interviewers, who have the responsibility of selecting those to be interviewed, since a quota sample is employed. Each interviewer must locate within a particular area an assigned number of readers who are 18 years of age and over, with various occupations, family sizes, and marital and economic statuses. The quotas are determined so that different characteristics will be represented in the sample in proportion to their representation in the population. Readers are included in the sample when they conform to the specified demographic characteristics and when they reply in the affirmative when asked if they have read the particular magazine issue in question. The size of the sample varies by publication. Most Starch studies are based on a minimum of 100 issue readers.

Starch readership reports are compiled issue by issue and include three features: (1) labeled issue, (2) summary report, and (3) adnorm tables. The target ads in each issue are labeled to indicate overall readership level as well as the noting or reading of the major components of the ads. The summary report lists all the ads that were measured in the issue. The ads are arranged by product category and show the percentages for the three degrees of ad readership: noted, associated, and read most, allowing the comparison of the readership of each ad versus the other target ads in the issue. The adnorm tables enable one to compare the readership of an ad in a given issue with the norm for ads of the same size and color that are for the same product category for that publication.

Starch readership data allow advertisers to compare their ads with competitors' ads, current ads with prior ads, current ads against competitors' prior ads, and current ads against Starch adnorm tables. This process can be effective in assessing changes in theme, copy, layout, use of color, and so on.

Multimedia Services

The Simmons Media/Marketing Service uses a national probability sample of over 19,000 respondents and serves as a comprehensive data source allowing the cross-referencing of product usage and media exposure. Four different interviews are conducted with each respondent so that magazine, television, newspaper, and radio can all be covered by the Simmons Service. Information is reported for total adults and for males and females separately.[14]

The service conducts two personal interviews, which obtain measures of respondent readership of individual magazines and newspapers. A self-administered questionnaire is used to gather product purchase and use information for over 800 product categories, which remain relatively fixed from year to year. Television-viewing behavior is ascertained by means of a personal viewing diary, while radio-listening behavior is gathered through both personal and telephone interviews. A probability sample is used in selecting respondents for the study. All households receive a premium for participating, and a minimum of six calls is made in the attempt to interview previously unavailable respondents. A large number of demographic characteristics are gathered from each respondent included in the study, which permits firms to identify the heavy purchasers of various products. By also taking into account the purchaser's media habits, the firms are better able to segment and target the most promising groups.

Simmons determines magazine readership using the *through-the-book*, or *editorial interest*, method. In the through-the-book method, respondents are screened to determine which magazines they might have read during the past six months. They are then shown actual issues of magazines stripped of confusing material (for identification purposes), such as advertising pages and recurring columns and features. Nine feature articles unique to the issue are exhibited, and an indirect approach, asking respondents to select the articles they personally find especially interesting, is employed. At the end, a qualifying question is asked: "Now that you have been through this magazine, could you tell me whether this is the first time you happened to look into this particular issue, or have you looked into it before?" Respondents must affirm prior exposure to the issue to qualify as readers. Expressions of doubt or uncertainty would disqualify them.

Mediamark Research also makes available information on exposure to various media and household consumption of various products and services. Its annual survey of 20,000 adult respondents covers more than 250 magazines, newspapers, radio stations, and television channels and over 450 products and services.[15] Information is gathered from respondents by two methods. First, a personal interview is used to collect demographics and data pertaining to media exposure. Magazine readership is measured by a recent-reading method that asks respondents to sort a deck of magazine logo cards according to whether they (1) are sure they have read, (2) are not sure they have read, and (3) are sure they have not read a given magazine within the previous six months.

Newspaper readership is measured using a *yesterday-reading* technique in which respondents are asked which of the daily newspapers on the list of papers that circulate in the area were read or looked at within the previous seven days. For Sunday and weekend papers, a four-week time span is used. Radio listening is determined through a *yesterday-*

recall technique in which respondents are shown a list of five day parts and are asked how much time was spent listening to a radio during each time period on the previous day. They are then asked what stations were listened to. Television-audience data are collected in a similar manner.

On completion of the interview, interviewers then leave a questionnaire booklet with respondents. The booklet, which covers personal and household usage of approximately 3,500 product and service categories and 5,700 brands, is personally picked up by the interviewer after a short time. The 20,000 respondents for the Mediamark reports are selected using probability sampling methods.

The difference in the procedures used by Simmons and Mediamark to measure media exposure, particularly magazine readership, can create a real dilemma for advertisers. Both firms interview approximately 20,000 people for each study, but the figures reported by them can be very different. In general, it seems that Mediamark's figures of readership are about 10 percent higher for weeklies and 35 percent higher for monthlies, but that can vary dramatically by publication.[16] This difference, of course, creates havoc for those attempting to buy media space in which to place ads.

Customized Measurements

In addition to the services mentioned previously, some firms supply customized rather than standardized marketing information. To discuss all of these suppliers of marketing intelligence would take us too far afield. We do wish to discuss mail panels, though, to give readers a sense of their operation. Although they are not a true source of secondary data, because the data collected using them are specifically designed to meet the clients needs, the studies are sufficiently standardized and have enough features in common to warrant their inclusion here.

NFO Research, Inc., is one of the major independent research firms specializing in custom-designed consumer surveys using mail panels. NFO maintains representative panels drawn from a sampling frame of more than 525,000 households representing nearly one million consumers who have agreed to cooperate without compensation in completing self-administered questionnaires on a variety of subjects. The topics may include specific product usage; reaction to the product or advertising supporting it; reaction to a product package; attitude toward or awareness of some issue, product, service, or ad; and so on.

The national panel is dissolved and rebuilt every two years so that it matches current family–population characteristics with respect to income, population density, age of homemaker, and family size for the continental United States and each of the nine geographic divisions in the census.

A current demographic profile is maintained for each family in the data bank. Included are such characteristics as size of family, education, age of family members, presence and number of children by sex, occupation of the principal wage earner, race, and so on. This information is used to generate highly refined population segments. If the user's needs require it, NFO can offer the client panels composed exclusively of mothers of infants, teenagers, elderly people, dog and cat owners, professional workers, mobile home residents, multiple-car owners, or other specialized types. Each of these panels can be balanced to match specific quotas dictated by the client.[17]

The Consumer Mail Panel (CMP), operated as part of Market Facts, Inc., also represents a sample of households that have agreed to respond to mail questionnaires and product tests. Samples of persons for each product test or use are drawn from the 290,000 households in the CMP pool. The pool is representative of the geographical divisions in the United States and Canada and is broken down, within these divisions, according to census data on total household income, population density and degree of urbanization, and age of panel member.

According to CMP, its mail panel is ideally suited for experimental studies because the samples are matched with respect to demographic characteristics. In particular, CMP is believed to be particularly valuable when

1. Large samples are required at low cost because the size of the subgroups is large or there are many subgroups to be analyzed.

2. Large numbers of households must be screened to find eligible respondents.

3. Continuing records are to be kept by respondents to report such data as products purchased, how products are used, television programs viewed, magazines read, and so on.

CMP has recorded a number of other characteristics with respect to each participating household that allow for cross tabulation of the client's criterion variable against such things as place of residence (state, county, and standard metropolitan area), marital status, occupation and employment status, household size, age, sex, home ownership, type of dwelling, and ownership of pets, dishwashers, washing machines, dryers, other selected appliances, and automobiles.[18]

Back to the Case

As the market for natural foods has expanded, so has the amount of data available to Whole Foods and its competitors.

Geodemographic data can tell Whole Foods about its customers. It needs to locate stores near the kinds of consumers who can afford to spend a little extra and who value natural products. A logical place to start is with the PRIZM cluster called "Urban Uptown"—young, affluent, mostly single professionals, artists, executives, and students. Thus, Whole Foods's first expansion stores in Texas were in neighborhoods of Dallas, Plano, and Richardson with a high concentration of these kinds of people. As the store broadens its appeal and builds customer loyalty, it expands into areas with young families that have rising or higher-than-average incomes.

As Whole Foods enters and serves these markets, it can work with firms such as Claritas, the source of PRIZM data, to define not only the demographics of its markets, but also the media usage and lifestyles of its target markets. This can enable the company to target its promotional activities.

Other sources of data can tell Whole Foods what natural and organic products sell best, at its own stores and nationwide. For example, SPINs is a San Francisco–based marketing research firm that monitors the sales of over 80,000 products sold by natural-food stores and supermarkets. It can tell that the fastest-growing natural products are nondairy beverages; chips, pretzels, and snacks; and cold cereals.

SPINs also identifies regions where sales of products are growing. Natural products once were primarily sold in the biggest cities, like Chicago and Los Angeles, but that has been changing over the past decade, according to SPINs. Now stores in Hartford and St. Louis are enjoying impressive performance.

Whole Foods can participate in research projects that gather panel data to monitor sales of particular products. ACNielsen's Homescan has recently expanded to collect data on some of Whole Foods's mainstays: produce, bulk foods, fresh meats, and deli fare. This type of data collection helps manufacturers evaluate which advertising and promotional activities are beneficial and where products sell most successfully. By sharing the data with Whole Foods, the manufacturers and research firms can help the chain tailor its stores' product mix to what customers want.

As an advertiser itself, Whole Foods can obtain data from firms that specialize in testing advertising. For instance, the retailer can use readership reports such as the Starch service to evaluate its advertising programs.

The explosion in the demand for natural and organic products is sending Whole Foods into the big league of retailing. Fortunately, big-league researchers offer plenty of help.

Sources: Worth Wren, Jr., "The Green Grocer: Markets Such as Whole Foods Are Pulling In a Wider Base of Customers," *Fort Worth Star-Telegram* (July 12, 1998, downloaded from Northern Light Internet site, www.northernlight.com, August 13, 1999); Len Lewis, "Natural Selection," *Progressive Grocer* (September 1998), pp. 74–75, 78, 80; Deborah L. Cohen, "Trotsky and Tofu Meet in Evanston: Shoppers Unite! Testing Lower-Cost Natural Foods Store," *Crain's Chicago Business* (August 9, 1999, downloaded from Dow Jones Publications Library at the Dow Jones Web site, www.dowjones.com, August 16, 1999); Whole Foods Market Web site (www.wholefoods.com, downloaded August 16, 1999); Whole Foods Market, Annual Report, 1998 (downloaded from Whole Foods Web site, www.wholefoods.com, August 16, 1999).

Summary

Learning Objective 1

List three common uses of the information supplied by standardized marketing information services.

The information supplied by standardized marketing information services is commonly used to (1) profile customers, (2) measure product sales and market share, and (3) measure advertising exposure and effectiveness.

Learning Objective 2

Define geodemography.
Geodemography refers to the availability of demographic, consumer-behavior, and lifestyle data by arbitrary geographic boundaries that are typically small.

Learning Objective 3

Describe the operation of a diary panel.

Diary panels are made up of families who use a preprinted diary to record the details of each purchase in a number of prespecified product categories. The details include the brand and amount bought, the price paid, whether the product was purchased on any deal and the type of deal if it was, the store where purchased, and so on. Families are recruited on a regular basis, often quarterly, to keep the panel balanced demographically.

Learning Objective 4

Describe the operation of store audits.

Store audits involve sending field workers, called auditors, to a select group of retail stores at fixed intervals. On each visit the auditors take a complete inventory of all products designated for the audit. The auditors also note the merchandise moving into the store by checking wholesale invoices, warehouse withdrawal records, and direct shipments from manufacturers, and from this information determine sales to consumers.

Learning Objective 5

Define UPC.

The Universal Product Code (UPC) is an 11-digit number imprinted on each product sold in a supermarket. The first digit, called the number system character, indicates the type of product (e.g., grocery or drug). The next five digits identify the manufacturer; and the last five, a particular product of the manufacturer, be it a different size, variety, or whatever.

Learning Objective 6

Define single-source measurement.

Single-source measurement refers to those organizations that have the capability to monitor product-purchase data and advertising-exposure data by household, and to relate that information to the demographic characteristics of the various households.

Learning Objective 7

Discuss the purpose and operation of people meters.

People meters attempt to measure which household members are watching which television channels at what times. Each member of the family has his or her own viewing number. Whoever turns on the set, sits down to watch, or changes the channel is supposed to enter his or her number into the people meter, which is an electronic device that stores and transmits this information to a central computer for processing.

Review Questions

1. What is the basic operation of a store audit?

2. Describe how a type of business can be more successfully identified using the Enhanced DMI.

3. If you were a product manager for Brand X detergent and you needed up-to-date market share information by small geographical sectors, would you prefer National Purchase Diary Panel data or ACNielsen data? Why?

4. For what types of studies would you prefer NPD consumer data rather than BehaviorScan consumption data? Vice versa?

5. What is the advantage of using single-source data?

6. How are Starch scores determined?

7. What is the basis for the Nielsen television ratings?

8. How do the multimedia services operate?

9. For what types of studies would you use mail panels?

Discussion Questions, Problems, and Projects

1. Several scenarios are presented below. In each case, there exists a need for standardized marketing information. Recommend a service or services that could provide the required information. Explain your choice.

   (a) As part of its advertising-sales strategy, radio KZZD wants to stress the fact that their programming appeals to young adults between the ages of 19 and 25. The advertising salespeople need "numbers" to back up this claim.

   (b) Pulitzer Peanut Company has developed a unique couponing and television ad campaign for their 36-ounce container of Spanish peanuts. They need to know the following in order to evaluate the campaign:
      (1) Are people more likely to use the coupon when they've also seen the television ad?
      (2) What is the median size of the households using the coupon?
      (3) What is the proportion of new purchasers to past purchasers among the users of the coupon?

   (c) A national manufacturer of a nutritional supplement for children between the ages of 2 and 4 is considering changing the current packaging to a recyclable glass container. The change will necessitate a 10 percent price increase. The manufacturer wants to know if its target market (parents with children between 2 and 4 years of age) will perceive the price increase as justified since the new package is more environmentally sound.

(d) EMM Advertising Agency assured one of its clients that despite the $200,000 cost of placing a half-page ad in one issue of a national magazine, the actual cost per reader of the ad would be less than two cents. EMM is preparing a report to the client and needs data to back its assurance.

(e) Eco-Soft, Inc., is introducing a software package that will make long-range forecasts of contaminant buildup levels in plants that manufacture polyester fibers. They need a current listing of potential customers, organized by plant sales volume, in order to prioritize their sales calls for the new package.

(f) MidTowne Shopping Mall wishes to know the demographic characteristics of its patrons. However, the mall's retail tenants recently voted to ban marketing research interviews in or around the mall area, due to numerous customer complaints about harassment by interviewers. Where might the mall obtain the desired information?

2. Interview representatives of your local media outlets (e.g., radio stations, television stations, and newspapers) and determine the extent to which they utilize sources of standardized marketing information. You may wish to use the following questions as a guideline for your interviews.

(a) Which sources do they use?

(b) What specific types of information do they obtain from the source?

(c) How do they use the information?

(d) How important is the information in the conduct of their business?

(e) How do they rate the accuracy of the information?

(f) Do they supplement the standardized information with locally collected primary data?

Endnotes

1. *Where & Who (Are the Customers)* (Detroit: R. L. Polk & Co., undated).

2. Eric Schine, "Computer Maps Pop Up All Over the Map," *Business Week*, July 26, 1993, pp. 75–76.

3. Pamela DeSmidt, "Claritas for Market Demographic Analysis," *Database* (June 1, 1999, downloaded from the Northern Light Internet site, www.northernlight.com, August 16, 1999).

4. For discussion of some of the marketing insights made possible by the availability of geodemographic data, see Martha Fransworth Riche, "The Business Guide to the Galaxy of Demographic Products and Services," *American Demographics* 7 (June 1985), p. 25; Lisa Del Priore, "Geomapping Tools for Market Analysis," *Marketing Communications* 12 (March 1987), pp. 91–94; Joe Schwartz, "Why They Buy," *American Demographics* 11 (March 1989), pp. 40–41; Howard Schlossberg, "Census Bureau's TIGER Seen as a Roaring Success," *Marketing News* 24 (April 30, 1990), p. 2; Richard K. Thomas and Russell J. Kirchner, *Desktop Marketing: Lessons From America's Best* (Ithaca, N.Y.: American Demographic Books, 1991; Diane Crispell, *The Insider's Guide to Demographic Know How* (Burr Ridge, IL.: Irwin Professional Publishing, 1992).

5. Bradley Johnson, "ZDNet Hones Targeting to Link Marketers, Prospects," *Advertising Age* (May 31, 1999), p. 60.

6. See *Insights* (New York: NPD Research, Inc., undated) for discussion of these and other analyses using diary-panel data.

7. Information Resources now also offers BehaviorScan for testing in mass merchandisers such as Wal-Mart, Kmart, and Target, in addition to grocery stores and drugstores. See *Testing Services* (Chicago: Information Resources, undated).

8. *Nielsen Household Panel* (Northbrook, Ill.: A. C. Nielsen Company, undated). For a specific example of the use of Homescan, see "Using the Numbers," *Progressive Grocer* 75 (May 1996), pp. 117–123.

9. Priscilla Donegan, "Completing the Picture," *Grocery Headquarters* (April 1999), pp. 100–102.

10. "Study Predicts Bigger Impact by Single-Source Data," *Marketing News* 22 (February 1, 1988), p. 13. See also John Phillip Jones, "Single-Source Begins to Fulfill Its Promise," *Journal of Advertising Research* 35 (May/June 1995), pp. 9–16.

11. Rick Wartzman, "A Push to Probe Buying Habits in Latino Homes," *The Wall Street Journal* (August 5, 1999, downloaded from Dow Jones Publications Library at the Dow Jones Web site, www.dowjones.com, August 10, 1999).

12. Greater detail about the Nielsen television rating can be found in *The Nielsen Ratings in Perspective* (Northbrook, Ill.: ACNielsen Company, undated). For discussion of the controversy surrounding the use of people meters for TV audience measurement, see Richard Mahler, "Grousing about People Meters," *Adweek Special Report* (December 5, 1988), pp. F.K. 10–11; Peter Barnes and Joanne Lipman, "Networks and Ad Agencies Battle over Estimates of TV Viewership," *The Wall Street Journal* (January 7, 1987), p. 21; Roland Soong, "The Statistical Reliability of People Meter Ratings," *Journal of Advertising Research* 26 (February–March 1988), pp. 50–56; J. Ronald Milavsky, "How Good Is the A. C. Nielsen People-Meter System? A Review of the Report by the Committee on Nationwide Television Audience Measurement," *Public Opinion Quarterly* 56 (Spring 1992), pp. 102–115; David Lieberman, "Static Over TV Ratings System," *USA Today*, February 10, 1996, p. 3B; Elizabeth Jensen, "Networks Blame Faulty Ratings for Drop in Viewerships," *The Wall Street Journal* (November 22, 1996), pp. A1, A8. ACNielsen is experimenting with a passive meter system that would require viewers to do nothing but turn on their sets. Those watching a particular program would be identified through computer-image recognition technology. For discussion of the opportunities and problems with this system, see Steve McClellan, "New Nielsen System Is Turning Heads," *Broadcasting* 122 (May 18, 1992), p. 8; Barry Cook, "Commercial Television: Dead or Alive? A Status Report on Nielsen's Passive People Meter," *Journal of Advertising Research* 35 (March/April 1995), pp. RC5–RC10.

13. *Starch Readership Report: Scope, Method, and Use* (Mamaroneck, N.Y.: Starch INRA Hooper, undated).

14. *Simmons Research: Your Key to Opportunity* (New York: Simmons Market Research Bureau, undated).

15. More detail about Mediamark's operations and the types of analysis the media-exposure and product-use databases allow can be found in the company's publications *Knowledge is Power, Winning the Marketing Game: How Syndicated Consumer Research Helps Improve the Odds*, or *Ready for the 90's*, or on the company's Web site.

16. Joanne Lipman, "Readership Figures for Periodicals Stir Debate in Publishing Industry," *The Wall Street Journal* (September 2, 1987), p. 21; Jeff Gremillion, "Reader Research Rumble," *Mediaweek* 6 (September 16, 1996), pp. 4–5; Jane Beresford, "A House of Cards," *Mediaweek* 6 (July 8, 1996), p. 13.

17. More detailed information about the mail panel can be found in the company's publication *NFO* (Toledo, Ohio: NFO Research, undated), or on the company's Web site.

18. More detail about the Market Facts mail panel can be found in the company's publications: *Why Consumer Mail Panel Is the Superior Option, Market Facts, Inc.: Data Collection and Analysis for Reducing Business Decision Risks, Consumer Mail Panel Reference Guide*, or on the company's Web site.

Suggested Additional Readings

The best source of additional readings with respect to the operation of, and the possible analyses with, standardized marketing information services are the brochures describing their services put out by the companies themselves. Complimentary copies are often available for the asking. Much information can also be found on the companies' Web sites.

Chapter 9

COLLECTING PRIMARY DATA

LEARNING OBJECTIVES

Upon Completing This Chapter, You Should Be Able to

1. List the kinds of demographic and socioeconomic characteristics that interest marketers.

2. Relate the premise on which lifestyle analysis rests.

3. Cite the three main approaches used to measure the effectiveness of magazine ads.

4. Give two reasons why researchers are interested in people's motives.

5. Describe the two basic means of obtaining primary data.

6. State the specific advantages of each method of data collection.

Case in Marketing Research

The numbers were glaring. American Express Financial Advisors (AEFA) was missing a major sales opportunity. Several years ago, company reports showed that of the customers receiving financial advice from AEFA, only 28 percent—barely more than one out of four—purchased life insurance.

Management at AEFA, a Minneapolis-based American Express subsidiary that offers investments, insurance, and financial planning services, appointed a team of employees to conduct exploratory research. Their mission: Find out why most customers were saying "no thanks" to life insurance.

The team talked to customers and planners, and they watched the selling process. Team members kept track of individual planners' performance. They also consulted with a research psychologist. They tried to understand, not just the outward behavior of a sales call, but what was going on in the heads of the company's clients.

Customers, they observed, are experiencing significant emotions during financial planning sessions. While considering their options, they feel some combination of worry, uncertainty, trust, security, and pride. In contrast, many of the financial planners were focusing on the objective, rational aspects of financial planning. They talked about numbers and made financial projections. "Look," they would say, "here are your estimated financial needs, and here is a product that can meet those needs." More often than not, this approach elicited the usual response: "No, thank you."

The team saw a mismatch between clients' motives and planners' selling methods. They concluded that customers were acting on emotional motives, whereas salespeople were trained to put emotions aside and focus on rational considerations. They generated a hypothesis that planners with greater emotional competency would sell more insurance. Based on this hypothesis, they recommended that sales training include development of "emotional intelligence," that is, understanding and managing one's own emotions and the emotions of others.

This was not the answer AEFA management was expecting. According to Kate Cannon, then director of leadership development at AEFA and a participant on the research team, "For years I talked to people [about the importance of emotional intelligence] and watched their eyes roll and witnessed snickering behind the scenes." Cannon and her teammates would have to test their recommendation and prove its merit.

Discussion Issues

1. The AEFA team concluded that clients select insurance based on emotional, rather than rational, motives. How could the company identify and test such motives?

2. Besides an understanding of clients' emotions, what other information does the company need?

3. How can AEFA test the team's hypothesis that planners with greater emotional intelligence will perform better?

In Chapter 7 we emphasized the advantages of using secondary data. Such research information is usually fast, inexpensive, and fairly easy to obtain. We also noted that researchers who give secondary data only a casual look are being reckless. However, as we have seen, such data also have certain shortcomings and rarely will provide a complete solution to a research problem. The units of measurement or classes used to report the data may be wrong; the data may be nearly obsolete by the time of their publication; the data may be incomplete; and so on. When these conditions occur, the researcher logically turns to primary data.

This chapter is the first of three dealing with primary data, and it serves as an introduction to the subject. In this chapter we will discuss the various types of primary data researchers collect from and about subjects, and we will examine the two main means they employ to do it: communication and observation. In subsequent chapters we will explore each of these methods in more detail.

Types of Primary Data

Demographic/Socioeconomic Characteristics

One type of primary data of great interest to marketers is the subject's demographic and socioeconomic characteristics, such as age, education, occupation, marital status, sex, income, and social class. Researchers often match these variables with the data they have collected to gain greater insight into the subject under investigation. They might be interested, for example, in determining whether people's attitudes toward ecology and pollution are related to their level of formal education. Alternatively, they may ask whether the use of a particular product is in any way related to a person's age, sex, education, income, and so on, and if so, in what way. These are questions of market segmentation. Demographic and socioeconomic characteristics are often used to delineate market segments.

Marketers also use demographic and socioeconomic data in planning advertising campaigns, so that the media and message are appropriate for reaching targeted market segments. A growing number of advertisers are considering placement of messages on the World Wide Web, and ad agencies therefore need demographic data on Web users. For example, Star Media commissioned a demographic study of Latin American visitors to the Web. Results of the study indicated that 67 percent are between the ages of 18 and 34, 78 percent are men, and 78 percent attended college. The Latin American country with the most widespread Internet access was Brazil.[1]

Demographic and socioeconomic characteristics are sometimes called "states of being," in that they represent attributes of people. Some of these states of being, such as a respondent's age, sex, and level of formal education, can be readily verified. Some, such as social class, cannot be verified except very crudely, since they are relative and not absolute measures of a person's standing in society. A person's income can also be a fairly difficult piece of information to verify. Although the amount a person earns in a given year is an absolute, not a relative, quantity, in our society money is such a sensitive topic that exact numbers may be hard to determine.

Psychological/Lifestyle Characteristics

Personality
Normal patterns of behavior exhibited by an individual; the attributes, traits, and mannerisms that distinguish one individual from another.

Another type of primary data of interest to marketers is the subject's psychological and lifestyle characteristics in the form of personality traits, activities, interests, and values. **Personality** refers to the normal patterns of behavior exhibited by an individual—the attributes, traits, and mannerisms that distinguish one individual from another. We often characterize people by the personality traits—aggressiveness, dominance, friendliness, sociability—they display. Marketers are interested in personality because it seems as if it would affect the way consumers and others in the marketing process behave. Many marketers maintain, for example, that personality can affect a consumer's choice of stores or products, or an individual's response to an advertisement or point-of-purchase display. Similarly, they believe that successful salespeople are more likely to be extroverted and understanding of other people's feelings than are unsuccessful salespeople. Although the empirical evidence regarding the ability of personality to predict consumption behavior or salesperson success is weak, personality remains a variable dear to the hearts of marketing researchers. Typically, it is measured by one of the standard personality inventories that have been developed by psychologists.[2]

Lifestyle analysis rests on the premise that the firm can plan more effective strategies to reach its target market if it knows more about its customers in terms of how they live, what interests them, and what they like. For example, Frito-Lay conducted research that identified two broad categories of snackers, which it called Compromisers and Indulgers. The Compromisers are typically female and are more likely to exercise, read health and fitness magazines, be concerned about nutrition, and read product labels. Frito-Lay appeals to this group with its Baked Lay's potato chip, a reduced fat snack. Frito-Lay's traditional potato chips are targeted to the other psychographic category, the Indulgers, who are mostly male, in their late teens and early twenties, snack heavily, feel unconcerned about what they eat, and hesitate to sacrifice taste for a reduction in fat.[3]

Psychographic analysis
A technique that investigates how people live, what interests them, and what they like; it is also called *lifestyle analysis*, since it relies on a number of statements about a person's AIO—activities (A), interests (I), and opinions (O).

The general thrust of such research, which is often called **psychographic analysis,** has been to develop a number of statements that reflect a person's AIO—activities (A), interests (I), and opinions (O)—and consumption behavior. The statements might include such things as "I like to watch football games on television," "I like stamp collecting," "I am interested in national politics." Such a psychographic test would typically contain a great many such statements for respondents to choose from and would be administered to a large sample of respondents.[4]

For example, the advertising agency of Needham, Harper, and Steers conducts an annual lifestyle study that asks 3,500 respondents to answer 700 questions. Exhibit 9.1 contains the list of characteristics that are usually assessed with AIO inventories. The analysis

EXHIBIT 9.1   Lifestyle Dimensions

Activities	Interests	Opinions
Work	Family	Themselves
Hobbies	Home	Social issues
Social events	Job	Politics
Vacation	Community	Business
Entertainment	Recreation	Economics
Club membership	Fashion	Education
Community	Food	Products
Shopping	Media	Future
Sports	Achievements	Culture

Source: Adapted from Joseph T. Plummer, "The Concept and Application of Life Style Segmentation," *Journal of Marketing* 38 (January 1974), p. 34. Published by the American Marketing Association. See also Ronald D. Michman, *Lifestyle Market Segmentation* (New York: Praeger Publishers, 1991).

attempts to identify groups of consumers who are likely to behave similarly toward a product, and who have similar lifestyle profiles. Research Window 9.1, for example, provides lifestyle descriptions of the five most common gasoline buyers identified by Mobil's marketing research. Finding that the Price Shopper spends no more than $700 annually, while the biggest spenders, the Road Warriors and True Blues, average at least $1,200 a year, Mobil decided to refocus its strategy to emphasize exceptional service over low prices.[5]

One problem that marketers experienced when using psychographics or AIO inventories was that the categories of users distinguished in one study focusing on one type of product would be very different from the categories of individuals identified in another study examining a different product. This meant that each product required a new data-collection and analysis exercise. Because the profiles across products were so unstable, it was impossible to develop demographic descriptions of the various groups that would be useful in planning marketing strategies for new products or brands.

The purpose of value and lifestyle (VALS) research is to avoid these problems by creating a standard psychographic framework that can be used for a variety of products. Exhibit 9.2, for example, shows the ten segments that have been identified from applying VALS in Japan.[6]

Attitudes/Opinions

Attitude
An individual's preference, inclination, views, or feelings toward some phenomenon.

Opinion
Verbal expression of an attitude.

Some authors distinguish between attitudes and opinions, while others use the terms interchangeably. Most typically **attitude** is used to refer to an individual's "preference, inclination, views or feelings toward some phenomenon," while **opinions** are "verbal expressions of attitudes." We shall not make the distinction between the terms in this text but will treat attitudes and opinions interchangeably as representing a person's ideas, convictions, or liking with respect to a specific object or idea.

Attitude is one of the more important notions in the marketing literature, since it is generally thought that attitudes are related to behavior.[7] In general, if a person has a positive attitude toward a product or brand, the person is more likely to buy that product or to choose that brand. Because attitudes influence behavior in this way, marketers want to shape attitudes or target people with favorable attitudes.

Thus, marketers often want to learn people's attitudes toward product categories, brands, and features of particular products or brands. For example, Ford Motor Company

---

Research Window 9.1   **Lifestyle Descriptions of the Five Most Common Types of Gasoline Buyers**

Road Warriors (16%)   Generally higher income, middle-aged men who drive 25,000 to 50,000 miles a year . . . buy premium with a credit card . . . purchase sandwiches and drinks from the convenience store . . . will sometimes wash their cars at the car wash.

True Blues (16%)   Usually men and women with moderate to high incomes who are loyal to a brand and sometimes to a particular station . . . frequently buy premium gasoline and pay in cash.

Generation F3 (for fuel, food and fast)   (27%) Upwardly mobile men and women—half under 25 years of age—who are constantly on the go . . . drive a lot and snack heavily from the convenience store.

Homebodies (21%)   Usually housewives who shuttle their children around during the day and use whatever gasoline station is based in town or along their route of travel.

Price Shoppers (20%)   Generally aren't loyal to either a brand or a particular station, and rarely buy the premium line . . . frequently on tight budgets . . . efforts to woo them have been the basis of marketing strategies for years.

Source: Allanna Sullivan, "Mobil Bets Drivers Pick Cappuccino over Low Prices," *The Wall Street Journal* (January 30, 1995), pp. B1, B4.

Dimension	Group	Percentage of Population	Description
Exploration	Integrators	4	Well-educated, modern people who enjoy the new and risky.
	Sustainers	15	People who resent changes.
Self-Expression	Self-Innovators	7	Young, active people who are interested in fashion and spend a lot of money on themselves.
	Self-Adapters	11	Shy people who are sensitive to others and pattern their buying after that of Self-Innovators.
Achievement	Ryoshiki ("social intelligence") Innovators	6	Career-oriented, highly educated, middle-aged people.
	Ryoshiki Adapters	10	Shy people who are sensitive to others and pattern their buying after that of Ryoshiki Innovators.
Tradition	Tradition Innovators	6	Middle-aged homeowners with middle-management jobs who are active in community affairs.
	Tradition Adapters	10	Affluent, young, well-educated managers who travel frequently.
Realist Orientation	High Pragmatics	14	Least likely to agree with any attitude statement; withdrawn; suspicious; unconcerned about self-improvement or preserving customs.
	Low Pragmatics	17	Attitudinally negative people with no psychological tendency who prefer inexpensive goods and established brands.

Source: Lewis C. Winters, "International Psychographics," *Marketing Research: A Magazine of Management & Applications* 4 (September 1992), pp. 48–49. Reprinted with permission of American Marketing Association.

learned about young adults' attitudes toward advertising and used that insight to shape its own advertising for its Focus subcompact. The company determined that its young target market has a favorable attitude toward what Ford's communications manager Jan Klug calls "taking risks and living in the moment" and that they are skeptical of polished corporate messages. The company addressed those attitudes with a series of live (rather than prerecorded) commercials featuring TV star Anabelle Gurwitch.[8] Attitude is such a pervasive notion in behavioral science, and particularly in marketing, that Chapter 14 is devoted to various types of instruments used to measure it.

Awareness/Knowledge

Awareness/knowledge
Insight into, or understanding of facts about, some object or phenomenon.

Awareness/knowledge as used in marketing research refers to what respondents do and do not know about some object or phenomenon. For instance, an issue of considerable importance is the effectiveness of magazine ads. One indicator of effectiveness is the "awareness" generated by the ad, which is measured using one of the three approaches described in Exhibit 9.3. All three approaches are aimed at assessing the respondent's awareness of and knowledge about the ad, although the three approaches can produce dramatically different results.

Retention rates are much higher when knowledge is measured by recognition rather than by recall and by aided rather than unaided recall. This, of course, raises the question of which method is the most accurate. There are problems with each method, not the least of which is separating true awareness from bogus recall.[9] The important thing to note is that when marketers speak of a person's awareness, they often mean the individual's knowledge of the advertisement. A person "very much aware" or possessing "high awareness" typically knows a great deal about the ad.

EXHIBIT 9.3   **Approaches Used to Measure Awareness**

Unaided Recall   Without being given any clues, consumers are asked to recall what advertising they have seen recently. Prompting is not used because, presumably, even if prompting for the general category were used (for example, laundry detergents), respondents would have a tendency to remember more advertisements in that product category.

Aided Recall   Consumers are given some prompting, typically in the form of questions about advertisements in a specific

product category. Alternatively, respondents might be given a list showing the names or trademarks of advertisers that appeared in a particular magazine issue, along with names or trademarks that did not appear, and would be asked to check those to which they were exposed.

Recognition   Consumers are shown copies of actual advertisements and are asked whether they remember seeing each one.

Awareness and *knowledge* are also used interchangeably when marketers speak of product awareness. Marketing researchers are often interested in determining whether the respondent is aware of the following:[10]

- The product
- Its features
- Where it is available
- Its price
- Its manufacturer
- Where it is made
- How it is used, and for what purpose
- Its specific distinctive features

Although framed in terms of awareness, these questions, to a greater or lesser degree, aim at determining the individual's knowledge of or beliefs about the product. For our purposes, then, *knowledge* and *awareness* will be used interchangeably to refer to what a respondent believes about an advertisement, product, retail store, and so on.

Intentions

Intentions
Anticipated or planned future behavior.

A person's **intentions** refer to the individual's anticipated or planned future behavior. Marketers are interested in people's intentions primarily with regard to purchase behavior. One of the better known studies regarding purchase intentions is that conducted by the Survey Research Center at the University of Michigan. The center regularly conducts surveys for the Federal Reserve Board to determine the general financial condition of consumers and their outlook with respect to the state of the economy in the near future. The center asks consumers about their buying intentions for big-ticket items such as appliances, automobiles, and a home during the next few months. The responses are then analyzed, and used as one indicator of future economic activity. In marketing, intentions are often gathered by asking respondents to indicate which of the following best describes their plans with respect to a new product or service:

- definitely would buy
- probably would buy
- undecided
- probably would not buy
- definitely would not buy

The number of people who answer that they definitely would buy or probably would buy are often combined into a "top box" to indicate likely reaction to the new product or service.

Intentions receive less attention in marketing than do other types of primary data, largely because there is often a great disparity between what people say they are going to do and what they actually do. This is particularly true with respect to purchase behavior.

Figure 9.1, for example, describes the results of one investigation of the relationship. In the experiment, consumers were given a questionnaire that described a new pricing option for a service to which customers already subscribed. The questionnaire asked the respondents to circle a number that best indicated how likely they were to buy the service when it became available. The scale anchors ranged from 1 (definitely would not buy) to 10 (definitely would buy). As Figure 9.1 indicates, only 45 percent of those indicating that they definitely would buy the service did so within the first three months of its availability. Further, some of the respondents who indicated that they would not buy it did so.

Researchers are most likely to use purchasing intentions when investigating the likelihood of consumers buying items that require a large sum of money. For a family this might be an automobile, a new house, or even a vacation trip. For a business, a study of purchase intentions would usually focus on a new plant or equipment.

The general assumption researchers make is that the more an item costs, the more time a consumer will spend in planning the purchase. If that assumption is true, then there should be a significant correlation between anticipated and actual behavior. Unfortunately, the evidence of such a correlation is weak.[11]

| FIGURE 9.1 | **Proportion of People Buying the Service versus Their Intention to Purchase It** |

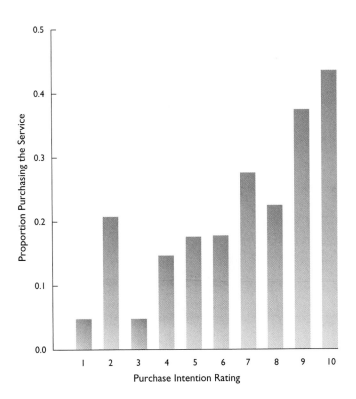

Source: William J. Infosino, "Forecasting New Product Sales from Likelihood of Purchase Ratings," *Marketing Science* 5 (Fall 1986), p. 375. See also Vicki G. Morwitz and David Schmittlein, "Using Segmentation to Improve Sales Forecasts Based on Purchase Intent: Which 'Intendees' Actually Buy," *Journal of Marketing Research* 29 (November 1990), pp. 391–405.

Motivation

The concept of motivation seem to contain more semantic confusion than most concepts in the behavioral sciences.

> Some writers insist that motives are different from drives and use the latter term primarily to characterize the basic physiological "tissue" needs (e.g., hunger, thirst, shelter, sex). Others distinguish between needs and wants, stating that needs are the basic motivating forces which translate themselves into more immediate wants which satisfy these needs (e.g., hunger needs give rise to wanting a good steak dinner).[12]

Motive
A need, a want, a drive, a wish, a desire, an impulse, or any inner state that energizes, activates, or moves and that directs or channels behavior toward goals.

For our purposes, a **motive** may refer to a need, a want, a drive, an urge, a wish, a desire, an impulse, or any inner state that directs or channels behavior toward goals. Ensuring the financial security of one's family is the motive behind the ad shown for life and health insurance.

A marketing researcher's interest in motives typically involves determining *why* people behave as they do. There are several reasons for this interest. In the first place, researchers believe that a person's motives tend to be more stable than an individual's behavior and therefore offer a better basis for predicting future behavior than does past behavior. For example, a young couple living in an apartment may say that they want to buy a house. Just because they did not buy a house last year, or the year before, does not mean that their motives have changed. Once they have saved enough for a down payment, or once a baby is on the way, they may be spurred to act on their motives, and past behavior will have no bearing on this action.

The second reason researchers are interested in motives is that by understanding what drives a person's behavior, it is easier to understand the behavior itself. A desire for status may motivate one car buyer to purchase a Mercedes-Benz, while a concern for safety may send another to the local Volvo showroom. If researchers understand the forces underlying consumer behavior, they are in a better position to influence future behavior, or at least to design products consistent with what they anticipate that behavior to be.

Behavior

Behavior
What subjects have done or are doing.

Behavior concerns what subjects have done or are doing. In marketing this usually means purchase and use behavior. Now, behavior is a physical activity. It takes place under specific circumstances, at a particular time, and involves one or more actors or participants. A marketing researcher investigating behavior would be interested in a

---

Ethical Dilemma 9.1

A national department store chain with a relatively sophisticated image is planning to open a store in an area inhabited by professionals. The marketing research director of the company wants a detailed profile of the residents' characteristics and lifestyles in order to tailor the new store to the tastes of this lucrative new market. He suggests that you, a member of his staff, contribute to the research effort by spending a month observing the residents going about their daily affairs of eating in restaurants, attending church, shopping in other stores, socializing with one another, and so on. You are then to prepare a report on what expenditures support their lifestyles.

- Are there ethical problems involved in observing people in public places? Do the ethical problems become more serious if you socialize with your subjects?

- Who has ethical responsibility for your behavior: the marketing research director? You? Both?

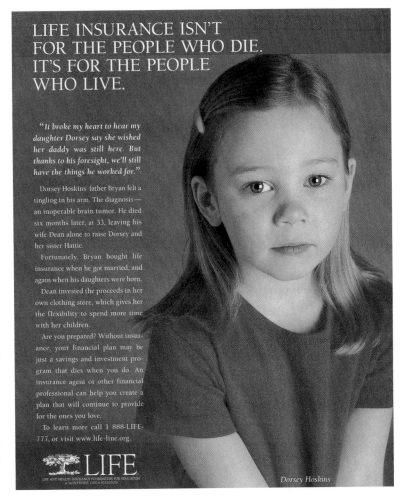

description of the activity and its various components. Exhibit 9.4 is a checklist of the key elements involved in purchase behavior. Researchers can use a checklist like this one to design data collection instruments.

As a researcher fills in each category, he or she must make a decision about what information to include or omit. Consider the "where" category, for example. The "where of purchase" may be specified with respect to kind of store, the location of the store by broad geographic area or specific address, size of the store, or even the name of the store. So it is with each of the many categories. The study of behavior, then, involves the development of a description of the purchase or use activity, either past or current, with respect to some or all of the characteristics contained in Exhibit 9.4.

EXHIBIT 9.4	**Behavior Checklist**	
	Purchase Behavior	**Use Behavior**
What and how much		
How		
Where		
When		
Who		

Behavior data is becoming more important to marketers in an increasingly competitive world. Fortunately, new technologies in the form of electronic capture via scanners or other means, mass storage capabilities, and more sophisticated systems and techniques are making the analysis of behavior data increasingly easy and insightful.[13]

Obtaining Primary Data

Communication

A method of data collection involving questioning of respondents to secure the desired information, using a data collection instrument called a questionnaire.

Observation

A method of data collection in which the situation of interest is watched and the relevant facts, actions, or behaviors are recorded.

The researcher attempting to collect primary data has a number of choices to make among the means that will be used. Figure 9.2 represents an overview of these choices. The primary decision is whether to employ communication, or observation. **Communication** involves questioning respondents to secure the desired information, using a data collection instrument called a questionnaire. The questions may be oral or in writing, and the responses may also be given in either form. **Observation** does not involve questioning. Rather, it means that the situation of interest is scrutinized and the relevant facts, actions, or behaviors are recorded. The observer may be one or more persons or a mechanical device. For instance, supermarket scanners may be used to determine how many boxes of a particular brand of cereal are sold in a given region in a typical week. Alternatively, a researcher interested in the brands of canned vegetables a family buys might arrange a pantry audit in which the family's shelves are checked to see which brands they have on hand.

Choosing a primary method of data collection necessitates a number of additional decisions. For example, should we administer questionnaires by mail, over the telephone, or in person? Should the purpose of the study be disguised or remain undisguised? Should the answers be open-ended, or should the respondent be asked to choose from a limited set of alternatives? While Figure 9.2 implies that these decisions are independent, they

FIGURE 9.2   Basic Choices among Means for Collecting Primary Data

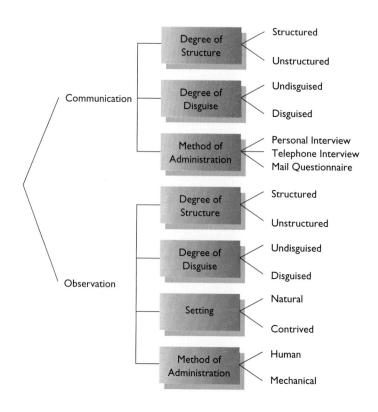

are actually intimately related. A decision with respect to method of administration, say, has serious implications regarding the degree of structure that must be imposed on the questionnaire.

Each method of obtaining primary data has its own advantages and disadvantages. For the remainder of this chapter we will review these general pluses and minuses. In the next chapter we will discuss the decisions that must be made when using the communication method; and in the chapter after that, the decisions involved in the observational method. In general, the communication method of data collection has the general advantages of versatility, speed, and cost, while observational data are typically more objective and accurate.

Versatility

Versatility is the ability of a technique to collect information on the many types of primary data of interest to marketers. A respondent's demographic/socioeconomic characteristics and lifestyle, the individual's attitudes and opinions, awareness and knowledge, intentions, the motivation underlying the individual's actions, and even the person's behavior may all be ascertained by the communication method. All we need to do is ask, although the replies will not necessarily be truthful.

Not so with observation. Observational techniques can provide us only with information about behavior and certain demographic/socioeconomic characteristics and even here there are certain limitations. Our observations are limited to present behavior, for example. We cannot observe a person's past behavior. Nor can we observe the person's intentions as to future behavior. If we are interested in past behavior or intentions, we must ask.

Some demographic/socioeconomic characteristics can be readily observed. Sex is the most obvious example. Others can be observed but with less accuracy. A person's age and income, for example, might be inferred by closely examining the individual's mode of dress and purchasing behavior. Clearly, though, both of these observations may be in error, with income likely to be the furthest off. Still others, such as social class, cannot be observed with any degree of confidence about the accuracy of the recorded data.

The other basic types of primary data cannot be measured by observation at all. We simply cannot observe an attitude or opinion, a person's awareness or knowledge, or motivation. Certainly we can attempt to make some inferences about these variables on the basis of the individual's observed behavior. For instance, a recent report by Media Matrix ranked the Web sites at which men and women spent the most time. The Media Matrix

---

Ethical Dilemma 9.2

A marketing research firm was hired by a candy manufacturer to gather data on the alternatives consumers consider when deciding to buy a candy bar. Sue Samuelson, the person in charge of the research, believed that the best way to collect accurate information was through an observation study done in major supermarkets, drugstores, and discount stores in a number of large cities. Unfortunately, at that time the personnel of the firm were stretched to the limit because of a number of other assignments. The company simply did not have sufficient personnel available to do the study using personal observation and still meet the client's deadline. Samuelson consequently decided that she would propose to the client a mail study utilizing the research firm's panel of households. Not only would this place fewer demands on the research firm's personnel, but the cost to the client would be about 25 percent less than with personal observation.

- Does Samuelson have an obligation to the client to disclose why she is recommending the mail panel?

- Is it ethical for a research firm to use alternative methods of gathering data because of internal constraints? What if the alternatives reduce the charges to the client?

- Who should make the decision as to the best way to approach the project—the client or the research supplier?

study found that men spent the most minutes at the eBay auction site, spending an average of almost 150 minutes per month at that site alone.[14] (Women spent slightly less time at eBay, which was the number three site among women.) While this observation tells something about the behavior of male Web users, it doesn't indicate why men spent more time at eBay than at any other site, whether they enjoyed that time on-line, whether they are aware of other on-line or live auctions, and whether they would prefer to meet their same objective in some other way, such as at a differently designed Web site or through the mail. Generalizing from behavior to states of mind is clearly risky, and researchers need to recognize this. Questioning clearly affords a broader base of primary data.

Speed and Cost

The speed and cost advantages of the communication method are closely intertwined. Assuming the data lend themselves to either means, communication is often a faster means of data collection than observation, because it provides a greater degree of control over data-gathering activities. With the communication method, researchers are not forced to wait for events to occur, as they are with the observation method. In some cases, it is impossible to predict when the event will occur precisely enough to observe it. For still other behaviors, the time interval between events can be substantial. For instance, an observer seeking to determine the brand purchased most frequently in one of several appliance categories might have to wait a long time to make any observations at all. Much of the time the observer would be idle. Such idleness is expensive, as the worker will probably be compensated on an hourly, rather than a per-contact, basis. Events that last a long time can also cause difficulty. An observational approach to studying the relative influence of a husband and a wife in the purchase of an automobile would be prohibitive in terms of both time and money.

There are also instances when observation is faster and costs less than communication. A primary one involves the purchase of consumer nondurables. The use of scanners, for example, allows many more purchases to be recorded and at less cost than if purchasers were questioned about what they bought.

Objectivity and Accuracy

Although the observation method has some serious limitations in terms of scope, time, and cost, it does have certain advantages with regard to objectivity and accuracy. Data that can be secured by either method will typically be more accurately secured by observation. This is because the observation method is independent of the respondent's unwillingness or inability to provide the information desired. For example, respondents are often reluctant to cooperate whenever their replies might place them in an unfavorable light. Sometimes respondents conveniently forget embarrassing events, while in other cases the events are not of sufficient importance for them to remember what happened. Since observation allows the recording of behavior as it occurs, it is not dependent on the respondent's memory or mood in reporting what occurred.

Observation typically produces more objective data than does communication. The interview represents a social interaction situation. Thus, the replies of the person being questioned are conditioned by the individual's perceptions of the interviewer. The same is true of interviewers' perceptions, but their training should afford a greater degree of control over their perceptions than would be true of the interviewee. With the observation method, the subject's perceptions play less of a role than in the communication method. Sometimes people are not even aware that they are being observed. Thus, they are not tempted to tell the interviewer what they think the interviewer wants to hear or to give socially acceptable responses that are not truthful. The problems of objectivity are concentrated in the observer's methods, and this makes the task easier. The observer's selection, training, and control, and not the subject's perceptions of the field worker, become the crucial elements.

Back to the Case

American Express Financial Advisors (AEFA) agreed to test the idea that planners with emotional intelligence would sell more insurance. The test involved setting up an experiment.

The company took financial planners with similar skills and backgrounds and divided the planners into two groups. The experimental group received 12 hours of training in one aspect of emotional intelligence: coping skills (managing one's own emotions and impulses). The control group received no training. The performance of the two groups was then tracked for three months.

At the end of the experimental period, the research team tallied the results. Planners in the experimental group performed 10 percent better than those in the control group. The experiment supported the hypothesis. Now there was evidence to support the idea that planners need to sell feelings as well as figures.

The team sent a report highlighting this difference to Jim Mitchell, the executive who had originally formed the team. Mitchell's reaction: "Do I understand that for the last 25 years, everything I've been doing is missing the point?"

These results convinced Mitchell to expand and change training, but research into the training's impact continued. The company would train more of its planners in more dimensions of emotional intelligence, and it would look for improvements in its sales. AEFA trained several dozen planners in awareness of their own emotions and those of clients. The objective was

that planners would be skilled not only in talking about financial goals but also in building clients' trust, pride, and sense of security.

Initial results showed that the financial planners who received the training significantly outperformed their untrained colleagues. By one measure, advisers with emotional intelligence training enjoyed 18.1 percent growth in their businesses, compared with 16.2 percent growth for those without training. At a company with over $200 billion in financial assets, a 2 percent difference translates into big dollars.

Follow-up research also asked planners about their attitudes toward emotional intelligence. Around 90 percent said competency in emotional intelligence is important to job performance.

Managers at AEFA are now sold on the idea. They have begun requiring every new financial adviser to complete a program in emotional intelligence as part of the company's initial training. Besides this six-day training session, executives are incorporating emotional intelligence training into sales conferences and performance reviews.

Sources: Scott Hays, "American Express Taps into the Power of Emotional Intelligence," *Workforce* (July 1, 1999, downloaded from Northern Light Web site, www.northernlight.com, September 22, 1999); Michelle Neely Martinez, "The Smarts That Count," *HR Magazine* (November 1997, downloaded from the Society for Human Resource Management Web site, www.shrm.org, May 28, 1999); American Express Web site, www.americanexpress.com, downloaded September 21, 1999.

Summary

Learning Objective 1

List the kinds of demographic and socioeconomic characteristics that interest marketers.

Marketers are interested in such socioeconomic and demographic characteristics as age, education, occupation, marital status, sex, income, and social class.

Learning Objective 2

Relate the premise on which lifestyle analysis rests.

Lifestyle analysis rests on the premise that the firm can plan more effective strategies to reach its target market if it knows more about its customers in terms of how they live, what interests them, and what they like.

Learning Objective 3

Cite the three main approaches used to measure the effectiveness of magazine ads.

The three main approaches used to measure awareness of magazine ads are (1) unaided recall, in which the consumer is given no cues at all; (2) aided recall, in which the consumer is given some prompting; and (3) recognition, in which the consumer is actually shown an advertisement and asked whether or not he or she remembers seeing it.

Learning Objective 4

Give two reasons why researchers are interested in people's motives.

First, researchers believe that motives tend to be more stable than behavior and therefore offer a better basis for predicting future behavior than does past behavior. Secondly, researchers believe that by understanding what drives a person's behavior, it is easier to understand the behavior itself.

Learning Objective 5

Describe the two basic means of obtaining primary data.

The two basic means of obtaining primary data are communication and observation. Communication involves questioning respondents to secure the desired information, using a data collection instrument called a questionnaire. Observation involves scrutinizing the situation of interest and recording the relevant facts, actions, or behaviors.

Learning Objective 6

State the specific advantages of each method of data collection.

In general, the communication method of data collection has the advantages of versatility, speed, and cost, while observation data are typically more objective and accurate.

Review Questions

1. What types of primary data interest marketing researchers most? How are they distinguished?

2. What are the general advantages and disadvantages associated with obtaining information by questioning? By observation? Which method provides more control over the sample?

Discussion Questions, Problems, and Projects

Should the communication or the observation method be used in the situations described in Questions 1 and 2? (Justify your choice.)

1. The Metal Product Division of Miracle Ltd. devised a special metal container to store plastic garbage bags. Plastic bags pose household problems, as they give off unpleasant odors, look disorderly, and provide a breeding place for insects. The container overcomes these problems, as it has a bag-support apparatus that holds the bag open for filling and seals the bag when the lid is closed. In addition, there is enough storage area for at least four full bags. The product is priced at $53.81

and is sold through hardware stores. The company has done little advertising and relies on in-store promotion and displays. The divisional manager is wondering about the effectiveness of these displays. She has called on you to do the necessary research.

2. Friendship is a national manufacturer and distributor of greeting cards. The company has recently begun distributing a lower-priced line of cards that is made possible by using a lower-grade paper. Quality differences between the higher- and lower-priced cards do not seem to be noticeable to consumers. The company follows a policy of printing its name and the price on the back of each card. The initial acceptance of the new line of cards has convinced the vice president of production, Sheila Howell, that the company should use this lower-grade paper for all its cards and increase its profit margin from 12.3 percent to 14.9 percent. The sales manager is strongly opposed to this move and has commented, "Sheila, consumers are concerned about the quality of greeting cards; a price difference of 5 cents on a card does not matter." The vice president has called upon you to undertake the study.

3. Stop-Buy, Inc., recently opened a new convenience store in Galveston, Texas. The store is open every day from 7:00 A.M. to 11:00 P.M. Management is interested in determining the trading area from which this store draws its customers, so that it can better plan the location of other units in the Galveston area.

    How would you determine this information by the questionnaire method? By the observation method? Which method would be preferred? Be sure to specify in your answer how you would define "trading area."

4. Following are several objectives for marketing research projects. For each objective, specify the type(s) of primary data that would be of use and a possible method of data collection.
    (a) assess "people flow" patterns inside a shopping mall
    (b) gauge the effectiveness of a new advertisement
    (c) gauge a salesperson's potential for success
    (d) segment a market
    (e) identify the shopper types that patronize a particular store
    (f) discover how people feel about a new package design

5. Lifestyle, or psychographic, analysis collects data concerning three dimensions of a respondent's lifestyle. Compare and contrast these dimensions. Are the three dimensions exhaustive, or can you suggest others that should be included?

Endnotes

1. Hope Katz Gibbs, "Latin American Marketing: Mediums for the Message," *Export Today* (June 1999), pp. 22–27.

2. There are a number of guides to the various personality inventories. Some of the more extensive ones are C. M. Bonjean, R. J. Hill, and S. D. McLemore, *Sociological Measurement: An Inventory of Scales and Indices* (San Francisco: Chandler, 1967); Ki-Taek Chun, Sidney Cobb, and J. R. P. French, *Measures for Psychological Assessment* (Ann Arbor, Mich.: Institute for Social Research, University of Michigan, 1975); Delbert C. Miller, *Handbook of Research Design and Social Measurement*, 5th ed. (Thousand Oaks, Calif.: Sage Publications, 1991).

3. Frito-Lay Profiles Salty Snack Consumers," *Supermarket News* (March 18, 1996), p. 39.

4. One of the more popular AIO inventories is the 300-question set that appears in William D. Wells and Douglas Tigert, "Activities, Interests, and Opinions," *Journal of Advertising Research* 11 (August 1971), pp. 27–35. For a general review of the origins, development, and thrust of lifestyle and psychographic research, see William D. Wells, ed., *Life Style and Psychographics* (Chicago: American Marketing Association, 1974). For evidence regarding the reliability and validity of psychographic inventories, see Alvin C. Burns and Mary Carolyn Harrison, "A Test of the Reliability of Psychographics," *Journal of Marketing Research* 16 (February 1979), pp. 32–38; John L. Lastovicka, "On the Validation of Lifestyle Traits: A Review and Illustration," *Journal of Marketing Research* 19 (February 1982), pp. 126–138; Ian Fenwick, D. A. Schellinck, and K. W. Kendall, "Assessing the Reliability of Psychographic Analyses,"

Marketing Science, 2 (Winter 1983), pp. 57–74; Thabet A. Edris and A. Meidan, "On the Reliability of Psychographic Research: Encouraging Signs for Measurement Accuracy and Methodology in Consumer Research," *European Journal of Marketing* 24 (No. 3, 1990), pp. 23–41; Faye W. Gilbert and William E. Warren, "Psychographic Constructs and Demographic Segments," *Psychology & Marketing* 12 (May 1995), pp. 223–237.

5. Allana Sullivan, "Mobile Bus Drivers Pick Cappuccino over Low Prices," *The Wall Street Journal* (January 30, 1995), pp. B1, B4.

6. The original VALS was a typology of the American population developed by Arnold Mitchell to provide a model of societal values. It is described in his book *The Nine American Lifestyles* (New York: Macmillan, 1983). It has been supplanted in the United States by VALS2, which is much more focused on predicting consumer behavior. Other value-based classification schemes include: Monitor, and The List of Values (LOV). For discussion of the use of value and lifestyle research, see Bickley Townsend, "Psychographic Glitter and Gold," *American Demographics* 7 (November 1985), pp. 22–29; Lynn R. Kahle, Sharon E. Beatty, and Pamela Homer, "Alternative Measurement Approaches to Consumer Values: The List of Values (LOV) and Values and Life Style (VALS)," *Journal of Consumer Research* 13 (December 1986), pp. 405–409; Rebecca Piirto, *Beyond Mind Games: The Marketing Power of Psychographics* (Ithaca, N.Y.: American Demographic Books, 1991); Wagner A. Kamakura and Thomas P. Novak, "Value-Based Segmentation: Exploring the Meaning of LOV," *Journal of Consumer Research* 19 (June 1992), pp. 129–132.

7. For a general discussion of the role of attitude in consumer behavior, see J. Paul Peter and Jerry C. Olson, *Consumer Behavior and Marketing Strategy*, 4th ed. (Burr Ridge, Ill.: Irwin, 1996), especially pages 155–190.

8. "Ford's Focus: Aim for Young Drivers," *Chicago Tribune* (August 13, 1999), sec. 3, p. 3.

9. See Herbert E. Krugman, "Point of View: Measuring Memory—An Industry Dilemma," *Journal of Advertising Research* 25 (August/September 1985), pp. 49–51; Charles E. Young and Michael Robinson, "Guideline: Tracking the Commercial Viewer's Wandering Attention," *Journal of Advertising Research* 27 (June/July 1987), pp. 15–22; Murphy A. Sewall and Dan Sarel, "Characteristics of Radio Commercials and Their Recall Effectiveness," *Journal of Marketing* 50 (January 1986), pp. 52–60; Myron Glassman and John B. Ford, "An Empirical Investigation of Bogus Recall," *Journal of the Academy of Marketing Science* 16 (Fall 1988), pp. 38–41; Robin Higie and Murphy A. Sewall, "Using Recall and Brand Preference to Evaluate Advertising Effectiveness," *Journal of Advertising Research* 31 (April/May, 1991), pp. 56–63; Erik du Plessis, "Recognition Versus Recall," *Journal of Advertising Research* 34 (May/June 1994), pp. 75–91; Joel S. Dubrow, "Recall Revisited: Recall Redux," *Journal of Advertising Research* 34 (May/June 1994), pp. 92–106.

10. Fred L. Schreier, *Modern Marketing Research: A Behavorial Science Approach* (Belmont, Calif: Wadsworth, 1963), pp. 269–273.

11. Manohar U. Kalwani and Alvin J. Silk, "On the Reliability and Predictive Validity of Purchase Intention Measures" *Marketing Science* 1 (Summer 1982), pp. 243–286; Gary M. Mullett and Marvin J. Karson, "Analysis of Purchase Intent Scales Weighted by Probability of Actual Purchase," *Journal of Marketing Research* 22 (February 1985), pp. 93–96; Vicki G. Morwitz and David Schmittlein, "Using Segmentation to Improve Sales Forecasts Based on Purchase Intent: Which 'Intendees' Actually Buy," *Journal of Marketing Research* 29 (November 1990), pp. 391–405; Richard H. Evans, "Analyzing the Potential of a New Market," *Industrial Marketing Management* 22 (February 1993), pp. 35–39; Albert C. Bemmaor, "Predicting Behavior from Intention-to-Buy Measures: The Parametric Case," *Journal of Marketing Research* 32 (May 1995), pp. 176–191. Those organizations that collect purchase-intentions data regularly often adjust the data based on their past experiences to how much bias a set of intentions data might contain.

12. James H. Myers and William H. Reynolds, *Consumer Behavior in Marketing Management* (Boston: Houghton Mifflin, 1967), p. 80.

13. See, for example, Don Schultz, "Losing Attitude," *Marketing Research: A Magazine of Management & Applications* 7 (Fall 1995), pp. 9–15, for discussion of some of the major changes taking place.

14. "'Sticky' Site-uations on the Net Vary by Gender," *Adweek* (April 5, 1999), p. 45.

Suggested Additional Readings

There are a number of guides to the various personality inventories. One of the better ones for marketers is Delbert C. Miller, Handbook of Research Design and Social Measurement, 5th ed. (Thousand Oaks, Calif.: Sage Publications, 1991).

For a general discussion of the purpose, procedures, and uses of lifestyle research, see
Arnold Mitchell, The Nine American Lifestyles (New York: Macmillan, 1983).
Rebecca Piirto, Beyond Mind Games: The Marketing Power of Psychographics (Ithaca, N.Y.: American Demographic Books, 1991).

Chapter 10

COLLECTING INFORMATION BY QUESTIONNAIRE

LEARNING OBJECTIVES

Upon Completing This Chapter, You Should Be Able to

1. Explain the concept of *structure* as it relates to questionnaires.

2. Explain what is meant by *disguise* in a questionnaire.

3. Discuss why structured-undisguised questionnaires are the type most frequently used by marketing researchers.

4. Cite three drawbacks of fixed-alternative questions.

5. Explain the reason why researchers use projective methods in conducting some studies.

6. List three common types of stimuli used in projective techniques.

7. Differentiate among the three methods of administering questionnaires.

8. Cite the points researchers generally consider when they compare the various methods of administering questionnaires.

Case in Marketing Research

"Do you know who your customers *really* are?" asked Rick Shanahan, the domestic sales manager for Clean-Rite appliances. He was sitting in the office of Tom Karlin, a successful appliance distributor who had a nine-county Clean-Rite franchise in booming central Florida.

"What do you mean?" asked Karlin, obviously intrigued.

"I mean that demographically, I can tell you who in your region has bought a Clean-Rite appliance within the last two years. I can tell you how old they are, how much money they make, what they like to do in their free time, and why they bought Clean-Rite rather than the competition."

"That's neat," replied Karlin, "but where's the information from? I didn't think Clean-Rite did a lot of heavy demographic research, especially not anything specific to central Florida."

"Well, we don't—at least not directly. We've started using a company that specializes in providing a consumer database that it generates from the information on product registration cards."

"You mean the cards the customers fill out and send back, saying where and when they bought their dishwasher and what the serial number is?"

"Yep. Not only does the registration card help us keep track of warranty information, but we also ask the consumers to answer some quick questions about their income, education, and interests. We already know their address. Most people don't even realize they're filling out a questionnaire."

"You're right, I never thought about product registration cards as questionnaires."

"Well," continued Shanahan, warming to his subject, "we pack a postage-paid registration card in with every appliance. The buyer fills it out and sends it directly to DLD, Demographics Life-Style Data, a company in Houston. DLD uses the information from the cards to generate a demographic database similar to U.S. Census information, but much more current. In addition, DLD's database has a lot more lifestyle information about the respondents. But the real beauty of the thing isn't in national projections—any marketer can send out 2,000 questionnaires and make national projections. DLD can break out specific *geographical regions*. They can make projections down to specific postal codes or neighborhoods. Like I said, I can tell you all about the consumers in your franchise area who, over the past two years, have bought an appliance from Clean-Rite."

"That's amazing," replied Karlin, "I'd love to see the information."

When the DLD computer printouts arrived several days later, Karlin spent some time studying the data. It really was interesting to see what kind of person bought Clean-Rite over other brands. Of course, he'd already had a picture of that customer in the back of his mind, based on his experience as a dealer. Clean-Rite had a reputation as a quality manufacturer and as a rule didn't go after the low end of the market. But this information was much more specific than just a salesman's gut response.

He learned that the typical Clean-Rite purchaser in his part of Florida had an income of $40,000 or greater, a college education, and a taste for outdoor recreation like golf, tennis, and boating.

"Great," thought Karlin as he tapped his pencil against the side of his coffee cup. "Now what?"

Discussion Issues

1. What are the limitations of product registration cards used as marketing research questionnaires?

2. Should someone make any major decisions based on the product registration data alone?

3. What kinds of additional research would you recommend?

In Chapter 9 we discussed the types of primary data that interest marketing researchers. We also briefly examined the two methods, communication and observation, that researchers employ to gather such data. In this chapter we will investigate communication techniques more closely, paying particular attention to the many types of questionnaires researchers use and the means by which they are administered.

Communication Methods

As we saw in Figure 9.2, if researchers choose to use the communication method of securing data, they must then decide on the kind of questionnaire that would best serve the problem at hand. They must determine the degree of **structure,** or standardization, to be imposed on the questionnaire, and the degree of **disguise** that is appropriate to the problem they are investigating.

In a highly structured questionnaire, the questions to be asked and the responses permitted the subjects are completely predetermined. In a highly unstructured questionnaire, the questions to be asked are only loosely predetermined, and the respondents are free to respond in their own words. A questionnaire in which the questions are fixed but the responses are open-ended would represent an intermediate degree of structure. A disguised questionnaire attempts to hide the purpose of the study, whereas an undisguised questionnaire makes the purpose of the research obvious by the questions posed.

Structure
The degree of standardization imposed on the data collection instrument. A highly structured questionnaire, for example, is one in which the questions to be asked and the responses permitted subjects are completely predetermined, while a highly unstructured questionnaire is one in which the questions to be asked are only loosely predetermined, and respondents are free to respond in their own words and in any way they see fit.

Disguise
The amount of knowledge about the purpose of a study communicated to the respondent. An undisguised questionnaire, for example, is one in which the purpose of the research is obvious.

Fixed-alternative questions
Questions in which the responses are limited to stated alternatives.

Structured-Undisguised Questionnaires

Marketing researchers often use structured-undisguised questionnaires in which questions are presented with exactly the same wording and in exactly the same order to all respondents when collecting data. The reason for standardizing the wording is to ensure that all respondents are replying to the same questions. If one interviewer asked, "Do you drink orange juice?" and another asked, "Does your family use frozen orange juice?" the replies would not be comparable.

In the typical structured-undisguised questionnaire, the responses as well as the questions are standardized. **Fixed-alternative questions,** in which the responses are limited to the stated alternatives, are used. Consider the following question regarding the subject's attitude toward pollution and the need for more government legislation to control it.

Do you feel the United States needs more or less antipollution legislation?

☐ Needs more

☐ Needs less

☐ Neither more nor less

☐ No opinion

This question is a good example of a structured-undisguised question for two reasons. First, its purpose is clear: It seeks to discover the subject's attitudes toward antipollution legislation in a very straightforward manner. Second, it employs a highly structured format. Respondents are limited to only one of four stated replies.

This e-poll "Is Travel Taking Its Toll?" from the Inc. Online World Wide Web site (www.inc.com) is an example of a structured-undisguised questionnaire. The questions are presented to each poll recipient with exactly the same wording and in exactly the same order. This ensures that all respondents will reply to the same question, reducing errors caused by interpretation.

Source: Copyright 1999. Goldhirsh Group, Inc. Inc. is a registered trademark of The Goldhirsh Group, which owns Inc. magazine and Inc. Online.

Probably the greatest advantages of structured-undisguised questionnaires are that they are simple to administer and easy to tabulate and analyze. Subjects should be reliable in that if they were asked the question again, they would answer in a similar fashion (assuming, of course, the absence of some attitude-changing event).

Such reliability is facilitated by the consistency of fixed-alternative questions. These questions help standardize responses by providing subjects with an identical frame of reference. In contrast, consider the question, "How often do you watch television?" If no alternatives were supplied, one respondent might say "every day," another might say "regularly," and still another might respond with the number of hours per day. Responses from such an open-ended question would be far more difficult to interpret than those from a fixed-alternative question limiting replies to the categories of "every day," "at least three times a week," "at least once a week," or "less than once a week."

Providing alternative responses also often helps to make the question clear. "What is your marital status?" is less clear in its intent than "Are you married, single, widowed, or divorced?" The latter question provides the dimensions in which to frame the reply.

Although fixed-alternative questions tend to provide the most reliable responses, they may also elicit misleading answers. For example, fixed alternatives may force an answer to a question on which the respondent has no opinion. Even when a "no opinion" category is provided, interviewers often try to keep the number of "no opinions" to a minimum by pressing the respondent for a reply. The individual may agree, under pressure, to one of the other alternatives offered, but the alternative may not accurately capture the individual's true position on the issue. For example, the antipollution example presented earlier makes no allowance for those who feel that something probably should be done about pollution and that more legislation may possibly be one answer, but who fundamentally favor other approaches.

Fixed-alternative responses may also produce inaccuracies when the response categories themselves introduce bias. This is particularly true when a reasonable response is omitted because of an oversight or insufficient prior research as to the response categories that are appropriate. The provision of an "other" category does not eliminate this bias either, since subjects are often reluctant to respond in the "other" category. In posing a fixed-alternative question, one should make sure the alternatives offered adequately cover the range of probable replies.

The fixed-alternative question is thus most productive when possible replies are well known, limited in number, and clear-cut. Thus they work well for securing factual information (age, education, home ownership, amount of rent, and so on) and for eliciting expressions of opinion about issues on which people hold clear opinions. They are not very appropriate for securing primary data on motivations but certainly could be used (at least sometimes) to collect data on attitudes, intentions, awareness, demographic/ socioeconomic characteristics, and behavior.

Unstructured-Undisguised Questionnaires

The unstructured-undisguised questionnaire is distinguished by the fact that the purpose of the study is clear but the response to the question is open-ended. Consider the following question:

"How do you feel about pollution and the need for more antipollution legislation?"

This initial question (which is often called a *stimulus* by researchers) is clear in its purpose. With it the interviewer attempts to get the subject to talk freely about his or her attitudes toward pollution. This is an **open-ended question,** and often leads to a very unstructured interview (called a **depth interview**). The respondent's initial reply, the interviewer's follow-up questions that seek elaboration, and the respondent's subsequent answers determine the direction of the interview. The interviewer may attempt to follow a rough outline. However, the order and the specific framing of the questions will vary from interview to interview, and the specific content will therefore vary.

The freedom permitted the interviewer in conducting these depth interviews reveals the major advantages and disadvantages of the method. By not limiting the respondent to a fixed set of replies, and by careful probing, an experienced interviewer should be able to derive a more accurate picture of the respondent's true position on some issue. This is particularly true with respect to sensitive issues in which there is social pressure to conform and to offer a "socially acceptable" response. Note, however, that we qualified our description of this method by specifying that "experienced interviewers" be used and "careful probing" be done. The depth interview requires highly skilled interviewers. They are hard to find and expensive to hire. But they are essential to accurate results with this type of questionnaire, in which the lack of structure allows the interviewer to strongly influence the result. Keen judgment as to when to probe and how to word the probes is required of the interviewer, and good depth interviews often take a long time to complete. This makes it difficult to secure the cooperation of respondents. It also means that a study using depth interviews, as opposed to fixed-alternative questions, will not only take longer to complete, but will involve fewer respondents or will require a greater number of interviewers. And the more interviewers there are, the more likely it will be that responses will vary based on each interviewer's personal technique in administering the questionnaire.

The depth interview also causes severe problems in analysis. One or more skilled researchers are typically required to interpret the responses—an expensive service. Further,

Open-ended question
A question characterized by the condition that respondents are free to reply in their own words rather than being limited to choosing from among a set of alternatives.

Depth interview
An unstructured personal interview in which the interviewer attempts to get the subject to talk freely and to express his or her true feelings.

the researcher's own background and frame of reference will affect the interpretation. This subjectivity raises questions about both the reliability and validity of the results. It also causes difficulty in determining what the correct interpretation is and thus presents problems when tabulating the replies.

Some of the problems with coding open-ended questions may be changing with new technology. Researchers today often feed respondents' answers into computers programmed to recognize a large vocabulary of words in their search for regularities in the replies. The computers are able to rank each word by the frequency of usage and then can print out sentences containing the key words. The detailed analysis of these sentences allows researchers to pick up on recurring themes.[1] Although these systems automate the coding of unstructured interviews, they still leave interpretation to the individual analyst. Nevertheless, the systems can achieve in hours what a purely human review might take weeks to accomplish.

The depth interview is probably best suited to exploratory research, since it is productive with respect to just about all of the common purposes of exploratory research.

Unstructured-Disguised Questionnaires

Unstructured-disguised questionnaires lie at the heart of what has become known as motivation research.

> A person needs only limited experience in questionnaire-type surveys to realize that many areas of inquiry are not amenable to exploration by direct questions. Many important motives and reasons for choice are of a kind that the consumer will not describe because a truthful description would be damaging to his ego. Others he cannot describe, either because he himself does not have the words to make his meaning clear or because his motive exists below the level of awareness. Very often such motives are of paramount importance in consumer behavior. If one tries to inquire into them with direct questions, especially categorical questions, one tends to get replies that are either useless or dangerously misleading.[2]

Projective method
The term used to describe questionnaires containing ambiguous stimuli that force subjects to rely on their own emotions, needs, motivations, attitudes, and values in framing a response.

Researchers have tried to overcome subjects' reluctance to discuss their feelings by developing techniques that are largely independent of the subjects' self-awareness and willingness to reveal themselves. The main thrust of these kinds of techniques, known as **projective methods,** has been to conceal the true subject of the study by using a disguised stimulus.

Though the stimulus is typically standardized, subjects are allowed to respond to it in a very unstructured form, which is why this method is known as an unstructured-disguised questionnaire. The basic assumption in projective methods is that the way an individual responds to a relatively unstructured stimulus provides clues as to how that person really perceives the subject under investigation and what his or her true reactions are to it.

> [T]he more unstructured and ambiguous a stimulus, the more a subject can and will project his emotions, needs, motivations, attitudes, and values. The structure of a stimulus . . . is the degree of choice available to the subject. A highly structured stimulus leaves very little choice: the subject has unambiguous choice among clear alternatives. . . . A stimulus of low structure has a wide range of alternative choices. It is ambiguous: the subject can "choose" his own interpretation.[3]

In general terms, then, a projective technique involves the use of a vague stimulus that an individual is asked to describe, expand upon, or build a structure around. Among the most common stimuli used are word association, sentence completion, and storytelling.

Word association
A questionnaire containing a list of words to which respondents are instructed to reply with the first word that comes to mind.

Word Association In the projective method of **word association,** subjects respond to a list of words with the first word that comes to mind. The test words are intermixed with neutral words to conceal the purpose of the study. In the study of pollution, some of the key words might be

- Water   _____

- Air   _____

- Lakes   _____

- Industry   _____

- Smokestack   _____

- City   _____

Responses to each of the key terms are recorded word-for-word and later analyzed for their meaning. The responses are usually judged in three ways: by the frequency with which any word is given as a response, by the average amount of time that elapses before a response is given, and by the number of respondents who do not respond at all to a test word after a reasonable period of time.

Any common responses that emerge are grouped to reveal patterns of interest, underlying motivations, or stereotypes. It is often possible to categorize the associations as favorable/unfavorable, pleasant/unpleasant, modern/old-fashioned, and so forth, depending upon the problem

To determine the amount of time that elapses before a response is given to a test word, a stopwatch may be used or the interviewer may count silently while waiting for a reply. Respondents who hesitate (which is usually defined as taking longer than three seconds to reply) are judged to be sufficiently emotionally involved in the word so as to provide not their immediate reaction but rather what they consider to be an acceptable response. If they do not respond at all, their emotional involvement is judged to be so high as to block a response. An individual's pattern of responses, along with the details of the response to each question, are then used to assess the person's attitudes or feelings on the subject.

Sentence completion

A questionnaire containing a number of sentences that subjects are directed to complete with the first words that come to mind.

Sentence Completion The method of **sentence completion** requires that the respondent complete a number of sentences similar to the following:

- Many people behave as if our natural resources were _____.

- A person who does not use our lakes for recreation is _____.

- The number-one concern for our natural resources is _____.

- When I think of living in a city, I _____.

Again, respondents are instructed to reply with the first thoughts that come to mind. The responses are recorded word-for-word and are later analyzed.

> In one study, Kassarjian and Cohen asked 179 smokers who believed cigarettes to be a health hazard why they continued to smoke. The majority gave responses such as "Pleasure is more important than health," "Moderation is OK," "I like to smoke." One gets the impression that smokers are not dissatisfied with their lot. However, in a portion of the study involving sentence-completion tests, smokers responded to the question, "People who never smoke are _____," with comments such as "better off," "happier," "smarter," "wiser," "more informed." To the question, "Teenagers who smoke are _____," smokers responded with "foolish," "crazy," "uninformed," "stupid," "showing off," "immature," "wrong."
>
> Clearly the impression one gets from the sentence completion test is that smokers are anxious, uncomfortable, dissonant, and dissatisfied with their habit. This is quite different from the results of a probed open-end question.[4]

One advantage of sentence completion over word association is that respondents can be provided with a more directed stimulus. There should be just enough direction to evoke some association with the concept of interest. The researcher needs to be careful not to convey the purpose of the study or provoke the "socially acceptable" response. Obviously, skill is needed to develop a good sentence-completion or word-association test.

Storytelling

A questionnaire method of data collection relying on a picture stimulus such as a cartoon, photograph, or drawing, about which the subject is asked to tell a story.

Thematic Apperception Test (TAT)

A copyrighted series of pictures about which the subject is asked to tell stories.

Storytelling Pictorial material such as cartoons, photographs, or drawings is often used in the **storytelling** approach, although other stimuli are also used. These pictorial devices are descendants of the psychologists' **Thematic Apperception Test (TAT).** The TAT consists of a copyrighted series of pictures about which the subject is asked to tell stories. Some of the pictures are of ordinary events and some of unusual events; in some of the pictures the persons or objects are clearly represented, and in others they are relatively obscure. The way a subject responds to these events helps researchers interpret that individual's personality. For example, the nature of the response might show a subject to be impulsive or controlled, creative or unimaginative, and so on.

When used in a marketing situation, the same pattern is followed. Respondents are shown a picture and asked to tell a story about the picture. However, the responses are used to assess attitudes toward the phenomenon under investigation rather than to interpret the subject's personality. For example,

> McCann-Erickson ad agency resorted to stick-figure sketches in research on its American Express Gold Card account. Focus group interviews hadn't made clear consumers' differing perceptions of gold-card and green-card holders.
> The drawings, however, were much more illuminating. In one set, for example, the gold-card user was portrayed as a broad-shouldered man standing in an active position, while the green-card user was a "couch potato" in front of a TV set. Based on such pictures and other research, the agency decided to market the gold card as a "symbol of responsibility for people who have control over their lives and finances."[5]

With respect to the pollution example, the stimulus might be a picture of a city, and the respondent might be asked to describe what it would be like to live there. The analysis of the individual's response would then focus on the emphasis given to pollution in its various forms. If no mention were made of traffic congestion, dirty air, noise, and so on, the person would be classified as displaying little concern for pollution and its control.

Each of the projective methods we have discussed differs somewhat in how structured its stimulus is. In the word-association and sentence-completion methods, researchers present each respondent with the same stimulus in the same sequence, and in this sense these methods are quite structured. However, both methods are typically categorized with storytelling as unstructured techniques, because, like the storytelling techniques, they allow very unstructured responses. Respondents are free to interpret and respond to the stimuli with their own words and in terms of their own perceptions.

Many of the same difficulties encountered with the unstructured-undisguised methods of data collection are also encountered with projective methods. Although having a standardized stimulus is a distinct advantage in interpreting the replies, the interpretation often reflects the researcher's frame of reference as much as it does the respondent's. Different researchers often reach different conclusions about the same response. This wreaks havoc with the editing, coding, and tabulating of replies and suggests that projective methods are also more suited for exploratory research than for descriptive or causal research.

Structured-Disguised Questionnaires

Structured-disguised questionnaires are the least used in marketing research. They were developed as a way of combining the advantages of disguise in uncovering subconscious motives and attitudes with the advantages of structure in coding and tabulating replies. Those who favor the structured-disguised approach usually base their support on the importance of a person's attitudes in his or her mental and psychological makeup.

One theory holds, for example, that an individual's knowledge, perception, and memory of a subject are conditioned by his or her attitudes toward it. Thus, in order to secure information about people's attitudes when a direct question would produce a biased answer, this theory suggests we simply ask them what they know, not what their opinion is. Presumably greater knowledge reflects the strength and direction of an attitude. Democratic voters, for example, could be expected to know more about Democratic candidates and the Democratic platform than would those intending to vote Republican. This argument is consistent with what we have learned about the process that psychologists call *selective perception*. That concept holds that individuals tend to selectively expose themselves to, selectively perceive, and selectively retain ideas, arguments, events, and phenomena that are consistent with their previously held beliefs. Conversely, people tend to avoid, see differently, and forget situations and items that are inconsistent with their previously held beliefs.

This theory would suggest that one way of discovering a respondent's true attitudes toward pollution and the need for antipollution legislation, for example, would be to ask the person what he or she knows about the subject. Thus, the researcher might ask, "What is the status of the antipollution legislation listed below?" and then present some actual and some hypothetical bills for the respondent to check: "In committee," "Passed by the House but not the Senate," "Vetoed by the president," and so on. Respondents' attitudes toward the need for more legislation would then be assessed by the accuracy of their responses.

The main advantages of this approach emerge in analysis. Responses are easily coded and tabulated and an objective measure of knowledge quickly derived. Whether this measure of knowledge can also be interpreted as a measure of the person's attitudes, though, is another matter. Is high legislative awareness indicative of a favorable or an unfavorable attitude toward the need for more antipollution legislation? Or is it simply indicative of someone who keeps abreast of current events? In general, the evidence suggests that it is possible to obtain results with a structured-disguised approach that are at least comparable to those obtained with unstructured-disguised approaches.

Methods of Administering Questionnaires

Questionnaires can also be classified by the method that will be used to administer them. The main methods are by personal interview, telephone interview, and mail questionnaire.

Personal interview
Direct, face-to-face conversation between a representative of the research organization, the interviewer, and a respondent, or interviewee.

A **personal interview** implies a direct face-to-face conversation between the interviewer and the respondent. The interview can take place in a home or office or at a central location like a mall where shoppers are stopped or intercepted and asked to participate. The **telephone interview** means that the conversation occurs over the phone. In all these cases, the interviewer asks the questions and records the respondent's answers either while the interview is in progress or immediately afterward. The **mail questionnaire** is sent to designated respondents with an accompanying cover letter. The respondents complete the questionnaire at their leisure and mail their replies back to the research organization.

Telephone interview
Telephone conversation between a representative of the research organization, the interviewer, and a respondent, or interviewee.

Mail questionnaire
A questionnaire administered by mail to designated respondents under an accompanying cover letter. The respondents return the questionnaire by mail to the research organization.

A number of variations are possible on these so-called pure methods of administration. Questionnaires for a mail administration may simply be attached to products or printed in magazines and newspapers. Questionnaires in a personal interview may be self-administered, meaning the respondents complete the questionnaire themselves as opposed to having the interviewer ask the questions and fill in the respondents' answers. This might be done in the interviewer's presence, in which case there would be an opportunity for the respondents to ask the interviewer to clarify any points that may be confusing. Or the respondents might complete the questionnaire in private for later pickup by a representative of the research organization, in which case the interaction would resemble a personal interview even less. Another possibility is for the interviewer to hand the designated respondent the questionnaire personally, but then have the respondent complete it in private and mail it directly to the research organization. In this case, the personal interview is indistinguishable from the mail-questionnaire method. Another way of administering

Ethical Dilemma 10.1

Pharmaceutical Supply Company derived its major source of revenue from physician-prescribed drugs. For quite some time, Pharmaceutical Supply had maintained a dominant position in the market. A new competitor had entered the market, however, and was quickly gaining market share.

In response to competitive pressure, Pharmaceutical Supply's management decided that it needed to conduct an extensive study concerning physician decision making with regard to selection of drugs. Janice Rowland, the marketing research director, decided that the best way to gather this information would be through the use of personal and telephone interviews. Rowland directed the interviewers to represent themselves as employees of a fictitious marketing research agency, as she believed that a biased response would result if the physicians were aware that Pharmaceutical Supply was conducting the study. In addition, the interviewers were

instructed to tell the physicians that the research was being conducted for the research agency's own purpose and not for a particular client.

- Was Rowland's decision to withhold the sponsor's true name and purpose a good one?

- Did the physicians have a right to know who was conducting the research?

- It has been argued that use of such deception prevents a respondent from making a rational choice about whether or not she or he wishes to participate in a study. Comment on this.

- What kind of results might have been obtained if the physicians had known the true sponsor of the study?

- What are the consequences for the research profession of using this form of deception?

questionnaires is via e-mail and the Web. In many ways, e-mail administration has features like mail administration. Similarly, telephone administration becomes very similar to mail administration when the telephone is used to fax the questionnaire to the respondent.[6]

Each of these methods of communication possesses some advantages and disadvantages. When discussing the pros and cons, the pure cases logically serve as a frame of reference. When a modified administration is used, the general advantages and disadvantages may no longer hold. They may also cease to hold in specific situations, in which case a general advantage may become a disadvantage, and vice versa. The advantages and disadvantages also may not apply when dealing with different countries with different cultures. For example, it is not culturally acceptable to answer questions from "strangers" over the telephone in Japan, while that is commonly done in the United States.

In Saudi Arabia, door-to-door interviewing is illegal, but not in the United States. Further, while the ability to develop a good mailing list is an important factor affecting the attractiveness of mail surveys in the United States, the Swedish government routinely publishes lists of every Swedish household, making mail studies very feasible there.[7] Therefore, it is not surprising that there are differences by country in the relative frequency with which the various data collection techniques are used. Figure 10.1 for example, highlights some of the country-by-country differences in Europe—differences that are particularly

FIGURE 10.1 **Relative Use of Various Data Collection Techniques in Selected European Countries**

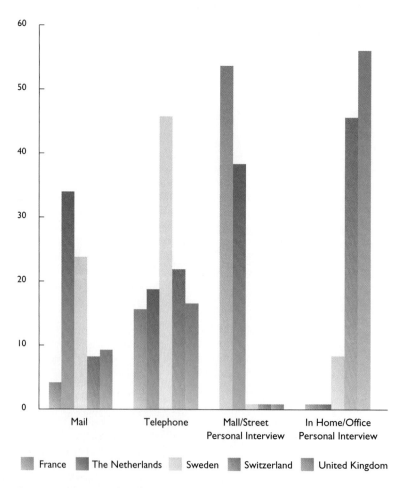

Source: Emanuel H. Demby, "ESOMAR Urges Changes in Reporting Demographics, Issues Worldwide Report," *Marketing News* 24 (January 8, 1990), pp. 24–25. Reprinted with permission of American Marketing Association.

dramatic with respect to when and where personal interviews are conducted. In Sweden, personal interviews are used very seldom. In Switzerland and the United Kingdom, they almost always take place in a home or office. In France and The Netherlands, researchers typically rely on intercepting the respondent in a mall or on the street.

The specific problem and culture then will actually dictate the benefits and weaknesses that are associated with each method. Nevertheless, a general discussion of advantages and disadvantages serves to highlight the various methods, issues, and criteria that need to be considered in deciding on the manner in which the data will be collected. Sampling control, information control, and administrative control are definite points to consider when comparing the methods.

Sampling Control

Sampling control
The term applied to studies relying on questionnaires and concerning the researcher's dual abilities to direct the inquiry to a designated respondent and to secure the desired cooperation from that respondent.

Sampling frame
The list of sampling units from which a sample will be drawn; the list could consist of geographic areas, institutions, individuals, or other units.

Sampling control involves the researcher's ability to direct the inquiry to a designated respondent and to get the desired cooperation from that respondent. The direction of the inquiry is guided by the **sampling frame**—that is, by the list of population elements from which the sample will be drawn. With the telephone method, for example, one or more phone books typically serve as the sampling frame. Respondents are selected by some random method from phone books serving the areas in which the study is to be done. Phone book sampling frames are inadequate because they do not include those without phones or those who have unlisted numbers.

Of course, a great percentage of the U.S. population has phones—almost 95 percent of all households. Yet there is some variation by region and by other demographic factors, both in the United States and worldwide. Research Window 10.1 shows the distribution of telephone ownership worldwide, while Exhibit 10.1 summarizes the evidence regarding the demographic factors affecting phone ownership. The differences in phone ownership by various demographic factors can bias the results of a telephone survey.

The proportion of households with telephones increases each year, however, and thus the problem of bias resulting from the exclusion of nontelephone households should diminish in the future.

Studies that rely on phone book sampling frames underrepresent transient households. Anywhere from 12 percent to 15 percent of the residential numbers in a typical telephone directory are disconnected when called. Phone book sampling frames also do not include numbers that were assigned after the current directory was published, as well as the segment of the population that has requested an unlisted telephone number. The voluntary unlisted segment has been growing steadily and now represents over 28 percent of all residential phones in the United States.[8] The problem is particularly acute in urban areas in general, and some urban areas in particular. Figure 10.2 for example, shows the ten metropolitan areas in the United States with the highest population of unlisted numbers.

A comparison of unlisted versus listed households indicates that unlisted households are younger than listed households, more likely to live in urban areas, nonwhite, more mobile, and either very high or very low income.

Random-digit dialing
A technique used in studies employing telephone interviews, in which the numbers to be called are randomly generated.

Some researchers attempt to overcome the sampling bias of unlisted numbers by using **random-digit dialing.** This approach entails the random generation of numbers to be called, and often the automatic dialing of these calls as well. The calls are typically handled through one central interviewing facility. This procedure allows geographically wide distribution or coverage.

One problem with the random generation of phone numbers is that it can increase survey costs. While there are approximately 340 million possible phone numbers that can be called in the continental United States, there are only about 80 million working residential telephone numbers. Hence, when using random dialing, interviewers may only make a residential contact in about one out of four calls. This makes random-digit dialing very costly both in dollars and in time.[9]

Plus-one sampling
A technique used in studies employing telephone interviews, in which a single, randomly determined digit is added to numbers selected from the telephone directory.

An alternative scheme to random-digit is **plus-one sampling,** where a probability sample of phone numbers is selected from the telephone directory and a single, randomly determined digit is added to each selected number.[10]

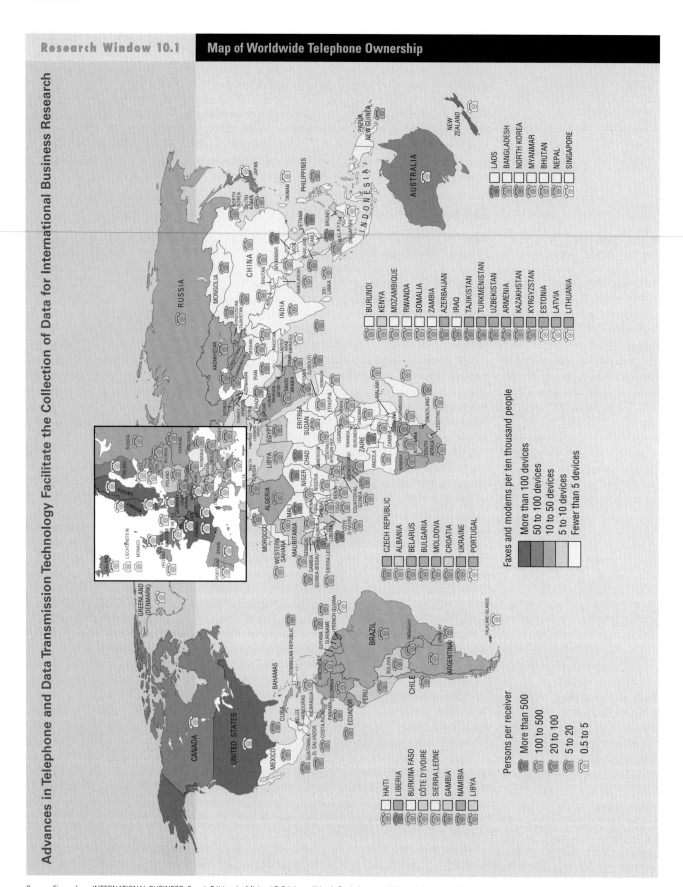

Source: Figure from INTERNATIONAL BUSINESS, Fourth Edition, by Michael R Czinkota, Ilkka A. Ronkainen, and Michael H. Moffett, © 1996 by Harcourt Brace & Company, reproduced by permission of the publisher.

EXHIBIT 10.1   **Summary of Studies of Demographic Factors Related to Telephone Ownership**

1. Telephone coverage is greater in urban areas than in rural areas, although in countries with very high overall telephone penetration (e.g., Canada, France, Denmark, and Norway) the difference is rather small.
2. In the United States, coverage is lower in the South. Similar regional differences prevail in at least some other countries (e.g., Ireland and Israel), but regional categorizations are country specific and are hard to compare cross-nationally.
3. In the United States, coverage is lower among nonwhites. No racial information was available from other countries.
4. Telephone coverage is always lower among those with lower incomes, the unemployed, those in manual or low-prestige occupations, and the less educated.
5. Telephone coverage is consistently lower for renters and people who live in apartments or trailers rather than in single-family homes. Only the relationship with renting has data from both the United States and other countries.
6. Households without telephones tend to be headed by younger people, unmarried people, and perhaps males (data exists only for the United States, and even in the United States, the relationship is uncertain).
7. Nontelephone households tend to be either smaller than average or larger than average.

Source: Tom W. Smith, "Phone Home? An Analysis of Household Telephone Ownership," *International Journal of Public Opinion Research* 2 (Winter 1990), p. 386.

FIGURE 10.2   **Ten Metro Areas with the Highest Proportion of Unlisted Telephone Numbers**

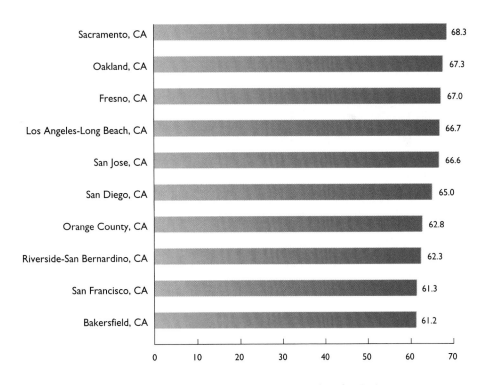

Source: "Sacramento Is Top Unlisted Market," *The Frame* (February 1995), p. 1, published by Survey Sampling, Inc.

One or more mailing lists typically serve as the sampling frame in mail questionnaires. The quality of these lists determines the sampling biases. If the list is a reasonably good one, the bias may be small. For example, some firms have established panels, which can be used to answer mail questionnaires and which are representative of the population in many important respects. Further, some mailing lists that may be ideally suited for certain types of studies can be purchased.

> Say you run a direct-mail business that specializes in selling monogrammed baby bibs. For a fee at any given time you can obtain a mailing list containing the names and addresses of up to one million pregnant women. And if it should suit your purposes, it's easy enough to get the list limited to women whose babies are expected in a certain month or who are expecting their first child.[11]

Sometimes the list is internally generated. When first-time customers order office furniture from National Business Furniture, the business-to-business catalog retailer sends along a questionnaire when it delivers their order. This survey inquires about the customers' satisfaction with National's products and service. In addition, when people call to ask for a catalog but never place an order afterward, National sends them a questionnaire to find out why they didn't buy.[12] On a more sophisticated level, many companies mine their customer databases to target questionnaires to buyers with certain demographics or purchase histories.

The fact remains, though, that the mailing list determines the sampling control in a mail study. If there is an accurate, applicable, and readily available list of population elements, the mail questionnaires allows a wide and representative sample, since it costs no more to send a questionnaire across country than it does to send one across town. Even ignoring costs, it is sometimes the only way of contacting the relevant population, such as busy executives who will not sit still for an arranged personal or telephone interview but may respond to a mail questionnaire. A key here, though, is the ability to address the questionnaire to a specific respondent rather than a position.

It is estimated that the average consumer has his or her name on anywhere from 25 to 40 separate mailing lists and receives 80 pieces of unsolicited mail per year. All those who think unsolicited mail is a bother, however, can send one letter to the Direct Mail Marketing Association, a trade group of more than 2,600 direct mail marketers, and that organization will remove the name from every member's list. The statistics indicate, however, that for every person requesting to have his or her name removed, two more request that their names be added.[13]

E-mail administered questionnaires are similar to mail questionnaires when it comes to sampling control. The sample, of course, is limited to those who own or have access to a computer and an e-mail account. However, if there is an accurate, applicable and readily available list of e-mail addresses, e-mail allows a geographically dispersed sample to be used. For example, e-mail administration has been used to survey college and university faculty since their e-mail addresses are often easy to obtain.[14] Similarly, Internet retailer Drugstore.com conducts on-line surveys of its customers, who are, by definition, Internet users. A more complex situation faced a consortium called Advanced General Aviation Transport Experiment (AGATE). The AGATE consortium first determined that the profile of people who buy and fly airplanes closely matches that of World Wide Web users. Having established that resemblance, AGATE went ahead with an Internet survey of pilots, former pilots, and potential pilots.[15] For many populations of interest, though, generating a list of relevant e-mail addresses is difficult.

Sampling control for personal interviewing is a bit more difficult than for telephone interviewing or mail questionnaires, but is still possible. For some populations, such as doctors, architects, or business firms, trade associations or directories will furnish names from which a sample can be drawn. For studies focused on consumers in which in-house interviews are to be conducted, however, there are few lists available, and those that are available are typically out-of-date. Instead of seeking names, researchers often choose their samples based on geographic areas and houses or apartments, termed *sampling units,* within the area. In this method, instead of inaccurate lists of people, interviewers use accurate, current lists of sampling units in the form of maps. In a later chapter we will discuss how such *area sampling,* as it is called, works.

Mall intercept

A method of data collection in which interviewers in a shopping mall stop or interrupt a sample of those passing by to ask them if they would be willing to participate in a research study; those who agree are typically taken to an interviewing facility that has been set up in the mall, where the interview is conducted.

Although there is still the problem of ensuring that the field interviewer will contact the right household and person, the personal interview does provide some sampling control in directing the questionnaire to specific sampling units.

A currently popular alternative for conducting personal interviews among consumers is to use **mall intercepts.** The technique involves exactly what the name implies.[16] Interviewers intercept, or stop, those passing by and ask if they would be willing to participate in a research study. Those who agree are typically taken to the firm's interviewing facility that has been set up in the mall, where the interview is conducted. With shopping mall intercepts, there are two issues affecting the ability to direct the inquiry to a randomly determined respondent. First, although a great many people do shop at malls, almost one in four people do not.[17] Moreover, only those who visit the particular mall in question have a chance of being included in the study. Second, a person's chances of being asked to participate depend on the likelihood of their being in the mall. That, in turn, depends on the frequency with which they shop there. One thing that is commonly done with respect to this second source of variation in the selection probabilities is to weight the replies of the respondent by the reciprocal of the number of visits made to the mall in a set amount of time.[18]

The experience of mall intercept researchers at the Hawthorn Center shopping mall illustrates some limitations of this type of personal interview. Quick Test, Inc., a marketing research firm based in Florida, conducts research at Hawthorn Center because the Chicago-area shopping mall primarily serves shoppers who have families and are in the 25-to-49 age group—demographics that interest many marketers. At the same time, choosing a particular mall also limits the population from which the sample will be drawn. In addition, the practice of asking people to participate is not entirely random. Recruiters know that many of the shoppers they invite to participate will decline—sometimes rudely—so they develop skill in identifying who to ask. For example, experience teaches they have a better chance with a shopper who maintains eye contact with them.[19] Because it is up to the recruiters to initiate contact personally, the process is very difficult to control, even through a rigid sampling design.

It is one thing to figure out whom to contact in a study; it is quite another to get that person to agree to participate. For example, of the three methods of data collection we have discussed, the personal interview affords the most sample control with respect to obtaining cooperation from the designated respondent. With a personal interview, the respondent's identity is known, and thus there is little opportunity for anyone else to reply. People are also less likely to refuse a personal interview than they are a telephone interview or a mail questionnaire. There is sometimes a problem with not-at-homes, but this can often be handled by calling back at a different time.

Telephone methods also suffer from not-at-homes or no-answers. In one very large study involving more than 259,000 telephone calls, it was found, for example, that over 34 percent of the calls resulted in a no-answer, a situation that has gotten worse since the study was conducted with the increased popularity of telephone screening techniques such as the answering machine and Caller ID.[20] Even more disturbing was the fact that the probability of making contact with an eligible respondent on the first call was less than 1 in 10 (see Exhibit 10.2). Of course, calling back by phone is much simpler and more economical than is trying to rearrange a personal interview. The relatively low expense of a telephone contact allows a number of follow-up calls to secure a needed response, while the high cost of field contact restricts the number of follow-ups that can be made in studies using personal interviews. However, making sure the intended respondent replies is somewhat more difficult with telephone interviews than with personal interviews, as is the problem of determining which person in the household should be interviewed.[21]

Mail questionnaires afford the researcher little control in securing a response from the intended respondent. Although the researcher can offer the individual some incentive for cooperating, a great many subjects may nevertheless refuse to respond. In many cases, only those most interested in the subject will respond. In other cases subjects will be incapable of responding because they are illiterate. For example, the International Reading Association estimates that some 20 million English-speaking, native-born American adults

EXHIBIT 10.2   **Results of First Dialing Attempts**

Result	Number of Dialings	Probability of Occurrence
No answer	89,829	.347
Busy	5,299	.020
Out-of-service	52,632	.203
No eligible person	75,285	.291
Business	10,578	.041
At home	25,465	.098
Refusal	3,707	.014 (.146)[a]
Completion	21,758	.084 (.954)
Total	259,088	1.000

[a]Probability of occurrence given eligible individual is at home.
Source: Roger A. Kerin and Robert A. Peterson, "Scheduling Telephone Interviews," *Journal of Advertising Research* 23 (April/May 1983), p. 44. See also Peter Tuckel and Harry W. O'Neill, "Screened Out," *Marketing Research: A Magazine of Management & Applications* 8 (Fall 1996), pp. 34–42.

read or write so poorly that they have trouble holding jobs, and the author of *Illiterate America* suggests that 60 million adult Americans are illiterate.[22] Since many of these people have difficulty with everyday tasks such as reading job notices, making change, or getting a driver's license, it is no wonder that they might not respond to a mail questionnaire!

Whatever the reason for nonresponse, it causes a bias of unknown size and direction. Lack of control also exists in respect to identifying who is responding to the mail questionnaire. The researcher cannot even ensure that the preferred respondent from the household replies.

E-mail administered questionnaires are somewhat better in these respects. For one thing, literacy is not a major problem because those owning and using computers are typically better educated. Moreover, there is much less likelihood that someone other than the intended respondents will reply since the questionnaires reside in their personal e-mail accounts. Fax surveys provide less control in terms of who responds, although they too are less subject to literacy problems because those who have access to and use fax machines are typically better educated.

Information Control

Information control A term applied to studies using questionnaires and concerning the amount and accuracy of the information that can be obtained from respondents.

Information control, which involves the kinds of questions that can be asked and the amount and accuracy of the information that can be obtained from respondents, varies according to the method of data collection that is used. The personal interview, for example, can be conducted using almost any form of questionnaire, from structured-undisguised through unstructured-disguised. The personal nature of the interaction allows the interviewer to show the respondent pictures, examples of advertisements, lists of words, scales, and so on, as stimuli. In contrast, the telephone interview rules out most aids. The mail questionnaire, however, allows the use of some of them.

Personal interviews also allow the automatic sequencing of questions; for example; if the answer to question 4 is positive, ask questions 5 and 6, whereas if it is negative, ask questions 7 and 8. Although automatic sequencing is also possible with telephone interviews, mail questionnaires permit much less of it.

There is a greater danger of *sequence bias* with mail, e-mail, and faxed questionnaires than with questionnaires administered in person or over the phone. Respondents can see the whole questionnaire, and thus their replies to any single question may not be independently arrived at but are more likely to be conditioned by their responses to other questions than if either personal interviews or telephone interviews were used.

Mail, e-mail, and faxed questionnaires permit control of the bias caused by the interviewee's perception of the interviewer. With each of these questionnaires, respondents are also able to work at their own pace. This may produce better-thought-out responses than would be obtained in personal or telephone interviews, where there is a certain urgency associated with giving a response. A thought-out response, however, is no guarantee of an appropriate reply. If the question is ambiguous, these self-administered surveys offer no opportunity for clarification. Each question must succeed or fail on its own merits. Because researchers cannot decipher differences in interpretation among respondents, they cannot impose a consistent frame of reference on the replies. Thus the responses to an open-ended question in a mail, e-mail or faxed questionnaire may be excessive or inadequate. With structured questions, the answers may simply reflect differences in the frame of reference being employed rather than any subject-to-subject variation in the particular characteristic being measured. The anonymity sometimes associated with a mail questionnaire does afford people an opportunity to be more frank on certain sensitive issues (for example, sexual behavior). Since replies to e-mail can often be traced to the sender, there is less anonymity with e-mail than with mail or faxed questionnaires.

Both personal and telephone interviews can cause interviewer bias because of the respondents' perception of the interviewer or because different interviewers ask questions and probe in different ways. Both of these biases can be more easily controlled in telephone surveys. There are fewer interviewer actions to which the respondent can react, and a supervisor can be present during telephone interviews to ensure that they are being conducted consistently. It is typically more difficult, though, to establish rapport over the phone than in person. The respondent in a telephone interview often demands more information about the purposes of the study, the credentials of the interviewer and research organization, and so on.

With regard to the length of the questionnaire or the amount of information to be collected, the general rule of thumb is that long questionnaires can be handled best by personal interview and least well by telephone interview. So much, though, depends on the subject of inquiry, the form of the questionnaire, and the approach used to secure cooperation that a rigid interpretation of this advice would be unwarranted and hazardous.

As with so many things, computers are changing the way surveys are conducted. Computers were first used in the early 1970s to assist with telephone interviews. Interviewers would read the questions displayed on the computer screen, then key in the answers to a file which was sent to a mainframe computer. The early systems saved so much time and money that they spawned a virtual revolution in data collection, helping to make telephone interviews the most popular data collection technique (see Research Window 10.2).

Greater computing power through personal computers and the Internet have since permitted broader applications of computers to research. Currently, there are at least four types of uses for micro-based, stand-alone, **computer-assisted interviewing (CAI)** software:

Computer-assisted interviewing (CAI)

The conduct of surveys using computers to manage the sequence of questions and where the answers are recorded electronically through the use of a keyboard.

1. Telephone surveys in which each interviewer has a personal computer from which to ask questions;

2. In-person interviews in which the interviewer transports a notebook computer to the interview site and uses it to interview the respondent, or places the computer in front of the respondent and lets the respondent answer questions as they appear on the screen;

3. Interviews in which the interviewee sits in front of the computer in a shopping mall or research laboratory and responds to questions as they are displayed on the monitor;

4. Mail or e-mail administration in which the questionnaire is sent by mail on diskette or attached to an e-mail message. Respondents answer the questions at their own computer and submit their responses by mailing back the diskette or attaching them to an e-mail reply.[23]

One of the most important advantages of computer-assisted interviewing is the information control it allows. First, the computer displays each question exactly as the researcher

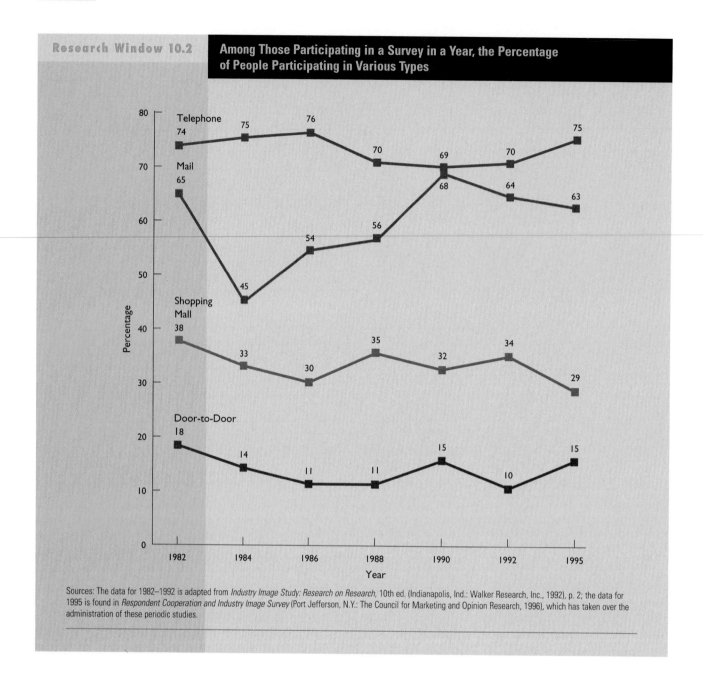

Research Window 10.2

Among Those Participating in a Survey in a Year, the Percentage of People Participating in Various Types

Sources: The data for 1982–1992 is adapted from *Industry Image Study: Research on Research*, 10th ed. (Indianapolis, Ind.: Walker Research, Inc., 1992), p. 2; the data for 1995 is found in *Respondent Cooperation and Industry Image Survey* (Port Jefferson, N.Y.: The Council for Marketing and Opinion Research, 1996), which has taken over the administration of these periodic studies.

intended. It will show only the questions and information that the respondent needs to, or should, see. Further, it will display the next question only when an acceptable answer to the current one is entered on the keyboard. If a respondent says that she or he bought a brand that is not available in that particular locale, for example, the computer can be programmed to reject the answer. This greatly simplifies skipping or branching procedures. The interviewer does not have to grapple with selecting the next question given the response to the current one; the computer does this automatically. This saves considerable time and confusion in administering the questionnaire and permits a more natural flow of the interview. It also ensures that there will be no variation in the sequence in which the questions are asked. Information control also manifests itself in the following:

1. *Personalization of the questions.* During the course of the interview, the computer is aware of all previous responses (e.g., name of wife, cars owned, supermarket

patronized) and can customize the wording of future questions—for example, "When your wife, Ann, shops at the Acme, does she usually use the Toyota or the Buick?" Such personalized questions can enhance rapport and thus provide for higher-quality interviews.

2. *Customized questionnaires.* Key information elicited early in the interview can be used to customize the questionnaire for each respondent. For example, only product attributes previously acknowledged by respondents as determinants of their decisions would be used to measure their brand perceptions, rather than using an a priori list of attributes common to all respondents.

In addition to the enhanced branching abilities and personalization of the questionnaires that they allow, computer-assisted interviews often produce increased accuracy in the results. There is evidence to suggest that people are more truthful when responding to a computer than to an interviewer or even when completing a self-administered, paper-and-pencil questionnaire. They seem to think that the computer is less judgmental and provides them greater anonymity. For example, Chevron's Ortho Consumer Products unit in San Francisco asked salespeople in two separate studies to assess the company's marketing strategy. Although both studies promised anonymity, salespeople had only kind words for their bosses when asked in the paper-and-pencil survey. "When the questions were posed by computer, in contrast, 'not all the responses were so favorable to management,' says Edward Evans, manager of planning and analysis."[24]

Computer-assisted interviewing certainly speeds the data collection and processing tasks. The preliminary tabulations of the answers are available at a moment's notice, because the replies are already stored in memory. One does not have the typical two-to-three-week delay caused by coding and data entry that happens when questionnaires are completed by hand.

Respondents also seem to enjoy the interviewing experience more when the questionnaire is administered by computer. That, in turn, seems to help response rates. For example, the return rate in disk-by-mail surveys often exceeds 50 percent.[25] Further, the whole notion of involving computers in the interviewing process has opened up some other capabilities with respect to managing the interviewing process, including making it easier to write the questionnaire, schedule the people to be contacted, monitor what happens to each attempted call, and prepare the research report.[26]

Even though computers have had a profound effect on interviewing techniques, they are not a panacea.

> There are limits to what the machines can do. They can't win over respondents with social chitchat or explain questions that are misunderstood. Unless the interviewees are good typists, the computers can't elicit lengthy responses. They can't recognize fuzzy or superficial answers and prod respondents to elaborate. They can't ask follow-up questions of interviewees who drop unexpected leads. And, the ones that ask questions by phone with mechanical voices have raised the ire of some people who consider unsolicited, randomly dialed calls an invasion of privacy.[27]

Further, disk-by-mail administration can be used only among those likely to own or to have access to a computer with the right software. Although they can be quite useful in industrial surveys, they are more limited in general consumer surveys unless the product or service at issue involves a population likely to own a microcomputer (e.g., a new software program).

Administrative Control

Administrative control
A term applied to studies relying on questionnaires and referring to the speed, cost, and control of the replies afforded by the mode of administration.

Administrative control involves the time and cost of administering the questionnaire, as well as the control of the replies afforded by the administrative method chosen. The telephone survey is one of the quickest ways of obtaining information. A number of calls can be made from a central exchange in a short period, perhaps as many as 15 or 20 per hour per interviewer if the questionnaire is short. An in-home personal interview affords no such time economies, since there is unproductive time between each interview in which the interviewer travels to the next respondent. If the researcher wishes to speed up the replies secured with in-home personal interviews, the size of the field force must be increased. However, as the number of interviewers increases, so do problems of interviewer-related variations in responses. By properly selecting and training interviewers, researchers can minimize some of the differences in approach that lead to variations, but personal interviews still present more problems of control than telephone interviews.

Personal interviews also give researchers little control over possible interviewer cheating. Since the researcher can supervise telephone interviewers directly when they are making their calls, problems of variation in administration and cheating should be minimized, although the ability to supervise telephone interviewers may be changing in response to worker complaints.[28]

While the mail questionnaire represents a standardized stimulus, and thus allows little variation in administration, it also affords little speed control. It often takes several weeks to secure the bulk of the replies, at which time a follow-up mailing is often begun. It, too, will involve a time lapse of several weeks for the questionnaires to reach the respondents, be completed, and find their way back. Depending on the number of follow-up mailings required, the total time needed to conduct a good mail study can often be substantial. With a mail study it also takes as long to get replies from a small sample as it does from a large sample. This is not so with personal and telephone interviews, where there is a direct relationship between the number of interviews and the time required to complete them. In general, in-home personal interviews tend to be the most expensive per completed contact, and the mail questionnaire tends to be the cheapest. However, many factors can change the cost picture dramatically. For example, it costs relatively little, per contact, to mail a questionnaire; but if the response rate is very low, the cost per return may actually be quite high. An advantage e-mail and faxed questions have over mail questionnaires is that they typically are returned more quickly.[29]

For the most part, the cost of the various methods hinges on the problem of ensuring quality control. It is generally true that the larger the field staff is, the greater the problems of control. Mail surveys require the fewest staffers. Telephone, mall, and in-home personal interview methods require progressively larger field staffs. Hence, a personal interview in the home is typically the most expensive method of data collection. Exhibit 10.3 summarizes the advantages and disadvantages of the primary communication methods.

Combining Administration Methods

Each method of data collection thus has its advantages and disadvantages, and none is superior in all situations. The research problem itself will often suggest one approach over the others, but the researcher should recognize that a combination of approaches is often the most productive. In one home product-use test, for example, interviewers distributed the product, self-administered questionnaires, and return envelopes to the respondents, while telephone interviews were used for follow-up. The combination of methods produced telephone cooperation from 97 percent of the testing families, while 82 percent of the mail questionnaires were returned.[30]

Another example demonstrating the advantages that can accrue through the creative use of a combination of data collection techniques is the locked-box approach, which has been used in several industrial surveys. Surveying the industrial market is a relatively expensive proposition. One has to contend with busy executives who have better things to do with their time than answer questionnaires, and with efficient secretaries and receptionists who prescreen executive mail, telephone calls, and personal visitors. Industrial surveys consequently produce very low response rates. The locked box has proved to be effective in getting through the prescreens and in generating executive cooperation. It is nothing more than a metal, shoe-sized box that is locked with a three-digit combination lock and that contains flash cards, interview exhibits, concept statements, or other survey materials. It is accompanied by a cover letter explaining the purpose of the survey and

ADVANTAGES	DISADVANTAGES

In-Home Personal Interview

ADVANTAGES	DISADVANTAGES
• Probably highest response rate	• Generally narrow distribution
• Best for getting response from specific, identified person	• Interviewer supervision and control difficult to maintain
• Allows use of any type of question/questionnaire	• Often difficult to identify individuals to include in sampling frame
• Sequencing of questions is easily changed	• Generally most expensive method of administration
• Allows probing of open-ended questions	• Costly to revisit "not-at-homes"
• Allows clarification of ambiguous questions	• Relatively slow method of administration
• Permits easy use of visuals	• Subject to interviewer bias

Mall Intercept (Same Advantages as In-Home Interview, Plus)

ADVANTAGES	DISADVANTAGES
• Relatively short project completion time	• Sample control is more difficult than with in-home personal interview in terms of identifying a representative sample
• Less expensive than in-home interview	• Interviews typically need to be shorter than in-home interview
• Much better interviewer supervision and control than in-home interview	

Mail

ADVANTAGES	DISADVANTAGES
• May be only method able to reach respondent	• Very little control in securing response from specific individual
• Sampling frame easily developed when mailing lists are available	• Cannot secure response from illiterates
• Not subject to interviewer bias	• Cannot control speed of response; long response time
• Respondents work at their own pace	• Researcher cannot explain ambiguous questions
• Ensures anonymity of respondents	• Does not allow probing with open-ended questions
• Wide distribution possible	• Difficult to change sequence of questions
• Best for personal, sensitive questions	• Sequence bias: respondents can view entire questionnaire as they respond
• Generally least expensive	

Telephone

ADVANTAGES	DISADVANTAGES
• Relatively low cost	• Difficult to establish representative sampling frame due to unlisted numbers
• Wide distribution possible	• Cannot use visual aids
• Interviewer supervision is strong; less interviewer bias	• More difficult to establish rapport over the telephone than in person
• Relatively strong response rates (much higher than mail surveys)	• Does not handle long interview well in most cases
• One of the quickest methods of data collection	• Subject to some degree of interviewer bias (but much less than with personal interview)
• Less difficulty and cost in handling "call-backs" than in-home interviews	• More difficult to determine that appropriate respondent is being interviewed than with personal interviews
• Allows easy use of computer support	
• Sequence of questions is easily changed	

telling the respondent that an interviewer will be contacting him or her in a few days. The box becomes a gift for cooperating. However, it is of no use unless one knows the combination, information that is given the executive after he or she cooperates in the follow-up telephone interview. Thus, mail is used to deliver the box; and the telephone, to conduct the actual interview. At the same time, the box provides an opportunity to use stimuli such as pictures, examples, lists of words, scales, and so on—stimuli that otherwise might be restricted to personal interviews. It remains to be seen, though, if the locked box will remain productive in the future, given the increase in terrorism such as the "Unabomber" and general reactions to suspicious packages in the mail.

Back to the Case

Tom Karlin had built a successful appliance distributorship by taking the initiative, so not surprisingly, it wasn't long before the information he received from Demographics Life-Style Data (DLD) gave him an idea. He made an appointment to see Peter Haraldsen, a Tampa real estate developer.

Haraldsen specialized in luxury developments built around golf courses. The homes in Haraldsen's latest development would start at around $200,000 when they were finished. Haraldsen had set up the meeting to take place at one of the finished model homes in that development.

"It really is beautiful," commented Karlin after he'd been given the tour.

"Thank you," replied Haraldsen, "but you know this is our fifth development, and I think we've really gotten the hang of what our clientele wants."

"What are your customers like?" asked Karlin.

"Successful businesspeople in their late 50s, early 60s. They're still active, still working. Often they buy a second home in Florida with the idea that within the next ten years they'll move down here permanently. These are active people, mind you. They could go anywhere. They come here for the golf and the tennis, the year-round good weather."

"Well," replied Karlin, launching into his pitch, "the reason I wanted to meet with you today was to have a chance to share some data with you. My data show that the profile of the high-end Clean-Rite appliances purchaser matches the profile of your potential customers perfectly."

Karlin and Haraldsen spent an hour going over the data, but in the end Haraldsen remained unconvinced. He'd had few complaints about the WasherMaid appliances he'd used in his previous developments, so even the sweet prices that Karlin was offering him didn't seem reason enough to change.

"I'll tell you what," Haraldsen concluded, "leave the data with me. I'll send the information over to my marketing director and let him take a look at it, and we'll get back to you."

Three weeks later, Karlin received a call from Haraldsen. "Tom, I've got to tell you—when I showed my marketing director that appliance-sale demographic data, he was a bit skeptical. So he asked 100 potential home buyers who came to one of our open houses to fill out a questionnaire about their appliance preferences. And you know what? Most of them preferred Clean-Rite. Let's set up a time this week to get together and talk dollars and cents."

Summary

Learning Objective 1

Explain the concept of structure as it relates to questionnaires.

The degree of structure in a questionnaire is the degree of standardization imposed on it. In a highly structured questionnaire the questions to be asked and the responses permitted the subjects are completely predetermined. In a highly unstructured questionnaire, the questions to be asked are only loosely predetermined, and the respondents are free to respond in their own words. A questionnaire in which the questions are fixed but the responses are open-ended would represent an intermediate degree of structure.

Learning Objective 2

Explain what is meant by disguise in a questionnaire.

The amount of disguise in a questionnaire is the amount of knowledge hidden from the respondent as to the purpose of the study. An undisguised questionnaire makes the purpose of the research obvious by the questions posed, while a disguised questionnaire attempts to hide the purpose of the study.

Learning Objective 3

Discuss why structured-undisguised questionnaires are the type most frequently used by marketing researchers.

Structured-undisguised questionnaires are the most popular type of data collection because they are simple to administer and easy to tabulate and analyze. They are also relatively reliable, since they typically use fixed-alternative questions.

Learning Objective 4

Cite three drawbacks of fixed-alternative questions.

Fixed-alternative questions may force a subject to respond to a question on which he or she does not really have an opinion. They may also prove inaccurate if none of the response categories allows the accurate expression of the respondent's opinion. The response categories themselves may introduce bias if one of the probable responses is omitted because of an oversight or insufficient prior research.

Learning Objective 5

Explain the reason why researchers use projective methods in conducting some studies.

Researchers use projective techniques as a way of overcoming subjects' reluctance to discuss their feelings. The main thrust of these techniques has been to conceal the true subject of the study by using a disguised stimulus. The basic assumption in projective methods is that the way an individual responds to a relatively unstructured stimulus provides clues as to how that person really perceives the subject under investigation and what his or her reactions are to it.

Learning Objective 6

List three common types of stimuli used in projective techniques.

Three common types of stimuli used in projective techniques are word association, sentence completion, and storytelling.

Learning Objective 7

Differentiate among the three methods of administering questionnaires.

Personal interviews imply a direct face-to-face conversation between the interviewer and the respondent, as opposed to the *telephone interview*. In both types, the interviewer asks the questions and records the respondents' answers, either while the interview is in progress or immediately afterward. *Mail questionnaires* are sent to designated respondents with an accompanying cover letter. The respondents complete the questionnaire at their leisure and mail their replies back to the research organization.

Learning Objective 8

Cite the points researchers generally consider when they compare the various methods of administering questionnaires.

Sampling control, information control, and administrative control are the points researchers generally consider when comparing the methods of personal interviewing, telephone interviewing, and mail questionnaires.

Review Questions

1. What is a disguised questionnaire? What is a structured questionnaire?

2. What are the advantages and disadvantages of structured-undisguised questionnaires? Of unstructured-undisguised questionnaires?

3. What is the rationale for employing unstructured-disguised stimuli? What is a word association test? A sentence completion test? A storytelling test?

4. What operating principle or assumption underlies the use of structured-disguised questionnaires? What are the advantages and disadvantages associated with structured-disguised questionnaires?

5. How do mail, telephone, and personally administered questionnaires differ with respect to the following:
   (a) sampling control
   (b) information control
   (c) administrative control

Discussion Questions, Problems, and Projects

1. Pick three of your friends and conduct a depth interview with each one of them to determine their feelings toward purchasing designer jeans.
   (a) What factors were mentioned in the first interview?
   (b) What factors were mentioned in the second interview?
   (c) What factors were mentioned in the third interview?
   (d) Based on the findings for Questions a, b, and c, what specific hypotheses would you suggest?
   (e) Briefly discuss the strengths and weaknesses of depth interviews.

2. Design and administer a word-association test to determine a student's feelings toward eating out.
   (a) List ten stimuli and the subject's responses and the amount of time that elapsed before the subject reacted to each stimulus.

Stimulus	Response	Time
1.		
2.		
3.		
4.		
5.		
6.		
7.		
8.		
9.		
10.		

   (b) On the basis of your mini-survey, what tentative conclusions can you infer regarding the person's feelings toward eating out?
   (c) Briefly discuss the strengths and weaknesses of this technique.

3. Design and administer a sentence-completion test to determine a student's feelings toward coffee consumption.
   (a) List at least eight sentences that are to be used in the sentence-completion exercise.
      1.
      2.
      3.
      4.
      5.
      6.
      7.
      8.
   (b) On the basis of the respondent's reactions, how would you describe the person's attitudes toward drinking coffee?
   (c) How would a researcher analyze the responses?

4. Design and administer a storytelling test to determine a student's reasons for not living in a residence hall, or dormitory.
   (a) Develop a stimulus (verbal or pictorial) for the story-completion exercise. (Hint: It might be easier to use a verbal stimulus.)
   (b) Based on this exercise, what are your findings as to the person's reasons for not living in a residence hall?

5. Suppose you were requested to design an appropriate communication method to find out students' feelings and opinions about the various food services available on campus.
   (a) What degree of structure would be appropriate? Justify your choice.
   (b) What degree of disguise would be appropriate? Justify your choice.
   (c) What method of administration would be appropriate? Justify your choice.

6. Which survey method (mail, telephone, or personal) would you use for the following situations? Justify your choice.
   (a) Administration of a questionnaire to determine the number of people who listened to the "100 Top Country Tunes in 1999," a program that aired on December 31, 1999.
   (b) Administration of a questionnaire to determine the number of households having a mentally ill individual in the household and the history of mental illness in the family.
   (c) Administration of a questionnaire by a national manufacturer of microwave ovens in order to test people's attitudes toward a new model.
   (d) Administration of a questionnaire by a local dry cleaner who wants to determine customers' satisfaction with a recent discount promotion.
   (e) Administration of a questionnaire by the management of a small local hotel that wants to assess customers' opinions of its service.

7. Arrange an interview with a professional researcher engaged in commercial marketing research. Discuss the objectives of the researcher's current project and what type of method(s) she or he is using to collect primary data. Report on the advantages and disadvantages of the data collection method(s) used in relation to the research objective. Try to determine if trade-offs have been necessary (e.g., cost against speed; structure against disguise) in order to collect the data, and if so, the reasons for those trade-offs. Be sure to address the broad issues of structure, disguise, sampling control, information control, and administrative control in your report.

8. Arrange an interview with a member of the marketing faculty at your school (other than your instructor in this course) who is actively engaged in academic marketing research. Discuss the objectives of the faculty member's research and what type of method(s) she or he uses to collect primary data. Report on the advantages and disadvantages of the data collection method(s) used in relation to the research objective. Try to determine if trade-offs have been necessary (e.g., cost against speed; structure against disguise) in order to collect the data, and if so, the reasons for those trade-offs. Be sure to address the broad issues of structure, disguise, sampling control, information control, and administrative control in your report.

Endnotes

1. Formally, the procedure is known as content analysis. For discussion of how to go about conducting a content analysis, see Robert P. Weber, *Basic Content Analysis* (Thousand Oaks, Calif.: Sage Publications, 1985). For discussion of recent advances in the automation of the analysis of verbatim responses, see David W. Stewart, "Making Use of Verbatim Response Analysis in Survey Research: New Solutions on the Horizon" (Paper presented at the American Marketing Association's 2nd Advanced Research Techniques Forum, Beaver Creek, Colorado, June 16–19, 1991); Robert Burbach and Roger Heeler, "Using Neural Nets to Analyze Qualitative Data," *Marketing Research: A Magazine of Management & Applications* 7 (Winter 1995), pp. 35–39.

2. F. P. Kilpatrick, "New Methods of Measuring Consumer Preferences and Motivation," *Journal of Farm Economics* (December 1957), p. 1314. See also Dennis Rook, "The Ritual Dimension of Consumer Behavior," *Journal of Consumer Research* 12 (December 1985), pp. 251–264.

3. Fred N. Kerlinger, *Foundations of Behavioral Research,* 3rd ed. (New York: Holt, Rinehart and Winston, 1986), p. 471. See also W. G. Klopfer and E. S. Taulkie, "Projective Tests," in M. R. Rosenzweig and L. W. Porter, eds., *Annual Review of Psychology* (1976), pp. 543–567; Sidney J. Levy, "Dreams, Fairy Tales, Animals, and Cars," *Psychology and Marketing* 2 (Summer 1985), pp. 67–82; Sidney Levy, "Interpreting Consumer Mythology: Structural Approach to Consumer Behavior Focuses on Story Telling," *Marketing Management* 2 (No. 4, 1994), pp. 4-9.

4. Harold H. Kassarjian, "Projective Methods," in Robert Ferber, ed., *Handbook of Marketing Research* (New York: McGraw-Hill, 1974), pp. 3–91. See also Eugene H. Fram and Elaine Cibotti, "The Shopping List Studies and Prospective Techniques: A 40-Year View," *Marketing Research: A Magazine of Management & Applications* 3 (December 1991), pp. 14–21.

5. Ronald Alsop, "Advertisers Put Consumers on the Couch," *The Wall Street Journal* (May 13, 1988). p. 17.

6. John P. Dickson and Douglas L. MacLachlan, "Fax Surveys?" *Marketing Research: A Magazine of Management & Applications* 4 (September 1992), pp. 26–30; Israel D. Nebenzahl and Eugene D. Jaffe, "Facsimile Transmission versus Mail Delivery of Self-Administered Questionnaires in Mail Surveys," *Industrial Marketing Management* 24 (June 1995), pp. 167–175.

7. Jeffrey Pope, *How Cultural Differences Affect Multi-Country Research* (Minneapolis, Minn.: Custom Research, Inc., 1991); Aimee Stern, "Do You Know What They Want?," *International Business* 6 (March 1993), pp. 102–103.

8. "More Households Dial 'U' for Unlisted," *The Wall Street Journal* (May 7, 1991), p. B1.

9. There is some evidence to suggest that certain sampling schemes can produce a higher proportion of working residential numbers without introducing any appreciable bias in the process. See, for example, Joseph Waksberg, "Sampling Methods for Random Digit Dialing," *Journal of the American Statistical Association* 73 (March 1978), pp. 40–46; Robert Groves and Robert L. Kahn, *Surveys by Telephone* (New York: Academic Press, 1979); Richard Pothoff, "Some Generalizations of the Mitofsky-Waksberg Technique of Random Digit Dialing," *Journal of the American Statistical Association* 82 (June 1987), pp. 409–418. For discussion of the services of firms supplying telephone samples, see Lewis C. Winters, "What's New in Telephone Sampling Technology," *Marketing Research: A Magazine of Management & Applications* 2 (March 1990), pp. 80–82.

10. E. Landon, Jr., and Sharon K. Banks, "Relative Efficiency and Bias of Plus-One Telephone Sampling," *Journal of Marketing Research* 14 (August 1977), pp. 294–299; Madhav N. Segal and Firooz Hekmat, "Random Digit Dialing: A Comparison of Laird Methods," *Journal of Advertising* 14 (No. 4, 1985), pp. 36–43.

11. "Mailing List Brokers Sell More than Names to Their Many Clients," *The Wall Street Journal* (February 19, 1974), pp. 1, 18; Bob Davis, "Baby-Goods Firms See Direct Mail as the Perfect Pitch for New

Moms," *The Wall Street Journal* (January 29, 1986), p. 31. For discussion of how firms go about developing mailing lists and their value, see Michael W. Miller, "Data Mills Delve Deep to Find Information About U.S. Consumers," *The Wall Street Journal* (March 14, 1991), pp. A1, A12.

12. Paul Miller, "How Are We Doing?" *Catalog Age* (June 1, 1999, downloaded from Northern Light Web site, www.northernlight.com); Hottest Markets of the '90s (Ithaca, N.Y.: American Demographics, 1990).

13. Bruce Shawkey, "Mail Order Peddlers Pan Gold in Them Thar Lists," *Wisconsin State Journal,* July 31, 1983, pp. 1 and 4; Melinda Grenier Guiles, "Why Melinda S. Gets Ads for Panty Hose, Melinda F., Porsches," *The Wall Street Journal* (May 6, 1988), pp. 1 and 4. Ellen E. Schultz. "When It's the Wrong Time for Big Financial Decisions," *The Wall Street Journal* (October 29, 1991), pp. C1, C17.

14. Barbara A. Schuldt and Jeff W. Totten, "Electronic Mail vs. Mail Survey Response Rates," *Marketing Research: A Magazine of Management & Applications* 6 (Winter 1994), pp. 36-39. See also Martin Opperman, "E-mail Surveys: Potentials and Pitfalls," *Marketing Research: A Magazine of Management & Applications* 7 (Summer 1995), pp. 28–33.

15. Beth Clarkson, "Research and the Internet: A Winning Combination," *Quirk's Marketing Research Review* (July 1999), pp. 46–51.

16. For general discussions of the mall intercepts as a data collection technique, see Roger Gates and Paul J. Solomon, "Research Using the Mall Intercept: State of the Art," *Journal of Advertising Research* 22 (August/September 1982), pp. 43–50; Alan J. Bush and Joseph F. Hair, Jr., "An Assessment of the Mall Intercept as a Data Collection Method," *Journal of Marketing Research* 22 (May 1985), pp. 158–167; Alan J. Bush, Ronald F. Bush, and Henry C. K. Chen, "Method of Administration Effects in Mall Intercept Interviews," *Journal of the Market Research Society* 33 (October 1991), pp. 309–319.

17. Tim Cavanaugh, "Mall Crawl Polls," *American Demographics* 18 (September 1996), pp. 14–16.

18. The weighting technique was suggested by Seymour Sudman, "Improving the Quality of Shopping Center Sampling," *Journal of Marketing Research* 17 (November 1980), pp. 423–431. For empirical assessments of the usefulness of the weighting, see Thomas D. Dupont, "Do Frequent Mall Shoppers Distort Mall-Intercept Survey Results?" *Journal of Advertising Research* 27 (August/September 1987), pp. 45–51; John P. Murry, Jr., John L. Lastovicka, and Guarav Bhalla, "Demographic and Life-style Selection Error in Mall-Intercept Data," *Journal of Advertising Research* 27 (February/March 1989), pp. 46–52. For information on the relationship between mall shopping behavior and various demographic characteristics, see Abhik Roy, "Correlates of Mall Visit Frequency," *Journal of Retailing* 70 (Summer 1994), pp. 139–161.

19. Randy Minkoff, "Matters of Opinion: Foot Soldiers of Marketing Research Battle for a Moment of Your Time in the Mall," *Chicago Tribune* (July 5, 1998, downloaded from the Dow Jones Publications Library at www.dowjones.com, August 4, 1999).

20. Roger A. Kerin and Robert A. Peterson, "Scheduling Telephone Interviews," *Journal of Advertising Research* 23 (April/May 1983), pp. 41–47. See also Michael F. Weeks, Richard A. Kulka, and Stephanie A. Pierson, "Optimal Call Scheduling for a Telephone Interview," *Public Opinion Quarterly* 51 (1987), pp. 540–549; Gautam Naik, "Big Brothers Inc.? Gizmos for Evading—Or Snooping On—Callers," *The Wall Street Journal* (September 3, 1996), p. B1; Peter Tuckel and Harry W. O'Neill, "Screened Out," *Marketing Research: A Magazine of Management & Applications* 8 (Fall 1996), pp. 34–42.

21. See Paul L. Erdos, *Professional Mail Surveys* (Malabar, Fla.: Robert E. Kreiger, 1983), or Donald A. Dillman, "The Design and Administration of Mail Surveys," *Annual Review of Sociology* 17 (1991), pp. 225–249, for a discussion of the problem of sample control in mail surveys and what can be done to overcome respondent resistance. For general references on conducting telephone, mail, or personal interview surveys, see A. B. Blankenship, *Professional Telephone Surveys* (New York: McGraw-Hill, 1977); Donald A. Dillman, *Mail and Telephone Surveys: The Total Design Method* (New York: Wiley-Interscience, 1978); Robert M. Groves, et al., eds., *Telephone Survey Methodology* (New York: Wiley-Interscience, 1988); Paul J. Lavrakas, *Telephone Survey Methods* (Thousand Oaks, Calif.: Sage Publications, 1993); James H. Frey and Sabine Martens Oishi, *How to Conduct Interviews by Telephone and in Person* (Thousand Oaks, Calif.: Sage Publications, 1995); Thomas W. Mangione, *Mail Surveys* (Thousand Oaks, Calif.: Sage Publications, 1995).

22. Daniel Machalaba, "Hidden Handicap: For Americans Unable to Read Well, Life Is a Series of Small Crises," *The Wall Street Journal* (January 17, 1984), pp. 1 and 12; Chris Martell, "Illiteracy Hurts All, Author Says," *Wisconsin State Journal* (April 3, 1985), pp. 1–2; Jock Elliott, "Our Inadequate, Uncompetitive System of Education," *Viewpoint* (July–August 1987), pp. 31–35; Janice C. Simpson, "A Shallow Labor Pool Spurs Businesses to Act to Bolster Education," *The Wall Street Journal* (September 28, 1987), pp. 1 and 19; Mogens Nygaard Christofferson, "The Educational Bias in Mail Questionnaires," *Journal of Official Statistics* 3 (No. 4, 1987), pp. 459–464; Robert Naylor, Jr., "Americans Test Poorly for

Literacy," *Wisconsin State Journal*, September 9, 1993, p. 1A. The illiteracy problem is also severe in England. See *Journal of the Market Research Society* 26 (April 1984), for a number of articles on the subject and its consequences for survey research. The illiteracy problem has gotten so severe that many businesses are setting up their own in-house programs to combat it. See, for example, Helene Cooper, "Carpet Firm Sets Up an In-House School to Stay Competitive," *The Wall Street Journal* (October 5, 1992), pp. A1, A5.

23. Edwin H. Carpenter, "Software Tools for Data Collection: Microcomputer Assisted Interviewing," *Applied Marketing Research* 29 (Winter 1989), pp. 23–32. This article also compares the available CAI software packages with respect to their capabilities. See also Michael F. Weeks, "Computer-Assisted Survey Information Collection: A Review of CASIC Methods and Their Implications for Survey Operation," *Journal of Official Statistics* 8 (No. 4, 1992), pp. 445–465.

24. Selwyn Feinstein, "Computers Replacing Interviewers for Personnel and Marketing Tasks," *The Wall Street Journal* (October 9, 1986), p. 35. See also John P. Liefeld, "Response Effects in Computer Administered Questioning," *Journal of Marketing Research* 25 (November 1988), pp. 397–404; Edith D. De Leeuw, Joop J. Hox, and Ger Smijkers, "The Effect of Computer-Assisted Interviewing on Data Quality: A Review," *Journal of the Market Research Society* 37 (October, 1995), pp. 325–344.

25. "Disks-by-Mail," *Sawtooth News* 5 (Spring 1989), pp. 4–5; Arthur Saltzman, "Improving Response Rates in Disk-by-Mail Surveys," *Marketing Research: A Magazine of Management & Applications* 5 (Summer 1993), pp. 32–39.

26. For general overviews of the effect of computer-assisted telephone interviewing systems, see William L. Nicholls II and Robert M. Groves, "The Status of Computer-Assisted Telephone Interviewing: Part I—Introduction and Impact on Cost and Timeliness of Survey Data," *Journal of Official Statistics* 2 (No. 2, 1986), pp. 93–115; Robert M. Groves and William L. Nicholls II, "The Status of Computer-Assisted Telephone Interviewing: Part II—Data Quality Issues," *Journal of Official Statistics* 2 (No. 2, 1986), pp. 117–134; William E. Saris, *Computer-Assisted Interviewing* (Thousand Oaks, Calif.: Sage Publications, 1991). For an annotated bibliography, see Edith D. De Leeuw and Joop J. Hox, "Computer Assisted Data Collection: Data Quality and Costs: An Annotated Bibliography," *The Survey Statistician* 32 (1995) pp. 5–10.

27. Feinstein, "Computers Replacing Interviewers."

28. Michael Allen, "Legislation Could Restrict Bosses from Snooping on Their Workers," *The Wall Street Journal* (September 24, 1991), pp. B1, B5; Diane K. Bowers, "Privacy at a Price," *Marketing Research: A Magazine of Management & Applications* 5 (Fall 1993), pp. 40–41.

29. John P. Dickson and Douglas L. MacLachlan, "Fax Surveys: Return Patterns and Comparisons with Mail Surveys," *Journal of Marketing Research* 33 (February 1996), pp. 108–113; Schuldt and Totlen, "Electronic Mail vs. Mail Survey Response Rates."

30. Stanley L. Payne, "Combination of Survey Methods," *Journal of Marketing Research* 1 (May 1964), p. 62. See also Kenneth C. Schneider and William C. Rodgers, "Differences between Nonrespondents and Refusers in Market Surveys Using Mixed Modes of Contact," *Journal of Business Research* 21 (September 1990), pp. 91–107.

Suggested Additional Readings

For a useful discussion of the advantages and disadvantages of structured, unstructured, disguised, and undisguised questions, see

Claire Selltiz, Lawrence S. Wrightsman, and Stuart W. Cook, *Research Methods in Social Relations,* 3rd ed. (New York: Holt, Rinehart and Winston, 1976).

For specific suggestions as to how to conduct mail, telephone, or personal studies, see

James H. Frey and Sabine Martens Oishi, *How to Conduct Interviews by Telephone and in Person* (Thousand Oaks, Calif.: Sage Publications, 1995).

Paul J. Lavrakas, *Telephone Survey Methods* (Thousand Oaks, Calif.: Sage Publications, 1993).

Thomas W. Mangione, *Mail Surveys* (Thousand Oaks, Calif.: Sage Publications, 1995).

Chapter 11

COLLECTING INFORMATION BY OBSERVATION

L E A R N I N G   O B J E C T I V E S

Upon Completing This Chapter, You Should Be Able to

1. List the different methods by which observational data can be gathered.

2. Cite the main reason researchers may choose to disguise the presence of an observer in a study.

3. Explain the advantages and disadvantages of conducting an observational experiment in a laboratory setting.

4. Discuss the principle that underlies the use of a galvanometer.

5. Explain the function of a tachistoscope.

6. Explain how researchers use eye cameras.

7. Define *response latency* and explain what it measures.

8. Define *voice-pitch analysis* and explain what it measures.

Case in Marketing Research

Tom Stemberg, chief executive of the Staples office supply retailer, likes to tell a story about Sam Walton, a fellow retailing
entrepreneur. Walton, according to Stemberg, believed he
could visit any competitor and learn from something that competitor did better than Wal-Mart. Stemberg says Walton visited a dismal store in Tennessee: "The produce smelled, and it
was just a disaster. And his associates were kidding each
other, saying, 'I wonder what Sam is going to say now.' And
Sam looked at the back of the store and saw this cigarette
rack and said, 'You know, that's the finest cigarette merchandising I've seen in a year.'"

For Stemberg, the principle behind this story is that a company can generate an endless stream of inspiration by observing the competition. Stemberg follows Walton's lead by
making it a practice to visit at least one of his stores and another company's store every week. He insists that he always
learns something from what he observes. These lessons have
helped him build an innovation (selling office supplies at
superstores) into a $5.2 billion retailing enterprise.

Stemberg has a set methodology for this research. He takes
note of how easy the store is to find. Then he walks in un-
announced and carrying a small notebook in which to record
his observations. He observes how much time passes before
an employee offers to help him. He looks for specific problem
areas, such as out-of-stock merchandise or incorrect price
tickets. He asks an employee a question, such as where to
find a particular item, and notes whether the employee rattles
off an aisle number or walks along to help him. He records

subjective data as well—his impressions of the shopping
experience, including whether prices seem high or low,
whether items are easy to find, and whether it is easy to get
questions answered.

Stemberg doesn't do all his own research; his mother-in-law
helps. He has asked her to shop the competition, the Office
Depot store near her home. Stemberg's mother-in-law bought
products there and then returned some of them. Stemberg
took note of the whole experience: how quickly the store delivered the items, their billing process, their promptness in
picking up items she wanted to return. His mother-in-law even
chatted with the truck driver to learn how many orders were
in the truck.

By a recent count, Stemberg had visited over 90 percent of the
740 Staples stores. And his research goes beyond Staples and
Office Depot to any retailer he thinks might have lessons for
him. He has visited—and learned from—Price Club, Costco,
Toys "R" Us, and even Mobil gas stations.

Discussion Issues

1. What kinds of information can a retailer's employees learn by
   observing their stores and competitors'?

2. What kinds of information can a manufacturing or services
   company learn from visiting the stores that sell its products?

3. What are some limitations of a company's executives
   gathering this information themselves, rather than delegating
   this activity to researchers?

In Chapter 10 we examined how researchers use communication techniques to collect data, specifically by questioning respondents. In this chapter we will look at another method by which researchers gather information—observation.

Methods of Observation

Observation is a fact of everyday life. We are constantly observing other people and events as a means of securing information about the world around us. Admittedly, some people make more productive use of those observations than do others. One of them is Paco Underhill, the anthropological researcher introduced in the story at the opening of this part (page 156). He has made a career out of watching people in stores and drawing conclusions that have escaped seasoned retailers. For example, he watched shoppers in a well-known women's apparel store. Women often brought men into the store with them, and while the women browsed, the men would look around for somewhere to sit down. However, the store didn't want to devote valuable selling space to chairs for nonshoppers, so the men had to improvise. Some of them regularly drifted toward a large window with a broad sill at a comfortable level. There they would sit and gaze at the scene before them—which in this case was a magnificent display of Wonderbras.

Needless to say, this arrangement was a retailing fiasco: Women would approach the lavish, carefully designed display, begin to study the products, and then notice their audience. On the day Underhill was watching, two elderly men engaged in a steady commentary about each shopper's need for a Wonderbra. Few were sold that day.[1]

Observation is also a tool of scientific inquiry. When used for that purpose, the observations are systematically planned and recorded so as to relate to the specific phenomenon of interest. Although planned, they do not have to be sophisticated to be effective. They can be as basic as United Airlines' study of the garbage gathered from its various flights, which prompted the airline to discontinue serving butter on many of its short-range flights because few people were eating it. Or take the method employed by the retailer who used a different color of promotional flyer for each ZIP Code to which he mailed. When customers came in the store with the flyers, he could then identify which trading areas the store was serving.

A more sophisticated scheme is used by many malls to determine their trading areas. People are hired to walk the parking lot of the mall and record every license number they find. A typical day yields 2,500 different numbers. The data are then fed into computers at R. L. Polk & Company of Detroit, specialists in auto industry statistics. Polk matches the license plates to ZIP Code areas or census tracts and returns a color-coded map showing customer density from the various areas. At a cost of anywhere from $5,000 to $25,000, these studies are not only less expensive, but they are quicker and more reliable, than store interviews or examinations of credit card records.

One of the reasons often cited for the Japanese success in new product development is that they are masters of the art of observation. Japanese marketers spend a good deal of time studying consumers as they make use of the goods they buy.

"I know of a Japanese shoe manufacturer who came to New York with a high-powered lens and a camera," says Johny K. Johansson, professor of marketing and international business at Georgetown University. "He rented a second-floor hotel room and took pictures of people's feet as they walked past." The hundreds of photographs the manufacturer took gave him a sense of how people walked.

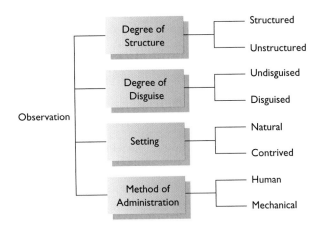

"This was New York City," Mr. Johansson says, "one of the biggest shoe markets in the world. The manufacturer wanted to see what kinds of shoes people wore who were in a hurry to get somewhere."[2]

Like communication methods, observation methods may be structured or unstructured, disguised or undisguised. Further, as Figure 11.1 shows, the observations may be made in a contrived or a natural setting and may be secured by a human or a mechanical observer.

Structured versus Unstructured Observation

Structured observation
The problem has been defined precisely enough so that the behaviors that will be observed can be specified beforehand, as can the categories that will be used to record and analyze the situation.

Unstructured observation
The problem has not been specifically defined, so a great deal of flexibility is allowed the observers in terms of what they note and record.

The distinction between structured and unstructured observation is similar to that between structured and unstructured communication methods. **Structured observation** applies when the problem has been defined precisely enough so that the behaviors that will be observed can be specified beforehand, as can the categories that will be used to record and analyze the situation. **Unstructured observation** is used for studies in which the problem has not been so specifically defined, so that a great deal of flexibility is allowed the observers in terms of what they note and record. For example, by peering from the catwalks, researchers for Marsh Supermarkets discovered to their dismay that people shopped heavily the periphery of the store—the produce, dairy, and meat sections—but often bypassed the core dry-goods section that accounted for the bulk of the store space.[3]

To distinguish between structured and unstructured observation, consider a study designed to investigate the amount of search and deliberation that a consumer goes through in buying a detergent. On the one hand, the observers could be told to stand at one end of a supermarket aisle and record whatever behavior they think is appropriate with respect to each sample customer's deliberation and search. This might produce the following record: "Purchaser first paused in front of ABC brand. He picked up a box of ABC, glanced at the price, and set it back down again. He then checked the label and price for DEF brand. He set that back down and after a slight pause, picked up a smaller box of ABC than originally looked at, placed it in his cart, and moved down the aisle." Alternatively, observers might simply be told to record the first detergent examined, the total number of boxes picked up by the customer, and the time in seconds that the customer spent in front of the detergent shelves—and to record these observations by checking the appropriate boxes on the observation form. The last situation represents a good deal more structure than the first.

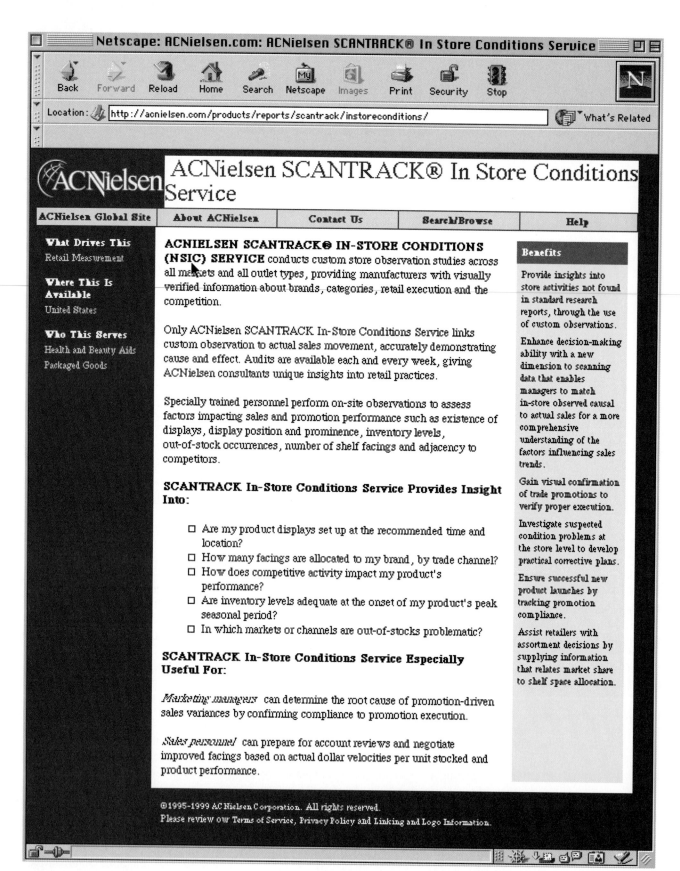

Back Forward Reload Home Search Netscape Images Print Security Stop

Location: http://acnielsen.com/products/reports/scantrack/instoreconditions/   What's Related

ACNielsen SCANTRACK® In Store Conditions Service

| ACNielsen Global Site | About ACNielsen | Contact Us | Search/Browse | Help |

What Drives This
Retail Measurement

Where This Is Available
United States

Who This Serves
Health and Beauty Aids
Packaged Goods

ACNIELSEN SCANTRACK® IN-STORE CONDITIONS (NSIC) SERVICE conducts custom store observation studies across all markets and all outlet types, providing manufacturers with visually verified information about brands, categories, retail execution and the competition.

Only ACNielsen SCANTRACK In-Store Conditions Service links custom observation to actual sales movement, accurately demonstrating cause and effect. Audits are available each and every week, giving ACNielsen consultants unique insights into retail practices.

Specially trained personnel perform on-site observations to assess factors impacting sales and promotion performance such as existence of displays, display position and prominence, inventory levels, out-of-stock occurrences, number of shelf facings and adjacency to competitors.

SCANTRACK In-Store Conditions Service Provides Insight Into:

- ☐ Are my product displays set up at the recommended time and location?
- ☐ How many facings are allocated to my brand, by trade channel?
- ☐ How does competitive activity impact my product's performance?
- ☐ Are inventory levels adequate at the onset of my product's peak seasonal period?
- ☐ In which markets or channels are out-of-stocks problematic?

SCANTRACK In-Store Conditions Service Especially Useful For:

Marketing managers can determine the root cause of promotion-driven sales variances by confirming compliance to promotion execution.

Sales personnel can prepare for account reviews and negotiate improved facings based on actual dollar velocities per unit stocked and product performance.

Benefits

Provide insights into store activities not found in standard research reports, through the use of custom observations.

Enhance decision-making ability with a new dimension to scanning data that enables managers to match in-store observed causal to actual sales for a more comprehensive understanding of the factors influencing sales trends.

Gain visual confirmation of trade promotions to verify proper execution.

Investigate suspected condition problems at the store level to develop practical corrective plans.

Ensure successful new product launches by tracking promotion compliance.

Assist retailers with assortment decisions by supplying information that relates market share to shelf space allocation.

ACNielsen SCANTRACK In-Store Conditions Service, a division of the ACNielsen Corporation, offers structured observation services to clients. It can help marketers by tracking sales movement, "accurately demonstrating cause and effect." The service is described on the ACNielsen.com Retail Measurement Web page.

Source: Courtesy of ACNielsen.

To use the more structured approach, researchers must decide precisely which behaviors are to be observed and which specific categories and units will be used to record the observations. In order to make such decisions, researchers must have specific hypotheses in mind. Thus, the structured approach is again more appropriate for descriptive and causal studies than for exploratory research. The unstructured approach would be useful in generating insights about the various aspects of the search and deliberation behavior in the preceding example. But it is less appropriate for testing hypotheses about it. Since so many different kinds of behaviors could be recorded, it would be difficult for researchers to code and quantify the data in a consistent manner.

One way to develop consistency in coding is to make sure that the coders are well trained. A number of trained coders were used, for example, in an observational study examining the patterns of interactions between parents and children in choosing breakfast cereals. The observers in this study recorded word for word the verbal exchanges between parent and child when making the choice. The coders then tried to assess

1. which party initiated the selection episode;

2. how the other party responded;

3. the content and tone of the communication;

4. the occurrence of unpleasant consequences such as arguments or unhappiness.

The ultimate aim of the study was to determine if the child was unhappy with the resolution of the situation.[4]

The advantages and disadvantages of structure in observation are very similar to those in communication. Structuring the observation reduces the potential for bias and increases the reliability of observations. However, the reduction in bias may be accompanied by a loss of validity, since the number of seconds spent in deliberation or the number of boxes of detergent picked up and examined may not represent the complete story of deliberation and search. What about the effort spent in simply looking at what is available but not picking them up, or the discussion between husband and wife as to which detergent to select? A well-trained, highly qualified observer might be able to interpret these kinds of behaviors and relate them in a meaningful way to search and deliberation.

> The major problem of behavioral observation is the observer himself. . . . In behavioral observation the observer is both a crucial strength and a crucial weakness. Why? The observer must digest the information derived from observations and then make inferences about constructs. . . . The strength and the weakness of the procedure is the observer's powers of inference. If it were not for inference, a machine observer would be better than a human observer. The strength is that the observer can relate the observed behavior to the constructs or variables of a study: he brings behavior and construct together.[5]

Nintendo, the computer game manufacturer, is one company that makes regular use of both structured and unstructured observation to keep abreast of playing trends and interests. The main mechanism by which it does this is through its Player-Support Program, which consists of "hotline" telephone numbers that provide tips on playing Nintendo games. In a typical week, some 16,000 people will call the toll-free number for recorded tips, and another 84,000 people will speak to more than 250 game counselors. In addition, the game counselors will respond to another 8,000 letters per week. Nintendo uses these hotlines not only to enhance customer satisfaction but also as a source of marketing intelligence. As Peter Main, the vice-president of marketing, comments: "It has kept us in close contact with the end user. . . . We use the data we collect to absolutely ensure that our game developers are aware of what's hot and what's not."[6] The game counselors and the unstructured observations they make, along with structured observations of the number of calls made to the recorded tips on each game, allow Nintendo to monitor changing player interests.

Disguised versus Undisguised Observation

Undisguised observation
The subjects are aware that they are being observed.

Disguised observation
The subjects are not aware that they are being observed.

In **undisguised observation,** the subjects know they are being observed; in **disguised observation,** they do not. In the search and deliberation study just described earlier, observers could assume a position well out of the way of shoppers' notice. Or the disguise could be accomplished by observers' becoming part of the shopping scene. For example, some firms use paid observers disguised as shoppers, or mystery shoppers as they are often called, to evaluate sales service and the attitudes and courtesy of the employees.[7] The reason the observer's presence is disguised, of course, is to control the tendency for people to behave differently when they know their actions are being watched. For example, although Envirosell's data gatherers generally don't buy anything, they try to blend in with the other shoppers so that they can make observations without altering behavior. An indicator of their success is that the company has sometimes recorded people in the act of shoplifting. Envirosell founder Paco Underhill recalls an instance when a well-dressed, middle-aged woman repeatedly sent a perfume salesclerk off on a variety of errands. Every time the clerk walked away, the woman deposited another bottle of perfume in her tote bag. In another store, an Envirosell employee watched a father slide a screwdriver set into his baby's diaper.[8]

At least two disadvantages are entailed in disguised observation, though. First, it is often very difficult to disguise an observation completely, and second, one cannot obtain other relevant information, such as background data, that can often be obtained by identifying oneself as a research worker. On the other hand, under what circumstances is disguised observation ethical?

Disguised observations may be *direct* or *indirect*. A direct observation, for example, might be a person at the checkout counter counting the number of boxes of each brand of detergent being purchased. An indirect observation might involve counting the inventory on hand by brand at the end of each day and adjusting the results for shipments received to determine how much of each brand was sold. The key difference is that the behavior itself is observed in direct observation, whereas the *effects* or *results* of that behavior are observed in indirect observation.

There are many types of indirect observation.[9] One could, for example, determine the market share held by each brand of detergent by conducting pantry audits. In a pantry audit, researchers would visit respondents' homes and ask permission to examine the "pantry inventory." Their goal would be to determine what brands the family had on hand and the amount of each. While it is rare that researchers would go to the expense of a pantry audit for one product, they might use this method if they wanted to determine consumption of a number of products at once.

Over the years a number of innovative, indirect measures of behavior have been developed. For example, a car dealer in Chicago checked the position of the radio dial of each car brought in for service. The dealer then used this as a way of determining the appropriate share of the listening audience each station held, and used that information to decide where to advertise. As further examples, the number of different fingerprints on a page has been used to assess the readership of various ads in a magazine, and the age and condition of the cars in the parking lot have been used to gauge the affluence of the group patronizing a given business establishment.

Observation is often more useful than surveys in sorting fact from fiction with respect to behaviors, particularly "desirable" behaviors. For example, a group of electric utilities had been accustomed to using pollsters' reports of consumer interviews to project energy usage. Despite their attempt to forecast demand scientifically, they found their projections continually fell short of reality. They asked a marketing research firm to investigate. The research firm put television cameras focused on the thermostat in 150 homes. The cameras revealed that what people said they did and what they actually did were vastly different. Many people claimed they set the thermostat at 68 degrees and left it there. It turned out that they fiddled with it all day. "Older relatives and kids—especially teenagers—tended to turn [it] up, and so did cleaning ladies. Even visitors did it. In a lot of homes, it was guerrilla warfare over the thermostat between the person who paid the bill and everyone else."[10]

Urban Outfitters has also found the use of video cameras helpful. The managers at Urban Outfitters rely on videotapes and snapshots of customers in their stores as well as people in their natural habitats to get ideas as to what people are wearing as information inputs to their merchandising decisions.[11] Similarly, Steelcase, the office furniture manufacturer, used video cameras to study how teams actually function when designing its very successful modular office units.[12]

Natural versus Contrived Setting for Observation

Natural setting
Subjects are observed in the environment where the behavior normally takes place.

Contrived setting
Subjects are observed in an environment that has been specially designed for recording their behavior.

Observations may be obtained in either **natural** or **contrived settings.** Sometimes the natural setting is altered to some degree for experimental purposes. In the search and deliberation study mentioned earlier, for example, researchers may choose to keep the setting completely natural and study only the extent of the activities that normally go into the purchase of detergents. Alternatively, they may wish to introduce some point-of-purchase display materials and measure their effectiveness. One measure of effectiveness might be the amount of search and deliberation the materials stimulate for the particular brand being promoted.

If a contrived setting is desired, the researcher could bring a group of people into a very controlled environment such as a multiproduct display in a laboratory and ask them to engage in some simulated shopping behavior. This controlled environment might contain, for example, a detergent display that would enable researchers to study the degree of search and deliberation each participant goes through as he or she decides what to buy.

An increasingly popular method for assessing customer reactions in a controlled environment is virtual reality, which enables marketers to display potential new products or product displays without going to the expense of physically building them. The technology originally relied on users wearing special goggles and gloves to see and manipulate objects. The advantage was that the objects appeared in three dimensions, as if they were actually there. For example, General Motors used virtual reality technology to test consumers' reactions to the view from the front seat of a new car.[13] The technology has also been used in consumer shopping experiments.[14]

The advantage of the laboratory environment is that researchers are better able to control outside influences that might affect the interpretation of what happened. For example, shoppers in a natural setting might pause to chat with neighbors in the midst of deciding what detergent to buy. If researchers were measuring the time spent in deliberation, this interruption could raise havoc with the accuracy of the measurement. The disadvantage of the laboratory setting is that the contrived setting itself may cause differences in behavior and thus raise real questions about the external validity of the findings.

A contrived setting also tends to speed the data collection process, result in lower-cost research, and allow the use of more objective measurements. For example, Fisher-Price, which used to take toy prototypes to local homes to test reactions, switched to a free nursery at its corporate headquarters. The nursery handles five groups of children who come for six-week periods. Designers watch as children play with Fisher-Price toys and those of competitors.[15] Another advantage of the contrived setting is that the researcher does not need to wait for events to occur but can instruct the participants to engage in the needed kind of behavior. This means that a great many observations can be made in a short period of time; perhaps an entire study can be completed in a couple of days or a week. This can substantially reduce costs.

The laboratory also may allow greater use of electrical and/or mechanical equipment than the natural setting does and thereby frees the measurement from the observer's selective processes. For example, IBM has used laboratories in which video cameras tape customers as they try out software. However, as electronic equipment becomes more portable and affordable, this advantage of the laboratory setting may be less significant. Lexant, for example, sells health-related information to employers, who make the information available to their employees at Lexant's DoHealth Web site. Lexant has tested its Web site by installing video cameras in the homes of a sample of customers' employees. The video cameras, placed near the home computers, record how much time the users spend on their computers, what they do with the computers, and what else is going on in that part of the house that might distract them. Lexant learned that users would move through a page on, say, smoking cessation or stress reduction, arrive at the bottom of the page, and realize in frustration that they couldn't click to another part of the site. They had to scroll back to the top of the page first. Lexant soon corrected this problem by adding links to the bottom of each Web page.[16]

Human versus Mechanical Observation

Much scientific observation is of the pencil-and-paper variety. One or more individuals are trained to observe a phenomenon systematically and to record on the observational form the specific events that took place—this is **human observation** as opposed to **mechanical observation.** Human observation can identify unexpected behaviors that defy preestablished response categories. The Envirosell research firm set up a test for a video game station that was to be installed in the play area of a fast-food restaurant. The designer of the fixtures sat with an Envirosell representative and observed, as, one at a time, children were invited in to try the game station. The first child sat down and played for a while, as did a second. The third child removed his shoes, leaned back, and proceeded to play by touching the screen with his toes. The fourth child approached the machine with a plastic toy he had received with his lunch and used it to pound on the video screen. Needless to say, the designer was taken aback.[17]

Electrical and/or mechanical observation also has its place in marketing research. Although it has been used for a long time, the development of new technologies is expanding the role and importance of electrical/mechanical observation. For example, in an effort to improve service and sales, Kmart relies on a radarlike system that tracks customer traffic. The system relies on sensors mounted over the store entrance and at certain locations inside the store to count customers as they interrupt the beams of light the sensors emit. Kmart uses the system "to improve service by sending salespeople to crowded departments and opening more checkout lanes before long lines form. . . . [It] also expects to be able to determine for the first time what percentage of shoppers actually make purchases. Until now, the company has only tracked transactions."[18]

Some of the earliest uses of electrical/mechanical observation focused on copy research and involved the *galvanometer, tachistoscope,* and *eye camera.* The **galvanometer** is used to measure the emotional arousal induced by an exposure to specific advertising copy. It belongs to the class of instruments that measure autonomic reactions, or reactions that are not under an individual's voluntary control. Because these responses are not controlled, it is not possible for individuals to mask or hide their true reactions to a stimulus.

Human observation

Individuals are trained to systematically observe a phenomenon and to record on the observational form the specific events that take place.

Mechanical observation

A mechanical device observes a phenomenon and records the events that take place.

Galvanometer

A device used to measure the emotion induced by exposure to a particular stimulus by recording changes in the electrical resistance of the skin associated with the minute degree of sweating that accompanies emotional arousal; in marketing research, the stimulus is often specific advertising copy.

Ethical Dilemma 11.1

A leading manufacturer of breakfast cereals was interested in learning more about the kinds of processes that consumers go through when deciding to buy a particular brand of cereal. To gather this information, an observational study was conducted in the major food chains of several large cities. The observers were instructed to assume a position well out of the shoppers' way, because it was thought that the individuals would change their behavior if they were aware of being observed.

- Was it ethical to observe another person's behavior systematically without that person's knowledge?

What if the behavior had been more private in nature? What if the behavior had been recorded on videotape?

- Does use of this method of data collection invade an individual's privacy?

- Even if there is no harm done to the individual, is there harm done to society?

- Does the use of such a method add to the concern over Big Brotherism?

- Can you suggest alternative methods for gathering the same information?

The galvanometer operates on the same principle as the lie-detector apparatus used in criminal investigations. Galvanometers record changes in the electrical resistance of the skin associated with the minute degree of sweating that accompanies emotional arousal. The subject is fitted with small electrodes on the palms or forearms to monitor this electrical resistance. As different advertising copy is shown, the strength of the current that results is used to gauge the subject's attitude.[19]

Tachistoscope

A device that provides the researcher timing control over a visual stimulus; in marketing research, the visual stimulus is often a specific advertisement.

The **tachistoscope** is a device that tells researchers how long it takes a subject to get the intended point of an ad. It does this by flashing the ad before the subject for an exposure interval that may range from less than a hundredth of a second to several seconds. After each exposure, the subject is asked to describe everything he or she saw and to explain what it meant. By systematically varying the exposure, the researcher is able to measure how quickly and accurately a particular stimulus—in this case, the ad—can be perceived and interpreted. Note, however, that since the subject is asked to respond verbally to what he or she saw, the tachistoscope is not a mechanical observer, but rather a mechanical means of presenting stimuli.

Eye camera

A device used by researchers to study a subject's eye movements while he or she is reading advertising copy.

The **eye camera** is now used by researchers to study a subject's eye movements while he or she is reading advertising copy. The original eye cameras, which were introduced at the Chicago World's Fair in 1890, established the fact that people's eyes do not move smoothly along a line of type as they read and that people's reading habits differ widely. Until recently, eye cameras used a light that was positioned to bounce off the cornea of the subject's eye onto a moving film. The reflected light traced eye movements on the film. The researcher had to then project the film, frame by frame, while manually recording eye movements on a sheet of paper. Since the mid-1970s, computers have been developed that can automatically perform this analysis for videotape. There have also been significant advances in the cameras themselves. Some of the new videocameras weigh only a few ounces and are so small that they can be clipped to a respondent's eyeglasses. The visual record produced as an individual reads an advertisement allows researchers to study the person's behavior in great detail. The eye camera can reveal the part of the ad the subject noticed first, how long his or her eyes lingered on a particular item, and whether the subject read all the copy or only part of it. The small videocameras that follow the path of the eye have also been used to analyze package designs, billboards, and displays in the aisles of supermarkets.[20]

Some of the newer electrical/mechanical observation devices include the optical scanner, which has automated the checkout process at many retail stores and in the process revolutionized the marketing research function, and the people meter, which is used to develop television-viewing statistics. Both of these were discussed in earlier chapters.

Two methods of mechanical observation are used to provide useful supplementary information in telephone interviews—response latency and voice-pitch analysis—owe their current popularity to mechanical/electronic recorders and the computer's ability to diagnose what is recorded. **Response latency** is the amount of time a respondent deliberates before answering a question. Since response time seems to be directly related to the respondent's uncertainty in the answer, it assists in assessing the individual's strength of preference when choosing among alternatives. It helps researchers judge how strongly an individual prefers one brand over another when asked to choose between alternatives. It also provides an unobtrusive way of measuring a subject's ambiguity in responding to a particular question.

Response latency

The amount of time a respondent deliberates before answering a question.

The measure of response depends upon a voice-operated relay that triggers an electronic stopwatch. When an interviewer approaches the end of a question, he or she simply presses a pedal that sets the stopwatch to zero and alerts the electronic mechanism to listen for the offset (end of the question) of the interviewer's voice. The stopwatch is automatically triggered at the offset. The moment the respondent begins answering, the watch is stopped by the voice-operated relay system, and a digital readout system indicates response latency to the interviewer, who can then record the deliberation time on the interview form.

There are several advantages in such a system. First, the method provides an accurate response latency measure without respondents' being aware that this dimension of behavior is being recorded. Second, since the time is measured by an automatic device, the technique does not make the interviewer's task any more difficult, nor does it appreciably lengthen the interview.[21]

In an otherwise routine research study, and with little additional effort, Du Pont, for example, used response latency to assess potential users' brand awareness and perception of quality of an industrial product compared to many competing brands.[22]

Voice-pitch analysis

Analysis that examines changes in the relative frequency of the human voice that accompany emotional arousal.

Voice-pitch analysis relies on the same basic premise as the galvanometer. Subjects experience a number of involuntary physiological reactions, such as changes in blood pressure, rate of perspiration, or heart rate when emotionally aroused by external or internal stimuli. Voice-pitch analysis examines changes in the relative vibration frequency of the human voice that accompanies emotional arousal. All individuals function at a certain physiological pace, called the *baseline*. The baseline in voice analysis is established by recording the respondent's speech while he or she is engaged in unemotional conversation. Deviations from the baseline level indicate that the respondent has reacted to the stimulus question. These deviations can be measured by special computer equipment adapted to hear abnormal frequencies in the voice caused by changes in the nervous system. Such changes may not be discernable to the human ear. The amount the individual was affected by the stimulus can be measured by comparing the person's abnormal frequency to his or her normal one. The greater the difference, the greater the emotional intensity of the subject's reaction is said to be.

Voice-pitch analysis has at least two advantages over other physiological-reaction techniques. First, unlike the other techniques, it measures not only the intensity but also the direction of the individual's feeling, since subjects are asked the nature of their opinions while the intensity of their emotions is being measured mechanically. Second, voice-pitch analysis allows a natural interaction between researcher and participant because subjects do not need to be connected to any equipment. This also tends to make it less time-consuming and expensive to use.[23]

Brain-wave research

Subjects are fitted with electrodes that monitor the electrical impulses emitted by the brain as the subject is exposed to various stimuli.

At the other extreme, **brain-wave research,** which is still in its infancy and surrounded by a good deal of controversy, requires a rather elaborate hookup of the subject to equipment. The purpose of this technique is to assess the stimuli that subjects find arousing or interesting. To do this, subjects are fitted with electrodes that monitor the

---

Ethical Dilemma 11.2

You are running a laboratory experiment for the promotion manager of a soft drink company. The promotion manager has read a journal article indicating that viewers' responses to upbeat commercials are more favorable if the commercials follow very arousing film clips, and he is interested in testing this proposition with respect to his firm's commercials. To establish whether film clips that induce high levels of arousal result in more extreme evaluations of ensuing commercials than film clips that induce low levels of arousal, you are pretesting film clips for their arousing capacity. To do this, you are recording subjects' blood pressure levels as they watch various film clips. The equipment is not very intrusive, consisting of a finger cuff attached to a recording device. You are satisfied that the procedure does not threaten the subject's physical safety in any way. In addition, you have made the subjects familiar with the equipment, with the result that they are relaxed and comfortable and absorbed in the film clips. On getting up to leave at the end of the session, one subject turns to you and asks, "Is my blood pressure normal, then?"

- Is it ethical to give respondents information about their physiological responses that they can interpret as an informed comment on the state of their health?

- What might be the result if you do not tell the subject the function of the equipment?

electrical impulses emitted by the brain as the subject is exposed to various stimuli. The evidence suggests that the two hemispheres of the brain respond differently to specific stimuli, with the right hemisphere responding more to emotional stimuli and the left to rational stimuli.[24]

As mentioned, electrical/mechanical equipment frees the observation from the observer's selective process. This is both its major strength and its major weakness. Certainly recording when a television set is turned on, to what channel it is tuned, and who is "watching" can be accomplished much more accurately by a people meter than by some other means. The fact that the set is tuned to a particular channel and that someone pushed the button indicating that he or she was in the room does not say anything, however, about the person's level of interest. A trained human observer's record might be more difficult to analyze, and it might be less objective, but his or her powers of integration could certainly produce a more valid assessment of what occurred. The essential point is that marketing researchers need to be aware of the electrical/mechanical equipment that is available so that they can make an informed choice as to the best technique for a particular study. Would a piece of equipment make a better observer than a human in a given instance, or vice versa? Or would a combination approach be more productive? These are difficult decisions that can greatly affect the quality of a study. A research who keeps abreast of the developments in the field is in the best position to make those decisions.

Back to the Case

Tom Stemberg credits his trips to stores with helping him correct misperceptions. For an executive sitting in an office and looking at numbers, customer complaints can seem isolated and minor. but walking around the aisles and talking to people gives Stemberg a customer's-eye view of his business.

For example, from his office he concluded that credit was not a challenge for his customers. The store's credit policy appeared liberal, and secondary data showed that credit card companies were handing out cards to almost everyone. However, on a visit to a South Carolina store, Stemberg listened as a store manager told about how his church couldn't obtain credit approval. As the manager detailed the experience, Stemberg realized that whereas he had seen easy credit terms, the manager saw an approval process that was so arduous some potential customers didn't even bother with it.

However, Stemberg freely acknowledges that his observational research has limitations. For one thing, shopping the competition narrows the focus of problem definition. Visiting stores can train attention on existing competitors, with the risk of devoting too little attention to understanding customers and future competitors. Stemberg illustrates the problem with an example: The Borders bookselling chain and its competitor, Barnes and Noble, look so much alike that they evidently go to great lengths to study one another. However, Stemberg believes, this competitive analysis may ignore potentially greater threats, such as the growing number of people buying books on-line at Amazon.com. In addition, the field of marketing research offers many techniques for studying shoppers and customers that provide in-depth information not available from walking around a store.

Stemberg also notes that his role as CEO limits his effectiveness as a researcher for his company. Although he tries to make surprise visits, his managers keep an eye out for him. This problem emerged on a visit to Pennsylvania and Ohio. Stemberg visited stores in Pittsburgh and Youngstown, and he was pleased with what he saw. The next stop was in New Kensington, Pennsylvania, and he was amazed by the excellent service: Three different employees approached him and offered to help. He commented to them, "I've got a funny feeling you were waiting for me." Indeed, they had been. The manger in Youngstown had called the manager in New Kensington to tip him off.

Certainly, a professional research team could devise many ways to record and observe the behavior of shoppers at Staples. Such a team also could expertly tabulate and analyze the results. But no matter how much research Staples might ever commission, it seems unlikely that Stemberg would use researchers' work as a replacement for his own visits. Joining his customers in his stores has been too great a learning opportunity. so that man next to you in the file folder aisle just might be the owner of the store.

Source: Stephanie Gruner, "Face-to-Face: Spies Like Us," *Inc.* (August 1998), pp. 45, 47, 49.

Summary

Learning Objective 1

List the different methods by which observational data can be gathered.

Observational data may be gathered using structured or unstructured methods that are either disguised or undisguised. The observations may be made in a contrived or a natural setting and may be secured by a human or an electrical/mechanical observer.

Learning Objective 2

Cite the main reason researchers may choose to disguise the presence of an observer in a study.

Most often an observer's presence is disguised in order to control the tendency of people to behave differently when they know their actions are being watched.

Learning Objective 3

Explain the advantages and disadvantages of conducting an observational experiment in a laboratory setting.

The advantage of a laboratory environment is that researchers are better able to control outside influences that might affect the interpretation of what happened. The disadvantage of the laboratory setting is that the contrived setting itself may cause differences in behavior and thus threaten the external validity of the findings. A contrived setting, however, usually speeds the data collection process, results in lower-cost research, and allows the use of more objective measurements.

Learning Objective 4

Discuss the principle that underlies the use of a galvanometer.

The galvanometer records changes in the electrical resistance of the skin associated with the minute degree of sweating that accompanies emotional arousal. When the subject is shown different advertising copy, the strength of the current that results is used to gauge his or her attitude toward the copy.

Learning Objective 5

Explain the function of a tachistoscope.

The tachistoscope is a device that tells researchers how long it takes a subject to get the intended point of an ad. It does this by flashing the ad before the subject for a short interval of time and then asking that subject to describe everything he or she saw and to explain what it meant.

Learning Objective 6

Explain how researchers use eye cameras.

Eye cameras are used by researchers to study a subject's eye movements while he or she is reading advertising copy. The visual record produced can allow researchers to determine the part of the ad the subject noticed first, how long his or her eyes lingered on a particular item, and whether the subject read all the copy or only part of it.

Learning Objective 7

Define response latency and explain what it measures.

Response latency is the amount of time a respondent deliberates before answering a question. Since response time seems to be directly related to the respondent's uncertainty in the answer, it assists in assessing the individual's strength of preference when choosing among alternatives.

Learning Objective 8

Define voice-pitch analysis and explain what it measures.

Voice-pitch analysis examines changes in the relative vibration frequency of the human voice that accompany emotional arousal. The amount an individual is affected by a stimulus question can be measured by comparing the person's abnormal frequency to his or her normal one. The greater the difference, the greater the emotional intensity of the subject's reaction is said to be.

Review Questions

1. How can observational methods be classified? What are the key distinctions among the various types?

2. What principle underlies the use of a galvanometer?

3. What is a tachistoscope?

4. What is an eye camera?

5. What is an optical scanner?

6. What does response latency assess? How is it measured?

7. What is voice-pitch analysis? What does it measure?

Discussion Questions, Problems, and Projects

1. Next time you go shopping (grocery or otherwise) do the following disguised observation study with a fellow student. The objective is to assess the service provided to customers while checking out purchases. One of you should complete the following structured observation table. The other should conduct an unstructured observation study by observing and recording all that seems relevant to the objective.

   (a) Store _____   Date _____

          Location _____   Time _____

Too few checkout counters	Yes	No
Long wait in line	Yes	No
Cashier: Quick and efficient	Yes	No
Cashier: Prices well recorded	Yes	No
Cashier: Friendly and pleasant	Yes	No
Purchases packed quickly	Yes	No
Purchases packed poorly	Yes	No
Bags carried to car	Yes	No
Bags provided were flimsy	Yes	No

Endnotes

1. Paco Underhill, *Why We Buy: The Science of Shopping* (New York: Simon & Schuster, 1999), pp. 88–89.

2. Jeff Shear, "The Japanese Excel at Gauging Public Reaction to a New Product," *The Washington Times* (March 15, 1990), p. C1.

3. Michael J. McCarthy, "James Bond Hits the Supermarket: Stores Snoop on Shoppers' Habits to Boost Sales," *The Wall Street Journal* (August 25, 1993), pp. B1, B5.

4. Charles K. Atkin, "Observation of Parent-Child Interaction in Supermarket Decision Making," *Journal of Marketing* 42 (October 1978), pp. 41–45. See also Langbourne Rust, "Parents and Children Shopping Together: A New Approach to the Qualitative Analysis of Observation Data," *Journal of Advertising Research* 33 (July/August 1993), pp. 65–70.

5. Fred N. Kerlinger, *Foundations of Behavioral Research,* 3rd ed. (New York: Holt, Rinehart and Winston, 1986), p. 487.

6. Joe Mandese, "Power Plays," *Marketing & Media Decisions* 24 (March 1989), p. 104. See also Lucie Juneau, "No More Playing Around on Nintendo's Help Desk," *Computerworld* 26 (June 1992), p. 68; Joan Indiana Rigdon, "Nintendo 64 Revitalizes Slumping Video-Game Market," *The Wall Street Journal* (December 17, 1996), pp. B1, B4.

7. Jolie Solomon, "Trying to Be Nice Is No Labor of Love," *The Wall Street Journal* (November 29, 1990), pp. B1, B6.

8. Underhill, *Why We Buy,* pp. 241–242.

9. For insight into some of the many ingenious ways that have been developed to make indirect measurements by observation, see Eugene J. Webb et al., *Unobtrusive Measures: Nonreactive Research in the Social Sciences* (Chicago: Rand McNally, 1966); Lee Sechrest, *New Directions for Methodology of Behavior Science: Unobtrusive Measurement Today* (San Francisco: Jossey-Bass, 1979); Thomas J. Bouchard, Jr., "Unobtrusive Measures: An Inventory of Uses," *Sociological Methods and Research* (February 1976), pp. 267–301.

10. Frederick C. Klein, "Researcher Probes Consumers Using 'Anthropological Skills,'" *The Wall Street Journal* (July 7, 1983), p. 21. See also John F. Sherry, Jr., ed., *Contemporary Marketing and Consumer Behavior: An Anthropological Sourcebook* (Thousand Oaks, Calif.: Sage Publications, 1995), for other examples.

11. Justin Martin, "Ignore Your Customer," *Fortune* 131 (May 1, 1995), pp. 121–126.

12. Ibid.

13. Phil Guarisco, "How GM Targets 'Mature' Market Niche," *Advertising Age* 64 (January 11, 1993), p. 26.

14. For other examples of the use of virtual reality, see Stephen Cohen and Mike Gadd, "Virtual Reality Shopping Simulation for the Modern Marketer," *Marketing & Research Today* 24 (February 1996), pp. 18–26; Raymond R. Burke, "Virtual Shopping: Breakthrough in Marketing Research," *Harvard Business Review* 74 (March/April 1996), pp. 120–131.

15. "Fisher-Price Built on Reputation," *Wisconsin State Journal* (March 17, 1986), p. B3. See also Allison Lucas, "When Every Penny Counts," *Sales & Marketing Management* 148 (February 1996), pp. 74–75, for further discussion of research at Fisher-Price.

16. Joshua Macht, "The New Market Research," *Inc.* (July 1998), pp. 87–94.

17. Underhill, *Why We Buy,* pp. 148–149.

18. Francine Schwadel, "Kmart Testing 'Radar' to Track Shopper Traffic," *The Wall Street Journal* (September 24, 1991), pp. B1, B7.

19. A review of 118 studies on involuntary responses to advertising found that pupil dilation, skin moisture, and heart rate are the most commonly used. See Paul J. Watson and Robert J. Gatchel, "Autonomic Measures of Advertising," *Journal of Advertising Research* 19 (June 1979), pp. 15–26. See also David W. Stewart and David H. Furse, "Applying Psychophysiological Measures to Marketing and Advertising Research Problems," in James H. Leigh and Claude R. Martin, Jr., eds., *Current Issues and Research in Advertising* (Ann Arbor: University of Michigan, 1982), pp. 1–38; Joanne M. Klebba, "Physiological Measures of Research: A Review of Brain Activity, Electrodermal Response, Pupil Dilation and Voice Analysis Methods and Studies," in Leigh and Martin, *Current Issues and Research in Advertising,* pp. 53–76; Priscilla A. La Barbera and Joel D. Tucciarone, "GSR Reconsidered: A Behavior-Based Approach to Evaluating and Improving the Sales Potency of Advertising," *Journal of Advertising Research* 35 (September/October 1995), pp. 33-53.

20. For discussions of the operation and use of eye camera technology to study the effectiveness of ads, packages, and displays, see J. E. Russo, "Eye Fixation Can Save the World," in H. K. Hunt, ed., *Advances in Consumer Research* (Ann Arbor, Mich.: Association for Consumer Research, 1978), pp. 561–570; J. Treistman and J. P. Gregg. "Visual, Verbal, and Sales Response to Print Ads," *Journal of Advertising Research* 19 (August 1979), pp. 41–47; Leo Bogart and B. Stuart Tolley, "The Search for Information in Newspaper Advertising," *Journal of Advertising Research* 28 (April/May 1988), pp. 9–19.

21. For general discussions of the use of response latency measures in marketing research, see James MacLachlan, John Czepiel, and Priscilla LaBarbera, "Implementation of Response Latency Measures," *Journal of Marketing Research* 16 (November 1979), pp. 573–577; James MacLachlan and Priscilla LaBarbera, "Response Latency in Telephone Interviews," *Journal of Advertising Research* 19 (June 1979), pp. 49–56; Tyzoon T. Tyebjee, "Response Latency: A New Measure for Scaling Brand Preference," *Journal of Marketing Research* 16 (February 1979), pp. 96–101; John N. Bassili and Joseph F. Fletcher, "Response-Time Measurement in Survey Research: A Method for CATI and a New Look at Nonattitudes," *Public Opinion Quarterly* 55 (Fall 1991), pp. 331–346; John N. Bassili, "Response Latency versus Certainty as Indexes of the Strength of Voting Intentions in a CATI Survey," *Public Opinion Quarterly* 57 (Spring 1993), pp. 54–61.

22. Robert C. Grass, Wallace H. Wallace, and Samuel Zuckerkandel, "Response Latency in Industrial Advertising Research," *Journal of Advertising Research* 20 (December 1980), pp. 63–65.

23. Nancy Nischwonger and Claude R. Martin, "On Using Voice Analysis in Marketing Research," *Journal of Marketing Research* 18 (August 1981), pp. 350–355. For general discussions of the use of voice-pitch analysis in marketing research, see Ronald G. Nelson and David Schwartz, "Voice Pitch Analysis," *Journal of Advertising Research* 19 (October 1979), pp. 55–59; Glen A. Buckman, "Uses of Voice-Pitch Analysis," *Journal of Advertising Research* 20 (April 1980), pp. 69–73; Linda Edwards, "Hearing What Consumers Really Feel," *Across the Board* 17 (April 1980), pp. 62–67; James Grant and Dean E. Allman, "Voice Stress Analyzer Is a Marketing Research Tool," *Marketing News* 22 (January 4, 1988), p. 22.

24. For general discussions of the status of brain-wave research, see F. Hansen, "Hemispherical Lateralization: Implications for Understanding Consumer Behavior," *Journal of Consumer Research* 8 (June 1981), pp. 23–36; Michael L. Rothschild et al., "Hemispherically Lateralized EEG as a Response to Television Commercials," *Journal of Consumer Research* 15 (September 1988), pp. 185–198; Michael L. Rothschild and Yong J. Hyun, "Micro Information Processing: Predicting Memory for Components of TV Commercials from EEG," *Journal of Consumer Research* 16 (December 1989), pp. 7–16; Michael L. Rothschild and Yong J. Hyun, "Predicting Memory for Components of TV Commercials from EEG," *Journal of Consumer Research* 6 (March 1990), pp. 472–478.

Suggested Additional Readings

For discussion of the strengths and weaknesses of observation as a data collection method, see
Fred N. Kerlinger, *Foundations of Behavioral Research,* 3rd. ed. (New York: Holt, Rinehart and Winston, 1986).

For discussion and examples of unobtrusive measurement techniques, see
Thomas J. Bouchard, Jr., "Unobtrusive Measures: An Inventory of Uses," *Sociological Methods and Research* (February 1976), pp. 267–301.
Lee Sechrest, *New Directions for Methodology of Behavioral Science: Unobtrusive Measurement Today* (San Francisco: Jossey-Bass, 1979).

For discussion of physiological measures to assess respondents' reactions to stimuli, see
Joanne M. Klebba, "Physiological Measures of Research: A Review of Brain Activity, Electrodermal Response, Pupil Dilation and Voice Analysis Methods and Studies," in James H. Leigh and Claude R. Martin, Jr., eds., *Current Issues and Research in Advertising* (Ann Arbor: University of Michigan, 1985), pp. 53–76.
David W. Stewart and David H. Furse, "Applying Psychophysiological Measures to Marketing and Advertising Research Problems," in James H. Leigh and Claude R. Martin, Jr., eds., *Current Issues and Research in Advertising* (Ann Arbor: University of Michigan, 1982), pp. 1–38.

The third stage in the research process is to determine the data collection method. As we have seen from the chapters in this section, two types of data may be useful in addressing the research problem: secondary data and primary data. While a beginning researcher's initial impulse may be to advocate a survey among respondent groups, the prudent and experienced researcher will always begin the study by investigating available secondary data first. Only if the answer the decision maker is seeking is unavailable in the secondary data should the researcher consider gathering primary data.

If a research study seems to be warranted, many other decisions must be made. In the data collection stage, one of the primary decisions is whether to collect information by questionnaire or by observation.

Researchers for CARA sought to determine whether differences existed in the attitudes of local businesspeople toward the advertising media or television, radio, and newspaper, and toward the sales representatives of those media. They also wanted to test the hypothesis that differences in attitudes were associated with differences in annual advertising budgets.

As the researchers told their clients, when the purpose of a study is to determine the association between variables, the most common research design is descriptive. Descriptive designs presuppose a good deal of knowledge about the phenomenon to be studied, and they are guided by one or more hypotheses. Knowledge about the phenomenon under investigation was gleaned from the exploratory research phase of the study. The hypotheses mentioned here and discussed in earlier parts of this textbook guided the descriptive design.

Researchers used secondary data—existing data gathered for some purpose other than the study at hand—during the exploratory research phase to help in understanding the topic of advertising and its perceived strengths and weaknesses.

The information gained from the descriptive phase of the study, however, was based on primary data (data collected to solve the particular problem under investigation) and was secured with a structured-undisguised questionnaire. This type of data collection instrument is characterized by standardized questions and responses, which simplify administration, make the purpose of the study clear, facilitate easy tabulation and analysis of the data, and provide reliable responses.

The researchers chose to administer the questionnaire by mail. This method was chosen partly to avoid the disadvantages posed by telephone and personal interviews and also because researchers wanted a tangible form that would allow a respondent to view all the alternative responses. The mail questionnaire's format was designed with standardized questions and responses for reporting attitudes.

While the mail questionnaire format had many advantages, researchers were also aware of its possible drawbacks. For one, researchers often find it difficult to get individuals to respond to this type of questionnaire. In many studies researchers find that offering respondents an incentive of some sort may help to increase the response rate. Nonetheless, the problem of determining how those who do respond differ from those who do not remains.

Despite these problems, mail questionnaires are often the least expensive method of administration per completed contact. Researchers for CARA estimated that the cost per contact for personal interviews would be about $25; the cost per contact for mail questionnaires was $1.70. When the cost of an incentive for return was added in, the cost jumped to between $4.50 and $5.50. While substantially higher than the base cost per contact, this cost was still much lower than the cost of a personal interview.

Besides lower cost and the opportunity for the respondent to mull over a list of possible alternative answers, what other advantages might the mail questionnaire have had over personal or telephone interviews in this study?

Case III.A   Suchomel Chemical Company

Suchomel Chemical Company was an old-line chemical company that was still managed and directed by its founder, Jeff Suchomel, and his wife, Carol. Jeff served as president and Carol as chief research chemist. The company, which was located in Savannah, Georgia, manufactured a number of products that were used by consumers in and around their homes. The products included waxes, polishes, tile grout, tile cement, spray cleaners for windows and other surfaces, aerosol room sprays, and insecticides. The company distributed its products regionally. It had a particularly strong consumer following in the northern Florida and southern Georgia areas.

The company had not only managed to maintain but had increased its market share in several of its key lines in the past half dozen years in spite of increased competition from the national brands. Suchomel Chemical had done this largely through product innovation, particularly innovation that emphasized modest product alterations rather than new technologies or dramatically new products. Jeff and Carol both believed that the company should stick to the things it knew best rather than try to be all things to all people and in the process spread the company's resources too thin, particularly given its regional nature. One innovation the company was now considering was a new scent for its insect spray, which was rubbed or sprayed on a person's body. The new scent had undergone extensive testing both in the laboratory and in the field. The tests indicated that it repelled insects, particularly mosquitoes, as well as or even better than the two leading national brands. One thing that the company was particularly concerned about as it considered the introduction of the new brand was what to call it.

The Insecticide Market

The insecticide market had become a somewhat tricky one to figure out over the past several years. Although there had been growth in the purchase of insecticides in general, much of this growth had occurred in the tank liquid market. The household spray market had decreased slightly during the same time span. Suchomel Chemical had not suffered from the general sales decline, however, but had managed to increase its sales of spray insecticides slightly over the past three years. The company was hoping that the new scent formulation might allow it to make even greater market share gains.

The company's past experience in the industry led it to believe that the name that was given to the new product would be a very important element in the product's success, because there seemed to be some complex interactions between purchase and usage characteristics among repellent users. Most purchases were made by married

women for their families. Yet repeat purchase was dependent on support by the husband that the product worked well. Therefore, the name must appeal to both the buyer and the end user, but the two people are not typically together at the time of purchase. To complicate matters further, past research indicated that a product with a name that appeals to both purchaser and end user would be rejected if the product's name and scent do not match. In sum, naming a product like this that is used on a person's body is a complex task.

Research Alternatives

The company followed its typical procedures in developing possible names for the new product. First, it asked those who had been involved in the product's development to suggest names. It also scheduled some informal brainstorming sessions among potential customers. Subjects in the brainstorming sessions were simply asked to throw out all the names they could possibly think of with respect to what a spray insecticide could or should be called. A panel of executives, mostly those from the product group but a few from corporate management as well, then went through the names and reduced the large list down to a more manageable subset based on their personal reactions to the names and subsequent discussion about what the names connoted to them. The subset of names was then submitted to the corporate legal staff, who checked them for possible copyright infringement. Those that survived this check were discussed again by the panel, and a list of 20 possibles was generated. Those in the product group were charged with the responsibility of developing a research design by which the final name could be chosen.

The people in the product group charged with the name test were considering two different alternatives for finding out which name was preferred. Both alternatives involved personal interviews at shopping malls. More specifically, the group was planning to conduct a set of interviews at one randomly determined mall in Atlanta, Savannah, Tallahassee, and Orlando. Each set of interviews would involve 100 respondents. The target respondents were married females, ages 21 to 54, who purchased the product category during the past year. Likely-looking respondents would be approached at random and asked if they had used any insect spray at all over the past year and then asked their age. Those that qualified would be asked to complete the insecticide-naming exercise using one of the two alternatives being considered.

Alternative 1 involved a sort of the 20 tentative names by the respondents. The sort would be conducted in the following way. First, respondents would be asked to sort the

20 names into two groups based on their appropriateness for an insect repellent. Group 1 was to consist of the 10 best names and Group 2 the 10 worst. Next, respondents would be asked to select the four best from Group 1 and the four worst from Group 2. Then they would be asked to pick the one best from the subset of the four best and the one worst from the subset of the four worst. Finally, all respondents would be asked why they picked the specific names they did as the best and the worst.

Alternative 2 also had several stages. All respondents would first be asked to rate each of the 20 names on a seven-point semantic differential scale with end anchors "Extremely inappropriate name for an insect repellent" and "Extremely appropriate name for an insect repellent." After completing this rating task, they would be asked to spray the back of their hands or arm with the product. They would then be asked to repeat the rating task using a similar scale, but this time it was be one in which the polar descriptors referred to the appropriateness of the name

with respect to the specific scent. Next they would be asked to indicate their interest in buying the product by again checking one of the seven positions on a scale that ranged from "Definitely would not buy it" to "Definitely would buy it." Finally, each respondent would be asked why she selected each of the names she did as being most appropriate for insect repellents in general and the specific scent in particular.

Questions

1. Evaluate each of the two methods being considered for collecting the data. Which would you recommend and why?

2. How would you use the data from each method to decide what the brand name should be?

3. Do you think that personal interviews in shopping malls are a useful way to collect these data? If not, what would you recommend as an alternative?

Case III.B   Wisconsin Power & Light (B)[1]

In response to the current consumer trend towards increased environmental sensitivity, Wisconsin Power & Light (WP&L) adopted several high-visibility environmental initiatives. These environmental programs fell under the BuySmart umbrella of WP&L's Demand-Side Management Programs and were intended to foster the conservation of energy among WP&L's residential, commercial, and industrial customers. Examples of specific programs include: Appliance Rebates, Energy Analysis, Weatherization Help, and the Home Energy Improvement Loan (HEIL) program. All previous marketing research and information gathering focused primarily on issues from the customers' perspective, such as an evaluation of net program impacts in terms of energy and demand savings, and an estimation of the levels of free ridership (individuals who would have undertaken the conservation actions promoted by the program, even if there was no program in place). In addition, a study has been designed and is currently being conducted to evaluate and identify customer attitudes and opinions concerning the design, implementation, features, and delivery of the residential programs. Having examined the consumer perspective, WP&L's next objective is to focus on obtaining information from other participants in the programs, namely employees and lenders.

WP&L's first step in shifting the focus of its research is to undertake a study of the Home Energy Improvement Loan

(HEIL) program of the BuySmart umbrella. The HEIL program had been introduced four years ago. It was designed to make low-interest-rate financing available to residential gas and electric WP&L customers for conservation and weatherization measures. The low-interest guaranteed loans are delivered through WP&L account representatives in conjunction with participating financial institutions and trade allies. The procedures for obtaining a loan begin with an energy "audit" of the interested customer's residence to determine the appropriate conservation measures. Once the customer decides on which measures to have installed, the WP&L representative assists in arranging low-interest-rate financing through one of the participating local banking institutions. At the completion of the projects, WP&L representatives conduct an inspection of the work by checking a random sample of participants. Conservation measures eligible under the HEIL program include the installation of natural gas furnaces/boilers, automatic vent dampers, intermittent ignition devices, heat pumps, and heat pump water heaters. Eligible structural improvements include the addition of attic/wall/basement insulation, storm windows and doors, sillbox insulation, window weather-stripping, and caulking.

Purpose

The primary goal of the current study is to identify ways of improving the HEIL program from the lenders' point of view. Specifically, the following issues need to be addressed:

- Identify the lenders' motivation for participating in the program.

[1]The contributions of Kavita Maini and Paul Metz to the development of this case are gratefully acknowledged as is the permission of Wisconsin Power & Light to use the material included.

- Determine how lenders get their information regarding various changes/updates in the program.

- Identify how lenders promote the program.

- Assess the current program with respect to administrative and program features.

- Determine the type of credit analysis conducted by the lenders.

- Identify ways of minimizing the default rate from the lenders' point of view.

- Assess the lenders' commitment to the program.

- Identify lenders' opinions of the overall program.

- Identify if the reason for loan inactivity in some lending institutions is due to lack of a customer base.

Methodology

WP&L decided to use a telephone survey of participating lending institutions to collect the data for its study. WP&L referenced two lists of lending institutions, which were supplied by its resident marketing staff, in order to select the sample for the survey. A total of 124 participating lending institutions were identified with the lists. However, it was found that one of the lists was shorter than the other by 15 names. Specifically, the names of some of the branches of major banks were not enumerated on one of the lists. Nevertheless, all 124 institutions, including the 15 discrepant ones, were included in the pool of names from which the sample was drawn.

The sample pool was classified into three groups based on loan activity in the 1998 calendar year. The groups fell out as follows:

Group	Number of Lenders	Loan Activity, 1998
1	44	0 loans
2	40	1 to 7 loans
3	40	8 to 54 loans

The rationale for the classification strategy was to allow analysis of key variables by three key groups: no loan activity, "light" loan activity, and "heavy" loan activity. The delineation between "light" and "heavy" activity was determined by the median number of loans issued by "active" participants.

The final sample for the survey consisted of 20 randomly chosen institutions from Groups 2 and 3, and 10 from Group 1. The samples of 20 lenders from both Groups 2 and 3 were identified by selecting every other listed respondent after a randomly determined starting point in each list. The 40 institutions selected from among Groups 2 and 3 formed the sample base in which WP&L was most interested (this was because each of these 40 institutions demonstrated loan activity in the past year). The sample size ($n = 40$) was based on judgment. The 10 randomly selected institutions from Group 1 were chosen primarily to explore the hypothesized reasons for zero-loan activity. These 10 zero-loan lenders received a shortened version of the telephone survey that focused only on their lack of activity.

All of the districts within WP&L's service territory were notified two weeks in advance that a survey was going to be conducted. The survey was pretested and modified prior to final administration. All interviewing was conducted over a one-week period by a project manager and research assistant, both employees of WP&L's marketing department.

Questions

1. Given the project's objectives, describe the best way to proceed in terms of data collection. Provide support for your conclusion.

2. What kind of sample was used by Wisconsin Power & Light in their research effort? What advantages did WP&L gain by using the sampling method they used? What were the disadvantages? Suggest possible sampling alternatives that WP&L could have used.

Case III.C   Office of Student Financial Services (A)[1]

Background

Magnus Pym, dean of Student Affairs at a midwestern university, developed a campuswide service quality initiative program that he was interested in implementing. As an initial measure, he fielded a quality service initiative (QSI)

[1]The contributions of Neeraj Bharadwaj to the development of this case are gratefully acknowledged.

campuswide survey designed to ascertain the level of satisfaction undergraduate students had with the various student services provided on campus. After analyzing the results of the survey instrument, he noticed that the Office of Student Financial Services (OSFS) received one of the lowest rankings among all the departments. Because the financing of a college education is a high-involvement issue for most students, Magnus felt that he needed to examine this area more closely.

Magnus contacted Susan Solacy, director of the OSFS for the past 10 years, to further discuss his preliminary concerns. After examining the QSI survey instrument, she defended the performance of her department by raising three issues:

- The campuswide QSI survey had only one question that pertained directly to satisfaction with the OSFS, and thus it may have provided a distorted view of what students were actually feeling.

- All the questions in the QSI survey were structured (closed-ended). This may have caused respondents to feel that they needed to provide an answer even when they did not have an opinion on the issue. This may be the case in this instance, as historically, only about 30 percent of the student body applies for financial aid through the OSFS. However, almost all the students completing the QSI survey had responded to the question regarding satisfaction with the OSFS.

- The majority of the funding guidelines regarding scholarships, grants, and loans are established by the federal government. Given that the role of the OSFS is simply to execute the procedures set forth at the national level, it has no control over the final allocation decision. In sum, students might be dissatisfied with issues over which the OSFS has no control.

Research Method

To address the aforementioned concerns, Susan recommended that the university commission a more focused study to better understand the factors contributing to the low satisfaction with the OSFS. Based upon her personal experience, she felt that a survey would be the best suited for gathering this descriptive information. In fact, she recently came across a financial aid survey fielded at Bond University that examined many of the same issues that applied to the OSFS. It contained 40 five-point Likert scale items pertaining to the application process (speed in receiving checks/awards, satisfaction with work study/scholarship/loan process, and so on), the

helpfulness of the staff/counselors, and demographic information of the respondents.

Susan hired three undergraduate students from a marketing research class to develop an instrument that addressed potential areas of dissatisfaction with the OSFS. In addition to the structured questions appearing in the Bond survey, she was interested in having some open-ended questions that tapped into concerns associated with picking up the checks/awards, generated a list of what students felt were the most important services provided by the OSFS, and ascertained suggestions/areas for improvement. Prior to letting the student research team begin developing the questionnaire, Susan identified several other issues that would influence the study:

- She highlighted the accessibility to the OSFS database, which consists of 13,000 students who had applied for financial aid within the last 12 months.

- She mentioned that she had a very limited budget.

- She wants to ensure that enough information is generated for each cell so that the results are statistically significant. This is key as she had witnessed previous surveys that had drawn conclusions from what she felt was insufficient data. Therefore, for the approximately 40 to 45 five-point Likert scale items that she envisions for the OSFS instrument, she feels that it is necessary to receive 1,000 completed surveys.

- She wants the completed research report citing results/recommended actions within four months, as she is up for a promotion next year.

Questions
1. In light of the parameters mentioned by Susan, what method of administration (personal interview, telephone interview, or mail questionnaire) would you recommend to her if you were part of the student team?

2. Given the method you prescribed in Question 1, what could be done to increase the response rate?

Case III.D   Premium Pizza Inc.[1]

The 1980s saw a sharp increase in the use of promotions (coupons, cents-off deals marked on the package, free gifts, etc.) because of their manifest success at increasing short-term purchase behavior. In fact, sales promotion is now estimated to account for over one-half of the typical promotion budget while advertising accounts for less than half. In many industries, however, the initial benefit of

[1]The contributions of Jacqueline C. Hitchon to this case are gratefully acknowledged.

increased sales has resulted in long-term escalation of competition. As firms are forced to "fight fire with fire," special offer follows special offer in a never-ending spiral of promotional deals.

The fast-food industry has been one of the most strongly affected by this trend. Pizzas come two for the price of one; burgers are promoted in the context of a double-deal involving cuddly toys for the kids; tacos are reduced in price some days—but not others. It is within this fiercely competitive, erratic environment that Premium Pizza Corporation has grown from a small local chain into an extensive midwestern network with national aspirations. Over the past few years, Jim Battaglia, vice president of marketing, has introduced a number of promotional offers, and Premium Pizza parlors have continued to flourish. Nevertheless, as the company contemplates further expansion, Jim is concerned that he knows very little about how his customers respond to his promotional deals. He believes that he needs a long-term strategy aimed at maximizing the effectiveness of dollars spent on promotions. And, as a first step, he thinks that it is important to assess the effectiveness of his existing offers.

Specific Objectives

In the past, Jim has favored the use of five types of coupons, and he now wishes to determine their independent appeal, together with their relation to several identifiable characteristics of fast-food consumers. The five promotional concepts are listed in Exhibit III.D.1. The consumer characteristics that Jim's experience tells him warrant investigation include number of children living at home, age of youngest child, propensity to eat fast food, propensity to eat Premium Pizza in particular, preference for slices over pies, propensity to use coupons, and occupation.

The specific objectives of the research study can therefore be summarized as follows:

- To evaluate the independent appeal of the five promotional deals to determine which deals are most preferred;

- To gain insight into the reasons that certain deals are preferred; and

- To examine the relationships between the appeal of each promotional concept and various consumer characteristics.

Proposed Methodology

After much discussion, Jim's research team finally decided that the desired information could best be gathered by means of personal interviews, using a combination of open-ended and closed-ended questions. A medium-sized shopping mall on the outskirts of a metropolitan area in the Midwest was selected as the research site. Shoppers were intercepted by professional interviewers while walking in the mall and asked to participate in a survey requiring five minutes of their time.

The sampling procedure employed a convenience sample in which interviewers were instructed to approach anyone passing by, provided that they met certain criteria (see Exhibit III.D.2). In sum, the sample of respondents was restricted to adult men and women between the ages of 18 and 49 who had both purchased lunch, dinner, or carry-

out food at a fast-food restaurant in the past seven days and had eaten restaurant pizza within the last 30 days, either at a restaurant or delivered to the home. In addition, interviewers were warned not to exercise any bias during the selection process, as they would do, for example, if they approached only those people who looked particularly agreeable or attractive. Finally, interviewers were asked to obtain as close as possible to a 50-50 split of male and female participants.

The questionnaire was organized into three sections (see Exhibit III.D.3). The first section contained the screening questions aimed at ensuring that respondents qualified for the sample. In the second section, respondents were asked to evaluate on 10-point scales the appeal of each of the five promotional concepts based on two factors: perceived value and likelihood of use. After they had evaluated a concept, interviewees were asked to give reasons for their likelihood-of-use rating. The third and final section consisted of the questions on consumer characteristics that Jim believed to be pertinent.

The questionnaire was to be completed by the interviewer based on the respondent's comments. In other words, the interviewer read the questions aloud and wrote down the answer given in each case by the interviewee. It was decided to show respondents an example of each coupon before they rated it. For this purpose, enlarged photographs of each coupon were produced. It was also thought necessary to depict the 10-point scales that consumers should use to evaluate the promotional offer. Coupons and scales were therefore assembled in a booklet so that, as the interviewer showed each double-page spread, the respondent would see the scales on the top page and the coupon in question on the bottom page (see Figure III.D.1).

Because the researcher wished to counterbalance the order in which the coupons were viewed and rated, the five coupons were organized into booklets of six different sequences. Each sequence was subsequently bound in one of six distinctly colored binders. A total of 96 questionnaires were then printed in six different colors to

EXHIBIT III.D.1	Five Promotional Concepts
Coupon A:	Get a medium soft drink for 5 cents with the purchase of any slice.
Coupon B:	Buy a slice and get a second slice of comparable value free.
Coupon C:	Save 50 cents on the purchase of any slice and receive one free trip to the salad bar.
Coupon D:	Buy a slice and a large soft drink and get a second slice free.
Coupon E:	Get a single-topping slice for only 99 cents.

EXHIBIT III.D.2   **Interviewer Instructions**

Below are suggestions for addressing each question. Please read all of the instructions before you begin questioning people.

Interviewer Instructions

Approach shoppers who appear to be between 18 and 49 years of age. Since we would like equal numbers of respondents in each age category and a 50 percent male-female ratio, please do not select respondents based on their appeal to you. The interview should take approximately five minutes. When reading questions, read answer choices *if indicated*.

Question 1:   Terminate any respondent who has not eaten lunch or dinner from any fast-food restaurant in the last seven days.

Question 2:   Terminate any respondent who has not eaten pizza within the last 30 days. This includes carry-out, drive-thru, or dining in.

Question 3:   Terminate respondent if not between 18 and 49 years of age. If between 18 and 49, circle the appropriate number answer. For this question, please read the question and the answer choices.

After completing questions 1 through 3, hand respondent the coupon booklet. *Make sure that the booklet and the response sheets are the same color.* Also check to see that the coupon booklet number indicated on the upper right-hand corner of the response sheet matches the coupon book number.

Question 4:   Ask the respondent to open the coupon booklet and read the first coupon concept. Read the first section of Question 4 showing the respondent that the scales are provided on the page above the coupon concept. Enter his or her answer in the box provided.

Read the second section of the question and enter respondent's answer in the second box provided.

When asking the respondent, "Why did you respond as you did for use," please record the first reason mentioned and use the lines provided to probe and clarify the reasons.

This set of instructions applies to Questions 5 through 8. Periodically remind the respondent to look at the scales provided on the page above the coupon concept that he or she is looking at.

Question 9:   Enter number of children living at home. If none, enter the number zero and proceed to Question 11.

Question 10:   Enter age of *youngest* child living at home in the box provided.

Question 11:   Read the question and each answer slowly. Circle the number corresponding to the appropriate answer.

Question 12:   Read the question and each answer slowly. Circle the number corresponding to the appropriate answer. If answer is never, proceed to Question 14. Otherwise, continue to Question 13.

Question 13:   Circle the number corresponding to the appropriate answer. Do not read answer choices.

Question 14:   Circle the number corresponding to the appropriate answer. Do not read answer choices.

Question 15:   Read the question and each answer slowly. Circle the number corresponding to the appropriate answer.

Question 16:   Read the question and each answer slowly. Circle the number corresponding to the appropriate answer.

Question 17:   If an explanation is requested for occupation, please tell respondent that we are looking for a broad category or title. "No occupation" is not an acceptable answer. If this should happen, please probe to see if the person is a student, homemaker, retired, unemployed, etc.

At the end of the questionnaire, you are asked to indicate whether the respondent was male or female. Please circle the appropriate answer. This is not a question for the respondent.

EXHIBIT III.D.3   **Questionnaire**

Response Number   _____
Coupon Book #   _____

(Approach shoppers who appear to be between the ages of 18 and 49 and say . . .)

Hi, I'm _____ from *Midwest Research Services. Many companies like to know your preferences and opinions about new products and promotions. If you have about 5 minutes, I'd like to have your opinions in this marketing research study.*

(If refused, terminate)

1. *Have you eaten lunch or dinner in, or carried food away from, a fast-food restaurant in the last seven days?*
   . . . (must answer yes to continue)

2. *Have you eaten restaurant pizza within the last thirty days, either at the restaurant or by having it delivered?*
   . . . (must answer yes to continue)

3. *Which age group are you in? (read answers, circle number)*
   1 18–24   2 25–34   3 35–49   4 Other—Terminate interview

I am now going to show you five different coupon concepts and ask you three questions for each. Please respond to each coupon independently of the others. Look at the next coupon only when I ask you to.

4. *Please read the first coupon concept. Using a ten-point scale as shown on the page above, how would you rate this concept if one represents very poor value and ten represents very good value?*

   ⬚ enter value

   Looking at the second scale, how would you rate this concept if one represents definitely would not use and ten represents definitely would use?

   ⬚ enter value

   Why did you respond as you did for use? _____
   _____
   _____

5. *Please turn the page and read the next coupon concept. Ignoring the last coupon and using the same scale, how would you rate this concept in terms of value?*

   ⬚ enter value

   Referring to the second scale, how would you rate this concept in terms of your level of use?

   ⬚ enter value

   Why did you respond as you did for use? _____
   _____
   _____

6. *Please turn the page and read the next coupon concept. Ignoring the last coupon and using the same scale, how would you rate this concept in terms of value?*

   ⬚ enter value

   Referring to the second scale, how would you rate this concept in terms of your level of use?

   ⬚ enter value

   Why did you respond as you did for use? _____
   _____
   _____

continued

EXHIBIT III.D.3 **Questionnaire,** *continued*

7. *Please turn the page and read the next coupon concept. Ignoring the last coupon and using the same scale, how would you rate this concept in terms of value?*

enter value

Referring to the second scale, how would you rate this concept in terms of your level of use?

enter value

Why did you respond as you did for use? _____

_____

_____

8. *Please turn the page and read the next coupon concept. Ignoring the last coupon and using the same scale, how would you rate this concept in terms of value?*

enter value

Referring to the second scale, how would you rate this concept in terms of your level of use?

enter value

Why did you respond as you did for use? _____

_____

_____

Thank you. The following questions will help us classify the preceding information.

9. *How many children do you have living at home?*
   If answer is none, proceed to question 11.

enter number
none = 0

10. *What is the age of your youngest child?*

11. *How often do you eat fast food for lunch or dinner?*
    (read answers, circle number) 1 Once per month or less
    2 Two to three times per month
    3 Once or twice a week
    4 More than twice a week

12. *How often do you eat at Premium Pizza?*
    (read answers, circle number) 1 Never visited Premium Pizza
    2 Once per month or less
    3 Two to three times per month
    4 Once a week or more
    If answer is never, proceed to question 14.

13. *Do you yourself usually buy whole pies or slices at Premium Pizza?*

1 whole pies
2 slices
(circle one)

14. *Have you used fast-food or restaurant coupons in the last 30 days?*

1 yes
2 no
(circle one)

15. *Have you ever used coupons for Premium Pizza?*
    (read answers, circle number) 1 Never
    2 I sometimes use them when I have them.
    3 I always use them when I have them.

EXHIBIT III.D.3   Questionnaire, *continued*

16. *What is your marital status:*
    (read answers, circle number)   1 Single
                                    2 Married
                                    3 Divorced, separated, widowed

17. *What is your occupation?* _____
    This is *not* a question for the respondent.
    Please circle appropriate answer—respondent was: 1 male
                                                       2 female
                                                       (circle number)

Thank you for your participation—Terminate interview at this time.

FIGURE III.D.1   Stimuli

match the binder. In this way, there were 16 questionnaires of each color, and the color of the respondent's questionnaire indicated the sequence that he or she had seen.

The questionnaire and procedure were pretested at a mall similar to the target mall and were found to be satisfactory.

Questions

1. Is the choice of mall intercept interviews an appropriate data collection method given the research objectives?

2. Do you think that there are any specific criteria that the choice of shopping mall should satisfy?

3. Evaluate the instructions to interviewers.

4. Evaluate the questionnaire.

5. Do you think that it is worthwhile to present the coupons in a binder, separate from the questionnaire? Why or why not?

6. Do you consider it advisable to rotate the order of presentation of coupons? Why or why not?

Data Collection Forms

Once the data collection method has been decided, the researcher needs to design the data collection forms that will be used. Chapter 12 discusses the construction of questionnaires and observation forms. Chapter 13 provides some measurement basics that researchers need to be aware of so that they do not mislead others. Chapter 14 then discusses the measurement of attitudes, perceptions, and preferences.

ARAMARK: SEEKING SATISFACTION IN THE COMPANY'S CAFETERIA If you've ever tried to plan a family meal or order pizza for a group of hungry students, you know it can be hard to satisfy everyone's tastes. But imagine that your job involves feeding millions of workers every day. That's the daily responsibility of ARAMARK Food and Support Services. This ARAMARK division provides cafeteria and other support services to businesses, sports facilities, government agencies, and health care and educational institutions throughout the Untied States and northern Mexico.

To negotiate and keep contracts with businesses such as Ford, General Motors, and Xerox, ARAMARK has to appeal to their employees' taste buds and meet their expectations for service. ARAMARK does this by incorporating customer and employee surveys into its regular practices. These surveys are intended to identify areas requiring improvement.

Each year the company distributes printed questionnaires to its dining facilities. The surveys are prepared by NCS, a Minneapolis research firm, as part of a kit that also includes posters and cash register displays to promote the surveys. When the managers of the food service facilities receive the kits, they set up the promotional materials and distribute the questionnaires. Most place the questionnaires near the cash registers; a few send them out via interoffice mail. Some facilities offer a free cookie as an incentive for completing the survey.

NCS prepares both English and Spanish versions of the questionnaires. In general, the questions fall into three categories:

1. *Food:* Questions about the overall quality, taste, and appearance of the food, as well as whether the food is a good value for the price

2. *Service:* Questions about the promptness of service and the courtesy of the staff, as well as their appearance and their knowledge about the menu

3. *Facilities:* Questions about the serving area and dining room, including cleanliness, seating availability, and ease of obtaining service; questions about the convenience of service hours

In addition, regional versions of the questionnaire address topics that apply only to certain areas. For example, facilities in an area that offers gourmet coffees or serves special dietary needs may ask about these offerings.

The employee questionnaires are similar. However, ARAMARK employees also answer questions about the quality of their work life, including ratings of their supervisors, coworkers, and the equipment they use. They also provide opinions about such work-related issues as their opportunities for advancement.

During the week-long survey period, customers and employees mark their opinions on the scannable survey forms. The facilities manager gathers the completed questionnaires, puts them in a preaddressed mailer, and forwards them to NCS. At the research firm's offices, a computer scans the responses. Two weeks later, NCS has already scanned and processed the data. It can do this so quickly because the responses are in a format that is readable by computer, and the survey header and address label are bar coded. When NCS receives the completed forms, it scans the bar codes so it knows where the data came from and where the results should be mailed.

Thus, two weeks after it receives the completed questionnaires, NCS sends a summary of the data to ARAMARK managers. Each facility manager gets a summary of the responses from his or her own facility, and ARAMARK managers at headquarters also get reports.

NCS then goes to work analyzing the data to identify major areas of concern. Three weeks later, it sends ARAMARK managers a Performance Improvement Planner. This report maps 25 major attributes of the menu, service, and dining environment in terms of their importance to customers and the facility's performance. Managers study these maps, focusing especially on attributes that rate high in importance and low in performance. These are the areas where action is most critical. The employee and customer responses are presented separately. This enables managers to identify both management and customer service concerns. In addition, gaps between employee and customer evaluations may signal problems—for example, a need to set higher quality standards.

With the Performance Improvement Planners in hand, company managers meet with the management of each facility to review performance ratings and areas requiring improvement. The importance rankings help the mangers to focus on the attributes that are most significant to customers and employees.

ARAMARK responds with a program called We Heard You, which is designed to show customers that the company is applying the results of the survey. The program uses posters and stationery with the We-Heard-You slogan to communicate the survey results and the actions ARAMARK is taking in response. Thus, if customers of a cafeteria complain about the location of the salad bar, ARAMARK materials can summarize the concern and specify the response: "Because you asked, starting next week, the salad bar will be located [in the desired spot]." When people arrive at the cafeteria, they can see concrete evidence that ARAMARK paid attention to their comments. This, in turn, encourages them to respond to the survey the next year it is administered.

Similarly, ARAMARK management uses the survey to demonstrate to its own employees that it is committed to customer satisfaction. First, it provides leadership in focusing on customer concerns. In addition, performance goals for managers often incorporate the employee and customer concerns raised in the surveys. Thus, if the survey shows that customer service or employee opportunity is lacking in some area, managers' goals will include improving performance in that area.

ARAMARK also uses the survey results to build its business. The company can present its existing corporate customers with data indicting that their employees are asking for additional services—say, additional service hours or broader menu offerings. Even more important, the company's track record of applying customer research shows current and prospective customers that ARAMARK has a tradition of caring about customer satisfaction.

Sources: Joseph Rydholm, "High Marks," *Quirk's Marketing Research Review* (May 1998, downloaded from the magazine's Web site, www.quirks.com, August 13, 1999); ARAMARK Web site (www.aramark.com, downloaded September 27, 1999).

Chapter 12

DESIGNING THE QUESTIONNAIRE OR OBSERVATION FORM

LEARNING OBJECTIVES

Upon Completing This Chapter, You Should Be Able to

1. Explain the role of research hypotheses in developing a questionnaire.

2. Define *telescoping error* and *recall loss* and explain how they affect a respondent's ability to answer questions accurately.

3. Cite some of the techniques researchers use to secure respondents' cooperation in answering sensitive questions.

4. Explain what an open-ended question is.

5. Name two kinds of fixed-alternative questions and tell the difference between them.

6. List some of the primary rules researchers should keep in mind in trying to develop bias-free questions.

7. Explain what the funnel approach to question sequencing is.

8. Explain what a branching question is and discuss when it is used.

9. Explain the difference between basic information and classification information and tell which should be asked first in a questionnaire.

Case in Marketing Research

Bill Hershey, a young staffer at Wright Communications Research, was leafing through the first batch of questionnaires that had been returned on the MedAccounts study. To anyone passing his desk, he presented a picture of frustration and bewilderment. This was supposed to be a very straightforward survey, and Hershey didn't understand what could have gone wrong.

MedAccounts was a company that provided specialized computer systems for doctors' offices. Its systems centralized all record-keeping and billing functions, which cut down on the cost and time devoted to updating charts and sending bills. However, when there was a service problem with the MedAccounts system, a doctor's office could be paralyzed. That was why the people at MedAccounts had hired Wright Communications Research to find out how quickly and effectively their service department was handling service calls.

It had been decided that the most cost-efficient method for the study would be to send out a questionnaire. Hershey had been picked to help draft it. He had taken the questionnaire through several versions and had fine-tuned it with more experienced staffers. Then the final version had been printed and mailed to the sample of 900 physicians listed by MedAccounts as using its system.

Hershey had thought that the hard part was over; all that remained was to tabulate the responses from the completed questionnaires. The stack of completed forms on his desk, however, constituted a rude surprise.

For one thing, it represented a much lower response rate than he'd counted on. He had expected that many of the physicians surveyed would be too busy to reply to the questionnaire, but he'd expected more responses than this.

Even more perplexing was the Jekyll and Hyde quality of the replies. About half of the questionnaires were intelligently completed. The other half were full of sketchy answers and questions left blank.

Hershey had no idea what was going on, but he was determined to find out. He picked up the phone and began dialing the number of one of the physicians whose half-filled-out questionnaire sat on the desk in front of him.

Discussion Issues

1. Do you think that a mail questionnaire was a good choice for the MedAccounts study? Why or why not?

2. Do you think that Hershey might have avoided some of the problems with a pretest of his questionnaire?

3. What are some of the possible explanations for the kinds of initial results Hershey received?

In the previous chapters we discussed the various types of questionnaires and observation forms researchers use and how they are administered, as well as the pros and cons of the specific types of questionnaires and observation methods. We also examined the various advantages and disadvantages of using communication and observation research techniques.

In this chapter we will build on that discussion by reviewing the procedures researchers can follow in developing a questionnaire or observation data collection form.

Questionnaire Design

Although much progress has been made, designing questionnaires is still an art and not a science. Much of the progress has been simply an awareness of what to avoid, for example, leading questions and ambiguous questions. Few guidelines exist, however, on how to develop questions that are not leading or ambiguous.

Figure 12.1 offers a method the beginning researcher might find helpful to develop questionnaires.[1] More experienced researchers would be expected to develop their own patterns, although the steps listed in Figure 12.1 would certainly be part of that pattern.

Although the stages of development are presented in the figure in sequence, researchers will rarely be so fortunate as to develop a questionnaire in that step-by-step fashion. A more typical development will involve circling back to clarify some aspects of earlier steps after they have been found to be faulty later on in the questionnaire's design. The researcher may find, for example, that the way a question is worded tends to elicit

FIGURE 12.1   **Procedure for Developing a Questionnaire**

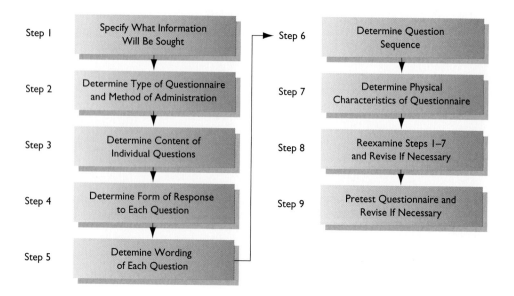

Step 1	Specify What Information Will Be Sought
Step 2	Determine Type of Questionnaire and Method of Administration
Step 3	Determine Content of Individual Questions
Step 4	Determine Form of Response to Each Question
Step 5	Determine Wording of Each Question
Step 6	Determine Question Sequence
Step 7	Determine Physical Characteristics of Questionnaire
Step 8	Reexamine Steps 1–7 and Revise If Necessary
Step 9	Pretest Questionnaire and Revise If Necessary

unhelpful responses. Researchers should not be surprised, then, if they find themselves working back and forth among some of the stages. That is natural.

Researchers should also be warned not to take the stages too literally. They are presented as a guide or a checklist. With questionnaires, the proof of the pudding is very much in the eating. Does the questionnaire produce accurate data of the kind needed? Blind adherence to procedure is no substitute for creativity in approach, nor is it any substitute for a pretest (Step 9 of Figure 12.1), with which one can discover if the typical respondent indeed understands each question and is able and willing to supply the information sought.

Step 1: Specify What Information Will Be Sought

The first step in questionnaire design, deciding what information will be sought, is easy, provided that researchers have been meticulous and precise at earlier stages in the research process. Careless earlier work will make this decision difficult.

Both descriptive and causal research require that researchers have enough knowledge about the problem to frame some specific hypotheses to guide the research. The hypotheses also guide the questionnaire. They determine what information will be sought, and from whom, because they specify what relationships will be investigated. If researchers have already established dummy tables to structure the data analysis, their job of determining what information is to be collected is essentially complete. You may remember that a dummy table is a table designed to catalog the data that will be collected. It is identical to the one that will be used in the actual research, but in this early stage it has no numbers.

Researchers must collect information on the variables specified in the dummy tables in order to investigate the hypotheses. Further, researchers must collect this information from the right people and in the right units. Hence, it is clear that hypotheses are not only guides to what information will be sought, but also affect the type of question and form of response used to collect it.

Of course, the preparation of the questionnaire may itself suggest further hypotheses and other relationships that might be investigated at slight additional effort and cost. A

Ethical Dilemma 12.1

A financial institution has developed a new type of savings bond. The marketing director of this institution has requested that a local research supply company design a questionnaire that will help quantify target consumers' interest in this new bond. However, the marketing director is concerned about the possibility of competitors hearing about the new product concept because of the survey. She requests that the questionnaire be written in such a way as to mask the true purpose of the study.

To mask the actual purpose of the study, the questionnaire primarily asks respondents for details of their holiday plans and budgets. Because respondents are asked questions about their finances only after multiple vacation-related questions, it is hoped that the respondents will assume the information is for a travel company.

Moreover, the marketing director of the financial institution asks that interviewers tell respondents that the information is being gathered for a travel-related company.

- Discuss the implications of deceiving respondents on a questionnaire in this way.

- If the interviewers had not been told to explicitly tell respondents that the information was for a travel-related corporation, would the deception be acceptable?

- Are there ways of gaining this type of information without resorting to deception while still protecting the institution's new product idea?

- Discuss the validity issues associated with respondents knowing the purpose of the survey as they are completing it.

most important warning is in order here: If the new hypothesis is indeed vital to understanding the phenomenon, by all means include it and use it to advantage when designing the questionnaire. On the other hand, and we are repeating ourselves, if it simply represents one of those potentially "interesting findings" but is not vital to the research effort, forget it. The inclusion of interesting but not vital items simply lengthens the questionnaire, causes problems in administration and analysis, and often increases non-response.

The exploratory research effort is, of course, aimed at the discovery of ideas and insights and not at their systematic investigation. The questionnaire for an exploratory study is therefore loosely structured, with only a rough idea of the kind of information that might be sought. This is particularly true at the earliest stages of exploratory research. It is also true, but to a lesser extent, at the later stages of exploratory research, when the emphasis is on determining the priorities that should be given to various hypotheses in guiding future research.

When Murray Simon was conducting exploratory research about a new medication for a pharmaceutical company, he found that the doctors he interviewed were unwilling to speculate about how they would use the medication. Thus, asking, "Would you write a prescription for this medicine?" was unproductive. The doctor would say, "I can't make a judgment until I see the clinical trials," or, "Send your rep around with samples. After I have some experience with it, we can talk about it." So Simon tried a less structured type of question in his one-on-one interviews. He asked the doctor to imagine he or she was playing the role of the salesperson calling on a doctor, and Simon would play the role of the doctor. Most of the doctors willingly participated, and Simon's client learned a great deal by evaluating what selling points the doctors-as-sales-reps incorporated into their sales pitches. For example, they indicated that a sizable share of patients were unhappy with the new drug's primary competitor. The drug company also learned that some of the claims it planned to make about the new drug were difficult to defend, so it modified those statements before launching the product.[2]

Step 2: Determine Type of Questionnaire and Method of Administration

After specifying the basic information that will be sought, the researcher needs to specify how it will be gathered. Decisions on the type of questionnaire and method of administering it constitute the second step. Such decisions center on the structure and disguise to be used in the questionnaire and whether it will be administered by mail, telephone, or personal interviews. We saw previously that these decisions are not independent of one another. If the researcher decides on a disguised-unstructured questionnaire in which subjects will be shown a picture and asked to tell a story about it, a telephone interview would be out of the question, and even a mail survey might pose serious problems. Similarly, it is probably not a good idea to use a mail survey for an unstructured-undisguised questionnaire that asks open-ended questions.

The type of data to be collected will have an important effect, of course, on the method of data collection. For example, the San Francisco research firm King, Brown & Partners had a client that wanted to know what proportion of Internet users had various multimedia plug-ins (for example, Shockwave or Acrobat for downloading and playing multimedia files). From experience, King, Brown knew that one-third or more users don't accurately know which plug-ins they have, especially when it comes to such detailed information as which version of the plug-in. It would have been a waste of time to call or write to computer users and pose such questions. Rather, the researchers set up an on-line survey that was structured to help the users answer accurately. They created a kind of multimedia test, in which they used a variety of plug-in file formats to display images. For each image, users who downloaded the survey were asked whether they could see the image. If they clicked "yes," the researchers knew, by the format used to create the image, precisely what plug-in they were using. This methodology let respondents provide data without knowing the technical details.[3]

Another influence on the data collection method is the culture of the country where the study is being done (see Research Window 12.1). A researcher investigating the

---

Research Window 12.1   **How Cultural Differences Affect Marketing Research in Different Countries**

Willingness to Cooperate

Compared with people around the world, Americans tend to be unusually helpful and friendly, which is reflected in their general willingness to cooperate in marketing research surveys. Quite often, Americans will answer the questions of a total stranger (in the research industry we call them "interviewers") about almost any subject—up to and including one's sex life. And Americans will agree to be interviewed anywhere: over the telephone, in a shopping mall, or at their place of business.

This climate of assumed cooperation can spoil Americans for doing research elsewhere in the world. Individual consumers in many other countries are less ready to answer any questions from an interviewer, let alone delicate or personal ones. Business people in many parts of the world have a more closed attitude than Americans about taking part in surveys.

In Korea, for example, business people are reluctant to answer any survey questions about their company—it is considered disloyal to divulge any type of information to "outsiders." And most Japanese business people are hesitant to take part in surveys during business hours—

taking time away from your work for a survey is like "stealing" from your employer.

Differences in Research Costs

The cost of doing exactly the same research can vary dramatically from country to country. Japan is generally regarded as the most expensive research market in the world; projects there usually cost several times what the same study would cost in the United States.

But even within a single region, such as the European community, costs can vary dramatically from country to country. ESOMAR, the European Society for Opinion and Marketing Research (the European equivalent of a combined American Marketing Association and Advertising Research Foundation), periodically studies differences in research costs from country to country within Europe. Here are examples of some of the cost differences ESOMAR found in its most recent study:

Source: Jeffrey Pope, *How Cultural Differences Affect Multi-Country Research* (Minneapolis, Minn.: Custom Research, Inc., 1991).

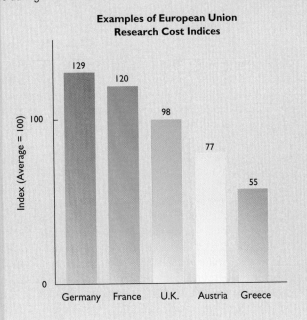

Examples of European Union Research Cost Indices

FIGURE 12.2   **Mail Questionnaire for Caffeinated Ground Coffee Study**

1.   What type of coffeemaker do you usually use to prepare your ground coffee at home? (CHECK *ONE* BOX)

   1 ☐ Automatic drip
   2 ☐ Electric percolator
   3 ☐ Stove top percolator
   4 ☐ Stove top dripolator
   ☐ Other (Specify): _____

2. a. Check all the brands of regular ground coffee that you have **ever used** at home. (CHECK *ALL* THAT APPLY)

    b. Check the **one** brand you **use most often.** (CHECK *ONE* BOX)

    c. Check all the brands you currently **have on hand.** (CHECK *ALL* THAT APPLY)

    d. Check the **one** brand you will probably **buy next.** (CHECK *ONE* BOX)

    e. For each brand please indicate how much you like the brand overall on a scale of 1 to 10 with "1" meaning **dislike it extremely** and "10" meaning **like it extremely.** Rate each brand, whether you have used the brand or not.

	"A" Ever Used	"B" Use Most Often	"C" Have On Hand	"D" Will Buy Next	Brand Rating "1" Dislike It Extremely ◄------------------► "10" Like It Extremely
Folgers	1☐	1☐	1☐	1☐	01☐ 02☐ 03☐ 04☐ 05☐ 06☐ 07☐ 08☐ 09☐ 10☐
Hills Brothers	2☐	2☐	2☐	2☐	01☐ 02☐ 03☐ 04☐ 05☐ 06☐ 07☐ 08☐ 09☐ 10☐
Maxwell House Regular	3☐	3☐	3☐	3☐	01☐ 02☐ 03☐ 04☐ 05☐ 06☐ 07☐ 08☐ 09☐ 10☐
Maxwell House Master Blend	4☐	4☐	4☐	4☐	01☐ 02☐ 03☐ 04☐ 05☐ 06☐ 07☐ 08☐ 09☐ 10☐
Yuban	5☐	5☐	5☐	5☐	01☐ 02☐ 03☐ 04☐ 05☐ 06☐ 07☐ 08☐ 09☐ 10☐
Other (Specify): _____	6☐	6☐	6☐	6☐	01☐ 02☐ 03☐ 04☐ 05☐ 06☐ 07☐ 08☐ 09☐ 10☐

3.   What do you usually add to the coffee you drink? (CHECK *ALL* THAT APPLY)

   1 ☐ Nothing (I drink it black)
   2 ☐ A dairy creamer, like milk, cream, or Half and Half
   3 ☐ A non-dairy creamer, powdered or liquid
   4 ☐ Sugar
   5 ☐ Artificial sweetener
   ☐ Something else (Specify): _____

4.   Are you the principal coffee **purchaser** for your household?

   1 ☐ Yes
   2 ☐ No

relationship between some behavior and a series of demographic characteristics in the United States (for example, How is dishwasher ownership related to income, age, family size, and so on?) might use mail, telephone, or in-home or mall personal interviews to gather the data. The methods would not be equally attractive because of cost and other considerations, but they all could be used. On the other hand, a researcher interested in measuring attitudes could not use all of the methods. The method that would be most appropriate would be largely determined by decisions made earlier about structure and disguise. If researchers decided to use a lengthy attitude scale, for example, they would probably have to rule out telephone interviews. Such data could be gathered best either by mail or in personal interviews. Likewise, an open-ended questionnaire on attitudes might be unsuitable for mail administration. Thus, the researcher must specify precisely what primary data are needed, how these data might be collected, what degree of structure and disguise will be used, and then how the questionnaire will be administered.

Figure 12.2 offers an example of a questionnaire. The primary data at issue are the use of caffeinated ground coffee and attitudes toward various brands. The questions are all very structured and undisguised. The questionnaire is to be administered by mail, using part of the National Family Opinion panel. Note the ease with which the responses could be tabulated.

FIGURE 12.2   *continued*

5. Please indicate how important it is to you that a ground coffee have each of the following characteristics. **(CHECK** *ONE* **BOX FOR** *EACH* **CHARACTERISTIC)**

	Not At All Important									Extremely Important
Rich taste	01☐	02☐	03☐	04☐	05☐	06☐	07☐	08☐	09☐	10☐
Always fresh	01☐	02☐	03☐	04☐	05☐	06☐	07☐	08☐	09☐	10☐
Gets the day off to a good start	01☐	02☐	03☐	04☐	05☐	06☐	07☐	08☐	09☐	10☐
Full–bodied taste	01☐	02☐	03☐	04☐	05☐	06☐	07☐	08☐	09☐	10☐
Rich aroma in the cup	01☐	02☐	03☐	04☐	05☐	06☐	07☐	08☐	09☐	10☐

	Not At All Important									Extremely Important
Good value for the money	01☐	02☐	03☐	04☐	05☐	06☐	07☐	08☐	09☐	10☐
The best coffee to drink in the morning	01☐	02☐	03☐	04☐	05☐	06☐	07☐	08☐	09☐	10☐
Rich aroma in the can/bag	01☐	02☐	03☐	04☐	05☐	06☐	07☐	08☐	09☐	10☐
Smooth taste	01☐	02☐	03☐	04☐	05☐	06☐	07☐	08☐	09☐	10☐
Highest quality coffee	01☐	02☐	03☐	04☐	05☐	06☐	07☐	08☐	09☐	10☐

	Not At All Important									Extremely Important
Premium brand	01☐	02☐	03☐	04☐	05☐	06☐	07☐	08☐	09☐	10☐
Not bitter	01☐	02☐	03☐	04☐	05☐	06☐	07☐	08☐	09☐	10☐
The coffee that brightens my day the most	01☐	02☐	03☐	04☐	05☐	06☐	07☐	08☐	09☐	10☐
Costs more than the other brands	01☐	02☐	03☐	04☐	05☐	06☐	07☐	08☐	09☐	10☐
Strong taste	01☐	02☐	03☐	04☐	05☐	06☐	07☐	08☐	09☐	10☐

	Not At All Important									Extremely Important
Has no aftertaste	01☐	02☐	03☐	04☐	05☐	06☐	07☐	08☐	09☐	10☐
Economy brand	01☐	02☐	03☐	04☐	05☐	06☐	07☐	08☐	09☐	10☐
Rich aroma while brewing	01☐	02☐	03☐	04☐	05☐	06☐	07☐	08☐	09☐	10☐
The best ground coffee available	01☐	02☐	03☐	04☐	05☐	06☐	07☐	08☐	09☐	10☐
Enjoy drinking with a meal	01☐	02☐	03☐	04☐	05☐	06☐	07☐	08☐	09☐	10☐
Costs less than other brands	01☐	02☐	03☐	04☐	05☐	06☐	07☐	08☐	09☐	10☐

Continued

Step 3: Determine Content of Individual Questions

The researcher's previous decisions regarding information needed, the structure and disguise to be imposed on its collection, and the method for administering the questionnaire will largely control the decisions regarding individual question content, which is the third step. But the researcher can and should ask some additional questions.[4]

Is the Question Necessary? Suppose an issue is important. Then the researcher needs to ask whether the point has been adequately covered by other questions. If not, a new question is in order. The question should then be framed to secure an answer with the required detail, but not an answer with more detail than needed. Very often in marketing, for example, we employ the concept of *stage in the life cycle* to explore family consumption behavior. Stage in the life cycle is a variable made up of several elements, including marital status, presence of children, and the ages of children. The presence of children is an important factor, because it most often indicates a dependency relationship. This is especially true if the youngest child is under 6 years old and thus represents one type of responsibility, whereas children over 6 but under 17 represent another type of responsibility

FIGURE 12.2   *continued*

6.   On a scale of **0** to **10** with **"0"** meaning **does not describe at all** and **"10"** meaning **describes completely,** please indicate how well the following statements describe **each** of the coffee brands listed below. Rate each brand, whether you have used the brand or not. Please write in the number which indicates your answer on the lines provided.

	Folgers	Hills Brothers	Maxwell House Regular	Maxwell House Master Blend	Yuban
Rich taste	____	____	____	____	____
Always fresh	____	____	____	____	____
Gets the day off to a good start	____	____	____	____	____
Full–bodied taste	____	____	____	____	____
Rich aroma in the cup	____	____	____	____	____

	Folgers	Hills Brothers	Maxwell House Regular	Maxwell House Master Blend	Yuban
Good value for the money	____	____	____	____	____
The best coffee to drink in the morning	____	____	____	____	____
Rich aroma in the can/bag	____	____	____	____	____
Smooth taste	____	____	____	____	____
Highest quality coffee	____	____	____	____	____

	Folgers	Hills Brothers	Maxwell House Regular	Maxwell House Master Blend	Yuban
Premium brand	____	____	____	____	____
Not bitter	____	____	____	____	____
The coffee that brightens my day the most	____	____	____	____	____
Costs more than the other brands	____	____	____	____	____
Strong taste	____	____	____	____	____

	Folgers	Hills Brothers	Maxwell House Regular	Maxwell House Master Blend	Yuban
Has no aftertaste	____	____	____	____	____
Economy brand	____	____	____	____	____
Rich aroma while brewing	____	____	____	____	____
The best ground coffee available	____	____	____	____	____
Enjoy drinking with a meal	____	____	____	____	____
Costs less than other brands	____	____	____	____	____

7.   Please indicate your **sex** and **age.**

     1 ☐ Male
     2 ☐ Female   Age:_____

Source: Contributed by NFO Research, Inc.

for the parents. In a study using stage in the life cycle as a variable, there is no need to ask the age of each child. Rather, all that is needed is one question aimed at securing the age of the youngest child if there are any children. Once again, the roles of the hypotheses and dummy tables are obvious when designing the questionnaire.

Are Several Questions Needed Instead of One? There will often be situations in which several questions are needed instead of one. Consider the question, "Why do you use Crest?" One respondent may reply, "To reduce cavities," while another may reply, "Because our dentist recommended it." Obviously two different frames of reference are being employed to answer this question. The first respondent is replying in terms of why he is using it now, while the second is replying in terms of how she started using it. It would be better to break this one question down into separate questions that reflect the possible frames of reference that could be used. For example:

How did you first happen to use Crest? ____

What is your primary reason for using it? ____

Do Respondents Have the Necessary Information? The researcher should carefully examine each issue to determine whether the typical respondent can be expected to have the information sought. Respondents will give answers; whether the answers mean anything, though, is another matter. In one public opinion survey, the following question was asked:[5]

Which of the following statements most closely coincides with your opinion of the Metallic Metals Act?

☐ It would be a good move on the part of the United States.

☐ It would be a good thing, but it should be left to the individual states.

☐ It is all right for foreign countries, but it should not be required here.

☐ It is of no value at all.

☐ No opinion.

The proportion of respondents checking each alternative was, respectively, 21.4 percent, 58.6 percent, 15.7 percent, 4.3 percent, and 0.3 percent. The second alternative captures the prevailing sentiment, right? Wrong! There was no Metallic Metals Act, and the point of the example is that *most questions will get answers, but the real concern is whether the answers mean anything.*[6] For the answers to mean anything, the questions need to mean something to the respondent. This means that, first, the respondent needs to be informed with respect to the issue addressed by the question, and, second, the respondent must remember the information.

Consider the question, "How much does your family spend on groceries in a typical week?" Unless the respondent does the grocery shopping or the family operates with a fairly strict budget, he or she is unlikely to know. In a situation like this, it might be helpful to ask "filter questions" before this question to determine if the individual is indeed likely to have this information. A filter question might be, "Who does the grocery shopping in your family?" It is not unusual, for example, to use filter questions of the sort, "Do you have an opinion on . . . ?" before asking about the specific issue in question in opinion surveys. The empirical evidence indicates that providing a filter like this will typically increase the proportion responding "no opinion" by 20 to 25 percentage points.[7]

Not only should the individual have the information sought, but he or she should remember it. Our ability to remember various events is influenced by the event itself and its importance, the length of time since the event, and the presence or absence of stimuli that assist in recalling it. Important events are more easily remembered than are unimportant events. While many older adults might be able to remember who shot President John F. Kennedy or the make of the first car they ever owned, many of them will be unable to recall the particular television shows they watched last Wednesday evening. Returning to our toothpaste example, many people will be unable to recall the first brand they ever used, when they switched to their current brand, or why they switched. While the switching and use information might be very important to a brand manager for toothpastes, it is unimportant to most individuals, a condition we have to keep in mind continually when designing questionnaires. We need to put ourselves in the shoes of the respondent, not those of the product manager, when deciding whether the information is important enough for the individual to remember.

We also need to recognize that an individual's ability to remember an event is influenced by how long ago it happened. While we might recall the television programs we watched last evening, we might have much greater difficulty remembering those we watched last week on the same evening, and might find it all but impossible to recall our viewing pattern of a month ago. The moral of this is that if the event could be considered relatively unimportant to most individuals, we should ask about very recent occurrences of it.[8] For more important events, there are two forces, operating in opposite directions, that affect a respondent's ability to provide accurate answers to questions referring to some specified time period. **Telescoping error** is one; it is the tendency to remember an event as having occurred more recently than it did. **Recall loss** is the other; it is the tendency to forget the relatively important event entirely. The degree to which the two sources of error affect the accuracy of the reported information depends on the length of the period in question. For long periods, the telescoping effect is smaller, while the recall loss is greater. For short periods, the reverse is true: "Thus, for short reference periods, the telescoping error may outweigh the recall loss, while for long periods the reverse will apply; in between there will be a length of reference periods at which the two effects counterbalance each other."[9] Unfortunately, there is no single reference period that can be used to frame questions for all events, because what is optimal depends on the importance of the event to those involved.

Will Respondents Give the Information? Even though respondents have the information, there is always a question of whether they will share it. Eastern Europeans are wonderful in this regard.

> [U]nlike blasé Western consumers, people in Eastern Europe are more than willing to answer questions. After years of directives from the top, people are flattered to be asked their opinions, even if they're just being asked about the taste of a toothpaste or the feel of a shaving cream. Gallup's Mr. Manchin [a regional vice president] recounts how an old lady in Hungary thanked the interviewer at the end of an hour-long session. "It was such a wonderful experience to have a chance to talk to you for so long," she said. "How much do I pay you?"[10]

Researchers in many other parts of the world are not as fortunate and sometimes encounter situations in which respondents have the necessary information, but they will not give it. Their unwillingness may be a function of the amount of work involved in producing an answer, their ability to articulate an answer, or the sensitivity of the issue.

Although a purchasing agent may be able to determine to the penny how much the company spent on cleaning compound last year, or the relative amount spent on each brand bought, the agent is unlikely to take the time to look up these data to reply to an unsolicited questionnaire. Questionnaire developers need to be constantly mindful of the amount of effort it might take respondents to give the information sought. When the effort is excessive, the respondent may either ignore the question or give only an approximate answer. It may be wiser to omit these types of questions, since they tend to irritate respondents and lessen their cooperation in responding to the rest of the survey.

Otherwise, the researcher needs to use a good deal of creative energy designing a mechanism that allows respondents to articulate their views. Although respondents might not be able to express their preferences in furniture styles, for example, they should be able to indicate the style they like best when shown pictures, prototypes, hardware samples, and fabric swatches. La-Z-Boy used this approach when it invited a panel of consumers to evaluate a line of new products, including fabrics and styles. The consumers liked all the fabrics except for two plaid designs, which they rated as not soft enough. La-Z-Boy dropped one of the patterns and asked the manufacturer to modify the other one to make it softer.[11]

When an issue is embarrassing or otherwise threatening to respondents, they are also apt to refuse to cooperate. Such issues should be avoided whenever possible. If that is impossible because the issue is very significant to the study, then the researcher needs to pay close attention to how the issue is addressed, particularly with respect to question location and question phrasing.

Telescoping error
A type of error resulting from the fact that most people remember an event as having occurred more recently than it did.

Recall loss
A type of error caused by a respondent's forgetting that an event happened at all.

La-Z-Boy
Furniture

How To Make The Rooms That Make A Home

Welcome to the La-Z-Boy Gallery Online. Here, you'll find the looks, fabrics and styles that can help you make your home everything you want it to be. We offer literally hundreds of choices -- so many that we can't even show you all of them here. So if you don't see exactly what you want on our web site, don't worry. Your nearest La-Z-Boy dealer can help you find exactly what you're looking for. Choose from any of the following menus to get started. Have fun!

WHAT MAKES A LA-Z-BOY A LA-Z-BOY?

- Why our furniture is better: the inside story
- Our company history

FURNITURE CATEGORY

- Sofas
- Modular Furniture
- Leather Upholstery
- Chairs
- Recliners

Leather Furniture   Recliners   Modular Furniture   Chairs   Sofas and Loveseats

The corporate Web site for La-Z-Boy gives consumers the opportunity to see its line of furniture in different fabrics and styles. In the future, consumers will be able to purchase their products on-line from traditional La-Z-Boy retailers. Not only will the company be able to satisfy customers who want to buy on-line, but it will be able to track customer choices and collect data to fine-tune its product offerings.

Source: La-Z-Boy Incorporated.

In general, it is better to address sensitive issues later, rather than earlier, in the survey. Most surveys will produce some initial mistrust in respondents. One has to overcome this skepticism and establish rapport. This is made easier when respondents have the opportunity to warm to the task by answering nonthreatening questions early in the interview, particularly questions that establish the legitimacy of the project.

When sensitive questions must be asked, it helps to consider ways to make them less threatening. Some helpful techniques in this regard follow:[12]

1. Hide the question in a group of other, more innocuous questions.

2. Before asking the specific question, state that the behavior or attitude is not unusual; for example, "Recent studies show that one of every four households has trouble meeting its monthly financial obligations." This technique, known as the use of counterbiasing statements, makes it easier for the respondent to admit the potentially embarrassing behavior.

3. Phrase the question in terms of others and how they might feel or act; for example, "Do you think most people cheat on their income taxes? Why?" While respondents

might readily reveal their attitudes toward cheating on income tax forms when asked about other people, they might be very reluctant to do so if *they* were asked outright if they ever cheat on their taxes and why.

4. State the response in terms of a number of categories that the respondent may simply check. Instead of asking respondents for their age, for example, one could simply hand them a card with the age categories,

A: 20–29   D: 50–59

B: 30–39   E: 60+

C: 40–49

and ask them to respond with the appropriate letter.

Randomized-response model

An interviewing technique in which potentially embarrassing and relatively innocuous questions are paired, and the question the respondent answers is randomly determined but is unknown to the interviewer.

5. Use the **randomized-response model,** in which the respondent answers one of several paired questions at random.[13] For example, the respondent may draw colored balls from an urn, being instructed to answer Question A if the ball is blue and Question B if the ball is red. The interviewer is unaware of the question being answered by the respondent, because he or she never sees the color of the ball drawn. Under these conditions the respondent is less likely to refuse to answer or to answer untruthfully. A study to investigate the incidence of shoplifting might pair the sensitive question, "Have you ever shoplifted?" with the innocuous question, "Is your birthday in January?" The incidence of shoplifting can still be estimated by using an appropriate statistical model, since the percentage of respondents answering each question is controlled by the proportion of red and blue balls in the urn. Since the researcher cannot determine specifically which respondents have admitted to shoplifting by this technique, though, there is no opportunity to examine such questions as whether shoplifting behavior was associated with any particular demographic characteristics.

Step 4: Determine Form of Response to Each Question

Once the content of the individual questions is determined, researchers must decide whether to use questions that are open-ended or that have multiple choices, two choices, or perhaps represent a scale.

Open-ended question

A question that respondents are free to answer in their own words rather than being limited to choosing from among a set of alternatives.

Open-Ended Questions Respondents are free to reply to **open-ended questions** in their own words rather than being limited to choosing from a set of alternatives. The following are examples:

How old are you? _____

Do you think laws requiring passengers in motor vehicles to wear seat belts are needed? _____

Can you name three sponsors of the Monday-night football games? _____

Do you intend to purchase an automobile this year? _____

Why did you purchase a Magnavox brand color television set? _____

Do you own a VCR? _____

These questions span the gamut of the types of primary data that could be collected—from demographic characteristics, through attitudes and intentions, to behavior. The open-ended question is indeed a versatile device.

Open-ended questions are often used to begin a questionnaire. The general feeling is that it is best to proceed from the general to the specific in constructing questionnaires. So an opening question like, "When you think of television sets, which brands come to mind?" gives some insight into the respondent's frame of reference and could be most helpful in interpreting the individual's replies to later questions. The open-ended question is also often used to probe for additional information. The probes "Why do you feel that way?" and "Please explain" are often used to seek elaboration of a respondent's reply.

In a fixed-alternative format, respondents choose their answer from a predetermined number of responses. Researchers generally use one of three types of fixed-alternative formats.

Multichotomous Questions Despite the daunting name, every college student is probably familiar with the **multichotomous question.** From grade school to graduate school, students answer questions in the same format on multiple-choice exams. In a multichotomous question, respondents are asked to choose the one alternative from several choices that most closely reflects their position on the subject. Exhibit 12.1, for example, presents some of the open-ended questions from the preceding list as multichotomous questions. Respondents would be instructed to check the box or boxes that apply.

The examples in Exhibit 12.1 illustrate some of the difficulties encountered in using multiple-choice questions. None of the alternatives in the seat belt question, for example, may correctly capture the respondent's true feeling on the issue. The individual's opinion may be more complex. He may feel that seat belts should be required on school buses but not in private vehicles. Or she may think that seat belts should be required but that tickets for noncompliance should be issued only in conjunction with another traffic violation. The multiple-choice question does not permit individuals to elaborate on their true position but requires them to condense their complex attitude into a single statement. Of course, a well-designed series of multiple-choice questions could allow for such elaborations. Researchers must be careful, however, not to allow so many possible choices that the questionnaire becomes too long to be used effectively.

The seat belt question also illustrates a general problem in question design: Should respondents be provided with a "don't know" or "no opinion" option? If a respondent truly does not know an answer, or has no opinion on an issue, he or she should obviously be allowed to state so. But should the option be explicitly provided to the respondent in the form of a "don't know" or "no opinion" category or by asking a filter question like, "Do you have an opinion . . . "? The arguments about the desirability of a neutral point or "no

Multichotomous question

A fixed-alternative question in which respondents are asked to choose the alternative that most closely corresponds to their position on the subject.

EXHIBIT 12.1 **Examples of Multichotomous Questions**

Age	**Television Purchase**
How old are you?	**Why did you purchase a Magnavox brand color TV?**
☐ Less than 20	☐ Price was lower than other alternatives
☐ 20–29	☐ Feel it represents the highest quality
☐ 30–39	☐ Availability of local service
☐ 40–49	☐ Availability of a service contract
☐ 50–59	☐ Picture is better
☐ 60 or over	☐ Warranty is better
	☐ Other

Seat Belt Legislation	**Telephone Use**
Do you think laws requiring passengers in motor vehicles to wear seat belts are needed?	**How many long-distance telephone calls do you make in a typical week?**
☐ Definitely needed	☐ Less than 5
☐ Probably needed	☐ 5–10
☐ Probably not needed	☐ More than 10
☐ Definitely not needed	
☐ No opinion	

opinion" category center on the need for data accuracy versus the desire to have as many respondents as possible answer the question at issue.

Those against including a "no opinion" answer argue that most respondents are unlikely to be truly neutral on an issue. Instead of providing them an easy way out, critics say, it is much better to have them think about the issues so that they can frame their preference, however slight it may be. That is much better than allowing the researcher to infer the majority opinion from the responses of those taking a stand on the issue. The argument for including a neutral or "no opinion" category among the responses claims that forcing a respondent to make a choice when his or her preference is fuzzy or nonexistent simply introduces response error into the results. Further, it makes it harder for respondents to answer, and it may turn them off to the whole survey. The jury is still out with respect to which form better captures respondents' true position on an issue.

There is no question, however, that the two alternatives can produce widely differing proportions regarding the number holding a neutral view, potentially in the range of 10 to 50 percent.[14] For example, in a national telephone survey of 1,422 adults, results differed according to whether respondents were given a "don't know" option. The poll, jointly sponsored by the Kaiser Family Foundation, National Public Radio, and Harvard's Kennedy School of Government, asked a variety of questions to guage public opinion about education issues.[15] Two questions asked about attitudes toward issues that have lately received media attention: school vouchers and charter schools. Half of the respondents were given two choices: whether they favor or oppose these programs. The other half of the respondents were given three choices: whether they favor or oppose the programs or haven't heard enough about the issue to have an opinion. As Figure 12.3 shows, people who heard this third choice were much more likely to say they didn't know enough to have an opinion.

The television set purchase question in Exhibit 12.1 illustrates a number of problems associated with multiple-choice questions. First, the list of reasons cited for purchasing a Magnavox color television may not exhaust the reasons that could have been used by the respondent. The person may have purchased a Magnavox out of loyalty to a friend who owns the local Magnavox distributorship or because she really supports the "buy locally" plea advanced by many small-town chambers of commerce. The "other" response category attempts to solve this problem. If a great many respondents check the "other" category, however, they could render the study useless. Thus, the burden is on the researcher to make the list of alternatives in a multiple-choice question exhaustive. This may entail a good deal of prior research into the phenomenon that is to serve as the subject of a multiple-choice question.

Unless the respondent is instructed to check all alternatives that apply, or is to rank the alternatives in order of importance, the multiple-choice question also demands that the alternatives be mutually exclusive. The income categories of $10,000–$20,000 and $20,000–$30,000 violate this principle. A respondent with an income of $20,000 would not know which alternative to check. A legitimate response with respect to the color television purchase question might include several of the alternatives listed. The respondent thought the picture, warranty, and price were all more attractive on the Magnavox than they were on other makes. Thus, the instructions would necessarily have to be "Check the most important reason," "Check all those reasons that apply," or "Rank all the reasons that apply from most important to least important."

A third difficulty with the television purchase question is its great number of alternative responses. The list should be exhaustive. Yet the number of alternative statements an individual can process simultaneously appears to be limited. In one early study, the researchers presented each respondent with a card with six alternative statements. After each respondent had made his or her choice, the card was immediately replaced with another. On the second card, two of the six statements had been changed, and one statement from the original list was omitted. Yet only one-half of the respondents "could identify the changes, and a mere handful located the omission."[16] The meaning of all this is that in designing multiple-choice questions, the researcher should remain aware of

FIGURE 12.3 **Differences in Response with Use of a "Don't Know" Option**

Questions about Vouchers

"Do you favor or oppose . . . 'vouchers' . . . ?"

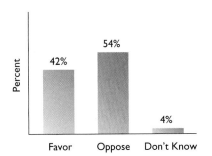

"Do you favor or oppose 'vouchers' . . . , or haven't you heard enough about that to have an opinion?"

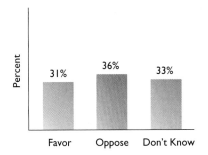

Questions about Charter Schools

After defining "charter schools": "Do you favor or oppose such a program?"

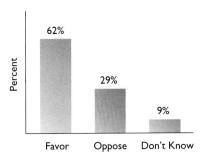

After defining "charter schools": "Do you favor or oppose such a program, or haven't you heard enough about that to have an opinion?"

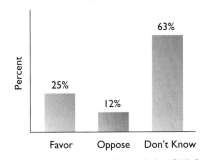

Note: The results are from a random telephone survey of 1,422 adults (18 and over) nationwide, developed jointly by National Public Radio, the Henry J. Kaiser Family Foundation, and Harvard University's Kennedy School of Government and administered by ICR/International Communications Research in June and July 1999.
Source: "NPR/Kaiser/Kennedy School Education Survey," National Public Radio Web site (www.npr.org, downloaded September 9, 1999).

human beings' limited data-processing capabilities. Perhaps a series of questions is more appropriate than one question. If there are a great many alternatives to a single question, then they should be shown to respondents using cards, and not simply read to them.

The fourth weakness of the television purchase question in Exhibit 12.1 is that it is susceptible to order bias. That is, the responses are likely to be affected by the order in which the alternatives are presented. Research Window 12.2, for example, shows how the distribution of responses to the same questions was affected by the order in which the alternatives were listed on two versions of a mail questionnaire. That the three questions produced statistically significant different distributions of replies is especially noteworthy because order bias is least likely to occur in mail questionnaires, because respondents can see all the response categories. In point of fact, response order bias is typically much greater in telephone surveys or interviews in which the structured responses are read to the respondents. The recommended procedure for combating this order, or position, bias is to prepare several forms of the questionnaire, or several cards, if cards are used to list the alternatives. The order in which the alternatives are listed is then altered from form to

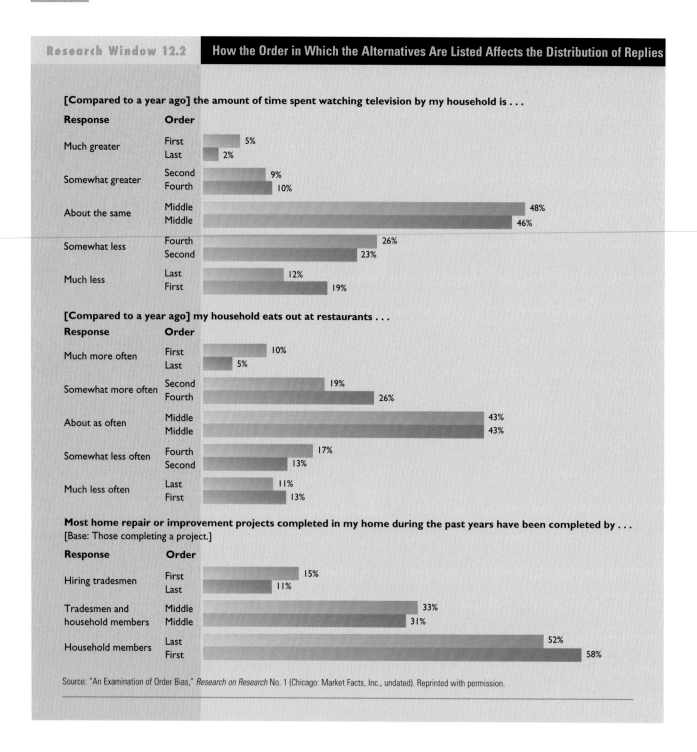

form. If each alternative appears once at the extremes of the list, once in the middle, and once somewhere in between, the researcher can feel reasonably comfortable that the possible effects of position bias have been neutralized.

The long-distance telephone call example in Exhibit 12.1 illustrates another problem with multiple-choice questions when they are used to get at the frequency of various behaviors. The range of the categories used in the question seems to cue respondents about how they should reply. That is, the response scale categories themselves affect subjects' reports of the frequency with which they engage in the behavior. A scale with the three categories

☐ Less than 10

☐ 10–20

☐ More than 20

would likely produce a different picture of the frequency with which these same respondents make long-distance telephone calls. It seems that respondents make judgments about the researcher's knowledge or expectations from the categories and then respond accordingly. Specifically, they seem reluctant to report behaviors that are unusual in the context of the response scale—namely, those that constitute the extreme categories.[17] A general strategy for combating this tendency is to use open-ended answer formats when obtaining data on behavioral frequencies.

Dichotomous question

A fixed-alternative question in which respondents are asked to indicate which of two alternative responses most closely corresponds to their position on a subject.

Dichotomous Questions Also a fixed-alternative question, the **dichotomous question** is one in which there are only two alternatives listed, as in the following examples:

Do you think laws requiring passengers in motor vehicles to wear seat belts are needed?

☐ Yes

☐ No

Do you intend to purchase an automobile this year?

☐ Yes

☐ No

We have already seen how the first of these questions could also be handled as a multiple-choice question. The second could also be given a multichotomous structure. Instead of simply presenting the yes-no alternatives, the list could be framed as "Definitely intend to buy," "Probably will buy," "Probably will not buy," "Definitely intend not to buy," and "Undecided." Dichotomous questions can often be framed as multichotomous questions, and vice versa. (The two possess similar advantages and disadvantages, which were reviewed earlier when discussing structured questions. The advantages and disadvantages will not be repeated here.) The dichotomous question offers the ultimate in ease of coding and tabulation, and this probably accounts for its being the most commonly used type of question in communication studies.

One special problem with the dichotomous question is that the response can well depend on how the question is framed. This is true, of course, of all questions, but with the dichotomous question it represents a special problem. Consider two alternative questions:

Do you think that gasoline will be more expensive or less expensive next year than it is now?

☐ More expensive

☐ Less expensive

Do you think that gasoline will be less expensive or more expensive next year than it is now?

☐ Less expensive

☐ More expensive

Now the questions appear identical, and certainly we might want to expand each to include categories for "no opinion" and "about the same." The fact remains, though, that the two questions will elicit different responses.[18] The simple switching of the positions of

"More expensive" and "Less expensive" can affect the response an individual gives. Which, then, is the correct wording?

As mentioned earlier, one generally accepted procedure for combating this order bias is to employ a split ballot. One phrasing is used on one-half of the questionnaires, and the alternative phrasing is employed on the other one-half of the questionnaires. The averaged percentages from the two forms should then cancel out any biases.

Scales Another type of fixed-alternative question is the question that employs a scale to capture the response. For instance, when inquiring about VCR use, the following question might be asked:

How often do you tape programs for later viewing with your VCR?

◻ Never

◻ Occasionally

◻ Sometimes

◻ Often

In this form, the question is a multichotomous question. However, the responses also represent a scale of use. The scale nature of the question would be more obvious, perhaps, if the following form were used to secure the replies:

Never	Occasionally	Sometimes	Often

The advantage of this scheme is that the descriptors or categories could be presented at the top of the page, and types of programs could be listed along the left margin—for example, films, sporting events, and network specials. The respondent would then be instructed to designate the frequency with which the VCR is used to record each type. The instruction would need to be given only once, at the beginning, and thus a great deal of information could be secured from the respondent in a short time.

Step 5: Determine Wording of Each Question

Step 5 in the questionnaire development process involves the phrasing of each question. This is a critical task, in that poor phrasing of a question can cause respondents to refuse to answer it even though they agreed to cooperate in the study. Poor phrasing may also cause respondents to answer a question incorrectly, either on purpose or because of misunderstanding. The first condition, known as **item nonresponse,** can create a great many problems in analyzing the data. The second condition produces measurement error in that the recorded or obtained score does not equal the respondent's true score on the issue.[19]

Experienced researchers know that the phrasing of a question can directly affect the responses to it. One humorous anecdote in this regard involves two priests, a Dominican and a Jesuit, who are discussing whether it is a sin to smoke and pray at the same time. "After failing to reach a conclusion, each goes off to consult his respective superior. The next week they meet again. The Dominican says, 'Well, what did your superior say?' The Jesuit responds, 'He said it was all right.' 'That's funny,' the Dominican replies, 'my superior said it was a sin.' Jesuit: 'What did you ask him?' Reply: 'I asked him if it was all right to smoke while praying,' 'Oh,' says the Jesuit, 'I asked my superior if it was all right to pray while smoking.'"[20]

Although researchers recognize that question wording can affect the answers obtained, there are, unfortunately, few basic principles researchers can rely upon to develop bias-free ways of framing a question. Instead, the literature is replete with rules of thumb. Although these rules of thumb are often easier to state than to practice, researchers need to be aware of them.

Item nonresponse
A source of nonsampling error that arises when a respondent agrees to an interview but refuses, or is unable, to answer specific questions.

Use Simple Words Because most researchers are more highly educated than the typical questionnaire respondent, they tend to use words with which they themselves are familiar but that are not understood by many respondents. This is a difficult problem because it is not easy to dismiss what one knows and put oneself instead in the respondent's shoes when trying to determine appropriate vocabulary. A significant proportion of the population, for example, does not understand the word *Caucasian*, although most researchers do, and a very serious problem in designing questionnaires to survey Hispanics is in developing an unambiguous ethnic identifier.[21] The researcher needs to be constantly aware that the average person in the United States has a high school, not a college, education and that many people have difficulty in coping with such routine tasks as making change, reading job notices, or completing a driver's license application blank. Even common words can cause difficulty on questionnaires as Research Window 12.3 indicates. The best advice is to keep the words simple.

Research Window 12.3 — **A Rogues' Gallery of Problem Words**

"Use Simple Words!" "Use unambiguous words!" Students of questionnaire design are accustomed to hearing those rules cited loudly and often. But, unfortunately, some of the simplest words may still be ambiguous in meaning. Here's a short list of words that may cause trouble if you're not sensitive to their possibilities for misinterpretation.

You

"You" is extremely popular with question worders, since it is implicated in every question they ask. In most cases "you" gives no trouble, since it is clear that it refers to the second person singular. However, and here is the problem, the word sometimes may have a collective meaning. Consider the question:

How many television sets did you repair last month?

The question seems to be straightforward, until it is asked of a repairman in a large shop, who counters with, "Who do you mean, me or the whole shop?"

Sometimes "you" needs the emphasis of "you yourself," and sometimes it just isn't the word to use, as in the above situation, where the entire shop is meant.

All

"All" is one of those dead-giveaway words. From your own experience with true-false exams, you probably know that it is safe to count almost every all-inclusive statement as false. That is, you have learned that in such tests it is safe to follow the idea that all statements containing "all" are false, including this one. Some people have the same negative reaction to opinion questions that hinge upon all-inclusive or all-exclusive words. They may be generally in agreement with a proposition, but nevertheless hesitate to accept the extreme idea of *all, always, each, every, never, nobody, only, none,* or *sure.*

Bad

In itself the word "bad" is not at all bad for question wording. It conveys the meaning desired and is

Grant Wood, *Dinner for Threshers*, 1934. The Fine Arts Museum of San Francisco. Gift of Mr. and Mrs. John D. Rockefeller 3rd, 1979.7.105.

satisfactory as an alternative in a "good or bad" two-way question. Experience seems to indicate, however, that people are generally less willing to criticize than they are to praise. Since it is difficult to get them to state their negative views, sometimes the critical side needs to be softened. For example, after asking, "What things are good about your job?" it might seem perfectly natural to ask, "What things are bad about it?" But if we want to lean over backwards to get as many criticisms as we can, we may be wise not to apply the "bad" stigma, but to ask, "What things are not so good about it?"

Dinner

"Dinner," the main meal of the day, comes at noon with some families and in some areas. Elsewhere it is the evening meal. The question should not assume that it is either the one or the other.

Government

"Government" is one of those words heavily loaded with emotional concepts. It is sometimes used as a definite word meaning the federal government, sometimes as an inclusive term for federal, state, and local government, sometimes as an abstract idea, and sometimes as the party in power as distinct from the opposition party. The trouble is that the respondent does not always know which "government" is meant. One person may have a different idea from another. It is best to specify if we want all respondents to answer with the same government in mind.

Like

"Like" is on the problem list only because it is sometimes used to introduce an example. The problem with bringing an example into a question is that the respondent's attention may be directed toward the particular example and away from the general issue which it is meant only to illustrate. The use of examples may sometimes be necessary, but the possible hazard should always be kept in mind. The choice of an example can affect the answers to the question—in fact, it may materially change the question, as in these two examples:

Do you think that leafy vegetables like spinach should be in the daily diet?
Do you think that leafy vegetables like lettuce should be in the daily diet?

Where

The frames of reference in answers to a "where" question may vary greatly. Consider the possible answers from this simple question:

Where did you read that?

Three of the many possible answers are,

In the New York Times.
At home in front of the fire.
In an advertisement.

Despite the seemingly wide variety of these three answers, some respondents could probably have stated them all: "In an ad in the *New York Times* while I was at home sitting in front of the fire."

Source: Stanley L. Payne, *The Art of Asking Questions* (Princeton: Princeton University Press, 1979), pp. 158–176.

Avoid Ambiguous Words and Questions Not only should the words and questions be simple, they should also be unambiguous. Consider again the multichotomous question:

How often do you tape programs for later viewing with your VCR?

☐ Never

☐ Occasionally

☐ Sometimes

☐ Often

For all practical purposes, the replies to this question would be worthless. The words *occasionally, sometimes,* and *often* are ambiguous. For example, to one respondent, the word often might mean "almost everyday." To another it might mean, "Yes, I use it when I have the specific need. This happens about once a week." The words *occasionally* and *sometimes* could also be interpreted differently by different respondents. Thus, although the question would get answers, it would generate little real understanding of the frequency of use of the VCR to tape programs. A much better strategy would be to provide concrete alternatives for the respondent, such as the following:

☐ Never use

☐ Use approximately once a month

☐ Use approximately once a week

☐ Use almost every day

Another way to avoid ambiguity in asking about the frequency of behavior is to ask when the behavior last occurred. Our earlier question might be framed in the following way:

Did you tape any programs with your VCR in the last two days?

☐ Yes

☐ No

☐ Can't recall

The proportion responding yes would then be used to infer the frequency with which the VCR was used, while the follow-up question among all those responding yes—"For what purpose?"—would give insight as to how respondents are using it. Among the people responding, there will be some who normally use their VCR but did not use it in the last two days. There will be others who do not normally use it but did use it within the last two days. These variations should cancel each other out if a large enough sample of respondents is used.

The total sample should provide a good indication of the proportion of times the VCR is used, and the proportion of times it is used to tape various types of programs. The researcher, in effect, relies on the sample to provide insight into how frequently the phenomenon occurs, rather than relying on a specific question that may contain ambiguous alternatives. In such cases it is important that the sample be large enough so that the proportions can be estimated with the appropriate degree of confidence.

Leading question
A question framed so as to give the respondent a clue as to how he or she should answer.

Avoid Leading Questions A question framed so as to give the respondent a clue as to how he or she should answer is a **leading question.** Consider this question:

Do you feel that limiting taxes by law is an effective way to stop the government from picking your pocket every payday?

☐ Yes

☐ No

☐ Undecided

This was one of three questions in an unsolicited questionnaire that the author received as part of a study sponsored by the National Tax Limitation Committee. The committee intended to make the results of the poll available to Congress and to state legislators. Given the implied purpose, it is probably not surprising to see the leading words "picking your pocket" being used in this question, or the leading word "gouge" being used in another question. What is especially unfortunate is that it is unlikely that the questions themselves accompanied the report to Congress. Rather, it is more likely that the report suggested that some high percentage (e.g., 90 percent of those surveyed) favored laws limiting taxes. Conclusion: Congress should pay attention to the wishes of the people and pass such laws.

One sees instances of this phenomenon every day in the newspaper. The public is treated to a discussion of the results of this or that study with respect to how the American people feel on issues but is not shown the questionnaire. Yet question wording makes a difference and it is important for researchers to realize that if one truly wants an accurate picture of the situation, one needs to avoid leading the respondent as to how he or she should answer

Implicit alternative

An alternative answer that is not expressed in a question's options.

Avoid Implicit Alternatives An alternative that is not expressed in the options is an **implicit alternative.** In one study, researchers wanted to know the attitudes of full-time homemakers toward the idea of having a job outside the home. They asked two random samples of homemakers the following two questions:[22]

Would you like to have a job, if this were possible? _____

Would you prefer to have a job, or do you prefer to do just your housework? _____

While the two questions appear very similar, they produced dramatically different responses. In the first version, 19 percent of the homemakers said they would not like to have a job. In the second version, 68 percent said they would prefer not to have one—over three and one-half times as many as in the first version. The difference in the two questions is that the second version makes explicit the alternative only implied in the first version. As a general rule, one should avoid implicit alternatives unless there is a special reason for including them. Thus, the second version is better than the first. Further, because the order in which the alternatives appear can affect the responses, one should rotate the order of the options in samples of questionnaires.

Implicit assumption

A problem that occurs when a question is not framed so as to explicitly state the consequences, and thus it elicits different responses from individuals who assume different consequences.

Avoid Implicit Assumptions Questions are frequently framed so that there is an **implicit assumption** as to what will happen as a consequence. The question "Are you in favor of placing price controls on crude oil?" will elicit different responses from individuals, depending on whether they think price controls will result in rationing, long lines at the pump, or lower prices. A better way of stating this question is to make explicit the possible consequence(s). For example, the question could be altered to ask, "Are you in favor of placing price controls on crude oil if it would produce gas rationing?"

Figure 12.4 shows what can happen when the consequences are explicitly stated in a question. Version B makes the implied consequence in Version A explicit; the only way the seat belt law could be effective would be if there were some penalty for not complying with it. Yet, when there was no explicit statement about what would happen if a person did not comply with the proposed law, 73 percent were in favor of it. When people faced the prospect of a fine for noncompliance, only 50 percent favored a mandatory seat belt law.

Avoid Generalizations and Estimates Questions should always be asked in specific, rather than general, terms. Consider the question "How many salespeople did you see last year?" which might be asked of a purchasing agent. To answer the question, the agent would probably estimate how many salespeople call in a typical week and would multiply this estimate by 52. This burden should not be placed on the agent. Rather, a more accurate estimate would be obtained if the purchasing agent were asked "How many representatives called last week?" and the researcher multiplied the answer provided by 52.

Double-barreled question

A question that calls for two responses and thereby creates confusion for the respondent.

Avoid Double-Barreled Questions A question that calls for two responses and thereby creates confusion for the respondent is a **double-barreled question.** The question "What is your evaluation of the price and convenience offered by XYZ's catalog showroom?" is asking respondents to react to two separate attributes by which the showroom could be described. The respondent might feel the prices are attractive but the location is not, for example, and thereby is placed in a dilemma as to how to respond. The problem is particularly acute if the individual must choose an answer from a fixed set of alternatives. One

FIGURE 12.4   **Illustration of What Can Happen When an Implied Assumption Is Made Explicit**

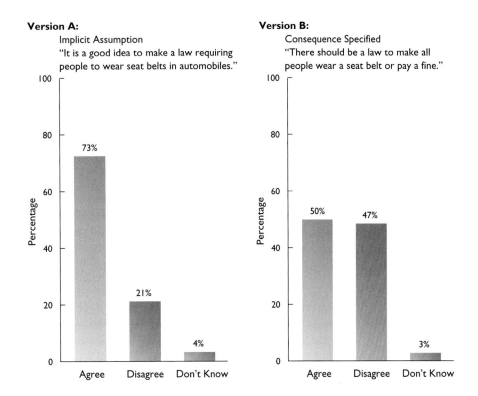

Version A:
Implicit Assumption
"It is a good idea to make a law requiring people to wear seat belts in automobiles."

Version B:
Consequence Specified
"There should be a law to make all people wear a seat belt or pay a fine."

Source: Albert J. Ungar, "Projectable Surveys: Separating Useful Data from Illusions," *Business Marketing* 71 (December 1986), p. 90. Reprinted with permission from the December 1986 issue of *Business Marketing.* Copyright, Crain Communications, Inc.

can and should avoid double-barreled questions by splitting the initial question into two separate questions. A useful indicator that two questions might be needed is the use of the word *and* in the initial wording of the question.

Step 6: Determine Question Sequence

Once the form of response and specific wording for each question have been decided, the researcher is ready to begin putting them together into a questionnaire. The researcher needs to recognize immediately that the order in which the questions are presented can be crucial to the success of the research effort. Again, there are no hard-and-fast principles but only rules of thumb to guide the researcher in this activity.

Use Simple and Interesting Opening Questions The first questions asked the respondent are crucial. If respondents cannot answer them easily or if they find them uninteresting or threatening in any way, they may refuse to complete the remainder of the questionnaire. Thus, it is essential that the first few questions be simple, interesting, and in no way threatening to respondents. Questions that ask respondents for their opinion on some issue are often good openers, as most people like to feel their opinion is important. Sometimes it is helpful to use such an opener even when responses to it will not be analyzed, since opinion questions are often effective in relaxing respondents and securing their cooperation.

Funnel approach
An approach to question sequencing that gets its name from its shape, starting with broad questions and progressively narrowing down the scope.

Use Funnel Approach One approach to question sequencing is the **funnel approach,** which gets its name from its shape, starting with broad questions and progressively narrowing down the scope. If respondents are to be asked, "What improvements are needed in the company's service policy?" and also, "How do you like the quality of service?" the first question needs to be asked before the second. Otherwise, quality of service will be emphasized disproportionately in the responses simply because it is fresh in the respondents' minds.

There should also be some logical order to the questions. This means that sudden changes in topics and jumping around from topic to topic should be avoided. Transitional devices are sometimes necessary to smooth the flow when a change in subject matter occurs. Sometimes researchers will insert filter questions as a way to change the direction of the questioning. Most often, however, researchers will insert a brief explanation as a way of bridging a change in subject matter.

Branching question
A technique used to direct respondents to different places in a questionnaire, based on their response to the question at hand.

Design Branching Questions with Care A direction as to where to go next in the questionnaire based on the answer to a preceding question is called a **branching question.** For example, the initial question might be, "Have you bought a car within the last six months?" If the respondent answers yes, he or she is then instructed to go to another place in the questionnaire, where questions are asked about specific details of the purchase. Someone replying no to the same question would be directed to skip the questions relating to the details of the purchase. The advantage to branching questions is that they reduce the number of alternatives that are needed in individual questions, while ensuring that those respondents capable of supplying the needed information still have an opportunity to do so. Those for whom a question is irrelevant are simply directed around it.

Branching questions and directions are much easier to develop for telephone or personal interviews, especially for those administered through computer-assisted interviewing, than for mail surveys. With mail questionnaires the number of branching questions needs to be kept to an absolute minimum so that respondents do not become confused when responding, or refuse to cooperate because the task becomes too difficult. While they can be used more liberally with telephone and personal interview surveys, branching questions still need to be designed with care, since the evidence indicates that branching instructions increase the rate of item nonresponse for items immediately following the branch.[23] When using branching questions, it is generally good practice to (1) develop a flow chart of the logical possibilities and then prepare the branching questions and instructions to follow the flow chart, (2) place the question that follows the branch as close as possible to the original question, so as to minimize the amount of page-flipping that is necessary, and (3) order the branching questions so that respondents cannot anticipate what additional information is required.[24]

The last point can be illustrated by a questionnaire seeking information about small appliance ownership. A skillfully designed questionnaire might begin by asking if a respondent owns any of a certain list of small appliances. If she answers yes to any, the researcher may then go on to ask the brand name, the store where purchased, and so on, for each. If instead the researcher had begun by asking, "Do you own a food processor?" and followed up with questions about brand, price, and so on, the respondent would soon recognize that "yes" answers to subsequent questions about the ownership of other appliances would inevitably lead to many other questions, and she may decide it is less taxing to say no in the first place.

Ask for Classification Information Last The typical questionnaire contains two types of information: basic information and classification information. *Basic information* refers to the subject of the study, for example, intentions or attitudes of respondents. *Classification information* refers to the other data we collect to classify respondents so as to extract more information about the phenomenon of interest. For instance, we might be interested in determining if a respondent's attitudes toward the need for seat belt legislation are in any way affected by the person's income. Income here would be a classification variable. Demographic/socioeconomic characteristics of respondents are often used as classification variables for understanding the results.

The proper questionnaire sequence is to present questions securing basic information first and those seeking classification information last. There is a logical reason for this. The basic information is most critical. Without it, there is no study. Thus, the researcher should not risk alienating the respondent by asking a number of personal questions before getting to the heart of the study, since it is not unusual for personal questions to alienate respondents most. Respondents who readily offer their opinions about television programming may balk when asked about their income. An early question aimed at determining their income may affect the whole tone of the interview or other communication. It is best to avoid this possibility by placing the classification information at the end.

Place Difficult or Sensitive Questions Late in the Questionnaire The basic information itself can also present some sequence problems. Some of the questions may be sensitive. Early questions should not be, for the reasons we mentioned earlier. If respondents feel threatened, they may refuse to participate in the study. Thus, sensitive questions should be placed in the body of the questionnaire and intertwined and hidden among some not-so-sensitive ones. Once respondents have become involved in the study, they are less likely to react negatively or refuse to answer when delicate questions are posed.

Step 7: Determine Physical Characteristics of Questionnaire

The physical characteristics of the questionnaire can affect the accuracy of the replies that are obtained.[25] The physical characteristics of a questionnaire can also affect how respondents react to it and the ease with which the replies can be processed. In determining the physical format of the questionnaire, a researcher wants to do those things that help get the respondent to accept the questionnaire, and facilitate handling and control by the researcher.

Securing Acceptance of the Questionnaire The physical appearance of the questionnaire can influence respondents' cooperation. This is particularly true with mail questionnaires, but it applies as well to questionnaires used in personal interviews. If the questionnaire looks sloppy, respondents are likely to feel the study is unimportant and hence refuse to cooperate despite researchers' assurance that it is important. If the study is important, and there is no reason to conduct it if it is not, make the questionnaire reflect that importance. This means that good-quality paper should be used for the questionnaires. It also means that the questionnaires should be printed, not mimeographed or otherwise photocopied.

The introduction to the research can also affect acceptance of the questionnaire. With mail questionnaires, the cover letter serves to introduce the study. It is very important the cover letter convince the designated respondent to cooperate. Good cover letters are rarely written in a hurry; rather, they usually require a series of painstaking rewrites to get the wording just so. Research Window 12.4 lists important content considerations in the construction of cover letters.[26] With personal and telephone interviews, the introduction to the research is necessarily shorter. Nonetheless, the introduction needs to convince respondents about the importance of the research and the importance of their participation. Typically, this means describing how they can benefit from it, the fact that their replies will be confidential, and the incentive, if any, that they will receive for participating.

It is also a good idea to include the name of the sponsoring organization and the name of the project on the first page or on the cover if the questionnaire is in book form. Both of these lend credibility to the study. However, since awareness of the sponsoring firm may bias respondents' answers, many firms use fictitious names for the sponsoring organization. This practice also helps eliminate phone calls or other inquiries from respondents asking for the results of the study.

Facilitate Handling and Control Several steps that facilitate handling and control by the researcher also contribute to acceptance of the questionnaire by respondents. These include questionnaire size and layout and question sequencing.

Research Window 12.4   Contents of and Sample Cover Letter for a Mail Questionnaire

Panel A: Contents

1. Personal communication

2. Asking a favor

3. Importance of the research project and its purpose.

4. Importance of the recipient.

5. Importance of the replies in general.

6. Importance of the replies when the reader is not qualified to answer most questions.

7. How the recipient may benefit from this research.

8. Completing the questionnaire will take only a short time.

9. The questionnaire can be answered easily.

10. A stamped reply envelope is enclosed.

11. How recipient was selected.

12. Answers are anonymous or confidential.

13. Offer to send report on results of survey.

14. Note of urgency.

15. Appreciation of sender.

16. Importance of sender.

17. Importance of the sender's organization.

18. Description and purpose of incentive.

19. Avoiding bias.

20. Style

21. Format and appearance.

22. Brevity.

Source: Paul L. Erdos, *Professional Mail Surveys* (Melbourne, Fla.: Robert E. Krieger Publishing Co., Inc., 1983), pp. 102–103. Reprinted with permission.

Questionnaire size is important.[27] Smaller questionnaires are better than larger ones if—and this is a big if—they do not appear crowded. Smaller questionnaires seem easier to complete; they appear to take less time and are less likely to cause respondents to refuse to participate. They are easier to carry in the field and are easier to sort, count, and file in the office than are larger questionnaires.

If, on the other hand, smaller size is gained at the expense of an uncluttered appearance, these advantages are lost. A crowded questionnaire has a bad appearance, leads to errors in data collection, and results in shorter and less informative replies for both self-administered and interviewer-administered questionnaires. Researchers have found, for example, that the more lines or space left for recording the response to open-ended questions, the more extensive the reply will be. Similarly, the more information a respondent is given about the kind of information being sought, the better the reply is apt to be. Both of these techniques, however, increase the physical size of the questionnaire needed for the study.

While post-card size probably represents the lower limit, letter size probably represents the upper limit to the size of an individual page in a questionnaire. When the questions will not all fit on the front and back of one sheet, multiple sheets need to be used. When this happens, one should make the questionnaire into a booklet rather than staple or paper-clip the pages together. The method of binding not only facilitates handling but also reinforces an image of quality. So does numbering the questions, which also promotes respondent cooperation, particularly when branching questions are employed. Without numbered questions, instructions as to how to proceed (e.g., "If the answer to Question 2 is yes, please go to Question 5") cannot be used. Even with numbered questions, though, it is helpful if the respondent can be directed by arrows to the appropriate next question after a branching question. Another technique researchers have found useful with branch-type questions is the use of color coding on the questionnaire, where the next question to which the respondent is directed matches the color of the space in which the answer to the branching or filter question was recorded.

The numbers refer to the corresponding items in Panel A.

Panel B: Sample

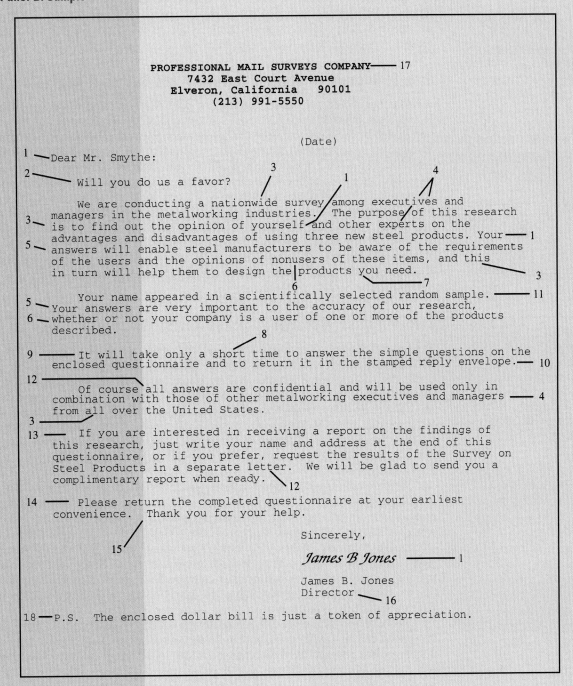

PROFESSIONAL MAIL SURVEYS COMPANY——— 17
7432 East Court Avenue
Elveron, California   90101
(213) 991-5550

(Date)

1 ——Dear Mr. Smythe:

2 ———— Will you do us a favor?

We are conducting a nationwide survey among executives and
managers in the metalworking industries. The purpose of this research
3 ——is to find out the opinion of yourself and other experts on the
advantages and disadvantages of using three new steel products. Your ——— 1
5 ——answers will enable steel manufacturers to be aware of the requirements
of the users and the opinions of nonusers of these items, and this
in turn will help them to design the products you need.
6   7   3

Your name appeared in a scientifically selected random sample. ——— 11
5 ——Your answers are very important to the accuracy of our research,
6 ——whether or not your company is a user of one or more of the products
described.

8
9 ————It will take only a short time to answer the simple questions on the
enclosed questionnaire and to return it in the stamped reply envelope.——— 10
12 ————
Of course all answers are confidential and will be used only in
combination with those of other metalworking executives and managers ——— 4
from all over the United States.
3 ————
13 —— If you are interested in receiving a report on the findings of
this research, just write your name and address at the end of this
questionnaire, or if you prefer, request the results of the Survey on
Steel Products in a separate letter. We will be glad to send you a
complimentary report when ready.
12

14 —— Please return the completed questionnaire at your earliest
convenience. Thank you for your help.

Sincerely,

15

James B Jones ——— 1

James B. Jones
Director —— 16

18 ——P.S. The enclosed dollar bill is just a token of appreciation.

Numbering the questions also makes it easier to edit, code, and tabulate the responses.[28] It also helps if the questionnaires themselves are numbered. This makes it easier to keep track of the questionnaires and to determine which ones, if any, are lost. It also makes it easier to monitor interviewer performance and to detect interviewer biases, if any. The research director will be able to develop a log listing which questionnaires were assigned to which interviewers. Mail questionnaires are an exception to the principle that the questionnaires themselves be numbered. Respondents often interpret an assigned number on a mail questionnaire as a mechanism by which their responses can be identified as theirs. The possible loss in anonymity is threatening to many of them, and they may refuse to cooperate or even distort their answers.

Step 8: Reexamine Steps 1 through 7 and Revise If Necessary

A researcher should not expect that the first draft will result in a usable questionnaire. Rather, reexamination and revision are staples in questionnaire construction. Each question should be reviewed to ensure that the question is easy to answer and not confusing, ambiguous, or potentially offensive to the respondent. Neither should any question be leading or bias-inducing. How can one tell? An extremely critical attitude and good common sense should help. The researcher should examine each word in each question. The literature on question phrasing is replete with examples of how some seemingly innocuous questions produced response problems.[29] When a potential problem is discovered, the question should be revised. After examining each question, and each word in each question, for its potential meanings and implications, the researcher might test the questionnaire in some role-playing situations, using others working on the project as subjects. This role playing should reveal some of the most serious shortcomings and should lead to further revision of the questionnaire.

Step 9: Pretest Questionnaire and Revise If Necessary

Pretest

Use of a questionnaire (or observation form) on a trial basis in a small pilot study to determine how well the questionnaire (or observation form) works.

The real test of a questionnaire is how it performs under actual conditions of data collection. For this assessment, the questionnaire **pretest** is vital. The questionnaire pretest serves the same role in questionnaire design that test-marketing serves in new product-development. While the product concept, different advertising appeals, alternative packages, and so on, may all have been tested previously in the product development process, test-marketing is the first place where they all come together. Thus, test-marketing provides the real test of customer reactions to the product and the accompanying marketing program. Similarly, the pretest provides the real test of the questionnaire and the mode of administration.

There are a number of interesting examples in the literature of questions with unintended implications that could have been avoided with an adequate pretest of the questionnaire. In one lifestyle study, for example, the following question was asked: "How would you like to be living two years from now?" While the question was intended to get at hoped-for lifestyles, a large group of the respondents simply replied "yes." In another study, a question about brands of deodorant was used on a self-administered questionnaire. It was only when a number of replies came back with the written response "AirWick" that the researchers realized that putting the word *personal* in front of *deodorant* would have eliminated the confusion caused by the question.[30]

Data collection should never begin without an adequate pretest of the questionnaire. The pretest can be used to assess both individual questions and their sequence.[31] It is best if there are two pretests. The first pretest should be done by personal interview, regardless of the actual mode of administration that will be used. An interviewer can watch to see if people actually remember data requested of them, or if some questions seem confusing or produce resistance or hesitancy among respondents for one reason or another. The pretest interviews should be conducted among respondents similar to those who will be used in the actual study, by the firm's most experienced interviewers.

The personal interview pretest should reveal some questions in which the wording could be improved or the sequence changed. If the changes are major, the revised questionnaire should again be pretested employing personal interviews. If the changes are minor, the questionnaire can be pretested a second time using mail, telephone, or personal interviews, whichever is going to be used for the full-scale study. This time, though, less experienced interviewers should also be used in order to determine if typical interviewers will have any special problems with the questionnaire. The purpose of the second pretest is to uncover problems unique to the mode of administration.

Finally, the responses that result from the pretest should be coded and tabulated. We have previously discussed the need for the preparation of dummy tables prior to the development of the questionnaire. The tabulation of pretest responses can check on our conceptualization of the problem and the data and method of analysis necessary to answer it.

> [T]he tables will confirm the need for various sets of data. If we have no place to put the responses to a question, either the data are superfluous or we omitted some contemplated analysis. If some part of a table remains empty, we may have omitted a necessary question. Trial tabulations show us, as no previous method can, that all data collected will be put to use, and that we will obtain all necessary data.[32]

The researcher who avoids a questionnaire pretest and tabulation of replies is either naive or a fool. The pretest is the most inexpensive insurance the researcher can buy to ensure the success of the questionnaire and the research project. A careful pretest along with proper attention to the dos and don'ts presented in this chapter and summarized in Exhibit 12.2 should make the questionnaire development process successful.

EXHIBIT 12.2   Some Dos and Don'ts When Preparing Questionnaires

Step 1: Specify What Information Will Be Sought

1. Make sure that you have a clear understanding of the issue and what it is that you want to know (expect to learn). Frame your research questions, but refrain from writing questions for the questionnaire at this time.
2. Make a list of your research questions. Review them periodically as you are working on the questionnaire.
3. Use the dummy tables that were set up to guide the data analysis to suggest questions for the questionnaire.
4. Conduct a search for existing questions on the issue.
5. Revise existing questions on the issue, and prepare new questions that address the issues you plan to research.

Step 2: Determine Type of Questionnaire and Method of Administration

1. Use the type of data to be collected as a basis for deciding on the type of questionnaire.
2. Use the degree of structure and disguise as well as cost factors to determine the method of administration.
3. Compare the special capabilities and limitations of each method of administration and the value of the data collected from each with the needs of the survey.

Step 3: Determine Content of Individual Questions

1. For each research question ask yourself, "Why do I want to know this?" Answer it in terms of how it will help your research. "It would be interesting to know" is not an acceptable answer.
2. Make sure each question is specific and addresses only one important issue.
3. Ask yourself whether the question applies to all respondents; it should, or provision should be made for skipping it.
4. Split questions that can be answered from different frames of reference into multiple questions, one corresponding to each frame of reference.
5. Ask yourself whether respondents will be informed about, and can remember, the issue that the question is dealing with.
6. Make sure the time period of the question is related to the importance of the topic. Consider using aided-recall techniques like diaries or written records.
7. Avoid questions that require excessive effort, that have hard-to-articulate answers, and that deal with embarrassing or threatening issues.
8. If threatening questions are necessary,
   (a) hide the questions among more innocuous ones.
   (b) make use of a counterbiasing statement.
   (c) phrase the question in terms of others and how they might feel or act.
   (d) ask respondents if they have ever engaged in the undesirable activity, and then ask if they are presently engaging in such an activity.

Continued

EXHIBIT 12.2   *continued*

(e) use categories or ranges rather than specific numbers.

(f) use the randomized-response model.

Step 4: Determine Form of Response to Each Question

1. Determine which type of question—open-ended, dichotomous, or multichotomous—provides data that fit the information needs of the project.
2. Use structured questions whenever possible.
3. Use open-ended questions that require short answers to begin a questionnaire.
4. Try to convert open-ended questions to fixed-response questions to reduce respondent work load and coding effort for descriptive and causal studies.
5. If open-ended questions are necessary, make the questions sufficiently directed to give respondents a frame of reference when answering.
6. When using dichotomous questions, state the negative or alternative side in detail.
7. Provide for "don't know," "no opinion," and "both" answers.
8. Be aware that there may be a middle ground.
9. Be sensitive to the mildness or harshness of the alternatives.
10. When using multichotomous questions, be sure the choices are exhaustive and mutually exclusive, and if combinations are possible, include them.
11. Be sure the range of alternatives is clear and that all reasonable alternative answers are included.
12. If the possible responses are very numerous, consider using more than one question to reduce the potential for information overload.
13. When using dichotomous or multichotomous questions, consider the use of a split-ballot procedure to reduce order bias.
14. Clearly indicate if items are to be ranked or if only one item on the list is to be chosen.

Step 5: Determine Wording of Each Question

1. Use simple words.
2. Avoid ambiguous words and questions.
3. Avoid leading questions.
4. Avoid implicit alternatives.
5. Avoid implicit assumptions.
6. Avoid generalizations and estimates.
7. Use simple sentences and avoid compound sentences.
8. Change long, dependent clauses to words or short phrases.
9. Avoid double-barreled questions.
10. Make sure each question is as specific as possible.

Step 6: Determine Question Sequence

1. Use simple, interesting questions for openers.
2. Use the funnel approach, first asking broad questions and then narrowing them down.

3. Ask difficult or sensitive questions late in the questionnaire, when rapport is better.
4. Follow chronological order when collecting historical information.
5. Complete questions about one topic before moving on to the next.
6. Prepare a flow chart whenever branching questions are being considered.
7. Ask filter questions before asking detailed questions.
8. Ask demographic questions last so that if respondent refuses, the other data are still usable.

Step 7: Determine Physical Characteristics of Questionnaire

1. Make sure the questionnaire looks professional and is relatively easy to answer.
2. Use quality paper and print; do not photocopy the questionnaire.
3. Attempt to make the questionnaire as short as possible while avoiding a crowded appearance.
4. Use a booklet format for ease of analysis and to prevent lost pages.
5. List the name of the organization conducting the survey on the first page.
6. Number the questions to ease data processing.
7. If the respondent must skip more than one question, use a "go to."
8. If the respondent must skip an entire section, consider color coding the sections.
9. State how the responses are to be reported, such as a check mark, number, circle, etc.

Step 8: Reexamine Steps 1–7 and Revise If Necessary

1. Examine each word of every question to ensure that the question is not confusing, ambiguous, offensive, or leading.
2. Get peer evaluations of the draft questionnaire.

Step 9: Pretest Questionnaire and Revise If Necessary

1. Pretest the questionnaire first by personal interviews among respondents similar to those to be used in the actual study.
2. Obtain comments from the interviewers and respondents to discover any problems with the questionnaire, and revise it if necessary. When the revisions are substantial, repeat Steps 1 and 2 of Step 9.
3. Pretest the questionnaire by mail or telephone to uncover problems unique to the mode of administration.
4. Code and tabulate the pretest responses in dummy tables to determine if questions are providing adequate information.
5. Eliminate questions that do not provide adequate information, and revise questions that cause problems.

Observation Forms

There are generally fewer problems in constructing observation forms than in constructing questionnaires, because the researcher is no longer concerned with the fact that the question and the way it is asked will affect the response. Through proper training of observers, the researcher can create the necessary expertise so that the data collection instrument is handled consistently. Alternatively, the researcher may simply use a mechanical device to measure the behavior of interest and secure complete consistency in measurement. This is not to imply that observation forms offer no problems of construction. Rather, the researcher needs to make very explicit decisions about what is to be observed and the categories and units that will be used to record this behavior. Figure 12.5, which is the observation form used by a bank to evaluate the service provided by its employees having extensive customer contact, shows how detailed some of these decisions can be. In this case the observers posed as shoppers.

The statement that "one needs to determine what is to be observed before one can make a scientific observation" seems trite. Yet this is exactly the case. Almost any event can be described in a number of ways. When we watch someone making a cigarette purchase, we might report that (1) the person purchased one package of cigarettes; (2) the woman purchased one package of cigarettes; (3) the woman purchased a package of Tareyton cigarettes; (4) the woman purchased a package of Tareyton 100s; (5) the woman, after asking for and finding that the store was out of Virginia Slims, purchased a package of Tareyton 100s; and so on.

A great many additional variations are possible, such as adding the type, name, or location of the store where this behavior occurred. In order for this observation to be productive for scientific inquiry, we must predetermine which aspects of this behavior are relevant. In this particular example, the decision as to what to observe requires that the researcher specify the following:

- Who should be observed? Anyone entering the store? Anyone making a purchase? Anyone making a cigarette purchase?

- What aspects of the purchase should be reported? Which brand they purchased? Which brand they asked for first? Whether the purchase was of king-size or regular cigarettes? What about the purchaser? Is the person's sex to be recorded? Is the individual's age to be estimated? Does it make any difference if the person was alone or in a group?

- When should the observation be made? On what day of the week? At what time of the day? Should day and time be reported? Should the observation be recorded only after a purchase occurs, or should an approach by a customer to a salesclerk also be recorded even if it does not result in a sale?

- Where should the observation be made? In what kind of store? How should the store be selected? How should it be noted on the observation form—by type, by location, by name? Should vending-machine purchases also be noted?

The careful reader will note that these are the same kinds of who, what, when, and where decisions that need to be made in selecting the research design. The why and how are also implicit. The research problem should dictate the why of the observation, while the how involves choosing the observation device or form that will be used. A paper-and-pencil form should be very simple to use. It should parallel the logical sequence of the purchase act (for example, a male approaches the clerk, asks for a package of cigarettes, and so on, if these behaviors are relevant) and should permit the recording of observations by a simple check mark if possible. Again, careful attention to detail, exacting examination of the preliminary form, and an adequate pretest should return handsome dividends with respect to the quality of the observations made.

Bank _____
Date _____ Time _____ Shopper's Name _____
Nature of Transaction: ☐ Personal ☐ Telephone
Details _____
_____
_____
_____

- -

A. FOR PERSONAL TRANSACTIONS

Bank Employee's Name _____

1. How was name obtained?
 ☐ Employee had name tag
 ☐ Nameplate on counter or desk
 ☐ Employee gave name
 ☐ Shopper had to ask for name
 ☐ Name provided by other employee
 ☐ Other _____
 _____

B. FOR TELEPHONE TRANSACTIONS

Bank Employee's Name _____

1. How was name obtained?
 ☐ Employee gave name upon answering the telephone
 ☐ Name provided by other employee
 ☐ Shopper had to ask for name
 ☐ Employee gave name during conversation
 ☐ Other _____
 _____

C. CUSTOMER RELATIONS SKILLS	YES	NO	DOES NOT APPLY
1. Did the employee notice and greet you immediately?	☐	☐	☐
2. Did the employee speak pleasantly and smile.	☐	☐	☐
3. Did the employee answer the telephone promptly?	☐	☐	☐
4. Did the employee find out your name?	☐	☐	☐
5. Did the employee use your name during the transaction?	☐	☐	☐

FIGURE 12.5   *continued*

		YES	NO	DOES NOT APPLY
6.	Did the employee ask you to be seated?	☐	☐	☐
7.	Was the employee helpful?	☐	☐	☐
8.	Was the employee's desk or work area neat and uncluttered?	☐	☐	☐
9.	Did the employee show a genuine interest in you as a customer?	☐	☐	☐
10.	Did the employee thank you for coming in?	☐	☐	☐
11.	Did the employee enthusiastically support the bank and its services.	☐	☐	☐
12.	Did the employee handle any interruptions (phone calls, etc.) effectively?	☐	☐	☐

Comment on any positive or negative details of the transaction that you found particularly noticeable.

_____

_____

_____

_____

_____

D. SALES SKILLS		YES	NO	DOES NOT APPLY
1.	Did the employee determine if you had any accounts with this bank?	☐	☐	☐
2.	Did the employee use "open-ended" questions in obtaining information about you?	☐	☐	☐
3.	Did the employee listen to what you had to say?	☐	☐	☐
4.	Did the employee sell you on the bank service by showing you what the service could do for you?	☐	☐	☐
5.	Did the employee ask you to open the service which you inquired about?	☐	☐	☐
6.	Did the employee ask you to bank with this particular bank?	☐	☐	☐
7.	Did the employee ask you to contact him/her when visiting the bank?	☐	☐	☐
8.	Did the employee ask you if you had any questions or if you understood the service at the end of the transaction?	☐	☐	☐

Continued

FIGURE 12.5   *continued*

9. Did the employee give you brochures about other services?   ☐   ☐   ☐

10. Did the employee give you his/her calling card?   ☐   ☐   ☐

11. Did the employee indicate that you might be contacted by telephone, engraved card, or letter as a means of follow-up?   ☐   ☐   ☐

12. Did the employee ask you to open or use other services? Check the following if they were mentioned.   ☐   ☐   ☐

    ☐ savings account

    ☐ checking account

    ☐ automatic savings

    ☐ Mastercharge

    ☐ Master Checking

    ☐ safe-deposit box

    ☐ loan services

    ☐ trust services

    ☐ automatic payroll deposit

    ☐ bank-by-mail

    ☐ automatic loan payment

    ☐ bank hours

    ☐ other _____

Comment on the overall effectiveness of the employee's sales skills.

_____

_____

_____

_____

_____

Source: Courtesy of Neil M. Ford.

Ethical Dilemma 12.2

A candy manufacturer tells you that he wants to raise the price of his gourmet chocolates and he needs you to establish the greatest price increase that shoppers will stand. He suggests that you interview patrons of gourmet candy shops without informing them of the sponsor or purpose of the research, describe the candy to them in general terms, and suggest prices that they might find acceptable, starting with the highest price.

◦ Is it ethical to ask people questions when their answer may be detrimental to their self-interest?

◦ Is it ethical not to reveal the purpose or sponsor of the research? If you did reveal the purpose of the research, would survey respondents give the same answers as otherwise?

Ethical Dilemma 12.3

As you supervise the sending out of a mail survey from a client's place of business, you notice some numbers printed on the inside of the return envelopes. You point out to the client that the cover letter promises survey respondents anonymity, which is not consistent with a policy of coding the return envelopes. She replies that she needs to identify those respondents who have not replied so that she can send a follow-up mailing. She also suggests the

information might be useful in the future in identifying those who might react favorably to a sales call for the product.

- Is it ethical to promise anonymity and then not adhere to your promise?

- Is it healthy for the marketing research profession if legitimate research becomes associated with subsequent sales tactics?

Back to the Case

It wasn't really funny, but Bill Hershey had to laugh. He had spent the afternoon on the phone with a random sample of the physicians that MedAccounts had earmarked to reply to its service questionnaire. The poor overall response to the questionnaire now made perfect sense. And while the whole situation was quite a screwup, he could laugh about it because his boss had taken it philosophically, and it was at least as much the client's fault as it was Hershey's.

In a nutshell, the problem was that MedAccounts didn't have a clear idea of who its customers were, at least in terms of service. True, its sales reps called on the physicians in a practice, and some physicians purchased the MedAccounts billing system. But in reality, the doctors spent their days treating patients, not billing them. While the doctors might have been the purchasers of the system, they were certainly not the users. Most of the doctors who purchased the MedAccounts system didn't even know where it was located in their office. They weren't the ones who called the service department: they had no idea of whether the service rep was punctual, polite, or quick to spot the problem.

It was the office manager who called MedAccounts when there was a problem, who knew the service rep's name and whether his or her appearance was neat and demeanor professional. Hershey's informal phone research explained a lot. Many of the doctors to whom the questionnaire had been sent had just thrown it away. Some of the doctors had given the questionnaire to their office manager or had filled it out with the office manager's assistance. Other doctors had taken a couple of minutes and filled it out as best as they could with their limited knowledge and had sent it off half finished.

In school Hershey had been taught the importance of checking one's hypothesis when formulating a questionnaire. Still, it had never occurred to him to question whether a client knew who its own customers were. As a result, the research firm and the client had wasted some money, and they'd wasted some time. Hershey was more than a little embarrassed, but he recognized that he'd learned an important lesson, albeit the hard way.

Summary

Learning Objective 1

Explain the role of research hypotheses in developing a questionnaire.

Research hypotheses guide the questionnaire by determining what information will be sought and from whom (since the hypotheses specify what relationships will be investigated). Hence, research hypotheses also affect the type of question and the form of response used to collect it.

Learning Objective 2

Define telescoping error *and* recall loss *and explain how they affect a respondent's ability to answer questions accurately*

Telescoping error refers to people's tendency to remember an event as having occurred more recently than it did. *Recall loss* means they forget it happened at all. The degree to which the two types of error affect the accuracy of the reported information depends on the length of the period in question. For long periods, the telescoping effect is smaller, while the recall loss is larger. For short periods, the reverse is true.

Learning Objective 3

Cite some of the techniques researchers use to secure respondents' cooperation in answering sensitive questions.

When asking sensitive questions, researchers may find it helpful to (1) hide the question in a group of other, more innocuous, questions; (2) state that the behavior or attitude is not unusual before asking the specific question of the respondent; (3) phrase the question in terms of others and how they might feel or act; (4) state the response in terms of a number of categories that the respondent may simply check; (5) use the randomized-response model.

Learning Objective 4

Explain what an open-ended question is.

An open-ended question is one in which respondents are free to reply in their own words rather than being limited to choosing from a set of alternatives.

Learning Objective 5

Name two kinds of fixed-alternative questions and tell the difference between them.

Two types of fixed-alternative questions are multichotomous and dichotomous questions. In a multichotomous question respondents are asked to choose from a list of alternatives the one that most closely reflects their position on the subject. In a dichotomous question, only two alternatives are listed.

Learning Objective 6

List some of the primary rules researchers should keep in mind in trying to develop bias-free questions.

Among the rules of thumb that researchers should keep in mind in developing bias-free questions are (1) use simple words, (2) avoid ambiguous words and questions, (3) avoid leading questions, (4) avoid implicit alternatives, (5) avoid implicit assumptions, (6) avoid generalizations and estimates, and (7) avoid double-barreled questions.

Learning Objective 7

Explain what the funnel approach to question sequencing is.

The funnel approach to question sequencing gets its name from its shape, starting with broad questions and progressively narrowing down the scope.

Learning Objective 8

Explain what a branching question is and discuss when it is used.

A branching question is one that contains a direction as to where to go next on the questionnaire based on the answer given. Branching questions are used to reduce the number of alternatives that are needed in individual questions, while ensuring that those respondents capable of supplying the needed information still have an opportunity to do so.

Learning Objective 9

Explain the difference between basic information and classification information and tell which should be asked first in a questionnaire.

Basic information refers to the subject of the study; classification information refers to the other data we collect to classify respondents so as to extract more information about the phenomenon of interest. The proper questionnaire sequence is to present questions securing basic information first and those seeking classification information last.

Review Questions

1. What role do the research hypotheses play in determining the information that will be sought?

2. Suppose you wanted to determine the proportion of men in a geographic area who use hair sprays. How could the information be obtained by open-ended question, by multiple-choice question, and by dichotomous question? Which would be preferable?

3. How does the method of administration of a questionnaire affect the type of question to be employed?

4. What criteria can a researcher use to determine whether a specific question should be included in a questionnaire?

5. What is telescoping error? What does it suggest about the period to be used when asking respondents to recall past experiences?

6. What are some recommended ways by which one can ask for sensitive information?

7. What is an open-ended question? A multichotomous question? A dichotomous question? What are some of the key things researchers must be careful to avoid in framing multichotomous and dichotomous questions?

8. What is a split ballot, and why is it employed?

9. What is an ambiguous question? A leading question? A question with implicit alternatives? A question with implied assumptions? A double-barreled question?

10. What is the proper sequence when asking for basic information and classification information?

11. What is the funnel approach to question sequencing?

12. What is a branching question? Why are such questions used?

13. Where should one ask for sensitive information in the questionnaire?

14. How can the physical features of a questionnaire affect its acceptance by respondents? Its handling and control by the researcher?

15. What is the overriding principle guiding questionnaire construction?

16. What decisions must the researcher make when developing an observational form for data collection?

Discussion Questions, Problems, and Projects

1. Evaluate the following questions.

   (a) **Which of the following magazines do you read regularly?**
      _____ *Time*
      _____ *Newsweek*
      _____ *Business Week*

   (b) **Are you a frequent purchaser of Birds Eye Frozen vegetables?**
      _____ Yes   _____ No

   (c) **Do you agree that the government should impose import restrictions?**
      _____ Strongly agree
      _____ Agree
      _____ Neither agree nor disagree
      _____ Disagree
      _____ Strongly disagree

   (d) **How often do you buy detergent?**
      _____ Once a week
      _____ Once in two weeks
      _____ Once in three weeks
      _____ Once a month

   (e) **Rank the following in order of preference:**
      _____ Kellogg's Corn Flakes
      _____ Quaker's Life
      _____ Post Bran Flakes
      _____ Kellogg's Bran Flakes
      _____ Instant Quaker Oatmeal
      _____ Post Rice Krinkles

   (f) **Where do you usually purchase your school supplies?**

   (g) **When you are watching television, do you also watch most of the advertisements?**

   (h) **Which of the following brands of tea are most similar?**
      _____ Lipton's Orange Pekoe
      _____ Twinings Orange Pekoe
      _____ Bigelow Orange Pekoe
      _____ Salada Orange Pekoe

   (i) **Do you think that the present policy of cutting taxes and reducing government spending should be continued?**
      _____ Yes   _____ No

   (j) **In a seven-day week, how often do you eat breakfast?**
      _____ Every day of the week
      _____ 5–6 times a week
      _____ 2–4 times a week
      _____ Once a week
      _____ Never

2. Make the necessary corrections to the above questions.

3. Evaluate the following multichotomous questions. Rephrase them as dichotomous or open-ended questions if you think it would be more appropriate.

   (a) **Which one of the following reasons is most important in your choice of stereo equipment?**
      _____ Price
      _____ In-store service
      _____ Brand name
      _____ Level of distortion
      _____ Guarantee/warranty

   (b) **Please indicate your education level.**
      _____ Less than high school

_____ Some high school
_____ High school graduate
_____ Technical or vocational school
_____ Some college
_____ College graduate
_____ Some graduate or professional school

(c) **Which of the following reflects your views toward the issues raised by ecologists?**
_____ Have received attention
_____ Have not received attention
_____ Should receive more attention
_____ Should receive less attention

(d) **With which of the following statements do you most strongly agree?**
_____ Delta Airlines has better service than Northwest Airlines.
_____ Northwest Airlines has better service than United Airlines.
_____ United Airlines has better service than Delta Airlines.
_____ United Airlines has better service than Northwest Airlines.
_____ Northwest Airlines has better service than Delta Airlines.
_____ Delta Airlines has better service than United Airlines.

4. Evaluate the following open-ended questions. Rephrase them as multichotomous or dichotomous questions if you think it would be more appropriate.
   (a) **Do you go to the movies often?**
   (b) **Approximately how much do you spend per week on groceries?**
   (c) **What brands of cheese did you purchase during the last week?**

5. Assume you are doing exploratory research to find out people's opinions about television advertising.
   (a) Specify the necessary information that is to be sought.
   You have decided to design a structured-undisguised questionnaire and employ the personal interview method.
   (b) List the individual questions on a separate sheet of paper.
   (c) Specify the form of the response for each question (i.e., open-ended, multichotomous, dichotomous, scale). Provide justification for selecting a particular form of response.
   (d) Determine the sequence of the questions. Reexamine and revise the questions.
   (e) Attach the final version of the questionnaire.
   (f) Pretest the questionnaire on a convenience sample of five students, and report the results of your pretest.

6. The objective of this study is to determine whether brand names are important for mothers purchasing children's clothing.
   (a) Specify the necessary information that is to be sought.
   You have decided to use a structured-undisguised questionnaire and to employ the telephone interview method.
   (b) List the individual questions on a separate sheet of paper.
   (c) Specify the form of the response for each question. Provide justification for selecting a particular form of response.
   (d) Determine the sequence of the questions. Reexamine and revise the questions.
   (e) Attach the final version of the questionnaire.
   (f) Using the phone book as a sampling frame, pretest the questionnaire on a sample of five respondents, and report the results of your pretest.

7. A small brokerage firm was concerned with its declining number of customers and decided to do a quick survey. The major objective was to find out the reasons for patronizing a particular brokerage firm and to find out the importance of customer service. The following questionnaire was to be administered by telephone.

Good Afternoon, Sir/Madam:

We are doing a survey on attitudes toward brokerage firms. Could you please answer the following questions? Thank you.

1. Have you invested any money in the stock market?
    _____ Yes   _____ No

If respondent replies "yes" continue; otherwise terminate interview.

2. Do you manage your own investments, or do you go to a brokerage firm?
    _____ Manage own investments   _____ Go to brokerage firm

If respondent replies "go to a brokerage firm," continue; otherwise terminate interview.

3. How satisfied are you with your brokerage firm?

VERY SATISFIED	SATISFIED	NEITHER SATISFIED NOR DISSATISFIED	DISSATISFIED	VERY DISSATISFIED
____	____	____	____	____

4. How important is personal service to you?

VERY IMPORTANT	IMPORTANT	NOT PARTICULARLY IMPORTANT	NOT AT ALL IMPORTANT
____	____	____	____

5. Which of the following reasons is the most important in patronizing a particular firm?

    _____ The commission charged by the firm
    _____ The personal service
    _____ The return on investment
    _____ The investment counseling

6. Approximately how long have you been investing through the brokerage firm you are currently using?

    _____ about 3 months   _____ about 9 months
    _____ about 6 months   _____ about 1 year or more

7. How much capital do you have invested?

    _____ $500–$750   _____ $1,000–$1,500
    _____ $750–$1,000   _____ $1,500 or more

Good-bye, and thank you for your cooperation.

Evaluate the above questionnaire.

8. Assume that a medium-sized manufacturer of candy employs you to conduct an observation study in determining children's influence on adults in the purchase of candy.
    (a) List the variables that are relevant in determining this influence.
    (b) List the "observations" that might reflect each of these variables.
    (c) Develop an observation form that will be able to collect the needed information.
    (d) Observe three such purchases in a store/supermarket or the location that you specified above.
    (e) Report your findings.

9. This observation task can be conducted near the vending machines in the cafeteria, library, or business school: The objective is to observe the deliberation time taken at the various machines and determine the factors that influence the deliberation time.
   (a) List the variables that would be relevant in achieving the above objective.
   (b) List the "observations" that would reflect each of these variables.
   (c) Develop an observation form that will be able to collect the needed information.
   (d) Do five such observations and report your findings.

10. Your employer, a commercial marketing research firm, has contracted to perform a study whose objective is the investigation of usage patterns and brand preferences for premixed infant formula among migrant farm workers in the southeastern United States. You have been assigned to develop a suitable questionnaire and method of administration to collect the desired information. What potential problems might arise in design and administration due to the unique nature of the population in question? List these problems and provide solutions. What method of administration will you recommend?

11. Discuss various reasons that a researcher might have for using an observation form as opposed to a questionnaire.

Endnotes

1. This procedure is adapted from one suggested by Arthur Kornhauser and Paul B. Sheatsley, "Questionnaire Construction and Interview Procedure," in Claire Selltiz, Lawrence S. Wrightsman, and Stuart W. Cook, *Research Methods in Social Relations,* 3rd ed. (New York: Holt, Rinehart and Winston, 1976), pp. 541–573. See also Arlene Fink, *How to Design Surveys* (Thousand Oaks, Calif.: Sage Publications, 1995).

2. Murray Simon, "Face/Off: A Pharmaceutical Projection Technique," *Quirk's Marketing Research Review* (December 1998), pp. 39–41.

3. Chris Grecco and Hal King, "Of Browsers and Plug-Ins: Researching Web Surfers' Technological Capabilities," *Quirk's Marketing Research Review* (July 1999), pp. 58–62.

4. These questions were suggested by Kornhauser and Sheatsley, "Questionnaire Construction." For a systematic treatment of questionnaire construction, see the classic work by Stanley L. Payne, *The Art of Asking Questions* (Princeton, N.J.: Princeton University Press, 1978). Other good general sources are Seymour Sudman and Norman M. Bradburn, *Asking Questions: A Practical Guide to Questionnaire Design* (San Francisco: Jossey-Bass, 1982); William Foddy, *Constructing Questions for Interviews and Questionnaires* (New York: Cambridge University Press, 1993); Arlene Fink, *How to Ask Survey Questions* (Thousand Oaks, Calif.: Sage Publications, 1995).

5. Sam Gill, "How Do You Stand on Sin?" *Tide* 21 (March 14, 1947), p. 72.

6. In a subsequent replication of the study on the Metallic Metals Act almost 40 years later, 64 percent of those interviewed had a definite opinion on the nonexistent act. See Daniel T. Seymour, "Numbers Don't Lie–Do They?" *Business Horizons* 27 (November/December 1984), pp. 36–37. There are a number of other examples in the literature that report findings of people having opinions about totally fictional issues like the Metallic Metals Act. See, for example, Del I. Hawkins and Kenneth A. Coney, "Uninformed Response Error in Survey Research," *Journal of Marketing Research* 18 (August 1981), pp. 370–374; Kenneth C. Schneider, "Uninformed Response Rates in Survey Research: New Evidence," *Journal of Business Research* 13 (August 1985), pp. 153–162; George F. Bishop, Alfred J. Tuchfarber, and Robert W. Oldendick, "Opinions on Fictitious Issues: The Pressure to Answer Survey Questions," *Public Opinion Quarterly* 50 (Summer 1986), pp. 240–250; Arthur Sterngold, Rex H. Warland, and Robert O. Herrmann, "Do Surveys Overstate Public Concern?" *Public Opinion Quarterly* 58 (Summer 1994), pp. 255–263. The phenomenon is not unique to opinions. It also applies when measuring brand awareness, where it has been observed that the more plausible sounding a brand name, the more likely consumers are to claim they are aware of it even though it does not exist. See "'Spurious Awareness' Alters Brand Tests," *The Wall Street Journal* (September 13, 1984), p. 29; See also Eric R. A. N. Smith and Peverill Squire, "The Effects of Prestige Names in Question Wording," *Public Opinion Quarterly* 54 (Spring 1990), pp. 97–116.

7. Howard Schuman and Stanley Presser, "The Assessment of 'No Opinions' in Attitude Surveys," in Karl F. Schnessler, ed., *Sociological Methodology, 1979* (San Francisco: Jossey-Bass, 1979), pp. 241–275. See also George F. Bishop, Robert W. Oldendick, and Alfred J. Tuchfarber, "Effects on Filter Questions in Public Opinion Surveys," *Public Opinion Quarterly* 47 (Winter 1983), pp. 528–546; Otis Dudley Duncan

and Magnus Stenbeck, "No Opinion or Not Sure?" *Public Opinion Quarterly* 52 (Winter 1988), pp. 513–525; Kenneth C. Schneider and James C. Johnson, "Link Between Response-Inducing Strategies and Uninformed Response," *Marketing Intelligence and Planning* 12 (No. 1, 1994), pp. 29–36.

8. Bruce Buchanan and Donald G. Morrison, "Sampling Properties of Rate Questions with Implications for Survey Research," *Marketing Science* 6 (Summer 1987), pp. 286–298; Scot Burton and Edward Blair, "Task Conditions, Response Formulation Processes, and Response Accuracy for Behavioral Frequency Questions in Surveys," *Public Opinion Quarterly* 55 (Spring 1991), pp. 50–79; Richard Nadeau and Richard G. Niemi, "Educated Guesses: The Process of Answering Factual Knowledge Questions in Surveys," *Public Opinion Quarterly* 59 (Fall 1995), pp. 323–346.

9. Graham Kalton and Howard Schuman, "The Effect of the Question on Survey Responses: A Review," *Journal of the Royal Statistical Society, Series A,* 145 (Part I, 1982), pp. 44–45. See also William A. Cook, "Telescoping and Memory's Other Tricks," *Journal of Advertising Research* 27 (February/March 1987), pp. RC5–RC8; Norman M. Bradburn, Lance J. Rip, and Steven K. Shevell, "Answering Autobiographical Questions: The Impact of Memory and Inference on Surveys," *Science* 236 (April 10, 1987), pp. 157–161; McKee J. McClendon, "Acquiescence and Recency Response Order Effects in Interview Surveys," *Sociological Methodology and Research* 20 (August 1991), pp. 60–103.

10. Lee Valeriano Lourdes, "Marketing: Western Firms Poll Eastern Europeans to Discern Tastes of Nascent Consumers," *The Wall Street Journal* (April 27, 1992), p. B1.

11. Stella M. Hopkins, "Furniture Makers Start Asking Customers What They Want," *Charlotte* (N.C.) *Observer* (October 12, 1998, downloaded from Dow Jones Publications Library, Dow Jones Web site, www.dowjones.com, August 16, 1999).

12. For general treatments on how to handle sensitive questions, see Kent H. Marquis et al., *Response Errors in Sensitive Topic Surveys: Estimates, Effects, and Correction Options* (Santa Monica, Calif.: Rand Corporation, 1981); Claire M. Renzetti and Raymond M. Lee, eds., *Researching Sensitive Topics* (Thousand Oaks, Calif.: Sage Publications, 1992); Raymond M. Lee, *Doing Research on Sensitive Topics* (Thousand Oaks, Calif.: Sage Publications, 1993).

13. James E. Reinmuth and Michael D. Geurts, "The Collection of Sensitive Information Using a Two-Stage Randomized Response Model," *Journal of Marketing Research* 12 (November 1975), pp. 402–407. For discussion of randomization devices and methodologies for self-administered and telephone interview applications of the randomized-response method, see Donald E. Stem, Jr., and R. Kirk Steinhorst, "Telephone Interview and Mail Questionnaire Applications of the Randomized Response Model," *Journal of the American Statistical Association* 79 (September 1984), pp. 555–564. For general treatments, see James Alan Fox and Paul E. Tracy, *Randomizing Response: A Method for Sensitive Surveys* (Beverly Hills, Calif.: Sage Publications, 1986); U. N. Umesh and Robert A. Peterson, "A Critical Evaluation of the Randomized Response Model: Applications, Validations, and Research Agenda," *Sociological Methods and Research* 20 (August 1991), pp. 104–138.

14. Kalton and Schuman, "The Effect of the Question on Survey Responses: A Review," pp. 51–52. See also Gail S. Poe et al., "Don't Know Box in Factual Questions in a Mail Questionnaire: Effects on Level and Quality of Response," *Public Opinion Quarterly* 52 (Summer 1988), pp. 212–222; Mikael Gilliam and Donald Granberg, "Should We Take Don't Know for an Answer," *Public Opinion Quarterly,* 57 (Fall 1993), pp. 348–357.

15. National Public Radio, "All Things Considered" (September 7, 1999, summary and audio downloaded from the NPR Web site, www.npr.org, September 9, 1999); National Public Radio, "Americans Willing to Pay for Improving Schools," NPR Web site (www.npr.org, downloaded September 9, 199); "NPR/Kaiser/ Kennedy School Education Survey," NPR Web site (www.npr.org, downloaded September 9, 1999).

16. Hadley Cantril and Edreta Fried, *Gauging Public Opinion* (Princeton, N.J.: Princeton University Press, 1944), Chapter 1, as reported in Payne, *The Art of Asking Questions,* p. 93. For a discussion of how to take account of people's information processing abilities when designing questionnaires, see Seymour Sudman, Norman M. Bradburn and Norbert Schwarz, *Thinking about Answers: The Application of Cognitive Process to Survey Methodology* (San Francisco, Calif.: Jossey-Bass, 1996).

17. Norbert Schwarz, Hans J. Hippler, Brigitte Deutsch, and Fritz Strack, "Response Scales: Effect of Category Range on Reported Behavior and Comparative Judgments," *Public Opinion Quarterly* 49 (Fall 1985), pp. 388–395; Norbert Schwarz et al., "The Range of Response Alternatives May Determine the Meaning of the Question: Further Evidence on Information Functions of Response Alternatives," *Social Cognition* 6 (No. 2, 1988), pp. 107–117; Eric A. Greenleaf, "Measuring Extreme Response Style," *Public Opinion Quarterly* 56 (Fall 1992), pp. 328–351.

18. Two of the best discussions of this are to be found in Payne, *The Art of Asking Questions,* and Howard Schuman and Stanley Presser, *Questions and Answers in Attitude Surveys* (Orlando, Fla.: Academic Press, 1981), especially pp. 56–77. See also Donald A. Dillman et al., "Effects of Category Order on Answers in Mail and Telephone Surveys," *Rural Sociology* (Winter 1995), pp. 674–687.

19. For a review of the literature on the quality of questionnaire data, including item omission, see Robert A. Peterson and Roger A. Kerin, "The Quality of Self-Report Data: Review and Synthesis," in Ben Enis and Kenneth Roering, eds., *Annual Review of Marketing* 1981 (Chicago: American Marketing Association, 1981), pp. 5–20. See also Floyd Jackson Fowler, Jr., "How Unclear Terms Affect Survey Data," *Public Opinion Quarterly* 56 (Summer 1992), pp. 218–231.

20. Sudman and Bradburn, *Asking Questions,* p. 1.

21. Gonzalo R. Soruco, "Sampling and Nonsampling Errors in Hispanic Population Telephone Surveys," *Applied Marketing Research* 29 (Summer 1989), pp. 11–15; Patrice Braus, "What Does 'Hispanic' Mean?" *American Demographics* 15 (June 1993), pp. 46–49, 58.

22. E. Noelle-Neumann, "Wanted: Rules for Wording Structural Questionnaires," *Public Opinion Quarterly* 34 (Summer 1970), p. 200. See also Philip Gendall and Janet Hoek, "A Question of Wording," *Marketing Bulletin* 1 (May 1990), pp. 25–36.

23. Donald J. Messmer and Daniel T. Seymour, "The Effects of Branching on Item Nonresponse," *Public Opinion Quarterly* 46 (Summer 1982), pp. 270–277.

24. Sudman and Bradburn, *Asking Questions,* pp. 223–227.

25. For examples, see Charles S. Mayer and Cindy Piper, "A Note on the Importance of Layout in Self-Administered Questionnaires," *Journal of Marketing Research* 19 (August 1982), pp. 390–391; Maria Elena Sanchez, "Effects of Questionnaire Design on the Quality of Survey Data," *Public Opinion Quarterly* 56 (Summer 1992), pp. 206–217.

26. Each of the parts listed in Research Window 12.4 is discussed in detail in Paul L. Erdos, *Professional Mail Surveys* (Melbourne, Fla.: Robert E. Krieger Publishing Co., 1983), pp. 101–117. See also Linda B. Bourque and Eve P. Fiedler, *How to Conduct Self-Administered and Mail Surveys* (Thousand Oaks, Calif.: Sage Publications, 1995).

27. A. Regula Herzog and Jerald G. Bachman, "Effects of Questionnaire Length on Response Quality," *Public Opinion Quarterly* 45 (Winter 1981), pp. 549–559; David Jobber, "An Examination of the Effects of Questionnaire Factors on Response to an Industrial Mail Survey," *International Journal of Research on Marketing* 6 (December 1989), pp. 129–140; Andrew G. Bean and Michale J. Rozkowski, "The Long and Short of It," *Marketing Research: A Magazine of Management & Applications* 7 (Winter 1995), pp. 21–26.

28. These elementary steps, which are involved in the processing of all questionnaires, are discussed in Chapter 19.

29. Payne's book, *The Art of Asking Questions,* is particularly good in this regard. Chapter 13, for example, is devoted to the development of a passable question. When one considers that an entire chapter can be devoted to the development of one passable question (not a great question, mind you), one can appreciate the need for reexamining each question under a microscope for its potential implications. A condensed treatment of the things to be avoided in a question is to be found in Lyndon O. Brown and Leland L. Beik, *Marketing Research and Analysis,* 4th ed. (New York: Ronald, 1969), pp. 242–262. See also Sudman and Bradburn, *Asking Questions,* which has recommendations specific to the type of question being asked (e.g., opinions versus demographic characteristics) and Floyd J. Fowler, Jr., *Improving Survey Questions* (Thousand Oaks, Calif.: Sage Publications, 1995).

30. Linda Kirby, "Bloopers," *Newspaper Research Council* (January/February 1989), p. 1.

31. Shelby D. Hunt, Richard D. Sparkman, Jr., and James B. Wilcox, "The Pretest in Survey Research: Issues and Preliminary Findings," *Journal of Marketing Research* 19 (May 1982), pp. 265–275. Ruth N. Bolton, Randall G. Chapman, and John M. Zych, "Pretesting Alternative Survey Administration Designs," *Applied Marketing Research* 30 (No. 3, 1990), pp. 8–13; Nina Reynolds, Adamantios Diamantopoulus, and Bodo Schlegelmich, "Pretesting in Questionnaire Design: A Review of the Literature and Suggestions for Further Research," *Journal of the Market Research Society* 35 (April 1993), pp. 171–182. For discussion of some of the things the Department of Commerce pretested as it prepared for the 2000 Census, see John Pierson, "Preparing for 2000, Census Bureau Tests Carrots vs. Sticks," *The Wall Street Journal,* May 2, 1996, pp. B1, B9.

32. Brown and Beik, *Marketing Research and Analysis,* pp. 265–266.

Suggested Additional Readings

For more elaborate treatments of how to go about constructing questionnaires, see

Patricia J. Labaw, *Advanced Questionnaire Design* (Cambridge, Mass.: Abt Books, 1981).

Stanley L. Payne, *The Art of Asking Questions* (Princeton, N.J.: Princeton University Press, 1979).

Howard Schuman and Stanley Presser, *Questions and Answers in Attitude Surveys* (Orlando, Fla.: Academic Press, 1981).

Seymour Sudman and Norman M. Bradburn, *Asking Questions: A Practical Guide to Questionnaire Design* (San Francisco: Jossey-Bass, 1982).

Chapter 13

MEASUREMENT BASICS

L E A R N I N G   O B J E C T I V E S

Upon Completing This Chapter, You Should Be Able to

1. Define the term *measurement* as it is used in marketing research.

2. List the four types of scales that can be used to measure an attribute.

3. Explain the primary difference between a ratio scale and an interval scale.

4. Cite some of the factors that may cause differences in two measures of the same attribute.

5. Name the two types of error that may affect measurement scores and define each.

6. Explain the concept of validity as it relates to measuring instruments.

7. Specify the two types of inferences a researcher makes in attempting to establish the validity of an instrument.

8. Cite the three types of direct assessment techniques used to infer the validity of a measure.

9. Outline the sequence of steps to follow in developing valid measures of marketing constructs.

Case in Marketing Research

On the first day that Teen Sport deodorant was being marketed in Middlefield, Ernie Henderson, the research analyst in charge of the project, had a meeting with Todd Whalen, from marketing. Henderson found Whalen in his office, feet up on his desk, looking at some of the promotional materials that had been produced for Teen Sport, Reliance Cosmetics' new deodorant, which was targeted to girls aged 12 to 17.

When Henderson entered the room, Whalen leapt to his feet and greeted the researcher with a hearty handshake.

"Well, Ernie," he said jovially, "I've done my job. Now it's your turn to do yours. The advertising is ready, the promotional coupons are in the pipeline, and we've got a lock on our shelf space in the retail outlets. As we speak, samples are being mailed to all the teenaged girls in Middlefield."

"I'm all set to go, too," replied Henderson. "We'll be running qualitative studies to find out what consumers like and dislike about Teen Sport. We'll also be doing awareness studies of both print and television advertising."

"So when do we get to hear whether we have the winner I think we have?"

"I know you're excited about the test market," answered Henderson cautiously, "and I'm not saying that we're not going to hit a home run with this one, but I think it's more likely that we're going to have to make some adjustments after we get the results from Middlefield."

"Don't be a wet blanket, Ernie," replied Whalen. "You don't know teenagers like I know teenagers. I handed out samples at my 14-year-old's slumber party, and the girls said Teen Sport was great."

"Teenagers are a very fickle and segmented market," countered Henderson. "Their tastes vary widely from one part of the country to the other, and what they think is great one day is passé six months later."

"So, then, how long is it going to be before we get results from the test market?"

"I figure we need to measure at 8, 14, and 20 weeks to get any valid reading. I'm also worried that we're going to run into problems with Christmas. . . ."

"Ernie, I think you're just a born worrier."

"Not really," replied Henderson. "You came here from snack foods. Wait until you've been in personal consumer products as long as I have—you'll be a worrier, too."

Discussion Issues

1. What kinds of problems might a marketer encounter in trying to measure consumers' attitudes toward a new product?

2. What assumption is Whalen making that could prove faulty? Why could it prove faulty?

3. What kinds of questions should Henderson ask to determine consumers' attitudes toward the new deodorant?

Without realizing it, most of us spend the day engaging in various forms of measurement. We stagger out of bed and hop onto the bathroom scale, hoping our midnight foray to the refrigerator will fail to register. We measure coffee into the coffee maker, or stir a teaspoonful of instant coffee into a cup of water. We keep an eye on the clock so that we will not miss the bus or leave too little time to negotiate the rush-hour traffic on our way to class. We check the sports page for the score of the previous night's game—and perhaps the business section for the closing price on a favorite investment.

Most of the things we measure are fairly concrete: pounds on a scale, teaspoons of coffee, the amount of gas in a tank. But how does one measure a person's attitude toward bubble gum? The likelihood of a teenager's using a certain brand of acne medication? A family's social class? Marketers are interested in measuring many attributes that laypeople rarely think of in terms of numerical values. In this chapter and the next, we will discuss how marketing researchers go about assigning numbers to various objects and phenomena.

Scales of Measurement

Measurement
Rules for assigning numbers to objects to represent quantities of attributes.

Measurement consists of "rules for assigning numbers to objects in such a way as to represent quantities of attributes."[1] Note two things about the definition. First, it indicates that we measure the attributes of objects and not the objects themselves. We do not measure a person, for example, but may choose to measure the individual's income, social class, education, height, weight, attitudes, or whatever, all of which are attributes of this person. Second, the definition is broad in that it does not specify how the numbers are to be assigned. In this sense, the rule is too simplistic and conveys a false sense of security, because there is a great temptation to read more meaning into the numbers than they actually contain. We often incorrectly attribute all the properties of the scale of numbers to the assigned numerals.

Consider the properties of the scale of numbers for a minute. Take the numbers 1, 2, 3, and 4. Now let the number 1 stand for one object, 2 for two objects, and so on. The scale of numbers possesses a number of properties. For example, we can say that 2 is larger than 1, and 3 is larger than 2, and so on. Also, we can say that the interval between 1 and 2 is the same size as the interval between 3 and 4, which is the same as that between 2 and 3, and so on. We can say still further that 3 is three times greater than 1, while 4 is four times greater than 1 and two times greater than 2, and so on.

When we assign numbers to attributes of objects, we must beware of the temptation to make these same arguments with the numbers in that it is *unlikely* that these relationships hold. We must determine the properties of the attribute and assign numbers in such a fashion that they accurately reflect the properties of the attribute. Errors at this point could mislead both the researchers and the users of the research.

There are four types of scales on which an attribute can be measured, namely, nominal, ordinal, interval, and ratio.[2] Exhibit 13.1 summarizes some of the more important features of these scales.

Nominal scale
Measurement in which numbers are assigned to objects or classes of objects solely for the purpose of identification.

Nominal Scale

One of the simplest properties of the scale of numbers is *identity*. A person's social security number is a **nominal scale,** as are the numbers on football jerseys, lockers, and so on.

EXHIBIT 13.1	Scales of Measurement			

Scale	Basic Comparisons[a]	Typical Examples	Measures of Average[b]
Nominal	Identity	Male/Female User/nonuser Occupations Uniform numbers	Mode
Ordinal	Order	Preference for brands Social class Hardness of minerals Graded quality of lumber	Median
Interval	Comparison of intervals	Temperature scale Grade point average Attitude toward brands	Mean
Ratio	Comparison of absolute magnitudes	Units sold Number of purchasers Probability of purchase Weight	Geometric mean Harmonic mean

[a]All the comparisons applicable to a given scale are permissible with all scales above it in the table. For example, the ratio scale allows the comparison of intervals and the investigation of order and identity, in addition to the comparison of absolute magnitudes.

[b]The measures of average applicable to a given scale are also appropriate for all scales below it in the table; e.g., the mode is also a meaningful measure of the average when measurement is on an ordinal, interval, or ratio scale.

These numbers simply identify the individual assigned the number. Similarly, if in a given study males are coded 1 and females 2, we have again made use of a nominal scale. The individuals are uniquely identified as male or female. All we need to determine an individual's sex is to know whether the person is coded as a 1 or as a 2. Note further that there is nothing implied by the numerals other than identification of the sex of the person. Females, although they bear a higher number, are not necessarily "superior" to males, or "more" than males or twice as many as males—as the numbers 2 and 1 might indicate—or vice versa. We could just as easily reverse our coding procedure so that each female is a 1 and each male a 2.

The reason we could reverse our codes is that the only property conveyed by the numbers is identity. With a nominal scale, the only permissible operation is counting. Thus, the mode is the only legitimate measure of central tendency or average. It does not make sense in a sample consisting of 60 men and 40 women to say that the average sex is 1.4, given males were coded 1 and females 2, even though the calculation 0.6 (1) + 0.4 (2) yields the number 1.4. All we can say is that there were more males in the sample than females, or that 60 percent of the sample was male.

Ordinal Scale

Ordinal scale
Measurement in which numbers are assigned to data on the basis of some order (for example, more than, greater than) of the objects.

A second property of the scale of number is that of *order.* Thus, we could say that the number 2 is greater than the number 1, that 3 is greater than both 2 and 1, and that 4 is greater than all three of these numbers. The numbers 1, 2, 3, and 4 are ordered, and the larger the number, the greater the property. Note that the **ordinal scale** implies identity, since the same number would be used for all objects that are the same. An example would be the assignment of the number 1 to denote freshmen, 2 to denote sophomores, 3, juniors, and 4, seniors. We could just as well use the numbers 10 for freshmen, 20 for sophomores, 25 for juniors, and 30 for seniors. This assignment would still indicate the class level of each person and the *relative standing* of two persons when compared in terms of who is further along in the academic program. Note that this is all that is conveyed by an ordinal scale. The difference in ranks says nothing about the difference in academic achievement between two ranks.

This is perhaps easier to see if we talk about the three top people in a graduating class. Assume that the top-ranked person's average grade is 3.85 on a four-point scale, the second-ranked person's average is 3.74, and the third-ranked person's is 3.56. While an ordinal scale will tell us that one person was ranked first and another was ranked second, it tells us nothing about the difference in academic achievement between the two. Nor does an ordinal scale imply that the difference in academic achievement between the first- and second-ranked people equals the difference between the second- and third-ranked people, even though the difference between 1 and 2 equals the difference between 2 and 3.

As suggested, we can transform an ordinal scale in any way we wish as long as we maintain the basic ordering of the objects. Again, whether we can use the ordinal scale to assign numerals to objects depends on the attribute in question. The attribute itself must possess the ordinal property to allow ordinal scaling that is meaningful. With ordinal scales, both the median and the mode are permissible, or meaningful, measures of average. Thus, if 20 people ranked Product A first in comparison with Products B and C, while 10 ranked it second and 5 ranked it third, we could say that (1) the average rank of Product A as judged by the median response was 1 (with 35 subjects, the median is given by the 18th response when ranked from lowest to highest) and that (2) the modal rank was also 1.

Interval Scale

A third property of the scale of numbers is that the *intervals* between the numbers are meaningful in the sense that the numbers tell us how far apart the objects are with respect to the attribute. This means that the differences can be compared. The difference between 1 and 2 is equal to the difference between 2 and 3. Further, the difference between 2 and 4 is twice the difference that exists between 1 and 2.

One classic example of an **interval scale** is the temperature scale, since it indicates what we can and cannot say when we have measured an attribute on an interval scale. Suppose the low temperature for the day was 40°F and the high was 80°F. Can we say that the high temperature was twice as hot (that is, represented twice the heat) as the low temperature? The answer is an unequivocal no. To see the folly in claiming 80°F is twice as warm as 40°F, one simply needs to convert these temperatures to their centigrade equivalents, where C = (5F − 160)/9. Now we see that the low was 4.4°C and the high was 26.6°C, a much different ratio between low and high than was indicated by the Fahrenheit scale.

The example illustrates that we cannot compare the absolute magnitude of numbers when measurement is made on the basis of an interval scale. The reason is that in an interval scale, the zero point is established arbitrarily. For example, the same natural phenomenon, the freezing point of water, is represented by zero on the Celsius scale but 32 on the Fahrenheit scale.[3] The zero position is therefore arbitrary.

What, then, can we say when measurement is made on an interval scale? First, we can say that 80°F is warmer than 40°F. Second, given a third temperature, we can compare the intervals; that is, we can say the difference in heat between 80°F and 120°F is the same as the difference between 40°F and 80°F, and that the difference between 40°F and 120°F is twice the difference between 40°F and 80°F. To see that this conclusion is legitimate, we can simply resort to the centigrade equivalents: The difference between 4.4°C (40°F) and 26.6°C (80°F) is the same as that between 26.6°C (80°F) and 48.8°C (120°F), namely, 22.2°. Further, the difference of 44.4° between 4.4°C and 48.8°C is twice as great as that between 4.4°C and 26.6°C, as it was when the Fahrenheit scale was used. The comparison of intervals is legitimate with an interval scale because the relationships among the differences hold regardless of the particular constants chosen. With an interval scale, the mean, median, and mode are all meaningful measures of average.

Interval scale
Measurement in which the assigned numbers legitimately allow the comparison of the size of the differences among and between members.

small business association dues: $450 (450 miles)

payroll & accounting software: $760 (760 miles)

office supplies: $150 (150 miles)

remembering who you work for:

When you get a MasterCard BusinessCard® with MasterCard Business Bonuses,℠
you'll earn one mile for every dollar you spend. Good on any airline. No blackouts.
For details and participating banks, call 1-800-788-1365.

there are some things money can't buy.
for everything else there's MasterCard.℠

Ratio Scales

Ratio scale
Measurement that has a natural, or absolute, zero and therefore allows the comparison of absolute magnitudes of the numbers.

The **ratio scale** differs from an interval scale in that it possesses a *natural,* or *absolute,* zero, one for which there is universal agreement as to its location. Height and weight are obvious examples. Because there is an absolute zero, comparison of the *absolute magnitude* of the numbers is legitimate. Thus, a person weighing 200 pounds is said to be twice as heavy as one weighing 100 pounds, and a person weighing 300 pounds is three times as heavy. The MasterCard ad shown uses a ratio scale; the MasterCard user receives three times as many miles by paying the small business association dues of $450 than buying $150 of office supplies with the MasterCard.

In a ratio scale, zero has an absolute empirical meaning—that is, that none of the property being measured exists. Further, we have already seen that the more powerful scales include the properties possessed by the less powerful ones. This means that with a ratio scale we can compare intervals, rank objects according to magnitude, or use the numbers to identify the objects (everything that interval, ordinal, and nominal scales do). And the geometric mean, as well as the more usual arithmetic mean, median, and mode, is a meaningful measure of average when attributes are measured on a ratio scale.

Scaling of Psychological Attributes

The attribute determines the most powerful scale that can be used to measure the characteristic. That is always the way it is in measurement. The characteristic and its qualities set the upper limit for the assignment of numerals to objects. Because of the procedures used in generating the instrument, it is always possible to end up with what we might call a less powerful measure of the attribute (for example, a nominal rather than an ordinal scale). However, we can never exceed the basic nature of the attribute with our measure; for example, we can never generate an interval scale for an attribute that is only ordinal

NOMINAL SCALE

Which of the soft drinks on the following list do you like? Check all that apply.

_____ Coke
_____ Dr Pepper
_____ Mountain Dew
_____ Pepsi
_____ Seven Up
_____ Sprite

ORDINAL SCALE

Please rank the soft drinks on the following list according to your degree of liking for each, assigning your most preferred drink rank = 1 and your least preferred drink rank = 6.

_____ Coke
_____ Dr Pepper
_____ Mountain Dew
_____ Pepsi
_____ Seven Up
_____ Sprite

INTERVAL SCALE

Please indicate your degree of liking of each of the soft drinks on the following list by checking the appropriate position on the scale.

	DISLIKE A LOT	DISLIKE	LIKE	LIKE A LOT
Coke	____	____	____	____
Dr Pepper	____	____	____	____
Mountain Dew	____	____	____	____
Pepsi	____	____	____	____
Seven Up	____	____	____	____
Sprite	____	____	____	____

RATIO SCALE

Please divide 100 points among each of the following soft drinks according to your degree of liking for each.

_____ Coke
_____ Dr Pepper
_____ Mountain Dew
_____ Pepsi
_____ Seven Up
_____ Sprite
100

in nature. Thus, it is critical to know something about the attribute itself before we assign numbers to it using some measurement procedure. For instance, there are few psychological constructs that can reasonably be assumed to have a natural or absolute zero.

> For example, what would an absolute zero of intelligence be? Or what is the absolute zero of attitude toward the Republican Party? There can be neutrality of feeling, and the neutral position is often used as the zero point on the scale, but it does not represent an absolute lack of the attitude.[4]

The problem is no less real in marketing. Many of our constructs, borrowed from psychology and sociology, possess no more than interval measurement and some even less. We have to be very careful in conceptualizing the construct or characteristic so as not to delude ourselves or mislead others with our measures and (more important) *with our interpretation of those measures.*

Further, the procedure used in constructing the scale determines the type of scale actually generated. The more powerful scales allow stronger comparisons and conclusions to be made. Thus, we can make certain types of comparisons that allow particular conclusions when measurement is on a ratio scale, for example, that we cannot make when measurement is on an interval, ordinal, or nominal scale. There is a great temptation to *assume* that our measures have the properties of the ratio or at least the interval scale. Whether they do in fact is another question, and the simple condition that the attributes of the objects have been assigned numbers should not delude us. Rather, we should critically ask: What is the basic nature of the attribute? Have we captured this basic nature by our measurement procedure?

Moreover, while ratio scales allow stronger comparisons, they are also more demanding on subjects. For example, Figure 13.1 uses the issue of a respondent's preferences for six different soft drinks to illustrate how questions about this issue might be framed to secure reactions on a nominal, an ordinal, an interval, and a ratio scale. Readers are encouraged to complete the exercise in light of their own preferences. Did you find it more difficult to complete the "more powerful" scales at the bottom of the figure than the nominal scale at the top? Thus, while we might like to capture a respondent's reaction on a ratio scale, there is often a question as to whether our measurement procedure will allow it.

Introduction to Psychological Measurement

Constitutive (conceptual) definition
A definition in which a given construct is defined in terms of other constructs in the set, sometimes in the form of an equation that expresses the relationship among them.

Operational definition
A definition of a construct that describes the operations to be carried out in order for the construct to be measured empirically.

A problem that marketers have in common with other scientists is how to go about measuring the variables that interest them. For example, marketers are well aware of the fact that consumers' spending can be affected by their general feelings as to "how good things are." But how do you measure this general affective state? *American Demographics* considered productivity and technology, leisure, consumer attitudes, social and physical environment, income, and employment opportunities in developing its "Well-Being Index," which it uses in comparing areas and preparing forecasts.[5]

The essence of the measurement problem is presented in Figure 13.2. The basic researcher or scientist uses theories in an attempt to explain phenomena. These theories or models consist of constructs (denoted by the circles with *C*'s in them), linkages among and between the constructs (single lines connecting the *C*'s), and data that connect the constructs with the empirical world (double lines). The single lines represent **conceptual** or **constitutive definitions,** in that a given construct is defined in terms of other constructs in the set. The definition may take the form of an equation that precisely expresses the interrelationship of the construct to the other constructs, such as the equation in mechanics that suggests that force equals mass times acceleration. Alternatively, the relationship may be only imprecisely stated, which is typically the case in the social sciences.

The double lines represent operational definitions. An **operational definition** describes how the construct is to be measured. It specifies the activities that the researcher

FIGURE 13.2   **Schematic Diagram Illustrating the Structure of Science and the Problem of Measurement**

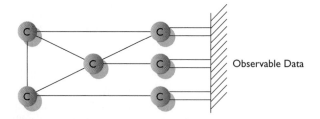

Observable Data

must complete in order to assign a value to the construct (e.g., sum the scores on the ten individual statements to generate a total score). In essence, the operational definition tells the investigator what to do and in what manner to measure the concept. Exhibit 13.2, for example, shows how consumer sentiment toward marketing was assessed in one large study using Market Facts' mail panel by measuring respondents' reactions to product quality, product prices, advertising, and retailing and personal selling. Conceptual definitions logically precede operational definitions and guide their development, for we must specify what a construct is before we can develop rules for assessing its magnitude.

The role of scientific inquiry is to establish the relationships that exist among the constructs of a model. It is necessary that some of the constructs be related to observable data if scientists are to accomplish their task. Otherwise, the model will be circular, with given unobservable constructs being defined in terms of other unobservable constructs. Since a circular model cannot be supported or refuted by empirical data, it is not legitimately considered a theory. Rather, a theory or system of explanation rests upon the condition that at least some of the constructs can be operationalized sufficiently so as to allow their measurement. Recall that measurement is defined as "rules for assigning numbers to objects to represent quantities of attributes." The rigor with which these rules are defined and the skill with which they are implemented determine whether the construct has been captured by the measure.

EXHIBIT 13.2	Illustration of Operational Definitions

Concept	Measurement[a]
	Sum of responses to the following items, each measured on a five-point disagree–agree scale.
Product Quality	The quality of most products I buy today is as good as can be expected. I am satisfied with most of the products I buy. Most products I buy wear out too quickly. (R) Products are not made as well as they used to be. (R) Too many of the products I buy are defective in some way. (R) The companies that make products I buy don't care enough about how well they perform. (R) The quality of products I buy has consistently improved over the years.
Price of Products	Most products I buy are overpriced. (R) Business could charge lower prices and still be profitable. (R) Most prices are reasonable considering the high cost of doing business. Competition between companies keeps prices reasonable. Companies are unjustified in charging the prices they charge. Most prices are fair. In general, I am satisfied with the prices I pay.
Advertising for Products	Most advertising provides consumers with essential information. Most advertising is very annoying. (R) Most advertising makes false claims. (R) If most advertising were eliminated, consumers would be better off. (R) I enjoy most ads. Advertising should be more closely regulated. Most advertising is intended to deceive rather than to inform consumers. (R)
Retailing or Selling	Most retail stores serve their customers well. Because of the way retailers treat me, most of my shopping is unpleasant. (R) I find most retail salespeople to be very helpful. Most retail stores provide an adequate selection of merchandise. In general, most middlemen make excessive profits. (R) When I need assistance in a store, I am usually *not* able to get it. (R) Most retailers provide adequate service.

[a]An (R) indicates that scoring of the item needs to be reversed so that higher scores indicate more positive attitudes.
Source: Developed from the information in John F. Gaski and Michael J. Etzel, "The Index of Consumer Sentiment Toward Marketing," *Journal of Marketing* 50 (July 1986), pp. 71–81. American Marketing Association.

You would undoubtedly scoff at the following measurement procedure: John has blue eyes and Bill has brown eyes; therefore, John is taller than Bill. You might reply that the color of a person's eyes has nothing to do with the person's height and, further, that if you wanted to see who was taller, the best procedure would be to measure them with a yardstick or to stand them side by side and compare their heights. You would be right on both counts. If I measured both John and Bill by asking them how tall they were, you would have probably voiced less objection to my procedure—unless John said he was taller while your observation of the two men showed that Bill was definitely the taller.

Now the interesting thing about most psychological constructs is that we cannot rely on visual comparisons to either confirm or refute a measure. We cannot see an attitude, a personality characteristic, a person's knowledge about or awareness of a particular product, or other psychological characteristics such as intelligence, mental anxiety, or whatever. These characteristics are all part of the consumer's black box. Their magnitude must be inferred from our measurements. Since we cannot resort to a visual check on the accuracy of our measures, we must rely on evaluating the procedures we used to determine the measure. Eye color is certainly not height, but can we capture sales representatives' satisfaction with their job if we ask them directly how satisfied they are? Probably not, for reasons that will become obvious as we continue our discussion.

Note that the problem of measuring the constructs is not unique to the researcher interested in scientific explanation. The practitioner shares this concern. A manufacturer, for example, interested in assessing customer reactions to a new product needs to know that the research is actually measuring consumers' attitudes toward the new product and that the accuracy of the data is not being influenced by the interviewers asking the questions or by one of the many other factors with which research must contend. The ability to make these assessments relies heavily on an understanding of measurement, measurement error, and the concepts of reliability and validity. Understanding these concepts is the task to which we now turn.

Variations in Measured Scares

You will recall that when we engage in measurement we are measuring the attributes of objects, not necessarily the objects themselves. Most measurement tasks present problems, but psychological measurement is particularly difficult at times since it usually involves a complex situation in which there are a great many factors that affect the attribute being measured. In addition, the measurement process itself may influence the results. For example, assume that certain tobacco companies are interested in measuring people's attitudes toward smoking in public places such as restaurants, office buildings, and medical waiting areas. An attitude scale to measure these feelings has been administered to a sample of respondents. A high score (maximum: 100) means that the respondent has a strong objection to smoking in public areas, while a low score (minimum: 25) indicates the opposite. If Mary scored 75 and Jane scored 40, we might conclude that Mary has a much more negative attitude toward smoking in public places than does Jane. But the validity of that conclusion would depend on the quality of the measurement. Let us consider some of the possible causes for the difference in the two scores.[6]

1. *A true difference in the characteristic we are measuring.* In an ideal situation, the difference in scores would reflect true differences in the attitudes of Mary and Jane and nothing else. This situation will rarely, if ever, occur. More likely, the different scores will also reflect some of the intruding factors that follow.

2. *True differences in other relatively stable characteristics of the individual.* Not only does a person's position on an issue affect his or her score, but other characteristics can also be expected to have an effect. For example, Research Window 13.1 illustrates the impact culture has on people's response styles. Perhaps the difference between Mary's and Jane's scores is simply due to the greater willingness of Mary to express negative feelings. Jane, by contrast, follows the adage, "If you can't say something nice, don't say anything at all." Her cooperation in the study has been requested, so she responds, but not truthfully.

3. *Differences due to transient personal factors.* A person's mood, state of health, fatigue, and so on, may all affect his or her responses. Yet these factors are temporary and can vary. Thus, if Mary, a nonsmoker, has just returned from a long wait in her dentist's smoke-filled waiting room, her responses may be decidedly different than if she had been interviewed several days earlier.

4. *Differences due to situational factors.* The situation surrounding the measurement also can affect the score. Mary's score might be different if her husband were there while

the scale was being administered. Incidentally, this problem is the bane of researchers studying the decision-making process of married couples. When the husband is asked for the respective roles of husband and wife in purchasing a new automobile, for instance, one set of responses is secured; when the wife is asked, the responses are different; when the two are asked together, still a third set is obtained. Which is correct? It is hard to say, since the fact remains that the situation surrounding a measurement can affect the scores that are obtained.

5. *Differences due to variations in administration.* Much measurement in marketing involves the use of questionnaires administered by phone or in person. Since interviewers can vary in the way they ask questions, the responses also may vary as a function of the interviewer. The same interviewer may even handle two interviews differently enough to trigger a variance in recorded answers, although the respondents do not really differ on the characteristic.

6. *Differences due to the sampling of items.* As we attempt to measure any construct, we typically tap only a small number of the items relevant to the characteristic being measured. Thus, our attitude scale for the tobacco companies will contain only a sample of all the items or statements we could possibly have included. In fact, often we will not even know what all the relevant items are. If we added, deleted, or

---

Research Window 13.1 | **Impact of Culture on Response Styles**

One of the most important and dramatic ways culture impacts multicountry research is in the different ways people in various countries respond to survey questions and use questionnaire scales. In a carefully controlled experiment, Custom Research, Inc. (CRI) explored the use of different kinds of scales in new product research. The result: *We found extraordinary differences from country to country in the way respondents use common survey scales.* For example: Survey respondents in the Philippines and Italy are four times more likely than respondents in Hong Kong or Japan to use the "top box" of a buying intent scale.

And these differences are clearly the result of culture, not economic levels. Japan and the United States, two of the most affluent countries in the world, are dramatically different on these measures. These differences must be understood and taken into account in analyzing multi-country studies. In the CRI experiment across 18 countries, here are a few of the differences we found on use of the buying intent scale:

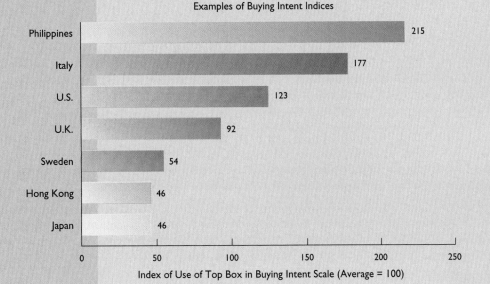

Examples of Buying Intent Indices

Country	Index
Philippines	215
Italy	177
U.S.	123
U.K.	92
Sweden	54
Hong Kong	46
Japan	46

Index of Use of Top Box in Buying Intent Scale (Average = 100)

Continued

Research Window 13.1   **Impact of Culture on Response Styles,** *continued*

But the effect of cultural differences on scale use is even more complex: Differences even exist within the same country from one scale to another.

That is illustrated by comparing the example below, showing use of the uniqueness scale, with the previous example on buying intent. Italians are less bullish in their use of the uniqueness scale, while respondents in the United Kingdom are more aggressive in using the uniqueness scale than in stating buying intent.

This means there is no single, simple way to adjust for country-to-country differences. It requires experience across countries and a thorough understanding of how each scale is used differently country by country.

Source: Jeffrey Pope, *How Cultural Differences Affect Multi-Country Research* (Minneapolis, Minn.: Custom Research Inc., 1991).

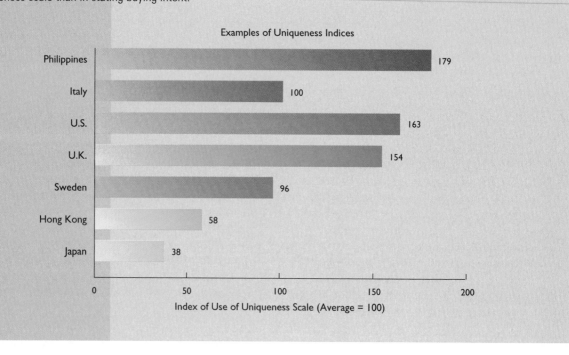

Examples of Uniqueness Indices

Country	Index
Philippines	179
Italy	100
U.S.	163
U.K.	154
Sweden	96
Hong Kong	58
Japan	38

Index of Use of Uniqueness Scale (Average = 100)

changed the wording of some items, we would undoubtedly change the outcome with respect to the scores of Mary and Jane. We must constantly be aware that our instrument reflects our interpretation of the construct and the items we use to measure it and that the resulting scores will vary according to the way in which items are chosen and the way those items are expressed.

Our final score is also influenced by the number of items presented. A man's height can serve as an indicator of his "size," but so can his weight, the size of his waistline, chest, and so on. We certainly could expect to have a better measure of a man's size if we included all these items. So it is with psychological measurements. Other things being equal, a one-item scale is a less adequate sample of the universe of items relevant to a characteristic than is a 25-item scale.

7. *Differences due to lack of clarity of the measuring instrument.* Sometimes a difference in response to a questionnaire or an item on a scale may represent differences in interpretation of an ambiguous or complex question rather than any fundamental differences in the characteristic one is attempting to measure. We saw in the last chapter how even simple words can be open to misinterpretation. In measuring complex concepts such as attitudes, the possibilities for misunderstanding increase

greatly. One of the researcher's main tasks is to generate items or questions that mean the same thing to all respondents, so that the observed differences in scores are not caused by differences in interpretation.

8. *Differences due to mechanical factors.* Mechanical factors can also affect obtained scores. Such things as a lack of space to record the responses, inadvertent check marks in the wrong box, and improper interpretation of a hard-to-read answer can all affect the scores that are assigned.

Classification and Assessment of Error

Systematic error
Error in measurement that is also known as constant error since it affects the measurement in a systematic way.

The ideal in any scale is to generate a score that reflects true differences in the characteristic one is attempting to measure, without interference from irrelevant factors. What we may in fact obtain is often something else. One type of error that may appear in our scores is **systematic error,** which is also called **constant error** since it affects the measurement in a constant way. One example would be the measurement of a man's height with a poorly calibrated wooden yardstick. Another example involves the federal government's collection of data about economic activity. The Department of Commerce routinely measures annual domestic growth by tallying the amount of goods and services sold in the United States, finding the difference from the previous year, and subtracting the amount contributed by inflation. However, until recently, the government did not include Internet commerce in its sales data. For instance, it would have counted Dell Computer's sales to retailers but not its on-line sales, thus understating each year's economic activity.[7]

Random error
Error in measurement due to the transient aspects of the person or measurement situation and which affects the measurement in irregular ways.

Another type of error, **random error,** is not constant but is instead due to transient aspects of the person or measurement situation, and which affects the measurement in irregular ways. A random error is present when we repeat a measurement on an individual or group of individuals and do not get the same scores as the first time we did the measurement, even though the characteristic being measured has not changed. For instance, if, unbeknownst to the researcher, a man who was measured once changes his shoes before being measured again, the two measures may not agree even though the man's actual height has not changed.

Validity
The extent to which differences in scores on a measuring instrument reflect true differences among individuals, groups, or situations in the characteristic that it seeks to measure, or true differences in the same individual, group, or situation from one occasion to another, rather than constant or random errors.

The distinction between systematic error and random error is critical because of the way the **validity,** or correctness, of a measure is assessed. Any scale or other measurement instrument that accurately measures what it was intended to measure is said to have validity. The validity of a measuring instrument is defined as "the extent to which differences in scores on it reflect true differences among individuals on the characteristic we seek to measure, rather than constant or random errors."[8] To accomplish this is a very difficult task. It is not accomplished by simply making up a set of questions or statements to measure a person's attitude toward smoking in public places, for example. The researcher must take the necessary steps to ensure the questionnaire does actually measure a person's attitude on this subject. This is never established unequivocally, but is always inferred. There are two types of inferences we make as we try to establish the validity of an instrument: (1) direct assessment of validity and (2) indirect assessment using reliability.[9]

Direct Assessment of Validity

There are three types of direct assessment techniques we can use to infer the validity of a measure. We can look for evidence of its predictive validity, content validity, and construct validity.

Predictive validity
The usefulness of the measuring instrument as a predictor of some other characteristic or behavior of the individual; it is sometimes called *criterion-related validity.*

Predictive Validity How well the measure actually predicts the criterion, whether it be a characteristic or specific behavior of the individual, is its **predictive validity.** An example would be the Graduate Management Admissions Test. The fact that this test is required by most of the major schools of business attests to its predictive validity; it has proved useful in predicting how well a student with a particular score on the exam will do in an accredited M.B.A. program. The test score is used to predict the criterion of performance. An attitude-scale example might be to use scores that sales representatives achieve on a measuring instrument designed to assess their job satisfaction in predicting their likelihood of quitting. Both of these examples illustrate *predictive validity*—in the true sense of the word—that is, the use of the score to predict some future occurrence.

However, there is another type of predictive validity known as **concurrent validity,** which is concerned with the relationship between the predictor variable and the criterion variable when both are assessed at the same point in time. For example, the common tuberculin tine test, which is a routine part of many physical exams, is not meant to predict whether a person is apt to contract tuberculosis at some point in the future, but whether the person has tuberculosis now.

Concurrent validity

The correlation between the predictor variable and the criterion variable when both are assessed at the same point in time.

Predictive validity is determined strictly by the correlation between the measuring instrument and the characteristic or behavior being measured. If the correlation is high, the measure is said to have predictive validity. "Thus if it were found that accuracy in horseshoe pitching correlated highly with success in college, horseshoe pitching would be a valid measure for predicting success in college."[10] This is not meant to imply that sound theory and common sense are not useful in selecting predictor instruments for investigation, but after the investigations are done, the entire proof of the pudding is in the correlations.

Predictive validity is relatively easy to assess. It requires, to be sure, a reasonably valid way of measuring the criterion with which the scores on the measuring instrument are to be compared. Given that such scores are available, though (for example, the grades the student actually achieves in an M.B.A. program or a tally of how many sales representatives actually quit), all that the researcher needs to do is to establish the degree of relationship, usually in the form of some kind of correlation coefficient, between the scores on the measuring instrument and the criterion variable. While easy to assess, predictive validity is rarely the most important kind of validity. We are often concerned with "what the measure in fact measures" rather than simply whether it predicts accurately or not.

Content Validity If the measurement instrument adequately covers the most important aspects of the construct that is being measured, it has **content validity**. Consider, for example, the characteristic of "spelling ability," and suppose that the following list of words was used to assess an individual's spelling ability: *catcher, shortstop, foul, strike, walk, pitcher.* Now, you would probably take issue with this spelling test. Further, the basis for your objection probably would be the fact that all the words relate to the sport of baseball. Therefore, you could argue that an individual who is basically a very poor speller could do well on this test simply because he or she is a baseball fan. You would be right, of course. A person with a good basic ability for spelling but little interest in baseball might, in fact, do worse on this spelling test than one with less native ability but a good deal more interest in baseball. The test could be said to lack content validity, since it does not properly sample the range of all possible words that could be used but is instead very selective in its emphasis.

Content validity

The adequacy with which the domain of the characteristic is captured by the measure; it is sometimes called *face validity.*

Theoretically, to capture a person's spelling ability (in English) most accurately, we would have to administer a test that includes all the words in the English language. The person who spelled the greatest number of these words correctly would be said to have the most spelling ability. This is an unrealistic procedure. It would take much of a person's lifetime to complete. We therefore resort to sampling the range of the characteristic by constructing spelling tests that consist of samples of all the possible words that could be used. Different samples of items can produce different comparative performances by individuals. We need to recognize that whether we have assessed the true characteristic depends on how well we have sampled the range of the characteristic. This is true not only for spelling ability, but also holds for psychological characteristics.

How can we ensure that our measure will possess content validity? We can never guarantee it, because it is partly a matter of judgment. We may feel quite comfortable with the items included in a measure, for example, while a critic may argue that we have failed to sample from some relevant aspect of the characteristic. While we can never guarantee the content validity of a measure, we can minimize the objections of the critics. The key to content validity lies in the *procedures* that are used to develop the instrument.

One way to define an appropriate domain, for example, is to search the literature and see how other researchers have defined the domain. The next step is to formulate a large number of items that broadly represent the range of attitudes that could be related to the topic in question. At this stage, the researcher may wish to include a wide variety of items with slightly different shades of meaning, since this original list will be narrowed down to produce the final instrument.

The collection of items must be large, so that after refinement the measure still contains enough items to adequately sample the entire range of the variable. In the example cited previously, a measure of a sales representative's job satisfaction would need to include items about each of the components of the job (duties, fellow workers, top management, sales supervisor, customers, pay, and promotion opportunities) if it is to be content-valid.

Construct validity

Assessment of how well the instrument captures the construct, concept, or trait it is supposed to be measuring.

Construct Validity The measurement of constructs is a vital task, and **construct validity** is the most difficult type of validity to establish. Not only must the instrument be internally consistent, but it must also measure what it was intended to measure. That is, each item in the instrument must reflect the construct and must also show a correlation with other items in the instrument.

Thus, a measuring instrument designed to measure attitude would be said to have construct validity if it indeed measured the attitude in question and not some other underlying characteristic of the individual that affects his or her score. Construct validity lies at the very heart of scientific progress. Scientists need constructs with which to communicate. So do you and I. In marketing we speak of people's socioeconomic class, their personality, their attitudes, and so on, because these are all constructs for explaining marketing behavior. And while vital, they also are unobservable. We can observe behavior related to these constructs but not the constructs themselves. Rather, we try to operationally define a construct in terms of things we can observe.

When we agree on the operational definition, precision in communication is advanced. Instead of saying that what is measured by these 75 items is the person's brand loyalty, we can speak of the notion of brand loyalty.

While the measurement of constructs is vital to scientific progress, construct validity is the most difficult type of validity to establish.[11] Research Window 13.2, for example, discusses the problems encountered historically when measuring the construct "discretionary income" and a proposed new measure. We need to ensure, through the plans and procedures used in constructing the instrument, that we have adequately sampled the domain of the construct and that there is internal consistency among the items of the domain.

Once researchers have specified the domain of the construct, generated a set of items relevant to the breadth of the domain, refined the items, and ensured that the remaining items are internally consistent, the final step is to see how well the measure relates to measures of other constructs to which the construct in question is theoretically related. Does it behave as expected? Does it fit the theory or model relating this construct to other constructs?

For example, consider our earlier example relating job satisfaction to job turnover among sales representatives. Suppose we had developed a measure to assess a sales representative's job satisfaction. The construct validity of the measure could be assessed by determining if there is indeed a relationship between job-satisfaction scores and company turnover. Those companies in which the scores are low (indicating less job satisfaction) should experience more turnover than those with high scores. If they do not, one would question the construct validity of the job-satisfaction measure. In other words, the construct validity of a measure is assessed by whether the measure confirms or denies the hypotheses predicted from the theory based on the constructs.

The problem, of course, is that the failure of the hypothesized relationship to hold true for the phenomenon being observed may be due either to a lack of construct validity or

Research Window 13.2   **Measuring the Construct "Discretionary Income"**

Along with sex and age, family income is among the most often collected and most effective predictors of consumer behavior. Virtually all marketing research instruments include an income question, and the answers to that question are used in many ways. Income describes consumers, segments markets, predicts or explains purchases, and provides reasons for purchasing pattern changes.

Although family income is a useful predictor, it is far from complete. Consumers with low incomes sometimes behave like consumers with high incomes and vice versa. Among the many reasons for such contradictions is that consumers differ greatly in their financial obligations and in their ability to manage the funds they have. When two families have exactly the same income, the amount remaining after the essentials have been purchased may leave one family relatively well off and the other relatively poor. Families with more "discretionary" income have more opportunity to purchase extras or luxury and convenience items, or to put the money away for future use. Knowledge of discretionary income, therefore, would be of considerable value in marketing research.

Despite its obvious benefits, the discretionary income concept has not been used much over the years. One author ascribed this neglect to the fact that consumers cannot determine and report their discretionary income objectively and precisely. Other scholars have cited the generally ambiguous ways in which consumers employ economic ideas. They have been especially bothered by the fact that what is "discretionary" and what is "essential" are to some degree a matter of individual taste.

One way to avoid such problems is to use a psychological approach in determining discretionary income. Instead of trying to get consumers to provide hard, objective economic data, the psychological approach focuses on an entirely subjective variable: how people think about what they have.

Our measure of subjective discretionary income (SDI) was created from three items already present on the DDB Needham advertising agency Life-style Questionnaire:

1. No matter how fast our income goes up, we never seem to get ahead.

2. We have more to spend on extras than most of our neighbors do.

3. Our family income is high enough to satisfy nearly all our important desires.

The statements are answered on a 6-point scale with definitely disagree (1) and definitely agree (6) as the anchor points. When the responses to the three items are summed, with the first item being reverse coded, the result is a score with a range from 3 to 18. Respondents who score high on this scale are indicating that they have enough money to buy what they think they need and then some. Respondents who score low are saying that they have a tough time simply making ends meet.

Each item taps an important aspect of the SDI construct. The first item measures an aspect of SDI very close to perceived economic well-being and also probably related closely to ability to manage money. The second item speaks of "extras" in relation to neighbors, an important reference group. The third item pertains to feelings of having enough income for things that are considered to be important but are still termed "desires." This item gets at the very essence of what "discretionary" means.

Source: Thomas C. O'Guinn and William D. Wells, "Subjective Discretionary Income," *Marketing Research: A Magazine of Management and Applications* 1 (March 1989), pp. 32–41. American Marketing Association. For estimates of the amount of discretionary income U.S. households have, see Cheryl Russell and Margaret Ambry, *The Official Guide to American Incomes* (Ithaca, N.Y.: New Strategist Publications & Consulting, 1993).

to incorrect theory. We often try to establish the construct validity of a measure, therefore, by relating it to a number of other constructs rather than only one. We also try to use those theories and hypotheses that have been tested by others and found to be sound.

Convergent validity
Confirmation of the existence of a construct determined by the correlations exhibited by independent measures of the construct.

If the trait or construct exists, it also should be measurable by more than one method. These methods should be independent insofar as possible. If they are all measuring the same construct, though, the measures should have a high level of correlation. This provides evidence of **convergent validity,** which is defined as "the confirmation of a relationship by independent measurement procedures." Another evidence of construct

Discriminant validity
Criterion imposed on a measure of a construct requiring that it not correlate too highly with measures from which it is supposed to differ.

Reliability
Similarity of results provided by independent but comparable measures of the same object, trait, or construct.

validity is **discriminant validity,** which requires that a measure not correlate too highly with measures from which it is supposed to differ.[12] Correlations that are too high suggest that the measure is not actually capturing a distinct or isolated trait.

Indirect Assessment via Reliability

Reliability refers to the ability to obtain similar results by measuring an object, trait, or construct with independent but comparable measures. If we gave a group of people two different measures of intelligence, and the two sets of scores from the two measures correlated highly with each other, we would say that the measures are reliable in that each is able to replicate the scores of the other.

Evaluating the reliability of any measuring instrument consists of determining how much of the variation in scores is due to inconsistencies in measurement.[13] The reliability of the instrument should be established before it is used for a substantive study and not after.

Before discussing how evidence of reliability is obtained, we need to make a few points. If a measure is reliable, it is not influenced by transitory factors. However, a measure could be reliable but not necessarily valid. For example, the Food Marketing Institute (FMI) annually conducts a survey of its member companies to estimate the causes of merchandise loss by supermarkets. It measures the extent of shoplifting by asking the stores how many shoplifters they caught and how much the merchandise they recovered was worth. Assuming stores keep records of such incidents, the data may be quite reliable. However, this method may not be a valid measure of the extent of shoplifting, because it does not count the number of shoplifters who were not caught or the value of merchandise not recovered. In fact, FMI's Charles Miller, vice president of loss prevention services, says organized shoplifters (called "boosters" in the industry) typically take over 60 items at a time, specialize in relatively high-ticket items like razors and film, and are rarely caught.[14] Some of this loss could be detected with scanner data to measure changes in inventory levels—but the use of scanner data suffers from a validity problem of its own: The data can show that inventory has disappeared but not that shoplifting was the cause of the disappearance.

Figure 13.3 illustrates the concept pictorially. The old rifle is unreliable. The new rifle is relatively reliable, but its sights are set incorrectly in the center diagram. The right-hand diagram shows the new rifle with its sights set correctly. Only in the right-hand diagram could a user of any of the rifles be expected to hit the center of the target with regularity.

Although a measure that is reliable may or may not be valid, if it is not reliable, it is surely not valid. Conversely, if it is valid, it is surely reliable. A valid measure of height will

FIGURE 13.3 **Illustration of Difference Between Random and Systematic Error**

Old Rifle

New Rifle That Is
Sighted in Poorly

New Rifle That Is
Sighted in Accurately

be reliable, since it is actually measuring the trait in question. Reliability thus provides only negative evidence; it can prove the lack of validity but not the presence of it. Reliability is more easily determined than validity, however, so there has been a greater emphasis on it historically for inferring the quality of measures.

Stability

Evidence of the reliability of a measure; determined by measuring the same objects or individuals at two different points in time and then correlating the scores; also known as *test-retest reliability assessment.*

Stability One of the more popular ways of establishing the reliability of a measure is to measure the same objects or individuals at two different points in time and to correlate the obtained scores. Assuming that the objects or individuals have not changed in the interim, the two scores should correlate perfectly. To the extent that they do not, random disturbances were operating in either one or both of the test situations to produce random error in the measurement. The procedure is known as *test-retest reliablity assessment*, and it establishes a measure's **stability.**

One of the critical decisions the researcher must face in determining the stability of a measure is how long to wait between successive administrations of the instrument. Suppose the researcher's instrument is an attitude scale. If the researcher waits too long, the person's attitude may change, thus producing a low correlation between the two scores. On the other hand, a short wait will likely produce test bias—people may remember how they responded the first time and be more consistent in their responses than is warranted by their attitudes.

To handle this problem, many researchers will use alternative forms for the two administrations. Instead of putting all the items in one form, the researcher generates two instruments that are as identical as possible in content. That is, each form should contain items from the same domains, and each domain of content should receive approximately the same emphasis in each form. Ideally, there would be a one-to-one correspondence between items on each of the two forms so that the means and standard deviations of the two forms would be identical and the intercorrelations among the items would be the same in both versions.[15] While it is next to impossible to achieve the ideal, it is possible to construct forms that are roughly parallel, and parallel forms can be correlated across time to measure stability. The recommended time interval between administrations is two weeks.[16]

Equivalence

Evidence of the reliability of a measure; determined in both single instruments and measurement situations. When applied to instruments, the equivalence measure of reliability is the internal consistency or internal homogeneity of the set of items forming the scale; when applied to measurement situations, the equivalence measure of reliability focuses on whether different observers or different instruments used to measure the same individuals or objects at the same point in time yield consistent results.

Equivalence In an attitude scale, every item is theoretically acting as a measure of the attitude, and a subject's score on one part of the scale should correlate with his or her score on another part of the scale. The **equivalence** measure of reliability focuses on the internal consistency of the set of items forming the scale.

The earliest measure of the internal consistency of a set of items was the *split-half reliability* of the scale. In assessing split-half reliability, the total set of items is divided into two equivalent halves; the total scores for the two halves are correlated; and this is taken as the measure of reliability of the instrument. Sometimes the division of items is made randomly, while at other times the even items are assumed to form one half and the odd the other half of the instrument. The total score on the even items is then correlated with the total score obtained from the odd items.

Pointed criticism has been directed at split-half reliability as the measure of the internal consistency of a scale. The criticism focuses on the necessarily arbitrary division of the items into equivalent halves. Each of the many possible divisions can produce different correlations between the two halves or different reliabilities. Which division is correct or, alternatively, what is then the reliability of the instrument? For example, a ten-item scale has 126 possible splits or 126 possible reliability coefficients.

A more appropriate way to assess the internal homogeneity of a set of items is to look at all of the items simultaneously, using coefficient alpha. One reason is that coefficient alpha has a direct relationship to the most accepted and conceptually appealing measurement model, the *domain sampling model*. The domain sampling model holds that the purpose of any particular measurement is to estimate the score that would be obtained if *all* the items in the domain were used. The score that any subject would obtain over the whole sample domain is the person's true score, X_T.

In practice, one typically does not use all of the items that could be used, but only a sample of them. To the extent that the sample of items correlates with true scores, it is good. According to the domain sampling model, then, a primary source of measurement error is the inadequate sampling of the domain of relevant items.

Basic to the domain sampling model is the concept of a very large correlation matrix showing all correlations among the items in the domain. No single item is likely to provide a perfect representation of the concept, just as no single word can be used to test for difference in subjects' spelling abilities and no single question can measure a person's intelligence.

The average correlation among the items in this large matrix, $\bar{r}$, indicates the extent to which some common core is present in the items. The dispersion of correlations about the average indicates the extent to which items vary in sharing the common core. The key assumption in the domain sampling model is that all items, *if they belong to the domain of the concept,* have an equal amount of common core. This statement implies that the average correlation in each column of the hypothetical matrix is the same, and in turn equals the average correlation in the whole matrix. That is, if all the items in a measure are drawn from the domain of a single construct, responses to those items should be highly intercorrelated. Low inter-item correlations, in contrast, indicate that some items are not drawn from the appropriate domain and are producing error and unreliability.

Coefficient alpha provides a summary measure of the intercorrelations that exist among a set of items. Alpha is calculated as[17]

$$\alpha = \left(\frac{k}{k-1} \right) \left(1 - \frac{\sum_{i=1}^{k} \sigma_i^2}{\sigma_t^2} \right)$$

where k = number of items in the scale,
σ_i^2 = variance of scores on item i across subjects, and
σ_t^2 = variance of total scores across subjects where the total score for each respondent represents the sum of the individual item scores.

Coefficient alpha routinely should be calculated to assess the quality of measure. It is pregnant with meaning because the *square root* of coefficient alpha is the *estimated correlation of the k-item test with errorless true scores.*

If alpha is low, what should the analyst do? If the item pool is sufficiently large, this outcome suggests that some items do not share equally in the common core and possibly should be eliminated. The easiest way to find them is to calculate the correlation of each item with the total score and to plot these correlations by decreasing order of magnitude. Items with correlations near zero would be eliminated. Further, items that produce a substantial or sudden drop in the item-to-total correlations would also be considered candidates for deletion.

If the construct had, say, five identifiable dimensions or components, coefficient alpha would be calculated for each dimension. The item-to-total correlations used to delete items would also be based on the items in the component and the total score for that dimension.

The preceding discussion deals with the equivalence measure of reliability when applied to a single instrument. An alternate equivalence measure is used when different observers or different instruments measure the same individuals or objects at the same point in time. Do these methods produce consistent results? Are they equivalent as measured by the correlations among the total scores? An example would be a beauty contest. Do the judges, using the established criteria of beauty, talent, poise, and so on, rank the women in the same order in terms of winner, first runner-up, second runner-up, and so on? The reliability of the measure is greater to the extent that the judges agree. Figure 13.4, for example, depicts a situation in which the judgments of two different observers do not agree. This type of equivalence is the basis of convergent validation when the measures are independent.[18]

Source: Reprinted with special permission of King Features Syndicate.

Developing Measures

For a beginning researcher, it is easy to get confused over the issue of how one goes about developing measures of marketing constructs. How does one contend with the basic issues of reliability and validity, and how does one make the choices among the various coefficients that can be computed? Figure 13.5 diagrams a sequence of steps that can be followed to develop valid measures of marketing constructs.[19]

Step 1 in the process involves specifying the domain of the construct that is to be measured. Researchers need to be careful in specifying what is included in the domain of the construct and what is excluded. Consider measuring customer satisfaction with a new space heater the family recently purchased. What attributes of the product and the purchase should be measured to assess accurately the family's satisfaction? Certainly one would want to be reasonably exhaustive in the list of product features to be included, incorporating such facets as cost, durability, quality, operating performance, and aesthetic features. But what about the purchaser's reaction to the sales assistance received? What about the family members' reactions to subsequent advertising for a competitor's product offering the same features at lower cost? Or what about the family's reactions to news of some negative environmental effects of using the product? To detail which of these factors should be included or how customer satisfaction should be operationalized is beyond the scope of this book. But, obviously, researchers need to be very careful in specifying what is to be included in the domain of the construct being measured and what is to be excluded.

Step 2 in the process is to generate items that capture the domain as specified. Those techniques that are typically productive in exploratory research, including literature searches, experience surveys, and insight-stimulating examples, are generally productive here. The literature should indicate how the variable has been defined previously and how many dimensions or components it has. The search for ways to measure customer satisfaction would include product brochures, articles in trade magazines and newspapers, or results of product tests such as those published by *Consumer Reports*. The experience survey might include discussions with people in the product group responsible for the product, sales representatives, dealers, persons in marketing research, consumers, and outsiders who have a special expertise in heating equipment. The insight-stimulating examples could involve a comparison of competitors' products or a detailed examination of some particularly vehement complaints in unsolicited letters about the performance of the product. Examples that reveal sharp contrasts or having striking features would be most productive. Focus groups also could be used to advantage at the item-generation stage.

FIGURE 13.5   **Suggested Procedure for Developing Measures**

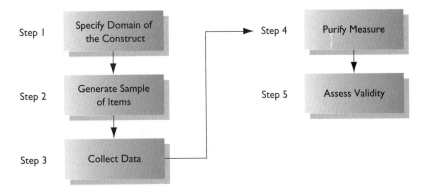

Source: Adapted from the procedure suggested by Gilbert A. Churchill, Jr., "A Paradigm for Developing Better Measures of Marketing Constructs," *Journal of Marketing Research* 16 (February 1979), p. 66. American Marketing Association.

Another potential source of items involves having respondents focus on the interactions that were crucial or critical in shaping their reactions to the phenomenon. For example, the following questions were asked of all respondents in an attempt to identify the features of service encounters that make them satisfactory or unsatisfactory.[20]

- Think of a time when, as a customer, you had a particularly *satisfying (dissatisfying)* interaction with an employee of an airline, hotel, or restaurant.

- When did the incident happen?

- What specific circumstances led up to this situation?

- Exactly what did the employee say or do?

- What resulted that made you feel the interaction was *satisfying (dissatisfying)?*

Ethical Dilemma 13.2

Susan Black has been given the assignment of measuring the quality of service provided by her employer, Valley Bank. She welcomes the assignment for several reasons. One important reason is that she saw a scale for measuring a bank's image in a recent issue of a bank trade magazine. She plans to use the scale as is. That will take care of the measurement issues, leaving only the sampling issues (e.g., who to sample, how many, how, and so on) with which to grapple, thereby simplifying the task.

Before using a scale of this type, does Black have any responsibility to investigate its reliability and validity properties?

Can she simply assume that because the scale has been published it is good? What are the publisher's responsibilities in this regard?

What if Black has no formal training in measurement? What should she do?

Note the emphasis on having respondents describe a specific instance in which a good or poor service interaction occurred. A similar procedure could be used among a sample of purchasers of the space heater to generate items.

Step 3 involves collecting data about the concept from a relevant sample of the target population—for example, all those who have purchased a space heater within the last six months.

Step 4 uses the data collected in Step 3 to purify the original set of items. The purification involves eliminating items that seemed to create confusion among respondents and items that do not discriminate between subjects with fundamentally different positions on the construct. The fundamental criterion that is used to eliminate items is how each item goes together with the other items. If all the items in a measure are drawn from the domain of a single construct, responses to those items should be highly correlated. If they are not, that is an indication that some of the items are not drawn from the appropriate domain and are producing error and unreliability, and those items should be eliminated. Several of the equivalence reliability coefficients mentioned earlier can be used to make this assessment, as can other statistical techniques.[21]

Step 5 in the process involves determining the validity of the purified measure. This involves assessing primarily its convergent, discriminant, and construct validity, since its content validity will have largely been addressed in Steps 1 through 4. The assessment of its construct validity involves determining whether it behaves as expected, which in turn involves determining its predictive validity.

Back to the Case

"Cheer up, Todd," urged Ernie Henderson. "It's not the end of the world. It's not even the end of Teen Sport. We just have to make some changes, that's all."

"I can't believe it," replied Todd Whalen, shaking his head. "I know that Teen Sport's a winner. I simply can't believe these test market results. I think you just ran into so much trouble with the holidays that it screwed up all of the results."

"It's true, we did run into problems with the holidays. At that time of year the stores are so full of promotional items that people tend to be distracted from everyday products like deodorant. We also had a lower response rate on our phone interviews than we usually like to have. People are very tense and busy during the holidays and are much less likely to say yes when a phone interviewer asks them for 10 minutes of their time."

"Like I said," snapped Whalen, "the test results are suspect."

"I don't think so," said Henderson calmly. "Besides, the test market study has turned up another problem that's completely unrelated to the holidays."

"I don't want to hear it."

"Well, here it is anyway: I think we're going to have to dump all the Teen Sport we have on hand and reformulate. Remember how I pushed for an additional round of open-ended focus groups when we were testing for packaging preferences?"

"We just didn't have time," replied Whalen. "You yourself said that teenagers are fickle. We needed to get the product on the shelves before they changed their minds about what they liked."

"Well, the problem is that while we addressed the usual issues of smell, odor protection, packaging, and price in the initial round of focus groups, we never considered one variable that's going to turn out to be very important."

"What's that?" asked Whalen.

"Color."

"Color? All your studies showed that teenaged girls love hot, neon colors. I thought that making the deodorant shocking pink would be the perfect way to get the message across that Teen Sport wasn't their mother's deodorant. It ties in perfectly with the advertising campaign."

"Yes, but maybe teenaged girls love neon colors only for the package," replied Henderson. "There's a lot of environmental awareness among kids this age. Maybe the girls don't want to use a product that contains artificial colors. Besides, I think that the neon craze has already peaked. . . ."

Not only should researchers be careful to not let their own biases affect the instrument, but they also need to be careful to design attitude scales that measure the total potential domain of the construct being measured. Only if the total domain is covered can the instrument be said to provide content validity.

Summary

Learning Objective 1

Define the term measurement *as it is used in marketing research.*

Measurement consists of rules for assigning numbers to objects in such a way as to represent quantities of attributes.

Learning Objective 2

List the four types of scales that can be used to measure an attribute.

The four types of scales on which an attribute can be measured are nominal, ordinal, interval, and ratio scales.

Learning Objective 3

Explain the primary difference between a ratio scale and an interval scale.

In an interval scale, the zero point is established arbitrarily. The ratio scale possesses a natural, or absolute, zero—one for which there is universal agreement as to its location.

Learning Objective 4

Cite some of the factors that may cause differences in two measures of the same attribute.

Some of the factors that may cause differences in two measures of the same attribute are (1) true differences in the characteristic being measured, (2) true differences in other relatively stable characteristics of the individual that affect the score, (3) differences due to transient personal factors, (4) differences due to situational factors, (5) differences due to variations in administration, (6) differences due to the sampling of items, (7) differences due to lack of clarity of the measuring instrument, and (8) differences due to mechanical factors.

Learning Objective 5

Name the two types of error that may affect measurement scores and define each.

Two types of error may affect scores. The first type is systematic error, which affects the measurement in a constant way. The second type is random error, which is due to transient aspects of the person or measurement situation, and which affects the measurement in irregular ways.

Learning Objective 6

Explain the concept of validity as it relates to measuring instruments.

Any scale or other measurement instrument that actually measures what it was intended to measure is said to have validity. The validity of a measuring instrument is defined as "the extent to which differences in scores on it reflect true differences among individuals on the characteristic we seek to measure, rather than constant or random errors."

Learning Objective 7

Specify the two types of inferences a researcher makes in attempting to establish the validity of an instrument.

The two types of inferences we make as we try to establish the validity of an instrument are based on (1) direct assessment of its validity and (2) indirect assessment of its validity using reliability.

Learning Objective 8

Cite the three types of direct assessment techniques used to infer the validity of a measure.

The three types of validity that can be directly assessed in a measure are predictive validity, content validity, and construct validity.

Learning Objective 9

Outline the sequence of steps to follow in developing valid measures of marketing research.

The following sequence of steps is helpful in developing better measures of marketing constructs: (1) specify the domain of the construct, (2) generate a sample of items, (3) collect data, (4) purify the measure, and (5) assess validity.

Review Questions

1. What is measurement?

2. What are the scales of measurement? What comparisons among scores can be made with each?

3. What are the factors that may produce differences in the scores held by two individuals with respect to measurement of the same trait?

4. What is reliability? What information does it contribute to determining if a measure is accurate?

5. What are the various types of reliability?

6. What is validity?

7. What are the various types of validity?

Discussion Questions, Problems, and Projects

1. Identify the type of scale (nominal, ordinal, interval, ratio) being used in each of the following questions. Justify your answer.
   (a) **During which season of the year were you born?**
      _____ winter _____ spring _____ summer _____ fall
   (b) **What is your total household income?**_____
   (c) **Which are your three most preferred brands of cigarettes? Rank them from 1 to 3 according to your preference, with 1 as most preferred.**
      _____ Marlboro   _____ Salem
      _____ Kent   _____ Kool
      _____ Benson and Hedges   _____ Vantage

(d) **How much time do you spend on traveling to school every day?**
    _____ under 5 minutes   _____ 16–20 minutes
    _____ 5–10 minutes   _____ 30 minutes and over
    _____ 11–15 minutes

(e) **How satisfied are you with *Newsweek* magazine?**
    _____ very satisfied   _____ dissatisfied
    _____ satisfied   _____ very dissatisfied
    _____ neither satisfied nor dissatisfied

(f) **On an average, how many cigarettes do you smoke in a day?**
    _____ over 1 pack   _____ less than 1/2 pack
    _____ 1/2 to 1 pack

(g) **Which of the following courses have you taken?**
    _____ marketing research   _____ sales management
    _____ advertising management   _____ consumer behavior

(h) **What is the level of education for the head of household?**
    _____ some high school   _____ some college
    _____ high school graduate   _____ college graduate and/or graduate work

2. The analysis for each of the preceding questions follows. Is the analysis appropriate for the scale used?

    (a) About 50 percent of the sample was born in the fall, while 25 percent of the sample was born in the spring, and the remaining 25 percent was born in the winter. It can be concluded that the fall is twice as popular as the spring and the winter seasons.

    (b) The average income is $25,000. There are twice as many individuals with an income of less than $9,999 than individuals with an income of $40,000 and over.

    (c) Marlboro is the most preferred brand. The mean preference is 3.52.

    (d) The median time spent on traveling to school is 8.5 minutes. There are three times as many respondents traveling less than 5 minutes as respondents traveling 16–20 minutes.

    (e) The average satisfaction score is 4.5, which seems to indicate a high level of satisfaction with *Newsweek* magazine.

    (f) Ten percent of the respondents smoke less than one-half pack of cigarettes a day, while three times as many respondents smoke over one pack of cigarettes a day.

    (g) Sales management is the most frequently taken course, since the median is 3.2.

    (h) The responses indicate that 40 percent of the sample have some high school education, 25 percent of the sample are high school graduates, 20 percent have some college education, and 10 percent are college graduates. The mean education level is 2.6.

3. You have developed a questionnaire designed to measure attitudes toward a set of television ads for a new snack food product. The respondents, as a group, will view the ads on a television set and then complete the questionnaire. Due to logistical circumstances beyond your control, you must split your sample of respondents into three groups and collect data on three separate days. What steps might you take in an effort to minimize possible variance in scores caused by the three separate administrations?

4. Many areas of marketing research rely heavily on measures of psychological constructs. What characteristics inherent in these constructs make them so difficult to measure? What tools can the marketing researcher bring to bear when evaluating the "correctness" of his or her measure? In other words, what things can we do that allow us to state with some degree of confidence that we are indeed measuring the construct of interest?

5. Discuss the notion that a particular measure could be reliable and still not be valid. In your discussion, distinguish between reliability and validity.

6. Feather-Tote Luggage is a producer of cloth-covered luggage, one of the primary advantages of which is its light weight. The company distributes its luggage through major department stores, mail-order houses, clothing retailers, and other retail outlets

such as stationery stores, leather good stores, and so on. The company advertises rather heavily, but it also supplements this promotional effort with a large field staff of sales representatives, numbering around 400. The number of sales representatives varies, and one of the historical problems confronting Feather-Tote Luggage has been the large number of sales representatives' resignations. It is not unusual for 10 to 20 percent of the sales force to turn over every year. Since the cost of training a new sales representative is estimated at $5,000 to $10,000, not including the lost sales that might result because of a personnel switch, Mr. Harvey, the sales manager, is rightly concerned. He has been concerned for some time and therefore has been conducting exit interviews with each departing sales representative. On the basis of these interviews, he has formulated the opinion that the major reason for this high turnover is general sales representatives' dissatisfaction with company policies, promotional opportunities, and pay. But top management has not been sympathetic to Harvey's pleas regarding the changes needed in these areas of corporate policy. Rather, it has tended to counter Harvey's pleas with arguments that too much of what he is suggesting is based on his gut reactions and little hard data. Before it would be willing to change things, top management desires more systematic evidence that job satisfaction, in general, and these dimensions of job satisfaction, in particular, are the real reasons for the high turnover.

Describe the procedures you would employ in developing a measure by which the job satisfaction of Feather-Tote Luggage sales representatives could be assessed. Indicate the type of scale you would use and why, and detail the specific steps you would undertake to assure the validity and reliability of this measure.

Endnotes

1. Peter D. Bennett, ed., *Dictionary of Marketing Terms*, 2nd ed. (Chicago: American Marketing Association, 1995), p. 173.

2. Our classification follows that of Stanley S. Stevens, "Mathematics, Measurement and Psychophysics," in Stanley S. Stevens, ed., *Handbook of Experimental Psychology* (New York: John Wiley, 1951), the most accepted classification in the social sciences.

3. The zero point on the Fahrenheit scale was originally established by mixing equal weights of snow and salt.

4. Wendell R. Garner and C. D. Creelman, "Problems and Methods of Psychological Scaling," in Harry Helson and William Bevan, eds., *Contemporary Approaches to Psychology* (New York: Van Nostrand, 1967), p. 4.

5. Elia Kacapyr, "Money Isn't Everything," *American Demographics* 18 (July 1996), pp. 10–11; Elia Kacapyr, "The Well-Being Index," *American Demographics* 18 (February 1996), pp. 32–35, 43.

6. These differences are adapted from Claire Selltiz, Lawrence S. Wrightsman, and Stuart W. Cook, *Research Methods in Social Relations*, 3rd ed. (New York: Holt, Rinehart and Winston, 1976), pp. 164–168. See also Duane F. Alwin and David J. Jackson, "Measurement Models for Response Errors in Surveys: Issues and Applications," in Karl F. Schuessler, ed., *Sociological Methodology* 1980 (San Francisco: Jossey-Bass, 1979), pp. 69–119; Frank E. Saal, Ronald G. Downey, and Mary Anne Lakey, "Rating the Ratings: Assessing the Psychometric Quality of Ratings Data," *Psychological Bulletin* 88 (September 1980), pp. 413–428; Ellen J. Wentland and Kent W. Smith, *Survey Responses: An Evaluation of Their Validity* (San Diego, Calif.: Academic Press, 1993).

7. Tom Benemann, "Feds Announce Collection of Information on E-Commerce," *Forbes* (June 8, 1999, downloaded from the Forbes Web site, www.forbes.com, June 8, 1999).

8. Selltiz, Wrightsman, and Cook, *Research Methods*, p. 169.

9. For detailed discussion of the conceptual relationships that should exist among the various indicants of reliability and validity and an empirical assessment of the evidence, see J. Paul Peter and Gilbert A. Churchill, Jr., "The Relationship among Research Design Choices and Psychometric Properties of Rating Scales: A Meta-Analysis," *Journal of Marketing Research* 23 (February 1986), pp. 1–10. See also Mark S. Litwin, *How to Measure Survey Reliability and Validity* (Thousand Oaks, Calif.: Sage Publications, 1995).

10. Jum C. Nunnally and Ira H. Bernstein, *Psychometric Theory*, 3rd ed. (New York: McGraw-Hill, 1994), p. 95.

11. See Gilbert A. Churchill, Jr., "A Paradigm for Developing Better Measures of Marketing Constructs," *Journal of Marketing Research* 16 (February 1979), pp. 64–73, for a procedure that can be used to

construct scales having construct validity. See J. Paul Peter, "Construct Validity: A Review of Basic Issues and Marketing Practices," *Journal of Marketing Research* 18 (May 1981), pp. 133–145, for an in-depth discussion of the notion of construct validity. See also Robert DeVellis, *Scale Development: Theory and Applications* (Thousand Oaks, Calif.: Sage Publications, 1991).

12. One convenient way of establishing the convergent and discriminant validity of a measure is through the multitrait-multimethod matrix of Campbell and Fiske. See Donald T. Campbell and Donald W. Fiske, "Convergent and Discriminant Validation by the Multitrait-Multimethod Matrix," *Psychological Bulletin* 56 (1959), pp. 81–105. For an example of its use, see Ronald E. Goldsmith and Janelle Emmert, "Measuring Product Category Involvement: A Multitrait-Multimethod Study," *Journal of Business Research* 23 (December 1991), pp. 363–371.

13. See J. Paul Peter, "Reliability: A Review of Psychometric Basics and Recent Marketing Practices," *Journal of Marketing Research* 16 (February 1979), pp. 6–17, for a detailed treatment of the issue of reliability in measurement. See Gilbert A. Churchill, Jr., and J. Paul Peter, "Research Design Effects on the Reliability of Rating Scales: A Meta-Analysis," *Journal of Marketing Research* 21 (February 1984), pp. 360–375, for an empirical assessment of the factors that seem to affect the reliability of rating scales.

14. Food Marketing Institute (FMI), "Shoplifting Remains Top Challenge for the Supermarket Industry," news release (May 3, 1998, downloaded from the FMI Web site, www.fmi.org, September 28, 1999); Steve Weinstein, "Loss Leaders," *Progressive Grocer* (September 1998), pp. 57–65.

15. George W. Bohrnstedt, "Reliability and Validity Assessment in Attitude Measurement," in Gene F. Summers, ed., *Attitude Measurement* (Chicago: Rand McNally, 1970), p. 85.

16. Nunnally and Bernstein, *Psychometric Theory*, pp. 252–255, argue strongly against using straight test-retest reliability and in favor of alternate forms of reliability.

17. See Nunnally and Bernstein, *Psychometric Theory*, Chapters 6 and 7, pp. 209–292, for the rationale behind coefficient alpha and more detailed discussion of the formula for computing it. For discussion of its use in marketing and psychology, see Robert A. Peterson, "A Meta-Analysis of Cronbach's Coefficient Alpha," *Journal of Consumer Research* 21 (September 1994), pp. 381–391.

18. For a general discussion of the measurement of interjudge reliability, see William D. Perreault, Jr., and Laurence E. Leigh, "Reliability of Nominal Data Based on Qualitative Judgments," *Journal of Marketing Research* 26 (May 1989), pp. 135–148; Marie Adele Hughes and Dennis E. Garrett, "Intercoder Reliability Estimation Approaches in Marketing: A Generalizability Theory Framework for Quantitative Data," *Journal of Marketing Research* 27 (May 1990), pp. 185–195. See also Roland T. Rust and Bruce Cooil, "Reliability Measures for Qualitative Data: Theory and Implications," *Journal of Marketing Research* 31 (February 1994), pp. 1–14.

19. The procedure is adapted from Gilbert A. Churchill, Jr., "A Paradigm," pp. 64–73.

20. Mary Jo Bitner, Bernard H. Booms, and Mary Stanfield Tetreault, "The Service Encounter: Diagnosing Favorable and Unfavorable Incidents," *Journal of Marketing* 54 (January 1990), pp. 71–84. See also Mary Jo Bitner, Bernard H. Booms, and Lois A. Mohr, "Critical Service Encounters: The Employee's Viewpoint," *Journal of Marketing* 58 (October 1994), pp. 95–106.

21. See Churchill, "A Paradigm," for detailed discussion of which coefficients should be used and the rationale for their use.

Suggested Additional Readings

For a procedure that can be used to construct scales having construct validity, see
Gilbert A. Churchill, Jr., "A Paradigm for Developing Better Measures of Marketing Constructs," *Journal of Marketing Research* 16 (February 1979), pp. 64–73.

For a treatment of the various types of reliability and the role of reliability in measurement, see
Gilbert A. Churchill, Jr., and J. Paul Peter, "Research Design Effects on the Reliability of Rating Scales: A Meta-Analysis," *Journal of Marketing Research* 21 (February 1984), pp. 360–375.
J. Paul Peter, "Reliability: A Review of Psychometric Basics and Recent Marketing Practices," *Journal of Marketing Research* 16 (February 1979), pp. 6–17.

For in-depth discussions of the notions of validity, see
J. Paul Peter, "Construct Validity: A Review of Basic Issues and Marketing Practices," *Journal of Marketing Research* 18 (May 1981), pp. 133–145.
J. Paul Peter and Gilbert A. Churchill, Jr., "The Relationship among Research Design Choices and Psychometric Properties of Rating Scales: A Meta-Analysis," *Journal of Marketing Research* 23 (February 1986), pp. 1–10.

Chapter 14

MEASURING ATTITUDES, PERCEPTIONS, AND PREFERENCES

L E A R N I N G   O B J E C T I V E S

Upon Completing This Chapter, You Should Be Able to

1. List the various ways by which attitudes can be measured.

2. Name the most widely used attitude scaling techniques in marketing research and explain why researchers prefer them.

3. Explain how a Stapel scale differs from a semantic-differential scale.

4. Cite the one feature that is common to all ratings scales.

5. List three of the most common types of ratings scales.

6. Explain the difference between a graphic-ratings scale and an itemized-ratings scale.

7. Explain how the constant-sum scaling method works.

8. Identify the key decisions an analyst must make in order to complete a multidimensional-scaling analysis.

9. Explain the basic principle behind conjoint analysis.

Case in Marketing Research

It's four o'clock in the afternoon of a typical working mother. What's that little rumble in her belly? Well, she barely had time to heat up her soup in the microwave for lunch, and now she's getting hungry. Better think about dinner.

This scene happens across America every workday, according to Angelo Iantosca, vice president of marketing for Nestlé Frozen Food. His company has asked working mothers how they handle meal planning and preparation. The research found that almost half plan dinner after 4 P.M. each workday.

By that time, the prospect of making dinner can be exhausting even to contemplate. What to prepare? Do we have the ingredients? Do we have the time, between runs to day care and soccer and homework, to shop for and prepare a meal?

Iantosca and his colleagues at Nestlé have their own questions. Nestlé, whose brands include Stouffer's and Lean Cuisine, wants consumers to choose these frozen-dinner lines when it is time to shop for a meal. Industry data show that dollar sales of frozen food have been on the rise, but the unit volume has not. How can the company persuade consumers to look for their dinner in the frozen-food aisle of the supermarket? When do consumers even consider this as an option? And when they do, how do they decide which product to buy?

Over at Nestlé's rival Vlasic Foods, marketing researchers are asking similar questions about their line of Swanson frozen foods. According to Vlasic Foods vice president Kevin Lowery, the company has established a focus: "to go after a significant segment of the [frozen dinner] business by improving our quality and advertising those improvements nationally." To do this effectively, Vlasic, too, seeks to know the mind of its consumers.

Knowing what's inside another person's head is never easy. Companies like Vlasic and Nestlé conduct their own research and join trade groups that sponsor research. For example, the National Frozen Food Institute sponsored a study called "Understanding the Frozen Food Consumer," conducted by The Alcott Group, Chicago. The study explored the reasons behind soft sales of frozen food. Researchers asked whether consumers were intentionally avoiding frozen foods and, when they did buy, what benefits they were seeking in frozen foods. In addition, the companies study consumers' attitudes toward their own brands and products.

Discussion Issues

1. How can marketers like Nestlé Frozen Food and Vlasic Foods benefit from gathering data about attitudes and preferences, as opposed to data about purchasing behavior?

2. What problems would you expect them to encounter in measuring attitudes and preferences?

3. How might the companies apply this information to their decisions about frozen dinners?

One of the most pervasive notions in all of marketing is that attitudes play a pivotal role in consumer behavior. Consequently, an attempt to measure attitudes is incorporated in most of the major marketing models and in many, if not most, investigations of consumer behavior that do not rely on formal integrated models.[1] Marketers tend to emphasize the importance of attitudes. "Attitudes directly *affect* purchase decisions and these, in turn, *directly affect* attitudes through experience in using the product or service selected. In a broad sense, purchase decisions are based *almost solely* upon attitudes existing at the time of purchase, however these attitudes might have been formed"[2] (emphasis added).

Practitioners are also interested in people's attitudes and use them for a variety of purposes, including determining the amount to pay employees. For example, the guiding premise for AT&T when it developed its credit-card service was quality. Quality was defined as delighting the customer—exceeding his or her expectations in every way. To make sure it is succeeding in this endeavor, AT&T measures customers' reactions to its service in several ways, including surveying customers every month to determine the features of its service that matter most and how AT&T is performing on these features. It uses these measurements of customer attitudes along with more than 150 measurements of the performance of its vendors and its own internal operations to determine employee pay, since employees in the credit-card division have their paychecks tied to quality performance.[3]

Still other common uses include the following: (1) The appliance manufacturer's interest in present dealer and prospective dealer attitudes toward the company's warranty policy. If the dealers support the policy, the company feels they are more likely to give adequate, courteous service and, in the process, produce more satisfied customers. (2) The cosmetic manufacturer's interest in consumers' attitudes toward the company's new shampoo as it debuts in test market. Based on an early assessment of consumers' reactions, the company may decide to revise or fine-tune its introductory marketing strategy before going national. (3) The industrial marketer's interest in the general job satisfaction of its highly trained, highly skilled field staff of sales representatives.

These examples indicate some of the many groups of people in whose attitudes the marketer typically is interested: the company's employees, its intermediaries, and its customers. Their attitude, stance, or predisposition to act can be important determinants of the company's success, and the marketer needs devices for measuring these attitudes. This chapter reviews some of those devices.

Although the attitude concept is one of the most widely used in social psychology, it is used inconsistently. Both researchers and practitioners have trouble agreeing on interpretations of its various aspects. However, there does seem to be substantial agreement on the following points:

1. Attitude represents a predisposition to act but does not guarantee that the actual behavior will occur. It merely indicates that there is a readiness to respond to an object. It is still necessary to do something to trigger the response. The Omega ad, for example, can help shape an attitude but does not guarantee a response.

2. Attitudes are relatively persistent and consistent over time. They can be changed, to be sure, but alteration of an attitude that is strongly held requires substantial intervention.

3. There is a consistency between attitudes and behavior, and people act in such a fashion as to maintain this consistency.

4. Attitudes connote a preference and evaluation of an idea or object. They result in either positive or neutral or negative feelings for the idea or object.

Omega watch advertises that its product is "James Bond's Choice," assuming that consumers' interest in and positive attitude toward the literary and movie character James Bond may transfer into purchase of a watch. The consumer's positive attitude, however, does not guarantee that he or she will actually purchase the watch.

James Bond's Choice

Seamaster Professional
Automatic chronometer.
Water-resistant to 300m/1000ft.
OMEGA ~ Swiss made since 1848.

The World Is Not Enough
007

Ω
OMEGA

SMART.
JEWELERS
Fine Watches and Jewelry of Distinction
3350 W. Devon Avenue Lincolnwood, IL 60712
(847) 673-6000

The consistencies noted in this list led to our definition of attitude as representing a person's ideas, convictions, or liking with regard to a specific object or idea, presented in Chapter 9.

In addition to attitudes, marketers also have a keen interest in perceptions and preferences, and in this chapter we will examine some of the techniques researchers use to measure attitudes, perceptions, and preferences.

Attitude-Scaling Procedures

Self-report
A method of assessing attitudes in which individuals are asked directly for their beliefs about or feelings toward an object or class of objects.

There are a number of ways in which attitudes have been measured, including self-reports, observation of overt behavior, indirect techniques, performance of objective tasks, and physiological reactions.[4] By far the most common approach has been **self-reports,** in which people are asked directly for their beliefs or feelings toward an object or class of objects. For example, Research Window 14.1 depicts the results of a study that used self-reports, which was conducted by Ogilvy & Mather to help the agency select media in various countries. A number of scales and scaling methods using self-reports have been devised to measure these feelings. The main types will be reviewed here, but first let us briefly review the other approaches to attitude determination.

	Hong Kong, % Agree	Brazil, % Agree	Colombia, % Agree	UK, % Agree	U.S., % Agree	West Germany, % Agree
NEWSPAPERS						
Informative	32	71	74	45	57	46
Entertaining	39	11	11	8	10	14
Boring	22	13	15	34	25	35
Irritating	7	5	—	13	8	5
RADIO						
Informative	23	51	19	23	33	17
Entertaining	39	21	30	18	28	31
Boring	22	19	32	30	23	45
Irritating	16	9	19	29	16	7
TV						
Informative	26	48	18	19	29	18
Entertaining	61	32	75	51	29	39
Boring	6	15	5	13	22	38
Irritating	7	5	2	17	20	5
BILLBOARDS						
Informative	24	51	36	33	32	21
Entertaining	50	20	43	33	21	21
Boring	22	20	15	26	26	52
Irritating	24	9	6	8	21	6
MAGAZINES						
Informative	33	71	31	41	52	32
Entertaining	40	14	62	22	19	21
Boring	23	10	6	25	18	40
Irritating	4	5	1	12	11	7
DIRECT MAIL						
Informative	24	62	60	10	16	19
Entertaining	18	2	17	3	5	7
Boring	24	26	19	23	35	57
Irritating	34	10	4	64	44	17

Informative, entertaining, boring, or irritating—pick *one* to describe advertising in each medium: newspapers, magazines, radio, TV, billboards, and direct mail.

If you're American, you're most likely to say newspaper and magazine advertising is "informative," and direct mail is "irritating." After that you can't decide. If you're British, you feel much the same, except you do also grant that TV advertising is "entertaining." For the West Germans, though, it's *all* pretty "boring." By complete contrast, unless you're talking about direct mail, it's all

"entertaining" in Hong Kong; and in Brazil, advertising, no matter where you find it, is likely to be "informative." The Colombians are more discriminating—newspaper and direct mail advertising is "informative"; TV, billboard and magazine advertising is "entertaining"; and radio advertising in Colombia is just as likely to be "boring" as "entertaining."

Source: *Listening Post, Number 64* (September 1987) (New York: Ogilvy & Mather), pp. 3 and 5. Reprinted with permission from Ogilvy & Mather.

Observation of Behavior

The observation approach to attitude determination rests on the presumption that a subject's behavior is conditioned by his or her attitudes, and that we can therefore use the observed behavior to infer these attitudes. Thus, from the fact that McDonald's heavily promoted McLean Deluxe hamburger was a marketing flop, observers inferred that consumers aren't looking for a low-fat meal when they enter McDonald's. Apparently, since the company spent $50 million to launch the product, consumers had responded differently when asked to directly state their attitudes toward a low-fat hamburger.[5]

The behavior that the researcher wishes to observe is often elicited by creating an artificial situation. For example, to assess a person's attitude toward mandatory seat belt legislation, the subject might be asked to sign a strongly worded petition in favor of making seat belt usage a law. The individual's attitude toward seat belts would be inferred based on whether or not he or she signed. Alternatively, subjects might be asked to participate in a group discussion of the seat belt issue, and the researcher would note whether the individuals supported or opposed seat belt legislation in the discussion.

Indirect Techniques

Indirect techniques
Methods of assessing attitudes that use unstructured or partially structured stimuli, such as word-association tests, sentence-completion tests, storytelling, and so on.

The **indirect techniques** of attitude assessment use some unstructured or partially constructed stimuli as discussed in Chapter 10, such as word-association tests, sentence-completion tests, storytelling, and so on. Since the arguments concerning the use of these devices were detailed there, they will not be repeated here.

Performance of Objective Tasks

Performance of objective tasks
A method of assessing attitudes that rests on the presumption that a subject's performance of a specific assigned task (for example, memorizing a number of facts) will depend on the person's attitude.

On the theory that people's **performance of objective tasks** will reflect their attitudes, one might ask a person to memorize a number of facts about an issue and then assess his or her attitude toward that issue from the facts that were successfully memorized. Thus, to assess a person's attitude toward seat belt legislation, one might ask him or her to memorize such facts as (1) the number of lives saved by seat belt usage, (2) the number of people who died in accidents because they could not remove their seat belts in time, and (3) the number of states that have adopted a mandatory seat belt law. The material should reflect both sides of the issue. The researcher then would determine what facts the person remembered. The assumption is that subjects would be more apt to remember those arguments that are most consistent with their own position.

Physiological Reaction

Physiological reaction
A method of assessing attitudes in which the researcher monitors the subject's response, by electrical or mechanical means, to the controlled introduction of some stimuli.

Another approach to attitude measurement involves **physiological reaction,** which was discussed in Chapter 11. Here, through electrical or mechanical means, such as the galvanic skin response technique, the researcher monitors the subject's response to the controlled introduction of some stimuli. One problem that arises in using these measures to assess attitude is that, with the exception of voice-pitch analysis, the individual's physiological response indicates only the intensity of the individual's feelings and not whether they are negative or positive.

Although self-report techniques for attitude assessment are the most widely used in marketing research studies because they are easy to administer, one should be aware of these other approaches, particularly when attempting to establish the validity of a self-report measure. They can provide useful insight into how the method of measurement, rather than differences in the basic attitudes of subjects, caused the scores to vary. This is consistent with the notion of using multiple indicators to establish the convergent and discriminant validity of a measure.

Self-Report Attitude Scales

Since attitude is one of the most pervasive concepts in all of social psychology, it is natural that researchers would devise a number of methods to measure it. Although many of the methods use self-reports, each method uses them in different ways. In this section, we shall review some of these self-report scales, particularly those that have novel features or have been used extensively in marketing studies. The discussion should give you an appreciation of the main types and their construction and use. Incidentally, in following the arguments, you will find it helpful to distinguish between how a scale is constructed and how it is used.

Summated-Ratings Scale

Summated-ratings scale

A self-report technique for attitude measurement in which the subjects are asked to indicate their degree of agreement or disagreement with each of a number of statements; a subject's attitude score is the total obtained by summing over the items in the scale.

The *Likert scale,* also called a **summated-ratings scale,** is one of the most widely used attitude-scaling techniques in marketing research. It is particularly useful since it allows respondents to express the intensity of their feelings.[6]

Scale Construction In developing a Likert, or summated-ratings scale, researchers devise a number of statements that relate to the issue or object in question. Subjects are asked to indicate their degree of agreement or disagreement with each and every statement in the series. Figure 14.1 is an example of a scale that might be used by a bank interested in comparing its image with that of its competitors.

In developing this type of scale, the researcher tries to generate statements about the characteristics of the object that could influence a person's attitude toward it. Each statement is then classified as either favorable or unfavorable.

Subjects are asked to indicate their degree of agreement or disagreement with each statement, and the various degrees of agreement are assigned scale values. For our purposes, let's assume the values 1, 2, 3, 4, and 5 are assigned to the respective response categories. Now, a subject could be considered to feel positively about the bank if he or she either agreed with a favorable statement or disagreed with an unfavorable statement. Consequently, it is necessary to reverse the scaling with negative statements; a "strongly agree" response to a favorable statement and a "strongly disagree" response to an unfavorable statement would both receive a score of 5.

Using this scoring procedure, a total attitude score is then calculated for each subject. Researchers then evaluate the responses to determine which of the items discriminate most clearly between the high scorers and low scorers on the total scale. Those statements that generate mixed responses are weeded out, since they may tend to produce ambiguous

FIGURE 14.1 **Example of Summated-Ratings Scale**

	STRONGLY DISAGREE	DISAGREE	NEITHER AGREE NOR DISAGREE	AGREE	STRONGLY AGREE
1. The bank offers courteous service.	——	——	——	——	——
2. The bank has a convenient location.	——	——	——	——	——
3. The bank has convenient hours.	——	——	——	——	——
4. The bank offers low-interest-rate loans.	——	——	——	——	——

results or, at the very least, may not be discriminating of attitude. In this way, the questionnaire is made internally consistent, so that every item relates to the same general attitude.[7]

Scale Use Once the list of statements has been refined, the remaining items are randomly ordered on the scale form so as to mix positive and negative statements. The scale is then ready to be administered to the desired sample of respondents. Once again, subjects are asked to indicate their degree of agreement with each statement. Subjects generally find it easy to respond, because the response categories allow the expression of the intensity of the feeling. The subject's total score is generated as the simple sum of the scores on each statement.

Unfortunately, interpretation of these summed scores is rarely simple. If, for example, the maximum favorable score on a particular 20-item scale is 100, what do we say about a score of 78? Can we assume that the person's attitude toward the bank is favorable? We cannot, since the raw scores assume meaning only when we compare them with some standard. This problem is not unique to psychological scaling. It arises every day of our lives in a variety of ways. We are always making judgments on the basis of comparisons with some standard. Most typically the standard is established via our experiences and rarely is rigorously defined. Thus, when we say, "The man is very tall," we are in effect saying that on the basis of the experience we have, the man is taller than average.

In psychological scaling, this is formalized somewhat by clearly specifying the standard. Very often the standard is taken as the average score for all subjects, although averages are also computed for certain predefined subgroups. The procedure is called *developing norms*. Comparison can then be made against the norms to determine whether the person has a positive or negative attitude toward the object.

Norms are not, of course, necessary for comparing subjects to determine which person has the more favorable attitude. Here one can simply compare the raw scores of the subjects. Nor are norms necessary when attempting to determine whether an individual's attitude has changed over time or whether a person likes one object better than another. One can simply compare the later and earlier scores or the difference in scores for the two objects. This is the approach taken by the National Quality Research Center (NQRC) in measuring customer satisfaction with the American Customer Satisfaction Index. NQRC researchers conduct telephone interviews of people who have recently bought or used a company's product or service, asking them about three determinants of satisfaction: their expectations, perception of quality, and perception of value. Using a multiequation model, NQRC uses their responses to rate organizations and industries on a 1–100 scale of satisfaction, as well as a national customer satisfaction score. An organization can track its own performance since the baseline measure was made in 1994, or it can compare its performance to industrywide numbers, or its industry to overall customer satisfaction. For example, customer satisfaction with TV broadcasting has fallen almost every year, from 77 in 1994 to 62 in 1999. In contrast, customer satisfaction with electric utilities and retailers has remained steady, at about 74 in both categories.[8]

Semantic-Differential Scale

Semantic-differential scale
A self-report technique for attitude measurement in which the subjects are asked to check which cell between a set of bipolar adjectives or phrases best describes their feelings toward the object.

One of the most popular techniques for measuring attitudes in marketing research is the **semantic-differential scale.** It has been found to be particularly useful in corporate, brand, and product-image studies.

This scale grew out of some research by Charles Osgood and his colleagues at the University of Illinois concerning the underlying structure of words.[9] The technique has been adapted, however, to make it suitable for measuring attitudes.

The original semantic-differential scale consisted of a great many bipolar adjectives, which were used to determine people's reactions to the objects of interest. Osgood found that most reactions could be categorized into one of three basic dimensions: (1) an *evaluation* dimension, represented by adjective pairs such as good-bad, sweet-sour, helpful-unhelpful; (2) a *potency* dimension, represented by adjective pairs such as powerful-powerless, strong-weak, deep-shallow; and (3) an *activity* dimension, represented by adjective pairs such as fast-slow, alive-dead, noisy-quiet. The same three dimensions tended to emerge regardless of the object being evaluated. Thus, the general thrust in using the semantic-differential technique to form scales was to select an appropriate sample of the accepted or basic adjective pairs so that a score could be generated for the object for each of the evaluation, potency, and activity dimensions. The object could then be compared to other objects using these scores.

Marketers have taken Osgood's general idea and adapted it to fit their own needs. First, instead of applying the *basic* adjective pairs to the objects of interest, marketers have generated pairs of their own. These pairs have not always been antonyms, nor have they been single words. Rather, marketers have used phrases to anchor the ends of the scale, and some of these phrases have been attributes possessed by the product. For example, one end of the scale may be "good value for the money," and its opposite end, "poor value for the money." Second, instead of attempting to generate evaluation, potency, and activity scores, marketers have been more interested in developing profiles for the brands, stores, companies, or whatever is being compared, and total scores by which the objects could be compared. In this respect, the use of the semantic-differential approach in marketing studies has tended to follow the summated-ratings approach to scale construction rather than the semantic-differential tradition.

Let us again use the bank attitude-scaling problem to illustrate the semantic-differential method. First, a researcher would generate a large list of bipolar adjectives or phrases. Figure 14.2 parallels Figure 14.1 in terms of the attributes used to describe the bank, but it is arranged in semantic-differential format. All we have done in Figure 14.2 is to try to express the things that could be used to describe a bank, and thus serve as a basis for attitude formation, in terms of positive and negative statements. Note that the negative phrase sometimes appears at the left side of the scale and other times at the right. This is to prevent a respondent with a positive attitude from simply checking either the right- or left-hand sides without even bothering to read the descriptions.

The scale would then be administered to a sample of subjects. Each respondent would be asked to read each set of bipolar phrases and to check the cell that best described his or her feelings toward the object. Respondents are usually instructed to consider the end positions in the scale as being *very descriptive* of the object, the center position as being *neutral,* and the intermediate positions as *slightly descriptive* and *quite descriptive.* Thus, for example, if the subject felt that Bank A's service was courteous, but only moderately so, he or she would check the sixth position reading from left to right.

The subject could be asked to evaluate two or more banks using the same scale. When several banks are rated, the different profiles can be compared. Figure 14.3, for example (which is sometimes referred to as a **snake diagram** because of its shape), illustrates that Bank A is perceived as having more courteous service and a more convenient location and as offering lower interest rates on loans, but as having less convenient hours than Bank B. Notice that in constructing these profiles, all positive descriptors were placed on the right. This practice makes it much easier to interpret the results. The plotted values represent the average score of all subjects on each descriptor. The profile that emerges gives a clear indication of how respondents perceive the differences between the two banks.

Rather than developing a profile, one can also total the scores on a semantic-differential scale in order to compare attitudes toward different objects (for example, al-

Snake diagram

A diagram (so called because of its shape) that connects with straight lines the average responses to a series of semantic-differential statements, thereby depicting the profile of the object or objects being evaluated.

FIGURE 14.2 **Example of Semantic-Differential Scaling Form**

Service is discourteous.	:——:——:——:——:——:——:	Service is courteous.
Location is convenient.	:——:——:——:——:——:——:	Location is inconvenient.
Hours are inconvenient.	:——:——:——:——:——:——:	Hours are convenient.
Loan interest rates are high.	:——:——:——:——:——:——:	Loan interest rates are low.

Contrasting Profiles of Banks A and B

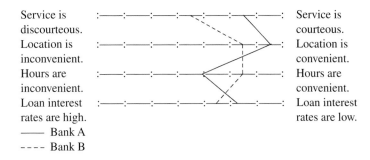

Service is discourteous.	: —: —: —: —: —: :	Service is courteous.
Location is inconvenient.	: —: —: —: —: —: :	Location is convenient.
Hours are inconvenient.	: —: —: —: —: —: :	Hours are convenient.
Loan interest rates are high.	: —: —: —: —: —: :	Loan interest rates are low.

—— Bank A
- - - - Bank B

ternative package designs). This score is arrived by totaling the scores for the individual descriptors.

The popularity of semantic-differential scales in marketing research may be due to the ease with which they can be developed and the clarity with which they reveal results. The technique also has the advantage of allowing subjects to express the intensity of their feelings toward company, product, package, advertisement, or whatever. When combined with proper item-analysis techniques, the semantic-differential technique offers the marketing researcher a most valuable research tool.

Stapel Scale

Stapel scale

A self-report technique for attitude measurement in which respondents are asked to indicate how accurately each of a number of statements describes the object of interest.

A modification of the semantic-differential scale that has received some attention in marketing literature is the **Stapel scale.** It differs from the semantic-differential scale in that (1) adjectives or descriptive phrases are tested separately instead of simultaneously as bipolar pairs, (2) points on the scale are identified by number, and (3) there are ten scale positions rather than seven. Figure 14.4 casts the same four attributes previously used to measure attitudes toward banks in a Stapel scale format. Respondents would be told to rate how accurately each of a number of statements describes the object of interest, Bank A. Instructions such as the following are given to respondents:

You would select a *plus* number for words that you think describe (Bank A) accurately. The more accurately you think the word describes it, the larger the *plus* number you would choose. You would select a *minus* number for words you think do not describe it accurately. The less accurately you think a word describes it, the larger the *minus* number you would choose. Therefore, you can select any number from +5, for words that you think are very accurate, all the way to −5, for words that you think are very inaccurate.[10]

Example of Stapel Scale

	−5	−4	−3	−2	−1	+1	+2	+3	+4	+5
Service is courteous.	□	□	□	□	□	□	□	□	□	□
Location is convenient.	□	□	□	□	□	□	□	□	□	□
Hours are convenient.	□	□	□	□	□	□	□	□	□	□
Loan interest rates are high.	□	□	□	□	□	□	□	□	□	□

Proponents of the Stapel scale point out that this method not only frees the researcher from the sometimes difficult task of developing bipolar adjectives for each of the items on the test, but also permits finer discriminations in measuring attitudes. Despite these advantages, the Stapel scale has not been as warmly embraced as the semantic-differential scale, judging by the number of published marketing studies using each.[11] One problem with the Stapel scale is that many of the descriptors used to evaluate an object can be phrased one of three ways—positively, negatively, or neutrally—and the particular choice of phrasing seems to affect the results as well as subjects' ability to respond. Nevertheless, it is a useful addition to the researcher's equipment arsenal, especially since it can be administered over the telephone.[12]

It should be pointed out that a total score on both the semantic-differential and Stapel scales is like a total score on a summated-ratings scale. The score 48, for example, is meaningless by itself but takes on meaning when compared with some norm or other score. There is a good deal of controversy as to whether semantic-differential, Stapel, or even summated-ratings total scores represent interval scaling, or, in actuality, ordinal scaling. While the controversy rages, marketers, like many psychological scaling specialists, have opted to assume that the scores represent interval scaling. While this assumption may not be entirely correct, it does allow researchers to use more powerful methods of analysis on the data generated.

Further, from a statistical point of view, the assumption of intervality often makes sense. Statistical tests of significance, for example, "do not care from where the numbers come" as long as the assumptions underlying the use of a particular statistical test are satisfied.[13] It is not necessary, therefore, to be overly concerned about the level of measurement from a *statistical* point of view. What we must be careful about, though, is the *interpretation* of the results (for example, arguing that a person with a score of 80 has twice as favorable an attitude toward an object as a person with a score of 40—unless, of course, the measurement scale is ratio).

Other Ratings Scales

The previous discussion dealt with some of the main scaling methods that have been used to measure attitudes. The treatment was by no means exhaustive. Particularly conspicuous by its absence was a discussion of the importance of the various attributes to the individ-

Ethical Dilemma 14.1

An independent researcher was hired by a national chain of department stores to develop a scale by which the chain could measure the image of each of its stores. The researcher thought that the best way to do this was through a semantic-differential scale. Since she was interested in establishing her credentials as an expert on store-image research, however, she decided to also develop items for a Likert scale and to administer both of the scales to designated participants. She realized that this might induce greater respondent fatigue and perhaps lower-quality responses, but she was willing to take the chance because she knew that the client would not sanction nor pay for administering the second survey to an independent sample of respondents.

- Was it ethical for the researcher to accept the risk of lowering the quality of the data addressing the client's issue so that she could further her own goals and career?

- What if the data collected by the two instruments provided stronger evidence that store image had indeed been measured adequately than if data had been collected through the sole use of the semantic-differential scale?

- Would it make any difference if there had been a reasonable chance that the Likert format would produce a better instrument for measuring retail image than a semantic-differential format?

ual. That is, in the bank example, even though the individual believes the bank has convenient hours, the person may not value this attribute, and, therefore, it may not affect his or her attitude toward the bank. On the other hand, if the individual places a strong emphasis on the convenience of a bank's location, and if he or she perceives the bank as being inconveniently located, this will have a negative, and perhaps a strongly negative, impact on his or her feelings toward the bank. To capture the differing emphases people place on specific attributes, researchers often try to measure their importance. Research Window 14.2, for example, depicts the importance of various attributes to people when shopping for microwave ovens, console color televisions, and portable video cameras or camcorders.

Admittedly, there is a good deal of controversy about how importance of various attributes should be incorporated in determining a person's attitude toward an object. We shall not delve into this controversy, because it involves some very complex arguments as to how one determines which attributes are salient (that is, used in forming an attitude) and how they should be measured. Rather, we shall simply use importance values as a way of focusing on the differences among the general types of ratings scales.[14] Knowledge of the basic types should help in developing special scales for particular purposes.

There is one feature that is common to all ratings scales: "The rater places the person or object being rated at some point along a continuum or in one of an ordered series of categories; a numerical value is attached to the point or the category."[15] The scales differ, though, in the fineness of the distinctions they allow and in the procedures involved in

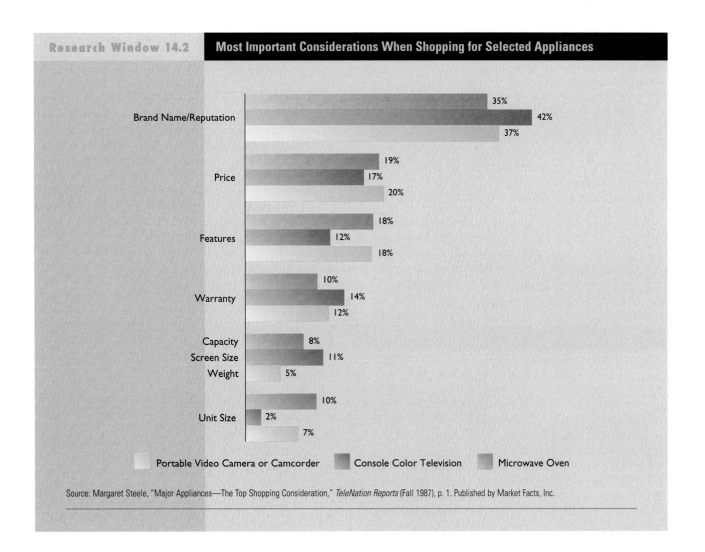

Research Window 14.2　**Most Important Considerations When Shopping for Selected Appliances**

Brand Name/Reputation: 35%, 42%, 37%
Price: 19%, 17%, 20%
Features: 18%, 12%, 18%
Warranty: 10%, 14%, 12%
Capacity: 8%
Screen Size: 11%
Weight: 5%
Unit Size: 10%, 2%, 7%

☐ Portable Video Camera or Camcorder　☐ Console Color Television　☐ Microwave Oven

Source: Margaret Steele, "Major Appliances—The Top Shopping Consideration," *TeleNation Reports* (Fall 1987), p. 1. Published by Market Facts, Inc.

assigning objects to positions. Three of the most common ratings scales are the graphic, the itemized, and the comparative.

Graphic-Ratings Scale

Graphic-ratings scale
A scale in which individuals indicate their ratings of an attribute by placing a check at the appropriate point on a line that runs from one extreme of the attribute to the other.

When using **graphic-ratings scales** individuals indicate their rating by placing a check at the appropriate point on a line that runs from one extreme of the attribute to the other. Many variations are possible. The line may be vertical or horizontal; it may be unmarked or marked; if marked, the divisions may be few or many as in the case of a *thermometer scale*, so called because it looks like a thermometer. Figure 14.5 is an example of a horizontal, end-anchored only, graphic-ratings scale. Each individual would be instructed to indicate the importance of the attribute by checking the appropriate position on the scale. The importance value would then be inferred by measuring the length of the line from the left origin to the marked position.

One of the great advantages of graphic-ratings scales is the ease with which they can be constructed and used. They provide an opportunity to make fine distinctions and are limited in this regard only by the discriminatory abilities of the rater. Yet, for their most effective use, the researcher is advised to avoid making the ends of the continuum too extreme, since extremes tend to force respondents into the center of the scale, resulting in little useful information.

Itemized-Ratings Scale

Itemized-ratings scale
A scale distinguished by the fact that individuals must indicate their ratings of an attribute or object by selecting one from among a limited number of categories that best describes their position on the attribute or object.

The **itemized-ratings scale** is similar to the graphic-ratings scale except that the rater must select from a limited number of categories instead of placing a mark on a continuous scale. In general, five to nine categories work best in that they permit fine distinctions and yet seem to be readily understood by respondents. Of course, more can be used.[16]

There are a number of possible variations with itemized scales. Figure 14.6, for example, depicts three different forms of itemized-ratings scales that have been used to measure customer satisfaction. Note that the categories are ordered in terms of their scale positions, and that while in some cases the categories have verbal descriptions attached, in other cases they do not. Category descriptions are not absolutely necessary in itemized-ratings scales, although their presence and nature does seem to affect the responses.[17] When they are used, it is important to ensure that the descriptors mean similar things to those responding. When they are not used, it is tempting to conclude that a graphic-ratings scale is being used. That is an erroneous conclusion, however. The distinguishing feature of an itemized scale is that the possible response categories are limited in number. Thus, a set of faces varying systematically in terms of whether they are frowning or smiling used to capture a person's satisfaction or preference (appropriately called a *faces scale*) would be considered an itemized scale, even when no descriptions are attached to the face categories.

FIGURE 14.5 **Graphic-Ratings Scale**

Please evaluate each attribute, in terms of how important the attribute is to you personally, by placing an "X" at the position on the horizontal line that most reflects your feelings.

ATTRIBUTE	NOT IMPORTANT	VERY IMPORTANT
Courteous service		
Convenient location		
Convenient hours		
Low-interest-rate loans		

A summated-ratings statement is an example of a five-point itemized-ratings scale, while a semantic-differential adjective pair is an example of a seven-point scale. Figure 14.7 is an itemized-ratings scale used to measure importance values; this four-point scale has the descriptor labels attached to the categories.

FIGURE 14.6   Three Different Forms of Itemized-Ratings Scales Used to Measure Satisfaction

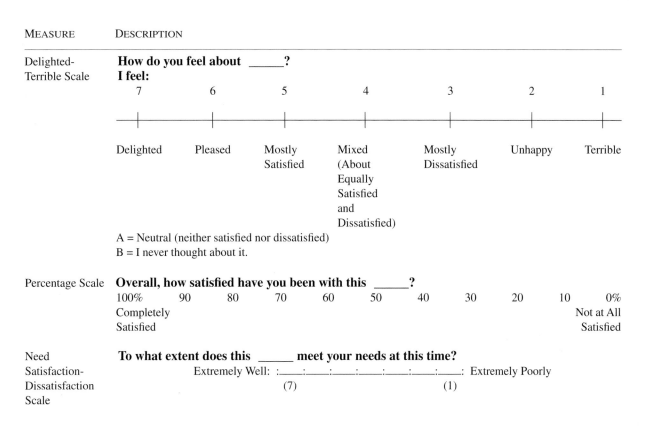

MEASURE	DESCRIPTION

Delighted-Terrible Scale

How do you feel about _____?
I feel:

7	6	5	4	3	2	1
Delighted	Pleased	Mostly Satisfied	Mixed (About Equally Satisfied and Dissatisfied)	Mostly Dissatisfied	Unhappy	Terrible

A = Neutral (neither satisfied nor dissatisfied)
B = I never thought about it.

Percentage Scale

Overall, how satisfied have you been with this _____?

100%   90   80   70   60   50   40   30   20   10   0%
Completely   Not at All
Satisfied   Satisfied

Need Satisfaction-Dissatisfaction Scale

To what extent does this _____ meet your needs at this time?
Extremely Well: :___:___:___:___:___:___:___: Extremely Poorly
                     (7)   (1)

Source: Adapted from Robert A. Westbrook, "A Rating Scale for Measuring Product/Service Satisfaction," *Journal of Marketing* 44 (Fall 1980), p. 69. Published by the American Marketing Association, Chicago, IL.

FIGURE 14.7   Itemized-Ratings Scale Used to Measure Importance Values

Please evaluate each attribute, in terms of how important the attribute is to you personally, by placing an "X" in the appropriate box.

ATTRIBUTE	NOT IMPORTANT	SOMEWHAT IMPORTANT	FAIRLY IMPORTANT	VERY IMPORTANT
Courteous service	☐	☐	☐	☐
Convenient location	☐	☐	☐	☐
Convenient hours	☐	☐	☐	☐
Low-interest-rate loans	☐	☐	☐	☐

FIGURE 14.8 **Comparative-Ratings Scale**

Please divide 100 points between the following two attributes in terms of the relative importance of each attribute to you.

Courteous service _____

Convenient location _____

The itemized-ratings scale is also easy to construct and use, and although it does not permit the fine distinctions possible with the graphic-ratings scale, the clear definition of categories generally produces more reliable ratings.

Comparative-Ratings Scale

In graphic and itemized scales, respondents are not asked to compare two attributes with each other or with a standard given by researchers. For example, respondents may be asked to indicate how important convenient location is to them in choosing a bank, but not if convenient location is more or less important than convenient hours. In **comparative-ratings scales,** however, respondents are asked to judge each attribute with direct reference to the other attributes being evaluated.

The constant-sum scaling method is an example of a comparative-ratings scale that can be used to measure importance values. In the **constant-sum method,** the individual is instructed to divide some given sum among two or more attributes on the basis of their importance to him or her. Thus, in Figure 14.8, if the subject assigned 50 points to courteous service and 50 points to convenient location, the attributes would be judged to be equally important; if the individual assigned 80 to courteous service and 20 to convenient location, courteous service would be considered to be four times as important. Note the difference in emphasis with this method. All judgments are now made in comparison to some other alternative.

Respondents are generally asked to compare two attributes in this method, although it is possible to compare more. The individual could also be asked to divide 100 points among three or more attributes.

Although comparative scales require more judgments from the individual than either graphic or itemized scales, they do tend to eliminate the **halo effect** that so often manifests itself in scaling. A halo effect occurs when there is carryover from one judgment to another.

The problem researchers may encounter in using graphic or itemized scales to measure importance values is that respondents may be inclined to indicate that all, or nearly all, of the attributes are important. Yet empirical research indicates that when individuals are confronted by decisions that are complex because many alternatives or attributes are involved, they tend to simplify the decision by reducing the number of alternatives or attributes they actually consider.[18] This is consistent with the notion that only certain attributes are salient when forming attitudes. The comparative scaling methods do allow more insight into the relative ranking, if not the absolute importance, of the attributes to each individual.

Comparative-ratings scale
A scale requiring subjects to make their ratings as a series of relative judgments or comparisons rather than as independent assessments.

Constant-sum method
A type of comparative-ratings scale in which an individual is instructed to divide some given sum among two or more attributes on the basis of their importance to him or her.

Halo effect
A problem that arises in data collection when there is carryover from one judgment to another.

Determining Which Scale to Use

When making the choice among scale types, number of scale points to use, whether to reverse some of the items, and so on, readers might find help in the findings of a very extensive study of the marketing measurement literature that examined these questions, and others, with respect to their impact on the reliability of measures.

The study, which reviewed the marketing literature over a 20-year period, examined measures for which at least two indicators of quality were reported, and it quantitatively assessed the impact of a measure's features on its reliability.[19] As you may recall from Chapter 13, reliability gauges whether different measures of the same object, trait, or construct produce similar results. It is an important indicator of a measure's quality because it determines the impact of inconsistencies in measurement on the results. The general conclusion that emerged from the study is that many of the characteristics do not seem to affect the quality of the measure in any significant way. The exceptions are the number of items and the number of scale points. For both of these characteristics, the reliability of the measure increases as they increase. For the other characteristics, though, no choices are superior in all instances. Many of the choices are, and will probably remain, in the domain of researcher judgment, including the choice among semantic-differential, summated-ratings, or other ratings scales. All the scales have proven useful at one time or another. All rightly belong in the researcher's measurement tool kit.

The nature of the problem and the planned mode of administration will affect the final choice. So will the characteristics of the respondents, their commitment to the task, and their experience and ability to respond. In some cultures, graphic-ratings scales may be unknown, and respondents with low levels of education may not even be able to conceptualize a continuous scale from extreme dissatisfaction to extreme satisfaction, say, that is divided into equal increments of satisfaction. In other cultures, such as Eastern Europe, the use of these scales may be a very new experience for most research participants, and interviewers may need to spend considerable time explaining the scale. In still other situations, it might be necessary to develop new scales. For example, the "sad-to-happy faces" scale that works in the United States does not work in Africa; rather, their culture requires some different-looking faces to depict the various stages of happiness. See Figure 14.9.

Perceptual Scaling

Thus far in this chapter, we have emphasized the measurement of people's attitudes toward objects. Marketing managers are also interested in determining how people perceive various objects, be they products or brands. In its constant quest for a differential advantage, a firm needs to correctly position its products against competitive offerings. To do this, the product manager needs to identify the following.[20]

1. The number of dimensions consumers use to distinguish products.

2. The names of these dimensions.

3. The positioning of existing products along these dimensions.

4. Where consumers prefer a product to be on the dimensions.

One way in which managers can grasp the positioning of their brand versus competing brands is through the study of perceptual maps. In a perceptual map, each product or brand occupies a specific point. Products or brands that are similar lie close together, and those that are different lie far apart. Perceptual maps provide managers with meaningful pictures of how their products and brands compare with other products and brands.

There are several ways by which perceptual maps can be created. The fundamental distinction is between nonattribute-based and attribute-based approaches. The attribute-based approaches rely on characteristic-by-characteristic assessments of the various objects using, for example, summated-ratings or semantic-differential scales. The ratings of the objects on each of the items are subsequently analyzed using various statistical techniques to identify the key dimensions or attributes consumers use to distinguish the objects.

In the nonattribute-based approaches, instead of asking a subject to rate objects on designated attributes (such as convenience, friendliness, or value for the money), one asks the individual to make some *summary* judgments about the objects. Then the

FIGURE 14.9   **Examples of "Sad-to-Happy Faces" Scales That Work in the United States versus Those That Work in Africa**

Source: The African faces can be found in C. K. Corder, "Problems and Pitfalls in Conducting Marketing Research in Africa," in Betsy Gelb, ed., *Marketing Expansion in a Shrinking World,* Proceedings of American Marketing Association Business Conference (Chicago: American Marketing Association, 1978), pp. 86–90. Reprinted with permission of American Marketing Association.

researcher attempts to infer which characteristics were used to form those judgments. This indirect approach is used because in many cases the attributes may be unknown and the respondents unable or unwilling to represent their judgments accurately.

Typically, subjects are asked for their *perceptions of the similarity* between various objects and their *preferences* among these objects. An attempt is then made to locate

Multidimensional scaling
An approach to measurement in which people's perceptions of the similarity of objects and their preferences among the objects are measured, and these relationships are plotted in a multidimensional space.

the objects in a multidimensional space where the number of dimensions corresponds to the number of characteristics the individual used in forming the judgments. **Multidimensional-scaling** analysis is the label that is used to describe the similarity- and preference-based approaches.

The preference-based approaches for perceptual mapping are not used nearly as much as the similarity-based approaches. Our discussion, therefore, will concentrate on the similarity-based approaches, and in particular on the decisions that must be made in order to conduct a multidimensional-scaling analysis.

The attribute-based approaches are discussed only briefly later in this chapter because a full appreciation of them requires understanding of the essential purposes and operation of factor and discriminant analyses, topics that are not discussed in this book.[21]

Key Decisions in Multidimensional Scaling

To complete a multidimensional-scaling analysis, an analyst must make a variety of decisions. Several of the key ones are pictured in Figure 14.10. The first of these is to specify the products or brands that will be used. While the purpose of the study will determine some of them, others will be left to the analyst to choose. In choosing, an analyst needs to recognize that the dimensions that appear in the perceptual map will be a direct result of the objects (known as a *stimulus set*) used to secure the judgments.

Suppose the study was being conducted to determine respondents' perceptions of various soft drinks. If no unsweetened or low-calorie soft drinks were included in the stimulus set, this very important dimension may not appear in the results. So as not to run such a risk, analysts may be tempted to include every conceivable product or brand in the stimulus set. This strategy, though, can place such a burden on respondents that their answers may be meaningless.

The burden on respondents is going to depend partly on the number of judgments each has to make and partly on the difficulty of each judgment. Both of these issues in turn depend on how the similarity judgments are to be secured. There are two main alternatives and a number of options under each alternative. The two major options are *direct* or *indirect similarity judgments,* two terms that are to some extent self-explanatory. The direct methods rely on data collection mechanisms in which respondents compare stimuli using whatever criteria they desire and, on the basis of that comparison, state which of the stimuli are most similar, least similar, and so on.

FIGURE 14.10 **Key Decisions When Conducting a Multidimensional-Scaling Analysis**

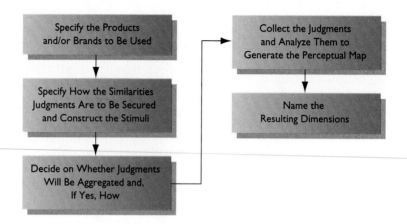

In our soft drink example, for instance, respondents might evaluate brands on the basis of their "colaness" or "dietness." All possible pairs of the brands being evaluated could be formed, and respondents could be asked to rank-order the various pairs from most similar to least similar using their own criteria. (For example, which pair is more similar: Pepsi–Coke, 7-Up–Coke, or Pepsi–7-Up?) Alternatively, a brand could be singled out as a focal brand, and respondents could be asked to rank-order each of the other brands in terms of their similarity to the focal brand (if, for example, Coke were the focal brand, respondents might be asked to rank-order Pepsi, RC Cola, 7-Up, and Dr Pepper as to their similarities to Coke). Each brand could serve, in turn, as the focal brand. While there are a number of alternative ways of collecting these judgments, they all have one thing in common: The respondents are asked to judge directly how similar the various alternatives are using criteria that they choose.

The indirect methods operate differently. Instead of respondents' selecting the criteria on which to compare the alternatives, they are asked to evaluate each brand using prespecified criteria chosen by the analyst. Some kind of measure of similarity is then calculated for each pair of brands (for example, the correlation between the ratings of the brands). Millward Brown International, the London-based marketing research arm of advertising agency WPP, used this approach in its giant international study of brand loyalty, titled Brandz. The study interviewed 70,000 consumers about 3,500 brands in 50 corporate and product categories. Millward Brown measured brand loyalty according to criteria it was already using for its clients' brands: presence (consumers' awareness of the brand), relevance, product performance, advantage, and bonding (percent of consumers who have an emotional and rational "bond" with the brand). Millward Brown can compare these criteria—together called a Brand Signature—for related brands, as in the case of Reebok and New Balance shoes at the top of Figure 14.11.[22]

The third decision analysts have to make is whether the judgments of individual respondents will be aggregated, or grouped together, so that group perceptual maps can be developed, or whether individual maps will be generated. The problem with individual maps is that they become very difficult for the marketing manager to use to develop marketing strategy. Managers typically look at marketing planning questions in terms of market segments, not individuals. Yet, as soon as the segment issue is raised, the question becomes one of deciding how the individual judgments will be aggregated. Is it likely that individuals used the same number of criteria (say, colaness, dietness, and sweetness) when evaluating the various brands? Even if they used the same number, are the criteria themselves likely to be the same? (What if some used colaness, dietness, and value for the

FIGURE 14.11 **Multidimensional Scaling Analysis Comparing Major Consumer Brands**

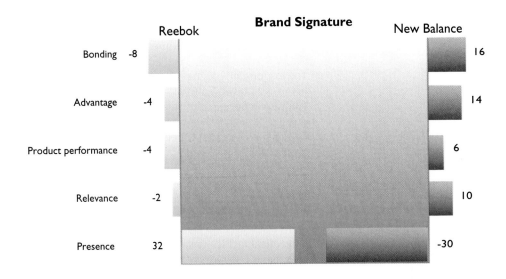

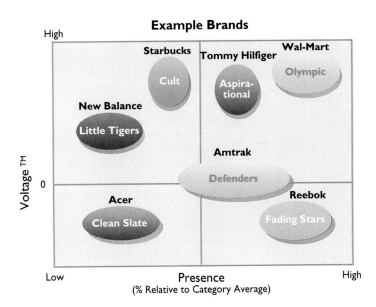

Source: Jean McDougall, "Building Brands for the Future," *Perspectives* (Millward Brown International), Winter 1998 (downloaded from Millward Brown Web site, www.millwardbrown.com, September 30, 1999).

money instead?) If they are not, what criteria should be used to group respondents? One of the most popular algorithms, INDSCAL, for example, assumes that all subjects use the same criteria to judge the similarity of objects but that they weight the dimensions differently when forming their judgments.[23]

Step 4 in Figure 14.10 involves the actual collection of the judgments and their processing. The processing involves two steps. First, an initial configuration must be determined for each of the dimensions. Different programs use different routines to generate an initial solution. Second, the points must be moved around until the fit is the best it can be in that dimensionality, using the criterion under which the program operates.

The last decision analysts have to make when conducting a similarity-based multi-dimensional-scaling analysis involves what to call the dimensions. Returning to the earlier example of Millward Brown's Brandz study, the researchers generate maps comparing brands in terms of various dimensions. The bottom of Figure 14.11 shows such a map for selected consumer brands. The dimensions are defined as presence (degree of consumer awareness) and Brand Voltage (an estimate of the likelihood the brand will grow).

There are several procedures for naming the dimensions:

- The respondent can be asked to evaluate each of the objects (for instance, soft drinks) in terms of several attributes (colaness, dietness, price) determined by the researcher. The researcher then correlates the attribute scores each object receives with the coordinates for each object on the plotted diagram. In this method, the size of the respective correlation coefficients between attributes and dimensions is used to attach labels.

- The manager or researcher can interpret the dimensions using his or her own experience and the visual configuration of points.

- The researcher can attempt to relate the dimensions to the physical characteristics of the soft drinks such as sweetness, color, or calories.

The practical fact is, however, that difficulty in naming the dimensions is one of management's major concerns with similarity-based multidimensional-scaling analysis.

Attribute-Based Approaches

One of the advantages of the attribute-based approaches to the development of perceptual maps is that they do make the naming of dimensions easier. They also seem to be easier for respondents to use. As mentioned earlier, the attribute-based approaches rely on having individuals rate various brands using (usually) either semantic-differential or summated-ratings scales. These judgments are usually then inputted to either discriminant analysis or factor analysis.

The emphasis in discriminant analysis is upon determining the combinations of attributes that best discriminate between the objects or brands. The dependent measures are the product rated (Coke, Pepsi, 7-Up), and the predictor variables are the attribute ratings. The analysis is typically run across groups of respondents to find a common structure. The dimensions are named by examining the weightings of the attributes that make up a discriminant dimension or by computing the correlations between the attributes and each of the discriminant scores. The use of discriminant analysis to develop perceptual maps seems to work particularly well when one is concerned with product design attributes that can be clearly and unequivocally perceived by consumers.[24]

Factor analysis relies on the assumption that there are only a few basic dimensions that underlie the attribute ratings. It examines the correlations among the attributes to identify these basic dimensions. The correlations are typically computed across brands and groups of consumers. The dimensions usually are named by examining the factor loadings that represent the correlations between each attribute and each factor. The use of factor analysis in the development of perceptual maps seems to be particularly useful when the marketing emphasis is on the formulation of communications strategy in which the linguistic relations between the attributes are key.

Comparison of Approaches to Perceptual Mapping

The advantages of the attribute-based approach versus the nonattribute-based approach to multidimensional scaling are summarized in Exhibit 14.1. Most of the nonattribute-based applications in marketing use similarity judgments. Similarity measurement has the advantage of not depending on a predefined attribute set. But this feature is a two-edged sword. Although it allows respondents to use only those dimensions they normally use in making judgments among objects, it creates difficulties in naming the dimensions. Fur-

EXHIBIT 14.1 **Comparison of the Nonattribute- and Attribute-based Approaches for Developing Perceptual Maps**

Technique	Respondent Measures	Advantages	Disadvantages
Nonattribute-based similarity judgments	Judged similarity of various products and/or brands	Does not depend on a predefined attribute set. Allows respondents to use their normal criteria when judging objects. Allows for condition that perception of the "whole" may not be simply the sum of the perceptions of the parts.	Difficult to name dimensions. Difficult to determine if, and how, the judgments of individual respondents should be combined. Criteria respondents use depend on the stimuli being compared. Requires special programs. Provides oversimplified view of perceptions when few objects are used.
Attribute-based discriminant or factor analysis	Ratings on various products and/or brands on pre-specified attributes	Facilitates naming the dimensions. Easier to cluster respondents into groups with similar perceptions. Easy and inexpensive to use. Computer programs are readily available.	Requires a relatively complete set of attributes. Rests on the assumption that overall perception of a stimulus is made up of the individual's reactions to the attributes making up the stimulus.

ther, different consumers may use different dimensions, and then one must grapple with how best to combine consumers when forming maps. Constructing a separate map for each individual is prohibitively costly. Aggregating all the responses and then developing one map distorts reality in that it implies a homogeneity in perceptions that probably does not exist. The middle ground of grouping consumers into segments raises the whole issue of how the aggregation should be effected. Even individual consumers have been known to vary the criteria they use when making a series of judgments, indicating that the criteria depend on the products or brands in the stimulus set.

The fact that the criteria can change as the series of similarity judgments are made makes the already difficult problem of naming the dimensions even harder. One must be especially careful in using the similarity-based programs if the number of objects being judged is less than eight, as it is then very easy to develop an oversimplified picture of the competitive environment.

As previously mentioned, the attribute-based approaches make naming the dimensions easier and they also make the task of clustering respondents into groups with similar perceptions easier to deal with. They presume, however, that the list of attributes used to secure the ratings are relatively accurate and complete and that a person's perception or evaluation of a stimulus is some combination of the individual's reactions to the attributes making up the stimulus. Yet, people may not perceive or evaluate objects in terms of underlying attributes but may instead perceive them as some kind of whole that is not decomposable in terms of separate attributes. (For example, Corvette owners may not buy the car because of its handling, gas mileage, or even styling, but because of some undefinable attribute, or attributes—status, image, sexiness, playfulness, power?—that together make up a quality uniquely held by Corvette.)

Further, the measures used to group people imply some assumptions about how consumers' reactions to the various attribute scales should be combined. The attribute-based approaches are easier to use than the similarity method, since the programs employed are more readily available and less expensive to run.

Regardless of the approach taken, the appeal of multidimensional scaling lies in the maps produced by the technique. These maps can be used to provide insight into some very basic questions about markets, including, for product markets, the following:

1. The salient product attributes perceived by buyers in the market.

2. The combination of attributes buyers most prefer.

3. The products that are viewed as substitutes and those that are differentiated from one another.

4. The viable segments that exist in a market.

5. Those "holes" in a market that can support a new product venture.

Further, the technique also appears suited for product life-cycle analysis, market segmentation, vendor evaluation, the evaluation of advertisements, test marketing, sales representative-image and store-image research, brand-switching research, and attitude scaling.[25]

Conjoint Analysis

Conjoint analysis
A technique in which respondents' utilities or valuations of attributes are inferred from the preference they express for various combinations of these attributes.

Like multidimensional-scaling analysis, **conjoint analysis** relies on the ability of respondents to make judgments about stimuli. In multidimensional-scaling analysis, the stimuli are existing products or brands, and respondents are asked to make judgments about their relative *similarity*. In conjoint analysis, the stimuli represent some *predetermined combinations of features, benefits, and attributes* offered by a product, and respondents are asked to make judgments about their *preference* for these various combinations. In essence, conjoint analysis seeks to determine which benefit or attributes buyers are willing to trade off to retain others. The basic aim is to determine which combinations of features respondents prefer most.

Respondents might use, for example, such attributes as miles per gallon, seating capacity, price, length of warranty, and so on, in making judgments about which automobile they prefer. Yet, if asked to do so directly, many respondents might find it very difficult to state which attributes they were using and how they were combining them to form overall judgments. Conjoint analysis attempts to handle this problem by estimating how much each of the attributes are valued on the basis of the choices respondents make among product concepts that are varied in systematic ways. In this type of analysis, researchers attempt to infer respondents' value systems based on their choices rather than on the respondents' own estimations.

Conjoint analysis presumes that the relative values of things considered jointly can be measured when they might not be measurable if taken one at a time. Quite often respondents are asked to express the relative value to them of various alternatives by ordering the alternatives from most desirable to least desirable. Researchers then attempt to assign values to the levels of each of the attributes in a way that is consistent with the respondents' rank-order judgments.

Example of Conjoint Analysis

Suppose we were considering introducing a new drip coffeemaker and wished to assess how consumers evaluated the following levels of each of these product attributes:

- Capacity—4, 8, and 10 cups

- Price—$28, $32, and $38

- Brewing time—3, 6, 9, and 12 minutes

All three of these attributes are *motherhood* attributes, meaning that, other things being equal, most consumers would prefer either the most or least of each property—in this instance, the largest-capacity maker with the shortest brewing time and the lowest price. Unfortunately, life is not that simple. The larger coffeemaker will cost more; faster brewing means a larger heating element for the same pot capacity, which also raises the cost. And a larger-capacity maker with no change in the heating element will require increased brewing time. In sum, a consumer is going to have to trade off one property to secure more of another. The manufacturer is interested in determining how consumers value these specific attributes. Is low price most valued, or are consumers willing to pay a higher price to secure some of the other properties? Which price? Which properties?

One way to answer these questions is to develop a set of index cards containing all possible combinations of these product attributes. If each card contained a combination of one possible aspect of each category (e.g., 4-cup capacity, $32 price, 6-minute brewing time), there would be 36 possible combinations.

Suppose we then asked a respondent to order these product descriptions or cards from least desirable (ranked 1) to most desirable (ranked 36), so that higher numbers reflected greater preference. The respondent could be instructed, for example, to sort the cards first into four categories labeled "very undesirable," "somewhat undesirable," "somewhat desirable," and "very desirable," and then, after completing the sorting task, to order the cards in each category from least to most desirable. Suppose the ordering contained in Exhibit 14.2 resulted from this process.

Note several things about these entries. First, the respondent least preferred the $38 maker with 4-cup capacity and 12-minute brewing time (ranked 1) and most preferred the 10-cup maker with 3-minute brewing time priced at $28 (ranked 36). Second, if the respondent cannot have her first choice, she is willing to trade off the short brewing time for a longer brewing time so that she could still get the 10-cup maker for $28 (ranked 35). She is not willing to trade off too much, however, as reflected by her third choice (ranked 34). Rather, she is willing to pay a little more to secure the faster 3-minute brewing time rather than having to endure an even slower 9-minute brewing time. In effect, she is willing to trade off price for brewing time.

The type of question that conjoint analysis attempts to answer is, What are the individual's utilities for price, brewing time, and pot capacity in determining her choices? How much value does the individual place on each of these attributes in making her choice of products?

Procedure in Conjoint Analysis

The procedure for determining the individual's *utilities,* or values, for each of several product attributes followed in conjoint analysis is quite similar to that followed in multidimensional-scaling analysis. Again the technique is dependent on the availability of a high-speed computer. Just as in multidimensional scaling, the computer program's emphasis is on generating an initial solution and subsequently on modifying that solution through a series of iterations to improve the goodness of fit.[26] More specifically, given a set of input judgments, the computer program will

EXHIBIT 14.2	**Respondent Ordering of Various Product Descriptions**								
Capacity		**4 Cups**			**8 Cups**			**10 Cups**	
Price	$28	$32	$38	$28	$32	$38	$28	$32	$38
Brewing Time									
3 minutes	17	15	6	30	26	24	36	34	28
6 minutes	16	12	5	29	25	22	35	33	27
9 minutes	9	8	3	21	20	8	32	31	23
12 minutes	4	2	1	14	13	7	19	18	11

1. Assign arbitrary utilities to each level of each attribute.

2. Calculate the utilities for each alternative by somehow combining, most typically adding, the individual utility values.

3. Calculate the goodness of fit between the ranking of the alternatives using these derived utility values and the original ordering of the input judgments.

4. Modify the utility values in a systematic way until the derived utilities produce evaluations that, when ordered, correspond as closely as possible to the order of the input judgments.

Based on the results determined by the computer, the researcher can determine the relative importance of each attribute. It is important to keep in mind that the importance values are dependent on the particular attributes chosen to structure the analysis. Thus, if higher prices had been used, the respondents' values may have been different, suggesting that price was relatively more important to the individual than if lower prices had been used. An analysis such as this can be used to identify the optimal levels and importance of each attribute in structuring product and service offerings.

General Comments on Conjoint Analysis

One can see that vital marketing questions in product design are being addressed by conjoint analysis. Further, the technique is not restricted to product evaluations. It can be used whenever one is making a choice among multi-attribute alternatives. With multi-attribute alternatives, one typically does not have the option of having more of everything that is desirable and less of everything that is not desirable. Instead, most decisions involve trading off part of something in order to get more of something else. Conjoint analysis attempts to mirror the trade-offs one is willing to make. Consequently, while it has most often been used for product-design issues, including concept evaluation, it is also used quite regularly as an aid in pricing decisions, market-segmentation questions, or advertising decisions. It has been used less frequently for making distribution decisions, for evaluating vendors, for determining the rewards that salespeople value, and for determining consumer preferences for various attributes of health organizations, among other things.

Back to the Case

If Vlasic Foods and Nestlé Frozen Food made their marketing decisions based strictly on observable behavior, they couldn't be responsive to consumers. They might spend many years and millions of dollars tinkering with a product until they stumbled on the combination that would increase sales. Therefore, despite the limitations of measuring attitudes and preferences, the companies use research that asks consumers' opinions, and they apply the response data to their marketing decisions.

Either company might start with existing data such as the National Frozen Food Association's "Understanding the Frozen Food Consumer" study, which found some general patterns in consumers' attitudes toward frozen food. Consumers are well aware that frozen food provides convenience, but they are less apt to think of frozen food as offering "peak taste and nutrition." Nevertheless, consumers tend to have a higher opinion of frozen food than boxed or canned alter-

natives. The study also grouped frozen-food buyers into five categories, based on their attitudes and buying behavior:

1. Good Meal Makers (26 percent of the sample): These confident cooks use frozen food as a meal component. They turn to frozen food for side dishes, vegetables, or selected cuts of meat and poultry.

2. Hectic Have To's (24 percent): Very busy and very pressed for time, they buy whatever will save the most time. This segment purchases the most frozen food.

3. Simply Content (19 percent): These less-than-competent cooks are looking for simple meals. They are very satisfied with frozen food.

4. Basic Cooks (19 percent): These cooks are practical and economical. They tend to prefer canned or boxed foods over frozen foods, which they view as being of lower quality.

Summary

Learning Objective 1

List the various ways by which attitudes can be measured.

Attitudes can be measured by self-reports, observation of overt behavior, indirect techniques, performance of objective tasks, and physiological reactions.

Learning Objective 2

Name the most widely used attitude scaling techniques in marketing research and explain why researchers prefer them.

The Likert scale, or summated-ratings scale, and the semantic-differential scale are the most widely used attitude scaling techniques in marketing research. Both are particularly useful because they allow respondents to express the intensity of their feelings.

Learning Objective 3

Explain how a Stapel scale differs from a semantic-differential scale.

A Stapel scale differs from a semantic-differential scale in that (1) adjectives or descriptive phrases are tested separately instead of simultaneously as bipolar

---

5. Frozen Rejecters (12 percent): They don't care about convenience and don't like frozen food. They use it only as a backup in a pinch.

These descriptions can help each company define market segments and create questions to ask when they conduct their own research.

Vlasic talked to consumers about their associations with the Swanson brand. They found that consumers in the 25–54 age bracket had strong memories of Swanson TV dinners. When these consumers were children, their parents would let them pick out a Swanson dinner to eat while the parents went out for the evening. This was a pleasant memory for these consumers, and Vlasic decided to capitalize on that positive relationship with the brand. it launched an advertising campaign with the theme "Make New Memories with Swanson." The advertising supports an improved fried chicken dinner—the perennial favorite.

Nestlé's Lean Cuisine brand, a later entry to the frozen-food aisle, does not have the same appeal to nostalgia. That company has used consumer data to find its own niche. Nestlé talked to its target market, working mothers, and learned that almost half of them plan dinner after 4 P.M. and

about the same number believe that six o'clock is too late to start preparing a meal with fresh ingredients. For these consumers, Nestlé developed Lean Cuisine Skillet Sensations, which combines frozen meat and frozen vegetables in a single bag. Consumers can pick up the whole meal without making trips to the meat counter and the frozen-vegetable case, yet they still can prepare fresh-tasting food.

Why not simply put everything on a tray and sell TV dinners as Swanson does? Then consumers wouldn't have to bother with a skillet on a stove. Nestlé positioned this offering based on its own research. The company talked to the household members who made decisions about dinner, asking them about the timing and factors considered in these decisions. Nestlé learned that most working mothers would be happy to cook but believe they don't have enough time. According to Nestlé's Angelo Iantosca, "Skillet Sensations is designed for . . . consumers who need a balance between convenience and fresh taste." Packaging indicates that preparation time is just 15 minutes.

Sources: David Wellman, "New Life in the Freezer Case," *Supermarket Business* (February 1999), pp. 34–36; Maryellen Lo Bosco, "NFFA Study: Target the Right Consumer," *Supermarket News* (November 2, 1998), p. 47.

pairs, (2) points on the scale are identified by number, and (3) there are ten scale positions rather than seven. Respondents are told to rate how accurately each of a number of statements describes the object of interest.

Learning Objective 4

Cite the one feature that is common to all ratings scales.

The one feature common to all ratings scales is that the rater places the person or object being rated at some point along a continuum or in one of an ordered series of categories; a numerical value is attached to the point or the category.

Learning Objective 5

List three of the most common types of ratings scales.

Three of the most common ratings scales are the graphic, the itemized, and the comparative scales.

Learning Objective 6

Explain the difference between a graphic-ratings scale and an itemized-ratings scale.

The itemized-ratings scale is similar to the graphic-ratings scale except that the rater must select from a limited number of categories instead of placing a mark on a continuous scale. In general, five to nine categories work well.

Learning Objective 7

Explain how the constant-sum scaling method works.

In the constant-sum method of comparative rating, the individual is instructed to divide some given sum among two or more attributes on the basis of their importance to him or her. Respondents are generally asked to compare two attributes in this method, although it is possible to compare more.

Learning Objective 8

Identify the key decisions an analyst must make in order to complete a multidimensional-scaling analysis.

In order to complete a multidimensional-scaling analysis, an analyst must (1) specify the products and/or brands to be used; (2) specify how the similarities judgments are to be secured and construct the stimuli; (3) decide on whether judgments will be aggregated and, if so, how; (4) collect the judgments and analyze them to generate the perceptual map; and (5) name the resulting dimensions.

Learning Objective 9

Explain the basic principle behind conjoint analysis.

In conjoint analysis, the stimuli represent some predetermined combinations of features, benefits, and attributes offered by a product, and respondents are asked to make judgments about their preference for these various combinations. In essence, conjoint analysis seeks to determine which benefits or attributes buyers are willing to trade off to obtain others. The basic aim is to determine which combinations of features respondents prefer most.

Review Questions

1. What are the major ways that have been used to measure attitudes?

2. How does one construct a Likert summated-ratings scale? How are subjects scaled with a Likert scale?

3. What is a semantic-differential scale? How is a person's overall attitude assessed with a semantic-differential scale?

4. How does a Stapel scale differ from a semantic-differential scale?

5. What is a graphic-ratings scale? An itemized scale? A constant-sum scale?

6. What is a perceptual map? What is the primary difference between the nonattribute- and attribute-based approaches in generating perceptual maps?

7. What is the purpose of conjoint analysis? How is this purpose accomplished?

Discussion Questions, Problems, and Projects

1. (a) List at least eight attributes that students might use in evaluating bookstores.
   (b) Using these attributes, develop eight summated-ratings items and eight semantic-differential items by which attitudes toward (i) the university bookstore and (ii) some other bookstore can be evaluated.
   (c) Administer each of the scales to ten students.
   (d) What are the average sample scores for the two bookstores using the scale of summated ratings? What can be said about students' attitudes toward the two bookstores?
   (e) Develop a profile analysis or snake diagram for the semantic-differential scale.
   (f) Based on the semantic-differential scale, what can be said about students' attitudes toward the two bookstores?

2. (a) Assume that a manufacturer of a line of cheese products wanted to evaluate customer attitudes toward the brand. A panel of 500 regular consumers of the brand responded to a questionnaire that was sent to them and that included several attitude scales, which produced the following results:
   (i) The average score for the sample on a 25-item summated-ratings scale was 105.
   (ii) The average score for the sample on a 20-item semantic-differential scale was 106.
   (iii) The average score for the sample on a 15-item Stapel scale was 52.
   The vice-president has requested you to indicate whether his customers have a favorable or unfavorable attitude toward the brand. What will you tell him? Please be specific.
   (b) Following your initial report, the vice-president has provided you with some more information. The following memo has been given to you: "The company has been using the same attitude measures over the past eight years. The results of the previous studies are as follows:

Year	Summated Ratings	Semantic-Differential	Stapel
1992	86	95	43
1993	93	95	48
1994	97	98	51
1995	104	101	55
1996	110	122	62
1997	106	112	57
1998	104	106	53
1999	105	106	52

We realize there may not be any connection between attitude and behavior, but it must be pointed out that sales peaked in 1996 and since then have been gradually declining." With this information, do your conclusions change? Can anything more be said about customer attitudes?

3. Generate eight attributes that assess students' attitudes toward "take-home exams." Use (i) graphic-, (ii) itemized-, and (iii) comparative-ratings scales to determine the importance of each of these attributes in students' evaluation of take-home exams. (Note: In the case of the comparative-ratings scale, use only five of the attributes.) Administer each of these scales to separate samples of five students.
   (a) What are your findings with the graphic-ratings scale? Which attributes are important?
   (b) What are your findings with the itemized-ratings scale? Which attributes are important?
   (c) What are your findings with the comparative-ratings scale? Which attributes are important?

4. Assume that you are a staff researcher for a manufacturer of three nationally branded laundry detergents. The research and development department has formulated a new type of detergent that the company has decided to introduce under a new brand name. The product manager for the laundry detergent line has expressed concern that the new brand, unless it is carefully positioned, may cannibalize sales of the firm's current brands. You have been assigned to provide research-based information that will assist management in properly positioning the new brand in order to minimize the possibility of cannibalization. What method of analysis should you employ and why? Given your choice of method, what are some fundamental decisions that you must make?

5. Find six print advertisements for different types of medium-sized automobiles (for example, Ford, Toyota, Dodge). Append the six advertisements to this exercise.
   (a) Form all possible pairs of these models. Using the advertisements as input, rank the pairs in decreasing order of similarity (rank the most similar pair as 1) according to the way you perceive them.
   (b) Complete the following table:

PERCEIVED SIMILARITY JUDGMENTS

Model	1	2	3	4	5	6
1. ___						
2. ___						
3. ___						
4. ___						
5. ___						
6. ___						

   (c) List the criteria that you used in determining the similarity of the models.
   (d) Now, rate the models on two attributes—(i) style and (ii) features—using a seven-point semantic-differential scale. For example, if you think that a particular model has a lot of style, you should give it a rating of 6 or 7, and so on. Do this for all six models on both the attributes.
   (e) Complete the following distance matrix by computing the distances between each pair of objects. The distances can be computed with the following formula:

$$D_{ij} = \sqrt{(x_i - x_j)^2 + (y_i - y_j)^2}$$

where

x_i = rating of Model i on Attribute 1 $i = 1 \ldots . 6$
y_i = rating of Model i on Attribute 2

$$x_j = \text{rating of Model } j \text{ on Attribute 1 } j = 1 \ldots . 6 \; i \neq j$$
$$y_j = \text{rating of Model } j \text{ on Attribute 2}$$

For example, the distance between Model 1 and Model 2 is

$$D_{12} = \sqrt{(x_1 - x_2)^2 + (y_1 - y_2)^2}$$

DISTANCE MATRIX

Model	1	2	3	4	5	6
1. ___						
2. ___						
3. ___						
4. ___						
5. ___						
6. ___						

Note: The pairs that are most similar on the two attributes have smaller distances. The pairs that are most dissimilar on the two attributes have larger distances.

(f) Convert the preceding distances to similarity values by assigning the rank of 1 to the two closest objects, the rank of 2 to the next closest objects, and so on. Assign the average of the ranks to those pairs in which the distances between the two objects are the same.

CALCULATED SIMILARITY JUDGMENTS

Model	1	2	3	4	5	6
1. ___						
2. ___						
3. ___						
4. ___						
5. ___						
6. ___						

(g) Compare the perceived similarity in part (b) of this question and the calculated similarity in part (f).

6. Suppose you are interested in introducing a new toaster oven and decide to use conjoint analysis to determine how people value different attributes.
   (a) List three product attributes that would be relevant to you.
   (b) List three levels of each of these product attributes you might use to assess respondents' utilities.
   (c) Assign utilities to each of these levels. For example, suppose size is one of the attributes. One might then assign higher utilities to each of the larger sizes.

ATTRIBUTE I		ATTRIBUTE II		ATTRIBUTE III	
Levels	Utility	Levels	Utility	Levels	Utility
1.					
2.					
3.					

(d) Calculate the utilities for each alternative by assuming that the utilities for each attribute will combine additively. Complete the following table:

UTILITIES FOR THE FEATURE COMBINATIONS
GIVEN THE ASSUMED VALUES

Attribute I		(1)			(2)			(3)	
Attribute II	(1)	(2)	(3)	(1)	(2)	(3)	(1)	(2)	(3)
Attribute III									
(1)									
(2)									
(3)									

(e) Request a respondent to rank-order those product descriptions from least desirable (rank of 1) to most desirable (rank of 27).
   Note: (i) There are 27 combinations.
         (ii) Writing each combination on a separate index card would ease the task.

(f) Now, complete the following table.

RESPONDENT'S ORDERING OF VARIOUS PRODUCT DESCRIPTIONS

Attribute I		(1)			(2)			(3)	
Attribute II	(1)	(2)	(3)	(1)	(2)	(3)	(1)	(2)	(3)
Attribute III									
(1)									
(2)									
(3)									

(g) Plot the original order of the input judgments against the assigned utilities.

(h) Are the assigned utilities appropriate?

7. Questionnaire design is, at best, guided by only generalized rules and procedures. As a result, two researchers with the same objective may design very different questionnaires. With this in mind, critically review the CARA questionnaire presented in the Part Four Research Project, on the following pages. What are its good points? What features would you change? Provide specific examples and justify them if you feel an alternative technique would provide more useful information.

Endnotes

1. See, for example, James F. Engel, Roger D. Blackwell, and Paul Miniard, *Consumer Behavior,* 8th ed. (Fort Worth, Tex.: Dryden Press, 1996).

2. James H. Myers and William H. Reynolds, *Consumer Behavior and Marketing Management* (Boston: Houghton Mifflin, copyright © 1967), p. 146. For discussion of the role of attitudes and their effects, see Alice H. Eagley and Chaiken Shelly, *The Psychology of Attitudes* (Fort Worth, Tex.: Harcourt Brace Jovanovich, 1993).

3. Kevin T. Keleghan, "Quality of Service: Dancing to the Customer's Tune," *Retail Control* 60 (March 1992), pp. 3–8. See also Robert Davis, Susan Rosengrant, and Michael Watkins, "Managing the Link between Measuement and Compensation," *Quality Progress* (February 1995), pp. 101–106.

4. This classification of approaches is taken from Stuart W. Cook and Claire Selltiz, "A Multiple Indicator Approach to Attitude Measurement," *Psychological Bulletin* 62 (1964), pp. 36–55. See also Dagmar Krebs and Peter Schmidt, eds., *New Directions in Attitude Measurement* (Berlin: Walter de Gruyter, 1993).

5. Hugh Graham, "Annals of Marketing: Don't Go Changin'," *Globe and Mail* (September 25, 1998, downloaded from Dow Jones Publications Library at the Dow Jones Web site, www.dowjones.com, August 10, 1999).

6. The scale was first proposed by Rensis Likert, "A Technique for the Measurement of Attitudes," *Archives of Psychology,* No. 140 (1932).

7. For a generalizable procedure on how to go about constructing scales, see Gilbert A. Churchill, Jr., "A Paradigm for Developing Better Measures of Marketing Constructs," *Journal of Marketing Research* 16 (February 1979), pp. 64–73.

8. "American Customer Satisfaction Index," American Society for Quality Web site (www.asq.org, downloaded September 30, 1999).

9. Charles E. Osgood, George J. Suci, and Percy H. Tannenbaum, *The Measurement of Meaning* (Champaign, Ill.: University of Illinois Press, 1957).

10. Irving Crespi, "Use of a Scaling Technique in Surveys," *Journal of Marketing* 25 (July 1961), p. 71.

11. One study that compared the performance of the Stapel scale with that of the semantic-differential found basically no difference between the results produced by, or respondents' ability to use, each. See Del I. Hawkins, Gerald Albaum, and Roger Best, "Stapel Scale or Semantic Differential in Marketing Research," *Journal of Marketing Research* 11 (August 1974), pp. 318–322. See also Grahame R. Dowling, "Measuring Corporate Images: A Review of Alternative Approaches," *Journal of Business Research* 17 (August 1988), pp. 27–34.

12. Gregory D. Upah and Steven C. Cosmas, "The Use of Telephone Dials as Attitudes Scales," *Journal of the Academy of Marketing Science* (Fall 1980), pp. 416–426; Barbara Loken et al., "The Use of 0–10 Scales in Telephone Surveys," *Journal of the Market Research Society* 29 (July 1987), pp. 353–362.

13. There is evidence that demonstrates, for example, that there is little difference in results when ordinal data are analyzed by procedures appropriate to interval data. See Stanford Labovitz, "Some Observations on Measurement and Statistics," *Social Forces* 46 (1967), pp. 151–160; Sanford Labovitz, "The Assignment of Numbers to Rank Order Categories," *American Sociological Review* 35 (1970), pp. 515–524; John Gaito, "Measurement Scales and Statistics: Resurgence of an Old Misconception," *Psychological Bulletin* 87 (1980), pp. 564–567.

14. For empirical comparisons involving various forms of self-report scales of attribute importance, see "Measuring the Importance of Attributes," *Research on Research,* No. 28 (Chicago: Market Facts, Inc., undated); "The Use of Concern Scales as an Alternative to Importance Ratings," *Research on Research,* No. 44 (Chicago: Market Facts, Inc., undated); "An Analysis of Importance Ratings," *Research on Research,* No. 60 (Chicago: Market Facts, Inc., undated).

15. Claire Selltiz, Lawrence S. Wrightsman, and Stuart W. Cook, *Research Methods in Social Relations,* 3rd ed. (New York: Holt, Rinehart and Winston, 1976), pp. 403–404.

16. Eli P. Cox III, "The Optimal Number of Response Alternatives for a Scale: A Review," *Journal of Marketing Research* 17 (November 1980), pp. 407–422. For discussion of the issue of number of scale points specifically with respect to customer satisfaction measurement, see the special session "Scales: A Weighty Debate," *Marketing Research: A Magazine of Management & Applications* 9 (Fall 1994), pp. 6–33.

17. Albert R. Wildt and Michael B. Mazis, "Determinants of Scale Response: Label versus Position," *Journal of Marketing Research* 15 (May 1978), pp. 261–267; H. H. Friedman and J. R. Liefer, "Label versus Position in Rating Scales," *Journal of the Academy of Marketing Science* (Spring 1981), pp. 88–92; Norbert Schwarz et al., "Rating Scales: Numeric Values May Change the Meanings of Scale Labels," *Public Opinion Quarterly* 55 (Winter 1991), pp. 570–582; Colm O'Muircheartaigh, George D. Gaskell, and Daniel B. Wright, "Weighing Anchors: Verbal and Numerical Labels for Response Scales," *Journal of Official Statistics* 11 (1995), pp. 295–307.

18. Jerome S. Bruner, Jacqueline J. Goodnow, and George R. Austin, *A Study of Thinking* (New York: John Wiley, 1956); James G. Miller, "Sensory Overloading," in Bernard E. Flaherty, ed., *Psychophysiological Aspects of Space Flight* (New York: Columbia University Press, 1961), pp. 215–224; Jacob Jacoby, "Perspectives on Information Overload," *Journal of Consumer Research* 10 (March 1984), pp. 432–435.

19. Gilbert A. Churchill, Jr., and J. Paul Peter, "Research Design Effects on the Reliability of Rating Scales: A Meta-Analysis," *Journal of Marketing Research* 21 (November 1984), pp. 360–375.

20. Glen L. Urban and John R. Hauser, *Design and Marketing of New Products,* 2nd ed. (Englewood Cliffs, N.J.: Prentice-Hall, 1993). For discussion of the usefulness of various techniques for answering these questions, see Michael D. Johnson and Elania J. Hudson, "On the Perceived Usefulness of Scaling Techniques in Market Analysis," *Psychology & Marketing* 13 (October 1996), pp. 653-675.

21. See John R. Hauser and Frank S. Koppelman, "Alternative Perceptual Mapping Techniques: Relative Accuracy and Usefulness," *Journal of Marketing Research* 16 (November 1979), pp. 495–506; Joel Huber and Morris B. Holbrook, "Using Attribute Ratings for Product Positioning: Some Distinctions Among Compositional Approaches," *Journal of Marketing Research* 16 (November 1979), pp. 507–516, for illustrations of the factor and discriminant analysis approaches to the generation of perceptual maps.

22. Jean McDougall, "Building Brands for the Future," *Perspectives* (Millward Brown International), Winter 1998 (downloaded from the Millward Brown Web site, www.millwardbrown.com, September 30,

1999); Mercedes M. Cardona, "WPP Brand Study Ranks Gerber 1st in U.S. Market," *Advertising Age* (October 5, 1998).

23. For an overview of some marketing studies that have used various algorithms, see Lee G. Cooper, "A Review of Multidimensional Scaling in Marketing Research," *Applied Psychological Measurement* 7 (Fall 1983), pp. 427–450. For a review of algorithms generally available on microcomputers, including INDSCAL, see Paul E. Green, Frank J. Carmone, Jr., and Scott M. Smith, *Multidimensional Scaling: Concepts and Applications* (Boston: Allyn and Bacon, 1989).

24. Huber and Holbrook, "Using Attribute Ratings for Product Positioning."

25. For a review of these applications, see Cooper, "A Review of Multidimensional Scaling in Marketing Research," p. 23.

26. There are a number of programs available. One of the historically more popular programs was MONANOVA. See J. B. Kruskal, "Analysis of Factorial Experiments by Estimating Monotone Transformations of the Data," *Journal of the Royal Statistical Society*, Series B, 27 (1965), pp. 251–263. For a review and comparison of currently popular programs, see the review by F. J. Carmone and C. M. Schaffer in the *Journal of Marketing Research* 32 (February 1995), pp. 113–120.

Suggested Additional Readings

For a general discussion of how to ask questions in attitude surveys, see
Howard Schuman and Stanley Presser, *Questions and Answers in Attitude Surveys* (Orlando, Fla.: Academic Press, 1981).

For discussion of a general procedure that can be followed to develop attitude scales having desirable qualities, see
Gilbert A. Churchill, Jr., "A Paradigm for Developing Better Measures of Marketing Constructs," *Journal of Marketing Research* 16 (February 1979), pp. 64–73.

For discussion of the various alternatives for perceptual mapping, see
Glen L. Urban and John R. Hauser, *Design and Marketing of New Products*, 2nd ed. (Englewood Cliffs, N.J.: Prentice-Hall, 1993).

For discussion of the various issues surrounding conjoint analysis, see
J. Douglas Carroll and Paul E. Green, "Psychometric Methods in Marketing Research: Part I, Conjoint Analysis," *Journal of Marketing Research* 32 (November 1995), pp. 385–391.
Paul E. Green and V. Srinivasan, "Conjoint Analysis in Marketing: New Developments with Implications for Research and Practice," *Journal of Marketing* 54 (October 1990), pp. 3–19.

The fourth stage in the research process is to design the data-collection form. As we learned from the chapters in this part, designing a questionnaire is still an art, not a science. Nonetheless, as we saw in Chapter 12, there is a pattern of steps that beginning researchers often find useful in developing questionnaires. The method outlined begins with specifying what information will be sought, and it ends with pretesting the questionnaire and revising it if necessary. As was pointed out in the chapter, however, only rarely will actual questionnaire development be so orderly. More often, researchers will find themselves circling back to revise an earlier part of the questionnaire after subsequent development has proven it to be faulty in some respect.

We also learned in these chapters that the typical questionnaire contains two types of information: basic information and classification information. Basic information refers to the subject of the study, while classification information refers to the data collected about respondents, such as demographic and socioeconomic characteristics, that help in understanding the results. As we saw, the proper questionnaire sequence is to secure basic information first and classification information last, since without the basic information, there is no study.

Researchers for CARA decided to use a self-report attitude scale to measure local businesspeople's feelings toward various advertising media and their sales representatives. In the chosen format, respondents were asked to indicate the extent to which they agreed or disagreed with statements about sales representatives and advertising media by checking one of the blanks ranging from strong agreement to strong disagreement. This format allowed the researchers two advantages: they could measure a respondent's intensity of feeling, and responses could be easily scored.

In the CARA study, the various degrees of agreement were assigned the values of 5, 4, 3, 2, and 1, with "strongly agree" representing the value of 5 and "strongly disagree" representing the value of 1. A total attitude score for each respondent could thereby be calculated by summing the ratings of the individual items.

Respondents were asked to rate the importance of the attributes and characteristics used to describe sales representatives and advertising media by checking the three most important items in each category. Researchers thought this was important because an individual may strongly agree or disagree with an item but may not value that characteristic or attribute.

Each of the three categories of sales representatives contained 12 descriptive attributes. The attributes were ordered randomly, and the identical order was then used in each category. By using identical items in identical order, researchers could compare total attitude scores between the sales representative categories. If different items, or a different ordering of items, within each category had been used, variation in the testing instrument might have been responsible for differences in resulting scores.

Respondents were also asked to indicate which 3 of the 12 attributes they felt were the most important. These attributes were listed in the same order as the items in the sales representatives' scales.

The advertising media of television, radio, and newspaper were also described by 12 characteristics. These characteristics were randomly ordered, and each category used the identical order of items for the reason just cited. The 12 attributes were also listed in an importance scale in the same order as the items in the media categories, and respondents were asked to select the 3 attributes they believed to be most important.

Questions regarding the sales representatives were asked first so as to generate interest in the questionnaire. This section was followed by questions about attitudes toward the various media. Finally, researchers added a section requesting classification information. This section was last because, while important, it was the least critical to the study.

Researchers chose the 12 specific attributes used to describe the sales representatives and the advertising media based on their review of the literature, discussions with CARA members, and experience surveys with local retailers.

CARA Questionnaire

Section 1

Please indicate your opinion as to the extent to which you agree or disagree with the following statements for your television, radio, and newspaper sales representatives by placing an "X" in the appropriate blank. If you have more than one sales representative in any of these media, your opinions should include your general impressions of the sales representatives calling on you. If you have never been in contact with a sales representative in one or more of these media, please omit that section (or those sections) and proceed to the next. Don't worry over individual responses. It is your first impression on each item that is important.

TELEVISION SALES REPRESENTATIVE

The television sales representatives calling on me are	Strongly Agree	Agree	Neither Agree nor Disagree	Disagree	Strongly Disagree
1. Creative	____	____	____	____	____
2. Reliable	____	____	____	____	____
3. Sincere	____	____	____	____	____
4. Results oriented	____	____	____	____	____
5. Knowledgeable about my business	____	____	____	____	____
6. Cooperative	____	____	____	____	____
7. Available when needed	____	____	____	____	____
8. Hardworking	____	____	____	____	____
9. Concerned about my particular advertising needs	____	____	____	____	____
10. Able to get my ads placed quickly	____	____	____	____	____
11. Aware of who my customers are	____	____	____	____	____
12. Concerned about follow-through after the service	____	____	____	____	____

RADIO SALES REPRESENTATIVE

The radio sales representatives calling on me are	Strongly Agree	Agree	Neither Agree nor Disagree	Disagree	Strongly Disagree
1. Creative	____	____	____	____	____
2. Reliable	____	____	____	____	____
3. Sincere	____	____	____	____	____
4. Results oriented	____	____	____	____	____
5. Knowledgeable about my business	____	____	____	____	____
6. Cooperative	____	____	____	____	____
7. Available when needed	____	____	____	____	____
8. Hardworking	____	____	____	____	____
9. Concerned about my particular advertising needs	____	____	____	____	____
10. Able to get my ads placed quickly	____	____	____	____	____
11. Aware of who my customers are	____	____	____	____	____
12. Concerned about follow-through after the service	____	____	____	____	____

NEWSPAPER SALES REPRESENTATIVE

The newspaper sales representatives calling on me are	Strongly Agree	Agree	Neither Agree nor Disagree	Disagree	Strongly Disagree
1. Creative	____	____	____	____	____
2. Reliable	____	____	____	____	____
3. Sincere	____	____	____	____	____
4. Results oriented	____	____	____	____	____
5. Knowledgeable about my business	____	____	____	____	____
6. Cooperative	____	____	____	____	____
7. Available when needed	____	____	____	____	____
8. Hardworking	____	____	____	____	____
9. Concerned about my particular advertising needs	____	____	____	____	____
10. Able to get my ads placed quickly	____	____	____	____	____
11. Aware of who my customers are	____	____	____	____	____
12. Concerned about follow-through after the service	____	____	____	____	____

Please indicate what you believe are the three most important characteristics of a sales representative by placing an "X" in the appropriate blank. For example, if you feel Items 4, 8, and 10 are the most important characteristics, you would place an "X" in the blank next to each of these items.

The three most important characteristics of a media sales representative are

1. Creativity   _____
2. Reliability   _____
3. Sincerity   _____
4. An orientation toward results   _____
5. A knowledge about my business   _____
6. Cooperation   _____
7. Availability when needed   _____
8. A willingness to work hard   _____
9. A concern about my particular advertising needs   _____
10. The ability to quickly place my ads   _____
11. Awareness of who my customers are   _____
12. Concern about follow-through after the service   _____

Section 2

Please indicate your opinion as to the extent to which you agree or disagree with the following statements about television, radio, and newspaper advertising, regardless of whether you use that form of advertising or not. Place an "X" in the appropriate blank. Again, don't worry about individual responses, since it is your first impression on each item that is important.

Television Advertising	Strongly Agree	Agree	Neither Agree nor Disagree	Disagree	Strongly Disagree
1. People pay attention to the ads.	___	___	___	___	___
2. The ads reach my target market.	___	___	___	___	___
3. The ads do not cost too much.	___	___	___	___	___
4. The ads improve my sales volume.	___	___	___	___	___
5. The ads are creative.	___	___	___	___	___
6. The ads do not have to be repeated frequently to be effective.	___	___	___	___	___
7. The ads reach a large number of people.	___	___	___	___	___
8. The ads build up recognition of my business.	___	___	___	___	___
9. There is evidence that ads reach a known market.	___	___	___	___	___
10. Buying the ads is not a difficult process.	___	___	___	___	___
11. It is easy to monitor when the ads are being run.	___	___	___	___	___
12. The quality of the ads is high (good).	___	___	___	___	___

Continued

Radio Advertising	Strongly Agree	Agree	Neither Agree nor Disagree	Disagree	Strongly Disagree
1. People pay attention to the ads.	_____	_____	_____	_____	_____
2. The ads reach my target market.	_____	_____	_____	_____	_____
3. The ads do not cost too much.	_____	_____	_____	_____	_____
4. The ads improve my sales volume.	_____	_____	_____	_____	_____
5. The ads are creative.	_____	_____	_____	_____	_____
6. The ads do not have to be repeated frequently to be effective.	_____	_____	_____	_____	_____
7. The ads reach a large number of people.	_____	_____	_____	_____	_____
8. The ads build up recognition of my business.	_____	_____	_____	_____	_____
9. There is evidence that ads reach a known market.	_____	_____	_____	_____	_____
10. Buying the ads is not a difficult process.	_____	_____	_____	_____	_____
11. It is easy to monitor when the ads are being run.	_____	_____	_____	_____	_____
12. The quality of the ads is high (good).	_____	_____	_____	_____	_____

Newspaper Advertising	Strongly Agree	Agree	Neither Agree nor Disagree	Disagree	Strongly Disagree
1. People pay attention to the ads.	_____	_____	_____	_____	_____
2. The ads reach my target market.	_____	_____	_____	_____	_____
3. The ads do not cost too much.	_____	_____	_____	_____	_____
4. The ads improve my sales volume.	_____	_____	_____	_____	_____
5. The ads are creative.	_____	_____	_____	_____	_____
6. The ads do not have to be repeated frequently to be effective.	_____	_____	_____	_____	_____
7. The ads reach a large number of people.	_____	_____	_____	_____	_____
8. The ads build up recognition of my business.	_____	_____	_____	_____	_____
9. There is evidence that ads reach a known market.	_____	_____	_____	_____	_____
10. Buying the ads is not a difficult process.	_____	_____	_____	_____	_____
11. It is easy to monitor when the ads are being run.	_____	_____	_____	_____	_____
12. The quality of the ads is high (good).	_____	_____	_____	_____	_____

Please indicate what you believe are the three most important attributes of advertising by placing an "X" in the appropriate blank. For example, if you feel Items 4, 8, and 10 are the most important attributes, you would place an "X" in the blank next to each of these items.

The three most important attributes of advertising are that

1. People pay attention to the ads.   _____
2. The ads reach my target market.   _____
3. The ads do not cost too much.   _____
4. The ads improve my sales volume.   _____
5. The ads are creative.   _____
6. The ads do not have to be repeated frequently to be effective.   _____

7. The ads reach a large number of people.   _____
8. The ads build up recognition of my business.   _____
9. There is evidence that ads reach a known market. _____
10. Buying the ads is not a difficult process.   _____
11. It is easy to monitor when the ads are being run. _____
12. The quality of the ads is high (good).   _____

Section 3: Classification Data

1. What types of advertising have you used over the last 12 months?

Outdoor   _____
Radio   _____
Television   _____
Newspaper   _____
Magazine   _____
Yellow Pages   _____
Direct Mail   _____
Shoppers   _____
Other   _____

2. Approximately what proportion of your total yearly advertising budget is spent on each of the following types of advertising?

Outdoor   _____
Radio   _____
Television   _____
Newspaper   _____
Magazine   _____
Yellow Pages   _____
Direct Mail   _____
Shoppers   _____
Other   _____
Total =   100%

3. How much do you spend annually on advertising?

0–$9,999   _____
$10,000–$24,999   _____
$25,000–$49,999   _____
$50,000 and over   _____

4. Which category best descibes your position?

Manager   _____
Owner/Manager   _____
Secretary   _____
Clerk   _____
Other   _____

5. Do you make decisions regarding advertising expenditures?

Yes   _____
No   _____

6. Do you use an advertising agency?

Yes   _____
No   _____

Case IV.A   Rumstad Decorating Centers (B)

Rumstad Decorating Centers was an old-line Rockford, Illinois, business. The company was originally founded as a small paint and wallpaper supply store in 1929 by Joseph Rumstad, who managed the store until his retirement in 1970, at which time Jack Rumstad, his son, took over. In 1974, the original downtown store was closed and a new outlet was opened on the city's rapidly expanding west side. In 1999, a second store was opened on the east side of the city, and the name of the business was changed to Rumstad Decorating Centers.

Jack Rumstad's review of 2000 operations proved disconcerting. Both stores had suffered losses for the year [see Case II.A, Rumstad Decorating Centers (A)]. The picture was far more dismal at the west side store. Losses at the east side store were 80 percent less than the previous year's, which was partially due to some major organizational changes. Further, the east side store had experienced a 25 percent increase in net sales and a 25 percent increase in gross profits over 1999. The west side store, in contrast, had shown a 21 percent decrease in net sales and a 31 percent decrease in gross profit.

Some preliminary research by Rumstad suggested that the problem at the west side store might be traced to the store's location or its advertising. Was the location perceived as convenient? Were potential customers aware of Rumstad Decorating Centers, the products they carried, and where they were located? Did people have favorable impressions of Rumstad? How did attitudes towards Rumstad compare with those toward Rumstad's major competitors?

Rumstad realized that he did not have the expertise to answer these questions. Consequently, he called in Sandra Parrett, who owned and managed her own marketing research service in the Rockford area. Parrett handled all liaison work with the client and assisted in the research design. In addition to Parrett, Lisa Parrett, her daughter, supervised the field staff of four, analyzed data, and prepared research reports. Although the company was small, it had an excellent reputation within the business community.

Research Design

Rumstad agreed with Sandra Parrett's suggestion that the best way to investigate Rumstad's concerns would be to use a structured, somewhat disguised questionnaire (see Exhibit IV.A.1). The sponsor of the research was to be hidden from the respondents to prevent them from answering "correctly" instead of honestly, so questions about two of Rumstad's main competitors, the Nina Emerson Decorating Center and the Wallpaper Shop, were introduced. Both of these stores offered products and services similar to those carried by Rumstad, and they were located in the same area as Rumstad's west side store. The study was to be confined to the west side store because of cost; loss of profits for the last several years had severely constrained Rumstad's ability to engage in research of this sort. However, the west side store was so critical to the very survival of Rumstad Decorating Centers that Rumstad was willing to commit funds to this investigation, although he repeatedly stressed to Parrett the need to keep the cost as low as possible.

EXHIBIT IV.A.1   Sample Questionnaire—Rumstad Decorating Centers

Section I

For Questions 1–8, please indicate your opinion about the importance of the following factors in choosing a decorating center. Place an X in the appropriate blank.

	Not Important	Slightly Important	Fairly Important	Very Important
1. *Saw or heard an advertisement*	_____	_____	_____	_____
2. *Special sale*	_____	_____	_____	_____
3. *Convenient location*	_____	_____	_____	_____
4. *Convenient hours*	_____	_____	_____	_____
5. *Knowledgeable sales personnel*	_____	_____	_____	_____
6. *Good quality products*	_____	_____	_____	_____
7. *Additional services (e.g., matching paints, decorator services, etc.)*	_____	_____	_____	_____
8. *Reasonable prices in relation to quality*	_____	_____	_____	_____

EXHIBIT IV.A.1   **Sample Questionnaire—Rumstad Decorating Centers,** *continued*

Below is a list of abbreviations for the three west side stores that will be referred to throughout the questionnaire:

Emerson Decorating Center—"Emerson"
Rumstad Decorating Center—"Rumstad"
Wallpaper Shop—"Wallpaper Shop"

Please indicate your response with an X in the appropriate blank.

9. *Do you know where any of the following west side stores are located? (i.e., could you find any of these stores without referring to another source?)*

	Yes	No
Emerson	_____	_____
Rumstad	_____	_____
Wallpaper Shop	_____	_____

10. *When was the last time you heard or saw any advertisements for the following stores?*

	Never	Within the Last Month	1–6 Months	More than 6 Months
Emerson	_____	_____	_____	_____
Rumstad	_____	_____	_____	_____
Wallpaper Shop	_____	_____	_____	_____

11. *Please indicate the source(s) of any advertisements you have seen or heard.*

	Have Not Seen/Heard	Shopper's World	Rockford Morning Star	Radio	TV	Other	Don't Recall
Emerson	_____	_____	_____	_____	_____	_____	_____
Rumstad	_____	_____	_____	_____	_____	_____	_____
Wallpaper Shop	_____	_____	_____	_____	_____	_____	_____

12. *Do you know which of the following items are available in these stores? If so, check the item(s) that apply.*

	Don't Know	Paint	Paneling	Carpeting	Draperies	Other
Emerson	_____	_____	_____	_____	_____	_____
Rumstad	_____	_____	_____	_____	_____	_____
Wallpaper Shop	_____	_____	_____	_____	_____	_____

13. *Which name brands of paint, if any, do you associate with the following stores?*

	Benjamin Moore	Dutch Boy	Glidden	Pittsburgh	Do Not Associate Any Listed
Emerson	_____	_____	_____	_____	_____
Rumstad	_____	_____	_____	_____	_____
Wallpaper Shop	_____	_____	_____	_____	_____

Continued

EXHIBIT IV.A.1 **Sample Questionnaire—Rumstad Decorating Centers,** *continued*

14. Have you ever visited any of these west side stores?

	Never	Within Last Year	1–5 Yrs. Ago	More than 5 Yrs. Ago
Emerson	_____	_____	_____	_____
Rumstad	_____	_____	_____	_____
Wallpaper Shop	_____	_____	_____	_____

Section II

If you have visited or have knowledge of one or more of the stores listed below, please indicate the extent to which you agree or disagree with the following statements for each store(s). For instance, if you have knowledge of only one store, please answer each question for that particular store. If you have not visited or have no knowledge of any of these stores, omit this section and proceed to Section III.

	Strongly Agree	Agree	Neither Agree nor Disagree	Strongly Disagree	Disagree
15. The location of the store is convenient.					
Emerson	_____	_____	_____	_____	_____
Rumstad	_____	_____	_____	_____	_____
Wallpaper Store	_____	_____	_____	_____	_____
16. The sales personnel are knowledgeable.					
Emerson	_____	_____	_____	_____	_____
Rumstad	_____	_____	_____	_____	_____
Wallpaper Store	_____	_____	_____	_____	_____
17. The store lacks additional services (e.g., matching paint, decorator services, etc.).					
Emerson	_____	_____	_____	_____	_____
Rumstad	_____	_____	_____	_____	_____
Wallpaper Store	_____	_____	_____	_____	_____
18. The store carries good-quality products.					
Emerson	_____	_____	_____	_____	_____
Rumstad	_____	_____	_____	_____	_____
Wallpaper Store	_____	_____	_____	_____	_____
19. The prices are reasonable in relation to the quality of the products.					
Emerson	_____	_____	_____	_____	_____
Rumstad	_____	_____	_____	_____	_____
Wallpaper Store	_____	_____	_____	_____	_____
20. The store hours are inconvenient.					
Emerson	_____	_____	_____	_____	_____
Rumstad	_____	_____	_____	_____	_____
Wallpaper Store	_____	_____	_____	_____	_____

EXHIBIT IV.A.1   Sample Questionnaire—Rumstad Decorating Centers, *continued*

Section III

1. Your sex: _____ Male   _____ Female

2. Your age: _____ Under 25   _____ 25–29 years   _____ 30–39 years
_____ 40–54 years   _____ 55 or over

3. How long have you lived in Rockford?
_____Less than 1 year   _____ 1–3 years   _____ 4 or more years

4. Do you: _____ Own a home or condominium _____ Rent a house
_____ Rent an apartment   _____ Other

5. When was the last time you painted or remodeled your residence?
_____ Never   _____ Within past year   _____ 1–5 years ago   _____ More than 5 years ago

6. Approximately how many times have you received the weekly Shopper's World *in the past 3 months?*
_____ Never   _____ 1–5 times   _____ 6–12 times

7. Do you read or page through the Shopper's World*?*
_____ Do not receive it   _____ Never   _____ Less than ½ the time
_____ About ½ the time   _____ More than ½ the time

Even though the Emerson Decorating Center and the Wall-paper Shop were similar to Rumstad, there were differences in their marketing strategies. Both stores seemed to advertise more than Rumstad, for example, although the exact amounts of their advertising budgets were not available. Emerson advertised in the *Shopper's World* (a weekly paper devoted exclusively to advertising that is distributed free), ran ads four times a year in the *Rockford Morning Star,* and did a small amount of radio and outdoor advertising. The Wallpaper Shop also advertised regularly in the *Shopper's World* but ran small ads daily in the *Morning Star* and had daily radio commercials as well. Rumstad had formerly advertised in the *Morning Star* but now relied exclusively on the *Shopper's World.*

Sample

Because of the financial constraints imposed on the study by Jack Rumstad, it was decided to limit the study to households within a two-mile radius of Rumstad, Emerson, and the Wallpaper Shop. Aldermanic districts within the two-mile radius were identified; there were four in all, and the wards within each district were listed. Two of the 12 wards were then excluded because they were outside of

the specified area. Blocks within each of the 10 remaining wards were enumerated, and 5 blocks were randomly selected from each ward. An initial starting point for each block was determined, and the questionnaires were then administered by the Parrett field staff at every sixth house on the block. All interviews were conducted on Saturday and Sunday. If there was no one at home or if the respondent refused to cooperate, the next house on the block was substituted; there was no one at home at 39 households, and 18 others refused to participate. The field work was completed within one weekend and produced a total sample of 123 responses.

Questions

1. Evaluate the questionnaire. Do you think the questionnaire adequately addresses the concerns raised by Rumstad?

2. How would you suggest the data collected be analyzed to best solve Rumstad's problem?

3. Do you think personal administration of the questionnaires was called for in this study, or would you suggest an alternative scheme? Why or why not?

Case IV.B   School of Business (A)[1]

The School of Business, one unit in a public university enrolling over 40,000 students, has approximately 2,100 students in its bachelor's, master's, and doctorate programs emphasizing such areas of business as accounting, finance, information and operations management, marketing, management, and others. Because the School of business must serve a diverse student population on limited resources, it feels it is important to measure accurately students' satisfaction with the school's programs and services.

Accurate measurement of student satisfaction will enable the school to target improvement efforts to those areas of greatest concern to students, whether that be by major, support services, or some other aspect of their educational experience. The school feels that improving its service to its customers (students) will result in more satisfied alumni, better community relations, additional applicants, and increased corporate involvement. Because graduate and undergraduate students are believed to have different expectations and needs, the school plans to investigate the satisfaction of these two groups separately.

[1]The contributions of Sara Pitterle to the development of this case are gratefully acknowledged.

In a previous survey of graduating seniors using open-ended questions, three primary areas of concern were identified: the faculty, classes/curriculum, and resources. Resources consisted of five specific areas: Undergraduate Advising Services, the Learning Center, Computer Facilities, the Library, and the Career Services Office. The research team for this project developed five-point Likert scale questions to measure students' satisfaction in each of these areas. In addition, demographic questions were included to determine whether satisfaction with the school was a function of a student's grade point average, major, job status upon graduation, or gender. Previous surveys used by the School of Business and other published satisfaction scales provided examples of questions and question formats. Exhibit IV.B.1 shows the questionnaire that was used.

Although the survey contained primarily Likert-scale questions, a few open-ended questions were also asked. Specifically, respondents were asked to list the Business School's strengths and weaknesses as well as their reasons for not using the various resource areas. The responses obtained to the question seeking the school's strengths and weaknesses were classified into four major subgroups: classes, reputation, resources, and professors. A sample of the actual verbatims are provided in Exhibit IV.B.2.

EXHIBIT IV.B.1   Survey of Graduating Business Students

In your opinion, what are the greatest strengths and weaknesses of the Business School?

Strengths

_____

_____

_____

_____

Weaknesses

_____

_____

_____

_____

CLASSES/CURRICULUM
Please indicate the extent to which you agree with the following statements.

Strongly Agree	Agree	Neither Agree/Dis.	Disagree	Strongly Disagree

I was satisfied with the quality of classes I took within my major.

(1) ____   (2) ____   (3) ____   (4) ____   (5) ____

EXHIBIT IV.B.1 Survey of Graduating Business Students, *continued*

I was able to take enough electives within my major.

        (1) _____   (2) _____   (3) _____   (4) _____   (5) _____

"Lecture-Driven" vs. "Project" or "Group" class formats are most useful for learning.

        (1) _____   (2) _____   (3) _____   (4) _____   (5) _____

The business school taught too much theory and not enough about real-life applications.

        (1) _____   (2) _____   (3) _____   (4) _____   (5) _____

Creative problem solving was encouraged in my classes.

        (1) _____   (2) _____   (3) _____   (4) _____   (5) _____

My classes were too large.

        (1) _____   (2) _____   (3) _____   (4) _____   (5) _____

I was challenged by my coursework.

        (1) _____   (2) _____   (3) _____   (4) _____   (5) _____

There were not enough group projects in my classes.

        (1) _____   (2) _____   (3) _____   (4) _____   (5) _____

More night courses should be offered.

        (1) _____   (2) _____   (3) _____   (4) _____   (5) _____

Overall, the material presented in my classes was current.

        (1) _____   (2) _____   (3) _____   (4) _____   (5) _____

FACULTY

Strongly Agree	Agree	Neither Agree/Dis.	Disagree	Strongly Disagree

My professors are concerned about my future success.

        (1) _____   (2) _____   (3) _____   (4) _____   (5) _____

Overall, the Business School professors are good teachers.

        (1) _____   (2) _____   (3) _____   (4) _____   (5) _____

The Business School places too much emphasis on research and not enough on teaching.

        (1) _____   (2) _____   (3) _____   (4) _____   (5) _____

Overall, my professors were accessible outside of class.

        (1) _____   (2) _____   (3) _____   (4) _____   (5) _____

The Business School takes my comments on professor evaluation forms seriously.

        (1) _____   (2) _____   (3) _____   (4) _____   (5) _____

Overall, my professors provided adequate office hours during the semester.

        (1) _____   (2) _____   (3) _____   (4) _____   (5) _____

Overall, my professors encouraged students to raise relevant questions during class.

        (1) _____   (2) _____   (3) _____   (4) _____   (5) _____

My professors tested memorization skills on exams more than my ability to apply concepts.

        (1) _____   (2) _____   (3) _____   (4) _____   (5) _____

Overall, the Business School professors interacted well with students.

        (1) _____   (2) _____   (3) _____   (4) _____   (5) _____

My professors showed creativity in their teaching methods.

        (1) _____   (2) _____   (3) _____   (4) _____   (5) _____

My professors are at the leading edge of knowledge in their fields.

        (1) _____   (2) _____   (3) _____   (4) _____   (5) _____

I approve of TA's teaching foundation courses.

        (1) _____   (2) _____   (3) _____   (4) _____   (5) _____

My professors were stimulating.

        (1) _____   (2) _____   (3) _____   (4) _____   (5) _____

Continued

EXHIBIT IV.B.1   **Survey of Graduating Business Students,** *continued*

<u>RESOURCES</u>

<u>Advising</u>

Did you ever use the undergraduate advising office?
        (1) _____ Yes   (2) _____ No

If not, why not?

_____
_____
_____
_____

If you answered yes to the question above, please complete the remainder of the questions regarding Advising. If you answered no, please proceed to the following section—Learning Center.

Strongly Agree	Agree	Neither Agree/Dis.	Disagree	Strongly Disagree

The undergraduate advising office played a big role in helping me plan my business curriculum.
        (1) _____   (2) _____   (3) _____   (4) _____   (5) _____
The undergraduate advising office should have more advisors.
        (1) _____   (2) _____   (3) _____   (4) _____   (5) _____
The advisor(s) in the undergraduate advising office was (were) helpful.
        (1) _____   (2) _____   (3) _____   (4) _____   (5) _____
The staff in the advising office was helpful.
        (1) _____   (2) _____   (3) _____   (4) _____   (5) _____
I felt like I was bothering the advisor(s) in the undergraduate advising office if I asked him/her a question.
        (1) _____   (2) _____   (3) _____   (4) _____   (5) _____
The advisor(s) in the undergraduate advising office was (were) concerned about my needs.
        (1) _____   (2) _____   (3) _____   (4) _____   (5) _____
If there were more undergraduate advisors, I would have utilized the advising services more often.
        (1) _____   (2) _____   (3) _____   (4) _____   (5) _____
Advice offered by the advising office was not helpful to me.
        (1) _____   (2) _____   (3) _____   (4) _____   (5) _____

<u>Learning Center</u>

Did you ever use The Learning Center?
        (1) _____ Yes   (2) _____ No

If not, why not?

_____
_____
_____
_____

If you answered yes to the question above, please complete the remainder of the questions regarding The Learning Center. If you answered no, please proceed to the following section—Career-Services Facilities/Staff.

EXHIBIT IV.B.1   Survey of Graduating Business Students, *continued*

	Strongly Agree	Agree	Neither Agree/Dis.	Disagree	Strongly Disagree
The Learning Center was useful to me.	(1) ___	(2) ___	(3) ___	(4) ___	(5) ___
The staff at the Learning Center are helpful.	(1) ___	(2) ___	(3) ___	(4) ___	(5) ___
The Learning Center needs to extend its hours.	(1) ___	(2) ___	(3) ___	(4) ___	(5) ___

<u>Career-Services Facilities/Staff</u>

Did you ever use the Career-Services office as a resource in your search for full- or part-time employment?
      (1) ___ Yes   (2) ___ No

If not, why not?

_____

_____

_____

_____

If you answered yes to the question above, please complete the remainder of the questions regarding Career-Services Facilities/Staff. If you answered no, please proceed to the following section—Computer Facilities/Staff.

	Strongly Agree	Agree	Neither Agree/Dis.	Disagree	Strongly Disagree
Overall, the Career-Services office has been a valuable resource in my job search.	(1) ___	(2) ___	(3) ___	(4) ___	(5) ___
The staff in the Career-Services office are helpful.	(1) ___	(2) ___	(3) ___	(4) ___	(5) ___
The Career-Services office is/was my main resource used in my search for my job.	(1) ___	(2) ___	(3) ___	(4) ___	(5) ___
In my opinion, the Career-Services office is understaffed.	(1) ___	(2) ___	(3) ___	(4) ___	(5) ___
I was pleased with the number of companies interviewing at the Career-Services office within my major.	(1) ___	(2) ___	(3) ___	(4) ___	(5) ___
The Career-Services office is successful at attracting desirable employers to interview on campus.	(1) ___	(2) ___	(3) ___	(4) ___	(5) ___
The sign-up process for interviews at the Career-Services office is fair.	(1) ___	(2) ___	(3) ___	(4) ___	(5) ___
The Career-Services office provides enough information on how to use the Resume Expert software.	(1) ___	(2) ___	(3) ___	(4) ___	(5) ___
The Career-Services office offers adequate interview training.	(1) ___	(2) ___	(3) ___	(4) ___	(5) ___

<u>Computer Facilities/Staff</u>

Did you ever use the Business School's computer facilities?
      (1) ___ Yes   (2) ___ No

Continued

EXHIBIT IV.B.1   Survey of Graduating Business Students, *continued*

If not, why not?

_____
_____
_____
_____

If you answered yes to the question above, please complete the remainder of the questions regarding Computer Facilities/Staff. If you answered no, please proceed to the following section—Library Facilities/Staff.

Strongly Agree	Agree	Neither Agree/Dis.	Disagree	Strongly Disagree

The computer room needs to extend its weekend hours.
(1) ____   (2) ____   (3) ____   (4) ____   (5) ____

The computer room needs to extend its night hours.
(1) ____   (2) ____   (3) ____   (4) ____   (5) ____

More computers are needed in the computer room.
(1) ____   (2) ____   (3) ____   (4) ____   (5) ____

More printers are needed in the computer facilities.
(1) ____   (2) ____   (3) ____   (4) ____   (5) ____

The computer-room staff is helpful.
(1) ____   (2) ____   (3) ____   (4) ____   (5) ____

A computer was available when I needed to use one.
(1) ____   (2) ____   (3) ____   (4) ____   (5) ____

Library Facilities/Staff

Did you use the Business School's library facilities?
(1) ____ Yes   (2) ____ No

If not, why not?

_____
_____
_____
_____

If you answered yes to the question above, please complete the remainder of the questions regarding Library Facilities/Staff. If you answered no, please proceed to the following section—Student Organizations.

Strongly Agree	Agree	Neither Agree/Dis.	Disagree	Strongly Disagree

The Library staff is helpful.
(1) ____   (2) ____   (3) ____   (4) ____   (5) ____

The Library has adequate study space.
(1) ____   (2) ____   (3) ____   (4) ____   (5) ____

Student Organizations

Were you a member of any Business School student organizations?
(1) ____ Yes   (2) ____ No

EXHIBIT IV.B.1   **Survey of Graduating Business Students,** *continued*

If not, why not?

_____

_____

_____

_____

If you answered yes to the question above, please complete the remainder of the questions regarding Student Organizations. If you answered no, please proceed to the following section—GENERAL.

How many organizations were you a member of?

       (1) _____ 1

       (2) _____ 2

       (3) _____ 3

       (4) _____ >3

Did you hold an office?   (1) _____ Yes   (2) _____ No

Do you believe the faculty and staff were supportive of the student organizations?

       (1) _____ Yes   (2) _____ No   (3) _____ Don't know

What were your reasons for joining?

_____

_____

_____

_____

GENERAL

	Strongly Agree	Agree	Neither Agree/Dis.	Disagree	Strongly Disagree
My Business School education has given me a sense of accomplishment.	(1) _____	(2) _____	(3) _____	(4) _____	(5) _____
The Business School is well respected nationally.	(1) _____	(2) _____	(3) _____	(4) _____	(5) _____
My undergraduate degree has prepared me well for a successful career in business.	(1) _____	(2) _____	(3) _____	(4) _____	(5) _____
The caliber of my classmates enhanced my learning.	(1) _____	(2) _____	(3) _____	(4) _____	(5) _____
The Business School should require more computer courses.	(1) _____	(2) _____	(3) _____	(4) _____	(5) _____
The copying facilities at the Business School are inadequate.	(1) _____	(2) _____	(3) _____	(4) _____	(5) _____
My undergraduate experience was disappointing.	(1) _____	(2) _____	(3) _____	(4) _____	(5) _____
The Business School placed too much emphasis on a high GPA and not enough on learning.	(1) _____	(2) _____	(3) _____	(4) _____	(5) _____
I felt like a number here at the Business School.	(1) _____	(2) _____	(3) _____	(4) _____	(5) _____
The Business School should have a mandatory class on ethics for undergraduates.	(1) _____	(2) _____	(3) _____	(4) _____	(5) _____

Continued

EXHIBIT IV.B.1 **Survey of Graduating Business Students,** *continued*

Please indicate the extent to which you agree that each of the following factors POSITIVELY CONTRIBUTED to the quality of your over-all undergraduate business education:

Strongly Agree	Agree	Neither Agree/Dis.	Disagree	Strongly Disagree

Class size in major classes:
    (1) _____ (2) _____ (3) _____ (4) _____ (5) _____

Class size in required courses:
    (1) _____ (2) _____ (3) _____ (4) _____ (5) _____

Group projects:
    (1) _____ (2) _____ (3) _____ (4) _____ (5) _____

Case studies:
    (1) _____ (2) _____ (3) _____ (4) _____ (5) _____

Multiple-choice exams:
    (1) _____ (2) _____ (3) _____ (4) _____ (5) _____

Use of creative thought:
    (1) _____ (2) _____ (3) _____ (4) _____ (5) _____

Guest lecturers:
    (1) _____ (2) _____ (3) _____ (4) _____ (5) _____

Required classes:
    (1) _____ (2) _____ (3) _____ (4) _____ (5) _____

Number of electives you can take:
    (1) _____ (2) _____ (3) _____ (4) _____ (5) _____

Number of required computer courses:
    (1) _____ (2) _____ (3) _____ (4) _____ (5) _____

Please indicate the extent to which you agree that each of the following core classes POSITIVELY CONTRIBUTED to the quality of your overall undergraduate business education:

	Strongly Agree	Agree	Neither Agree/Dis.	Disagree	Strongly Disagree
Comp Sci	(1) _____	(2) _____	(3) _____	(4) _____	(5) _____
Managerial Acctg 302	(1) _____	(2) _____	(3) _____	(4) _____	(5) _____
Financial Acctg 200	(1) _____	(2) _____	(3) _____	(4) _____	(5) _____
Communications 320	(1) _____	(2) _____	(3) _____	(4) _____	(5) _____
Business Law 330	(1) _____	(2) _____	(3) _____	(4) _____	(5) _____
Corporate Finance 510	(1) _____	(2) _____	(3) _____	(4) _____	(5) _____
Marketing 520	(1) _____	(2) _____	(3) _____	(4) _____	(5) _____
Org. Behavior 530	(1) _____	(2) _____	(3) _____	(4) _____	(5) _____
Business Statistics 570	(1) _____	(2) _____	(3) _____	(4) _____	(5) _____
Mgt of Serv-Mfg Op 574	(1) _____	(2) _____	(3) _____	(4) _____	(5) _____
OVERALL	(1) _____	(2) _____	(3) _____	(4) _____	(5) _____

GENERAL INFORMATION

Please mark the number corresponding to your gender:
    (1) _____ Female   (2) _____ Male

Are you a state resident?
    (1) _____ Yes   (2) _____ No

Please mark the number(s) corresponding to your major(s).

    (1) _____ Accounting   (7) _____ Marketing
    (2) _____ Actuarial Science   (8) _____ Quantitative Analysis
    (3) _____ Diversified   (9) _____ Real Estate
    (4) _____ Finance   (10) _____ Risk Management
    (5) _____ Information Systems   (11) _____ Transportation and Public Utilities
    (6) _____ Management and Human Resources

EXHIBIT IV.B.1   Survey of Graduating Business Students, *continued*

Please mark the number corresponding to your GPA.

(1) _____ 3.5–4.0   (2) _____ 3.0–3.49   (3) _____ 2.5–2.99   (4) _____ 2.0–2.49

Please mark the number of years it will take you to graduate.

(1) _____ 3 1/2   (2) _____ 4   (3) _____ 4 1/2   (4) _____ 5   (5) _____ >5 1/2

During the program (excluding summers), have you been employed?

(1) _____ Employed full time   (2) _____ Employed part-time   (3) _____ Not employed

What do you plan to do upon graduation?

(1) _____ full-time employment
(2) _____ part-time employment
(3) _____ graduate school
(4) _____ other, please specify

If you intend to work full time, please specify if you:

(1) _____ have already accepted a position
(2) _____ are still in the process of interviewing
(3) _____ other, please specify

THANK YOU FOR COMPLETING THE SURVEY OF GRADUATING BUSINESS STUDENTS

EXHIBIT IV.B.2   A Sample of the Survey Responses to Question 1 Regarding Strengths and Weaknesses

Strengths	Weaknesses
"Breadth of courses and disciplines."	"Not enough real-life applications"
"The increase in group projects was also helpful."	"Core classes tedious."
"Classes in your major are relatively small."	"Too much emphasis on GPA."
"Excellent faculty advising (not undergrad advising)."	"Lack of advisors."
"Good Faculty" "Excellent Profs"	"Lack of support facilities."
"Has a good reputation."	"Awful Undergraduate advising."
"Required some thought-provoking classes (literature, philosophy)."	"Classes are too much on theory."
"Free laser printing in the computer lab."	"The computer classes are a waste of time."
"The resources for information gathering are great."	"Too many unnecessary core requirements that could be used for
"The options of resources available are great."	another class or elective."
"The competitiveness, quality of students."	"Too many exams scheduled in the 6th and 12th weeks."
"Nice that classes aren't greatly dependent on Fridays	"Too many required group projects."
(open to work or volunteering)."	"Can't get classes when needed."
"Clear curriculum of what classes are needed if in Pre-	"Too few resources for the number of students."
Business or Business—although there are a lot of	"Students not treated as individuals."
them, the core classes allow you to touch all majors."	"Not enough computers."
"A well-respected and less costly route to a business	"Makes students take core classes in each function of business."
undergrad degree than other alternatives available."	"Need more case studies & seminar type classes with fewer
"A few good professors that make up for all the bad ones."	students."
"Some of the professors are terrific and really care	"There is too much memorization and not enough
about the students."	practical application of knowledge."
"National Reputation."	"Making appointments to see advisors."
	"Professors expect too much."
	"Computer courses are too technical."

Questions

1. Considering customer satisfaction as it applies to a university setting, what are some other areas in addition in those identified for the project that may contribute to students' satisfaction/dissatisfaction with their education experience?

2. Does the current questionnaire provide information on students' overall satisfaction with their undergraduate degree program? Explain. What revisions are necessary to this questionnaire to obtain an overall satisfaction rating?

3. Can the School of business use the results of this study to target the most important areas for improvement? Explain. Identify changes to the questionnaire that would allow the school to target areas based on importance.

4. What are the advantages and disadvantages of using open-ended questions to identify the school's strengths and weaknesses? Taking the responses in Exhibit IV.B.2, what system would you use for coding these responses?

Case IV.C   Young Ideas Publishing Company (A)[1]

How does a company go about marketing products to a specific niche of the teenage market? That is the question confronting Linda Halley, co-owner of Young Ideas Publishing Company. Halley is convinced that her unconventional novels for young people would be very attractive to at least a segment of the teenaged market. She is unsure, however, about how to reach this "nonconformist" segment of the market.

Background

Three years ago, Halley wrote her first novel, a youth-oriented book (ages 15–18) entitled *Illusions of Summer*. None of the major publishers would publish the book, however, primarily because it dealt with several controversial social and political concerns. Most publishers simply felt that such topics would not be of interest to enough high school teenagers to justify publication, although many agreed that the novel was of publication quality in other respects.

Frustrated in her efforts to publish her novel, Halley and a business partner, Teresa Martinez, decided to form their own publishing company and publish the book themselves. Both believed that teenagers would be interested in social and political topics and would buy the book. Thus, Young Ideas Publishing Company was born. Halley hoped that effective marketing of the book on a local basis by the company might encourage national distributors to alter their positions toward the novel.

When *Illusions of Summer* was released, it was very well received by several literary critics, winning promising reviews and awards. Despite its critical success, however, commercial acceptance has been much harder to find. During the first 24 months after publication, only about 1,500 copies of the book have been sold, mostly through local bookstores and mail orders. Most distributors were unwilling to handle the book because it was not from an established publisher. With few channels through which to market the product, it remains virtually unknown outside of a limited local market.

Even with this poor showing from a commercial standpoint, Halley continued to believe that so-called "nonconformist" teenagers would be willing to buy books of this nature. Accordingly, she wrote and published a second novel, *Ultimate Choices*. Once again, the novel dealt with several controversial issues for teens and social and political concerns; once again, the critics reacted favorably. Initial sales for *Ultimate Choices* have been better than they were for *Illusions of Summer;* currently (two months after publication), about 250 copies have been sold. By talking to clerks in local bookstores, Halley has learned that most of the books are being sold to teenagers.

Nature of the Problem

Although encouraged by the good reviews and increased sales of the second book, Halley and Martinez are concerned about the future of Young Ideas Publishing Company. Even though the company has managed to break even during the past two years by contracting for outside printing jobs, Martinez has indicated that the survival of the company may well depend on the success of the new novel.

Both partners are still convinced that a market exists for the novels. They now recognize, however, that they may not know enough about the teenage market to effectively market the novels. For example, they believe that insights are needed in the following areas:

- Will high school teenagers specifically select young adult novels, or do they think that these are written for younger teens?

- Are teenagers interested in social and political issues?

- Where do high school teenagers usually obtain books for pleasure reading?

[1]The contribution of Tom J. Brown to the development of this case are gratefully acknowledged.

- Do teens purchase books for themselves, or do parents purchase books for them?

- What types of promotional items do high school teens enjoy most?

- What advertising media are most effective in reaching teens?

- How do "nonconformist" teens differ on these issues from other teens?

You have been hired by Young Ideas Publishing Company to develop and implement a research project to investigate these ideas. Resources are limited; Halley would like the results of the research within 60 days.

Questions

1 Based on the information provided and your knowledge of marketing and marketing research, define the research problem.

2. What is the target population for your study?

3. Discuss your proposed sampling plan, including the implications for the implementation of the project.

Case IV.D   CTM Productions (A)[1]

CTM Productions, formerly Children's Theatre of Madison, was formed in 1965 to "produce theater of the highest quality." CTM's mission is to "ensure that our [CTM's] efforts are inclusive of all the human family, rather than parts of it." In order to measure its present and future achievement of this goal, CTM must learn who its audience actually is.

CTM's research team decided to study the audience of CTM's production *To Kill a Mockingbird*. The study had

[1]The contribution of Sara L. Pitterle to this case are gratefully acknowledged.

three major objectives: (1) to develop an audience profile including demographic and media exposure data; (2) to provide a framework and data collection instrument for future marketing research; and (3) to supply a list of potential season subscribers. Since CTM had never undertaken any marketing research prior to this study, internal secondary information did not exist. External secondary information provided guidance as to the types of questions to be asked on this type of questionnaire and the appropriate phrasing for such questions. The questionnaire is shown in Exhibit IV.D.1.

EXHIBIT IV.D.1   CTM Questionnaire

Introduce Yourself to CTM

Welcome to CTM's production of *To Kill a Mockingbird*. CTM Productions has been around for a long time—since 1965. And in this time we have had over 33,000 people in our audience. People to whom we have never been introduced. Real people like you that presently exist as numbers in our records. Now you have a chance to change your status. Introduce yourself to us by taking two minutes to answer the following questions to help us understand who you really are.

Let's start out with the basics. Your name is _____
and you live at (please include mailing address with Zip Code) _____

How many CTM productions have you attended?   [ ] this is my first CTM production

1999–2000 Season
[ ] season subscriber
[ ] *Wind in the Willows*
[ ] *A Christmas Carol*
[X] *To Kill a Mockingbird*
[ ] *Babar II* (plan to attend)

1998–1999 Season
[ ] season subscriber
[ ] *Red Shoes*
[ ] *A Christmas Carol*
[ ] *Anne of Green Gables*
[ ] *Narnia*

1997–1998 Season
[ ] season subscriber
[ ] *Beauty and the Beast*
[ ] *A Christmas Carol*
[ ] *I Remember Mama*
[ ] *Babar the Elephant*

Who is with you today? **(check all that apply)**
[ ] myself
[ ] adult friend(s)
[ ] my spouse/partner
[ ] unrelated kids
[ ] my kids
[ ] other families

Continued

EXHIBIT IV.D.1   CTM Questionnaire, *continued*

Who have you attended with in the past? (again, check all that apply)

[ ] myself [ ] my spouse/partner [ ] my kids
[ ] adult friend(s) [ ] unrelated kids [ ] other families

Have you or any of your family participated in any of these CTM activities? (check all that apply)

[ ] after-school drama classes [ ] auditions [ ] have not participated
[ ] summer school [ ] performances [ ] did not know I could

How did you find out about our production of To Kill a Mockingbird? (check all that apply)

[ ] season brochure [ ] poster

Read story in:
[ ] *State Journal* [ ] *Capitol Times* [ ] *Isthmus* [ ] other

Saw ad in:
[ ] *State Journal* [ ] *Capitol Times* [ ] *Isthmus* [ ] other

[ ] radio (which station) _____
[ ] television (which station) _____
[ ] magazine (which one) _____
[ ] word of mouth [ ] other

Did you come to this performance because you knew someone in the cast?   [ ] yes   [ ] no

What other events have you attended in the last six months? (check all that apply)

With your family or friends:
[ ] sports [ ] movies [ ] live musical performances
[ ] museums [ ] lectures [ ] other live theatrical performances

Alone:
[ ] sports [ ] movies [ ] live musical performances
[ ] museums [ ] lectures [ ] other live theatrical performances

Your answers to the following demographic questions will help us understand who you are.

Are you a female or male?   [ ] female   [ ] male

Which age category do you belong to?

[ ] 16–20 [ ] 31–40 [ ] 51–60 [ ] 71–80
[ ] 21–30 [ ] 41–50 [ ] 61–70 [ ] 81–100

How did you get here today?

[ ] walked [ ] car [ ] bus [ ] other

From how far away did you come?

[ ] within Madison [ ] less than 5 miles [ ] 6–10 miles [ ] over 10 miles

How long have you lived in the Madison/south-central Wisconsin area?

[ ] do not live here [ ] just arrived [ ] 1–3 years [ ] 4–7 years [ ] more

What is your highest level of education?

[ ] some high school [ ] some college [ ] some graduate school [ ] more
[ ] high school graduate [ ] college graduate [ ] graduate school graduate

CTM Questionnaire, *continued*

What is your annual household income?
[ ] below $20,000   [ ] $31–40,000   [ ] more than $50,000   [ ] do not wish to reply
[ ] $21–30,000   [ ] $41–50,000   [ ] not sure

Does this represent a dual income household?   [ ] yes   [ ] no

How many people live in your household? (circle only one, include yourself)
1   2   3   4   5   6   more

If you have children, how many are in each grade category?
[ ] not in school yet   [ ] 4th–5th grade   [ ] high school   [ ] other
[ ] kindergarten–3rd grade   [ ] 6th–8th grade   [ ] college

Would you like to be on our mailing list to keep informed of CTM activities?   [ ] yes   [ ] no

| Case IV.E   Caldera Industries[1]

Chris Totten has just begun a summer internship at Caldera Industries, a national supplier of electronics components. Caldera's clients include OEM (original equipment manufacturers) firms that market televisions, home stereo and audio, and computer products to the general public. Returning from lunch, Chris finds the following memo and questionnaire in her mailbox.

[1]This case was prepared by Michael R. Luthy, Ph.D., Associate Professor of Marketing, W. Fielding Rubel School of Business, Bellarmine College, 2001 Newburg Road, Louisville, KY 40205. Reprinted with permission.

EXHIBIT

Caldera Industries

Serving our Customers' Electronics Needs For Over 15 Years

CI

Internal Memorandum

TO: Chris Totten
           Marketing Analyst Intern

cc: Caren Menlo
           Marketing Manager

From: Manuel Ortega
           Vice President for Sales and Marketing

Date: May 23, 2000

Regarding: Evaluation of Market Research Questionnaire

In three weeks I will be meeting with executives from a number of our client companies. One of the items on the agenda is the research project our company has agreed to undertake on their behalf. At that meeting, the final version of our questionnaire will be distributed and approved.

Continued

On the attached pages is an initial draft of the Consumer Electronics Questionnaire we plan on using for the study. As the newly hired Marketing Intern, and because of your marketing research coursework experience, I suggested to our Marketing Manager, Caren Menlo that reviewing the questionnaire would make an ideal first assignment for you. She agreed.

Please examine the attached questionnaire and provide me with a written memo of your analysis, comments, and suggestions for improvement (if you believe any are warranted) within two (2) weeks. More specifically, I am interested in your comments to the following issues:

- the type and amount of information being sought

- appropriateness of the type of questionnaire designed and its method of administration

- the content of questions in the draft document

- response formats used for the various questions

- question wording

- question sequencing

- physical characteristics and layout of the instrument

I am also interested in any comments or suggestions you have on pretesting the questionnaire. I look forward to reading your memo.

Consumer Electronics Research Questionnaire

Directions: This questionnaire has been developed for a consortium of computer and home entertainment company's (who wish to remain anonymous). Complete all questions and mail this questionnaire to us today.

Quality Research Associates
5716 N. Woodlawn Court
Champaign, IL 61820

1. Name: _____   _____ Mr.   _____ Mrs.

2. Sex: _____

3. How old are you: _____

4. Intelligence: _____ Only completed college degree (Bachelor's)
   _____ Completed some graduate work
   _____ Completed graduate degree
   _____ Completed graduate degree beyond masters

5. Ethnic Status: _____ White   _____ Asian
   _____ Black   _____ Indian
   _____ Asian   _____ Other   What? _____

6. Political Party Support: _____ Democrat
   _____ Republican
   _____ Independent
   _____ Other

7. Your Occupation: _____

8. Spouse's Name and Age: _____

EXHIBIT *continued*

9. Number of Children: _____

10. Your Company: _____

11. Your Work Fax Number: (__ __ __) __ __ __ - __ __ __ __

12. How Long Have You Been Married: _____ Never married
    _____ Less than a year
    _____ Between 1 and 5 years
    _____ Over 5 but less than 10 years
    _____ Over 15 years but less than 20 years
    _____ More than 20 years

13. Your Annual Income: $ _____

14. Social Security Number: __ __ __ - __ __ - __ __ __ __

15. The sponsors of this research are constantly introducing new products that they believe you (and your loved one, if any) will be interested in. In order to better make you aware of these offerings, please provide your telephone number below.

    (__ __ __) __ __ __ - __ __ __ __

16. Do you own a computer at home or at work?
    _____ Yes   _____ No

17. During an average week, how much time do you spend on it?
    _____ Hours   _____ Minutes

18. Doing what mostly?
    _____

For each of the products listed below, please indicate the extent of your satisfaction with it, ceteris paribus, by either circling or placing an "X" on the line to the right of each statement.

Mild Satisfaction .... Extremely Satisfied

19. Apple Computers and Peripherals.
20. Gateway Computers and Peripherals.
21. Dell Computers and Peripherals.
22. IBM Computers and Peripherals
24. Hewlett-Packard Computers and Peripherals.
25. MacIntosh Computers and Peripherals.
26. Hitachi, Ltd. Computers and Peripherals.
27. Unisys Computers and Peripherals.
28. Tandy Computers and Peripherals.

29. Without being too loquacious, what emerging trends or technologies do you see as important to you that computer manufacturers (both hardware and software) should consider in developing new products?
    _____
    _____

30. How many different computer chattrooms have you visited in the last month?
    _____ 1-2
    _____ 2-3
    _____ 3-4
    _____ more than four

Continued

Below is a listing of ways in which people interact with consumer electronics on a quasi regular basis. What percentage of your time do you typically spend with each?

Check Below If You Do Not Use	Do Use			On Average, Number of "Others" Present During Your Usage
31. _____	_____ %	Work related computer activities		_____
32. _____	_____ %	Entertainment related computer activities		_____
33. _____	_____ %	Watching Network Television		_____
34. _____	_____ %	Watching Cable Television		_____
35. _____	_____ %	Watching Premium Cable Services		_____
36. _____	_____ %	Watching Rented Movies on VCR		_____
37. _____	_____ %	Watching Rented Movies on DVD		_____
38. _____	_____ %	Listening to Music on Radio or on CD's		_____
39. _____	_____ %	Other (specify)		_____
		_____		_____
		_____		

Referencing the music you listen to, vis `a vis your response to question #38 above (see question #38 if needed), which are your favorite musical periods or types? Please indicate your first 10 choices in numerical order.

40. Earlier than renaissance   _____
41. Renaissance   _____
42. Baroque   _____
43. Classical   _____
44. Romantic   _____
45. Impressionistic   _____
46. Neo-Classical   _____
47. Contemporary   _____
48. Contemporary Christian   _____
49. Rock   _____
50. Hard Rock   _____
51. Grung Rock   _____
52. Jazz   _____
53. Easy Listening   _____
54. Jazz/Rock Fusion   _____
55. Bluegrass   _____
56. Contemporary   _____
57. Folk Music   _____
58. Country   _____
59. Western   _____
60. Other   _____

61. Chart your child's usage of the following computer-related activities in 1998: (A = never, B = once to twice a per month, C = once to twice a week, D = every week, E = twice or more per week, F = daily, G = multiple times a day)

	Word Processing	EXCEL	Database Programs	E-Mail	Internet "Surfing"	Internet Chattrooms	Games
Jan 1–Jan 15							
Jan 16–Jan 31							
Feb 1–Feb 15							
Feb 16–Feb 28							
Mar 1–Mar 15							
Mar 16–Mar 30							
Apr 1–Apr 15							
Apr 16–Apr 30							
May 1–May 15							
May 16–May 30							
Jun 1–Jun 15							
Jun 16–Jun 30							
Jul 1–Jul 15							
Jul 16–Jul 31							
Aug 1–Aug 15							
Aug 16–Aug 31							
Sep 1–Sep 15							
Sep 16–Sep 30							
Oct 1-Oct 15							
Oct 16–Oct 31							
Nov 1–Nov 15							
Nov 16–Nov 30							

What is the *most* you would be willing to spend to purchase the following consumer electronic products if you were going to purchase them within the next year? and why?

Why?

62. $ _____ DVD player _____
63. $ _____ External Zip drive _____
64. $ _____ Big Screen Television _____
65. $ _____ Portable Stereo or Television _____
66. $ _____ Digital Camera _____

Note: On question #61 previously, if you have more than one child, use the computer usage of the oldest. ◀━━━━━━━━━━▶

67. To what degree do you believe that access to the Internet
    is important to your family's entertainment needs?   A   B   C   D   E

68. What emerging trends or technologies do you see as important to you that computer manufacturers (both hardware and software)
    should consider in developing new products?

_____

_____

Continued

EXHIBIT   *continued*

69. On a separate sheet of paper, please provide the names and addresses of at least three (3) friends or relatives that have recently (within the last two years) purchased an advanced consumer electronics product so that we may contact them.

Mail your completed questionnaire in a standard business size envelope to:

Quality Research Associates
4518 North Trails End
Cleveland, OH 34454
(a single 33-cent stamp will be needed)

Questions

1. Evaluate the questionnaire in relation to the issues raised by Manuel Ortega.

2. How would you recommend the instrument be pretested?

Case IV.F   Calamity-Casualty Insurance Company[1]

Calamity-Casualty is an insurance company located in Dallas, Texas, that deals exclusively with automobile coverage. Its policy offerings include the standard features offered by most insurers, such as collision, comprehensive, emergency road service, medical, and uninsured motorist. The unique aspect of Calamity-Casualty Insurance is that all policies are sold through the mail. Agents do not make personal calls on clients, and the company does not operate district offices. As a result, Calamity-Casualty's capital/labor requirements are greatly reduced at a substantial cost savings to the company. A great portion of these savings are passed on to the consumer in the form of lower prices. The data indicate that Calamity-Casualty offers its policies at 20 to 25 percent below the average market rate.

The company's strategy of selling automobile insurance by mail at low prices has been very successful. Calamity-Casualty has traditionally been the third largest seller of automobile insurance in the Southwest. During the past five years, the company has consistently achieved an average market share of some 14 percent in the four states it serves: Arizona, New Mexico, Nevada, and Texas. This compares favorably to the 19 percent and 17 percent market shares realized by the two leading firms in the region. However, Calamity-Casualty has never been highly successful in Arizona. The largest market share gained by Calamity-Casualty in Arizona for any one year was 4 percent, which placed the company seventh among firms competing in that state.

The company's poor performance in Arizona greatly concerns Calamity-Casualty's board of executives.

Demographic experts estimate that during the next six to ten years, the population in Arizona will increase some 10 to 15 percent, the largest projected growth rate of any state in the Southwest. Thus, for Calamity-Casualty to remain a major market force in the area, the company needs to improve its sales performance in Arizona.

In response to this matter, Calamity-Casualty sponsored a study that was conducted by the Automobile Insurance Association of America (AIAA), the national association of automobile insurance executives, to determine Arizona residents' attitudes toward and perception of the various insurance companies selling policies in that state. The results of the AIAA research showed that Calamity-Casualty was favorably perceived across most categories measured. Calamity-Casualty received the highest ratings with respect to service, pricing, policy offering, and image. Although these findings were well received by the company's board of executives, they provided little strategic insight into how Calamity-Casualty might increase sales in Arizona.

Because the company was committed to obtaining information useful for developing a more effective Arizona sales campaign, the executive board sought the services of Aminbane, Pedrone, and Associates, a marketing research firm specializing in insurance consulting, to help with the matter. After many discussions between members of the research team and executives at Calamity-Casualty, it was decided that the most beneficial approach toward designing a more appropriate sales campaign would be to ascertain the psychographic profiles of nonpurchasers and direct-mail purchasers of Calamity-Casualty insurance. This would help the company better understand the personal factors influencing people's decision to respond or not respond to direct-mail solicitation.

[1]The contributions of David M. Szymanski to the development of this case are gratefully acknowledged.

Research Design

To learn more about which psychographic factors are important in describing purchasers of automobile insurance, some exploratory research was undertaken. In-depth interviews were held with two insurance salespersons, who offered various insights on the subject. These experience interviews were followed by a focus group meeting with Arizona residents who had received a direct-mail offer from Calamity-Casualty. Finally, the research team consulted university professors in both psychology and mass communications to uncover other determinants of buyer behavior. Output from these procedures revealed three primary factors that could be used to describe purchasers of insurance by mail—namely, risk aversion, powerlessness, and convenience orientation. It was believed that people who were risk averse, had a low sense of powerlessness, and were convenience-oriented would be more favorably disposed toward direct-mail marketing efforts and thus would be more likely to purchase Calamity-Casualty automobile insurance.

Method of Data Collection

Given these factors of interest, the list of items contained in Exhibit 1 was generated to form the basis of a questionnaire to be administered to Arizona residents. Two samples of subjects were to be used—one of direct-mail buyers and one of nonbuyers. The research team estimated that 175 subjects would be required from both samples to adequately assess the three constructs. Because a mail questionnaire dealing with psychographic subject matter might have a very low response rate, and because attitude toward direct mail was one of the attributes being measured, a telephone interview was believed to be best suited to the needs at hand.

EXHIBIT 1   **Calamity-Casualty Marketing Research Questionnaire Items**

Risk Aversion

1. It is always better to buy a used car from a dealer than from an individual.
2. Generally speaking, I avoid buying generic drugs at the drugstore.
3. It would be a disaster to be stranded on the road due to a breakdown.
4. It would be important to me to plan a long road trip very carefully and in great detail.
5. I would like to try parachute jumping sometime.
6. Before buying a new product, I would first discuss it with someone who had already used it.
7. Before deciding to see a new movie in a theater, it is important to read the critical reviews.
8. If my car needed even a minor repair, I would first get cost estimates from several garages.

Powerlessness

1. Persons like myself have little chance of protecting our personal interests when they conflict with those of strong pressure groups.
2. A lasting world peace can be achieved by those of us who work toward it.
3. I think each of us can do a great deal to improve world opinion of the United States.
4. This world is run by the few people in power, and there is not much the little guy can do about it.

5. People like me can change the course of world events if we make ourselves heard.
6. More and more, I feel helpless in the face of what's happening in the world today.

Convenience Orientation

1. I like to buy things by mail or catalog because it saves time.
2. I think that it is not worth the extra effort to clip coupons for groceries.
3. I would rather wash my own car than pay to have it washed at a car wash.
4. I would prefer to have an automatic transmission rather than a stick shift in my car.
5. When choosing a bank, I believe that location is the most important factor.
6. When shopping for groceries, I would be willing to drive a longer distance in order to buy at lower prices.

Note: Each item requires one of the following responses:

Responses	Code
S.A.—Strongly Agree	5
A.—Agree	4
N.—Neither Agree nor Disagree	3
D.—Disagree	2
S.D.—Strongly Disagree	1

Questions

1. Conceptually, what are the constructs risk aversion, convenience, and powerlessness?

2. Do you think that the sample of items adequately assesses each construct? Can you think of any additional items that could or should be used?

Sampling and Data Collection

Part Five focuses on the collection of data needed to answer a problem. Chapter 15 overviews the various types of sampling plans that can be used to determine the population elements from which data should be collected. It also describes nonprobability sampling and simple random sampling, one of the probability sampling plans. Chapter 16 then discusses two popular, but more complex, probability sampling schemes—stratified and cluster sampling. Chapter 17 treats the question of how many of the population elements are needed to answer the problem with precision and confidence in the results. Chapter 18 discusses the many nonsampling errors that can arise in completing the data collection task.

MARKETING RESEARCH PREPARES PENN STATE FOR A LAUNCH INTO CYBERSPACE Our fast-changing world and the demands of an information economy make lifelong learning more important than it ever has been. To respond to the needs of these lifelong learners, Penn State offers "independent learning" in the form of correspondence courses using textbooks, audio- and videotapes, CD-ROMs, and video-conferencing. In addition, the school set out to create a World Campus—a worldwide community of learners linked by the Internet to Penn State's educational resources. The administration wanted to maintain the university's high standards and reputation by creating programs in which it could excel and meet students' needs. So Penn State started by asking its Outreach Office of Marketing Research to investigate possible strategies.

The Penn State researchers began by evaluating the kinds of questions they would need to cover. They determined that they should ask about the level of demand for on-line courses in various disciplines, the readiness of students to try an on-line course, the readiness of faculty members to provide this type of instruction, the ability and willingness of students to pay for on-line instruction, the extent of on-line instruction available from other schools, the reputation of the program, and the potential for creating partnerships with other organizations. The researchers recognized that answering this broad range of questions required collection of objective and subjective data through broad-ranging and open-ended discussions as well as precise questionnaires. In addition, they needed to talk to a variety of community members, from students to faculty to potential business partners. Thus, the researchers crafted a multiphase research plan involving several methods for collecting data.

The first phase of data collection examined the strengths of Penn State's programs and the demographics of Internet users. The researchers then turned to students and prospective students. They conducted telephone surveys of students who were enrolled in an independent learning certificate program. They also conducted on-line surveys of students enrolled in Internet courses that Penn State was already testing. Another survey was e-mailed to people who had given an e-mail address when they submitted inquiries about Penn State's independent-learning program.

The results of the e-mail survey indicated that a potential student body existed for the World Campus. Of the people who desired to continue their education as independent learners, 82 percent were seeking convenience of study, 53 percent were interested in a Penn State education, 85 percent had access to the necessary technology, and 43 percent expected to receive some reimbursement from their employers. The researchers therefore continued by exploring in greater detail the prospects for offering courses in the nine subject areas selected in the initial phase of research.

For each of the nine programs under consideration, the marketing researchers gathered data to answer the following questions:

- *What is Penn State's reputation?* To answer this question, the researchers conducted secondary research, including Internet searches and a study of rankings by the national media. They also conducted internal assessments and interviews with other universities and associations.

- *How ready is each department for on-line instruction?* The researchers conducted in-depth interviews in which they asked faculty members about their experience in and attitudes about on-line instruction. They also asked whether the new program would contribute to achieving the department's strategic goals.

- *What are the conditions of the population to be served by the World Campus?* This area of questioning took the form of surveys addressed to about 100 professionals practicing in each of the fields covered by the courses under consideration. The surveys asked whether respondents thought others in their field would be interested in the proposed courses, as well as about their access to the necessary technology.

The data gathered through this combination of methods enabled the researchers to make specific recommendations. They learned, for example, that Penn State has a strong reputation in the fields of engineering, agriculture, health care, business, and science. They learned that many faculty members had a limited understanding of the capabilities of on-line instruction (for example, that it could be interactive). Surveys of the potential student body showed the greatest interest in and readiness for courses in engineering, geographic information systems (GIS), turfgrass management, and chemical dependency counseling. Access to technology was greatest for those in the fields of GIS and nutrition. Technology was less available for chemical dependency counseling, but the expected growth in this field, coupled with the fast spread of Internet technology, made this content area attractive as well. Some fields were also attractive because trade groups were willing to support the educational program. For example, the Golf Course Superintendents Association of America was enthusiastic about partnering with Penn State to deliver courses in turfgrass management. After analyzing such data, the Outreach Office of Marketing Research recommended that Penn State's World Campus start by offering certificate programs in turfgrass management, chemical dependency counseling, and noise control engineering. Penn State has since added courses in GIS, fundamentals of engineering, business logistics, nutrition, and numerous other subject areas.

The research provided a good road map for Penn State's journey into cyberspace. In the first year, the program admitted 41 students; just a year later, their number had grown to 526 students from South America, Europe, and Asia, as well as the United States. Students who obtain an access account can download course materials, submit completed assignments, correspond with their instructors and classmates, and link to experts via e-mail, chats, and bulletin boards. Penn State predicts that by 2002, it will offer over 300 courses to 10,000 students at the World Campus.

Sources: James Fong, "Turning to a Virtual Campus for a Real Education," *Quirk's Marketing Research Review* (July 1998, downloaded form the *Quirk's* Web site, www.quirks.com, August 13, 1999); Penn State University Web site (www.psu.edu, downloaded October 4, 1999).

Chapter 15

TYPES OF SAMPLES AND SIMPLE RANDOM SAMPLING

L E A R N I N G   O B J E C T I V E S

Upon Completing This Chapter, You Should Be Able to

1. Distinguish between a census and a sample.

2. List the six steps researchers use to draw a sample of a population.

3. Define *sampling frame.*

4. Explain the difference between a probability sample and a nonprobability sample.

5. Distinguish between a fixed and a sequential sample.

6. Explain what a judgment sample is and describe its best use and its hazards.

7. Define *quota sample.*

8. Explain what a parameter in a sampling procedure is.

9. Explain what the derived population is.

10. Explain why the concept of sampling distribution is the most important concept in statistics.

Case in Marketing Research

There's a ratings war going on, and it's not the war of the TV networks. Rather, it's a war for dominance in measuring what people are doing on the Internet.

The major contenders are Media Metrix, a New York company that pioneered the tabulation of Web usage, and Nielsen/NetRatings, an enterprise cosponsored by NetRatings and Nielsen Media Research, the longtime leader of television ratings. Each is trying to claim dominance based on the quality of its data.

Victory in this war requires that the winner persuade clients and potential clients that it provides more reliable data. Many of those clients are advertising agencies. Agencies buy the data so that they can help marketers place advertising on the Web sites where it will be seen by as many members of the target market as possible. In addition, media companies use the data for selling advertising on their Web sites, and marketers with an Internet presence use the data for measuring the success of their on-line activities.

Suppose, for example, that you work for Sony. You have set up a Web site, and you want to buy banner advertisements that Web surfers can click on for a link to your Web site. Where should you place those ads? Preferably on Web sites that generate a lot of traffic from people in your target market. You want your advertising agency to be able to tell you which sites are most visited by people whose demographics and buying behavior match what you know about your target market. To obtain this information, you or your ad agency might subscribe to Media Metrix, Nielsen/NetRatings, or both.

The war between Media Metrix and Nielsen/NetRatings started at the end of the 1990s, following a merger of two former rivals, Media Metrix and RelevantKnowledge. Each of the two had formerly claimed it had the superior methodology. After the merger forming the new Media Metrix (with the slogan "The Power of Relevant Knowledge"), the company said it was combining the best features of both methods. Just two weeks following that merger announcement, Nielsen Media Research and Silicon Valley–based NetRatings announced they had formed an alliance to measure Internet usage. Nielsen/NetRatings claimed that its methodology was better than that of Media Metrix.

One difference is the size of the samples used for each company's panel. Media Metrix uses a panel of 40,000 home and office users, versus 9,000 panel members, all of them home computer users, for Nielsen/NetRatings. However, Nielsen/NetRatings maintains that its methodology for recruiting panel members creates a more representative sample. Another difference is that Media Metrix tracks all of its panel members' activities, whereas NetRatings' specialty is Web sites and the banner ads of the biggest advertisers on the Web.

Jim Nail, a senior analyst at Forrester Research, told *Adweek* that NetRatings' smaller sample won't prevent it from posing a challenge to Media Metrix: "Just get the product to the marketing guys, show them that they can see all the banners [ads on the Web] and all the sites that their competitors are running on. Then tell them, by the way, we have all the methodology stuff buttoned up so you know that this is accurate data." Nail predicts that this pitch is enough to convert some marketers to Nielsen.

Discussion Issues

1. If your company sells software to consumers, what information would you want to have about Internet usage?

2. If your company sells software to businesses, how would your needs for Internet usage data differ from those identified in question 1?

3. What questions would you have about the samples used by Media Metrix and Nielsen NetRatings? How would you decide which service to subscribe to (or ask your ad agency to subscribe to)?

Once the researcher has clearly specified the problem and developed an appropriate research design and data collection instruments, the next step in the research process is to select those elements from which the information will be collected. One way to do this is to collect information from each member of the population of interest by completely canvassing this population. A complete canvass of a population is called a **census.** Another way would be to collect information from a portion of the population by taking a **sample** of elements from the larger group and, on the basis of the information collected from the subset, to infer something about the larger group. One's ability to make this inference from subset to larger group depends on the method by which the sample of elements was chosen. A major part of this chapter is devoted to the "why" and "how" of taking a sample.

Incidentally, **population** here refers not only to people but also to manufacturing firms, retail or wholesale institutions, or even inanimate objects such as parts produced in a manufacturing plant; it is defined as the totality of cases that conform to some designated specifications. The specifications define the elements that belong to the target group and those that are to be excluded. A study aimed at establishing a demographic profile of frozen-pizza eaters requires specifying who is to be considered a frozen-pizza eater. Anyone who has ever eaten a frozen pizza? Those who eat at least one such pizza a month? A week? Those who eat a certain minimum number of frozen pizzas per month? Researchers need to be very explicit in defining the target group of interest. They also need to be very careful that they have actually sampled the target population and not some other population due to an inappropriate or incomplete **sampling frame,** which is the listing of the elements from which the actual sample will be drawn.

One might choose to sample rather than to canvass a whole population for several reasons. First, complete counts on populations of even moderate size are very costly and time-consuming. Often the information will be obsolete by the time the census is completed and the information processed. In some cases, a census is impossible. If, for example, researchers sought to test the life of a company's electric light bulbs by leaving all its inventory of bulbs on until they burned out, they would have reliable data, but no product to sell.

Finally—and to novice researchers, surprisingly—one might choose a sample over a census for purposes of accuracy. Censuses involve larger field staffs, which in turn introduce greater potential for nonsampling error. This is one of the reasons the Bureau of the Census uses sample surveys to check the accuracy of various censuses. That is correct; samples are used to infer the accuracy of the census.[1]

Census
A complete canvass of a population.

Sample
Selection of a subset of elements from a larger group of objects.

Population
The totality of cases that conform to some designated specifications.

Sampling frame
The list of sampling units from which a sample will be drawn; the list could consist of geographic areas, institutions, individuals, or other units.

Required Steps in Sampling

Figure 15.1 outlines a useful six-step procedure that researchers can follow when drawing a sample of a population. Note that it is first necessary to define the population, or the collection of elements, about which the researcher wishes to make an inference. For example, when the preferences of children are involved, researchers have to decide whether the population to be measured is the kids, their parents, or both.

> One company tested its slotless road racing sets only with children. Kids loved 'em. But moms said they didn't like the sets because they were teaching children to crash cars, and dads didn't like the fact that the product was made into a toy.

FIGURE 15.1   **Six-Step Procedure for Drawing a Sample**

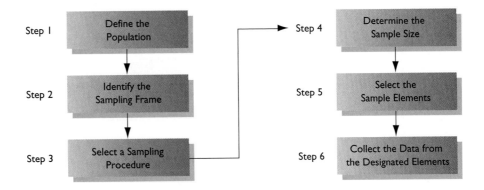

It can work the other way, too. One company introduced a food product with a national ad campaign that starred a rather precocious child. The company tested the campaign only with mothers, who thought it was great. Kids thought the precocious child was obnoxious—and the product, too. End of product.[2]

The researcher must decide if the relevant population consists of individuals, households, business firms, other institutions, credit card transactions, or whatever. In making these decisions, the researcher also has to be careful to specify what units are to be excluded. Geographic boundaries and a time period for the study must always be specified, although additional restrictions are often placed on the elements. When the elements are individuals, for example, the relevant population may be defined as all those over 18 years of age, or females only, or those with a high school education only.

The problem of specifying the geographic boundaries for the target population is sometimes more difficult in international marketing research studies because of the additional complexity an international perspective introduces. For example, urban versus rural areas may be significantly different from each other in various countries. Also, the composition of the population can vary depending on the location within the country. For example, in Chile, the north has a highly centralized Indian population, whereas the south has high concentrations of individuals of European descent.

In general, the simpler the definition of the target population, the higher the incidence and the easier and less costly it is to find the sample.[3] **Incidence** refers to the percent of the general population or group that qualifies for inclusion in the sample using some criteria. Incidence has a direct bearing on the time and cost it takes to complete studies. When incidence is high (i.e., most population elements qualify for the study because only one or very few easily satisfied criteria are used to screen potential respondents), the cost and time to collect data are minimized. Alternatively, as the number of criteria used to describe what constitutes eligible respondents for the study increases, so do the cost and time necessary to find them.

Figure 15.2, for example, shows the percentage of adults who are estimated to participate in various sports. The data in Figure 15.2 suggest that it would be more difficult and costly to focus a study on people who motorcycle, only 3.6 percent of all adults, than people who walk for health, 27.4 percent of all adults. The most important thing is that the researcher be precise in specifying exactly what elements are of interest and what elements are to be excluded. A clear statement of research purpose helps immeasurably in determining the appropriate elements of interest.

The second step in the sample-selection process is identifying the sampling frame, which, you will recall, is the listing of the elements from which the actual sample will be

Incidence

The percent of the general population or group that qualifies for inclusion in the sample using some criteria.

FIGURE 15.2   **Percentage of Adults Estimated to Participate in Various Sports**

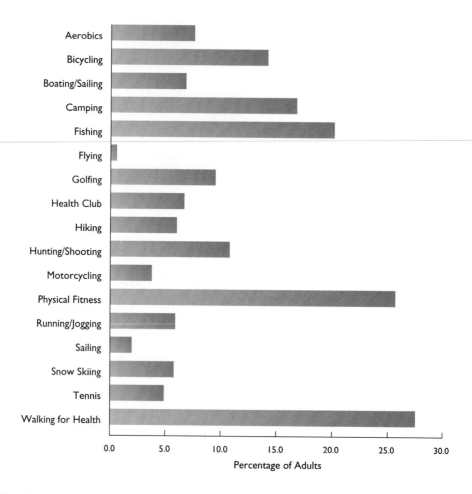

Source: Developed from the information in "SSI-*LITe*™: *Low Incidence Targeted Sampling*" (Fairfield, Conn.: Survey Sampling, Inc., 1994).

drawn. Say that the target population for a particular study is all the households in the metropolitan Dallas area. At first glance, the Dallas phone book would seem an easy and good example of a sampling frame. However, upon closer examination it becomes clear that the telephone directory provides an inaccurate listing of Dallas households, omitting those with unlisted numbers (and, of course, those without phones) and double-counting those with multiple listings. People who have recently moved and thus received new phones not yet listed are also omitted.

Experienced researchers have found that only rarely is there a perfect correspondence between the sampling frame and the target population in which they are interested. One of the researcher's more creative tasks in sampling is developing an appropriate sampling frame when the list of population elements is not readily available. This may require sampling working blocks of numbers and exchanges, as when random digit dialing is used with telephone surveys because of the inadequacies of directory samples. However, the dramatic increase in the number of working blocks over the last 10 years has made this task more difficult. See Research Window 15.1. Or it sometimes means sampling geographic areas or institutions and then subsampling within these units when, say, the target population is individuals but a current, accurate list of appropriate individuals is not available.

Research Window 15.1   **Changes in the Structure of Telephone Numbers**

Since 1986, the estimated number of telephone households in the United States has increased by 14.2 percent, while the number of working residential exchanges has increased by 27.1 percent and the number of working blocks by 182.4 percent. See the chart below. During the same time period, the number of directory-listed households has increased by only 10.4 percent, causing the continuing decline in listed rates.

	1986	**1996**	**Growth**
Telephone households	80,900,000	92,366,039	14.2%
Directory-listed households	59,788,590	66,016,760	10.4%
Working residential exchanges	31,530	40,083	27.1%
Working blocks	1,391,237	3,928,200	182.4%

Definitions

Block or bank: the first two digits of the last four digits of the telephone number

Working block: any block with at least one listed number

Exchange/prefix: "Exchange" designates the city, town, or community in which the number originates. "Prefix" is the 3-digit number assigned to an exchange area. The terms are often used interchangeably.

Technological changes, particularly the explosive growth of cellular and mobile phones, paging equipment modems, and fax machines, have dramatically increased the demand for telephone numbers. This has not only spurred the introduction of new area codes, but has also reduced the density of listed numbers in the working blocks because some of the numbers are dedicated to modems and fax machines.

The new competitive telephone market is also contributing to the declining working block density. Multiple telephone companies are serving smaller markets and are assigned exclusive exchanges. More exchanges are being assigned to more telephone companies, but the working blocks are not being filled out as completely.

What's the significance for sampling? The most obvious change concerns the working phone rate (WPR) of a random digit (RDD) sample. As the number of listed phones per working block decreases, the probability of selecting a listed number in an RDD sample decreases, which may decrease the WPR. Samples that include metropolitan areas are more likely to be affected by this trend.

Source: "Working Block Density Declines" (Fairfield, Conn.: Survey Sampling, Inc., 1996).

The third step in the procedure for drawing a sample is closely intertwined with the identification of the sampling frame. Choosing a sampling method or procedure depends largely on what the researcher can develop for a sampling frame. Different types of samples require different types of sampling frames. This chapter and the next review the main types of samples employed in marketing research. The connection between sampling frame and sampling method should become obvious from these discussions.

The fourth step in the sample-selection process requires that sample size be determined. Chapter 17 discusses this question. The fifth step indicates that the researcher needs to actually pick the elements that will be included in the study. How this is done depends upon the type of sample being used, and consequently we will explore the topic of sample selection when we discuss sampling methods. Finally, the researcher needs to actually collect data from the designated respondents. A great many things can go wrong with this task. These problems are reviewed, and some methods for handling them are discussed, in Chapter 18.

Types of Sampling Plans

Probability sample
A sample in which each population element has a known, nonzero chance of being included in the sample.

Nonprobability sample
A sample that relies on personal judgment somewhere in the element selection process and therefore prohibits estimating the probability that any population element will be included in the sample.

Fixed sample
A sample for which size is determined *a priori* and needed information is collected from the designated elements.

Sequential sample
A sample formed on the basis of a series of successive decisions. If the evidence is not conclusive after a small sample is taken, more observations are taken; if it is still inconclusive after these additional observations, still more observations are taken. At each stage, then, a decision is made as to whether more information should be collected or whether the evidence is sufficient to draw a conclusion.

Sampling techniques can be divided into the two broad categories of **probability** and **nonprobability samples.** In a probability sample, each member of the population has a *known, nonzero* chance of being included in the sample. The chances of each member of the population being included in the sample may not be equal, but everyone has a known probability of inclusion. That probability is determined by the specific mechanical procedure that is used to select sample elements.

With nonprobability samples, on the other hand, there is no way of estimating the probability that any population element will be included in the sample. Thus, there is no way of ensuring that the sample is representative of the population. For example, Allstate Corporation has been developing a system for mining the claims data of its 14 million customer households. The company plans to use the data to identify patterns in the demand for its products—say, the likelihood that a household with a Mercedes Benz would own a vacation home (which would require insurance). Although the data base is huge, the company has no way of estimating the probability of any individual customer making a claim. It therefore cannot be positive that data about customers who file claims are representative of all its customers, much less its potential customers.[4]

All nonprobability samples rely on personal judgment somewhere in the sample-selection process rather than on a mechanical procedure to select sample members. While these judgments may sometimes yield good estimates of a population characteristic, there is no way of determining objectively if the sample is adequate. It is only when the elements have been selected with known probabilities that one is able to evaluate the precision of a sample result. For this reason, probability sampling is usually considered to be the superior method, in terms of being able to estimate the amount of sampling error present.

Samples can also be categorized by whether they are **fixed** or **sequential samples.** In fixed samples, the sample size is decided before the study begins, and all the needed information is collected before the results are analyzed. In our discussion we shall emphasize fixed samples since they are the type most commonly used in marketing research. Nevertheless, you should be aware that sequential samples can also be taken, and they can be used with each of the basic sampling plans we will discuss.

In a sequential sample, the number of elements to be sampled is not decided in advance but is determined by a series of decisions as the data are collected. For example, if, after a small sample is taken, the evidence is not conclusive, more observations will be made. If the results are still inconclusive, the size of the sample will be expanded further. At each stage, a decision is made as to whether more information should be collected or whether the evidence is now sufficient to permit a conclusion. The sequential sample al-

---

FIGURE 15.3   **Classification of Sampling Techniques**

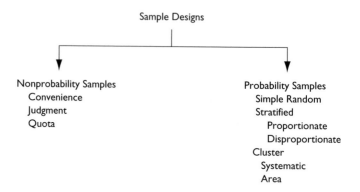

lows trends in the data to be evaluated as the data are being collected, and this affords an opportunity to reduce costs when additional observations show diminishing usefulness.

Both probability and nonprobability sampling plans can be further divided by type. Nonprobability samples, for instance, can be classified as *convenience, judgment,* or *quota,* while probability samples can be *simple random, stratified,* or *cluster,* and some of these can be further divided. Figure 15.3 shows the types of samples we shall discuss in this chapter and the next. You should be aware that the basic sample types can be combined into more complex sampling plans. If you understand the basic types, though, you should well understand the more complex designs.

Nonprobability Samples

As we stated earlier, nonprobability samples involve personal judgment somewhere in the selection process. Sometimes this judgment is imposed by the researcher, while in other cases the selection of population elements to be included is left to individual field-workers. Since the elements are not selected by a mechanical procedure, it is impossible to assess the probability of any population member being included and, thus, the degree of sampling error involved. Without knowing how much error results from a particular sampling procedure, researchers cannot gauge the accuracy of their estimates with any precision.

Convenience Samples

Convenience sample

A nonprobability sample sometimes called an *accidental sample* because those included in the sample enter by accident, in that they just happen to be where the study is being conducted when it is being conducted.

Convenience samples are sometimes called *accidental samples* because those composing the sample enter by "accident"—they just happen to be where the information for the study is being collected. Examples of convenience samples abound in our everyday lives. We talk to a few friends, and on the basis of their reactions, we infer the political sentiment of the country; our local radio station asks people to call in and express their reactions to some controversial issue, and the opinions expressed are interpreted as prevailing sentiment; we ask for volunteers in a research study and use those who come forward.

The problem with convenience samples, of course, is that we have no way of knowing if those included are representative of the target population. And while we might hesitate to infer that the reactions of a few friends indicate prevailing political sentiment, we are often tempted to conclude that large samples, even though selected conveniently, are representative. The fallacy of this assumption is illustrated by a personal incident.

One of the local television stations in the city where the author resides conducted a daily public opinion poll several years ago on topics of interest to the local community. The polls were labeled the "Pulse of Madison" and were conducted in the following way. During the six o'clock news every evening, the station would ask a question about some controversial issue to which people could reply with a yes or no. Persons in favor would call one number; persons opposed would call another. The number of viewers calling each number was recorded electronically. Percentages of those in favor and opposed would then be reported on the ten o'clock news. With some 500 to 1,000 people calling in their opinions each night, the local television commentator seemed to interpret these results as reflecting the true state of opinion in the community.

On one six o'clock broadcast, the following question was posed: "Do you think the drinking age in Madison should be lowered to 18?" The existing legal limit was 21. Would you believe that almost 4,000 people called in that night and that 78 percent were in favor of lowering the drinking age requirement? Clearly, 4,000 responses in a community of 180,000 people "must be representative"! Wrong. As you may have suspected, certain segments of the population were more vitally interested in the issue than others. Thus, it was no surprise, when discussing the issue in class a few weeks later, to find that students had taken half-hour phone shifts on an arranged basis. Each person would call the yes number, hang up, call again, hang up, and so on, until it was the next person's turn. Thus, neither the size of the sample nor the proportion favoring the age change was surprising. The sample was simply not representative.

Further, increasing a sample's size does not make it representative. The representativeness of a sample must be ensured by the sampling procedure. When participation is voluntary or sample elements are selected because they are convenient, the sampling plan provides no assurance that the sample is representative. Empirical evidence, as a matter of fact, is much to the contrary. Rarely do samples selected on a convenient basis, regardless of size, prove representative. Telephone polls using 800 and 900 numbers represent a particularly common example of large but unrepresentative samples. What is especially unfortunate is that a great many people believe the results of these polls are accurate.[5]

An all too common use of convenience samples in international marketing research is to use foreigners from the countries being studied who are currently residing in the country where the study is being conducted (e.g., Scandinavians currently residing in the United States). Even though such convenience samples can shed some light on certain country conditions, it must be recognized that these individuals typically represent the elite class, often are already "westernized," and may not be in touch with current developments in their own country. Convenience samples are not recommended for descriptive or causal research. They may be used with exploratory designs in which the emphasis is on generating ideas and insights, but even here the judgment sample seems superior.

Judgment Samples

Judgment sample
A nonprobability sample that is often called a *purposive sample;* the sample elements are handpicked because they are expected to serve the research purpose.

Judgment samples are often called *purposive samples;* the sample elements are handpicked because it is expected that they can serve the research purpose. Procter & Gamble used this method when it advertised for "interns" aged 13 to 17 from the area around its Cincinnati headquarters. The company's food and beverage division hired this group of teenagers to serve as a kind of consumer panel. Working 10 hours a week in exchange for $1,000 and a trip to a concert, they reviewed television commercials, visited the mall with P&G managers to study retail displays, tested new products, and discussed their purchasing behavior. By selecting the panel members through a "hiring" process rather than randomly, the company could focus on traits it considered helpful—say, the teenagers' ability to articulate their views clearly—at the risk that their views might not be representative of their age group.[6]

As mentioned, the key feature of judgment sampling is that population elements are purposively selected. In some cases, sample elements are chosen not because they are representative but rather because they can offer researchers the information they need. When the courts rely on expert testimony, they are in a sense using judgment samples. The same kind of philosophy may prevail in creating exploratory designs. When searching for ideas and insights, the researcher is not interested in sampling a cross section of opinion but rather in sampling those who can offer some perspective on the research question.

Snowball sample
A judgment sample that relies on the researcher's ability to locate an initial set of respondents with the desired characteristics; these individuals are then used as informants to identify still others with the desired characteristics.

The **snowball sample** is a judgment sample that is sometimes used to sample special populations.[7] This sample relies on the researcher's ability to locate an initial set of respondents with the desired characteristics. These individuals are then used as informants to identify others with the desired characteristics.

Imagine, for example, that a company wanted to determine the desirability of a certain product that would enable deaf people to communicate over telephone lines. Researchers might begin by identifying some key people in the deaf community and asking them for names of other deaf people who might be used in the study. Those asked to participate would also be asked for names of others who might cooperate.[8] In this way the sample "snowballs" by getting larger as participants identify still other possible respondents.

As long as the researcher is at the early stages of research when ideas or insights are being sought—and when the researcher realizes its limitations—the judgment sample can be used productively. It becomes dangerous, though, when it is employed in descriptive or causal studies and its weaknesses are conveniently forgotten. The Consumer Price Index (CPI) provides a classic example of this. As Sudman points out, "the CPI is in only fifty-six cities and metropolitan areas selected judgmentally and to some extent on the basis of political pressure. In reality, these cities represent *only themselves* although the index is called the *Consumer Price Index for Urban Wage Earners and Clerical Workers,* and most people believe the index reflects prices everywhere in the United States. Within cities, the selection of retail outlets is done judgmentally, so that the *possible size of sample bias is unknown*" (emphasis added).[9]

Quota Samples

Quota sample

A nonprobability sample chosen in such a way that the proportion of sample elements possessing certain characteristics is approximately the same as the proportion of the elements with the characteristics in the population; each field-worker is assigned a quota that specifies the characteristics of the people he or she is to contact.

A third type of nonprobability sample, the **quota sample,** attempts to be representative of the population by including the same proportion of elements possessing certain characteristics as is found in the population (see Research Window 15.2). Consider, for example, an attempt to select a representative sample of undergraduate students on a college campus. If the eventual sample of 500 contained no seniors, one would have serious reservations about the representativeness of the sample and the generalizability of the conclusions beyond the immediate sample group. With a quota sample, the researcher could ensure that seniors would be included and in the same proportion as they occur in the entire undergraduate student body.

Assume that a researcher was interested in sampling the undergraduate student body in such a way that the sample would reflect the composition of the student body by class and sex. Suppose further that there were 10,000 undergraduate students in total and that 3,200 were freshmen, 2,600 sophomores, 2,200 juniors, and 2,000 seniors, and further that 7,000 were males and 3,000 females. In a sample of 1,000, the quota sampling plan would require that 320 sample elements be freshmen, 260 sophomores, 220 juniors, and 200 seniors, and further that 700 of the sample elements be male and 300 be female. The researcher would accomplish this by giving each field-worker a quota—thus the name *quota sample*—specifying the types of undergraduates he or she is to contact. Thus, one field-worker assigned 20 interviews might be instructed to find and collect data from

- Six freshmen—five male and one female
- Six sophomores—four male and two female
- Four juniors—three male and one female
- Four seniors—two male and two female

Note that the specific sample elements to be used would not be specified by the research plan, but would be left to the discretion of the individual field-worker. The field-worker's personal judgment would govern the choice of specific students to be interviewed. The only requirement would be that the interviewer diligently follow the established quota and interview five male freshmen, one female freshman, and so on.

Note further that the quota for this field-worker accurately reflects the sex composition of the student population, but does not completely parallel the class composition; 70 percent (14 of 20) of the field-worker's interviews are with males but only 30 percent (6 of 20) are with freshmen, whereas freshmen represent 32 percent of the undergraduate student body. It is not necessary or even usual with a quota sample that the quotas per field-worker accurately mirror the distribution of the control characteristics in the population; usually only the total sample has the same proportions as the population.

Note finally that quota samples still rely on personal, subjective judgment rather than objective procedures for the selection of sample elements. Here the personal judgment is that of the field-worker rather than the designer of the research, as it might be in the case of a judgment sample. This raises the question of whether quota samples can indeed be considered representative even though they accurately reflect the population with respect to the proportion of the sample possessing each control characteristic. Three points need to be made in this regard.

First, the sample could be very far off with respect to some other important characteristic likely to influence the result. Thus, if the campus study is concerned with racial

Every year advertisers spend millions of dollars producing the ads that appear in publications ranging from *Advertising Age* to *Yankee* magazine. While a certain amount of copy and art testing can be done in-house at the agency before the ad is published, the real test of its success is when it appears in a publication, alongside dozens of other ads designed equally carefully, and fights for a reader's attention.

Roper Starch Worldwide is a company that measures advertising readership in consumer, business, trade, and professional magazines and newspapers and reports its findings to advertisers and agencies—for a fee, of course. Since large sums are being gambled daily by advertisers seeking to get their message across to consumers, the Starch organization has been careful to design a sample for its research that can give subscribers fast—and accurate—information about the success of its advertising. Each year Starch interviews more than 50,000 people on their reading of over 20,000 advertisements. Approximately 500 individual issues are studied annually.

Starch uses a quota sample comprised of a minimum of 100 readers per sex. Starch has determined that at this sample size, major fluctuations in readership levels stabilize. Adults, eighteen years and older, are personally interviewed face-to-face for all publications except those that are directed exclusively to special groups (e.g., for *Seventeen* magazine they would interview teenaged girls).

Interviews are arranged to parallel the publication's geographic circulation. For *Los Angeles* magazine, for example, the study would focus on readers in southern California. A study of *Time* magazine would parallel its national circulation. Interviews are conducted in between 20 and 30 cities for each issue under study.

Each interviewer is assigned only a small quota of interviews in order to minimize interviewer bias. Interviews are distributed among people of varied ages, income

levels, and occupations so that collectively each study is broadly representative of the publication's audience. For certain business, trade, and professional publications, interviewing assignments are also designed to parallel the circulation by field of industry and job responsibility. For publications with small circulations, subscriber lists are used to help locate eligible respondents.

In each interview, interviewers ask respondents, who are permitted to look through the publication at the time of the interview, if they have seen or read any part of a particular advertisement. If the respondent answers yes, the interviewer follows up with more questions to determine the extent to which the respondent has read the ad.

Three degrees of readership are measured:

- *Noted:* The percent who remember having previously seen the ad in the issue.

- *Associated:* The percent who saw any part of the ad that clearly indicated the brand or advertiser.

- *Read Most:* The percent who read 50% or more of the written material in the ad.

After all the ads are asked about, interviewers record basic classification data on sex, age, occupation, marital status, race, income, family size and composition, so that sampling can be checked and cross tabulations of readership can be made.

Properly used, Starch data help advertisers and agencies to identify the types of advertisement layouts that attract and retain the highest readership and those that result in average or poor readership. For advertisers, this kind of information can be invaluable in designing an effective campaign for their products.

Source: "Roper Starch Worldwide" (Mamaroneck, NY 10543).

prejudice existing on campus, it may very well make a difference whether field-workers interview students from urban or rural areas. Since a quota for the urban-rural characteristic was not specified, it is unlikely that those participating will accurately reflect this characteristic. The alternative, of course, is to specify quotas for all potentially important characteristics. The problem is that increasing the number of control characteristics makes specifications more complex. This in turn makes the location of sample elements more difficult—perhaps even impossible—and certainly more expensive. If, for example,

You are designing an experiment to compare the effectiveness of different types of commercials and need to recruit a large group of subjects of varying ages to watch television for an hour every night for a week. You approach your local church minister and tell her that you will make a donation to the church restoration fund for every member of the congregation who agrees to participate.

- When might incentives be coercive?
- Is it ethical to coerce people to participate in research?
- Will the quality of the data suffer from the coercive recruitment of participants?

geographic origin and socioeconomic status were also important characteristics in the study, the field-worker might be assigned to find an upper-middle-class male freshman from an urban area. This is obviously a much more difficult task than simply locating a male freshman.

Also, it is difficult to verify whether a quota sample is representative. Certainly one can check the distribution of characteristics in the sample not used as controls to determine whether the distribution parallels that of the population. However, this type of comparison provides only negative evidence. It can indicate that the sample does not reflect the population if the distributions on some characteristics are different. If the sample and population distributions are similar for each of these characteristics, it is still possible for the sample to be vastly different from the population on some characteristic not explicitly compared.

Finally, interviewers left to their own devices are prone to follow certain practices. They tend to interview their friends in excessive proportion. Since their friends are often similar to themselves, this can introduce bias. The empirical evidence from England, for example, indicates that quota samples are biased (1) toward the accessible, (2) against small households, (3) toward households with children, (4) against workers in manufacturing, (5) against extremes of income, (6) against the less educated, and (7) against low-status individuals.[10] Interviewers who fill their quotas by stopping passersby are likely to concentrate on areas where there are large numbers of potential respondents, such as business districts, railway and airline terminals, and the entrances to large department stores. This practice tends to overrepresent the kinds of people who frequent these areas. When home visits are required, interviewers often succumb to the lures of convenience and appearance. They may conduct interviews only during the day, for example, resulting in an underrepresentation of working people. They often avoid dilapidated buildings and the upper stories of buildings without elevators.

Depending on the subject of the study, all these tendencies have the potential for bias. They may or may not in fact actually bias the result, but it is difficult to correct them when analyzing the data. When the sample elements are selected objectively, on the other hand, researchers have certain tools they can rely on to make the question of whether a particular sample is representative less difficult. In these probability samples, one relies on the sampling procedure and not on the composition of the specific sample to solve the problem of representation.

Probability Samples

In a probability sample, researchers can calculate the likelihood that any given population element will be included, because the final sample elements are selected objectively by a specific process and not according to the whims of the researcher or field-worker. Since the elements are selected objectively, researchers are then able to assess the reliability of the sample results, something not possible with nonprobability samples regardless of the careful judgment exercised in selecting individuals.

This is not to say that probability samples will always be more representative than nonprobability samples. Indeed, a nonprobability sample may be more representative. The advantage of probability samples is that they allow an assessment of the amount of sampling error likely to occur, because a sample rather than a census was employed when gathering the data. Nonprobability samples, on the other hand, allow the investigator no objective method for evaluating the adequacy of the sample.

Simple Random Sampling

Most people have had experience with simple random samples either in beginning statistics courses or in reading about the results of such samples in newspapers or magazines. In a simple random sample, each unit included in the sample has a known and equal chance of being selected for study, and every combination of population elements is a sample possibility. For example, if we wanted a simple random sample of all students enrolled in a particular college, we might assign a number to each student on a comprehensive list of all those enrolled and then have a computer pick a sample randomly.

Parent Population

Parent population
The totality of cases that conform to some designated specifications; also called a *target population*.

Parameter
A fixed characteristic or measure of a parent, or target, population.

The **parent population,** or *target population,* is the population from which the simple random sample will be drawn. This population can be described by certain **parameters,** which are characteristics of the parent population, each representing a fixed quantity that distinguishes one population from another. For example, suppose the parent population for a study were all adults in Cincinnati. A number of parameters could be used to describe this population: the average age, the proportion with a college education, the range of incomes, and so on. Note that these quantities are fixed in value. Given a census of this population, we can readily calculate them. Rather than relying on a census, we usually select a sample and use the values calculated from the sample observations to estimate the required population values.

To see how this is done, consider the hypothetical population of 20 individuals shown in Exhibit 15.1. There are several advantages in working with a small hypothetical population like this. First, the population's small size makes it easy to calculate the population parameters that might be used to describe it. Second, its size makes it relatively easy to see

EXHIBIT 15.1	Hypothetical Population						
Element	Income (Dollars)	Education (Years)	Newspaper Subscription	Element	Income (Dollars)	Education (Years)	Newspaper Subscription
1 A	5,600	8	X	11 K	9,600	13	X
2 B	6,000	9	Y	12 L	10,000	13	Y
3 C	6,400	11	X	13 M	10,400	14	X
4 D	6,800	11	Y	14 N	10,800	14	Y
5 E	7,200	11	X	15 O	11,200	15	X
6 F	7,600	12	Y	16 P	11,600	16	Y
7 G	8,000	12	X	17 Q	12,000	16	X
8 H	8,400	12	Y	18 R	12,400	17	Y
9 I	8,800	12	X	19 S	12,800	18	X
10 J	9,200	12	Y	20 T	13,200	18	Y

what might happen under a particular sampling plan. Both of these features make it easier to compare the sample results to the "true," but now known, population value than would be the case in the typical situation where the actual population value is unknown. The comparison of the estimate with the "true" value is thus more vivid than it otherwise would be.

Suppose we wanted to estimate the average income in this population from two elements selected randomly. Then the *population mean income* would be a parameter. To estimate a population mean, denoted by μ, we would divide the sum of all the values by the number of values making up the sum. That is,

$$\text{population mean } \mu = \frac{\text{sum of population elements}}{\text{number of population elements}}$$

In this case the calculation yields

$$\frac{5,600 + 6,000 + \ldots + 13,200}{20} = 9,400$$

Another parameter that might be used to describe the incomes in this population would be the *population variance,* which is one measure of the spread of incomes. To compute the population variance, we would calculate the deviation of each value from the mean, square these deviations, sum them, and divide by the number of values making up the sum. Letting σ^2 denote the populating variance, the calculation yields

$$\text{population variance } \sigma^2 = \frac{\begin{array}{c}\text{sum of squared differences of each}\\ \text{population element from the population mean}\end{array}}{\text{number of population elements}}$$

$$= \frac{(5,600 - 9,400)^2 + (6,000 - 9,400)^2 + \ldots + (13,200 - 9,400)^2}{20}$$

$$= 5,320,000$$

Derived Population

The **derived population** consists of all the possible samples that can be drawn from the parent population under a given sampling plan. A **statistic** is a characteristic or measure of a sample. The value of a statistic used to estimate a particular parameter depends on the particular sample selected from the parent population under the sampling plan specified. Different samples yield different statistics and different estimates of the same population parameter.

Consider the derived population of *all* the possible samples that could be drawn from our hypothetical parent population of 20 individuals, under a sampling plan that specifies that a sample size of $n = 2$ be drawn by simple random sampling without replacement.

Let us assume, for the time being, that the information for each population element—in this case, the person's name and income—is written on a disk, placed in a jar, and shaken thoroughly. The researcher then reaches into the jar, pulls out one disk, records the information on it, and puts it aside. She does the same with a second disk. Then she places both disks back in the jar and repeats the process. Exhibit 15.2 shows the many possible results of following this procedure. There are 190 possible combinations of the 20 disks.

For each combination, one could calculate the sample mean income. Thus, for the sample AB, $(k = 1)$,

$$k^{\text{th}} \text{ sample mean} = \frac{\text{sum of sample elements}}{\text{number of elements in sample}} = \frac{5,600 + 6,000}{2} = 5,800$$

Figure 15.4 displays the estimates of population mean income and the amount of error in each estimate when samples $k = 25, 62, 108, 147,$ and 189 are drawn.

EXHIBIT 15.2   Derived Population of All Possible Samples of Size $n = 2$ with Simple Random Selection

K	Sample Identity	Mean	K	Sample Identity	Mean	K	Sample Identity	Mean	K	Sample Identity	Mean
1	AB	5,800	51	CQ	9,200	101	GI	8,400	151	KQ	10,800
2	AC	6,000	52	CR	9,400	102	GJ	8,600	152	KR	11,000
3	AD	6,200	53	CS	9,600	103	GK	8,800	153	KS	11,200
4	AE	6,400	54	CT	9,800	104	GL	9,000	154	KT	11,400
5	AF	6,600	55	DE	7,000	105	GM	9,200	155	LM	10,200
6	AG	6,800	56	DF	7,200	106	GN	9,400	156	LN	10,400
7	AH	7,000	57	DG	7,400	107	GO	9,600	157	LO	10,600
8	AI	7,200	58	DH	7,600	108	GP	9,800	158	LP	10,800
9	AJ	7,400	59	DI	7,800	109	GQ	10,000	159	LQ	11,000
10	AK	7,600	60	DJ	8,000	110	GR	10,200	160	LR	11,200
11	AL	7,800	61	DK	8,200	111	GS	10,400	161	LS	11,400
12	AM	8,000	62	DL	8,400	112	GT	10,600	162	LT	11,600
13	AN	8,200	63	DM	8,600	113	HI	8,600	163	MN	10,600
14	AO	8,400	64	DN	8,800	114	HJ	8,800	164	MO	10,800
15	AP	8,600	65	DO	9,000	115	HK	9,000	165	MP	11,000
16	AQ	8,800	66	DP	9,200	116	HL	9,200	166	MQ	11,200
17	AR	9,000	67	DQ	9,400	117	HM	9,400	167	MR	11,400
18	AS	9,200	68	DR	9,600	118	HN	9,600	168	MS	11,600
19	AT	9,400	69	DS	9,800	119	HO	9,800	169	MT	11,800
20	BC	6,200	70	DT	10,000	120	HP	10,000	170	NO	11,000
21	BD	6,400	71	EF	7,400	121	HQ	10,200	171	NP	11,200
22	BE	6,600	72	EG	7,600	122	HR	10,400	172	NQ	11,400
23	BF	6,800	73	EH	7,800	123	HS	10,600	173	NR	11,600
24	BG	7,000	74	EI	8,000	124	HT	10,800	174	NS	11,800
25	BH	7,200	75	EJ	8,200	125	IJ	9,000	175	NT	12,200
26	BI	7,400	76	EK	8,400	126	IK	9,200	176	OP	11,400
27	BJ	7,600	77	EL	8,600	127	IL	9,400	177	OQ	11,600
28	BK	7,800	78	EM	8,800	128	IM	9,600	178	OR	11,800
29	BL	8,000	79	EN	9,000	129	IN	9,800	179	OS	12,000
30	BM	8,200	80	EO	9,200	130	IO	10,000	180	OT	12,200
31	BN	8,400	81	EP	9,400	131	IP	10,200	181	PQ	11,800
32	BO	8,600	82	EQ	9,600	132	IQ	10,400	182	PR	12,000
33	BP	8,800	83	ER	9,800	133	IR	10,600	183	PS	12,200
34	BQ	9,000	84	ES	10,000	134	IS	10,800	184	PT	12,400
35	BR	9,200	85	ET	10,200	135	IT	11,000	185	QR	12,200
36	BS	9,400	86	FG	7,800	136	JK	9,400	186	QS	12,400
37	BT	9,600	87	FH	8,000	137	JL	9,600	187	QT	12,600
38	CD	6,600	88	FI	8,200	138	JM	9,800	188	RS	12,600
39	CE	6,800	89	FJ	8,400	139	JN	10,000	189	RT	12,800
40	CF	7,000	90	FK	8,600	140	JO	10,200	190	ST	13,000
41	CG	7,200	91	FL	8,800	141	JP	10,400			
42	CH	7,400	92	FM	9,000	142	JQ	10,600			
43	CI	7,600	93	FN	9,200	143	JR	10,800			
44	CJ	7,800	94	FO	9,400	144	JS	11,000			
45	CK	8,000	95	FP	9,600	145	JT	11,200			
46	CL	8,200	96	FQ	9,800	146	KL	9,800			
47	CM	8,400	97	FR	10,000	147	KM	10,000			
48	CN	8,600	98	FS	10,200	148	KN	10,200			
49	CO	8,800	99	FT	10,400	149	KO	10,400			
50	CP	9,000	100	GH	8,200	150	KP	10,600			

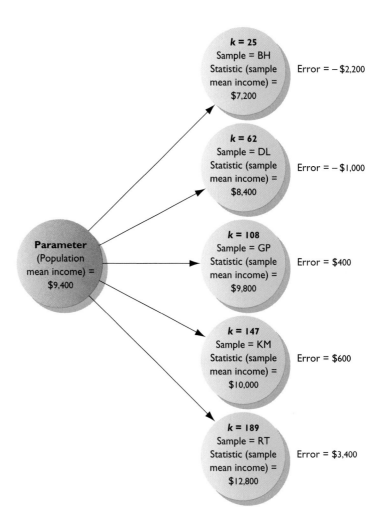

Before discussing the relationship between the sample mean income (a statistic) and the population mean income (the parameter to be estimated), a few words are in order regarding the notion of derived population. First, note that, in practice, we do not actually generate the derived population. This would be extremely wasteful of time and data. Rather, the practitioner merely generates one sample of the needed size. But the researcher will make use of the *concept* of a derived population and the associated notion of sampling distribution in making inferences. We shall see how in just a moment.

Second, note that the derived population is defined as the population of all possible distinguishable samples that can be drawn under a *given sampling plan.* Change any part of the sampling plan, and the derived population will also change. Thus, when selecting disks, if the researcher is to replace the first disk drawn, the derived population will include the sample possibilities *AA, BB,* and so on. With samples of Size 3 instead of 2, drawn without replacement, *ABC* is a sample possibility, and there are a number of additional possibilities as well—1,140 versus the 190 with samples of Size 2. Change the method of selecting elements by using something other than simple random sampling, and the derived population will also change.

Finally, note that picking a sample of a given size from a parent population is equivalent to picking a single element (1 of the 190 disks) out of the derived population. This fact is basic in making statistical inferences.

Sample Mean versus Population Mean

If we want to evaluate the income of those in a simple random sample, can we assume that the sample mean will equal the parent population mean? To a large extent we generally assume there is a relationship. Sometimes we know *a priori* that the estimate could be in error. We might expect information gathered from a sample of Internet users, for example, to vary greatly from the population as a whole (see the e-centives ad). In other cases, we think the sample mean should fairly accurately estimate the population mean; otherwise, it would be senseless to use the sample value to estimate the population value. But how much error is there likely to be?

Suppose we added up all the sample means in Exhibit 15.2 and divided by the number of samples; that is, suppose we were to average the averages. By doing this, we would get the following:

$$\frac{5,800 + 6,000 + \ldots + 13,000}{190} = 9,400$$

This is the mean of the parent population also. And this is what is meant by an *unbiased statistic*. A statistic is unbiased when its average value equals the population parameter that it is supposed to estimate. Note that the fact that it is unbiased says nothing about any particular value of the statistic. Even though unbiased, a particular estimate may be very far from the true population value—for example, if either sample *AB* or sample *ST* were selected. In some cases, the true population value may even be impossible to achieve with any possible sample even though the statistic is unbiased; this is not true in the example, though, since a number of sample possibilities—for example, *AT*—yield a sample mean that equals the population average.

The Internet is a source of information for marketers, who can track people's browsing and purchasing habits. Programs such as e-centives reward browsers with online coupons and other offers for filling out personal profiles. A sample mean of the Net-savvy public, however, would differ from that of the general population, who are less technologically proficient and may be more cautious about providing information online. So marketers would need to be careful about making projections to the general population based on information they can gather on-line.

Next it is useful to take a look at the spread of these sample estimates, and particularly the relationship between this spread of estimates and the dispersion of incomes in the population. We saw previously that in order to compute the population variance, we needed to calculate the deviation of each value from the mean, square these deviations, sum them, and divide by the number of values making up the sum.

The variance of mean incomes could be calculated similarly. That is, we could calculate the variance of mean incomes by taking the deviation of each mean around its overall mean, squaring and summing these deviations, and then dividing by the number of cases.

Alternatively, we could determine the variance of mean incomes indirectly by using the variance of incomes in the parent population, since there is a direct relationship between the two quantities. More specifically, it turns out that when the sample is only a small part of the parent population, the variance of sample mean incomes is equal to the parent population variance divided by the sample size. In symbols, this means that

$$\sigma_{\bar{x}}^2 = \frac{\sigma^2}{n}$$

where $\sigma_{\bar{x}}^2$ is the variance of sample mean incomes, while σ^2 is the variance of incomes in the population, and n is the sample size.[11]

Third, consider the distribution of the estimates in contrast to the distribution of the variable in the parent population. Figure 15.5 indicates that the parent population distribution, depicted by Panel A, is spiked—each of the 20 values occurs once—and is symmetrical about the population mean value of 9,400. The distribution of estimates, displayed in Panel B, was constructed from Exhibit 15.3, which in turn was generated by placing each of the estimates in Exhibit 15.2 in categories according to size and then counting the number contained in each category. Panel B is the traditional histogram discussed in beginning statistics courses and represents the **sampling distribution** of the statistic. Note this: The notion of sampling distribution is the single most important notion in statistics; it is the cornerstone of statistical inference procedures. If one knows the sampling distribution for the statistic in question, one is in a position to make an inference about the corresponding population parameter. If, on the other hand, one knows only that a particular sample estimate will vary with repeated sampling and has no information as to *how* it will vary, then it will be impossible to devise a measure of the sampling error associated with that estimate. Since the sampling distribution of an estimate describes how

Sampling distribution
The distribution of values of some statistic calculated for each possible distinguishable sample that could be drawn from a parent population under a specific sampling plan.

FIGURE 15.5   **Distribution of Variable in Parent Population and Distribution of Estimates in Derived Population**

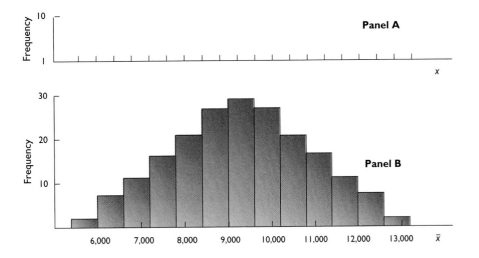

EXHIBIT 15.3	Classification of Estimates by Size

Sample Mean	Number of Samples
$6,000 or less	2
$6,100 to 6,600	7
$6,700 to 7,200	11
$7,300 to 7,800	16
$7,900 to 8,400	20
$8,500 to 9,000	25
$9,100 to 9,600	28
$9,700 to 10,200	25
$10,300 to 10,800	20
$10,900 to 11,400	16
$11,500 to 12,000	11
$12,100 to 12,600	7
$12,700 or more	2

that estimate will vary with repeated sampling, it provides a basis for determining the reliability of the sample estimate. This is why probability sampling plans are so important to statistical inference. With known probabilities of inclusion of any population element in the sample, statisticians are able to derive the sampling distribution of various statistics. Researchers then rely on these distributions—be they for a sample mean, sample proportion, sample variance, or some other statistic—in making their inferences from single samples to population values. Note also that the distribution of sample means is mound-shaped and symmetrical about the population mean with samples of Size 2.

Recapitulating, we have shown that

1. The mean of all possible sample means is equal to the population mean.

2. The variance of sample means is related to the population variance.

3. The distribution of sample means is mound-shaped, whereas the population distribution is spiked.

Central-limit theorem

A theorem that holds that if simple random samples of size n are drawn from a parent population with mean μ and variance σ^2, then when μ is large, the sample mean $\bar{x}$ will be approximately normally distributed with mean equal to μ and variance equal to σ^2/n. The approximation will become more and more accurate as n becomes larger.

Central-Limit Theorem The mound-shaped distribution of estimates provides preliminary evidence of the operation of the **central-limit theorem,** which holds that if simple random samples of a given size n are drawn from a parent population with mean equal to μ, and variance equal to σ^2, then when the sample size n is large, the *distribution of sample means* will be approximately normally distributed with its mean equal to the population mean and its variance equal to the parent population variance divided by the sample size; that is,

$$\sigma_{\bar{x}}^2 = \frac{\sigma^2}{n}$$

The approximation will become more and more accurate as n becomes larger. Note the impact of this. It means that regardless of the shape of the parent population, the distribution of sample means *will be normal* if the sample is large enough. How large is large enough? If the distribution of the variable in the parent population is normal, then the distribution of means of samples of size $n = 1$ will be normal. If the distribution of the variable is symmetrical but not normal, then samples of very small size will produce a distribution in which the means are normally distributed. If the distribution of the variable is highly skewed in the parent population, then samples of a larger size will be needed.

The fact remains, though, that the distribution of the statistic, sample mean, can be assumed normal if only we work with a sample of sufficient size. We do not need to rely on the assumption that the variable is normally distributed in the parent population in order to make inferences using the normal curve. Rather, we rely on the central-limit theorem and adjust the sample size according to the population distribution so that the normal curve can be assumed to hold. Fortunately, the normal distribution of the statistic occurs with samples of relatively small size, as Figure 15.6 indicates.

FIGURE 15.6   Distribution of Sample Means for Samples of Various Sizes and Different Population Distributions

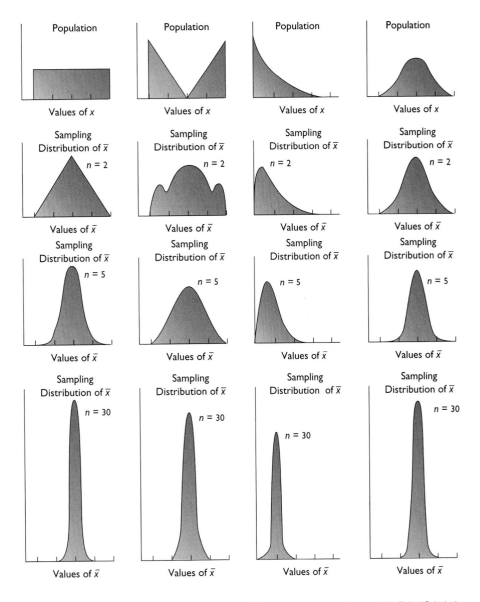

Source: Ernest Kurnow, Gerald, J. Glasser, and Frederick R. Ottman, *Statistics for Business Decisions* (Homewood, Ill.: Richard D. Irwin, Inc., © 1959), pp. 182–183. Used with permission.

Confidence Interval Estimates How does all of the preceding help us in making inferences about the parent population mean? After all, in practice we do not draw all possible samples of a given size, but only one, and we use the results obtained in it to infer something about the target group. It all ties together in the following way.

It is known that with any normal distribution, a specific percentage of all observations is within a certain number of standard deviations of the mean; for example, 95 percent of the values are within ±1.96 standard deviations of the mean. The distribution of sample means is normal if the central-limit theorem holds and thus is no exception. Now, the mean of this sampling distribution is equal to the population mean μ, and its standard deviation is given by the square root of the variance of means, which is called the standard error of the mean, specifically $\sigma_{\bar{x}} = \sigma \sqrt{n}$. Therefore, it is true that

- 68.26 percent of the sample means will be within $\pm 1 \, \sigma_{\bar{x}}$ of the population mean

- 95.45 percent of the sample means will be within $\pm 2 \, \sigma_{\bar{x}}$ of the population mean

- 99.73 percent of the sample means will be within $\pm 3 \, \sigma_{\bar{x}}$ of the population mean

and in general that $\mu \pm z\sigma_{\bar{x}}$ will contain some certain proportion of all sample means depending on the selected value of z. This expression can be rewritten as an inequality relation that

$$\binom{\text{population}}{\text{mean}} - z\binom{\text{standard error}}{\text{of the mean}} \leq \binom{\text{sample}}{\text{mean}} \leq \binom{\text{population}}{\text{mean}} + z\binom{\text{standard error}}{\text{of the mean}}$$

or

$$\mu - z\sigma_{\bar{x}} \leq \bar{x} \leq \mu + z\sigma_{\bar{x}} \tag{15.1}$$

which is held to be true a certain percentage of the time, and which implies that the sample mean will be in the interval formed by adding and subtracting a certain number of standard deviations to the mean value of the distribution. This inequality can be transferred to the equivalent inequality:

$$\binom{\text{sample}}{\text{mean}} - z\binom{\text{standard error}}{\text{of the mean}} \leq \binom{\text{population}}{\text{mean}} \leq \binom{\text{sample}}{\text{mean}} + z\binom{\text{standard error}}{\text{of the mean}}$$

or

$$\bar{x} - z\sigma_{\bar{x}} \leq \mu \leq \bar{x} + z\sigma_{\bar{x}} \tag{15.2}$$

And, if Equation 15.1 is true, say, 95 percent of the time ($z = 1.96$), then Equation 15.2 is also true 95 percent of the time. *When we make an inference on the basis of a single sample mean, we make use of Equation 15.2.*

It is important to note that Equation 15.2 says *nothing about the interval constructed from a particular sample as including the population mean.* Rather, the interval addresses the *sampling procedure.* The interval around a single mean may or may not contain the true population mean. Our confidence in our inference rests on the property that 95 percent of all the intervals we could construct under that sampling plan would contain the true value. We trust or hope that our sample is one of those 95 out of 100 that does (when we are 95 percent confident) include the true value.

To illustrate this important point, suppose for the moment that the distribution of sample means of size $n = 2$ for our hypothetical example was normal. Exhibit 15.4 illustrates the outcome pictorially for the first 10 out of the possible 190 samples that could be drawn under the specified sampling plan. Note that only 7 of the 10 intervals contain the true population mean. Confidence in the estimate arises because of the *procedure,* therefore, and not because of a particular estimate. The procedure suggests that with, say, a 95 percent confidence interval, if 100 samples were to be drawn and the sample mean and the confidence interval computed for each, 95 of the constructed intervals would include the true population value. The accuracy of a specific sample is evaluated only by reference to the procedure by which the sample was obtained. A sampling plan that is representative

			Confidence Interval		

Sample Number	**Sample Identity**	**Mean**	**Lower Limit**	**Upper Limit**	**Pictorial True $\mu = 9,400$ (represented by vertical line)**
1	AB	5,800	2,689	8,911	
2	AC	6,000	2,889	9,111	
3	AD	6,200	3,089	9,311	
4	AE	6,400	3,289	9,511	
5	AF	6,600	3,489	9,711	
6	AG	6,800	3,689	9,911	
7	AH	7,000	3,889	10,111	
8	AI	7,200	4,089	10,311	
9	AJ	7,400	4,289	10,511	
10	AK	7,600	4,489	10,711	

EXHIBIT 15.4 Confidence Intervals for First Ten Samples Assuming the Distribution of Sample Means Was Normal

does not guarantee that a particular sample is representative. Statistical inference procedures rest on the representativeness of the sampling plan, and this is why probability samples are so critical to those procedures. Probability samples allow an estimate of the *precision* of the results in terms of how closely the estimates will tend to cluster about the true value. The greater the standard error of the statistic, the more variable the estimates and the less precise the procedure.

If it disturbs you that the confidence level applies to the procedure and not a particular sample result, you can take comfort in the fact that you can control the level of confidence with which the population value is estimated. Thus, if you do not wish to take the risk that you might have 1 of the 5 sample intervals in 100 that does not contain the population value, you might employ a 99 percent confidence interval, in which the risk is that only 1 in 100 sample intervals will not contain the population mean. Further, if you are willing to increase the size of the sample, you can increase your confidence and at the same time maintain the precision with which the population value is estimated. This will be explored more fully in Chapter 17.

There is one other perhaps disturbing ingredient in our procedure: The confidence interval estimate made use of three values: $\bar{x}$, z, and $\sigma_{\bar{x}}$. Now the sample mean x is computed from the selected sample, and z is specified to produce the desired level of confidence. But what about the standard error of the mean, $\sigma_{\bar{x}}$? It is equal to $\sigma_{\bar{x}} = \sigma/\sqrt{n}$, and thus, in order to calculate it, we need to know the standard deviation of the variable in the population—that is, σ. What do we do if the population standard deviation, σ, is unknown? There is no problem, for two reasons. First, variation typically changes much more slowly than level for most variables of interest in marketing. Thus if the study is a repeat, we can use the previously discovered value for σ. Second, once the sample is selected and the information gathered, we can calculate the sample variance to estimate the population variance. The unbiased sample variance $\hat{s}^2$ is calculated as

$$\text{sample variance } \hat{s}^2 = \frac{\text{sum of deviations around sample mean squared}}{\text{sample size} - 1}$$

To compute the sample variance, then, we first calculate the sample mean. We then calculate the difference between each of our sample values and the sample mean, square these differences, sum them, and divide the sum by one less than the number of sample observations. The sample variance not only provides an estimate of the population variance, but it can also be used to secure an estimate of the standard error of the mean. When the population variance, σ^2, is known, the standard error of the mean, $\sigma_{\bar{x}}$, is also known, since $\sigma_{\bar{x}} = \sigma/\sqrt{n}$. When the population variance is unknown, the standard error of the mean can only be estimated. The estimate is given by $s_{\bar{x}}$, which equals the sample standard deviation divided by the square root of the sample size—that is, $\hat{s}/\sqrt{n}$. The estimate calculation parallels that for the true value with the sample standard deviation substituted for the population standard deviation. Thus, if we draw sample AB, with a mean of 5,800,

$$\hat{s} = \frac{(5,600 - 5,800)^2 + (6,000 - 5,800)^2}{1} = 80,000$$

and thus $\hat{s} = 283$ and $s_{\bar{x}} = \hat{s}/\sqrt{n} = 283/\sqrt{2} = 200$, and the 95 percent confidence interval is now

$$5,800 - 1.96(200) \leq \mu \leq 5,800 + 1.96(200) = 5,408 \leq \mu \leq 6,192$$

which is somewhat smaller than before.

Exhibit 15.5 summarizes the computational formulas for the various means and variances used in this chapter.

Drawing the Simple Random Sample Although it was useful for illustrating the concepts of derived population and sampling distribution, the selection of sample elements from a jar containing all the population elements is not particularly recommended because of its great potential for bias. It is unlikely that the disks would be exactly uniform in size or feel, and slight differences here could affect the likelihood that any single element would be drawn. The national draft during the Vietnam War using a lottery serves as an example. Draft priorities were determined by drawing disks with birth dates stamped on them from a large container in full view of a television audience. Unfortunately, the dates of the year had initially been poured into the bowl systematically, January first and December last. Although the bowl was then stirred vigorously, December dates tended to be chosen first and January dates last. The procedure was later revised to produce a more random selection process.

EXHIBIT 15.5   **Symbols and Formulas Used for Means and Variances with Simple Random Samples**

	Mean	**Variance**
Population	$\mu = \dfrac{\text{sum of population elements}}{\text{number of population elements}}$	$\sigma^2 = \dfrac{\text{sum of squared differences of each population element from the population mean}}{\text{number of population elements}}$
Sample	$\bar{x} = \dfrac{\text{sum of sample elements}}{\text{number of sample elements}}$	$s^2 = \dfrac{\text{sum of squared differences of each sample element from the sample mean}}{\text{number of sample elements} - 1}$
Derived Population of Sample Means	average value = unknown population mean	$\sigma_{\bar{x}}^2 = \dfrac{\sigma^2}{n}$ (when population variance is known) $s_{\bar{x}}^2 = \dfrac{\hat{s}^2}{n}$ (when population variance is unknown)

The preferred way of drawing a simple random sample is through the use of a table of random numbers. Using a random-number table involves the following sequence of steps: First, the elements of the parent population are numbered serially from 1 to N; for the hypothetical population, the element A would be numbered 1, B as 2, and so on. Next, the numbers in the table are treated so as to have the same number of digits as N. With $N = 20$, two-digit numbers would be used; if N were between 100 and 999, three-digit numbers would be required, and so on. Third, a starting point is determined randomly. We might simply open the table to some arbitrary place and point to a position on the page with our eyes closed. Since the numbers in a random-number table are in fact random—that is, without order—it makes little difference where we begin.[12] Finally, we proceed in some arbitrary direction, for example, up, down, or across, and select those elements for the sample for which there is a match of serial number and random number.

To illustrate, consider the partial list of random numbers contained in Exhibit 15.6. Since $N = 20$, we need work with only two digits, and therefore we can use the entries in Exhibit 15.6 as is, instead of having to combine columns to produce numbers covering the range of serial numbers. Suppose we had previously decided to read down and that our arbitrary start indicated the eleventh row, fourth column, specifically the number 77. This number is too high and would be discarded. The next two numbers would also be discarded, but the fourth entry, 02, would be used, since 2 corresponds to one of the serial numbers in the list, Element B. The next five numbers would also be passed over as too large, whereas the number 05 would designate the inclusion of Element E. Elements B and E would thus represent the sample of two from whom we would seek information on income.

An alternative strategy would be to use a computer program to generate the random numbers. Although there is some recent evidence that suggests the numbers generated by computer programs are not as random as is commonly believed, their accuracy is sufficient for most applied marketing research studies, although perhaps not for complex mathematical model building.[13]

You should note that a simple random sample requires a serial numbered list of population elements. This means that the identity of each member of the population must be known. For some populations this is no problem—for example, if the study is to be conducted among *Fortune* magazine's list of the 500 largest corporations in the United States. The list is readily available, and a simple random sample of these firms could be easily selected. For many other populations of interest (for example, all families living in a particular city), the list of universe elements is much harder to come by, and applied researchers often resort to other sampling schemes.

EXHIBIT 15.6   **Abridged List of Random Numbers**

10 09 73 25 33	76 52 01 35 86	34 67 35 48 76	80 95 90 91 17	39 29 27 49 45
37 54 20 48 05	64 89 47 42 96	24 80 52 40 37	20 63 61 04 02	00 82 29 16 65
08 42 26 89 53	19 64 50 93 03	23 20 90 25 60	15 95 33 47 64	35 08 03 36 06
99 01 90 25 29	09 37 67 07 15	38 31 13 11 65	88 67 67 43 97	04 43 62 76 59
12 80 79 99 70	80 15 73 61 47	64 03 23 66 53	98 95 11 68 77	12 17 17 68 33
66 06 57 47 17	34 07 27 68 50	36 69 73 61 70	65 81 33 98 85	11 19 92 91 70
31 06 01 08 05	45 57 18 24 06	35 30 34 26 14	86 79 90 74 39	23 40 30 97 32
85 26 97 76 02	02 05 16 56 92	68 66 57 48 18	73 05 38 52 47	18 62 38 85 79
63 57 33 21 35	05 32 54 70 48	90 55 35 75 48	28 46 82 87 09	83 49 12 56 24
73 79 64 57 53	03 52 96 47 78	35 80 83 42 82	60 93 52 03 44	35 27 38 84 35
98 52 01 77 67	14 90 56 86 07	22 10 94 05 58	60 97 09 34 33	50 50 07 39 98
11 80 50 54 31	39 80 82 77 32	50 72 56 82 48	29 40 52 42 01	52 77 56 78 51
83 45 29 96 34	06 28 89 80 83	13 74 67 00 78	18 47 54 06 10	68 71 17 78 17
88 68 54 02 00	86 50 75 84 01	36 76 66 79 51	90 36 47 64 93	29 60 91 10 62
99 59 46 73 48	87 51 76 49 69	91 82 60 89 28	93 78 56 13 68	23 47 83 41 13
65 48 11 76 74	17 46 85 09 50	58 04 77 69 74	73 03 95 71 86	40 21 81 65 44
80 12 43 56 35	17 72 70 80 15	45 31 82 23 74	21 11 57 82 53	14 38 55 37 63
74 35 09 98 17	77 40 27 72 14	43 23 60 02 10	45 52 16 42 37	96 28 60 26 55
69 91 62 68 03	66 25 22 91 48	36 93 68 72 03	76 62 11 39 90	94 40 05 64 18
09 89 32 05 05	14 22 56 85 14	46 42 75 67 88	96 29 77 88 22	54 38 21 45 98
91 49 91 45 23	68 47 92 76 86	46 16 28 35 54	94 75 08 99 23	37 08 92 00 48
80 33 69 45 98	26 94 03 68 58	70 29 73 41 35	53 14 03 33 40	42 05 08 23 41
44 10 48 19 49	85 15 74 79 54	32 97 92 65 75	57 60 04 08 81	22 22 20 64 13
12 55 07 37 42	11 10 00 20 40	12 86 07 46 97	96 64 48 94 39	28 70 72 58 15
63 60 64 93 29	16 50 53 44 84	40 21 95 25 63	43 65 17 70 82	07 20 73 17 90
61 19 69 04 46	26 45 74 77 74	51 92 43 37 29	65 39 45 95 93	42 58 26 05 27
15 47 44 52 66	95 27 07 99 53	59 36 78 38 48	82 39 61 01 18	33 21 15 94 66
94 55 72 85 73	67 89 75 43 87	54 62 24 44 31	91 19 04 25 92	92 92 74 59 73
42 48 11 62 13	97 34 40 87 21	16 86 84 87 67	03 07 11 20 59	25 70 14 66 70
23 52 37 83 17	73 20 88 98 37	68 93 59 14 16	26 25 22 96 63	05 52 28 25 62
04 49 35 24 94	75 24 63 38 24	45 86 25 10 25	61 96 27 93 35	65 33 71 24 72
00 54 99 76 54	64 05 18 81 59	96 11 96 38 96	54 69 28 23 91	23 28 72 95 29
35 96 31 53 07	26 89 80 93 54	33 35 13 54 62	77 97 54 00 24	90 10 33 93 33
59 80 80 83 91	45 42 72 68 42	83 60 94 97 00	13 02 12 48 92	78 56 52 01 06
46 05 88 52 36	01 39 09 22 86	77 28 14 40 77	93 91 08 36 47	70 61 74 29 41
32 17 90 05 97	87 37 92 52 41	05 56 70 70 07	86 74 31 71 57	85 39 41 18 38
69 23 46 14 06	20 11 74 52 04	15 95 66 00 00	18 74 39 24 23	97 11 89 63 38
19 56 54 14 30	01 75 87 53 79	40 41 92 15 85	66 67 43 68 06	84 96 28 52 07
45 15 51 49 38	19 47 60 72 46	43 66 79 45 43	59 04 79 00 33	20 82 66 95 41
94 86 43 19 94	36 16 81 08 51	34 88 88 15 53	01 54 03 54 56	05 01 45 11 76
98 08 62 48 26	45 24 02 84 04	44 99 90 88 96	39 09 47 34 07	35 44 13 18 80
33 18 51 62 32	41 94 15 09 49	89 43 54 85 81	88 69 54 19 94	37 54 87 30 43
80 95 10 04 06	96 38 27 07 74	20 15 12 33 87	25 01 62 52 98	94 62 46 11 71
79 75 24 91 40	71 96 12 82 96	69 86 10 25 91	74 85 22 05 39	00 38 75 95 79
18 63 33 25 37	98 14 50 65 71	31 01 02 46 74	05 45 56 14 27	77 93 89 19 36
74 02 94 39 02	77 55 73 22 70	97 79 01 71 19	52 52 75 80 21	80 81 45 17 48
54 17 84 56 11	80 99 33 71 43	05 33 51 29 69	56 12 71 92 55	36 04 09 03 24
11 66 44 98 83	52 07 98 48 27	59 38 17 15 39	09 97 33 34 40	88 46 12 33 56
48 32 47 79 28	31 24 96 47 10	02 29 53 68 70	32 30 75 75 46	15 02 00 99 94
69 07 49 41 38	87 63 79 19 76	35 58 40 44 01	10 51 82 16 15	01 84 87 69 38

Source: This table is reproduced from page 1 of The Rand Corporation, *A Million Random Digits with 100,000 Normal Deviates* (New York: The Free Press, 1955). Copyright © 1955 and 1983 by The Rand Corporation. Used by permission.

Back to the Case

Both sides in the ratings war are optimistic that clients will see the superiority of their methods. Mary Ann Packo, chief operating officer of Media Metrix, says, "With our sample being 40,000, it's significantly larger than Nielsen/NetRatings', and a large sample is really critical here." Tim Meadows, vice president of marketing for NetRatings, counters, "If you're talking abut providing valuable information to advertisers, then I would argue that the top 100 Web sites are what counts."

Let's take a closer look at each company's methodology.

Media Metrix gathers data from a panel of over 50,000 Internet users. Panel members are recruited via mail and telephone techniques. Meters on panel members' computers collect data measuring which sites they visit and how long they spend on each site. Media Metrix sorts the data according to whether the computers are at home or at work. It counts the number of unique visitors to each Web site (meaning that if you were to visit a site twice in the measurement period, you would be counted only once). The data cover usage of over 21,000 Web sites and other on-line services.

Nielsen Media Research uses an Internet panel of 9,000 home computer users recruited over the phone. The company uses random digit dialing to contact people at their residences and encourage them to participate in the panel. The caller from Nielsen determines whether they are eligible (based on having a personal computer and Internet access) and, if so, asks them to participate. Those who agree are sent a package including tracking software to be installed on their computer. If a household is not eligible or refuses to participate, Nielsen contacts them again six months later, to see if they are eligible and willing at this time. This is to improve the quality of the sample. Nielsen also calls panel members every two months to thank them for participating and ask if the family is having any difficulties related to participation. This follow-up is designed to encourage continuing participation from panel members.

Nielsen/NetRatings has determined that constructing a truly representative sample of the work population would be difficult to do, in light of differing company policies for maintaining computer security. However, the company is exploring the possibility of setting up a panel of workplace users.

Which approach is better? Some companies—including advertising's OgilvyOne, Internet portal Yahoo!, and on-line retailer Amazon.com—are hedging their bets. They all subscribe to both services.

Sources: Kipp Cheng, "Measurement's Tangled Web," *Adweek* (March 29, 1999), pp. 47–48; Nielsen/NetRatings Web site (www.nielsennetratings.com, downloaded August 18, 1999); Media Metrix Web site (www.mediametrix.com, downloaded October 4, 1999); Media Metrix, "A Comparison of World Wide Web Audience Estimates Utilizing Two Different Approaches," paper (downloaded from the Media Metrix Web site, October 4, 1999).

Summary

Learning Objective 1

Distinguish between a census and a sample.

A complete canvass of a population is called a *census*. A *sample* is a portion of the population taken from the larger group.

Learning Objective 2

List the six steps researchers use to draw a sample of a population.

The six steps researchers use in drawing a sample are (1) define the population, (2) identify the sampling frame, (3) select a sampling procedure, (4) determine the sample size, (5) select the sample elements, and (6) collect the data from the designated elements.

Learning Objective 3

Define sampling frame.

A sampling frame is the listing of the elements from which the actual sample will be drawn.

Learning Objective 4

Explain the difference between a probability sample and a nonprobability sample.

In a probability sample, each member of the population has a known, nonzero chance of being included in the sample. The chances of each member of the population being included in the sample may not be equal, but everyone has a known probability of inclusion.

With nonprobability samples, on the other hand, there is no way of estimating the probability that any population element will be included in the sample. Thus, there is no way of ensuring that the sample is representative of the population. All nonprobability samples rely on personal judgment at some point in the sample-selection process. While these judgments may yield good estimates of a population characteristic, there is no way of determining objectively if the sample is adequate.

Learning Objective 5

Distinguish between a fixed and a sequential sample.

In a fixed sample, the sample size is decided before the study begins, and all the needed information is collected before the results are analyzed. In a sequential sample, the number of elements to be sampled is not decided in advance but is determined by a series of decisions as the data are collected.

Learning Objective 6

Explain what a judgment sample is and describe its best use and its hazards.

A judgment sample is that in which sample elements are handpicked because it is expected that they can serve the research purpose. Sometimes, the sample elements are selected because it is believed that they are representative of the population of interest.

As long as the researcher is at the early stages of research, when ideas or insights are being sought—or when the researcher realizes its limitations—the judgment sample can be used productively. It becomes dangerous, though, when it is employed in descriptive or causal studies and its weaknesses are conveniently forgotten.

Learning Objective 7

Define quota sample.

The quota sampling technique attempts to ensure that the sample is representative of the population by selecting sample elements in such a way that the proportion of the sample elements possessing a certain characteristic is approximately the same as the proportion of the elements with the characteristic in the population. This is accomplished by assigning each field-worker a quota that specifies the characteristics of the people the interviewer is to contact.

Learning Objective 8

Explain what a parameter in a sample procedure is.

A parameter is a characteristic of the parent population; it is a fixed quantity that distinguishes one population from another.

Learning Objective 9

Explain what the derived population is.

The derived population consists of all the possible samples that can be drawn from the parent population under a given sampling plan.

Learning Objective 10

Explain why the concept of sampling distribution is the most important concept in statistics.

The notion of the sampling distribution of the statistic is the cornerstone of statistical inference procedures. If one knows the sampling distribution for the statistic in question, one is in a position to make an inference about the corresponding population parameter. If, on the other hand, one knows only that a particular sample estimate will vary with repeated sampling and has no information as to how it will vary, then it will be impossible to devise a measure of the sampling error associated with that estimate. Since the sampling distribution of an estimate describes how that estimate will vary with repeated sampling, it provides a basis for determining the reliability of the sample estimate.

Review Questions

1. What is a census? What is a sample?

2. Is a sample ever preferred to a census? Why?

3. What distinguishes a probability sample from a nonprobability sample?

4. What is a convenience sample?

5. What is a judgment sample?

6. Explain the operation of a quota sample. Why is a quota sample a nonprobability sample? What kinds of comparisons should one make with the data from quota samples to check their representativeness, and what kinds of conclusions can one legitimately draw?

7. What are the distinguishing features of a simple random sample?

8. What is a derived population? How is it distinguished from a parent population?

9. Consider the estimation of a population mean. What is the relation between the mean of the parent population and the mean of the derived population? Between the variance of the parent population and the variance of the derived population?

10. What is the central-limit theorem? What roles does it play in making inferences about a population mean?

11. What procedure is followed in constructing a confidence interval for a population mean when the population variance is known? When the population variance is unknown? What does such an interval mean?

12. How should a simple random sample be selected? Describe the procedure.

Discussion Questions, Problems, and Projects

1. For each of the following situations identify the appropriate target population and sampling frame.

   (a) A local chapter of the American Lung Association wants to test the effectiveness of a brochure titled "12 Reasons for Not Smoking" in the city of St. Paul, Minnesota.

   (b) A medium-sized manufacturer of cat food wants to conduct an in-home usage test of a new type of cat food in Sacramento, California.

   (c) A large wholesaler dealing in household appliances in the city of New York wants to evaluate dealer reaction to a new discount policy.

   (d) A local department store wants to assess the satisfaction with a new credit policy offered to charge account customers.

   (e) A national manufacturer wants to assess whether adequate inventories are being held by wholesalers in order to prevent shortages by retailers.

   (f) Your school cafeteria wants to test a new soft drink manufactured and sold by the staff of the cafeteria.

   (g) A manufacturer of cake mixes selling primarily in the Midwest wants to test-market a new brand of cake mix.

2. The management of a popular tourist resort on the West Coast had noticed a decline in the number of tourists and length of stay over the past three years. An overview of industry trends indicated that the overall tourist trade was expanding and growing rapidly. Management decided to conduct a study to determine people's attitudes toward the particular activities that were available at the resort. It wanted to cause the minimum amount of inconvenience to its customers and hence adopted the following plan: A request was deposited in each hotel room of the two major hotels in the resort, indicating the nature of the study and encouraging customers to participate. The customers were requested to report to a separate desk located in the lobby of the hotels. Personal interviews, lasting 20 minutes, were conducted at this desk.

   (a) What type of sampling method was used?

   (b) Critically evaluate the method used.

3. A national manufacturer of baby food was planning to enter the Canadian market. The initial thrust was to be in the provinces of Ontario and Quebec. Prior to the final decisions of launching the product, management decided to test-market the products in two cities. After reviewing the various cities in terms of such external criteria as demographics, shopping characteristics, and so on, the research department settled on the cities of Hamilton, Ontario, and Sherbrooke, Quebec.

   (a) What type of sampling method was used?

   (b) Critically evaluate the method used.

4. The Juno Company, a manufacturer of clothing for large-size consumers, was in the process of evaluating its product and advertising strategy. Initial efforts consisted of a number of focus-group interviews. The focus groups consisted of 10 to 12 large men and women of different demographic characteristics who were selected by the company's research department using on-the-street observations of physical characteristics.

   (a) What type of sampling method was used?

   (b) Critically evaluate the method used.

5. The Hi-Style Company is a chain of beauty salons in San Diego, California. During the past five years the company has witnessed a sharp increase in the number of outlets it operates and in the company's gross sales and net profit margin. The owner plans to offer a free service of hair analysis and consultation, a service for which competing salons charge a substantial price. In order to offset the increase in operating expenses, the owner plans to raise the rates on other services by 5 percent. Prior to introducing this new service and increasing rates, the owner wants to do a survey

using her customers as a sample and employing the method of quota sampling. Your assistance is required in planning the study.

(a) On what variables will you suggest the quotas be based? Why? List the variables with their respective levels.

(b) The owner has kept close track of the demographic characteristics of her customers over a five-year period and decides that these would be most relevant in identifying the sample elements to be used.

Variable	Level	Percent of Customers
Age	0–15 years	5
	16–30 years	30
	31–45 years	30
	46–60 years	15
	61–75 years	15
	76 years and over	5
Sex	Male	24
	Female	76
Income	$0–$9,999	10
	$10,000–$19,999	20
	$20,000–$29,999	30
	$30,000–$39,999	20
	$40,000 and over	20

Based on these three quota variables, indicate the characteristics of a sample of 200 subjects.

(c) Discuss the possible sources of bias with the sampling method.

Endnotes

1. The fact that sample information is used to gauge the accuracy of the census has embroiled the Census Bureau in a debate about whether census counts should be adjusted on the basis of the sample results. For discussion of the controversy surrounding adjustment, see Eugene Carlson, "Census Debate: Is an Estimate More Accurate than a Count?" *The Wall Street Journal* (August 4, 1987), p. 35; Timothy Noah, "Census Bureau Says It Missed 2% of Population," *The Wall Street Journal* (April 19, 1991), p. 1. Partly because of the accuracy controversy, sampling was proposed as the better way to conduct the 2000 census, but this idea was rejected by Congress.

2. Cyndee Miller, "Researching Children Isn't Kids Stuff Anymore," *Marketing News* 24 (September 3, 1990), p. 32.

3. Seymour Sudman, "Applied Sampling," in Peter H. Rossi, James D. Wright, and Andy B. Anderson, eds., *Handbook of Survey Research* (Orlando: Academic Press, 1983), p. 145–194. See also "SSI Lowers the Cost of Finding Rare Groups," *The Frame* (October 1991), p. 3.

4. Julie Johnsson, "Writing a New Policy," *Crain's Chicago Business* (June 7, 1999), pp. E47, E49.

5. Kathy Gardner Chadwick, "Some Caveats Regarding the Interpretation of Data from 800 Number Callers," *Journal of Services Marketing* 5 (Summer 1991), pp. 55–61; Jack Honomichl, "It's Time to 86 the 900-Number Poll Plague," *Marketing News* 25 (September 2, 1991), p. 33.

6. Jack Neff, "P&G Enlists 13-Year-Olds in Summer Intern Jobs," *Advertising Age* (June 28, 1999), p. 20.

7. The technique was originally suggested by Leo A. Goodman, "Snowball Sampling," *Annuals of Mathematical Statistics* 32 (1961), pp. 148–170.

8. AT&T used such a process for this communications problem, according to Robert Whitelaw, division manager for market research, in a speech "Research Solutions and New High Technology Service Concepts," which was delivered at the American Marketing Association's 1981 Annual Conference, held in San Francisco, California, June 14–17, 1981.

9. Seymour Sudman, *Applied Sampling* (San Francisco: Academic Press, 1976), p. 10. For discussion of the makeup of the CPI, see John R. Dorfman, "U.S. to Give More Emphasis to Costs of Housing in the Consumer Price Index," *The Wall Street Journal* (February 26, 1987), p. 8; Christina Duff, "Is the CPI

Accurate? Ask the Federal Sleuths Who Get the Numbers," *The Wall Street Journal* (January 16, 1997), pp. A1, A6.

10. Catherine Marsh and Elinor Scarbrough, "Testing Nine Hypotheses About Quota Sampling," *Journal of the Market Research Society* 32 (October 1990), pp. 485–506. For an example, see Gunter Schweiger, Gerald Haubl, and Geroen Friederes, "Consumer Evaluations of Products Labeled 'Made in Europe,'" *Marketing & Research Today* 23 (February 1995), pp. 25–34.

11. In the example at hand, the sample is 10 percent of the population, since the procedure specifies samples of size $n = 2$ be drawn from a population of size $n = 20$. In a situation such as this, in which the sample is a relatively large part of the population, the correct formula relating the two variances contains an additional term. Specifically it equals

$$\sigma_{\bar{x}}^2 = \frac{\sigma^2}{n} \frac{N-n}{N-1}$$

The additional term $\dfrac{N-n}{N-1}$ is called the *finite population correction factor*. It is, of course, close to 1 when the population is very large in comparison to the sample, and can then safely be ignored. The variance of mean incomes for the example using the formula turns out to be

$$\sigma_{\bar{x}}^2 = \frac{5,320,000}{2} \frac{20-2}{20-1} = 2,520,000$$

12. There are two major errors to avoid when using random-number tables: (1) starting at a given place because one knows the distribution of numbers at that place, and (2) discarding a sample because it does not "look right" in some sense and continuing to use random numbers until a "likely looking" sample is selected. Sudman, "Applied Sampling," p. 165.

13. Malcolm W. Browne, "Coin-Tossing Computers Found to Show Subtle Bias," *The New York Times* (January 13, 1993), pp. B5–B6.

Suggested Additional Readings

For a good exposition of the principles and advantages of sequential sampling versus fixed samples, see
E. J. Anderton and R. Tudor, "The Application of Sequential Analysis in Market Research," *Journal of Marketing Research* 17 (February 1980), pp. 97–105.

For a discussion of the use of snowball samples, see
Patrick Biernacki and Dan Waldorf, "Snowball Sampling: Problems and Techniques of Chain Referred Sampling," *Sociological Methods and Research* 10 (November 1981), pp. 141–163.

For a more in-depth discussion of some of the more fundamental issues in sampling, see
Martin Frankel, "Sampling Theory," in Peter H. Rossi, James D. Wright, and Andy B. Anderson, eds., *Handbook of Survey Research* (Orlando: Academic Press, 1983), pp. 21–67.
Richard L. Schaeffer and William Mendenhall, *Elementary Survey Sampling*, 5th ed. (Belmont, Calif.: Wadsworth Publishing, 1996).

Chapter 16

STRATIFIED AND CLUSTER SAMPLING

L E A R N I N G   O B J E C T I V E S

Upon Completing This Chapter, You Should Be Able to

1. Specify the two procedures that distinguish a stratified sample.

2. Cite two reasons why researchers might opt to use a stratified sample rather than a simple random sample.

3. Note what points investigators should keep in mind when dividing a population into strata for a stratified sample.

4. Explain what a proportionate stratified sample is.

5. Explain what a disproportionate stratified sample is.

6. List the steps followed in drawing a cluster sample.

7. Explain the difference between a one-stage cluster sample and a two-stage cluster sample.

8. Explain why cluster sampling, though far less statistically efficient than comparable stratified samples, is the sampling procedure used most in large-scale field surveys employing personal interviews.

9. Distinguish between one-stage area sampling and simple two-stage area sampling.

10. Note the quality that distinguishes probability-proportional-to-size sampling and explain when it is used.

Case in Marketing Research

Pam Heisler looked across the table at the two researchers whose efforts had allowed her to keep a pulse on the mood of the electorate during the early months of her campaign for state senator. She had the highest respect for their judgment. They had helped her keep the Heisler for Senate campaign focused on issues that mattered most to her constituents. The only problem was that right now, they were giving her conflicting advice.

"Every day, the people on the Internet look more and more like the overall population," said one researcher, Terry Shapiro. "If you want to know what your people are thinking right now, this minute, you will ask them on-line. You'll build your reputation for being someone who listens to the people and cares about what they think."

"That may be where we're headed," cautioned Jim Lovesey, the other researcher. "But we're not there yet. The current statistics show that Internet users are more educated than the general population. They also overrepresent whites and males. You just can't draw inferences about the general population by drawing a sample from the cyberpopulation. Pam, what you'll build is a reputation for caring about what the *techies* think."

"Aren't there ways to adjust your methods to account for the discrepancies between the groups?" asked Pam.

"Sure there are," said Terry confidently. "For example, we can set some quotas—you know, get so many women, so many blacks, so many whites. Or we could take random samples from those different groups."

"But you can't be sure that that will make your results more accurate," added Jim.

"Why not?" Pam asked.

"Well, for example, you can survey the right percentage of blacks to mirror that group's share of the population, but you can't be sure that the black people who go on-line have the same opinions as the blacks who don't. And the same problem exists for any other subgroup—women, Republicans, whatever. You can't be sure that the people in cyberspace see the world the same way as everyone else."

"Then before we go any further with this experiment, find out what the experience has been so far with polling on the Internet. Are those polls valid or not? Get back to me next week, and we'll make a decision at that point."

Discussion Issues

1. If you were Pam Heisler, what would you want to know about the sampling methods available for on-line polling?

2. What might be the advantages of this information source?

3. What pitfalls will you need to avoid? How might you avoid them?

In the preceding chapter we discussed the basic types of samples and how they are drawn. Simple random samples were used to illustrate the basis of statistical inference in which a parameter is estimated from a statistic. In this chapter we will take these concepts a bit further to explore two other types of probability samples: stratified samples and cluster samples.

Stratified Sample

Sometimes a simple random sample is not the most useful way to answer a research question. A Westport, Connecticut, retail marketing agency called TradeZone, for example, wanted to compare different kinds of retailers' experiences with promotions. More specifically, TradeZone wanted to compare the opinions of supermarkets, drugstores, and mass merchandisers regarding the success of various promotional activities, from frequent-shopper programs to in-store demonstrations. The agency wondered if some promotional activities were more appropriate for one category of retailers than for the others.[1] A simple random sample would not ensure that each category of retailer was well represented. A more targeted approach would be to use some form of stratified sample. A **stratified sample** is a probability sample that is distinguished by the following two-step procedure:

Stratified sample

A probability sample that is distinguished by a two-step procedure in which (1) the parent population is divided into mutually exclusive and exhaustive subsets, and (2) a simple random sample of elements is chosen independently from each group or subset.

1. The parent population is divided into mutually exclusive and exhaustive subsets.

2. A simple random sample of elements is chosen independently from each group or subset.

In the case of the TradeZone study, the parent population would be retailers, and the subsets would be supermarkets, drugstores, and mass merchandisers.

Note that the definition says nothing about what criteria are used to separate the universe elements into subsets. That is because it is not the criteria that determine whether a stratified sample has been drawn. Admittedly, those criteria will make a difference as to the ultimate usefulness of the particular sample in question. But as long as the sample reflects the two-stage process, it is a stratified sample. Keep this distinction in mind. It will be useful later when distinguishing cluster samples from stratified samples.

The subsets into which the universe elements are divided are called *strata* or *subpopulations*. Note that our definition specified that this division be mutually exclusive and exhaustive. This means that every population element must be assigned to one, and only one, stratum and that no population elements are omitted in the assignment procedure.

To illustrate the process, suppose we again used the hypothetical population of 20 people used in the preceding chapter and shown again in Exhibit 16.1. That population could be described by several parameters, such as the average income, the range in education, and the proportion subscribing to various newspapers. Now assume we divide the group into two strata on the basis of educational level. Exhibit 16.2 shows the results of this stratification procedure. Elements A though J form the *first stratum* (education of 12 years or less) and Elements K through T form the *second stratum* (education of more than 12 years). There is no particular reason to choose two strata. The parent population can be divided into any number of strata. We chose two as a convenient way of illustrating the technique.

EXHIBIT 16.1	Hypothetical Population						
Element	**Income (Dollars)**	**Education (Years)**	**Newspaper Subscription**	**Element**	**Income (Dollars)**	**Education (Years)**	**Newspaper Subscription**
1 A	5,600	8	X	11 K	9,600	13	X
2 B	6,000	9	Y	12 L	10,000	13	Y
3 C	6,400	11	X	13 M	10,400	14	X
4 D	6,800	11	Y	14 N	10,800	14	Y
5 E	7,200	11	X	15 O	11,200	15	X
6 F	7,600	12	Y	16 P	11,600	16	Y
7 G	8,000	12	X	17 Q	12,000	16	X
8 H	8,400	12	Y	18 R	12,400	17	Y
9 I	8,800	12	X	19 S	12,800	18	X
10 J	9,200	12	Y	20 T	13,200	18	Y

EXHIBIT 16.2	Stratification of Hypothetical Population by Education		
Stratum I Elements		**Stratum II Elements**	
A	F	K	P
B	G	L	Q
C	H	M	R
D	I	N	S
E	J	O	T

The second step in the process requires that a simple random sample be drawn independently from *each* stratum. Let us again work with samples of Size 2, formed in this case by selecting one element from each stratum. (The number of elements from each stratum does not have to be equal, however.)

The procedure that would be used to select the two elements for the stratified sample would be the same as that used in drawing a simple random sample. Within each stratum, the population elements would be serially numbered from 1 to 10. A table of random numbers would be consulted. The first number encountered between 1 and 10 would designate the element from the first stratum. The element from the second stratum could be selected from another independent start or by continuing from the first randomly determined start. In either case, it would again be designated by the first encounter with a number between 1 and 10.

Derived Population

Although only one sample of Size 2 will in fact be selected, let us look briefly at the derived population of all possible samples of Size 2 that could be selected under this sampling plan. This derived population along with the mean of each sample is displayed in Exhibit 16.3.

Note that in this sampling plan there are only 100 possible sample combinations of elements, whereas with simple random sampling there were 190 possible combinations. That is because this type of sampling specified that one element be drawn from each stratum. In simple random sampling, you will recall, any two elements could be drawn from the population of items. In this sense, stratified sampling is always more restrictive than simple random sampling. Note further that every element has an equal chance of being included in the sample—1 in 10—since each can be the single element selected from the stratum that it is in. This explains why we specified an additional requirement to define a

EXHIBIT 16.3   Derived Population of All Possible Samples of Size 2 with Stratified Sampling

k	Sample Identity	Mean	k	Sample Identity	Mean	k	Sample Identity	Mean	k	Sample Identity	Mean
1	AK	7,600	26	CP	9,000	51	FK	8,600	76	HP	10,000
2	AL	7,800	27	CQ	9,200	52	FL	8,800	77	HQ	10,200
3	AM	8,000	28	CR	9,400	53	FM	9,000	78	HR	10,400
4	AN	8,200	29	CS	9,600	54	FN	9,200	79	HS	10,600
5	AO	8,400	30	CT	9,800	55	FO	9,400	80	HT	10,800
6	AP	8,600	31	DK	8,200	56	FP	9,600	81	IK	9,200
7	AQ	8,800	32	DL	8,400	57	FQ	9,800	82	IL	9,400
8	AR	9,000	33	DM	8,600	58	FR	10,000	83	IM	9,600
9	AS	9,200	34	DN	8,800	59	FS	10,200	84	IN	9,800
10	AT	9,400	35	DO	9,000	60	FT	10,400	85	IO	10,000
11	BK	7,800	36	DP	9,200	61	GK	8,800	86	IP	10,200
12	BL	8,000	37	DQ	9,400	62	GL	9,000	87	IQ	10,400
13	BM	8,200	38	DR	9,600	63	GM	9,200	88	IR	10,600
14	BN	8,400	39	DS	9,800	64	GN	9,400	89	IS	10,800
15	BO	8,600	40	DT	10,000	65	GO	9,600	90	IT	11,000
16	BP	8,800	41	EK	8,400	66	GP	9,800	91	JK	9,400
17	BQ	9,000	42	EL	8,600	67	GQ	10,000	92	JL	9,600
18	BR	9,200	43	EM	8,800	68	GR	10,200	93	JM	9,800
19	BS	9,400	44	EN	9,000	69	GS	10,400	94	JN	10,000
20	BT	9,600	45	EO	9,200	70	GT	10,600	95	JO	10,200
21	CK	8,000	46	EP	9,400	71	HK	9,000	96	JP	10,400
22	CL	8,200	47	EQ	9,600	72	HL	9,200	97	JQ	10,600
23	CM	8,400	48	ER	9,800	73	HM	9,400	98	JR	10,800
24	CN	8,600	49	ES	10,000	74	HN	9,600	99	JS	11,000
25	CO	8,800	50	ET	10,200	75	HO	9,800	100	JT	11,200

simple random sample. Although simple random samples provide each element an equal chance of selection, other techniques can also. Thus, equal probability of selection is a necessary but not a sufficient condition for simple random sampling; in addition, each combination of n elements must be a sample possibility and as likely to occur as any other combination of n elements.

Sampling Distribution

Exhibit 16.4 contains the classification of sample means by size, and Figure 16.1 displays the plot of this sample statistic. Note that in relation to Figure 15.4, for simple random sampling, stratified sampling can produce a more concentrated distribution of estimates. This suggests one reason why we might choose a stratified sample; stratified samples can produce sample statistics that are more precise, or that have smaller error due to sampling, than simple random samples. With education as a stratification variable, there is a marked reduction in the number of sample means that deviate widely from the population mean.

A second reason for drawing a stratified sample is that stratification allows the investigation of the characteristic of interest for particular subgroups. Thus, by stratifying, one is able to guarantee representation of those with a high school education or less, and those with more than a high school education. This can be extremely important when sampling from populations with rare segments. Suppose, for example, that a manufacturer of diamond rings wants to conduct a study of sales of the product by social class. Unless special precautions are taken, it is likely that the upper class—which represents only 3 percent of the total population—will not be represented at all, or will be represented by

EXHIBIT 16.4   **Classification of Sample Means by Size with Stratified Sampling**

Sample Mean	Number of Samples
7,300 to 7,800	3
7,900 to 8,400	12
8,500 to 9,000	21
9,100 to 9,600	28
9,700 to 10,200	21
10,300 to 10,800	12
10,900 to 11,400	3

FIGURE 16.1   **Distribution of Sample Means with Stratified Sampling**

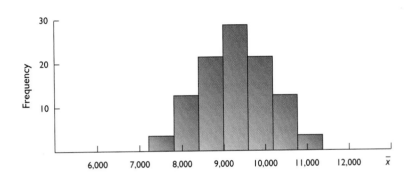

too few cases. Yet this may be an extremely important segment to the ring manufacturer. It is often true in marketing that a small subset of the population of interest will account for a large proportion of the behavior of interest—for example, consumption of the product. It then becomes critical that this subgroup be adequately represented in the sample. Stratified sampling is one way of ensuring adequate representation from each subgroup of interest.

Confidence Interval Estimate

In establishing a confidence interval with a simple random sample, we saw that we need three things to complete the confidence interval specifications given by

$$\bar{x} - zs_{\bar{x}} \leq \mu \leq \bar{x} + zs_{\bar{x}}$$

1. The degree of confidence desired so that a z value can be selected.

2. A point estimate of the population mean given by the sample mean $\bar{x}$.

3. An estimate of the amount of sampling error associated with the sample mean, which was given by the standard error of the mean, $s_{\bar{x}} = \hat{s}/\sqrt{n}$, when the population variance was unknown.

The same three quantities are required for making inferences with a stratified sample. The only difference in the procedure occurs in the way Items 2 and 3 are generated. With stratified sampling, the sample estimate of the population mean and the standard error of estimate associated with this statistic are determined by weighting the individual strata results.

More specifically, the analyst needs to compute the sample mean and the sample variance for each stratum. These would be calculated exactly as before, since a simple random sample is being taken from each stratum. The mean for the sample as a whole is then determined by weighting each of the respective strata means by the relative proportion of elements in the population that belong to the stratum. For example, if the population is divided into groups in such a way that one stratum contains one-fourth of all the population members, the sample mean for that stratum receives a weight of .25 when one is determining the mean for the total sample. Similarly, the sample mean for a stratum that contains 10 percent of the population elements is weighted .10 when one is estimating the overall sample mean.

The process to get the overall standard error of the mean is slightly more complex. The relative sizes of the respective strata are again used but the ratios are squared; for example, a stratum containing 10 percent of the population members would be weighted $(.10)^2 = .01$. Further, one needs to weight the variances of means by strata to get the overall variance of the mean. Then one takes the square root of the overall result to get the standard error of the mean for the overall sample. The variance of means for each stratum is obtained just as it was for a simple random sample—that is, by dividing the sample variance for the stratum by the sample size from that stratum.

Exhibit 16.5 illustrates the procedure assuming Elements B and E were randomly selected from the first stratum and Elements N and S from the second stratum. Since each stratum contains 10 of the 20 population elements, the sample mean for each stratum is weighted by one-half $(10 \div 20)$ when one is determining the overall sample mean, while each variance of estimate is weighted .25. With the overall sample mean of 9,200 and standard error of estimate of 583, the 95 percent confidence interval $(z = 1.96)$ is 9,200 $\pm$

EXHIBIT 16.5   **Computation of Mean and Standard Error of Estimate for Stratified Sample**

STRATUM 1		STRATUM 2	
Element	**Income**	**Element**	**Income**
B	6,000	N	10,800
E	7,200	S	12,800

Mean: $\bar{x}_1 = \dfrac{6,600 + 7,200}{2} = 6,600$

$\bar{x}_2 = \dfrac{10,800 + 12,8000}{2} = 11,800$

Variance: $\hat{s}_1^2 = \dfrac{(6,000 - 6,600)^2 + (7,200 - 6,600)^2}{2 - 1}$

$\hat{s}_1^2 = \dfrac{(10,800 - 11,800)^2 + (12,800 - 11,800)^2}{2 - 1}$

$= 720,000$

$= 2,000,000$

Variance of estimate: $s_{\bar{x}_1}^2 = \dfrac{\hat{s}_1^2}{n_1} = \dfrac{720,000}{2} = 360,000$

$s_{\bar{x}_2}^2 = \dfrac{\hat{s}_2^2}{n_2} = \dfrac{2,000,000}{2} = 1,000,000$

OVERALL SAMPLE

Mean: $\bar{x} = \dfrac{10}{20}(6,600) + \dfrac{10}{20}(11,800) = 9,200$

Variance of estimate: $s_{\bar{x}}^2 = \left(\dfrac{10}{20}\right)^2 (360,000) + \left(\dfrac{10}{20}\right)^2 (1,000,000) = 340,000$

Standard error of estimate: $s_{\bar{x}} = \sqrt{s_{\bar{x}}^2} = 583$

(1.96)583 or $8{,}057 \leq \mu \leq 10{,}343$. This interval is interpreted as before. The true mean may or may not be in the interval, but since 95 of 100 intervals constructed by this process will contain the true mean, we are 95 percent confident that the true population mean income is between $8,057 and $10,343.[2]

Increased Precision of Stratified Samples We mentioned previously that one might choose a stratified sample because such samples offer an opportunity for reducing sampling error or increasing precision. When estimating a mean, sampling error is given by the size of the standard error of the mean, $s_{\bar{x}}$; the smaller $s_{\bar{x}}$ is, the less the sampling error and the more precise the estimate will be, as indicated by the narrower confidence interval associated with a specified degree of confidence.

Consider the example in Exhibit 16.1 again. The total size of the population and the population within each stratum are fixed. The only way, therefore, for total sampling error to be reduced is for the variance of the estimate within each stratum to be made smaller. Now the variance of the estimate by strata in turn depends on the variability of the characteristic within the strata. Thus, the estimate of the mean can be made more precise to the extent that the population can be partitioned so that there is little variability within each stratum—that is, to the extent the strata can be made internally homogeneous.

A characteristic of interest will display a certain amount of variation in the population. The investigator can do nothing about this total variation because it is a fixed characteristic of the population. In the population in Exhibit 16.1, for example, there is variation in incomes which the investigator can do nothing about. But the analyst can do something when dividing the elements of the population into strata so as to increase the precision with which the average value of the characteristic (i.e., average income) can be estimated. Specifically, the goal is to divide the population into strata so that the elements within any given stratum are as similar in value as possible and the values between any two strata are as disparate as possible. In this case, the division of the population between those who have more than a high school education and those who do not was a good way of separating the population into two strata since the elements within each stratum have similar incomes.

In the limit, if the investigator is successful in partitioning the population so that the elements in each stratum are exactly equal, there will be no error associated with the estimate of the population mean. That is right! The population mean could then be estimated without error because *the variability that exists between strata does not enter into the calculation of the standard error of estimate with stratified sampling.*

One can see this readily in a simple case with a limited number of values. Suppose that in a population of 1,000 elements, 200 had the value 5; 300 had the value 10; and 500 had the value 20. Now the mean of this population is $\mu = 14$, and the variance is $\sigma^2 = 39$. If a simple random sample of size $n = 3$ is employed to estimate this mean, then the standard error of estimate is

$$\sigma_{\bar{x}} = \frac{\sigma}{\sqrt{n}} = \frac{\sqrt{39}}{\sqrt{3}} = 3.61$$

and the width of confidence interval would be $\pm z$ times this value, 3.61. Suppose, on the other hand, a researcher employed a stratified sample and was successful in partitioning the total population so that all the elements with a value of 5 on the characteristic were in one stratum, those with the value 10 in the second stratum, and those with the value 20 in the third stratum. To generate a completely precise description of the mean of each stratum, the researcher would then need only to take a sample of one from each stratum. Further, when the investigator combined these individual results into a global estimate of the overall mean, the standard error of the estimate is zero. The population mean value would be determined exactly.

Bases for Stratification The fact that variation among strata does not enter into the calculation of the standard error of estimate suggests the kinds of criteria that should be used to partition the population. The values assumed by the characteristic will be unknown, for if they were known, there would be no need to take a sample to estimate their mean level. What the investigator attempts to do, therefore, is to partition the population according to one or more criteria that are expected to be related to the characteristic of interest. It was no accident, therefore, that in our hypothetical example, education was employed to divide the population elements into strata. As Exhibit 16.1 indicates, there is a relationship between educational level and income level: the more years of school, the higher the income tends to be. Newspaper subscriptions, on the other hand, would have made a poor variable for partitioning the population into segments, since there is almost no relation between the paper to which a person subscribes and the individual's income. Whether one selects a "good" or a "bad" variable to partition the population does not affect whether a stratified sample is selected or not. It is significant in determining whether a good or poor sample is selected, but the two features defining a stratified sample are still (1) the partitioning of the population into subgroups and (2) the random selection of elements from each subgroup.

The calculation of the standard error of estimate provides some clue as to the number of strata that should be used. Since the standard error of estimate depends only on variability within strata, the various strata should be made as homogeneous as possible. One way of doing this is to employ many, very small strata. In our education example, for instance, additional strata could be grade school education or less, some high school education, some college education, and graduate school education. Or even finer distinctions could be made. There are practical limits, though, to the number of strata that should be and are used in actual research studies. First, the creation of additional strata is often expensive in terms of sample design, data collection, and analysis. Second, there is an upper limit to the amount of variation that can be accounted for by any practical stratification. Regardless of the criteria by which the population is partitioned, a certain amount of variation is likely to remain unaccounted for, and thus the additional strata will serve no productive purpose.

Proportionate and Disproportionate Stratified Samples

Whether one chooses a stratified sample over a simple random sample depends in part on the trade-off between cost and precision. Although stratified samples typically produce more precise estimates, they also usually cost more than simple random samples. If the decision is made in favor of a stratified sample, the researcher must still decide whether to select a proportionate or disproportionate one.

Proportionate stratified sample
A stratified sample in which the number of observations in the total sample is allocated among the strata in proportion to the relative number of elements in each stratum in the population.

Disproportionate stratified sample
A stratified sample in which the individual strata or subsets are sampled in relation to both their size and their variability; strata exhibiting more variability are sampled more than proportionately to their relative size, while those that are very homogeneous are sampled less than proportionately.

With a **proportionate stratified sample,** the number of observations in the total sample is allocated among the strata in proportion to the *relative* number of elements in each stratum in the population. A stratum containing one-fifth of all the population elements would account for one-fifth of the total sample observations, and so on. Proportionate sampling was employed in our education example, since each stratum contained one-half of the population and they were sampled equally.

One advantage of proportionate allocation is that the investigator needs to know only the relative sizes of each stratum in order to determine the number of sample observations to select from each stratum with a given sample size. A **disproportionate stratified sample,** however, can produce still more efficient estimates. It involves balancing the two criteria of strata size and strata variability. With a fixed sample size, strata exhibiting more variability are sampled more than proportionately to their relative size. Conversely, those strata that are very homogeneous are sampled less than proportionately. Research Window 16.1, for example, describes the disproportionate stratified sampling scheme used by Nielsen in developing its SCANTRAK service, described in Chapter 8.[3]

While a full discussion of how the sample size for each stratum should be determined would take us too far afield and would be much too technical for our purpose, some feel for the rational behind disproportionate sampling is useful. Consider at the extreme a stratum with zero variability. Since all the elements are identical in value, a single observation

Disproportionate Stratified Sampling Scheme Used by Nielsen

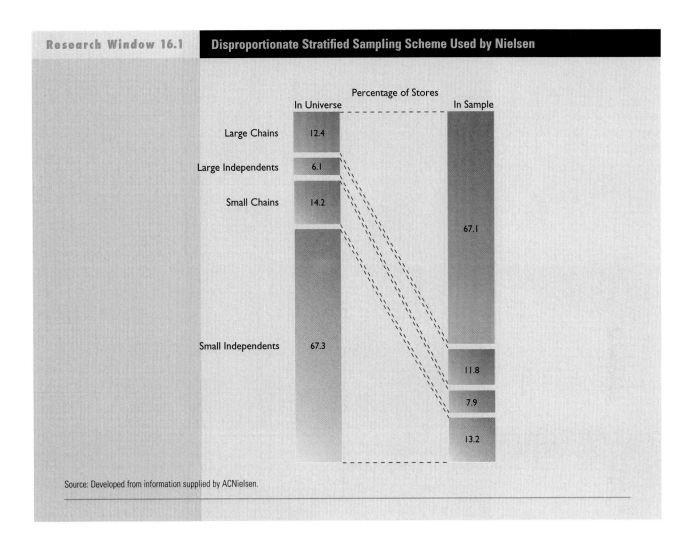

Percentage of Stores

In Universe — In Sample

	In Universe	In Sample
Large Chains	12.4	67.1
Large Independents	6.1	
Small Chains	14.2	
Small Independents	67.3	11.8
		7.9
		13.2

Source: Developed from information supplied by ACNielsen.

tells all. On the other hand, a stratum that is characterized by great variability will require a large number of observations to produce a precise estimate of the stratum mean. One would expect, for example, great variability among the income levels of those people subscribing to *Newsweek* but much less among people subscribing to the glossy society magazine *Town and Country* (see another example in the ads for sport-utility vehicles). One can expect greater precision when the various strata are sampled proportionate to the relative variability of the characteristic under study rather than proportionate to their relative size in the population.

A disproportionate stratified sample requires more knowledge about the population of interest than does a proportionate stratified sample. To sample the strata in relation to their variability, one needs knowledge of relative variability. Sampling theory is a peculiar phenomenon in that knowledge begets more knowledge. Disproportionate sampling can produce more efficient estimates than proportionate sampling, but the former method also requires that some estimate of the relative variation within strata be known. One can sometimes anticipate the relative homogeneity likely to exist within a stratum on the basis of past studies and experience. Sometimes the investigator may have to rely on logic and intuition in establishing sample sizes for each stratum. For example, one might expect that large retail stores would show greater variation than small stores in sales of some products. That is one reason why the large stores are sampled more heavily in the Nielsen's SCANTRAK service.

These two magazine ads are both for four-wheel-drive vehicles. One would expect greater variability among the income levels of consumers purchasing a Toyota 4Runner, which advertises the potential to save money, and lesser income level variability for those interested in the Range Rover, whose ad states, "A Range Rover will make you feel like a million dollars. Unless, of course, you're worth more."

Stratified versus Quota Sample

Inexperienced researchers sometimes confuse stratified samples with quota samples. There are similarities. In each case, the population is divided into segments, and elements are selected from each segment. There is one key difference, though. In stratified samples, sample elements are selected by probability methods; in quota samples, elements are chosen based on a researcher's judgment. This difference has important implications. Since elements in a stratified sample are selected probabilistically, researchers can establish the sampling distribution of the statistic in question, and hence a confidence interval judgment. In a quota sample there is no objective way to assess the degree of sampling error. Therefore there is also no way to arrive at confidence interval estimates and statistical tests of significance.

Cluster Sample

Cluster sample

A probability sample distinguished by a two-step procedure in which (1) the parent population is divided into mutually exclusive and exhaustive subsets, and (2) a random sample of subsets is selected. If the investigator then uses all the population elements in the selected subsets for the sample, the procedure is one-stage cluster sampling; if a sample of elements is selected probabilistically from the subsets, the procedure is two-stage cluster sampling.

Cluster samples are another probability sampling technique often used by researchers. Cluster sampling shares some similarities with stratified sampling, but also has some key differences. Cluster sampling involves the following steps:

1. The parent population is divided into mutually exclusive and exhaustive subsets.

2. A random sample of the subsets is selected.

If the investigator then uses all the population elements in the selected subsets for the sample, the procedure is one-stage cluster sampling. If, on the other hand, a sample of elements is selected probabilistically from the selected subsets, the procedure is known as two-stage cluster sampling.

Note the similarities and differences between cluster sampling and stratified sampling. Although in each case the population is divided into mutually exclusive and exhaustive subgroups, in stratified sampling a sample of elements is selected *from each subgroup*. With cluster sampling, one chooses a *sample of subgroups*.

Remember that in stratified sampling, the goal is to separate the population into strata that are fairly homogeneous for a certain characteristic. In cluster sampling, the goal is to form subgroups that are similar to each other and are each small-scale models of the population. Each cluster should reflect the diversity of the whole population.

In our earlier example relating income to level of education, we noted that dividing the population into subgroups based on newspaper subscriptions was probably not a good idea for stratified sampling because that characteristic is not a good predictor of income. However, since the goal in cluster sampling is to form subgroups that are as heterogeneous as possible, newspaper subscriptions might be a good basis for dividing the population for this form of sample.

If all those subscribing to Paper X were considered to form one subgroup and all those subscribing to Paper Y a second subgroup, then one could be relatively safe in randomly selecting either subgroup to estimate the mean income in the population. While the distribution of incomes within each subgroup is not exactly the same as it is in the population, the range of incomes is such that there would be only a slight error if one were to estimate the mean income and variance of incomes of the population with the elements from either subset.

Admittedly, in practice clusters are not always formed to be as heterogeneous as possible. Because of the way cluster samples are often drawn, the defined clusters are homogeneous rather than heterogeneous in regard to the characteristic of interest. Beginning researchers often mistakenly then call the procedure *stratified sampling*, since it involves the construction of homogeneous subgroups of population elements. But as long as subgroups are subsequently selected for investigation randomly, the procedure is *cluster sampling* regardless of how the subgroups are formed. Admittedly, however, homogeneous subgroups produce less ideal cluster samples from a statistical efficiency viewpoint than do heterogeneous subgroups.

Statistical efficiency
A measure used to compare sampling plans; one sampling plan is said to be superior (more statistically efficient) to another if, for the same size sample, it produces a smaller standard error of estimate.

Statistical efficiency is a relative notion by which sampling plans can be compared. One sampling plan is said to be more statistically efficient than another if, for the same size sample, it produces a smaller standard error of estimate. When the characteristic of interest is the mean, for example, the sampling plan that produces the smallest value of the standard error of the mean, $s_{\bar{x}}$, for a given-size sample is most statistically efficient. Cluster samples are typically much less statistically efficient than comparable stratified samples or even simple random samples because the probable margin of error with a fixed-size sample is often greatest with cluster sampling.

Even with its typically lower statistical efficiency, cluster sampling is probably the sampling procedure used most in large-scale field surveys employing personal interviews, particularly those involving in-home personal interviews. Why? Simply because cluster sampling is often more *economically efficient* in that the cost per observation is less. The economies permit the selection of a larger sample at a smaller cost. Since cluster sampling allows researchers to secure so many more observations for a given cost than they would be able to secure with stratified sampling, the margin of error associated with the estimate may actually be smaller for cluster sampling. That is, cluster sampling is often more *efficient overall* than the other forms of sampling. Although it requires a larger sample for the same degree of precision, and is thus less statistically efficient, the smaller cost per observation allows samples so much larger that estimates with a smaller standard error can be produced for the same cost.

Systematic Sample

Systematic sample
A form of cluster sampling in which every *k*th element in the population is designated for inclusion in the sample after a random start.

The **systematic sample** is a form of cluster sampling that offers one of the easiest ways of sampling many populations of interest. It involves selecting every *k*th element after a random start. For example, a database technology firm called Informix wanted to gather basic data about the preferences of visitors to its Web site, including what they were looking for at the site and what they liked or disliked about the site. To gather this information, Informix set up its software to count visitors to the site and invite every fourth visitor to take a survey. Although the company was well aware that this method would not generate a random sample of all potential customers, the survey was a low-cost way to identify areas in which the Web site could be improved.[4]

Consider again the hypothetical population of 20 individuals, and suppose a sample of 5 is to be selected from this population. Number the elements from 1 to 20. With 20 population elements and a sample size of 5, the sampling fraction is $f = \dfrac{n}{N} = \dfrac{5}{20} = \dfrac{1}{4}$, meaning that 1 element in 4 will be selected. The sampling interval $i = \dfrac{1}{f}$ will be 4. This means that, after a random start, every fourth element will be chosen. The random start, which must be some number between 1 and 4—1 and *i* in general—is determined from a random-number table. Thus if the random start were 1, the first, fifth, ninth, thirteenth, and seventeenth items would be the sample. If it were 2, the second, sixth, tenth, fourteenth, and eighteenth items would be the sample, and so on.

Systematic sampling is one-stage cluster sampling since the subgroups are not sub-sampled, but rather all the elements in the selected clusters are used. The subgroups or clusters in this case are

- Cluster I: A, E, I, M, Q

- Cluster II: B, F, J, N, R

- Cluster III: C, G, K, O, S

- Cluster IV: D, H, L, P, T

and one of these clusters is selected randomly for investigation. The random start, of course, determines the cluster that is to be used.

One can readily see the ease with which a systematic sample can be drawn. It is much easier to draw a systematic sample than it is to select a simple random sample of the same size, for example. With a systematic sample one needs to enter the random-number table only once. The problem of checking for the duplication of elements, which is cumbersome with simple random samples, does not occur with systematic samples. All the elements are uniquely determined by the selection of the random start.[5]

A systematic sample can often be made more representative than a simple random sample. With our hypothetical population, for example, we are guaranteed representation from the low-income segment and the high-income segment with our systematic sampling plan. Regardless of which of the four clusters is chosen, one element must have an income of $6,800 or less; another must have an income of $12,000 or more; and the remaining three elements must have incomes between these two values. A simple random sample of Size 5 might or might not include low-income or high-income people.

The same is true when sampling from other populations. Thus, if we are sampling retail stores, we can guarantee representation of both small and large stores by employing a systematic sample, if the stores can be arrayed from smallest to largest according to some criteria such as annual sales or square footage. The ability to guarantee representation from each size segment depends on the availability of knowledge about the size of each store so that they can be arrayed from smallest to largest and numbered serially. A simple random sample of stores would be apt to represent large stores inadequately since there are fewer large stores than small stores. Yet the fewer large stores account for a great proportion of all sales.

The degree to which the systematic sample will be more representative than a simple random sample thus depends on the clustering of objects within the list from which the sample will be drawn. The ideal list for a systematic sample will have elements similar in value on the characteristic (for example, similar levels of income, sales, education, and so on) close together and elements diverse in value spread apart.

At least one danger with systematic samples is that if there is a natural periodicity in the list of elements, the systematic sample can produce estimates seriously in error. For example, suppose we have the annual ticket sales of an airline by day and wish to analyze these sales in terms of length of trip. To analyze all 365 days may be prohibitively costly, but suppose the research budget does allow the investigation of 52 days of sales. A systematic sample of days using a sampling interval of 7 (365 ÷ 52) would obviously produce some misleading conclusions, since the day's sales would reflect all Monday trips, Friday trips, or Sunday trips, for example.[6] Of course, any other sampling interval would be acceptable, and in general, an enlightened choice of the sampling interval can do much to eliminate the problems associated with natural periodicities in the data. An appropriate choice of sampling interval, of course, depends on knowledge of the phenomenon and the nature of the periodicity.

Area Sample

In every probability sampling plan discussed so far, the investigator needs a list of population elements in order to draw the sample. A list identifying each population element is a necessary requirement for simple random samples, stratified samples, and systematic samples. The latter two procedures also require knowledge about some other characteristic of the population if they are to be designed optimally. For many populations of interest, however, such detailed lists are unavailable. Further, it will often prove prohibitively costly to construct them. When this condition arises, the cluster sample offers the researcher another distinct benefit—he or she needs only the list of population elements for the selected clusters.

Suppose, for example, that an investigator wishes to measure certain characteristics of industrial sales representatives, such as their earnings, attitudes toward the job, hours worked, and so on. It would be extremely difficult, if not impossible, and certainly costly to develop an up-to-date roster listing each industrial sales representative. Yet such a list would be required for a simple random sample. A stratified sample would further require that the investigator possess knowledge about some additional characteristics of each sales representative (for example, education or age) so that the population could be divided into mutually exclusive and exhaustive subsets. With a cluster sample, on the other hand, one could use the companies as sampling units. The investigator would generate a sample of business firms from the population of firms of interest. The business firms would be primary **sampling units** where a sampling unit is defined as "that element or set of elements considered for selection in some stage of sampling."[7] The investigator could then compile a list of sales representatives working for each of the selected firms, a much more realistic assignment. If the investigator then studied each of the sales representatives in each of the selected firms, it would be one-stage cluster sampling. If the researcher subsampled sales representatives from each company's list, it would be two-stage cluster sampling. Exhibit 16.6 lists some other possible clusters that could be used to sample various types of population elements.

The same principle underlies **area sampling.** Current, accurate lists of population elements are rarely available. Directories of all those living in a city at a particular moment simply do not exist for many cities, and when they do exist, they are obsolete when published: people move, others die, new households are constantly being formed.[8] Although lists of families are nonexistent, relatively accurate lists of primary sampling units are available in the form of city maps, if the area divisions of the city serve as the primary sampling units. Although the complex details of area sampling are not relevant here, an appreciation for the rationale underlying the various approaches is.

One-Stage Area Sample Suppose the investigator is interested in estimating the amount of wine consumed per household in the city of Chicago, and how consumption is related to family income. An accurate listing of all households is unavailable for the Chicago area. A phone book when published is already somewhat obsolete, in addition to having the other inadequacies previously mentioned. One approach to this problem would be to

1. Choose a simple random sample of n city blocks from the population of N blocks.

2. Determine wine consumption and income for all households in the selected blocks and generalize the sample relationships to the larger population.

The probability of any household being included in the sample can be calculated. It is given simply as $\frac{n}{N}$ since it equals the probability that the block on which it is located

Sampling units

Nonoverlapping collections of elements from the population.

Area sampling

A form of cluster sampling in which areas (for example, census tracts, blocks) serve as the primary sampling units. The population is divided into mutually exclusive and exhaustive areas using maps, and a random sample of areas is selected. If all the households in the selected areas are used in the study, it is one-stage area sampling; if the areas themselves are subsampled with respect to households, the procedure is two-stage area sampling.

EXHIBIT 16.6   **Possible Clusters to Use to Sample Various Types of Population Elements**

Population Elements	Possible Clusters
College seniors	Colleges
Elementary school students	Schools
Manufacturing firms	Counties
	Localities
	Plants
Airline travelers	Airports
	Planes
Hospital patients	Hospitals

Source: Adapted from Seymour Sudman, *Applied Sampling* (San Francisco: Academic Press, 1976), p. 70.

will be selected. Since the probabilities are known, the procedure is indeed probability sampling. Here, though, blocks have been substituted for households when selecting primary sampling units. The substitution is made because the list of blocks in the Chicago area can be developed from city maps. Each block can be identified, and the existence of this universe of blocks permits the calculation of the necessary probabilities.

Since each household on the selected blocks is included in the sample, the procedure is one-stage area sampling. Note that the blocks serve to divide the parent population into mutually exclusive and exhaustive subsets. Note further that the blocks do not serve very well as ideal subsets statistically for cluster samples; households on a given block can be expected to be somewhat similar with respect to their income and wine consumption rather than heterogeneous as desired. On the other hand, the data collection costs will be very low because of the concentration of households within each block.

Two-Stage Area Sample The distinguishing feature of the one-stage area sample is that all the households in the selected blocks (or other areas) are enumerated and studied. It is not necessary to employ all items in a selected cluster; the selected areas themselves can be subsampled, and it is often quite advantageous to do so. Two types of two-stage sampling need to be distinguished:

1. Simple, two-stage area sampling.

2. Probability-proportional-to-size area sampling.

Simple two-stage area sampling

A form of cluster sampling in which a certain proportion of second-stage sampling units (e.g., households) is selected from each first-stage unit (e.g., blocks).

With **simple two-stage area sampling,** a certain proportion of second-stage sampling units (e.g., households) is selected from each first-stage unit (e.g., a block). Consider a universe of 100 blocks; suppose there are 20 households per block; assume that a sample of 80 households is required from this total population of 2,000 households. The overall sampling fraction is thus $\frac{8}{2,000} = \frac{1}{25}$. There are a number of ways by which the sample can be completed, such as by (1) selecting 10 blocks and 8 households per block, (2) selecting 8 blocks and 10 households per block, (3) selecting 20 blocks and 4 households per block, or (4) selecting 4 blocks and 20 households per block. The last alternative would, of course, be one-stage area sampling, while the first three would all be two-stage area sampling.

The probability with which the blocks are selected is called the *block,* or *first-stage, sampling fraction* and is given as the ratio of n_B/N_B, where n_B and N_B are the number of blocks in the sample and in the population, respectively. For the first three schemes illustrated above, the first-stage sampling fractions would be, in order, 1 in 10, 1 in 12.5, and 1 in 5.

The probability with which the households are selected is called the *household,* or *second-stage, sampling fraction.* Since there must be a total of 80 households in the sample, the second-stage sampling fraction differs for each alternative. The second-stage sampling fraction is given as $n_{H/B}/N_{H/B}$, where $n_{H/B}$ and $N_{H/B}$ are the number of households per block in the sample and in the population. For the first sampling scheme, the household sampling fraction is calculated to be $\frac{8}{20} = \frac{2}{5}$, while for the second scheme, it is $\frac{10}{20} = \frac{1}{2}$, and for the third scheme, $\frac{4}{20} = \frac{1}{5}$. Note that the product of the first-stage and second-stage sampling fractions in each case equals the overall sampling fraction of $\frac{1}{25}$.

Which scheme would be preferable? Although it is beyond the scope of this text to present the detailed calculation for determining this, we would like to illustrate the general principle. Economies of data collection would dictate that the second-stage sampling fraction be high. This means that a great many households would be selected from each designated block, as with the second scheme. Statistical efficiency would dictate a small second-stage sampling fraction, since it can be expected that the blocks would be relatively homogeneous and thus it would be desirable to have a very few households from any one block. The third scheme would be preferred on statistical grounds. Statistical sampling theory would suggest the balancing of these two criteria. There are formulas for this purpose that reflect essentially the cost of data collection and the variability of the characteristic within and between clusters, although a useful rule of thumb is that clusters of three to eight households per block or segment are near optimum for most social science variables.[9]

Simple two-stage area sampling is quite effective when there is approximately the same number of second-stage units (e.g., households) per first-stage unit (e.g., a block). When the second-stage units are decidedly unequal, simple two-stage area sampling can cause bias in the estimate. To pursue our hypothetical example, some blocks in Chicago may contain multistoried low-income housing. Blocks in more affluent parts of the city may contain relatively few, single-family houses. In such a case, the number of second-stage units per first-stage unit would be vastly different. Sometimes this problem can be overcome by combining areas. When this option is not available or is cumbersome to implement, *probability-proportional-to-size sampling* can be employed.

Consider, for example, the data of Exhibit 16.7 and suppose a sample of 20 elements is to be selected from this population of 2,000 households. With **probability-proportional-to-size sampling,** a *fixed* number of second-stage units is selected from each first-stage unit. Suppose after balancing economic and statistical considerations that the number of second-stage units per first-stage unit is determined to be 10. Two first-stage units must be selected to produce a total sample of 20. The procedure gets its name from the way these first-stage units are selected. The probability of selection is variable in that it depends on the size of the first-stage unit. In this particular case, a table of four-digit random numbers will be consulted. The first two numbers encountered between 1 and 2,000 will be employed to indicate the blocks that will be used. All numbers between 1 and 800 will indicate the inclusion of Block 1; those from 801 to 1,200, Block 2; from 1,201 to 1,400, Block 3; and so on.

The probability that any particular household is included in the sample is equal, since the unequal first-stage selection probabilities are balanced by unequal second-stage selection probabilities. Consider, for example, Blocks 1 and 10, the two extremes. The first-stage selection probability for Block 1 is $\frac{800}{2000} = \frac{1}{25}$, since 800 of the permissible 2,000 random numbers correspond to Block 1. Only 25 of the permissible random numbers (1,976 to 2,000) correspond to Block 10, on the other hand, and thus the first-stage sampling fraction for Block 10 is $\frac{25}{2000} = \frac{1}{80}$. Since 10 households are to be selected from each block, the second-stage sampling fraction for Block 1 is $\frac{10}{800} = \frac{1}{80}$, while for Block

Probability-proportional-to-size sampling
A form of cluster sampling in which a fixed number of second-stage units is selected from each first-stage unit. The probabilities associated with the selection of each first-stage unit are in turn variable because they are directly related to the relative sizes of the first-stage units.

EXHIBIT 16.7   Illustration of Probability-Proportional-to-Size Sampling

Block	Households	Cumulative Number of Households
1	800	800
2	400	1,200
3	200	1,400
4	200	1,600
5	100	1,700
6	100	1,800
7	100	1,900
8	50	1,950
9	25	1,975
10	25	2,000

10 it is $\dfrac{10}{25} = \dfrac{1}{25}$. The products of the first- and second-stage sampling thus compensate, since

$$\frac{800}{2,000} \times \frac{10}{800} = \frac{25}{2,000} \times \frac{10}{25}$$

which is also true for the remaining blocks.

Probability-proportional-to-size sampling is another illustration of how information begets information with applied sampling problems. One can avoid the bias of simple two-stage area sampling and can also produce estimates that are more precise when there is great variation in the number of second-stage units per first-stage unit. The price one pays, of course, is that probability-proportional-to-size sampling requires that one have detailed knowledge about the size of each first-stage unit. This is not quite as high a price as it might be, since the Census Bureau has reported the number of households per block for all cities of over 50,000 in population as well as for a number of other urbanized areas.[10] Maps are included in each report. Although somewhat obsolete when published, these map and block statistics can be updated. The local electrical utility will have records of connections current to the day, and so will the telephone company. In many cases, these statistics will be broken down by blocks.

Combining Sample Types

As you can probably begin to appreciate, sample design is a very detailed subject. Our discussion has concentrated on only a few of the fundamentals and, in particular, the basic types of probability samples. You should be aware, though, that the basic types can be, and are, combined in large-scale field studies to produce some very complex designs.

The Gallup Poll, for example, is probably one of the best known of all the polls. The sample for the Gallup Poll for each survey "consists of 1,500 adults selected from 320 locations, using area sampling methods. At each location the interviewer is given a map with an indicated starting point and is required to follow a specified direction. At each occupied dwelling unit, the interviewer must attempt to meet sex quotas."[11] In sum, the Gallup Poll uses a combination of area and quota sampling. Further, it is not uncommon to have several levels of stratification, such as by geographic area and density of population, precede several stages of cluster sampling. Thus, you cannot expect to be a sampling expert with the brief exposure to the subject contained here.[12] But you should be able to communicate effectively about the sample design and use effectively the available microcomputer software for selecting samples. Further, although you may not understand completely, say, why n_1 observations were taken from one stratum and n_2 from another, you should appreciate the basic considerations determining the choice.

Back to the Case

When Pam Heisler assembled with her researchers the next week, they were both ready to tell her about earlier attempts at Internet polling.

Terry Shapiro started by reporting on polls conducted by Harris Black International. That research firm had tracked voters' preferences in the months leading up to several elections for governor and U.S. Senate. In 21 out of 22 races that Harris had followed, it predicted the winners accurately.

"That's very impressive," said Pam. "What happened in the 22nd race?"

"That was the Georgia governor's race," said Terry. "The Harris Black poll predicted that Guy Millner, a Republican, would capture the governor's seat. What they didn't know was that Democrats would be so upset with the effort to impeach President Clinton that they would turn out in big numbers. They voted for Roy Barnes, the Democratic gubernatorial candidate, and he won."

"Didn't the poll uncover the Democrats' anger?"

"It appears that it didn't. But you know, you can get unexpected turnout in certain groups, no matter what kind of poll you conduct."

"True," said Jim Lovesey. "But the Republican Party in Atlanta hired Whit Ayres to do a telephone poll, and that poll picked the winner in the Georgia governor's race."

"What else did you learn, Jim?" asked Pam.

"America Online has been doing on-line polls, too. They asked over 100,000 of their subscribers about their opinions of President Clinton before the impeachment hearings. Over half of them thought Clinton should resign. Telephone polls of the general population conducted at that time showed that over half thought he should *not* resign."

"True," interjected Terry, "but the AOL researchers didn't even try to correct for the differences between their demographics and the U.S. population overall."

"That's right," Jim agreed. "But some polling experts say that adjusting for those demographics doesn't really get at the differences between Internet users and nonusers. You're looking not just at economic or racial differences, but at differences in attitudes toward technology—and that can be driven by so many factors."

"Wouldn't we be better off to start with a sample that really represents my constituents," asked Pam, "rather than trying to make the numbers fit?"

"You're the customer, Pam," said Terry.

"That's right," said Jim, finally agreeing. "You tell us what you want to know, and we'll get you the best answers we can."

Source: This case is based on the discussion of on-line political polls in John Simons, "Is a Web Political Poll Reliable? Yes? No? Maybe?" *The Wall Street Journal* (April 13, 1999), pp. B1, B4.

Summary

Learning Objective 1

Specify the two procedures that distinguish a stratified sample.

A stratified sample is a probability sample that is distinguished by the following two-step procedure: (1) the parent population is divided into mutually exclusive and exhaustive subsets, and (2) a simple random sample of elements is chosen independently from each group or subset.

Learning Objective 2

Cite two reasons why researchers might opt to use a stratified sample rather than a simple random sample.

Stratified samples can produce sample statistics that are more precise, meaning they have smaller error due to sampling, than simple random samples. Stratification also allows the investigation of the characteristics of interest for particular subgroups.

Learning Objective 3

Note what points investigators should keep in mind when dividing a population into strata for a stratified sample.

Investigators should divide the population into strata so that the elements within any given stratum are as similar in value as possible and so that the values between any two strata are as disparate as possible.

Learning Objective 4

Explain what a proportionate stratified sample is.

With a proportionate stratified sample, the number of observations in the total sample is allocated among the strata in proportion to the relative number of elements in each stratum in the population.

Learning Objective 5

Explain what a disproportionate stratified sample is.

Disproportionate stratified sampling involves balancing the two criteria of strata size and variability. With a fixed sample size, strata exhibiting more variability are sampled more than proportionately to their relative size. Conversely, those strata that are very homogeneous are sampled less than proportionately.

Learning Objective 6

List the steps followed in drawing a cluster sample.

Cluster sampling involves the following steps: (1) the parent population is divided into mutually exclusive and exhaustive subsets, and (2) a random sample of the subsets is selected.

Learning Objective 7

Explain the difference between a one-stage cluster sample and a two-stage cluster sample.

If an investigator uses all the population elements in the selected subsets for the sample, the procedure is one-stage cluster sampling. If, on the other hand, a sample of elements is selected probabilistically from the selected subsets, the procedure is known as two-stage cluster sampling.

Learning Objective 8

Explain why cluster sampling, though far less statistically efficient than comparable stratified samples, is the sampling procedure used most in large-scale field surveys employing personal interviews.

Cluster sampling is the sampling procedure used most in large-scale field surveys using personal interviews because it is often more economically efficient in that the cost per observation is less. The economies permit the selection of a larger sample at a smaller cost. Although cluster sampling requires a larger sample for the same degree of precision, and is thus less statistically efficient, the smaller cost per observation allows samples so much larger that estimates with a smaller standard error can be produced for the same cost.

Learning Objective 9

Distinguish between one-stage area sampling and simple two-stage area sampling.

The distinguishing feature of the one-stage area sample is that all of the households in the selected blocks (or other areas) are enumerated and studied. With simple two-stage area sampling, a certain proportion of second-stage sampling units is selected from each first-stage unit.

Learning Objective 10

Note the quality that distinguishes probability-proportional-to-size sampling and explain when it is used.

With probability-proportional-to-size sampling, a fixed number of second-stage units is selected from each first-stage unit. This type of sampling is particularly useful when the number of second-stage units is unequal and simple two-stage area sampling could cause bias in the estimate.

Review Questions

1. What is a stratified sample? How is a stratified sample selected?

2. Is a stratified sample a probability or nonprobability sample? Why?

3. What principle should be followed in establishing the strata for a stratified sample? Why? How can this principle be implemented in practice?

4. Describe the procedure that is followed in developing a confidence interval estimate for a population mean with a stratified sample. Be specific.

5. Which sampling method typically produces more precise estimates of a population mean—simple random sampling or stratified sampling? Why?

6. What is a proportionate stratified sample? What is a disproportionate stratified sample? What must be known about the parent population to select each?

7. What is a cluster sample? How is a cluster sample selected?

8. What are the similarities and differences between a cluster sample and a stratified sample?

9. What is a systematic sample? How are the random start and sampling interval determined with a systematic sample?

10. What are the advantages and disadvantages associated with systematic samples?

11. What is an area sample? Why are area samples used?

12. How does a two-stage area sample differ from a one-stage area sample?

Discussion Questions, Problems, and Projects

1. The Minnesota National Bank, headquartered in Minneapolis, Minnesota, has some 400,000 users of its credit card scattered throughout the state of Minnesota. The application forms for the credit card asked for the usual information on name, address, phone, income, education, and so on, that is typical of such applications. The bank is now very much interested in determining if there is any relationship between the uses to which the card is put and the socioeconomic characteristics of the using party; for example, is there a difference in the characteristics of those people who use the credit card for major purchases only, such as appliances, and those who use it for minor as well as major purchases?
   (a) Identify the population and sampling frame that would be used by Minnesota National Bank.
   (b) Indicate how you would draw a simple random sample from the above sampling frame.
   (c) Indicate how you would draw a stratified sample from the above sampling frame.
   (d) Indicate how you would draw a cluster random sample from the above sampling frame.
   (e) Which method would be preferred? Why?

2. Exclusive Supermarkets is considering entering the Boston market. Before doing so, though, management wishes to estimate the average square feet of selling space among potential competitors, so as to plan better the size of the proposed new outlet. A stratified sample of supermarkets in Boston produced the following results:

Size	Total Number in City	Number of This Size in Sample	Mean Size of Stores in Sample	Standard Deviation of Stores in Sample
Small supermarkets	1,000	20	4,000 sq. ft.	2,000 sq. ft.
Medium supermarkets	600	12	10,000 sq. ft.	1,000 sq. ft.
Large supermarkets	400	8	60,000 sq. ft.	3,000 sq. ft.

   (a) Estimate the average-sized supermarket in Boston. Show your calculations.
   (b) Develop a 95 percent confidence interval around this estimate. Show your calculations.
   (c) Was a proportionate or disproportionate stratified sample design used in determining the number of sample observations for each stratum? Explain.

3. Store-More is a large department store located in Lansing, Michigan. The manager is worried about the constant overstocking of a number of items in the various departments. Approximately 3,000 items ranging from small multipurpose wrenches to lawn mowers are overstocked every month. The manager is uncertain whether the surpluses are primarily due to poor purchasing policies or poor store layout and shelving practices. The manager realizes the difficulty of scrutinizing the purchase orders, invoices, and inventory cards for all the items that are overstocked. She decides on choosing a sample of items but does not know how to proceed.
   (a) Identify the population elements and sampling frame.
   (b) What sampling method would you recommend? Why? Be specific.
   (c) How would you draw the sample based on this sampling method?

4. The university housing office has decided to conduct a study to determine what influence living in dormitories versus off-campus housing has on the academic performance of the students. You are required to assist the housing office.
   (a) What sampling method will you recommend? Why? Be specific.
   (b) How would you draw the sample based on this sampling method?

5. Maxwell Federated operates a chain of department stores in the greater Chicago metropolitan area. The management of Maxwell Federated has been concerned of late with tight money conditions and the associated deterioration of the company's accounts

receivable. It appears on the surface that more and more customers are becoming delinquent each month. Management wishes to assess the current state of delinquencies, to determine if the delinquencies are concentrated in any stores, and to determine if they are concentrated among any particular types of purchases or purchasers.
(a) What sampling method would you recommend? Why? Be specific.
(b) How would you draw the sample based on this sampling method?

6. A retailer of household appliances is planning to introduce a new brand of dishwashers to the local market and wishes to estimate demand for the product. He has decided to use two-stage area sampling and has secured an up-to-date map of your area, but he does not know how to proceed and requires your assistance. Outline a step-by-step approach you will recommend for conducting the study.

7. In February, a midwestern city instituted a mandatory recycling plan for certain types of household waste. A marketing research firm was hired to evaluate the progress of the plan in July. Among several measures of effectiveness to be employed, the researchers wished to compare the weight of recyclables collected per household per week with a pre-implementation estimate of ten pounds per week. In order to do this, the following sampling procedure was used. First, the city was divided into 840 blocks. The blocks were then arrayed from largest to smallest based on the estimated number of households they contained and, based on the selection of a random number, every twelfth block was selected. Researchers then accompanied collectors on their weekly round and weighed each bag of recyclables collected on the specified blocks. (Assume each household puts out one bag per week.)
(a) What are the population elements and the sampling frame?
(b) What are the primary sampling units?
(c) Describe the sampling plan used by the researchers?
(d) What is the approximate probability that a household will be included in the sample?

8. A researcher is interested in studying the job satisfaction of salespeople in the automatic milking machine industry. She has decided to use probability-proportional-to-size sampling to select a sample. Preliminary work has identified only eight companies that manufacture automatic milkers. Each company is considered to be one first-stage unit. The researcher has determined that she wants to draw four second-stage units per first-stage unit. The total sample size desired is 16. The following table has been generated:

Unit	Salespeople	Cumulative Salespeople
1	6	6
2	10	16
3	7	23
4	12	35
5	8	43
6	8	51
7	14	65
8	9	74

(a) How many first-stage units must be selected?
(b) Refer to Exhibit 15.6, "Abridged List of Random Numbers," in the preceding chapter. Entering at the first column, first row and moving downward, which first-stage units will be selected for second-stage sampling?
(c) Demonstrate that the probability of any salesperson's being included in the sample is equal.

Endnotes

1. Cecelia Blalock, "Selling Sales," *Grocery Headquarters* (December 1998), pp. 43–46.

2. Note that we are again assuming that the normal distribution applies in making this inference. While this assumption is not strictly correct in this instance because of the size of the sample taken from each stratum, we are making it to allow more direct comparison with the interval constructed using simple random sampling. In most situations the normal distribution would hold because the central-limit theorem also applies to the individual strata means, and the linear combination of these means produces a normally distributed overall sample mean.

3. The Census Bureau also uses disproportionate stratified sampling in its surveys. For descriptions of the strata and the sampling rates, see "Eighteen Million Households Will Receive Sample Question-naire in '90 Census," *Census and You* 24 (January 1989), p. 2.

4. Joseph Rydholm, "On the Front Line of On-Line," *Quirk's Marketing Research Review* (July 1998, downloaded from the *Quirk's* Web site, www.quirks.com, August 13, 1999).

5. See J. Michael Brick, Joseph Waksberg, Dale Kulp, and Amy Starer, "Bias in List-Assisted Telephone Samples," *Public Opinion Quarterly* 59 (Summer 1995), pp. 218–235, for discussion of the use of systematic samples in telephone surveys.

6. Sudman suggests that when the "sampling interval i is not a whole number, the easiest solution is to use as the interval the whole number just below or above i. Usually, this will result in a selected sample that is only slightly larger or smaller than the initial sample required, and this new sample size will have no noticeable effect on either the accuracy of the results or the budget. For samples in which the interval i is small (generally for i less than 10), so that the rounding has too great an effect on the sample size, it is possible to add or delete the extra cases. . . . It is usually easier to round down in computing i so that the sample is larger, and then to delete systematically." Seymour Sudman, *Applied Sampling* (San Francisco: Academic Press, 1976), p. 54.

7. Earl R. Babbie, *The Practice of Social Research,* 7th ed. (Belmont, Calif.: Wadsworth Publishing, 1995), p. 198.

8. R. L. Polk and Company, in Taylor, Michigan, publishes some 1,400 directories for most medium-sized cities in the range of 50,000 to 800,000 people. The directories contain both an alphabetical list of names and businesses and a street address directory of households. While the alphabetic list can contain a large percentage of inaccurate listings at any one time, the address directory is reasonably accurate since it omits only new construction after the directory is published and the directories are revised every two or three years.

9. Sudman, *Applied Sampling,* p. 81.

10. *U.S. Census of Housing: Vol. III, City Blocks,* HC(3)—No. (city number).

11. Sudman, *Applied Sampling,* p. 71.

12. Those interested in pursuing the subject further should see one of the excellent books on the subject, such as William G. Cochran, *Sampling Techniques,* 3rd ed. (New York: John Wiley, 1977); Morris H. Hansen, William N. Hurwitz, and William G. Madow, *Sample Survey Methods and Theory, Vol. I, Methods and Applications* (New York: John Wiley, 1953); Gary T. Henry, *Practical Sampling* (Thousand Oaks, Calif.: Sage Publications, Inc., 1990); Leslie Kish, *Survey Sampling* (New York: John Wiley, 1995); Paul S. Levy and Stanley Lemeshow, *Sampling of Populations: Methods and Applications* (New York: John Wiley and Sons, Inc., 1991); Richard L. Schaeffer and William Mendenhall, *Elementary Survey Sampling,* 5th ed. (Belmont, Calif.: Wadsworth Publishing Company, 1996).

Suggested Additional Readings

There are a number of excellent books that discuss in more detail than here the rationale for and various types of stratified and cluster samples. Three of the better and more extensive treatments are
William Cochran, *Sampling Techniques,* 3rd ed. (New York: John Wiley, 1977).
Morris H. Hansen, William N. Hurwitz, and William G. Madow, *Sample Survey Methods and Theory, Vol. 1, Methods and Applications* (New York: John Wiley, 1993).
Leslie Kish, *Survey Sampling* (New York: John Wiley, 1995).

For more abbreviated but still useful treatments of the principles underlying survey sampling, see
Graham Kalton, *Introduction to Survey Sampling* (Thousand Oaks, Calif.: Sage Publications, 1982).
Richard L. Schaeffer and William Mendenhall, *Elementary Survey Sampling,* 5th ed. (Belmont, Calif.: Wadsworth Publishing Company, 1996).

Chapter 17

SAMPLE SIZE

L E A R N I N G   O B J E C T I V E S

Upon Completing This Chapter, You Should Be Able to

1. Specify the key factor a researcher must consider in estimating sample size using statistical principles.

2. Cite two other factors researchers must also take into account when estimating a sample size and explain their relationship.

3. Explain in what way the size of the population influences the size of the sample.

4. Specify the circumstances under which the finite population correction factor should be used.

5. Explain the impact that cost has on sample size in stratified or cluster samples.

6. Cite the general rule of thumb for calculating sample size when cross-classification tables are used.

Case in Marketing Research

"How was your dinner this evening?" inquired Rosemary Malgieri of William and Emily Bader as they finished off their veal picata.

"It was wonderful, as always," answered Emily. Her husband, still chewing, nodded appreciatively.

"I've asked Vincent to bring you some cannoli and cappuccino for dessert, with my compliments."

"How lovely, thank you," replied Emily.

"I feel a little bit awkward intruding on your dinner," began Rosemary, "but I remember Mr. Bader telling me one evening that he works for a marketing research company. I was wondering if there might be a time that I could discuss a little idea of mine. . . ."

"No time like the present," replied William, wiping his mouth and motioning to the empty chair next to him. "That is, if you can manage to leave your duties in the restaurant for a few minutes."

Rosemary motioned to the busboys to clear the Baders' table while she sat down. Vincent appeared at double speed with frothing cups of hot cappuccino and crisp tubes of pastry filled with ricotta cream.

"As I'm sure you know, the restaurant business is a very competitive one. Customer satisfaction is everything. Careless service, a change in the kitchen, can spell death for a restaurant. We have been very lucky here at Malgieri's. We have done very well ever since we opened three years ago. We've had very little turnover in our wait staff, and our chef, while temperamental, has been very loyal to us."

"So what is it you want my help with?" asked William.

"You know that my husband, Michael, and I are partners in this restaurant. I manage the dining room and oversee the kitchen. He handles the financial end. We both agree that it is time to expand. He would like to see us open a second location. He has his eye on a restored storefront in Bentleyville."

"On the west side?" asked Emily. "Where they're doing all the renovations in the old warehouse district?"

"Exactly. Michael feels that the area has a big potential for attracting the after-work crowd from downtown. He's probably right. On the other hand, I'm not convinced that another location is the right way to expand. I feel that Michael and I are the reason Malgieri's is a success. One of us is in the restaurant at all times. With two locations some distance apart, we will have to hire a manager, which will dilute our level of personal control."

"So how would you like to expand?" inquired Emily. "Do you want to increase the size of the existing restaurant?"

"No. I'd like to start a take-out and delivery service. When I was in Chicago for the restaurant show, I noticed that there is a big trend toward restaurant meals at home. I'd like to see us tap into that market. The problem is, I don't know whether to gear the service toward young professionals who don't have time to cook and want an elegant, restaurant-style meal at home or toward busy families who would see our take-out and delivery service as an alternative to a home-cooked meal."

"Well, one way to find out what people want and are willing to pay is to do a survey. A good start would be to survey people who've dined at Malgieri's during the past six months," William replied.

"But how many people would you want to survey?" asked the restaurateur. "I can't afford to spend a lot of money on marketing research. Restaurants operate on a very slim margin. Besides, my husband is determined to open a second restaurant. While solid marketing research might convince him that my plan is the better one, he's not going to agree to invest a lot of money in studying an option he's not particularly interested in."

Discussion Issues

1. What factors might influence sample size for a study that William Bader would do for Malgieri's Restaurant?

2. If you were William Bader, what information might you want to have about the patrons of Malgieri's Restaurant?

Thus far, our discussion of sampling has concentrated on sample type. Another important consideration is sample size. Unless the researcher is going to use a sequential sample, he or she needs some means of determining the necessary size of the sample before beginning data collection.

Beginning researchers might suppose that the sample should be as large as the client can afford, but the question of sample size is complex. It depends on, among other things, the type of sample, the statistic in question, the homogeneity of the population, and the time, money, and personnel available for the study. We cannot discuss all of these issues adequately in one chapter, but we will present the important statistical principles that determine sample size, using only simple random samples and a few of the more popular statistics. Readers interested in how sample size is determined for stratified or cluster samples should consult one of the standard references on sampling theory. Readers who would like to be able to use a simple random sample to estimate such things as population variance, which is beyond the scope of this chapter, will find help in a good intermediate-level statistics text. The principles are the same in each case, but the formulas differ since they depend on the sampling plan and the statistic in question.

Basic Considerations in Determining Sample Size

Not surprisingly, the sampling distribution of the statistic is the key to determining sample size. You will recall that the sampling distribution of the statistic indicates how the sample estimates vary as a function of the particular sample selected. If a researcher knows the spread of the sampling distribution, he or she can then determine the amount of error that can be associated with any estimate. For instance, in Chapter 15, we saw that the error associated with the estimation of a population mean by a sample mean was given by the standard error of the mean $\sigma_{\bar{x}} = \sigma/\sqrt{n}$, or the population standard deviation divided by the square root of the sample size when the population variance was known, and $\hat{s}_{\bar{x}} = \hat{s}/\sqrt{n}$, or the sample standard deviation divided by the square root of the sample size when the population variance was unknown. The first factor one must consider in estimating sample size, then, is the standard error of the estimate obtained from the known sampling distribution of the statistic.

A second consideration is how precise the estimate must be. For example, a researcher investigating mean income might want the sample estimate to be within ±$100 of the true population value. Or a less precise estimate might be required—say, one within ±$500 of the true value. When the problem involves estimating a population parameter, **precision** can be said to be measured by the magnitude of error, or the size of the estimating interval.

The degree of precision required will be greatly influenced by the importance of the decision involved in the study from a managerial perspective. If millions of dollars and hundreds of employees' jobs ride on the results of the study, the acceptable range of error is likely to be small. *Absolute precision* is expressed as within plus or minus so many units. *Relative precision* is expressed relative to the level of the estimate of the parameter.

Another factor that affects sample size is the degree of **confidence** the researcher requires in the estimate. With a sample of fixed size, there is a trade-off between degree of confidence and degree of precision. One can specify either the degree of precision or the degree of confidence, but not both. It is only when sample size is allowed to vary that one can achieve both a specified precision and a specified degree of confidence in the result.

Precision
The degree of error in a study, or the size of the estimating interval. *Absolute precision* is expressed as within plus or minus so many units. *Relative precision* is expressed relative to the level of the estimate of the parameter.

Confidence
The degree to which one can feel confident that an estimate approximates the true value.

Actually, the determination of sample size using statistical principles involves balancing the two considerations against each other.[1]

To understand the distinction between confidence and precision, suppose that we need to know the mean income of a certain population. The most precise measure of that particular parameter would be a point estimate of the mean, which is an estimate that involves a single value with no associated bounds of error. In the case of our study, calculations may show that the population mean income as estimated by the sample mean is $19,243. This point estimate is most assuredly wrong, and thus we can have no confidence in it despite its preciseness. On the other hand, we can have complete confidence in an estimate that the population mean income is between zero and $1 million, but that estimate is too imprecise to be of value.

Sample Size Determination When Estimating Means

We can best see the interrelationship of the basic factors affecting the determination of sample size by looking at an example. Imagine that the Division of Tourism in a certain state wants to know the average amount that fishermen spend each year on food and lodging while on fishing trips within the state. Our job as researchers is to use a simple random sample to estimate the mean annual expenditure of those fishermen, using a list of all those who applied for fishing licenses within the year.[2] The central-limit theorem suggests that the distribution of sample means will be normal for samples of reasonable size regardless of the distribution of expenditures in the population of fishermen. Consider, then, the sampling distribution of sample means in Figure 17.1 and distinguish two cases: Case I, in which the population variance is known, and Case II, in which the population variance is unknown.

Case I: Population Variance Known

The population variance, σ^2, might be known from past studies, even though the average expenditures for food and lodging might be unknown, since variation typically changes much more slowly than level.[3] This means that the spread of the distribution given by the standard error of estimate, $\sigma_{\bar{x}}$, as shown in Figure 17.1, is also known up to a proportionality

Suppose that one wished to estimate the mean annual expenditure by fishermen in a certain state. The central-limit theorem suggests that the distribution of sample means will be normal for samples of reasonable size regardless of the distribution of expenditures in the population of fishermen.

FIGURE 17.1   **Sampling Distribution of Sample Means**

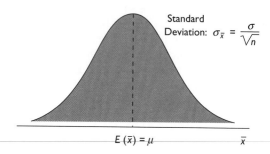

Standard Deviation: $\sigma_{\bar{x}} = \dfrac{\sigma}{\sqrt{n}}$

$E(\bar{x}) = \mu$ $\bar{x}$

Ethical Dilemma 17.1

Researchers in the laboratory of a regional food manufacturer recently developed a new dessert topping. This topping was more versatile than those currently on the market because it came in a variety of flavors and thus had more potential uses than a product like Dream Whip, for instance. Although the manufacturer believed that the product had great promise, management also thought it would be necessary to convince the trade of its sales potential in order to get wholesalers and retailers to handle it. The manufacturer consequently decided to test-market the product in a couple of areas where it had especially strong distribution. It selected several stores with which it had a long working relationship to carry the product. During the planned two-month test period, product sales did not begin to compare with sales of other dessert toppings. Feeling that such evidence would make it very difficult to gain distribution, the manufacturer decided to do two things: (1) run the test for a longer period, and (2) increase the number of accounts handling the test product. Four months later, the results were much

more convincing and management felt more comfortable in approaching the trade with the test market results.

- Is it ethical to conduct a test market in an area where a firm's distribution or reputation is especially strong?

- Is it ethical not to report this fact to the trade, thereby causing it to misinterpret the market response to the item?

- Is it ethical to increase the size of the sample until one secures a result one wants? What if the argument for increasing sample size was that the product was so novel that two months simply was not enough time for consumers to become sufficiently familiar with it?

- Would it have been more ethical to plan initially for a larger and longer test than to adjust the length and scope of the test on the basis of early results? Why or why not?

---

constant, the square root of the sample size, since $\sigma_{\bar{x}} = \sigma/\sqrt{n}$. Thus we have some idea of the first ingredient in sample size determination, the standard error of estimate.

Suppose the director of tourism wanted the estimate to be within ±\$25 of the true population value. Total precision would thus be \$50, and half-precision, call it H, would be \$25. The reason we work with H instead of the full length of the interval is that the normal curve is symmetrical about the true population mean, and it simplifies the calculations to work with only one-half of the curve.

The remaining item that needs to be specified is the degree of confidence desired in the result. Suppose the director of tourism wants to be 95 percent confident that the interval the researcher constructs will contain the true population mean. This implies that z is approximately equal to 2.[4]

Now we have all we need for determining sample size, since it is known that a number of standard deviations on each side of the mean will include a certain proportion of all observations with a normal curve and, in particular, that two standard deviations will include 95 percent of all observations. In Figure 17.1, each observation is a sample mean; the distribution of these sample means is centered about the population mean; and two standard deviations are $2\sigma_{\bar{x}}$ or $z\sigma_{\bar{x}}$ in the general case. Note that the standard deviation for this distribution is the standard error of the mean since the distribution at issue is the distribution of sample means. Since we want our estimate to be no more than \$25 ($=H$) removed from the true population value, we can simply equate the size of the specified half-interval with the number of standard deviations ($= z\sigma_{\bar{x}}$) to yield

$$H = z\sigma_{\bar{x}} \qquad\qquad (17.1)$$

$$= z\,\frac{\sigma}{\sqrt{n}}$$

This equation can be solved for n, since H and z have been specified and σ is known from past studies. Specifically, n can be shown to be equal to

$$n = \frac{z^2}{H^2}\sigma^2 \qquad\qquad (17.2)$$

or, in words,

$$\text{sample size} = \frac{\begin{array}{c}z,\ \text{corresponding to desired}\\ \text{degree of confidence, squared} \times \text{population variance}\end{array}}{\text{desired level of precision squared}}$$

To illustrate, suppose the historic variation in expenditures on food and lodging as measured by the population standard deviation, σ, was \$100. Then

$$n = \frac{(2)^2}{(25)^2}\,(100)^2$$

and $n = 64$. Thus only a relatively small sample needs to be taken to estimate the mean expenditure level when the population standard deviation is \$100 and the allowed precision is plus or minus \$25.

Another way to solve estimation problems is to develop a *nomograph* for the equation and read off the sample size rather than calculate it. A nomograph, or *alignment chart,* is simply a graphical solution to an equation. When values of all but one of the variables in the equation are specified, the value of the remaining variable can be read from the graph. Figure 17.2 is a nomograph for Equation 17.2 when a 95 percent confidence level is desired. By placing a ruler, preferably a clear plastic ruler, on the values $H = 25$ and $\sigma = 100$, we can read the sample size from the column of sample sizes. For a 95 percent confidence level, the nomograph shows that $n = 64$.

Note what happens, however, if the estimate must be twice as precise: \$25 is the total width of the desired interval and $H = 12.5$. Reading from Figure 17.2 or substituting in Equation 17.2,

$$n = \frac{(2)^2}{(12.5)^2}\,(100)^2$$

and $n = 256$; doubling the precision (halving the total width of the interval) increased the required sample size by a factor of 4. This is the basic trade-off between precision and sample size. Whenever precision is increased by a factor, c, sample size is increased by a factor of c^2. Thus, if the desired precision were \$10 instead of \$50—the estimate must be five times more precise ($c = 5$)—the sample size would be 1,600 instead of 64 ($c^2 = 25$).

Standard Deviation—σ	Sample Size—n	Half Precision—H
500	40000 / 35000	5
450	30000 / 25000	
400	20000	6
	15000	
350	10000 / 9000 / 8000 / 7000	7
300	6000 / 5000	8
	4000 / 3500 / 3000	9
250	2500	
	2000	10
	1500	11
200	1000 / 900 / 800 / 700	12
		13
175	600	14
	500	
	400	15
150	350 / 300	16
	250	
	200	18
125	150	20
	100 / 90 / 80 / 70	
100	60	25
	50	
90	40 / 35	
80	30	30
75	25	
70	20	35
	15	
65		
60	10	40
55		45
50	5 / 4	50

One also pays dearly for increases in the degree of confidence. Suppose, for example, that 99 percent confidence is desired rather than 95 percent. We could use the nomograph for a 99 percent confidence interval as shown in Figure 17.3, or we could calculate the result directly, using Equation 17.2, but now letting $z = 3$ instead of 2 as before. Suppose $H = 25$ and $\sigma = 100$ as in the original situation. Then

$$n = \frac{(3)^2}{(25)^2} \, (100)^2$$

and $n = 144$, whereas $n = 64$ when $z = 2$. When z was increased by a factor of $d(d = \frac{3}{2}$ in the example), sample size increased by a factor of $d^2 (d^2 = \frac{9}{4}$ in the example).

The bottom line in all these calculations is that you should be well aware of the price that must be paid for increased precision and confidence. Although we often desire very precise estimates in which we have a great deal of confidence, in the real world somebody must foot the bill incurred by each added degree of precision and confidence.

Case II: Population Variance Unknown

In our first case we used examples in which the population variance was known. What happens in the more typical case, when the population variance is unknown? The procedure in estimating the sample size is the same except that an *estimated* value of the population standard deviation, σ, is used in place of the previously known value. Once the sample is selected, the variance calculated from the sample is *used in place of the originally estimated variance* when establishing confidence intervals.

Suppose, for example, that there were no past studies to base an estimate of the population standard deviation of σ. How does one then generate an estimate of the population standard deviation? One could do a pilot study.[5] Alternatively, sometimes the variance can be estimated from the conditions surrounding the approach to the problem. Research Window 17.1, for example, discusses the estimation of the variance when rating scales are being used to measure the important variables. Still a third possibility is to take into account the fact that for a normally distributed variable, the range of the variable is approximately equal to plus or minus three standard deviations. Thus, if one can estimate the range of variation, one can estimate the standard deviation by dividing by 6. A little a priori knowledge of the phenomenon is often enough to estimate the range. If the estimate is in error, the consequence is a confidence interval more or less precise than desired. Let us illustrate.

Certainly there would be some licensed fishermen who would spend zero dollars on food and lodging while on fishing trips, since they would only be making one-day trips. Some might also be expected to go on several one-week trips a year. Suppose that 15 days a year were considered typical of the upper limit, and food and lodging expenses were calculated at $30 per day; the total dollar upper limit would be $450. The range would also be 450 (since they could not spend less than zero); and the estimated standard deviation would then be $\frac{450}{6} = 75$.

With desired precision of ±$25 and a 95 percent confidence interval, the calculation of sample size is now

$$n = \frac{z^2}{H^2} \, (\text{est. } \sigma)^2$$

$$= \frac{(2)^2}{(25)^2} \, (75)^2$$

and $n = 36$. The nomograph in Figure 17.2 could also be used to get the same result.

FIGURE 17.3 **Nomograph to Determine Sample Size to Estimate a Mean with 99 Percent Confidence Level**

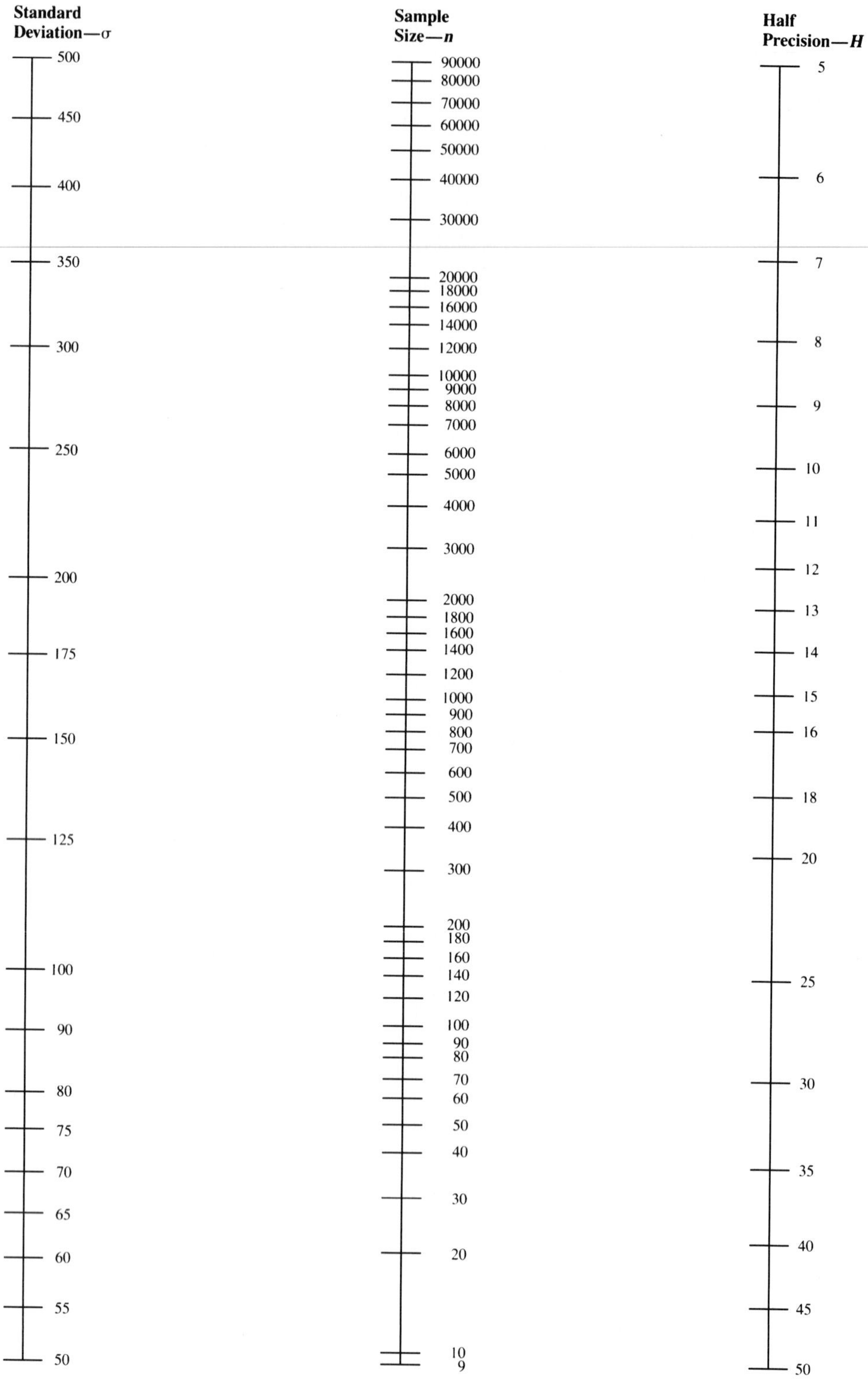

Rating scales are doubly bounded: on a 5-point scale, for instance, responses cannot be less than 1 or greater than 5. This constraint leads to a relationship between the mean and the variance. For example, if a sample mean is 4.6 on a 5-point scale, there must be a large proportion of responses of 5, and it follows that the variance must be relatively small. On the other hand, if the mean is near 3.0, the variance can be potentially much greater. The nature of the relationship between the mean and the variance depends on the number of scale points and on the "shape" of the distribution of responses (e.g., approximately normal or symmetrically clustered around some central scale value, or skewed, or uniformly spread among the scale values). By considering the types of distribution shapes typically encountered in practice, it is possible to estimate variances for use in calculating sample size requirements for a given number of scale points.

The table lists ranges of variances likely to be encountered for various numbers of scale points. The low end of the range is the approximate variance when data values tend to be concentrated around some middle point of the scale, as in a normal distribution. The high end of the range is the variance that would be obtained if responses were uniformly spread across the scale points. Although it is possible to encounter distributions with larger variances than those listed (such as distributions with modes at both ends of the scale), such data are rare.

In most cases, data obtained using rating scales tend to be more uniformly spread out than in a normal distribution. Hence, to arrive at conservative sample size estimates (i.e., sample sizes that are *at least* large enough to accomplish the stated objectives), it is advisable to use a variance estimate at or near the high end of the range listed.

Table 1

Number of Scale Points	Typical Range of Variances
4	0.7–1.3
5	1.2–2.0
6	2.0–3.0
7	2.5–4.0
10	3.0–7.0

Source: *Research on Research*, No. 37 (Chicago: Market Facts, Inc., undated).

A sample of size 36 would then be selected and the information collected. Suppose these observations generated a sample mean, $\bar{x} = 35$, and a sample standard deviation, $\hat{s} = 60$. The confidence interval is calculated as before,[6] using the expression sample mean $\pm z$ (standard error of the mean), where now the standard error of the mean is estimated using the sample standard deviation, or in symbols, $\bar{x} \pm z s_{\bar{x}}$, or

$$35 \pm 2\,\frac{\hat{s}}{\sqrt{n}} = 35 \pm 2\frac{60}{\sqrt{36}} = 35 \pm 20$$

or

$$15 \leq \mu \leq 55$$

Note what has happened. The desired precision was $\pm$\$25; the obtained precision is $\pm$\$20. The interval is narrower than planned (a bonus) because we overestimated the population standard deviation as judged by the sample standard deviation. If we had underestimated the standard deviation, the situation would have been reversed, and we would have ended up with a wider confidence interval than desired.

Case of Multiple Objectives

Researchers rarely conduct a study to determine only one parameter. It is much more typical for a study to involve multiple objectives. For example, BAI Global, a Tarrytown, New York, marketing research firm, tracks the type and amount of credit card offers sent to U.S. households. The firm studies the mail received by a sample of households, then extrapolates the results to the overall U.S. population and credit card industry. BAI gathers such data as the volume of credit card solicitations, the interest rates being offered, and the proportion of households that accept any of these offers.[7]

Because multiple objectives are typical, let us return to our previous example of fishermen and assume more realistically that the researcher has been asked also to estimate the annual mean level of expenditures on tackle and equipment by licensed fishermen, and the number of miles traveled in a year on fishing trips. There are now three means to be estimated. Suppose each is to be estimated with 95 percent confidence and that the desired absolute precision and estimated standard deviation are as given in Exhibit 17.1. Exhibit 17.1 also contains the sample sizes needed to estimate each variable, which were calculated using Equation 17.2.

The three requirements produce conflicting sample sizes. Depending on the variable being estimated, n should equal 36, 16, or 100. The researcher must somehow reconcile these values to come up with a sample size suitable for the study as a whole. The most conservative approach would be to choose $n = 100$, the largest value. This would ensure that each variable would be estimated with the required precision, assuming that the estimates of the standard deviations were accurate.

However, let us assume that of the three means to be determined, the estimate of miles traveled is the least critical. In such a case, it would be wasteful of resources to use a sample size of 100. A better approach would be to focus on those variables that are most critical and to select a sample sufficient in size to estimate them with the required precision and confidence. The variables for which a larger sample size is needed would then be estimated with either a lower degree of confidence or less precision than planned. Suppose in this case that the expenditure data are most critical and that the analyst, therefore, decides on a sample size of 36. Suppose also that the information from this sample of 36 fishermen produced a sample mean of $\bar{x} = 300$ and a sample deviation of $\hat{s} = 500$ miles traveled. The sample result is thus seen to agree with the original estimate of the population standard deviation, and so the confidence interval estimate will not be affected by inaccuracies here.

Using the standard expression, sample mean $\pm z$ (standard error of the mean), the confidence interval for miles traveled is calculated as

$$\bar{x} \pm zs_{\bar{x}} = \bar{x} \pm \frac{z\hat{s}}{\sqrt{n}} = 300 \pm 2\frac{500}{\sqrt{36}}$$

or $133.3 \leq \mu \leq 466.7$. Whereas the desired precision was ± 100 miles, the obtained precision is ≤ 166.7 miles. In order to produce an estimate with the desired precision, the degree of confidence would have to be lowered from its present 95 percent level.

EXHIBIT 17.1   Sample Size Needed to Estimate Each of Three Means

	VARIABLE		
	Expenditures on Food and Lodging	Expenditures on Tackle and Equipment	Miles Traveled
Confidence level	95 percent ($z = 2$)	95 percent ($z = 2$)	95 percent ($z = 2$)
Desired precision	$\pm\$25$	$\pm\$10$	± 100 miles
Estimated standard deviation	$\pm\$75$	$\pm\$20$	± 500 miles
Required sample size	36	16	100

Sample Size Determination When Estimating Proportions

The preceding examples all concern mean values. Marketers are also often interested in estimating other parameters, such as the population proportion, π. In our example, the researcher might be interested in determining the proportion of licensed fishermen who are from out of state, or from rural areas, or who took at least one overnight trip.

At the beginning of this chapter we suggested three things were needed to determine sample size: a specified degree of confidence, specified precision, and knowledge of the sampling distribution of the statistic. As we noted earlier, the specific requirements of the research problem determine how the first two items will be specified. With percentages, though, absolute precision means that the estimate will be within plus or minus so many percentage points of the true value, as, for example, within ±5 percentage points of the true value. For example, when the *Chicago Tribune* conducted a poll of local suburbanites to learn their sense of economic well-being, it sampled 930 residents of the counties surrounding Chicago. The newspaper reported that the degree of precision was plus or minus 3 percentage points. Thus, whereas the paper said 50 percent of residents of the Chicago suburbs believed they will be better off in five years, the true percentage could be anywhere between 47 and 53 percent.[8]

The remaining consideration then is the sampling distribution of the sample proportion. If the sample elements are selected independently, as can reasonably be assumed if the sample size is small relative to the population size, then the theoretically correct distribution of the sample proportion is the binomial. But the binomial becomes indistinguishable from the normal with large samples or when the population proportion is close to one-half.[9] It is convenient to use the normal approximation when estimating sample size. After the sample is drawn and the sample proportion determined, the researcher can always fall back on the binomial distribution to determine the confidence interval if the normal approximation proves to be in error.

The distribution of sample proportions is centered about the population proportion (Figure 17.4). The sample proportion is an unbiased estimate of the population proportion. The standard deviation of the normal distribution of sample proportions, that is, the standard error of the proportion, denoted by σ_p, is equal to $\sqrt{\pi(1-\pi)/n}$. Since we are working again with the normal curve, the level of precision is again equated to the number of standard deviations the estimate can be removed from the mean value. But now the mean value is the population proportion, while the standard deviation is the standard error of the proportion; that is,

$$H = z\sigma_p.$$ (17.3)

Substituting $\sqrt{\pi(1-\pi)/n}$ for σ_p and solving for n yields

Approximate Sampling Distribution of the Sample Proportion

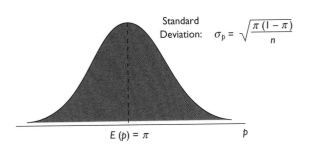

$$n = \frac{z^2}{H^2} \, \pi(1 - \pi) \qquad\qquad \textbf{(17.4)}$$

or, in words,

$$\text{sample size} = \frac{\begin{array}{c} z, \text{ corresponding to desired} \\ \text{degree of confidence, squared} \end{array} \times \begin{array}{c} \text{population} \\ \text{proportion} \end{array} \times \begin{array}{c} (1 - \text{population} \\ \text{proportion}) \end{array}}{\text{desired level of precision squared}}$$

Suppose the Division of Tourism is interested in knowing the proportion of all fishermen who took at least one overnight fishing trip in the past year. Suppose also that they wanted this estimate within ± 2 percentage points, and they wanted to be 95 percent confident ($z = 2$) in the result. Substituting these values in the formula (Equation 17.4) yields

$$n = \frac{(2)^2}{(.02)^2} \, \pi(1 - \pi)$$

This equation contains two unknowns: the population proportion being estimated and the sample size. Thus, it is not solvable as it stands. In order to determine sample size, the researcher needs to estimate the population proportion. That is right! *The researcher must estimate the very quantity the study is being designed to discover in order to determine sample size.*

This fact is often bewildering, and certainly disconcerting, to decision makers and beginning researchers alike. Nevertheless, it is true that with proportions one is forced to make some judgment about the approximate value of the parameter in order to determine sample size. This is another example of how information begets information in sample design. To arrive at an initial estimate, researchers might consult past studies or other published data. Alternatively, they might conduct a pilot study. If neither of these options is available, they might simply use informed judgment—a best guess—as to the approximate likely value of the parameter.

A poor estimate will make the confidence interval more or less precise than desired. Suppose, for example, that the best considered judgment was that 20 percent of all licensed fishermen could be expected to take an overnight fishing trip during the year. Sample size is then calculated to be

$$n = \frac{(2)^2}{(.02)^2} \, (.20)(1 - .20)$$

and $n = 1{,}600$. After data are collected from the designated 1,600 fishermen, suppose that the sample proportion, p, actually turns out to be equal to 0.40. The confidence interval is then established, employing the sample standard error of the proportion, s_p, to estimate the unknown population standard error of the proportion, σ_p, where

$$s_p = \sqrt{\frac{pq}{n}}$$

where p is the proportion engaging in the behavior in the particular sample selected, and $q = 1 - p$. In the example,

$$s_p = \sqrt{\frac{0.40(0.60)}{1{,}600}} = \sqrt{\frac{0.24}{1{,}600}} = 0.012$$

The confidence interval for the population proportion is given by the expression, sample proportion $\pm$ (z) (standard error of the proportion), or

$$p \pm zs_p = 0.40 \pm 2(0.012)$$

or

$$0.376 \le \pi \le 0.424$$

Note the interval is wider than desired. This is because the sample proportion turned out to be larger than the *estimated* population proportion.

Suppose a wider interval than planned was unacceptable. One way of preventing it is to choose the sample size so as to reflect the "worst of worlds." Note from the formula that the largest sample size will be obtained when the product $\pi(1 - \pi)$ is greatest, since sample size is directly proportional to this quantity. This product is in turn greatest when the population proportion $\pi = 0.5$, as might be intuitively expected, since, if one-half the population behaves one way and the other half the other way, then one would require more evidence for a valid inference than if a substantial proportion all behaved in the same way.

In the absence of any other information about the population proportion, then, one can always conservatively assume that π is equal to 0.5. The established confidence interval will simply be more precise to the extent that the sample estimate deviates from the assumed 0.5 value. Figures 17.5 and 17.6 are the nomographs for determining sample size to estimate a population proportion with 95 percent confidence level and 99 percent confidence level, respectively.

Population Size and Sample Size

Although you may not have noticed it before, note it now: *The size of the population does not enter into the calculation of the size of the sample.* Except for one slight modification we will discuss shortly, the size of the population has *no direct effect* on the size of the sample.

Although this statement may initially seem strange, consider it carefully and you will see why it is true. When estimating a mean, if all population elements have exactly the same value of the characteristic (for example, if each of our fishermen spent exactly $74 per year on food and lodging), then a sample of one is all that is needed to determine the mean. This is true whether there are 1,000, 10,000, or 100,000 elements in the population. What directly affects the size of the sample is the variability of the characteristic in the population.

Suppose that our example state offered some of the best fishing in the country and drew fishermen from across the nation as well as happy locals. If the parameter we sought to measure was mean number of miles traveled annually on fishing trips, there would be great variation in the characteristic. The more variable the characteristic, the larger the sample needed to estimate it with some specified level of precision. This idea not only makes intuitive sense, but we can see it directly expressed in the formulas for determining sample size to estimate a population mean. (See Equation 17.2.) Thus, population size affects sample size only indirectly through variability. In most cases, the larger the population, the greater the *potential* for variation of the characteristic.

It is also true that population size does not affect sample size when estimating a proportion. With a proportion, the determining factor, as we have seen, is the estimated proportion of the population possessing the characteristic; the closer the proportion is to 0.5, the larger the sample that will be needed, regardless of the size of the population. A value of 0.5 signifies greatest variability because one-half of the population possesses the characteristic and one-half does not.

The procedures we have discussed so far apply to situations where the target population is essentially infinite. This is the case in most consumer goods studies. However, when we first began our discussion, we mentioned that there was one modification to the general rule that population size has no direct effect on sample size. In cases where the

FIGURE 17.5   Nomograph to Determine Sample Size to Estimate a Proportion with 95 Percent Confidence Level

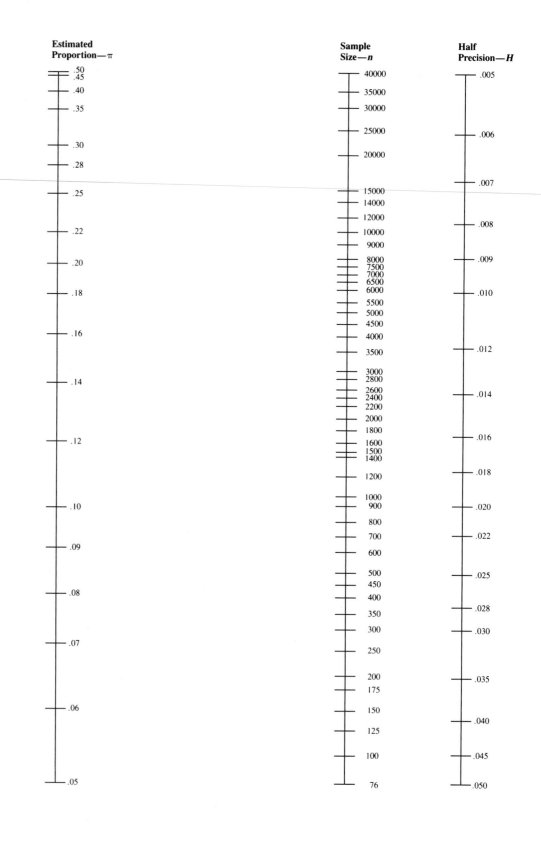

FIGURE 17.6   **Nomograph to Determine Sample Size to Estimate a Proportion with 99 Percent Confidence Level**

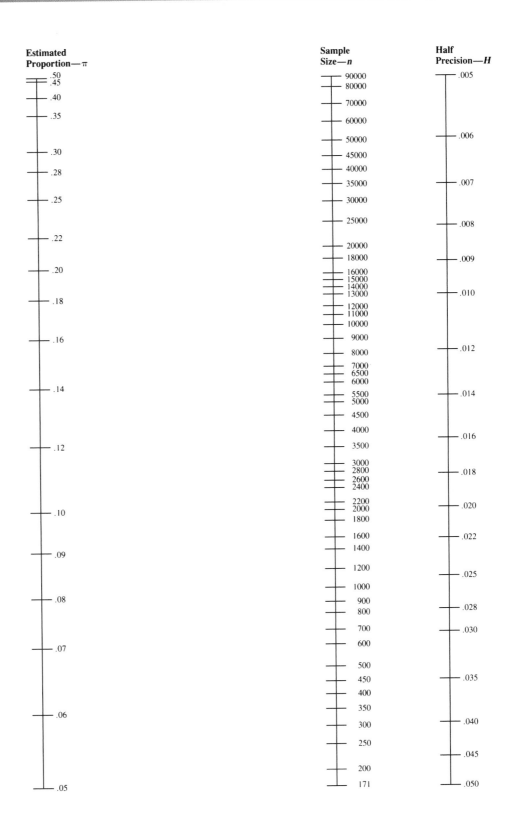

sample represents a large portion of the population, the formulas must be altered or they will overestimate the required sample. Since the larger the sample, the more expensive the study, the finite population correction factor should be employed.

As we have seen previously, the formula for the standard error of the mean is $\sigma_{\bar{x}} = \sigma/\sqrt{n}$ for most sampling problems. When the finite population correction factor is required, the formula becomes

$$\sigma_{\bar{x}} = \frac{\sigma}{\sqrt{n}} \sqrt{\frac{N-n}{N-1}}$$

where N denotes the size of the population and n denotes the size of the sample. The factor $(N-n)/(N-1)$ is the finite population correction factor.

When the estimated sample represents more than 5 percent of the population, the calculated size should be reduced by the finite population correction factor.[10] If, for example, the population contained 100 elements and the calculation of sample size indicated that a sample of 20 was needed, fewer than 20 observations would, in fact, be taken if the finite population correction factor were employed.

The required sample would be given as $n' = n [N/(N + n - 1)]$, where n was the originally determined size and n' was the revised size. Thus, with $N = 100$ and $n = 20$, only 17 sample elements would, in fact, be employed.

Other Probability Sampling Plans

So far, the discussions of sample size have been based on simple random samples. You should be aware, though, that there are also formulas for determining sample size when other probability sampling plans are used. The formulas are more complex, to be sure, but the same underlying principles apply. One still needs a knowledge of the sampling distribution of the statistic in addition to the research specifications regarding level of precision and degree of confidence.

The issue of sample size is compounded, though, by the fact that one now has a number of strata or a number of clusters with which to work. This means that one must deal with within-strata variability and within- and between-cluster variability in calculating sample size, whereas with simple random sampling only total population variability entered the picture. As before, the more variable the stratum or cluster, the larger the sample that needs to be taken from it, other things being equal. This is precisely the basis for disproportionate stratified sampling discussed in Chapter 16.

Something else that must be equal, though, is cost. Cost did not enter directly into the calculation of sample size with simple random sampling, although it often does affect sample size. If the cost of data collection with a sample of the calculated size would exceed the research budget, the cost could be the factor keeping the sample size below what was indicated by the formulas. In fact, it is not unusual for the size of a simple random sample to be determined by dividing the data collection budget by the estimated cost per observation. From a strictly statistical viewpoint, however, cost per observation does not enter into the formulas for calculating sample size with simple random samples.

With stratified or cluster samples, cost exerts a direct impact. In calculating sample size, one has to allow for unequal costs per observation by strata or by cluster, and in implementing the sample size calculation, one has to have some initial estimate of these costs. The task then becomes one of balancing variability against costs and assessing the trade-off function relating the two. With a stratified sample, for example, if cost were the same by strata, one would want to sample most heavily the stratum that was most variable. On the other hand, if there were little variation within strata, one might choose to sample more heavily those strata in which the cost per observation was less. Since it is unlikely that the cost per observation or variability will be the same for each stratum, the challenge becomes one of determining sample size by considering the precision likely to result from sampling each stratum at a given rate. Formulas are available for this purpose, as for cluster samples. We shall not go into these formulas here, as they are readily available in the standard works on sampling theory and fall largely in the domain of the sampling specialist.[11] You should be aware, though, that when dealing with stratified or cluster samples, cost per observation by subgroup enters directly into the calculation of sample size.

You should also be aware that there are formulas for determining sample size when the problem is one of hypothesis testing and not confidence interval estimation. Once again, the principles are the same, although there are some additional considerations such as the levels of Type I and Type II errors to be tolerated and the issue of whether it is necessary to detect subtle differences or only obvious differences. We shall not deal with these formulas, since they are also readily available in standard statistical works and their discussion would take us too far afield.[12]

Sample Size Determination Using Anticipated Cross Classifications

Thus far, our discussion of how sample size is determined has been based primarily on the use of statistical principles, with a particular focus on the sampling error involved and the trade-off between degree of confidence and degree of precision. Until now we have limited ourselves to a discussion of these considerations since they are the most important ones theoretically. But in applied problems, the size of the sample is also going to be affected by certain practical considerations. In our discussion of stratified and cluster samples we already mentioned that the size of the budget for the study and the anticipated cost per observation would affect sample size. In addition to that, the size of the sample may also be affected by other, quite subjective factors. For example, researchers may find themselves increasing the size of the sample beyond what is required statistically in order to convince skeptical executives, who have little understanding of sampling theory, that they can have confidence in the results of the study.

One of the more important practical bases for determining the size of sample that will be needed is the cross classifications to which researchers plan to subject the data. Suppose that in our task of estimating the proportion of all fishermen who took at least one overnight fishing trip in the past year, we also proposed to determine whether this pattern of behavior was somehow related to an individual's age and income. Assume that the age categories of interest were as follows: younger than 20, 20–29, 30–39, 40–49, and 50 and older. Assume the income categories of interest were as follows: less than $10,000, $10,000–$19,999, $20,000–$29,999, $30,000–$39,999, and $40,000 and over. There are thus five age categories and five income categories for which the proportion of fishermen taking an overnight trip would be estimated.

While we could estimate proportions for each of these variables separately, we should also recognize that the two variables are interrelated in that increases in incomes are typically related to increases in age. To allow for this interdependence, we need to consider the impact of the two variables simultaneously. The way to do this is through a cross-classification table in which age and income jointly define the cells or categories in the table.[13]

Exhibit 17.2, for instance, is a cross-classification table that could be used for the example at hand. Note that this dummy table is complete in all respects except for the numbers that actually go in each of the cells. These would, of course, be determined by the data actually collected on the number and proportion of all those sampled who actually made at least one overnight trip. In the table there are 25 cells that need estimation. It is unlikely, however, that the decision maker for whom our study is designed is going to be comfortable with an estimate based on only a few cases of the phenomenon. Yet even with a sample of, say, 500 fishermen, there is only a potential of 20 cases per cell (i.e., 500 cases divided by 25 cells) if the sample is evenly divided with respect to the age and income levels considered. Further, it is very unlikely that the sample would split this way, which would put the researcher in the awkward position of estimating the proportion in a cell engaging in this behavior on the basis of fewer than 20 cases.

			AGE		
Income	**Younger than 20**	**20–29**	**30–39**	**40–49**	**50 and older**
Less than $10,000					
$10,000–$19,999					
$20,000–$29,999					
$30,000–$39,999					
$40,000 and over					

EXHIBIT 17.2 Number and Proportion of Fishermen Staying Overnight as a Function of Age and Income

One can reverse this argument to estimate how large a sample should be taken. First, the researcher would calculate the number of cells in the intended cross classifications. That number can be found by multiplying the number of levels of the characteristics forming each of the cross classifications. In our study, researchers would multiply five levels of income by five levels of age to get 25 cells. If it was felt that the decision maker might need at least 30 observations per cell in order to feel comfortable with the cell's estimate, that would mean a sample of 750 subjects would be needed. However, the sample of 750 is unlikely to be evenly distributed across the cells of the table, so the researchers would need to determine how the variables are likely to be distributed. Once the most important cells have been identified, the researcher can compute a sample size large enough to satisfy concerns about sufficient sampling. One general rule of thumb is that "the sample should

Ethical Dilemma 17.1

A recent discussion between the account manager for an independent research agency and the marketing people for the client left the account manager feeling perplexed. After numerous discussions, the account manager believed that she had a good handle on the client's problem and major concerns. On the basis of this understanding, she had developed a set of dummy tables by which the client's concerns could be investigated. During the most recent meeting, she had presented these to the client. The client had completely accepted the account manager's recommendation about how the data would be viewed, and closed the meeting by asking how large a sample the account manager would recommend and how much the study would cost. The account manager's anxiety was caused by the fact that she believed from the earlier discussions and some preliminary investigation that two of the seven hypotheses were especially promising. The sample size that was needed to investigate these two hypotheses was almost 60 percent smaller than that needed to address some of

the other hypotheses because of the fewer cells in the cross-classification table. The account manager was in a dilemma about whether she should take the safe route and recommend the larger sample size to the client and thereby assure that all the planned cross-classifications could be completed or whether she should go with her instinct and recommend the smaller sample size and save the client some money.

What would you recommend that the account manager do?

Is it ethical for the account manager to recommend the larger sample size when she is fairly certain that the smaller one will provide the answers the client needs? Is it ethical to do the reverse and recommend the smaller sample when there is some risk that the smaller sample will not adequately answer the problem that the firm was hired to solve?

What are the account manager's responsibilities to the client in a case like this?

be large enough so that there are 100 or more units in each category of the major break-downs and a minimum of 20 to 50 in the minor breakdowns."[14] Major breakdowns refer to the cells in the most critical cross tabulations for the study, and minor breakdowns refer to the cells in the less important cross classifications.

Through all of this one has to make allowances for nonresponses, since some individuals designated for inclusion in the sample will be unavailable and others will refuse to participate. The researcher "builds up" the sample, so to speak, from the size of the cross-classification table with due allowance for these considerations.

Perhaps cross classification will not be the basic method used to analyze the data. Perhaps, instead, other statistical techniques will be used. If so, the same arguments for determining sample size apply. That is, one needs a sufficient number of cases to satisfy the requirements of the technique, so as to inspire confidence in the results. Different techniques have different sample size requirements, often expressed by the degrees of freedom required for the analysis. Readers interested in using a particular statistical technique for analysis should pay close attention to the sample size requirements for the technique to be used safely. For now, we merely wish to reiterate the important point made earlier when introducing the research process—that the stages are very much related, and a decision with respect to one stage can affect all the other stages. In this case a decision with respect to Stage 6 regarding the method of analysis can have an important impact on Stage 5, which precedes it, with respect to the size of the sample that should be selected. Therefore, the researcher needs to think through the entire research problem, including how the data will be analyzed, before beginning the data collection process.

Determining Sample Size Using Historical Evidence

A final method by which an analyst can determine the size of the sample to employ is to use the size that others have used for similar studies in the past. Although this may be different from the ideal size in a given problem, the fact that the contemplated sample size is in line with that used for similar studies is psychologically comforting, particularly to inexperienced researchers. Exhibit 17.3, which summarizes the evidence, provides a crude yardstick in this respect. Note that national studies typically involve larger samples than regional or special studies. Note further that the number of subgroup analyses has a direct impact on sample size.

EXHIBIT 17.3	Typical Sample Sizes for Studies of Human and Institutional Populations			
NUMBER OF SUBGROUP ANALYSES	**PEOPLE OR HOUSEHOLDS**		**INSTITUTIONS**	
	National	**Regional or Special**	**National**	**Regional or Special**
None or few	1,000–1,500	200–500	200–500	50–200
Average	1,500–2,500	500–1,000	500–1,000	200–500
Many	2,500+	1,000+	1,000+	500+

Source: Seymour Sudman, *Applied Sampling* (San Francisco, Academic Press, 1976), p. 87.

Back to the Case

At three o'clock in the afternoon Malgieri's Restaurant looked very different than it did at night when it was filled with people. Without tablecloths, the tables were revealed to be pitted and worn. In one corner, busboys in shirtsleeves sat folding napkins while they watched soap operas on a small black-and-white television.

Michael and Rosemary Malgieri were seated at another table going over what looked like receipts. They greeted William Bader warmly, and if Michael objected to his wife's exploring a business alternative that he didn't support, he certainly didn't show it.

"I've been giving Rosemary's idea of a take-out and delivery service a good deal of thought," began William. "In order to know whether it would be a profit-making venture for you, I think the single most important thing to find out is where your customers live relative to the restaurant. People won't go too far to pick up food, for fear that it'll be cold when they get home and because the whole idea of takeout is convenience. And if you're going to add a delivery service, you'll have the same concerns about hot food, as well as time and fuel costs for deliveries far away."

"So how about if tonight we instruct the wait staff to ask all patrons where they live and how far it is from the restaurant? They can ask when the patrons pay their check. We'll serve at least a hundred people tonight: that should give us a pretty good idea," suggested Michael.

"It would be a start, but not a particularly accurate one. I'd feel more comfortable if you would let me write out a little question-and-answer sheet for each waiter to read to the patrons on a given night. That way we'd be sure that everyone was responding to the same questions, and I'd be able to tabulate the results with some confidence. Also, I know that a hundred people sounds like a lot, but I'm not sure of how reliable an estimate of average miles traveled would be, based on that number of respondents. I'd feel much more comfortable if you'd be willing to repeat the survey on one or two more nights if it turned out to be necessary."

"That seems reasonable," replied Rosemary.

"Then, I propose that if the simple location survey shows enough patrons clustered within a comfortable radius of the restaurant, we do another patron survey. The focus of this one would be to explore age, income, and interest in a take-out and delivery service. That way we'd be able to see whether it would be better to gear your out-of-restaurant menu toward people wanting restaurant meals or those wanting family-style meals."

"How many people would you like to survey in the second stage?" asked Michael.

"Again, I'd like to keep that open-ended," replied William. "In any sample there's a trade-off between degree of confidence and degree of precision. If we allow ourselves to vary the sample size to produce an estimate with precision and confidence levels that we want, then you're going to feel confident putting your time and dollars behind the decision you make."

Summary

Learning Objective 1

Specify the key factor a researcher must consider in estimating sample size using statistical principles.

The key factor a researcher must consider in estimating sample size is the standard error of the estimate obtained from the known sampling distribution of the statistic.

Learning Objective 2

Cite two other factors researchers must also take into account when estimating a sample size and explain their relationship.

When estimating a sample size, researchers must consider both how precise the estimate must be and the degree of confidence that is required in the estimate. With a sample of fixed size, there is a trade-off between degree of confidence and degree of precision. One can specify either the degree of precision or the degree of confidence, but not both. It is only when sample size is allowed to vary that one can achieve both a specified precision and a specified degree of confidence in the result. The determination of sample size involves balancing the two considerations against each other.

Learning Objective 3

Explain in what way the size of the population influences the size of the sample.

In most instances, the size of the population has no direct effect on the size of the sample but only affects it indirectly through the variability of the characteristic; and sample size is directly proportional to variability.

Learning Objective 4

Specify the circumstances under which the finite population correction factor should be used.

In general, when the estimated sample represents more than 5 percent of the population, the calculated sample size should be reduced by the finite population correction factor.

Learning Objective 5

Explain the impact that cost has on sample size in stratified or cluster samples.

With stratified or cluster samples, cost exerts a direct impact. In calculating sample size, one has to allow for unequal costs per observation by strata or by cluster; and in implementing the sample size calculation, one has to have some initial estimate of these costs. The task, then, becomes one of balancing variability against costs and assessing the trade-off function relating the two.

Learning Objective 6

Cite the rule of thumb for calculating sample size when cross-classification tables are used.

When calculating sample size by using cross-classification tables, the rule of thumb is that the sample should be large enough so that there are 100 or more units in each category of the major breakdowns and a minimum of 20 to 50 in the minor breakdowns.

Review Questions

1. In determining sample size, what factors must an analyst consider?

2. When estimating a population mean, what is meant by absolute precision? What is meant by relative precision?

3. What is the difference between degree of confidence and degree of precision?

4. Suppose that the population variance is known. How do you then determine the sample size necessary to estimate a population mean with some desired degree of

precision and confidence? Given that the sample has been selected, how do you generate the desired confidence interval?

5. How does the procedure in Question 4 differ when the population variance is unknown?

6. What effect would relaxing by 25 percent the absolute precision with which a population mean is estimated have on sample size? Decreasing the degree of confidence from 95 percent to 90 percent? ($z = 1.64$)

7. Suppose that you wanted to estimate a population mean within ±10 percent at the 95 percent level of confidence. How would you proceed? What quantities would you need to estimate?

8. Suppose that you wanted to estimate a population proportion within ±3 percentage points at the 95 percent level of confidence. How would you proceed and what quantities would you need to estimate?

9. What happens if the sample proportion is larger than the estimated population proportion used to determine sample size? If it is smaller? What value of the population proportion should be assumed if you wish to take no chance that the generated interval will be larger than the desired interval?

10. What is the correct procedure for treating multiple study objectives when calculating sample size?

11. How is sample size determined based on anticipated cross classifications of the data?

Discussion Questions, Problems, and Projects

1. A survey was being designed by the marketing research department of a medium-sized manufacturer of household appliances. The general aim was to assess customer satisfaction with the company's dishwashers. As part of this general objective, management wished to measure the average maintenance expenditure per year per household, the average number of malfunctions or breakdowns per year, and the number of times a dishwasher is cleaned within a year. Management wished to be 95 percent confident in the results. Further, the magnitude of the error was not to exceed ±$4 for maintenance expenditures, ±1 for malfunctions, and ±4 for cleanings. The research department noted that while some households would spend nothing on maintenance expenditures per year, others might spend as much as $120. Also, while some dishwashers would experience no breakdowns within a year, the maximum expected would be no more than three. Finally, while some dishwashers might not be cleaned at all during the year, others might be cleaned as frequently as once a month.
   (a) How large a sample would you recommend if each of the three variables were considered separately? Show all your calculations.
   (b) What size sample would you recommend *overall* given that management felt that the expenditure on repairs was most important and the number of cleanings least important to know accurately?
   (c) The survey indicated that the average maintenance expenditure was $30, and the standard deviation was $15. Estimate the confidence interval for the population parameter μ. What can you say about the degree of precision?

2. The management of a major dairy wanted to determine the average ounces of milk consumed per resident in the state of Montana. Past trends indicated that the variation in milk consumption (σ) was 4 ounces. A 95 percent confidence level is required and the error is not to exceed ±½ ounce.
   (a) What sample size would you recommend? Show your calculations.

    (b) Management wanted to double the level of precision and increase the level of confidence to 99 percent. What sample size would you recommend? Show your calculations. Comment on your results.

3. The manager of a local recreational center wanted to determine the average amount each customer spent on traveling to and from the center. On the basis of the findings, the manager was planning on raising the entrance fee. The manager noted that customers living near the center would spend nothing on traveling. On the other hand, customers living at the other side of town had to travel about 15 miles and spent about 20 cents per mile. The manager wanted to be 95 percent confident of the findings and did not want the error to exceed ± 10 cents.
    (a) What sample size should the manager use to determine the average travel expenditure? Show your calculations.
    (b) After the survey was conducted, the manager found the average expenditure to be $1.00, and the standard deviation was $0.60. Construct a 95 percent confidence interval. What can you say about the level of precision?

4. A large manufacturer of chemicals recently came under severe criticism from various environmentalists for its disposal of industrial effluent and waste. In response, management launched a campaign to counter the bad publicity it was receiving. A study of the effectiveness of the campaign indicated that about 20 percent of the residents of the city were aware of the campaign and the company's position. In conducting the study, a sample of 400 was used and a 95 percent confidence interval was specified. Three months later, it was believed that 30 percent of the residents were aware of the campaign. However, management decided to do another survey and specified a 99 percent confidence level and a margin error of ± 2 percentage points.
    (a) What sample size would you recommend for this study? Show all your calculations.
    (b) After doing the survey it was found that 50 percent of the population was aware of the campaign. Construct a 99 percent confidence interval for the population parameter.

5. Score-It, Inc., is a large manufacturer of video games. The marketing research department is designing a survey to determine attitudes toward the products. Additionally, the percentage of households owning video games and the average usage rate per week are to be determined. The department wants to be 95 percent confident of the results and does not want the error to exceed ± 3 percentage points for video game ownership and ± 1 hour for average usage rate. Previous reports indicate that about 20 percent of the households own video games and the average usage rate is 15 hours with a standard deviation of 5 hours.
    (a) What sample size would you recommend, assuming only the percentage of households owning video games is to be determined? Show all your calculations.
    (b) What sample size would you recommend, assuming only the average usage rate per week is to be determined? Show all your calculations.
    (c) What sample size would you recommend, assuming both the above variables are to be determined? Why?
After the survey was conducted, the results indicated that 30 percent of the households owned video games and the average usage rate was 13 hours with a standard deviation of 4 hours.
    (d) Compute the 95 percent confidence interval for the percentage of individuals owning video games. Comment on the degree of precision.
    (e) Compute the 95 percent confidence interval for the average usage rate. Comment on the degree of precision.

6. The local gas and electric company in a city in the northeast United States recently started a campaign to encourage people to reduce unnecessary use of gas and electricity. To assess the effectiveness of the campaign, management wanted to do a survey to determine the proportion of people that had adopted the recommended energy-saving measures.
   (a) What sample size would you recommend if the error was not to exceed ±0.025 percentage points and the confidence level was to be 90 percent? Show your calculations.
   (b) The survey indicated that the proportion adopting the measures was 40 percent. Estimate the 90 percent confidence interval. Comment on the level of precision. Show your calculations.

7. Assume you are a marketing researcher analyst for TV Institute, and you have just been given the assignment of estimating the percentage of all American households that watched the ABC movie last Sunday night. You have been told that your estimate should have a precision ±1 percentage point and that there should be a 95 percent "probability" of your being "correct" in your estimate. Your first task is to choose a sample of the appropriate size. Make any assumptions that are necessary.
   (a) Recast the problem in a statistical format.
   (b) Compute the sample size that will satisfy the required specifications.
   (c) What is the required sample size if the precision is specified as ±2 percentage points?
   (d) What would be the sample size if the probability of being "correct" were decreased to 90 percent, keeping the precision at ±1 percentage points?
   (e) If you had only enough time to take a sample of Size 100, what precision could you expect from your estimate? (Assume a 95 percent confidence interval.)
   (f) Assume that instead of taking a sample from the entire country (60 million households), you would like to restrict yourself to one state with one million households. Would the sample size computed in (b) be too large? Too small? Explain.

8. Assume TV Institute has hired you to do another study, this time estimating the average number of hours of television viewing per week per family in the United States. You are asked to generate an estimate within ±5 hours. Further, there should be 95 percent confidence that the estimate is correct. Make any assumptions that are necessary.
   (a) Compute the sample size that will satisfy the required specifications.
   (b) What would be the required sample size if the precision were changed to ±10 hours?

9. The manager of a local bakery wants to determine the average expenditure per household on bakery products. Past research indicates that the standard deviation is $10.
   (a) Calculate the sample size for the various levels of precision and confidence. Show your calculations:

	Desired Precision (±)	Desired Confidence	Estimated Sample Size
1	0.50	0.95	
2	1.00	0.99	
3	0.50	0.90	
4	0.25	0.90	
5	0.50	0.99	
6	0.25	0.95	
7	1.00	0.90	
8	1.00	0.95	
9	0.25	0.99	

   (b) Which alternative gives the largest estimate for sample size? Explain.

10. A manufacturer of liquid soaps wishes to estimate the proportion of individuals using liquid soaps as opposed to bar soaps. Prior estimates of the proportions are listed below.
    (a) For the various levels of precision and confidence indicated, calculate the needed size of the sample.

	Desired Precision in Percentage Points (±)	Desired Confidence	(%) Estimated Proportion	Estimated Sample Size
1	6	0.99	20	
2	2	0.90	10	
3	6	0.99	10	
4	4	0.95	30	
5	2	0.90	20	
6	2	0.99	30	
7	6	0.90	30	
8	4	0.95	10	
9	4	0.95	20	

   (b) Which alternative gives the largest estimate of the sample size? Explain.

11. Your World, Inc., is a large travel agency located in Cincinnati, Ohio. Management is concerned about its declining leisure travel-tour business. It believes that the profile of those engaging in leisure travel has changed in the past few years. To determine if that is indeed the case, management decides to conduct a survey to determine the profile of the current leisure travel-tour customer. Three variables are identified that require particular attention. Prior to conducting the survey, the following three dummy tables are developed.

	Age			
Income	18–24	25–34	35–54	55+
0–$9,999				
$10,000–$19,999				
$20,000–$29,999				
$30,000–$39,999				
$40,000 and over				

	Education			
Age	Some High School	High School Graduate	Some College	College Graduate
18–24				
25–34				
35–54				
55+				

	Education			
Income	Some High School	High School Graduate	Some College	College Graduate
0–$9,999				
$10,000–$19,999				
$20,000–$29,999				
$30,000–$39,999				
$40,000 and over				

(a) How large a sample would you recommend be taken? Justify your answer.

(b) The survey produced the following incomplete table for the variables of age and education. Complete the table on the basis of the assumption that the two characteristics are independent (even though that assumption is wrong). On the basis of the completed table, do you think an appropriate sample size was used? If yes, why? If no, why not?

| | **Education** | | | | |
Age	Some High School	High School Graduate	Some College	College Graduate	Total
18–24					100
25–34					200
35–54					350
55+					350
Total	200	400	300	100	1,000

12. You are the assistant director of political research for the ABC television network. It is 1996, and Marge Simpson and Ethan Martin are running for president of the United States of America. You need to furnish a prediction of the percentage of the vote going to Martin, assuming the election was held today, for tomorrow's evening newscast. You want to be 95 percent confident in your prediction and desire a total precision of 6 percent.

(a) Assume that you have no reliable information concerning the percentage of the population that prefers Martin. What sample size will you use for the project?

(b) Assume that a similar poll, taken 30 days ago, revealed that 40 percent of the respondents would vote for Martin. Taking this information into account, what sample size will you use for the project?

(c) Which of the two sample sizes you have just calculated would you prefer to use for your study? Why?

(d) Most polls of this type are conducted by telephone. When a potential respondent answers the phone, what is the *first* question you should ask? Why?

13. A city is considering implementing a "pay as you throw" billing system for residential garbage pickup. Under the plan, a household would be charged by the pound for garbage removal. As part of its proposal to the city council, the sanitation department needs to calculate an average monthly bill per household under the proposed system. To do so, the sanitation department plans to weigh the garbage collected from a random sample of households over the next two months. Based on an informal poll of route drivers, the department estimates that a household throws away between 30 and 90 pounds of garbage a month. The department wants the estimate to be within ±2 pounds of the true population average, and the city council insists that it will accept only a figure that has a 99 percent probability of being correct.

(a) What sample size would you recommend?

(b) You have just been informed that the budget has been cut and the size of the sample must be cut by 20 percent. However, a 99 percent confidence level must be maintained. What is the new sample size? What does this mean in terms of the precision of the estimate?

Endnotes

1. Bayesian analysts also consider the cost of wrong decisions when determining sample size. For a comparison of classical and Bayesian procedures for determining sample size, see Seymour Sudman, *Applied Sampling* (San Francisco: Academic Press, 1976), pp. 85–105.

2. The problem would be of interest to the tourist industry, and it also could be of interest to the division of state government concerned with economic development. The problem was chosen because the availability of a list of population elements allows a simple random sample to be selected.

3. See Morris H. Hansen, William N. Hurwitz, and William G. Madow, *Sample Survey Methods and Theory: Vol. I, Methods and Applications* (New York: John Wiley, 1993), for one of the best treatments on securing variance estimates from past data, especially pp. 450–455.

4 The variable *z* more correctly equals 1.96 for a 95 percent confidence interval. The approximation $z = 2$ is used since it simplifies the calculations.

5. See Raphael Gillett, "Confidence Interval Construction by Stein's Method: A Practical and Economical Approach to Sample Size Determination," *Journal of Marketing Research* 26 (May 1989), pp. 237–240, for discussion of how the pilot study results can be used not only to develop an estimate of the population variance but also to produce an estimate of the population mean corresponding to the specified confidence level and desired interval size.

6. One would more strictly use the *t* distribution to establish the interval, since the population variance was unknown. The example was framed using the approximate $z \pm 2$ value for a 95 percent confidence interval to better illustrate the consequence of a poor initial estimate of σ.

7. Joseph B. Cahill, "Credit Cards Get a Record Level of Solicitations," *The Wall Street Journal* (April 9, 1999), p. B10.

8. Ted Gregory, "Suburbanites a Study in Optimism," *Chicago Tribune* (August 29, 1999), sec. 1, pp. 1, 16.

9. The strict requirement is that $n\pi$ must be above a certain level if the normal curve is to provide a good approximation to the binomial, where π is the population proportion and n is the sample size. Some books hold that $n\pi$ must be greater than 5, while others suggest that the product must be greater than 10.

10. The 5 percent correction factor is not a hard-and-fast rule. Some books contend that the finite population correction factor should be ignored if the sample includes no more than 10 percent of the population. Cochran suggests that the finite population correction can be ignored whenever the "sampling fraction does not exceed 5 percent and for many purposes even if it is as high as 10 percent." William G. Cochran, *Sampling Techniques,* 3rd ed. (New York: John Wiley, 1977), p. 25. See also Richard L. Schaeffer, William Mendenhall, and Lyman Ott, *Elementary Survey Sampling,* 4th ed. (Boston: PWS-Kent Publishing Co., 1990). Ignoring the finite population correction will result in overestimating the standard error of estimate.

11. See, for example, Cochran, *Sampling Techniques*; Hansen, Hurwitz, and Madow, *Sample Survey Methods*; Leslie Kish, Survey Sampling (New York: John Wiley, 1965); R. L. Jensen, Statistical Survey Techniques (New York: John Wiley, 1978); Paul S. Levy and Stanley Lemeshaw, *Sampling of Populations: Methods and Applications* (New York: John Wiley and Sons, Inc., 1991).

12. Computer-based expert systems that rely on artificial intelligence techniques also exist for determining sample size. These systems guide the researcher through a series of questions about the needed degree of confidence, precision, variability, and so on, and, based on the answers, perform the tedious computations concerning the needed sample size. See, for example, Ex-Sample, which is available from the Idea Works in Columbia, Missouri.

13. Chapter 19 discusses the procedures for setting up and analyzing cross-classification tables so that the proper inferences can be drawn.

14. Sudman, *Applied Sampling,* p. 30.

Suggested Additional Readings

For a more thorough discussion of the estimation of sample size for different types of samples and characteristics other than the mean and proportion, see
William Cochran, *Sampling Techniques,* 3rd ed. (New York: John Wiley, 1977).
Morris H. Hansen, William N. Hurwitz, and William G. Madow, *Sample Survey Methods and Theory, Vol. I, Methods and Applications* (New York: John Wiley, 1953).
Leslie Kish, Survey Sampling (New York: John Wiley, 1995).
Richard L. Schaeffer, William Mendenhall, and Lyman Ott, *Elementary Survey Sampling,* 5th ed. (Belmont, Calif.: Wadsworth Publishing Co., 1996).

Chapter 18

COLLECTING THE DATA: FIELD PROCEDURES AND NONSAMPLING ERRORS

LEARNING OBJECTIVES

Upon Completing This Chapter, You Should Be Able to

1. Explain what sampling error is.

2. Cite the two basic types of nonsampling errors and describe each.

3. Outline several ways in which noncoverage bias can be reduced.

4. Explain what error due to nonresponse is.

5. Cite the standard definition for *response rate*.

6. Identify the two main sources of nonresponse bias.

7. Define *contact rate*.

8. Cite some of the factors that may contribute to a respondent's refusal to participate in a study.

9. Identify three factors that may be a source of bias in the interviewer-interviewee interaction.

10. Discuss the types of interviewer behaviors that may lead to response bias.

Case in Marketing Research

Lucy Lindenbloom was dressed for combat, or at least that's how she thought of it as she prepared herself to go to work. Lindenbloom was employed by the U.S. government, but not as a soldier. She was an official field interviewer for the U.S. Census Bureau, and her years on the job had taught her to be prepared for the worst.

She was dressed neatly but plainly, incorporating several layers because of the uncertain March weather. She had a raincoat in the trunk of her car and comfortable shoes on her feet. On the front seat of her aging Honda lay a map of the greater Plainfield area, a dozen No. 2 pencils, a ponderous manual of instructions, and a box of Kleenex tissues.

While most people thought that all the Census Bureau did was count noses every ten years, Lindenbloom had been involved in any number of other information-collection operations. Presently, she was gathering data for the Current Population Survey, a continuing program on which national unemployment figures are based. She had a list of people to contact that week in order to ask them about their work status during the previous week.

Her assignment that day was to interview a list of people in one of the city's most affluent suburbs, Moreland Heights. Early on in her career she might have looked forward to a day spent in a neighborhood where large houses were set back on deep, manicured lawns. Instead, she now foresaw a day filled with trekking up long driveways.

The first address on her list was 2720 Shelley Drive. When Lindenbloom rang the doorbell, she heard the sound of dogs barking within, but there was no response. Seeing cars parked behind the house and lights on in the upstairs windows, she went around to the side door and rang the bell. After still receiving no response, she opened the storm door and made vigorous use of the door knocker. Inside, the dogs were getting hysterical.

Finally, the face of a young woman appeared at the window and she opened the door.

"Oh, hi," she said. "I hope you haven't been at the door long. I was upstairs riding the exercise bike and I didn't hear the bell. What can I do for you?"

"I'm a field interviewer for the U.S. Census Bureau," said Lindenbloom, showing her official ID card, "and I'm trying to locate Suzanne Cooper to ask her some questions about her employment during the last week."

"Suzanne—employed?" asked the young woman with a laugh. "Not unless you count tennis and shopping as employment."

"I take it you're not Mrs. Cooper," said Lindenbloom.

"No, I'm her sister. I'm just staying here to keep an eye on the dogs."

"Could you tell me when I might be able to find Mr. or Mrs. Cooper at home?"

"I'm not sure. They're in Italy right now. Rick had some business there, and Suzanne went along. I don't know—I think they're due back the middle of April."

Lindenbloom thanked the young woman for her time and continued down the street to 2722. When an older woman in a white uniform came to the door, Lindenbloom introduced herself and asked to speak to Mr. or Mrs. Evans.

"Mr. Evans doesn't live here anymore," said the woman. "He ran off with some woman from his office. He and Mrs. Evans are getting a divorce."

"I see," replied Lindenbloom. "Is Mrs. Evans at home?"

"No, she's at work. She's a lawyer downtown."

"Do you know when I might be able to catch her at home?"

"It's hard to say. Some nights she's back home by supper time; other nights she's got a meeting. I know the baby-sitter's coming tonight, so I guess she won't be home."

"Thanks for your time," replied Lindenbloom.

By midafternoon Lindenbloom had been to every house on Shelley Drive. She had talked to six housekeepers, one window cleaner, and three nannies. She felt as if she'd walked about 20 miles.

Discussion Issues

1. Besides not-at-homes and problems in coverage of the specified sampling areas, what other problems might field interviewers expect to encounter when gathering data?

2. What procedures might be helpful in alleviating such problems?

3. What problems might interviewers encounter in personal or telephone surveys that may not be a problem in mail surveys? What particular problems might mail surveys pose?

The data collection task is the one that most often comes to mind when people think of marketing research. At this stage in the research process, some kind of a field force is used, operating either in the field or from an office as in a phone or mail, e-mail, or fax survey. In this chapter we will focus on the various things that can go wrong in conducting a field study, with a special emphasis on sources of error we have not discussed in earlier chapters. A person who understands the potential sources of error in data collection will have insights that will be useful in evaluating the research information upon which decisions must be based.

Impact and Importance of Nonsampling Errors

Sampling error
The difference between the observed values of a variable and the long-run average of the observed values in repetitions of the measurement.

Two basic types of errors arise in research studies: *sampling errors* and *nonsampling errors*. The concept of **sampling error** underlies much of the discussion in Chapters 15, 16, and 17. Basic to that discussion was the concept of the sampling distribution of some statistic, be it the sample mean, sample proportion, or whatever. The sampling distribution arises because of sampling error. The sampling distribution reflects the fact that the different possible samples that could be drawn under the sampling plan will produce different estimates of the parameter. The statistic varies from sample to sample simply because we are only sampling part of the population in each case. Sampling error then is "the difference between the observed values of a variable and the long-run average of the observed values in repetitions of the measurement."[1] As we saw, sampling errors can be reduced by increasing sample size. The distribution of the sample statistic becomes more and more concentrated about the long-run average value, as the sample statistic is more equal from sample to sample, when it is based on a larger number of observations.

Nonsampling error
Error that arises in research and that is not due to sampling; nonsampling error can occur because of errors in conception, logic, interpretation of replies, statistics, arithmetic, tabulating, coding, or reporting.

Nonsampling errors reflect the many other kinds of error that arise in research, even when the survey is not based on a sample. They can be *random* or *nonrandom*. Nonrandom nonsampling errors are the more troublesome of the two. Random errors produce estimates that vary from the true value; sometimes these estimates are above and sometimes below the true value, but on a random basis. The result is that, if there are no sampling errors, the sample estimate will equal the population value. Nonrandom nonsampling errors, on the other hand, tend to produce mistakes only in one direction. They tend to bias the sample value away from the population parameter. Nonsampling errors can occur because of errors in conception, logic, interpretation of replies, statistics, arithmetic, tabulation, coding, or reporting. They are so pervasive that they caused one writer to lament:

> The roster of possible troubles seems only to grow with increasing knowledge. By participating in the work of a specific field, one can, in a few years, work up considerable methodological expertise, much of which has not been and is not likely to be written down. *To attempt to discuss every way a study can go wrong would be a hopeless venture.*[2] (Emphasis added.)

Not only are nonsampling errors pervasive, but they are not as manageable as sampling errors. Sampling errors decrease with increases in sample size. Nonsampling errors do not necessarily decrease with increases in sample size. They may, in fact, increase. Also, sampling errors can be estimated if probability sampling procedures are used. With nonsampling errors, it is difficult even to predict the direction, much less the size, of the error.

People may report different behaviors than they actually practice—a type of nonsampling error. In today's health-conscious society, some people might overstate their consumption of fresh fruit and vegetables or believe they are living healthier lifestyles than they actually are.

Source: © Roy Morsch/The Stock Market

True, nonsampling errors bias the sample value away from the population parameter, but in many studies it is hard to see whether they cause underestimation or overestimation of the parameter. Nonsampling errors also distort the reliability of sample estimates. The bias they cause may increase the error of estimates of particular statistics to such an extent that the confidence interval estimates turn out to be faulty.

One study, the Consumer Savings Project, conducted at the University of Illinois, demonstrated striking evidence of this phenomenon. In that study, researchers contrasted consumers' reports of financial assets and debts with known data.

> The empirical studies presented . . . indicate in striking fashion that nonsampling errors are not simply a matter of theory, but do in fact exist and are mainly responsible for the pronounced tendency of survey data to understate aggregates. . . . Not only was this bias present in the survey data, but in many instances the contribution of nonsampling errors to the total variance in the data was so large as to *render meaningless confidence intervals computed by the usual statistical formulas.* . . . The magnitude of this type of error tends, *if anything, to increase with sample size.*[3] (Emphasis added.)

Further, more sophisticated samples are not the answer to eliminating nonsampling errors.

> If the findings of this project are any indication, increasing attention must be given to the detection and correction of nonsampling errors. Such attention will be needed particularly in the conduct of large-scale, well-designed probability samples, for as the efficiency of a sample design increases and the size of sampling variances decreases, the effect of nonsampling errors becomes progressively more important. Since nonsampling variances are virtually unaffected by sample size, we are faced with the paradoxical situation that the more efficient is the sample design, the more important are nonsampling errors likely to be and the more meaningless are confidence interval computations based on the usual error formulas.[4]

In the University of Illinois study, the amount of nonsampling error could be calculated since the reports consumers gave of their financial assets and debts could be contrasted with actual data regarding their financial condition. But suppose such data were not available. Researchers may suspect that the responses they are eliciting are not accurate, but how are they to predict the direction of the error? Should they assume consumers are overstating their assets, for example, to impress the interviewer, or understating them for fear the IRS may get wind of the information? And if they are misrepresenting their assets, how is a researcher to determine the magnitude of this amount? Is it $10,000 over the real figure or $2,000 under? Or vice versa?

As you can begin to see, nonsampling errors are frequently the most important errors that arise in research. No responses from some and poor responses from others targeted for inclusion in a study, two types of nonsampling errors, can literally wreak havoc with survey results. In special Census Bureau investigations of their size, for example, nonsampling errors were found to be ten times the magnitude of sampling errors.[5] This is not an unusual finding. Rather, a consistent finding is that nonsampling error is the major contributor to total survey error, while random sampling error has minimal impact.[6] Nonsampling errors can be reduced, but their reduction depends on improving method rather than increasing sample size. By understanding the sources of nonsampling errors, the analyst is in a better position to reduce them.

Types of Nonsampling Errors

Nonobservation error

Nonsampling error that arises because of nonresponse from some elements designated for inclusion in the sample.

Observation error

Nonsampling error that arises because inaccurate information is secured from the sample elements or because errors are introduced in the processing of the data or in reporting the findings.

Figure 18.1 offers a general overview of nonsampling errors. They are of two basic types—errors due to nonobservation or to observation. **Nonobservation errors** result from a failure to obtain data from parts of the survey population. Nonobservation errors can happen because part of the population of interest was not included, or because some elements designated for inclusion in the sample did not respond.[7] According to an anecdote told by Marsh Faber, an executive for Hewlett-Packard, this type of problem plagued new-product research at an HP laboratory. A team of engineers, all of them men, were developing a switch to be used in manufacturing. To activate the switch, the production worker would move two mechanical arms together. The engineering team was reviewing a prototype of the switch when a female product engineer suggested that a woman try it out, since many users of the product would be women. The team invited the product engineer to try. Even after a struggle, she was unable to move the switch's arms together. The surprised engineers had to redesign the switch to make it usable by women, who on average have less upper-body strength than men.[8] In this situation, women were part of the population of interest (that is, potential users), and uncovering the design problem required adding a woman to the group of people evaluating the new product. **Observation errors** occur because inaccurate information is secured from the sample elements or because errors are introduced in the processing of the data or in reporting the findings. In many ways, they are more troublesome than nonobservation errors. With nonobservation errors, we at least know we have a problem because of noncoverage or nonresponse. With observation errors, we may not even be aware that a problem exists. The very notion of an

FIGURE 18.1   **Overview of Nonsampling Errors**

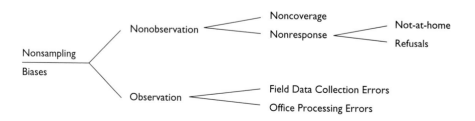

observation error rests on the presumption that there is indeed some "true" value for the variable or variables. An observation error, then, is simply the difference between the reported value and the "true" value. You can readily see that detection of an observation error places the researcher in the awkward position of knowing the very quantity the study is designed to estimate.

Nonobservation Errors

As is evident from Figure 18.1, there are two types of nonobservation errors: noncoverage errors and nonresponse errors. Each is capable of introducing significant bias in the results of a study, but analysts skilled enough to recognize the potential problem have several options for compensating for, or adjusting for, possible error.

Noncoverage error

Nonsampling error that arises because of a failure to include some units, or entire sections, of the defined target population in the sampling frame.

Noncoverage Errors A source of significant error in a study can be noncoverage, but **noncoverage error** does not refer to sections of a population that are deliberately excluded from the survey, but to those that were mistakenly excluded. Noncoverage, then, is essentially a sampling frame problem.

Researchers realize that the telephone directory, for instance, does not provide a complete sampling frame for most general surveys. Not every family has a phone, and not all those people who have telephones have their numbers listed in the directory. Further, some variation exists between those having and not having phones in terms of certain important demographic characteristics. These conditions are compounded for fax surveys of the general population. They are less of a problem, though not eliminated, in surveys of businesses or other institutions.

Noncoverage is also a problem in mail and e-mail surveys. The mailing and e-mail lists dictate the sampling frame. If the lists inadequately represent segments of the population, the survey will also suffer from the bias of noncoverage, and rare is the mailing list or list of e-mail addresses that exactly captures the population that the researcher wishes to study, even though mailing lists are available for very specific population groups, as Exhibit 18.1 indicates.

When the data are to be collected by personal interview in the home, some form of area sample is typically used to pinpoint respondents. In this case, the sampling frame is one of areas, blocks, and dwelling units, rather than a list of respondents. However, this does not eliminate the incomplete frame problem. Maps of the city may not be totally current, and so the newest areas may not have a proper chance of being included in the sample. The instructions to the interviewer may not be sufficiently detailed. The direction, "Start at the northwest corner of the selected blocks, generate a random start, and take every fifth dwelling unit thereafter," may be inadequate to handle those blocks with a number of apartment units. The evidence indicates, for example, that lower-income households are avoided when the selection of households is made by the field staff rather than the home office. Further, interviewers typically select the most accessible individuals within the household, contrary to instructions for random selection. This again means that a portion of the intended population is underrepresented in the study, while the accessible segment is overrepresented.

There are also sampling frame problems when personal interviews in shopping malls are to be used to collect the data. For one thing, there is no list of population elements. Rather, only those who shop in a particular mall have a chance of being included in the study, and their chances of being included depend on how often they shop there. That is why quota samples are often used in mall intercept studies.

However, noncoverage bias is not eliminated in quota samples, whether conducted in a mall or elsewhere. Rather, the interviewers' flexibility in choosing respondents can open the door to substantial noncoverage bias. Interviewers typically underselect in both the high- and low-income classes. The research director may not discover this bias, since field staffers also have a tendency to falsify characteristics so that it appears that they interviewed the appropriate number of cases per cell. Further, the more elaborate and complex the quota sample, the more critical this "forcing" problem becomes. With three or

EXHIBIT 18.1 Some Population Groups for Which Mailing Lists Are Available

Quantity		Price
12,900	Babies' Wear Retail	$45/M
800	Bagel Shops	$85
30,200	Bakeries, Retail	$45/M
2,400	Bakery Products Mfrs	$45/M
600	Ballet/Dance Companies	$85
2,450	Balloon (Hot Air) Owners	$45/M
10,500	Band Directors, High School	$45/M
16,100	Bankers, Mortgage, Executives	$45/M
4,100	Bankers, Mortgage, Firms	$45/M
Banks		
13,790	Banks, Main Offices	$45/M
324	Banks with Assets $1 Billion or more	$85
538	Banks with Assets $500 Million or more	$85
1,278	Banks with Assets $200 Million or more	$85
3,582	Bank with Assets $75 Million or more	$45/M
8,835	Banks with Assets $25 Million or more	$45/M
12,400	Banks with Assets $10 Million or more	$45/M
13,245	Banks with Assets $5 Million or more	$45/M
200	Banks with Assets less than $5 Million	$85
40,100	Banks, Branches	$45/M
20,000	Banks, Cashiers	$45/M
209,600	Banks, Executives	$45/M
66,700	Banks, Executives, Women	$45/M
3,490	Banks, Savings & Loans (HQ)	$45/M
16,800	Banks, Savings & Loans (Branches)	$45/M
6,000	Banks, Trust Officers	$45/M
11,030	Banks, Loan Offices	$45/M
243	Bankruptcy, Judges	$85
8,400	Barber & Beauty Supplies	$45/M
64,200	Barber Shops	$45/M
81,900	Bars, Taverns, Cocktail Lounges	$45/M
2,800	Beauty Schools	$45/M
200,000	Beauty Shops	$45/M
315	Beekeepers	$85
90	Beer Brewers	$85
11,900	Beer Distributors	$45/M
37,000	Behavioral Scientists	$45/M

Quantity		Price
170	Better Business Bureaus	$85
4,000	Beverage Bottlers & Distributors	$45/M
26,000	Beverage Industry Executives	$45/M
11,700	Bicycle Dealers & Repairs	$45/M
2,500	Billiard Parlors & Poolrooms	$45/M
1,380	Billion Dollar Companies	$85
5,700	Biological Chemists	$45/M
23,700	Biologists	$45/M
3,900	Birth Control Centers	$45/M
6,400,000	Black Families	Inquire
4,600	Blood Banks	$45/M
3,000,000	Blue Collar Workers	Inquire
Boats		
5,250	Boat Basins (Marinas)	$45/M
12,350	Boat Dealers	$45/M
21,000	Boat & Marine Supplies	$45/M
567,400	Boat Owners (Select by Type, Length, Power)	$50/M
10,000	Boat Yards, Building & Repairing	$45/M
14,000	Boards of Education	$45/M
67,700	Body & Top Repair, Automobile	$45/M
5,000	Boiler Contractors	$45/M
135	Book Clubs	$85
6,300	Book Publishers	$45/M
1,725	Book Publishers (Major)	$85
850	Book Wholesalers	$85
24,000	Bookkeeping Services	$45/M
20,100	Bookstores	$45/M
588	Bookstores, Chains	$85
3,100	Bookstores, College	$45/M
3,300	Bookstores, Religious	$45/M
132	Botanical Gardens	$85
2,700	Botanists	$45/M
2,600	Bottlers, Soft Drink	$45/M
4,600	Boutiques	$45/M
7,500	Bowling Alleys	$45/M
6,000	Box & Container Mfrs	$45/M

Source: Zeller List Corp., 15 East 26th Street, New York, NY 10010. Reprinted with permission.

four variables defining the individual cells, the interviewer may find it difficult to locate respondents who have all the prescribed characteristics, so he or she may "cheat" a little bit on the characteristics defining difficult cells to fill.

Overcoverage error
Nonsampling error that arises because of the duplication of elements in the list of sampling units.

Overcoverage error can arise because of duplication in the list of sampling units. Units with multiple entries in the sampling frame—for example, families with several phone listings—have a higher probability of being included in the sample than do sampling units with one listing. For most surveys, though, noncoverage is much more common and troublesome than overcoverage.

Noncoverage bias is not a problem in every survey. For some studies, clear, convenient, and complete sampling frames exist. For example, the department store wishing to conduct a study among its charge-account customers should have little trouble with frame bias. The sampling frame is simply those with charge accounts. There might be some difficulty in distinguishing active accounts from inactive accounts, but this problem can be addressed during the design stage of the study.

Similarly, the credit union in a firm should experience little noncoverage bias in conducting a study among its potential clientele. The population of interest here would be the firm's employees, and it could be expected that the list of employees would be current and accurate since it is needed to generate the payroll.

Noncoverage bias raises two questions for the researcher: (1) How pervasive is it likely to be? (2) What can be done to reduce it? One difficulty is that its magnitude can be estimated only by comparing the sample survey results with some outside criterion. The outside criterion can in turn be established through an auxiliary quality check of a portion of the results, or it may be available from another reliable and current study, such as the population census. Comparison with the census or another large sample, though, means that the basic sampling units must be similar in terms of operational definitions. If researchers plan to make such comparisons, they may want to plan the study in such a way that the bases used (e.g., dwellings or persons) lend themselves to effective comparisons.

Given that noncoverage bias is likely, what can the researcher do to lessen its effect? The most obvious step, of course, is to improve the quality of the sampling frame. This may mean taking the time to bring available city maps up to date, or it may mean taking a sample to check the quality and representativeness of a mailing list with respect to a target population. The unlisted-number problem common to telephone surveys can be handled by random-digit or plus-one dialing, although this will not provide adequate sample representation of those without phones.

There are usually limits to the degree to which an imperfect sampling frame can be improved. Once these limits are reached, the researcher can attempt to reduce noncoverage bias still further through the selection of sampling units or the adjustment of the results. When sampling from lists, for example, analysts often encounter the problem that unwanted ineligibles and duplicates are included on the list, while some members of the target population are excluded. The first corrective step for this problem is to update the list, using supplementary sources if possible. While this would help reduce one aspect of the problem (excluded members), it might do little to eliminate ineligibles and duplicates. When the sample is drawn, however, all ineligibles can be ignored. Beware of the temptation to substitute the next name on the list, since this would bias selection toward those elements that follow ineligible listings. The correct procedure is to draw another element randomly, if simple random selection procedures are being used. If systematic sampling procedures are being used, the sampling interval should be adjusted before the fact to allow for the percentage of ineligibles.

The problem of duplicates is handled by adjustment. Specifically, the results are weighted by the inverse of the probability of selection. In a study using a list of car registrations, for example, each contracted respondent would be asked, "How many cars do you own?" The response of someone who said two would be weighted by $\frac{1}{2}$, while that of someone who said three would be weighted by $\frac{1}{3}$.[9]

The appropriate sampling and adjustment procedures to account for inadequate sampling frames can become quite technical in complex sample designs and fall largely in the domain of the sampling specialist. We shall consequently not delve into these processes but shall simply note that noncoverage bias

1. Is a nonsampling error and is therefore not dealt with in the standard statistical formulas.

2. Is *not* likely to be eliminated by increasing the sample size.

3. Can be of considerable magnitude.

4. Can be reduced, but not necessarily eliminated, by recognizing its existence, working to improve the sampling frame, and employing a sampling specialist to help reduce,

through the sampling procedure, and adjust, through analysis, the remaining frame imperfections.

Nonresponse error

Nonsampling error that represents a failure to obtain information from some elements of the population that were selected and designated for the sample.

Nonresponse Errors Another source of nonobservation bias is **nonresponse error,** which represents a failure to obtain information from some elements of the population that were selected and designated for the sample. The first hurdle to overcome in dealing with nonresponse errors is simply anticipating all the things that can go wrong with an attempt to contact a designated respondent. Figure 18.2, for example, depicts the various outcomes of an attempted telephone contact. There is such a bewildering array of alternatives that even calculating a measure of the extent of the nonresponse problem becomes difficult.

In the late 1970s, several researchers became concerned that the marketing research industry had no uniform standard for measuring rates of response and nonresponse. Because the various research organizations used widely differing definitions and methods for calculating nonresponse, it was impossible to get an accurate assessment of the nonresponse problem. In an attempt to get a handle on the problem, the researchers conducted a study among a sample of members of the Council of American Survey Research Organizations (CASRO) and leading user companies. Each member was mailed a questionnaire that displayed actual contact and response data from three different telephone surveys—a telephone directory sample, a random-digit sample, and a list sample. Respondents were asked to calculate the response, contact, completion, and refusal rates for each of the three surveys.[10] (Each of these rates is defined later in this chapter.) The difference in results was rather startling. The upper part of Exhibit 18.2 displays the raw data from the telephone directory sample. Using the very same data, one responding organization reported the **response rate**—which is the number of interviews divided by the number of contacts—as 12 percent, while another reported 90 percent. Nor was there agreement among the other firms. No more than 3 firms out of 40 agreed on any single de-

Response rate

The number of completed interviews with responding units divided by the number of eligible responding units in the sample.

FIGURE 18.2 **Possible Outcomes When Attempting to Contact Respondents for Telephone Surveys**

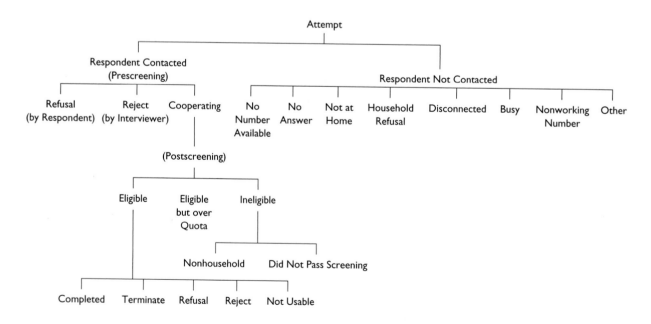

Source: Frederick Wiseman and Philip McDonald, *Toward the Development of Industry Standards for Response and Nonresponse Rates* (Cambridge, Mass.: Marketing Science Institute, 1980), p. 29. Reprinted with permission. American Marketing Association.

EXHIBIT 18.2	**Response Rate Calculations for Telephone Directory Sample**

Panel A: Outcome of Telephone Call

Disconnected/nonworking telephone number	426
Household refusal	153
No answer, busy, not at home	1,757
Interviewer reject (language barrier, hard of hearing . . .)	187
Respondent refusal	711
Ineligible respondent	366
Termination by respondent	74
Completed interview	501
Total	4,175

Panel B: Most Frequent, Minimum, and Maximum Response Rates

Most frequent

$$\frac{\text{Household refusals} + \text{Rejects} + \text{Refusals} + \text{Ineligibles} + \text{Terminations} + \text{Completed interviews}}{\text{All}} = \qquad (1)$$

$$\frac{153 + 187 + 711 + 366 + 74 + 501}{4,175} = 48\%$$

$$\frac{\text{Rejects} + \text{Refusals} + \text{Ineligibles} + \text{Terminations} + \text{Completed interviews}}{\text{All}} = \qquad (2)$$

$$\frac{187 + 711 + 366 + 74 + 501}{4,175} = 44\%$$

$$\frac{\text{Completed interviews}}{\text{All}} = \frac{501}{4,175} = 12\% \qquad (3)$$

Minimum

$$\frac{\text{Completed interviews}}{\text{All}} = \frac{501}{4,175} = 12\%$$

Maximum

$$\frac{\text{Refusals} + \text{Ineligibles} + \text{Termination} + \text{Completed interviews}}{\text{Rejects} + \text{Refusals} + \text{Ineligibles} + \text{Termination} + \text{Completed interviews}} =$$

$$\frac{711 + 366 + 74 + 501}{187 + 711 + 366 + 74 + 501} = 90\%$$

Source: Frederick Wiseman and Philip McDonald, *Toward the Development of Industry Standards for Response and Nonresponse Rates* (Cambridge, Mass.: Marketing Science Institute, 1980), pp. 12 and 19. Reprinted with permission. See also M. A. Hidiroglu, J.D. Drew, and G. B. Gray, "A Framework for Measuring and Reducing Nonresponse in Surveys," *Survey Methodology* 19 (1993), pp. 81–94.

finition of the response rate, and those firms used three different definitions to arrive at their answers. The lower part of Exhibit 18.2 displays the three most frequently used definitions and the definitions producing the minimum and maximum response rates.

Not only does the variation in definitions cause confusion when nonresponse rates are reported for a survey, but it also makes the treatment of the nonresponse error problem more difficult. It becomes hard to discern, for instance, whether a particular method proved effective, or whether a different definition was responsible for a lower nonresponse error in a particular study. In an attempt to standardize findings to improve the practice of survey research, a special CASRO task force developed the following definition of response rate that the industry is being encouraged to embrace as the standard definition:[11]

$$\text{response rate} = \frac{\text{number of completed interviews with responding units}}{\text{number of eligible responding units in the sample}}$$

The key requirement in accurately calculating the response rate is to properly handle eligibles. Exhibit 18.3 shows how to calculate the response rate properly depending on whether there is or is not an eligibility requirement for inclusion in the sample.

Nonresponse is a problem in any survey in which it occurs because it raises the question of whether those who did respond are different in some important way from those who did not respond. This is, or course, a question we cannot answer, although study af-

---

EXHIBIT 18.3   The Impact of an Eligibility Requirement on the Calculation of the Response Rate

Example 1. Single-Stage Sample, No Eligibility Requirement

Suppose a survey is conducted to obtain 1,000 interviews with subscribers of a particular magazine. A random sample of $n = 1,000$ is selected, and the initial data collection effort produces the following results:

Complete interviews	= 660
Refusals	= 115
Respondents not contacted	= 225

For each of the 340 nonrespondents, substitute subscribers are selected until a completed interview is obtained. Assume that in this follow-up data collection effort 600 substitute names are required to secure the 340 interviews. The recommended response rate is

$$660/1,000 = 66.0\%$$

and not

$$1,000/1,600 = 62.5\%.$$

Example 2. Single-Stage Sample, Eligibility Requirement

From a list of registered voters, a sample of $n = 900$ names is selected. Eligible respondents are defined as those planning to vote in an upcoming election. Assume the data collection effort produces the following results:

Completed interviews	= 300
Not contacted	= 250
Refused, eligibility not determined	= 150
Ineligible	= 200

The recommended response rate is

$$\frac{300}{300 + \left[\dfrac{300}{300 + 200}\right](250 + 150)} = \frac{300}{300 + 240} = 55.5\%$$

As indicated, when using an eligibility requirement one first must estimate the number of eligibles among the nonrespondents. This is done by using the eligibility percentage, $(330/500) = 60\%$, obtained among persons successfully screened and applying this percentage to the nonrespondents. Thus, of the 400 nonrespondents, 60% (240) are estimated to have been eligible and the estimated response rate becomes 300/540, or 55.5%.

Source: Frederick Wiseman and Maryann Billington, "Comment on a Standard Definition of Response Rates," *Journal of Marketing Research* 21 (August 1984), p. 337. Reprinted from *Journal of Marketing Research*, published by the American Marketing Association, Chicago, IL 60606.

ter study has indicated that the assumption that those who did not respond were in fact equal to those who did is risky.

The two main sources of nonresponse bias are not-at-homes and refusals. Nonresponse bias can arise with studies using personal interviews, telephone, or mail surveys to secure the data. With mail surveys, though, the not-at-home problem becomes one of nonreceipt of the questionnaire. The questionnaire may simply have been lost in the mail, in which case the nonsampling error could be considered random and nonbiasing, or there may be more fundamental reasons for nonreceipt: the addressee may have moved or died. These latter conditions would be a source of systematic nonsampling error.

Not-at-homes

Nonsampling error that arises when replies are not secured from some designated sampling units because the respondents are not at home when the interviewer calls.

Not-at-Homes Replies will not be secured from some designated sampling units because the respondents will not be at home when the interviewer calls. The empirical evidence indicates that the percentage of **not-at-homes** has been increasing for a long time. Obviously, much depends upon the nature of the designated respondent and the time of the call. Married women with young children are more apt to be at home during the day on weekdays than are men, married women without children, or single women. The probability of finding someone home is also greater for low-income families and for rural families. Seasonal variations, particularly during the holidays, occur, as do weekday-to-weekend variations.[12] Further, it is much easier to find a "responsible adult" at home than a specific respondent, and thus the choice of the elementary sampling unit is key in the not-at-home problem.

Several things can be done to reduce the incidence of not-at-homes. For example, in some studies the interviewer might make an appointment in advance with the respondent. Although this approach is particularly valuable in surveys of busy executives, it may not be justifiable in an ordinary consumer survey. A commonly used technique in the latter instance is the callback, which is particularly effective if the callback (preferably callbacks) is made at a different time than the original call. As a matter of fact, the nonresponse problem due to not-at-homes is so acute and so important to the accuracy of most surveys that one leading expert has suggested that small samples with four to six callbacks are more efficient than large samples without callbacks, unless the percentage of initial response can be increased considerably above normal levels.[13] Some data indicate, for example, that four to five calls are often needed to reach three-fourths of the sample of households (see Exhibit 18.4).

| EXHIBIT 18.4 | Percentage of Sample Homes Reached with Each Call in Personal Interview and Telephone Surveys |

	PERSONAL INTERVIEW		TELEPHONE	
Call	Percent	Cumulative Percent	Percent	Cumulative Percent
1	25	25	24	24
2	25	50	18	42
3	18	68	14	56
4	11	79	11	67
5	7	86	8	75
6	5	91	6	81
7	3	94	5	86
8	6	100	3	89[a]

[a]It took 17 calls to reach all the homes in the telephone survey.
Source:Robert M. Groves and Robert L. Kahn, *Surveys by Telephone* (Orlando, Fla: Academic Press, 1979), pp. 56 and 58.

An alternative to the *straight callback* is the *modified callback*. If the initial contact attempt and first few callbacks were made by an interviewer and a contact was not established, the interviewer might simply mail a self-administered questionnaire with a stamped, self-addressed envelope (or leave one at the door if an in-person survey is being made). If the not-at-home is simply a "designated-respondent-absent" rather than a "nobody-at-home," the interviewer can use the opportunity to inquire about the respondent's hours of availability.

One technique that is sometimes naively suggested for handling the not-at-homes is to substitute the neighboring dwelling unit or, in a telephone survey, to call the next name on the list. This is a very poor way of handling the not-at-home condition. All it does is substitute more at-homes (who may be different from the not-at-homes in a number of important characteristics) for the population segment the interviewer is in fact trying to reach. This increases the proportion of at-homes in the sample and, in effect, aggravates the problem instead of solving it.

The proportion of reported not-at-homes is likely to depend on the interviewer's skill and the judgment used in scheduling initial contacts and callbacks. This suggests that one way of reducing not-at-home nonresponse bias is by better interviewer training, particularly with respect to how to schedule callbacks more efficiently.

The fact that interviewer effectiveness affects the number of not-at-homes also suggests one measure by which interviewers themselves can be compared and evaluated: by calculating the **contact rate (K),** which is the percentage of the eligible assignments in which the interviewer makes contact with the designated respondent; that is,

Contact rate(*K*)
A measure used to evaluate and compare the effectiveness of interviewers in making contact with designated respondents; *K* = number of sample units contacted divided by total number of eligible sample units approached.

$$K = \frac{\text{number of sample units contacted}}{\text{total number of eligible sample units approached}}$$

The contact rate measures the interviewer's persistence. Interviewers can be compared with respect to their contact rates, and corrective measures can often be taken on that basis. The field supervisor may want to investigate the reasons for any individual interviewer's low contact rate. Perhaps this interviewer is operating in a traditionally high not-at-home area, such as a high-income section of an urban area. Alternatively, by examining the call reports for the time of each call, the trouble may be traced to poor follow-up procedures. This condition would suggest additional training is necessary, which might then be provided by the field supervisor while the study is still in progress. The contact rate can also be used to evaluate an entire study with respect to the potential nonresponse caused by not-at-homes.

Not-at-home nonresponse bias can also be addressed by statistical adjustment of the results using a scheme developed by Politz and Simmons.[14] Rather than relying on callbacks, their scheme depends on a single attempted contact with each sample member at a randomly determined time. During this contact, the respondent is asked if he or she was at home at the time of the interview for the five preceding days. These five answers and the time of the interview provide information on the time the respondent was at home for six different days. The responses from each informant are then weighted by the reciprocal of their self-reported probability of being at home; for example, the answers of a respondent who was at home one out of six times would receive a weight of six. The basic rationale is that people who are usually not at home are more difficult to catch for an interview and therefore will tend to be underrepresented in the survey. Consequently, the less a subject reports being at home, the more that subject's responses should be weighted.

Refusals In almost every study, some respondents will refuse to participate. In one of the most extensive investigations of the magnitude of this problem, 46 field research companies sponsored a study called "Your Opinion Counts," which involved almost 1.4 million phone and personal interviews. The study indicated that 38 percent of the people asked to participate declined to do so, with 86 percent of those people refusing to participate before or during the introduction. The rest of those who declined broke away before the survey was completed.[15] Research Window 18.1 depicts what is happening to refusal rates in general and some of the major reasons respondents give for having refused to participate in surveys.

Panel A: Percentage of Those Contacted Who Had Refused to Participate
in a Survey in the Past Year

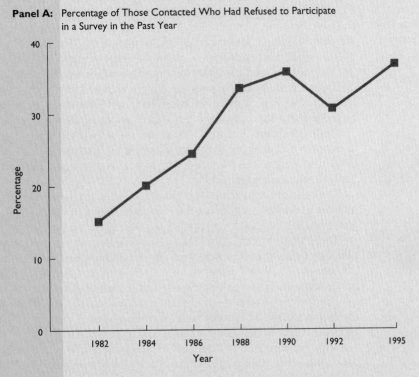

Panel B: Reasons Given for Having Refused to Participate*

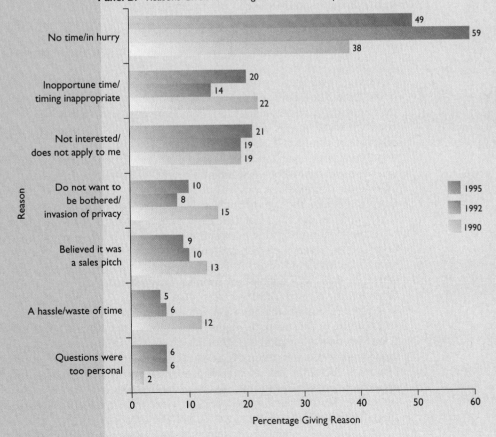

Source: *Respondent Cooperation and Industry Image Survey* (Port Jefferson, N.Y.: The Council for Marketing and Opinion Research, 1996), pp. 36–37.

Refusals

Nonsampling error that arises because some designated respondents refuse to participate in the study.

The rate of **refusals** depends, among other things, on the nature of the respondent, the nature of the organization sponsoring the research, the circumstances surrounding the contact, the nature of the subject under investigation, and the skill of the interviewer. Even the culture of the country can affect the refusal rate. For example, in some cultures like Saudi Arabia, it is nearly impossible to interview women.

The method used to collect the data also makes a difference. The empirical evidence indicates, for example, that personal interviews are most effective, and mail questionnaires least effective, in generating response. Telephone interviews are somewhat less successful on the average than personal interviews in getting target respondents to cooperate.

Although different data collection techniques will influence the types of people likely to cooperate in a survey, there does seem to be a tendency for females, nonwhites, and those who are less well educated, who have lower incomes, and who are older to be more likely to refuse to participate.[16]

The type of organization sponsoring the research can also make a difference in the number of refusals. People not only report differently to different sponsors, but they may also make their decision on whether to respond on the basis of who the sponsor is.

Sometimes the circumstances surrounding the contact can cause a refusal. A respondent may be busy, tired, or sick when contacted. And the subject of the research also affects the refusal rate. Those interested in the subject are most likely to respond. On the other hand, nonresponse tends to increase with the sensitivity of the information being sought.

Finally, interviewers themselves can have a significant impact on the number of refusals they obtain. Their approach, manner, and even their own demographic characteristics can affect a respondent's willingness to participate.

What can be done to correct the nonresponse bias introduced when designated respondents refuse their participation? There seem to be three available strategies:

1. The initial response rate can be increased.

2. The impact of refusals can be reduced through follow-up.

3. The obtained information can be extrapolated to allow for nonresponse.

Increasing Initial Response Rate   Improving the circumstances surrounding an interview or increasing the training of interviewers are logical ways to increase the response rate, but the nature of the respondent would seem to be one factor strictly beyond the researcher's control. After all, the problem dictates the target population, and this population is likely to contain households with different education levels, income levels, cultural and occupational backgrounds, and so forth. However, the task is not as hopeless as it might seem. As will be shown later when we examine a model for interviewer-interviewee interaction, the interviewee's cooperation can be encouraged by an "appropriate choice" of interviewer. Cooperation can also be encouraged by convincing respondents of the value of the research and the importance of their participation. Advance notice may help, too.

If the identification of the organization sponsoring the research is likely to increase nonresponse, researchers can overcome this bias by concealing that information or by hiring a professional research organization to conduct the field study. This is one reason why companies with established, sophisticated research departments of their own sometimes employ research firms to collect data.

Evidence suggests that the more information interviewers provide about the content and purpose of the survey, the higher the response rate will be in both personal and telephone interviews. A guarantee of confidentiality will secure further responses, since some individuals refuse to participate because they do not wish to be identified with their responses. Moreover, the research suggests that monetary incentives are effective in increasing response rates in mail surveys.[17] Interestingly, they are not effective when personal interviews are being used, except when the interviewing is being conducted at shopping malls.

The ability to generalize what might happen if a particular inducement technique is used to increase the cooperation rate in a survey is clouded by the fact that the effects are different from survey to survey. When one looks across surveys, the picture becomes somewhat clearer, even though the many review articles do not completely agree on the impact of various response inducement techniques. This is due partially to the articles and time periods included in their reviews.[18] The results of one of the most extensive reviews of mail-survey response involvement techniques are shown in Figure 18.3. The average effect of the facilitation technique is shown by the weighted correlation coefficient across studies where the weights reflect the size of the various samples on which the individual correlations were based. The larger the weighted mean correlation, the more

FIGURE 18.3   **Impact of Selected Response Inducement Technique on Mail Survey Response Rates**

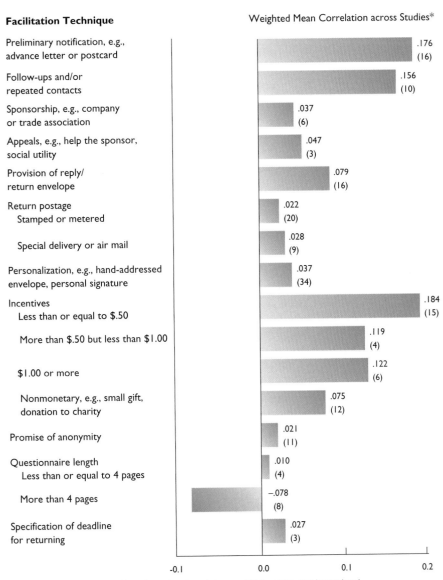

*The numbers shown in brackets indicate the number of correlations on which the average correlation is based.

Source: Developed from the inforamtion in Frances J. Yammarino, Steven J. Skinner, and Terry L. Childers, "Understanding Mail Survey Response Behavior: A Meta-Analysis," *Public Opinion Quarterly* 55 (Winter 1991), pp. 613–639. Reprinted with permission University of Chicago Press.

impact the particular facilitation technique has. The results in Figure 18.3 indicate that, on average, the most successful response inducement techniques in mail surveys are the use of incentives, preliminary notification that the survey is coming, and follow-ups or repeated mailings.

Increasing Response Rate by Follow-up   In some cases, the circumstances surrounding a contact are responsible for a respondent's refusal to participate. Since these circumstances may be temporary or changeable, follow-up actions may elicit a later response and thus increase the overall response rate. If a respondent declined participation because he or she was busy or sick, a callback at a different time or using a different approach may be enough to secure cooperation. In a mail survey, this may mean a follow-up mailing at a more convenient time. The key to the success of this follow-up may be appropriate training and control of the field staff.

Less can be done with the subject of the research itself if it is the source of nonresponse bias, since it is dictated by the problem to be solved. A sensitive research subject or one of little interest to the respondents is likely to elicit a high rate of refusals. However, the researcher should not overlook any opportunities for making the study more interesting—for example, by eliminating unnecessary questions.

If a respondent has refused to participate in a personal interview or a telephone survey for reasons other than circumstances, callbacks will be less successful. This is not so with mail surveys. Frequently responses are obtained with the second and third mailings from those who did not respond to the initial mailing. Of course, follow-up in a mail survey requires identification of those not responding earlier, which in turn requires identification of those who did respond, and we have already seen that reluctance to be identified may cause a refusal. Thus, identification of the respondents, which may serve to decrease one source of nonresponse, may increase another. The alternative, which is to send each new mailing to each designated sample member without screening those who have responded previously, can be expensive for the research organization and frustrating for the respondent.

Adjusting Results to Correct for Nonresponse   A third strategy for treating nonresponse bias involves estimating its effects and then adjusting the results.[19] Suppose that in estimating the mean income for some population, one secured responses from only a portion (p_r) of some designated sample. The proportion not responding could then be denoted p_{nr}. If $\bar{x}_r$ is the mean income of those responding, and $\bar{x}_{nr}$ the mean income of those *not* responding, then the overall mean would be

$$\bar{x} = p_r\bar{x}_r + p_{nr}\bar{x}_{nr}$$

This computation, of course, assumes that $\bar{x}_{nr}$ is known or at least can be estimated. An intensive follow-up of a sample of the nonrespondents is sometimes used to generate this estimate. The follow-up may be a modified callback (described earlier). While this rarely generates a response from each nonrespondent designated for the follow-up, it does allow a crude adjustment of the initial results. Ignoring the initial nonresponse is equivalent to assuming that $\bar{x}_{nr}$ is equal to $\bar{x}_r$, which is usually incorrect.

A second way to adjust the results is to keep track of those responding to the initial contact, the first follow-up, the second follow-up, and so on. The mean of the variable (or other appropriate statistic) is then calculated, and each subgroup is compared to determine whether any statistically significant differences emerge as a function of the difficulty experienced in making contact. If not, the variable mean for the nonrespondents is assumed equal to the mean for those responding. If a discernible trend is evident, the trend is extrapolated to allow for nonrespondents. This method is particularly valuable in mail surveys, where it is an easy task to identify those responding to the first mailing, the second mailing, and so on.

Evidence accumulated in past surveys also sometimes serves as the basis of the adjustment for nonresponse. Organizations that frequently conduct surveys using similar sampling procedures find this approach particularly useful. While no method of adjustment is perfect, any of them is better than assuming that nonrespondents are similar to respondents on the characteristics of interest. Yet this is the very assumption we make if no attempt is made to correct for nonresponse.

Item Nonresponse   The preceding discussions all deal with *total nonresponse. Item nonresponse,* which can also be a problem, occurs when the respondent agrees to the total interview but refuses, or is unable, to answer some specific questions because of the content or form of the questions, or the amount of work required to produce the requested information. As we discussed earlier, researchers usually attempt to address these problems when developing the questionnaire and planning the methods for administering it. Sometimes, however, item nonresponses occur in spite of researchers' best efforts to avoid them.

Whether anything can then be done about item nonresponse depends on its magnitude. Here we must distinguish between flagrant item nonresponse and isolated or sporadic nonresponse. If too many questions are left unanswered, the reply becomes unusable, and the treatment, or at least adjustment, is the same as that for a complete nonresponse. On the other hand, if only a few items are left unanswered on any questionnaire, the reply can often be made usable. At the very minimum, the "don't know" and "no answers" can be treated as separate categories when reporting the results. In many ways this is the best strategy because the little evidence that is available on item nonresponse suggests that the problem is extensive and nonrandom. Alternatively, the information from the missing item or items can sometimes be inferred from other information in the questionnaire. This is especially true if there are other questions on the questionnaire that relate to the same issue. The other questions are checked, and a consistent answer is formulated for the unanswered item. In the absence of such consistency checks, the statistical technique known as *regression analysis,* which measures the relationship between two or more variables, is sometimes used. The missing item is treated as the criterion variable, and the functional relationship is established between it and a priori related questions through regression analysis for those cases for which the item was answered. The equation is then used to estimate a response for the remaining questionnaires given the information they contain on the predictor variables.

Finally, a third way by which item nonresponse is handled is by substituting the average response for the item of those who did respond. This technique, of course, carries the assumption that those who did not respond to the item are similar to those who did. As we have suggested many times, this assumption may be risky, and therefore substituting the average should be done with caution.

Response Rates versus Completeness Rate   Just as the contact rate can be used to compare and evaluate interviewers with respect to not-at-homes, at least two ratios have been suggested for comparing interviewers with respect to refusals: the response rate, R, and the **completeness rate, C.** As explained earlier, the response rate equals the ratio of the number of completed interviews with responding units divided by the number of eligible responding units in the sample. The response rate reflects the interviewer's effectiveness at the door or on the phone.

The completeness rate applies to the individual items in the study. Most typically it will be used to evaluate interviewers with respect to the crucial questions involved in the study, for example, a respondent's income, debt, or asset position, although it can also be used to evaluate the whole contact. The completeness rate simply determines whether the response is complete or not, either with respect to the crucial questions or the whole questionnaire.

Completeness rate (C)
A measure used to evaluate and compare interviewers with respect to their ability to secure needed information from contacted respondents; the completeness rate measures the proportion of complete contacts by interviewer.

Observation Errors

Observation errors, defined earlier, may be more insidious than nonobservation errors, since the research analyst may not even be aware that they exist.

Field Error
Nonsampling error that arises during the actual collection of the data.

Field Errors   By far the most prevalent type of observation error is the **field error,** which arises after the individual has agreed to participate in a study. Instead of cooperating fully, the individual refuses to answer specific questions or provides an untruthful response. These errors have been referred to, respectively, as *errors of omission* and *errors of commission.*[20] In the preceding section we discussed errors of omission and item nonresponse. Now we wish to turn our attention to errors of commission, which are usually categorized as response errors.

When considering response errors, it is useful to keep in mind what occurs when respondents answer questions. First, they need to understand what is being asked. Second, they need to engage in a reasoning process to arrive at an answer. Typically, the respondent will try to assess the information needed for an accurate answer and then remember the attitudes, facts, or experiences that would be relevant to the question. He or she will then try to organize a response based on this information. Third, respondents need to evaluate the response in terms of its accuracy. Fourth, they need to evaluate the response in terms of other goals they might have, such as preserving their self-image or attempting to please the interviewer. Finally, they need to put into words the response that results from all this mental processing. Reaching the final step is the object of the survey process. However, breakdowns can occur at any of the preceding steps, resulting in an inaccurate answer—a response error.

The factors that can cause response errors are so numerous that they almost defy categorization. One seemingly useful scheme for dealing with data collection errors, though, is the interviewer-interviewee interaction model proposed by Kahn and Cannell (Figure 18.4).[21] The model suggests several things. First, each person brings certain background characteristics and psychological predispositions to the interview. While some of the background characteristics (such as age and sex) are readily observable, others are not, nor can the psychological state of the other person be seen. Yet both interviewer and in-

FIGURE 18.4   **A Model of Bias in the Interview**

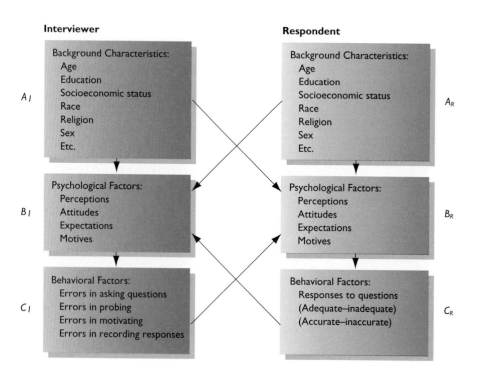

Source: Robert L. Kahn and Charles F. Cannell, *The Dynamics of Interviewing* (New York: John Wiley and Sons, Inc., © 1957), p. 193. See also Wendy Sykes and Martin Collins, "Anatomy of the Survey Interview," *Journal of Official Statistics* 8 (No. 3, 1992), pp. 277–291.

terviewee will form some attitudes toward, and expectations of, the other person on the basis of their initial perceptions. Second, the interview is an interactive process, and both interviewer and interviewee are important determinants of the process. Each party perceives and reacts to the specific behaviors of the other. Note, though, that there is no direct link between the boxes labeled behavior. Rather, the linkage is more complicated, "involving a behavior on the part of the interviewer or respondent, the perception of this behavior by the other principal in the interview, a cognitive or attitudinal development from that perception, and finally a resultant motivation to behave in a certain way. Only at this point is a behavioral act carried out, which in turn may be perceived by and reacted to by the other participant in the interview."[22]

The perceptions of this behavior may not be correct, just as the initial perceptions of each party may be in error. Nevertheless, such inferences will inevitably be made as both interviewer and respondent search for cues to help them understand each other and carry out the requirements imposed by the interview situation. In sum, not only do the specific behaviors of each party to the interaction affect the outcome, but so do the background characteristics and psychological predispositions of both interviewer and respondent.

The interviewer-interviewee interaction model is appealing for several reasons. One, it is consistent with the empirical evidence. Two, it offers some valuable insight on how response errors (as well as nonresponse errors due to refusals) can potentially be reduced. The model also applies to telephone and mail surveys, thereby further increasing its value. For example, the respondent's perceptions of the background characteristics and behavior of a telephone interviewer will likely affect the answers he or she provides. The respondent's background is certainly going to affect his or her reported responses. So will the person's suspicions regarding the true purpose of the study, or the individual's assumption of how confidential his or her responses will truly be. These factors can distort the respondent's answers regardless of the manner used to collect the data, and it is unlikely these distortions would be random. At any rate, the model suggests certain actions that the researcher can take to generate accurate information.

Background Factors The empirical evidence supports the notion that background factors affect reported responses. More specifically, the evidence suggests that the interviewer is likely to get better cooperation and more information from the respondent when the two share similar backgrounds than if they are different. This is particularly true for readily observable characteristics, such as race, age, and sex, but applies as well to more unobservable characteristics, such as social class and income. Consequently, it may be prudent to match the background characteristics of the interviewer and respondent as closely as possible, since the more characteristics the two have in common, the greater the probability of a successful interview.

Unfortunately, researchers have found it difficult to implement this practice. Most interviewers are married women who work part-time from home. The job by no means attracts a balanced demographic cross section of people. So what can the researcher do to minimize such biases? He or she may be restricted to merely computing a measure of interviewer variability when analyzing the results. Possibly the field supervisor could revise interviewers' schedules in a specific project so as to improve background matches, but the most effective measure would be to recruit interviewers with diverse socioeconomic backgrounds.

Psychological Factors Respondents don't want to embarrass themselves, even with a stranger. They may sometimes say what they think sounds most appropriate in the situation. For example, James Sorensen has told about a study in which interviewers for his firm, Sorensen Associates, talked to shoppers in grocery stores. An interviewer approached a man who had finished paying for his purchases and asked the man some questions. The shopper said he was using a shopping list that day and that an item the interviewer asked about was on the list. To get the wording the shopper used on the list, the interviewer asked to see it. The shopper declined to show the list. The interviewer probed for a reason, and the shopper admitted the truth: "The item I just purchased was not on the list. I lied."[23]

The evidence regarding the impact of psychological factors on responses tends to support the notion that interviewers' opinions, perceptions, expectations, and attitudes affect the responses they receive.[24] Certainly these attitudes, opinions, expectations, and so on, are going to be conditioned by the interviewers' backgrounds, and since that is something we cannot control, how are we to control for these psychological factors? The primary way is through training. The fact that interviewers will have psychological predispositions is not critical, since these psychological factors are not observed by the respondent. What is critical is that these factors not be allowed to affect interviewers' behavior during the interview and thereby contaminate the responses.

Most surveys, therefore, are conducted using a rather rigid set of procedures that interviewers must follow. The instructions should be clear and should be written. Further, they should state the purpose of the study clearly. They should describe the materials to be used, such as questionnaires, maps, time forms, and so on. They should describe how each question should be asked, the kinds of answers that are acceptable, and the kinds and timing of probes that are to be used, if any. The instructions should also specify the number and identity of respondents that interviewers need to contact and the time constraints under which they will be operating. It is also important that the instructions be well organized and unambiguous.

The instructions must be clearly articulated; however, it is even more important that interviewers understand and can follow them. This suggests that practice training sessions will be necessary. It might also be necessary to actually examine the interviewers with respect to study purposes and procedures. Finally, interviewers might also be required to complete the questionnaire so that if there is a pattern between the interviewers' answers and the answers they get when administering the questionnaire, it can be discerned.

Behavioral Factors   The respondents' background, attitudes, motives, expectations, and so on are also potentially biasing. Whether they actually do introduce bias depends on how the interviewer and respondent interact. In other words, the predispositions to bias become operative only in behavior. Some researchers try to correct for this problem with carefully structured surveys. To study people who buy and fly airplanes, the Advanced General Aviation Transport Experiment (AGATE) conducted on-line surveys. The developers of the AGATE questionnaire noted that when surveys ask how much people are willing to pay for some item, respondents typically give an answer near the bottom of the true acceptable range, whereas asking a yes/no question like "Are you willing to pay $200?" generates more accurate responses but only about that particular price. So the AGATE researchers set up a questionnaire format that used random numbers to select prices to present to respondents. Thus, no respondent would have the burden of evaluating all the price points. Rather, each person answered a few dozen randomly selected questions, and the results were pooled to create graphs showing the percentages of respondents who said each choice was acceptable.[25]

In the realm of in-person and telephone interviews, the evidence indicates that even when the rules are rigid and the questionnaires relatively simple and structured, interviewers do not follow the rules. They thereby introduce bias. In one classic study, 15 college-educated interviewers interviewed the same respondent, who had previously been instructed to give identical answers to all 15 interviewers.[26] All the interviews were recorded and were later analyzed for the incidence of errors by type and frequency. One of the most startling findings of the study was the sheer number of errors. For example, there were 66 failures to ask supplementary questions when inadequate responses were given, and the number of errors per interviewer varied from 12 to 36. In another study, it was found that "one-third of the . . . interviewers deviated frequently and markedly from their instructions, sometimes failing to explain the key terms or to repeat them as required, sometimes leaving them out altogether, shortening questions, or failing to follow up certain ambiguous answers in the manner required."[27]

At least three interviewer behaviors led to response bias: (1) errors in asking questions and in probing when additional information is required, (2) errors in recording the answers, and (3) errors due to cheating.

While errors in asking questions can arise with any of the basic question types, the problem is particularly acute with open-ended questions where probing follows the initial response. No two interviewers are likely to employ the same probes. The content, as well as the timing, of the probes may differ. This raises the possibility that the differences in answers may be due to the probes that are used rather than any "true" differences in the position of the respondents.

The manner in which the initial question is phrased can also introduce error. Interviewers often reword the question to fit their perceptions of what the respondent is capable of understanding. They may also change the wording in a way that reflects their own opinion of what constitutes an appropriate answer.

Surprisingly, questions that include alternative answers possess great potential for interviewer bias. This bias occurs because the interviewer places undue emphasis on one of the alternatives in stating the question. Slight changes in tone can change the meaning of the entire question. In one of the most comprehensive studies to investigate interviewer errors in asking questions, it was found, for example, that the average number of errors per question by type was[28]

- Reading error   0.293
- Speech variations   0.116
- Probes   0.140
- Feedbacks to respondents 0.161

One of the interviewer's main tasks is keeping the respondent interested and motivated. At the same time, the interviewer must try to record what the respondent is saying by dutifully writing down the person's answers to open-ended questions or checking the appropriate box with closed questions. These dual, sometimes incompatible, responsibilities can also be a source of error. Interviewers may not correctly "hear" what the respondent is actually saying. This may be because the respondent is inarticulate and the response is garbled, or because an interviewer's own selective processes are operating. Interviewers may hear what they want to hear and retain what they want to retain. This is a common failing with all of us, and, in spite of interviewer training, recording errors in the interview are all too common. Lest we be too hard on interviewers, we need to recognize that their job is a difficult one. It demands a good deal of ingenuity, creativity, and dogged determination.

Interviewer cheating can also be a source of response error. Cheating may range from the fabrication of a whole interview to the fabrication of one or two answers to make the response complete. The Advertising Research Foundation (ARF), for example, conducts validation studies for its members upon request by reinterviewing a sample of those who were reported to have been interviewed previously. Foundation researchers check to see if the interview actually took place and the designated questions were asked. In one of its studies, ARF found that 5.4 percent of the interviews across 33 separate studies could not be verified, and that an additional 7.9 percent contained at least two performance errors.[29] What is especially disturbing about these results is that it is generally believed that the surveys submitted for verification are among the best executed in the advertising area. Even the Census Bureau, commonly recognized as the most sophisticated and careful collector of data in the world, must contend with the fabrication of interviews. See Research Window 18.2.

Most commercial research firms validate 10 to 20 percent of the completed interviews through follow-up telephone calls or by sending postcards to a sample of "respondents" to verify that they have in fact been contacted. The validation usually covers such general areas as:

1. Method of contact—to be sure a personal interview wasn't actually handled on the telephone, for example.

Research Window 18.2   **Even the Census Bureau Must Contend with Interviewer Cheating**

Terry Ghazey and Mary Beth Scully used to believe in the census. They started working in the district office here last winter. Ghazey at one point made three visits after dark to a motel for the homeless to try to count everyone. In time she was promoted to supervise 100 enumerators.

Scully led a quality-control team of 25. "If I thought people in the field were making things up, we'd fight it," she said.

Then came the weekend of June 22. Hackensack was under pressure from the Philadelphia regional census office to finish its count. Of the 45,000 district households that hadn't mailed in forms, enumerators still had no data for 4,500.

Scully, Ghazey, and six others interviewed said that on Friday, June 22, the Hackensack district manager, Michael Rodak, ordered the staff to begin making up numbers, alternating "one, two, and three" occupants on questionnaires.

"Everyone was sitting around falsifying questionnaires," Scully said. "They were laughing. People were being paid overtime to work all weekend making up forms. They'd say, 'We need 300 more to finish this section' and they'd fill out 300."

"It went on for days," said Ghazey, who estimates that 3,500 forms were falsified. "There were piles and piles."

Kristin Veleber said she was one of 50 workers Rodak told to do the "one-two-three" forms. "Everybody available did them," she said. "I did a big stack, probably 300 in two days." She was asked to work overtime to do more, but refused. "When I realized what was going on, I was disturbed."

The Census Bureau began an inquiry two weeks ago, after *The Record of Hackensack* reported some of these events. John Connelly, a Census Bureau spokesman, said there could be "no legitimate explanation for a one-two-three rotation. No way you could authorize that."

Scully was so upset on that Friday in June that she tracked down the regional manager for central New Jersey, Medell Ford. "I was livid," she said. "I had just spent three months doing quality control and here they were falsifying data. I told Medell I had refused to take part. He said the Bureau

appreciated my concern, but it was fine, other offices were doing the same thing. He acted as if it was common practice in the region."

Ford refused to comment, saying he had been told not to speak to reporters. Rodak would say only, "I followed procedures and I did nothing wrong."

There had been considerable turmoil in the central New Jersey operation. Directors of three of the area's four district offices—Hackensack, Bergenfield, and Wayne—resigned in the midst of the count last spring. Rodak, who is 24 years old and had been the sixth ranking person in Hackensack, was promoted to run the office in April. With much of the census over, he now works part-time for a local state assemblyman and is a substitute teacher.

Former supervisors say much of the problem was lack of experience from top to bottom. Hackensack is one of the more urban areas of this largely suburban district. "It was hard to find adult enumerators to do Hackensack," Ghazey said. "They wound up with almost all high school students."

Murray Rubenstein, who was a crew leader, said questionnaires were constantly being lost. "Some forms were misplaced twice. We don't know how much was lost." He said at the end of the count the office was training hundreds of new enumerators at a time when there wasn't enough work for existing enumerators.

"So much tax money was wasted," Scully said.

Ghazey said that even as office workers were falsifying questionnaires in June, enumerators were out trying to count households legitimately. "They'd bring in the correct forms and we tried to process them. But the computer would reject them because there was already a falsified form for that address."

Bob Fuchs, a former supervisor, said that when he tried to enter accurate forms, "they were rejected as duplicates." What happened to the correct forms? "They were taken outside and thrown away," Ghazey said.

Source: Michael Winerip, "How to Finish a Census: Just Make It Up," *New York Times* (November 19, 1990), p. A18. Copyright © 1990 by the New York Times Company. Reprinted by permission.

2. Questions asked—to verify that no important questions, such as qualifying or demographic questions, were skipped.

3. Exhibits/products shown—to make sure people saw any concept boards or products that they were supposed to see.

4. Respondent's familiarity with interviewer—to determine that the interviewer did not contact friends or acquaintances.

5. General reactions to the interview—to check on the general quality of the contact.[30]

Another form of cheating, which is not exactly response error but which has a strong effect on all nonsampling errors, is padding bills. The interviewer may falsify the number of hours worked or the number of miles traveled. The problem is widespread because of the nature of the interviewing situation. The interviewer works without direct supervision in a basically low-paying job. Further, the supervisor's pay is normally geared to the interviewer's charges, so that the higher the interviewer's bills, the higher the supervisor's compensation. Bill padding drains resources from other parts of the study and thereby decreases the efficiency (value) of the information because it is obtained at higher cost.

As suggested previously, it is much more difficult to adjust for response errors than for nonresponse errors. Both their direction and their magnitude are unknown because, in order to estimate their effects, the true value must be known. The researcher's main hope lies in prevention rather than subsequent adjustment of the results. The various sources of errors themselves suggest preventives. For example, training can help reduce errors in asking questions and recording answers. Similarly, the way interviewers are selected, paid, and controlled could reduce cheating. Overall interviewer performance can be assessed by rating the quality of the work with respect to appropriate characteristics such as costs, types of errors, ability to follow instructions, and so on. We shall not elaborate on the recommended procedures for assessing these factors, since that would be a book in its own right. For our purposes, we need to recognize the existence of response errors, their sources, and their potentially devastating impact. The interviewer-interviewee interaction model is helpful in visualizing these sources and in indicating some methods of prevention.

Office Errors

Our problems with nonsampling errors do not end with data collection. Errors can and do arise in the editing, coding, tabulating, and analyzing of the data.[31] For the most part, these errors can be reduced, if not eliminated, by exercising proper controls in data processing. These questions are discussed in the chapters dealing with analysis.

Total Error Is Key

By this time the reader should understand the warning that total error, rather than any single type of error, is the key in a research investigation. The admonition particularly applies to sampling error. With a course in statistics behind them, students beginning their studies in research methods often argue for the "largest possible sample," reasoning that a large sample is much more likely to produce a statistic close to the population parameter being estimated than a small sample is. What the student fails to appreciate, though, is that the argument applies only to sampling error. Increasing the sample size does, in fact, decrease sampling error. However, it may also increase nonsampling error because the large sample requires more interviews, for instance, and this creates additional burdens in selection, training, and control. Further, nonsampling error is a much more insidious and troublesome error than sampling error. Sampling error can be estimated. Many forms of nonsampling error cannot. Sampling error can be reduced through more sophisticated sample design or by using a larger sample. The path is clear and relatively well-traveled,

A well-known car agency needed to make a decision about whether to import a relatively unknown line of foreign cars to complement its domestic line. To aid in its decision making, the agency contracted a research firm to conduct a study to determine potential consumer interest and demand for this foreign car line. The results indicated that substantial awareness and interest existed, and consequently the decision was made to take on the new line.

To publicize the new line, a special preview was arranged for interested community members such as local newspaper and radio people, executives in related automotive industries, filling station and repair shop owners, and leaders of men's and women's clubs. The agency's owners also wanted to invite the survey participants who had expressed an interest in the car and consequently asked the research firm to make known to them the respondents' names. The research firm refused to comply

with this request, arguing that to do so would be a violation of the respondents' promised anonymity.

- Should the research firm have complied with the agency's request?
- Did the car agency have the right to receive the participants' names since it had paid for the research?
- Would it have made a difference if the study had not been one to determine sales potential?
- What would be some of the consequences of making the respondents' names known to the car agency?
- If the question had been anticipated before the survey was begun, could the interview structure have avoided the dilemma in which the research company and the agency now find themselves?

so the researcher should have little difficulty keeping sampling error within bounds. Not so with nonsampling errors. The path is not paved. New sources of nonsampling error are being discovered all the time, and even though known, many of these sources defy reduction by any automatic procedure. "Improved method" is critical, but what this ideal method should be is unknown. This chapter has attempted to highlight some of the better-known sources of nonsampling error and ways of dealing with them.

Exhibit 18.5 attempts to summarize what we have been saying about nonsampling errors and how they can be reduced and controlled. The table can be used as a sort of checklist for marketing managers and other users of research to evaluate the quality of the research prior to making substantive decisions on the basis of the research results.

Although not all the methods for handling nonsampling errors will be applicable in every study, a systematic analysis of the research effort, using the table guidelines, should provide the proper appreciation for the quality of research information that is obtained.

EXHIBIT 18.5   Overview of Nonsampling Errors and Some Methods for Handling Them

Type	Definition	Methods for Handling
Noncoverage	Failure to include some units or entire sections of the defined target population in the sampling frame.	1. Improve basic sampling frame using other sources. 2. Select sample in such a way as to reduce incidence, for example, by ignoring ineligibles on a list. 3. Adjust the results by appropriately weighting the subsample results.

EXHIBIT 18.5	Overview of Nonsampling Errors and Some Methods for Handling Them, *continued*	
Type	**Definition**	**Methods for Handling**
Nonresponse	Failure to obtain information from some elements of the population that were selected for the sample	
Not-at-homes	Designated respondent is not home when the interviewer calls.	1. Have interviewers make advance appointments. 2. Call back at another time, preferably at a different time of day. 3. Attempt to contact the designated respondent using another approach (e.g., use a modified callback).
Refusals	Respondent refuses to cooperate in the survey.	1. Attempt to convince the respondent of the value of the research and the importance of his or her participation. 2. Provide advance notice that the survey is coming. 3. Guarantee anonymity. 4. Provide an incentive for participating. 5. Hide the identification of the sponsor by using an independent research organization. 6. Try to get a foot in the door by getting the respondent to comply with some small task before getting the survey. 7. Use personalized cover letters. 8. Use a follow-up contact at a more convenient time. 9. Avoid unnecessary questions. 10. Adjust the results to account for the nonresponse.
Field	Although the individual participates in the study, he or she refuses to answer specific questions or provides incorrect answers to them.	1. Match the background characteristics of interviewer and respondent as closely as possible. 2. Make sure interviewer instructions are clear and written down. 3. Conduct practice training sessions with interviewers. 4. Examine the interviewers' understanding of the study's purposes and procedures. 5. Have interviewers complete the questionnaire and examine their replies to see if there is any relationship between the answers they secure and their own answers. 6. Verify a sample of each interviewer's interviews.
Office[a]	Errors that arise when coding, tabulating, or analyzing the data.	1. Use a field edit to detect the most glaring omissions and inaccuracies in the data. 2. Use a second edit in the office to decide how data collection instruments containing incomplete answers, obviously wrong answers, and answers that reflect a lack of interest are to be handled. 3. Use closed questions to simplify the coding, but when open-ended questions need to be used, specify the appropriate codes that will be allowed before collecting the data. 4. When open-ended questions are being coded and multiple coders are being used, divide the task by questions and not by data collection forms. 5. Have each coder code a sample of the other's work to ensure that a consistent set of coding criteria is being employed. 6. Follow established conventions; for example, use numeric codes and not letters of the alphabet when coding the data for computer analysis. 7. Prepare a codebook that lists the codes for each variable and the categories included in each code. 8. Use appropriate methods to analyze the data.

[a]Steps to reduce the incidence of office errors are discussed in more detail in the analysis chapters.

Ethical Dilemma 18.2

"These new computer-voiced telephone surveys are wonderful!" your friend enthuses over lunch. "Because we don't have to pay telephone interviewers, we can afford to have target numbers automatically redialed until someone answers. Of course, the public finds the computer's voice irritating and the whole notion of being interviewed by a machine rather humiliating. Nevertheless, we can overcome most people's reluctance to participate by repeatedly calling them until they give in and complete the questionnaire."

- Is it ethical to contact respondents repeatedly until they agree to participate in a research study? How many contacts are legitimate?

- If an industry is unable to constrain its members to behave ethically, should the government step in with regulations?

- If the public reacts against this kind of telephone survey, what are the results likely to be for researchers using traditional, more considerate telephone surveys?

Back to the Case

Rosemont was not that far geographically from affluent Moreland Heights, but economically it was a world away. Rosemont was a low-income neighborhood with a high crime rate, and it was literally on the other side of the tracks. But to Lucy Lindenbloom, gathering information in Rosemont wasn't any worse than gathering it in Moreland Heights. As a census interviewer, she was always faced with problems: In Rosemont the problems were just a little different. Besides, Lindenbloom always felt a special mission when she went into low-income neighborhoods. These were the people that many government programs were designed to help. If the government couldn't find these people to count them, then it would never be able to find them to help them.

Her first stop was a run-down brownstone with a broken doorbell and a busted lock on the front door. Lindenbloom stepped into the vestibule. It was crammed with strollers and smelled faintly of cabbage. On one wall was a bank of mailboxes. She found the name she was looking for on the box marked 4D. "Great," she thought to herself, "the fourth floor and no elevator."

Lindenbloom knew that it was buildings like this that sometimes drove interviewers to skip the stairs and just fill in the interview forms themselves. The temptation to cheat was always there, and interviewers had been known to fabricate data in a number of ways, from making up entire interviews to more subtle methods such as interviewing respondents in groups rather than separately. "But no matter how you did it," thought Lindenbloom as she plodded up the uneven stairs, "it would still be cheating. When one interviewer cheats, it affects the work of all the others by introducing response error into the data."

Lindenbloom, slightly out of breath, knocked on the door of apartment 4D.

"Who is it?" inquired a frightened voice.

"U.S. Census Bureau, ma'am," Lindenbloom responded. "I'm trying to locate Mary Porter to ask her some questions."

"Wait there," said the voice.

Lindenbloom waited and waited. After ten minutes, she knocked on the door again. "Ms. Porter?" she asked. "Are you all right?"

Just then Lindenbloom heard footsteps on the stairway. Two uniformed policemen approached her and demanded to know what she was doing.

"I'm a census interviewer," Lindenbloom said, showing her ID.

"Sorry to trouble you," one of the officers said, "but there have been a lot of robberies in the neighborhood. It makes folks around here real suspicious of people trying to gain access to their apartments."

"It's okay, Mrs. Porter," one of the policemen shouted through the locked door. "This is Ms. Lindenbloom. She really is with the Census Bureau. She just wants to ask you a few questions."

Lindenbloom sighed as she heard the sound of the chain lock being slipped aside. She had been a Census interviewer for more than ten years. This wasn't the first time she had begun an interview with a police escort.

Summary

Learning Objective 1

Explain what sampling error is.

Sampling error is the difference between the observed values of a variable and the long-run average of the observed values in repetitions of the measurement.

Learning Objective 2

Cite the two basic types of nonsampling errors and describe each.

There are two basic types of nonsampling errors: errors due to nonobservation and errors due to observation. Nonobservation errors result from a failure to obtain data from parts of the target population. They occur because part of the population of interest was not included or because some elements designated for inclusion in the sample did not respond. Observation errors occur because inaccurate information was secured from the sample elements or because errors were introduced in the processing of the data or in reporting the findings.

Learning Objective 3

Outline several ways in which noncoverage bias can be reduced.

Noncoverage bias can be reduced, although not necessarily eliminated, by recognizing its existence, working to improve the sampling frame, and employing a sampling specialist to help reduce (through the sampling procedure) and adjust (through analysis) the remaining frame imperfections.

Learning Objective 4

Explain what error due to nonresponse is.

Error due to nonresponse represents a failure to obtain information from some elements of the population that were selected and designated for the sample.

Learning Objective 5

Cite the standard definition for response rate.

Response rate may be defined as the number of completed interviews with responding units divided by the number of eligible responding units in the sample.

Learning Objective 6

Identify the two main sources of nonresponse bias.

The two main sources of nonresponse bias are not-at-homes and refusals.

Learning Objective 7

Define contact rate.

The *contact rate* is the percentage of eligible assignments in which the interviewer makes contact with the designated respondents; that is,

$$K = \frac{\text{number of sample units contacted}}{\text{total number of eligible sample units approached}}$$

Learning Objective 8

Cite some of the factors that may contribute to a respondent's refusal to participate in a study.

The rate of refusals in a study will depend on, among other things, the nature of the respondent, the nature of the organization sponsoring the research, the circumstances surrounding the contact, the nature of the subject under investigation, and the skill of the interviewer. The method used to collect the data may also make a difference.

Learning Objective 9

Identify three factors that may be a source of bias in the interviewer-interviewee interaction.

The interviewer-interviewee interaction may be biased by background characteristics, psychological factors, and behavioral factors on the part of either the interviewer or the respondent, or both.

Learning Objective 10

Discuss the types of interviewer behaviors that may lead to response bias.

At least three interviewer behaviors can lead to response bias: (1) errors in asking questions and in probing when additional information is required, (2) errors in recording the answers, and (3) errors due to cheating.

Review Questions

1. Distinguish between sampling error and nonsampling error. Why is the distinction important?

2. What are noncoverage errors? Are they a problem with telephone surveys? How? With mail surveys? How? With personal interview studies? How?

3. How can noncoverage bias be assessed? What can be done to reduce it?

4. What is nonresponse error?

5. What are the basic types of nonresponse error? Are they equally serious for mail, telephone, or personal interview studies? Explain.

6. What can be done to reduce the incidence of not-at-homes in the final sample?

7. What is the contact rate? What role does it play in evaluating the results?

8. What are the typical reasons why designated respondents refuse to participate in a study? What can be done to reduce the incidence of refusals? Do refusals generally introduce random error or systematic biases into studies?

9. What is item nonresponse? What alternatives are available to the researcher for treating item nonresponse?

10. What is the response rate? What is the completeness rate? Is there any relation between the two?

11. What are observation errors? What are the basic types of observation errors?

12. Are observation errors likely to be a more serious or less serious problem than nonobservation errors? Explain.

13. Describe the interviewer-interviewee interaction model, including its basic propositions.

14. What does the interviewer-interviewee interaction model suggest with respect to the background characteristics of interviewers? With respect to their psychological characteristics?

15. What basic types of interviewer behaviors can lead to response bias?

16. Explain the statement, "Total error is key."

Discussion Questions, Problems, and Projects

1. J. Hoffman was the owner of a medium-sized supermarket located in St. Cloud, Minnesota. She was considering altering the layout of the store so that, for example, the frozen food section would be near the section with fresh fruit and vegetables. These changes were designed to better accommodate customer shopping patterns and thereby increase customer patronage. Prior to making the alterations, she decided to administer a short questionnaire in the store to a random sample of customers. For a period of two weeks, three of the store cashiers were instructed to stand at the end of selected aisles and conduct personal interviews with every fifth customer. Hoffman gave specific instructions that on no account were customers to be harassed or offended. Identify the major sources of noncoverage and nonresponse errors. Explain.

2. Tough-Grip Tires was a large manufacturer of radial tires located in New Orleans, Louisiana, and it was experiencing a problem common to tire manufacturers. The poor performance of the auto industry was having a severe negative impact on the tire industry. To try to maintain sales and competitive positions, the various manufacturers were offering wholesalers additional credit and discount opportunities. Tough-Grip's management was particularly concerned about wholesaler reaction to a new discount policy it was considering. The first survey the company conducted to explore this reaction was unsatisfactory to management. Management felt it was conducted in a haphazard manner and contained numerous nonsampling errors. Tough-Grip's management decided to conduct another study, containing the following changes:

   • The sampling frame was defined as a list of 1,000 of the largest wholesalers that stocked Tough-Grip tires, and the sample elements were to be randomly selected from this list.

   • A callback technique was to be employed, with the callbacks being made at different times than the original attempted contact.

   • The sample size was to be doubled, from 200 to 400 respondents.

   • The sample elements that were ineligible or refused to cooperate were to be substituted by the next element from the list.

   • An incentive of $1.00 was to be offered to respondents.

   Critically evaluate the steps that were being considered to prevent the occurrence of nonsampling errors. Do you think they were appropriate? Be specific.

3. A major publisher of a diverse set of magazines was interested in determining customer satisfaction with three of the company's leading publications: *Style Update, Business Profiles,* and *Hi-Tech Review.* The three magazines dealt, respectively, with women's fashions, business trends, and computer technology developments. Three sampling frames, consisting of lists of subscribers residing in Chicago, were formulated. Three random samples were to be chosen from these lists. Personal interviews using an unstructured-undisguised questionnaire were to be conducted. The publishing company had a regular pool of interviewers that it called upon whenever interviews were to be conducted. The interviewers had varying educational backgrounds, though 95 percent were high school graduates and the remaining 5 percent had some college education. In terms of age and sex, the range varied from 18 years to 45 years with 70 percent females and 30 percent males. The majority of interviewers were housewives and students. Prior to conducting a survey the company sent the necessary information and requested that the interviewers indicate whether they were interested. The questionnaires, addresses, and other details were then sent to those interviewers replying affirmatively. After an interviewer completed his or her quota of interviews, the replies were sent back to the company. The company then mailed the interviewer's remuneration.
   (a) Using the guidelines in Exhibit 18.5, critically evaluate the selection, training, and instructions given to the field interviewers.
   (b) Using Kahn and Cannell's model (Figure 18.4), identify the major sources of bias that would affect the interviews.

4. The placement office at your university has asked you to assist it in the task of determining the size of starting salaries and the range of salary offers received by graduating seniors. The placement office has always gathered some information in this regard in that historically some seniors come in to report the name of the company for which they are going to work and the size of their starting salary. The office feels that these statistics may be biased, and thus it wishes to approach the whole task more systematically. This is why it has hired your expertise to determine what the situation was with respect to last year's graduating seniors.
   (a) Describe how you would select a sample of respondents to answer the question of starting salaries. Why would you use this particular sample?
   (b) What types of nonsampling errors might you expect to encounter with your approach, and how would you control for them?

5. An executive recruitment firm utilized a lengthy mail survey to gather information on the job mobility of midlevel managers. A sample of 500 eligible middle managers was selected, using a simple random sampling procedure. The firm used three waves of mailings. After the third mailing, each of the nonresponding sample units was contacted by phone and asked to answer only four questions regarding variables that the recruitment firm thought were particularly important, given the objective of the study. The table below gives mean values for these variables.

Wave	Number of Responses	Age	Income ($)	Years in Current Position	Total Years of Management Experience
1	125	30	22,000	1.2	5.1
2	100	37	27,000	4.0	9.4
3	75	42	32,500	5.1	15.1
N.R.	200	50	31,250	10.2	24.2

   (a) What was the response rate for the completed questionnaire?
   (b) Furnish some rough estimates for the *overall* sample means of the four variables. Show your work.
   (c) Which variables seem to be most affected by potential nonresponse bias? Does this tell you anything about the sample selection procedure?

6. Arrange to interview a researcher at a local marketing research firm or in-house research department. How large a problem is nonresponse for the firm? What are the typical response rates for the firm's research projects? Discuss the method(s) used to handle nonresponse bias. Does the firm compensate for nonresponse in ways that are not addressed in the text? Prepare a written report of your findings.

7. Prepare a brief questionnaire regarding the television-viewing habits of adults in your city. Administer this instrument to a sample of subjects using at least ten telephone interviews and ten personal interviews. Discuss the extent of the nonresponse bias with each method.

8. For this exercise you will need to use the questionnaire on television-viewing habits developed in Exercise 7. In addition, develop questions designed to measure a respondent's attitude toward the television medium. Add these questions to the questionnaire on television-viewing habits. Administer this new questionnaire to one of your classmates. Then request that this classmate administer the questionnaire so that you will be the interviewee. Refer to Figure 18.4, and discuss the background factors, psychological factors, and behavioral factors that might have led to bias in the interview. (Hint: After the interview it would be useful to discuss these aspects with your classmate. Explain what you meant by the various questions, and find out how your classmate interpreted these questions.)

Endnotes

1. Frederick Mosteller, "Nonsampling Errors," *Encyclopedia of Social Sciences* (New York: Macmillan, 1968), p. 113. See also the special issue of the *Journal of Official Statistics* 4 (No. 3, 1987), edited by Lars Lyberg, which is devoted to nonsampling errors, and Elizabeth Hervey Stephen and Beth J. Soldo, "How to Judge the Quality of a Survey," *American Demographics* 12 (April 1990), pp. 42–43; Tom Corlett, "Sampling Results in Practice," *Journal of the Market Research Society* 38 (October 1996), pp. 307–318.

2. Mosteller, "Nonsampling Errors," p. 113.

3. Robert Ferber, *The Reliability of Consumer Reports of Financial Assets and Debts* (Urbana, Ill.: Bureau of Economic and Business Research, University of Illinois, 1966), p. 261. There was a series of studies with respect to the single objective. Ferber's monograph provides an overview of the studies and results, although there are six monographs in all. See also Floyd J. Fowler, Jr., *Survey Research Methods*, 2nd ed. (Thousand Oaks, Calif.: Sage Publications 1993) for further discussion of the importance of minimizing nonsampling errors and how to go about this task.

4. Ibid., p. 266. Wiseman and McDonald make a similar point with the comment, "The use of very sophisticated sampling schemes when other aspects of the data collection effort are much less sophisticated may result in higher costs than are justified for the resultant data quality." See Frederick Wiseman and Philip McDonald, "Noncontact and Refusal Rates in Consumer Telephone Surveys," *Journal of Marketing Research* 16 (November 1979), p. 483. See also Robert Groves, *Survey Errors and Survey Costs* (New York: John Wiley and Sons, Inc., 1989).

5. W. H. Williams, "How Bad Can 'Good' Data Really Be?" *The American Statistician* 32 (May 1978), p. 61. See also Judith T. Lessler and William D. Kalsbeek, *Nonsampling Errors in Surveys* (New York: John Wiley and Sons, Inc., 1992).

6. See, for example, Ronald Andersen, Judith Kasper, Martin R. Frankel, and Associates, *Total Survey Error* (San Francisco: Jossey-Bass, 1979), or Henry Assael and John Keon, "Nonsampling vs. Sampling Errors in Survey Research," *Journal of Marketing* 46 (Spring 1982), pp. 114–123.

7. Leslie Kish, *Survey Sampling* (New York: John Wiley, 1995), Chapter 13, "Biases and Nonsampling Errors," is particularly recommended for discussion of the biases arising from nonobservation.

8. Tia O'Brien, "Women on the Verge of a High-Tech Breakthrough," *West* (magazine supplement to *San Jose Mercury News*) (May 9, 1999), pp. 10–14, 19.

9. The general adjustment procedure for dealing with the problem of duplicates on a list is to weight sample elements discovered to have been listed k times by $1/k$. Seymour Sudman, *Applied Sampling* (San Francisco: Academic Press, 1976), p. 63. Most of the standard computer packages for statistically analyzing the data contain mechanisms by which the analyst can specify the weight to be applied to each sample observation.

10. Frederick Wiseman and Philip McDonald, *Toward the Development of Industry Standards for Response and Nonresponse Rates* (Cambridge, Mass.: Marketing Science Institute, 1980).

11. "On the Definition of Response Rates," *CASRO Special Report* (Port Jefferson, N.Y.: The Council of American Survey Research Organizations, 1982). See also M. A. Hidiroglu, J. D. Drew, and G. B. Gray, "A Framework for Measuring and Reducing Nonresponse in Surveys," *Survey Methodology* 19 (1993), pp. 81–94.

12. There are several studies that contain data about when particular types of individuals are likely to be home. See, for example, M. F. Weeks, B. L. Jones, R. E. Folsum, Jr., and C. H. Benrud, "Optimal Times to Contact Sample Households," *Public Opinion Quarterly* 44 (Spring 1980), pp. 101–114; Michael F. Weeks, Richard W. Kulka, and Stephanie A. Pierson, "Optimal Call Scheduling for a Telephone Survey," *Public Opinion Quarterly* 51 (Winter 1987), pp. 540–549; Gideon Vigderhaus, "Scheduling Telephone Interviews: A Study of Seasonal Patterns," *Public Opinion Quarterly* 45 (Summer 1981), pp. 250–259. The report "Identifying Monthly Response Rates Aids in Mail Planning," *Specialty Advertising Report* 15 (4th Quarter, 1979), contains a useful table for scheduling mail studies to coincide with the months in which people are most likely to respond.

13. W. Edwards Deming, "On a Probability Mechanism to Attain an Economic Balance between the Resultant Error of Response and the Bias of Nonresponse," *Journal of the American Statistical Association* 48 (December 1953), pp. 766–767. See also Benjamin Lipstein, "In Defense of Small Samples," *Journal of Advertising Research* 15 (February 1975), pp. 33–40; William C. Dunkelburg and George S. Day, "Nonresponse Bias and Callbacks in Sample Surveys," *Journal of Marketing Research* 10 (May 1973), pp. 160–168; Lorna Opatow, "Some Thoughts about How Interview Attempts Affect Survey Results," *Journal of Advertising Research* 31 (February/March 1991), pp. RC6–RC9.

14. The technique can be used with telephone interviews, although it was designed for personal interviews because of the tremendous expense of personal interview callbacks. Moreover, probing on the phone about when a respondent was home during the last five days can cause mistrust. See Alfred Politz and Willard Simmons, "An Attempt to Get the Not-at-Homes into the Sample Without Callbacks," *Journal of the American Statistical Association* 44 (March 1949), pp. 9–32, for explanation of the technique. For an empirical investigation of the effect of weighting on bias, see James Ward, Bertram Russick, and William Rudelius, "A Test of Reducing Callbacks and Not-at-Homes Bias in Personal Interviews by Weighting At-Home Respondents, *Journal of Marketing Research* 22 (February 1985), pp. 66–73. See also I-Fen Lin and Nora Cate Schaeffer, "Using Survey Participants to Estimate the Impact of Nonparticipation," *Public Opinion Quarterly* 59 (Summer 1995), pp. 236–258.

15. *Your Opinion Counts: 1986 Refusal Rate Study* (Chicago: Marketing Research Association, 1986). See also Tom W. Smith, "Trends in Nonresponse Rates," *International Journal of Public Opinion Research* 7 (1995), pp. 157–171.

16. T. De Maio, "Refusals: Who, Where, and Why," *Public Opinion Quarterly* 44 (Summer 1980), pp. 223–233. See also Jolene M. Strubbe, Jerome B. Kernan, and Thomas J. Grogan, "The Refusal Problem in Telephone Surveys," *Journal of Marketing Research* 26 (June/July 1986), pp. 29–37; Kathy E. Green, "Sociodemographic Factors and Mail Survey Response," *Psychology & Marketing* 13 (March 1996), pp. 171–184.

17. James R. Chromy and Daniel G. Horowitz, "The Use of Monetary Incentives in National Assessment Household Surveys," *Journal of the American Statistical Association* 73 (September 1978), pp. 473–478; Lee Harvey, "Factors Affecting Response Rates to Mailed Questionnaires: A Comprehensive Literature Review," *Journal of the Market Research Society* 29 (July 1987), pp. 341–353; Mike Brennan, "The Effect of a Monetary Incentive on Mail Survey Response Rates: New Data," *Journal of the Market Research Society* 34 (April 1992), pp. 173–177; Jeannine M. James and Richard Bolstein, "Large Monetary Incentives and Their Effect on Mail Survey Response Rates," *Public Opinion Quarterly* 56 (Winter 1992), pp. 442–453; Allan H. Church, "Estimating the Effect of Incentives on Mail Survey Response Rates: A Meta-analysis," *Public Opinion Quarterly* 57 (Spring 1993), pp. 62–79; Diane K. Willimack, Howard Schuman, Beth-Ellen Pennel, and James M. Lepkowski, "Effecs of a Prepaid Nonmonetary Incentive on Response Rates and Response Quality in a Face-to-Face Survey," *Public Opinion Quarterly* 59 (Spring 1995), pp. 78–92.

18. Leslie Kanuk and Conrad Berenson, "Mail Surveys and Response Rates: A Literature Review, *Journal of Marketing Research* 12 (November 1975), pp. 440–453; T. A. Heberlein and R. A. Baumgartner, "Factors Affecting Response Rates to Mailed Questionnaires: A Quantitative Analysis of the Published Literature," *American Sociological Review* 43 (August 1978), pp. 447–462; Julie Yu and Harris Cooper, "A Quantitative Review of Research Design Effects on Response Rates to Questionnaires," *Journal of Marketing Research* 20 (February 1983), pp. 36–44; Richard J. Fox, Melvin R. Crask, Jonghoon Kim, "Mail Survey Response Rate: A Meta-Analysis of Selected Techniques for Inducing Response," *Public Opinion Quarterly* 52 (Winter 1989), pp. 467–491; Francis J. Yammarino, Steven J. Skinner, and Terry L. Childers, "Understanding Mail Survey Response Behavior: A Meta-Analysis," *Public Opinion Quarterly* 55 (Winter 1991), pp. 613–639.

19. *Statistical Adjustment for Nonresponse in Sample Surveys: A Selected Bibliography with Annotations* (Monticello, Ill.: Vance Bibliographies, 1979); J. Scott Armstrong and Terry S. Overton, "Estimating

Nonresponse Bias in Mail Surveys," *Journal of Marketing Research* 14 (August 1977), pp. 396–402; Michael J. O'Neil, "Estimating the Nonresponse Bias Due to Refusals in Telephone Surveys," *Public Opinion Quarterly* 40 (Summer 1976), pp. 218–232; David Elliott and Roger Thomas, "Further Thoughts on Weighting Survey Results to Compensate for Nonresponse," *Survey Methodology Bulletin* 15 (February 1983), pp. 2–11; Valentine Appel and Julian Baim, "Predicting and Correcting Response Rate Problems Using Geodemography," *Marketing Research: A Magazine of Management & Applications* 4 (March 1992), pp. 22–28.

20. Robert A. Peterson and Roger A. Kerin, "The Quality of Self-Report Data: Review and Synthesis," in Ben Enis and Kenneth Roering, eds., *Annual Review of Marketing 1981* (Chicago: American Marketing Association, 1981), pp. 5–20.

21. Robert L. Kahn and Charles F. Cannell, *The Dynamics of Interviewing* (New York: John Wiley, © 1957), p. 193. The figure is used by permission of John Wiley and Sons, Inc. See also Wendy Sykes and Martin Collins, "Anatomy of the Survey Interview," *Journal of Official Statistics* 8 (No. 3, 1992), pp. 277–291.

22. Kahn and Cannell, *The Dynamics of Interviewing*, p. 194.

23. Art Shulman, "War Stories: True-Life Tales in Marketing Research," *Quirk's Marketing Research Review* (December 1998), p. 16.

24. Seymour Sudman, Norman Bradburn, Ed Blair, and Carol Stocking, "Modest Expectations: The Effects of Interviewers' Prior Expectations and Response," *Sociological Methods & Research* 6 (November 1977), pp. 177–182; Eleanor Singer, Martin R. Frankel, and Marc B. Glassman, "The Effect of Interviewer Characteristics and Expectations on Response," *Public Opinion Quarterly* 47 (Spring 1983), pp. 68–83; Stanley Presser and Shanyang Zhao, "Attributes of Questions and Interviewers as Correlates of Interviewing Performance," *Public Opinion Quarterly* 56 (Summer 1992), pp. 236–240.

25. Beth Clarkson, "Research and the Internet: A Winning Combination," *Quirk's Marketing Research Review* (July 1999), pp. 46, 48–51.

26. L. L. Guest, "A Study of Interviewer Competence," *International Journal of Opinion and Attitude Research* 1 (March 1947), pp. 17–30; P. Davis and A. Scott, "The Effect of Interviewer Variance on Domain Comparisons," *Survey Methodology* 21 (1995), pp. 99–106; Pamela Kiecker and James E. Nelson, "Do Interviwers Follow Survey Instructions?" *Journal of the Market Research Society* 38 (April 1996), pp. 161–176.

27. W. A. Belson, "Increasing the Power of Research to Guide Advertising Decisions," *Journal of Marketing* 29 (April 1965), p. 38. See also Martin Collins and Bob Butcher, "Interviewer and Clustering Effects in an Attitude Survey," *Journal of the Market Research Society* 25 (January 1983), pp. 39–58.

28. Norman M. Bradburn and Seymour Sudman, *Improving Interview Method and Questionnaire Design* (San Francisco: Jossey-Bass, 1979), p. 29.

29. Benjamin Lipstein, "In Defense of Small Samples," *Journal of Advertising Research* 15 (February 1975), pp. 33–40.

30. Jeffrey L. Pope, *Practical Marketing Research* (New York: American Management Association, 1993), p. 57. See also pages 56–59 for some effective validation questions for getting at these issues.

31. The reader who believes that analysis errors should be no problem should see Mosteller, "Nonsampling Errors," in which he devotes 9 of 19 pages to the discussion of potential errors in analysis. See also John G. Keane, "Questionable Statistics," *American Demographics* 7 (June 1985), pp. 18–21. Paul Lavrakas, "To Err Is Human," *Marketing Research: A Magazine of Management & Applications* 8 (Spring 1996), pp. 30–36.

Suggested Additional Readings

For general discussions of data quality, the differences between sampling and nonsampling error, and steps that can be taken to improve the quality of information gathered in marketing research studies, see
Ronald Andersen, Judith Kasper, Martin R. Frankel, and Associates, *Total Survey Error* (San Francisco: Jossey-Bass, 1979).
Henry Assael and John Keon, "Nonsampling vs. Sampling Errors in Survey Research," *Journal of Marketing* 46 (Spring 1982), pp. 114–123.
Judith T. Lessler and William D. Kalsbeek, *Nonsampling Errors in Surveys* (New York: John Wiley and Sons, Inc., 1992).
Robert A. Peterson and Roger A. Kerin, "The Quality of Self-Report Data: Review and Synthesis," in Ben Enis and Kenneth Roering, eds., *Annual Review of Marketing 1981* (Chicago: American Marketing Association, 1981), pp. 5–20.

The fifth stage in the research process is to design the sample and collect the data. As we learned from the chapters in this part, researchers generally prefer to use a sample of a population rather than a census of a population, not only because a sample is less costly to obtain, but because it is generally more accurate.

In these chapters we learned that researchers generally follow a six-step procedure for drawing a sample, which includes defining the population, identifying the sampling frame, selecting a sampling procedure, determining the sample size, selecting the sample elements, and collecting the data from the designated elements. We investigated the different types of samples that researchers use and the advantages and disadvantages of each.

In the last chapter we investigated the second type of error that affects research studies: nonsampling error. As we discussed, there are two types of nonsampling errors: those due to nonobservation and those due to observation. Nonobservation errors include coverage errors and nonresponse errors, while observation errors include field errors and office errors.

The problem with nonsampling error, we learned, is that, unlike sampling error, it generally cannot be accurately estimated and corrected for. Like viruses for the common cold, new sources of nonsampling error are being discovered all the time—and, again like the common cold, are proving resistant to cure. A researcher's best tactic is to know as much as possible about the types of nonsampling errors that can occur and try to design a study that will prevent them.

Researchers for CARA were interested in assessing the attitudes of local businesspeople for their study. They decided to define the *local area* as the Fairview County area. *Businesspeople* were defined as individuals who made decisions regarding advertising expenditures for their firms. The researchers decided to exclude from the sample any firms that used an advertising agency or showed minimal interest in using any of the three major advertising media. They excluded these firms because CARA was interested in obtaining responses from firms that were likely to be targeted directly by sales representatives. Companies that use advertising agencies will normally have little direct contact with sales representatives; very small companies offer little potential for ad revenues.

The researchers decided to use the latest Centerville Telephone Directory Yellow Pages as their sampling frame. Recall that a sampling frame is the list of elements from which the sample is drawn. They identified ten major categories of business from which to select the sample: building materials and hardware; automotive sales and service; apparel; furniture and home furnishings; eating and drinking establishments; health and fitness; financial institutions; home entertainment; professional services; and a miscellaneous category including florists, jewelers,

printers, book dealers, and retail photographic sales and service.

By further winnowing the list to eliminate those firms employing advertising agencies or expressing little interest in advertising, the researchers compiled a final list of 3,086 businesses.

A systematic sampling plan was chosen for this study. Recall that in this type of sampling plan each element has a known a priori chance of inclusion in the sample. Each of the 3,086 businesses identified as a part of the sampling frame was classified as a member of one of the ten categories of business and was placed in alphabetical order within that category. The ten categories were then randomly ordered, and the businesses were numbered from 1 to 3,086.

The researchers decided on a sample size of 600 and then determined two measures: the sampling interval and a random start. The sampling interval involved dividing the number of elements in the population (3,086) by the desired sample size (600). This number (5.14) was then rounded down to 5. A random-number table was used to select the initial number between 1 and 5, and every fifth element was selected thereafter until the desired sample size was achieved. This process ensured that the sample was representative of the sampling frame; the proportion of various categories of business included in the sample equaled the proportion of these types of business in the sampling frame.

The researchers then pretested the questionnaire by mailing 20 questionnaires to businesses selected by the systematic sampling plan. Half of the respondents were given a dollar for their cooperation; half were given nothing except thanks. Eight of those receiving the incentive returned the questionnaire; only one of the others complied. Since eight of the nine questionnaires that were returned were fully completed, the researchers decided that no changes needed to be made to the questionnaire. Since CARA was interested in whether offering respondents an incentive would increase response similarly in the larger group, the researchers decided to offer half the sample a dollar for responding and nothing to the other half.

A general rule for selecting sample size is that there should be 100 or more units for each category of the major breakdowns and 20 to 50 for the minor breakdowns. The researchers assumed that the section of the questionnaire requesting attitudes toward sales representatives would have the highest percentage of incomplete subsections. Based on the responses to that section in the pretest, they estimated that 150 questionnaires were necessary to fulfill the requirement for the major breakdowns. They also assumed that if the returned forms were evenly distributed among the four categories of annual advertising budgets,

25 units per minor breakdown should result, thus fulfilling the second general rule.

Since there was no assurance that an even distribution would occur, they decided to increase the number of returns to increase the probability that the desired number of units in the minor breakdowns would approach the desired level. They estimated the rates of return conservatively at 10 percent for those individuals not receiving a dollar and 50 percent for those receiving a dollar. Hence, a sample size of 300 for each group should have resulted in 30 and 150 returns for the no-dollar and dollar groups, respectively, which would be enough to satisfy the general rules mentioned.

CARA researchers recognized the sources of nonsampling error in their study. They knew, for example, that coverage errors in their sampling frame were inevitable because the Centerville Yellow Pages was not a complete list of all local businesses. Some of the businesses listed were no longer in existence, others were too new to have been listed, and others may have chosen not to be listed. Nevertheless, no alternative offered a better list of businesses at a reasonable cost.

By using only ten major categories of businesses, the researchers also recognized that they had probably included some businesses that should not have been on the list and excluded others that should have been. Errors of inclusion and exclusion were also likely in their attempts to select only businesses not employing an advertising agency and businesses that would be interested in using the three major advertising media. Because of these biases, the researchers cautioned CARA representatives about generalizing the study's results to all businesses in Fairview County.

Nonresponse errors were evident in the response rates. Of the 600 questionnaires initially mailed, a total of 212 were returned. Of these, 165 were from the 300 that received a dollar, and 47 were from the 300 that received no incentive. Thirty-four of the returned questionnaires were unusable, however, either because none of the pages were completed or because only classification data were given.

The researchers were interested in sampling from among firms that did not use an advertising agency, individuals who were involved in making advertising decisions, and individuals who held the position of manager and/or owner. The results of the study seemed to indicate that the questionnaire generally secured responses from the population of interest. Of the 178 respondents submitting usable questionnaires, 149 companies (84 percent) did not use an advertising agency, 166 respondents (93 percent) were decision makers, and 160 respondents (90 percent) were owners and/or managers.

To further ensure that the data used for analyses were representative of the desired population, mean scores on attitudes toward the various advertising media and advertising media sales representatives were compared for those companies using an advertising agency versus those not using an advertising agency, those respondents who made decisions about advertising versus those who did not, and those who were owners and/or managers versus those who were not. No significant differences (alpha = 0.05) were found, except for the attitudes of those who used an advertising agency versus those who did not. Therefore, when analyzing the attitude scores, only those scores of those companies who did not use advertising agencies were considered.

Field errors occur when an individual who has agreed to participate in a study either refuses to answer specific questions or provides untruthful answers. CARA researchers noticed several instances of probable field errors in the completed questionnaires. For example, on the scale measuring attitudes toward the advertising media of television, radio, and newspaper, 453 subsections were completed. Of this number, 133 were from the television category, 153 from the radio category, and 167 from the newspaper category. Since individuals were asked to fill out each subsection regardless of whether they used that type of advertising or not, there should not have been differences in these numbers. The researchers speculated that the respondents may have been confused as to what their task was on this section, or they may merely have decided not to complete this section.

Respondents were also asked to approximate the proportion of their yearly advertising budget spent on nine different types of advertising. The researchers took the responses and determined the mean percentage scores for each category. The percentages did not add up to 100 percent, however, which indicated that some respondents had had difficulty determining these proportions.

Case V.A St. Andrews Medical Center[1]

The Eating Disorders Clinic of the St. Andrews Medical Center has been operating since 1985 to treat anorexia nervosa and bulimia. Anorexia nervosa, often characterized by intense obsession with dieting and weight loss, and bulimia, also known as the "binge and purge syndrome," typically afflict young women between the ages of 14 and 22 years. Both conditions can result in very serious health problems (or even death) if left untreated.

In recent years, the clinic has experienced a dramatic decline in patients, while, officials believe, a competing program offered by City Hospital has continued to grow. The programs are comparable in terms of staffing and cost of treatment. Patients are normally referred to an eating disorders program by their primary-care physician or other health-care professional.

Officials at St. Andrews were very concerned about the downward trend in the number of patients being referred to and treated at the Eating Disorders Clinic. Initially, they believed that the decrease might simply be a reflection of a decrease in the prevalence of anorexia nervosa and bulimia in the population. However, a review of the medical literature and discussions with administrators of eating disorders programs from across the country strongly suggested that this was not the case. Furthermore, conversations with the medical director at City Hospital confirmed that the number of cases of the disorders treated by the City Hospital program has continued to increase during recent years.

St. Andrews' officials next turned to the marketing department for the development and implementation of some type of research designed to uncover the reasons behind the decreasing enrollment in the eating disorders program.

Sampling Plan

Because more than 80 percent of the cases treated at the Eating Disorders Clinic are referred to the program by other health-care providers, St. Andrews' marketing staff believed that the research should be directed at these health-care providers. In particular, they wanted to obtain attitudes and opinions about the St. Andrews program specifically and about eating disorders programs in general.

The population for which a sample frame was to be developed included all health-care professionals in the market area of St. Andrews Medical Center who may treat female patients between the ages of 14 and 22 years.

A review of admittance records showed that referrals were most likely to come from primary care practitioners, including physicians in general medicine, family medicine, internal medicine, and gastroenterology. In addition, referrals have been received from pediatricians, obstetricians/gynecologists, psychiatrists, and psychologists. Although the names and addresses of physicians in these specialties were available from several sources, the marketing staff believed that the telephone directory provided the easiest and least expensive listing. The sampling frame thus included all physicians (or psychologists) from each of these specialties and was drawn from the Yellow Pages of the current telephone directory. The exhibit below provides the breakdown of the number of professionals of each type included in the sampling frame. All health-care providers on the list were to be contacted.

Administration

The marketing department staff decided to conduct a mail survey and constructed a three-page structured questionnaire that was sent to the 699 health-care providers on the list using the addresses obtained from the telephone directory. An appropriate cover letter was also included. Although neither the cover letter nor the questionnaire identified St. Andrews Medical Center as the sponsor of the survey, no attempt was made to disguise the purpose of the survey. In addition to questions related specifically to the St. Andrews' program, the marketing staff included questions about City Hospital's competing program and about eating disorders programs in general.

Of the 699 questionnaires distributed, 56 (8 percent) were returned as undeliverable by the postal service, while 119 were completed and returned by respondents (a 17 percent response rate). Although St. Andrews' officials were displeased with the low response rate—they had anticipated at least a 25 percent return rate—they thought that the data would provide useful information for the management of the Eating Disorders Clinic.

EXHIBIT V.A.1 Sampling Frame

Specialty	Number of Practitioners
Pediatricians	63
Obstetricians/Gynecologists	63
Psychiatrists	124
Psychologists	128
Primary-Care Practitioners*	321
Total	699

*Includes specialists in family medicine, general medicine, internal medicine, and gastroenterology.

[1]The contributions of Tom J. Brown to the development of this case are gratefully acknowledged.

Questions

1. What is the appropriate target population given the hospital's interest?

2. Evaluate the sampling frame given the target population chosen by the hospital staff. What other sources might exist for use in developing the sampling frame?

3. Evaluate the use of a mail questionnaire for this research.

Case V.B   Riverside County Humane Society (B)

The demands on the Riverside County Humane Society (RCHS) had increased rather dramatically over the past several years, while the tax dollars the society received to provide services had remained relatively unchanged. In an effort to halt further decline in the quality of its services and to provide better care for the pets at the center, the Membership Committee of the board of directors began making plans for a member/contributor drive. The organized drive was to be the first of its kind for the local chapter and the committee members wanted it to be as productive as possible.

As the plans began to evolve, the committee realized that the organization had only scattered bits and pieces of information about its current members. It did have a list of members and contributors for the last five years that had been compiled by the RCHS staff. In addition, it had access to the results of a survey that had been done by a staff member several years previous that focused on member usage of shelter facilities and their opinions of shelter services and programs. However, the organization had only sparse knowledge of the profile of its typical member and contributor, why they belonged or contributed, how long they had been associated with the humane society, how the services of the humane society could be improved, and so on. The committee members believed information on these issues was important to the conduct of a successful membership drive, and thus they commissioned some research to secure it.

Some initial contacts with other humane society chapters and interviews with some RCHS staff and board members produced a number of hypotheses regarding who is likely to become a member or contributor, why, how much people are likely to give, and so on. The researchers are interested in examining these hypotheses through a mail survey sent to current members and contributors. (See Case II.B Riverside County Humane Society [A] for details.)

Sampling Plan

For the last five years, the RCHS had maintained a master list of members and contributors. Contributors were those who had sent a donation to RCHS but had not opted to fill out an official form making them members, which essentially entitled them to receive RCHS's newsletter. The separate list of members contained all those who had expressed interest in membership and who were receiving the newsletter. Both lists were alphabetical. The contributor list included the amount received from each person or business, but not the number of times the person or business gave during the last five years. The member list showed the number of years each organization or person had belonged.

For purposes of the study, all names of businesses or other organizations were deleted and a separate sample was taken from each list. There were approximately 1,050 people on the member list and 300 on the contributor list. The researchers decided to take 120 names from the member list and 50 from the contributor list. They identified those to be sent questionnaires by drawing two random numbers—3 and 5—using a random number table. They then sent questionnaires to the 3rd, 11th, 19th, etc., person on the member list, and the 5th, 11th, 17th, etc., person on the contributor list.

Questions

1. What is the sampling frame and is it a good frame for the target population?

2. What type of sample is being used?

3. Can you think of some ways in which the sample could be improved?

Case V.C PartyTime, Inc.[1]

Andrew Todd, chief executive officer of PartyTime, Inc., a manufacturer of specialty paper products, is preparing to make an important decision. In the 14 years since he founded the company, sales and profits have increased over tenfold to all-time highs of $7,000,000 and $1,150,000, respectively, during the current year. Industry analysts predict continued stable growth during the upcoming year. Despite his firm belief in the adage, "If it's not broken, don't fix it," Todd thinks that it might be time for the addition of a new channel of distribution, based on information he has recently received.

About the Company

PartyTime manufactures a variety of specialty paper products that can be grouped into three basic categories: gift wrap (all types), party goods (printed plates, cups, napkins, party favors, etc.), and other paper goods (specialty advertising, calendars, etc.). When Todd founded the company, he purchased and renovated an existing paper mill located in the Pacific Northwest. Today, company headquarters and production facilities remain at the original location. During the heavy production season, the company employs approximately 200 people.

As shown in the exhibit below, gift wrap accounts for about 60 percent of revenues (50 percent of profits), and party goods amount to about 30 percent of sales (40 percent of profits). All other paper products sold by the company produce about 10 percent of revenues and an equivalent percentage of profits. Sales of gift wrap and other paper goods have been stable, increasing 3 to 4 percent per year during the previous five years. Interestingly (and as Todd is pleased to note), total sales of party goods have been increasing at about a 9 percent annual rate.

The Distribution Decision

Given the profitability of the party-goods line and its substantial sales growth in recent years, Todd is very interested

[1]The contribution of Tom J. Brown to the development of this case are gratefully acknowledged.

in further increasing sales of specialty party goods. A recent publication of the National Association of Paper and Party Retailers (NAPPR) indicated that industrywide sales of party goods are expected to increase some 10 to 20 percent during the upcoming year. Of particular interest is the projection that sales of party goods through independent party goods (IPG) shops will increase more than 25 percent. Currently, PartyTime party goods are distributed only through mass merchandisers and chain drugstores.

Although sales have been increasing steadily using existing channels, Todd wondered if the time was right to add the IPG channel. Any decision to include the new channel would have to be made early in the year, however, before orders for the holiday season begin arriving (a large percentage of total sales of party goods at the retail level occur during the holiday season).

Independent Party Goods (IPG) Shops

IPG retailers typically operate small to moderate-sized stores that are often located in malls or strip shopping centers. The label "independent" indicates that the stores are not owned or franchised by major manufacturers, such as Hallmark. In recent years, the number of IPG shops has grown tremendously, to the point where it is not unusual to have 15 to 20 shops in larger cities. Growth has been particularly strong in California, Florida, the upper Midwest, and the East.

Competitive Issues

Competition within traditional channels of distribution for party goods is intense. Within these channels, PartyTime must compete against major producers, such as C.A. Reed, Beach Products, Unique, Hallmark, and Ambassador. The major competitors within the IPG channel, in contrast, are fewer in number; only AMSCAM, Contempo, and Paper Art serve as primary suppliers. Competition within the IPG channel is thought to be much less intense than that in the traditional channels.

EXHIBIT V.C.1	Current-Year Sales and Profit Breakdown by Category			
Category	Sales	Percentage	Profit	Percentage
Gift wrap	$4,302,300	61	$ 564,700	49
Party goods	2,045,500	29	472,300	41
Other paper goods	705,200	10	115,000	10
Total	$7,053,000	100	$1,152,000	100

December 13 Todd is leaning strongly toward committing the resources necessary to enter the IPG channel and has called a meeting of his managers to discuss the proposed move. He believes that there is room for at least one more supplier, because the competition is less intense than in the traditional distribution channels. In addition, he regards this as an opportunity to further expand the most profitable area of PartyTime's business.

At the meeting, most of PartyTime's managers seem to agree with Todd, although Kim Shinoda, the company's chief accountant, suggests that the company should learn more about IPG retailers before a decision is made. In a memorandum distributed at the meeting, she details the following areas in which more information is needed before a decision is reached:

- *Competitive Products*   Are IPG retailers satisfied with current product offerings on the market? Do they receive a satisfactory level of service from the current suppliers?

- *Purchase Criteria*   In addition to price and product considerations, what other characteristics of suppliers and product lines do retailers think are important?

- *Supplier Loyalty*   To what extent are retailers willing to carry product lines of more than one supplier?

Todd agrees that more information would be useful in making a decision, but he realizes that time constraints will force him to make a decision within the next few weeks. Along with his managers, he decides to bring in a marketing research team.

January 16   The marketing research team is now ready to share the results of the research project with the managers at PartyTime. To implement the research, they had developed an undisguised, semistructured telephone questionnaire designed to obtain the information that Shinoda had suggested.

Officials at PartyTime are particularly interested in the responses of retailers located in those geographic areas in which growth is expected to be strongest over the next year; therefore, a sampling frame was developed using telephone directories in the major cities within these geographic regions. Because many types of stores could conceivably be considered IPG shops, two criteria were established for inclusion in the sampling frame: (1) the shop must devote more than 50 percent of its shelf space to paper and party goods, and (2) the shop must carry products from more than one supplier. A total of 110 shops were identified using the telephone directories. Although attempts were made to contact each of these shops during business hours, only 82 could be reached. Thirty-two of these met the two criteria, and 23 agreed to participate in the interview.

January 19   Based on the results of the marketing research project and the input of his managers, Todd has decided to increase production of party goods and market these products through the IPG channel.

Questions

1. Evaluate the research team's development of the sample of store owners. How would you have recommended the research team develop the sampling frame?

2. Do you think that a telephone survey was the best way to collect the needed information?

Case V.D   Student Computer Lab (B)[1]

Rod Stevenson, director of the Student Computer Center (SCC), opened a new computer lab in the business school at a major university in the fall of 2000. The new lab was designed to meet the needs of all business school students. It offered specialized software required by student courses, both IBM compatible and Macintosh machines, and the latest technology in hardware and software. After operating for six months, Mr. Stevenson recognized some potential problems with the new computer lab. Although the number of computers had doubled with the new lab, student

suggestions and complaints indicated that the demand for computers at times exceeded the available resources.

To address this problem, in January 2001, Mr. Stevenson established a task force to investigate the level of student satisfaction with the computer lab. The task force was made up of four business graduate students. They aimed to (1) help the computer lab identify students needs and (2) provide suggestions on how student needs could be most effectively met. After reviewing available information on the lab, the students in the task force decided to conduct some research before making recommendations on the services offered. (See Case II.D, Student Computer Lab [A] for more information.)

---

[1]The contributions of Monika E. Wingate to the development of this case are gratefully acknowledged.

Student Survey

Using the input from several focus groups, the students developed a questionnaire they felt addressed all the important computer lab issues. Before presenting this survey to Mr. Stevenson, the task force also needed to propose a method to administer the questionnaire. They defined the target population as students enrolled in the School of Business. Since there was not adequate time or funding to administer the questionnaire to all these students, the task force members all agreed they should take a sample. To achieve a 90 percent confidence level, the task force estimated they needed to collect 100 surveys. They came up with five possible sampling plans to achieve this.

Plan 1   Since all the task force members had classes in the business school, each student in the task force could administer the survey to students before and after classes, or in the hallways of the business school. Each task force member would be responsible for completing 25 surveys.

Plan 2   The university publishes a list of courses offered in the business school. The course listing could be used as a sampling frame. A random-number table could be used to select the classes, and all students in those classrooms would be sampled. Since the average class size is about 45 students, a total of 3 classes would be selected for sampling.

Plan 3   A list of all business school students was available from the dean's office. This list had student names, ID numbers, and addresses. The task force could use a random-number table to pull a sample of students by their ID number, and then mail the survey including a return envelope, to the address listed. Enough surveys would be mailed to receive 100 responses.

Plan 4   Each task force member could be assigned to collect 25 surveys from either undergraduate or graduate students. Because 75 percent of the business school students are undergraduates, three task force members would collect surveys from undergraduates and one from graduate students.

Plan 5   Both the graduate and undergraduate offices have lists of students enrolled in their program. The listing includes name, ID number, address, and phone. A sample could be pulled from each list separately, using a random-number table. Because 75 percent of the business school students are undergraduates, the task force would telephone enough students to receive 75 undergraduate and 25 graduate student responses.

The SCC task force had three questions they felt were pertinent to deciding the appropriate sampling plan. First, was it necessary to take a random sample of students? Second, since both undergraduate and graduate students used the lab, did the task force need to insure responses from both groups? Third, would the method of data collection impact student responses?

Questions

1. What type of sampling plan is being proposed in each case?

2. How do you think the SCC task force should address each of the questions they listed for deciding the appropriate sampling plan?

3. What are the strengths and weaknesses of each proposed sampling plan? Which plan would you recommend and why?

Case V.E   First Federal Bank of Bakersfield

The Equal Credit Opportunity Act, which was passed in 1974, was partially designed to protect women from discriminatory banking practices. It forbade, for example, the use of credit evaluations based on gender or marital status. Although adherence to the law has changed the way many bankers do business, women's perception that there is a bias against them by a particular financial institution often remains unless some specific steps are taken by the institution to counter that perception.

Close to a dozen "women's banks"—that is, banks owned and operated by and for women—opened their doors during the 1980s with the specific purpose of targeting and promoting their services to this otherwise underdeveloped market. Although women's banks currently are evolving into full-service banks serving a wide range of clients, a number of traditional banks are moving in the other direction by attempting to develop services that are targeted specifically to-

ward women. Many of these institutions see such a strategy as a viable way to attract valuable customers and to increase their market share in the short term while gaining a competitive advantage by which they can compete in the long term as the roles of women in the labor force gain in importance. One can find, with even the most cursory examination of the trade press, examples of credit-card advertising that depicts single, affluent, and head-of-the-household female card holders; financial seminar programs for wives of affluent professional men; informational literature that details how newly divorced and separated women can obtain credit; and entire packages of counseling, educational opportunities, and special services for women.

The First Federal Bank of Bakersfield was interested in developing its own program of this kind. The executives were curious about a number of issues. Were women's financial needs being adequately met in the Bakersfield area? What additional financial services would women especially like to have? How do Bakersfield's women feel about banks and bankers? Was First Federal in a good position to take advantage of the needs of women? What channels of communication might be best to reach women who might be interested in the services that First Federal had to offer?

The executives believed that First Federal might have some special advantages if it did try to appeal to women. For one thing, the Bakersfield community seemed to be quite sensitive to the issues being raised by the feminist movement. For another, First Federal was a small, personal bank. The executives thought that women might be more comfortable in dealing with a smaller, more personalized institution and that the bank might not have the traditional "image problem" among women that larger banks might have.

Research Objectives

One program the bank executives were considering that they believed might be particularly attractive to women was a series of financial seminars. The seminars could cover a number of topics, including money management, wills, trusts, estate planning, taxes, insurance, investments, financial services, and establishing a credit rating. The executives were interested in determining women's reactions to each of these potential topics. They were also interested to know what the best format might be in terms of location, frequency, length of each program, and so on, if there were a high level of interest. Consequently, they decided that the bank should conduct a research study that had the assessment of the financial seminar series as its main objective but that also shed some light on the other issues they had been debating. More specifically, the objectives of the research were as follows:

1. To determine the interest that exists among women in the Bakersfield area for seminars on financial matters.

2. To identify the reasons why Bakersfield women would change, or have changed, their banking affiliations.

3. To examine the attitudes of Bakersfield women toward financial institutions and the people who run them.

4. To determine if there was any correlation between the demographic characteristics of women in the Bakersfield area and the services they might like to have.

5. To analyze the media usage habits of Bakersfield-area women.

Method

The assignment to develop a research strategy by which these objectives could be assessed was given to the bank's internal marketing research department. The department consisted of only five members—Beth Anchurch, the research director, and four project analysts. As Anchurch pondered the assignment, she was concerned about the best way to proceed. She was particularly concerned with the relatively short time horizon she was given for the project. Top executives thought that there was promise in the seminar idea. If they were right, they wanted to get on with designing and offering the seminars before any of their competitors came up with a similar idea. Thus, they specified that they would like the results of the research department's investigation to be available within 45 to 50 days.

As Anchurch began to contemplate the data collection, she became particularly concerned with whether the study should use mail questionnaires or telephone interviews. She had tentatively ruled out personal interviews because of the short deadline that had been imposed. After several days of contemplating the alternatives, she finally decided that it would be best to collect the information by telephone. Further, she decided that it would be better to hire out the telephone interviewing than to use her four project analysts to make the calls.

Anchurch believed that the multiple objectives of the project required a reasonably large sample of women so that the various characteristics of interest would be sufficiently represented to enable some conclusions to be drawn about the population of Bakersfield as a whole. After pondering the various cross tabulations in which the bank executives would be interested, she finally decided that a sample of 500 to 600 adult women would be sufficient. The sample was to be drawn from the white pages of the Bakersfield telephone directory by the Bakersfield Interviewing Service, the firm that First Federal had hired to complete the interviews.

The sample was to be drawn using a scheme in which two names were selected from each page of the directory, first by selecting two of the four columns on the page at random and then by selecting the fifteenth name in each of the selected columns. The decision to sample names from each page was made so that each interviewer could operate with certain designated pages of the directory, since each was operating independently out of her home.

The decision to sample every fifteenth name in the selected columns was determined in the following way. First, there were 328 pages in the directory with four columns of names per page. There were 80 entries per column on average, or approximately 26,240 listings. Using Bureau of the Census data on household composition, it was estimated that 20 percent of all households would be ineligible for the study because they did not contain an adult female resident. This meant that only 20,992 ($0.80 \times 26,240$) of the listings would probably qualify. Since 500 to 600 names were needed, it seemed easiest to select two columns on each page at random and to take the same numbered entry from each column. The interviewer could then simply count or measure down from the top of the column. The number 15 was determined randomly; thus, the fifteenth listing in the randomly selected columns on each page was called. If the household did not answer or if the women of the house refused to participate, the interviewers were instructed to select another number from that column through the use of an abbreviated table of random numbers that each was given. They were to use a similar procedure if the household that was called did not have an adult woman living there.

First Federal decided to operate without callbacks because the interviewing service charged heavily for them. Anchurch did think it would be useful to follow up with a sample of those interviewed to make sure that they indeed had been called, since the interviewers for Bakersfield Interviewing Service operated out of their own homes and it was impossible to supervise them more directly. She did this by selecting at random a handful of the surveys completed by each interviewer. She then had one of her project assistants call that respondent, verify that the interview had taken place, and check the accuracy of the responses of a few of the most important questions. This audit revealed absolutely no instances of interviewer cheating.

The completed interview forms were turned over to First Federal for its own internal analysis. As part of this analysis, the project analyst compared the demographic characteristics of those contacted to the demographic characteristics of the population in the Bakersfield area as reported in the 2000 census. The comparison is shown in Exhibit V.E.1. The analyst also prepared a summary of the nonresponses and refusals by interviewer. This comparison is shown in Exhibit V.E.2.

EXHIBIT V.E.1   Selected Demographic Comparison of Survey Respondents with Bureau of Census Data

| | PERCENTAGE OF WOMEN | |
Characteristic/Category	Survey	Census
Marital Status		
Married	53	42
Single	30	40
Separated	1	2
Widowed	9	9
Divorced	7	7
Age		
18–24	23	23
25–34	30	28
35–44	16	14
45–64	18	21
65+	13	14
Income		
Less than $10,000	9	29
$10,000–$19,999	19	29
$20,000–$50,000	58	36
More than $50,000	2	6
Refused	12	

EXHIBIT V.E.2   Results of Calls by Interviewer

	NUMBER OF NONRESPONSES			NUMBER OF REFUSALS		
Interviewer	Line Busy	No Answer	Ineligibles*	Initial	After Partial Completion	Number of Completions
1	7	101	36	15	0	30
2	2	45	13	16	0	30
3	11	71	23	17	7	30
4	14	56	47	35	6	39
5	9	93	10	23	13	30
6	5	102	28	63	14	35
7	6	36	17	16	0	18
8	7	107	23	13	0	30
9	11	106	36	47	0	30
10	10	55	6	35	9	30
11	38	83	48	92	0	30
12	5	22	3	8	0	9
13	23	453	102	65	7	99
14	12	102	27	31	0	19
15	7	173	29	66	0	34
16	2	65	9	33	0	22
Total	169	1,670	457	575	56	515
		1,839			631	

*No adult female resident.

Questions

1. Compare the advantages and disadvantages of using telephone interviews rather than personal interviews or mail questionnaires to collect the needed data.

2. Compare the advantages and disadvantages of using in-house staff versus a professional interviewing service to collect the data.

3. Do you think that the telephone directory provided a good sampling frame given the purposes of the study, or would you recommend an alternative sampling frame?

4. What type of sample is being used here? Still using the white pages of the telephone directory as the sampling frame, would you recommend some other sampling scheme? Why or why not?

5. If you were Anchurch, would you be happy with the performance of the Bakersfield Interviewing Service? Why or why not?

Case V.F   Holzem Business Systems

Holzem Business Systems serviced a number of small-business accounts in the immediate area surrounding its Madison, Wisconsin, location. The company, which was headed by Claude Holzem, a certified public accountant, specialized in the preparation of financial statements, tax forms, and other reports required by various governmental units. Since its founding, the company had experienced steady, and sometimes spectacular, growth. Holzem, whose policy was high-quality service at competitive rates, was so successful in Dane County that it was far and away the dominant firm serving small businesses in the area. Further growth seemed to depend more on expansion into new areas than on further penetration of the Madison market.

Faced with such a prospect, Holzem conceived a plan that would capitalize on the substantial talent at the company's main office. What he envisioned was an operation in which area field representatives would secure raw data from clients. At the end of each day, they would transmit this information to headquarters using microcomputers with modems. There it would be coded and processed and the necessary forms prepared. These income statements, balance sheets, or tax forms would then be returned to the area representative. The field person would go over them with clients and would answer any questions that clients might have.

In Holzem's mind, the system had a number of advantages. First, it allowed Holzem Business Systems to capitalize on the substantial expertise it had in its Madison office. The quality control for which the company had become noted could be maintained, as could the company's record of quick service. Second, the company would not need to hire CPAs as field representatives, because these area managers would not actually be preparing financial statements. The prospect of using general business-college graduates who understood financial statements and could explain their significance to clients had cost advantages for Holzem since CPAs were commanding higher salaries.

The big question confronting Holzem was whether there would be a demand for such a service. There was no

question in his mind that there was a need for accounting services among small businesses. His Madison experience had demonstrated this. But he was concerned that the physical distance between the client and the office might prove to be a psychological barrier for clients. If it proved to be necessary to establish full-service branches in each area, then geographic expansion was less attractive to him.

To help him decide whether to go ahead, Holzem commissioned a research study that had as its objectives identifying the perceived problems and the need for CPA services in general and, in particular, potential client attitudes toward the type of service arrangement he envisioned.

Hathaway Research Associates, headed by James and Nancy Hathaway, was retained to do the study. It was to be conducted using personal interviews among a representative sample of small businesses within the state. For purposes of the study, a small business was defined as one employing fewer than 50 people. The study was to be confined to small businesses in the industries designated contract construction, manufacturing, wholesale trade, retail trade, and commercial services. These categories represented approximately 95 percent of all Holzem accounts, 85 percent of the total small businesses, and 81 percent of all businesses in the state.

Sampling Plan

The businesses serving as the sample were to be selected in the following way. First, the state was to be divided into the three regions depicted in Figure V.F.1. Next, five counties were to be selected from each region by the following scheme.

1. The cumulative number of businesses was to be calculated from Exhibit V.F.1. The accumulation for the first ten counties in Region 1, for example, is as follows:

FIGURE V.F.1   Regional Breakdown of Wisconsin Counties

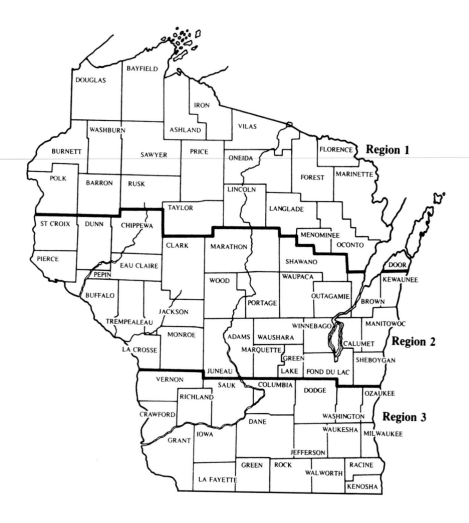

County	Number of Businesses	Cumulative Number of Businesses
Douglas	668	668
Burnett	147	815
Polk	488	1,303
Washburn	282	1,585
Barron	565	2,150
Baysfield	178	2,328
Sawyer	324	2,652
Rusk	229	2,881
Ashland	307	3,188
Iron	122	3,310

2. A table of random numbers would be employed to determine which five counties would be selected. For example, if a number between 816 and 1,303 came up, Polk county would be used.

Hathaway Research Associates then planned to contact the state Department of Industry, Labor, and Human Relations (DILHR) for a list of individual firms within each county. DILHR used the unemployment computer tape to prepare such lists. This tape was compiled each year and reflected payments by firms into the state's unemployment compensation system. The records within the tape were maintained county by county, by SIC (Standard Industrial Classification) code within county, and in alphabetical order within the SIC code. Since the number of employees of each firm was indicated, DILHR could screen the master list and print out only those firms that satisfied the location, industry, and geographic criteria Hathaway Research Associates specified. DILHR would sell these lists of firms to interested clients, but they would only provide the name, address, and phone number of the selected businesses.

Hathaway Research Associates proposed to select 40 businesses from each county by the following procedure:

| EXHIBIT V.F.1 | Number of Small Businesses by Major Industry Category | | | | | |

County	Contract Construction	Manufacturing	Wholesale Trade	Retail Trade	Commercial Services	Total
Adams	14	10	3	49	27	103
Ashland	26	37	26	127	91	307
Barron	88	52	82	295	48	565
Bayfield	20	25	8	85	40	178
Brown	387	187	330	871	804	2,579
Buffalo	23	14	22	92	47	198
Burnett	22	12	7	82	24	147
Calumet	62	47	48	162	128	447
Chippewa	105	67	94	300	216	782
Clark	60	76	82	203	101	522
Columbia	98	55	84	360	208	805
Crawford	33	25	32	119	64	273
Dane	638	314	493	1,800	1,705	4,950
Dodge	143	98	119	370	258	988
Door	76	27	27	206	168	504
Douglas	49	30	43	339	207	668
Dunn	37	21	55	187	110	410
Eau Claire	122	39	113	415	331	1,020
Florence	4	6	1	29	6	46
Fond du Lac	178	94	131	546	374	1,323
Forrest	9	25	8	116	27	185
Grant	88	60	125	341	200	814
Green	71	49	82	234	122	558
Green Lake	60	28	28	150	84	350
Iowa	41	23	55	135	65	319
Iron	11	15	10	60	26	122
Jackson	27	14	29	120	49	239
Jefferson	120	88	111	400	283	1,002
Juneau	38	28	27	172	79	344
Kenosha	159	75	105	624	167	1,130
Kewaunee	44	35	32	112	76	299
La Crosse	167	91	159	573	450	1,440
Lafayette	31	29	50	106	58	274
Langlade	29	53	59	135	92	368
Lincoln	50	43	38	184	109	424
Manitowoc	161	102	119	464	338	1,184
Marathon	244	148	196	520	432	1,540
Marinette	63	75	56	253	153	600
Marquette	27	11	9	68	34	149
Menominee	1	5	2	4	6	18
Milwaukee	1,200	1,238	1,711	4,914	5,708	14,771
Monrow	49	37	67	235	115	503
Oconto	49	43	50	143	97	382
Oneida	101	40	45	305	180	671
Outagamie	273	117	227	697	568	1,882
Ozaukee	151	109	95	313	245	915
Pepin	12	7	18	61	31	129
Pierce	50	27	29	206	104	416
Polk	59	44	51	234	100	488

Continued

EXHIBIT V.F.1	Number of Small Businesses by Major Industry Category, *continued*					
Portage	83	42	71	280	171	647
Price	19	44	32	92	59	246
Racine	292	285	178	853	738	2,346
Richland	29	20	35	108	67	259
Rock	236	118	148	811	570	1,883
Rusk	24	34	34	95	42	229
St. Croix	80	44	61	225	144	554
Sauk	104	58	91	376	223	852
Sawyer	36	25	16	128	119	324
Shawano	65	58	61	232	110	526
Sheboygan	204	151	118	523	433	1,429
Taylor	29	28	36	93	57	243
Trempeleau	51	43	60	192	98	444
Vernon	37	39	52	154	85	367
Vilas	72	30	17	175	113	407
Walworth	144	106	90	522	345	1,207
Washburn	41	27	18	136	60	282
Washington	173	110	97	369	262	1,011
Waukesha	694	506	501	1,147	1,097	3,945
Waupaca	81	70	72	328	201	752
Waushara	26	22	30	114	71	263
Winnebago	244	157	151	759	632	1,943
Wood	141	83	104	427	303	1,058
Totals	8,475	5,995	7,466	26,655	20,957	69,548

Source: County Business Patterns.

1. The total number of businesses within the county was to be divided by 40 to get a sampling interval. The sampling interval would be different, of course, for each county.

2. A random start was to be generated for each county, using a table of random numbers. The random number was to be some number between one and the sampling interval, and this number was to be used to designate the first business to be included in the sample.

3. The sampling interval was to be added repeatedly to the random start, and every number generated in this manner was to designate a business to be included in the sample.

This procedure was to be followed for all counties except Milwaukee and Dane. Holzem believed that if he were to expand into the Milwaukee market at all, he wanted to do it with a completely self-sufficient branch and not with a satellite office tied to the Madison headquarters. He consequently instructed Hathaway Research Associates to exclude Milwaukee County from this part of the research investigation. Dane County was to be excluded because of the company's already successful penetration of this market.

Once the total sample of 600 businesses had been specified, Hathaway Research Associates would contact each firm by phone to set up an appointment for a personal interview with one of its highly trained field interviewers.

Questions

1. What kind of sample is being proposed by Hathaway Research Associates? Is this a good choice?

2. Is the sample a true probability sample (i.e., does every small business in Wisconsin have a known chance of selection)?

3. What is the probability that a small business in Menominee County (the county with the fewest small businesses) will be included in the sample? What is the probability that a small business in Waukesha County (of those counties eligible, the one with the most small businesses) will be included in the sample? Will this discrepancy cause any problems in analysis?

4. Are businesses within each of the Standard Industrial Classifications likely to be represented properly in the sample?

Case V.G   The Dryden Press

The Dryden Press was established in the mid-1960s by Holt, Rinehart and Winston, which had traditionally been a strong social science publisher, as a response to the growth in enrollments that business schools were experiencing and the explosion in enrollments that was predicted they would experience in the future. The venture represented one of the first forays by a traditional nonbusiness text publisher into the college business market. The experiment turned out to be very successful, and The Dryden Press became one of the top six publishers in the business area in sales. Company executives believed that one of the key reasons for Dryden's success was its ability to target books for specific market segments. The company was one of the first to recognize the potential growth in courses in consumer behavior and managerial economics, for example, and introduced the successful texts by Engel, Kollat, and Blackwell in consumer behavior and by Brigham and Pappas in managerial economics in response. Through careful management of the revisions, these books maintained strong market positions more than 25 years after they had been introduced.

The Dryden Press editorial staff tried to maintain a posture of extreme sensitivity to changing market conditions brought about by the publication of new research findings or the changing demands placed on students as a result of changes in the environment and the needs of businesses. The editors made it a point to keep up with these changes so that the company would be prepared with new products when the situation demanded it. This was no small task, because the lead time on a book typically ran from three to four years from the time the author was first signed to a contract to when the book was actually published. It seemed to take most authors almost two years to develop a first draft of a book manuscript. The typical manuscript was then reviewed by a sample of experts in the field. Based on their reactions, most manuscripts would undergo some revision before being placed in production. The production process, which included such things as copyediting the manuscript, setting type, drawing all figures, preparing promotional materials, proofreading, and so on, usually took about a year.

Research Questions and Objectives

So that it would not be caught short if the needs and desires of the market in consumer behavior texts changed, the editorial staff decided to find out the current level of use of the various texts in consumer behavior and the directions in which the market was moving. What were the market shares of the respective texts? What features of the various books were liked and disliked? Did the use of the various texts and the preference for certain features

vary by class of school? Did four-year colleges have different requirements for consumer behavior texts than two-year schools? After a good deal of discussion among the members of the editorial staff, these general concerns were translated into specific research objectives. More specifically, the staff decided to conduct a research investigation that attempted to determine the following:

1. the importance of various topical areas in the teaching of consumer behavior within the next two to five years;

2. the importance and treatment of managerial applications in consumer behavior courses;

3. the level of satisfaction with the textbooks currently in use;

4. the relative market shares of the major consumer behavior textbooks.

5. the degree of switching of texts that goes on in consumer behavior courses from year to year;

6. the importance of various pedagogical aids, such as glossaries, cases, learning objectives, and so on, in the textbook selection decision; and

7. the importance of supplementary teaching tools, such as student study guides, overhead transparency masters, or an instructor's manual, among others, in the textbook selection decision.

The editorial staff thought it was important that the needed information be obtained from those who were actively involved in teaching consumer behavior courses. The staff also thought it imperative that only one respondent be used from any given school, even though the editors realized that some schools had multiple sections of the consumer behavior course and that different books might be used in different sections. For the most part, however, the editors believed that the same book would be used across sections, though not across courses, in the sense that the introductory courses at the undergraduate and graduate levels would use different books. The editors decided that it would be better to target the questionnaires to one individual at each of the selected institutions and to simply have that person indicate on the questionnaire whether he or she normally taught a graduate or undergraduate course. Dryden could then analyze the responses to determine if there were any differences in them that could be attributed to the level at which the course was taught.

Method

There were several reasons why the editorial staff decided to use a mail questionnaire to collect the data. For one thing, the target population was geographically dispersed. Even though it was decided to limit the study only to those actively involved in teaching consumer behavior domestically, that still meant respondents could come from all over the United States, which in turn meant that it could be prohibitive to collect this information by personal interview. At the same time, professors had no standard working schedule. Some might teach in the morning and some in the evening. When they were not teaching, some might work in their offices while others might work elsewhere. This variety of schedules and work conditions required that the questionnaires be available when the professors might be inclined to fill them out. Also, the objectives finally decided on allowed the use of a relatively structured and undisguised questionnaire.

The big question facing the Dryden staff was how to draw a sample from the target population of those actively teaching a consumer behavior course, either at the undergraduate or graduate levels. For purposes of the study, "actively teaching" was operationally defined as having taught a consumer behavior course at least once in the last two years or being scheduled to teach one within the next year.

The company was considering drawing the sample from one of two lists that it had at its disposal. One of the lists was an internal list consisting of all those professors whom the salespeople's reports indicated were interested in teaching specific courses, such as financial planning, introductory accounting, marketing management, or consumer behavior. This meant that the salesperson had indicated on his or her report that the professor was to receive sample copies of all those books in, say, consumer behavior that The Dryden Press published. Most of the entries on the list were developed from salespeople's calls, although some of them arose at the national association meetings at which Dryden displayed its list of titles. Professors would often request sample copies of selected titles at the meetings so that they could review them before making an adoption decision. All requests for complimentary copies were sent for authorization to the salesperson serving the school. By approving the request, the salesperson

was aware of the professor's interest and could follow it up in an attempt to get the adoption. Because of how it was developed and used, the internal list paralleled the salesperson territory structure.

Although most salespeople operated within one state and often within only part of a state, some operated across several states. Each salesperson was responsible for all the schools in his or her territory, including the universities with graduate programs, four-year colleges without graduate programs, and two-year institutions. The schools were listed alphabetically by salesperson, and each school had a computer code associated with it, designating its type. Each professor on the list had a set of computer codes associated with the name that identified his or her interest areas.

The alternate list The Dryden Press considered using was the printed membership directory of the Association for Consumer Research (ACR). ACR is an organization formed in the late 1960s that was designed for the pursuit of knowledge in the area of consumer behavior. Its membership is dominated by marketing professors (almost 80 percent of the total), although it also includes interested members from business and government as well as members representing other academic disciplines, such as sociology and psychology. The ACR directory was organized alphabetically by name of the member. Along with each member's name, the directory provided either the office or home address, depending on which the individual preferred to use, and both the office and the home phone numbers. While about one-half of the addresses listed only the college at which the individual worked, the other 50 percent also listed the department. There were 64 pages in the directory, and all pages except the last one had 16 names. A small percentage of the addresses were international.

Questions
1. Given the purposes of the study, how would you recommend a sample be drawn from
   (a) Dryden's internal computer list?
   (b) the ACR printed membership directory?
2. Which approach would you recommend and why?

Case V.H   School of Business (B)[1]

The School of Business, one unit in a public university enrolling over 40,000 students, has approximately 2,100 students in its bachelor's, master's, and doctorate degree programs in all areas of business, including accounting,

finance, operations and information management, marketing, management, and others. Because the School of Business must serve a diverse student population on limited resources, it is important to accurately measure students' satisfaction with the school's services.

Accurate measurement of student satisfaction will enable the school to target improvement efforts to those areas of greatest concern to students, whether that be by major,

[1]The contributions of Sara Pitterle to the development of this case are gratefully acknowledged.

support services, or some other aspect of their educational experiences. The school feels that improving its service to its customers (students) will result in more satisfied alumni, better community relations, additional applicants, and increased corporate involvement. Since graduate and undergraduate students are believed to have different expectations and needs, the school plans to investigate the satisfaction of these two groups separately.

In a previous survey of graduating seniors using open-ended questions, three primary areas of concern were identified: the faculty, classes/curriculum, and resources. Resources consisted of five specific areas: Undergraduate Advising Services, the Learning Center, Computer Facilities, the Library, and the Career Services Office. The research team for this project developed five-point Likert scale questions to measure students' satisfaction in each of these areas. In addition, demographic questions were included to determine whether satisfaction with the school was a function of a student's grade point average, major, job status upon graduation, or gender. Previous surveys used by the School of Business and other published satisfaction scales provided examples of questions and wording for the survey.

A random sample of the 400 graduating School of Business seniors was selected to receive the questionnaire. Random sampling for this project was possible because the school maintains a computer list of all seniors graduating at the end of the current semester. The list of graduating seniors contains home phone numbers and addresses. Numbers were assigned to each student and a random number generator was used to select the respondents. Because the research team was working under a tight deadline (seniors were graduating and leaving), a modified mail format was used to increase the response rate.

Questionnaires were mailed to each of the respondents on a Friday. Over the weekend, the research team called each respondent and explained the purpose and importance of the survey. A verbal commitment to complete the survey was obtained from each respondent. One week after mailing the survey, the research team again telephoned each respondent. Those respondents who had already completed the questionnaire were thanked for their prompt response. Those who had not yet completed the questionnaire were reminded of the importance to the school of their candid responses.

In addition to the telephone calls, the team used the following strategies to increase the response rate:

• The respondents were promised anonymity.

• The questionnaire included a 10 percent off coupon from area Pizza Huts.

• Two of the respondents were randomly selected to receive a $15 cash prize.

• Convenient drop-off locations for the surveys were provided within the School of Business.

The collected information was analyzed using cross tabulations.

Questions

1. Currently, more students apply for admission to the School of Business than there are places available. Since there are more than enough applicants, is it necessary for the school to measure student satisfaction?

2. Describe how satisfaction information is useful for marketing and promoting the School of Business.

3. For the research team to determine the appropriate sample size for this research project, what other information is required?

4. The research team has put considerable effort and money into improving the response rate for this study. Discuss why it is important to obtain responses from the entire sample of respondents.

5. The School of Business has hypothesized that satisfaction levels may vary depending on certain demographic characteristics of respondents. Is simple random sampling the most appropriate sampling method to investigate these hypotheses? Explain. What are other sampling methods that may have been useful for this project?

Case V.I   Rockway Publishing Company, Inc.[1]

The Problem

Rockway Publishing Company publishes telephone directories for suburban and rural communities. Headquartered in a large midwestern metropolitan area, Rockway publishes directories for over 80 markets, mostly in the midwestern and southern parts of the United States. The

[1]This case was prepared by Paul D. Boughton, Ph.D., Associate Professor of Marketing, Saint Louis University, 3674 Lindell Blvd., St. Louis, MO 63108. Reprinted with permission.

telephone directories are published as an alternative to, and in competition with, directories published by the local telephone companies serving these markets. Rockway has been very successful in offering yellow-page advertisers a quality product at competitive rates. However, there have been some problems with distribution.

The distribution of the directories is handled in one of two ways. Winston Delivery Company has been under contract

EXHIBIT V.I.1   **Survey Results**

	HAND DELIVERED			MAIL DELIVERED	
	Area 1	Area 2	Area 3	Area 4	Area 5
Total area population	35,000	50,000	69,000	85,000	155,000
City	24,000	45,700	52,000	43,000	100,000
Rural	11,000	4,300	17,000	42,000	55,000
Total Sample	525	750	1,035	1,275	2,325
City	325	650	775	685	1,325
Rural	200	100	260	590	1,000
Overall percentage receiving directory	88%	90%	95%	85%	92%

for the past two years to hand deliver directories in suburban areas and small cities. Winston hires college students, at minimum wage plus car expenses, to make the deliveries. Each student is given an assigned area of streets and rural routes to cover. For some locations, particularly where the households are heavily rural, the directories are sent through the mail. Recently, Rockway's salespeople have been receiving complaints from advertisers that some of their customers have not received a directory. It is believed by some of the salespeople that as much as 10 to 15 percent of households, in any given market, are not receiving a directory.

Survey Method

Faced with the prospect that not all of the directories intended for households are being delivered, Ron Combs, president of Rockway, instituted a plan for measuring the discrepancy. Approximately three weeks after a directory is delivered in an area, a sample of households is telephoned, and respondents are asked if the directory has been received. The results are tabulated according to whether the household has a city or rural address. To be counted, the respondent must be sure that the book has been received or has not been received. Respondents who are uncertain or don't know are given more information about the time of delivery, what the face of the book looks like, and how it was delivered (by mail or by hand). If they are still uncertain, they are replaced in the sample and not included in the tally. The respondent may be anyone in the household who answers the phone or is available at the time of the call. Combs wants to ensure that sampling error is not greater than plus or minus two percentage points.

The Sampling Plan

The sampling frame is an internally produced cross directory of white-page listings by street. The interviewer goes through the pages, arbitrarily pulling names from the listings. If a respondent says a directory has not been received, additional calls are made on that street to determine if the entire street was missed. However, these additional calls are not included in the survey results.

The exhibit above shows the results of the survey for areas distributed to in the most recent months.

The total sample size for each area was determined by taking 1.5 percent of the area population. The breakdown between city and rural sample is arbitrary and the result of actual calls completed.

Combs wants to determine three things: (1) the overall soundness of the sampling plan; (2) the amount of sampling error in the results; and (3) the amount of response error by respondents.

Questions

1. What type of sample is being taken? Are city and rural residents being represented adequately? What other approach would you recommend and why?

2. What is the range of sampling error experienced from Area 1 to Area 5? (Assume 95 percent level of confidence.) How can Combs's error goal of plus or minus two percentage points be achieved?

3. What would you recommend as a sample size for each of the five areas?

4. Does Combs have enough information to determine respondent error? What would you recommend he do to obtain this information?

Data Analysis

After the data have been collected, the emphasis in the research process logically turns to analysis, which is the search for meaning in the collected information. This search involves many questions and several steps. Chapter 19 reviews the common steps of editing, coding, and tabulating the data. Some studies stop with these steps. Many involve additional analyses, however, particularly the testing for statistical significance, and Appendix 19a reviews some of the fundamentals regarding the testing for statistical significance. Chapter 20 and Appendix 20a then discuss the statistical procedures appropriate for determining whether some observed differences between and among groups are statistically significant.

Finally, Chapter 21 and Appendix 21a discuss procedures for assessing the degree of association between variables.

SALES DATA GET NEW-PRODUCT LAUNCHES OFF THE GROUND Research psychologist Neil Rackham was fascinated by a pattern he saw when new products were launched at Xerox: First the company announced the new product. With high expectations and enthusiasm, it trumpeted all the product's great features and innovations. Then salespeople headed out to spread the good news to their customers, but initial sales figures were disappointing. Finally, some time after salespeople had given up on the new product's potential, the orders started to come in, and the product made a recovery.

The pattern was puzzling. Why did the product not succeed when it had the enthusiastic backing of salespeople and management? Why did it perform better when attention had turned to later offerings? Rackham considered and then abandoned some hypotheses:

- Customers might resist innovation. But when Rackham talked to potential customers during Xerox's launch of its first "mega-copier," the 9200 model, he learned that only a few were threatened by the new technology; the others were very interested but then didn't buy. This didn't fit the normal pattern of change resistance, in which customers would initially resist change and then eventually lower their resistance.

- Salespeople might resist the innovation. During the launch of the 9200 copier, Rackham administered a questionnaire to each salesperson to measure their attitude toward the new product. He found a correlation between enthusiasm and success—a *negative* correlation. The more enthusiastic salespeople were, the less they sold.

If the problem wasn't attitudes toward technology or the copier itself, what could cause the poor sales associated with a product launch? Rackham decided to research the problem further. He decided to find out what was happening during sales calls to potential customers.

Rackham made this investigation part of a broader research study being conducted by his firm, Huthwaite Inc. By observing 35,000 sales calls, the researchers were looking for the behaviors that had the greatest correlation with sales success. The researchers already had collected data on Xerox salespeople's behavior during sales calls. The next step was to compare this past behavior with what the same sample of salespeople did when pitching a new product, the 9200 copier.

Members of the Huthwaite research team accompanied Xerox salespeople on sales calls and recorded data about their interactions with customers. Compared with the baseline data about Xerox salespeople, the researchers found two notable differences in how they sold the new copiers:

1. During calls to sell the new product, salespeople asked 40 percent fewer questions than they had on their previous sales calls. This was a significant area of difference, because earlier research had shown that the success of a sales call went up in proportion to the number of questions salespeople asked.

2. During calls to sell the new product, salespeople provided three times as many product details as they had on their previous sales calls. Rackham calls this method of selling a "feature dump." To the prospect, it feels as if the salesperson is dumping a bucketful of data over the prospect's head. In fact, earlier studies associated feature dumps with selling failure.

These patterns in the data gave Rackham some new ways to explain the pattern of sales at Xerox. Salespeople weren't selling the new product as effectively because they were using a less effective sales approach. They were spending less time on the activities that worked best, like learning customer needs, and spending more time on relatively unproductive activities, like describing product features. Rackham hypothesized that the salespeople's behavior was the cause of the poor initial sales.

His hypothesis had the virtue that it fit with widely accepted principles of selling. Successful salespeople agree that it is important to learn about customer wants and needs and to focus on how products can meet those wants and needs. The approach has a strategic advantage. It positions the salesperson's organization as a company that responds to customer needs, rather than as a company that has some particular technology, which competitors can eventually copy.

To test his hypothesis, Rackham set up an experiment with another sample of salespeople. This time, he worked with a different Huthwaite client, Kodak. The situation was just right: Kodak was launching a blood analyzer, a machine with so many innovations that, as Rackham put it, "We knew it would be a magnet for feature dumps." In fact, Kodak's salespeople had already attended the main product launch, where they witnessed the usual hoopla about the product's bells and whistles.

The research team randomly selected a dozen of Kodak's salespeople to be the test group and another group to serve as a control group. The researchers gave the salespeople in the test group training in how to introduce the blood analyzer to prospective customers by emphasizing benefits rather than features. The salespeople learned ways that the new product solved problems typically experienced by doctors, clinicians, technicians, and administrators. Salespeople identified which of their customers were experiencing these various problems. They practiced uncovering and discussing these problems. The training of the salespeople in the test group didn't include any coverage of product features. The demonstration model was even covered up during the training.

For a year the research team collected data on the sales history of the salespeople handling the blood analyzer. Compared with the control group, the group with the special training averaged 54 percent greater sales volume for the new product.

These results make good business sense for Kodak, as well as Xerox and the other companies for which Huthwaite has performed research. The companies can apply the data about sales methods to win customers in the early months of a product's life, before competitors move in. For instance, when Xerox introduced the 9200 copier, the company estimated it had about three and a half years to gain market share before competitors could offer a comparable product. Nowadays, the competition moves even faster. When companies launch a new product, they need to know how to sell it right away, and marketing research can help them do it right.

Source: Neil Rackham, "What's New: Why Do New Product Launches Often Rise, Fall and Rise Again?" *Selling Power* (January/February 1999), pp. 90, 92–93.

Chapter 19

DATA ANALYSIS: PRELIMINARY STEPS

L E A R N I N G   O B J E C T I V E S

Upon Completing This Chapter, You Should Be Able to

1. Explain the purpose of the field edit.

2. Define what coding in the research process is.

3. List the three steps in the coding process.

4. Outline the conventions that are customarily followed when data are to be analyzed by a computer.

5. Describe the kinds of information contained in a codebook.

6. Define what tabulation is and distinguish between the two types of tabulation.

7. Explain the various ways in which one-way tabulation can be used.

8. Assess the particular importance of cross tabulation.

9. Describe a method by which a researcher can determine what impact one variable has on another in a cross-tabulation table.

10. Describe what banners are and how they are useful.

Case in Marketing Research

You're enjoying a night out on the town with some friends when you notice you're down to your last $5. No problem. You head for the nearest automated teller machine (ATM) and slide in your ATM card. Press a few buttons, and out slips another $40 from your checking account. As long as you have money in your account, an ATM can give you some for your wallet.

You enjoy the convenience, and the owner of that ATM is glad you do. Shared electronic services networks like PULSE EFT Association and NYCE set up networks of ATMs for banks and other depository institutions. The banks issue ATM cards to their customers and typically receive a steady stream of income from fees they charge ATM users. Naturally, they want to attract and keep more cardholders, and they encourage them to use their ATMs.

To achieve such marketing objectives, the networks commission research. For example, both PULSE and NYCE work with Richard R. Batsell's research firm, Analytica Inc., based in Houston. Analytica studies ATM usage and generates data on the demographics of ATM users.

In a study that involved interviewing 3,000 consumers nationwide, Analytica determined that almost 71 percent have an ATM card and 50 percent use it as their main way of obtaining cash. The Analytica study broke the data down according to consumers' racial and ethnic background. It found some differences in patterns of usage:

Racial/Ethnic Group	Have an ATM Card	ATM Card Is Main Way to Get Cash
African-American	76%	58%
Native American	75%	54%
Asian-American	74%	59%
Hispanic	82%	64%
White	68%	47%

From the data, it is easy to draw some general conclusions. For instance, we can see that many Americans are aware of ATM cards (the majority already have one) and that there is room for growth in usage of the cards.

The data also raise questions. For example, why are Hispanic consumers more likely than non-Hispanic whites to own an ATM card and use it as the primary way to get cash? For the data to be useful for marketing decisions, ATM owners need to explain the difference in usage levels.

One approach would be to simply assume that something about Hispanic culture makes ATM cards more attractive. Marketers that rely on this explanation might target most marketing efforts to Hispanic consumers. However, that is the group with the least potential for growth, since almost two-thirds of Hispanics already use the cards as the main way to get cash. Some ATM owners might prefer to expand their market by broadening the appeal of cards to consumers in other groups. This requires them to study the data further and learn more about what characteristics are associated with use of ATM cards.

Discussion Issues

1. If you owned an ATM network, what else would you want to know about ATM users?

2. What other ways of segmenting the data would interest you?

3. What further research would you request?

Imagine yourself as the director of a marketing research project. For weeks you have supervised a massive field study in numerous shopping malls. Now the foot soldiers in your data collecting army have moved on to other projects, and you are left in your office surrounded by stacks of completed questionnaires. The battle to get the information may be over, but you have not yet won the war until you can determine what all those data really mean.

In this chapter, we will begin to explore how analysts obtain meaning from raw data. All previous steps in the research process have been undertaken to support this search for meaning. The specific analytical procedures involved are closely related to the preceding steps, because the careful analyst looked ahead to this moment when he or she designed those other steps. The most astute researchers developed dummy tables as well, indicating how each item of information would be used. Thorough preparatory work probably revealed some undesirable data gaps and some "interesting" but not vital items that might have posed problems if they had not been dealt with at that time.

The search for meaning can take many forms. However, the preliminary analytical steps of editing, coding, and tabulating the data are common to most studies, so a review of what they are and how they are used is warranted.

Editing

The basic purpose of editing is to impose some minimum quality standards on the raw data. Editing involves the inspection and, if necessary, correction of each questionnaire or observation form. Inspection and correction are often done in two stages: the field edit and the central-office edit.

Field Edit

Field edit

A preliminary edit, typically conducted by a field supervisor, which is designed to detect the most glaring omissions and inaccuracies in a completed data collection instrument.

The **field edit** is a preliminary edit designed to detect the most glaring omissions and inaccuracies in the data. It is also useful in helping to control the behavior of the field force personnel and to clear up any misunderstandings they may have about directions, procedures, specific questions, and so on. For example, in a Roper survey conducted in Ukraine, the field edit revealed that an employee had left the questionnaire with the respondents instead of interviewing them as instructed. The tip-off was the different ways the answers were circled.[1]

Ideally, the field edit is done as soon as possible after the questionnaire or other data collection form has been administered. In that way, problems can be corrected before the interviewing or observation staff is disbanded, and while the particular contacts that were the source of trouble are still fresh in the interviewer's or observer's mind. The preliminary edit is usually conducted by a field supervisor. Some of the items checked are described in Exhibit 19.1.

Central-Office Edit

Central-office edit

Thorough and exacting scrutiny and correction of completed data collection forms, including a decision about what to do with the data.

The field edit is typically followed by a **central-office edit,** which involves more complete and exacting scrutiny and correction of the completed returns. The work calls for the keen eye of a person well versed in the objectives and procedures of the study. To ensure consistency of treatment, it is best if one individual handles all completed instruments. If the

EXHIBIT 19.1 **Items Checked in the Field Edit**

1. **Completeness:** The check for completeness involves scrutinizing the data form to ensure that no sections or pages were omitted, and it also involves checking individual items. A blank for a specific question could mean that the respondent refused to answer; alternatively, it may simply reflect an oversight on the respondent's part or that he or she did not know the answer. It may be very important for the purposes of the study to know which reason is correct. It is hoped that by contacting the field-worker while the interview is fresh in his or her mind, the field editor can obtain the needed clarification.

2. **Legibility:** It is impossible to code a questionnaire that cannot be deciphered because of illegible handwriting or obscure abbreviations. It is a simple matter to correct this now, whereas it is often extremely time-consuming later.

3. **Comprehensibility:** Sometimes a recorded response is incomprehensible to all but the field interviewer. By detecting this now, the field editor can obtain the necessary clarification.

4. **Consistency:** Marked inconsistencies within an interview or observation schedule typically indicate errors in collecting or recording the data and may indicate ambiguity in the instrument or carelessness in its administration. For instance, if a respondent indicated that he or she saw a particular commercial on television last night on one part of the questionnaire, and later indicated that he or she did not watch television last night, the analyst would indeed be in a dilemma. Such inconsistencies can often be detected and corrected in the field edit.

5. **Uniformity:** It is very important that the responses be recorded in uniform units. For instance, if the study is aimed at determining the number of magazines read per week per individual, and the respondent indicates the number of magazines for which he or she has monthly subscriptions, the response base is not uniform, and the result could cause confusion in the later stages of analysis. If the problem is detected now, perhaps the interviewer can recontact the respondent and get the correct answer.

work must be divided because of length and time considerations, the division should be by parts of the data collection instruments rather than by respondents. That is, one editor would edit Part A of all questionnaires while the other would edit Part B.

Unlike the field edit, the central-office edit depends less on follow-up procedures and more on deciding just what to do with the data. Accurate follow-up is now more difficult because of the time that has elapsed. The editor must decide how data collection instruments containing incomplete answers, obviously wrong answers, and answers that reflect a lack of interest will be handled. Since such problems are more prevalent with questionnaires than with observation forms, we will discuss these difficulties from that perspective, although our discussion applies generally to all types of data collection forms.

The study in which all the returned questionnaires are completely filled out is rare. Some will have complete sections omitted. Others will reflect sporadic item nonresponse. The editor's decision on how to handle these incomplete questionnaires depends on the severity of the omission. Questionnaires that omit complete sections are obviously suspect. Yet they should not automatically be thrown out. It might be, for example, that the omitted section refers to the influence of the spouse in some major durable purchase, whereas the respondent is not married. This type of reply is certainly usable in spite of the incomplete section. If there is no logical justification for the large number of unanswered questions, the total reply will probably be thrown out, increasing the nonresponse rate for the study. Questionnaires containing only isolated instances of item nonresponse will be retained, although they might undergo some *data cleaning* after coding, a subject discussed later in this chapter.

Careful editing of the questionnaire will sometimes show that an answer to a question is obviously incorrect. For example, a researcher at a consumer panel research company once came upon data that 45 percent of the households in the panel had purchased dog food, but only 40 percent of the households reported that they owned a dog.[2] Presumably, data on some of the panel questionnaires indicated a dog food purchase but not dog ownership. One explanation for this seeming inconsistency is that some of the questionnaires contain incorrect answers. The editor may be able to determine which of the two answers is correct from other information in the questionnaire. Alternatively, the editor may need to establish policies as to which answer, if either, will be treated as correct when these inconsistencies or other types of inaccuracies arise. These policies will reflect the purposes of the study. As an example, consider the quandary of Susan Hooper, the Eastern Europe marketing director for Pepsi Cola International, who was given results of a survey conducted in Hungary that said drugstores are an outlet for soft drinks. Susan could not take this information at face value for she knew full well that drugstores didn't exist in Hungary and that the information had been forced into a structure developed in the West.[3]

Editors must also be on the alert to spot completed questionnaires that have failed to engage the respondent's interest. Evidence of this lack of interest may be obvious or quite subtle. Consider, for example, a subject who checked the "5" position on a five-point scale for each of 40 items in an attitude questionnaire, even though some items were expressed negatively and some positively. Obviously, that person did not take the study seriously, and the editor should probably throw out such a response. A discerning editor might also be able to pick up more subtle indications of disinterest, such as check marks that are not within the boxes provided, scribbles, spills on the questionnaire, and so on. An editor may not want to throw out these responses, but they should be coded so that it is later possible to run separate tabulations for the questionable instruments and obviously good questionnaires. Then the two groups could be compared to see whether lack of interest makes any difference in the results.

Coding

Coding
The technical procedure by which raw data are transformed into symbols; it involves specifying the alternative categories or classes into which the responses are to be placed and assigning code numbers to the classes.

Coding is the technical procedure by which raw data are transformed into symbols. Most often the symbols are numerals, since they can be tabulated and counted more easily. The transformation is not automatic, however, but involves judgment on the part of the coder.

The first step in coding is specifying the categories or classes into which the responses are to be placed.[4] There is no magic number of categories. Rather, the number will depend on the research problem being investigated and the specific items used to generate the information. Response choices should be mutually exclusive and exhaustive, so that every response logically falls into one and only one category. Multiple responses are legitimate for some questions—for example, if the question is "For what purposes do you use Jell-O?" and the responses include such things as "a dessert item," "an evening snack," "an afternoon snack," and so on. Another example of legitimate multiple responses is with high-tech electronic devices, which are used for many purposes, as shown in the ad for the Nokia 6100 Series wireless phone. On the other hand, if the question focuses on the person's age, then only one age category is, of course, acceptable, and the code should indicate clearly which category.

Coding closed questions and most scaling devices is simple because the coding is established when the data collection instrument is designed. Respondents then code themselves with their responses, or the interviewer codes them in recording the responses on the checklist provided. For example, the Association of European Airlines gathers data on the flight delays at European airports. It codes a flight as delayed if the flight departs at least 15 minutes beyond the scheduled time.[5]

Coding open-ended questions can be very difficult and is often much more expensive than coding closed questions. The coder has to determine appropriate categories on the basis of answers that are not always anticipated. International studies can create their own special coding problems because different labels may mean different things. For example, a conservative in the former Soviet Union is someone who wishes to adhere to or return to the "old Communism," which in turn might be seen as very left-wing in Western countries. Liberal Russians, in turn, are the ones who wish to introduce market perspectives into economics and politics, a perspective that usually will be held by conservatives in the West.

If there are so many questionnaires that several coders are needed, inconsistency in coding may be an additional problem. To ensure consistency of treatment, the work

This ad for the Nokia 6100 Series wireless phone lists twelve reasons (such as client phone list, calendar, e-mail, calculator, clock, pager, even a source of a son or daughter's electronic games) why the Nokia digital phone should be "your own personal assistant." When there are many possible reasons for choosing a product, a question about buying the product would have to allow for multiple responses.

It adds six ounces to your pocket while lifting considerably more from your shoulders.

Consider the Nokia 6100 Series wireless phone your own personal assistant. This digital wonder is loaded with features to help you get through your busy day: up to 199-name phone directory,

one-touch dialing, calendar, clock, calculator, caller ID, text messaging, reminder messages, call waiting, up to four hours of talk time, up to 200 hours of standby time, four games and profile settings that let you silence your phone during important meetings. So if you feel as if you're carrying the weight of the world, try carrying the Nokia 6100 Series wireless phone instead.

NOKIA
CONNECTING PEOPLE
www.NokiaUSA.com

should be divided by task, not by dividing the questionnaires equally among the coders. By allowing coders to focus their energies on one or a few questions, researchers can ensure that a consistent set of standards is being applied to each question. This approach is also more efficient, because coders can easily memorize just a few codes and thus do not have to consult the codebook for each instrument. When several persons do, in fact, code the same question on different batches of questionnaires, it is important that they also code a sample of the other's work to ensure that a consistent set of coding criteria is being employed.[6]

The second step in coding involves assigning code numbers to the classes. For example, sex might be assigned the letter *M* for male and *F* for female. Alternatively, the classes could be denoted by 1 for male and 2 for female. Generally, it is better to use numbers rather than letters to denote the classes. It is also better at this stage to use numerical data as it was reported on the data collection form, rather than to collapse it into smaller categories. For example, it is not advisable to code age as 1 = under 20 years, 2 = 20–29, 3 = 30–39, and so on, if actual ages of the people were provided. This would result in an unnecessary sacrifice of information in the original measurement and could just as easily be done at later stages in the analysis.

When a computer is being used to analyze the data, it is necessary to code the data so that they can be readily inputted to the machine. Regardless of how that input will be handled, whether by mark-sense forms or directly through a keyboard on a terminal, it is helpful to visualize the input in terms of a multiple-column record. Further, it is advisable to follow certain conventions when coding the data.

1. Locate only one character in each column. When the question allows multiple responses, allow separate columns in the coding for each answer. Thus in our Jell-O example, the coder should provide a separate column for those who use the product as a dessert item, those who use it as an evening snack, and so on.

2. Use only numeric codes, not letters of the alphabet or special characters, like @, or blanks. Most computer statistical programs have trouble manipulating anything but numerals.

3. Use as many columns for the field assigned to a variable as are necessary to capture the variable. Thus, if the variable is such that the ten codes from 0 to 9 are not sufficient to exhaust the categories, then one should use two columns, providing one hundred codes from 00 through 99. Moreover, no more than one variable should be assigned to any field.

4. Use standard codes for "no information." Thus, all "don't know" responses might be coded as 8, "no answers" as 9, and "does not apply" as 0. It is best if the same code is used throughout the study for each of these types of "no information."

5. Code in a respondent identification number on each record. This number need not, and typically will not, identify the respondent by name. Rather, the number simply ties the questionnaire to the coded data. This is often useful information in data cleaning (discussed later). If the questionnaire will not fit on one record, then code the respondent identification number and a sequence number into each record. Column 10 in the first record might then indicate how the respondent answered Question 2, while Column 10 in the second record might indicate whether the person is male or female.[7]

Codebook

A book that describes each variable, gives it a code name, and identifies its location in the record.

The final step in the coding process is to prepare a **codebook,** which contains the general instructions indicating how each item of data was coded. It lists the codes for each variable and the categories included in each code. It further indicates where on the computer record the variable is located and how the variable should be read—for example, with a decimal point or as a whole number. The latter information is provided by the format specifications.

Tabulation

Simple tabulation
A count of the number of cases that fall into each category when the categories are based on one variable.

Cross tabulation
A count of the number of cases that fall into each of several categories when the categories are based on two or more variables considered simultaneously.

Tabulation consists simply of counting the number of cases that fall into the various categories. The tabulation may take the form of a *simple tabulation* or a *cross tabulation*. **Simple tabulation** involves counting a single variable. It may be repeated for each of the variables in the study, but the tabulation for each variable is independent of the tabulation for the other variables. In **cross tabulation,** two or more of the variables are treated simultaneously. For instance, coding the number of people who bought Campbell's soup at a Kroger store is an example of a cross tabulation, since it measures two related characteristics.

The tabulations may be done entirely by hand, entirely by machine, or partially by machine and partially by hand. Which is more efficient depends both on the number of tabulations necessary and on the number of cases in each tabulation. The number of tabulations is a direct function of the number of variables, while the number of cases is a direct function of the size of the sample. The fewer the number of tabulations required and the smaller the sample, the more attractive hand methods become. However, the attractiveness of either alternative also is highly dependent on the complexity of the tabulations. Complexity increases as the number of variables receiving simultaneous treatment in a cross tabulation increases. Complexity also increases as the number of categories per variable increases.

Although the hand tabulation might be useful in very simple studies involving a few questions and a limited number of responses, most studies rely on computer tabulation using packaged programs. A great many such programs are available. Some will calculate summary statistics and will plot a histogram of the values in addition to reporting the number of cases in each category.

The basic input to these statistical analyses will be the *data array,* which lists the value of each variable for each sample unit. Each variable occupies a specific place in the record for a sample unit, thereby making it easy to pick off the values for it from all the cases. The location of each variable is given in the codebook. Figure 19.1 shows an abbreviated version of a questionnaire that was sent to customers of a sporting goods retailer to

FIGURE 19.1　**Part of the Questionnaire for Avery Sporting Goods**

The following questionnaire was designed to give a well-known sporting goods company a better idea of people's perceptions of buying sporting goods and other general merchandise through catalogs. The first three columns of the data listed in Table 19.3 contain the customers' survey identification numbers.

1. **During the past year, what percentage of the sporting goods you purchased were ordered through a catalog?**

   _____ 0 percent

   _____ 1–10 percent

   _____ 11–15 percent

   _____ 16–20 percent

   _____ 21+ percent

2. **How willing are you to purchase merchandise offered through the Avery Sporting Goods catalog?**

   _____ Not at all willing

   _____ Somewhat willing

   _____ Very willing

continued

3. **Have you ever ordered any merchandise from the Avery Sporting Goods catalog?**

_____ Never ordered

_____ Ordered before, but not within the last year

_____ Ordered within the last year

	NOT AT ALL CONFIDENT	SLIGHTLY CONFIDENT	SOMEWHAT CONFIDENT	CONFIDENT	VERY CONFIDENT

4. **How confident are you that the following sporting goods purchased through a catalog would be of high quality?**
   (a) Athletic clothing (shirts, warm-up suits, etc.)
   (b) Athletic shoes
   (c) Fishing equipment
   (d) Balls (basketballs, footballs, etc.)
   (e) Skiing equipment

5. **How confident are you that the following sporting goods would be of high quality if purchased in a retail sporting goods store?**
   (a) Athletic clothing (shirts, warm-up suits, etc.)
   (b) Athletic shoes
   (c) Fishing equipment
   (d) Balls (basketballs, footballs, etc.)
   (e) Skiing equipment

EXHIBIT 19.2   **Listing of Raw Data**

```
0011115554344434
0021214455545453
0034135544245321
0043225543554324
0052115355453542
```

determine their perceptions of buying sporting goods through the mail. Exhibit 19.2 is an example of the data array that could result from such a study. Exhibit 19.3 is the codebook to the study, describing what is contained in each column. Note that only one line had to be devoted to each sample unit or observation. If the amount of information sought from each sample unit were greater, so that it would not fit on one line, additional lines would be devoted to each observation. The codebook would still indicate where the information for any particular variable was located.

There are a number of important questions concerning the analysis of data that can be illustrated using one-way tabulations and cross tabulations as vehicles. Consider, therefore, the data in Exhibit 19.4. Suppose that the data were collected for a study fo-

EXHIBIT 19.3   **Portion of Codebook for Avery Sporting Goods Questionnaire**

Column(s)	Question Number	Variable (Variable Number)	Coding Specification
1–3	—	Questionnaire identification number (V1)	—
4	1	Percentage of products purchased through a catalog (V2)	1 = 0 percent 2 = 1–10 percent 3 = 11–15 percent 4 = 16–20 percent 5 = 21+ percent
5	2	Willingness to purchase merchandise from the Avery Sporting Goods catalog (V3)	1 = Not at all willing 2 = Somewhat willing 3 = Very willing
6	3	Ever ordered from the Avery Sporting Goods catalog (V4)	1 = Never ordered 2 = Ordered before, but not within the last year 3 = Ordered within the last year
			Coding Specifications 4(a)–5(e) 1 = Not at all confident 2 = Slightly confident 3 = Somewhat confident 4 = Confident 5 = Very confident
7	4(a)	Confidence in buying athletic clothing through a catalog (V5)	
8	4(b)	Confidence in buying athletic shoes through a catalog (V6)	
9	4(c)	Confidence in buying fishing equipment through a catalog (V7)	
10	4(d)	Confidence in buying balls through a catalog (V8)	
11	4(e)	Confidence in buying skiing equipment through a catalog (V9)	
12	5(a)	Confidence in buying athletic clothing in a retail store (V10)	
13	5(b)	Confidence in buying athletic shoes in a retail store (V11)	
14	5(c)	Confidence in buying fishing equipment in a retail store (V12)	
15	5(d)	Confidence in buying balls in a retail store (V13)	
16	5(e)	Confidence in buying skiing equipment in a retail store (V14)	

cusing on car ownership. Suppose, in particular, that the following questions were of research interest:

- What characteristics distinguish families owning two or more cars from families owning one car?

- What are the distinguishing characteristics of those who buy station wagons? Foreign economy cars? Vans?

- Are there differences in the characteristics of families who financed their automobile purchase and those who did not?

Suppose that the data were collected from a probability sample of respondents using mailed questionnaires, and that the 100 people to whom the questionnaire was sent all replied. Thus, there are no problems of nonresponse with which to contend.

EXHIBIT 19.4   Raw Data for Car Ownership Study

Family Ident. No.	(1) Income in Dollars	(2) Number of Members in Family	(3) Education of Household Head in Yrs.	(4) Region Where Live N = North S = South	(5) Lifestyle Orientation L = Liberal C = Conservative	(6) Number of Cars Family Owns	(7) Did Family Finance the Car Purchase?	(8) Does Family Own Station Wagon?	(9) Does Family Own Foreign Economy Car?	(10) Does Family Own Van?	(11) Does Family Own Some Other Kind of Car?
1001	26,800	3	12	N	L	1	N	N	N	Y	N
1002	17,400	4	12	N	L	1	N	N	N	N	Y
1003	14,300	2	10	N	L	1	N	N	N	N	Y
1004	35,400	4	9	N	L	1	N	N	N	N	Y
1005	24,000	3	8	N	L	1	N	N	N	N	Y
1006	17,200	2	12	N	L	1	N	N	Y	N	N
1007	27,000	4	12	N	L	1	N	N	N	N	Y
1008	16,900	3	10	N	L	1	N	N	N	N	Y
1009	26,700	2	12	N	L	1	N	N	N	N	Y
1010	13,800	4	6	N	C	1	Y	N	N	N	Y
1011	34,100	3	8	N	C	1	N	N	N	N	Y
1012	16,300	3	11	N	C	1	N	N	N	N	Y
1013	14,700	2	12	N	C	1	N	N	N	N	Y
1014	25,400	4	12	N	C	1	N	N	N	N	Y
1015	15,400	4	12	N	C	1	N	N	N	N	Y
1016	25,900	3	11	N	C	1	Y	N	N	N	Y
1017	36,300	3	12	N	C	1	N	N	N	N	Y
1018	27,400	2	12	N	C	2	N	N	N	N	Y
1019	17,300	2	12	N	C	1	N	N	N	N	Y
1020	13,700	3	8	N	C	1	N	N	N	N	Y
1021	26,100	2	12	N	C	1	N	N	Y	N	N
1022	16,300	4	12	N	C	1	Y	N	N	N	Y
1023	33,800	3	6	N	C	1	N	N	N	N	Y
1024	34,400	4	8	N	C	1	N	N	N	N	Y
1025	15,300	2	9	N	C	1	Y	N	N	N	Y
1026	35,900	3	12	N	C	1	N	N	N	N	Y
1027	15,100	4	12	S	L	1	N	N	N	Y	N
1028	17,200	2	12	S	L	1	N	N	N	N	N
1029	35,400	4	10	S	L	1	N	N	N	N	Y
1030	15,600	3	12	S	L	1	N	N	N	N	Y
1031	24,900	3	12	S	L	1	N	N	N	N	Y
1032	34,800	4	11	S	C	1	N	N	N	Y	N
1033	14,600	4	12	S	C	1	N	N	N	N	Y
1034	23,100	3	9	S	C	1	N	N	N	N	Y
1035	15,900	3	12	S	C	1	N	N	N	Y	N
1036	26,700	4	12	S	C	1	N	N	N	N	Y
1037	17,300	4	12	S	C	1	N	N	N	Y	N
1038	37,100	3	12	S	C	1	N	N	N	Y	N
1039	14,000	3	10	S	C	1	N	N	N	N	Y
1040	23,600	3	10	S	C	1	N	N	N	N	Y
1041	16,200	3	12	S	C	1	N	N	N	N	Y
1042	24,100	4	10	S	C	1	N	N	N	Y	N
1043	12,700	2	8	S	C	1	N	N	N	N	Y
1044	26,000	4	13	S	L	1	N	Y	N	N	N
1045	15,400	3	16	N	L	2	N	Y	Y	N	N
1046	16,900	4	16	N	L	1	N	N	N	N	Y
1047	23,800	6	10	S	C	1	Y	Y	N	N	N
1048	37,100	8	16	N	L	2	Y	N	Y	N	Y
1049	16,800	5	15	S	C	2	Y	N	N	N	Y
1050	22,900	5	8	N	L	1	N	Y	N	N	N
1051	13,700	6	8	N	L	1	Y	Y	N	N	N
1052	26,800	8	12	S	C	2	N	Y	N	N	Y
1053	16,100	8	12	N	L	2	N	Y	N	N	Y
1054	25,700	5	12	N	C	1	N	N	N	N	Y
1055	38,200	2	12	N	L	1	N	N	N	N	Y
1056	49,800	3	12	N	L	1	Y	N	N	N	Y
1057	60,400	4	12	N	L	1	Y	N	N	N	Y
1058	39,000	2	12	N	L	1	N	N	N	Y	Y
1059	57,600	4	12	N	L	1	Y	N	N	N	Y
1060	42,000	3	12	N	L	1	N	N	N	N	Y
1061	38,600	3	12	N	L	1	N	N	N	Y	N
1062	66,400	4	12	N	L	2	Y	N	Y	N	Y

EXHIBIT 19.4 **Raw Data for Car Ownership Study,** *continued*

Family Ident. No.	(1) Income in Dollars	(2) Number of Members in Family	(3) Education of Household Head in Yrs.	(4) Region Where Live N = North S = South	(5) Lifestyle Orientation L = Liberal C = Conservative	(6) Number of Cars Family Owns	(7) Did Family Finance the Car Purchase?	(8) Does Family Own Station Wagon?	(9) Does Family Own Foreign Economy Car?	(10) Does Family Own Van?	(11) Does Family Own Some Other Kind of Car?
1063	71,200	2	12	N	L	1	Y	N	N	N	Y
1064	49,300	4	10	N	C	1	Y	N	N	N	Y
1065	37,700	4	10	N	C	1	Y	N	N	N	Y
1066	72,400	3	12	N	C	2	N	N	Y	N	Y
1067	88,700	3	12	N	C	1	N	N	N	Y	N
1068	44,200	2	12	S	L	1	Y	N	N	N	Y
1069	55,100	3	12	S	L	2	N	N	N	Y	Y
1070	73,300	4	12	S	L	1	N	N	N	Y	N
1071	80,200	2	12	S	L	1	Y	N	N	N	Y
1072	39,300	3	10	S	C	2	N	N	N	Y	Y
1073	48,200	4	12	S	C	1	N	N	N	N	Y
1074	57,800	2	12	S	C	1	Y	N	N	N	Y
1075	38,000	3	10	S	C	1	Y	N	N	Y	N
1076	81,300	4	16	N	L	1	N	Y	N	N	N
1077	96,900	4	16	N	L	2	N	N	N	N	Y
1078	44,700	3	14	N	L	1	N	N	N	N	Y
1079	107,300	3	17	N	L	1	N	N	N	N	Y
1080	38,100	2	13	N	L	2	Y	N	N	N	Y
1081	304,200	2	14	N	L	1	N	N	N	N	Y
1082	46,100	3	16	S	L	1	N	N	N	Y	N
1083	49,300	4	13	S	L	1	N	N	N	N	Y
1084	160,800	4	16	S	L	9	N	N	N	N	Y
1085	39,100	4	16	S	L	1	N	N	N	Y	N
1086	46,400	2	14	S	C	1	N	N	N	Y	N
1087	58,300	6	10	N	L	2	Y	N	N	N	Y
1088	47,800	5	10	N	L	2	Y	Y	N	N	Y
1089	58,000	7	8	N	L	2	Y	Y	N	N	Y
1090	69,600	9	12	N	L	2	Y	Y	N	N	Y
1091	44,200	11	12	N	L	2	N	N	Y	N	Y
1092	62,100	6	10	N	L	2	Y	Y	N	N	Y
1093	99,000	5	12	S	L	3	Y	N	Y	Y	Y
1094	53,300	6	12	S	L	2	N	Y	N	Y	Y
1095	72,200	9	10	S	C	2	N	Y	N	Y	N
1096	64,700	7	12	S	C	2	Y	Y	N	Y	N
1097	77,300	6	16	N	L	2	Y	Y	Y	N	N

One-way Tabulation

The one-way tabulation, in addition to communicating the results of a study, can be used for several other purposes: (1) to determine the degree of item nonresponse, (2) to locate *blunders* (defined later), (3) to locate *outliers* (defined later), (4) to determine the empirical distribution of the variable in question, and (5) to calculate summary statistics. The first three of these are often referred to as *data cleaning*.

Item nonresponse is a significant problem in most surveys. Some percentage of the survey instruments invariably suffer from it. As a matter of fact, the degree of item nonresponse often serves as a useful indicator of the quality of the research. When it is excessive, it calls the whole research effort into question and suggests that the research objectives and procedures should be examined critically. When it is in bounds, it is still necessary for the research director to make a decision regarding what should be done about the missing items before analyzing the data. There are several possible strategies:

1. Leave the items blank, and report the number as a separate category. Although this procedure works well for simple one-way and cross tabulations, it does not work well for a number of other statistical techniques.

2. Eliminate the case with the missing item in analyses using the variable. When using this approach, the analyst must continually report the number of cases on which the analysis is based, since the sample size is not constant across analyses. It also ignores the fact that a significant degree of nonresponse on a particular item might be informative in that it suggests respondents do not care very deeply about the issue being addressed by the question.

3. Substitute values for the missing items. Typically, the substitution will involve some measure of central tendency such as the mean, median, or mode. Alternatively, sometimes the analyst attempts to estimate the answer using other information contained in the questionnaire. The substitution of values makes maximum use of the data, since all the reasonably good cases are used. At the same time, it requires more work from the analyst, and it contains some potential for bias. It also raises the question of which statistical technique should be used to generate the estimate.[8]

There is no "right" or simple answer as to how missing items should be handled. It all depends on the purposes of the study, the incidence of missing items, and the methods that will be used to analyze the data.

As mentioned earlier, another purpose of one-way tabulation is to locate **blunders,** which are simply errors that occur during editing, coding, or entering the data into the computer. Consider the one-way tabulation of the number of cars owned per family in Exhibit 19.5. A check of the original questionnaire indicates the family reporting ownership of nine cars had, in fact, one car. The 9 is a blunder. The simple one-way tabulation has revealed the error, and it can now be corrected at a very early stage in the analysis with a minimum of difficulty and expense.

The number of cases serving as a base for the one-way tabulation in Exhibit 19.5 is 100, and thus the number entries are easily converted to percentages. In most cases, conversion will not be this simple. However, it is a good practice always to indicate percentages in the table, since they aid communication. Hence, a more typical way of presenting our car study data, corrected for blunders, is shown in Exhibit 19.6.

Blunder
An error that arises when editing, coding, keypunching, or tabulating the data.

EXHIBIT 19.5 **Cars per Family**

Number of Cars per Family	Number of Families
1	74
2	23
3	2
9	1

EXHIBIT 19.6 **Cars per Family**

Number of Cars per Family	Number of Families	Percent of Families
1	75	75
2	23	23
3	2	2
	100	100

Note that the percentages are presented to zero decimal places. In this case the percentages are whole numbers to begin with, because the sample size was 100, but in most cases they would have to be rounded off. Whole numbers should almost always be used, since they are easier to read and also because decimals may convey a greater accuracy than the figures can support, especially in a small sample. While in some cases the analyst might be justified in reporting percentages to one decimal place (rarely two decimal places, though), the general rule in reporting percentages is, *unless decimals have a special purpose, they should be omitted.*[9]

Sometimes the percentages are presented in parentheses (see Exhibit 19.7) immediately to the right or below the actual count entry in the table. Sometimes only the percentages are presented. In this case it is imperative that the total number of cases on which the percentages are based be provided.

Outlier

An observation so different in magnitude from the rest of the observations that the analyst chooses to treat it as a special case.

Still another use of the one-way tabulation is to locate **outliers,** which are not errors but rather observations so different in magnitude from the rest of the observations that the analyst chooses to treat them as special cases. This may mean eliminating the observation from the analysis or determining the specific factors that generate this unique observation. For instance, if the family in our earlier example had really owned nine cars, this figure would be considered an outlier, since it is highly unusual for a family to own that many cars.

For another case, consider the tabulation of incomes contained in Exhibit 19.7, but ignore the right-hand column for the moment. The tabulation indicates there are four families with incomes greater than $105,000 and Exhibit 19.4 indicates that only one family had an annual income greater than $161,000, namely Number 1081 with an income of $304,200. This is clearly out of line with the rest of the sample and is properly considered an outlier. What the analyst chooses to do with this observation depends on the objectives of the study. In this case, it is not unreasonable for a family to have such an income, and so the observation will be retained in the analysis.

A fourth use of the one-way frequency tabulation is to determine the *empirical distribution* of the characteristic in question. Some analysts ignore the distribution of the variables and automatically calculate summary statistics such as the mean. Ignoring the distribution of the variables can be a serious mistake. Consider the case of a new sauce product:

On the average, consumers wanted it neither really hot nor really mild. The mean rating of the test participants was quite close to the middle of the scale, which had "very mild" and "very hot" as its bipolar adjectives. This happened to fit the client's preconceived notion.

EXHIBIT 19.7 **Income Distribution of Respondents in Car Ownership Study**

Income	Number of Families		Cumulative Number of Families	
Less than $15,000	8	(8.0)	8	(8.0)
$15,000 to $24,900	25	(25.0)	33	(33.0)
$25,000 to $34,900	15	(15.0)	48	(48.0)
$35,000 to $44,900	18	(18.0)	66	(66.0)
$45,000 to $54,900	8	(8.0)	74	(74.0)
$55,000 to $64,900	8	(8.0)	82	(82.0)
$65,000 to $74,900	7	(7.0)	89	(89.0)
$75,000 to $84,900	3	(3.0)	92	(92.0)
$85,000 to $94,900	1	(1.0)	93	(93.0)
$95,000 to $104,900	3	(3.0)	96	(96.0)
More than $105,000	4	(4.0)	100	(100.0)
Total number of families	100	(100.0)		

However, examination of the distribution of the ratings revealed the existence of a large proportion of consumers who wanted the sauce to be mild and an equally large proportion who wanted it to be hot. Relatively few wanted the in-between product, which would have been suggested by looking at the mean rating alone.[10]

Histogram

A form of bar chart on which the values of the variable are placed along the abscissa, or X axis, and the absolute frequency or relative frequency of occurrence of the values is indicated along the ordinate, or Y axis.

Frequency polygon

A figure obtained from a histogram by connecting the midpoints of the bars of the histogram with straight lines.

Cumulative distribution function

A function that shows the number of cases having a value less than or equal to a specified quantity; the function is generated by connecting points representing the given combinations of X's (values) and Y's (cumulative frequencies) with straight lines.

It is always a good idea to get a sense for a variable's distribution before performing any analysis with it. The distribution of a variable can be visualized through a **histogram,** a form of bar chart in which successive values of the variable are placed along the abscissa, or X axis, and the absolute frequency or relative frequency of occurrence of the values is indicated along the ordinate, or Y axis. The histogram for the income data in Exhibit 19.7 appears as Figure 19.2, with the incomes over $105,000 omitted because their inclusion would have required an undue extension of the income axis. It is readily apparent that the distribution of incomes is skewed to the right. The actual distribution can be compared to some theoretical distribution to determine whether the data are consistent with some a priori model. Further insight into the empirical distribution of income can be obtained by constructing the **frequency polygon,** which is obtained from the histogram by connecting the midpoints of the bars with straight lines. The frequency polygon for incomes is superimposed on the histogram in Figure 19.2.

An alternative way of gaining insight into the empirical distribution is through the empirical **cumulative distribution function.** Once again, the one-way tabulation is the source of the data. In this case, though, the number of observations with a value less than or equal to a specified quantity is determined; that is, the cumulative frequencies are generated. Thus, in the right-hand column of Exhibit 19.7, we see that there are 8 families with incomes less than $15,000, whereas there are 33 families (8 + 35) with incomes of $24,900 or less and 48 families (8 + 25 + 15) with incomes of $34,900 or less. These cumulative frequencies are denoted along the ordinate in Figure 19.3, while the abscissa again contains incomes. The empirical cumulative distribution function is generated by connecting the points representing the given combinations of X's (values) and Y's (cumulative frequencies) with straight lines.

The cumulative distribution function can also be used to determine whether the distribution of observed incomes is consistent with some theoretical or assumed distribu-

FIGURE 19.2   Histogram and Frequency Polygon of Incomes of Families in Car Ownership Study

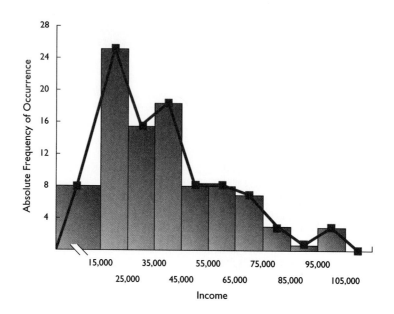

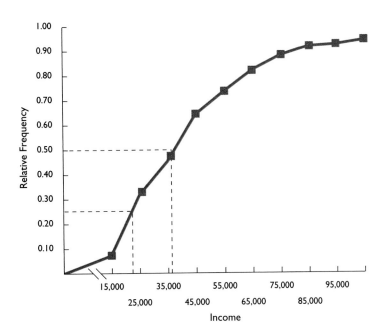

tion. In addition, it can be used to calculate some of the commonly used measures of location, such as the median, quartiles, and percentiles. These can simply be read from the
plot once the cumulative relative frequencies are entered. In our case, the cumulative relative frequencies are equal to the cumulative absolute frequencies divided by 100, since
there are 100 cases.

By definition, the sample median is that value for which 50 percent of the values lie
below it and 50 percent are above it. To read the sample median from the plot of the cumulative distribution, simply extend a horizontal line from 0.50 on the relative frequency
ordinate until it intersects the graph, and then drop a vertical line from the point of intersection to the X axis. The point of intersection with the X axis is the approximate sample
median. In the case at hand, the sample median equals $35,700. The quality of the ap-
proximation could be checked by actually determining the median using the detailed
data.

Sample quartiles could be determined in similar fashion. The first sample quartile
(also known as the 25th percentile) is that value for which 25 percent of the observations
are below it. The first sample quartile is determined by drawing a horizontal line from 0.25
on the relative frequency ordinate until it intersects the graph, dropping a vertical line
from the point of intersection to the horizontal axis, and reading off the value of the first
quartile at the point of intersection with the X axis. The first quartile is thus found to be
$17,300. The procedure for the third quartile (75th percentile) or any other percentile
would be the same as that for the median or first quartile. The only change would be
where the horizontal line began.

The one-way tabulation is also useful in calculating other summary measures, like the
mode, mean, and standard deviation. The mode, or the most frequently occurring item,
can be read directly from the one-way tabulation. Thus, Exhibit 19.6 suggests that most
families own one car.

The mean, or "average" response, can be calculated from a one-way tabulation by
weighting each value by its frequency of occurrence, summing these products, and

dividing by the number of cases. The average number of cars per family given the data in Exhibit 19.6 would thus be estimated as follows:

Value	Frequency	Value × Frequency
1	75	75
2	23	46
3	2	6
	100	127

The result is $\dfrac{127}{100}$ = 1.27 cars per family.

The standard deviation provides a measure of spread in the data. It is calculated from the one-way tabulation by taking the deviation of each value from the mean and squaring these deviations. The squared deviations are then multiplied by the frequency with which each occurs, these products are summed, and the sum is divided by one less than the number of cases to yield the sample variance. The square root of the sample variance then yields the sample standard deviation. The calculation of the standard deviation is thus very similar to that for ungrouped data, except for the fact that each value is weighted by the frequency with which it occurs. The standard deviation for the data in Exhibit 19.7 is thus calculated as follows:

Value	Value − Mean	(Value − Mean)²	Frequency	Frequency Times Difference Squared
1	−.27	.0729	75	5.4675
2	.73	.5329	23	12.2567
3	1.73	2.9929	2	5.9858
				23.7100

This yields a variance of 23.7100/99 = .2395 and a standard deviation of $\sqrt{.2395}$ = .4894.

The one-way tabulation as a communication vehicle for the results has not been discussed. The reader needs only to look at Exhibit 19.4 to see how much insight can be gathered about the variable income and then compare that with the insight generated in the one-way tabulation contained in Exhibit 19.7. Considering that one-way tabulations also serve as a basic input to the histogram, frequency polygon, empirical cumulative distribution function, and in calculating summary statistics, it is an unwise analyst indeed who does not take the time to develop the one-way tabulations of the variables in the study and to plot the results so as to get a sense of how they are distributed.[11]

Cross Tabulation

While the one-way tabulation is useful for examining the variables of the study separately, cross tabulation is a most important mechanism for studying the relationships among and between variables. In cross tabulation the sample is divided into subgroups so as to learn how the dependent variable varies from subgroup to subgroup. It is clearly the most used data-analysis technique in marketing research. Some would call it the bread and butter of applied research. Most marketing research studies go no further than cross tabulation, while many of the studies that do use more sophisticated analytical methods still contain cross tabulation as a significant component. Thus, the analyst and the decision maker both need to understand how cross tabulations are developed and interpreted.

Consider the question of the relationship, if any, between the number of cars that a family owns and family income. To keep the example simple, suppose the analyst is simply interested in determining if a family above average in income is more likely to own two or more cars than a family below average in income. Suppose further that $37,500 is the median income in the population and that this figure is to be used to split the families in the sample into two groups, those with below-average and those with above-average incomes.

Exhibit 19.8 presents the two-way classification of the sample families by income and number of cars. Looking at the marginal totals, we see that 75 families have one car or less, while 25 families have two cars or more. We also see that the sample is fairly representative of the population, at least as far as income is concerned—54 families fall into the below-average income group using the $37,500 cutoff.

Does the number of cars depend on income? It certainly seems so on the basis of Exhibit 19.8, since 19 of the families owning two or more cars are in the upper-income group. Is there anything that can be done to shed additional light on the relationship? The answer is yes. Compute percentages. Exhibits 19.9 and 19.10 are mathematically equivalent to Exhibit 19.8 but are based on percentages calculated in different directions: horizontally in Exhibit 19.9 and vertically in Exhibit 19.10. The tables contain quite different messages. Exhibit 19.9 suggests that multiple-car ownership is affected by family income: 41 percent of the families with above-average incomes had two or more automobiles, while only 11 percent of the below-average-income families did. This is an unambiguous finding. Exhibit 19.10, on the other hand, conveys a different story. It suggests that 64 percent of those who owned one car had below-average incomes, while only 24 percent of those who owned two or more cars were below average in income. Does this mean that multiple-car ownership paves the way to higher incomes? Definitely not. Rather, it simply illustrates a fundamental rule of percentage calculations: *Always calculate percentages in the direction of the causal factor, or across the effect factor.* In this case, income is logically considered the cause, or independent variable, and multiple-car ownership the effect, or dependent variable. The percentages are correctly calculated, therefore, in the direction of income as in Exhibit 19.9.

EXHIBIT 19.8 **Family Income and Number of Cars Family Owns**

	NUMBER OF CARS		
Income	1 or None	2 or More	Total
Less than $37,500	48	6	54
More than $37,500	27	19	46
Total	75	25	100

EXHIBIT 19.9 **Number of Cars by Family Income**

	NUMBER OF CARS			
Income	1 or None	2 or More	Total	Number of Cases
Less than $37,500	89%	11%	100%	54
More than $37,500	59%	41%	100%	46

EXHIBIT 19.10 **Family Income by Number of Cars**

Income	1 or None	2 or More
Less than $37,500	64%	24%
More than $37,500	36%	76%
Total	100%	100%
(Number of cases)	(75)	(25)

Conditional Probability
Probability that is assigned to Event A when it is known that Event B has occurred, or probability that would be assigned to Event A if it were known that Event B would occur.

One very useful way to determine the direction in which to calculate percentages is to think about the problem in terms of **conditional probabilities,** or the probability of one event occurring given that another event has occurred or will occur. Thus, the notion that a family is likely to have two or more cars *given* that it is a high-income family makes sense, while the notion that a family is likely to have a high income *given* that it has two or more cars does not.

The two-way cross tabulation, although it provides some insight into a dependency relationship, is not the final answer. Rather, it represents a start. Consider the relationship between multiple-car ownership and size of family. Exhibit 19.11 indicates the number of small and large (five or more members) families that possess two or more cars. Now, analysts would logically consider family size a cause of multiple-car ownership, and not vice versa. Thus, the percentages would be properly computed *in the direction of size of family, or across number of cars.* Exhibit 19.12 presents these percentages and suggests that the number of cars a family owns is affected by the size of the family—77 percent of the large families have two or more cars, while only 10 percent of the small families do.

This result raises the question, Does multiple-car ownership depend on family size or, as previously suggested, on family income? The proper way to answer this question is through the *simultaneous* treatment of income and family size. In effect, the two-way cross-classification table needs to be partitioned and a three-way table of income, family size, and multiple-car ownership formed. One way of doing this is illustrated in Exhibit 19.13. This table is, in one sense, two cross-classification tables of multiple-car ownership versus income—one for small families of four or fewer members, and one for large families of five or more members.

EXHIBIT 19.11   Number of Cars and Size of Family

	NUMBER OF CARS		
Size of Family	1 or None	2 or More	Total
4 or less	70	8	78
5 or more	5	17	22
Total	75	25	100

EXHIBIT 19.12   Number of Cars by Size of Family

	NUMBER OF CARS			
Size of Family	1 or None	2 or More	Total	Number of Cases
4 or less	90%	10%	100%	(78)
5 or more	23%	77%	100%	(22)

EXHIBIT 19.13   Number of Cars by Income and Size of Family

	4 MEMBERS OR LESS: NUMBER OF CARS			5 MEMBERS OR MORE: NUMBER OF CARS			TOTAL NUMBER OF CARS		
Income	1 or None	2 or More	Total	1 or None	2 or More	Total	1 or None	2 or More	Total
Less than $37,500	44	2	46	4	4	8	48	6	54
More than $37,500	26	6	32	1	13	14	27	19	46
Total	70	8	78	5	17	22	75	25	100

Once again we would want to compute percentages in the direction of income within each table. Exhibit 19.14 contains these percentages, which indicate that multiple-car ownership depends both on income and on family size. For small families of four or less, 19 percent of those with above-average incomes have two or more cars, while only 4 percent of those with below-average incomes have more than one automobile. For large families, 93 percent of those with above-average incomes and 50 percent of those with below-average incomes have more than one vehicle.

The preceding comparisons highlight the effect of income on multiple-car ownership, holding family size constant. We could also compare the effect of family size on multiple-car ownership, holding income constant. We would still find that each provides a partial explanation for multiple-car ownership. Now, you may have felt a bit uncomfortable with the presentation of the data in Exhibits 19.13 and 19.14. The information is there to be mined, but perhaps you may have wondered whether it could not be presented in a more revealing manner. It can, if you are willing to accept a couple of refinements in the manner of presentation. Look specifically at the first row of the first section of Exhibit 19.14 as it is reproduced as Exhibit 19.15. All the information contained in this table can be condensed into one figure, 4 percent. This is the percentage of small, below-average-income families that have two or more cars. It follows that the complementary percentage, 96 percent, represents those that have one automobile or none.

Exhibit 19.16 shows the rest of the data in Exhibit 19.14 treated in the same way. The entry in each case is the percentage of families in that category that own two or more

EXHIBIT 19.14 Number of Cars by Income and Size of Family

Income	4 MEMBERS OR LESS: NUMBER OF CARS			5 MEMBERS OR MORE: NUMBER OF CARS			TOTAL NUMBER OF CARS		
	1 or None	2 or More	Total	1 or None	2 or More	Total	1 or None	2 or More	Total
Less than $37,500	96%	4%	100% (46)	50%	50%	100% (8)	89%	11%	100% (54)
More than $37,500	81%	19%	100% (32)	7%	93%	100% (14)	59%	41%	100% (46)

EXHIBIT 19.15 Car Ownership for Small, Below-Average-Income Families

Income	4 MEMBERS OR LESS: NUMBER OF CARS		
	1 or None	2 or More	Total
Less than $37,500	96%	4%	100% (46)

EXHIBIT 19.16 Percentage of Families Owning Two or More Cars by Income and Size of Family

Income	SIZE OF FAMILY		
	4 or Less	5 or More	Total
Less than $37,500	4%	50%	11%
More than $37,500	19%	93%	41%

automobiles. Exhibit 19.16 conveys the same information as Exhibit 19.14, but it delivers the message with much greater clarity. The separate effect of income on multiple-car ownership, holding family size constant, can be determined by reading down the columns, while the effect of family size, holding income constant, can be determined by reading across the rows. Omitting the complementary percentages has helped reveal the structure of the data. Consequently, we will use this form of presentation whenever we attempt to determine the effect of several explanatory variables, considered simultaneously, in the pages that follow.

The original association between number of cars and family income reflected in Exhibit 19.9 is called the **total** (or *zero-order*) **association** between the variables. Exhibit 19.16, which depicts the association between the two variables within categories of family size, is called a *conditional table* that reveals the **conditional association** between variables. Family size here is a *control variable*. Conditional tables that are developed on the basis of one control variable are called *first-order* conditional tables, while those developed using two control variables are called *second-order* conditional tables, and so on.

Which variable has the greater effect on multiple-car ownership: income or family size? A useful method for addressing this question is to calculate the *difference in proportions* as a function of the level of the variable.[12] This can be done for the zero-order tables as well as the conditional tables of higher order. Consider again Exhibit 19.9, concentrating on the impact of income on the probability of the family's having multiple cars. The proportion of low-income families that have two or more cars is 0.11, while the proportion of high-income families is 0.41. The probability of having multiple cars is clearly different depending on the family's income; specifically, high income increases the probability of having two or more cars by 0.30 (0.41 − 0.11) over low income. A similar analysis applied to Exhibit 19.12 suggests the probability of multiple-car ownership is clearly different depending on family size. While 0.10 of the small families have multiple cars, 0.77 of the large families do. Thus, large family size increases the probability of having two or more cars by 0.67 (0.77 − 0.10) over small family size.

To determine whether income or family size has the greatest impact, it is necessary to consider them simultaneously using a similar analysis. Exhibit 19.16 contains the data that are necessary for this analysis. Let us first consider the impact of income. The proper way to determine the effect of income is to hold family size constant, which means, in essence, that we must investigate the relationship between income and multiple-car ownership for small families and then again for large families. Among small families, having high income increases the probability of having multiple cars by 0.15 (0.19 − 0.04). Among large families, having high income increases the probability of having multiple cars by 0.43 (0.93 − 0.50). The size of the associations between income and multiple-car ownership are different for different family sizes. This means there is a statistical interaction between the independent variables, and in order to generate a single estimate of the effect of income on car ownership, some kind of *average* of the separate effects needs to be computed. The appropriate average is a weighted average that takes account of the sizes of the groups on which the individual effects were calculated. There were 78 small families in the sample of 100 and 22 large families; the weight for small families is thus 0.78 and for large families 0.22. The weighted average is thus

$$0.15(0.78) + 0.43(0.22) = 0.21$$

which suggests that, on average, high versus low income increases the probability of owning multiple cars by 0.21.

To investigate the impact of family size, it is necessary to hold income constant or, alternatively, to investigate the impact of family size on multiple-car ownership for low-income families, then for high-income families, and then to generate a weighted average of the two results if they are not the same. Among low-income families, being large in size increases the probability of having multiple cars by 0.46 (0.50 − 0.04) compared with small size. Among high-income families, large size increases the probability by 0.74 (0.93 − 0.19) versus small size. Since there were 54 low-income families and 46 high-income families, the appropriate weights for weighting the two effects are 0.54 and 0.46, respectively. The calculation yields

$$0.46(0.54) + 0.74(0.46) = 0.59$$

as the estimate for the impact of family size on multiple-car ownership.

Family size has a more pronounced effect on multiple-car ownership than does income. It increases the probability of having two or more cars by 0.59, whereas income increases it by 0.21.

The preceding example highlights an important application of cross tabulation—the use of an additional variable to refine an initial cross tabulation. In this case, family size was used to refine the relationship between multiple-car ownership and income. This is only one of the many applications of successive cross tabulation of variables, and, in fact, a number of conditions can occur when additional variables are introduced into a cross tabulation, as shown in the various panels of Exhibit 19.17. The two-way tabulation may initially indicate the existence or nonexistence of a relationship between the variables. The introduction of a third variable may occasion no change in the initial conclusion, or it may indicate that a substantial change is in order.

Panel I: Initial Relationship Is Modified by Introduction of a Third Variable Now that we have considered Panel I-A ("Refine explanation") in the preceding discussion, let us turn to an analysis of the alternative conditions. Consider Panel I-B ("Reveal spurious explanation"). One of the purposes of the automobile ownership study was to determine the kinds of families that purchase specific kinds of automobiles. Consider vans. It was expected that van ownership would be related to lifestyle and, in particular, that those with a liberal orientation would be more likely to own vans than would those who are conservative by nature. Exhibit 19.18 was constructed, employing the raw data on car ownership in Exhibit 19.4, to test this hypothesis. Contrary to expectation, conservatives are more apt than liberals to own vans; 24 percent of the conservatives and only 16 percent of the liberals in the sample owned vans.

EXHIBIT 19.17 Conditions That Can Arise with the Introduction of an Additional Variable into a Cross Tabulation

Initial Conclusion	WITH THE ADDITIONAL VARIABLE	
	Change Conclusion	**Retain Conclusion**
Some relationship	I A. Refine explanation B. Reveal spurious explanation C. Provide limiting conditions	II
No relationship	III	IV

EXHIBIT 19.18 Van Ownership by Lifestyle

Lifestyle	OWN VAN?		Total
	Yes	**NO**	
Liberal	9 (16%)	46 (84%)	55 (100%)
Conservative	11 (24%)	34 (76%)	45 (100%)

Is there some logical explanation for this unexpected finding? Consider the addition of a third variable, the region of the country in which the family resides, to the analysis. A clear picture of the relationship among the three variables considered simultaneously can be developed employing our previously agreed-upon convention; that is, simply report the percentage in each category. The complement, 100 minus the percentage, then indicates the proportion not owning vans.

As Exhibit 19.19 indicates, van ownership is not related to lifestyle. Rather, it depends on the region of the country in which the family resides. When region is held constant, there is no difference in van ownership between liberals and conservatives. Families living in the South are much more likely to own a van than are families who live in the northern states. It just so happens that people in the South are more conservative with regard to their lifestyle than people in the North. The original relationship is therefore said to be spurious.

While it seems counterproductive to calculate the difference in proportions to determine the impact of each variable for each of the potential conditions in Exhibit 19.17, it does seem useful to do it for this case to demonstrate what is meant by a *main effect* without a statistical interaction. The example is also useful in reinforcing how the difference-in-proportion calculation can be used to isolate the causal relationships that exist in cross-tabulation data. Consider first the zero-order association between van ownership and lifestyle contained in Exhibit 19.18. Being a conservative increases the probability of van ownership by 0.08 (0.24 − 0.16) compared to being liberal. Yet Exhibit 19.19 shows that this is a spurious effect that is due to region of the country, since it disappears when region is held constant. Among those living in the North, the partial association between van ownership and lifestyle is 0.00 (0.05 − 0.05). Among those living in the South, there is a slightly higher probability of van ownership among conservatives, namely, 0.02 (0.43 − 0.41). This effect is so small that it can be attributed to rounding error, particularly since the proportions were carried to only two decimal places and the number of cases is so small. Regardless of the region of the country in which the family resides, their liberal or conservative orientation has no effect on whether they own a van.

Note, conversely, that the effect of region is pronounced and consistent. Among liberal families, living in the South increases the probability of van ownership 0.36 (0.41 − 0.05) compared to living in the North. Among conservative families, living in the South increases the probability by 0.38 (0.43 − 0.05). Within rounding error, the effect is the same for families with both philosophical orientations, which means there is no interaction among the two predictor variables. Rather, there is only a main effect of region on van ownership, and the best estimate of its size is given by either of these estimates or their average.

Consider now the question of ownership of foreign economy cars (Panel I-C, "Provide limiting conditions"). Does it depend on the size of the family? Exhibit 19.20 suggests it does. Smaller families are *less* likely to own a foreign economy car than are larger families! Only 8 percent of the small families, but 27 percent of the large families, have such automobiles. This relationship is interesting because it runs counter to what we might intuitively expect to find. Can it be accounted for?

Let us expand this cross classification by adding a variable for the number of cars the family owns. Exhibit 19.21 presents the percentage data, which indicate that it is only when large families have two or more cars that they own a foreign economy car. No large

EXHIBIT 19.19	Van Ownership by Lifestyle and Region of Country		
	REGION OF COUNTRY		
Lifestyle	**North**	**South**	**Total**
Liberal	5%	41%	16%
Conservative	5%	43%	24%

EXHIBIT 19.20 Foreign Economy Car Ownership by Family Size

Size of Family	OWN FOREIGN ECONOMY CAR?		Total
	Yes	No	
4 or less	6 (8%)	72 (92%)	78 (100%)
5 or more	6 (27%)	16 (73%)	22 (100%)

EXHIBIT 19.21 Foreign Economy Car Ownership by Family Size and Number of Cars

Size of Family	NUMBER OF CARS		Total
	1 or None	2 or More	
4 or less	6%	25%	8%
5 or more	0%	35%	27%

EXHIBIT 19.22 Station Wagon Ownership by Family Size

Size of Family	OWN STATION WAGON?		Total
	Yes	No	
4 or less	3 (4%)	75 (96%)	78 (100%)
5 or more	15 (68%)	7 (32%)	22 (100%)

EXHIBIT 19.23 Station Wagon Ownership by Family Size and Income

Size of Family	INCOME		Total
	Less than $37,500	More than $37,500	
4 or less	4%	3%	4%
5 or more	63%	71%	68%

families with one car owned such an automobile. The introduction of the third variable has revealed a condition that limits foreign economy car ownership—multiple-car ownership where large families are concerned.

Panel II: Initial Conclusion of a Relationship Is Retained Consider now the analysis of station wagon ownership based on the data in Exhibit 19.4. At first, it would seem to be related to family size. A case could be made that larger families have a greater need for station wagons than smaller families.

The cross tabulation of these two variables in Exhibit 19.22 suggests that larger families are indeed more likely to own station wagons: 68 percent of the large families and only 4 percent of the small families own them.

Consider, however, whether income might also affect station wagon ownership. As Exhibit 19.23 indicates, income has an effect over and above family size. As one goes from a small to a large family, there is a substantial increase in the likelihood of owning a station wagon. With high-income families, however, the increase is larger. Alternatively, if one focuses solely on large families, there is an increase in station wagon ownership from below-average to above-average income groups. The initial conclusion, though, is retained: Large families do display a greater tendency to purchase station wagons. Further, the effect of family size on station wagon ownership is much larger than the effect of income.

Panel III: Relationship Is Established with Introduction of a Third Variable Suppose one purpose of the study is to determine the characteristics of families who financed the purchase of their automobiles. Consider the cross tabulation of installment debt versus education of the household head. Exhibit 19.24 results when the families included in Exhibit 19.4 are classified into one of two educational categories—those with a high school education or less and those with some college training. As is evident, there is no relationship between education and installment debt; the percentage of families with outstanding car debt is 30 percent in each case.

Exhibit 19.25 illustrates the situation when income is also considered in the analysis. For below-average incomes, the presence of installment debt increases with education. For above-average incomes, installment debt decreases with education. The effect of education was obscured in the original analysis because the effects canceled each other. When income is also considered, the relationship of installment debt to education is quite pronounced.

Panel IV: Conclusion of No Relationship Is Retained with Addition of a Third Variable Consider once again the question of station wagon ownership. We have seen previously that it is related to family size. Let us forget this result for a minute and begin the analysis with the question, Is station wagon ownership affected by region of the country in which the family lives? Exhibit 19.26 provides an initial answer. Station wagon ownership does not

EXHIBIT 19.24   Financed Car Purchase by Education of Household Head

Education of Household Head	FINANCED CAR PURCHASE?		
	Yes	No	Total
High school or less	24 (30%)	56 (70%)	80 (100%)
Some college	6 (30%)	14 (70%)	20 (100%)

EXHIBIT 19.25   Financed Car Purchase by Education of Household Head and Income

Education of Household Head	INCOME		
	Less than $37,500	More than $37,500	Total
High school or less	12%	58%	30%
Some college	40%	27%	30%

EXHIBIT 19.26   Station Wagon Ownership by Region

Region	OWN STATION WAGON?		
	Yes	No	Total
North	11 (18%)	49 (82%)	60 (100%)
South	7 (18%)	33 (82%)	40 (100%)

depend on region; 18 percent of the sample families living both in the North and in the South own wagons.

Let us now consider the relationship when family size is again taken into account. Exhibit 19.27 presents the data. Once again the percentages are constant across regions. There is a minor variation, but this is due to round-off accuracy. Small families display a low propensity to purchase station wagons, regardless of whether they live in the North or the South. Large families have a high propensity, and this, too, is independent of where they live. The original lack of relationship between station wagon ownership and region of residence is confirmed with the addition of the third variable, family size.

Summary Comments on Cross Tabulation The previous examples should confirm the tremendous usefulness of cross tabulation as a tool in analysis. We have seen applications in which a third variable (1) helped to uncover a relationship not immediately discernible and (2) triggered the modification of conclusions drawn on the basis of a two-variable classification. You may have paused to ask yourself, Why stop with three variables? Would the conclusion change with the addition of a fourth variable? A fifth? Indeed it might. The problem is that one never knows for sure when to stop introducing variables. The conclusion is always susceptible to change with the introduction of the "right" variable or variables.

For example, there is currently a great deal of concern about the disappearance of the middle class and what that portends for the United States economically and socially. Yet there is a very real question as to whether the nation's middle class is in fact disappearing. Research Window 19.1 overviews the concern and highlights what happens when other factors, such as age and marital status, are taken into account.

Thus, the analyst is always in the position of "inferring" that a relationship exists. Later research may demonstrate that the inference was incorrect. This is why the accumulation

EXHIBIT 19.27 **Station Wagon Ownership by Region and Family Size**

	SIZE OF FAMILY		
Region	**4 or Less**	**More than 4**	**Total**
North	4%	69%	18%
South	3%	67%	18%

Research Window 19.1 **The Disappearance of the Middle Class: Fact or Fancy?**

In recent years, there has been a growing and uncritical acceptance of the view that the United States is becoming an increasingly polarized society—with rich and poor growing more numerous, and the middle class becoming an endangered species.

The proponents of this thesis maintain that those developments are the consequence of significant structural changes in our economy and hence will become increasingly aggravated. We are warned that this will eventually have alarming political and social consequences as the middle class—"the glue that holds society together"—continues to wither away.

But this bleak outlook is curiously inconsistent with many of the nation's principal economic indicators. Over the past decade and a half alone, the U.S. economy generated more than 30 million new jobs, an increase of an imposing third in the size of the labor force. Today, close to 80 percent of all working-age men and women are earning a paycheck, up from about 70 percent 20 years ago. Over those years, real per capita income rose at an average annual pace of 1.9 percent—which has added up to almost a 50 percent increase in the real living standards of the average American. Certainly, this is not arithmetic that lends credibility to the notion that the poor are growing poorer, and that the middle class is shrinking.

continued

Research Window 19.1   **The Disappearance of the Middle Class: Fact or Fancy?,** *continued*

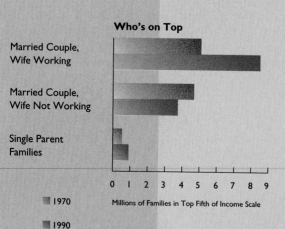

Who's on Top

Married Couple,
Wife Working

Married Couple,
Wife Not Working

Single Parent
Families

0 1 2 3 4 5 6 7 8 9

Millions of Families in Top Fifth of Income Scale

■ 1970

■ 1990

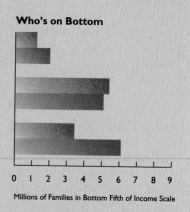

Who's on Bottom

Married Couple,
Wife Working

Married Couple,
Wife Not Working

Single Parent
Families

0 1 2 3 4 5 6 7 8 9

Millions of Families in Bottom Fifth of Income Scale

Precisely how the fortunes of the nation's middle class have changed over the years varies according to which earning brackets are selected to define middle income. But whatever the definition selected, the middle class is clearly not "disappearing." It has, in fact, been growing—but less rapidly than the nation's total household population and hence has declined in relative importance.

The affluent earning brackets have increased significantly over the years, as millions of families moved up from middle class. Contributing powerfully to this process has been the growing prevalence of working wives. In fact, over the past two decades, the entire increase in the number of families in the highest fifth of the income scale was accounted for by working-wife families. As of last year, two thirds of all wives in that bracket brought home a paycheck, up from only one in two 20 years ago.

With millions of families moving from the middle to the affluent brackets, the pertinent issue is why so many households have crowded into the lower brackets. Again, demographic and related social developments provide the answer.

By the early 1970s, the baby-boom generation began to come to age, which made for an extraordinary surge in the number of young adults. That generation has been inclined to marry late. Today, more than two out of every five women aged 20 to 30 are still single, compared with only one in four in 1970. Thus, over the past two decades, the number of husband-wife families in the nation increased by a mere 15 percent, but the number of single-person homes increased by an awesome 90 percent, and young singles by considerably more than that.

Not surprisingly, of the entire increase in the number of households in the lower-income brackets, a large proportion was accounted for by single-person households, and because the young are more likely to divorce than those further along in age, the nation also experienced a sharp rise in the number of single-parent families.

Clearly, it's been primarily demographic and social currents, not structural changes in the nation's economy, that have made for some polarization of income in recent years. In fact, over the longer run, we have experienced a continuous upward trend in earnings at all levels of the income scale. Many in the lower brackets moved into the middle, and those in the middle into the upper. Since the mid-1970s, however, while many middle-class homes swelled into the upper-income tiers, the proportion of households with marginal earnings remained stubbornly high. The latter development was not due to a polarization of jobs and wages, as alleged, but principally to the increase in the number of young homes and the rapid growth in the number of single-parent families.

In summary, then, what the proponents of the income-polarization thesis have demonstrated is that the young earn less than at later stages in life, that single-parent families experience financial stress, and that two people working earn more than one.

Source: Fabian Linden, "How We Live," *Across the Board* 27 (December 1990), pp. 9–10. Reprinted with permission of The Conference Board, New York City. For alternate perspectives, see R. C. Longworth and Sharman Stein, "The Unmaking of the Middle Class," *The Chicago Tribune* (August 20, 1995), pp. 1, 14; W. Bradford Fay, "The Fading Post-War Middle Class," *Marketing Research: A Magazine of Management & Applications* 8 (Fall 1996), pp. 47–48.

of studies, rather than a single study, supporting a particular relationship is so vital to the advancement of knowledge.

Exhibit 19.28 is an overview of the dilemma the researcher faces. The true situation is always unknown. If it were known, there would be no need to research it. Instead, the researcher is always in the position of making statements about an unknown true situation. The analyst may conclude that there is no relationship, or that there is some relationship, between two or more variables when in fact there is none or there is some. Only one of the four possibilities in Exhibit 19.28 *necessarily* corresponds to a correct conclusion—when the analyst concludes there is no relationship and in fact there is no relationship. Two of the other possibilities are necessarily incorrect, while one contains the possibility for error. That is, suppose the true situation is one of some relationship between or among the variables. The analyst has reached a correct conclusion only if he or she concludes that there is some relationship and, further, discovers its correct form.

Spurious noncorrelation means that the analyst concludes there is no relationship when, in fact, there is one. *Spurious correlation* occurs when there is no relationship among the variables but the analyst concludes that a relationship exists.

The opportunities for error are great. Consequently, one may be tempted to continue adding variables to the analysis ad infinitum. Fortunately, both theory and data will prevent the anxious—or overly ambitious—analyst from pursuing this course. Theory will constrain him or her because certain tabulations simply will not make any sense. The data will also act as a barrier to endless cross tabulations for several reasons. First, note that the analyst will want to add variables successively to the analysis in the form of higher-dimensional cross-classification tables. This can be accomplished only if the analyst has correctly anticipated the tabulations that would be desirable. This is most important. It is too late to say, "If only we had collected information on variable *X!*" once the analysis has begun. The relationships to be investigated, and thus the cross tabulations that should be appropriate, must be specified before the data are collected. Ideally, the analyst would construct dummy tables before beginning to collect the data. The dummy tables would be complete in all respects except for the number of observations falling in each cell. As a practical matter, it is usually impossible to anticipate all the cross tabulations one will want to develop. Nevertheless, careful specification of these tables at problem-definition time can return substantial benefits.

The analyst also is going to be limited by the size of the sample. In our example, since we started with 100 observations, the two-way tables were not particularly troublesome. Yet as soon as we introduced the third variable, cell sizes became extremely small. This occurred even though we treated all variables as dichotomies. Families were either below average or above average in income; they were either small or large; they lived in the North or in the South, and so on. This was done purposely so as to simplify the presentation. Yet even here the three-way tabulation offers eight cells ($2 \times 2 \times 2 \times 2$) into which the observations may be placed. Assuming an even allocation of the cases to the cells, this only allows 12.5 cases per cell. This is clearly a small number upon which to base any kind of conclusion.

EXHIBIT 19.28   The Researcher's Dilemma

Researcher's Conclusion	TRUE SITUATION	
	No Relationship	**Some Relationship**
No relationship	Correct decision	Spurious noncorrelation
Some relationship	Spurious correlation	Correct decision if concluded relationship is of proper form

The problem, of course, would have been compounded if a greater number of levels had been used for any of the variables. Consider what would have happened if the families had been divided into four income groups rather than two, given that the number of cells is the product of the number of levels for the variables being considered. For example, four income levels, three educational levels, and four family size levels would generate a cross-tabulation table with 48 separate cells (4 × 3 × 4). One would need a much larger sample than 100 to have any confidence in the suggested relationships.

Presenting Tabular Data

Banner

A series of cross tabulations between a criterion, or dependent variable, and several (sometimes many) explanatory variables in a single table.

Tabular results for commercial marketing research studies are seldom presented using the tabulation and cross-tabulation procedure discussed so far in this chapter. Rather, the use of banners has become increasingly popular. A **banner** is a series of cross tabulations between a criterion or dependent variable and several (sometimes many) explanatory variables in a single table on a single page. The dependent variable, or phenomenon to be explained, typically serves as the row variable, which is also known as the *stub*. The predictor or explanatory variables serve as the column variables, with each category of these variables serving as a banner point. Exhibit 19.29, for example, shows what the banner format might look like for the car ownership study. Although only two explanatory variables are shown, many more could be. The top line in each row of the table indicates the absolute number possessing the characteristic, whereas the second line indicates the percentage. All percentages have been rounded to zero decimal places in keeping with recommended practice.

The advantages of banner tables are several. In the first place, they allow a great amount of information to be conveyed in a very limited space. Second, their display format makes it easy for nonresearch managers to understand. Managers simply need to look at how the responses to the actual questions that were asked are distributed. A difficulty with these tables is that they tend to hide relationships in which it is necessary to consider several variables simultaneously (e.g., the joint effect of income and family size on multiple car ownership). They consequently make it more difficult to probe alternative explanations for what is producing the results. Banners also make it more difficult to detect data errors caused by improper coding or editing. Although popular, they should not be considered as a substitute for careful cross-tabulation analysis but more as an efficient form of data presentation.

EXHIBIT 19.29   Banner Format for Car Ownership Data

Question: How many cars does your family own?

	Total Sample	INCOME		FAMILY SIZE	
		Less than $37,500	More than $37,500	4 or Less	5 or More
Total	100	54	46	78	22
	(100)	(100)	(100)	(100)	(100)
1	75	48	27	70	5
	(75)	(89)	(59)	(90)	(23)
2	23	6	17	8	15
	(23)	(11)	(37)	(10)	(68)
3	2	0	2	0	2
	(2)	(0)	(4)	(0)	(9)

Ethical Dilemma 19.1

A manufacturer of aspirin had its marketing research department conduct a national survey among doctors to investigate what common household remedies doctors would be most likely to recommend when treating a patient with a cold. The question asked doctors to pick the one product they would most likely prescribe for their patients from among the choices Advil, Tylenol, aspirin, or none of the above. The distribution of responses was as follows:

Advil	100
Tylenol	100
Aspirin	200
None of the above	600
Total	1,000

The firm used the results of the survey as a basis for an extensive ad campaign that claimed, "In a national survey, doctors recommended aspirin two to one over Advil and Tylenol as the medicine they would most likely recommend to their patients suffering from colds."

Was the firm's claim legitimate?

Was it ethical for the firm to omit reporting the number of doctors that expressed no preference?

What would be the fairest way to state the ad claim? Do you think stating the claim in this way would be as effective as stating it in the way the firm did?

Back to the Case

Fortunately for his clients, Richard Batsell, a research pro (he is also a marketing professor at Rice University), did not stop by gathering ethnic data. He has also explored other patterns in ATM usage.

Batsell's firm, Analytica, also looked at age distributions and noted that age is associated with usage of ATM cards. In general, younger consumers are more likely to use ATMs, and younger consumers are also more heavily represented in ethnic minority groups than among non-Hispanic whites. In a study of Texas consumers, Analytica found that about 60 percent of people between the ages of 18 and 24 had an ATM card. Among those 65 and older, just 10 percent had a card.

Batsell judged that the age relationship provided a better explanation than the racial/ethnic categories. He hypothesized that older Americans had formed banking habits in the days before ATMs existed, so they were less likely to perceive a need for an ATM card.

Later, Batsell was startled by the results of a study he conducted for the Magic Line ATM network (since renamed NYCE) in the Midwest. In a single year, ATM usage among older Americans jumped from 8 percent—comparable to the findings of the Texas study—to 26 percent.

He found the likely answer to that surprise when he presented the results to a conference sponsored by Magic Line. After Batsell's presentation, the representatives of two large Michigan banks drew him aside to chat. They told him

that they had tried to apply his earlier findings to their marketing programs. The banks defined the lower ATM usage rates of older customers as a signal the banks needed to learn more about these customers' banking habits and needs. They held focus groups with their older customers and discovered an unmet need. Many of their customers spent winters in the South and believed they needed separate checking accounts for their winter homes.

The Michigan banks began touting their cards as a more convenient alternative to dual checking accounts. The banks explained to their customers that they could use their Michigan ATM cards to access their funds while they were in Florida or Texas. Once the older customers realized this benefit, many started using ATM cards. The banks had used the research data to convert a marketing weakness into an opportunity.

Batsell routinely looks at a number of demographic variables when he studies ATM usage. Although other variables such as education level and income are important, age has been the most significant in predicting ATM usage. However, if more banks are as savvy as the ones in Michigan in marketing to their nonusers, that pattern may change. And Analytica will be right there measuring the new trends.

Sources: "Knowledge = Power," *ATM Magazine* (September 24, 1999, downloaded from the *ATM Magazine* Web site, www.atmmagazine.com, October 7, 1999); "PULSE Study: Minorities Use ATM Cards More," *ATM Magazine* (May 5, 1999, downloaded from the *ATM Magazine* Web site, www.atmmagazine.com, October 7, 1999).

Summary

Learning Objective 1

Explain the purpose of the field edit.

The field edit is a preliminary edit designed to detect the most glaring omissions and inaccuracies in the data. It is also useful in helping to control the actions of the field force personnel and to clear up any misunderstanding they may have about directions, procedures, specific questions, and so on.

Learning Objective 2

Define what coding in the research process is.

Coding is the technical procedure by which data are categorized. Through coding, the raw data are transformed into symbols—usually numerals—that may be tabulated and counted. The transformation is not automatic, however; it involves judgment on the part of the coder.

Learning Objective 3

List the three steps in the coding process.

The coding process involves the three steps of (1) specifying the categories or classes into which the responses are to be placed, (2) assigning code numbers to the classes, and (3) preparing the codebook.

Learning Objective 4

Outline the conventions that are customarily followed when data are to be analyzed by a computer.

When data are to be analyzed by computer, a number of conventions should be followed in assigning the code numbers, including the following:
1. Locate only one character in each column.
2. Use only numeric codes.
3. Assign as many columns as are necessary to capture the variable.
4. Use the same standard codes throughout for "no information."
5. Code in a respondent identification number on each record.

Learning Objective 5

Describe the kinds of information contained in a codebook.

The codebook contains the general instructions indicating how each item of data was coded. It lists the codes for each variable and the categories included in each code. It further indicates where on the computer record the variable is located and how the variable should be read.

Learning Objective 6

Define what tabulation is and distinguish between the two types of tabulation.

Tabulation consists simply of counting the number of cases that fall into the various categories. The tabulation may take the form of a simple tabulation or a cross tabulation. Simple tabulation involves counting a single variable. In cross tabulation, two or more of the variables are treated simultaneously.

Learning Objective 7

Explain the various ways in which one-way tabulation can be used.

In addition to communicating the results of a study, one-way tabulation can be used (1) to determine the degree of item nonresponse, (2) to locate blunders, (3) to locate outliers, (4) to determine the empirical distribution of the variable in question, and (5) to calculate summary statistics.

Learning Objective 8

Assess the particular importance of cross tabulation.

Cross tabulation is one of the more useful devices for studying the relationships among and between variables since the results are easily communicated; further, cross tabulation can provide insight into the nature of a relationship since the addition of one or more variables to a two-way cross-classification analysis is equivalent to holding each of the variables constant.

Learning Objective 9

Describe a method by which a researcher can determine what impact one variable has on another in a cross-tabulation table.

A useful method for determining the impact one variable has on another variable in a cross-tabulation table is to compute the difference in proportions with which the dependent variable occurs as a function of the levels of the independent variable. This can be done for the zero-order tables as well as the conditional tables of higher order. The higher-order tables are used to remove the effects of other variables that might be affecting the dependent variable.

Learning Objective 10

Describe what banners are and how they are useful.

A banner is a series of cross tabulations between a criterion or dependent variable and several, sometimes many, explanatory variables in a single table. The dependent variable, or phenomenon to be explained, typically serves as the row variable, which is also known as the stub. The predictor or explanatory variables serve as the column variables, with each category of these variables serving as a banner point. Banners allow a great amount of information to be conveyed in a very limited space and are easy for managers to understand.

Review Questions

1. Distinguish among the preliminary data analysis steps of editing, coding, and tabulation.

2. What are the differences in emphasis between a field edit and a central-office edit?

3. What should an editor do with incomplete answers? Obviously wrong answers? Answers that reflect a lack of interest?

4. What are the principles that underline the establishment of categories so that collected data may be properly coded?

5. Suppose that you have a large number of very long questionnaires, making it impossible for one person to handle the entire coding task. How should the work be divided?

6. What is the difference between a one-way tabulation and a cross tabulation? Illustrate through an example.

7. When should you use machine tabulation? Manual tabulation?

8. What are the possible ways for treating item nonresponse? Which strategy would you recommend?

9. What is a blunder?

10. What is an outlier?

11. With how many digits should percentages be reported?

12. What is a histogram? A frequency polygon? What information do they provide?

13. What is the cumulative distribution function? Of what value is it?

14. How is the mean calculated from the one-way tabulation? The standard deviation?

15. What is the proper procedure for investigating the following hypotheses using cross-tabulation analysis?
    (a) Consumption of Product X depends on a person's income.
    (b) Consumption of Product X depends on a person's education.
    (c) Consumption of Product X depends on both.

16. How would you determine whether income or education had the greater effect on the consumption of Product X?

17. Illustrate the procedure from Questions 15 and 16 with data of your own choosing; that is, develop the tables, fill in the assumed numbers, and indicate the conclusions to be drawn from each table.

18. What is meant by the statement: the introduction of an additional variable
    (a) refined the original explanation?
    (b) revealed a spurious explanation?
    (c) provided limiting conditions?

19. How do you explain the condition in which a two-way cross tabulation of Variables X and Y revealed no relationship between X and Y but the introduction of Z revealed a definite relationship between X and Y?

20. What is the researcher's dilemma with respect to cross-tabulation analysis?

21. What constraints operate on researchers that prevent them from adding variables to cross-classification tables ad infinitum?

22. What are banners?

Discussion Questions, Problems, and Projects

1. The KIST television station was conducting research in order to help develop programs that would be well received by the viewing audience and would be considered dependable sources of information. A two-part questionnaire was administered by personal interviews to a panel of 3,000 respondents residing in the city of Houston. The field and office edits were simultaneously done, so that the deadline of May 1 could be met. A senior supervisor, Marlene Howe, was placed in charge of the editing tasks and was assisted by two junior supervisors and two field-workers. The two field-workers were instructed to discard instruments that were illegible or incomplete. Each junior supervisor was instructed to scrutinize 1,500 of

the instruments for incomplete answers, wrong answers, and responses that indicated a lack of interest. They were instructed to discard instruments that had more than five incomplete or wrong answers (the questionnaire contained 30 questions). In addition, they were asked to use their judgment in assessing whether the respondent showed a lack of interest and, if so, to discard the questionnaire.
(a) Critically evaluate the above editing tasks. Please be specific.
(b) Make specific recommendations to George Kist, the owner of the KIST television station, as to how the editing should be done.

2. (a) Establish response categories and codes for the question, "What do you like about this new brand of cereal?"
   (b) Code the following responses using your categories and codes.
       (1) "$1.50 is a reasonable price to pay for the cereal."
       (2) "The raisins and nuts add a nice flavor."
       (3) "The sizes of the packages are convenient."
       (4) "I like the sugarcoating on the cereal."
       (5) "The container does not tear and fall apart easily."
       (6) "My kids like the cartoons on the back of the packet."
       (7) "It is reasonably priced compared with other brands."
       (8) "The packet is attractive and easy to spot in the store."
       (9) "I like the price; it is not so low that I doubt the quality, and at the same time it is not so high as to be unaffordable."
       (10) "The crispness and lightness of the cereal improve the taste."

3. (a) Establish response categories and codes for the following question, which was asked of a sample of business executives: "In your opinion, which types of companies have not been affected by the present economic climate?"
   (b) Code the following responses using your categories and codes.
       (1) Washington Post   (9) Marine Midlands Banks
       (2) Colgate Palmolive   (10) Zenith Radio
       (3) Gillette   (11) Holiday Inn
       (4) Hilton Hotels   (12) The Dryden Press
       (5) Chase Manhattan   (13) Singer
       (6) Prentice-Hall   (14) Saga
       (7) Hoover   (15) Bank America
       (8) Fabergé

4. A large manufacturer of electronic components for automobiles recently conduced a study to determine the average value of electronic components per automobile. Personal interviews were conducted with a random sample of 400 respondents. The following information was secured with respect to each subject's "main" vehicle when he or she had more than one.

AVERAGE DOLLAR VALUE OF ELECTRONIC EQUIPMENT PER AUTOMOBILE

Dollar Value of Electronic Equipment	Number of Automobiles
Less than or equal to $50	35
$51 to $100	40
$101 to $150	55
$151 to $200	65
$201 to $250	65
$251 to $300	75
$301 to $350	40
$351 to $400	20
More than $400	5
Total number of automobiles	400

(a) Convert the above information into percentages.
(b) Compute the cumulative absolute frequencies.
(c) Compute the cumulative relative frequencies.
(d) Prepare a histogram and frequency polygon with the average value of electronic equipment on the X axis and the absolute frequency on the Y axis.
(e) Graph the empirical cumulative distribution function with the average value on the X axis and the relative frequency on the Y axis.
(f) Locate the median, first sample quartile, and third sample quartile on the cumulative distribution function graphed in Part (e) of this project.
(g) Calculate the mean and standard deviation and variance for the frequency distribution. (Hint: Use the midpoint of each class interval and multiply that by the appropriate frequency. For the interval starting at $401, assume the midpoint is 425.5.)

5. Select a convenience sample of 50 students on your campus and ask them the following two questions: Are you a part-time or full-time student? How many hours did you spend studying last week?
(a) Compute the average number of hours spent studying. Show your calculations.
(b) Complete the following cross-classification table.

HOURS SPENT STUDYING

Status	Less than Average	More than Average	Total
Full-time			
Part-time			
Total			

(c) Do your findings confirm the hypothesis that the hours spent studying depend on the status of the student? Compute the necessary percentages.

6. A social organization was interested in determining if there were various demographic characteristics that might be related to people's propensity to contribute to charities. The organization was particularly interested in determining if individuals above 40 years of age were more likely to contribute larger amounts than individuals below 40. The average contribution in the population was $1,500, and this figure was used to divide the individuals in the sample into two groups: those that contributed large amounts or more than average versus those that contributed less than average. The following table presents a two-way classification of the sample of individuals by contributions and age.

EXHIBIT 1   Personal Contributions by Age

Personal Contribution	AGE		Total
	39 or Less	40 or More	
Less than or equal to $1,500	79	50	129
More than $1,500	11	60	71
Total	90	110	200

In addition, the social organization wanted to determine if contributions depended on income and/or age. The following table presents the simultaneous treatment of age and income. The median income in the population was $18,200, and this figure was used to split the sample into two groups.

| EXHIBIT 2 | Personal Contributions by Age and Income | | | | | |

	INCOME					
	Less than or Equal to $18,200		More than $18,200		Total	
	AGE		AGE		AGE	
Personal Contributions	39 or Less	40 or More	39 or Less	40 or More	39 or Less	40 or More
Less than or equal to $1,500	63	22	16	28	79	50
More than $1,500	7	18	4	42	11	60
Total	70	40	20	70	90	110

(a) Does the amount of personal contributions depend on age? Generate the necessary tables to justify your answer.
(b) Does the amount of personal contributions depend on age alone? Generate the necessary tables to justify your answer.
(c) Present the percentage of contributions of more than $1,500 by age and income in tabular form. Interpret the table.

7. A large toy manufacturer wants to determine the characteristics of families who have purchased a new electronic game that is designed and marketed for all age groups. Management needs your assistance in interpreting the following two cross-classification tables.

| EXHIBIT 1 | Purchased Electronic Games versus Number of Children | | |

| | PURCHASED ELECTRONIC GAMES | | |
Number of Children	Yes	No	Total
Less than or equal to 1	63	87	150
More than 1	21	29	50

| EXHIBIT 2 | Purchased Electronic Games versus Number of Children and Age of Head of Household | | |

| | AGE OF HEAD OF HOUSEHOLD | | |
Number of Children	Less than or Equal to 45	More than 45	Total
Less than or equal to 1	14%	46%	42%
More than 1	38%	19%	42%

(a) What does Exhibit 1 indicate? Explain and show calculations where necessary.
(b) What does Exhibit 2 indicate? Have your conclusions changed or remained the same? Explain.

8. A local telephone company wants to determine the demographic characteristics of users of answering services. Management needs your help in interpreting the following two tables.
   (a) What does Exhibit 1 indicate? Explain and provide calculations where necessary.
   (b) What does Exhibit 2 indicate? Have your conclusions changed or remained the same? Explain.

EXHIBIT 1   Use of Answering Services versus Education

Education of Household Head	USE OF ANSWERING SERVICE		
	Yes	No	Total
High school or less	48	72	120
Some college or more	20	60	80

EXHIBIT 2   Use of Answering Services versus Education and Income

Education of Household Head	INCOME		
	Less than $18,200	More than $18,200	Total
High school or less	15%	45%	40%
Some college or more	15%	42%	25%

9. A study on television ownership patterns, undertaken by your research firm, has produced the following zero-order tables, among others. You have been asked to make a presentation of your findings to the study sponsor's vice-president of marketing. Your supervisor has told you that "the guy hates to look at a bunch of little tables. Combine all the zero-order stuff on one transparency." Complete a table that will fulfill your supervisor's instructions.

EXHIBIT 1   Household Income and Number of Televisions Owned

Income	NUMBER OF TELEVISIONS				
	1 or Less	2	3	4 or More	Total
Less than $20,000	89	43	11	1	144
$20,000 or more	41	49	10	6	106
Total	130	92	21	7	250

EXHIBIT 2   Household Size and Number of Televisions Owned

Household size	NUMBER OF TELEVISIONS				
	1 or Less	2	3	4 or More	Total
2 or less people	116	34	10	0	160
3 or more people	14	58	11	7	90
Total	130	92	21	7	250

EXHIBIT 3	Dwelling Size and Number of Televisions Owned				
			NUMBER OF TELEVISIONS		
Dwelling Size (sq. ft.)	**1 or Less**	**2**	**3**	**4 or More**	**Total**
1,500 or less	79	40	3	1	123
1,501 or more	51	52	18	6	127
Total	130	92	21	7	250

10. Visit your school's library and find examples of banner, zero-order, first-order, and second-order tables. Look for these in such publications as *Business Week, Fortune, Newsweek,* and *The Wall Street Journal.* Make a copy of each of the tables you find and analyze them, answering the following questions:
    (a) For the banner: What is the stub? What are the predictor variables? How many banner points are used for each predictor?
    (b) For the zero-order table: List the variables named in the table.
    (c) For the first-order table: List the variables named in the table: What is the control variable?
    (d) For the second-order table: List the variables named in the table. What are the control variables?
    (e) For each of the tables: Is the table presented in the format recommended in this textbook? How was the information presented in the table gathered? What table-based claims are made in the accompanying article? Does the table fully support these claims? Are there other variables that should have been considered? Are there alternative interpretations of the table that aren't mentioned in the article? If so, why aren't they mentioned in the article?

 NFO Applications NFO Research, Inc. (NFO), recently conducted a study of the ground caffeinated coffee market because several of its clients operate in this market. The study was undertaken with several objectives in mind, including the identification of benefits that consumers seek and the comparison of consumer opinions regarding several of the brands offered in the market.

The questionnaire in Figure 12.2 (pages 318–319) was designed to accomplish these objectives. This questionnaire was mailed to 400 individuals previously identified as consumers of ground caffeinated coffee (personally drinking at least one cup per day). Of those mailed out, 328 were returned; 299 of these were judged to be usable responses.

The data collected from these consumers are stored in a free-field format (space delimited) ASCII file named "coffee.dat" on the computer disk. The coding format of the data is shown below. Missing data are coded –99 for all items and should be disregarded for all analyses. While the data included are basically the data collected, some times or responses were generated to complete the data set.

11. (a) Produce a histogram for the age variable. Does it appear that anything has been obviously miscoded? If so, explain.
    (b) Produce a histogram for the variable "brand used most often." Determine an estimate of market share for the various brands based on this data set.
12. (a) Cross-tabulate "brand used most often" with "age," when the age variable has been recoded into the following categories:
    35 years or less
    36–45 years
    46–59 years
    60 years or more

Coding Format for NFO Coffee Study

Question Number	Variable (Variable Number)	Coding Specification
—	Questionnaire ID (VAR1)	—
1	Usual Method of Preparation (VAR2)	1 = automatic drip 2 = electric percolator 3 = stove-top percolator 4 = stove-top dripolator
2a	Ever Use: Folgers (VAR3) Hills Bros. (VAR4) Maxwell House Regular (VAR5) Maxwell House Master Blend (VAR6) Yuban (VAR7) Other (VAR8)	0 = no 1 = yes
2b	Brand Used Most Often (VAR9)	1 = Folgers 2 = Hills Bros. 3 = Maxwell House Regular 4 = Maxwell House Master Blend 5 = Yuban 6 = Other
2c	On Hand: Folgers (VAR10) Hills Bros. (VAR11) Maxwell House Regular (VAR12) Maxwell House Master Blend (VAR13) Yuban (VAR14) Other (VAR15)	0 = no 1 = yes
2d	Brand Will Buy Next (VAR16)	1 = Folgers 2 = Hills Bros. 3 = Maxwell House Regular 4 = Maxwell House Master Blend 5 = Yuban 6 = Other
2e	Overall Rating: Folgers (VAR17) Hills Bros. (VAR18) Maxwell House Regular (VAR19) Maxwell House Master Blend (VAR20) Yuban (VAR21) Other (VAR22)	Rating 1–10, where 1 = dislike it extremely 10 = like it extremely
3	Add Nothing (VAR23) Add Dairy Creamer (VAR24) Add Nondairy Creamer (VAR25) Add Sugar (VAR26) Add Artificial Sweetener (VAR27) Add Something Else (VAR28)	0 = no 1 = yes
4	Are You Primary Coffee Purchaser (VAR29)?	0 = no 1 = yes

5

Rich Taste (VAR30)
Always Fresh (VAR31)
Gets Day Off to Good Start (VAR32)
Full-Bodied Taste (VAR33)
Rich Aroma in the Cup (VAR34)
Good Value for the Money (VAR35)
Best Coffee in the Morning (VAR36)
Rich Aroma in the Can/Bag (VAR37)
Smooth Taste (VAR38)
Highest Quality Coffee (VAR39)
Premium Brand (VAR40)
Not Bitter (VAR41)
Coffee That Brightens Day Most (VAR42)
Cost More Than Other Brands (VAR43)
Strong Taste (VAR44)
Has No Aftertaste (VAR45)
Economy Brand (VAR46)
Rich Aroma While Brewing (VAR47)
Best Ground Coffee Available (VAR48)
Enjoy Drinking with Meal (VAR49)
Cost Less Than Other Brands (VAR50)

Importance Ratings, 0–10, where
  0 = not at all important
  10 = extremely important

Special Coding Instructions, Question 6:
All variables are rating scales coded 0–10, where
    0 = does not describe at all
    10 = describes completely

Variable	FOLGERS Var. No.	HILLS BROS. Var. No.	MAXWELL HOUSE REGULAR Var. No.	MAXWELL HOUSE MASTER BLEND Var. No.	YUBAN Var. No.
Rich Taste	VAR51	VAR72	VAR93	VAR114	VAR135
Always Fresh	VAR52	VAR73	VAR94	VAR115	VAR136
Good Start	VAR53	VAR74	VAR95	VAR116	VAR137
Full-Bodied Taste	VAR54	VAR75	VAR96	VAR117	VAR138
Rich Aroma/Cup	VAR55	VAR76	VAR97	VAR118	VAR139
Good Value	VAR56	VAR77	VAR98	VAR119	VAR140
Best Coffee in A.M.	VAR57	VAR78	VAR99	VAR120	VAR141
Rich Aroma/Can	VAR58	VAR79	VAR100	VAR121	VAR142
Smooth Taste	VAR59	VAR80	VAR101	VAR122	VAR143
Highest Quality	VAR60	VAR81	VAR102	VAR123	VAR144
Premium Brand	VAR61	VAR82	VAR103	VAR124	VAR145
Not Bitter	VAR62	VAR83	VAR104	VAR125	VAR146
Brightens Day Most	VAR63	VAR84	VAR105	VAR126	VAR147
Cost More	VAR64	VAR85	VAR106	VAR127	VAR148
Strong Taste	VAR65	VAR86	VAR107	VAR128	VAR149
No Aftertaste	VAR66	VAR87	VAR108	VAR129	VAR150
Economy Brand	VAR67	VAR88	VAR109	VAR130	VAR151
Rich Aroma/Brewing	VAR68	VAR89	VAR110	VAR131	VAR152
Best Available	VAR69	VAR90	VAR111	VAR132	VAR153
Enjoy with Meal	VAR70	VAR91	VAR112	VAR133	VAR154
Cost Less	VAR71	VAR92	VAR113	VAR134	VAR155

Question Number	Variable (Variable Number)	Coding Specifications
7a	Gender (VAR156)	1 = male 2 = female
7b	Age (VAR157)	Actual Age Coded

Generate percentages as well as frequency counts for each cell. What general conclusions might be drawn based on this information?

(b) How is the perceived relationship between brand used most often and age affected by the addition of a third variable, "sex of the respondent," to the analysis? Explain.

13. Suppose that it is your job to compare Folgers with Maxwell House Regular. Produce a snake diagram profiling these brands on the 21 attributes included in question 6 of the questionnaire. What do your results indicate?

Endnotes

1. Lourdes Lee Valeriano, "Marketing: Western Firms Poll Eastern Europeans to Discern Tastes of Nascent Consumers," *The Wall Street Journal* (April 27, 1992), p. B1.

2. Art Shulman, "War Stories: True-Life Tales in Marketing Research," *Quirk's Marketing Research Review* (December 1998), p. 16.

3. Valeriano, "Marketing: Western Firms Poll," p. B1.

4. Some writers would make the specification of categories part of the editing rather than the coding function. Its placement in one or the other function is not nearly as important as the recognition that it is an extremely critical step with significant ramifications for the whole research effort.

5. Carol Matlack, "What Unites Europe? Delayed Flights," *Business Week* (August 2, 1999), pp. 98, 100.

6. For discussion of a set of indices that can be used to investigate coder reliability as well as to determine which questions might prove to be particularly troublesome, see Martin Collins and Graham Kalton, "Coding Verbatim Answers to Open Questions," *Journal of the Market Research Society* 22 (October 1980), pp. 239–247; William D. Perreault, Jr., and Laurence E. Leigh, "Reliability of Nominal Data Based on Qualitative Judgments," *Journal of Marketing Research* 26 (May 1989), pp. 135–148.

7. Philip S. Siedl, "Coding," in Robert Ferber, ed., *Handbook of Marketing Research* (New York: McGraw-Hill, 1974), pp. 2–178 to 2–199. This article provides an excellent overview of the issues that arise in coding data and how they can be handled. See also Linda B. Bourque and Virginia A. Clark, *Processing Data: The Survey Example* (Thousand Oaks, Calif.: Sage Publications, Inc., 1992).

8. David W. Stewart, "Filling the Gap: A Review of the Missing Data Problem," unpublished manuscript, provides an excellent review of the literature on the problem of missing data, including various methods for eliminating cases and estimating answers. On the basis of this review, he concludes several things: Missing data points should be estimated regardless of whether the data are missing randomly or nonrandomly; for very small amounts of missing data, almost any of the estimation procedures work reasonably well; when larger amounts of data are missing and the average intercorrelation of variables is .20 or less, the substitution of the mean seems to work best; and when the average intercorrelation of the variables exceeds .20, a regression or principal-components procedure is the preferred choice when linearity among the variables may be assumed. For a study that empirically examines the question of whether or not missing items are random, see Richard M. Durand, Hugh J. Guffey, Jr., and John M. Planchon, "An Examination of the Random versus Nonrandom Nature of Item Omissions," *Journal of Marketing Research* 20 (August 1983), pp. 305–313. See also Roderick J. A. Little and Philip J. Smith, "Editing and Imputation for Quantitative Survey Data," *Journal of the American Statistical Association* 82 (March 1987), pp. 58–68; Roderick J. Little and Donald B. Rubin, "The Analysis of Social Science Data with Missing Values," *Sociological Methods and Research* 18 (November 1989), pp. 292–326; Philip L. Roth, "Missing Data: A Conceptual Review for Applied Psychologists," *Personnel Psychology* 47 (Autumn 1994), pp. 537–560.

9. See the classic book by Hans Zeisel, *Say It with Figures*, 5th ed. (New York: Harper and Row, 1968), pp. 16–17, for conditions that would support reporting percentages with decimal-place accuracy.

10. Robert J. Lavidge, "How to Keep Well-Intentioned Research from Misleading New-Product Planners," *Marketing News* 18 (January 6, 1984), p. 8. The more recent evidence suggests consumers want their sauces hot. See Kathleen Deveny, "Rival Hot Sauces Are Breathing Fire at Market Leader Tabasco," *The Wall Street Journal* (January 7, 1993), pp. B1, B6.

11. Box and whisker plots can also be used to get a sense for the distribution of the variable. They possess the attractive feature of including information about the variable mean, median, 25th and 75th percentiles, and outliers. For discussion of how they are constructed, see "Graphic Displays of Data: Box and Whisker Plots," *Research on Research*, No. 17 (Chicago: Market Facts, Inc., undated).

12. See Ottar Hellevik, *Introduction to Causal Analysis: Exploring Survey Data by Cross-tabulation*, 2nd ed. (Cambridge, Mass.: Scandinavian University Press, 1995).

Suggested Additional Readings

For useful discussion of the purposes and procedures to follow when editing and coding data, see
John A. Sonquist and William C. Dunkelberg, *Survey and Opinion Research: Procedures for Processing and Analysis* (Englewood Cliffs, N.J.: Prentice-Hall, 1977), especially pp. 41–196.

For especially insightful discussions of the use of cross-tabulation analysis to reveal the underlying patterns in data, see the classic works
Hans Zeisel, *Say It with Figures*, 5th ed. (New York: Harper and Row, 1968).
Ottar Helevik, *Introduction to Causal Analysis: Exploring Survey Data by Cross-tabulation*, 2nd ed. (Cambridge, Mass.: Scandinavian University Press, 1995).

HYPOTHESIS TESTING

In Chapter 19 we discussed the preliminary data-analysis steps of editing, coding, and tabulation. That chapter demonstrated the importance and potential value of these preliminary procedures, which are common to almost all research studies. Some studies stop with tabulation and cross tabulation. However, many others involve additional analyses, particularly the formal test of a statistical hypothesis or the establishment of a confidence interval. This appendix reviews these procedures.

When marketers prepare to launch a research study, they generally begin with a speculation, or guess, about a phenomenon in their environment. "I'll bet," the advertising manager might say to the marketing director, "that if we hired a sultry celebrity to promote our shampoo, sales would increase." Or the sales manager might say to the company's financial officer, "If my department only had more money to spend on training, our people would be more productive."

In marketing, as in other scientific fields, such unproven propositions are called *hypotheses*. Through the use of statistical techniques, we are often able to determine whether there is empirical evidence to confirm such hypotheses. Many of the procedures discussed in the next few chapters are used to test specific hypotheses. It is therefore useful to review some basic concepts that underlie hypothesis testing in classical statistical theory, such as framing the null hypothesis, setting the risk of error in making a wrong decision, and the general steps involved in testing the hypothesis.[1]

Null Hypothesis

Marketing research studies are unable to prove results. At best, they can indicate which of two mutually exclusive hypotheses are more likely to be true on the basis of observed results. The general forms of these two hypotheses and the symbols attached to them are as follows:

- H_0, the hypothesis that our results do not show any significant differences between population groups over whatever factors have been measured

- H_a, the alternate hypothesis that differences shown in our results reflect real differences between population groups

The first of these hypotheses, H_0, is known as the *null hypothesis*. One simple fact underlies the statistical test of a hypothesis: A hypothesis may be rejected but can never be accepted except tentatively, since further evidence may prove it wrong. In other words, one *rejects* the hypothesis or *does not reject* the hypothesis on the basis of the evidence at hand. It is wrong to conclude, however, that since the hypothesis was not rejected, it can be *accepted* necessarily as valid.

A naive qualitative example should illustrate the issue.[2] Suppose we are testing the hypothesis that John Doe is a poor man. We observe that Doe dines in cheap restaurants, lives in the slum area of the city in a run-down building, wears worn and tattered clothes, and so on. Although his behavior is certainly consistent with that of a poor man, we cannot accept the hypothesis that he is poor. It is possible that Doe may in fact be rich, but extremely frugal. We can continue gathering information about him, but for the moment we must decide *not to reject* the hypothesis. One single observation, for example, that indicates he has a six-figure bank account or that he owns 100,000 shares of AT&T stock would allow the immediate rejection of the hypothesis and would lead to the conclusion that John Doe is rich.

Thus, researchers need to recognize that in the absence of perfect information (such as is the case when sampling), the best they can do is form hypotheses or conjectures about what is true. Further, their conclusions about these conjectures can be wrong, and thus there is always some probability of error in accepting any hypothesis. Statistical parlance holds that researchers commit a Type I error when they reject a true null hypothesis and thereby accept the alternative; they commit a Type II error when they do not reject a false null hypothesis, which they should, given that it is false. The null hypothesis is assumed to be *true* for the purpose of the test. Such an assumption is used to generate knowledge about how the various sample estimates produced under the sampling plan might vary. Further, researchers need to be aware that Type I errors can be specified to be no more than some specific amount (e.g., ≤ 0.05), whereas Type II errors are functions.[3]

The upshot of this discussion is that the researcher needs to frame the null hypothesis in such a way that its rejection leads to the acceptance of the desired conclusion, that is, the statement or condition he or she wishes to verify. For example, suppose a firm was considering introducing a new product if it could be expected to secure more than 10 percent of the market. The proper way to frame the hypotheses then would be

$$H_0: \pi \leq 0.10$$
$$H_a: \pi > 0.10$$

If the evidence led to the rejection of H_0, the researcher would then be able to "accept" the alternative that the product could be expected to secure more than 10 percent of the market, and the product would be introduced, since such a result would have been unlikely to occur if the null was indeed true. If H_0 could not be rejected, though, the product would not be introduced unless more evidence to the contrary became available. The example as framed involves the use of a *one-tailed* statistical test in that the alternate hypothesis is expressed directionally, that is, as being greater then 0.10. The one-tailed test is most commonly used in marketing research, although there are research problems that warrant a *two-tailed* test; for example, the market share achieved by the new formulation of Product X is no different from that achieved by the old formulation, which was 10 percent. A two-tailed test would be expressed as

$$H_0: \pi = 0.10$$
$$H_a: \pi \neq 0.10$$

There is no direction implied with the alternate hypothesis; the proportion is simply expressed as not being equal to 0.10.

The one-tailed test is more commonly used than the two-tailed test in marketing research for two reasons. First, there is typically some preferred direction to the outcome, for example, the greater the market share, the higher the product quality, or the lower the expenses, the better. The two-tailed alternative is used when there is no preferred direction in the outcome or when the research is meant to demonstrate the existence of a difference but not its direction. Second, the one-tailed test, when it is appropriate, is more powerful statistically than the two-tailed alternative.

Types of Errors

Since the result of statistically testing a null hypothesis is to reject it or not reject it, two types of errors may occur. First, the null hypothesis may be rejected when it is true. Second, it may not be rejected when it is false and, therefore, should have been rejected. These two errors are, respectively, termed *Type I error* and *Type II error*, or α *error* and β *error*, which are the probabilities associated with their occurrence. The two types of errors are not complementary in that $\alpha + \beta \neq 1$.

To illustrate each type of error and to demonstrate that the errors are not complementary, consider a judicial analogy.[4] Since, under U.S. criminal law, a person is innocent until proven guilty, the judge and jury are always testing the hypothesis of innocence. The defendant may, in fact, be either innocent or guilty, but based on the evidence, the court may reach either verdict regardless of the true situation. Exhibit 19a.1 displays the possibilities. If the defendant is innocent and the jury finds him innocent, or if the defendant is guilty and the jury finds him guilty, the jury has made a correct decision. If, however, the defendant truly is innocent and the jury finds the person guilty, they have made an error, and similarly if the defendant is guilty and they find him innocent. The jury must find one way or the other, and thus the probabilities of the jury's decision must sum vertically to 1. Thus if we let α represent the probability of incorrectly finding the person guilty when he is innocent, then $1 - \alpha$ must be the probability of correctly finding him innocent. Similarly, β and $1 - \beta$ represent the probabilities of findings of innocence and guilt when he is guilty. It is intuitively obvious that $\alpha + \beta$ is not equal to 1, although later discussion will indicate that β must increase when α is reduced if other things remain the same. Since our society generally holds that finding an innocent person guilty is more serious than finding a guilty person innocent, α error is reduced as much as possible in our legal system by requiring proof of guilt "beyond any reasonable doubt."

Exhibit 19a.2 contains the corresponding research situation. Just as the defendant's true status is unknown to the jury, the true situation regarding the null hypothesis is unknown to the researcher. The researcher's dilemma parallels that of the jury in that the researcher has limited information with which to work. Suppose the null hypothesis is true. If the researcher concludes it is false, a Type I (α) error has been made. The significance level associated with a statistical test indicates the probability with which this error may be made. Since sample information will always be somewhat incomplete, there will always be some a error. The only way it can be avoided is by never rejecting the null hypothesis (never finding anyone guilty, in the judicial analogy). The *confidence level* of a statistical test is $1 - \alpha$, and the more confident we want to be in a statistical result, the lower we must set α error. The *power* associated with a statistical test is the probability of correctly rejecting a false null hypothesis. One-tailed tests are more powerful than two-tailed tests because, for the same α error, they are simply more likely to lead to a rejection of a false null hypothesis. β error represents the probability of not rejecting a false null hypothesis. There is no unique value associated with β error.

EXHIBIT 19a.1 **Judicial Analogy Illustrating Decision Error**

	TRUE SITUATION: DEFENDANT IS	
Verdict	**Innocent**	**Guilty**
Innocent	Correct decision: probability $= 1 - \alpha$	Error: probability $= \beta$
Guilty	Error: probability $= \alpha$	Correct decision: probability $= 1 - \beta$

EXHIBIT 19a.2 **Types of Errors in Hypothesis Testing**

	TRUE SITUATION: NULL HYPOTHESIS IS	
Research Conclusion	**True**	**False**
Do not reject H_0	Correct decision Confidence level Probability $= 1 - \alpha$	Error: Type II Probability $= \beta$
Reject H_0	Error: Type I Significance level Probability $= \alpha$	Correct decision Power of test Probability $= 1 - \beta$

Procedure

The relationship between the two types of errors is best illustrated through example, and the example would be most productive if developed following the general format of hypothesis testing. Research Window 19a.1 shows the typical sequence of steps that researchers follow in testing hypotheses. Suppose the problem was indeed one of investigating the potential for a new product and that the research centered around testing consumer preferences. Suppose that, in the judgment of management, the product should not be introduced unless at least 20 percent of the population could be expected to prefer it, and that the research calls for 625 respondents to be interviewed for their preferences.

Step 1

The null and alternate hypotheses would be

$$H_0: \pi \le 0.20$$
$$H_a: \pi > 0.20$$

The hypotheses are framed so that if the null hypothesis is rejected, the product should be introduced.

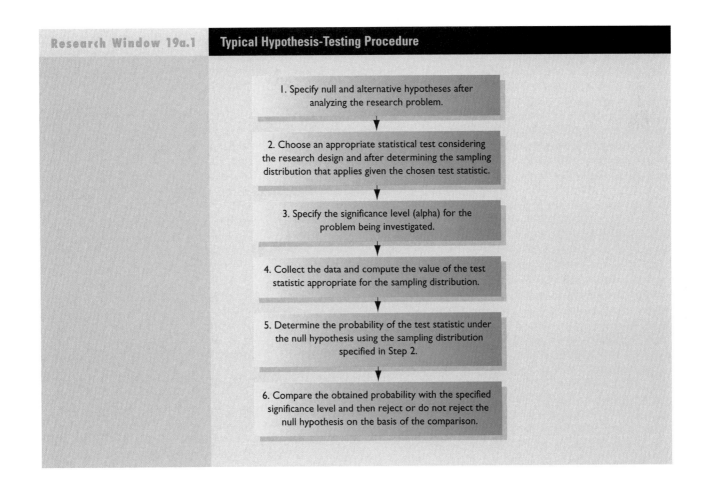

Research Window 19a.1 | **Typical Hypothesis-Testing Procedure**

1. Specify null and alternative hypotheses after analyzing the research problem.

2. Choose an appropriate statistical test considering the research design and after determining the sampling distribution that applies given the chosen test statistic.

3. Specify the significance level (alpha) for the problem being investigated.

4. Collect the data and compute the value of the test statistic appropriate for the sampling distribution.

5. Determine the probability of the test statistic under the null hypothesis using the sampling distribution specified in Step 2.

6. Compare the obtained probability with the specified significance level and then reject or do not reject the null hypothesis on the basis of the comparison.

Step 2

The appropriate sample statistic is the sample proportion, and the distribution of all possible sample proportions under the sampling plan is based on the assumption that the null hypothesis is true. Although the distribution of sample proportions is theoretically binomially distributed, the large sample size permits the use of the normal approximation.[5] The z test therefore applies. The z statistic in this case equals

$$z = \frac{p - \pi}{\sigma_p}$$

where p is the sample proportion preferring the product, σ_p is the standard error of the proportion, or the standard deviation of the distribution of sample p's. And σ_p in turn equals

$$\sqrt{\frac{\pi(1 - \pi)}{n}} = \sqrt{\frac{0.20(0.80)}{625}} = 0.0160$$

where n is the sample size. Note this peculiarity of proportions. As soon as we have hypothesized a population value, we have said something about the standard error of the estimate. The proportion is the most clear-cut case of "known variance," since the variance is specified automatically with an assumed π. The researcher thus knows all of the values for calculating z except p before ever taking the sample and further knows a priori the distribution to which the calculated statistic will be related. This is true in general, and the researcher should have these conditions clearly in mind before taking the sample.

Step 3

The researcher selects a significance level (α) using the following reasoning: In this situation α error is the probability of rejecting H_0 and concluding that $\pi > 0.2$, when in reality $\pi \leq 0.2$. This conclusion will lead the company to market the new product. However, since the venture will be profitable only if $\pi > 0.2$, a wrong decision to market would be financially unprofitable, possibly disastrous. The probability of Type I error should, therefore, be minimized as much as possible. The researcher recognizes, though, that the probability of a Type II error increases as α is decreased, other things being equal. Type II error in this case implies concluding $\pi \leq 0.2$ when in fact $\pi > 0.2$, which in turn suggests that the company would table the decision to introduce the product when it could be profitable. The opportunity lost from making such an error could be quite serious. Although, as explained later, the researcher does not know what β would be, he or she knows that α and β are interrelated and that an extremely low value of α, say 0.01 or 0.001, would produce intolerable β errors. The researcher decides, therefore, on an α level of 0.05 as an acceptable compromise.[6]

Step 4

Since Step 4 involves the computation of the test statistic, it can be completed only after the sample is drawn and the information collected. Suppose 140 of the 625 sample respondents preferred the product. The sample proportion is thus $p = \dfrac{140}{625} = 0.224$. The basic question that needs to be answered is conceptually simple: Is this value of p too large to have occurred by chance from a population with π assumed to be equal to 0.2? Or, in other words, What is the probability of getting $p = 0.224$ when $\pi = 0.2$? The test statistic, z, equals

$$\frac{p - \pi}{\sigma_p} = \frac{0.224 - 0.20}{0.0160} = 1.500$$

FIGURE 19a.1   **Probability of $z = 1.500$ with a One-Tailed Test**

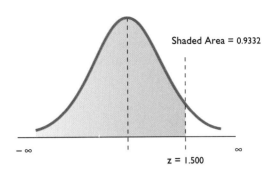

Step 5

The probability of occurrence of a z value of 1.500 can be found from standard tabled values of areas under the normal curve. (See Exhibit 1 at the end of the book.) Figure 19a.1 shows the procedure. The shaded area between $-\infty$ and 1.500 equals 0.9332; this means the area to the right of $z = 1.500$ is $1.000 - 0.9332$, or 0.0668. This is the probability of securing a z value of 1.500 under a true situation of $\pi = 0.2$.

Step 6

Since the calculated probability of occurrence is higher than the specified significance level of $\alpha = 0.05$, the null hypothesis is not rejected. The product would not be introduced because, while the evidence is in the right direction, it is not sufficient to conclude beyond "any reasonable doubt" that $\pi > 0.2$. If the decision maker had been able to tolerate a 10 percent chance of committing a Type I error, the null hypothesis would have been rejected and the product marketed, since the probability of getting a sample $p = 0.224$ when the true $\pi = 0.20$ is, as we have seen, 0.0668.

Power

The example illustrates the importance of correctly specifying the risk of error. If a 10 percent chance of an α error were tolerable and the researcher specified $\alpha = 0.05$, a potentially profitable opportunity would have been bypassed. The choice of the proper significance level involves weighing the costs associated with the two types of error, which is unfortunately a procedure that most researchers ignore, choosing out of habit $\alpha = 0.10$ or 0.05. Perhaps this lapse is due to the difficulty encountered in specifying β error, or Type II error.

The difficulty arises because β error is not constant. Recall that it is the probability of not rejecting a false null hypothesis. Therefore, the probability of committing a Type II error depends on the size of the difference between the *true*, but unknown, population value and the value assumed to be true under the null hypothesis. Other things being equal, we would prefer a test that minimized such errors. Alternatively, since the power of a test equals $1 - \beta$, we would prefer the test with the greatest power so that we would have the best chance of rejecting a false null hypothesis.[7] Now, clearly our ability to do this depends on "how false H_0 truly is." It could be "just a little bit false" or "way off the mark," and the probability of an incorrect inclusion would certainly be higher in the first case. The difference between the assumed value under the null and the true, but unknown, value is known as the *effect size*. As intuition suggests, large effects are easier to distinguish than small effects.

Consider again the hypotheses

$$H_0: \pi \leq 0.20$$
$$H_a: \pi > 0.20$$

where $\sigma_p = 0.0160$ and $\alpha = 0.05$, as before. Any calculated z value greater than 1.645 will cause us to reject this hypothesis, since this is the z value that cuts off 5 percent of the normal curve. The z value can be equated to the *critical* sample proportion through the formula

$$z = \frac{p - \pi}{\sigma_p}$$

$$1.645 = \frac{p - 0.20}{0.0166}$$

or $p = 0.2263$. Thus, any sample proportion greater than $p = 0.2263$ will lead to the rejection of the null hypothesis that $\pi \leq 0.2$. This means that if 142 or more [$0.2263(625) = 141.4$] of the sample respondents prefer the new product, the null hypothesis will be rejected and the product introduced, while if 141 or less of the sample respondent prefer it, the null hypothesis will not be rejected and the new product will not be introduced.

The likelihood of a sample proportion of $p = 0.2263$ is much greater for certain values of π than for others. Suppose, for instance, that the true but unknown value of π is 0.22. The sampling distribution of the sample proportion is again normal, but now it is centered about 0.22. The probability of obtaining the critical sample proportion $p = 0.2263$ under this condition is found again from the normal curve table, where now[8]

$$z = \frac{p - \pi}{\sigma_p} = \frac{0.2263 - 0.22}{0.0166} = 0.380$$

The shaded area between $-\infty$ and $z = 0.380$ is given in Exhibit 1 at the end of the book as 0.6480, and thus the area to the right of $z = 0.380$ is equal to $1.000 - 0.6480 = 0.3520$ (see Panel B in Figure 19a.2). This is the probability that a value as large or larger than $p = 0.2263$ would be obtained if the true population proportion was $\pi = 0.22$. It is also the power of the test in that if π is truly equal to 0.22, the null hypothesis is false and 0.3520 is the probability that the null will be rejected. Conversely, the probability that $p < 0.2263$ equals $1 - 0.3520 = 0.6480$, which is β error. The null hypothesis is false, and yet the false null hypothesis is not rejected from any sample for which the proportion $p < 0.2263$.

Suppose that the true population condition was $\pi = 0.21$ instead of $\pi = 0.22$, and the null hypothesis was again $H_0: \pi \leq 0.20$. Since the null hypothesis is less false in this second case, we would expect power to be lower and the risk of β error to be higher because the null hypothesis is less likely to be rejected. Let us see if that is indeed the case. The z value corresponding to the critical $p = 0.2263$ is 1.000. Power given by the area to the right of $z = 1.000$ is 0.1587 (the β error is 0.8413), and the expected result is obtained (see Figure 19a.2, Panel C).

Consider one final value, true $\pi = 0.25$. The null hypothesis of $\pi = 0.20$ would be "way off the mark" in this case, and we would expect there would be only a small chance that it would not be rejected and a Type II error would be committed. The calculations are displayed in Figure 19a.2, Panel D; $z = -1.368$, and the area to the right of $z = -1.368$ is 0.9144. The probability of β error is 0.0856, and the a priori expectation is confirmed.

Exhibit 19a.3 contains the power of the test for other selected population states, and Figure 19a.3 shows these values graphically. Figure 19a.3 is essentially the power curve for the hypotheses

$$H_0: \pi \leq 0.20$$
$$H_a: \pi > 0.20$$

FIGURE 19a.2   **Computation of β Error and Power for Several Assumed True Population Proportions for the Hypothesis $\pi \leq 0.2$**

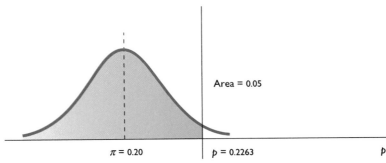

Area = 0.05

$\pi = 0.20$ $p = 0.2263$ p

Panel A: Critical Proportion under Null Hypothesis

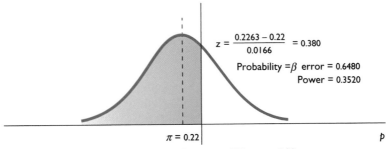

$$z = \frac{0.2263 - 0.22}{0.0166} = 0.380$$

Probability $= \beta$ error = 0.6480
Power = 0.3520

$\pi = 0.22$ p

Panel B: Probability of Realizing Critical Proportion When $\pi = 0.22$,
Which Means Null Hypothesis Is False

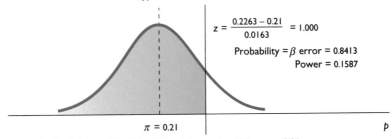

$$z = \frac{0.2263 - 0.21}{0.0163} = 1.000$$

Probability $= \beta$ error = 0.8413
Power = 0.1587

$\pi = 0.21$ p

Panel C: Probability of Realizing Critical Proportion When $\pi = 0.21$,
Which Means Null Hypothesis Is False

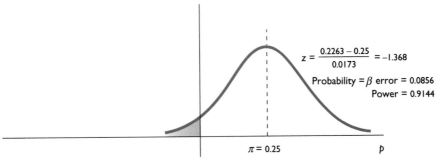

$$z = \frac{0.2263 - 0.25}{0.0173} = -1.368$$

Probability $= \beta$ error = 0.0856
Power = 0.9144

$\pi = 0.25$ p

Panel D: Probability of Realizing Critical Proportion When $\pi = 0.25$,
Which Means Null Hypothesis Is False

EXHIBIT 19a.3 β **Error and Power for Different Assumed True Values of** π **and the Hypotheses** H_0: $\pi \leq 0.20$ **and** H_a: $\pi > 0.20$

Value of π	Probability of Type II, or β, Error	Power of the Test: $1 - \beta$
0.20	$(0.950) = 1 - \alpha$	$(0.05) = \alpha$
0.21	0.8413	0.1587
0.22	0.6480	0.3520
0.23	0.4133	0.5867
0.24	0.2133	0.7867
0.25	0.0856	0.9144
0.26	0.0273	0.9727
0.27	0.0069	0.9931
0.28	0.0014	0.9986
0.29	0.0005	0.9995
0.30	0.0000	1.0000

FIGURE 19a.3 Power Function for Data of Exhibit 19a.3

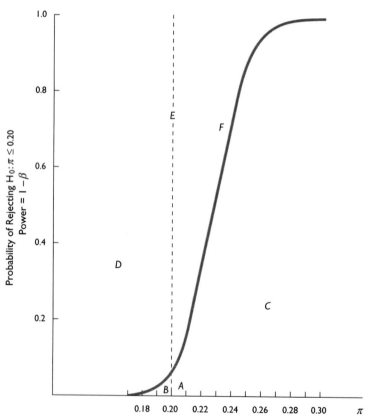

A — Type I error; true null hypothesis is rejected; significance level.
B — Type I error; true null hypothesis is rejected.
C — No error; false null hypothesis is rejected.
D — No error; true null hypothesis is not rejected.
E — No error; true null hypothesis is not rejected; confidence level.
F — Type II error; false null hypothesis is not rejected.

and it confirms that the further away the true π is from the hypothesized value in the direction indicated by the alternate hypothesis, the higher the power. Note that power is not defined for the hypothesized value, because if the true value in fact equals the hypothesized value, a β error cannot be committed.

Note that since power is a function rather than a single value, the researcher attempting to balance Type I and Type II errors logically needs to ask how false the null hypothesis is likely to be and to establish his or her decision rule accordingly. The way to control both errors within predetermined bounds for a given size effect is to vary the sample size.[9] The need to specify all three items—α error (or degree of confidence), β error (or power), and the size of the effect it is necessary to detect—possibly explains why so many researchers content themselves with the specification of Type I, or α, error and allow β error to fall where it may. The example provides an excellent opportunity to illustrate the dangers in this approach.

The failure to even worry about, much less explicitly take into account, the power of the statistical test represents one of the fundamental problems with the classical statistics hypothesis-testing approach as it is commonly practiced in marketing research. Moreover, Type II errors are often more costly than Type I errors. Another common problem is the widespread tendency to misinterpret a "statistically significant result." There are several common misinterpretations.[10] One of the most frequent is to view a p value as representing the probability that the results occurred because of sampling error. Thus, the commonly used $p = 0.05$ is taken to mean that there is a probability of only 0.05 that the results were caused by chance, and thus there must be something fundamental causing them. In actuality, a p value of 0.05 means that if, and this is a big if, the null hypothesis is true, the odds are only 1 in 20 of getting a sample result of the magnitude that was observed. Unfortunately, there is no way in classical statistical significance testing to determine whether the null hypothesis is true.

> A p value reached by classical methods is not a summary of the data. Nor does the
> p value attached to a result tell how strong or dependable the particular result is. . . .
> Writers and readers are all too likely to read .05 as $p(H/E)$, "the probability that the
> *H*ypothesis is true, given the *E*vidence." As textbooks on statistics reiterate almost in vain,
> p is $p(E/H)$, the probability that this *E*vidence would arise if the (null) *H*ypothesis is true.[11]

Another common misinterpretation is to equate statistical significance with practical significance. Many fail to realize that a difference can be of practical importance and not statistically significant if the power of the test is weak. Conversely, a result may be of no practical importance, even if highly significant, if the sample is very large.

A third very frequent misinterpretation is to hold that α or p level chosen is in some way related to the probability that the research hypothesis, typically captured in the alternative hypothesis, is true. Most typically, this probability is taken as the complement of the α level. Thus, a p value of 0.05 is interpreted to mean that its complement, $1 - 0.05 = 0.95$, is the probability that the research hypothesis is true. "Related to this misinterpretation is the practice of interpreting p values as a measure of the degree of validity of research results, i.e., a p value such as $p < .0001$ is 'highly statistically significant' or 'highly significant' and therefore much more valid than a p value of, say, 0.05."[12] Both of these related interpretations are wrong.

The only logical conclusion that can be drawn when a null hypothesis is rejected at some predetermined p level is that sampling error is an unlikely explanation of the results, given that the null hypothesis is true. In many ways that is not saying very much, because, as we just argued, the null hypothesis is a weak straw man; it is set up to be false. The null, as typically stated, holds that there is no relationship between a certain two variables, say, or that the groups are equal with respect to some particular variable. Yet, we do not really believe that. Rather, we investigate the relationship between variables because we believe there is some association between them, and we contrast the groups because we believe they are different with respect to the variable. Further, we can control our ability to reject the null hypothesis simply by the power we built into the statistical test, primarily through the size of the sample used to test it. "Given sufficiently high statistical power, one would expect virtually *always* to conclude the exact null hypothesis is false."[13]

Marketing researchers, then, need to be wary when interpreting the results of their hypothesis-testing procedures so that they do not mislead themselves and others. They need constantly to keep in mind both types of errors that it is possible to make. Further, they need to make sure they do not misinterpret what a test of significance reveals. It represents no more than a test against the null hypothesis. One useful way of avoiding misinterpretation is to calculate confidence intervals when possible, as this gives decision makers a much better feel for how much faith they can have in the results.

A test of significance is very much a yes-no affair: either the sample result is statistically significant or it is not. On the other hand, "the confidence interval not only gives a yes or no answer, but also, by its width, gives an indication of whether the answer should be whispered or shouted."[14] While not every test of significance can be put in the form of a confidence interval estimate, many of them can, and it is advisable to put them in that form when the opportunity arises.

Endnotes

1. Bayesian statistical theory assumes a different posture with respect to hypothesis testing than does classical statistics. Because classical statistical significance-testing procedures are much more commonly used in marketing research, though, only the basic elements underlying classical statistical theory are presented here.

2. The author expresses his appreciation to Dr. B. Venkatesh, of Burke Marketing Institute, for suggesting this example to illustrate the rationale behind the framing of hypotheses.

3. We will have more to say about Type I and Type II errors later.

4. R. W. Jastram, *Elements of Statistical Inference* (Berkeley, Calif.: Book Company, 1947), p. 44.

5. The binomial distribution tends toward the normal distribution for a fixed π as sample size increases. The tendency is most rapid when $\pi = 0.5$. With sufficiently large samples, normal probabilities may be used to approximate binomial probabilities with π's in this range. As π departs from 0.5 in either direction, the normal approximation becomes less adequate, although it is generally held that the normal approximation may be used safely if the smaller of $n\pi$ or $n(1 - \pi)$ is 10 or more. If this condition is not satisfied, binomial probabilities can either be calculated directly or found in tables that are readily available. In the example, $n\pi = 625(0.2) = 125$, and $n(1 - \pi) = 500$, and thus there is little question about the adequacy of the normal approximation to binomial probabilities.

6. We shall have more to say about the choice of $\alpha = 0.05$ and its interpretation after we have introduced the notion of power.

7. See Alan G. Sawyer and A. Dwayne Ball, "Statistical Power and Effect Size in Marketing Research," *Journal of Marketing Research* 18 (August 1981), pp. 275–290, for a persuasive argument about why marketing researchers need to pay more attention to power in their research designs. The article also offers some suggestions on how to improve statistical power. For a general discussion, see Jacob Cohen, *Statistical Power Analysis for the Behavioral Sciences*, 2d ed. (Hillsdale, N.J.: Lawrence Erlbaum Associates, 1988); M. W. Lipsey, *Design Sensitivity: Statistical Power for Experimental Research* (Thousand Oaks, Calif.: Sage Publications, Inc., 1990).

8. Note that σ_p is now $\sqrt{0.22(0.78)/625} = 0.0166$, because a different specification of π implies a different standard error of estimate.

9. See Helena Chumura Kraemer and Sue Thiemann, *How Many Subjects?* (Thousand Oaks, Calif.: Sage Publications, 1988), for discussion of the use of power to determine sample size.

10. For an excellent discussion of some of the most common misinterpretations of classical significance tests and some recommendations on how to surmount the problems, see Alan G. Sawyer and J. Paul Peter, "The Significance of Statistical Significance Tests in Marketing Research," *Journal of Marketing Research* 20 (May 1983), pp. 122–133. See also Jacob Cohen, "Things I Have Learned (So Far)," *American Psychologist* 45 (December 1990), pp. 1304–1312; Jacob Cohen, "The Earth is Round ($p<.05$)," *American Psychologist* 49 (December 1994), pp. 997–1003.

11. Lee J. Cronbach and R. E. Snow, *Aptitudes and Instructional Methods: A Handbook for Research on Interactions* (New York: Irvington, 1977), p. 52.

12. Sawyer and Peter, "The Significance," p. 123. For other useful discussions of what statistical tests of significance mean, see Mick Alt and Malcolm Brighton, "Analyzing Data or Telling Stories?" *Journal of*

the Market Research Society 23 (October 1981), pp. 209–219; Siu L. Chow, *Statistical Significance: Rationale Validity, and Utility* (Thousand Oaks, Calif.: Sage Publications, Inc., 1996).

13. Sawyer and Peter, "The Significance," p. 125.

14. Mary G. Natrella, "The Relation between Confidence Intervals and Tests of Significance," *American Statistician* 14 (1960), p. 22. See also G. R. Dawling and P. K. Walsh, "Estimating and Reporting Confidence Intervals for Marketing Opinion Research," *European Research* 13 (July 1985), pp. 130–133; Charles Cowan, "Testing versus Description: Confidence Intervals and Hypothesis Testing," *Marketing Research: A Magazine of Management & Applications* 2 (September 1990), pp. 59–61.

Chapter 20

DATA ANALYSIS: EXAMINING DIFFERENCES

L E A R N I N G   O B J E C T I V E S

Upon Completing This Chapter, You Should Be Able to

1. Explain the basic use of a chi-square goodness-of-fit test.

2. Discuss the similarities and differences between the chi-square goodness-of-fit test and the Kolmogorov-Smirnov test.

3. Specify which test is appropriate if one is testing a hypothesis about a single mean, given that the variance is known. Which is appropriate if the variance is unknown?

4. Identify the tests that are appropriate if the analysis involves two means from independent samples.

5. Specify the appropriate test if the analysis involves the difference between two parent-population proportions.

Case in Marketing Research

Angie Karlin followed Chuck Zellmer through the lunchtime crowd at the newest Omni Software store in Washington, D.C.

"The store is really sharp," remarked Karlin once they'd arrived at Zellmer's office, at the rear of the sales floor. "You certainly aren't having any trouble bringing in customers, not at this location anyway."

"Oh, no, we're doing a phenomenal business in the retail division. We're opening three more stores this year. Hopefully we'll be as successful at choosing the new locations as we were at choosing this one."

"So how's the catalog division doing?" asked Karlin. Zellmer was the director of catalog sales for Omni Software.

"Catalog sales are really flat. It's strange. You know that we started out as a catalog business and that the retail end was really an experiment that we could afford to make because we were doing so well in mail-order business. Now that we're making big bucks in retail, our mail orders are going nowhere. It troubles me because I can't explain it."

"Which is why you called me," filled in Karlin.

"Right. That is why I called you. We at Omni are committed to our catalog operation. It allows us to reach a national market at a fairly low cost. Besides, we think there is a fundamental difference between our catalog customers and our retail customers."

"What's that?" asked Karlin.

"You buy software from a catalog when you already know what you want. For example, if you're looking for a certain home finance program, let's say Thompson's Money Manager, then you look in the Omni catalog, call the 800 number, and order it. But if you're looking for a home finance program and you're not sure which one you need, then you go into an Omni store, where a salesperson can explain the different features of each program and help you decide."

"I understand why you see the market as being segmented," remarked Karlin.

"Our goal over the next year," continued Zellmer, "is to revitalize our catalog division. We'd like your firm to do a survey of our past customers so that we can gain an understanding of how to improve catalog sales."

"You know we'd love to do it," said Karlin. "It sounds like you guys have a pretty good idea of what you want."

"Yes. To begin with, we'd like to know what our mail-order customers think about our products and services. We'd also like to get a better feel for who our customers really are—how old they are, how much money they make, how computer literate they are," said Zellmer.

"I think that's a great start," replied Karlin. "But you know, there's a fixed cost to doing any kind of mail survey, and from my experience, I think we might as well take it one step further. I think we should take a look at how your customers feel about buying merchandise, especially computer software, through the mail as opposed to through a retail outlet. I think that perception might be important in how you subsequently formulate your marketing strategy."

"Great," said Zellmer. "Why don't you go ahead and draft a proposal for the study. I'll have Sid Green, at the mailing house, run out a list of the names of our catalog customers."

"Fine," answered Karlin. "How much have you budgeted for this study?"

"I don't know. How much is it going to cost?" asked Zellmer. "And don't think that by asking you that question I'm giving you a blank check. We're in a competitive business, and we're very sensitive to unnecessary expenditures. On the other hand, to do a study like this but not budget enough to do more than a half-baked job would be a total waste of money."

"Chuck," replied Karlin with feeling, "I wish all my clients were as intelligent as you are. . . ."

Discussion Issues

1. If you were the marketing research director on this survey, what variables would you want to investigate in the study?

2. How might some of those variables be interrelated?

3. Assuming a mail survey were to be used, what might you do to increase the response rate?

A question that arises regularly in the analysis of research data is, Are the research results statistically significant? Could the result have occurred by chance due to the fact that only a sample of the population was contacted, or does it actually indicate an underlying condition in the population? For example, a research firm called rsc, The Quality Measurement Company, studied the relationship between advertising of toothbrushes and toothbrush sales. The company collected data on the ARS Persuasion scores for various toothbrush ads (a measure of the shift in brand choice of consumers in a simulated-purchase environment before and after they watch television ads), as well as on the sales of toothbrushes during the time the ads were aired. The objective of the study was to test the hypothesis that high ARS Persuasion scores would be associated with a higher level of sales. The study indeed found that sales and market share were greatest for brands with the highest scores.[1] Researchers would also want to know whether that result was a coincidence (occurred by chance because of the sample from which the ARS scores were calculated) or showed an actual link between ad characteristics and sales.

To answer questions such as these, we use one of several tests of statistical significance. This chapter reviews some of the more important tests for examining the statistical significance of differences. The difference at issue might be the difference between some sample result and some expected population value, or the difference between two or more

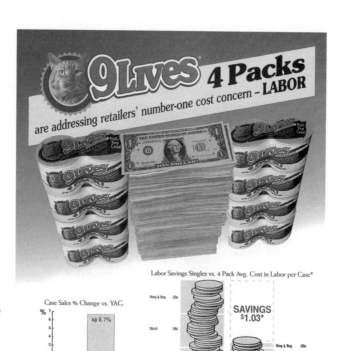

In this ad, which is directed to grocery retailers, Heinz Pet Products Company compares two sample averages to promote its 9Lives 4 Pack form of cat food packaging. The ad compares the average labor costs to handle cases containing single cans ($1.56) to those containing 4 packs ($.53), for a savings of $1.03 per case. The sample averages are shown graphically in the stacked-coin bar charts below the product.

sample results (see the 9Lives ad for an example). Different types of tests are applicable for different types of problems. The first part of the chapter reviews the χ^2 (chi-square) goodness-of-fit test, which is especially useful with nominal data. The second part reviews the Kolmogorov-Smirnov test, which is useful with ordinal data. The latter sections focus on the tests that are applicable when examining differences in means or proportions.

Goodness of Fit

It is often the case in marketing studies that an analyst must determine whether a certain pattern of behavior shown by the data corresponds to the pattern that was expected when the study was devised. As an illustration, consider a breakfast food manufacturer who has recently developed a new cereal called Score. The cereal will be packaged in the three standard sizes: small, large, and family size. In the past, the manufacturer has found that for every small package, three of the large and two of the family size are also sold. The manufacturer wishes to see if this same tendency will hold with this new cereal, since a change in consumption patterns could have significant production implications. The manufacturer therefore decides to conduct a market test to determine the relative frequencies with which consumers will purchase the various sizes.

Suppose that, in an appropriate test market, over a one-week period, 1,200 boxes of the new cereal are sold and that the distribution of sales by size is as follows:

NUMBER BUYING

Small	Large	Family	Total
240	575	385	1,200

As some quick multiplication would show, these figures do not match the pattern established earlier with other cereal brands. Does this preliminary evidence indicate that the firm should expect a change in the purchase patterns of the various sized packages with Score?

Chi-square goodness-of-fit test
A statistical test to determine whether some observed pattern of frequencies corresponds to an expected pattern.

This is the type of problem for which the **chi-square goodness-of-fit test** is ideally suited. (Note that *chi* is a Greek letter that rhymes with *sky.*) The variable of interest has been broken into k mutually exclusive categories ($k = 3$ in the example), and each observation logically falls into one of the k classes or cells. The trials (purchases) are independent, and the sample size is large.

All that is necessary to employ the test is to calculate the *expected* number of cases that would fall in each category and to compare that with the *observed* number actually falling in the category, using the equation

$$\chi^2 = \sum_{i=1}^{k} \frac{[O_i - E_i]^2}{E_i}$$

where

- O_i is the observed number of cases falling in the ith category
- E_i is the expected number of cases falling in the ith category
- k is the number of categories

The expected number falling into a category is generated from the null hypothesis, which in this case is that the composition of sales of Score by package size will follow the manufacturer's normal sales (that is, for every small package, three large and two family sizes will be sold). In terms of the proportion of all sales, that means

$$\text{small size: } \frac{1}{1+3+2} = 1/6$$

$$\text{large size: } \frac{3}{1+3+2} = 3/6$$

$$\text{family size: } \frac{2}{1+3+2} = 2/6$$

or that one-sixth of the sales could be expected to be in the small package size, one-half in the large size, and one-third in the family size if sales of the new cereal follow traditional patterns. If the 1,200 boxes sold in test market followed the normal or expected pattern, then 200 ($1/6 \times 1,200$) would have been the small size, 600 ($1/2 \times 1,200$) would have been the large size, and 400 ($1/3 \times 1,200$) would have been the family size. How does the observed pattern compare with the expected pattern? The appropriate χ^2 statistic is computed as

$$\chi^2 = \frac{(240-200)^2}{200} + \frac{(575-600)^2}{600} + \frac{(385-400)^2}{400} = 9.60$$

The chi-square distribution is one of the statistical distributions that is completely determined by its degree of freedom, ν. The term *degrees of freedom* refers to the number of things that can vary independently. For example, suppose you had five numbers for which you calculated an average. Then, by knowing any four of the numbers and the average, you would be able to determine the fifth number. In effect, you have used up one degree of freedom in the numbers by calculating the average. The degrees of freedom in the chi-square test are determined by how many cells in a table are free to vary. For example, suppose we had the following table,

	B_1	B_2	
A_1	x	x	5
A_2	x	x	7
	4	8	

and were given one of the cell values, say, the upper left value.

	B_1	B_2	
A_1	1	④	5
A_2	③	④	7
	4	8	

Then the circled values are all fixed, given that we know the marginal totals. If we know $A_1B_1 = 1$, then every other value is automatically determined. Because of this, we say that only one cell is free to vary.

In the cereal example, the number of degrees of freedom is one less than the number of categories (k), that is, $\nu = k - 1 = 2$, because the sum of the differences between the observed and expected frequencies is zero; both the expected and observed frequencies must sum to the total number of cases; given any $k - 1$ differences, the remaining difference is thus fixed, and this results in the loss of one degree of freedom.

Suppose the researcher has chosen a significance level of $\alpha = 0.05$ for this test. The tabled value of χ^2 for two degrees of freedom and $\alpha = 0.05$ is 5.99 (see Exhibit 2 in the appendix at the end of the book). Since the calculated value ($\chi^2 = 9.60$) is larger, the conclusion is that the sample result would be unlikely to occur by chance alone. Rather, the preliminary market-test results suggest that sales of Score will follow a different pattern than is typical. The null hypothesis of sales in the ratio of $1:3:2$ is rejected.

The chi-square test outlined here is an approximate test.[2] The approximation is relatively good if, as a rule of thumb, the expected number of cases in each category is five or more, although this value can be as low as 1 for some situations.[3]

The previous example illustrated the use of the chi-square distribution to test a null hypothesis regarding k population proportions, $\pi_1, \pi_2, \ldots, \pi_k$. The proportions were needed to generate the expected number of cases in each of the k categories. Viewed in this light, the test of a single proportion discussed when reviewing the logic of hypothesis testing in the appendix to Chapter 19 is a special case; in the goodness-of-fit test, the single parameter π is replaced by the k parameters $\pi_1, \pi_2, \ldots, \pi_k$.

Another use of the chi-square goodness-of-fit test is in determining whether a population distribution has a particular form. For instance, we might be interested in finding out whether a sample distribution of scores might have arisen from a normal distribution of scores. To investigate, we could construct the sample frequency histogram. The intervals would correspond to the k cells of the goodness-of-fit test. The observed cell frequencies would be the number of observations falling in each interval. The expected cell frequencies would be the number falling in each interval, if indeed the sample came from a normal distribution with mean μ and variance σ^2. If the population mean and variance were unknown, the sample and variance could be used as estimates. This would result in the loss of two additional degrees of freedom, but the basic test procedure would remain unchanged.

Kolmogorov-Smirnov Test

Kolmogorov-Smirnov test
A statistical test employed with ordinal data to determine whether some observed pattern of frequencies corresponds to some expected pattern; also used to determine whether two independent samples have been drawn from the same population or from populations with the same distribution.

The **Kolmogorov-Smirnov test** is similar to the chi-square goodness-of-fit test in that it uses a comparison between observed and expected frequencies to determine whether observed results are in accord with a stated null hypothesis. But the Kolmogorov-Smirnov test takes advantage of the ordinal nature of the data.

Consider, for example, a manufacturer of cosmetics who is testing four different shades of a foundation compound: very light, light, medium, and dark. The company has hired a marketing research firm to determine whether any distinct preference exists toward either extreme. If so, the company will manufacture only the preferred shades. Otherwise, it will market all shades. Suppose that in a sample of 100, 50 persons prefer the very light shade, 30 the light shade, 15 the medium shade, and 5 the dark shade. Do these results indicate some kind of preference?

Since shade represents a natural ordering, the Kolmogorov-Smirnov test can be used to test the preference hypothesis. The test involves specifying the cumulative distribution function that would occur under the null hypothesis and comparing that with the observed cumulative distribution function. The point at which the two functions show the maximum deviation is determined, and the value of this deviation is the test statistic.

The null hypotheses for the cosmetic manufacturer would be that there is no preference for the various shades. Thus it would be expected that 25 percent of the sample would prefer each shade. The cumulative distribution function resulting from this assumption is presented as the last column of Exhibit 20.1.

Kolmogorov-Smirnov D, which is equal to the *absolute value of this maximum deviation* between the observed cumulative proportion and the theoretical cumulative proportion, is $0.80 - 0.50 = 0.30$. If the researcher chooses an $\alpha = 0.05$, the critical value of D for large samples is given by $1.36/\sqrt{n}$, where n is the sample size. In our case of a sample size of 100, the critical value is 0.136. Calculated D exceeds the critical value, and thus the null hypothesis of no preference among shades is rejected. The data indicate a statistically significant preference for the lighter shades.

			Observed		**Theoretical**
Shade	**Observed Number**	**Observed Proportion**	**Cumulative Proportion**	**Theoretical Proportion**	**Cumulative Proportion**
Very light	50	0.50	0.50	0.25	0.25
Light	30	0.30	0.80	0.25	0.50
Medium	15	0.15	0.95	0.25	0.75
Dark	5	0.05	1.00	0.25	1.00

EXHIBIT 20.1   Observed and Theoretical Cumulative Distributions of Foundation Compound Preference

The careful reader will have noticed that the hypothesis of no preference could also have been tested with the chi-square goodness-of-fit test. When the data are ordinal though, the Kolmogorov-Smirnov test is the preferred procedure. It is more powerful than chi-square in almost all cases, is easier to compute, and does not require a certain minimum expected frequency in each cell as does the chi-square test.

The Kolmogorov-Smirnov test can be used to determine whether two independent samples have been drawn from the same population or from populations with the same distribution. An example would be a manufacturer interested in determining whether consumer preference among sizes for a new brand of laundry detergent was the same as for the old brand. To apply the test, we would simply need to create a cumulative frequency distribution for each sample of observations using the same intervals. The test statistic would be the value of the maximum deviation between the two observed cumulative frequencies.[4]

Hypotheses about One Mean

A recurring problem in marketing research studies is the need to make some statement about the parent-population mean. Recall that when sampling from a parent population with known variance that the distribution of sample means is equal to the population mean, and the variance of the sample means, $\sigma_{\bar{x}}^2$, is equal to the population variance divided by the sample size; that is, $\sigma_{\bar{x}}^2 = \sigma^2/n$. Thus, it should not prove surprising to find that the appropriate statistic for testing a hypothesis about a mean when the population variance is *known* is

$$z = \frac{\bar{x} - \mu}{\sigma_{\bar{x}}}$$

where

- $\bar{x}$ is the sample mean

- μ is the population mean

- $\sigma_{\bar{x}}$ is the standard error of the mean, which is equal to $\sigma/\sqrt{n}$, where n is the sample size and σ is the population standard deviation

The z statistic is appropriate if the sample comes from a normal population, or if the variable is not normally distributed in the population but the sample is large enough for the central-limit theorem to be operative. What happens, though, in the more realistic case, in which the population variance is *unknown*?

When the parent-population variance is unknown, then, of course, the standard error of the mean, $\sigma_{\bar{x}}$, is unknown, since it is equal to $\sigma/\sqrt{n}$. The standard error of mean must then be estimated from the sample data. The estimate is $s_{\bar{x}} = \hat{s}/\sqrt{n}$, where $\hat{s}$ is the unbiased sample standard deviation; that is,

$$\hat{s} = \sqrt{\frac{\sum_{i=1}^{n}(X_i - \bar{x})^2}{n-1}}$$

Or, in words,

$$\hat{s} = \sqrt{\frac{\text{the sum of the deviations of the sample observations around the sample mean squared}}{\text{sample size} - 1}}$$

The test statistic now becomes

$$\frac{\text{sample mean minus hypothesized value of population mean}}{\text{estimated standard error of the mean}}$$

or $(\bar{x} - \mu)/s_{\bar{x}}$, which is t distributed with $n-1$ degrees of freedom if the conditions for the t test are satisfied.

To use the t statistic appropriately for making inferences about the mean, two basic questions need to be answered:

- Is the distribution of the variable in the parent population normal, or is it asymmetrical?

- Is the sample size large or small?

If the variable of interest is normally distributed in the parent population, then the test statistic $(\bar{x} - \mu)/s_{\bar{x}}$ is t distributed with $n-1$ degrees of freedom. This is true whether the sample size is large or small. For small samples, we actually use t with $n-1$ degrees of freedom when making an inference. Although t with $n-1$ degrees of freedom is also the theoretically correct distribution for large n, the distribution approaches and becomes indistinguishable from the normal distribution for samples of 30 or more observations. The test statistic $(\bar{x} - \mu)/s_{\bar{x}}$ is therefore referred to a table of normal deviates when one is making inferences with large samples. Note, though, that this is because the theoretically correct t distribution (since σ is unknown) has become indistinguishable from the normal curve.

What happens if the variable is not normally distributed in the parent population when σ is unknown? If the distribution of the variable is symmetrical or displays only moderate skew, or asymmetry, there is no problem. The t test is quite robust to departures from normality. However, if the variable is highly skewed in the parent population, the appropriate procedure depends upon the sample size. If the sample is small, the t test is inappropriate. Either the variable has to be transformed so that it is normally distributed, or one of the distribution-free statistical tests must be used. If the sample is large, the normal curve could be used for making the inference, provided the following two assumptions are satisfied:

1. The sample size is large enough so that the distribution of the sample means, $\bar{x}$, is normal because of the operation of the central-limit theorem. The greater the degree of asymmetry in the distribution of the variable, the larger the size of the sample that is needed to satisfy this assumption.

2. The sample standard deviation, $\hat{s}$, is a close estimate of the parent-population standard deviation, σ. The higher the degree of variability is in the parent population, the larger the size of the sample needed to justify this assumption.

Research Window 20.1 summarizes the situation for making inferences about a mean for known and unknown parent-population standard deviation, σ, and normally distributed and asymmetrical parent-population distributions.

To illustrate the application of the t test, consider a supermarket chain that is investigating the desirability of adding a new product to the shelves of its associated stores. Since many products must compete for limited shelf space, the store has determined that it must sell 100 units per week in each store in order for the item to be sufficiently profitable to warrant handling it. Suppose that the research department decides to investigate the item's turnover by putting it in a random sample of ten stores for a limited period of time. Suppose further that the average sales per store per week were as shown in Exhibit 20.2.

Since the variance of sales per store is unknown and has to be estimated, the t test is the correct parametric test if the distribution of sales is normal. The normality assumption seems reasonable and could be checked using one of the goodness-of-fit tests. The little sales evidence available does not indicate any real asymmetry, so let us assume that the normality assumption is satisfied.

A one-tailed test is appropriate, since it is only when the sales per store per week reach at least 100 units that the product will be introduced on a national scale. The null and alternate hypotheses are

$$H_0: \mu \leq 100$$
$$H_a: \mu > 100$$

and suppose the significance level is to be $\alpha = 0.05$. From the data in Exhibit 20.2,

$$\text{sample mean} = \frac{\text{sum of observations}}{\text{sample size}}$$

EXHIBIT 20.2   **Store Sales of Trial Product per Week**

Store i	Sales X_i	Store i	Sales X_i
1	86	6	93
2	97	7	132
3	114	8	116
4	108	9	105
5	123	10	120

Research Window 20.1	Testing Hypotheses about a Single Mean	
	σ Known	**σ Unknown**
Distribution of variable in parent population is normal or symmetrical.	Small n: Use $z = \dfrac{\bar{x} - \mu}{\sigma_{\bar{x}}}$ Large n: Use $z = \dfrac{\bar{x} - \mu}{\sigma_{\bar{x}}}$	Small n: Use $$t = \frac{\bar{x} - \mu}{s_{\bar{x}}}$$ where $$s_{\bar{x}} = \hat{s}/\sqrt{n}$$ and $$\hat{s} = \sqrt{\frac{\sum\limits_{i=1}^{n}(X_i - \bar{x})^2}{n-1}}$$ and refer to t table for $n-1$ degrees of freedom. Large n: Since the t distribution approaches the normal as n increases, use $$z = \frac{\bar{x} - \mu}{s_{\bar{x}}}$$ for $n > 30$.
Distribution of variable in parent population is asymmetrical.	Small n: There is no theory to support the parametric test. Either one must transform the variate so that it is normally distributed and then use the z test, or one must use a distribution-free statistical test. Large n: If the sample is large enough so that the central-limit theorem is operative, use $$z = \frac{\bar{x} - \mu}{\sigma_{\bar{x}}}$$	Small n: There is no theory to support the parametric test. Either one must transform the variate so that it is normally distributed and then use the t test, or one must use a distribution-free statistical test. Large n: If sample is large enough so that (1) the central-limit theorem is operative and (2) $\hat{s}$ is a close estimate of σ, use $$z = \frac{\bar{x} - \mu}{\hat{s}_{\bar{x}}}$$

or

$$\bar{x} = \frac{\sum_{i=1}^{n} X_i}{n} = 109.4$$

and

$$\text{sample standard deviation} = \sqrt{\frac{\text{square root of sum of deviations around sample mean squared}}{\text{sample size} - 1}}$$

or

$$\hat{s} = \sqrt{\frac{\sum_{i=1}^{n} (X_i - \bar{x})^2}{n - 1}} = 14.40$$

and therefore the estimated standard error of the mean is $s_{\bar{x}} = \hat{s}/\sqrt{n} = 4.55$. Calculations yield

$$t = \frac{\bar{x} - \mu}{s_{\bar{x}}} = \frac{109.4 - 100}{4.55} = 2.07$$

Critical t as read from the t table with $\nu = n - 1 = 9$ degrees of freedom is 1.833 ($p = .95$). (See Exhibit 3 in the appendix at the end of the book.) It is unlikely that the calculated value would have occurred by chance if the sales per store in the population were indeed less than or equal to 100 units per week.

Some insight into the sales per store per week that might be expected if the product were introduced on a national scale can be obtained by calculating the confidence interval. The appropriate formula is

$$\text{sample mean} \pm t \text{ (estimated standard error of the mean)}$$

or

$$\bar{x} \pm t s_{\bar{x}}$$

For a 95 percent confidence interval and 9 degrees of freedom, $t = 1.833$, as we have already seen. The 95 percent confidence interval is thus $109.4 \pm (1.833)(4.55)$, or 109.4 ± 8.3, or, alternatively, $101.1 \leq \mu \leq 117.7$.

Suppose the product is placed in 50 stores and that the sample mean and sample standard deviation are the same, that is, $\bar{x} = 109.4$, $\hat{s} = 14.40$. The test statistics would now be $z = 4.62$, which would be referred to a normal table since the t is indistinguishable from the normal for samples of this size. Calculated z is greater than critical $z = 1.645$ for $\alpha = 0.05$, and, as expected, the same conclusion is warranted. The evidence is stronger now because of the larger samples of stores; the product could be expected to sell at a rate greater than 100 units per store per week.

The impact of the larger sample and the opportunity it provides to use the normal curve can also be seen in the smaller confidence interval the larger sample produces. When the normal curve rather than t distribution applies, the formula $x \pm t s_x$ for calculating the confidence interval changes to $\bar{x} \pm z s_{\bar{x}}$, where the appropriate z value is read from the normal curve table. Since for a 95 percent confidence interval, $z = 1.645$, the interval is $109.4 \pm (1.645)(4.55)$ or 109.4 ± 7.5, which yields the estimate $101.9 \leq \mu \leq 116.9$, a slightly narrower interval than that produced when 10 stores rather than 50 were in the sample.

Hypotheses about Two Means

Consider testing a hypothesis about the difference between two population means. An example is a nationwide consumer survey that was sponsored by the National Restaurant Association. The study gathered demographic data and data about preferences for takeout foods. The results showed that patrons of gourmet coffee shops have an average household income of $48,520, compared with a mean of $47,660 for all customers of takeout establishments.[5] A relevant question is whether the two means are significantly different; that is, are coffee shop customers richer than others who buy takeout?

The methodology for testing a hypothesis about two means will vary according to whether the samples are independent or related. Assuming the samples are independent, there are three cases to consider.

- The two parent-population variances are known

- The parent-population variances are unknown but can be assumed to be equal

- The parent-population variances are unknown and cannot be assumed to be equal

After exploring these alternatives, we will see how to test a hypothesis about two means when the samples are related.

Variances Are Known

Experience has shown that the population variance usually changes much more slowly than does the population mean. This means that the "old" variance can often be used as the "known" population variance for studies that are being repeated. For example, we may have annually checked the per capita soft drink consumption of people living in different regions of the United States. If we were now to test a hypothesis about the differences in per capita consumption of a new soft drink, we could use the previously determined variances as "known" variances for our new soft drink. Consider that our problem is indeed one of determining whether there are any differences between northerners and southerners in their consumption of a new soft drink our company has recently introduced, called Spark. Further, past data indicate that per capita variation in the consumption of soft drinks is 10 ounces per day for northerners and 14 ounces per day for southerners as measured by the standard deviation, that is, $\sigma_N = 10$ and $\sigma_S = 14$.

The null hypothesis is that there is no difference between northerners and southerners in their consumption of Spark, or that their mean consumption is equal (H_0: $\mu_N = \mu_S$), while the alternate hypothesis is that there is a difference (H_a: $\mu_N \neq \mu_S$). It so happens that if $\bar{x}_N$ and $\bar{x}_S$, the sample means, are normally distributed random variables, then their sum or difference is also normally distributed. The two sample means could be normally distributed because per capita consumption is normally distributed in each region or because the two samples are large enough that the central-limit theorem is operative. In either case, the test statistic is $z = $ the sample mean of the first sample minus the sample mean of the second sample minus the quantity, the hypothesized population mean in the first sample minus the hypothesized population mean in the second sample, all divided by the standard error of the difference in the two means; that is,

$$z = \frac{(\bar{x}_1 - \bar{x}_2) - (\mu_1 - \mu_2)}{\sigma_{\bar{x}_1 - \bar{x}_2}}$$

where

- $\bar{x}_1$ is the sample mean for the first (northern) sample

- $\bar{x}_2$ is the sample mean for the second (southern) sample

- μ_1 and μ_2 are the unknown population means for the northern and southern samples

- $\sigma_{\bar{x}_1 - \bar{x}_2}$ is the standard error of estimate for the difference in means and is equal to the square root of the sum of the two variances in means, specifically,

$$\sqrt{\sigma_{\bar{x}_1}^2 + \sigma_{\bar{x}_2}^2}$$

where, in turn $\sigma_{\bar{x}_1}^2 = \sigma_1^2/n_1$ and $\sigma_{\bar{x}_2}^2 = \sigma_2^2/n_2$. Now σ_1^2 and σ_2^2 are the "known" population variances of $\sigma_1^2 = (10)^2 = 100$ and $\sigma_2^2 = (14)^2 = 196$.

Suppose that a random sample of 100 people from the North and 100 people from the South indicates that $\bar{x}_1 = 20$ ounces per day and $\bar{x}_2 = 25$ ounces per day. Does this result indicate a real difference in consumption rates? The standard error of estimate is

$$\sigma_{\bar{x}_1 - \bar{x}_2} = \sqrt{\frac{100}{100} + \frac{196}{100}} = \sqrt{2.96} = 1.720$$

and the calculated z is

$$z = \frac{(20 - 25) - (\mu_1 - \mu_2)}{1.720} = \frac{-5 - 0}{1.720} = -2.906$$

Calculated z exceeds the critical tabled value of -1.96 for $\alpha = 0.05$, and the null hypothesis is rejected. There is a statistically significant difference in the per capita consumption of Spark by northerners and southerners.

The confidence interval for the difference in the two means is given by the formula

$$(\bar{x}_1 - \bar{x}_2) \pm z\sigma_{\bar{x}_1 - \bar{x}_2}$$

For a 95 percent confidence interval, $z = 1.96$, and the interval estimate of the difference in consumption of Spark by the two groups is $-5 \pm (1.96)(1.720) = -5 \pm 3.4$. Northerners, on average, are estimated to drink 1.6 to 8.4 ounces less of Spark per day than southerners.

Variances Are Unknown

When the two parent-population variances are unknown, the standard error of the test statistic $\sigma_{\bar{x}_1 - \bar{x}_2}$ is also unknown, since $\sigma_{\bar{x}_1}$ and $\sigma_{\bar{x}_2}$ are unknown and have to be estimated. As was true with one sample, the sample standard deviations are used to estimate the population standard deviations;

$$\hat{s}_1^2 = \frac{\sum_{i=1}^{n_1} (X_{i1} - \bar{x}_1)^2}{(n_1 - 1)}$$

is used to estimate σ_1^2 and

$$\hat{s}_2^2 = \frac{\sum_{i=1}^{n_1} (X_{i2} - \bar{x}_2)^2}{(n_2 - 1)}$$

is used to estimate σ_2^2, and the estimates of the standard error of the means become

$$s_{\bar{x}_1} = \hat{s}_1/\sqrt{n_1} \text{ and } s_{\bar{x}_2} = \hat{s}_2/\sqrt{n_2}$$

The general estimate of the standard error of the difference in two means, $\sigma_{\bar{x}_1 - \bar{x}_2}$, is then

$$s_{\bar{x}_1 - \bar{x}_2} = \sqrt{s_{\bar{x}_1}{}^2 + s_{\bar{x}_2}{}^2} = \sqrt{\frac{\hat{s}_1^2}{n_1} + \frac{\hat{s}_2^2}{n_2}}$$

Although unknown, if the two parent-population variances *can be assumed equal,* a better estimate of the common population variance can be generated by pooling the samples to calculate

$$\hat{s}^2 = \frac{\sum_{i=1}^{n_1}(X_{i1} - \bar{x}_1)^2 + \sum_{i=1}^{n_2}(X_{i2} - \bar{x}_2)^2}{(n_1 + n_2 - 2)}$$

where $\hat{s}^2$ is the pooled sample variance used to estimate the common population variance. Note that the calculation of the pooled sample variance involves summing the squares of the deviations of the first sample around their mean and adding that total to the sum of the squares of the deviations of the second sample around their mean. In this case the estimated error of the test statistic $s_{\bar{x}_1 - \bar{x}_2}$ reduces to

$$s_{\bar{x}_1 - \bar{x}_2} = \sqrt{\frac{\hat{s}_1^2}{n_1} + \frac{\hat{s}_2^2}{n_2}} = \sqrt{\frac{\hat{s}^2}{n_1} + \frac{\hat{s}^2}{n_2}} = \sqrt{\hat{s}^2 \left(\frac{1}{n_1} + \frac{1}{n_2} \right)}$$

If the distribution of the variable in each population can further be assumed to be normal, the appropriate test statistic is

$$t = \frac{(\bar{x}_1 - \bar{x}_2) - (\mu_1 - \mu_2)}{s_{\bar{x}_1 - \bar{x}_2}}$$

which is t distributed with $\nu = n_1 + n_2 - 2$ degrees of freedom.

Suppose, for example, that a manufacturer of floor waxes has recently developed a new wax. The company is considering two different containers for the wax, one plastic and one metal. The company decides to make the final determination on the basis of a limited sales test in which the plastic containers are introduced in a random sample of ten stores and the metal containers are introduced in an *independent* random sample of ten stores. The test results are contained in Exhibit 20.3.

$$\text{Calculated } t = \frac{(\bar{x}_1 - \bar{x}_2) - (\mu_1 - \mu_2)}{s_{\bar{x}_1 - \bar{x}_2}} = \frac{(403.0 - 390.3) - (0)}{8.15} = 1.56$$

This value is referred to a t table for $\nu = n_1 + n_2 - 2 = 18$ degrees of freedom. The test is two-tailed because the null hypothesis is that the preferences for the containers are equal; there was no a priori expectation in the alternate hypothesis that one was expected to sell better than the other. For $\alpha = 0.05$, say, and 18 degrees of freedom, critical $t = 2.101$. (One

	EXHIBIT 20.3	**Store Sales of Floor Wax in Units**			
Store	**Plastic Container**	**Metal Container**	**Store**	**Plastic Container**	**Metal Container**
1	432	365	6	380	372
2	360	405	7	422	378
3	397	396	8	406	410
4	408	390	9	400	383
5	417	404	10	408	400

needs to look in the column headed $1 - \alpha = .975$ rather than at .95 in Exhibit 3 in the appendix, since this is a two-tailed test.) Since calculated t is less than critical t, the null hypothesis of no difference would not be rejected. The sample data do not indicate that the plastic container could be expected to outsell the metal container in the total population, even though it did so in this limited experiment.

The example again demonstrates the importance of explicitly determining the statistical significance level by appropriately balancing Type I and Type II errors. Here α error was set arbitrarily equal to 0.05. This led to nonrejection of the null hypothesis and the conclusion that the plastic container would not be expected to outsell the metal container in the total population. Yet if the decision maker had been able to tolerate an α error of 0.20, say, just the opposite conclusion would have been warranted, since interpolating in Exhibit 3 in the appendix for 18 degrees of freedom indicates that the probability of getting calculated $t = 1.56$ under an assumption of no difference in the population means is approximately 15 percent. Assuming the production and other costs were the same, it would clearly seem that the final packaging decision should favor the plastic container. If the production and other costs were not the same, then these costs should be reflected in the statistical decision rule.[6]

The preceding discussion assumes that the samples are independent and that the variable of interest is normally distributed in each of the parent populations. The normality assumption was again necessary to justify the use of the t distribution. What happens, though, if the variable is not normally distributed or the samples are not independent? The lower half of Research Window 20.2 summarizes the approach for non-normal parent distributions for known and unknown σ, while the next section treats the case of **related samples.**

Related samples
Samples that are not drawn independently so that the observations are related in some way.

Samples Are Related

A manufacturer of camping equipment wished to study consumer color preferences for a sleeping bag it had recently developed. The bag was of medium quality and price. Traditionally, the high-quality, high-priced sleeping bags used by serious campers and backpackers came in the earth colors, such as green and brown. Previous research indicated that the low-quality, low-priced sleeping bags were frequently purchased for children, to be used at slumber parties. Vivid colors were preferred by this market segment, with bright reds and oranges leading the way. Production capacity restrictions would not allow the company to produce the new sleeping bag in both types of colors. To make the comparison, it selected a random sample of five stores into which it introduced bags of both types. The sales per store are indicated in Exhibit 20.4. Do the data present sufficient evidence to indicate a difference in the average sales for the different colors of bags?

An analysis of the data indicates a difference in the two means $(\bar{x}_1 - \bar{x}_1) = (50.2 - 45.2) = 5.0$. This is a rather small difference, considering the variability in sales that exists across the five stores. Further, application of the procedures of the preceding section suggests that the difference is not statistically significant. The pooled estimate of the common variance is

EXHIBIT 20.4 **Pre-Store Sales of Sleeping Bags**

Store	Bright Colors	Earth Colors
1	64	56
2	72	66
3	43	39
4	22	20
5	50	45

Testing Hypothesis about the Differences in Two Means

	σ Known	**σ Unknown**
Distribution of variables in parent populations is normal or symmetrical.	Small n: Use $$z = \frac{(\bar{x}_1 - \bar{x}_2) - (\mu_1 - \mu_2)}{\sigma_{\bar{x}_1 - \bar{x}_2}}$$ where $\sigma_{\bar{x}_1 - \bar{x}_2} = \sqrt{\dfrac{\sigma_1^2}{n_2} + \dfrac{\sigma_2^2}{n_2}}$ Large n: Use: $$z = \frac{(\bar{x}_1 - \bar{x}_2) - (\mu_1 - \mu_2)}{\sigma_{\bar{x}_1 - \bar{x}_2}}$$	Small n: Can you assume $\sigma_1 = \sigma_2$? 1. Yes: Use pooled variance t test where $$t = \frac{(\bar{x}_1 - \bar{x}_2) - (\mu_1 - \mu_2)}{s_{\bar{x}_1 - \bar{x}_2}}$$ and $s_{\bar{x}_1 - \bar{x}_2} =$ $$\sqrt{\frac{\sum\limits_{i=1}^{n_1}(X_{i1} - \bar{x}_1)^2 + \sum\limits_{i=1}^{n_2}(X_{i2} - \bar{x}_2)^2}{n_1 + n_2 - 2}\left(\frac{1}{n_1} + \frac{1}{n_2}\right)}$$ with $(n_1 + n_2 - 2)$ degrees of freedom. 2. No: Approach is shrouded in controversy. Several approaches have been suggested. Large n: Use $$z = \frac{(\bar{x}_1 - \bar{x}_2) - (\mu_1 - \mu_2)}{s_{\bar{x}_1 - \bar{x}_2}}$$ and use pooled variance if variances can be assumed equal, and unpooled variance is equality assumption is not warranted.
Distribution of variables in parent populations is asymmetrical.	Small n: There is no theory to support the parametric test. Either one must transform the variates so that they are normally distributed and then use the z test, or one must use a distribution-free statistical test. Large n: If the individual samples are large enough so that the central-limit theorem is operative for them separately, it will also apply to their sum or difference. Use $$z = \frac{(\bar{x}_1 - \bar{x}_2) - (\mu_1 - \mu_2)}{\sigma_{\bar{x}_1 - \bar{x}_2}}$$	Small n: There is no theory to support the parametric test. Either one must transform the variates so that they are normally distributed and then use the t test, or one must use a distribution-free statistical test. Large n: One must assume that n_1 and n_2 are large enough so that the central-limit theorem applies to the individual sample means. Then it can also be assumed to apply to their sum or difference. Use $$z = \frac{(\bar{x}_1 - \bar{x}_2) - (\mu_1 - \mu_2)}{s_{\bar{x}_1 - \bar{x}_2}}$$ employing a pooled variance if the unknown parent-population variances can be assumed equal, and use an unpooled variance if the equality assumption is not warranted.

$$\hat{s}^2 = \frac{\sum\limits_{i=1}^{n_1}(X_{i1} - \bar{x}_1)^2 + \sum\limits_{i=1}^{n_2}(X_{i2} - \bar{x}_2)^2}{(n_1 + n_2 - 2)} = \frac{1512.8 + 1222.8}{8} = 341.95$$

and

$$s_{\bar{x}_1 - \bar{x}_2} = \sqrt{\hat{s}^2\left(\frac{1}{n_1} + \frac{1}{n_2}\right)} = \sqrt{341.95\left(\frac{1}{5} + \frac{1}{5}\right)} = 11.70$$

Calculated t is thus

$$t = \frac{(\bar{x}_1 - \bar{x}_2)(\mu_1 - \mu_2)}{s_{\bar{x}_1 - \bar{x}_2}} = \frac{(50.2 - 45.2) - 0}{11.70} = 0.427$$

which is less than the critical value $t = 2.306$ found in the table for $\alpha = 0.05$ and $\nu = n_1 + n_2 - 2 = 8$ degrees of freedom. The null hypothesis of there being no difference in sales of the two types of colors cannot be rejected on the basis of the sample data.

But wait a minute! A closer look at the data indicates a marked inconsistency with this conclusion. The bright-colored sleeping bags outsold the earth-colored ones in each store, and indeed an analysis of the per-store differences (the procedure is detailed further on) indicates that there is a statistically significant difference in the sales of the two bags. The reason for the seeming difference in conclusions—the difference is not significant versus it is significant—arises because the t test for the difference in two means is *not appropriate* for the problem. The difference-in-means test assumes that the samples are independent. These samples are not. Sales of bright-colored and earth-colored bags are definitely related, since they are both found in the same stores. Note how this example differs from the floor wax example, in which the metal containers were placed in one sample of stores and the plastic containers were located in an independent sample of stores. We need a procedure that takes into account the fact that the observations are related.

The appropriate procedure is the t test for related samples. The procedure is as follows. Define a new variable d_i, where d_i is the difference between sales of the bright-colored bags and the earth-colored bags for the ith store. Thus

$$d_1 = 64 - 56 = 8$$

$$d_2 = 72 - 66 = 6$$

$$d_3 = 43 - 39 = 4$$

$$d_4 = 22 - 20 = 2$$

$$d_5 = 50 - 45 = 5$$

Now calculate the mean difference by averaging the individual store-to-store differences

$$\bar{d} = \frac{\sum\limits_{i=1}^{n} d_i}{n} = \frac{8 + 6 + 4 + 2 + 5}{5} = 5.0$$

and the standard deviation of the difference by determining the sum of the deviations around the mean squared, specifically

$$s_d = \sqrt{\frac{\sum\limits_{i=1}^{n}(d_i - \bar{d})^2}{n - 1}} = \sqrt{\frac{20}{4}} = 2.24$$

The test statistic is the sample mean difference minus the hypothesized population mean difference, divided by the standard deviation of the difference, divided by the square root of the sample size, or symbolically,

$$t = \frac{\bar{d} - D}{s_d/\sqrt{n}}$$

where D is the difference that is expected under the null hypothesis. Since there is no a priori reason why one color would be expected to sell better than the other, the appropriate null hypothesis is that there is no difference, while the alternate hypothesis is that there is; thus,

$$H_0: D = 0$$
$$H_a: D \neq 0$$

Calculated t is therefore

$$t = \frac{5.0 - 0}{2.24/\sqrt{5}} = 5.0$$

This value is referred to a t table for ν = (number of differences minus 1) degrees of freedom; in this case, there are five paired differences, and thus $\nu = 4$. Critical t for $\nu = 4$ and $\alpha = 0.05$ is 2.776, and thus the hypothesis of no difference is rejected. The sample evidence indicates that the bright-colored sleeping bags are likely to outsell the earth-colored ones.

An estimate of how greatly the sales per store of the bright-colored sleeping bags would exceed those of the earth-colored bags can be calculated from the confidence interval formula, sample mean difference $\pm$ t(standard error of the mean difference), or

$$\bar{d} \pm t(s_d/\sqrt{n})$$

The 95 percent confidence interval is

$$5.0 \pm (2.776)(2.24/\sqrt{5}) = 5.0 \pm 2.8$$

suggesting that sales of the bright-colored bags would be in the range of 2.2 to 7.8 bags greater per store on average.

Hypotheses about Two Proportions

The appendix to Chapter 19 reviewed the essential nature of hypothesis testing, employing as an example the testing of a hypothesis about a single population proportion. In this section, we want to illustrate the procedure for testing for the difference between two population proportions.[7] A situation where this would arise is the Mail Monitor survey, which tracks consumer responses to direct-mail offers of credit cards. Each quarter, Mail Monitor determines what percentage of consumers in the sample responded to such a mailing, and it compares those percentages from quarter to quarter. For example, in a recent report, Mail Monitor announced that the credit card response rate had fallen to 0.6 percent, a record low in 10 years of the study.[8] Was this rate truly the lowest level of consumer response in a decade, or was the result due to sampling and not statistically significant?

The test for the difference between two population proportions is basically a large sample problem. The samples from each population must be large enough so that the normal approximation to the exact binomial distribution of sample proportions can be used. As a practical matter, this means that np and nq should be greater than 10 for each sample, where p is the proportion of "successes" and q is the proportion of "failures" in the sample and n is the sample size.

To illustrate, suppose a cosmetics manufacturer is interested in comparing male college students and male nonstudents in terms of their use of hair spray. Suppose random samples of 100 male students and 100 male nonstudents in Austin, Texas, are selected and their use of hair spray in the last three months is determined. Suppose further that 30 of these students and 20 of these nonstudents have used hair spray within this period. Does this evidence indicate that a significantly higher percentage of male college students than male nonstudents use hair spray?

Since we are interested in determining whether the two parent-population proportions are different, the null hypothesis is that they are the same, that is,

$$H_0: \pi_1 = \pi_2$$
$$H_a: \pi_1 \neq \pi_2$$

where Population 1 is the population of male college students and Population 2 is the population of male nonstudents. The sample proportions are $p_1 = 0.30$ and $p_2 = 0.20$ and therefore $n_1 p_1 = 30$, $n_1 q_1 = 70$, $n_2 p_2 = 20$, $n_2 q_2 = 80$, and the normal approximation to the binomial distribution can be used. The test statistic is $z =$ first sample proportion minus second sample proportion minus the quantity, hypothesized proportion for the first population minus hypothesized proportion for the second population, divided by the standard error of the difference in the two sample proportions, or

$$z = \frac{(p_1 - p_2) - (\pi_1 - \pi_2)}{\sigma_{p_1 - p_2}}$$

where $\sigma_{p_1 - p_2}$ is the standard error of the difference in the two sample proportions. The one question that still remains in the calculation of z is, what does $\sigma_{p_1 - p_2}$ equal?

A general statistical result that is useful for understanding the calculation of $\sigma_{p_1 - p_2}$ is that *the variance of the sum or difference of two independent random variables is equal to the sum of the individual variances.* For a single proportion, the variance is $\pi(1 - \pi)/n$, and thus the variance of the difference is

$$\sigma^2_{p_1 - p_2} = \sigma^2_{p_1} + \sigma^2_{p_2} = \frac{\pi_1(1 - \pi_1)}{n_1} + \frac{\pi_2(1 - \pi_2)}{n_2}$$

Note that the variance of the difference is given in terms of the two unknown population proportions, π_1 and π_2. Although unknown, the two population proportions have been assumed equal, and thus we have a "natural" case of a *pooled variance* estimate; $s^2_{p_1 - p_2}$ is logically used to estimate $\sigma^2_{p_1 - p_2}$, where

$$s^2_{p_1 - p_2} = pq\left(\frac{1}{n_1} + \frac{1}{n_2}\right)$$

and

$$p = \frac{\text{total number of successes in the two samples}}{\text{total number of observations in the two samples}}$$

$$q = 1 - p$$

For the example,

$$p = \frac{30 + 20}{100 + 100} = \frac{50}{200} = 0.25,$$

$$s^2_{p_1 - p_2} = (0.25)(0.75)\left(\frac{1}{100} + \frac{1}{100}\right) = 0.00375,$$

and

$$s_{p_1 - p_2} = 0.061$$

Calculated z is found as follows:

$$z = \frac{(0.30 - 0.20) - (0)}{0.061} = \frac{0.10}{0.061} = 1.64$$

while critical $z = 1.96$ for $\alpha = 0.05$. The sample evidence does not indicate that there is a difference in the proportion of male college students and male nonstudents using hair spray.

The 95 percent confidence interval is calculated by the formula (first sample proportion − second sample proportion) $\pm z$(estimated standard error of the difference in the two proportions), or $(p_1 - p_2) \pm zs_{p_1 - p_2}$, which is $(.30 - .20) \pm 1.96(0.061) = .10 \pm .12$, and which yields a similar conclusion. The interval includes zero, suggesting that there is no difference in the proportions using hair spray in the two groups.

Back to the Case

"I know you didn't want to wait for a written report," said Angie Karlin, making herself comfortable in Chuck Zellmer's office, "so even though I've just finished analyzing the data, I'd be glad to fill you in on our findings so far."

"Wonderful," replied Zellmer. "What did you find?"

"Well, as you know, we mailed our questionnaire to 225 randomly chosen individuals from the mailing list Sid Green gave us. To encourage response, we offered these people a five-dollar coupon toward their next catalog purchase. We received 124 usable surveys, for a 55 percent response

rate. To conduct the analysis, we used a program called SPSS, which is short for —"

"Statistical Package for the Social Sciences. Sure, I know the package," said Zellmer.

"Take a look at this," said Karlin, handing Zellmer a data sheet. "This is a table of two variables: the willingness of individuals on the Omni mailing list to purchase from the catalog, and whether or nor those same individuals ever purchased from the catalog in the past. Willingness to buy

continued

| EXHIBIT 1 | Cross Tabulation of Willingness to Purchase from Omni's Catalog (V3) with Whether Respondent Has Purchased from It Before (V4) |

		V4			
Count **Row Percent** **Column Percent** **Total Percent**		**Never Ordered** **1**	**Ordered Before but Not within Past Year** **2**	**Ordered within Past Year** **3**	**Row Total**
V3 Unwilling	1	20 40.0 46.5 16.1	20 40.0 51.3 16.1	10 20.0 23.8 8.1	50 40.3
Somewhat Willing	2	7 20.0 16.3 5.6	11 31.4 28.2 8.9	17 48.6 40.5 13.7	35 28.2
Very Willing	3	16 41.0 37.2 12.9	8 20.5 20.5 6.5	15 38.5 35.7 12.1	39 31.5
Column Total		43 34.7	39 31.5	42 33.9	124 100.0

Raw chi-square = 10.997 with 4 degrees of freedom; significance = 0.027

through the Omni catalog is the dependent variable we are interested in explaining." (See Exhibit 1.)

"Look at the column percentages," Karlin instructed. "They suggest that the 'most willing' group of purchasers among the catalog recipients are those who ordered from Omni within the last year. Over 75 percent of these people (40.5 plus 35.7 percent) are somewhat willing to order from Omni again. At the same time, almost 25 percent of those who bought within the last year are not willing to place another order.

"Now, take a look at the figure given where it says 'raw chi-square.' Basically, that figure measures whether the results of our analysis are statistically significant or just a matter of chance. In this case, the value is such that we can say with some certainty that the two variables we measured are indeed related. That is, a customer's willingness to purchase through the Omni catalog appears to be influenced by whether or not he or she has purchased from it before."

"That may be true," replied Zellmer, "but telling me that people who bought once from the Omni catalog are somewhat willing to do it again doesn't give me a tremendous amount of insight into how to revitalize my flat catalog sales."

"Wait, there's more," explained Karlin. "There's a lot of valuable information hidden in these questionnaires. For example, take a look at Question 11. We asked people how confident they felt purchasing various types of software by mail. Now the beauty of this is that we generated an index called CATCON—short for 'catalog confidence'—which is designed to measure the amount of confidence people have when purchasing products from a catalog. The CATCON index in this case is what you would get if you added up the scores assigned to the response categories regarding how confident subjects were in buying each type of software by mail. The scores by question ranged from 1 (not at all confident) to 5 (very confident). Look at this table," Karlin said, handing Zellmer a small chart. (See Exhibit 2.)

continued

EXHIBIT 2 **Difference in Means for CATCON Index between Males and Females**

Variable/ Group	Number of Cases	Mean	Standard Deviation	Standard Error	POOLED VARIANCE ESTIMATE			SEPARATE VARIANCE ESTIMATE		
					t Value	Degrees of Freedom	Two-Tail Probability	t Value	Degrees of Freedom	Two-Tail Probability
CATCON 1. Males	65	21.462	2.001	.248	33.87	121	.000	33.87	119.42	.000
2. Females	58	9.224	2.000	.263						

"I assume you're going to tell me what this all means," Zellmer replied good-naturedly.

"Well, the really interesting thing we found is that the score differs based on the customer's sex. The table shows that the mean score for men is higher than it is for women. Since our sample was fairly small, you may well ask whether that difference is statistically significant," Karlin said.

"Sure," answered Zellmer. "The question was right on the tip of my tongue."

"It is significant," replied Karlin. "Look at the value of t."

The CATCON index is an example of a hypothesis about two means, since its goal was to assess whether there was a difference in the degree of confidence between males and females when buying software from catalogs. A two-tailed test was used, since the alternate hypothesis was that they were unequal but there was no belief beforehand that one sex would be more confident than the other. In this case, the null hypothesis is rejected, since there indeed is a statistically significant difference between men's and women's confidence when buying computer software through catalogs.

Summary

Learning Objective 1

Explain the basic use of a chi-square goodness-of-fit test.

The chi-square goodness-of-fit test is appropriate when a nominally scaled variable falls naturally into two or more categories and the analyst wishes to determine whether the observed number of cases in each cell corresponds to the expected number.

Learning Objective 2

Discuss the similarities and differences between the chi-square goodness-of-fit test and the Kolmogorov-Smirnov test.

The Kolmogorov-Smirnov test is similar to the chi-square goodness-of-fit test in that it uses a comparison between observed and expected frequencies to determine whether observed results are in accord with a stated null hypothesis. But the Kolmogorov-Smirnov test takes advantage of the ordinal nature of the data.

Learning Objective 3

Specify which test is appropriate if one is testing a hypothesis about a single mean, given that the variance is known. Which is appropriate if the variance is unknown?

In testing a hypothesis about a single mean, the z test is appropriate if the variance is known, while the t test applies if the variance is unknown.

Learning Objective 4

Identify the tests that are appropriate if the analysis involves two means from independent samples.

In an analysis that involves two means from independent samples, the z test is used if the variances are known. If the variances are unknown but assumed equal, a t test using a pooled sample variance applies.

Learning Objective 5

Specify the appropriate test if the analysis involves the difference between two parent-population proportions.

The test of the equality of proportions from two independent samples involves a "natural" pooling of the sample variances. The z test applies.

R e v i e w   Q u e s t i o n s

1. What is the basic use of a chi-square goodness-of-fit test? How is the value of the test statistic calculated? How are the expected frequencies determined?

2. If the data are ordinal and the analyst wishes to determine whether the observed frequencies correspond to some expected pattern, what statistical test is appropriate? What is the basic procedure to follow in implementing this test?

3. What is the appropriate test statistic for making inferences about a population mean when the population variance is known? When the population variance is unknown? Suppose that the population variance is unknown, but the sample is large. What is the appropriate procedure then?

4. Suppose you are testing for the statistical significance of the observed difference between the sample means from two independent samples. What is the appropriate procedure when the two parent-population variances are
   (a) known
   (b) unknown but can be assumed to be equal
   (c) unknown and cannot be assumed to be equal
   What conditions must occur in each case regarding the distribution of the variable?

5. Would your response to Question 4 change if the samples were related? Explain.

6. How do you test whether two parent-population proportions differ?

D i s c u s s i o n   Q u e s t i o n s ,   P r o b l e m s ,   a n d   P r o j e c t s

1. A large publishing house recently conducted a survey to assess the reading habits of senior citizens. The company published four magazines specifically tailored to suit the needs of senior citizens. Management hypothesized that there were no differences in the preferences for the magazines. A sample of 1,600 senior citizens interviewed in the city of Albuquerque, New Mexico, indicated the following preferences for the four magazines:

Publication	Frequency of Preference
1. *Golden Years*	350
2. *Maturation*	500
3. *High Serenity*	450
4. *Time of Living*	300
Total	1,600

Management needs your expertise to determine whether there are differences in senior citizens' preferences for the magazines.
(a) State the null and alternate hypotheses.
(b) How many degrees of freedom are there?
(c) What is the chi-square critical table value at the 5 percent significance level?
(d) What is the calculated χ^2 value? Show all your calculations.
(e) Should the null hypothesis be rejected? Explain.

2. Silken-Shine Company is a medium-sized manufacturer of shampoo. During the past years the company has increased the number of product variations of Silken-Shine shampoo from three to five to increase its market share. Management conducted a survey to compare sales of Silken-Shine shampoo with sales of Rapunzel and So-Soft, its two major competitors. A sample of 1,800 housewives indicated the following frequencies with respect to most recent shampoo purchased:

Shampoo	Number Buying
1. Silken-Shine	425
2. Rapunzel	1,175
3. So-Soft	200
Total	1,800

Experience had indicated that three times as many households preferred Rapunzel to Silken-Shine and that, in turn, twice as many households preferred Silken-Shine to So-Soft. Management wants to determine if the historic tendency still holds, given that Silken-Shine Company has increased the range of shampoos available.
(a) State the null and alternate hypotheses.
(b) How many degrees of freedom are there?
(c) What is the chi-square critical table value at the 5 percent significance level?
(d) What is the calculated χ^2 value? Show all your calculations.
(e) Should the null hypothesis be rejected? Explain.

3. A manufacturer of music cassettes wants to test four different cassettes varying in tape length: 30 minutes, 60 minutes, 90 minutes, and 120 minutes. The company has hired you to determine whether customers show any distinct preference toward either extreme. If there is a preference toward any extreme, the company will manufacture only cassettes of the preferred length; otherwise, the company is planning to market cassettes of all four lengths. A sample of 1,000 customers indicated the following preferences:

Tape Length	Frequency of Preference
30 minutes	150
60 minutes	250
90 minutes	425
120 minutes	175
Total	1,000

(a) State the null and alternate hypotheses.
(b) Compute the Kolmogorov-Smirnov D by completing the following table:

Tape Length	Observed Number	Observed Proportion	Observed Cumulative Proportion	Theoretical Proportion	Theoretical Cumulative Proportion
30 minutes					
60 minutes					
90 minutes					
120 minutes					

(c) Compute the critical value of D at $\alpha = 0.05$. Show your calculations.
(d) Would you reject the null hypothesis? Explain.
(e) What are the implications for management?
(f) Explain why the Kolmogorov-Smirnov test would be used in this situation.

4. Liberty Foods markets vegetables in six different sized cans: A, B, C, D, E, and F. Through the years the company has observed that sales of all its vegetables in the six can sizes are in the proportion $6:4:2:1.5:1.5:1$, respectively. In other words, for every 1 case of size F that is sold, 6 cases of size A, 4 of size B, 2 of size C, 1.5 of size D, and 1.5 of size E are also sold.

The marketing manager would like the sales data for a new canned vegetable—pureed carrots—compared with the pattern for the rest of Liberty's product line to see if there is any difference. Based on a representative sample of 600 cases of pureed carrots, he observes that 30 percent were Size A, 20 percent B, 10 percent C, 10 percent D, 15 percent E, and 15 percent F.

(a) The marketing manager has asked you to determine whether the pureed carrots' sales pattern is similar to the pattern for other vegetables by using the chi-square goodness-of-fit test. Show all your calculations clearly.
(b) You are now asked to determine the above with the use of the Kolmogorov-Smirnov test. Show all your calculations clearly.
(c) What can you conclude from the use of the two test statistics? Are your results from the two tests conflicting or similar?
(d) Which test statistic would you prefer? Why?

5. A medium-sized manufacturer of paper products was planning to introduce a new line of tissues, hand towels, and toilet paper. However, management had stipulated that the new products should be introduced only if average monthly purchases per household would be $2.50 or more. The product was market tested, and the diaries of the 100 panel households living in the test market area were checked. They indicated that average monthly purchases were $3.10 per household with a standard deviation of $0.50. Management is wondering what decision it should make and has asked for your recommendation.

(a) State the null and alternate hypotheses.
(b) Is the sample size considered large or small?
(c) Which test should be used? Why?
(d) At the 5 percent level of significance, would you reject the null hypothesis? Support your answer with the necessary calculations.

6. The president of a chain of department stores had promised the managers of the various stores a bonus of 8 percent if the average monthly sales per store increased $300,000 or more. A random sample of 12 stores yielded the following sales increases:

Store	Sales	Store	Sales
1	$320,000	7	$380,000
2	$230,000	8	$280,000
3	$400,000	9	$420,000
4	$450,000	10	$360,000
5	$280,000	11	$440,000
6	$320,000	12	$320,000

The president is wondering whether this random sample of stores indicates that the population of stores has reached the goal. (Assume the distribution of the variable in the parent population is normal.)
(a) State the null and alternate hypotheses.
(b) Is the sample size considered small or large?
(c) Which test should be used? Why?
(d) Would you reject the null hypothesis at the 5 percent level of significance? Support your conclusion with the necessary calculations.

7. Joy Forever is the owner of two jewelry stores located in Corpus Christi and San Antonio. Last year the San Antonio store spent a considerable amount on in-store displays as compared with the Corpus Christi store. Forever wants to determine if the in-store displays resulted in increased sales. The average sales for a sample of 100 days for the San Antonio and Corpus Christi stores were $21.8 million and $15.3 million. (Past experience has shown that $\sigma_{SA} = 8$ and $\sigma_{CC} = 9$ where σ_{SA} is the standard deviation in sales for the San Antonio store and σ_{CC} is the standard deviation for the Corpus Christi store.)
(a) State the null and alternate hypotheses.
(b) What test would you use? Why?
(c) What is the calculated value of the test statistic? Show your calculations.
(d) What is the critical tabled value at the 5 percent significance level?
(e) Would you reject the null hypothesis? Explain.
(f) What can Forever conclude?

8. Come-and-Go Company, a large travel agency located in Portland, Oregon, wants to study consumer preferences for its packaged tours to the East. For the past five years Come-and-Go has offered two similarly priced packaged tours to the East that differ only in the places included in the tour. A random sample of five months' purchases from the past five years has been selected. The numbers of consumers that purchased the tours during these five months are listed below:

Month	Packaged Tour I	Packaged Tour II
1	90	100
2	70	60
3	120	80
4	110	90
5	60	80

The management of Come-and-Go needs your assistance to determine whether there is a difference in preference for the two tours.
(a) State the null and alternate hypotheses.
(b) What test would you use? Why?
(c) What is the calculated value of the test statistic? Show your calculations.
(d) What is the critical tabled value at the 5 percent significance level?
(e) Would you reject the null hypothesis? Explain.
(f) What can the management of Come-and-Go Company conclude about preferences for the two tours?

9. Wet Noodle, a manufacturer of fresh refrigerated pasta products, is not happy with sales of its products. Management suspects that sales might improve if the product were displayed in a freestanding refrigerated case next to the dry pasta, rather than in the dairy case as it is now. To test this assumption, the marketing research department has arranged for six stores that currently carry Wet Noodle to allow placement of the freestanding case in addition to the regular display. Packages have been specially bar-coded so sales generated from each display can be tracked. After a three-week trail period, the following sales figures are assembled:

Store	New Display	Old Display
1	230	195
2	187	185
3	250	220
4	157	130
5	99	80
6	295	245

(a) What is the appropriate test to determine if the two displays differ in effectiveness?

(b) State the null and alternate hypotheses.

(c) What is the value of the test statistic?

(d) If $\alpha = 0.05$, what is your conclusion?

10. The manager of the Budget Department Store recently increased the store's use of in-store promotions in an attempt to increase the proportion of entering customers who made a purchase. The effort was prompted by a study made a year ago that showed 65 percent of a sample of 1,000 parties entering the store made no purchase. A recent sample of 900 parties contained 635 who made no purchases. Management is wondering whether there has been a change in the proportion of entering parties who make a purchase.

(a) State the null and alternate hypotheses.

(b) What is the calculated value? Show your calculations clearly.

(c) Based on your results, would you reject the null hypothesis? Explain.

11. The creative shop at Impact Advertising developed two different approaches, labeled A and B, for a new direct mail solicitation for a major client. In order to test the effectiveness of the different solicitations, the research department was directed to conduct a test mailing. Two independent random samples of size $n = 2,000$ were selected, and after a one-month waiting period, the number of orders received from each sample was tabulated. Approach A resulted in 257 orders, and Approach B generated 230 orders.

(a) What is the appropriate test to determine if Approach A and Approach B differ in effectiveness?

(b) State the null and alternate hypotheses.

(c) What is the value of the test statistic?

(d) If $\alpha = 0.05$, what is your conclusion?

Refer to the NFO Research, Inc., coffee study described on pages 621–624 in Chapter 19 for the next two problems.

12. Compare the overall ratings (from question 2) of Folgers and Yuban. Is there a difference in the ratings for the two brands of coffee ($\alpha = 0.05$)? If so, which brand is rated more highly?

13. Compute a "taste" index score on the following features of Question 6 for Maxwell House Regular: rich taste, always fresh, full-bodied taste, smooth taste, not bitter, has no aftertaste. Is there a difference in this overall score for individuals who add nothing to their coffee versus those who do add something ($\alpha = 0.05$)?

Endnotes

1. Michael J. Rabuck, "Persuasive Advertising Drives Toothbrush Sales," *Quirk's Marketing Research Review* (July 1999), pp. 80, 82–86.

2. The correct distribution to test the hypothesis is the hypergeometric. The hypergeometric distribution, however, is unwieldy for anything but very small samples. The chi-square distribution approximates the hypergeometric for large sample sizes. For a discussion of this point as well as the other condi-

tions surrounding a goodness-of-fit test, see Leonard A. Marascuilo and Maryellen McSweeney, *Non-parametric and Distribution Free Methods for the Social Sciences* (Belmont, Calif.: Brooks/Cole, 1977), pp. 243–248. See also Wayne W. Daniel, *Applied Nonparametric Statistics*, 2d ed. (Boston: PWS-Kent Publishing, 1990); Jean D. Gibbons, *Nonparametric Statistics: An Introduction* (Thousand Oaks, Calif.: Sage Publications, Inc., 1992).

3. W. G. Cochran, "The χ^2 Test of Goodness of Fit," *Annuals of Mathematical Statistics* 23 (1952), pp. 315–345.

4. See Marascuilo and McSweeney, *Nonparametric and Distribution Free Methods*, pp. 250–251. See also Jean Dickinson Gibbons and Subhabrata Chakraborti, *Nonparametric Statistical Inference*, 3rd ed. (New York: Marcel Dekker, Inc., 1992).

5. "Coffee-Bar Patrons Are a Richer Blend: Study," *Supermarket News* (October 26, 1998), p. 27.

6. The Bayesian posture would be to introduce the plastic container even with the obtained sample results if the opportunity costs associated with each alternative were the same. If they were not the same, then the Bayesian approach would incorporate these costs directly into the decision rule regarding which container should be produced.

7. The tests for population proportions are logically considered with nominal data because they apply in situations in which the variable being studied can be divided into those cases *possessing* the characteristic and those cases *lacking* it, and the emphasis is on the number or proportion of cases falling into each category. Marketing examples abound: "prefer A" versus "do not prefer A"; "buy" versus "do not buy"; "brand loyal" versus "not brand loyal"; "sales representatives meeting quota" versus "sales representatives not meeting quota." The test for the significance of the difference between two proportions is treated here because the hypothesis is examined using the z test, and the procedure relies on an "automatic pooled sample variance" estimate. It was thought that these notions would be better appreciated after the discussion of the test of means rather than before.

8. BAIGlobal, "Credit Card Response Rate at Record Low for 1999's Second Quarter," press release by BAIGlobal (September 1999, downloaded from the company's Web site, www.baiglobal.com, October 7, 1999). (Mail Monitor is a service provided by BAIGlobal.)

Suggested Additional Readings

Most of the statistical tests discussed in this chapter can be found in any introductory statistics text, and readers are encouraged to refer to the text they used in their introductory statistics course for more details on any of the methods that are discussed.

ANALYSIS OF VARIANCE

In Chapter 20 we used the example of packaging floor wax in plastic and metal containers to examine the statistical test of the difference in two population means. Let us now reconsider the data of Exhibit 20.3 to demonstrate an alternate approach to the problem. Known as the **analysis of variance (ANOVA),** it has the distinct advantage of being applicable when there are more than two means being compared. The basic idea underlying the analysis of variance is that the parent-population variance can be estimated from the sample in several ways, and comparisons among these estimates tell us a great deal about the population. Recall that the null hypothesis involving the two types of containers was that the two parent-population means were equal; that is, $\mu_1 = \mu_2$. If the null hypothesis is true, then, except for sampling error, the following three estimates of the population variance should be equal:

Analysis of variance (ANOVA)
A statistical test employed with interval data to determine if k $(k \geq 2)$ samples come from populations with equal means.

1. The *total variation,* computed by comparing each of the 20 sales figures with the grand mean.

2. The *between-group variation,* computed by comparing each of the two treatment means with the grand mean.

3. The *within-group variation,* computed by comparing each of the individual sales figures with the mean of its own group.

If, however, the hypothesis is not true, and there is a difference in the means, then the between-group variation should produce a higher estimate than the within-group variation, which considers only the variation within groups and is independent of differences between groups.

These three separate estimates of the population variation are computed in the following way when there are k treatments or groups.

1. Total variation: sum of squares total SS_T, given by the sum of the squared deviations of each observation from the grand mean. Now the grand mean of all n observations turns out to be equal to

$$\frac{432 + \ldots + 408 + 365 + \ldots + 400}{20} = 396.7$$

and the sum of squares total equals

$$SS_T = (432 - 396.7)^2 + \ldots + (408 - 396.7)^2 \\ + (365 - 390.7)^2 + \ldots + (400 - 396.7)^2$$

The difference between *each observation* and the *grand mean* is determined; the differences are squared and then summed.

2. Between-group variation: sum of squares between groups SS_B. To calculate between-group variation, it is first necessary to calculate the means for each group. The mean sales of the plastic container turn out to be equal to 403.0, and those for the metal container turn out to be equal to 390.3. The sum of squares between groups is thus

$$SS_B = 10(403.0 - 396.7)^2 + 10(390.3 - 396.7)^2$$

The difference between each *group mean* and the *overall mean* is determined; the difference is squared; each squared difference is weighted by the number of observations making up the group, and the results are summed.

3. Within-group variation: sum of squares within groups SS_W. The calculation of the sum of squares within groups involves calculating the difference between each observation and the mean of the group to which it belongs, specifically,

$$SS_W = (432 - 403.0)^2 + \ldots + (408 - 403.0)^2$$
$$+ (365 - 390.3)^2 + \ldots + (400 - 390.3)^2$$

The difference between *each observation* and its *group mean* is determined; the differences are squared and then summed.

Let us take a closer look at the behavior of these three sources of variation. First, SS_T measures the overall variation of the n observations. The more variable the n observations, the larger SS_T becomes. Second SS_B reflects the total variability of the means. The more nearly alike the k means are, the smaller SS_B becomes. If they differ greatly, SS_B will be large. Third, SS_W measures the amount of variation within each column or treatment. If there is little variation among the observations making up a group, SS_W is small. When there is great variability, SS_W is large.

It can be shown that $SS_T = SS_B + SS_W$ and that each of these sums of squares, when divided by the *appropriate number of degrees of freedom,* generates a mean square that is essentially an unbiased estimate of the population variance.[1] Further, if the null hypothesis of no difference among population means is true, they are all estimates of the same variance and should not differ more than would be expected because of chance. If the variance between groups is significantly greater than the variance within groups, the hypothesis of equality of population means will be rejected.

In other words, we can view the variance within groups as a measure of the amount of variation in sales of containers that may be expected on the basis of chance. It is the *error variance* or *chance variance.* The between-group variance reflects error variance plus any group-to-group differences occasioned by differences in popularity of the two containers. Therefore, if it is found to be significantly larger than the within-group variance, this difference may be attributed to group-to-group variation, and the hypothesis of equality of means is discredited.

But what are these degrees of freedom? The total number of degrees of freedom is equal to $n - 1$, since there is only a single constraint, the grand mean, in the computation of SS_T. For within-group sum of squares, there are n observations and k constraints, one constraint for each treatment mean. Hence, the degrees of freedom for the within-group sum of squares equals $n - k$. There are k values, one corresponding to each treatment mean, in the calculation of SS_B, and there is one constraint imposed by the grand mean; hence, the degrees of freedom for the between-group sum of squares is $k - 1$.

The separate estimates of the population variance or the associated mean squares are

$$MS_T = \frac{SS_T}{df_T} = \frac{SS_T}{n-1}$$

$$MS_B = \frac{SS_B}{df_B} = \frac{SS_B}{k-1}$$

$$MS_W = \frac{SS_W}{df_W} = \frac{SS_W}{n-k}$$

The mean squares computed from the sample data are merely estimates of the true mean squares. The true mean squares are in turn given by the expected values of the corresponding sample mean squares. Given that the samples are independent, that the population variances are equal, and that the variable is normally distributed in the parent population, it can be shown that these expected values are

$$E(MS_W) = \sigma^2 = \text{error variance or chance variance}$$

EXHIBIT 20a.1   **Analysis of Variance of Sales of Plastic versus Metal Containers**

Source of Variation	Sum of Squares	Degrees of Freedom	Mean Square	F Ratio
Between group	806.5	1	806.5	2.43
Within group	5,978.1	18	332.1	
Total	6,784.6	19		

and

$$E(MS_B) = \sigma^2 + \text{treatment effect}$$

The ratio $E(MS)_B/E(MS_W)$ will equal 1 if there is no treatment effect. It will be greater than 1 if there is a difference in the sample means. Since the two expected values are not known, the sample mean squares are used instead to yield the ratio

$$\frac{MS_B}{MS_W} = F$$

which follows the F distribution. The F distribution depends on two degrees of freedom, one corresponding to the mean square in the numerator and one corresponding to the mean square in the denominator. Since MS_B and MS_W are only sample estimates of the true variances, one should not expect the ratio MS_B/MS_W to be exactly 1 when the treatment effect is zero, nor should one immediately conclude that there is a difference among the group means when the ratio is greater than 1. Rather, given a significance level and the respective degrees of freedom for the numerator and denominator, a critical value of F may be read from standard tables. The critical value indicates the magnitude of the ratio that can occur because of random sampling fluctuations, even when there is no difference in the group means, that is, $E(MS_B)/E(MS_W) = 1$. The entire analysis is conveniently handled in an analysis-of-variance table.

Exhibit 20a.1 is the analysis-of-variance table for the plastic and metal container sales data. The calculated F value is referred to an F table for 1 and 18 degrees of freedom (see Table 4 in the appendix at the back of this textbook). Using the same α as before, $\alpha = 0.05$, critical F is found to be 4.41, and again the sample evidence is not sufficient to reject the hypothesis of the equality of the two means. This should not be surprising since it can be shown[2] that when the comparison is between two means (the degrees of freedom in the numerator of the F ratio are then $v_1 = k - 1 = 1$), $F = t^2 = (1.56)^2 = 2.43$. Both tests are identical in this special case, and if one test does not indicate a significant difference between the two means, neither will the other.[3]

Randomized-Block Design

Randomized-block design
An experimental design in which (1) the test units are divided into blocks, or homogeneous groups, using some external criterion, and (2) the objects in each block are randomly assigned to treatment conditions. The randomized-block design is typically employed when there is one extraneous influence to be explicitly controlled.

Imagine what might have happened if, by chance, the stores selected to handle the plastic containers were all substantially larger than those handling the metal containers. Any difference in sales between the two groups could have been because the larger stores routinely have more traffic and hence greater sales.

If a closer analysis of the situation shows that such outside influences may distort the results of an experiment, a **randomized-block design** can be employed. This design involves the grouping of "similar" test units into blocks and the random assignment of treatments to test units in each block. Similarity is determined by matching the test units on the expected extraneous source of variation, for example, store size in the container example. The hope is that the units within each block will be more alike than will units selected completely at random. Since the difference between blocks can be taken into account in the variance analysis for the same number of observations, the error mean square should be smaller than it would be if a completely randomized design had been used. The test should therefore be more efficient.

Latin-Square Design

Latin-square design
An experimental design in which (1) the number of categories for each extraneous variable one wishes to control is equal to the number of treatments, and (2) each treatment is randomly assigned to categories according to a specific pattern. The Latin-square design is appropriate where there are two extraneous factors to be explicitly controlled.

The **Latin-square design** is appropriate when there are two extraneous factors that can cause serious distortion in the results. Suppose a company wanted to test the effectiveness of three different plans for frequency of sales calls by their sales representatives on potential customers. The plans varied with regard to how often the sales rep would be required to call on various sizes of accounts. The manufacturer wanted to know which of the three would produce the most sales.

In order to test the plan, the firm chose a sample of 30 salespeople from among its sales staff of 500. The company was concerned that differences in sales ability might affect the results of the test. Consequently, it decided to match the sales representatives in terms of their ability, employing their past sales as the matching criterion. The company thus formed ten blocks of three relatively equal sales representatives each. The call-frequency plans were then assigned randomly to each of the sales representatives within a block, resulting in a randomized-block design.

Now suppose further that the firm decided to conduct the investigation not only with sales reps of different ability but also among sales representatives having different sizes of territories. Suppose, in fact, that it divided the sales representatives into three classes on the basis of ability—outstanding, good, and average—and three classes on the basis of territory size—large, average, and small. Thus there would be nine different conditions with which to cope. One way of proceeding would be to use randomized blocks and test each of the three call plans under each of the nine conditions. This would require a sample of 27 sales representatives. An alternative approach would be to try each call plan only once with each size of territory and each level of ability. This would require a sample of only 9 test units or sales representatives. The primary gain in this case would be administrative control. In other cases, there may be cost advantages associated with the use of fewer test units. The interesting point is that if differences in territory size do indeed have an effect, the Latin-square design with 9 test units could be as efficient as the randomized-block design with many more test units.

The Latin-square design requires that the number of categories for each of the extraneous variables we wish to control be equal to the number of treatments. With three call plans to investigate, it was no accident that the sales representatives were divided into three ability levels and the territories into three size categories. The Latin-square design also requires that the treatments be randomly assigned to the resulting categories. This is typically accomplished by selecting one of the published squares at random and then randomizing the rows, columns, and treatments using this square.[4]

Factorial Designs

So far we have considered designs that involve only one experimental variable, although it may have had multiple levels, for example, three different call plans. It is often desirable to investigate the effects of two or more factors in the same experiment. For instance, it might be desirable to investigate the sales impact of the shape as well as the construction material of containers for floor wax. Suppose that in addition to packaging a new floor wax in metal or plastic containers, two shapes, A and B, were being considered for the containers. Package shape and package type would both be called *factors*. There would be two different levels of each factor, four different treatments in all since they can be used

Factorial design
An experimental design that is used when the effects of two or more variables are being simultaneously studied; each level of each factor is used with each level of each other factor.

in combination, and a factorial design would be used. A **factorial design** is one in which the effects of two or more independent variables are considered simultaneously.

There are three very good reasons why one might want to use a factorial design.[5] First, it allows the interaction of the factors to be studied. The plastic container might sell better in Shape A, while the metal container sells better in Shape B. This type of effect can be investigated only if the factors are considered simultaneously. Second, a factorial design allows a saving of time and effort since all the observations are employed to study the effects of each of the factors. Suppose separate experiments were conducted, one to study the effect of container type and another to study the effect of container shape. Then some of the observations would yield information about type and some about shape. By combining the two factors in one experiment, all the observations bear on both factors. "Hence one two-factor experiment is more economical than two one-factor experiments."[6] Third, the conclusions reached have broader application since each factor is studied with varying combinations of the other factors.[7] This result is much more useful than it would be if everything else had been held constant.

The factorial design may be used with any of the single-factor designs previously discussed—completely randomized, randomized-block, and Latin-square. The underlying model changes, as does the analysis of variance table, but the principle remains the same.

Endnotes

1. See Geoffrey Keppel, *Design and Analysis: A Researcher's Handbook,* 3rd ed. (Englewood Cliffs, N.J.: Prentice-Hall, 1991). See also Richard Harris, *An Analysis of Variance Primer* (Itasea, Ill.: Peacock Publishers, 1994). For a more complete discussion of the various designs discussed in this appendix, see B. J. Winer, Donald R. Brown, and Kenneth M. Michels, *Statistical Principles in Experimental Design,* 3rd ed. (New York: McGraw-Hill, Inc., 1991).

2. It can be shown mathematically that if a random variable is t distributed with ν degrees of freedom, then t^2 is F distributed with $\nu_1 = 1$, $\nu_2 = \nu$ degrees of freedom.

3. For an insightful discussion of how one should set up hypotheses for analysis of variance, see Richard K. Burdick, "Statement of Hypotheses in the Analysis of Variance," *Journal of Marketing Research* 20 (August 1983), pp. 320–324.

4. See R. A. Fisher and F. Yates, *Statistical Tables* (Edinburgh: Oliver and Boyd, 1948), for Latin squares from 4×4 to 12×12.

5. William C. Guenther, *Analysis of Variance* (Englewood Cliffs, N.J.: Prentice-Hall, 1964), pp. 99–100; John Neter, William Wasserman, and Michael H. Kutner, *Applied Linear Statistical Models,* 4th ed. (Burr Ridge, Ill.: Richard D. Irwin, 1990, pp. 673–677.

6. Guenther, *Analysis of Variance,* p. 100. For examples of factorial experiments, see J. B. Wilkinson, J. Barry Mason, and Christie H. Paksoy, "Assessing the Impact of Short-Term Supermarket Strategy Variables," *Journal of Marketing Research* 19 (February 1982), pp. 72–86; Susan M. Petroshius and Kent B. Monroe, "Effect of Product-Line Pricing Characteristics on Product Evaluations," *Journal of Consumer Research* 13 (March 1987), pp. 511–519; Paul M. Herr, Frank R. Kardes, and John Kim, "Effects of Word-of-Mouth and Product Attribute Information on Persuasion: An Accessibility-Diagnosticity Perspective," *Journal of Consumer Research* 17 (March 1991), pp. 454–462; Syed Saad Andaleeb, "An Experimental Investigation of Satisfaction and Commitment in Marketing Channels: The Role of Trust and Dependence," *Journal of Retailing* 72 (Spring 1996), pp. 77–93.

7. One can often use select combinations of factor levels rather than every possible combination, which greatly simplifies the experiment. See Charles W. Holland and David W. Cravens, "Fractional Factorial Experimental Designs in Marketing Research," *Journal of Marketing Research* 10 (August 1973), pp. 270–276. See also Raghu N. Kacker, and Kwock-Leung Tsui, "Interaction Graphs: Graphical Aids for Planning Experiments," *Journal of Quality Technology* 22 (January 1990), pp. 1–14, for discussion of graphical aids to plan factorial experiments. For an example of the use of fractional factorials, see Paul D. Berger and Gerald E. Smith, "The Effect of Direct Mail Framing Strategies and Segmentation Variables on University Fundraising Performance," *Journal of Direct Marketing* 11 (Winter 1997), pp. 30–43.

Chapter 21

DATA ANALYSIS: INVESTIGATING ASSOCIATIONS

LEARNING OBJECTIVES

Upon Completing This Chapter, You Should Be Able to

1. Explain the difference between regression and correlation analysis.

2. List the three assumptions that are made about the error term in the least-squares solution to a regression problem.

3. Discuss what the Gauss-Markov theorem says about the least-squares estimators of a population parameter.

4. Define *standard error of estimate*.

5. Specify the relationship that a correlation coefficient is designed to measure.

6. Discuss the difference between simple regression analysis and multiple-regression analysis.

7. Explain what is meant by multicollinearity in a multiple-regression problem.

8. Describe when a partial-regression coefficient is used and what it measures.

9. Explain the difference between the coefficient of multiple determination and the coefficient of partial determination.

10. Describe how the use of dummy variables and variable transformations expands the scope of the regression model.

Case in Marketing Research

Lovelace Lingerie, Inc., had pioneered the sales of women's upscale lingerie—some called it "boudoir fashion"—by marketing it in tastefully decorated mall boutiques. But while women loved the lace curtains and antiques of the Lovelace retail outlets, most men were afraid to venture inside. That reluctance had given impetus for the company's mail-order catalog, which was geared toward men purchasing gifts.

Christmas catalog sales had been good, but Angela Spaulding, vice president for Lovelace catalog sales, felt that the company was tapping into only a small segment of a potentially large market. She had hired Michael Wyse's marketing research firm to conduct a study of 400 men who had placed orders from the Christmas catalog. The idea was to find out about these men, in the hopes of finding ways to expand catalog sales.

Now Wyse was on his way to meet with Spaulding to discuss the results of the study. When he located the Lovelace boutique in the Plainview Mall, he understood why most men had second thoughts about venturing inside. The windows were heavily draped with chintz, providing a backdrop for a black lace negligee suspended from a padded satin hanger. Huge arrangements of orchids flanked the display. It wasn't that there was anything racy or offensive about the store; it was just that it was so . . . well, feminine.

But an intrepid researcher to the end, Wyse took a deep breath and entered the world of Lovelace Lingerie. He marched resolutely past racks of silk robes and satin nightgowns and, directed by one of the sales staff, located Spaulding in a surprisingly spacious conference room tucked behind the store. From behind a table stacked with computer printouts and lingerie, Spaulding rose to greet him.

"Michael, so glad you were able to meet here," she said cheerfully, extending her hand. "We're just so busy putting together the merchandise for our spring catalog. What do you think of our store?"

"It's a lot different from my favorite place to shop," he replied apologetically.

"Where's that?" asked Spaulding.

"The hardware store around the corner from where I live," replied Wyse.

Spaulding laughed. "So tell me what you found in your study. We're having a big strategy meeting next week, and I'd like to have a firm plan for how best to expand our catalog sales."

"I know you're no slouch when it comes to numbers, Angela," said Wyse, "so I'd like to take you through some of the underlying statistical analyses, as well as the results of the study. I know you'll find the results interesting, but I think you'll have more confidence in our findings if you have an understanding of how we came up with them."

"I'm all ears," said Spaulding.

"In the survey we sent to our sample of 400 male catalog customers, Questions 7 through 11 were designed to get at how these men felt about making purchases from the Lovelace catalog. To determine that factor, we came up with an "Attitude toward Lovelace" index, called ATTLOVE, using responses to Questions 7 through 11." (See Exhibit A.)

"ATTLOVE was formed in such a way that higher scores implied more favorable attitudes about buying from Lovelace. The responses to the five questions were summed to produce the ATTLOVE score for each subject," Wyse said.

"We also wanted to know if that attitude was related to the respondent's demographic characteristics. This second table that we compiled shows whether the ATTLOVE index varies as a function of a person's occupation," he said, laying the relevant table in front of Spaulding.

"We coded blue-collar workers as 0 and white-collar workers as 1. Using simple regression analysis, we determined that the results are both statistically and practically significant. You see where it says the adjusted R-squared value is .752?" Wyse asked, pointing to the third line in Exhibit B.

Spaulding nodded her head.

"That means that approximately 75 percent of the variation in the ATTLOVE index can be accounted for or explained by the variation in occupation. There is a positive relationship between the two variables (B equals 11.534)," Wyse said.

"So white-collar workers have a much more favorable attitude toward Lovelace than blue-collar workers do," mused Spaulding. "Very interesting. Very interesting indeed."

Discussion Issues

1. In Wyse's study, regression analysis was used to study the relationship between two variables. What were they? Which was the dependent variable? Which was the independent?

2. While the regression analysis demonstrated a relationship between the two variables, did it demonstrate which one caused the other?

	Strongly Disagree	Disagree	Neither Agree nor Disagree	Agree	Strongly Agree
7. In general, Lovelace Lingerie sells a high-quality line of merchandise.	_____	_____	_____	_____	_____
8. Lovelace Lingerie carries a complete line of lingerie.	_____	_____	_____	_____	_____
9. Lovelace Lingerie has a very high-quality catalog.	_____	_____	_____	_____	_____
10. The Lovelace Lingerie catalog displays the merchandise attractively.	_____	_____	_____	_____	_____
11. It should be easy to find a nice gift in the Lovelace Lingerie catalog.	_____	_____	_____	_____	_____

Dependent variable . . . ATTLOVE
Variable(s) entered on step number 1: $V41$

		Analysis of Variance	DF	Sum of Squares	Mean Square	F
Multiple R	.869	Regression	1	4071.174	4071.174	374.512
R-squared	.754	Residual	122	1326.213	10.871	
Adjusted R-squared	.752					
Standard error	3.297					

VARIABLES IN THE EQUATION

Variable	B	Beta	Standard Error B	F
$V41$	11.534	.869	.596	374.512
(Constant)	9.727			

In the discussion of data analysis so far, we have been primarily concerned with testing for the significance of *differences* obtained under various research conditions, whether between a sample result and an assumed population condition or between two or more sample results. Quite often, however, the researcher must determine whether there is any *association* between two or more variables and, if so, the strength and functional form of the relationship. For example, to model Kmart's inventory needs for car batteries, the retailer compared two years' worth of national weather data with car battery sales during the same period. The retailer found relationships between weather patterns and battery sales (for example, sales rise when temperatures dip below a certain level). Kmart used the information to build a decision-making model for ordering car batteries based on weather forecasts. Following the success of this effort, the company planned to extend it to other products as well.[1]

Typically, we try to predict the value of one variable (for example, consumption of a specific product by a family) on the basis of one or more other variables (for example, income and number of family members). The variable being predicted is called the *dependent* or, more aptly, *criterion, variable.* The variables that form the basis of the prediction are called the *independent,* or *predictor,* variables. In the example of inventory management at Kmart, the dependent variable (what managers wanted to predict from the data) was sales of car batteries. The independent variable was the weather.

Simple Regression and Correlation Analysis

Correlation analysis
A statistical technique used to measure the closeness of the linear relationship between two or more intervally scaled variables.

Regression analysis
A statistical technique used to derive an equation that relates a single criterion variable to one or more predictor variables; when there is one predictor variable, it is simple regression analysis, while it is multiple-regression analysis when there are two or more predictor variables.

Regression analysis and *correlation analysis* are widely used among marketing researchers for studying the relationship between two or more variables. Although the two terms are often used interchangeably, there is a difference in purpose. **Correlation analysis** measures the *closeness* of the relationship between two or more variables (see the example in the milk ad shown). The technique considers the joint variation of two measures, neither of which is restricted by the experimenter. **Regression analysis,** on the other hand, is used to derive an *equation* that relates the criterion variable to one or more predictor variables. It considers the frequency distribution of the criterion variable when one or more predictor variables are held fixed at various levels.[2]

It is perfectly legitimate to measure the closeness of the relationship between variables without deriving an estimating equation. Similarly, one can perform a regression analysis without investigating the closeness of the relationship between the variables. But, since it is common to do both, the body of techniques, rather than one or the other, is usually referred to as either regression or correlation analysis.

As regards correlation analysis, we should also comment on the distinction between correlation and causation. The use of the terms *dependent* (criterion) and *independent* (predictor) *variables* to describe the measures in correlation analysis stems from the mathematical functional relationship between the variates and is in no way related to dependence of one variable on another in a causal sense. For example, while the techniques may show some correlation between high income and a tendency to take winter vacations to the Caribbean, it would be a mistake to assume that having a high income *causes* a person to head south when the thermometer plummets.

There is nothing in correlation analysis, or any other mathematical procedure, that can be used to establish causality. All these procedures can do is measure the nature and

The National Fluid Milk Processors Promotion Board is responsible for the celebrity milk-mustache ads. One of its current promotions is a yearly "Milk Mustache Celebrity Calendar Event," when calendars are sent to households. The board was interested in finding the correlation of its celebrity calendar event and gallon milk sales. Nielsen Homescan Data reported a 3.6 percent surge in gallon milk sales versus year-ago sales among households that received the 1999 calendar, plus a 9.7 percent boost in gallon milk sales among households with kids 6 to 12 years of age.

Kroger's no stranger to the benefits of the Milk Mustache Celebrity Calendar Event. And for those of you who like the numbers; Nielsen Homescan Data reported a 3.6% lift in gallon milk sales vs Year Ago among households who received the '99 calendar. Plus a 9.7% boost in gallon milk sales vs Year Ago among households with kids 6-12.* Near-pack premium displays like this one are a proven way to help drive multiple gallon purchases and move the milk meter. Celebrity Calendar 2000? Sign me up!

got milk?

JUD WELLS, DAIRY CATEGORY MANAGER-KROGER COLUMBUS
©1999 NATIONAL FLUID MILK PROCESSOR PROMOTION BOARD

degree of *association* or *covariation* between variables. Statements of causality must spring from underlying knowledge and theories about the phenomena under investigation. They in no way spring from the mathematics.[3] In Research Window 21.1, the former director of marketing research at General Mills urges researchers to look beyond the welter of data they devote their energies to collecting and consider the theory that directs marketing inquiry. Without the theory, the mathematics are useless.

For example, in analyzing the results of a survey it sponsored, Bank Network News drew upon its editors' understanding of consumer behavior and trends in the banking industry. The study found that monthly usage of automated teller machines (ATMs) fell

---

Research Window 21.1 | **The Importance of Theory in Marketing Research**

If marketing researchers want to acquire true marketing "knowledge" they should devote more time and effort to developing and validating marketing theories, according to Lawrence D. Gibson, former director of marketing research, General Mills, Inc., Minneapolis.

"There's a funny notion around that theories are vague, ephemeral, and useless, and data are nice, hard, real things. And that somehow knowledge is associated with facts and data. This is nonsense. Knowledge is an interrelated set of validated theories and established facts, not just facts. In marketing, we are profoundly ignorant of what we're doing because we're woefully short on theory while we're drowning in data."

Deploring the lack of validated marketing theories and the overabundance of marketing "facts," Gibson quoted the scientist, R. B. Braithwaite: "The world is not made up of empirical facts with the addition of the laws of nature. What we call the laws of nature are simply theories, the conceptual devices by which we organize our empirical knowledge and predict the future."

And he quoted Albert Einstein: "The grand aim of all science is to cover the maximum number of empirical facts, by logical deduction, into the smallest number of axioms, axioms which represent that remainder which is not comprehended."

In other words, Gibson said, "the axioms and theories are not our knowledge, they are our ignorance. They're part of the problem we assume away." A theory, he said, is how "scientists choose to organize their knowledge and perceptions of the world. Theories are pretty well laid out, simplistic, general, have predicted usefulness, and fit the facts.

"Theory is basic to what data you choose to collect," he said. "You can't observe all the veins of all the leaves of all the branches of all the trees of all the forests in the world. You've got to choose what facts you choose to observe, and you're going to be guided in some sense by some kind of theory. And when you turn around to use the data, you're also going to be guided by theory. It will have a profound effect on what you do."

This shows up in the way researchers go about analyzing different kinds of data. For example, when working with observational data, people simply don't realize the weak theoretical ground on which they stand. They wander around the data, merrily trying to find out what makes sense.

"Perhaps you've seen some fairly typical versions of this. The creative analyst looks at the data and the survey and they don't make sense. 'Make sense' means the findings are congenial to his prior judgment. But the world isn't working the way he thought it was supposed to be working.

"So he cross-tabs by big cities versus little cities. Still doesn't make sense. But he is very creative, and observes there are more outer-directed people in big cities than in little cities, so he now cross-tabs by inner-directed versus outer-directed by city size, and—lo and behold—he finds out he was right all along!

"Now, obviously, as long as you keep analyzing when you don't like what you see, and stop analyzing when you do like what you see, the world always will look to you the way it's supposed to look. You'll never learn anything."

Source: Larry Gibson, "Marketing Research Needs Validated Theories," *Marketing News* 17 (January 21, 1983), p. 14. Reprinted with permission from *Marketing News* published by the American Marketing Association, Chicago, IL 60606. For an example of the danger associated with continuing to analyze data when you don't like what you see, see Ralph T. King, Jr., "The Tale of a Dream Drug and Data Dredging," *The Wall Street Journal* (February 7, 1995), pp. B1, B6.

during the period studied. At the same time, point-of-sale transactions using debit cards (using a debit card to pay at the cash register) rose by a striking 35 percent. The editors attributed this inverse correlation to consumers' disenchantment with ATM service charges. They noted that many retailers allow customers not only to pay for their purchase with a debit card, but also to get cash back. And the retailers, unlike a growing share of ATMs, do not charge for this service.[4]

The subject of regression and correlation analysis is best discussed through example. Consider, therefore, the national manufacturer of a ballpoint pen, Click, which is interested in investigating the effectiveness of the firm's marketing efforts. The company uses wholesalers to distribute Click and supplements their efforts with company sales representatives and spot television advertising. The company plans to use annual territory sales as its measure of effectiveness. These data and information on the number of sales representatives serving a territory are readily available in company records. The other characteristics to which the manufacturer seeks to relate sales—television spot advertising and wholesaler efficiency—are more difficult to determine. To obtain information on television spot advertising in a territory, researchers must analyze advertising schedules and study area coverage by channel to determine what areas each broadcast might reach. Wholesaler efficiency requires rating the wholesalers on a number of criteria and aggregating the ratings into an overall measure of wholesaler efficiency, where 4 is outstanding, 3 is good, 2 is average, and 1 is poor. Because of the time and expense required to generate these advertising and distribution characteristics, the company has decided to analyze only a sample of sales territories. The data for a simple random sample of 40 territories are contained in Exhibit 21.1.

The effect of each of the marketing mix variables on sales can be investigated in several ways. One very obvious way is to simply plot sales as a function of each of the variables. Figure 21.1 contains these plots, which are called *scatter diagrams*. Panel A suggests that sales increase as the number of television spots per month increases. Panel B suggests sales increase as the number of sales representatives serving the territory increases. Finally, Panel C suggests that there is little relationship between sales in a territory and the efficiency of the wholesaler serving the territory.

A close look at Panels A and B also suggests that it would be possible to summarize the relationship between sales and each of the predictor variables by drawing a straight line through the data points. One way to generate the relationship between sales and either television spots or number of sales representatives would be to "eyeball" it; that is, one could visually draw a straight line through the points in the graphs. Such a line would represent the line of "average" relationship. It would indicate the average value of the criterion variable, sales, for given values of either of the predictor variables, television spots or number of sales representatives. One could then enter the graph with, say, the number of television spots in a territory, and could read off the average level of sales expected in the territory. The difficulty with the graphic approach is that two analysts might generate different lines to describe the relationship. This simply raises the question of which line is more correct or fits the data better.

An alternative approach is to mathematically fit a line to the data. The general equation of a straight line is $y = \alpha + \beta X$, where α is the Y intercept and β is the slope coefficient. In the case of sales Y and television spots X_1, the equation could be written as $Y = \alpha_1 + \beta_1 X_1$, while for the relationship between sales Y and number of sales representatives X_2, it could be written as $Y = \alpha_2 + \beta_2 X_2$, where the subscripts indicate the predictor variable being considered. As written, each of these models is a *deterministic model*. When a value of the predictor variable is substituted in the equation with specified α and β, a unique value for Y is determined, and no allowance is made for error.

When investigating social phenomena, there is rarely, if ever, zero error. Thus in place of the deterministic model, we might substitute a *probabilistic model* and make some assumptions about the error. For example, let us work with the relationship between sales and number of television spots and consider the model

$$Y_i = \alpha_1 + \beta_1 X_{i1} + \epsilon_i$$

EXHIBIT 21.1   Territory Data for Click Ballpoint Pens

Territory	Sales (in Thousands) Y	Advertising (TV Spots per Month) X_1	Number of Sales Representatives X_2	Wholesaler Efficiency Index X_3
005	260.3	5	3	4
019	286.1	7	5	2
033	279.4	6	3	3
039	410.8	9	4	4
061	438.2	12	6	1
082	315.3	8	3	4
091	565.1	11	7	3
101	570.0	16	8	2
115	426.1	13	4	3
118	315.0	7	3	4
133	403.6	10	6	1
149	220.5	4	4	1
162	343.6	9	4	3
164	644.6	17	8	4
178	520.4	19	7	2
187	329.5	9	3	2
189	426.0	11	6	4
205	343.2	8	3	3
222	450.4	13	5	4
237	421.8	14	5	2
242	245.6	7	4	4
251	503.3	16	6	3
260	375.7	9	5	3
266	265.5	5	3	3
279	620.6	18	6	4
298	450.5	18	5	3
306	270.1	5	3	2
332	368.0	7	6	2
347	556.1	12	7	1
358	570.0	13	6	4
362	318.5	8	4	3
370	260.2	6	3	2
391	667.0	16	8	2
408	618.3	19	8	2
412	525.3	17	7	4
430	332.2	10	4	3
442	393.2	12	5	3
467	283.5	8	3	3
471	376.2	10	5	4
488	481.8	12	5	2

where Y_i is the level of sales in the ith territory, X_{i1} is the level of advertising in the ith territory, and ϵ_i is the error associated with the ith observation. This is the form of the model that is used for regression analysis. The error term is part and parcel of the model. It represents a failure to include all factors in the model, the fact that there is an unpredictable element in human behavior, and the condition that there are errors of measurement.[5] The

FIGURE 21.1   Scatter Diagrams of Sales versus Marketing Mix Variables

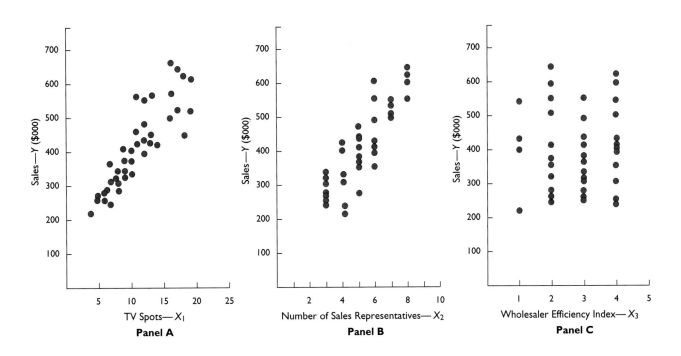

FIGURE 21.1   Scatter Diagrams of Sales versus Marketing Mix Variables

FIGURE 21.2   Relationship Between *Y* and *X$_i$* in the Probabilistic Model

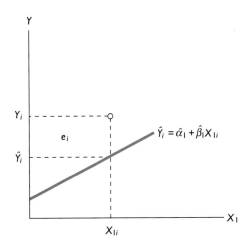

probabilistic model allows for the fact that the *Y* value is not uniquely determined for a given *X$_i$* value. Rather, all that is determined for a given *X$_i$* value is the "average value" of *Y*. Individual values can be expected to fluctuate above and below this average.

The mathematical solution for finding the *line of best fit* for the probabilistic model requires that some assumptions be made about the distribution of the error term. The line of best fit could be defined in a number of ways. The typical way is in terms of the line that minimizes the sum of the deviations squared about the line (the *least-squares solution*). Consider Figure 21.2 and suppose that the line drawn in the figure is the estimated equation. Employing a caret (ˆ) to indicate an estimated value, the error for the *i*th observation is the difference between the actual Y value, Y_i, and the estimated Y value, $\hat{Y}_i$, that is, $e_i = Y_i - \hat{Y}_i$. The least-squares solution is based on the principle that the sum of these squared errors should be made as small as possible; that is, $\sum_i^n e_i^2$ should be minimized. The sample estimates $\hat{\alpha}_1$ and $\hat{\beta}_1$ of the true population parameters α_1 and β_1 are determined so that this condition is satisfied.

There are three simplifying assumptions made about the error term in the least-squares solution:

1. The mean or average value of the error term is zero.

2. The variance of the error term is constant and is independent of the values of the predictor variable.

3. The values of the error term are independent of one another.

Given the assumptions, it is possible to solve formulas to secure estimates for the population parameters, $\hat{\alpha}_1$, the intercept, and $\hat{\beta}_1$, the slope, by hand, although it is much more common to use a computer to estimate them.[6]

If we used the data in Exhibit 21.1 for sales (Y) and television spots per month (X_1), it would turn out that the estimate for $\hat{\alpha}_1$ would be 135.4, and $\hat{\beta}_1$ would be 25.3.[7] The equation is plotted in Figure 21.3. The slope of the line is given by $\hat{\beta}_1$. The value 25.3 for $\hat{\beta}_1$ suggests that sales increase by \$25,300 for every unit increase in television spots. As mentioned previously, this is an estimate of the true population condition based on our particular sample of 40 observations. A different sample would most assuredly generate a different estimate. Further, we have not yet asked whether this is a statistically significant result or whether it could have occurred by chance. Nevertheless, it is a most vital item of information that helps in determining whether advertising expense is worth the estimated return. The estimate of the intercept parameter is $\hat{\alpha}_1 = 135.4$; this indicates where the line crosses the Y axis, since it represents the estimated value of Y when the predictor variable equals zero.

FIGURE 21.3   **Plot of Equation Relating Sales to Television Spots**

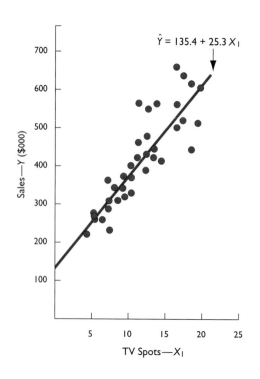

Standard Error of Estimate

An examination of Figure 21.3 shows that while the line seems to fit the points fairly well, there is still deviation in the points about the line. The size of these deviations measures the goodness of the fit. We can compute a numerical measure of the variation of the points about the line in much the same way as we compute the standard deviation of a frequency distribution.

Just as the sample mean is an estimate of the true parent-population mean, the line given by $\hat{Y}_i = \hat{\alpha}_1 + \hat{\beta}_1 X_{i1} + e_i$ is an estimate of the true regression line $Y_i = \alpha_1 + \beta_1 X_{i1} + \epsilon_i$. Consider the variance of the random error ϵ around the true line of regression, that is, σ_ϵ^2 or $\sigma_{Y/X}^2$. When the population variance σ^2 is unknown, an unbiased estimate is given by the square of the sample standard deviation, $\hat{s}$,

$$\hat{s} = \sqrt{\frac{\sum_{i=1}^{n}(X_i - \overline{x})^2}{(n-1)}}$$

Similarly, let $s_{Y/X}^2$ be an unbiased estimate of the population variance about the regression line, $\sigma_{Y/X}^2$. Now it can be shown that the sample estimate of the variance about the regression line is related to the sum of the squared errors; specifically, it equals

$$s_{Y/X}^2 = \frac{\sum_{i=1}^{n} e_i^2}{(n-2)} = \frac{\sum_{i=1}^{n}(Y_i - \hat{Y}_i)^2}{(n-2)}$$

where n is again the sample size, and $s_{Y/X}^2$ is an unbiased estimator of $\sigma_{Y/X}^2$, where Y_i and $\hat{Y}_i$ are, respectively, the observed and estimated values of Y for the ith observation. The square root of the above quantity, $s_{Y/X}$, is often called the **standard error of estimate,** although the term *standard deviation from regression* is more meaningful.

The interpretation of the standard error of estimate parallels that for the standard deviation. Consider an X_{i1} value. The standard error of estimate means that for any such value of television spots X_{i1}, Y_i (sales) tends to be distributed about the corresponding $\hat{Y}_i$ value—the point on the line—with a standard deviation equal to the standard error of estimate. Further, the variation about the line is the same throughout the entire length of the line. The point on the line, the arithmetic mean, changes as X_{i1} changes, but the distribution of Y_i values around the line does not change with changes in the number of television spots. Figure 21.4 depicts the situation under the assumption that the error term is

Standard error of estimate
A term used in regression analysis to refer to the absolute amount of variation in the criterion variable that is left "unexplained," or unaccounted for, by the fitted regression equation.

FIGURE 21.4   **Rectangular Distribution of Error Term**

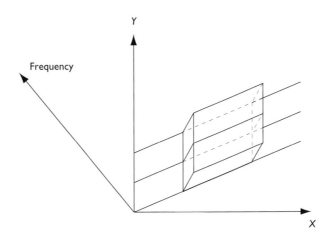

rectangularly distributed, for example.[8] Note that the assumption of constant $s_{Y/X}$, irrespective of the value of X_{i1}, produces parallel bands around the regression line.

The smaller the standard error of estimate, the better the line fits the data. For the line relating sales to television spots, it is $s_{Y/X} = 59.6$.

Inferences about the Slope Coefficient

Earlier we calculated the value of the slope coefficient, $\hat{\beta}_1$ to be 25.3. At that time we did not yet raise the question of whether that result was statistically significant or could have been due to chance. To deal with that question requires an additional assumption, namely, that the errors are normally distributed rather than rectangularly distributed as previously assumed. Before proceeding, though, let us emphasize that the least-squares estimators of the parent-population parameters are BLUE, that is, they are the *best linear unbiased* estimators of the true population parameters regardless of the shape of the distribution of the error term. All that is necessary is that the previous assumptions be satisfied. This is the remarkable result of the Gauss-Markov theorem. It is only if we wish to make statistical inferences about the regression coefficients that the assumption of normally distributed errors is required.

It can be shown that if the ϵ_i are normally distributed random variables, then $\hat{\beta}_1$ is also normally distributed. That is, if we were to take repeated samples from our population of sales territories and calculate a $\hat{\beta}_1$ for each sample, the distribution of these estimates would be normal and *centered* around the *true population* parameter β_1. Further, the variance of the distribution of $\hat{\beta}_1$'s, or $\sigma_{\hat{\beta}_1}^2$, can be shown to be equal to

$$\sigma_{\hat{\beta}_1}^2 = \frac{\sigma_{Y/X_1}^2}{\sum_{i=1}^{n}(X_{i1} - \overline{x}_1)^2}$$

Since the population σ_{Y/X_1}^2 is unknown, $\sigma_{\hat{\beta}_1}^2$ is also unknown and has to be estimated. The estimate, denoted as $s_{\hat{\beta}_1}^2$, is generated by substituting the standard error of estimate $s_{Y/X}$ for $\sigma_{Y/X}$

$$s_{\hat{\beta}_1}^2 = \frac{s_{Y/X_1}^2}{\sum_{i=1}^{n}(X_{i1} - \overline{x}_1)^2}$$

The situation so far is as follows: Given the assumption of normally distributed errors, $\hat{\beta}_1$ is also normally distributed with a mean of β_1 and unknown variance $\sigma_{\hat{\beta}_1}^2$. Since the variance of the distribution of the sample is unknown, we need to use a procedure similar to that used when making an inference about the mean when the population variance is unknown. That set of conditions requires a *t* test to examine statistical significance. The test for the significance of β_1 has a similar requirement. The null hypothesis is that there is no linear relationship between the variables, while the alternate hypothesis is that a linear relationship does exist; that is,

$$H_0: \beta_1 = 0$$
$$H_a: \beta_1 \neq 0$$

The test statistic is $t = (\hat{\beta}_1 - \beta_1)/s_{\hat{\beta}_1}$; that is, the slope estimated from the sample minus the hypothesized slope, divided by the standard error of estimate, which is *t* distributed with $n - 2$ degrees of freedom. In the example,

$$s_{\hat{\beta}_1}^2 = \frac{s_{Y/X_1}^2}{\sum_{i=1}^{n}(X_{i1} - \overline{x}_1)^2} = \frac{(59.6)^2}{723.6} = 4.91$$

$$s_{\hat{\beta}_1} = \sqrt{4.91} = 2.22$$

$$t = \frac{\hat{\beta}_1 - \beta_1}{s_{\hat{\beta}_1}} = \frac{25.3 - 0}{2.22} = 11.4$$

For a 0.05 level of significance, the tabled t value for $v = n - 2 = 38$ degrees of freedom is 2.02. Since calculated t exceeds critical t, the null hypothesis is rejected; $\hat{\beta}_1$ is sufficiently different from zero to warrant the assumption of a linear relationship between sales and television spots. Now this does not mean that the true relationship between sales and television spots is *necessarily* linear, only that the evidence indicates that Y (sales) changes as X_1 (television spots) changes, and that we may obtain a better prediction of Y using X_1 and the linear equation than if we simply ignored X_1.

What if the null hypothesis is not rejected? As we have noted, β_1 is the slope of the assumed line over the region of observation and indicates the linear change in Y for a one-unit change in X_1. If we do not reject the null hypothesis that β_1 equals zero, it does not mean that Y and X_1 are unrelated. There are two possibilities. First, we may simply be committing a Type II error by not rejecting a false null hypothesis. Second, it is possible that Y and X_1 might be perfectly related in some curvilinear manner and we have simply chosen the wrong model to describe the physical situation.

Correlation Coefficient

Coefficient of correlation
A term used in regression analysis to refer to the strength of the linear association between the criterion variable and a predictor variable.

So far we have been concerned with the functional relationship of Y to X. Suppose we were also concerned with the *strength of the linear relationship* between Y and X. This leads to the notion of the **coefficient of correlation.** Two additional assumptions are made when discussing the correlation model. First, X_i is also assumed to be a random variable. A sample observation yields both an X_i and Y_i value. Second, it is assumed that the observations come from a bivariate normal distribution, that is, one in which the X variable is normally distributed and the Y variable is also normally distributed.

Now consider the drawing of a sample of n observations from a bivariate normal distribution. Let ρ represent the strength of the linear association between the two variables in the parent population. Let r represent the sample estimate of ρ. Suppose the sample of n observations yielded the scatter of points shown in Figure 21.5 and consider the division

FIGURE 21.5   **Scatter of Points for Sample of *n* Observations**

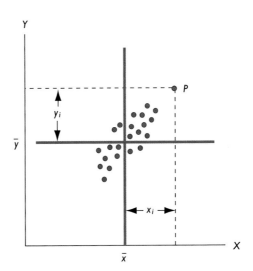

of the figure into the four quadrants formed by erecting perpendiculars to the two axes at $\bar{x}$ and $\bar{y}$.

Consider the deviations from these bisectors. Take any point P with coordinates (X_i, Y_i) and define the deviations

$$x_i = X_i - \bar{x}$$
$$y_i = Y_i - \bar{y}$$

where the small letters indicate deviations around a mean. It is clear from an inspection of Figure 21.5 that the product $x_i y_i$ is

- Positive for all points in Quadrant I
- Negative for all points in Quadrant II
- Positive for all points in Quadrant III
- Negative for all points in Quadrant IV

Hence, it would seem that the quantity $\sum_{i=1}^{n} x_i y_i$ could be used as a measure of the linear association between X and Y,

- For if the association is positive so that most points lie in the Quadrants I and III, $\sum_{i=1}^{n} x_i y_i$ tends to be positive
- While if the association is negative so that most points lie in the Quadrants II and IV, $\sum_{i=1}^{n} x_i y_i$ tends to be negative
- While if no relation exists between X and Y, the points will be scattered over all four quadrants and $\sum_{i=1}^{n} x_i y_i$ will tend to be very small

The quantity $\sum_{i=1}^{n} x_i y_i$ has two defects, though, as a measure of linear association between X and Y. First, it can be increased arbitrarily by adding further observations—that is, by increasing the sample size. Second, it can also be arbitrarily influenced by changing the units of measurement for either X or Y or both—for example, by changing feet to inches. These defects can be removed by making the measure of the strength of linear association a dimensionless quantity and dividing by n. The result is the *Pearsonian*, or *product-moment, coefficient of correlation*, that is,

$$r = \frac{\sum_{i=1}^{n} x_i y_i}{n s_X s_Y}$$

where s_X is the standard deviation of the X variable and s_Y is the standard deviation of the Y variable.

The correlation coefficient computed from the sample data is an estimate of the parent-population parameter ρ, and part of the job of the researcher is to use r to test hypotheses about ρ. It is unnecessary to do so for the example at hand because the test of the null hypothesis H_0: $\rho = 0$ is equivalent to the test of the null hypothesis H_0: $\beta_1 = 0$. Since we have already performed the latter test, we know that the sample evidence leads to the rejection of the hypothesis that there is no linear relationship between sales and television spots; that is, it leads to the rejection of H_0: $\rho = 0$.

The product-moment coefficient of correlation may vary from -1 to $+1$. Perfect positive correlation, where an increase in X determines exactly an increase in Y, yields a coefficient of $+1$. Perfect negative correlation, where an increase in X determines exactly a decrease in Y, yields a coefficient of -1. Figure 21.6 depicts these situations and several other scatter diagrams and their resulting correlation coefficients. An examination of these diagrams will provide some appreciation of the size of the correlation coefficient associated with a particular degree of scatter. The square of the correlation coefficient is the

FIGURE 21.6 **Sample Scatter Diagrams and Associated Correlation Coefficients**

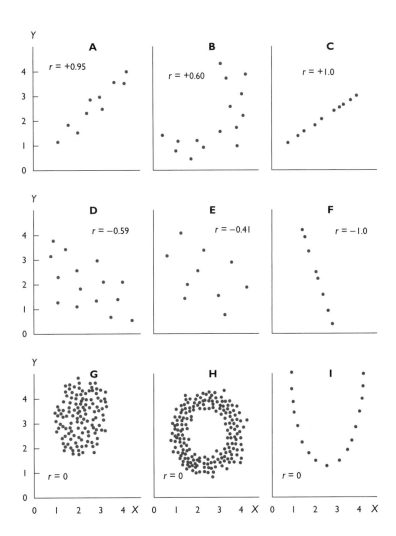

Source: Ronald E. Frank, Alfred A. Kuehn, and William F. Massy, *Quantitative Techniques in Marketing Analysis* (Homewood, Ill.: Richard D. Irwin, Inc., 1962), p. 71. Used with permission.

Coefficient of determination
A term used in regression analysis to refer to the relative proportion of the total variation in the criterion variable that can be explained or accounted for by the fitted regression equation.

coefficient of determination. By some algebraic manipulation, it can be shown to be equal to

$$r^2 = 1 - \frac{s_{Y/X}^2}{s_Y^2}$$

that is, $r^2 = 1$ minus the standard error of estimate squared, divided by the sample variance of the criterion variable. In the absence of the predictor variable, our best estimate of the criterion variable would be the sample mean. If there were low variability in sales from territory to territory, the sample mean would be a good estimate of the expected sales in any territory. However, high variability would render it a poor estimate. Thus, the variance in sales s_Y^2 is a measure of the "badness" of such an estimating procedure. The introduction of the covariate X might produce an improvement in the territory sales estimates. It depends on how well the equation fits the data. Since $s_{Y/X}^2$ measures the scatter of the points about the regression line, $s_{Y/X}^2$ can be considered a measure of the "badness" of an estimating procedure that takes account of the covariate. Now if $s_{Y/X}^2$ is small in relation to s_Y^2, the introduction of the covariate via the regression equation can be said to have substantially improved the predictions of the criterion variable, sales. Conversely, if $s_{Y/X}^2$ is approximately equal to s_Y^2, the introduction of the covariate X can be considered not to have helped in improving the predictions of Y. Thus, the ratio $s_{Y/X}^2/s_Y^2$ can be considered to be the ratio of variation left unexplained by the regression line divided by the total variation; that is,

$$r^2 = 1 - \frac{\text{unexplained variation}}{\text{total variation}}$$

The right side of the equation can be combined in a single fraction to yield

$$r^2 = \frac{\text{total variation} - \text{unexplained variation}}{\text{total variation}}$$

Total variation minus unexplained variation leaves "explained variation"—that is, the variation in Y that is accounted for or explained by the introduction of X. Thus, the coefficient of determination can be considered to be equal to

$$r^2 = \frac{\text{explained variation}}{\text{total variation}}$$

where it is understood that total variation is measured by the variance in Y. For the sales and television spot example, $r^2 = 0.77$. This means that 77 percent of the variation in sales from territory to territory is accounted for, or can be explained, by the variation in television spot advertising across territories. Consequently, we can do a better job of estimating sales in a territory if we take account of television spots than if we neglect this advertising effort.

Multiple-Regression Analysis

The basic idea behind multiple-regression analysis is the same as that behind simple regression: to determine the relationship between independent and dependent, that is, predictor and criterion, variables. Multiple-regression analysis allows the introduction of additional variables, so the equation constructed reflects the values of several rather than one predictor variable. The objective in introducing additional variables is to improve our predictions of the criterion variable.

A wry observer of many a research project once offered some astute insights on the behavior of variables and the way in which they may be correlated (see Research Window 21.2). You may want to keep them in mind while you read this section on multiple-regression analysis.

Revised Nomenclature

A more formal, revised notational framework is valuable for discussing multiple-regression analysis. Consider the general regression model with three predictor variables. The regression equation is

$$Y = \alpha + \beta_1 X_1 + \beta_2 X_2 + \beta_3 X_3 + \epsilon$$

which is a simplified statement of the more elaborate and precise equation,

Research Window 21.2   **Walkup's Laws of Statistics**

Law No. 1

Everything correlates with everything, especially when the same individual defines the variables to be correlated.

Law No. 2

It won't help very much to find a good correlation between the variable you are interested in and some other variable that you don't understand any better.

Law No. 3

Unless you can think of a logical reason why two variables should be connected as cause and effect, it doesn't help much to find a correlation between them. In Columbus, Ohio, the mean monthly rainfall correlates very nicely with the number of letters in the names of the months!

Source: Lewis E. Walkup, "Walkup's First Five Laws of Statistics," *The Bent*, Summer 1974, publication of Tau Beta Pi, National Engineering Honor Society, University of Missouri Alumni Magazine; as quoted in Robert W. Joselyn, *Designing the Marketing Research Project* (New York: Petrocelli/Charter, 1977), p. 175.

Ethical Dilemma 21.1

The newly appointed analyst in the firm's marketing research department was given the responsibility of developing a method by which market potential for the firm's products could be estimated by small geographic areas. The analyst went about the task by gathering as much secondary data as he could. He then ran a series of regression analyses using the firm's sales as the criterion and the demographic factors as predictors. He realized that several of the predictors were highly correlated (e.g., average income in the area and average educational level), but he chose to ignore this fact when presenting the results to management.

- What is the consequence when the predictors in a regression equation are highly correlated?

- Is a research analyst ethically obliged to learn all he or she can about a particular technique before applying it to a problem in order to avoid incorrectly interpreting the results?

- Is a research analyst ethically obliged to advise those involved to be cautious in interpreting results because of violations of the assumptions in the method used to produce the results?

- What are the researcher's responsibilities if management has no interest in the technical details by which the results are achieved?

$$Y_{(123)} = \alpha_{(123)} + \beta_{Y1.23} X_1 + \beta_{Y2.13} X_2 + \beta_{Y3.12} X_3 + \epsilon_{(123)}$$

Coefficient of partial (or net) regression
A quantity resulting from a multiple-regression analysis, which indicates the average change in the criterion variable per unit change in a predictor variable, holding all other predictor variables constant; the interpretation applies only when the predictor variables are independent, as required for a valid application of the multiple-regression model.

In this more precise system, the following holds true:

- $Y_{(123)}$ is the value of Y that is estimated from the regression equation, in which Y is the criterion variable and X_1, X_2, and X_3 are the predictor variables

- $\alpha_{(123)}$ is the intercept parameter in the multiple-regression equation, in which Y is the criterion variable and X_1, X_2, and X_3 are the predictor variables

- $\beta_{Y1.23}$ is the coefficient of X_1 in regression equation, in which Y is the criterion variable and X_1, X_2, and X_3 are the predictor variables. It is called the **coefficient of partial (or net) regression.** Note the subscripts. The two subscripts to the left of the decimal point are called *primary subscripts*. The first identifies the criterion variable, and the second identifies the predictor variable of which this β value is the coefficient. There are always two primary subscripts. The two subscripts to the right of the decimal point are called *secondary subscripts*. They indicate which other predictor variables are in the regression equation. The number of secondary subscripts varies from zero for simple regression to any number, $k - 1$, where there are k predictor variables in the problem. In this case, the model contains three predictor variables, $k = 3$, and there are two secondary subscripts throughout.

- $\epsilon_{(123)}$ is the error associated with the prediction of Y when X_1, X_2, and X_3 are the predictor variables

When the identity of the variables is clear, it is common practice to use the simplified statement of the model. The more elaborate statement is helpful, though, in interpreting the solution to the regression problem.

Multicollinearity Assumption

The assumptions that we made about the error term for the simple regression model also apply to the multiple-regression equation. And the multiple-regression model requires the additional assumption that the predictor variables are not correlated among themselves. When the levels of the predictor variables can be set by the researcher, the assumption is easily satisfied. When the observations result from a survey rather than an experiment, the assumption is often violated, because many variables of interest in marketing vary together. For instance, higher incomes are typically associated with higher education levels. Thus, the prediction of purchase behavior employing both income and education would violate the assumption that the predictor variables are independent of one another. **Multicollinearity** is said to be present in a multiple-regression problem when the predictor variables are correlated among themselves.

Multicollinearity
A condition said to be present in a multiple-regression analysis when the predictor variables are not independent as required but are correlated among themselves.

Coefficients of Partial Regression

Consider what would happen if we introduced a number of sales representatives into our problem of predicting territory sales. We could investigate the two-variable relationship between sales and the number of sales representatives. This would involve, of course, the calculation of the simple regression equation relating sales to the number of sales representatives. The calculations would parallel those for the sales and television spot relationship. Alternatively, we could consider the simultaneous influence of television spots and number of sales representatives on sales using multiple-regression analysis. Assuming that is indeed the research problem, the regression model would be written

$$Y_{(12)} = \alpha_{(12)} + \beta_{Y1.2}X_1 + \beta_{Y2.1}X_2 + \epsilon_{(12)}$$

indicating that the criterion variable, sales in a territory, is to be predicted employing two predictor variables, X_1 (television spots per month) and X_2 (number of sales representatives).

Once again, the parameters of the model could be estimated from sample data employing least-squares procedures. Let us again distinguish the sample estimates from the true, but unknown, population values by using a caret to denote an estimated value. Let us not worry about the formulas for calculating the regression coefficients. They typically will be calculated on a computer anyway and can be found in almost any introductory statistics book. The marketing analyst's need is how to interpret the results provided by the computer.

For this problem, the equation turns out to be

$$\hat{Y} = \hat{\alpha}_{(12)} + \hat{\beta}_{Y1.2}X_1 + \hat{\beta}_{Y2.1}X_2 = 69.3 + 14.2\,X_1 + 37.5X_2$$

This regression equation may be used to estimate the level of sales to be expected in a territory, given the number of television spots and the number of the sales representatives serving the territory. Like any other least-squares equation, the line (a plane in this case, since three dimensions are involved) fits the points in such a way that the sum of the deviations about the line is zero. That is, if sales for each of the 40 sales territories were to be estimated from this equation, the positive and negative deviations about the line would exactly balance.

The level at which the plane intercepts the Y axis is given by $\hat{\alpha}_{(12)} = 69.3$. Consider now the coefficients of partial regression, $\hat{\beta}_{Y1.2}$ and $\hat{\beta}_{Y2.1}$. *Assuming the multicollinearity assumption is satisfied,* these coefficients of partial regression can be interpreted as the average change in the criterion variable associated with a unit change in the appropriate predictor variable while holding the other predictor variable constant. Thus, assuming there is no multicollinearity, $\hat{\beta}_{Y1.2} = 14.2$ indicates that on the average, an increase of $14,200 in sales can be expected with each additional television spot in the territory if the number of sales representatives is not changed. Similarly $\hat{\beta}_{Y2.1} = 37.5$ suggests that each additional sales representative in a territory can be expected to produce $37,500 in sales, on the average, if the number of television spots is held constant.

In simple regression analysis, we tested the significance of the regression equation by examining the significance of the slope coefficient employing the t test. Calculated t was 11.4 for the sales and television spot relationship. The significance of the regression could also have been checked with an F test. In the case of a two-variable regression, calculated F is equal to calculated t squared; that is, $F = t^2 = (11.4)^2 = 130.6$, while in general calculated F is equal to the ratio of the mean square due to regression to the mean square due to residuals. In simple regression, the calculated F value would be referred to an F table for $v_1 = n - 2$ degrees of freedom. The conclusion would be exactly equivalent to that derived by testing the significance of the slope coefficient employing the t test.

In the multiple-regression case, *it is mandatory that the significance of the overall regression be examined using an F test.* The appropriate degrees of freedom are $v_1 = k$ and $v_2 = n - k - 1$, where there are k predictor variables. Critical F for $v_1 = 2$ and $v_2 = 40 - 2 - 1 = 37$ degrees of freedom, and a 0.05 level of significance is 3.25. Calculated F for the regression relating sales to television spots and the number of sales representatives is 128.1. Since calculated F exceeds critical F, the null hypothesis of no relationship is rejected. There is a statistically significant linear relationship between sales and the predictor variables, number of television spots and number of sales representatives.

The slope coefficients can also be tested individually for their statistical significance in a multiple-regression problem, given the overall function is significant. The t test is again used, although the validity of the procedure is highly dependent on the multicollinearity that exists within the data. If the data are highly multicollinear, there will be a tendency to commit Type II errors; that is, many of the predictor variables will be judged as not being related to the criterion variable when in fact they are. It is even possible to conclude that the overall regression is statistically significant but that none of the coefficients are significant. The difficulty with the t tests for the significance of the individual slope coefficients arises because the standard error of estimate of the least-square coefficients, $s_{\hat{\beta}}$, increases as the dependence among the predictor variables increases. And, of course, as the denominator of calculated t gets larger, t itself decreases, occasioning the conclusion of no relationship between the criterion variable and the predictor variable in question.

Is multicollinearity a problem in our example? Consider again the simple regression of sales on television spots: $\hat{\beta}_1$ ($\hat{\beta}_{Y1}$ in our more formal notation system) was equal to 25.3. Thus, when the number of sales representatives in a territory was not considered, the average change in sales associated with an additional television spot was $25,300. Yet when the number of sales representatives was considered, the average change in sales associated with an additional television spot was $14,200, $\hat{\beta}_{Y1.2} = 14.2$. Part of the sales effect that we were attributing to television spots was in fact due to the number of sales representatives in the territory. We were thus overstating the impact of the television spot advertising because of the way decisions have historically been made in the company. Specifically, those territories with the greater number of sales representatives have received more television advertising support (or vice versa). Perhaps this was logical since they contained a larger proportion of the consuming public. Nevertheless, the fact that the two predictor variables are not independent (the coefficient of simple correlation between television spots and number of sales representatives is 0.78) has caused a violation of the assumption of independent predictors. Multicollinearity is present within this data set.

A multicollinear condition within a data set reduces the efficiency of the estimates for the regression parameters. This is because the amount of information about the effect of each predictor variable on the criterion variable declines as the correlation among the predictor variable increases. The reduction in efficiency can be easily seen in the limiting case as the correlation between the predictor variables approaches 1 for a two-predictor model. Such a situation is depicted in Figure 21.7, where it is assumed that there is a perfect linear relationship between the two predictor variables, television spots and number of sales representatives, and also that there is a strong linear relationship between the criterion variable sales and television spots. Consider the change in sales from $75,000 to $100,000. This change is associated with a change in the number of television spots, from three to four. This change in television spots is also associated with a change in the number of sales representatives, from four to five. What is the effect of a television spot on sales? Can we say it is 100 − 75 = 25, or $25,000? Most assuredly not, for historically a sales representative has been added to a territory whenever the number of television spots has been increased by one (or vice versa). The number of television spots and of sales repre-

---

FIGURE 21.7   **Hypothetical Relationship between Sales and TV Spots and between TV Spots and Number of Sales Representatives**

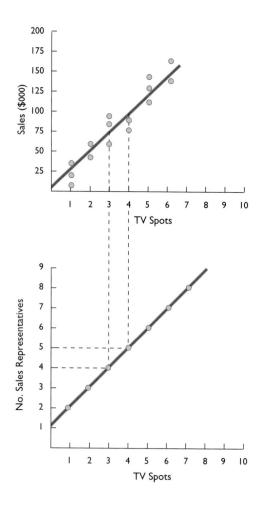

sentatives varies in perfect proportion, and it is impossible to distinguish their separate influences on sales, that is, their influence when the other predictor variable is held constant.

Very little meaning can be attached to the coefficients of partial regression when multicollinearity is present, as it is in our example. The "normal" interpretation of the coefficients of partial regression as "the average change in the criterion variable associated with a unit change in the appropriate predictor variable while holding the other predictor variables constant" simply does not hold.[9] The equation may still be quite useful for prediction, assuming conditions are stable. That is, it may be used to predict sales in the various territories for given levels of television spots and number of sales representatives *if* the historical relationship between sales and each of the predictor variables, and between or among the predictor variables themselves, can be expected to continue.[10] The partial-regression coefficients should not be used, though, as the basis for making marketing strategy decisions when significant multicollinearity is present.[11]

Coefficients of Multiple Correlation and Determination

One item of considerable importance in simple regression analysis is the measure of the closeness of the relationship between the criterion and predictor variables. The coefficient of correlation and its square, the **coefficient of multiple determination,** are used for this purpose. In multiple regression, there are similar coefficients for the identical purpose.

The **coefficient of multiple correlation** is formally denoted by $R_{Y.123}$, where the primary subscript identifies the criterion variable and the secondary subscripts identify the predictor variables. When the variables entering into the relationship are obvious, the abbreviated form, R, is used. The coefficient of multiple determination is denoted formally by $R_{Y.123}{}^2$ and informally by R^2. It represents the proportion of variation in the criterion variable that is accounted for by the covariation in the predictor variables. In the investigation of the relationship between sales and television spots and number of sales representatives, $R_{Y.12}{}^2 = 0.874$. This means that 87.4 percent of the variation in sales is associated with variation in television spots and number of sales representatives. The introduction of the number of sales representatives has improved the fit of the regression line; 87.4 percent of the variation in sales is accounted for by the two-predictor variable model, whereas only 77.5 percent was accounted for by the one-predictor model. The square root of this quantity, $R_{Y.12} = 0.935$, is the coefficient of multiple correlation. It is always expressed as a positive number.

Coefficients of Partial Correlation

There are two additional quantities to consider when interpreting the results of a multiple-regression analysis that were not present in simple regression analysis: the coefficient of partial correlation and its square, the *coefficient of partial determination.*

Recall that in the simple regression analysis relating sales Y to television spots X_1 the coefficient of simple determination could be written

$$r_{Y.1}{}^2 = 1 - \frac{\text{unexplained variation}}{\text{total variation}}$$

and recall also that the unexplained variation was given by the square of standard error of estimate, $s_{Y.1}{}^2$, since the standard error of estimate measures the variation in the criterion variable that was unaccounted for by the predictor variable X_1. Total variation, of course, was given by the variation in the criterion variable $s_Y{}^2$. Thus,

$$r_{Y.1}{}^2 = 1 - \frac{s_{Y.1}{}^2}{s_Y{}^2}$$

Coefficient of multiple determination

In multiple-regression analysis, the proportion of variation in the criterion variable that is accounted for by the covariation in the predictor variables.

Coefficient of multiple correlation

In multiple-regression analysis, the square root of the coefficient of multiple determination.

The last term in this formula is the ratio of the variation remaining in the criterion variable, after taking account of the predictor variable X_1, to the total variation in the criterion variable. It measures the relative degree to which the association between the two variables can be used to provide information about the criterion variable.

Now consider the multiple-regression case with two predictor variables, X_1 and X_2. Denote the standard error of estimate by $s_{Y.12}$ and its square by $s_{Y.12}{}^2$. The standard error of estimate measures the variation still remaining in the criterion variable Y after the two predictor variables X_1 and X_2 have been taken into account. Since $s_{Y.1}{}^2$ measures the variation in the criterion variable that remains after the first predictor variable has been taken into account, the ratio $s_{Y.12}{}^2/s_{Y.1}{}^2$ can be interpreted as measuring the relative degree to which the association among the three variables Y, X_1, and X_2 provides information about Y over and above that provided by the association between the criterion variable and the first predictor variable, X_1, alone. In other words, the ratio $s_{Y.12}{}^2/s_{Y.1}{}^2$ measures the *relative degree* to which X_2 adds to the knowledge about Y after X_1 has already been fully utilized. The ratio is the basis for the **coefficient of partial determination,** which in the sales (Y) versus television spots (X_1) and number of sales representatives (X_2) example is

$$r_{Y2.1}{}^2 = 1 - \frac{s_{Y.12}{}^2}{s_{Y.1}{}^2} = 1 - \frac{(45.2)^2}{(59.6)^2} = 1 - 0.576 = 0.424$$

This means that 42.4 percent of the variation in sales that is not associated with television spots is incrementally associated with the number of sales representatives. Alternatively, the errors made in estimating sales from television spots are, as measured by the variance, reduced by 42.4 percent when the number of sales representatives X_2 is added to X_1 as an additional predictor variable. The square root of the coefficient of partial determination is the **coefficient of partial correlation.**

In our example there were two predictors. Thus, we defined the coefficient of partial determination for the number of sales representatives X_2 as $r_{Y2.1}{}^2$. We could have similarly defined a coefficient of partial determination for television spots. It would be denoted as $r_{Y1.2}{}^2$, and it would represent the percentage of the variation in sales not associated with X_2 that is incrementally associated with X_1; this latter coefficient would show the incremental contribution of X_1 after the association between Y and X_2 had already been considered.

When there are more than two predictors, we could define many more coefficients of partial determination. Each would have two primary subscripts indicating the criterion variable and the newly added predictor variable. There could be a great many secondary subscripts, as they always indicate which predictor variables have already been considered. Hence, if we had three predictor variables, we could calculate $r_{Y2.1}$, $r_{Y3.1}$, $r_{Y1.2}$, $r_{Y3.2}$, $r_{Y1.3}$, and $r_{Y2.3}$. These would all be first-order partial-correlation coefficients since they have one secondary subscript indicating that one other predictor variable is taken into account. We could also calculate $r_{Y1.23}$, $r_{Y2.13}$, and $r_{Y3.12}$. These are all *second-order* partial-correlation coefficients. Each has two secondary subscripts indicating that the incremental contribution of the variable is being considered after two other predictor variables have already been taken into account. Simple correlation coefficients, of course, have no secondary coefficients; they are, therefore, often referred to as *zero-order* partial-correlation coefficients.

Dummy Variables

The analysis of the sales data of Exhibit 21.1 is still not complete. No attention has yet been given to the effect of distribution on sales, particularly as measured by the wholesaler efficiency index. One way of considering the effect of wholesaler efficiency on sales would be to introduce the index directly; that is, the X_3 value for each observation would simply be the value recorded in the last column of Exhibit 21.1. Letting X_3 represent the wholesaler efficiency index, the multiple-regression equation, using the informal notation scheme, would be

$$Y = \alpha + \beta_1 X_1 + \beta_2 X_2 + \beta_3 X_3 + \epsilon$$

Coefficient of partial determination

A quantity resulting from a multiple-regression analysis that indicates the proportion of variation in the criterion variable that is not accounted for by an earlier variable or variables and that is accounted for by the addition of a new variable into the regression equation.

Coefficient of partial correlation

In multiple-regression analysis, the square root of the coefficient of partial determination.

The least-squares estimate of β_3 in this equation turns out to be $\hat{\beta}_3 = 11.5$. Note what this number implies if the predictor variables are independent. It means that the estimated average change in sales is $11,500 for each unit change in the wholesaler efficiency index. This means that a fair distributor could be expected to sell $11,500 more on the average than a poor one; a good one could be expected to average $11,500 more than a fair one; and an excellent one could be expected to sell $11,500 more on the average than a good one. The sales increments are assumed constant for each change in wholesaler rating. The implication is that the wholesaler efficiency index is an intervally scaled variable and that the difference between a poor and a fair wholesaler is the same as the difference between a fair and a good one. This is a questionable assumption with an index that reflects ratings.

An alternative way of proceeding would be to convert the index into a set of **dummy variables** or, more appropriately, **binary variables.** A binary variable is one that takes on one of two values, 0 (zero) or 1. Thus, it can be represented by a single binary digit. Binary variables are used mainly because of the flexibility one has in defining them. They can provide a numerical representation for attributes or characteristics that are not essentially quantitative. For example, one could introduce sex into a regression equation using the dummy variable X_i, where

$$X_i = 0 \qquad \text{if the person is a female}$$
$$X_i = 1 \qquad \text{if the person is a male}$$

Dummy (or binary) variable
A variable that is given one of two values, 0 or 1, and that is used to provide a numerical representation for attributes or characteristics that are not essentially quantitative.

The technique is readily extended to handle multichotomous as well as dichotomous classifications. For instance, suppose one wanted to introduce the variable social class into a regression equation, and suppose there were three distinct class levels: upper class, middle class, and lower class. This could be handled using two dummy variables, say X_1 and X_2, as follows:

	X_1	X_2
• If a person belongs to the upper class	1	0
• If a person belongs to the middle class	0	1
• If a person belongs to the lower class	0	0

There are several other logically equivalent coding schemes—for example, the following:

	X_1	X_2
• If a person belongs to the upper class	0	0
• If a person belongs to the middle class	1	0
• If a person belongs to the lower class	0	1

It is therefore most important that the analyst interpreting the output from a regression run employing dummy variables pay close attention to the coding of the variables. It should be clear that an m category classification is capable of unambiguous representation by a set of $m - 1$ binary variables and that an mth binary would be entirely superfluous. As a matter of fact, the use of m variables to code an m-way classification variable would render most regression programs inoperative.

Suppose that we were to employ three dummy variables to represent the four-category wholesaler efficiency index in the Click ballpoint pen example as follows:

	X_3	X_4	X_5
• If a wholesaler is poor	0	0	0
• If a wholesaler is fair	1	0	0
• If a wholesaler is good	0	1	0
• If a wholesaler is excellent	0	0	1

The regression model is

$$Y = \alpha + \beta_1 X_1 + \beta_2 X_2 + \beta_3 X_3 + \beta_4 X_4 + \beta_5 X_5 + \epsilon$$

The least-squares estimates of the wholesaler efficiency parameters are as follows:

$$\hat{\beta}_3 = 9.2$$
$$\hat{\beta}_4 = 20.3$$
$$\hat{\beta}_5 = 33.3$$

These coefficients indicate that on the average a fair wholesaler could be expected to sell $9,200 more than a poor one; a good wholesaler could be expected to sell $20,300 more than a poor one; and an excellent wholesaler, $33,300 more than a poor one. Note that all these coefficients are interpreted with respect to the "null" state, that is, with respect to the classification for which all the dummy variables are defined to be zero—the classification "poor" in this case.[12]

The analyst wishing to determine the difference in sales effectiveness between other classifications must look at coefficient differences. Thus, if the researcher wanted to calculate the estimated difference in expected sales from a good wholesaler and a fair wholesaler, the appropriate difference would be $\hat{\beta}_4 - \hat{\beta}_3 = 20.3 - 9.2 = 11.1$ thousand dollars ($11,100). Similarly, an excellent wholesaler could be expected on the average to sell $\hat{\beta}_5 - \hat{\beta}_4 = 33.3 - 20.3 = 13.0$ thousand dollars ($13,000) more than a good one.

The use of dummy variables indicates that the relationship between sales and the wholesaler efficiency index is not linear as was assumed when the index was introduced as an intervally scaled variable. Instead of an across-the-board increase of $11,500 with each rating change, the respective increases are 9.2 ($9,200) from poor to fair, 11.1 ($11,100) from fair to good, and 13.0 ($13,000) from good to excellent.

Variable Transformations

The use of dummy variables greatly expands the scope of the regression model. They allow the introduction of classificatory and nominally scaled variables in regression problems. As we have seen, they also allow nonlinear criterion variable/predictor variable relationships to be dealt with. Another technique that expands the obvious scope of the regression model is that of variable transformations.

Variable transformation
A change in the scale in which a variable is expressed.

A **variable transformation** is simply a change in the scale in which the given variable is expressed. Consider the model

$$Y = \alpha Y_1^{\beta_1} X_2^{\beta_2} X_3^{\beta_3} \epsilon$$

in which the relationship among the predictors and between the predictors and the error is assumed to be multiplicative. At first glance, it would seem that it would be impossible to estimate the parameters α, β_1, β_2, and β_3 using our normal least-squares procedures. Now consider the model

$$W = \alpha' + \beta_1 Z_1 + \beta_2 Z_2 + \beta_3 Z_3 + \epsilon'$$

This is a linear model, and so it can be fitted by the standard least-squares procedures. But consider the fact that it is exactly equivalent to our multiplicative model if we simply let

$$W = \ln Y \qquad\qquad Z_2 = \ln X_2$$
$$\alpha' = \ln \alpha \qquad\qquad Z_3 = \ln X_3$$
$$Z_1 = \ln X_1 \qquad\qquad \epsilon' = \ln \epsilon$$

Sarah was absolutely convinced that there was a relationship between the firm's product sales to a household and the household's total disposable personal income. She was consequently very disappointed when her first pass through the diary panel data that she had convinced her superior to purchase revealed virtually no relationship between household purchases of the product and household income in the simple regression of one on the other. A series of additional passes in which a variety of transformations were tried proved equally disappointing. Finally, Sarah decided to break the income variable into classes through a series of dummy variables. When she regressed household purchases of the product against the income categories, she found a very irregular but strong relationship as measured by R^2. Purchases rose as income increased up to $24,999, then decreased as

income went from $25,000 to $59,999, increased again for income between $60,000 and $104,999, and seemed to be unaffected by incomes greater than $105,000.

- How would you evaluate Sarah's approach?

- Do you think it is good procedure to continue searching data for support for a hypothesis that you absolutely believe is true, or would you recommend a single pass through the data with the procedure that a priori you thought was best?

- What are Sarah's ethical responsibilities when reporting the results of her analysis? Is she obliged to discuss all the analyses she ran, or is it satisfactory for her to report only the results of the dummy variable regression?

We have converted a nonlinear model to a linear model using variable transformations. To solve for the parameters of our multiplicative model, we simply (1) take the natural log of Y and each of the X's, (2) solve the resulting equations by the normal least-squares procedures, (3) take the antilog of α' to derive an estimate of α, and (4) read the values of the β_i since they are the same in both models.

The transformation to natural logarithms involves the transformation of both the criterion and predictor variables. It is also possible to change the scale of either the criterion or predictor variables. Transformations to the exponential and logarithmic are some of the most useful since they serve to relax the constraints imposed by the following assumptions:[13]

- The relationship between the criterion variable and the predictor variables is additive

- The relationship between the criterion variable and the predictor variables is linear

- The errors are *homoscedastic* (i.e., are equal to a constant for all values of the predictors)

Dummy variables are one form of transformation, and we have already seen how they allow the treatment of nonlinear relationships.

Summary Comments on Data Analysis

We have now come to the end of our section on data analysis. As we have seen, there are many sophisticated techniques analysts use to determine the meaning of collected data. Although the computer has made data analysis much easier and has provided researchers with many more opportunities for examining various facts of the data, we would be remiss if we did not close this chapter on a note of caution.

That caution is to incorporate good sense and business judgment when making any marketing decision. Doing so can prevent many errors, such as the one made by a commercial bank that was trying to increase the income generated by its branches. The bank decided it would expand by adding to its line of financial products and services. It invested in extensive marketing research to determine which of the many possibilities to offer. Armed with statistically significant data, the bank launched its new services—and they were a flop. Only then did management think to ask customers to define what they wanted from a bank branch. "That's easy," customers replied. "We don't want to stand in line." The bank finally realized it would improve performance not by adding to its product mix, but by making the branches more convenient.[14] The original data had been analyzed carefully, but the researchers had asked the wrong questions.

Similarly, in Research Window 21.3 a well-known writer of the pre-computer era points out the hazards inherent in forecasting the future based on data collected in the past. For those of you who will be researchers, or even simply users of data, equations and statistical techniques will be important, but no more important than a heavy dose of common sense.

Life on the Mississippi—742 Years from Now

Mark Twain may not have been a statistician, but he knew enough about the tricks numbers can play to write this little spoof for those who would predict "logical" outcomes based on past data.

"In the space of one hundred and seventy-six years the Lower Mississippi has shortened itself two hundred and forty-two miles. This is an average of a trifle over one mile and a third per year. Therefore, any calm person, who is not blind or idiotic, can see that in the Old Oölitic Silurian Period, just a million years ago next November, the Lower Mississippi River was upward of one million three hundred thousand miles long, and stuck out over the Gulf of Mexico like a fishing-rod. And by the same token any person can see that seven hundred and forty-two years from now the Lower Mississippi will be only a mile and three-quarters long, and Cairo and New Orleans will have joined their streets together, and be plodding comfortably along under a single mayor and a mutual board of aldermen. There is something fascinating about science. One gets such wholesale returns of conjecture out of such a trifling investment of fact."

Source: From *Life on the Mississippi*, p. 156, by Mark Twain.

Mark Twain knew about the tricks numbers can play.

Source: UPI/Bettmann

Back to the Case

"The fact that white-collar men have a more favorable attitude about shopping through the Lovelace catalog is incredibly useful," said Angela Spaulding, "but there were other things I was interested in, too. For example, what's the breakdown of married versus nonmarried men? What about how long they've been employed?"

"If you've got the stomach for some more tables, I've got the answers," declared Michael Wyse.

"Go ahead," replied Spaulding.

"Okay, you asked about marital status and years worked. Well, we used a multiple-regression analysis to determine if the ATTLOVE index was related to those demographic characteristics.

"Since marital status can be broken into a variety of categories, we had to convert the categories into four dummy variables. Take a look at this table," he continued, handing Spaulding Exhibit C.

"Once again, we determined that the overall regression equation was statistically significant. Further, we discovered that the variables, taken together, account for 93 percent of the variation in the ATTLOVE index, as you can see from the adjusted R-squared value of .931," Wyse said.

"These results are particularly interesting, since they give us a chance to see the values for each of the categories of marital status, as they are keyed to the dummy variables. Look at this list," Wyse said, handing a small table to Spaulding. (See Exhibit D on page 630.)

"If we consider single people as the null state, we can see that marriage—even if it ends in divorce or the wife's death—seems to predispose men toward buying from Lovelace. Look at the $D2$ value, for example. It shows that there is an increase in the ATTLOVE index of 2.85 on average if the man is married rather than single," Wyse said.

"What if I want to know the difference between married men and divorced men?" asked Spaulding.

"Easy," replied Wyse. "Just subtract one from the other. Divorced men have an ATTLOVE index approximately 4.16 higher on average than married men, since $D4$ minus $D2$ equals 4.155."

"This is great stuff, Michael," exclaimed Spaulding. "Now all I need to do is figure out the best way to get my hands on a huge list of divorced white-collar men, and I'll be all set!"

EXHIBIT C Multiple-Regression Analysis of ATTLOVE Index versus Several Demographic Characteristics

Dependent variable . . . ATTLOVE
Variable(s) entered on step number 1: $D2$
$V41$
$V42$
$D5$
$D4$
$D3$

		Analysis of Variance	DF	Sum of Squares	Mean Square	F
Multiple R	.967	Regression	6	5042.459	840.410	277.036
R-squared	.934	Residual	117	354.928	3.034	
Adjusted R-squared	.931					
Standard error	1.742					

VARIABLES IN THE EQUATION

Variable	B	Beta	Standard Error B	F
$D2$	2.851	.165	.627	20.668
$V41$	3.753	.283	.600	39.081
$V42$	.213	.368	.029	55.626
$D5$	7.577	.550	.935	65.625
$D4$	7.006	.391	.948	54.618
$D3$	4.387	.267	.646	46.076
(Constant)	4.491			

EXHIBIT D	Relationship between ATTLOVE Index and Respondents' Marital Status When Converted to Dummy Variables

$D2 = 2.851$
$D3 = 4.387$
$D4 = 7.006$
$D5 = 7.577$
where the various D's are defined thus:

V43 =	Implying	D2	D3	D4	D5
1	Single	0	0	0	0
2	Married	1	0	0	0
3	Separated	0	1	0	0
4	Divorced	0	0	1	0
5	Widowed	0	0	0	1

Summary

Learning Objective 1

Explain the difference between regression and correlation analysis.

Analysts use correlation analysis to measure the *closeness* of the relationship between two or more variables. The technique considers the joint variation of two measures, neither of which is restricted by the experimenter.

Regression analysis refers to the techniques used to derive an *equation* that relates the criterion variable to one or more predictor variables. It considers the frequency distribution of the criterion variable when one or more predictor variables are held fixed at various levels.

Learning Objective 2

List the three assumptions that are made about the error term in the least-squares solution to a regression problem.

There are three simplifying assumptions made about the error term in the least-squares solution:
1. The mean or average value of the error term is zero.
2. The variance of the error term is constant and is independent of the values of the predictor variable.
3. The values of the error term are independent of one another.

Learning Objective 3

Discuss what the Gauss-Markov theorem says about the least-squares estimators of a population parameter.

According the Gauss-Markov theorem, the least-squares estimators are BLUE, that is, they are the *best linear unbiased estimators* of the true population parameters regardless of the shape of the distribution of the error term.

Learning Objective 4

Define standard error of estimate.

The standard error of estimate is an absolute measure of the lack of fit of the equation to the data.

Learning Objective 5

Specify the relationship that a correlation coefficient is designed to measure.

A correlation coefficient measures the strength of the linear relationship between Y and X.

Learning Objective 6

Discuss the difference between simple regression analysis and multiple-regression analysis.

The basic idea behind multiple-regression analysis is the same as that behind simple regression: to determine the relationship between independent and dependent, that is, predictor and criterion, variables. In multiple-regression analysis, however, several predictor variables are used to estimate a single criterion variable.

Learning Objective 7

Explain what is meant by multicollinearity in a multiple-regression problem.

Multicollinearity is said to be present in a multiple-regression problem when the predictor variables are correlated among themselves.

Learning Objective 8

Describe when a partial-regression coefficient is used and what it measures.

If the predictor variables are not correlated among themselves, each partial-regression coefficient indicates the average change in the criterion variable per unit change in the predictor variable in question, holding the other predictor variables constant.

Learning Objective 9

Explain the difference between the coefficient of multiple determination and the coefficient of partial determination.

The coefficient of multiple determination measures the proportion of the variation in the criterion variable accounted for, or "explained," by all the predictor variables, while the coefficient of partial determination measures the relative degree to which a given variable adds to our knowledge of the criterion variable over and above that provided by other predictor variables.

Learning Objective 10

Describe how the use of dummy variables and variable transformation expands the scope of the regression model.

Dummy, or binary, variables allow the introduction of classificatory or nominally scaled variables in the regression equation, while variable transformations considerably increase the scope of the regression model, since they allow certain nonlinear relationships to be considered.

Review Questions

1. What is the basic nature of the distinction between tests for group differences and tests to investigate association?

2. What is the difference between regression analysis and correlation analysis?

3. What is the difference between a deterministic model and a probabilistic model? Which type of model underlies regression analysis? Explain.

4. What assumptions are made about the error term in the least-squares solution to the regression problem? What is the effect of the assumption; that is, what is the Gauss-Markov theorem? When the analyst wishes to make an inference about a regression population parameter, what additional assumption is necessary?

5. What is the standard error of estimate?

6. Suppose that an analyst wished to make an inference about the slope coefficient in a regression model. What is the appropriate procedure? What does it mean if the null hypothesis is rejected? If it is not rejected?

7. What is the correlation coefficient, and what does it measure? What is the coefficient of determination, and what does it measure?

8. What is a coefficient of partial or net regression, and what does it measure? What condition must occur for the usual interpretation to apply? What happens if this condition is not satisfied?

9. What is the coefficient of multiple determination?

10. What is a coefficient of partial determination? What does it measure?

11. What is a dummy variable? When is it used? How is it interpreted?

12. What is a variable transformation? Why is it employed?

Discussion Questions, Problems, and Projects

1. The chancellor of Enormous State University has decided that ESU needs to develop a new marketing plan in order to attract the best students. The objective is to attract students who will have the best chance of graduating within four years of their matriculation. The administration has assigned you, the associate vice-chancellor, the responsibility for carrying out this project. You have decided that, as part of the research to be performed in designing the new marketing plan, it would be helpful to know what, if any, characteristics possessed by high school seniors are associated with success in college. After devoting some thought to the problem, you decide that a multiple-regression approach seems to be the way to proceed. Your task is simplified by the existence of a large, comprehensive database that contains the results of several broad-based surveys of high school seniors, many of whom later attended ESU. However, you know that simply mining the database is not likely to be much help. Accordingly, your first task is to develop a theory of why students succeed in college. After explaining your theory, specify the criterion variable and predictor variables that you will use in the regression equation. How serious a problem is multicollinearity in the data likely to be, given your objective?

2. The Crystallo Bottling Company, which provides glass bottles to various soft drink manufacturers, has the following information pertaining to the number of cases per shipment and the corresponding transportation costs:

Number of Cases per Shipment	Transportation Costs in Dollars
1,500	200
2,200	260
3,500	310
4,300	360
5,800	420
6,500	480
7,300	540
8,200	630
8,500	710
9,800	730

The marketing manager is interested in studying the relationship between the number of cases per shipment and the transportation costs. Your assistance is required in performing a simple regression analysis.

(a) Plot the transportation costs as a function of the number of cases per shipment.
(b) Interpret the scatter diagram.
(c) Calculate the coefficients $\hat{\alpha}$ and $\hat{\beta}$ and develop the regression equation.
(d) What is the interpretation of the coefficients $\hat{\alpha}$ and $\hat{\beta}$?
(e) Calculate the standard error of estimate.
(f) What is the interpretation of the standard error of estimate you calculated?
(g) Compare the t value with $n - 2$ degrees of freedom with the use of the following formula for the square root of the variance of the distribution of β's

$$ s_{\hat{\beta}} = \sqrt{\frac{s_{Y/X}^2}{\sum_{i=1}^{10}(X_i - \overline{X})^2}} $$

$$ t = \frac{\hat{\beta}_1 - \beta_1}{s_{\hat{\beta}}} $$

where β is assumed to be zero under the null hypothesis of no relationship; that is,

$$ H_0: \beta_1 = 0 $$
$$ H_a: \beta_1 \neq 0 $$

(h) What is the tabled t value at a 0.05 significance level?
(i) What can you conclude about the relationship between transportation costs and number of cases shipped?

3. Refer to the previous question for information on the transportation costs per shipment.

(a) Calculate the correlation coefficient.
(b) Interpret the correlation coefficient.
(c) Calculate the coefficient of determination.
(d) Interpret the coefficient of determination.

4. The marketing manager of Crystallo Bottling Company is considering multiple-regression analysis with the number of cartons per shipment and the size of cartons as predictor variables and transportation costs as the criterion variable (refer to the previous problem). He has devised the following regression equation:

$$ \hat{Y} = \hat{\alpha}_{(12)} + \hat{\beta}_{Y1.2}X_1 + \hat{\beta}_{Y2.1}X_2 = -41.44 - 3.95\,X_1 + 24.44X_2 $$

where X_1 is the number of cartons per shipment and X_2 is the size of the cartons.

(a) Interpret $\hat{\alpha}_{(12)}$, $\hat{\beta}_{Y1.2}$, and $\hat{\beta}_{Y2.1}$.
(b) Is multiple regression appropriate in this situation? If yes, why? If no, why not?

5. An analyst for a large shoe manufacturer developed a formal linear regression model to predict sales of its 122 retail stores located in different MSAs (Metropolitan Statistical Areas) in the United States. The model was as follows:

$$Y_{(123)} = \alpha_{(123)} + \beta_{1.23}X_1 + \beta_{2.13}X_2 + \beta_{3.12}X_3$$

where

X_1 = population in surrounding area in thousands
X_2 = marginal propensity to consume
X_3 = median personal income in surrounding area in thousands of dollars
Y = sales in thousands of dollars

Some empirical results were as follows:

Variable	Regression Coefficient	Coefficient Standard Errors ($s_{\beta i}$)
X_1	$\hat{\beta}_{1.23} = 0.49$	0.24
X_2	$\hat{\beta}_{2.13} = -0.40$	95
X_3	$\hat{\beta}_{3.12} = 225$	105
$R^2 = 0.47$	$\hat{\alpha} = -40$	225

(a) Interpret each of the regression coefficients.
(b) Are X_1, X_2, and X_3 significant at the 0.05 level? Show your calculations.
(c) Which independent variable seems to be the most significant predictor?
(d) Provide an interpretation of the R^2 value.
(e) The marketing research department of the shoe manufacturer wants to include an index that indicates whether the service in each store is poor, fair, or good. The coding scheme is as follows:

$$1 = \text{poor service}$$
$$2 = \text{fair service}$$
$$3 = \text{good service}$$

(1) Indicate how you would transform this index so that it could be included in the model. Be specific.
(2) Write out the regression model, including the preceding information.
(3) Suppose two of the parameters for the index are 4.6 and 10.3. Interpret these values in light of the scheme you adopted.

6. A survey was commissioned by Beyond the Blue Horizon (BBH) Travel Agency to help the agency better target its promotional efforts. BBH specializes in cruise ship tours that typically cost between $7,000 and $8,000 per couple. One objective of the research project is to predict the amount of money that couples spend on a vacation package, based on several socioeconomic characteristics (e.g., income level). BBH's rational is that if such a relationship can be discovered, the agency can buy mailing lists designed to cover individuals that have the desired socioeconomic profile. One part of the survey asked respondents to indicate their type of employment. Given the following categories, respondents were asked to check the one category that best described their job or profession.

Attorney	Physician
Business Management	Accountant
Dentist	University Faculty
Sales	Other

(a) Develop a coding scheme that will allow the employment variable to be introduced into a multiple-regression equation.

(b) Assume that the analyst wishes to run a regression model that includes only the employment data. Write the regression model.

7. (a) List the assumptions underlying regression analysis.
   (b) List the possible limitations of regression analysis.
   (c) Identify one important practical application of regression analysis for a marketing manager.

 Refer to the NFO Research, Inc., coffee study described on pages 621–624 in Chapter 19 for the next three problems.

8. Use simple linear regression to investigate the association between the predictor variable age (as a continuous variable) and the criterion variable "value" index score composed of the following attributes from Question 6 for Folgers: good value for the money, economy brand, costs less than other brands.

9. Repeat the previous analysis using dummy codes for age in the following categories:

> 35 years or less
> 36–45 years
> 46–59 years
> 60 years or more

Compare these results with those obtained previously.

10. Investigate the association between the "taste" index score for Yuban and the use (or nonuse) of the various additives from Question 3 using multiple regression. The "taste" index will serve as the dependent variable and is composed of the following items from Question 6: rich taste, always fresh, full-bodied taste, smooth taste, not bitter, has no aftertaste.

Endnotes

1. Denise Power, "Kmart Puts Weather to Work in Planning," *Executive Technology* (May 1999), p. 9.

2. Although the regression model theoretically applies to fixed levels of the predictor variables (X's), it can also be shown to apply when the X's themselves are random variables, assuming certain conditions are satisfied. See John Neter, Michael H. Kutner, and William Wasserman, *Applied Linear Regression Models*, 2d ed. (Burr Ridge, Ill.: Irwin/McGraw Hill, 1996), pp. 84–85; Thomas H. Wonnacott and Ronald J. Wonnacott, *Regression: A Second Course in Statistics* (Malabar, Fla.: Robert E. Krieger Publishing Co., 1986), pp. 48–50.

3. See the classic little book by Darrell Huff, *How to Lie with Statistics* (New York: Norton, 1954), pp. 87–99, for a discussion of this point using some rather humorous anecdotes.

4. "Consumers Hit Back at ATM Surcharges," *San Jose Mercury News* (August 3, 1999, downloaded from Mercury Center Web site, www.mercurycenter.com, August 4, 1999).

5. Strictly speaking, the regression model requires that errors of measurement be associated only with the criterion variable and that the predictor variables be measured without error. See Wonnacott and Wonnacott, *Regression*, pp. 293–299, for a discussion of the problems and solutions when the predictor variables also have an error component.

6. For those who would like to try solving for each of these values, the formulas are

$$\hat{\alpha} = \hat{y} - \hat{\beta}\bar{x},$$

$$\hat{\beta} = \frac{n\sum_{i=1}^{n} X_i Y_i - \left(\sum_{i=1}^{n} X_i\right)\left(\sum_{i=1}^{n} Y_i\right)}{n\sum_{i=1}^{n} X_i^2 - \left(\sum_{i=1}^{n} X_i\right)^2}$$

where

$$\bar{y} = \sum_{i=1}^{n} \frac{Y_i}{n} \text{ and } \bar{x} = \sum_{i=1}^{n} \frac{X_i}{n}.$$

7. Many of the results contained in the discussion were determined by computer and thus may differ slightly from those generated using hand calculations because of the rounding errors associated with the latter method.

8. This assumption will be modified shortly to that of normally distributed errors. It is made this way now in order to make more vivid the fact that the assumption of normally distributed errors is only necessary if statistical inferences are to be made about the coefficients.

9. M. G. Kendall, *A Course in Multivariate Analysis* (London: Charles Griffin, 1957), p. 74. See also Douglas C. Montgomery and Elizabeth A. Peck, *Introduction to Linear Regression Analysis,* 2d ed. (New York: Wiley, 1992); Thomas P. Ryan, *Modern Regression Methods* (New York: Wiley, 1996).

10. There are some things that the analyst faced with multicollinear data can do. See R. R. Hocking, "Developments in Linear Regression Methodology: 1959–1982," *Technometrics* 25 (August 1983), pp. 219–230, and Ronald D. Snee, "Discussion," *Technometrics* 25 (August 1983), pp. 230–237, for a discussion of the problem and some alternative ways of handling it. See also Charlotte H. Mason and William D. Perreault, Jr., "Collinearity, Power and Interpretation of Multiple Regression Analysis," *Journal of Marketing Research* 28 (August 1991), pp. 268–280; R. Carter Hill, Phillip A. Cartwright, and Julia F. Arbaugh, "The Use of Biased Predictors in Marketing Research," *International Journal of Forecasting* 7 (November 1991), pp. 271–282; Peter Kennedy, *A Guide to Econometrics,* 3rd ed. (Cambridge, Mass.: The MIT Press, 1992), pp. 176–187; Geore C. S. Wang, "How to Handle Multicollinearity in Regression Modeling," *Journal of Business Forecasting* 15 (Spring 1996), pp. 23–27.

11. There is another interpretation danger in the example that was not discussed. It is not unreasonable to assume that both the number of sales representatives serving a territory and the number of television spots per month were both determined on the basis of territorial potential. If this is the case, the implied causality is reversed or at least confused; instead of the number of sales representatives and number of television spots determining sales, sales in a sense (potential sales anyway) determine the former qualities, and they in turn could be expected to affect realized sales. If this is actually the case, the coefficient-estimating procedure needs to take into account the two-way "causation" among the variables. See Wonnacott and Wonnacott, *Regression,* pp. 284–292, for a discussion of the problems and the logic underlying the estimation of simultaneous equation systems.

12. For a useful discussion of some alternative ways to code dummy variables and the different insights that can be provided by the various alternatives, see Jacob Cohen and Patricia Cohen, *Applied Multiple Regression/Correlation Analysis for the Behavioral Sciences,* 2d ed., (Mahwah, N.J.: Lawrence Erlbaum, 1983), pp. 181–222; Melissa A. Hardy, *Regression with Dummy Variables* (Thousand Oaks, Calif.: Sage Publications, Inc, 1993).

13. See Ronald E. Frank, "Use of Transformations," *Journal of Marketing Research* 3 (August 1966), pp. 247–253, for a discussion of these conditions and how the proper transformation can serve to fulfill them. See also James G. Mackinnon and Lonnie Magee, "Transforming the Dependent Variable in Regression Models," *International Economic Review* 31 (May 1990), pp. 315–339; Richard A. Johnson and Dean W. Wichern, *Applied Multivariate Statistical Analysis,* 3rd ed. (Englewood Cliffs, N.J.: Prentice-Hall, Inc., 1992).

14. Peter F. Drucker, *Management Challenges for the 21st Century* (New York: HarperBusiness, 1999), p. 81.

Suggested Additional Readings

For a detailed discussion of regression and correlation analysis, see
Jacob Cohen and Patricia Cohen, *Applied Multiple Regression/Correlation Analysis for the Behavioral Sciences,* 2d ed. (Mahwah, N.J.: Lawrence Erlbaum, 1983).
Melissa A. Hardy, *Regression with Dummy Variables* (Thousand Oaks, Calif.: Sage Publications, Inc., 1993).
Thomas P. Ryan, *Modern Regression Methods* (New York: Wiley, 1996).
John Neter, Michael H. Kutner, and William Wasserman, *Applied Linear Regression Models,* 2d ed. (Burr Ridge, Ill.: Irwin, McGraw Hill, 1996).
Thomas H. Wonnacott and Ronald J. Wonnacott, *Regression: A Second Course in Statistics* (Malabar, Fla.: Robert E. Krieger Publishing Co., 1986).

NONPARAMETRIC MEASURES
OF ASSOCIATION

Chapter 21 focused on the product-moment correlation as the measure of association. While the product-moment correlation coefficient was originally developed to deal with continuous variables, it has proven quite robust to scale type and can sometimes handle variables that are ordinal or dichotomous as well as those that are interval.[1] Though widely applicable, it is not universally applicable. This appendix therefore treats some alternate measures of association—namely, the contingency table and coefficient that are appropriate for nominal data and also the Spearman's rank-order correlation coefficient and the coefficient of concordance, which are suited to the analysis of rank-order data.

Contingency Table

One problem researchers often encounter in analyzing nominal data is the independence of variables of classification. In Chapter 19, for example, we examined a number of questions involving the relationship between automobile purchases and family characteristics. At that time, we conducted no statistical tests of significance, thus avoiding the question of whether the results reflected sample aberrations or represented true population conditions. If statistical tests had been run at that time, they would have been primarily of the chi-square contingency-table type, which is ideally suited for investigating the independence of variables in cross classifications.

Consider, for example, a consumer study involving the preferences of families for different sizes of washing machines. A priori, it would seem that larger families would be more prone to buy the larger units and smaller families the smaller units. To investigate this question, suppose the manufacturer checked a random sample of those purchasers who returned their warranty cards. Included on the warranty cards was a question on the size of the family. Although not a perfect population for analysis, the manufacturer felt it was good enough for this purpose since some 85 percent of all warranty cards are returned. Furthermore, it was a relatively economical way to proceed, since the data were internal. The study could be carried out by checking a random sample of warranty cards for family size and machine purchased.

A random sample of 300 of these cards provided the data in Exhibit 21a.1. The assignment is to determine if family size affects the size of the machine that is purchased. The null hypothesis is that the variables are independent; the alternate is that they are not. Suppose a significance level of $\alpha = 0.10$ was chosen for the test. To calculate a χ^2 statistic, one needs to generate the expected number of cases likely to fall into each category. *The expected number is generated by assuming that the null hypothesis is indeed true*—that is, that there is no relationship between size of machine purchased and family size. Suppose size of machine purchased is denoted by the variable A and size of family by the variable B and that

$$A_1 = \text{purchase of an 8-lb. load washing machine}$$
$$A_2 = \text{purchase of an 10-lb. load washing machine}$$
$$A_3 = \text{purchase of an 12-lb. load washing machine}$$
$$B_1 = \text{family of one to two members}$$
$$B_2 = \text{family of three to four members}$$
$$B_3 = \text{family of five or more members}$$

If variables A and B are indeed independent, then the probability of occurrence of the event A_1B_1 (a family of one to two members purchased an 8-lb. load machine) is given as the product of the separate probabilities for A_1 and B_1; that is,

Size of Washing Machine Purchased	SIZE OF FAMILY IN MEMBERS			
	1 to 2	3 to 4	5 or More	Total
8-lb. load	25	37	8	70
10-lb. load	10	62	53	125
12-lb. load	5	41	59	105
Total	40	140	120	300

$$P(A_1B_1) = P(A_1)P(B_1)$$

by the multiplication law of probabilities for independent events. Now $P(A_1)$ is given by the number of cases possessing the characteristic A_1, n_{A1}, over the total number of cases n. $P(A_1)$ is thus

$$\frac{n_{A_1}}{n} = \frac{70}{300} = \frac{7}{30}$$

Similarly, $P(B_1)$ is given by the number of cases having the characteristic B_1, n_{B_1}, over the total number of cases, or $P(B_1)$

$$\frac{n_{B_1}}{n} = \frac{40}{300} = \frac{2}{15}$$

The joint probability $P(A_1B_1)$ is

$$P(A_1B_1) = P(A_1)P(B_1) = \left(\frac{7}{30}\right)\left(\frac{2}{15}\right) = \frac{7}{225}$$

Given a total of 300 cases, the number expected to fall in the cell A_1B_1, E_{11}, is given as the product of the total number of cases and the probability of any one of these cases falling into the A_1B_1 cell; that is,

$$E_{11} = nP(A_1B_1) = 300\left(\frac{7}{225}\right) = 9.33$$

Although this is the underlying rationale for generating the expected frequencies, there is an easier computational form. Recall that $P(A_1) = \dfrac{n_{A_1}}{n}$ and that $P(B_1) = \dfrac{n_{B_1}}{n}$ and that $P(A_1B_1) = P(A_1)P(B_1)$. The formula for E_{11} upon substitution then reduces to

$$E_{11} = nP(A_1B_1) = nP(A_1)P(B_1)$$
$$= n\frac{n_{A_1}}{n}\frac{n_{B_1}}{n} = \frac{n_{A_1}n_{B_1}}{n}$$
$$= \frac{70 \times 40}{300} = 9.33$$

Thus, to generate the expected frequencies for each cell, one needs merely to multiply the marginal frequencies and divide by the total. The remaining expected frequencies, which are calculated in like manner, are entered in the lower right-hand corner of each cell in Exhibit 21a.2. The calculated χ^2 value is thus

EXHIBIT 21a.2   **Size of Washing Machine versus Size of Family: Observed and Expected Frequencies**

SIZE OF FAMILY IN MEMBERS

Size of Washing Machine Purchased	B_1 1 to 2		B_2 3 to 4		B_3 5 or More		Total
A_1—8-lb. load	25		37		8		70
		9.33		32.67		28.00	
A_2—10-lb. load	10		62		53		125
		16.67		58.33		50.00	
A_3—12-lb. load	5		41		59		105
		14.00		49.00		42.00	
Total	40		140		120		300

$$\chi^2 = \sum_{i=1}^{3} \sum_{j=1}^{3} \frac{(O_{ij} - E_{ij})^2}{E_{ij}}$$

$$= \frac{(25 - 9.33)^2}{9.33} + \frac{(37 - 32.67)^2}{32.67} + \frac{(8 - 28.00)^2}{28.00}$$

$$+ \frac{(10 - 16.67)^2}{16.67} + \frac{(62 - 58.33)^2}{58.33} + \frac{(53 - 50.00)^2}{50.00}$$

$$+ \frac{(5 - 14.00)^2}{14.00} + \frac{(41 - 49.00)^2}{49.00} + \frac{(59 - 42.00)^2}{42.00}$$

$$= 26.318 + 0.574 + 14.286 + 2.669 + 0.231 + 0.180 + 5.786 + 1.306 + 6.881$$
$$= 58.231$$

where O_{ij} and E_{ij}, respectively, denote the actual number and expected number of observations that fall in the ij cell. Now the expected frequencies in any row add to the marginal total. This must be true because of the way the expected frequencies were calculated. Thus, as soon as we know any two expected frequencies in a row, say, 9.33 and 32.67 in Row A_1, for example, the third expected frequency is fixed, because the three must add to the marginal total. This means that there are only $(c - 1)$ degrees of freedom in a row, where c is the number of columns. A similar argument applies to the columns; that is, there are $r - 1$ degrees of freedom per column, where r is the number of rows. The degrees of freedom in total in a two-way contingency table are thus given by

$$v = (r - 1)(c - 1)$$

In our problem $v = (3 - 1)(3 - 1) = 4$. Using our assumed $\alpha = 0.10$, the tabled critical value of χ^2 for four degrees of freedom is 7.78 (see Table 2 in the appendix). Computed $\chi^2 = 58.321$ thus falls in the critical region. The null hypothesis of independence is rejected. Family size is shown to be a factor in determining size of washing machine purchased.

In one form or another, the chi-square test is probably the most widely used test in marketing research, and the serious student is well advised to become familiar with its requirements.

Contingency Coefficient

While the χ^2 contingency-table test indicates whether two variables are independent, it does not measure the strength of association when they are dependent. The contingency coefficient can be used for this latter purpose. Since the contingency coefficient is directly related to the χ^2 test, it can be generated by the researcher with relatively little additional computational effort. The formula for the contingency coefficient, call it C, is

$$C = \sqrt{\frac{\chi^2}{n + \chi^2}}$$

where n is the sample size and χ^2 is calculated in the normal way.

Recall that calculated χ^2 for the data in Exhibit 21a.1 was 58.23, and that since the calculated value was larger than the critical tabled value, the null hypothesis of independence was rejected. While the conclusion that naturally follows—that family size affects the size of washing machine purchased—is an interesting finding, it is only part of the story. Although the variables are dependent, what is the strength of the association between them? The contingency coefficient helps answer this question. The contingency coefficient is

$$C = \sqrt{\frac{58.23}{300 + 58.23}} = 0.403$$

Does this value indicate strong or weak association between the variables? We cannot say without comparing the calculated value against its limits. When there is no association between the variables, the contingency coefficient will be zero. Unfortunately though, the contingency coefficient does not possess the other attractive property of the Pearsonian product-moment correlation coefficient of being equal to 1 when the variables are completely dependent or perfectly correlated. Rather, its upper limit is a function of the number of categories. When the number of categories is the same for each variable, that is, when the number of rows r equals the number of columns c, the upper limit on the contingency coefficient for two perfectly correlated variables is

$$\sqrt{(r - 1)/r}$$

In the example at hand, $r = c = 3$, and thus the upper limit for the contingency coefficient is

$$\sqrt{\frac{2}{3}} = 0.816$$

The calculated value is approximately halfway between the limits of zero for no association and 0.816 for perfect association, suggesting there is moderate association between size of family and size of washing machine purchased.

Spearman's Rank-Order Correlation Coefficient

The Spearman correlation coefficient, denoted r_s, is one of the best-known coefficients of association for rank-order data. The coefficient is appropriate when there are two variables per object, both of which are measured on an ordinal scale so that the objects may be ranked in two ordered series.[2]

Suppose, for instance, that a company wishes to determine whether there is any association between the overall performance of a distributor and the distributor's level of service. Again, there are many measures of overall performance: sales, market share, sales growth, profit, and so on. The company in our example feels that no single measure adequately defines distributor performance, but that overall performance is a composite of all these measures. Thus, the marketing research department is assigned the task of developing an index of performance that effectively incorporates all these characteristics. The department is also assigned the responsibility of evaluating each distributor in terms of the service he or she provides. This evaluation is to be based on customer complaints, customer compliments, service turnaround records, and so on. The research department feels that the indices it develops to measure these characteristics could be employed to rank-order the distributors with respect to overall performance and service.

Exhibit 21a.3 contains the ranks of the company's 15 distributors with respect to each of the performance criteria. One way to determine whether there is any association between service and overall performance would be to look at the differences in ranks based on each of the two variables. Let X_i be the rank of the ith distributor with respect to service and Y_i be the rank of the ith distributor with regard to overall performance, and let $d_i = X_i - Y_i$ be the difference in rankings for the ith distributor. Now if the rankings on the two variables are exactly the same, each d_i will be zero. If there is some discrepancy in ranks, some of the d_i's will not be zero. Further, the greater the discrepancy, the larger will be some of the d_i's. Therefore, one way of looking at the association between the variables would be to examine the sum of the d_i's. The difficulty with this measure is that some of the negative d_i's would cancel some of the positive ones. To circumvent this difficulty, the differences are squared in calculating the Spearman rank-order correlation coefficient. The calculation formula is as follows:[3]

$$r_s = 1 - \frac{6 \sum_{i=1}^{n} d_i^2}{n(n^2 - 1)}$$

EXHIBIT 21a.3 **Distributor Performance**

Distributor	Service Ranking X_i	Overall Performance Ranking Y_i	Ranking Difference $D_i = X_i - Y_i$	Difference Squared D_i^2
1	6	8	−2	4
2	2	4	+2	4
3	13	12	+1	1
4	1	2	−1	1
5	7	10	−3	9
6	4	5	−1	1
7	11	9	+2	4
8	15	13	+2	4
9	3	1	+2	4
10	9	6	+3	9
11	12	14	−2	4
12	5	3	+2	4
13	14	15	−1	1
14	8	7	+1	1
15	10	11	−1	1

$$\sum_{i=1}^{15} d_i^2 = 52$$

In the example at hand,

$$\sum_{i=1}^{15} d_i^2 = 52$$

and

$$r_s = 1 - \frac{6(52)}{15(15^2 - 1)} = 1 - \frac{312}{3,360} = 0.907$$

Now the null hypothesis for the example would be that there is no association between service level and overall distributor performance, while the alternate hypothesis would suggest there is a relationship. The null hypothesis that $r_s = 0$ can be tested by referring to tables of critical values of r_s or, when the number of sample objects is greater than 10, by calculating the t statistic

$$t = r_s \sqrt{\frac{n - 2}{1 - r_s^2}}$$

which is referred to a t table for $v = n - 2$ degrees of freedom. Calculated t is

$$t = 0.907 \sqrt{\frac{15 - 2}{1 - (0.907)^2}} = 7.77$$

while critical t for $\alpha = 0.05$ and $v = 13$ degrees of freedom is 2.16. Calculated t exceeds critical t, and the null hypothesis of no relationship is rejected. Overall distributor performance is related to service level. The upper limit for the Spearman rank-order correlation coefficient is 1, since if there were perfect agreement in the ranks, $\sum_{i=1}^{n} d_i^2$ would be zero. Thus the relationship is significant and relatively strong.

Coefficient of Concordance

So far we have been concerned with the correlation between *two* sets of rankings of n objects. There has been an X and Y measure in the form of ranks for each object. There will be cases in which we wish to analyze the association among three or more rankings of n objects or individuals. When there are k sets of rankings, Kendall's *coefficient of concordance,* W, can be employed to examine the association among the k variables.

One particularly important use of the coefficient of concordance is in examining interjudge reliability. Consider a computer equipment manufacturer interested in evaluating its domestic sales branch managers. Many criteria could be used: sales of the branch office, sales in relation to the branch's potential, sales growth, and sales representative turnover are just a few. Assume that the company feels that different executives in the company would place different emphasis on the various criteria and that a consensus with respect to how the criteria should be weighted would be hard to achieve. The company therefore decides that the vice president in charge of marketing, the general sales manager, and the marketing research department should all attempt to rank the ten branch managers from best to worst, and that these rankings will be examined to determine whether there is agreement among them (see Exhibit 21a.4).

The right-hand column of Exhibit 21a.4 contains the sum of ranks assigned to each branch manager. Now if there were perfect agreement among the three rankings, the sum of ranks, R_i, for the top-rated branch manager would be $1 + 1 + 1 = k$, where $k = 3$. The second-rated branch manager would have the sum of ranks $2 + 2 + 2 = 2k$, and the nth-

EXHIBIT 21a.4   Branch Manager Rankings

Branch Manager	RANK ADVOCATED BY Vice-President of Marketing	General Sales Manager	Marketing Research Department	Sum of Ranks R_i
A	4	4	5	13
B	3	2	2	7
C	9	10	10	29
D	10	9	9	28
E	2	3	3	8
F	1	1	1	3
G	6	5	4	15
H	8	7	7	22
I	5	6	6	17
J	7	8	8	23

rated branch manager would have the sum of ranks $n + n + n = nk$. Accordingly, when there is perfect agreement among the k sets of rankings, the R_i would be $k, 2k, 3k, \ldots, nk$. If there is little agreement among the k ratings, the R_i would be approximately equal. Thus, the degree of agreement among the k rankings could be measured by the variance of the n sums of ranks; the greater the agreement, the larger would be the variance in the n sums.

The coefficient of concordance, W, is a function of the variance in the sums of ranks. It is calculated in the following way. First, the sum of the R_i for each of the n rows is determined. Second, the average R_i, $\bar{R}$, is calculated by dividing the sum of the R_i by the number of objects. Third, the sum of the squared deviations is determined; call this quantity s, where

$$s = \sum_{i=1}^{n} (R_i - \bar{R})^2$$

The coefficient of concordance is then computed as

$$W = \frac{s}{\frac{1}{12}k^2(n^3 - n)}$$

The denominator of the coefficient represents the maximum possible variation in sums of ranks if there were perfect agreement in the rankings. The numerator, of course, reflects the actual variation in ranks. The larger the ratio, the greater the agreement among the evaluations. For the example,

$$\bar{R} = \frac{\sum_{i=1}^{n} R_i}{n} = \frac{13 + 7 + \ldots + 23}{10} = \frac{165}{10} = 16.5$$

$$s = (13 - 16.5)^2 + (7 - 16.5)^2 + \ldots + (23 - 16.5)^2 = 720.5$$

and

$$\frac{1}{12}k^2(n^3 - n) = \frac{1}{12}(3)^2(10^3 - 10) = 742.5$$

Thus

$$W = \frac{720.5}{742.5} = 0.970$$

The significance of W can be examined by using special tables when the number of objects ranked is small, in particular, when $n \le 7$. When there are more than seven objects, the coefficient of concordance is approximately chi-square distributed where $\chi^2 = k(n-1)W$ with $v = n - 1$ degrees of freedom. The null hypothesis is that there is no agreement among the rankings, while the alternate hypothesis is that there is some agreement. For an assumed $\alpha = 0.05$, critical χ^2 for $v = n - 1 = 9$ degrees of freedom is 16.92, while calculated χ^2 is

$$\chi^2 = k(n-1)W = 3(9)(0.970) = 26.2$$

Calculated χ^2 exceeds critical χ^2, and the null hypothesis of no agreement is rejected, because there indeed is agreement. Further, the agreement is good, as is evidenced by the calculated coefficient of concordance. The limits of W are zero with no agreement and 1 with perfect agreement among the ranks. The calculated value of W of 0.970 suggests that while the agreement in the ranks is not perfect, it is certainly good. The marketing vice-president, the general sales manager, and the marketing research department are applying essentially the same standards in ranking the branch managers.

Kendall has suggested that the best estimate of the true ranking of n objects is provided by the order of the various sums of ranks, R_i, when W is significant.[4] Thus, the best estimate of the true ranking of the sales managers is that F is doing the best job, B the next best job, and C the poorest job.

Endnotes

1. Jum Nunnally and Ira Bernstein, *Psychometric Theory,* 3rd ed (New York: McGraw-Hill, 1994), especially pp. 114–158. For an empirical comparison of how various correlation coefficients perform with rating scale data, see Emin Babakus and Carl E. Ferguson, Jr., "On Choosing the Appropriate Measure of Association When Analyzing Rating Scale Data," *Journal of the Academy of Marketing Science* 16 (Spring 1988), pp. 95–102.

2. The Spearman rank correlation coefficient is a shortcut version of the product-moment correlation coefficient, in that both coefficients produce the same estimates of the strength of association between two sets of ranks. The rank correlation coefficient is easy to conceptualize and calculate, so it is often used when the data are ranked. See Nunnally and Bernstein, *Psychometric Theory,* pp. 131–132.

3. See Leonard A Marascuilo and Maryellen McSweeney, *Nonparametric and Distribution-Free Methods for the Social Sciences* (Belmont, Calif.: Brooks/Cole, 1977), pp. 250–251. See also Maurice G. Kendall and Jean D. Gibbons, *Rank Correlation Methods,* 5th ed. (New York: Oxford University Press, 1990); Jean D. Gibbons, *Nonparametric Measures of Association* (Thousand Oaks, Calif.: Sage Publications, Inc., 1993).

4. M. G. Kendall, *Rank Correlation Methods* (London: Griffin, 1948), p. 87.

The sixth stage in the research process is to analyze and interpret the data. All the earlier steps in the research process were undertaken to support this search for meaning. Most data analysis begins with the preliminary steps of editing, coding, and tabulating the data. The results are often analyzed further to determine if the differences are statistically significant, or if there is any correlation between the variables.

CARA researchers had begun their study with two objectives:

1. Identify business decision makers' attitudes toward the advertising media of newspaper, radio, and television.

2. Identify business decision makers' attitudes toward the advertising sales representatives of those media.

In analyzing the data collected from the questionnaires, researchers calculated the percentage of respondents who agreed that their sales representatives possessed the attributes listed on the questionnaire and who agreed that the categories of advertising media were characterized by the listed items. They calculated this by determining what proportion of the total number of respondents checked the "strongly agree" or "agree" category for each item.

Business Decision Makers' Attitudes Toward Advertising Media

CARA researchers found that the characteristics of television advertising that garnered the highest percentage of agreement were (1) that the ads reached many people (86 percent), (2) that they built up recognition (80 percent), and (3) that people paid attention (67 percent). The highest categories for radio advertising were (1) that the ads reached many people (73 percent), (2) that they built up recognition (67 percent), and (3) that they were easy to buy (54 percent). Respondents agreed that newspaper ads (1) were easy to monitor (77 percent), (2) built up recognition (70 percent), (3) reached many people (70 percent), and (4) were easy to buy (70 percent). The items on which respondents expressed the lowest percentage of agreement for television advertising were (1) that few repeats were necessary (20 percent), and (2) that the ads were not costly (10 percent). For radio advertising, the items of lowest agreement were (1) that the ads were not costly (34 percent) and (2) that few repeats were necessary (17 percent). For newspaper advertising the lowest categories were (1) that the ads were creative (27 percent) and (2) that few repeats were necessary (27 percent).

Business Decision Makers' Attitudes Toward Advertising Sales Representatives

When analyzing the data, CARA researchers found that 68 percent, 62 percent, and 62 percent of respondents felt their television sales representatives were cooperative, knowledgeable, and available, respectively, and these rep-

resented the items with the highest percentage of agreement in this category. For radio representatives, the highest percentage of agreement was found concerning their cooperation (72 percent), ability to quickly place ads (68 percent), and availability (64 percent). The highest rated items for newspaper representatives were cooperation (73 percent), the ability to place ads quickly (64 percent), and reliability (62 percent). The items with the lowest percent of agreement for television sales representatives were creativity (42 percent), awareness of client's customers (40 percent), and follow-through (37 percent). For radio representatives, the lowest items were follow-through (35 percent), awareness of client's customers (43 percent), and knowledgeability (28 percent). Follow-through, awareness, and knowledgeability were also the lowest items for newspaper representatives, with, respectively, 33 percent, 30 percent, and 29 percent of respondents agreeing.

Importance Scales

A chi-square test of independence was used to test whether respondents differed on the number of times they checked a given attribute or characteristic and to see whether these frequencies differed from the theoretical (expected) frequencies. Comparisons of the observed and expected frequencies for each individual attribute of sales representatives and characteristic of advertising media indicated that no significant differences existed between respondents who were decision makers and respondents who were not. The same type of comparison also revealed no significant differences between respondents who were owners and/or managers and those who were not.

A chi-square goodness-of-fit test was used to assess whether respondents ascribed different values to the attributes and characteristics listed in the sales-representatives and advertising-media sections of the study. Significant differences were found in the observed and expected frequencies of the attributes of sales representatives (see Exhibit 1). Not all attributes were rated equally important. Figure 1 portrays graphically the number of times each attribute was chosen as one of the three most important attributes. The most important attributes were creativity, knowledge about the client's business, concern about particular advertising needs, and an orientation toward results. The least important attributes were sincerity, concern about follow-through, a willingness to work hard, availability, ability to place ads quickly, and cooperation.

Significant differences were also noted when the observed and expected frequencies of the characteristics of advertising media were tested (see Exhibit 2). The hypothesis that each of the characteristics was of equal importance was rejected. Figure 2 displays the observed frequencies associated with each characteristic. The most important characteristics were whether the ads improved sales volume, whether they built recognition of the business, whether they were costly, and whether people paid attention to them. The least important characteristics were whether the ads were of high quality, whether there was evidence that the ads reached a known market, whether they were cre- ative, whether repetition was necessary for effectiveness, whether they were easy to monitor, and whether the ad-buying process was difficult.

EXHIBIT 1	Chi-Square Test: Attributes of Sales Representatives											
Item No.	1	2	3	4	5	6	7	8	9	10	11	12
Observed Frequencies	75	98	28	122	15	8	47	99	17	1	5	23
Expected Frequencies	All cells = 43.83		$df = 1$		$\chi^2 = 444.35$[a]							

[a]Statistically significant, $p < 0.001$.

FIGURE 1 Number of Times an Attribute Was Chosen as One of the Three Most Important

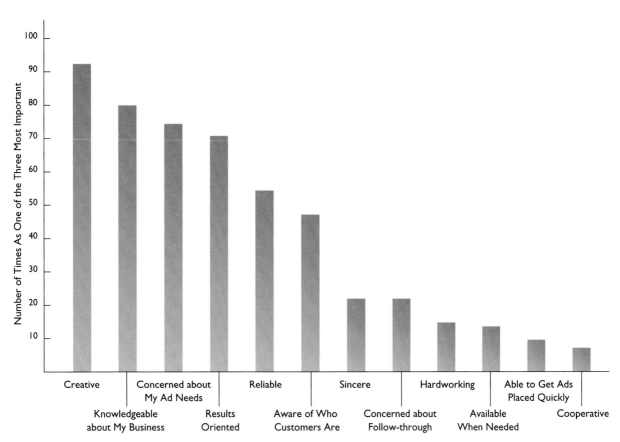

EXHIBIT 2	Chi-Square Test: Characteristics of Advertising											
Item No.	1	2	3	4	5	6	7	8	9	10	11	12
Observed Frequencies	91	54	23	73	80	11	17	18	75	13	48	23
Expected Frequencies	All cells = 43.83		df = 11		$\chi^2 = 222.67$[a]							

[a]Statistically significant, $p < 0.001$.

FIGURE 2	Number of Times a Characteristic Was Chosen as One of the Three Most Important

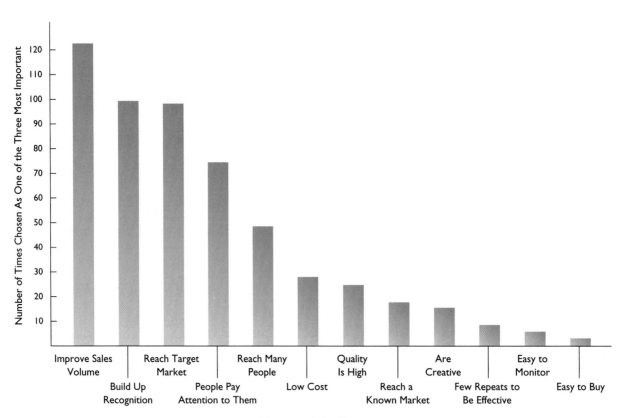

Case VI.A   Wisconsin Power & Light[1] (C)

In response to the current consumer trend towards increased environmental sensitivity, Wisconsin Power & Light (WP&L) adopted several high-visibility environmental initiatives. These environmental programs fell under the BuySmart umbrella of WP&L's Demand-Side Management Programs and were intended to foster the conservation of energy among WP&L's residential, commercial, and industrial customers. Examples of specific programs include: Appliance Rebates, Energy Analysis, Weatherization Help, and the Home Energy Improvement Loan (HEIL) program. All previous marketing research and information gathering focused primarily on issues from the customers' perspective, such as an evaluation of net program impacts in terms of energy and demand savings and an estimation of the levels of free ridership (individuals who would have undertaken the conservation actions promoted by the program, even if there was no program in place). In addition, a study has been designed and is currently being conducted to evaluate and identify customer attitudes and opinions concerning the design, implementation, features, and delivery of the residential programs. Having examined the consumer perspective, WP&L's next objective is to focus on obtaining information from other participants in the programs, namely employees and lenders.

WP&L's immediate research focus is to undertake a study of the Home Energy Improvement Loan (HEIL) program of the BuySmart umbrella. The HEIL program was introduced in 1987 and was designed to make low-interest-rate financing available to residential gas and electric WP&L customers for conservation and weatherization measures. The low-interest guaranteed loans are delivered through WP&L account representatives in conjunction with participating financial institutions and trade allies. The procedures for obtaining a loan begin with an energy "audit" of the interested customer's residence to determine the appropriate conservation measures. Once the customer decides on which measures to have installed, the WP&L representative assists in arranging low-interest-rate financing through one of the participating local banking institutions. At the completion of the projects, WP&L representatives conduct an inspection of the work by checking a random sample of participants. Conservation measures eligible under the HEIL program include the installation of natural gas furnaces/boilers, automatic vent dampers, intermittent ignition devices, heat pumps, and heat pump water heaters. Eligible structural improvements include the addition of attic/wall/basement insulation, storm windows and doors, sillbox insulation, window weather-stripping, and caulking.

[1] The contributions of Kavita Maini and Paul Metz to the development of this case are gratefully acknowledged as is the permission of Wisconsin Power & Light to use the material included.

Purpose

The primary goal of the current study is to identify ways of improving the HEIL program from the lenders' point of view. Specifically, the following issues need to be addressed:

- Identify the lenders' motivation for participating in the program.
- Determine how lenders get their information regarding various changes/updates in the program.
- Identify how lenders promote the program.
- Assess the current program with respect to administrative and program features.
- Determine the type of credit analysis conducted by the lenders.
- Identify ways of minimizing the default rate from the lenders' point of view.
- Assess the lenders' commitment to the program.
- Identify lenders' opinions of the overall program.
- Identify if the reason for loan inactivity in some lending institutions is due to lack of a customer base.

Methodology

WP&L decided to use a telephone survey of participating lending institutions to collect the data for their study. WP&L referenced two lists of lending institutions, which were supplied by their residential marketing staff, in order to select the sample for the survey. A total of 124 participating lending institutions was identified with the lists. However, it was found that one of the lists was shorter than the other by 15 names. Specifically, the names of some of the branches of major banks were not enumerated on one of the lists. Nevertheless, all 124 institutions, including the 15 discrepant ones, were included in the pool of names from which the sample was drawn.

The sample pool was stratified into three groups based on loan activity in the 2000 calendar year. The groups fell out as follows:

Group	Number of Lenders	Loan Activity, 2000
1	44	0 loans
2	40	1 to 7 loans
3	40	8 to 54 loans

The final sample for the survey consisted of 20 systematically chosen lenders from Groups 2 and 3, and 10 randomly chosen institutions from Group 1. The 40 institutions selected from among Groups 2 and 3 formed the sample base in which WP&L was most interested (this was because each of these 40 institutions demonstrated loan activity in the past year). Consequently, WP&L used a systematic selection procedure for this key group in order to ensure that the sample was representative of the population and to improve the statistical efficiency of the sample. The sample size ($n = 40$) was based on judgment. The 10 randomly selected institutions from Group 1 were chosen primarily to explore the hypothesized reasons for zero-loan activity. These 10 zero-loan lenders received a shortened version of the telephone survey that focused only on their lack of activity.

All the districts within WP&L's service territory were notified two weeks in advance that a survey was going to be conducted. A survey was designed to address the research objectives and included both closed- and open-ended questions. The survey was pretested and modified prior to

final administration. All interviewing was conducted over a one-week period by a project manager and research assistant, both employees of WP&L's marketing department.

One of the open-ended questions in the survey asked lenders to identify the benefits gained by participating in the HEIL program. The actual wording of the question follows:

Q.6 Does your bank benefit in any way by participating in this program?
  1 Yes
  2 No

Q.7 Would you please explain your answer?

Data from this question, it was hypothesized, could be used to address several of the aforementioned research objectives. First, the responses would provide qualitative insights into the lenders' motivation for participating in the program. Second, they would help explain lenders' level of commitment to the program as well as help identify rea-

---

EXHIBIT VI.A.1 **Verbatim Responses Regarding the Benefits Conveyed to Lenders by Participation in the HEIL Program**

1. We acquire a new loan customer. The customer likes the fact that the loan is guaranteed.
2. It's good public relations to be associated with WP&L. Also, we have nothing to lose on it. It is a risk-free program.
3. It fulfills the CRA (Credit Reinvestment Act) requirement.
4. We got some new customers. People from other towns cannot get into the HEIL program from their bank.
5. We make some money through the buydown.
6. We have access to more customers and can therefore cross-sell other services. We stay competitive this way. It's also good PR to be associated with WP&L.
7. We provide another service to the customer. It helps us to stay competitive.
8. We improve on customer service by providing an additional service. It helps us stay competitive.
9. We can provide another service. We have also built customer contact a lot more.
10. We earn interest income. Customers look on us more favorably because this program is really good.
11. We got some new customers. In addition, the HEIL program helps us make more loans, which is helping us to make revenue.
12. We get money out of the interest buydowns.
13. Another service to provide our customers.
14. It is an added service that enriches our offerings. People come back for other loans.
15. If fulfills CRA. Also, good public relations to be associated with WP&L.
16. It fulfills CRA. Also, more loans implies more income for the bank and a higher proportion can be reinvested back into the community.
17. Another service to provide our customers.
18. It fulfills CRA.
19. Another service to provide for our customers.
20. Good public relations.
21. We can provide another service to our customers.
22. We got some new customers.
23. It's good for our customers.
24. No benefits anymore. There are so many restrictions. There should be more types of options.
25. We are in it for the CRA.
26. We can provide another service to our customers.
27. No benefits because too many good options are excluded.
28. It fulfills the CRA requirement. We are providing the customers a service that has very good rates.
29. We got some new customers.
30. Financially, we get more money by lending without the program.
31. We provide another service to our customers.
32. We are in it for the CRA.
33. We get money through the buydowns.
34. We gain new customers.
35. Good public relations.
36. We provide another service and it allows us to help people who really need the loan.
37. We provide another service to our clients and community.
38. It helps us provide another service to our clients and community.
39. We don't have a high enough volume to be able to say that there has been a benefit.
40. We provide another service to our customers.

sons why banks promote (or fail to promote) the HEIL program. Finally, the benefits cited could provide WP&L with an understanding of the lenders' overall opinion of the program. Exhibit VI.A.1 contains a list of the verbatim responses to this open-ended question.

Questions

1. Synthesize the verbatim responses by developing a set of codes and then grouping them into categories that would help WP&L understand the perceived benefits of the HEIL program.

2. What advantages does the researcher gain by coding open-ended data?

3. What recommendations would you make to WP&L about the HEIL program based on what the open-ended data suggest?

Case VI.B   Star Equipment[1]

Star Equipment is a *Fortune* 500 company that manufactures technologically advanced equipment for a variety of applications. Star Equipment's office-products division is one of the three largest manufacturers of office equipment in the world. Traditionally, its largest competitor in the office-equipment category has been Vetra—a domestic manufacturer of advanced office equipment. However, beginning in the 1980s and continuing into the 1990s, Calt, a large foreign manufacturer of office equipment, achieved major gains in the U.S. market. Star also faces significant competition from a number of smaller, specialized office-equipment manufacturers.

In order for Star Equipment's office-products division to remain profitable with the increased competition, division managers outlined four strategies to promote sales: (1) identify key accounts for Star's office products, (2) examine the purchase decision process within these key accounts, (3) determine the critical vendor services sought by these accounts, and (4) assess the performance of Star and its two main competitors on these critical characteristics.

[1]The contributions of Sara L. Pitterle to this case are gratefully acknowledged.

Research Method

Star's marketing research team designed a two-stage research project involving both secondary and primary research to gather the information identified in the four strategies. The first stage of the project involved exhaustive secondary research along with internal and external depth interviews to identify the vendor attributes important to office-equipment customers. Thirteen vendor characteristics were identified as being of some importance to customers.

The thirteen characteristics were incorporated in a survey in which respondents were asked to select the four most- and four least-important characteristics. Respondents were also asked to rate the vendors considered for their company's most recent office-equipment purchase on each of the attributes. Since Star was interested primarily in its own performance ratings along with its two major competitors, Calt and Vetra, these three vendors were explicitly specified in Question 3 in the survey; an "other" column was provided to capture the ratings of smaller vendors that may have been considered.

The survey in Exhibit VI.B.1 was mailed to 812 respondents who were either considering an office-equipment purchase

continued

EXHIBIT VI.B.1   Star Office Equipment Questionnaire

Q1. Thinking specifically about your most recent equipment purchase decision, list all the vendors considered in this decision. By vendor we mean companies that manufacture the equipment.

_____	7–8
_____	9–10
_____	11–12
_____	13–14

Q2. Listed below are vendor characteristics that could be used to make a decision about which equipment to purchase. Thinking about your most recent purchase decision:
   A. Check (✓) the four (4) _most_ important vendor characteristics in your purchase decision.
   B. Check (✓) the four (4) _least_ important vendor characteristics in your purchase decision.

EXHIBIT VI.B.1	Star Office Equipment Questionnaire, *continued*

		A		B	
Vendor Characteristics		**Most Important (Check 4)**		**Least Important (Check 4)**	
a.	Vendor values a long-term relationship and works to meet my organization's unique needs	01 ☐	15–16/	01 ☐	23–24/
b.	My relationships with the vendor's sales and support representatives are easy and productive	02 ☐	17–18/	02 ☐	25–26/
c.	Vendor enables my organization to have a smooth decision process	03 ☐	19–20/	03 ☐	27–28/
d.	The vendor establishes fair pricing policies for products and services	04 ☐	21–22/	04 ☐	29–30/
e.	The vendor's service organization is responsive to my organization's needs	05 ☐		05 ☐	
f.	The vendor offers an extensive line of reliable products meeting the needs of my organization	06 ☐		06 ☐	
g	The vendor's solutions enable my organization to use people, space, and resources efficiently	07 ☐		07 ☐	
h.	The vendor offers software to increase the productivity and satisfaction of my department and employees	08 ☐		08 ☐	
i	Vendor's products are easy to use	09 ☐		09 ☐	
j	The vendor's solutions help my business grow	10 ☐		10 ☐	
k.	The vendor's solutions give me the ability to offer quick response to my customers' needs	11 ☐		11 ☐	
l.	The vendor provides my company with solutions that protect the safety and legality of information	12 ☐		12 ☐	
m.	The vendor provides my firm with technological advantages today that can be leveraged to meet our future requirements	13 ☐		13 ☐	

Q3. Using the following scale, write the number (in each box) that best describes how well each of the vendors fulfilled your expectations during your _most recent purchase_ decision.

1 = Completely Fulfilled	2 = Somewhat Fulfilled	3 = Neither Fulfilled nor Unfulfilled	4 = Somewhat Unfulfilled	5 = Not at All Fulfilled	0 = Not Appropriate

Vendor Characteristics		Calt		Star		Vetra		Other	
a.	Vendor values a long-term relationship and works to meet my organization's unique needs	☐	31/	☐	44/	☐	57/	☐	70/
b.	My relationships with the vendor's sales and support representatives are easy and productive	☐	32/	☐	45/	☐	58/	☐	71/
c.	Vendor enables my organization to have a smooth decision process	☐	33/	☐	46/	☐	59/	☐	72/
d.	The vendor establishes fair pricing policies for products and services	☐	34/	☐	47/	☐	60/	☐	73
e.	The vendor's service organization is responsive to my organization's needs	☐	35/	☐	48/	☐	61/	☐	74/
f.	The vendor offers an extensive line of reliable products meeting the needs of my organization	☐	36/	☐	49/	☐	62/	☐	75/
g.	The vendor's solutions enable my organization to use people, space, and resources efficiently	☐	37/	☐	50/	☐	63/	☐	76/
h.	The vendor offers software to increase the productivity and satisfaction of my department and employees	☐	38/	☐	51/	☐	64/	☐	77/
i.	Vendor's products are easy to use	☐	39/	☐	52/	☐	65/	☐	78/
j.	The vendor's solutions help my business grow	☐	40/	☐	53/	☐	66/	☐	79/

EXHIBIT VI.B.1 Star Office Equipment Questionnaire, *continued*

Vendor Characteristics		Calt	Star	Vetra	Other
k.	The vendor's solutions give me the ability to offer quick response to my customers' needs	☐ 41/	☐ 54/	☐ 67/	☐ 80/
l.	The vendor provides my company with solutions that protect the safety and legality of information	☐ 42/	☐ 55/	☐ 68/	☐ 81/
m.	The vendor provides my firm with technological advantages today that can be leveraged to meet our future requirements	☐ 43/	☐ 56/	☐ 69/	☐ 82/

Q4. How often do you acquire new equipment?
- 1 ☐ Less than 1 year
- 2 ☐ 1 year to less than 3 years
- 3 ☐ 3 years to less than 6 years   83/
- 4 ☐ 6 years or more

Q5. From whom do you acquire your equipment? (Check all that apply.)
- 1 ☐ Directly from manufacturers
- 2 ☐ Dealer
- 3 ☐ Broker   84–87/
- 4 ☐ Other (Specify): _____

Q6. From whom do you acquire your supplies and software? (Check all that apply.)
- 1 ☐ Manufacturer
- 2 ☐ Mail order
- 3 ☐ Contract dealer
- 4 ☐ Buying group
- 5 ☐ Supplies merchant
- 6 ☐ Small storefront   88–98/
- 7 ☐ Super stores
- 8 ☐ Warehouse club
- 9 ☐ Dealer
- 10 ☐ Other (Specify): _____

Q7. What are the reasons for using these suppliers and software? (Check all that apply.)
- 1 ☐ Reputation of supplier
- 2 ☐ Product-quality
- 3 ☐ Product-performance/yield
- 4 ☐ Ease of ordering
- 5 ☐ Recommendation   99–106/
- 6 ☐ Delivery time
- 7 ☐ Price
- 8 ☐ Other (Specify): _____

Q8. Do you purchase, rent, and/or lease your equipment? (Check all that apply.)
- 1 ☐ Purchase
- 2 ☐ Rent
- 3 ☐ Lease   107–110/
- 4 ☐ Other (Specify): _____

Q9. Which of the following best describes where these types of purchase decisions are made in your company?   111/
- 1 ☐ At corporate headquarters for all locations
- 2 ☐ At each company location or branch office
- 3 ☐ Departmental level within each location
- 4 ☐ My company has only one office or location
- 5 ☐ Other (Specify): _____

or had purchased this type of equipment within the last two years. The sample was drawn from the customer lists of both Star and its office-equipment dealers. A $10 incentive was used to encourage responses. The research sponsor was not identified, and data collection was coordinated through an independent research-supply firm. Three hundred usable surveys were returned from the initial mailing. Exhibit VI.B.2 displays the coding of the questionnaires.

The Sample

Star was able to identify the primary office-equipment manufacturer for each of the 300 respondents. This information is contained in Exhibit VI.B.3. Exhibit VI.B.4 lists the equipment vendors considered by these respondents for their most recent equipment purchase. Exhibit VI.B.5 summarizes the variables chosen as *Most Important* and *Least Important* by the respondents.

EXHIBIT VI.B.2   Coding Format for Star Office Equipment Questionnaire

Columns	Contents
1–5	Respondent identification number
6	Current primary equipment manufacturer for respondent: precoded, not a survey question.
	Manufacturers:
	1 = Star
	2 = Vetra
	3 = Calt
	4 = Snap
	5 = Reggies
	Q1. Vendors considered in most recent purchase
7–8	Vendor 1 (See vendor code list below)
9–10	Vendor 2
11–12	Vendor 3
13–14	Vendor 4
	Vendor codes:
	1 = Calt
	2 = Star
	3 = Reggies
	4 = Snap
	5 = Vetra
	94 = No selection made
	95 = Other vendor
	98 = Don't know
15–22	Q2. Four most important vendor characteristics
	(See Questionnaire for definition of codes 01–13)
23–30	Q2. Four least important vendor characteristics
	(See Questionnaire for definition of codes 01–13)
31	Q3a, Calt rating of how well vendor fulfilled expectations
	(See Questionnaire for definition of characteristics a–m and scale values)
32	Q3b
33	Q3c
34	Q3d
35	Q3e
36	Q3f
37	Q3g
38	Q3h
39	Q3i
40	Q3j
41	Q3k
42	Q3l
43	Q3m
44	Q3a, Star rating of how well vendor fulfilled expectations
	(See Questionnaire for definition of characteristics a–m and scale values)
45	Q3b
46	Q3c
47	Q3d
48	Q3e
49	Q3f
50	Q3g
51	Q3h

EXHIBIT VI.B.2   **Coding Format for Star Office Equipment Questionnaire,** *continued*

52	Q3i
53	Q3j
54	Q3k
55	Q3l
56	Q3m
57	Q3a, Vetra rating of how well vendor fulfilled expectations
	(See Questionnaire for definition of characteristics a–m and scale values)
58	Q3b
59	Q3c
60	Q3d
61	Q3e
62	Q3f
63	Q3g
64	Q3h
65	Q3i
66	Q3j
67	Q3k
68	Q3l
69	Q3m
70	Q3a, "Other vendor" rating of how well the vendor fulfilled expectations
	(See Questionnaire for definition of characteristics a–m and scale)
71	Q3b
72	Q3c
73	Q3d
74	Q3e
75	Q3f
76	Q3g
77	Q3h
78	Q3i
79	Q3j
80	Q3k
81	Q3l
82	Q3m
83	Q4. How often do you purchase this equipment?
84	Q5. Acquire equipment from manufacturers
85	from dealers
86	from brokers
87	from other
88–96	Q6. Where acquire supplies
	1 = Manufacturer
	2 = Mail order
	3 = Contract dealer
	4 = Buying group
	5 = Supplies merchant
	6 = Small storefront
	7 = Super stores
	8 = Warehouse club
	9 = Dealer
97–98	10 = Other

continued

EXHIBIT VI.B.2   Coding Format for Star Office Equipment Questionnaire, *continued*

99–106	Q7. Reasons use suppliers
	1 = Reputation of supplier
	2 = Product-quality
	3 = Product-performance/yield
	4 = Ease of ordering
	5 = Recommendation
	6 = Delivery time
	7 = Price
	8 = Other
107	Q8. Purchase equipment
108	Rent equipment
109	Lease equipment
110	Other
111	Q9. Where purchase decisions made

EXHIBIT VI.B.3   Primary Manufacturers

Manufacturer	Frequency	% Sample
Vetra	98	33
Star	87	29
Calt	61	20
Snap	32	11
Reggies	22	7

EXHIBIT VI.B.4   Vendors Considered in Most Recent Equipment Purchase

Manufacturer	Frequency	% Sample
Vetra	166	55
Star	109	36
Calt	109	36
Other Vendors	97	32
Snap	57	19
Reggies	46	15

Questions

1. Star wants the questionnaire in Exhibit VI.B.1 to be completed by the person responsible for purchasing office equipment. Is a mail survey the most appropriate way to reach these people? Why or why not?

2. Was conducting secondary research followed by depth interviews an appropriate means of generating the primary vendor characteristics for this survey? Why or why not?

3. Read each of the 13 vendor-characteristic statements carefully. Are these statements appropriate for a mail survey? Are there particular statements that may pose problems for respondents? Why?

4. Star's sample for this study was generated from its own sales lists and those of its dealers. Did the use of these lists as sampling frames lead to a biased sample? Explain.

5. Using the questionnaire and coding format provided in Exhibits VI.B.1 and VI.B.2, how many variables are necessary to capture completely the responses to Questions 6 and 7? Identify the problems that may arise from this particular coding format.

6. Using data supplied by your instructor, generate one-way tabulations for Survey Questions 6 and 7 (columns 88–106). How can these frequencies be explained? Is there a better way of coding these questions to avoid these types of problems?

EXHIBIT VI.B.5   Attributes Chosen as Most and Least Important

Attribute	MOST IMPORTANT				LEAST IMPORTANT			
	1	2	3	4	1	2	3	4
a	183	0	0	0	33	0	0	0
b	48	75	0	0	44	8	0	0
c	8	13	5	0	110	32	3	0
d	37	101	40	2	4	7	0	0
e	12	71	104	26	1	5	1	1
f	2	16	47	29	26	35	12	0
g	4	6	16	5	37	62	21	1
h	1	10	30	21	9	29	25	8
i	2	3	31	102	4	10	16	4
j	3	2	11	23	13	49	45	5
k	0	3	9	24	4	37	54	11
l	0	0	6	1	0	7	91	130
m	0	0	0	62	0	0	3	104
Total	300	300	299	295	285	281	271	264

7. Can the data in columns 88–106 still be used in this analysis? Justify your decision.

8. Star's research team wants to group respondents based on the similarity of attributes chosen as either important or not important. Thus, Question 2 is critical to the success of this project. Looking at Exhibit VI.B.5, did respondents answer this question correctly? What should be done with those cases that are incorrect? Justify your answer.

9. How would you recode the data from Question 3 to facilitate interpretation? How would you handle the 0 ("Not Appropriate") ratings in this question?

Case VI.C   CTM Productions (B)[1]

CTM Productions, formerly Children's Theatre of Madison, was formed in 1965 to "produce theater of the highest quality." CTM's mission is to ensure that the theatre's efforts are inclusive of the entire family. For CTM to fulfill its role in the community, the organization must identify its present audience in terms of demographic, psychographic, and media-exposure characteristics.

The research team decided to study the audience of CTM's production To Kill a Mockingbird. The study had three major objectives: (1) to develop an audience profile including demographic and media-exposure data; (2) to provide a framework and data collection instrument for future marketing research; and (3) to supply a list of potential season subscribers.

CTM had never undertaken marketing research prior to this study, so internal secondary information about previous audiences did not exist. External secondary information provided guidance as to the types of questions to be asked in a survey and the appropriate phrasing of these questions. The questionnaire is shown in Exhibit IV.D.1 of CTM Productions (A)—Case IV.D.

CTM's volunteer ushers distributed the survey at each of the 15 performances of To Kill a Mockingbird. The number of completed surveys for each show varied with the size of the audience for that show. A total of 1,016 usable surveys were collected during the course of the study. The data coding scheme for the survey is shown in Exhibit VI.C.1. The research team wishes to analyze the data in order to understand the profile of CTM audiences in general as well as how the audience profiles vary between different performances of the same production.

Questions

1. Discuss the implications for CTM's marketing team if there are significant differences in the demographic profiles of those people attending the afternoon versus evening shows.

2. Generate a priori hypotheses about the demographic profiles for the To Kill a Mockingbird performances.

[1]The contributions of Sara L. Pitterle to this case are gratefully acknowledged.

EXHIBIT VI.C.1   Coding Format for CTM Productions Questionnaire

Column(s)	Question Number	Variable	Coding Specification
1	—	Weekend of performance	1 = First weekend 2 = Second weekend 3 = Third weekend
2	—	Day and time of performance	1 = Friday, 7:30 P.M. 2 = Saturday, 3:30 P.M. 3 = Saturday, 7:30 P.M. 4 = Sunday, 1:00 P.M. 5 = Sunday, 3:30 P.M.
3–4	—	Performance in production	1 = Weekend 1, Show 1 2 = Weekend 1, Show 2 3 = Weekend 1, Show 3 4 = Weekend 1, Show 4 5 = Weekend 1, Show 5 6 = Weekend 2, Show 1 7 = Weekend 2, Show 2 8 = Weekend 2, Show 3 9 = Weekend 2, Show 4 10 = Weekend 2, Show 5 11 = Weekend 3, Show 1 12 = Weekend 3, Show 2 13 = Weekend 3, Show 3 14 = Weekend 3, Show 4 15 = Weekend 3, Show 5
5–7	1	Zip code—last three digits	999 = No response 000 = Outside of 53XXX XXX = other digit combos
8	2a	Attending first CTM production	1 = Yes, box checked 2 = No, box checked
9–22		Past Attendance of CTM productions	Questions 2b–2o
9	2b	Season subscriber 1999/2000	1 = Yes, box checked
10	2c	*Wind in the Willows*	2 = No, box checked
11	2d	*A Christmas Carol* 1999	
12	2e	*Babar II*—Plan to attend	
13	2f	Season subscriber 1998/1999	
14	2g	*Red Shoes*	
15	2h	*A Christmas Carol* 1998	
16	2i	*Anne of Green Gables*	
17	2j	*Narnia*	
18	2k	Season subscriber 1997/1998	
19	2l	*Beauty and the Beast*	
20	2m	*A Christmas Carol* 1997	
21	2n	*I Remember Mama*	
22	2o	*Babar the Elephant*	
23–28		Who attending with today	Questions 3a–3f
23	3a	By myself	1 = Yes, box checked
24	3b	Adult friends	2 = No, box checked
25	3c	Partner/spouse	9 = All blank = No response
26	3d	Unrelated kids	

EXHIBIT VI.C.1   **Coding Format for CTM Productions Questionnaire,** *continued*

Column(s)	Question Number	Variable	Coding Specification
27	3e	My kids	
28	3f	Other families	
29–34		Who attended with in past	Questions 4a–4f
29	4a	By myself	1 = Yes, box checked
30	4b	Adult friends	2 = No, box checked
31	4c	Partner/spouse	9 = All blank = No response
32	4d	Unrelated kids	
33	4e	My kids	
34	4f	Other families	
35–40		CTM activity participation	Questions 5a–5f
35		After-school drama classes	1 = Yes, box checked
36		Summer school	2 = No, box checked
37		Auditions	9 = All blank = No response
38		Performances	
39		Have not participated	
40		Did not know I could	
41–55		Media Exposure for *To Kill a Mockingbird*	Questions 6a–6o
41	6a	Season brochure	1 = Yes, box checked
42	6b	Poster	2 = No, box checked
43	6c	*State Journal* story	9 = All blank = No response
44	6d	*Capital Times* story	
45	6e	*Isthmus* story	
46	6f	Other story	
47	6g	*State Journal* ad	
48	6h	*Capital Times* ad	
49	6i	*Isthmus* ad	
50	6j	Other ad	
51	6k	Radio	
52	6l	Television	
53	6m	Magazine	
54	6n	Word of mouth	
55	6o	Other media/exposure	
56	7	Attending because knew cast member	1 = Yes; 2 = No; 9 = No response
57–62		Events attended in the last 6 months	Questions 8a–8f
57	8a	Sports	1 = Yes, box checked
58	8b	Museums	2 = No, box checked
59	8c	Movies	9 = All blank = No response
60	8d	Lectures	
61	8e	Live musical performances	
62	8f	Other live theatrical performances	
63	9	Gender of survey respondent	1 = Female; 0 = Male; 9 = No response
64	10	Age category of respondent	1 = 16–20 6 = 61–70
			2 = 21–30 7 = 71–80
			3 = 31–40 8 = 81–100
			4 = 41–50 9 = No response
			5 = 51–60
65	11	Method of transport to performance	1 = Walk 4 = Other
			2 = Car 9 = No response
			3 = Bus

continued

EXHIBIT VI.C.1 **Coding Format for CTM Productions Questionnaire,** *continued*

Column(s)	Question Number	Variable	Coding Specification
66	12	Distance traveled to performance	1 = Within Madison 2 = Less than 5 miles 3 = 6–10 miles 4 = Over 10 miles 9 = No response
67	13	Time lived in Madison/SC Wis.	1 = Do not live here 2 = Just arrived 3 = 1–3 years 4 = 4–7 years 5 = More 9 = No response
68	14	Level of education	1 = Some high school 2 = High school graduate 3 = Some college 4 = College graduate 5 = Some graduate school 6 = Graduate school graduate 7 = More 9 = No response
69	15	Annual household income	1 = Below $20,000 2 = $21–$30,000 3 = $31–$40,000 4 = $41–$50,000 5 = More than $50,000 6 = Not sure 7 = Do not wish to reply 9 = No response
70	16	Dual-income household	1 = Yes; 2 = No; 9 = No response
71	17	Number of people in household	1 = 1 (person) 5 = 5 2 = 2 6 = 6 3 = 3 7 = More 4 = 4 9 = No response
72–78		Number of children in grade categories	Questions 18a–18g
72	18a	Not in school yet	1, 2, . . . = Yes, # = Quantity
73	18b	Kindergarten–3rd grade	0 = None, box not checked
74	18c	4th–5th grade	9 = All blank = No response
75	18d	6th–8th grade	
76	18e	High school	
77	18f	College	
78	18g	Other	
79	19	Like to be on mailing list?	1 = Yes; 0 = No; 9 = No response
80	20	CTM member	1 = Yes; 0 = No; 9 = No response

Identify the cross tabulations necessary to test your hypotheses. Explain why these particular cross tabulations are necessary.

3. Using data provided by your instructor, run one-way tabulations on this data. Discuss the general findings from these tabulations.

4. Run the cross tabulations that you chose. What recommendations would you make to CTM based on these tables? Are the recommendations actionable? Explain.

5. What are the limitations of these profiles? Explain.

Case VI.D   Young Ideas Publishing Company (B)[1]

Young Ideas Publishing Company was founded three years ago by Linda Halley and her business partner, Teresa Martinez. Thus far, the company has published two novels, *Illusions of Summer* and *Ultimate Choices*, both of which were written by Halley. The novels address several controversial social and political topics and are targeted toward high-school-age teenagers (ages 15 to 18 years). Both books have received critical praise but have not fared well commercially. Distributors have been unwilling to carry the books, believing that no real market demand exists for novels of this type. Halley, however, maintains that her novels would appeal to teens, particularly "nonconformist" teens—by her definition, teens who take an interest in social and political issues.

In an effort to generate insights into the local teen market, Halley has retained the services of a young marketing researcher. A research project has been designed to focus on the potential demand for the product among teens as well as potential marketing-mix elements. A questionnaire has been designed and administered to 166 teens in the target age group. A portion of the questionnaire is shown in Exhibit VI.D.1; note that a scale to measure the nonconformity construct is included.

Questions

1. Items 13 through 25 in Exhibit VI.D.1 attempt to measure nonconformity. Define "nonconformity" based on these items. How well do these items tap into the construct? What other items could (or should) have been included?

2. Analyze the data provided on the computer disk using cross-tabulations or other analyses. Summarize your findings and make recommendations. Include descriptions of the student market in general, the most likely student market for books of this nature (if one exists), and the "nonconformist" student market.

[1]The contributions of Tom J. Brown to the development of this case are gratefully acknowledged.

EXHIBIT VI.D.1   Partial Questionnaire/Coding

The following is a portion of a questionnaire administered to teens ages 15 to 18 years. The questionnaire was designed to gather information and opinions pertaining to reading habits, subject matter preferences, and related issues.

NOTE: Nonresponses were coded as "9" or "99."

For the first group of questions, respondents were asked to check the appropriate box.

1. *On average, how many books do you read for pleasure outside of school in one month?*
   - ☐ Less than one
   - ☐ One
   - ☐ Two
   - ☐ Three
   - ☐ Four
   - ☐ Five
   - ☐ Six
   - ☐ I never read any.

2. *In the last 12 months, where have you usually gotten the books you have read for pleasure?*
   - ☐ I never read any.
   - ☐ Public library
   - ☐ School library
   - ☐ Home
   - ☐ Borrow from another person
   - ☐ Book store
   - ☐ Store other than book store
   - ☐ Book club
   - ☐ Mail order other than book club
   - ☐ Receive as gifts
   - ☐ Other

3. *On average, what would you pay for a new paperback book?*
   - ☐ Less than $3.00
   - ☐ $3.00 to $3.99
   - ☐ $4.00 to $4.99
   - ☐ $5.00 to $5.99
   - ☐ $6.00 to $6.99
   - ☐ $7.00 to $7.99
   - ☐ $8.00 or more

continued

EXHIBIT VI.D.1 Partial Questionnaire/Coding, *continued*

In the following section, the teens were asked to judge the importance of various features of books in their decision process of purchasing a book.

	Very Important	Somewhat Important	Neither Important nor Unimportant	Somewhat Unimportant	Very Unimportant
4. The story description	☐	☐	☐	☐	☐
5. The author	☐	☐	☐	☐	☐
6. The price	☐	☐	☐	☐	☐

Next, respondents were asked to circle the appropriate number corresponding to how likely they were to read books within various subject-matter categories.

	Extremely Likely			Neither Likely nor Unlikely			Extremely Unlikely
7. Science fiction	1	2	3	4	5	6	7
8. Humor/comedy	1	2	3	4	5	6	7
9. Mystery/suspense	1	2	3	4	5	6	7
10. Political	1	2	3	4	5	6	7
11. Romance	1	2	3	4	5	6	7
12. Social issues/problems	1	2	3	4	5	6	7

To determine the degree to which a teen was "nonconformist," he/she was asked to indicate his/her level of agreement with each of the following statements.

	Strongly Agree	Agree	Disagree	Strongly Disagree
13. When I make decisions, I like to get other people's opinions.	1	2	3	4
14. I would lead a demonstration for a social cause if I felt strongly about it.	1	2	3	4
15. I fit in well with society.	1	2	3	4
16. I respect the opinions of most adults.	1	2	3	4
17. I like to try to change society.	1	2	3	4
18. It's important to me that I fit in well with other students my age.	1	2	3	4

EXHIBIT VI.D.1   Partial Questionnaire/Coding, *continued*

19. I would participate in a local/national campaign to promote a candidate who represented my views.	1	2	3	4
20. My lifestyle is different than most students my own age.	1	2	3	4
21. I keep up with current events.	1	2	3	4
22. I don't like to call attention to myself.	1	2	3	4
23. If I feel strongly about something, I need to make my statement even if my friends disagree.	1	2	3	4
24. I try to avoid conflict with my parents.	1	2	3	4
25. Keeping up with the trends is important to me.	1	2	3	4

Finally, two of the classification questions from the questionnaire are presented.

26. What is your age? _____ years old.
   [actual age was coded}

27. Are you male or female?
   ☐ Male
   ☐ Female

Case VI.E   Office of Student Financial Services (B)[1]

Background

As part of a quality service initiative (QSI) program at a midwestern university, the Office of Student Affairs fielded a questionnaire designed to ascertain the level of satisfaction that undergraduate students had with the various student services provided on campus. Among its findings, which were distributed to all the relevant departments on campus, was that the Office of Student Financial Services (OSFS) was one of the lowest ranking departments. Susan Solacy, director of the OSFS, raised several issues that she felt were problematic with the QSI survey:

1. The QSI survey had only one question that pertained directly to satisfaction with the OSFS, and thus it may have provided a distorted view of what students were actually feeling. Moreover, the question may have captured dissatisfaction with issues over which the OSFS has no control in that the majority of the funding guidelines regarding scholarships, grants, and loans are established by the federal government. Given that the role of the OSFS is simply to execute the procedures set forth at the national level, it controls neither the amount of aid available nor the amount allocated to each applicant. In addition, the application processing time is also out of the OSFS's jurisdiction, as the materials are submitted by the students directly to the federal government.

2. All the questions in the QSI survey were structured (close-ended). This may have caused respondents to feel that they needed to provide an answer even when they did not have an opinion on the issue. This may be the case in this instance as historically only about 30 percent of the student body applies for financial aid through the OSFS. However, almost all the students completing the QSI survey had responded to the question regarding satisfaction with the OSFS.

Methodology

Susan felt that it was necessary to address any misconceptions that may have arisen from the QSI findings. She

[1]The contributions of Neeraj Bhardawaj to the development of this case are gratefully acknowledged.

therefore elected to develop her own study dealing specifically with the OSFS. The objectives of the study were to:

1. Determine the relative importance of the services provided by the OSFS that are listed in Exhibit VI.E.1, and

2. Ascertain the level of satisfaction with these services.

Susan hired several marketing research students to develop a mail questionnaire that would tap into the factors which contribute to the level of satisfaction with the OSFS. The direction provided to the students was based upon Susan's ten years of experience with the OSFS, and several financial aid surveys fielded at other universities that dealt with many of the same issues with which the OSFS is concerned.

To address the objectives set forth by Susan, the student marketing research team developed the mail questionnaire that appears in Exhibit VI.E.2. It contains five-point Likert scale items designed to ascertain the level of satisfaction students have with the various services provided by the OSFS, and the helpfulness of its staff. Of the 5,000 questionnaires mailed to students who had applied for financial aid within the last 12 months, 943 usable surveys were returned. Regarding the analysis, the OSFS has historically been most interested in looking at the top-two box score, along with its cumulative percentage. This top-two box score is obtained by simply combining the agree and strongly agree responses for each of the Likert scale items. For example, for question 14 ("I have no problem with picking up any financial aid check"), the top-two box score frequency is 448 and the top-two box cumulative percentage is 47.5%.

EXHIBIT VI.E.1   Services Provided by OSFS

Application process	Fee waivers
Dispensing checks	Federal Pell Grants
Scholarships	Summer financial aid
Federal work-study	Study abroad
Loans	Student job center

EXHIBIT VI.E.2   OSFS Survey

INSTRUCTIONS: Please read the statements below and select the responses that best describe your experience with the Office of Student Financial Services (OSFS)

	Strongly Disagree (1)	Disagree (2)	Neutral (3)	Agree (4)	Strongly Agree (5)
Application Process					
1. OSFS provided me with adequate information about my rights and responsibilities involved in the financial aid process.	____	____	____	____	____
2. The application instructions are clear, concise, and easy to understand.	____	____	____	____	____
3. Information concerning filing procedures and deadlines is clearly presented in the instruction sheet.	____	____	____	____	____
4. After filing the application, I always receive follow-up letters from OSFS informing me what documents are received, which are required to complete the application, and what forms are submitted incorrectly.	____	____	____	____	____
5. I open all mail from OSFS as soon as I receive it.	____	____	____	____	____
6. The follow-up letters I receive are useful in making sure I submit requested documents on time.	____	____	____	____	____

EXHIBIT VI.E.2   OSFS Survey, continued

	Strongly Disagree (1)	Disagree (2)	Neutral (3)	Agree (4)	Strongly Agree (5)
7. I usually get notified about missing documents just before deadlines.	____	____	____	____	____
8. OSFS does a good job in keeping track of my application process and informing me of my current status.	____	____	____	____	____
9. I do most of the job of keeping track of my own financial status by calling or visiting OSFS.	____	____	____	____	____
10. Not being able to fill out forms correctly is my biggest problem with the financial aid process.	____	____	____	____	____
11. Not being able to submit requested documents on time is my biggest problem with the financial aid application process.	____	____	____	____	____
12. OSFS mislocating submitted documents is the biggest problem with the financial aid application process.	____	____	____	____	____
13. I feel I am overwhelmed by the complexity of the entire financial aid process.	____	____	____	____	____

Receiving Checks

Please answer question 14 only if you received financial aid checks.

14. I have no problems with picking up my financial aid check.	____	____	____	____	____

General Information

15. How do you get most of your financial aid questions answered?
    (Please circle only one answer.)
    a. Telephone
    b. Walk ins/Counter help
    c. Appointments with counselors
    d. Financial aid publications
    e. Fellow students
    f. Public information sessions
    g. Other financial assistance agencies (banks, governments, etc.)
    h. High school counselor
    i. Other:

16. I prefer to contact OSFS by:

a. Telephone	____	____	____	____	____
b. Walk ins/Counter help	____	____	____	____	____
c. Appointments with counselors	____	____	____	____	____
d. Financial aid publications	____	____	____	____	____
e. Fellow students	____	____	____	____	____

continued

EXHIBIT VI.E.2   **OSFS Survey,** *continued*

	Strongly Disagree (1)	Disagree (2)	Neutral (3)	Agree (4)	Strongly Agree (5)
f. Public information sessions	———	———	———	———	———
g. Other financial assistance agencies (banks, governments, etc.)	———	———	———	———	———
h. High school counselor	———	———	———	———	———
i. Other	———	———	———	———	———

17. How many times have you called OSFS in the past year?
    a. 0–5
    b. 6–10
    c. 11–15
    d. More than 15

18. In reference to your telephone experience with the OSFS:

	Strongly Disagree (1)	Disagree (2)	Neutral (3)	Agree (4)	Strongly Agree (5)
a. The person was informative.	———	———	———	———	———
b. The person was courteous.	———	———	———	———	———
c. The person did not clearly explain the information.	———	———	———	———	———
d. I received correct information pertaining to my file.	———	———	———	———	———
e. I usually wait on hold for less than 5 minutes.	———	———	———	———	———
f. OSFS was easily accessible by telephone (not busy).	———	———	———	———	———

	Strongly Disagree (1)	Disagree (2)	Neutral (3)	Agree (4)	Strongly Agree (5)
19. I rely on the FINFONE service to check on the status of my financial aid.	———	———	———	———	———
20. The FINFONE service provided the information needed.	———	———	———	———	———

21. How many times have you visited OSFS in the past year?
    a. 0–5
    b. 6–10
    c. 11–15
    d. More than 15

22. In reference to your experience with the front desk personnel:

	Strongly Disagree (1)	Disagree (2)	Neutral (3)	Agree (4)	Strongly Agree (5)
a. The person was informative.	———	———	———	———	———
b. The person was courteous.	———	———	———	———	———
c. The person did not clearly explain the information.	———	———	———	———	———
d. I received correct information pertaining to my file.	———	———	———	———	———
e. The person was efficient.	———	———	———	———	———
f. I usually wait in line for less than 5 minutes.	———	———	———	———	———

	Strongly Disagree (1)	Disagree (2)	Neutral (3)	Agree (4)	Strongly Agree (5)
23. I rely on OSFS publications for financial aid information.	———	———	———	———	———

EXHIBIT VI.E.2 **OSFS Survey,** *continued*

	Strongly Disagree (1)	Disagree (2)	Neutral (3)	Agree (4)	Strongly Agree (5)
24. In reference to the publication(s) read:					
a. The material was informative.	___	___	___	___	___
b. The material was confusing.	___	___	___	___	___
c. The material was complete.	___	___	___	___	___
d. The material was sent in a timely manner when requested.	___	___	___	___	___
e. I usually find the information I need.	___	___	___	___	___

Counselors

25. Have you seen a counselor at the OSFS?
   (1) No (If no, please skip to question 27.)
   (2) Yes

	Strongly Disagree (1)	Disagree (2)	Neutral (3)	Agree (4)	Strongly Agree (5)
26. a. It was easy to reach the counselor by phone.	___	___	___	___	___
b. The counselor did not return my phone calls promptly.	___	___	___	___	___
c. It was easy to get in to see a counselor.	___	___	___	___	___
d. The counselor(s) spent enough time on me.	___	___	___	___	___
e. The counselor(s) was (were) friendly and courteous.	___	___	___	___	___
f. The counselor(s) was (were) knowledgeable about my financial aid concerns.	___	___	___	___	___
g. The counselor(s) did not explain the information clearly.	___	___	___	___	___
h. I received the necessary information during the FIRST visit.	___	___	___	___	___
i. Overall, the counselor(s) was (were) helpful.	___	___	___	___	___

Scholarships

Please answer questions in this section if your interaction with OSFS involved Scholarships. (Otherwise, skip to question 28.)

	Strongly Disagree (1)	Disagree (2)	Neutral (3)	Agree (4)	Strongly Agree (5)
27. a. The OSFS provided helpful publications and information on applying for scholarships.	___	___	___	___	___
b. The services provided by the Scholarship Office in the OSFS were useful to me.	___	___	___	___	___
c. The personnel in the office were unable to answer questions I asked concerning scholarships.	___	___	___	___	___
d. The amount of scholarships available through the OSFS were adequate.	___	___	___	___	___

continued

EXHIBIT VI.E.2   **OSFS Survey,** *continued*

	Strongly Disagree (1)	Disagree (2)	Neutral (3)	Agree (4)	Strongly Agree (5)

Federal Work-Study

Please answer questions in this section if your interaction with OSFS involved Federal Work-Study. (Otherwise, skip to question 29.)

		Strongly Disagree (1)	Disagree (2)	Neutral (3)	Agree (4)	Strongly Agree (5)
28.	a. The OSFS provided helpful publications and information on opportunities for federal work-study.	____	____	____	____	____
	b. The services regarding federal work-study provided by the OSFS were useful to me.	____	____	____	____	____
	c. The personnel in the office were unable to answer questions I asked concerning federal work-study.	____	____	____	____	____
	d. The amount of federal work-study available through the OSFS was adequate.	____	____	____	____	____

Loans

Please answer questions in this section if your interaction with OSFS involved Loans. (Otherwise, skip to question 30.)

		Strongly Disagree (1)	Disagree (2)	Neutral (3)	Agree (4)	Strongly Agree (5)
29.	a. The OSFS provided helpful publications and information on opportunities for loans.	____	____	____	____	____
	b. The service provided by the Loan Office of OSFS was useful to me.	____	____	____	____	____
	c. The personnel in the office were unable to answer questions I asked concerning loans.	____	____	____	____	____
	d. The amount of loans available through OSFS was adequate.	____	____	____	____	____
	e. The office was accurate and effective in servicing the loans (for example, informing when checks were in, payments, debt information.	____	____	____	____	____

Please answer questions in this section if your interaction with OSFS involved Fee Waivers. (Otherwise, skip to question 31.)

		Strongly Disagree (1)	Disagree (2)	Neutral (3)	Agree (4)	Strongly Agree (5)
30.	a. The OSFS provided helpful information on fee waivers.	____	____	____	____	____
	b. The personnel in the office were unable to answer questions I asked concerning fee waivers.	____	____	____	____	____
	c. The services for fee waivers provided by OSFS were useful to me.	____	____	____	____	____

EXHIBIT VI.E.2   OSFS Survey, *continued*

	Strongly Disagree (1)	Disagree (2)	Neutral (3)	Agree (4)	Strongly Agree (5)

Federal Pell Grants

Please answer questions in this section if your interaction with OSFS involved Federal Pell Grants. (Otherwise, skip to question 32.)

	Strongly Disagree (1)	Disagree (2)	Neutral (3)	Agree (4)	Strongly Agree (5)
31. a. The OSFS provided helpful publications and information on applying for federal Pell Grants.	——	——	——	——	——
b. The service provided by the Pell Grant Office of OSFS was useful to me.	——	——	——	——	——
c. The personnel in the office were unable to answer questions I asked concerning federal Pell Grants.	——	——	——	——	——
d. The amount of federal Pell Grants available through the OSFS was adequate.	——	——	——	——	——

Summer Financial Aid

Please answer questions in this section if your interaction with OSFS involved Summer Financial Aid. (Otherwise, skip to question 33.)

	Strongly Disagree (1)	Disagree (2)	Neutral (3)	Agree (4)	Strongly Agree (5)
32. a. The OSFS provided helpful publications and information on applying for summer financial aid.	——	——	——	——	——
b. The personnel in the office were unable to answer questions I asked concerning summer financial aid.	——	——	——	——	——
c. The amount of summer financial aid available through the OSFS was adequate.	——	——	——	——	——

Study Abroad

Please answer questions in this section if your interaction with OSFS involved Study Abroad. (Otherwise, skip to question 34.)

	Strongly Disagree (1)	Disagree (2)	Neutral (3)	Agree (4)	Strongly Agree (5)
33. a. The OSFS provided helpful publications and information on applying for study abroad.	——	——	——	——	——
b. The personnel in the office were unable to answer questions I asked concerning study abroad.	——	——	——	——	——
c. The amount of aid available for study abroad through the OSFS was adequate.	——	——	——	——	——

Student Job Center

Please answer questions in this section if your interaction with OSFS involved the Student Job Center. (Otherwise, skip to question 35.)

	Strongly Disagree (1)	Disagree (2)	Neutral (3)	Agree (4)	Strongly Agree (5)
34. a. The OSFS provided helpful publications and information on applying for jobs.	——	——	——	——	——

continued

EXHIBIT VI.E.2   **OSFS Survey,** *continued*

	Strongly Disagree (1)	Disagree (2)	Neutral (3)	Agree (4)	Strongly Agree (5)
b. The service provided by the Student Job Center of the OSFS was useful to me.	——	——	——	——	——
c. The personnel in the office were unable to answer questions I asked concerning jobs.	——	——	——	——	——
d. The amount of job opportunities available through the Student Job Center was adequate.	——	——	——	——	——

35. The following is a list of some of the services provided by the OSFS. Please identify what you feel are the five most important services by placing a "1" in front of the most important service, a "2" in front of the second most important service, a "3" in front of the third most important service, a "4" in front of the fourth most important service, and a "5" in front of the fifth most important service.

_____ a. Assistance in filling out financial aid forms
_____ b. Assistance with scholarship information
_____ c. The federal work-study program
_____ d. Assistance in obtaining loans
_____ e. Assistance with fee waivers
_____ f. Obtaining federal Pell Grants
_____ g. Assistance in obtaining summer financial aid
_____ h. The Study Abroad program
_____ i. Receiving a financial aid award in a timely fashion
_____ j. The FINFONE telephone service
_____ k. Loan servicing (for example, informing when checks are in, payments, debt information)
_____ l. Speed in obtaining financial aid check
_____ m. Counselor assistance
_____ n. Receiving printed informational material
_____ o. Other (please specify) _____

Please Circle or Complete as Appropriate

36. Gender:
    (1) Female
    (2) Male
37. Age:_____
38. Marital Status:
    (1) Single
    (2) Married
39. a. Do you have any children?
    (1) No (if no, please skip to question 40)
    (2) Yes
    b. If you have children, please circle the appropriate reply.
    (1) = 1 to 3 children
    (2) = 4 to 6 children
    (3) = 7 or more children

Exhibit VI.E.3 provides a tabulation of the rankings of all the services provided by the OSFS. This summary of frequencies is based on Question 35, which asks students to identify the five most important services provided by the OSFS (1 = most important, 2 = second most important, through 5 = fifth most important).

EXHIBIT VI.E.3   Ranking of Services Provided by OSFS (Summary of Question 35)

		FREQUENCY RANKING OF SERVICES					
Question	Service	1st	2nd	3rd	4th	5th	Not Ranked
35a	Assistance in filling out financial aid forms	191	117	73	78	80	404
35b	Assistance with scholarship information	101	85	87	71	47	552
35c	The federal work-study program	26	38	41	53	50	735
35d	Assistance in obtaining loans	112	117	98	73	74	469
35e	Assistance with fee waivers	4	13	25	29	29	843
35f	Obtaining federal Pell Grants	102	98	65	73	41	564
35g	Assistance in obtaining summer financial aid	3	10	26	19	35	850
35h	The Study Abroad Program	7	16	14	24	32	850
35i	Receiving a financial aid award in a timely fashion	134	114	105	110	89	391
35j	The FINFONE telephone service *	23	34	36	47	73	730
35k	Loan servicing	61	76	103	102	84	517
35l	Speed in obtaining financial aid check	62	98	98	99	83	503
35m	Counselor assistance	36	56	73	64	73	641
35n	Receiving printed information material	52	46	66	62	93	624
35o	Other	13	3	2	2	17	906

*FINFONE is a 24-hour touchtone system that students can call to check on the status of their financial aid applications. The information is part of Dean of Student Affairs Magnus Pym's Quality Service Initiative Program that enables students to have their most frequently asked questions about all the student services provided on campus to be answered by a preprogrammed telephone system.

Questions

1. On the basis of Exhibit VI.E.3, what do students feel are the most important services provided by the OSFS?

2. Using the top-two box cumulative percentage for the relevant five-point Likert scale items as a guide along with the raw data supplied by your instructor, are there any facets within the three most important services that are especially problematic?

3. Based upon the cross tabulation of most important services provided by OSFS (Question 35) with student classification (Question 42), are there any differences among the student classes regarding the most important services provided by the OSFS?

4. Given that the OSFS has limited resources, what would you recommend to Susan if you were part of the student marketing research team?

Case VI.F   Transitional Housing, Inc. (B)[1]

Transitional Housing Inc. (THI) is a nonprofit organization located in Madison, Wisconsin. THI provides assistance to homeless and very low income individuals and families in finding emergency shelter, food, employment, transitional housing, and affordable apartment housing (see Case I.B, Transitional Housing, Inc. [A], for more details). As part of its planning, the board of directors of THI was interested in finding ways to improve the organization's services. They decided to assemble a task force to evaluate THI's current

[1]The contributions of Monika Wingate to the development of this case are gratefully acknowledged.

facilities and services, and to determine what future facilities and services it should provide.

Methodology

The task force was assembled in February. After evaluating external information on the homeless situation in Dane County and internal information on THI, the task force submitted a proposal to the board outlining their methodology and time frame (see Exhibit VI.F1). The proposal consisted of three surveys, conducted on the organization's paid staff, volunteers, and guests (the homeless staying at THI or using its facilities/services).

EXHIBIT VI.F.1   **Research Proposal to Transitional Housing**

Purpose and Limits of the Project:

THI is interested in knowing how services provided enable them to meet community needs and if the services are aiding the clients in their struggle to "get out of the loop." Specifically, Transitional Housing, Inc. (THI), would like to address the following questions:

1. What are the needs of the homeless community?
2. Are current services meeting the homeless community's needs?
3. How could the homeless community's needs better be met?

As discussed in earlier meetings, this project will focus on the services provided by the Drop-In Shelter and the Hospitality House, as it is used in conjunction with the Drop-In Shelter.

Data Sources and Research Methodology:

The primary source of data collection will be through the use of a questionnaire. Focus groups will be conducted in order to facilitate development of the questions asked of the target populations. Secondary data collection sources will be: statistics on the current homeless population in Dane County, and internal information provided by THI, such as statistics of the guest services and previous/simultaneous studies conducted by THI.

The target population to be surveyed are current guests (at the Drop-In Shelter and Hospitality House), staff, volunteers, and previous guests of the Drop-In Shelter or Hospitality House who are currently in Transitional Housing. Sample sizes for the target population will be determined as follow:

- The current guest sample will be based on the number of guests staying at the Drop-In Shelter on two separate nights.

- The staff and volunteers sample sizes will be based on the number of years of service to the organization and will be adjusted for sample population mortality.

- The previous guests sample will be taken from the actual number of guests currently in one of the Transitional Housing facilities who were previous guests of the Drop-In Shelter and/or Hospitality House.

These groups were chosen because they are representative of the population who use THI services and who administer them.

Estimate of Time and Personnel Requirements:

The study will be conducted by the five research team members. Additional personnel may be required for administration of the questionnaire. They will be recruited from the THI volunteer base not included in the sample population. The projected time frame for the project is listed below:

- Focus groups and questionnaire development: 4–5 weeks

- Sample selection: 1 week

- Administration of the survey: 3–4 weeks

- Analysis of data and presentation to agency: 2 weeks

Given the exploratory nature of the research project, the task force decided to use a nonprobability convenience sample for guests and volunteers, and a census for the small number of staff members. Three separate questionnaires were used, with volunteers and staff being surveyed using self-administered questionnaires and guests being surveyed using structured in-person interviews.

Questionnaire

The initial research done by the task force suggested several areas of interest, including the need for adding staff members and services at the drop-in shelter, and the addition of personal sleeping and storage areas for guests. However, in order to create more directed questions, separate focus groups were conducted with staff, volunteers, and guests. Individual survey questions were based on the focus group responses.

The final questionnaire was broken out into four sections: physical facilities, current services, potential future services, and demographics (Exhibit VI.F2). Most questions for the three surveys were identical. Exceptions included demographic questions that were unique for guests, staff, and volunteers, and physical facilities questions that were applicable only to guests.

Both closed- and open-ended questions were asked to all three groups. After all the questionnaires were complete, open-ended responses were evaluated to determine representative categories. A coding sheet was then created to facilitate data entry (see Exhibit VI.F3). A total of 68 guests, 33 volunteers, and 11 staff members completed questionnaires. Two of the volunteer surveys were discarded due to incomplete responses. The raw data are contained in file THI.dat.

EXHIBIT VI.F.2   Questionnaires

Guest Questionnaire

Physical Facilities of the Drop-In Shelter:

The following questions relate to potential future facilities of the Drop-In Shelter. Please circle the number which most closely represents your opinion of the need for the following facilities.

	Definitely Needed	Needed	Neutral	Not Needed	Definitely Not Needed
1. Personal Storage Areas	1	2	3	4	5
2. Study Areas	1	2	3	4	5
3. Library	1	2	3	4	5
4. Separate Areas for Guests with Contagious Diseases (e.g., flu, cold, etc.)	1	2	3	4	5
5. Wheelchair Accessibility	1	2	3	4	5

6. Often there is limited funding, and choices on where to spend these funds must be made. Please rank the following items in order of importance using 1 through 5 (1 being most important and 5 being least important). Please use each number only once.

_____ Personal Storage Areas
_____ Study Areas
_____ Library
_____ Separate Areas for Guests with Contagious Diseases
_____ Wheelchair Accessibility

7. If the option existed for you to stay in a room by yourself for the night, what is the most that you would be willing (and able) to pay for this room? Would you be willing to pay . . . (CHECK HIGHEST AMOUNT YOU WOULD BE WILLING TO PAY)

_____ $2-$3 per night
_____ $4–$5 per night
_____ $6–$8 per night
_____ More than $8 per night
_____ I would not be willing to pay for my own room (skip to question 10)

8. If the option existed for you to stay in a room by yourself for the night, what is the farthest you would be willing to walk from the Capitol?

_____ under 1 block
_____ 1–2 blocks
_____ 3–4 blocks
_____ 5–6 blocks
_____ 7–8 blocks

If the option existed for you to stay in a room by yourself for the night, the following list of features are items that might be included in such a facility. On a scale of 1 to 5, where 1 is "very important" and 5 is "not at all important," please rate the need for the following facilities.

continued

EXHIBIT VI.F.2   Questionnaires, *continued*

	Very Important	Somewhat Important	Neutral	Not Very Important	Not at All Important
9. Personal storage areas in the room	1	2	3	4	5
10. Cafeteria/food service	1	2	3	4	5
11. Private bathroom	1	2	3	4	5

12. What other features, if any, do you think should be included in this type of facility?

_____

_____

_____

13. Would you be willing to pay for personal storage facilities at the Drop-In Shelter if they were available?

_____ Yes

_____ No

Services at the Drop-In Shelter

The questions in this section of the survey relate to the services available to guests of the Drop-In Shelter. The first section relates to services that are already provided at the Drop-In Shelter. The second section relates to potential services that may be provided at the Drop-In Shelter in the future.

Current Services

14. I find the social worker at the Drop-In Shelter helpful.

Strongly Agree	Agree	Neutral	Disagree	Strongly Disagree
1	2	3	4	5

15. There are enough social workers available to meet the guests' needs.

Strongly Agree	Agree	Neutral	Disagree	Strongly Disagree
1	2	3	4	5

IF GUEST ANSWERS WITH A 4 OR 5: How many social workers do you think would be better? _____

16. How do you think the counseling services could be improved, if at all, to better serve the needs of the Drop-In Shelter guests?

_____

_____

_____

17. I find the medical services at the Drop-In Shelter useful.

Strongly Agree	Agree	Neutral	Disagree	Strongly Disagree
1	2	3	4	5

18. There are enough staff people available for the medical services to meet the guests' needs.

Strongly Agree	Agree	Neutral	Disagree	Strongly Disagree
1	2	3	4	5

19. How do you think the medical services could be improved, if at all, to better serve the needs of the Drop-In Shelter guests?

_____

_____

_____

20. There are enough staff people available for the legal services to meet the guests' needs.

Strongly Agree	Agree	Neutral	Disagree	Strongly Disagree
1	2	3	4	5

EXHIBIT VI.F.2   Questionnaires, *continued*

21. How do you think the legal services could be improved, if at all, to better serve the needs of the Drop-In Shelter guests?

_____

22. One Mental Health worker (like Axel) is enough to meet the guests' needs.

Strongly Agree	**Agree**	**Neutral**	**Disagree**	**Strongly Disagree**
1	2	3	4	5

23. How do you think the mental health services could be improved, if at all, to better serve the needs of the Drop-In Shelter guests?

_____

24. There are enough volunteers available to meet the guests' needs.

Strongly Agree	**Agree**	**Neutral**	**Disagree**	**Strongly Disagree**
1	2	3	4	5

Potential Future Services

The following questions relate to potential future services of the Drop-In Shelter. Please circle the number which most closely represents your opinion of the need for the following services.

	Definitely Needed	**Needed**	**Neutral**	**Not Needed**	**Definitely Not Needed**
25. On-Duty Drug and Alcohol Counselor	1	2	3	4	5
26. Dental Services	1	2	3	4	5
27. Optical Services	1	2	3	4	5
28. Tutors for Guests	1	2	3	4	5
29. Assistance with Social Service Agencies	1	2	3	4	5
30. Seasonal clothing	1	2	3	4	5
31. Interview clothing	1	2	3	4	5
32. Haircuts	1	2	3	4	5

33. Are there any services that are offered during the day by the Hospitality House that you would like offered at the Drop-In Shelter at night?

_____

34. What other services do you think should be offered at the Drop-In Shelter?

_____

_____

Demographics Section:

35. On average, how many times a week do you stay at the Drop-In Shelter?
    _____ once a week or less
    _____ 2–3 times a week
    _____ 4–5 times a week
    _____ 6–7 times a week
36. Which months during the year do you usually stay at the Drop-In Shelter? (CHECK ALL THAT APPLY)

_____ January	_____ July
_____ February	_____ August
_____ March	_____ September
_____ April	_____ October
_____ May	_____ November
_____ June	_____ December

continued

EXHIBIT VI.F.2   **Questionnaires,** *continued*

37. On average, how many times a week do you visit the Hospitality House?
    _____ I don't use the Hospitality House
    _____ Only once per week
    _____ 2–3 times a week
    _____ 4–5 times a week
    _____ 6–7 times a week
38. If you do not use the Hospitality House when you stay at the Drop-In Shelter, why not? (DO NOT READ LIST; CHECK ALL THAT APPLY)
    _____ Not Applicable, I use the HH.
    _____ Too crowded/I don't feel safe.
    _____ Too far.
    _____ Don't like staff.
    _____ Don't feel it meets my service needs.
    _____ Don't want to participate in clean-up.
    _____ Not open on weekends.
    _____ Don't know about Hospitality House.
    _____ Other _____

Volunteer Questionnaire

Questions 1–6 are identical to Guest Questions 1–6
Questions 7–27 are identical to Guest Questions 14–34

Demographics Section:

28. How many years have you been a volunteer at the Drop-In Shelter?
    _____ This is my first night volunteering at the Drop-In Shelter.
    _____ 1 year or less
    _____ 2–3 years
29. On average, how often do you volunteer at the Drop-In Shelter?
    _____ At least once a month
    _____ 4 times a year
    _____ 2 times a year
    _____ Once a year
    _____ Less than once a year
30. How did you initially come to volunteer at the Drop-In Shelter?
    _____ Church group
    _____ Work group
    _____ Mandatory community service for a university class
    _____ Mandatory community service for some other reason
    _____ Personal interest
    _____ Other
31. What volunteer shift do you normally work?
    _____ Breakfast
    _____ 8 pm to midnight
    _____ midnight to 4 am

Staff Questionnaire

Questions 1–6 are identical to Guest Questions 1–6
Questions 7–27 are identical to Guest Questions 14–34

EXHIBIT VI.F.2   Questionnaires, *continued*

Demographics Section:

28. How long have you worked for Transitional Housing, Inc.?
    ____ Less than 1 year
    ____ 1–2 years
    ____ 3–4 years
    ____ 5 or more years
29. At which THI facility do you work?
    ____ Hospitality House
    ____ Drop-In Shelter
30. Are you a full-time or part-time employee?
    ____ Full-time
    ____ Part-time

EXHIBIT VI.F.3   THI Coding Scheme

Column(s)	Question #	Contents
1–3	N/A	Questionnaire I.D. #
4	N/A	Type: 1 - Guest
		2 - Volunteer
		3 - Staff
5	1	Personal Storage
6	2	Study Areas
	3	Library
8	4	Separate Areas for Guests with Contagious Diseases
9	5	Wheelchair Accessibility
10	6a	Personal Storage
11	6b	Study Areas
12	6c	Library
13	6d	Separate Areas
14	6e	Wheelchair Accessibility
15	7 (G14)	Social Worker Helpful
16	8a (G15a)	Enough Social Workers
17	8b (G15b)	How Many Social Workers
18–19, 20–21	9 (G16)	Counseling Services Improved OPEN-ENDED
(2 ideas)		01 - Make guess aware of counseling services
		02 - More individual one-on-one (case) interaction
		03 - Should give referrals
		04 - More structured and enforced rules
		05 - Better trained/new staff
		06 - More AODA counseling
		07 - Be available more often
		08 - Job opportunities advice
		09 - More time with social workers
		10 - Better help with handicapped/special needs
		11 - Other
22	10 (G17)	Medical Services Helpful
23	11 (G18)	Enough Medical Staff

continued

EXHIBIT VI.F.3   THI Coding Scheme, *continued*

Column(s)	Question #	Contents

24–25, 26–27
(2 ideas)
	12 (G19)	Medical Services Improved OPEN-ENDED
		    01 - Services offered more often
		    02 - Better trained people or "real" doctors/nurses
		    03 - More medicine available
		    04 - Offer dental care
		    05 - Offer eye doctor services
		    06 - Better equipment and/or facilities (clinic)
		    07 - Keep medical records of guests
		    08 - Get rid of it—use other existing programs
		    09 - Offer medical tests (TB, etc.)
		    10 - Offer more staff—more doctors
		    11 - More emphasis on preventive medicine
		    12 - Other

28	13 (G20)	Enough Staff—Legal Services

29, 30
(2 ideas)
	14 (G21)	Legal Services Improved OPEN-ENDED
		    1 - Longer appointments—more time with lawyers
		    2 - More staff (lawyers) available
		    3 - Offered more nights (accessibility)
		    4 - Schedule lawyers ahead of time by appt.
		    5 - Give guests info about legal rights, rental, etc.
		    6 - Other

31	15 (G22)	One Mental Health Worker Is Enough

32, 33
(2 ideas)
	16 (G23)	Mental Health Services Improved OPEN-ENDED
		    1 - Awareness (communicate availability to guests)
		    2 - Offer classes
		    3 - Network with existing agencies (referrals)
		    4 - More staff (one-female; one-male)
		    5 - Separate the mentally ill
		    6 - More individual counseling
		    7 - More hours of service
		    8 - More structured rules at Drop-In
		    9 - Other

34	17 (G24)	Enough Volunteers Available
35	18 (G25)	On-Duty Drug & Alcohol Counselor
36	19 (G26)	Dental Services
37	20 (G27)	Optical Services
38	21 (G28)	Tutors for Guests
39	22 (G29)	Assistance with Social Service Agencies
40	23 (G30)	Seasonal Clothing
41	24 (G31)	Interview Clothing
42	25 (G32)	Haircuts

43–44, 45–46,
47–48
(Maximum 3 ideas)
	26 (G33)	Any services offered at Hospitality House that
		could be offered? (OPEN-ENDED)
		    01 - Doesn't use Hospitality House/Unaware
		    02 - Counseling services
		    03 - Job listings
		    04 - Telephone and/or long distance
		    05 - Drug/alcohol referrals
		    06 - More staff available

EXHIBIT VI.F.3 **THI Coding Scheme,** *continued*

Column(s)	Question #	Contents
		07 - Newspaper
		08 - Computer/typewriter access
		09 - Mailboxes
		10 - Bus tickets/transportation
		11 - Rental/housing lists
		12 - Activities/game room
		13 - Cooking facilities
		14 - Nothing/should use Hospitality House
		15 - Other
49–50, 51–52, 53–54, 55–56 (Maximum: 4 ideas)	27 (G34)	What Other Services Should Be Offered?
		01 - More laundry facilities (& ironing board)
		02 - Daily newspaper
		03 - More counseling services
		04 - More showers/sinks
		05 - Additional entertainment
		06 - Bible study
		07 - Answering/message service
		08 - Telephone
		09 - Chiropractor
		10 - Better ventilation
		11 - More beds
		12 - Drug/alcohol treatment
		13 - Better food & more variety
		14 - Enforce rules (drinking)
		15 - Extended shelter hours in winter
		16 - VCR/movies/stereo
		17 - Offer Bible counseling/priests
		18 - Skills training/jobs
		19 - Check for weapons
		20 - Transportation (bus passes)
		21 - More blankets
		22 - More staff (more accommodating staff)
		23 - Mailing address/mail service
		24 - Other

GUEST-ONLY QUESTIONS: (For volunteer & staff, put spaces in)

57	G7	Own Room by Yourself Willing to Pay
58	G8	Own Room—Farthest Willing to Walk
59	G9	Personal Storage
60	G10	Cafeteria/Food Service
61	G11	Private Bathroom
62–63, 64–65 (2 ideas)	G12	What other features should be included? OPEN-ENDED
		01 - Warm blankets
		02 - A good bed
		03 - TV
		04 - Radio/stereo
		05 - Kitchenette
		06 - Telephone
		07 - Social room

continued

EXHIBIT VI.F.3 **THI Coding Scheme,** *continued*

Column(s)	Question #	Contents
		08 - Separate smoking room
		09 - Laundry facilities
		10 - Job training courses
		11 - Games/entertainment
		12 - Counseling services (all types)
		13 - Workout facilities/gym
		14 - Good ventilation
		15 - Refrigerator
		16 - First aid
		17 - Rules/policies enforcement
		18 - Other
66	G13	Would you be willing to pay for personal storage facilities . . .?
67	G35	On average, how many times a week do you stay . . .?
68–69, 70–71,	G36	Which months during the year?
72–73, 74–75		
76–77, 78–79		
ROW 2: 1–2,		
3–4, 5–6, 7–8,		
9–10, 11–12		
(12 possible months)		
ROW 2:		
13	G37	On average, how many times a week do you visit HH?
14–15, 16–17	G38	If you do not use HH, why not?
(2 ideas)		

Month codes for G36:

01 - January	07 - July
02 - February	08 - August
03 - March	09 - September
04 - April	10 - October
05 - May	11 - November
06 - June	12 - December

G38 codes:

01 - N/A; I use HH
02 - Too crowded
03 - Don't feel safe
04 - Don't like staff
05 - Don't feel meets service needs
06 - Don't want to take part in clean-up
07 - Not open on weekends
08 - Don't know about HH
09 - Busy doing other things
10 - Should have area for sleeping
11 - Too far away
12 - Too noisy
13 - Other

VOLUNTEER-ONLY QUESTIONS: (For guests & staff, put in spaces)

Column(s)	Question #	Contents
18	V28	How many years have you been a volunteer?
19	V29	On average, how often . . .?
20	V30	How did you initially come to volunteer at the Drop-In?
21	V31	What volunteer shift do you work?

STAFF-ONLY QUESTIONS: (For guests & volunteers, put in spaces)

Column(s)	Question #	Contents
22	S28	How long have you worked for?
23	S29	At which THI facility . . .?
24	S30	Are you full-time/part-time?

Questions

1. One of the research objectives was to determine what *new services* are needed by the homeless men. Which survey questions best address this research objective? Why?

2. Using the data provided on the computer disk, run one-way tabulations on the survey questions you recommended in Question 1. Discuss the general findings from these tabulations.

3. Using the data provided on the computer disk, run cross tabulations on the survey questions you recommended in Question 1 against the type of respondent. Are there significant differences among guests, volunteers, and staff? If yes, what are the implications for THI's board of directors?

4. What recommendations would you make to THI based on your findings? Why?

Case VI.G   Fabhus Inc.

Fabhus, Inc., a manufacturer of prefabricated homes located in Atlanta, Georgia, had experienced steady, sometimes spectacular, growth since its founding in the early 1950s. By the late 1990s, however, things were not so rosy. Sales fell off 8 percent from 1997 to 1998 and another 6 percent from 1998 to 1999, in spite of a very attractive interest-rate environment for home building.

In an attempt to offset the decline in sales, company management decided to use marketing research to get a better perspective on their customers so that they could better target their marketing efforts. After much discussion, the members of the executive committee finally determined that the following questions would be important to address in this research effort.

1. What is the demographic profile of the typical Fabhus customer?

2. What initially attracts these customers to a Fabhus home?

3. Do Fabhus home customers consider other factory-built homes when making their purchase decision?

4. Are Fabhus customers satisfied with their homes? If they are not, what particular features are unsatisfactory?

Method

The research firm that was called in on the project suggested conducting a mail survey to past buyers. Preliminary discussions with management revealed that Fabhus had the greatest market penetration near its factory. As one moved farther from the factory, the share of the total new housing business that went to Fabhus declined. The company suspected that this might result from the higher prices of the units due to shipping charges. Fabhus relied on a zone-price system in which prices were based on the product delivered at the construction site.

Local dealers actually supervised construction. Each dealer had pricing latitude and could charge more or less than Fabhus's suggested list price. Individual dealers were responsible for seeing that customers were satisfied with

their Fabhus home, although Fabhus also had a toll-free number that customers could call if they were not satisfied with the way their dealer handled the construction or if they had problems moving in.

Considering the potential impact distance and dealers might have, the research team thought it was important to sample purchasers in the various zones as well as customers of the various dealers. Since Fabhus's records of houses sold were kept by zone and by date sold within zone, sample respondents were selected in the following way. First, the registration cards per zone were counted. Second, the sample size per zone was determined so that the number of respondents per zone was proportionate to the number of homes sold in the zones. Third, a sample interval, k, was chosen for each zone, a random start between 1 and k was generated, and every kth record was selected. The mail questionnaire shown in Exhibit VI.G.1 was sent to the 423 households selected.

A cover letter informing Fabhus's customers of the general purpose of the survey accompanied the questionnaire, and a new one-dollar bill was included with each survey as an incentive to respond. Further, the anonymity of the respondents was guaranteed by enclosing a self-addressed postage-paid postcard in the survey. Respondents were asked to mail the postcard when they mailed their survey. All those who had not returned their postcards in two weeks were sent a notice reminding them that their survey had not been returned. The combination of incentives, guaranteed anonymity, and follow-up prompted the return of 342 questionnaires for an overall response rate of 81 percent.

A complete list of the data is available on the computer disk.

Questions

1. Using the data provided on the computer disk and analytic techniques of your own choosing, address as best you can the objectives that prompted the research effort in the first place.

2. Do you think the research design was adequate for the problems posed? Why or why not?

EXHIBIT VI.G.1   **Factory-Built Home Owners Survey**

1. How did you first learn of the factory-built home that you bought? (check one, please)

☐ Friend or relative   ☐ Direct mail

☐ Another customer   ☐ Newspaper

☐ Realtor   ☐ Radio

☐ Model home   ☐ TV

☐ Yellow pages   ☐ Don't remember

☐ National magazine   ☐ Other _____

(please specify)

2. Did you own the land your home is on before you first visited your home builder?

☐ Yes   ☐ No

3. How long have you lived in your home? _____ years

4. Where did you live before purchasing your factory-built home? (please check one)

☐ Rented a house, apartment, or mobile home

☐ Owned a mobile home

☐ Owned a conventionally built home

☐ Owned another factory-built home

☐ Other _____

(please specify)

5. Please rate your overall level of satisfaction with your home. (please check one)

☐ Very satisfied

☐ Somewhat satisfied

☐ Somewhat dissatisfied

☐ Very dissatisfied

6. How important to you were each of the following considerations in purchasing your factory-built home? (please check a box for each item)

Considerations	Extremely Important	Important	Slightly Important	Not Important
Investment value	☐	☐	☐	☐
Quality	☐	☐	☐	☐
Price	☐	☐	☐	☐
Energy features	☐	☐	☐	☐
Dealer	☐	☐	☐	☐
Exterior style	☐	☐	☐	☐
Floor plan	☐	☐	☐	☐
Interior features	☐	☐	☐	☐
Delivery schedule	☐	☐	☐	☐

7. Below, please list any other homes you looked at before purchasing the home you chose. Please state the reason you did not purchase the other home.

Name of Home	Factory-Built?	Reason for Not Purchasing
_____	☐ Yes ☐ No	_____
_____	☐ Yes ☐ No	_____
_____	☐ Yes ☐ No	_____
_____	☐ Yes ☐ No	_____

EXHIBIT VI.G.1   **Factory-Built Home Owners Survey,** *continued*

Now we would like you to please tell us about yourself and your family.

8. *How many children do you have living at home?* _____ children

9. *What is the age of the head of your household? (check one, please)*
- ☐ Under 20   ☐ 35–44   ☐ 55–64
- ☐ 20–24   ☐ 45–54   ☐ 65 or over
- ☐ 25–34

10. *What is the occupation of the head of the household? (check one, please)*
- ☐ Professional or official   ☐ Labor or machine operator
- ☐ Technical or manager   ☐ Foreman
- ☐ Proprietor   ☐ Service worker
- ☐ Farmer   ☐ Retired
- ☐ Craftsperson   ☐ Other _____
- ☐ Clerical or sales   (please specify)

11. *Which of the following categories includes your family's total annual income? (check one, please)*
- ☐ Less than $20,000   ☐ $50,000–$59,999
- ☐ $20,001–$29,999   ☐ $60,000–$69,999
- ☐ $30,000–$39,999   ☐ $70,000–$79,999
- ☐ $40,000–$49,999   ☐ $80,000 or over

12. *Is the spouse of the head of the household employed? (check one, please)*
- ☐ Spouse employed full-time   ☐ Spouse not employed
- ☐ Spouse employed part-time   ☐ Not married

One final question:

13. *Would you recommend your particular factory-built home to someone interested in building a new home?*
- ☐ Yes   ☐ No

Thank you very much for completing this survey.
Your help in this study is greatly appreciated.

Case VI.H   Como Western Bank[1]

Como Western Bank is one of several commercial lending institutions located in the Colorado community of Brentwood Hills. The bank maintains four branch offices with one branch each located in the east, west, north, and south districts of town. Its main office is located in downtown Brentwood Hills.

During the past decade, changes in the banking industry in Brentwood Hills have paralleled those taking place nationally, in that the environment has become increasingly complex and competitive. Deregulation, technological innovation, and changing interest rates have all made it difficult for banks to attract and keep customers. Local banks must now compete with insurance companies, multiservice investment firms, and even the government for clients. As a result, lending institutions are focusing increased attention on meeting consumer needs and developing strategies to increase their client base. Como Western is no exception.

[1]The contributions of David M. Szymanski to the development of this case are gratefully acknowledged.

A 1992 study of commercial banking in Brentwood Hills showed Como Western to have an above-average proportion of older households, long-time residents of the community, and middle-income persons as customers. The bank appeared to be less successful in attracting younger households, college graduates, and new residents of Brentwood Hills. In addition, the study found noncustomers of Como Western to have a weak image of the bank, even though customers held a very positive image. Bank officials sensed that these results typified the current situation as well. However, because the officials were in the process of developing a comprehensive marketing plan, they desired more up-to-date and detailed information to aid in formulating an appropriate marketing strategy. Therefore, bank officials contracted with the Mestousis Research Agency to study current bank customers. This small, local agency was led by its founder, Mike Mestousis, and Kathy Rendina, who served as the principal investigator on most projects. In addition, it employed six clerical people. The objectives of the study given to the Mestousis Agency were: (1) to determine the demographic profiles of present bank customers; (2) to determine customer awareness, use, and overall perception of current bank services; and (3) to identify new bank services desired by customers.

Research Method

The Mestousis Agency proposed and the bank's directors agreed that the study should be conducted in two phases. The first phase was designed to increase the research team's familiarity with Como Western's current clientele and service offerings. Several methods of inquiry were used. They included personal interviews with customers, bank employees, and members of the bank's board of directors, as well as a literature search of studies relating to the banking industry. Based on information gathered through these procedures, a questionnaire was developed to be used in the second portion of the project.

Because the information being sought was general yet personal in nature, the mail survey was deemed appropriate for data-collection purposes. To encourage a high response rate, a cover letter describing the research objectives and importance of responding was written by the bank president and mailed with each questionnaire, along with a stamped, self-addressed envelope. Furthermore, those who returned the questionnaire became eligible to participate in a drawing to win one of five $50 bills. To ensure anonymity, the name and address of the respondent was to be sealed in a separate envelope, which was supplied, and returned with the questionnaire.

The questionnaire shown in Exhibit VI.H.1 was also designed to encourage high response. The instructions made it clear that the information would be held in strict confidence, and the more sensitive questions were asked last. In addition, the questionnaire was extensively pretested using bank customers of various ages and backgrounds.

Several weeks before the questionnaire was mailed, customers were notified by means of the bank's newsletter of the possibility that they would be receiving the questionnaire.

Sampling Plan

The relevant population for the study was defined as all noncommercial customers of Como Western Bank who lived in Brentwood Hills and who were not employees of

---

EXHIBIT VI.H.1   Como Western Bank Customer Questionnaire

Please have the person who normally does the banking for your household fill out this questionnaire. The following information will be strictly confidential and is used ONLY for statistical analysis.

1. How many years have you been banking at the Como Western Bank?
   _____ years

2. Why did you choose to bank at Como Western Bank?
   _____
   _____
   _____

3. How often do you use the following to do your banking?

	Sometimes	Almost Always	Never
Lobby	_____	_____	_____
TYME machine	_____	_____	_____
Drive-up	_____	_____	_____
Walk-up	_____	_____	_____
Bank-by-mail	_____	_____	_____
Telephone	_____	_____	_____

EXHIBIT VI.H.1   Como Western Bank Customer Questionnaire, *continued*

4. The following is a list of GENERAL banking services. If you believe a service is available at Como Western Bank, please check whether you use the service. Otherwise, check if you believe a service is not available or if you are not certain.

	Available Used	Available Not Used	Not Available	Not Certain
Regular Checking	____	____	____	____
Regular Savings	____	____	____	____
Partnership Savings	____	____	____	____
NOW Account	____	____	____	____
Repurchase Agreement	____	____	____	____
IRA	____	____	____	____
Certificate of Deposit	____	____	____	____
U.S. Savings Bond	____	____	____	____
Personal Loan	____	____	____	____
Auto Loan	____	____	____	____
Mortgage Loan/Home Improvement Loan	____	____	____	____

5. How important are the following to you in selecting and staying with a bank? For each item, please place an X in the box which indicates the level of importance you assign to that item. For example, with the first item, "Close to my shopping areas," an X under "Extremely Important" means the item is extremely important to you in selecting and staying with a bank.

	Extremely Important	Very Important	Somewhat Important	Not Important But Desirable	Unimportant
Close to my shopping areas	____	____	____	____	____
Close to home	____	____	____	____	____
Close to work	____	____	____	____	____
Makes few errors	____	____	____	____	____
Friendly tellers	____	____	____	____	____
Leader with new services	____	____	____	____	____
Availability of personal loans	____	____	____	____	____
Low service charges	____	____	____	____	____
Convenient parking	____	____	____	____	____
Charges low rates for loans	____	____	____	____	____
Convenient hours	____	____	____	____	____
Is a large bank	____	____	____	____	____
Handles my complaints well	____	____	____	____	____
Pays high interest on savings	____	____	____	____	____
Has a wide variety of services	____	____	____	____	____
Fast service	____	____	____	____	____
Gives me enough information	____	____	____	____	____
Friendly personnel	____	____	____	____	____
Concerned about the community	____	____	____	____	____
Modern	____	____	____	____	____

6a. Please rate the COMO Western Bank on the following PAIRS of characteristics. Make an X in the box which you feel best describes the Como Western Bank. In the first item, for example, an X on the LEFT side under "Very Descriptive" means that you feel the bank is very close to your shopping areas. An X under "Very Descriptive" on the RIGHT side of the scale means you feel the bank is very far from the areas where you do your shopping.

continued

EXHIBIT VI.H.1   Como Western Bank Customer Questionnaire, *continued*

The Como Western Bank:

	Very Descriptive	Somewhat Descriptive	Neither	Somewhat Descriptive	Very Descriptive	
Is close to my shopping areas	____	____	____	____	____	Is far from my shopping areas
Is close to home	____	____	____	____	____	Is far from home
Is close to work	____	____	____	____	____	Is far from work
Makes a lot of errors	____	____	____	____	____	Makes few errors
Has friendly tellers	____	____	____	____	____	Has unfriendly tellers
Is a leader with new services	____	____	____	____	____	Is a follower with new services
Has personal loans available	____	____	____	____	____	Does not have personal loans available
Has low service charges	____	____	____	____	____	Has high service charges
Has inconvenient parking	____	____	____	____	____	Has convenient parking
Charges high rates for loans	____	____	____	____	____	Charges low rates for loans
Has convenient hours	____	____	____	____	____	Has inconvenient hours
Is large	____	____	____	____	____	Is small
Handles my complaints poorly	____	____	____	____	____	Handles my complaints well
Pays high interest on savings	____	____	____	____	____	Pays low interest on savings
Offers a wide variety of services	____	____	____	____	____	Offers limited services
Gives fast service	____	____	____	____	____	Gives slow service
Gives me enough information	____	____	____	____	____	Does not give me enough information
Has unfriendly personnel	____	____	____	____	____	Has friendly personnel
Is concerned about the community	____	____	____	____	____	Is not concerned about the community
Is old-fashioned	____	____	____	____	____	Is modern

6b. Since there are many financial institutions in the Brentwood Hills area, we are interested in knowing whether you feel the Como Western Bank is above average or below average. Using the scales from question 6a, mark an O on each line where you think other financial institutions as a whole rate.

7. Which of the following services would you use if they were offered at the Como Western Bank?

Discount brokerage ____   Tax preparation ____   Travel service ____

Insurance ____   Financial counseling ____   In-home banking ____
(Using personal computers)

Branch bank if it were located:

East ____   West ____   North ____   South ____

8. The following is a list of SPECIAL banking services. If you believe a service is available at the Como Western Bank, please check whether you use or do not use the service. Otherwise check if you believe a service is not available or if you are not certain.

	Available Used	Available Not Used	Not Available	Not Certain
Safe deposit	____	____	____	____
VISA/MASTERCARD	____	____	____	____
Priority Service for Seniors	____	____	____	____
24-Hour Depository	____	____	____	____
Overdraft Protection	____	____	____	____
Investment Management	____	____	____	____
Notary Public	____	____	____	____
Estate and Financial Planning	____	____	____	____

EXHIBIT VI.H.1   Como Western Bank Customer Questionnaire, *continued*

	Available Used	Available Not Used	Not Available	Not Certain
Trust Services	____	____	____	____
Utility Payments	____	____	____	____
Traveler's Cheques	____	____	____	____
Foreign Currency Exchange	____	____	____	____
TYME Card	____	____	____	____
Telephone Transfer	____	____	____	____
Wire Transfer	____	____	____	____
Direct Deposit	____	____	____	____
U.S. Treasury Bills and Notes	____	____	____	____

9. How do you obtain your local banking and financial information? (Please check all that apply.)

Newspaper ____   Friends ____   Bank Personnel ____

Television ____   Magazines ____   Bank Statement Stuffers ____

Radio ____   Bank Newsletter ____   Other (please write in) ____

_____

10. Is the information you obtain from the above sources sufficient?

Yes ____ No ____

If No, why not? _____

_____

11. Do you maintain accounts with other financial institutions (savings & loan, credit union, other bank, etc.)?

Yes ____ No ____

__ If Yes, please answer the next two questions (11a & 11b) before going on.

__ If No, go on to question 12.

11a. Which services do you use at other financial institutions?

Checking Account ____   VISA/MASTERCARD ____   U.S. Treasury Bills and Notes ____

Regular Savings ____   Trust Services ____   Safe Deposit Box ____

Certificate of Deposit ____   Money Market Funds ____   Personal Loan ____

Repurchase Agreement ____   Stocks and Bonds ____   Mortgage Loan ____

IRA ____   Auto Loan ____   Other (please write in) ____

_____

11b. Why do you use services at other financial institutions rather than the Como Western Bank?

_____

_____

12. Would you recommend the Como Western Bank to a friend?

Yes ____ No ____ Don't Know ____

13. Overall, how do you rate the service you have received from the Como Western Bank?

Excellent	Good	Acceptable	Poor	Unacceptable
____	____	____	____	____

14. Do you have any comments about or suggested changes for the Como Western Bank?

_____

_____

_____

15. Please check your sex and marital status.

Male ____   Single ____   Widowed ____

Female ____   Married ____   Divorced/Separated ____

continued

EXHIBIT VI.H.1   **Como Western Bank Customer Questionnaire,** *continued*

16. How many dependents do you have in your household?

    0 _____   1–2 _____   3–5 _____   6 or more _____

17. Are you the primary wage earner in your household?

    Yes _____   No _____

18. Please check your age and the highest level of education you reached. (If applicable, please check your spouse's age and highest level of education.)

Age	Self	Spouse	Education	Self	Spouse
Under 18	_____	_____	Grade School	_____	_____
18–21	_____	_____	Some High School	_____	_____
22–30	_____	_____	High School Graduate	_____	_____
31–40	_____	_____	Vocational/Technical	_____	_____
41–50	_____	_____	Attended College	_____	_____
51–64	_____	_____	College Graduate	_____	_____
65 or over	_____	_____	Post-Graduate Study	_____	_____

19. Please check the occupation which best applies to you. (If applicable, please check your spouse's occupation.)

	Self	Spouse		Self	Spouse
Professional/Technical	_____	_____	Craftsman	_____	_____
Farmer	_____	_____	Serviceworker	_____	_____
Manager, Administrator	_____	_____	Laborer	_____	_____
Proprietor	_____	_____	Retired	_____	_____
Clerical	_____	_____	Student	_____	_____
Sales	_____	_____	Not Currently Working	_____	_____

20. Please check the estimated total household income before taxes in 1997.

    $0–19,999 _____ $40,000–49,999 _____ $70,000–79,999 _____
    $20,000–29,999 _____ $50,000–59,999 _____ $80,000 or more _____
    $30,000–39,999 _____ $60,000–69,999 _____

21. How many people in your household work outside the home? _____

22. How many years have you lived in the Brentwood Hills area?

    Less than 1 year _____   6–10 years _____
    1–3 years _____   more than 10 years _____
    4–5 years _____

Thank you for taking the time to complete this questionnaire.

---

the bank. The total number of customers meeting these requirements was 10,300. A printout of bank customers revealed that bank records list customers in blocks according to ZIP codes.

The researchers were of the opinion that 500 survey responses were required to adequately perform the analysis. Anticipating a 30 to 35 percent response rate, 1,500 to 1,600 surveys needed to be mailed. Given 10,300 population elements and the estimated sample size of

1,600, the researchers decided to send a questionnaire to one of every six names on the list. They generated the first name randomly using a table of random numbers. It was the fourth name on the list. They consequently sent questionnaires to the fourth, tenth, sixteenth, and so on names on the list. In all, 1,547 questionnaires were sent and 673 were returned for a response rate of approximately 44 percent. Exhibit VI.H.2 displays the coding form while the raw data are contained in file COMOWEST.DAT.

EXHIBIT VI.H.2 **Coding Form**

RECORD 1

Columns	Description (Question)	Coding
1–3	Subject ID	
4–5	Years banking at Como Western (#1)	
6	Reason for choosing Como Western (#2)	1 = location
		2 = convenience
		3 = recommendation/reputation
		4 = previous contact
		5 = quality of service
		6 = free checking
		7 = variety of accounts
		8 = loan
		9 = other reasons
	Frequency with which services are used (#3)	1 = sometimes
		2 = almost always
		3 = never
7	Lobby	
8	TYME Machine	
9	Drive-up	
10	Walk-up	
11	Bank-by-mail	
12	Telephone	
	Use of services (4)	1 = available/used
		2 = available/not used
		3 = not available
		4 = not certain
13	Regular checking	
14	Regular savings	
15	Partnership savings	
16	NOW account	
17	Repurchase agreement	
18	IRA	
19	Certificate of deposit	
20	U.S. Savings Bond	
21	Personal loan	
22	Auto loan	
23	Mortgage/home improvement loan	
	Importance of various features (#5)	1 = extremely important
		2 = very important
		3 = somewhat important
		4 = not important but desirable
		5 = unimportant

continued

EXHIBIT VI.H.2   Coding Form, *continued*

Columns	Description (Question)	Coding
24	Close to my shopping areas	
25	Close to home	
26	Close to work	
27	Makes few errors	
28	Friendly tellers	
29	Leader with new services	
30	Availability of personal loans	
31	Low service charges	
32	Convenient parking	
33	Charges low rates for loans	
34	Convenient hours	
35	Is a large bank	
36	Handles my complaints well	
37	pays high interest on savings	
38	Has a wide variety of services	
39	Fast service	
40	Gives me enough information	
41	Friendly personnel	
42	Concerned about the community	
43	Modern	

Rating of Como on various features (#6A)

1 = very descriptive
2 = somewhat descriptive
3 = neither
4 = somewhat descriptive
5 = very descriptive

Columns	Description (Question)
44	Close to my shopping areas/far from my shopping areas
45	Close to home/far form home
46	Close to work/far from work
47	Makes a lot of errors/makes few errors
48	Friendly tellers/unfriendly tellers
49	A leader with new services/a follower with new services
50	Personal loans available/personal loans not available
51	Low service charges/high service charges
52	Inconvenient parking/convenient parking
53	Charges high rates for loans/charges low rates for loans
54	Convenient hours/inconvenient hours
55	Large/small
56	Handles my complaints poorly/handles my complaints well
57	Pays high interest on savings/pays low interest on savings
58	Wide variety of services/limited services
59	Fast service/slow service
60	Gives me enough information/does not give me enough information
61	Unfriendly personnel/friendly personnel
62	Concerned about the community/not concerned about the community
63	Old-fashioned/modern

EXHIBIT VI.H.2   **Coding Form,** *continued*

Columns	Description (Question)	Coding
	Services that would be used if available (#7)	1 = yes; 2 = no
64	Discount brokerage	
65	Insurance	
66	Tax preparation	
67	Financial counseling	
68	Travel service	
69	In-home banking	
70	East side branch	
71	West side branch	
72	North side branch	
73	South side branch	

RECORD 2

Columns	Description (Question)	Coding
1–3	Subject ID	
	Use of special services at Como Western (#8)	1 = available/used
		2 = available/not used
		3 = not available
		4 = not certain
4	Safe deposit	
5	VISA/MASTERCARD	
6	Priority service for seniors	
7	24-hour depository	
8	Overdraft protection	
9	Investment management	
10	Notary public	
11	Estate and financial planning	
12	Trust services	
13	Utility payments	
14	Traveler's cheques	
15	Foreign currency exchange	
16	TYME card	
17	Telephone transfer	
18	Wire transfer	
19	Direct deposit	
20	U.S. Treasury Bills and Notes	
	Source of local banking and financial information (#9)	1 = use
		2 = do not use
21	Newspaper	
22	Television	
23	Radio	
24	Bank personnel	
25	Friends	
26	Magazines	
27	Bank newsletter	

continued

EXHIBIT VI.H.2   **Coding Form,** *continued*

Columns	Description (Question)	Coding
28	Bank statement stuffers	
29	Other	
30	Is information sufficient (#10)	1 = yes; 2 = no
31	Maintain accounts with other financial institutions (#11)	1 = yes; 2 = no
	Services used at other institutions (#11a)	1 = use; 2 = do not use
32	Checking account	
33	Regular savings	
34	Certificate of Deposit	
35	Repurchase agreement	
36	IRA	
37	VISA/MASTERCARD	
38	Trust services	
39	Money market funds	
40	Stocks and bonds	
41	U.S. Treasury bills and notes	
42	Safe deposit box	
43	Personal loan	
44	Mortgage loan	
45	Auto loan	
46	Other	
47–48	Why use services at other institutions (#11b)	1 = branch location 2 = convenience 3 = already had account 4 = special services unavailable 5 = charges/balance 6 = savings interest rates 7 = low loan rates 8 = loan availability 9 = risk diversification 10 = service quality 11 = need separate accounts 12 = other
49	Recommend Como to a friend (#12)	1 = yes; 2 = no; 3 = don't know
50	Quality of service overall (#13)	1 = excellent 2 = good 3 = acceptable 4 = poor 5 = unacceptable
51–52	Comments and suggested changes (#14)	1 = branches 2 = personnel 3 = service charge

EXHIBIT VI.H.2   Coding Form, *continued*

Columns	Description (Question)	Coding
		4 = hours
		5 = general-negative
		6 = error rate
		7 = general-favorable
		8 = neutral
		9 = other
53	Sex (#15)	1 = male; 2 = female
54	Marital status (#15)	1 = single
		2 = married
		3 = widowed
		4 = divorced/separated
55	Number of dependents (#16)	1 = none
		2 = 1–2
		3 = 3–5
		4 = 6 or more
56	Primary wage earner (#17)	1 = yes; 2 = no
57–58	Age of self; age of spouse (#18)	1 = under 18
		2 = 18-21
		3 = 22–30
		4 = 31–40
		5 = 41–50
		6 = 51–64
		7 = 65 or over
59–60	Education of self; education of spouse (#18)	1 = grade school
		2 = some high school
61–62; 63–64	Occupation of self; occupation of spouse (#19)	1 = professional technical
		2 = farmer
		3 = manager/administrator
		4 = proprietor
		5 = clerical
		6 = sales
		7 = craftsman
		8 = serviceworker
		9 = laborer
		10 = retired
		11 = student
		12 = not currently working
65	Estimated household income (#20)	1 = $0–$19,999
		2 = $20,000–$29,999
		3 = $30,000–$39,999
		4 = $40,000–$49,999
		5 = $50,000–$59,999

continued

EXHIBIT VI.H.2   **Coding Form,** *continued*

Columns	Description (Question)	Coding
		6 = $60,000–$69,999
		7 = $70,000–$79,999
		8 = $80,000 or more
66	Number of people working outside home (#21)	1 = 0
		2 = 1
		3 = 2
		4 = 3 or more
67	Years lived in area (#22)	1 = less than 1
		2 = 1–3
		3 = 4–5
		4 = 6–10
		5 = more than 10

Questions

1. Evaluate the general research design.

2. Evaluate the sampling plan.

3. What do the results suggest with respect to the following:
   (a) The demographic characteristics of Como Western's customers?
   (b) Customer awareness, use, and perceptions of the various services provided by Como Western?
   (c) The relationship, if any, between age and income of the respondents and their overall evaluation of the services provided by Como Western?

4. What new services, if any, should Como Western offer?

Case VI.I   Joseph Machine Company

The Joseph Machine Company, which was named after its founder and longtime owner/manager Gerald Joseph, produced pumps and air compressors. Joseph Machine had for some time been concerned with improving the procedures by which its sales force was selected. The company had always hired engineering graduates for this work because an equipment sale demanded some technical sophistication on the part of sales representative. A sales representative simply had to be able to respond to a customer's technical questions about the equipment, and also to explain how the customer's processing system might be better designed. Assuming that a prospective sales candidate had an engineering degree (mechanical or electrical degrees were preferred, but others were accepted as well), the hiring decision was made primarily on the basis of a personal interview with several executives in the company. Those doing the interviewing often disagreed as to what kinds of credentials and candidates were acceptable.

The company was interested in determining whether there were some more objective criteria that could be employed in the hiring decision. An examination of sales performance literature suggested that a sales representative's personality and intellectual abilities are often primary determinants of success. The company therefore decided to administer personality and IQ tests to each of its sales representatives to determine whether there was any association between these characteristics and the representatives' performance. Total sales for the past year in relation to territory quota, expressed as an index, were to be employed as the performance criterion, and Joseph Machine wished to control for any differences in performance that might be attributable to time on the job.

The following data resulted from the investigation:

Sales Represen- tative	Per- formance Index	IQ Test	Personality Score	Time on the Job (in months)	Sales Represen- tative	Per- formance Index	IQ Test	Personality Score	Time on the Job (in months)
1	122	130	86	78	21	99	116	69	53
2	105	100	62	48	22	102	113	82	89
3	103	93	85	81	23	98	109	81	75
4	95	81	72	62	24	100	86	68	71
5	97	98	78	98	25	99	92	61	74
6	106	114	68	63	26	99	92	75	79
7	100	87	79	72	27	113	81	71	87
8	115	82	67	85	28	114	103	79	84
9	78	115	70	59	29	110	114	76	106
10	101	114	64	55	30	98	92	83	109
11	115	92	84	117	31	92	105	81	80
12	120	81	84	103	32	106	81	79	85
13	88	89	56	49	33	103	81	84	95
14	110	82	87	110	34	111	85	55	67
15	96	92	82	77	35	102	98	54	61
16	93	85	65	60	36	102	84	74	83
17	92	85	70	74	37	88	109	65	45
18	103	114	64	82	38	105	85	66	93
19	121	85	83	115	39	94	91	62	64
20	95	99	84	102	40	108	81	79	63
					41	84	101	59	41

Questions

1. Is there any relationship between a sales representative's performance and IQ? Performance and personality score?

2. Do the relationship changes when time on the job is held constant?

3. What amount of performance can be attributed to all three factors considered simultaneously?

4. Evaluate your method of analysis and also evaluate the procedure being employed by Joseph Machine Company to improve its sales representative selection procedures.

Research Reports

Part Seven consists of two chapters and an epilogue. Chapter 22 discusses one of the most important parts of the whole research process: the research report. The research report often becomes the standard by which the entire research effort is assessed, and it is important that the report contribute positively to the evaluation of the effort. Chapter 22 deals with the criteria a research report should satisfy and the form a research report can follow so that it does contribute positively to the research effort. Chapter 23 then discusses how to deliver effective oral reports and also reviews some of the graphic devices that can be employed to communicate important findings more forcefully. The epilogue ties together the parts of the research process. It reinforces the points made early in the text, that the steps in the research process are highly interrelated and a decision made at one stage has implications for the others, by demonstrating the nature of some of these interrelationships.

MINT MUSEUM OF ART USES RESEARCH TO PAINT A PICTURE OF ITS FUTURE Charlotte, North Carolina's Mint Museum of Art was at a crossroads that is familiar to many organizations. Its environment was changing, and it faced new opportunities. If the museum could correctly interpret and act on those opportunities, its future looked bright.

Although the museum is a nonprofit organization, not a business, the challenge was really a marketing challenge. It had to answer the basic marketing questions, Who are our customers, and what do they want? The Mint, as the museum is known, formed a marketing committee and hired a research firm, InterActive Research, to find the answers.

The Mint has a solid reputation as a cultural institution of the Southeast. It boasts an eclectic collection of historic costumes; paintings by European and American artists; pre-Columbian, African, and Spanish Colonial works; regional pottery and other crafts; and European and American porcelain and pottery. The Mint also enjoys a location in a growing city, and it was to receive the gift of a new space. NationsBank donated to the Mint a historic five-story building, the former Montaldo's clothing store.

Decision makers at the Mint looked at all these assets—the wide-ranging collection, growing population, and new space—and saw many pressing questions: What did the public want? How could it manage its collection and focus future acquisitions? Did the public even understand what the Mint had to offer?

The team from InterActive Research, based in Atlanta, designed a two-part study to measure awareness of, attitudes toward, and usage of the museum. The first part of the study involved 15 focus groups to uncover relevant issues and attitudes. The second part of the study consisted of mail questionnaires to gather quantitative data.

The focus groups brought together a sample of participants designed to be representative of the Mint's current and potential visitors: Mint members and nonmembers, young professionals who fit the typical demographics of a member, and Charlotte residents who differed from that typical-member profile.

The questionnaire was mailed to 10,000 residents of the Charlotte area. Of those residents, 1,300 replied.

In reporting the results, InterActive contrasted the data with the museum's preconceptions. For example, it compared its sample of Mint visitors with the museum's membership data, giving the institution a clearer picture of its public and its potential membership base. The comparison also helped the Mint pinpoint why some visitors had not (yet) become members.

The research report discussed respondents' attitudes and expectations. It indicated that many members of the public were intimidated by the Mint's elegance. Some felt it was an elite institution that would not necessarily welcome them. The museum's cold marble lobby reinforced this impression.

Decision makers at the Mint applied these findings to plans for the original museum and for the new space in the Montaldo's Building. To make the original museum more engaging, the Mint decided to reorganize its collections in terms of the theme "Art in the Americas." It began reinstalling its collections so that items are grouped according to their age. Exhibits move in chronological order from pre-Columbian art and artifacts through modern art. European pieces are arranged to show their influence on American artists of the time.

The museum decided to auction off pieces that did not fit the theme. This further supports the Mint's strategy by providing funds for additional acquisitions.

For the Montaldo's Building, the Mint planned to create a new museum to be called the Mint Museum of Craft and Design. The research showed the public was favorable to this idea but didn't fully understand it. In particular, there was no consensus about the meaning of "craft." The Mint therefore recognized it would have to plan an educational program along with the museum itself. In addition, it decided to make the facility feel welcoming by creating a visually warm entrance area featuring wood floors.

InterActive's research also addressed practical issues related to a museum: admission charges, parking, and food service. The researchers reported that people were concerned about the cost, safety, and availability of parking convenient to the uptown Montaldo's Building. The museum therefore realized it would have to include plans for public parking in the development of the craft and design museum.

Using responses to questions about what the public would pay, the researchers developed specific recommendations. They reported that people would be willing to pay an entrance fee between $5 and $7. In addition, they found significant interest in joint membership packages with other museums, which would grant members entrance to multiple institutions.

The research report also indicated solid support for facilities offering refreshments at both Mint museums. However, the museums operate in existing structures, so the museum staff had to weigh this information against the limitations of both buildings. Neither building was equipped to offer restaurant services, so the Mint initially planned to offer visitors to the Mint Museum of Craft and Design a map of nearby restaurants.

Finally, InterActive reported that the public wanted to see national touring shows, not just permanent collections. So the Mint met that need with the first exhibit in its new museum of Craft and Design. It opened the museum with an exhibit titled "The White House Collection of American Craft," presented at the end of a national tour. Following its exhibition at the Mint, the collection would be installed permanently at the Smithsonian. With shows such as this, the Mint put the Museum of Craft and Design on the map of worthy public museums—and ensured itself a place in the heart of North Carolinians for years to come.

Source: Michael Straus, "Minting a New Mint," *Quirk's Marketing Research Review* (February 1998, downloaded from *Quirk's* Web site, www.quirks.com, August 13, 1999).

Chapter 22

THE WRITTEN RESEARCH REPORT

LEARNING OBJECTIVES

Upon Completing This Chapter, You Should Be Able to

1. Specify the fundamental criterion by which all research reports are evaluated.

2. Identify and discuss the four criteria that a report should meet if it is to communicate effectively with readers.

3. Outline the main elements that make up a standard report form.

4. Explain the kind of information that is contained in the summary.

5. Distinguish between a conclusion and a recommendation.

6. Describe the kind of information that should be contained in the introduction.

7. Describe the kind of information that should be contained in the body.

8. Describe the kind of information that should be contained in the appendix.

Case in Marketing Research

Eric O'Donnell had spent a glorious summer weekend in the office, at his desk, working on the report for Oakhurst Hospital. To make matters worse, his boss, Caroline Sords, had asked him to drop off the first draft at her house when he'd finished. That was how he came to be sitting in his mentor's living room Sunday evening, studying her face for signs of a reaction.

"You know," said Sords, finally looking up from the report, "your writing has gotten a lot clearer since you first started, but you're still not writing to your audience. Tell me, who is going to read this report?"

"George Scanlon," replied O'Donnell promptly.

"And who else?"

"Probably Anthony Walsh."

"You'd better believe Walsh is going to read it," exclaimed Sords, "not to mention the hospital's chief financial officer, the board of directors, some of the trustees, the department heads, and, for all we know, the members of the Ladies Auxiliary."

"You think the report is too technical," groaned O'Donnell.

"You know it is," replied his boss kindly. "Eric, we're talking about a group of people—with the exception of Scanlon, who's got an M.B.A. in marketing—who think that a cross tab is something that holds your tie in place."

"I'll just scrap it and start over," said O'Donnell, determined to do a good job.

"You don't have to scrap the technical sections. Just move them into the appendix, where Scanlon can pore over them to his heart's content. And don't be discouraged. It's hard to keep in mind that most people are mystified by anything mathematical.

"But the truth is, our ultimate goal is to enable the hospital to improve its care delivery by acting on our findings. If they can't understand what we found out because they're confused by our complex analysis or turned off by your jargon, then we've failed—no matter how strong our research or how valid our findings."

"I don't know why I'm having such a hard time with this," said O'Donnell.

"You're having a hard time because it is really hard. But it'll be a whole lot easier if you go home and get a good night's sleep. I know you'll get it right if you tackle it fresh tomorrow morning."

Discussion Issues

1. What is the primary danger of an overly technical research report?

2. How might a research report like the one that O'Donnell is writing, which will be read by a wide audience with varying backgrounds, differ from one targeted to a smaller, more homogeneous audience?

A frustrated executive of a large corporation once remarked that "he is convinced reports are devices by which the informed ensure that the uninformed remain that way."[1] To avoid creating the kind of report that executive was thinking of requires considerable amounts of knowledge, skill, and attention to detail. If length were the criterion of importance of a chapter, there would be an inverse relationship between this chapter and the criterion. This chapter is short, but its subject is vital to the success of the research effort. Regardless of the sophistication displayed in other portions of the research process, the project is a failure if the research report fails.

The empirical evidence indicates that the research report is one of the five most important variables affecting the use of research information.[2] The research steps discussed in the preceding chapters of this text determine the content of the research report, but since the report is all that many executives will see of the project, it becomes the yardstick for evaluation. The writer must ensure that the report informs without misinforming.

The report must tell readers what they need and wish to know. Typically, executives must be convinced of the usefulness of the findings. They are more interested in results than methods. However, to act on the report effectively, they must know enough about the methods that were used to recognize the methods' weaknesses and bounds of error. It is the researcher's responsibility to convey this information to the decision maker in sufficient detail and in understandable form.

In this chapter and the next, we will offer some guidelines for developing successful research reports. In this chapter we will focus on the criteria by which research reports are evaluated and the parts and forms of the written research report.

Research Report Criteria

Research reports are evaluated by one fundamental criterion—how well they communicate with the reader. The "iron law" of marketing research holds, for example, that "people would rather live with a problem they cannot solve than accept a solution they cannot understand."[3] The reader is not only the reason that the report is prepared, but also the standard by which its success is measured. This means that the report must be tailor-made for its reader or readers, with due regard for their technical sophistication, their interest in the subject area, the circumstances under which they will read the report, and the use they will make of it.

The technical sophistication of the readers determines their capacity for understanding methodological decisions, such as experimental design, measurement device, sampling plan, analysis technique, and so on. Readers with little technical sophistication will more than likely take offense at the use of unexplained technical jargon. "The readers of your reports are busy people, and very few of them can balance a research report, a cup of coffee, and a dictionary at one time."[4] Unexplained jargon may even make such persons suspicious of the report writer. Researchers should try to be particularly sensitive to this hazard, because, being technical people, they may fail to realize that they are using technical language unless they remind themselves to watch for it.

While the readers' backgrounds and need for methodological detail will determine the upper limit for the technical content of the report, it is the readers' individual preferences that must guide the report writer.

Some executives demand a minimum report; they want only the results—not a discussion of how the results were obtained. Others want considerable information on the research methods used in the study. Many executives place a premium on brevity, while others demand complete discussion. Some are interested only in the statistical results and not in the researcher's conclusions and recommendations.

Thus, the audience determines the type of report. Researchers must make every effort to acquaint themselves with the specific preferences of their audience. They should not consider these preferences as unalterable, but *any deviations from them should be made with reason and not from ignorance!*[5] (Emphasis added.)

The report writer's difficulties in tailoring the report are often compounded by the existence of several audiences. The marketing vice president might have a different technical capacity and level of interest than the product manager responsible for the product discussed in the report. There is no easy solution to this problem of "many masters." The researcher must recognize the potential differences that may arise and may have to exercise a great deal of ingenuity to reconcile them. Occasionally, a researcher may find it necessary to prepare several reports, each designed for a specific audience, although more often the conflicting demands can be satisfied by one report that contains both technical and nontechnical sections for different readers.

In the experience of Ron Sellers, president of Ellison Research, researchers can best tailor their reports if they have earlier asked their clients what they are looking for. Sellers recommends asking the people for whom the report will be prepared to answer a few questions:

- What are the five or ten most important items you want the study to focus on (for example, satisfaction with product quality, intent to buy from a competitor)?

- What do you hope the research will show?

- What do you think the research will show?

The report then would highlight comparisons between the actual results and the audience's hopes and expectations for the key data items. Such a focus is almost certain to be significant to the audience—and grab their attention.[6]

Writing Criteria

A report that achieves the goal of communicating effectively with readers is generally one that meets the specific criteria of completeness, accuracy, clarity, and conciseness.[7] These criteria are intimately related. An accurate report, for example, is also a complete report. For discussion purposes, however, it is helpful to discuss the criteria as if they were distinct.

Completeness

Completeness
A criterion used to evaluate a research report; specifically, whether the report provides all the information readers need in language they understand.

A report is **complete** when it provides all the information readers need in language they understand. This means that the writer must continually ask whether every question in the original assignment has been addressed. What alternatives were examined? What was found? An incomplete report implies that supplementary reports, which are annoying and delay action, will be forthcoming.

The report may be incomplete because it is too brief or too long. The writer may omit necessary definitions and short explanations. On the other hand, the report may be lengthy but not profound, due to a reluctance to waste any collected information. In a report full of nonvital information, the main issues are often lost in the clutter. Also, if the report is big, it may discourage readers from even attempting to digest its contents.

Readers are thus the key to determining completeness. Their interest and abilities determine what clarification should be added and what findings should be omitted. In general, the amount of detail should be proportionate to the amount of direct control users can exercise over the areas under discussion. For example, if the intended reader is a product's advertising manager, it would generally be wise to omit a lengthy discussion of possible improvements to production techniques.

This principle would have prevented some frustration if it had been applied to some research that a firm conducted for the Turner Entertainment Group. Turner had hired the firm to conduct studies to support the development of Web sites for some of its entities, which include TBS, TNT, and the Cartoon network. Having demonstrated its ability to provide useful information for Web site development, the research firm urged Turner to try a new service that involved collecting ongoing, real-time data from visitors to the Web sites, including their demographics, satisfaction, and media consumption habits. The research firm pointed out that these ongoing reports, based on 100 surveys per week, would enable Webmasters to tweak sites in response to the most recent feedback. However, the Webmasters were appalled at the idea of having to review a continuous stream of research reports and add to their already heavy workload of maintaining Web sites. Under those conditions, Turner backed away from the idea of real-time research reporting. Dan Coates, a member of the research firm, explains the decision this way: "Just because you can incorporate all of this stuff and create one large on-line report that encompasses everything, doesn't mean you should." Turner instead opted to receive research updates once or twice a year.[8]

Accuracy

The previously discussed steps in the research process are obviously vital to accuracy, but, given accurate input, the research report may generate inaccuracies because of careless-

---

EXHIBIT 22.1   **Some Examples of Sources of Inaccuracy in Report Writing**

A. Simple Errors in Addition or Subtraction

"In the United States, 14 percent of the population has an elementary school education or less, 51 percent has attended or graduated from high school, and 16 percent has attended college."

An oversight such as this (14 + 51 + 16 does not equal 100 percent) can be easily corrected by the author, but not so easily by the reader, because he or she may not know if one or more of the percentage values is incorrect or if a category might have been left out of the tally.

B. Confusion between Percentages and Percentage Points

"The company's profits as a percentage of sales were 6.0 percent in 1990 and 8.0 percent in 1995. Therefore, they increased only 2.0 percent in five years."

In this example, the increase is, of course, 2.0 percentage points, or 33 percent.

C. Inaccuracy Caused by Grammatical Errors

"The reduction in the government's price supports for dairy products has reduced farm income $600 million to $800 million per year."

To express a range of reduction, the author should have written, "The reduction in the government's price supports for dairy products has reduced farm income $600–800 million per year."

D. Confused Terminology Resulting in Fallacious Conclusions

"The Joneses' household annual income increased from $10,000 in 1969 to $30,000 in 1999, thereby tripling the family's purchasing power."

While the Joneses' household income annual may have tripled in 30 years, the family's purchasing power certainly did not, as the cost of living, as measured by the consumer price index, more than tripled in the same period.

Accuracy
A criterion used to evaluate a research report; specifically, whether the reasoning in the report is logical and the information correct.

ness in handling the data, illogical reasoning, or inept phrasing.[9] Thus, **accuracy** is another writing criterion. Exhibit 22.1 illustrates some examples of sources of inaccuracy in report writing.

The possession of advanced degrees is no safeguard against the hazards detailed in Exhibit 22.1. In fact, the more educated a person is, the more apt he or she may be to sink into the morass of excess verbiage. Consider the president of a major university who, in the late 1960s, wrote a letter to soothe anxious alumni after a spell of campus unrest. "You are probably aware," he began, "that we have been experiencing very considerable potentially explosive expressions of dissatisfaction on issues only partially related." He meant that the students had been hassling the university about different things.[10] In Research Window 22.1, Jock Elliott, chairman emeritus of the advertising agency Ogilvy & Mather, shows how one corporate vice president also sank into the quicksand of his own words.

Inaccuracies also arise because of grammatical errors in punctuation, spelling, tense, subject and verb agreement, and so on.[11] Careful attention to detail in these areas is essential for any report writer.

Research Window 22.1 | **How to Write Your Way Out of a Job**

Jock Elliott, the chairman emeritus of the Ogilvy & Mather advertising agency, is a man who appreciates good writing. After all, his business is built on his employees' ability to communicate with clients and consumers.

Elliott makes no bones about the importance of being able to write well in order to advance in a career. "As you sail along on your career," he writes, "bad writing acts as a sea anchor, pulling you back, good writing as a spinnaker, pulling you ahead."

In the following excerpt from an article he wrote, he tells about one prospective employee who sank beneath the waves, weighted down by the anchor of his own words.

"Last month I got a letter from a vice president of a major management consulting firm. Let me read you two paragraphs. The first:

> Recently, the companies of our Marketing Services Group were purchased by one of the largest consumer research firms in the U.S. While this move well fits the basic business purpose and focus of the acquired MSG units, it is personally restrictive. I will rather choose to expand my management opportunities with a career move into industry.

"What he meant was: The deal works fine for my company, but not so fine for me. I'm looking for another job.

"Second paragraph:

> The base of managerial and technical accomplishment reflected in my enclosed resumé may suggest an opportunity to meet a management need for one of your clients. Certainly my experience promises a most productive pace to understand the demands and details of any new situation I would choose.

"What he meant was: As you can see in my resumé, I've had a lot of good experience. I am a quick study. Do you think any of your clients might be interested in me?

"At least, that's what I think he meant.

"This fellow's letter reveals him as pompous. He may not be pompous. He may only be a terrible writer. But I haven't the interest or time to find out which. There are so many people looking for jobs who don't sound like pompous asses.

"Bad writing done him in—with me, at any rate."

Jock Elliott, "How Hard It Is to Write Easily," *Viewpoint: By, For, and About Ogilvy & Mather* 2 (1980), p. 18. The use of jargon and imprecise expression have become so commonplace that computer programs that analyze grammar, readability, and sentence structure and suggest alternative wordings have been developed to deal with it. Microsoft Office 97, for example, contains a grammar checker, as do many of the most popular word processing programs. See Stephen H. Wildstrom, "Good Help Gets Easier to Find," *Business Week* (February 10, 1997), p. 21.

Clarity

Clarity
A criterion used to evaluate a research report; specifically, whether the phrasing in the report is precise.

The writing criterion of **clarity** is probably failed more than any other. Clarity is produced by clear and logical thinking and precision of expression. When the underlying logic is fuzzy or the presentation imprecise, readers experience difficulty in understanding what they read. They may be forced to guess, in which case the corollary to Murphy's law applies: "If the reader is offered the slightest opportunity to misunderstand, he probably will."[12] Achieving clarity, however, requires effort.

The first, and most important, rule is that the report be well organized.[13] For this to happen, you must first clarify for yourself the purpose of your report and how you intend to accomplish it. Make an outline of your major points. Put the points in logical order and place the supporting details in their proper position. Tell the reader what you are going to cover in the report and then do what you said you were going to do. Use short paragraphs and short sentences. Do not be evasive or ambiguous; once you have decided what you want to say, come right out and say it. Choose your words carefully, making them as precise and understandable as possible. See Research Window 22.2 for some specific suggestions when choosing words.

Do not expect your first draft to be satisfactory. Expect to rewrite it several times. When rewriting, attempt to reduce the length by half. That forces you to simplify and remove the clutter. It also forces you to think about every word and its purpose, to evaluate whether each word is helping you say what you wish to say. Jock Elliott has some very pointed comments on writing clearly:

> Our written and spoken words reflect what we are. If our words are brilliant, precise, well ordered and human, then that is how we are seen.
>
> When you write, you must constantly ask yourself: What am I trying to say? If you do this religiously, you will be surprised at how often you don't know what you are trying to say.
>
> You have to think before you start every sentence, and you have to think about ever word.
>
> Then you must look at what you have written and ask: Have I said it? Is it clear to someone encountering the subject for the first time? If it's not, it is because some fuzz has worked its way into the machinery. The clear writer is a person clearheaded enough to see this stuff for what it is: fuzz.

Source: Cartoon by Harley Schwadron.
Reprinted with permission.

" WE GOT THE ASPIRIN ACCOUNT! A STUDY SHOWED OUR ADS GIVE PEOPLE HEADACHES. "

1. *Use short words.* Always use short words in preference to long words that mean the same thing.

Use this	Not this
Now	Currently
Start	Initiate
Show	Indicate
Finish	Finalize
Use	Utilize
Place	Position

2. *Avoid vague modifiers.* Avoid lazy adjectives and adverbs and use vigorous ones. Lazy modifiers are so overused in some contexts that they have become clichés. Select only those adjectives and adverbs that make your meaning precise.

Lazy modifiers	Vigorous modifiers
Very good	Short meeting
Awfully nice	Crisp presentation
Basically accurate	Baffling instructions
Great success	Tiny raise
Richly deserved	Moist handshake
Vitally important	Lucid recommendation

3. *Use specific, concrete language.* Avoid technical jargon. There is always a simple, down-to-earth word that says the same thing as the show-off fad word or the vague abstraction.

Jargon	Down-to-earth English
Implement	Carry out
Viable	Practical, workable
Suboptimal	Less than ideal
Proactive	Active
Bottom line	Outcome

4. *Write simply and naturally—the way you talk.* Use only those words, phrases, and sentences that you might actually say to your reader if you were face-to-face. If you wouldn't say it, if it doesn't sound like you, don't write it.

Stiff	Natural
The reasons are fourfold	There are four reasons
Importantly	The important point is
Visitation	Visit

5. *Strike out words you don't need.* Certain commonly used expressions contain redundant phrasing. Cut out the extra words.

Don't write	Write
Advance plan	Plan
Take action	Act
Study in depth	Study
Consensus of opinion	Consensus
Until such time as	Until

Source: Table adapted from Chapter 2 of *Writing That Works* by Kenneth Roman and Joel Raphaelson. Copyright © 1981 by Kenneth Roman and Joel Raphaelson. Reprinted by permission of HarperCollins Publishers Inc.

It is not easy to write a simple declarative sentence. Here is one way to do it. Think what you want to say. Write your sentence. Then strip it of all adverbs and adjectives. Reduce the sentence to its skeleton. Let the verbs and nouns do the work.

If your skeleton sentence does not express your thoughts precisely, you've got the wrong verb or noun. Dig for the right one. Nouns and verbs carry the guns in good writing; adjectives and adverbs are decorative camp followers.[14]

Conciseness

Conciseness
A criterion used to evaluate a research report; specifically, whether the writing in the report is crisp and direct.

Although the report must be complete, it must also be **concise.** This means that the writer must be selective in what is included. The researcher must avoid trying to impress the reader with all that has been found. If something does not pertain directly to the subject, it should be omitted. The writer must also avoid lengthy discussions of commonly known methods. Given that the material is appropriate, conciseness can still be violated by writing style. This commonly occurs when the writer is groping for the phrases and words that capture an idea. Instead of finally coming to terms with the idea, the writer writes around it, restating it several times, in different ways, hoping that repetition will overcome poor expression. Concise writing, on the other hand, is effective because "it makes maximum use of every word. . . . No word in a concise discussion can be removed without impairing or destroying the function of the whole composition. . . . To be concise is to express a thought completely and clearly in the fewest words possible."[15]

One helpful technique for ensuring that the report is concise is reading the draft aloud. This often reveals sections that should be pruned or rewritten.[16]

Silent reading allows him [the writer] to skim over the familiar material and thus impose an artificial rapidity and structural simplicity on something that is in reality dense and tangled. The eye can grow accustomed to the appearance of a sentence, but it is much more difficult for the tongue, lips, and jaw to deal with what the eye might accept readily.

Forms of Report

The organization of the report influences all the criteria of report writing. While good organization cannot guarantee clarity, conciseness, accuracy, and completeness, poor organization can preclude them. There is no single acceptable organization for a report. Once again, the writer should be guided by the nature and needs of the reader in choosing the most appropriate format for the report. The following format is sufficiently flexible to allow the inclusion or exclusion of elements to satisfy particular needs:

1. Title page
2. Table of contents

Ethical Dilemma 22.1

As a member of an independent research team, it is your job to write the final report for a client. One of your colleagues whispers to you in passing, "Make it sound very technical. Lots of long words and jargon—you know the sort of thing. We want to make it clear that we earned our money on this one."

- Is it ethical to obscure the substance of a report beneath complex language?
- Will some clients be impressed by words that they do not fully understand?

3. Summary
    a. Introduction
    b. Results
    c. Conclusions
    d. Recommendations

4. Introduction

5. Body
    a. Methodology
    b. Results
    c. Limitations

6. Conclusions and recommendations

7. Appendix
    a. Copies of data collection forms
    b. Detailed calculations supporting sample size, test statistics, and so on
    c. Tables not included in the body
    d. Bibliography

Title Page

The title page indicates the subject of the report, the name of the organization for whom the report is made, the name of the organization submitting it, and the date. If the report is done by one department within a company for another, the names of organizations or companies are replaced by those of individuals. Those for whom the report is intended are listed on the title page, as are the departments or people preparing the report. If a report is confidential, it is especially important to list on the title page the names of the individuals authorized to see it.

Table of Contents

The table of contents lists, in order of appearance, the divisions and subdivisions of the report with page references. In a short report, the table of contents may simply contain the main headings. The table of contents will also typically include tables and figures and the pages on which they may be found. For most reports, exhibits will be labeled as either tables or figures, with maps, diagrams, and graphs falling into the latter category.

Summary

The summary is the *most important* part of the report. It is the heart and core. Many executives will read only the summary. Others will read more, but even they will use the summary as a guide to those questions about which they would like more information.

The true summary is not an abstract of the whole report in which everything is restated in condensed form, nor is it a simple restatement of the subject, nor is it a brief statement of the significant results and conclusions. A true summary gives the high points of the entire body of the report. A properly written summary saves the time of busy executives without sacrificing their understanding. A good test of a summary is self-sufficiency. Can it stand on its own, or does it collapse without the full report?

A good summary contains the necessary background information as well as the important results and conclusions. Whether it contains recommendations is determined to an extent by the reader. Some managers prefer that the writer suggest appropriate action, while others prefer to draw their own conclusions on the basis of the evidence contained in the study. Although the good summary contains the necessary information, it will rarely be broken down through the use of headings and subheadings. The summary that requires such subdivisions is probably too long.

The summary begins with an introduction that should provide the reader with enough background to appreciate the results, conclusions, and recommendations of the study.

The introduction should state who authorized the research and for what purpose. It should state explicitly the problems or hypotheses that guided the research.

Following the introduction should be a section in which the study's significant findings or results are presented. The results presented in the summary must agree, of course, with those in the body of the report, but only the key findings are presented here. A useful approach is to include one or several statements reporting what was found with regard to each problem or objective mentioned in the introduction.

The final two sections of the summary are conclusions and recommendations, which follow a discussion of the results. Conclusions and recommendations are not the same. A conclusion is an opinion based on the results. A recommendation is a suggestion as to appropriate future action.

Conclusions should be included in the summary section. The writer is in a much better position to base conclusions on the evidence than is the reader, as the writer has greater familiarity with the methods used to generate and analyze the data. The writer is at fault if conclusions are omitted and readers are allowed to draw their own. Recommendations, though, are another matter. Some managers simply prefer to determine the appropriate courses of action themselves and do not want the writer to offer recommendations. Others hold that the writer, being closest to the research, is in the best position to suggest a course of action. For example, the Lipton Company has the philosophy that it is the responsibility of the marketing research people to interpret the findings. As Dolph von Arx, the executive vice president, comments: "We feel strongly that our market research people must go beyond reporting the facts. We want them to tell us what *they* think the facts mean—both in terms of conclusions, and, if possible, indicated actions. Those who are responsible for making the decisions may or may not accept those conclusions or recommendations, but we want this input from our market research people."[17] The Lipton Company's philosophy is consistent with industry trends. Increasingly marketing researchers are being asked to interpret the findings in terms of what they mean to the business and to make recommendations as to appropriate courses of action.

Introduction

Whereas in the summary the readers' interests are taken into account, in the report's formal introduction their education and experience are considered. The introduction provides the background information readers need to appreciate the discussion in the body of the report. Some form of introduction is almost always necessary. Its length and detail, though, depend upon the readers' familiarity with the subject, the report's approach to it, and the treatment of it.[18] As a general rule, a report with wide distribution will require a more extensive introduction than a report for a narrow audience.

The introduction often serves to define unfamiliar terms or terms that are used in a specific way in the report. For instance, in a study of market penetration of a new product, the introduction might be used to define the market and name the products and companies considered "competitors" in calculating the new product's market share.

The introduction may provide some pertinent history, answering such questions as the following: What similar studies have been conducted? What findings did they produce? What circumstances led to the present study? How was its scope and emphasis determined? Clearly, if readers are familiar with the history of this project and related research or the circumstances that inspired the current research, these items can be omitted. A report going to executives with little background in the particular product or service dealt with would probably have to include them.

The introduction should state the specific objectives of the research. If the project was part of a larger, overall project, this should be mentioned. Each of the subproblems or hypotheses should be explicitly stated. After reading the introduction, readers should know just what the report covers and what it omits. They should appreciate the overall problem and how the subproblems relate to it. They should be aware of the relationship between this study and other related work. And they should appreciate the need for the study and its importance. Through all of this, the introduction should serve to win the readers' confidence and dispel any prejudices they may have.

Body

The details of the research—its method, results, and limitations—are contained in the body of the report. One of the hardest portions of the report to write is that giving the details of the method. The writer has a real dilemma here. Sufficient information must be presented so that readers can appreciate the research design, data collection methods, sample procedures, and analysis techniques that were used without being bored or overwhelmed. Technical jargon, which is often a succinct way of communicating a complex idea, should be omitted though, since many in the audience will not understand it.

Readers must be told whether the design was exploratory, descriptive, or causal. They should also be told why the particular design was chosen and what its merits are in terms of the problem at hand. Readers should also be told whether the results are based on secondary or primary data. If primary, are they based on observation or questionnaire? And if the latter, were the questionnaires administered in person, or by mail or telephone? Once again it is important to mention why the particular method was chosen. What were its perceived advantages over alternative schemes? This may mean discussing briefly the perceived weaknesses of the other data collection schemes that were considered.

Sampling is a technical subject, and the writer cannot usually hope to convey all the nuances of the sampling plan in the body of the report, but must be somewhat selective in this regard. At the very minimum, the researcher should answer the following questions:

1. How was the population defined? What were the geographical, age, sex, or other bounds?

2. What sampling units were employed? Were they business organizations or business executives? Were they dwelling units, households, or individuals within a household? Why were these particular sampling units chosen?

3. How was the list of sampling units generated? Did this produce any weaknesses? Why was this method used?

4. Were any difficulties experienced in contacting designated sample elements? How were these difficulties overcome, and was bias introduced in the process?

5. Was a probability or nonprobability sampling plan employed? Why? How was the sample actually selected? How large a sample was selected? Why was this size of sample chosen?

In essence, the readers need to understand at least three things with respect to the sample: What was done? How was it done? Why was it done?

There is very little that can be said about the method of analysis when discussing research methods, since the results tend to show what has been done in this regard. It often proves quite useful, though, to discuss the method in general before detailing the results. Thus, if statistical significance is established through chi-square analysis, the writer might provide the general rationale and calculation procedure for the chi-square statistic, as well as the assumptions surrounding this test and how well the data supported the assumptions. This enables readers to separate what was found from how it was determined. The distinction may not only help the readers' understanding but also prevent repetition in the report. The procedure is outlined with its key components once, and the results are then simply reported in terms of these components.

The results section of the body of the report presents the findings of the study in some detail, often including supporting tables and figures, and accounts for the bulk of the report. The results need to address the specific problems posed and must be presented with some logical structure.[19] The first of these requirements directs that information that is interesting but irrelevant in terms of the specific problems that guided the research be omitted. The second requirement directs that the tables and figures not be a random collection but reflect some psychological ordering.[20] This may mean ordering by subproblem, geographic region, time, or another criterion that served to structure the investigation.

Tables and figures should be used liberally when presenting the results. This is especially important in today's environment, where most clients are used to visual and even multimedia content, thanks to the ability of computer programs to translate data into charts and graphs. Clients will expect to see keys points illustrated clearly. At Ames Department Stores, for example, managers use their computers to look up colorful graphs displaying financial and merchandising data, as well as customer demographics and even weather data, rather than deciphering columns of numbers.[21] Similarly, the marketing team at NextCard, which offers credit cards strictly through on-line marketing (see the Web pages), tracks the performance of NextCard's on-line banner ads by watching a monitor in a San Francisco office. There, the performance of each ad is reported on a graph that uses colored lines to record the number of new accounts and new balances. The report is updated automatically every 15 minutes. If a line is trending downward, the marketing team must spring into action.[22]

While the tables in the appendix are complex, detailed, and apply to a number of problems, the tables in the body of the report should be simple summaries of this information. Each table should address only a single problem, and it should be specially constructed to shed maximum light on this problem. Guidelines for constructing tables follow:[23]

1. Order the columns or rows of the table by the marginal averages or some other measure of size. If there are many similar tables, keep the same order in each one.

2. Put the figures to be compared into columns rather than rows, and, if possible, put the larger numbers at the top of the columns.

3. Round the numbers to two effective digits.

4. For each table, give a brief verbal summary that will guide the reader to the main patterns and exceptions.

Exhibit 22.2 gives an example of how these guidelines can yield better tables.

The home page of NextCard gives consumers the opportunity to upgrade their current Visa card, save time while accessing available credit, and even learn more about the corporate structure of NextCard. The company, whose mission statement is to "redefine the banking experience for the Internet consumer," transacts business solely on the Internet and uses written reports of the marketing information gathered electronically to inform its in-house marketers of performance levels. It also uses electronic database information to prepare another form of written report, the NextCard eCommerce Index, which each month reports the "Top 25 places where people bought online."

Source: NextCard, the first true Internet Visa (www.nextcard.com).

NextCard eCommerce Index℠

Top 25 places where people bought online ℠

The NextCard eCommerce Index℠ is a monthly listing of the top 25 online merchants with the greatest number of online transactions by our customers. For more information, check out our FAQ section.

Rank	1 Month Movement	3 Month Movement	Merchant	Comment
1	--	+1	AMAZON.COM	AMZN beaks away from the pack for the eHoliday! Gains 70% volume over last month!
2	--	-1	AOL ONLINE SERVICE	
3	--	+4	BARNESANDNOBLE.COM*	Gains 50% over last month but AMZN still pulling away!
4	--	-1	BUY.COM	
5	+9	+10	REEL.COM	The eHoliday blitz is on - jumping 130%
6	-1	-1	CD NOW	
7	+2	-1	ONSALE	
8	-2	-4	EARTHLINK NETWORK	
9	+13	+44	ETOYS	Mosterious start to the eHolidays! Up almost 200% from October!
10	-2	-1	UBID	
11	-1	--	PRODIGY	
12	-5	-4	EGGHEAD.COM	
13	-1	+3	E BAY INC	
14	-1	-2	MINDSPRING	
15	--	-5	MSN ONLINE	
16	+5	-2	DRUGSTORE.COM	Online beauty keeps growing
17	-1	-4	COMPUSERVE	
18	-7	--	NETWORK SOLUTIONS	
19	-2	--	AT&T WORLDNET	
20	+6	+6	PLANETRX	Online beauty keeps growing
21	+8	+133	PETS.COM	Gifts for pets this eHoliday
22	-2	+5	1-800-FLOWERS	
23	--	-3	DVD EXPRESS	
24	+10	+46	KBKIDS.COM	eHolidays!!
25	+2	-3	BEYOND.COM	

Also seen at

EXHIBIT 22.2   **Guidelines for Producing Better Tables**

Table A displays some sales figures for a product being sold in ten U.S. cities. At first glance it seems fairly laid out, but look again. How would you summarize the information in the table to someone over the phone?

Table A
Quarterly Sales of Product Y in Ten Cities

City	SALES IN THOUSANDS OF DOLLARS			
	Quarter 1	Quarter 2	Quarter 3	Quarter 4
Atlanta	540.4	507.6	528.4	833.2
Chattanooga	68.9	64.0	55.4	64.5
Des Moines	65.7	61.1	52.9	61.5
Hartford	61.1	71.5	59.0	70.5
Indianapolis	153.2	162.8	122.8	185.7
Los Angeles	700.2	660.3	580.8	662.7
Miami	553.6	517.2	446.0	672.4
Omaha	78.3	72.8	63.0	73.3
Phoenix	196.8	227.6	198.5	235.2
San Antonio	168.2	179.3	166.9	207.1

The table seems to be a jumble when looked at more carefully. It appears that no thought was given to communicating what the numbers really mean. The main difficulty is that the cities for which the numbers are given are listed alphabetically. There is no apparent pattern in each column. Now look at the same information as presented in Table B.

Table B
Quarterly Sales of Product Y in Ten Cities Ordered by Population Size (Rounded and with Averages)

City	Quarter 1	Quarter 2	Quarter 3	Quarter 4	Average
Los Angeles	700	660	580	660	650
Miami	550	520	450	670	550
Atlanta	540	510	530	830	600
Phoenix	200	230	200	240	220
San Antonio	170	180	170	210	180
Indianapolis	150	160	120	190	160
Hartford	60	70	60	70	70
Omaha	80	70	60	70	70
Chattanooga	70	60	60	60	60
Des Moines	70	60	50	60	60
Average	260	250	230	310	260

Note how ordering the information by following the recommended steps improves the table's readability.

Table B's heading informs the reader that the cities are ordered by population size. Having this information and examining the table as it's laid out, we can begin to see major patterns emerge: the bigger the cities, the higher the sales, as might be expected. The single exception is Atlanta, where sales are relatively high given its population size.

Trends over time are also easier to see. Although not typical, the column averages help us see that sales in each city were relatively steady quarter by quarter, but that they were lower in Quarter 3 and Quarter 4. We can also see that the fourth-quarter increases were largest in Miami and Atlanta.

The difference between Tables A and B is the difference between a good table and a poor one. In a good table, the patterns and exceptions should be obvious at a glance, at least once one knows what they are.

Next time you have trouble reading a table, ask yourself if the information could be better ordered. The fault may not be in your ability to comprehend the information but in the table itself.

Source: Adapted from A. S. C. Ehrenberg, "The Problem of Numeracy," *The American Statistician* 35 (May 1981), pp. 67–71. Reprinted from *The American Statistician.* Copyright 1981 by the American Statistical Association. All rights reserved.

Figures, like tables, should address only one subproblem. Further, they should be chosen carefully for the type of message they can most effectively convey. This subject will be discussed in the next chapter.

It is impossible to conduct the "perfect" study, because every study has its limitations. The researcher knows what the limitations of his or her efforts are, and these limitations should not be hidden from the reader. Researchers sometimes fear that a frank admission of the study's limitations may diminish the reader's opinion of the quality of the research. Often the contrary is true. If some limitations are not stated and readers discover them, they may begin to question the whole report and assume a much more skeptical, critical posture than they would have had, had the limitations been stated explicitly. Stating them also allows the writer to discuss whether, and by how much, the limitations might bias the results. Their exclusion, and later discovery, encourages readers to draw their own conclusions in this regard.

When discussing the limitations, the writer should provide some idea of the accuracy with which the work was done. The writer should specifically discuss the sources of non-sampling error and the suspected direction of their biases. This often means that the researcher provides some limits by which the results are distorted due to these inaccuracies. Readers should be informed specifically as to how far the results can be generalized. To what populations can they be expected to apply? If the study was done in Miami, readers should be warned not to generalize the results to the southern states or all the states. The writer should provide the proper caveats for readers and not make readers discover the weaknesses themselves. However, *the writer should not overstate the limitations either, but should assume a balanced perspective.*

Conclusions and Recommendations

The results lead to the conclusions and recommendations. In this section, the writer shows the step-by-step development of the conclusions and states them in greater detail than in the summary. There should be a conclusion for each study objective or problem. As one book puts it, "readers should be able to read the objectives, turn to the conclusions section, and find specific conclusions relative to each objective."[24] If the study does not provide evidence sufficient to draw a conclusion about a problem, this should be explicitly stated.

Researchers' recommendations should follow the conclusions. In developing the recommendations, researchers need to focus on the value of the information that has been gathered. They need to interpret this information in terms of what it means for the business. One of the best ways of doing this is by offering specific recommendations as to the appropriate courses of action—along with reasons why—given the evidence. While not all managers want the researcher's recommendations, many do, and the researcher needs to be prepared to offer and support them.

Appendix

The appendix contains material that is too complex, too detailed, too specialized, or not absolutely necessary for the text. The appendix will typically contain as an exhibit a copy of the questionnaire or observation form used to collect the data. It will also contain any maps used to draw the sample as well as any detailed calculations used to support the determination of the sample size and sample design. The appendix may include detailed calculations of test statistics and will often include detailed tables from which the summary tables in the body of the report were generated. The writer should recognize that the appendix will be read by only the most technically competent and interested reader. Therefore, the writer should not put material in the appendix if its omission from the body of the report would create gaps in the presentation.

Synopsis

Exhibit 22.3 can serve as a checklist of things to include in reports. The checklist reflects the guidelines that have been developed to evaluate research that is to be put to a public

EXHIBIT 22.3   **Checklist for Evaluating Research Reports**

A. Origin: What Is Behind the Research

Does the report identify the organizations, divisions, or departments that initiated and paid for the research?
Is there a statement of the purpose of the research that says clearly what it was meant to accomplish?
Are the organizations that designed and conducted the research identified?

B. Design: The Concept and the Plan

Is there a full, nontechnical description of the research design?
Is the design consistent with the stated purpose for which the research was conducted?
Is the design evenhanded? That is, is it free of leading questions and other biases?
Have precautions been taken to avoid sequence or timing bias or other factors that might prejudice or distort the findings?
Does it address questions that respondents are capable of answering?
Is there a precise statement of the universe or population that the research is meant to represent?
Does the sampling frame fairly represent the population under study?
Does the report specify the kind of sample used and clearly describe the method of sample selection?
Does the report describe the plan for the analysis of the data?
Are copies of all questionnaire forms, field and sampling instructions, and other study materials available in the appendix or on file?

C. Execution: Collecting and Handling the Information

Does the report describe the data collection and data processing procedures?
Is there an objective report on the care with which the data were collected?
What procedures were used to minimize bias and ensure the quality of the information collected?

D. Stability: Sample Size and Reliability

Was the sample large enough to provide stable findings?
Are sampling error limits shown if they can be computed?
Are methods of calculating the sampling error described, or, if the error cannot be computed, is this stated and explained?
Does the treatment of sampling error limits make clear that they do not cover nonsampling error?
For the major findings, are the reported error tolerances based on direct analysis of the variability of the collected data?

E. Applicability: Generalizing the Findings

Does the report specify when the data were collected?
Does the report say clearly whether its findings do or do not apply beyond the direct source of the data?
Is it clear who is underrepresented by the research, or not represented at all?
If the research has limited application, is there a statement covering who or what it represents and the time or conditions under which it applies?

F. Meaning: Interpretations and Conclusions

Are the measurements described in simple and direct language?
Does it make logical sense to use such measurements for the purpose to which they are being put?
Are the actual findings clearly differentiated from the interpretation of the findings?
Have rigorous objectivity and sound judgment been exercised in interpreting the research findings?

G. Candor: Open Reporting and Disclosure

Is there a full and forthright disclosure of how the research was done?
Has the research been fairly presented?

Source: Adapted from *Guidelines for the Public Use of Market and Opinion Research* © 1981 by the Advertising Research Foundation. Adapted with permission.

purpose. Public-purpose research can affect the interests of people and organizations who have had no part in its design, execution, or funding. Consequently, the criteria on which it is evaluated tend to be stricter than those applied to research done for private use. Still, the general issues and questions serve as useful criteria by which all research reports can be judged.

Ethical Dilemma 22.2

A colleague confides in you: "I've just run a survey for a restaurant owner who is planning to open a catering service for parties, weddings, and the like. He wanted to know the best way to advertise the new service. In the questionnaire, I asked respondents where they would expect to see advertisements for catering facilities, and the most common source was the newspaper. I now realize that my question only established where people are usually exposed to relevant ads, not where they would like to see relevant ads or where they could most productively be exposed to an ad. All we know

is where other caterers advertise! Yet I'm sure my client will interpret my findings as meaning that the newspaper is the most effective media vehicle. Should I make the limitations of the research explicit?"

- What are the costs of making the limitations of the research explicit?
- What are the costs of not doing so?
- Isn't promoting the correct use of the research one of the researcher's prime obligations?

Back to the Case

"Eric, this is a 100 percent improvement," beamed Caroline Sords as she finished his latest draft of the research report for Oakhurst Hospital. "I think everyone, from the hospital's chief financial officer to the chairman of pediatrics, will be able to read it and understand it."

"Thanks, Caroline," replied Eric O'Donnell, breathing an internal sigh of relief.

"There is one thing that troubles me, though," said Sords. "I don't see any mention of the problems we had with data collection. In your first draft, they were mentioned in the results section."

"Yes, they were. I really went back and forth over whether to keep those in," responded O'Donnell. "Finally I thought they'd just confuse the people who read the report and erode their confidence in our findings."

"I admit our field interviewers had a lot of trouble reaching families in which both spouses worked," said Sords. "They also were turned down a good deal when they tried to interview the elderly. Now, I grant you that most of the people who are going to read this report wouldn't notice that we glossed over these problems, but George Scanlon's got a mind like a steel trap. He'd be sure to pick up on the fact that we failed to note the sources of nonsampling bias, and it would make our whole report suspect."

"Of course, you're right, Caroline. All those late nights working on the report must have been clouding my judgment. Any other changes?"

"Just a couple of editing changes that I've penciled in here and there. Otherwise it looks great. By the way, would you like to come with me when I present the results to Scanlon on Thursday? I'd like to have you there as a resource, and it'll give me a chance to show you off a little."

Summary

Learning Objective 1

Specify the fundamental criterion by which all research reports are evaluated.

> Research reports are evaluated by one fundamental criterion—communication with the reader. The reader is not only the reason that the report is prepared but also the standard by which its success is measured.

Learning Objective 2

Identify and discuss the four criteria that a report should meet if it is to communicate effectively with readers.

> A report that achieves the goal of communicating effectively with readers is generally one that meets the specific criteria of completeness, accuracy, clarity, and conciseness.

Learning Objective 3

Outline the main elements that make up a standard report form.

> A standard report generally contains the following elements: title page, table of contents, summary, introduction, body, conclusions and recommendations, and appendix.

Learning Objective 4

Explain the kind of information that is contained in the summary.

> A true summary gives the high points of the entire body of the report, including necessary background information, as well as important results and conclusions.

Learning Objective 5

Distinguish between a conclusion and a recommendation.

> A conclusion is an opinion based on the results. A recommendation is a suggestion as to appropriate future action.

Learning Objective 6

Describe the kind of information that should be contained in the introduction.

> An introduction provides background information, defines unfamiliar terms, outlines pertinent history, and states the specific objectives of the research. Through all this, the introduction should serve to win the readers' confidence and dispel any prejudices they may have.

Learning Objective 7

Describe the kind of information that should be contained in the body.

The details of the research are contained in the body of the report. This includes details of method, results, and limitations.

Learning Objective 8

Describe the kind of information that should be contained in the appendix.

The appendix contains material that is too complex, too detailed, too specialized, or not absolutely necessary for the text. The appendix will typically contain as an exhibit a copy of the questionnaire or observation form used to collect the data.

Review Questions

1. What is the fundamental report criterion? Explain.

2. What is meant by the report criteria of completeness, accuracy, clarity, and conciseness?

3. On the one hand, it is argued that the research report must be complete and, on the other, that it must be concise. Are these two objectives incompatible? If so, how do you reconcile them?

4. What is the essential content of each of the following parts of the research report?
   (a) title page
   (b) table of contents
   (c) summary
   (d) introduction
   (e) body
   (f) conclusions and recommendations
   (g) appendix

Discussion Questions, Problems, and Projects

1. It should be clear from your reading of this chapter that a professional marketing researcher must possess a well-developed ability to write effectively. Many colleges and universities offer a variety of programs designed to help students hone their writing skills. These programs may take a variety of forms, such as writing labs, special seminars, word-processing tutorials, one-on-one writing tutors, and regular written communication classes. Prepare a research report of the resources available at your school that can be used to enhance written communication skills. Assume that your report will be furnished to incoming first-year students as part of their orientation materials. Be sure to structure your report in the manner presented in this chapter.

2. The owner of a medium-sized home-building center specializing in custom-designed and do-it-yourself bathroom supplies requested the Liska and Leigh Consulting Firm to prepare a report on the customer profile of the bathroom design segment of the home-improvement market. Evaluate the following excerpts from the report:
   Research report excerpts
   The customer market for the company can be defined as the do-it-yourself and bathroom design segments. A brief profile of each follows.
   The do-it-yourself (DIY) market consists of individuals in the 25–45 age-group living in a single dwelling. DIY customers are predominantly male, although an increasing number of females are becoming active DIY customers. The typical DIY customer has an income in excess of $20,000 and the median income is $22,100 with a standard deviation of 86. The DIY customer has an increasing amount of leisure time, is strongly value- and convenience-conscious, and displays an increasing desire for self-gratification.

The mean age of the custom bathroom design segment is 41.26 and the annual income is in the range of $25,000 to $35,000. The median income is $29,000 with a standard deviation of 73. The custom bathroom design customers usually live in a single dwelling. The wife is more influential and is the prime decision maker about bathroom designs.

3. Discuss the difference between conclusions and recommendations in research reports.

4. Assume that Wendy's International, Inc., wants to diversify into another fast food area. You are required to prepare a brief report for the company executives outlining an attractive opportunity. In preparing the report, go through the following steps:
   (a) Decide on the particular fast food area you think is most appropriate.
   (b) Collect secondary data relating to the area and analyze consumption trends over the past five years (or ten years).
   (c) Decide on the outline of the report and its various sections.
   (d) Develop the appropriate tables and charts to support your analysis.
   (e) Write the report.

5. Describe the information that should be contained in the summary, and discuss why this is the most important part of the research report.

6. In presenting a report to a group of grocery store managers, a researcher stated the following: "The data from the judgment sample of 10 grocery stores was analyzed and the results show that the 95 percent confidence interval for average annual sales in the population of grocery stores is $1,000,000 ± $150,000."
   (a) As far as the audience is concerned, what is wrong with this statement?
   (b) Rewrite the statement. Be sure to include all the relevant information while correcting the problem.

7. Your marketing research firm is preparing the final written report on a research project commissioned by a major manufacturer of lawn mowers. One objective of the project was to investigate seasonal variations in sales, both on an aggregate basis and by each of the company's sales regions individually. Your client is particularly interested in the width of the range between maximum and minimum seasonal sales. Exhibit 1 was submitted by one of your junior analysts. Critique the table and prepare a revision suitable for inclusion in your report.

EXHIBIT 1   **Seasonal Sales Variation**

SALES IN THOUSANDS OF DOLLARS

Sales Region	Spring	Summer	Fall	Winter
Northeast	120.10	140.59	50.90	30.00
East-central	118.80	142.70	61.70	25.20
Southeast	142.00	151.80	134.20	100.10
Midwest	100.20	139.42	42.90	20.00
South-central	80.77	101.00	90.42	78.20
Plains	95.60	120.60	38.50	19.90
Southwest	105.40	110.50	101.60	92.10
Pacific	180.70	202.41	171.54	145.60

Endnotes

1. Reprinted by special permission from William J. Gallagher, *Report Writing for Management*, p. 1. Addison-Wesley Publishing Company, Inc., Reading, Massachusetts. Copyright © 1969. All rights reserved. Much of this introductory section is also taken from this excellent book. See also Pnenna Sageev, *Helping Researchers Write, So Managers Can Understand* (Columbus, Ohio: Batelle Press, 1995).

2. The other variables are the extent of interaction that researchers have with managers, the research objectives, the degree of surprise in the results, and the stage of the product or service in its life cycle. See Rohit Deshpande and Gerald Zaltman, "A Comparison of Factors Affecting Researcher and Manager Perceptions of Market Research Use," *Journal of Marketing Research* 21 (February 1984), pp. 32–38. The understandability of the research report also affects managers' trust and that, in turn, affects what they do with the information. See, for example, Christine Moorman, Rohit Deshpande, and Gerald Zaltman, "Factors Affecting Trust in Market Research Relationships," *Journal of Marketing* 57 (January 1993), pp. 81–101.

3. Walter B. Wentz, *Marketing Research: Management, Method, and Cases,* 2d ed. (New York: Harper and Row, 1979), p. 61. See also Edward P. Bailey and Philip A. Powell, *The Practical Writer,* 6th ed. (Orlando, Fla: Harcourt Brace College Publishers, 1994).

4. Stewart Henderson Britt, "The Communication of Your Research Findings," in Robert Ferber, ed., *Handbook of Marketing Research* (New York: McGraw-Hill, 1974), pp. 1–90. See also Edward P. Bailey, *The Plain English Approach to Business Writing* (New York: Oxford University Press, 1990).

5. Harper W. Boyd, Jr., Ralph Westfall, and Stanley F. Stasch, *Marketing Research: Text and Cases,* 7th ed. (Homewood, Ill.: Richard D. Irwin, 1989), p. 657.

6. Ron Sellers, "Interpreting Research Data: It All Depends on the Context," *Quirk's Marketing Research Review* (January 1998, downloaded from the *Quirk's* Web site, www.quirks.com, October 27, 1999).

7. Gallagher, *Report Writing*, p. 78.

8. Joseph Rydholm, "Are We Getting Ahead of Ourselves?" *Quirk's Marketing Research Review* (July 1999), pp. 19, 95–97.

9. See Gallagher, *Report Writing*, pp. 80–83, for a number of examples that display some of the inaccuracies that may arise. The examples are particularly interesting because they have been extracted from actual company reports.

10. Taken from William Zinsser, *On Writing Well*, 3rd ed. (New York: Harper and Row, 1985), pp. 7–8, a modern classic for writers that is as helpful as it is fun to read.

11. Gallagher, *Report Writing*, Chapter 10, "Reviewing for Accuracy: Grammar," pp. 156–177, has examples of how these inaccuracies can confuse and misinform.

12. Gallagher, *Report Writing*, p. 83.

13. Kenneth Roman and Joel Raphaelson, *Writing That Works* (New York: Harper and Row, 1981). This book gives some excellent advice on how to write more effective reports, memos, letters, and speeches. See also Simon Mort, *Professional Report Writing* (Brookfield, Vt.: Ashgate Publishing Company, 1995). The little book by William Strunk, Jr., and E. B. White, *The Elements of Style*, 3rd ed. (New York: Macmillan, 1979), is a classic on how to write clearly.

14. Jock Elliott, "How Hard It Is to Write Easily," *Viewpoint: By, For, and About Ogilvy & Mather* 2 (1980), p. 18.

15. Gallagher, *Report Writing*, p. 87.

16. Ibid., p. 84.

17. Dolph von Arx, "The Many Faces of Market Research," paper delivered at the meeting of the Association of National Advertisers, Inc., New York, April 3, 1985. See also Arthur Shapiro, "Downsizing and Its Effects on Corporate Marketing Research," *Marketing Research: A Magazine of Management & Application* 2 (December 1990), pp. 56–59.

18. Gallagher, *Report Writing*, p. 54.

19. Some of the many structures and the conditions under which they can be used are contained in Jessamon Dawe, *Writing Business and Economic Papers: Theses and Dissertations* (Totowa, N.J.: Littlefield, Adams, 1975), pp. 75–86. See also David Morris and Satish Chandra, *Guidelines for Writing a Research Report* (Chicago: American Marketing Association, 1992).

20. See Gallagher, *Report Writing,* pp. 50–68, for a discussion of the psychological order of things in research reports.

21. Jean Thilmany, "Ames' Gains," *Executive Technology* (May 1999), pp. 14–15.

22. "6: Direct Marketing: NextCard," *Fortune* (May 24, 1999), pp. 122–123.

23. See A. S. C. Ehrenberg, "Rudiments of Numeracy," *Journal of the Royal Statistical Society,* Series A, 140 (1977), pp. 277–297, and A. S. C. Ehrenberg, "The Problem of Numeracy," *American Statistician* 35 (May 1981), pp. 67–71, for particularly informative discussions using examples of how adherence to these principles can dramatically improve readers' abilities to comprehend the information being presented in tables. For a general discussion of the problem of numeracy in interpreting economic data, see Ingrid H. Rima, ed., *Measurement, Quantification, & Economic Analysis: Numeracy in Economics* (New York: Routledge, 1995).

24. Boyd, Westfall, and Stasch, *Marketing Research,* p. 663.

Suggested Additional Readings

For excellent, succinct treatments of how to write better, see
Edward P. Bailey, *The Plain English Approach to Business Writing* (New York: Oxford University Press, 1990).
Kenneth Roman and Joel Raphaelson, *Writing That Works* (New York: Harper and Row, 1981).
William Strunk, Jr., and E. B. White, *The Elements of Style,* 3rd ed. (New York: Macmillan, 1979).
William Zinsser, *On Writing Well,* 6th ed. (New York: Harperreference, 1998).

Chapter 23

THE ORAL RESEARCH REPORT

L E A R N I N G   O B J E C T I V E S

Upon Completing This Chapter, You Should Be Able to

1. Specify the first rule to keep in mind when preparing an oral report.

2. Describe the two most common forms of organization for oral reports.

3. Discuss the key points a presenter should keep in mind regarding the use of visual aids.

4. Explain how the time allotted for an oral presentation should be organized.

5. Describe the circumstances in which a pie chart is most effective.

6. Explain the best use of a line chart.

7. Describe the circumstances in which a stratum chart is most effective.

8. Cite the reason why bar charts are so widely used.

9. Describe the circumstances in which a grouped-bar chart is most effective.

Case in Marketing Research

If there's one thing George Kerns cares about, it's keeping his customers happy. Kerns is the executive in charge of Network Operations at GTE Internetworking (GTEI), which installs, maintains, and operates Internet services for other organizations. These customers hire GTEI to provide them with reliable Internet connections, prevent unauthorized external access to their systems, and deliver a variety of Web site services.

As good managers know, you need to measure the things you believe to be important. When employees know their boss is going to study certain areas of their performance, they focus on doing their best in those areas. Because Kerns wants his people to focus on customer satisfaction and, by extension, service quality, he institutes regular measurement of these important performance areas.

To achieve superior customer satisfaction, GTEI combines research with a system for applying the results. The company regularly conducts surveys of its customers' satisfaction. GTEI conducts an initial survey by contacting every new customer 30 days after the customer's GTEI service begins. The survey asks about the timeliness and quality of the installation, as well as the customer's initial impressions of the service. Other questions address customer interactions with GTEI employees: their perception of customer support, communications with GTEI personnel, and any other issues the customer considers important.

Two months later, GTEI conducts another survey of the same customers, focusing on the quality and performance of the system GTEI installed. After that, GTEI contacts the customers once a year, continuing to ask about system quality and customer service. Thus, the survey uses a census of all customers, rather than a sample. Because the company keeps adding new customers, the research is ongoing.

For each area of service to be evaluated, the survey asks whether customers are totally satisfied, somewhat satisfied, somewhat dissatisfied, or totally dissatisfied. When customers indicate less than total satisfaction, the interviewer asks a series of questions designed to probe for the reasons that the customer's satisfaction was less than complete. The specific areas of service included on the survey may be modified monthly to reflect areas of concern raised by customers answering previous surveys. Although this makes the survey less useful for measuring trends over time, it supports the primary objective of the survey: identifying areas of service requiring improvement.

Once a month, the researchers present the results orally to a team of GTEI executives and distribute their findings in writing to other managers. At the meeting with executives, the researchers report satisfaction in terms of the percentage of customers who say they are totally satisfied with each area of service. GTEI considers 70 percent totally satisfied to be the minimum acceptable level. Anything less is a signal for corrective action.

Discussion Issues
1. If you were conducting this research for GTEI, what would be some advantages of reporting the results orally?

2. How might you combine speaking with visual aids to convey the results effectively?

3. How might your oral report differ from your written report?

In addition to the written report, most marketing research investigations require one or more oral reports. Often clients, or those in the company for whom the study is being undertaken, want progress reports during the course of the project. Almost always they require a formal oral report at the conclusion of the study. The principles surrounding the preparation and delivery of the oral report parallel those for the written report.

That means report preparers and presenters need to realize that many listeners will not truly understand the technical ramifications involved in research and certainly will not be able to judge whether the research done is "quality research." However, they can judge whether the research was presented in a professional, confidence-inspiring manner or in a disorganized, uninformed one. A quality presentation can disguise poor research, but quality research cannot improve a poor presentation.

Preparing the Oral Report

As we emphasized in the preceding chapter, the first requirement is to know the audience. What is their technical level of sophistication? What is their involvement in the project? Their interest? Once again, researchers may want to present more detailed reports to those who are deeply involved in the project or who have a high level of technical sophistication than to those who are only slightly involved or interested.

Learning about the audience comes more naturally with the modern emphasis on teamwork. Kellogg, for example, has tried to improve new-product development by establishing cross-functional teams that bring together marketing researchers with food technologists and engineers. The objective is to develop products that appeal to customers, and are financially and technologically feasible.[1] Researchers who are assigned to such teams should use their participation as an opportunity to learn the technical sophistication and interests of their teammates. This understanding should enable researchers to target their reports and increase their value to the team.

In general, it is better to err on the side of too little technical detail rather than too much. Executives want to hear and see what the information means to them as managers of marketing activities. What do the data suggest with respect to marketing actions? They can ask for the necessary clarification with respect to the technical details if they want it. Paco Underhill, noted for his use of observational research in stores, emphasizes marketing implications. In one instance, Underhill told a group of (mostly male) Wal-Mart executives that he could tell whether any of their stores had a male or female manager, based only on how recently the women's dressing room had been painted. Over the months following that meeting, Underhill says, he noticed a lot of newly painted dressing rooms at Wal-Mart stores.[2]

Another important consideration is how the presentation is organized. There are two popular forms of organization. Both begin by stating the general purpose of the study and the specific objectives that were addressed. They differ, however, with respect to when the conclusions are introduced. In the most popular structure, the conclusions are introduced after all of the evidence supporting a particular course of action is presented. This allows the presenter to build a logical case in sequential fashion. By progressively disclosing the facts, the presenter has the opportunity to deal with audience concerns and biases as they arise, and thus lead listeners to the conclusion that the case builds.

In the alternative structure, conclusions are presented immediately after the purpose and main objectives. This structure tends to involve managers immediately in the findings.

Research Window 23.1

Ten Tips for Preparing Effective Presentation Visuals

Keep it simple. Deliver complex ideas in a manner that your audience can understand. Present one point per slide, with as few words and lines as possible.

Use lots of slides as you talk, rather than lots of talk per slide. Less is more when you are speaking.

Use one minute per visual. Slides and overheads should make their impact quickly, then move on. No more than ten words per slide.

Highlight significant points. Bullets work for black-and-white transparencies; slides are better suited for color and graphics.

Use a graphic on every page. One is usually enough. Take advantage of "white space," and don't overcrowd.

Build complexity. If you have a complicated concept to communicate, start with the ground level and use three or four slides to complete the picture.

Be careful with color. Color can add interest and emphasis. It can also detract if used without planning. Plan your color scheme and use it faithfully throughout.

Prepare copies of overheads or slides. Hand them to the audience before or after your presentation. If people have to take notes, they won't be watching or listening closely.

Number your pages. You will have a better reference for discussion or a question-and-answer period.

Make visuals easy to read. Use large, legible typefaces. You can use up to three sizes of type, but use only one or two typefaces. Bold and italics can be used freely for emphasis. With slides, use light type against a dark background.

Source: Colleen Paul, "You're in Show Biz! 10 Tips for Presenters," *Micro Monitor* 6 (May 1989), pp. 12–13.

It not only gets them to think about what actions the results suggest, but also alerts them to pay close attention to the evidence supporting the conclusions. This format allows managers to evaluate the strength of the evidence supporting an action, since they know beforehand the conclusions that have been drawn from it.

The structure a presenter decides to use should depend on the particular company's style and preferences and on the presenter's own level of comfort with each form of organization. In either case, the evidence supporting the conclusions must be presented systematically, and the conclusions drawn must be consistent with the evidence.

A third important element in an effective oral presentation is the use of appropriate visual aids. Depending on the size of the group and the physical facilities in which the meeting is held, flip charts, transparencies, slides, computerized graphics, and even whiteboards and markers can all be used to advantage. Regardless of which type of visual is used, make sure it can be read easily by those in the back of the room. Keep the visuals simple so they can be understood at a glance. Whenever possible, use figures rather than tables to make the points, as figures are more easily understood. In addition, obey the other principles of effective visual aid design listed in Research Window 23.1.

Delivering the Oral Report

Honor the time limit set for the meeting. Use no more than a third to a half of the time for the formal presentation. But be careful not to rush the presentation of the information contained in the charts. Remember, the audience is seeing them for the first time. Order your presentation in such a way that there is enough time to both present and discuss the most critical findings. Reserve the remaining time for questions and further discussion.

One of the unique benefits of the oral presentation is that it allows interaction. A question-and-answer period may be the most important part of your presentation. It allows you to clear up any confusion that may have arisen during the course of your talk, to emphasize points that deserve special attention, and to get a feeling for the issues that are of particular concern or interest to your audience. The nature of the questions raised during a progress report may help you structure your final report to best advantage.

Researcher Michele Holleran has experienced these benefits first hand at small to midsized companies, where her audience is apt to include a marketing director or vice president who sees the research in terms of the company's overall objectives. For example, she presented the results of a multifaceted study to management of a company that makes products for home builders. The study addressed a mix of issues, from what the company's advertising should emphasize to how the company's product mix should be expanded. The researchers managed to combine the findings of interviews and focus groups into a single report. In their oral presentation, the researchers emphasized what they concluded were the key pieces of information. They summarized what they learned, then asked the managers how it fit with what they already knew. The result was an interactive presentation, with all the parties contributing knowledge. At various points, managers asked the researchers to document findings that were counter to their expectations. Through this process, the company's management abandoned some misconceptions about the market and developed several growth strategies.[3]

When delivering the message, use the time-honored principles of public speaking: Keep the presentation simple and uncluttered so that the audience does not have to backtrack mentally to think about what was said, and choose words and sentences that are appropriate for the tongue. That means spoken speech, your usual vocabulary, and simple phrases.[4]

Graphic Presentation of the Results

The old adage that a picture is worth a thousand words is equally true for business reports. A picture, called a *graphic illustration* in the case of the research report, can indeed be worth a thousand words when it is appropriate to the presentation and well designed. When inappropriate or poorly designed, such an illustration may actually detract from the value of the written or oral research report. In this section, we will review briefly some of the most popular forms of graphics and when each is best used.[5]

In a research report, graphic illustration generally involves the presentation of quantities in graph form. To be effective, it must be more than simply converting a set of numbers into a drawing; the picture must give the readers an accurate understanding of the comparisons or relationships that they would otherwise have to search for in the numbers in the report and perhaps fail to see. If well done, the graphic illustration will give the readers this understanding more quickly, more forcefully, more completely, and more accurately than could be done in any other way.[6]

Graphic presentation is not the only way to present quantitative information, nor is it always the best. Sometimes text and tables are better used. Graphics should be used only when they serve the purpose better than do these other modes. Written textual material is generally the most useful in explaining, interpreting, and evaluating results, while tables are particularly good for providing emphasis and for vivid demonstrations of important findings. Particularly since some readers tend to shy away from graphic presentation as "too technical," it should be used with discretion and designed with care.

At one time graphic presentation was expensive and often delayed the presentation of reports because the visuals had to be drawn by graphic artists. Computer graphics have changed that. The development of computer software for graphically portraying the results of a study now makes the preparation of visuals fast and inexpensive. There is no longer any excuse for not using graphics when appropriate.

The results of a research study you supervised are disappointing. Only one of the four basic questions motivating the study has been clearly answered. The answers to the other three questions are rather equivocal in spite of careful planning of the study and a sizable expenditure of money to carry it out. Unanticipated difficulties in contacting people by telephone raised the cost of each contact, which meant the obtained sample was smaller than the planned sample, which in turn made the evidence less clear-cut. You are concerned that you and your research team will be evaluated unfavorably because of this. Members of your research team are arguing that when you deliver the oral report to management, you should attempt to somewhat hide the fact that

only one of the four basic questions has been answered satisfactorily. The team members propose a multimedia presentation with lots of glitz, with maximum time devoted to the formal presentation and minimum time allowed for questions.

- Is it ethical to hide disappointing results in this way?

- What are the consequences of doing so?

- Is it okay to use so much glitz to generate interest in the topic being presented that the glitz overwhelms the substance of the findings? Should you not use glitz at all?

There are three basic kinds of graphics: charts that show how much, maps that show where, and diagrams that show how. Since charts are generally the most useful of the three types, the following discussion focuses on some of the more common chart types.

Pie Chart

Pie chart
A circle representing a total quantity and divided into sectors, with each sector showing the size of the segment in relation to that total.

Probably one of the more familiar charts, the **pie chart** is simply a circle divided into sections, with each of the sections representing a portion of the total. Since the sections are presented as part of a whole, or total, the pie chart is particularly effective for depicting relative size or emphasizing static comparisons. Figure 23.1 (resulting from the data of Exhibit 23.1), for instance, shows the breakdown of personal consumption expenditures by

FIGURE 23.1   Personal Consumption Expenditures by Major Category for 1996

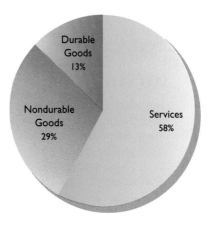

		DURABLE GOODS			NONDURABLE GOODS			SERVICES	
Year	Total Personal Consumption Expenditures	Total Durable Goods	Motor Vehicles & Parts	Furniture & Household Equipment	Total Nondurable Goods	Food	Clothing and Shoes	Gasoline and Oil	
1975	976.4	132.2	55.8	53.5	407.3	213.6	69.6	40.4	437.0
1976	1,084.3	156.8	72.6	59.1	441.7	230.6	75.3	44.0	485.7
1977	1,204.4	178.2	84.8	65.7	478.8	249.8	82.6	48.1	547.4
1978	1,346.5	200.2	95.7	72.8	528.2	275.9	92.4	51.2	618.0
1979	1,507.2	213.4	96.6	81.8	600.0	311.6	99.1	66.6	693.7
1980	1,668.1	214.7	90.7	86.3	668.8	345.1	104.6	84.8	784.5
1981	1,849.1	235.4	101.9	92.3	730.7	373.9	114.3	94.6	883.0
1982	2,050.7	252.7	108.9	95.7	771.0	398.8	124.4	89.1	1,027.0
1983	2,234.5	289.1	130.4	107.1	816.7	421.9	135.1	90.2	1,128.7
1984	2,430.5	335.5	157.4	118.8	867.3	448.5	146.7	90.0	1,227.6
1985	2,629.0	372.2	179.1	129.9	911.2	471.6	156.4	90.6	1,345.6
1986	2,797.4	406.0	196.2	139.7	942.0	500.0	166.8	73.5	1,449.5
1987	3,009.4	423.4	197.9	148.8	1,001.3	530.7	178.4	75.3	1,584.7
1988	3,238.2	457.5	212.2	161.8	1,060.0	562.6	191.1	77.3	1,720.7
1989	3,450.1	474.6	215.5	171.4	1,130.0	595.3	204.6	83.8	1,845.5
1990	3,659.3	480.3	213.0	176.4	1,193.7	624.7	213.2	93.8	1,983.3
1991	3,887.7	446.1	185.4	170.4	1,251.5	617.7	209.0	105.5	2,190.1
1992	4,095.8	480.4	203.7	180.9	1,290.7	630.9	221.8	105.4	2,324.7
1993	4,378.2	538.0	228.0	208.9	1,339.2	649.7	235.4	105.6	2,501.0
1994	4,628.4	591.5	251.2	229.7	1,394.3	679.6	246.5	107.2	2,642.7
1995	4,957.7	608.5	254.8	240.2	1,475.8	735.1	254.7	114.4	2,873.4
1996	5,207.6	634.5	261.3	252.6	1,534.7	756.1	264.3	122.6	3,038.4

major category for 1996. The conclusion is obvious. Expenditures for services account for the largest proportion of total consumption expenditures. Further, expenditures for services and nondurable goods completely dwarf expenditures for durable goods.

Figure 23.1 has three slices, and it is easy to interpret. Had the information been broken into finer categories (for example, if the separate components of durable and nondurable goods had been depicted), a greater number of sections would have been required. Although more information would have been conveyed, emphasis would have been lost. As a rule of thumb, no more than six slices should be generated; the division of the pie should start at the twelve o'clock position; the sections should be arrayed clockwise in decreasing order of magnitude; and the exact percentages should be provided on the graph.[7]

Line Chart

Line chart
A two-dimensional chart constructed on graph paper with the X axis representing one variable (typically time) and the Y axis representing another variable.

The pie chart is a one-scale chart, which is why it is best used for static comparisons of a phenomenon at a point in time. The **line chart** is a two-dimensional chart that is particularly useful in depicting dynamic relationships such as time-series fluctuations of one or more series. For example, Figure 23.2 (produced from the data of Exhibit 23.2) shows that, for 1975–1994, new car sales of imports were subject to much less fluctuation than were domestic sales.

The line chart is probably used even more often than the pie chart. It is typically constructed on graph paper with the X axis representing time and the Y axis representing values of the variable or variables. When more than one variable is presented, it is

FIGURE 23.2   **Retail Sales of New Passenger Cars, 1975–1994**

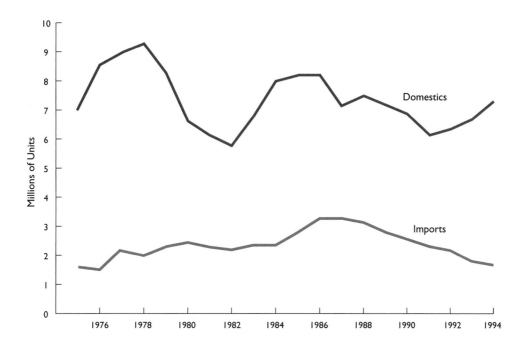

EXHIBIT 23.2   **Retail Sales of New Passenger Cars (millions of units)**

Year	Domestics	Imports	Total
1975	7.0	1.6	8.6
1976	8.5	1.5	10.0
1977	9.0	2.1	11.1
1978	9.2	2.0	11.2
1979	8.2	2.3	10.5
1980	6.6	2.4	9.0
1981	6.2	2.3	8.5
1982	5.8	2.2	8.0
1983	6.8	2.4	9.2
1984	8.0	2.4	10.4
1985	8.2	2.8	11.0
1986	8.2	3.2	11.4
1987	7.1	3.2	10.3
1988	7.5	3.1	10.6
1989	7.1	2.8	9.9
1990	6.9	2.6	9.5
1991	6.1	2.3	8.4
1992	6.3	2.1	8.4
1993	6.7	1.8	8.5
1994	7.3	1.7	9.0

Source: *Statistical Abstract of the United States.*

recommended that the lines for different items be distinctive in color or form (dots and dashes in suitable combinations) with identification of the different forms given in a legend.

Stratum Chart

Stratum chart
A set of line charts in which quantities are aggregated or a total is disaggregated so that the distance between two lines represents the amount of some variable.

The **stratum chart** serves in some ways as a dynamic pie chart, in that it can be used to show relative emphasis by sector (for example, quantity consumed by user class) and change in relative emphasis over time. The stratum chart consists of a set of line charts whose quantities are grouped together (or a total that is broken into its components). It is also called a *stacked line chart*. For example, Figure 23.3 (resulting from the data of Exhibit 23.1) shows personal consumption expenditures by major category for the 1975–1996 period. The lowest line shows the expenditures just for durable goods; the second lowest line shows the total expenditures for durable plus nondurable goods. Personal consumption expenditures for nondurable goods are thus shown by the area between the two lines. So it is with the remaining areas. We would need multiple pie charts (one for each year) to capture the same information, and the message would not be as obvious.

The X axis typically represents time in the stratum chart, and the Y axis again captures the value of the variables. The use of color or distinctive cross-hatching is strongly recommended to distinguish the various components in the stratum chart. As was true for the pie chart, no more than six components should be depicted in a stratum chart.

Bar Chart

Bar chart
A chart in which the relative lengths of the bars show relative amounts of variables or objects.

The **bar chart** can be either a one-scale or a two-scale chart. This feature, plus the many other variations it permits, probably accounts for its wide use. Figure 23.4, for example, is a one-scale chart. It also shows personal consumption expenditures by major category at a single point in time. Figure 23.4 presents the same information as Figure 23.1 but is, in at least one respect, more revealing; it not only offers some appreciation of the relative

FIGURE 23.3 **Stratum Chart Showing Personal Consumption Expenditures by Major Category, 1975–1996**

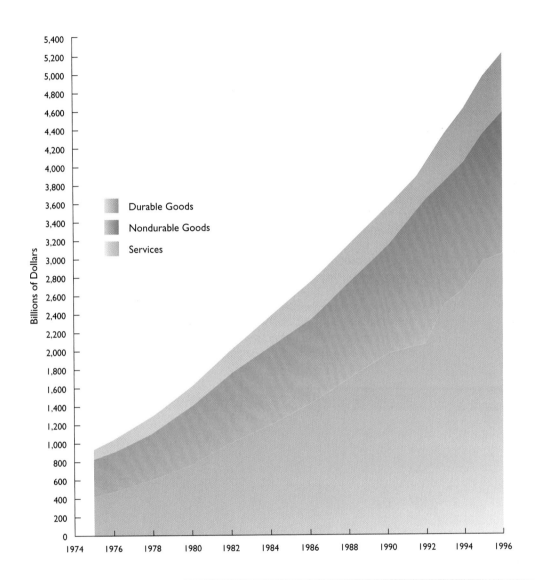

FIGURE 23.4 **Bar Chart Showing Personal Consumption Expenditures by Major Category for 1996**

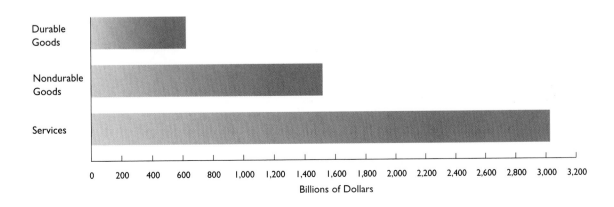

expenditures by major category, but also indicates the magnitude of the expenditures by category. Given the total amount of personal consumption expenditures for 1996, readers could, of course, also generate this information from the pie chart. However, it would involve additional calculations on their part.

Figure 23.5, on the other hand, is a two-scale bar chart. It uses the data contained in Exhibit 23.2 and shows total automobile sales for the period 1976–1994. The Y axis represents quantity, and the X axis, time.

Figures 23.4 and 23.5 show that the bar chart can be drawn either vertically or horizontally. When emphasis is on the change in the variable through time, the vertical form is preferred, with the X axis as the time axis. When time is not a variable, either the vertical or the horizontal form is used.

Bar Chart Variations

Pictogram
A bar chart in which pictures represent amounts—for example, piles of dollars for income, picture of cars for automobile production, people in a row for population.

As previously suggested, bar charts are capable of great variation. One variation is to convert them to **pictograms.** Instead of using the length of the bar to capture quantity, amounts are shown by piles of dollars for income, pictures of cars for automobile production, people in a row for population, and so on. This can be a welcome change of pace for the reader if there are a number of graphs in the report. (However, pictograms are especially susceptible to perceptual distortions. Report users have to be especially careful when reading them so that they are not led to incorrect conclusions.)

A variation of the basic bar chart—the grouped-bar chart—can be used to capture the change in two or more series through time. Figure 23.6, for example, shows the change in consumption expenditures by the three major categories for the period 1988–1996. Just as distinctive symbols are effective in distinguishing the separate series in a line chart, distinctive coloring and/or cross-hatching is equally helpful in a grouped-bar chart.

FIGURE 23.5 **Bar Chart Showing Total Automobile Sales, 1976–1994**

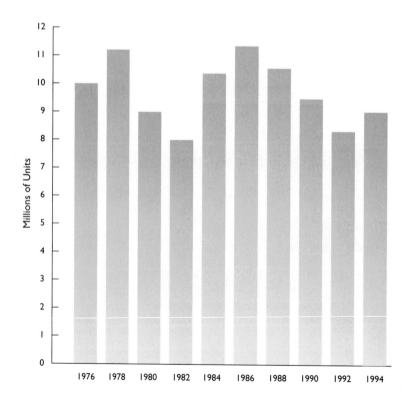

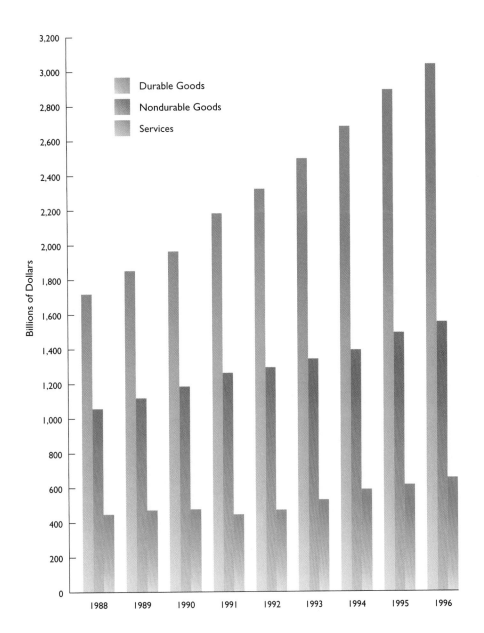

There is also a bar chart equivalent to the stratum chart—the divided-bar chart or, as it is sometimes called, the stacked-bar chart. Its construction and interpretation are similar to those for the stratum chart. Figure 23.7, for example, is a divided-bar chart of personal consumption expenditures by major category. It shows both total and relative expenditures through time, and it makes use of distinctive color for each component.

Maps

Maps focus attention on geographic areas. When used for the geographic display of quantitative or statistical information, they are usually called *data maps*.

FIGURE 23.7   **Divided Bar Chart Showing Personal Consumption Expenditures by Major Category, 1976–1996**

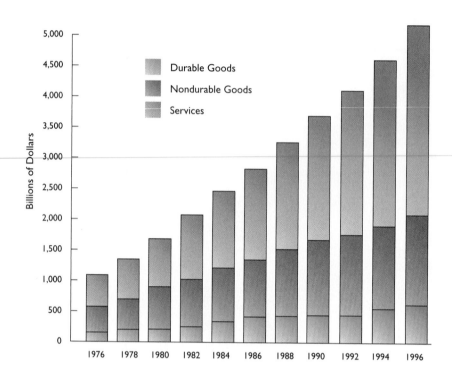

Ethical Dilemma 23.2

You are preparing to deliver the final report to top management to make the case that your new advertising campaign has increased sales dramatically in trial areas. Your conceptual arguments on behalf of the new campaign are very convincing, but although there has been a consistent rise in sales in trial areas, the bar charts look rather disappointing: 61,500 units the first month, 61,670 units the next, 61,820 the next. Why, the increase is barely visible! Then you realize how much more exciting your results would look if the Y axis were broken above the origin so that the plots started at 50,000 units.

• Where does salesmanship stop and deception start?

   Data maps are especially suited to the presentation of rates, ratios, and frequency-distribution data by areas. In constructing data maps, the quantity of interest is typically broken into groups, and cross-hatching, shading, or color is used to display the numerical group in which each area belongs. In general, it is helpful to keep the group intervals approximately equal and to use a limited number of shadings—four to seven and certainly no more than ten. Moreover, the shadings should run progressively from light to dark, and all areas should have some shading. Leaving an area blank or white tends to weaken its importance. For example, Figure 23.8 shows how employment, a sign of economic vitality, grew over a ten-year period in various countries.

   Research Window 23.2 offers some suggestions on using graphics in slide presentations.

FIGURE 23.8   **Growth in Employment, 1983–1993**

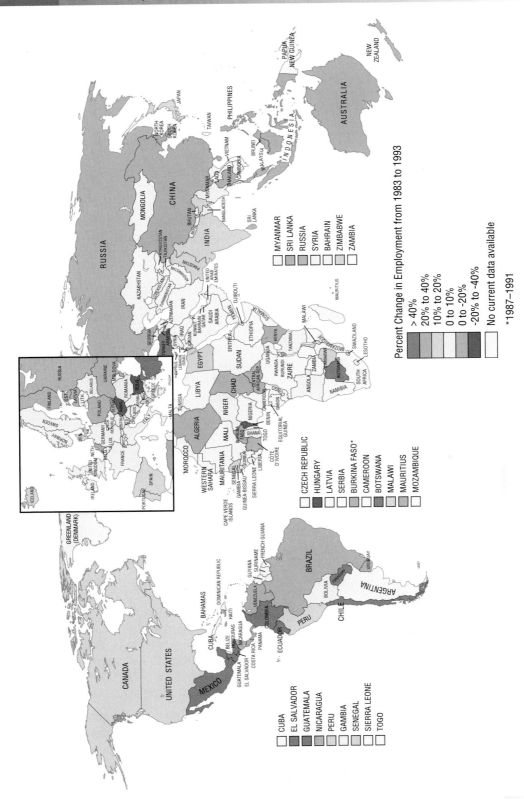

Source: Michael R. Czinkota, Ilkka A. Ronkainene and Michael H. Moffett, *International Business*, 4th ed. (Forth Worth, Tex.: The Dryden Press, 1996).

Word slides
- Keep word slides brief: use key words only.
- Use bullets and color to highlight key points.
- Break up the information to make a series of slides (a progressive or "build" series). Use color to show the new line added to each slide.

Tabular slides
- Use tabular slides to show lists.
- Keep items as brief as possible; arrange them to fill the slide area so the type can be as large as possible.

Box charts
- Use box charts for organization charts, flow charts.
- Simplify to keep them legible.
- Break up complex charts into a series. (Show flow chart divided by time periods; show organization chart with the overall chart and departmental "close-up.")

Bar charts
- Use bar charts for data arranged in segments (by month, year, etc.).
- Choose vertical or horizontal bars (both within horizontal slide format).
- Add drop shadows for dimensional bars.

- Show complex facts clearly by using multiple or segmented bars.
- Divide extensive data into a progressive disclosure series.

Pie charts
- Use pie charts to emphasize the relationship of the parts to the whole.
- Select single pie or double pie.
- Consider options such as drop shadow for dimensional effect, pulled-out slices, etc.
- Arrange the slices to make your point most effectively.
- Divide the slice into a series if that improves effectiveness.

Line graphs and area graphs
- Use line graphs and area graphs to display trends or continuous data.
- Decide whether line graph or area graph shows your point better.
- Select baseline and scale for maximum effectiveness.
- Use call-outs to identify key points in graph.
- Divide extensive data into a series of graphs.

Source: Leslie Blumberg, "For Graphic Presentations, Managers Focus on Slides," *Data Management* (May 1983), p. 22.

Back to the Case

At the beginning of each month, representatives from the research firm present the past month's results to the executives responsible for providing GTEI's services. They go over the statistics for each measurement category, as well as the comments made by customers.

Together, the participants in the meeting discuss the implications of the results. They look at trends and suggest factors that may have caused certain results. The executives use this discussion as the starting point for making improvements. They meet with their staff to discuss the results, set goals, and formulate plans.

GTEI considers even partial dissatisfaction to be unacceptable. If even one customer expresses total dissatisfaction with an area of service, or if at least three customers say they are somewhat dissatisfied, the person who handles that area of service is charged with attending to the problem immediately.

The process of discussing the results helps the researchers and GTEI management diagnose problems, even when the explanations are not obvious. For example, consider GTEI's Internet Advantage service, which provides companies with Internet connections. Internet Advantage includes the equipment for the site, but the dedicated phone line is installed by the local telephone company rather than GTEI personnel. Surveys of initial customer satisfaction showed that only 48 percent of customers were totally satisfied with the line installation—far below GTEI's minimum acceptable level of 70 percent.

The researchers and managers discussed the reasons behind the low satisfaction. Customer comments indicated they were unhappy about the time required to install the lines, sometimes 45 days or more. Should GTEI look for a way to reduce installation time? Researchers suggested the managers look elsewhere for a solution. They analyzed the data using a sophisticated technique called neural network analysis, which not only ranked sources of satisfaction but showed how much impact changing one of these factors would have on customers' overall satisfaction. This analysis showed that something else actually had more of an impact on satisfaction with installation: communication with GTEI's Network Operations Center, which coordinates Network Advantage.

The managers were initially puzzled by this relationship, but through discussion, they arrived at a hypothesis: GTEI personnel were giving customers an incorrect impression about the installation time. Customers were disappointed because their expectations were unrealistic. To test this idea, the researchers modified the next month's survey to ask about expectations related to installation.

Sure enough, at the next meeting, the results showed a notable difference between expectations and reality. As a re-sult, many customers were dissatisfied with installation. GTEI couldn't control the phone company, but it could control its own communications. It began establishing more realistic expectations, and within the year, overall satisfaction with installation soared to 83 percent.

This collaborative approach to reviewing and applying research has generated impressive results. In some areas of performance, the percentage of customers saying they are totally satisfied is over 90 percent. Such customer ratings are rare in the realm of marketing research—and are a tribute to George Kerns's passion for quality.

Source: Robert Brass, "A Strong Connection," *Quirk's Marketing Research Review* (October 1998, downloaded from the *Quirk's* Web site, www.quirks.com, October 27, 1999).

Summary

Learning Objective 1

Specify the first rule to keep in mind when preparing an oral report.

As with written reports, the first rule when preparing an oral report is to know your audience.

Learning Objective 2

Describe the two most common forms of organization for oral reports.

There are two popular forms of organization for oral reports. Both begin by stating the general purpose of the study and the specific objectives that were addressed. In the most popular structure, the conclusions are introduced after all of the evidence supporting a particular course of action is presented. This allows the presenter to build a logical case in sequential fashion. In the alternative structure, conclusions are presented immediately after the purpose and main objectives. This format allows managers to evaluate the strength of the evidence supporting an action, since they know beforehand the conclusions that have been drawn from it.

Learning Objective 3

Discuss the key points a presenter should keep in mind regarding the use of visual aids.

The visual aids used in an oral report should be easily understood and should be easily seen by those in the back of the room.

Learning Objective 4

Explain how the time allotted for an oral presentation should be organized.

Honor the time limit set for the meeting. Use no more than a third to a half of the time for the formal presentation. Reserve the remaining time for questions and discussion.

Learning Objective 5

Describe the circumstances in which a pie chart is most effective.

A pie chart is a one-scale chart, which is particularly effective in communicating a static comparison.

Learning Objective 6

Explain the best use of a line chart.

A line chart is a two-dimensional chart that is particularly useful in depicting dynamic relationships such as time-series fluctuations of one or more series.

Learning Objective 7

Describe the circumstances in which a stratum chart is most effective.

A stratum chart is in some ways a dynamic pie chart, in that it can be used to show relative emphasis by sector and change in relative emphasis over time.

Learning Objective 8

Cite the reason why bar charts are so widely used.

The bar chart can be either a one-scale or a two-scale chart. This feature, plus the many other variations it permits, probably accounts for its wide use.

Learning Objective 9

Describe the circumstances in which a grouped-bar chart is most effective.

A variation of the basic bar chart, the grouped-bar can be used to capture the change in two or more series through time.

Research Questions

1. What are the key considerations in preparing an oral report?

2. What is a pie chart? For what kinds of information is it particularly effective?

3. What is a line chart? For what kinds of information is it generally employed?

4. What is a stratum chart? For what kinds of information is it particularly appropriate?

5. What is a bar chart? For what kinds of problems is it effective?

6. What is a pictogram?

7. What is a grouped bar chart? When is it used?

8. What is a data map? For what kinds of information is it particularly effective?

Discussion Questions, Problems, and Projects

1. The management of the Seal-Tight Company, a manufacturer of metal cans, has presented you with the following information:

THE SEAL-TIGHT COMPANY:
A COMPARATIVE STATEMENT OF PROFIT AND LOSS FOR THE FISCAL YEARS 1995–1999

	1995	1996	1997	1998	1999
Net sales	$40,000,000	$45,000,000	$48,000,000	$53,000,000	$55,000,000
Cost and expenses	$28,000,000	$32,850,000	$33,600,000	$39,750,000	$40,150,000
Cost of goods sold					
Selling and admin. expenses	4,000,000	4,500,000	4,800,000	5,300,000	5,500,000
Depreciation	1,200,000	1,350,000	1,440,000	1,590,000	1,650,000
Interest	800,000	900,000	960,000	1,060,000	1,100,000
	$34,000,000	$39,600,000	$40,800,000	$47,700,000	$48,400,000
Profits from operations	6,000,000	5,400,000	7,200,000	5,300,000	6,600,000
Estimated taxes	$ 2,400,000	$ 2,160,000	$ 2,880,000	$ 2,120,000	$ 2,640,000
Net profits	$ 3,600,000	$ 3,240,000	$ 4,320,000	$ 3,180,000	$ 3,960,000

(a) Develop a visual aid to present the company's distribution of sales revenues in 1995.
(b) Develop a visual aid that would compare the change in the net profit level with the change in the net sales level.
(c) Develop a visual aid that will present the following expenses (excluding cost of goods sold) over the five-year period: selling and administration expenses and depreciation and interest expenses.
(d) The management of Seal-Tight has the following sales data relating to its two major competitors.

	1995	1996	1997	1998	1999
Metalmax Co.	$35,000,000	$40,000,000	$42,000,000	$45,000,000	$48,000,000
Superior Can Co.	$41,000,000	$43,000,000	$45,000,000	$46,000,000	$48,000,000

You are required to prepare a visual aid to facilitate the comparison of the sales performance of Seal-Tight Company with its major competitors.

2. Most universities and colleges offer a wide variety of computer graphics software for student use in campus microcomputer labs. Investigate the availability of graphics software on your campus. Prepare a report outlining your findings. Be sure to include the following information for each available package:
(a) Name of package and basic capabilities
(b) Location(s) of access point(s)
(c) Times available for use
(d) Name of contact person(s) for further information
(e) Any special skills required for use and availability of training if needed
(f) Access fees, if any
(g) Hard-copy formats available (e.g., dot matrix printers, laser printers, color plotters, transparencies, slides)

3. Visit your school's library and find examples of each of the graphic illustrations described in this chapter. Look for these in such publications as *Business Week*,

Fortune, Newsweek, and *The Wall Street Journal.* Make a copy of each chart and critique it, using the criteria noted in the text. For example, does the pie chart you found exceed the recommended maximum number of divisions? Are the exact percentages displayed? In each case, is the chart appropriate for its intended purpose, or would another type of chart be more informative? Are there any changes you might recommend if the chart were to be used in an oral presentation?

Endnotes

1. Alex Taylor III, "Kellogg Cranks Up Its Idea Machine," *Fortune* (July 5, 1999, downloaded from the Northern Light Web site, www.northernlight.com, August 6, 1999).

2. Paco Underhill, *Why We Buy: The Science of Shopping* (New York: Simon & Schuster, 1999), p. 241.

3. Michele Holleran, "Research Should Be Integrated and Lead to Strategic Decision-Making," *Quirk's Marketing Research Review* (June 1998, downloaded from the *Quirk's* Web site, www.quirks.com, October 27, 1999).

4. There are a number of excellent books available on making effective oral presentations. See, for example, Dorothy Sarnoff, *Make the Most of Your Best: A Complete Program for Presenting Yourself and Your Ideas with Confidence and Authority* (Garden City, N.Y.: Doubleday, 1983); Jan D'Arcy, *Technically Speaking: Proven Ways to Make Your Next Presentation a Success* (New York: AMACOM, 1992); Rudolph F. Verderber, *The Challenge of Effective Speaking,* 10th ed. (Belmont, Calif.: Wadsworth Publishing Company, 1997).

5. The presentation should by no means include all the graph forms that could be used, but rather just some of the more common ones. Those interested in more detail should see Mary E. Spear, *Practical Charting Techniques* (New York: McGraw-Hill, 1969); Edward R. Tufte, *The Visual Display of Quantitative Information* (Cheshire, Conn.: Graphics Press, 1983); Edward R. Tufte, *Envisioning Information* (Cheshire, Conn.: Graphics Press, 1991).

6. American Management Association, *Making the Most of Charts: An ABC of Graphic Presentation,* Management Bulletin, 28 (New York: American Telephone and Telegraph Company, 1960). See also J. M. Chambers, W. J. Cleveland, B. Kleiner, and P. A. Tukey, *Graphical Methods for Data Analysis* (Boston: Duxbury Press, 1983); William S. Cleveland, *The Elements of Graphing Data,* rev. ed. (Murray Hill, N.J.: AT&T Bell Laboratories, 1994).

7. Jessamon Dawe and William Jackson Lord, Jr., *Functional Business Communication,* 3rd ed. (Englewood Cliffs, N.J.: Prentice-Hall, 1983). See also Gene Zelazny, *The Executive's Guide to Visual Communication,* 3rd ed. (Burr Ridge, Ill.: Irwin Professional Publishing, 1996).

Suggested Additional Readings

For an excellent discussion of how to make effective oral presentations, see
Jan D'Arcy, *Technically Speaking: Proven Ways to Make Your Next Presentation a Success* (New York: AMACOM, 1992).
Dorothy Sarnoff, *Make the Most of Your Best: A Complete Program for Presenting Yourself and Your Ideas with Confidence and Authority* (Garden City, N.Y.: Doubleday, 1983).
Rudolph F. Verderber, *The Challenge of Effective Speaking,* 10th ed. (Belmont, Calif.: Wadsworth Publishing Company, 1997).

For discussion of how to develop effective graphics, see
William S. Cleveland, *The Elements of Graphing Data,* rev. ed. (Murray Hill, N.J.: AT&T Bell Laboratories, 1994).
Edward R. Tufte, *Envisioning Information* (Cheshire, Conn.: Graphics Press, 1990).
Leland Wilkinson, *SYGRAPH* (Evanston, Ill.: Systat, Inc., 1990), especially pp. 38–61.

EPILOGUE

The subject of marketing research can be approached in a number of ways. In this book we have used a *project emphasis* as the basis for our discussion. Using this perspective, we focused on how to define a problem and then develop the research needed to answer it. Because we have broken the research process down into components small enough to be discussed in the space of a chapter, it may seem to be a series of disconnected bits and pieces. However, as pointed out in Chapter 3, the research process is anything but a set of disconnected parts. All the steps are highly interrelated, and a decision made at one stage has implications for the others as well. Now that we have closely examined each of the individual components of the research process, in this epilogue we will look once again at how they work together. We will also review some of the key decisions that must be made as the process unfolds.

A research project should not be viewed as an end in itself. Projects arise because managerial problems need solving. The problems themselves may concern the identification of market opportunities, the evaluation of alternative courses of action, or control of marketing operations. Since these activities, in turn, are the essence of the managerial function, research activity can also be viewed from the broader perspective of the firm's marketing intelligence system. Chapter 2, therefore, focused on the nature and present status of the supply of marketing intelligence.

The Research Process Revisited

Earlier in this text, we suggested that marketing research involves the systematic gathering, recording, and analyzing of data about problems relating to the marketing of goods and services. We pointed out that these activities are logically viewed as a sequence of steps called the research process. The stages of the process were identified as follows:

1. Formulate the problem.

2. Determine the research design.

3. Determine the data collection method.

4. Design the data collection forms.

5. Design the sample and collect the data.

6. Analyze and interpret the data.

7. Prepare the research report.

The decision problem logically comes first. It dictates the research problem and design of the project. However, the transition from problem to project is not an automatic one. It is not unusual for a researcher to go from problem specification to tentative research design and then back to problem respecification and modified research design. This back-and-forth process is perfectly natural, and, in fact, reflects one of the researcher's more important roles: to help to define and redefine the problem so that it can be researched, and, more important, answer the decision maker's problem.

While this task might appear to be simple in principle, in practice it can be formidable, as it requires a clear specification of objectives, alternatives, and environmental constraints and influences. The decision maker may not readily provide these to the researcher, who then must dig them out in order to design effective research.

In some cases research may not even be necessary. If the decision maker's views are so strongly held that no amount of information might change them, the research will be wasted. It is up to the researcher to determine this before, rather than after, conducting the research. Often this can be accomplished by asking "what if" questions. What if consumer reaction to the product concept is overwhelmingly favorable? What if it is unfavorable? What if it is only slightly favorable? If the decision maker indicates that he or she will make the same decision in each case, there may be important objectives that have never been explicitly stated. This is a critical finding. Every research project should have one or more objectives, and one should not proceed to the other steps in the process until these can be explicitly stated.

It is also important to ask at this point whether the anticipated benefits of the research are likely to exceed the expected costs. It is a mistake to assume that simply because something might change as a result of the research, the research is warranted. It may be that the likelihood of finding something that might warrant a change in the decision is so remote that the research still will be wasted. Researchers and decision makers alike constantly need to ask: Why should this research be conducted? What could we possibly find out that we do not already know? Will the expected benefits from the research exceed its costs? If the answers indicate research, then the question logically turns to, what kind?

If the problem cannot be formulated as some specific "if-then" conjectural relationships, exploratory research is in order. The primary purpose of exploratory research is gathering some ideas and insights into the phenomenon. The output of an exploratory study will not be answers but more specific questions or statements of tentative relationships. The search for such insights demands a flexible research design. Structured questionnaires and probability sampling plans are not used in exploratory research, since the emphasis is not on gathering summary statistics but on gaining insight into the problem. The personal interview is much more appropriate than the telephone interview, and that in turn is more appropriate than a mail survey, since the unstructured question is most useful in the experience survey. Interviewees should be handpicked because they can provide the wanted information. In such cases, a convenience or judgment sample is very much in order, whereas it would be completely out of place in descriptive or causal research. Focus groups can also be productive.

The researcher may also want to conduct a survey of the literature or an analysis of selected cases. These steps can be advantageous in exploratory research, particularly if the researcher remembers that the goal of exploratory research is to discover ideas and tentative explanations of the phenomenon, and not to fix on one idea as being the sole definitive explanation. The analysis of published data may be particularly productive if it reveals sharp contrasts or other striking features that may help to illuminate the reasons behind the phenomenon under investigation.

If exploratory research has succeeded in generating one or more specific hypotheses to be investigated, the next research step would logically be descriptive or causal research. The design the researcher actually selects depends largely on how convinced he or she is that the tentative explanation is indeed the correct explanation for the phenomenon. Of course, the feasibility and cost of conducting an experiment are also important factors in determining research design. While experiments typically provide more convincing proof of causal relationships, they also usually cost more then descriptive designs. This is one of the reasons why descriptive designs are the most commonly employed type in marketing research.

Whereas exploratory designs are flexible, descriptive designs are rigid. Descriptive designs demand a clear specification of the who, what, when, where, how, and why of the research before data collection begins. They generally employ structured questionnaires or scales because these forms provide advantages in coding and tabulating. In descriptive designs, the emphasis is on generating an accurate picture of the relationships between and among variables. Probability sampling plans are desirable, but if the sample is to be drawn using nonprobabilistic methods, it is important that a quota sample be used. Descriptive studies typically rely heavily on cross-tabulation analysis or other means of investigating the association among variables, such as regression analysis, although the emphasis can also be on the search for differences. The great majority of descriptive studies are cross-sectional, although some do use longitudinal information.

Experiments are the best means we have for making inferences about cause-and-effect relationships, since, if designed properly, they provide the most compelling evidence regarding concomitant variation, time order of occurrence of variables, and elimination of other factors. A key feature of the experiment is that the researcher is able to control who will be exposed to the experimental stimulus (the presumed cause). Depending on the nature of the experiment, subjects may be individual consumers, members of panels, or other elements from the population of interest. Sampling plays little role in experiments other than in determining which objects are going to be assigned to which treatment conditions.

Because the goal is to test a specific relationship, causal designs also demand a clear specification of what is to be measured and how it is to be measured. Structured data collection instruments such as questionnaires and scales are often used. Researchers also rely heavily on the observation method for collecting data, because this method tends to produce more objective and accurate information.

The major objective in analyzing experimental results is to determine if there are differences between those exposed to the experimental stimulus and those not exposed. Although researchers generally use analysis of variance to investigate and measure these differences, other techniques (for example, the *t* test for the difference in means of independent or correlated samples) are used as well.

The previous paragraphs should indicate how significantly the steps are interrelated and, in particular, how the basic nature of the research design implies a number of things with respect to the structure of the data collection form, design of the sample, collection, and analysis of the data. A decision about appropriate research does not completely determine the latter considerations, of course, but simply suggests their basic nature. The analyst still has to determine their specific format. For example, is the structured questionnaire to be disguised or undisguised? Is the probability sample to be simple, stratified, or cluster? How large a sample is needed? Does the data collection instrument dictate a data-analysis procedure for nominal, ordinal, interval, or ratio data? These questions, too, will be determined in large part by the way the research question is framed, although the ingenuity displayed by the designer of the research will determine their final form. The researcher will have to balance the various sources of error that can arise in the process when determining this final form. In effecting this balance, the researcher must be concerned with assessing and minimizing total error; this often means assuming additional error in one of the parts of the process so that total error can be decreased.

The seventh and final stage in the research process is to prepare the research report. As we noted in the chapters in this part, despite the sophistication that may have been displayed in the earlier stages in the research process, the project will be a failure if the research report fails. Since the research report is all that most executives will see of the project, it is the yardstick by which the research will be evaluated.

A standard research report generally contains the following elements: title page, table of contents, summary, introduction, body, conclusions and recommendations, and appendix. Most marketing research projects also conclude with an oral report. Most effective oral presentations keep their technical detail to a minimum and make use of appropriate visual aids.

Both written and oral reports are judged by one fundamental criterion: how well they communicate with the audience, be it a reader or a listener. The report must be tailor-made for the reader or readers, with due regard for their technical sophistication, their interest in the subject area, the circumstances under which they will read the report, and the use they will make of it.

In the continuing case we have featured at the end of each part, we have discussed much of the material that would appear in a research report on such a project. For example, much of the information that would normally appear in an introduction appears at the end of Part I, where the first stage in the research process, problem formulation, is discussed. Information about the design of the study that would be included in the body of the report appears in subsequent sections that discuss the research design, the method of data collection, the design of the data collection form, the design of the sample, and the data collection process. Information that would generally appear in the section of the report devoted to conclusions was discussed at the end of Part VI. Certain items such as test statistics and calculations, tables, and a bibliography have been omitted because of length restrictions.

It is important, however, for students to see what the executive summary to such a research report would look like, since in many ways it encapsulates the rest of the document. A good executive summary contains necessary background information as well as the important results and conclusions, and it is thus the one part of the study that can truly stand alone.

This marketing research project was sponsored by the Centerville Area Radio Association (CARA). Its purpose was to identify specific problems that area businesses had with regard to advertising so that CARA advertising sales representatives could work to solve these through their marketing actions. The research objectives were as follows:

1. Identify business decision makers' attitudes toward the advertising media of newspaper, radio, and television.

2. Identify business decision makers' attitudes toward the advertising sales representatives of newspaper, radio, and television.

A five-page questionnaire was developed to measure these attitudes. The questionnaire was designed to test several hypotheses, the first being that different types of advertising media were perceived differently. CARA members were interested in investigating the different perceptions of newspaper, radio, and television as advertising media, since these three were the primary competitors for advertising budgets among Centerville-area businesses.

Another hypothesis was that the advertising sales representatives for the three types of media were also perceived differently from one another. Perceptions were measured through use of scaled ratings of itemized individual attributes of (1) the medium and (2) the sales representatives for each medium. It was hypothesized that attitudes would be further differentiated by the level of annual advertising expenditures made by the respondent's company. Moreover, the particular attributes of sales representatives and advertising media were tested to determine their importance to the respondents.

Also, it was hypothesized that the differences in businesspeople's attitudes toward the three media would be reflected in the differences in their attitudes toward the sales representatives of each of the media.

The position title of the respondent, whether the respondent made advertising decisions, and whether the business used an advertising agency were used to categorize and, if necessary, exclude individuals from the final data analysis.

The research method consisted of mailing a questionnaire to 600 area businesses. A systematic probability sample of 600 was drawn from a yellow pages listing of businesses identified by CARA as representative of those with which they did business or would have liked to do business. These businesses fell into ten broad categories: (1) building materials and hardware; (2) automotive sales and service; (3) apparel; (4) furniture and home furnishings; (5) eating and drinking establishments; (6) health and fitness; (7) financial institutions; (8) home entertainment; (9) professional services; and (10) a miscellaneous category consisting of florists, printers, bookstores, jewelers, and photographic sales and service.

In an effort to ensure an adequate response rate, a one-dollar bill was enclosed in 300 of the mailed questionnaires. The remaining 300 did not receive a dollar. The questionnaires were color coded (cream-color for the ones that received the dollar bill and white for the others) so that response rates for the two groups could be calculated. Systematic probability sampling was also used to determine which businesses would receive a questionnaire with a one-dollar bill inside.

The questionnaires were mailed April 8. The cutoff date for accepting returned questionnaires was April 24. One hundred sixty-five (165) of the cream-color questionnaires were returned, while 47 of the white ones were returned, for a total of 212. The results indicated that the inclusion of the dollar bill made a difference. Thirty-four (25 cream, 9 white) of the questionnaires returned were unusable due to incompleteness.

The hypothesis that there were differences in attitudes toward the three advertising media was not supported by the data. There were no significant differences in respondents' attitudes toward newspaper, radio, and television as advertising media.

With regard to the hypothesis that there were differences in attitudes toward newspaper, radio, and television sales representatives, there were no significant differences except when individuals whose business used an advertising agency were included with those who did not.

The classification of attitude scores by advertising expenditures revealed an inverse linear relationship: As advertising expenditures increased, attitudes toward advertising sales representatives became increasingly negative.

There were significant differences in the ratings of the *importance* of the different characteristics of the media and the various attributes of sales representatives. More particularly, the analysis of the item-importance scores indicated that it would be worthwhile for radio sales representatives to become more knowledgeable about their clients' areas of business and more aware and concerned about their clients' particular advertising needs. Radio representatives should make it clear to business clients that radio advertising can build up recognition of a business as well as, or better than, television advertising. Further, if radio advertising can improve a business's sales volume and can reach its target market better than television advertising, and as well as or better than newspaper advertising, this should be clearly indicated to business clients.

APPENDIX

TABLE 1   Cumulative Standard Unit Normal Distribution

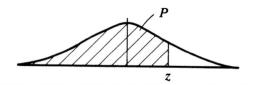

Values of P corresponding to Z for the normal curve. Z is the standard normal variable. The value of P for $-Z$ equals one minus the value of P for $+Z$, (e.g., the P for -1.62 equals $1 - .9474 = .0526$).

Z	.00	.01	.02	.03	.04	.05	.06	.07	.08	.09
.0	.5000	.5040	.5080	.5120	.5160	.5199	.5239	.5279	.5319	.5359
.1	.5398	.5438	.5478	.5517	.5557	.5596	.5636	.5675	.5714	.5753
.2	.5793	.5832	.5871	.5910	.5948	.5987	.6026	.6064	.6103	.6141
.3	.6179	.6217	.6255	.6293	.6331	.6368	.6406	.6443	.6480	.6517
.4	.6554	.6591	.6628	.6664	.6700	.6736	.6772	.6808	.6844	.6879
.5	.6915	.6950	.6985	.7019	.7054	.7088	.7123	.7157	.7190	.7224
.6	.7257	.7291	.7324	.7357	.7389	.7422	.7454	.7486	.7517	.7549
.7	.7580	.7611	.7642	.7673	.7704	.7734	.7764	.7794	.7823	.7852
.8	.7881	.7910	.7939	.7967	.7995	.8023	.8051	.8078	.8106	.8133
.9	.8159	.8186	.8212	.8238	.8264	.8289	.8315	.8340	.8365	.8389
1.0	.8413	.8438	.8461	.8485	.8508	.8531	.8554	.8577	.8599	.8621
1.1	.8643	.8665	.8686	.8708	.8729	.8749	.8770	.8790	.8810	.8830
1.2	.8849	.8869	.8888	.8907	.8925	.8944	.8962	.8980	.8997	.9015
1.3	.9032	.9049	.9066	.9082	.9099	.9115	.9131	.9147	.9162	.9177
1.4	.9192	.9207	.9222	.9236	.9251	.9265	.9279	.9292	.9306	.9319
1.5	.9332	.9345	.9357	.9370	.9382	.9394	.9406	.9418	.9429	.9441
1.6	.9452	.9463	.9474	.9484	.9495	.9505	.9515	.9525	.9535	.9545
1.7	.9554	.9564	.9573	.9582	.9591	.9599	.9608	.9616	.9625	.9633
1.8	.9641	.9649	.9656	.9664	.9671	.9678	.9686	.9693	.9699	.9706
1.9	.9713	.9719	.9726	.9732	.9738	.9744	.9750	.9756	.9761	.9767
2.0	.9772	.9778	.9783	.9788	.9793	.9798	.9803	.9808	.9812	.9817
2.1	.9821	.9826	.9830	.9834	.9838	.9842	.9846	.9850	.9854	.9857
2.2	.9861	.9864	.9868	.9871	.9875	.9878	.9881	.9884	.9887	.9890
2.3	.9893	.9896	.9898	.9901	.9904	.9906	.9909	.9911	.9913	.9916
2.4	.9918	.9920	.9922	.9925	.9927	.9929	.9931	.9932	.9934	.9936
2.5	.9938	.9940	.9941	.9943	.9945	.9946	.9948	.9949	.9951	.9952
2.6	.9953	.9955	.9956	.9957	.9959	.9960	.9961	.9962	.9963	.9964
2.7	.9965	.9966	.9967	.9968	.9969	.9970	.9971	.9972	.9973	.9974
2.8	.9974	.9975	.9976	.9977	.9977	.9978	.9979	.9979	.9980	.9981
2.9	.9981	.9982	.9982	.9983	.9984	.9984	.9985	.9985	.9986	.9986
3.0	.9987	.9987	.9987	.9988	.9988	.9989	.9989	.9989	.9990	.9990
3.1	.9990	.9991	.9991	.9991	.9992	.9992	.9992	.9992	.9993	.9993
3.2	.9993	.9993	.9994	.9994	.9994	.9994	.9994	.9995	.9995	.9995
3.3	.9995	.9995	.9995	.9996	.9996	.9996	.9996	.9996	.9996	.9997
3.4	.9997	.9997	.9997	.9997	.9997	.9997	.9997	.9997	.9997	.9998

Source: Paul E. Green, *Analyzing Multivariate Data* (Chicago: Dryden Press, 1978).

TABLE 2   Selected Percentiles of the χ^2 Distribution

Values of χ^2 corresponding to P

ν	$\chi^2_{.005}$	$\chi^2_{.01}$	$\chi^2_{.025}$	$\chi^2_{.05}$	$\chi^2_{.10}$	$\chi^2_{.90}$	$\chi^2_{.95}$	$\chi^2_{.975}$	$\chi^2_{.99}$	$\chi^2_{.995}$
1	.000039	.00016	.00098	.0039	.0158	2.71	3.84	5.02	6.63	7.88
2	.0100	.0201	.0506	.1026	.2107	4.61	5.99	7.38	9.21	10.60
3	.0717	.115	.216	.352	.584	6.25	7.81	9.35	11.34	12.84
4	.207	.297	.484	.711	1.064	7.78	9.49	11.14	13.28	14.86
5	.412	.554	.831	1.15	1.61	9.24	11.07	12.83	15.09	16.75
6	.676	.872	1.24	1.64	2.20	10.64	12.59	14.45	16.81	18.55
7	.989	1.24	1.69	2.17	2.83	12.02	14.07	16.01	18.48	20.28
8	1.34	1.65	2.18	2.73	3.49	13.36	15.51	17.53	20.09	21.96
9	1.73	2.09	2.70	3.33	4.17	14.68	16.92	19.02	21.67	23.59
10	2.16	2.56	3.25	3.94	4.87	15.99	18.31	20.48	23.21	25.19
11	2.60	3.05	3.82	4.57	5.58	17.28	19.68	21.92	24.73	26.76
12	3.07	3.57	4.40	5.23	6.30	18.55	21.03	23.34	26.22	28.30
13	3.57	4.11	5.01	5.89	7.04	19.81	22.36	24.74	27.69	29.82
14	4.07	4.66	5.63	6.57	7.79	21.06	23.68	26.12	29.14	31.32
15	4.60	5.23	6.26	7.26	8.55	22.31	25.00	27.49	30.58	32.80
16	5.14	5.81	6.91	7.96	9.31	23.54	26.30	28.85	32.00	34.27
18	6.26	7.01	8.23	9.39	10.86	25.99	28.87	31.53	34.81	37.16
20	7.43	8.26	9.59	10.85	12.44	28.41	31.41	34.17	37.57	40.00
24	9.89	10.86	12.40	13.85	15.66	33.20	36.42	39.36	42.98	45.56
30	13.79	14.95	16.79	18.49	20.60	40.26	43.77	46.98	50.89	53.67
40	20.71	22.16	24.43	26.51	29.05	51.81	55.76	59.34	63.69	66.77
60	35.53	37.48	40.48	43.19	46.46	74.40	79.08	83.30	88.38	91.95
120	83.85	86.92	91.58	95.70	100.62	140.23	146.57	152.21	158.95	163.64

Source: Adapted with permission from *Introduction to Statistical Analysis,* 2nd ed., by W. J. Dixon and F. J. Massey, Jr., © 1957 McGraw-Hill.

TABLE 3   **Upper Percentiles of the *t* Distribution**

ν	.75	.90	.95	.975	.99	.995	.9995
1	1.000	3.078	6.314	12.706	31.821	63.657	636.619
2	.816	1.886	2.920	4.303	6.965	9.925	31.598
3	.765	1.638	2.353	3.182	4.541	5.841	12.941
4	.741	1.533	2.132	2.776	3.747	4.604	8.610
5	.727	1.476	2.015	2.571	3.365	4.032	6.859
6	.718	1.440	1.943	2.447	3.143	3.707	5.959
7	.711	1.415	1.895	2.365	2.998	3.499	5.405
8	.706	1.397	1.860	2.306	2.896	3.355	5.041
9	.703	1.383	1.833	2.262	2.821	3.250	4.781
10	.700	1.372	1.812	2.228	2.764	3.169	4.587
11	.697	1.363	1.796	2.201	2.718	3.106	4.437
12	.695	1.356	1.782	2.179	2.681	3.055	4.318
13	.694	1.350	1.771	2.160	2.650	3.012	4.221
14	.692	1.345	1.761	2.145	2.624	2.977	4.140
15	.691	1.341	1.753	2.131	2.602	2.947	4.073
16	.690	1.337	1.746	2.120	2.583	2.921	4.015
17	.689	1.333	1.740	2.110	2.567	2.898	3.965
18	.688	1.330	1.734	2.101	2.552	2.878	3.922
19	.688	1.328	1.729	2.093	2.339	2.861	3.883
20	.687	1.325	1.725	2.086	2.528	2.845	3.850
21	.686	1.323	1.721	2.080	2.518	2.831	3.819
22	.686	1.321	1.717	2.074	2.508	2.819	3.792
23	.685	1.319	1.714	2.069	2.500	2.807	3.767
24	.685	1.318	1.711	2.064	2.492	2.797	3.745
25	.684	1.316	1.708	2.060	2.485	2.787	3.725
26	.684	1.315	1.706	2.056	2.479	2.779	3.707
27	.684	1.314	1.703	2.052	2.473	2.771	3.690
28	.683	1.313	1.701	2.048	2.467	2.763	3.674
29	.683	1.311	1.699	2.045	2.462	2.756	3.659
30	.683	1.310	1.697	2.042	2.457	2.750	3.646
40	.681	1.303	1.684	2.021	2.423	2.704	3.551
60	.679	1.296	1.671	2.000	2.390	2.660	3.460
120	.677	1.289	1.658	1.980	2.358	2.617	3.373
∞	.674	1.282	1.645	1.960	2.326	2.576	3.291

Column header: $1 - \alpha$; row label: ν = degrees of freedom

Source: Taken from Table III of R. A. Fisher and F. Yates: *Statistical Tables for Biological, Agricultural, and Medical Research,* published by Longman Group UK Ltd., London, 1974.

TABLE 4   Selected Percentiles of the *F* Distribution

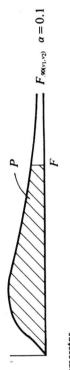

$F_{.90(\nu_1, \nu_2)}$ $\alpha = 0.1$

ν_1 = degrees of freedom for numerator

ν_2	1	2	3	4	5	6	7	8	9	10	12	15	20	24	30	40	60	120	∞
1	39.86	49.50	53.59	55.83	57.24	58.20	58.91	59.44	59.86	60.19	60.71	61.22	61.74	62.00	62.26	62.53	62.79	63.06	63.33
2	8.53	9.00	9.16	9.24	9.29	9.33	9.35	9.37	9.38	9.39	9.41	9.42	9.44	9.45	9.46	9.47	9.47	9.48	9.49
3	5.54	5.46	5.39	5.34	5.31	5.28	5.27	5.25	5.24	5.23	5.22	5.20	5.18	5.18	5.17	5.16	5.15	5.14	5.13
4	4.54	4.32	4.19	4.11	4.05	4.01	3.98	3.95	3.94	3.92	3.90	3.87	3.84	3.83	3.82	3.80	3.79	3.78	3.76
5	4.06	3.78	3.62	3.52	3.45	3.40	3.37	3.34	3.32	3.30	3.27	3.24	3.21	3.19	3.17	3.16	3.14	3.12	3.10
6	3.78	3.46	3.29	3.18	3.11	3.05	3.01	2.98	2.96	2.94	2.90	2.87	2.84	2.82	2.80	2.78	2.76	2.74	2.72
7	3.59	3.26	3.07	2.96	2.88	2.83	2.78	2.75	2.72	2.70	2.67	2.63	2.59	2.58	2.56	2.54	2.51	2.49	2.47
8	3.46	3.11	2.92	2.81	2.73	2.67	2.62	2.59	2.56	2.54	2.50	2.46	2.42	2.40	2.38	2.36	2.34	2.32	2.29
9	3.36	3.01	2.81	2.69	2.61	2.55	2.51	2.47	2.44	2.42	2.38	2.34	2.30	2.28	2.25	2.23	2.21	2.18	2.16
10	3.29	2.92	2.73	2.61	2.52	2.46	2.41	2.38	2.35	2.32	2.28	2.24	2.20	2.18	2.16	2.13	2.11	2.08	2.06
11	3.23	2.86	2.66	2.54	2.45	2.39	2.34	2.30	2.27	2.25	2.21	2.17	2.12	2.10	2.08	2.05	2.03	2.00	1.97
12	3.18	2.81	2.61	2.48	2.39	2.33	2.28	2.24	2.21	2.19	2.15	2.10	2.06	2.04	2.01	1.99	1.96	1.93	1.90
13	3.14	2.76	2.56	2.43	2.35	2.28	2.23	2.20	2.16	2.14	2.10	2.05	2.01	1.98	1.96	1.93	1.90	1.88	1.85
14	3.10	2.73	2.52	2.39	2.31	2.24	2.19	2.15	2.12	2.10	2.05	2.01	1.96	1.94	1.91	1.89	1.86	1.83	1.80
15	3.07	2.70	2.49	2.36	2.27	2.21	2.16	2.12	2.09	2.06	2.02	1.97	1.92	1.90	1.87	1.85	1.82	1.79	1.76
16	3.05	2.67	2.46	2.33	2.24	2.18	2.13	2.09	2.06	2.03	1.99	1.94	1.89	1.87	1.84	1.81	1.78	1.75	1.72
17	3.03	2.64	2.44	2.31	2.22	2.15	2.10	2.06	2.03	2.00	1.96	1.91	1.86	1.84	1.81	1.78	1.75	1.72	1.69
18	3.01	2.62	2.42	2.29	2.20	2.13	2.08	2.04	2.00	1.98	1.93	1.89	1.84	1.81	1.78	1.75	1.72	1.69	1.66
19	2.99	2.61	2.40	2.27	2.18	2.11	2.06	2.02	1.98	1.96	1.91	1.86	1.81	1.79	1.76	1.73	1.70	1.67	1.63
20	2.97	2.59	2.38	2.25	2.16	2.09	2.04	2.00	1.96	1.94	1.89	1.84	1.79	1.77	1.74	1.71	1.68	1.64	1.61
21	2.96	2.57	2.36	2.23	2.14	2.08	2.02	1.98	1.95	1.92	1.87	1.83	1.78	1.75	1.72	1.69	1.66	1.62	1.59
22	2.95	2.56	2.35	2.22	2.13	2.06	2.01	1.97	1.93	1.90	1.86	1.81	1.76	1.73	1.70	1.67	1.64	1.60	1.57
23	2.94	2.55	2.34	2.21	2.11	2.05	1.99	1.95	1.92	1.89	1.84	1.80	1.74	1.72	1.69	1.66	1.62	1.59	1.55
24	2.93	2.54	2.33	2.19	2.10	2.04	1.98	1.94	1.91	1.88	1.83	1.78	1.73	1.70	1.67	1.64	1.61	1.57	1.53
25	2.92	2.53	2.32	2.18	2.09	2.02	1.97	1.93	1.89	1.87	1.82	1.77	1.72	1.69	1.66	1.63	1.59	1.56	1.52
26	2.91	2.52	2.31	2.17	2.08	2.01	1.96	1.92	1.88	1.86	1.81	1.76	1.71	1.68	1.65	1.61	1.58	1.54	1.50
27	2.90	2.51	2.30	2.17	2.07	2.00	1.95	1.91	1.87	1.85	1.80	1.75	1.70	1.67	1.64	1.60	1.57	1.53	1.49
28	2.89	2.50	2.29	2.16	2.06	2.00	1.94	1.90	1.87	1.84	1.79	1.74	1.69	1.66	1.63	1.59	1.56	1.52	1.48
29	2.89	2.50	2.28	2.15	2.06	1.99	1.93	1.89	1.86	1.83	1.78	1.73	1.68	1.65	1.62	1.58	1.55	1.51	1.47
30	2.88	2.49	2.28	2.14	2.05	1.98	1.93	1.88	1.85	1.82	1.77	1.72	1.67	1.64	1.61	1.57	1.54	1.50	1.46
40	2.84	2.44	2.23	2.09	2.00	1.93	1.87	1.83	1.79	1.76	1.71	1.66	1.61	1.57	1.54	1.51	1.47	1.42	1.38
60	2.79	2.39	2.18	2.04	1.95	1.87	1.82	1.77	1.74	1.71	1.66	1.60	1.54	1.51	1.48	1.44	1.40	1.35	1.29
120	2.75	2.35	2.13	1.99	1.90	1.82	1.77	1.72	1.68	1.65	1.60	1.55	1.48	1.45	1.41	1.37	1.32	1.26	1.19
∞	2.71	2.30	2.08	1.94	1.85	1.77	1.72	1.67	1.63	1.60	1.55	1.49	1.42	1.38	1.34	1.30	1.24	1.17	1.00

ν_2 = degrees of freedom for denominator

continued

TABLE 4   **Selected Percentiles of the _F_ Distribution, _continued_**

$F_{.95}(\nu_1, \nu_2)$ α = 0.05

ν_1 = degrees of freedom for numerator

ν_2 = degrees of freedom for denominator

$\nu_2 \backslash \nu_1$	1	2	3	4	5	6	7	8	9	10	12	15	20	24	30	40	60	120	∞
1	161.4	199.5	215.7	224.6	230.2	234.0	236.8	238.9	240.5	241.9	243.9	245.9	248.0	249.1	250.1	251.1	252.2	253.3	254.3
2	18.51	19.00	19.16	19.25	19.30	19.33	19.35	19.37	19.38	19.40	19.41	19.43	19.45	19.45	19.46	19.47	19.48	19.49	19.50
3	10.13	9.55	9.28	9.12	9.01	8.94	8.89	8.85	8.81	8.79	8.74	8.70	8.66	8.64	8.62	8.59	8.57	8.55	8.53
4	7.71	6.94	6.59	6.39	6.26	6.16	6.09	6.04	6.00	5.96	5.91	5.86	5.80	5.77	5.75	5.72	5.69	5.66	5.63
5	6.61	5.79	5.41	5.19	5.05	4.95	4.88	4.82	4.77	4.74	4.68	4.62	4.56	4.53	4.50	4.46	4.43	4.40	4.36
6	5.99	5.14	4.76	4.53	4.39	4.28	4.21	4.15	4.10	4.06	4.00	3.94	3.87	3.84	3.81	3.77	3.74	3.70	3.67
7	5.59	4.74	4.35	4.12	3.97	3.87	3.79	3.73	3.68	3.64	3.57	3.51	3.44	3.41	3.38	3.34	3.30	3.27	3.23
8	5.32	4.46	4.07	3.84	3.69	3.58	3.50	3.44	3.39	3.35	3.28	3.22	3.15	3.12	3.08	3.04	3.01	2.97	2.93
9	5.12	4.26	3.86	3.63	3.48	3.37	3.29	3.23	3.18	3.14	3.07	3.01	2.94	2.90	2.86	2.83	2.79	2.75	2.71
10	4.96	4.10	3.71	3.48	3.33	3.22	3.14	3.07	3.02	2.98	2.91	2.85	2.77	2.74	2.70	2.66	2.62	2.58	2.54
11	4.84	3.98	3.59	3.36	3.20	3.09	3.01	2.95	2.90	2.85	2.79	2.72	2.65	2.61	2.57	2.53	2.49	2.45	2.40
12	4.75	3.89	3.49	3.26	3.11	3.00	2.91	2.85	2.80	2.75	2.69	2.62	2.54	2.51	2.47	2.43	2.38	2.34	2.30
13	4.67	3.81	3.41	3.18	3.03	2.92	2.83	2.77	2.71	2.67	2.60	2.53	2.46	2.42	2.38	2.34	2.30	2.25	2.21
14	4.60	3.74	3.34	3.11	2.96	2.85	2.76	2.70	2.65	2.60	2.53	2.46	2.39	2.35	2.31	2.27	2.22	2.18	2.13
15	4.54	3.68	3.29	3.06	2.90	2.79	2.71	2.64	2.59	2.54	2.48	2.40	2.33	2.29	2.25	2.20	2.16	2.11	2.07
16	4.49	3.63	3.24	3.01	2.85	2.74	2.66	2.59	2.54	2.49	2.42	2.35	2.28	2.24	2.19	2.15	2.11	2.06	2.01
17	4.45	3.59	3.20	2.96	2.81	2.70	2.61	2.55	2.49	2.45	2.38	2.31	2.23	2.19	2.15	2.10	2.06	2.01	1.96
18	4.41	3.55	3.16	2.93	2.77	2.66	2.58	2.51	2.46	2.41	2.34	2.27	2.19	2.15	2.11	2.06	2.02	1.97	1.92
19	4.38	3.52	3.13	2.90	2.74	2.63	2.54	2.48	2.42	2.38	2.31	2.23	2.16	2.11	2.07	2.03	1.98	1.93	1.88
20	4.35	3.49	3.10	2.87	2.71	2.60	2.51	2.45	2.39	2.35	2.28	2.20	2.12	2.08	2.04	1.99	1.95	1.90	1.84
21	4.32	3.47	3.07	2.84	2.68	2.57	2.49	2.42	2.37	2.32	2.25	2.18	2.10	2.05	2.01	1.96	1.92	1.87	1.81
22	4.30	3.44	3.05	2.82	2.66	2.55	2.46	2.40	2.34	2.30	2.23	2.15	2.07	2.03	1.98	1.94	1.89	1.84	1.78
23	4.28	3.42	3.03	2.80	2.64	2.53	2.44	2.37	2.32	2.27	2.20	2.13	2.05	2.01	1.96	1.91	1.86	1.81	1.76
24	4.26	3.40	3.01	2.78	2.62	2.51	2.42	2.36	2.30	2.25	2.18	2.11	2.03	1.98	1.94	1.89	1.84	1.79	1.73
25	4.24	3.39	2.99	2.76	2.60	2.49	2.40	2.34	2.28	2.24	2.16	2.09	2.01	1.96	1.92	1.87	1.82	1.77	1.71
26	4.23	3.37	2.98	2.74	2.59	2.47	2.39	2.32	2.27	2.22	2.15	2.07	1.99	1.95	1.90	1.85	1.80	1.75	1.69
27	4.21	3.35	2.96	2.73	2.57	2.46	2.37	2.31	2.25	2.20	2.13	2.06	1.97	1.93	1.88	1.84	1.79	1.73	1.67
28	4.20	3.34	2.95	2.71	2.56	2.45	2.36	2.29	2.24	2.19	2.12	2.04	1.96	1.91	1.87	1.82	1.77	1.71	1.65
29	4.18	3.33	2.93	2.70	2.55	2.43	2.35	2.28	2.22	2.18	2.10	2.03	1.94	1.90	1.85	1.81	1.75	1.70	1.64
30	4.17	3.32	2.92	2.69	2.53	2.42	2.33	2.27	2.21	2.16	2.09	2.01	1.93	1.89	1.84	1.79	1.74	1.68	1.62
40	4.08	3.23	2.84	2.61	2.45	2.34	2.25	2.18	2.12	2.08	2.00	1.92	1.84	1.79	1.74	1.69	1.64	1.58	1.51
60	4.00	3.15	2.76	2.53	2.37	2.25	2.17	2.10	2.04	1.99	1.92	1.84	1.75	1.70	1.65	1.59	1.53	1.47	1.39
120	3.92	3.07	2.68	2.45	2.29	2.17	2.09	2.02	1.96	1.91	1.83	1.75	1.66	1.61	1.55	1.50	1.43	1.35	1.25
∞	3.84	3.00	2.60	2.37	2.21	2.10	2.01	1.94	1.88	1.83	1.75	1.67	1.57	1.52	1.46	1.39	1.32	1.22	1.00

continued

TABLE 4 — Selected Percentiles of the *F* Distribution, *continued*

$F_{.975}(\nu_1, \nu_2)$ $\alpha = 0.025$

ν_1 = degrees of freedom for numerator

ν_2 = degrees of freedom for denominator

$\nu_2 \backslash \nu_1$	1	2	3	4	5	6	7	8	9	10	12	15	20	24	30	40	60	120	∞
1	647.8	799.5	864.2	899.6	921.8	937.1	948.2	956.7	963.3	968.6	976.7	984.9	993.1	997.2	1001	1006	1010	1014	1018
2	38.51	39.00	39.17	39.25	39.30	39.33	39.36	39.37	39.39	39.40	39.41	39.43	39.45	39.46	39.46	39.47	39.48	39.49	39.50
3	17.44	16.04	15.44	15.10	14.88	14.73	14.62	14.54	14.47	14.42	14.34	14.25	14.17	14.12	14.08	14.04	13.99	13.95	13.90
4	12.22	10.65	9.98	9.60	9.36	9.20	9.07	8.98	8.90	8.84	8.75	8.66	8.56	8.51	8.46	8.41	8.36	8.31	8.26
5	10.01	8.43	7.76	7.39	7.15	6.98	6.85	6.76	6.68	6.62	6.52	6.43	6.33	6.28	6.23	6.18	6.12	6.07	6.02
6	8.81	7.26	6.60	6.23	5.99	5.82	5.70	5.60	5.52	5.46	5.37	5.27	5.17	5.12	5.07	5.01	4.96	4.90	4.85
7	8.07	6.54	5.89	5.52	5.29	5.12	4.99	4.90	4.82	4.76	4.67	4.57	4.47	4.42	4.36	4.31	4.25	4.20	4.14
8	7.57	6.06	5.42	5.05	4.82	4.65	4.53	4.43	4.36	4.30	4.20	4.10	4.00	3.95	3.89	3.84	3.78	3.73	3.67
9	7.21	5.71	5.08	4.72	4.48	4.32	4.20	4.10	4.03	3.96	3.87	3.77	3.67	3.61	3.56	3.51	3.45	3.39	3.33
10	6.94	5.46	4.83	4.47	4.24	4.07	3.95	3.85	3.78	3.72	3.62	3.52	3.42	3.37	3.31	3.26	3.20	3.14	3.08
11	6.72	5.26	4.63	4.28	4.04	3.88	3.76	3.66	3.59	3.53	3.43	3.33	3.23	3.17	3.12	3.06	3.00	2.94	2.88
12	6.55	5.10	4.47	4.12	3.89	3.73	3.61	3.51	3.44	3.37	3.28	3.18	3.07	3.02	2.96	2.91	2.85	2.79	2.72
13	6.41	4.97	4.35	4.00	3.77	3.60	3.48	3.39	3.31	3.25	3.15	3.05	2.95	2.89	2.84	2.78	2.72	2.66	2.60
14	6.30	4.86	4.24	3.89	3.66	3.50	3.38	3.29	3.21	3.15	3.05	2.95	2.84	2.79	2.73	2.67	2.61	2.55	2.49
15	6.20	4.77	4.15	3.80	3.58	3.41	3.29	3.20	3.12	3.06	2.96	2.86	2.76	2.70	2.64	2.59	2.52	2.46	2.40
16	6.12	4.69	4.08	3.73	3.50	3.34	3.22	3.12	3.05	2.99	2.89	2.79	2.68	2.63	2.57	2.51	2.45	2.38	2.32
17	6.04	4.62	4.01	3.66	3.44	3.28	3.16	3.06	2.98	2.92	2.82	2.72	2.62	2.56	2.50	2.44	2.38	2.32	2.25
18	5.98	4.56	3.95	3.61	3.38	3.22	3.10	3.01	2.93	2.87	2.77	2.67	2.56	2.50	2.44	2.38	2.32	2.26	2.19
19	5.92	4.51	3.90	3.56	3.33	3.17	3.05	2.96	2.88	2.82	2.72	2.62	2.51	2.45	2.39	2.33	2.27	2.20	2.13
20	5.87	4.46	3.86	3.51	3.29	3.13	3.01	2.91	2.84	2.77	2.68	2.57	2.46	2.41	2.35	2.29	2.22	2.16	2.09
21	5.83	4.42	3.82	3.48	3.25	3.09	2.97	2.87	2.80	2.73	2.64	2.53	2.42	2.37	2.31	2.25	2.18	2.11	2.04
22	5.79	4.38	3.78	3.44	3.22	3.05	2.93	2.84	2.76	2.70	2.60	2.50	2.39	2.33	2.27	2.21	2.14	2.08	2.00
23	5.75	4.35	3.75	3.41	3.18	3.02	2.90	2.81	2.73	2.67	2.57	2.47	2.36	2.30	2.24	2.18	2.11	2.04	1.97
24	5.72	4.32	3.72	3.38	3.15	2.99	2.87	2.78	2.70	2.64	2.54	2.44	2.33	2.27	2.21	2.15	2.08	2.01	1.94
25	5.69	4.29	3.69	3.35	3.13	2.97	2.85	2.75	2.68	2.61	2.51	2.41	2.30	2.24	2.18	2.12	2.05	1.98	1.91
26	5.66	4.27	3.67	3.33	3.10	2.94	2.82	2.73	2.65	2.59	2.49	2.39	2.28	2.22	2.16	2.09	2.03	1.95	1.88
27	5.63	4.24	3.65	3.31	3.08	2.92	2.80	2.71	2.63	2.57	2.47	2.36	2.25	2.19	2.13	2.07	2.00	1.93	1.85
28	5.61	4.22	3.63	3.29	3.06	2.90	2.78	2.69	2.61	2.55	2.45	2.34	2.23	2.17	2.11	2.05	1.98	1.91	1.83
29	5.59	4.20	3.61	3.27	3.04	2.88	2.76	2.67	2.59	2.53	2.43	2.32	2.21	2.15	2.09	2.03	1.96	1.89	1.81
30	5.57	4.18	3.59	3.25	3.03	2.87	2.75	2.65	2.57	2.51	2.41	2.31	2.20	2.14	2.07	2.01	1.94	1.87	1.79
40	5.42	4.05	3.46	3.13	2.90	2.74	2.62	2.53	2.45	2.39	2.29	2.18	2.07	2.01	1.94	1.88	1.80	1.72	1.64
60	5.29	3.93	3.34	3.01	2.79	2.63	2.51	2.41	2.33	2.27	2.17	2.06	1.94	1.88	1.82	1.74	1.67	1.58	1.48
120	5.15	3.80	3.23	2.89	2.67	2.52	2.39	2.30	2.22	2.16	2.05	1.94	1.82	1.76	1.69	1.61	1.53	1.43	1.31
∞	5.02	3.69	3.12	2.79	2.57	2.41	2.29	2.19	2.11	2.05	1.94	1.83	1.71	1.64	1.57	1.48	1.39	1.27	1.00

continued

TABLE 4   **Selected Percentiles of the *F* Distribution, *continued***

$F_{.99}(\nu_1, \nu_2)$ α = 0.01

ν_1 = degrees of freedom for numerator

ν_2 = degrees of freedom for denominator

ν_2 \ ν_1	1	2	3	4	5	6	7	8	9	10	12	15	20	24	30	40	60	120	∞
1	4052	4999.5	5403	5625	5764	5859	5928	5982	6022	6056	6106	6157	6209	6235	6261	6287	6313	6339	6366
2	98.50	99.00	99.17	99.25	99.30	99.33	99.36	99.37	99.39	99.40	99.42	99.43	99.45	99.46	99.47	99.47	99.48	99.49	99.50
3	34.12	30.82	29.46	28.71	28.24	27.91	27.67	27.49	27.35	27.23	27.05	26.87	26.69	26.60	26.50	26.41	26.32	26.22	26.13
4	21.20	18.00	16.69	15.98	15.52	15.21	14.98	14.80	14.66	14.55	14.37	14.20	14.02	13.93	13.84	13.75	13.65	13.56	13.46
5	16.26	13.27	12.06	11.39	10.97	10.67	10.46	10.29	10.16	10.05	9.89	9.72	9.55	9.47	9.38	9.29	9.20	9.11	9.02
6	13.75	10.92	9.78	9.15	8.75	8.47	8.26	8.10	7.98	7.87	7.72	7.56	7.40	7.31	7.23	7.14	7.06	6.97	6.88
7	12.25	9.55	8.45	7.85	7.46	7.19	6.99	6.84	6.72	6.62	6.47	6.31	6.16	6.07	5.99	5.91	5.82	5.74	5.65
8	11.26	8.65	7.59	7.01	6.63	6.37	6.18	6.03	5.91	5.81	5.67	5.52	5.36	5.28	5.20	5.12	5.03	4.95	4.86
9	10.56	8.02	6.99	6.42	6.06	5.80	5.61	5.47	5.35	5.26	5.11	4.96	4.81	4.73	4.65	4.57	4.48	4.40	4.31
10	10.04	7.56	6.55	5.99	5.64	5.39	5.20	5.06	4.94	4.85	4.71	4.56	4.41	4.33	4.25	4.17	4.08	4.00	3.91
11	9.65	7.21	6.22	5.67	5.32	5.07	4.89	4.74	4.63	4.54	4.40	4.25	4.10	4.02	3.94	3.86	3.78	3.69	3.60
12	9.33	6.93	5.95	5.41	5.06	4.82	4.64	4.50	4.39	4.30	4.16	4.01	3.86	3.78	3.70	3.62	3.54	3.45	3.36
13	9.07	6.70	5.74	5.21	4.86	4.62	4.44	4.30	4.19	4.10	3.96	3.82	3.66	3.59	3.51	3.43	3.34	3.25	3.17
14	8.86	6.51	5.56	5.04	4.69	4.46	4.28	4.14	4.03	3.94	3.80	3.66	3.51	3.43	3.35	3.27	3.18	3.09	3.00
15	8.68	6.36	5.42	4.89	4.56	4.32	4.14	4.00	3.89	3.80	3.67	3.52	3.37	3.29	3.21	3.13	3.05	2.96	2.87
16	8.53	6.23	5.29	4.77	4.44	4.20	4.03	3.89	3.78	3.69	3.55	3.41	3.26	3.18	3.10	3.02	2.93	2.84	2.75
17	8.40	6.11	5.18	4.67	4.34	4.10	3.93	3.79	3.68	3.59	3.46	3.31	3.16	3.08	3.00	2.92	2.83	2.75	2.65
18	8.29	6.01	5.09	4.58	4.25	4.01	3.84	3.71	3.60	3.51	3.37	3.23	3.08	3.00	2.92	2.84	2.75	2.66	2.57
19	8.18	5.93	5.01	4.50	4.17	3.94	3.77	3.63	3.52	3.43	3.30	3.15	3.00	2.92	2.84	2.76	2.67	2.58	2.49
20	8.10	5.85	4.94	4.43	4.10	3.87	3.70	3.56	3.46	3.37	3.23	3.09	2.94	2.86	2.78	2.69	2.61	2.52	2.42
21	8.02	5.78	4.87	4.37	4.04	3.81	3.64	3.51	3.40	3.31	3.17	3.03	2.88	2.80	2.72	2.64	2.55	2.46	2.36
22	7.95	5.72	4.82	4.31	3.99	3.76	3.59	3.45	3.35	3.26	3.12	2.98	2.83	2.75	2.67	2.58	2.50	2.40	2.31
23	7.88	5.66	4.76	4.26	3.94	3.71	3.54	3.41	3.30	3.21	3.07	2.93	2.78	2.70	2.62	2.54	2.45	2.35	2.26
24	7.82	5.61	4.72	4.22	3.90	3.67	3.50	3.36	3.26	3.17	3.03	2.89	2.74	2.66	2.58	2.49	2.40	2.31	2.21
25	7.77	5.57	4.68	4.18	3.85	3.63	3.46	3.32	3.22	3.13	2.99	2.85	2.70	2.62	2.54	2.45	2.36	2.27	2.17
26	7.72	5.53	4.64	4.14	3.82	3.59	3.42	3.29	3.18	3.09	2.96	2.81	2.66	2.58	2.50	2.42	2.33	2.23	2.13
27	7.68	5.49	4.60	4.11	3.78	3.56	3.39	3.26	3.15	3.06	2.93	2.78	2.63	2.55	2.47	2.38	2.29	2.20	2.10
28	7.64	5.45	4.57	4.07	3.75	3.53	3.36	3.23	3.12	3.03	2.90	2.75	2.60	2.52	2.44	2.35	2.26	2.17	2.06
29	7.60	5.42	4.54	4.04	3.73	3.50	3.33	3.20	3.09	3.00	2.87	2.73	2.57	2.49	2.41	2.33	2.23	2.14	2.03
30	7.56	5.39	4.51	4.02	3.70	3.47	3.30	3.17	3.07	2.98	2.84	2.70	2.55	2.47	2.39	2.30	2.21	2.11	2.01
40	7.31	5.18	4.31	3.83	3.51	3.29	3.12	2.99	2.89	2.80	2.66	2.52	2.37	2.29	2.20	2.11	2.02	1.92	1.80
60	7.08	4.98	4.13	3.65	3.34	3.12	2.95	2.82	2.72	2.63	2.50	2.35	2.20	2.12	2.03	1.94	1.84	1.73	1.60
120	6.85	4.79	3.95	3.48	3.17	2.96	2.79	2.66	2.56	2.47	2.34	2.19	2.03	1.95	1.86	1.76	1.66	1.53	1.38
∞	6.63	4.61	3.78	3.32	3.02	2.80	2.64	2.51	2.41	2.32	2.18	2.04	1.88	1.79	1.70	1.59	1.47	1.32	1.00

Source: Adapted with permission from *Biometrika Tables for Statisticians*, Vol. 1, 2nd ed., edited by E. S. Pearson and H. O. Hartley, Cambridge University Press, 1958.

INDEX

Index

824

Index